Auto Electricity and Electronics

Principles, Diagnosis, Testing, and Service of All Major Electrical, Electronic, and Computer Control Systems

by

James E. Duffy
Automotive Writer

Publisher
The Goodheart-Willcox Company, Inc.
Tinley Park, Illinois

The Goodheart-Willcox Company, Inc. Brand Disclaimer: Brand names, company names, and illustrations for products and services included in this text are provided for educational purposes only and do not represent or imply endorsement or recommendation by the author or the publisher.

The Goodheart-Willcox Company, Inc. Safety Notice: The reader is expressly advised to carefully read, understand, and apply all safety precautions and warnings described in this book or that might also be indicated in undertaking the activities and exercises described herein to minimize risk of personal injury or injury to others. Common sense and good judgment should also be exercised and applied to help avoid all potential hazards. The reader should always refer to the appropriate manufacturer's technical information, directions, and recommendations; then proceed with care to follow specific equipment operating instructions. The reader should understand these notices and cautions are not exhaustive.

The publisher makes no warranty or representation whatsoever, either expressed or implied, including but not limited to equipment, procedures, and applications described or referred to herein, their quality, performance, merchantability, or fitness for a particular purpose. The publisher assumes no responsibility for any changes, errors, or omissions in this book. The publisher specifically disclaims any liability whatsoever, including any direct, indirect, incidental, consequential, special, or exemplary damages resulting, in whole or in part, from the reader's use or reliance upon the information, instructions, procedures, warnings, cautions, applications, or other matter contained in this book. The publisher assumes no responsibility for the activities of the reader.

Library of Congress Cataloging-in-Publication Data

Duffy, James E.
    Auto electricity and electronics / by James E. Duffy.
      p. cm.
   Includes index.
    ISBN 1-59070-271-9 (Softcover)
    ISBN 1-59070-272-7 (Hardcover)
  1. Automobiles—Electric Equipment
  2. Automobiles—Electronic Equipment
 I. Title.
  TL272 .D8297 2004
  629.2'7—dc21

Introduction

Automobiles and light trucks are now as much "electronic" as they are "mechanical." Look under the hood of any late-model car and you will find a maze of wires connecting dozens of devices. In fact, electronics can be found in almost every major system of a car, including the suspension, transmission, fuel, ignition, emission control, and braking systems. Some cars have four or five separate on-board computers.

The day of the "backyard mechanic" is over; this is the era of the well-trained electronic technician. Conventional electrical systems, when combined with newer computer-controlled systems, make it necessary to have a sound background in electricity and electronics. This knowledge will allow you to do competent repair work. Anyone versed in auto electronics will have no problem finding and keeping a good job in the automotive service industry.

Auto Electricity and Electronics Technology was designed to make the complex seem simple. Short sentences, abundant illustrations, and easy-to-follow procedures are used to make learning easier and more fun. All technical terms are printed in *italic type* and clearly defined in the first sentence of paragraphs so that you can quickly learn the "language" of the automotive electronic technician.

The text is divided into 30 chapters that are grouped into four sections. The first section reviews fundamentals: electrical principles and components, electronic components, wiring repairs, soldering, wiring diagrams, special tools and equipment, basic electrical tests, and safety. The second section summarizes the construction and operation of major electrical/electronic systems. The third section explains how to diagnose, test, and repair these electrical/electronic systems. The last section contains ASE information, useful tables, and an index-glossary reference.

Each chapter starts with Learning Objectives so you know what you are expected to learn in the chapter. A Summary at the end of each chapter allows you to quickly review the most important topics. Know These Terms sections are also given so you can make sure you grasp new technical words. A good mix of Review Questions allows you to determine how well you understand the material in the chapters. A separate section of ASE-Type Questions is presented at the end of each chapter to help you prepare for the types of questions that will be encountered on the ASE Certification Tests.

Auto Electricity and Electronics Technology stresses the use of on-board diagnostics, as well as conventional meter tests, to find electrical/electronic problems in all major automotive systems. Information on OBD II diagnostic systems has been strategically placed throughout the text. Additionally, electrical and electronic terminology has been updated to conform to the latest SAE standards (J1930).

This text is designed to help you pass the ASE Test A6, Electrical/Electronic Systems. However, it will also help you pass other ASE tests since they also contain questions requiring a knowledge of electricity and electronics.

Auto Electricity and Electronics Technology is a valuable "tool" for anyone wanting to know more about modern automobiles. It will help the experienced technician learn about new technology, review principles, and prepare for ASE certification. It will guide the student through a sequential program of study to prepare for employment. It will also help the car owner who just wants to know more about what is going on inside all those "wires and black boxes."

James E. Duffy

Contents

Section III—System Diagnosis and Repair

Section IV—ASE Certification/Reference Section

This text will explain and illustrate the operation, troubleshooting, and service of all major automotive electrical and electronic systems. It will explain how a computer system works (A); discuss the operation and construction of both electrical and electronic devices, such as heads-up windshield displays (B); and describe the basic procedures for testing electrical and electronic systems, such as using a digital voltmeter to pinpoint faulty components (C). It will also summarize the service procedures for both electrical and electronic components, such as replacing an ignition coil module (D).

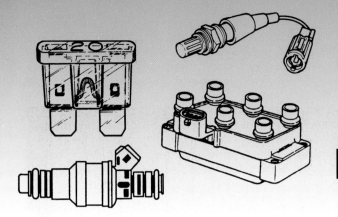

Chapter 1

Introduction to Electrical-Electronic Systems

After studying this chapter, you will be able to:
- *Explain why electronic devices are being used to increase vehicle efficiency.*
- *Summarize the operation of major electrical-electronic systems of an automobile.*
- *Describe the basic parts of major electrical-electronic systems.*
- *Locate major electrical-electronic components.*
- *Explain how modern automotive systems interact.*
- *Describe the purpose of a computer control system.*
- *Comprehend later textbook chapters more completely.*

Welcome to the exciting world of automotive electronics! You have wisely chosen to study a very rewarding and profitable specialized area of automotive service. Technicians trained in this area will be in demand well into the future.

This chapter will provide you with an overview of the most important electrical and electronic systems of a car. You will review the basic purpose of these systems and learn how many systems interact. You will also learn the general location of major electrical-electronic parts.

As a result, you will be better prepared to understand information given in following text chapters. By obtaining a ''mental image'' of the whole car as related to electricity and electronics, you will have a better ''mental framework'' on which to build your skills at doing automotive electrical-electronic tests and repairs.

Note! If you have already had previous courses in automotive technology, much of this chapter may be review. However, you should quickly scan through the chapter to refresh your memory. If this is one of your first classes in auto technology, study this chapter carefully!

THE ELECTRONIC REVOLUTION

The automotive industry is experiencing an ''electronic revolution.'' Electrical and electronic devices are now being used in almost every major system of the car. Open the hood or look under the dash of any new car and you will find a ''mind-boggling'' maze of wires and electrical devices.

Computers are commonplace and are being used to monitor and control almost all critical assemblies. The computer can be tied to the engine, fuel system, ignition system, emission systems, brakes, suspension, transmission, and many other systems. This can make electrical diagnosis and repair very challenging.

Electrical vs electronic

An *electrical device* is generally a more conventional component, such as an electric motor, mechanical switch, light bulb, etc. This term refers to devices that were used before the invention of electronics.

An *electronic device* is a more modern component that does not use moving parts for operation. Examples include transistors, diodes, vehicle sensors, computers, etc. Electronic devices normally operate off of low voltage.

Note! For simplicity, this book will use the term, either ''electrical'' or ''electronic,'' that best describes the situation. There is some overlap and confusion as to when an electrical component or system should be classified as electronic because most automotive devices operate on low voltage (around 12 volts). The voltage in a home wall outlet or an appliance is much higher (120 volts) and would always be classified as electrical.

Mechanical vs electrical

Electrical devices have replaced many mechanical devices in the automobile. Electrical devices can do the job of mechanical devices more efficiently. Since electricity moves at almost the speed of light, very fast and accurate operations or adjustments can be made to keep the car performing at maximum efficiency.

With electronics, the car can be designed for higher fuel economy and fewer emissions. The car can be made to be lighter, ride more smoothly, stop more quickly, and provide more comfort and convenience for its passengers. Some cars have a voice alert system that will even talk and explain vehicle conditions or troubles.

The electronic technician

The *electronic technician* is trained to diagnose and repair the many systems of a car that use electrical-electronic devices. With the influx of electronics into the passenger car, this type of specialized technician is in great demand. Of all service areas, the electronic service technician (mechanic) is predicted to be needed more than in any other area of auto repair.

Mechanics are finding it very difficult to keep up with this rapidly changing technology. Some have fallen behind and are not totally competent to work on modern computer systems. If not educationally prepared, a mechanic can waste time and money trying to find electrical problems. The untrained mechanic could replace parts one at a time using a trial-and-error method of repair. This is a terrible way to fix a car. It is not fair to the customer or the shop owner.

This text will help you become a productive and talented electrical-electronic technician. It will give you the "basics" needed to do competent repair work. By learning the fundamental methods to approach and solve electrical-electronic problems, this type of repair work can be relatively simple and fun. You can then satisfy your customers and employer.

System interaction

In the past, automotive systems worked almost independently of each other. For instance, the ignition system would "fire" the spark plugs based solely on engine speed and engine vacuum. Mechanical devices in the distributor would control when each spark plug fired. The fuel system would also operate independently of other systems. This made diagnosis and repair easy. Once a problem was isolated to a specific system, it was not difficult to find and correct the trouble.

Presently, all major engine and vehicle systems *interact* or *interface,* which means they work together. Using electrical-electronic devices, information from the ignition system (speed sensor) can be used by the computer to operate the fuel system. An electronic device on the transmission can also be used to feed data to the computer, improving the efficiency of both the fuel and ignition systems. As a result, these systems interface. As a result, more knowledge and skill are required to work on these systems.

A fault in one system can appear to be a problem in a completely different system. If not properly trained, this can be a service "nightmare" for an auto mechanic. He or she can become very frustrated when trying to service today's cars.

Remember! A sound background in electricity and electronics is absolutely necessary if you are to properly troubleshoot and repair today's complex, interacting vehicle systems.

The future of auto electronics

We are just seeing the beginning of electronics in the automobile. Studies show that the computer and electronic devices will be used even more in the future.

In perspective, only a few years ago the computer was seldom used in passenger cars. First came the electronic ignition system where a pickup coil and a small electronic amplifier replaced the mechanical breaker points. From there, more electronics has been gradually introduced. All late-model cars are equipped with one or more computers and various sensors and actuators that monitor and control almost every vehicle system.

THE COMPUTER NETWORK

The automotive *computer network* consists of electrical-electronic devices that perform specific functions. Instead of using old, heavy, mechanical switches, linkages,

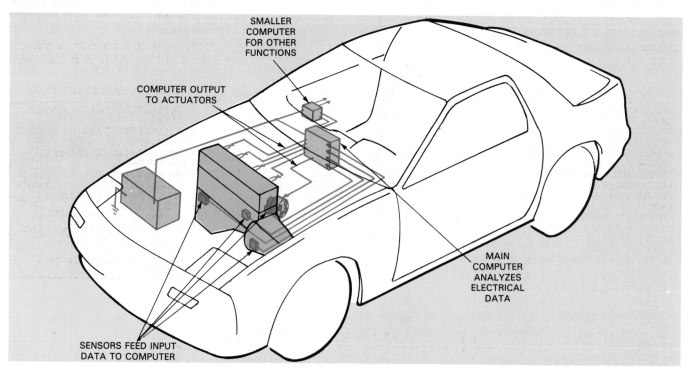

SMALLER COMPUTER FOR OTHER FUNCTIONS

COMPUTER OUTPUT TO ACTUATORS

MAIN COMPUTER ANALYZES ELECTRICAL DATA

SENSORS FEED INPUT DATA TO COMPUTER

Fig. 1-1. All late-model cars have one or more on-board computers, or electronic control units. The computer is a complex electronic circuit that produces pre-programmed electrical outputs when fed electrical inputs from sensors. This capability allows the computer to make super-fast adjustments for keeping the car performing at maximum efficiency. Normally, the computers, or controllers, are located under the car dash. Sensors and actuators can be located almost anywhere in vehicle.

and other components, very small electronic components are frequently used to do specific tasks, Fig. 1-1.

A computer network, also called *computer system,* uses three basic components:

1. VEHICLE SENSORS (devices for converting a condition into an electrical signal for the computer).
2. COMPUTER (complex electronic circuit that can use sensor signals to produce known electrical outputs for actuators).
3. ACTUATORS (electrical-electronic components that can do the work for the computer system).

During operation, the vehicle sensors produce varying electrical signals depending upon conditions. For example, if the engine is cold, a temperature sensor might have high resistance. Only a small amount of current would flow through the temperature sensor circuit to the computer. The computer could utilize this electrical data. The computer could change the output to the electronic fuel injectors (actuators) for cold engine operation. More fuel would be injected to keep the engine running in cold weather.

This same basic principle is used with dozens of vehicle sensors and actuators. Just as the temperature sensor and computer have replaced the mechanical carburetor choke and bi-metal choke spring, the sensors, computer, and actuators can do a more efficient job of controlling vehicle operation.

Vehicle sensors

The vehicle *sensors* serve as the "eyes, ears, and nose" of the computer network. They can detect part movement, temperature changes, pressure variance, chemical content of exhaust gases, part location, speed of rotation, sounds, and other conditions, Fig. 1-2.

The sensors act as *input devices* for the computer. They provide *data* (information) concerning how well each system is functioning for the conditions. Sensors can be found almost anywhere in a late model car.

As you will learn, there are several categories of

sensors and sensors can also be classified by system. This will be detailed in later chapters.

Vehicle computer

The car's *computer,* also called *microprocessor* or *electronic control unit,* is a super-complex set of electronic circuits that use sensor inputs to produce *programmed* (predetermined) outputs. The computer circuitry is usually encased in a sheetmetal housing. The unit frequently mounts under the dash but it can also be found in the engine compartment. Some cars use more than one computer or control unit. One is pictured in Fig. 1-3.

As you will find out in later chapters, the computer is commonly nicknamed the *"black box."* This is because the internal circuits are sealed and cannot be repaired in the field. The electronic technician may never see the inside of the computer nor understand all of its circuitry.

Vehicle actuators

An *actuator* is a device that uses electrical energy and engine vacuum, pressure, or a combination of each to do work. In the computer network, actuators use electric current to produce movement. Magnetic attraction in a solenoid or a small electric motor produce this movement. For example, an actuator might move the throttle to control engine speed or move a lever to unlock the car's doors.

Detailed in later chapters, actuators serve as the "hands" for a computer. They let the computer use current or voltage output to perform various functions. Another name for actuator is *output device.*

On-board diagnostics

On-board diagnostics refers to a vehicle computer's ability to analyze the operation of its circuits and to output data showing any problems. All new cars and light trucks have this self-test feature.

If the vehicle's computer detects a problem, it will turn on a dash warning light to tell the driver and technician

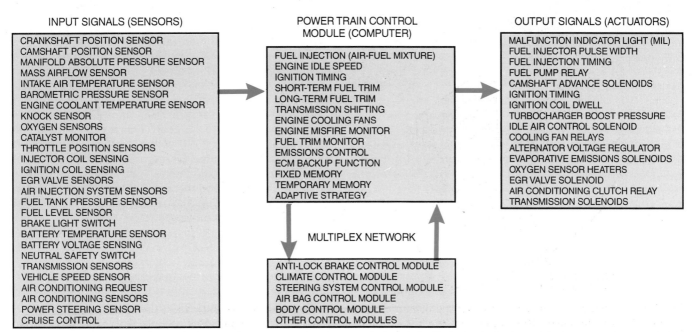

Fig. 1-2. This block diagram shows how input signals feed data to the main computer, or the power train control module. The computer can then use preprogrammed data to calculate the correct output signals. These output signals are sent to the actuators, which are used to control various systems. The multiplex network allows several other modules to communicate with the power train control module so all systems work in harmony.

Fig. 1-3. As you can see, the inside of a computer contains advanced electronic circuit chips that can make complex calculations using electrical signals from sensors. Only a few years ago, a computer with this "brain power" would fill a room in your house. (Delco Electronics)

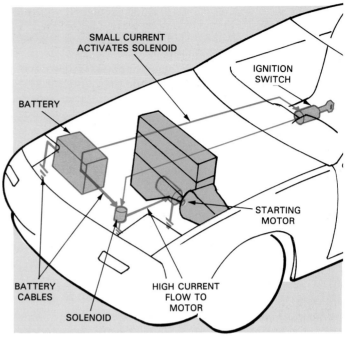

Fig. 1-4. Starting system uses four major components. Battery provides electrical power for system. When ignition switch is turned, small current flows to solenoid. This energizes solenoid and it closes battery to starting motor circuit. High current then flows to starting motor for engine cranking.

that something is wrong. It also places a diagnostic trouble code in its memory.

A *scan tool* is generally used to communicate with the vehicle's computers. It can retrieve trouble codes, display circuit and sensor electrical values, run tests, and give helpful hints for finding problem sources. This can all be done without disconnecting wires or removing parts.

The scan tool information tells the technician which circuits or parts are not operating properly. This helps the technician quickly find and correct problems in today's complex computer systems.

STARTING SYSTEM

The *starting system* uses battery power and a powerful electric motor to rotate the engine crankshaft. When the driver turns the ignition key switch to start, current flows through the starting system. Electricity from the *ignition switch* energizes the starter solenoid. The *starter solenoid* then energizes the starting motor, Fig. 1-4.

A small gear on the *starting motor* engages and turns a large ring gear on the engine flywheel. As the flywheel turns, it rotates the engine crankshaft and the engine goes through its four-stroke cycle. This pulls fuel and air into the cylinders and operates the ignition system.

When the engine begins to run on its own power, the driver releases the ignition key and the starting system no longer functions.

The starter usually bolts to the lower rear of the engine. The starter solenoid can mount on the motor or elsewhere in the engine compartment.

CHARGING SYSTEM

The starting system draws a tremendous amount of current from the battery. This runs down, or *discharges,* the battery. A system is needed to recharge the battery. Look at Fig. 1-5.

The *charging system* forces current back through the battery for recharging and also provides electricity for all of the electrical devices when the engine is running. This system serves as the "electrical power supply" under normal operating conditions, Fig. 1-6.

With the engine running, a belt is used to rotate the alternator pulley. The *alternator,* sometimes called *generator,* produces the current output. This current is fed to the battery and to other electrical-electronic systems.

The *voltage regulator* maintains an alternator output of approximately 13 to 15 volts. This is higher than battery voltage, which is 12.6 volts (12 volt battery). This higher voltage is needed to recharge the battery.

The alternator usually bolts near the front of the engine. Modern voltage regulators are located on or inside the alternator. Older regulators are mounted to one side of the engine compartment.

IGNITION SYSTEM

An *ignition system* is needed on gasoline engines to ignite the air-fuel mixture. It produces an extremely high voltage surge that operates the spark plugs. A very hot electric arc jumps across the tip of each spark plug at the correct time. This causes the engine's air-fuel mixture to burn, expand, and produce power. Study Fig. 1-7.

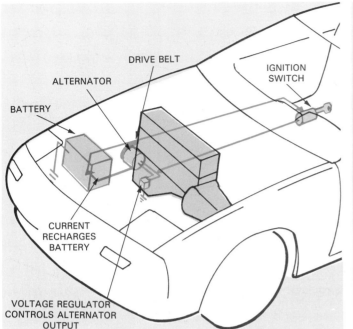

Fig. 1-5. Charging system uses belt driven alternator to feed current back into battery and to other electrical-electronic devices. With engine running, engine belt spins and powers alternator. Voltage regulator, usually mounted on alternator on newer cars, keeps voltage output at about 13 to 15 volts.

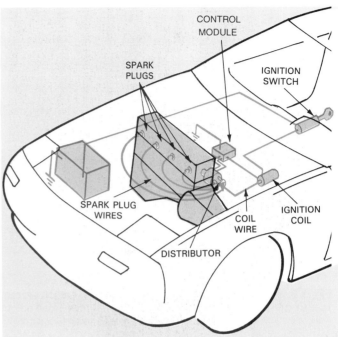

Fig. 1-7. New car ignition systems vary considerably. This is a basic system using electronic switching circuit that reacts to engine speed sensor or pick-up unit in distributor. Switching circuit controls when ignition coil fires and produces high voltage for spark plugs.

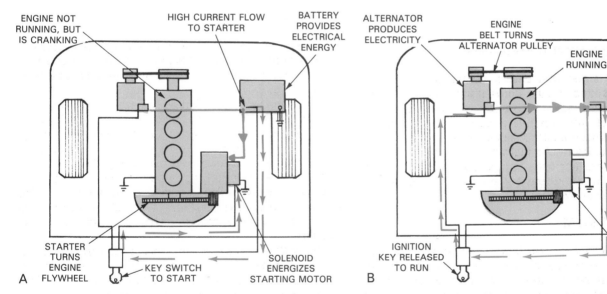

Fig. 1-6. A—Note current flow during engine cranking. Small current flows through ignition switch and to solenoid. Solenoid engages starter gear with flywheel ring gear and engine cranks. B—After engine starting, alternator action recharges battery. It also provides electrical power for other components.

With the ignition switch ON and the engine running, the system uses sensors to determine engine speed and other variables. Sensor signals are fed to a control module or an electronic switching circuit. The control module then modifies and *amplifies* (increases) these signals into on-off current pulses that trigger the ignition coil.

When triggered, the *ignition coil* can produce a high voltage output to "fire" the spark plugs. When the ignition key is turned off, the coil stops functioning and the spark-ignition engine stops running.

Ignition system designs vary. Some use a distributor to send voltage to each spark plug wire at the right time. Others use engine sensors, the computer, and multiple ignition coils without a distributor. Most ignition system parts mount on or near the engine.

Fig. 1-8 illustrates the basic action of an ignition system for a one-cylinder engine. When the switching device opens, the ignition coil fires and produces high

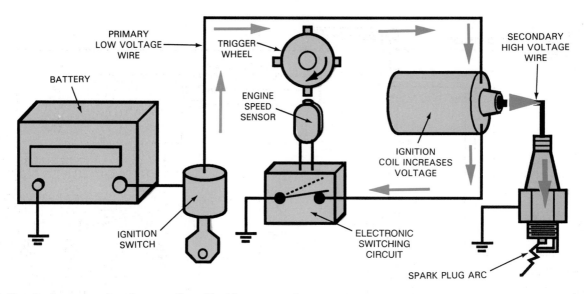

Fig. 1-8. Simple circuit drawing shows action of ignition system for one-cylinder engine. Small toothed wheel rotates with engine rpm to signal engine speed. Pick-up unit produces small electrical pulses for electronic switching circuit. Switching circuit can then cause ignition coil to "fire" and operate the spark plug.

voltage for the spark plug. This will be detailed in later chapters.

FUEL SYSTEM ELECTRONICS

Only a few years ago, new cars came equipped with carburetors, which were primarily mechanical. Most older fuel systems also had a mechanical fuel pump, which was bolted to the side of the engine block.

Today all new cars have electronic fuel injections. An electric fuel pump feeds fuel to the engine from the fuel tank, Fig. 1-9. Various engine sensors feed data to the computer. The computer then uses data to control fuel injection.

The fuel injectors are actuators that simply open and close small fuel spray nozzles into the engine intake

manifold. Fuel pressure from the electric pump, NOT vacuum as with a carburetor, forces fuel into the engine intake manifold. The sensors feed electrical data to the computer concerning vehicle operating conditions. Then, the computer can calculate when and how long to energize the injectors.

Electronic fuel injection provides much more precise control of how much fuel is metered into the engine. The sensors and computer react almost instantaneously to changes that affect engine operation. The sensors feed electrical data on engine temperature, engine speed, throttle position, engine vacuum (intake manifold pressure), transmission/transaxle gear selection, turbocharger boost, etc. for maximizing engine power and fuel economy.

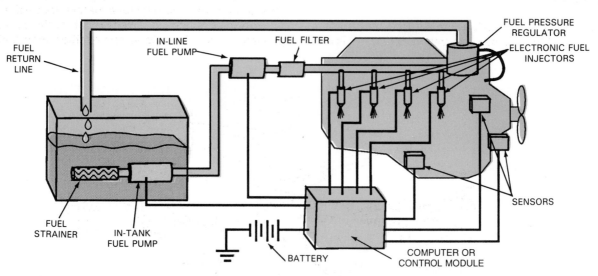

Fig. 1-9. Modern fuel systems now use electronics extensively. This diagram represents electronic fuel injection system. Electric fuel pump(s) force fuel to injectors and pressure regulator. Sensors feed data to computer about engine operating conditions. Computer can then activate injectors on each engine intake stroke. Pressure regulator maintains constant fuel pressure at injectors. Excess fuel is metered back into fuel tank.

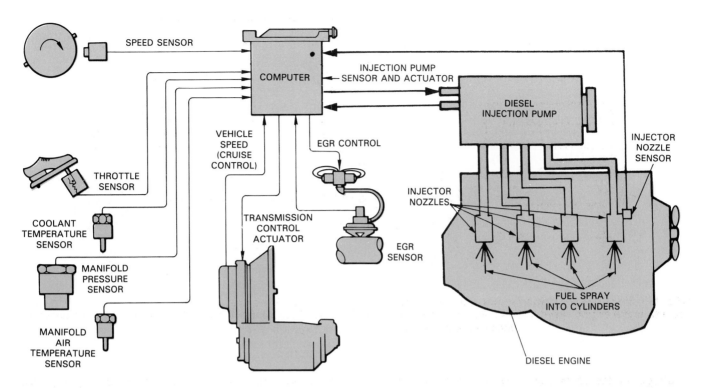

Fig. 1-10. Previously, diesel injection systems were mechanical. A high pressure mechanical pump forced diesel fuel directly into the engine combustion chambers. Then, compression stroke heat, not spark plugs, ignited the fuel. Now, electronic devices are being used to improve diesel efficiency. Sensors monitor operating conditions for the computer. Actuators on the injection pump can operate mechanical devices to more accurately control fuel metering.

Even diesel fuel systems are now using electronics, Fig. 1-10. Previously considered a mechanical system, sensors and actuators are now used on the injection pump to help control fuel delivery. However, the inner workings of the diesel injection pump are still mechanical because of the "super-high" pressures required for diesel fuel injection. This will be detailed later.

LIGHTING SYSTEM

The *lighting system* obviously provides illumination for night driving. Most of the components (bulbs, switches, etc.) are considered electrical in nature. However, some electronics is now being used in digital dashes, automatic light dimming systems, graphic displays (television type picture tube displays), etc.

Fig. 1-11 shows a basic lighting system. It uses various switches to control the operation of the bulbs. A large amount of wiring is needed to carry current to the numerous switches and bulbs.

In the future, *fiber optics* (light carrying strands of plastic) and *multiplexing* (one metal wire carries several control signals) should replace much of the conventional wiring in cars. A single strand of fiber optic material or

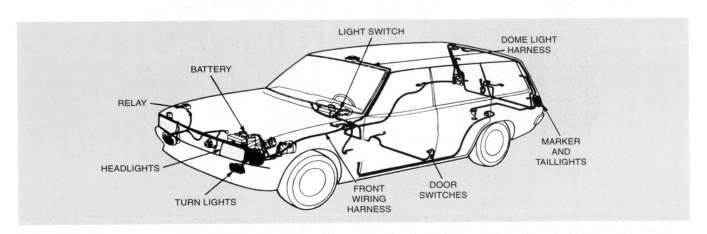

Fig. 1-11. Light systems have not changed very much over the years. However, some cars have digital dash displays that use a computer for operation.

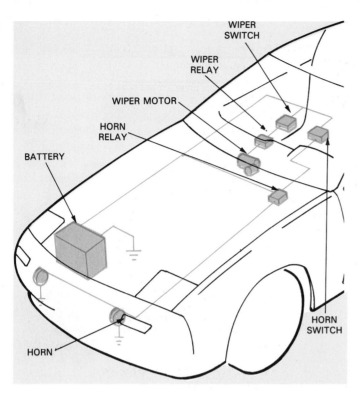

Fig. 1-12. Horn and wiper systems are fairly simple. Switches control current flow to other devices. Relays are sometimes used between switch and device.

one metal wire can replace a large bundle of wires. Remote units use the single-wire signals and activate other devices. This will be discussed in later chapters.

WIPER-WASHER AND HORN SYSTEMS

The *wiper-washer system* is still primarily electrical. Dash or steering column mounted switches allow the driver to activate the wipers in rain and the washer mechanism for windshield cleaning. Shown in Fig. 1-12,

an electric motor operates the wiper. It is a small DC (direct current) motor wired to the wiper switch.

The washer system normally uses a tiny electric motor in the bottom of the washer fluid reservoir. Pushing a button switch activates the small motor and fluid pump to force solution onto the windshield. Some washer pump mechanisms are mounted on the wiper motor.

The *horn system* uses a steering wheel mounted switch and a relay to send current to the horn. This is a fairly simple system that will be detailed in later chapters.

POWER LOCKS, SEATS, AND WINDOWS

Many new cars are ordered with optional power door locks and power seats. Again, these are relatively simple systems unless they are tied into the computer system. On some cars, the computer activates the door locks when the car begins to move forward or is shifted into drive.

A *power lock system* uses solenoids (electric plunging mechanisms) to move the door lock knobs up or down. Door mounted switches normally control the lock solenoids. Fig. 1-13 shows a basic door lock system.

A *power seat system* has small electric motors under each seat. Multiposition switches control the rotation and engagement of the motors to move the seats into various positions.

Power windows also use small electric motors and a gear system to raise or lower the side windows. Again, door-mounted switches control the motors.

SOUND SYSTEMS

A *sound system* can include an AM-FM stereo, a tape player, and even a compact disc player. New cars can come equipped with very exotic sound systems, which may include numerous speakers, a power booster, etc. Fig. 1-14 shows a sound system with six speakers. Sound systems are covered fully in later chapters.

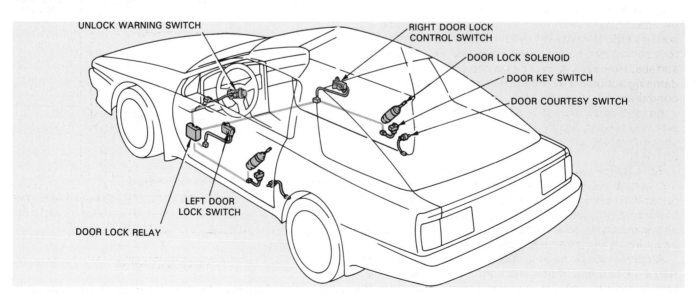

Fig. 1-13. Power door locks and power windows are becoming more common. This simple diagram shows basic parts in power door lock system. (Toyota)

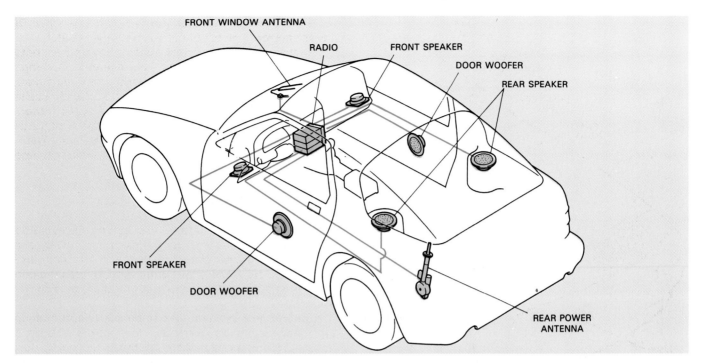

Fig. 1-14. Sound systems are becoming more complex. New cars have numerous speakers, electronic tuning, power antenna, and even digital disc player.

VOICE ALERT SYSTEMS

A *voice alert system* uses a small speaker, computer, and numerous sensors to inform the driver of vehicle conditions. Fig. 1-15 shows a voice alert system that tells the driver about 24 functions.

Some systems make an audible beep and then display the trouble as an *alpha-numeric* (letters or words and numbers) in the dash. Others actually talk and say things like—"door ajar, your fuel is low, etc."

SUSPENSION SYSTEM ELECTRONICS

Electronics can be used to improve the ride of a car tremendously. Conventionally, springs and shock absorbers are the method of allowing the wheels and tires to move up and down over bumps and dips in the road surface. However, it would be more efficient if different damping actions could be used on different road surface conditions.

An *automatic damping system* uses a computer, a steering sensor, the throttle sensor, speed sensor, and shock damping actuators to control shock stiffness. See Fig. 1-16.

For example, when cruising on a smooth highway at a constant speed, the computer can adjust the shocks for soft damping. Then, if the car is cornering on a highway ramp, for instance, the computer can use the shock actuators to increase shock stiffness. This provides for better cornering stability.

An *active suspension system* does NOT use conventional springs and shock absorbers. It uses a hydraulic ram, computer, sensors, and ram actuators to make the wheels follow the road surface. This can make the car ride almost perfectly smooth, on even the roughest

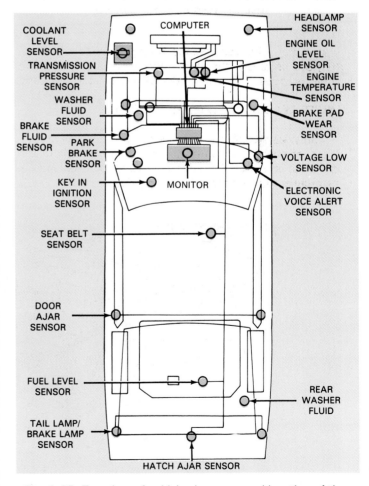

Fig. 1-15. Top view of vehicle shows general location of the many sensors used in this voice alert system. It will inform driver of numerous conditions.

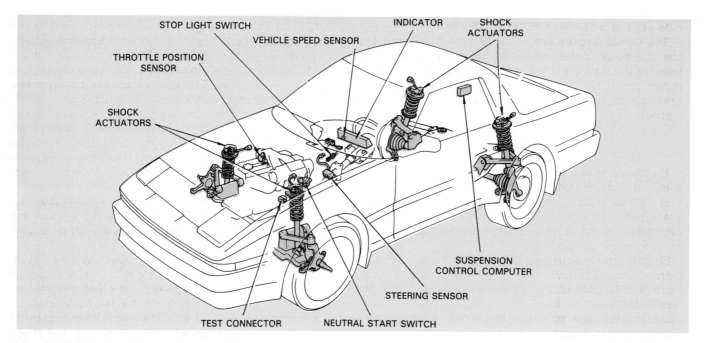

Fig. 1-16. This computer controlled suspension system can automatically adjust shock stiffness depending upon driving and road conditions. For instance, it will produce a soft, smooth ride when traveling down a straight highway. However, it will stiffen shock damping when cornering on a country road. (Toyota)

roads. The sensors, actuators, and computer can react so quickly that the ram can move the suspension system to follow the road surface. This prevents shocks from being transmitted to the car body. Several auto makers are experimenting with active suspension. Once perfected, it should revolutionize car ride and suspension technology.

BRAKE SYSTEM ELECTRONICS

Electronics is also being used in modern braking systems at an increasing rate. Sensors and the computer can monitor brake fluid level or even prevent wheel lock up and loss of maximum tire adhesion with the road during panic stops.

An *antilock brake system* uses wheel speed sensors, a hydraulic actuator, and a computer to maintain directional stability and steerability during braking. This is a tremendous breakthrough in braking technology and can increase passenger safety considerably. See Fig. 1-17.

With antilock brakes, the car can be stopped quickly in a straight line, even if two wheels are on dry pavement and the two on the other side of the car on snow or wet pavement. This prevents the car from skidding

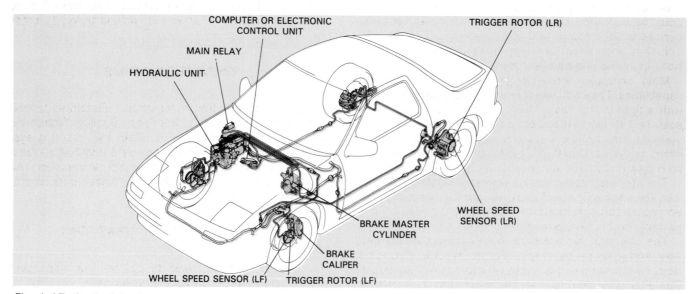

Fig. 1-17. Antilock brakes use wheel speed sensors, computer, and hydraulic actuator to prevent wheel and tire lockup. If a tire slows down too much and is ready to skid, the hydraulic unit cycles pressure on and off to that wheel. This system decreases stopping distance and improves vehicle directional stability during panic stops.

sideways in an emergency stop situation.

The wheel sensors send a pulsing electrical signal to the computer. If the sensor signal shows that one or more of the tires are slowing down too much, the computer cycles the hydraulic actuator to reduce brake pressure to prevent tire lockup and loss of braking traction.

SUMMARY

Electronic devices can be found almost everywhere on a modern car. Electrical devices are more conventional and include motors, relays, mechanical switches, etc. Electronic devices are solid state and do NOT have moving parts. Electronic devices include transistors, diodes, most sensors, computers, etc.

Electric and electronic components have replaced many mechanical devices. They are lighter and provide more precise control. For example, an ignition system distributor used to have mechanical weights and a vacuum diaphragm to alter ignition timing with engine speed and load. Now the computer and sensors control when each spark plug fires in the engine cylinder.

Because of the electronics influx into the passenger car, many systems now interact or interface. For instance, the fuel injection system now uses engine sensors that are common to both the ignition, emission control, and fuel systems. This makes it much more challenging to find and correct problems. A fault in one system can appear to be a problem in a completely different system.

A computer system consists of three basic components: sensors, actuators, and computer.

The sensors change physical conditions (temperature, motion, pressure, etc.) into an electrical signal for the computer.

The computer is a complicated electronic circuit that can analyze input signals and produce programmed output signals for the actuators.

An actuator is a device that uses electrical signals to produce motion. A small electric motor or a solenoid could be classified as actuators. The computer can send current to an actuator to do work—open a fuel injector, unlock a door, return a power seat to a previous position, increase engine idle speed, etc.

Most computer systems have on-board diagnostic capabilities. They will detect problems and warn the driver with a light in the dash. Then, the technician can use a scan tool to retrieve trouble codes from the computer's memory. The trouble code numbers will indicate which circuit or system is at fault. This narrows down the possible problems and makes diagnosis much easier.

The starting system uses a powerful electric motor to turn the engine flywheel and crankshaft. This makes the engine go through its four-stroke cycle for starting and running on its own power.

The charging system is used to re-energize the battery and provide electricity for all electric-electronic devices. It uses a belt-driven alternator or AC generator. The alternator produces an electrical output. A voltage regulator is used to keep alternator output at about 13 to 15 volts. Battery voltage is lower or about 12 volts (actually 12.5 volts).

Ignition system designs vary. Some still use a distributor to activate the ignition coil and feed high voltage to the spark plugs. Others use a computer and multiple ignition coils without a distributor. With any design, the ignition system must fire the spark plugs at the right time depending upon engine operating conditions.

Fuel systems are now using electronics extensively. Electronic fuel injection has replaced carburetion. Vehicle sensors "report" to the computer. Then, the computer can energize the injectors at the right instant and for the correct duration to maximize fuel efficiency and engine power.

Diesel systems, previously totally mechanical, are beginning to use electronics. Injection pump sensors and actuators are now being used to improve diesel engine operation.

Conventional systems (lighting, wiper-washer, horn, sound, etc.) vary slightly from car to car. Voice alert systems, digital dash displays, and other systems all require the talents of a properly trained technician.

Electronics is even used in the suspension system of a few makes of cars. Sensors, the computer, and shock damping actuators can be used to soften straight ahead driving or stiffen the shock action in corners for better handling.

Experimental active suspension systems do NOT use springs or shock absorbers. Computer controlled hydraulic rams support the wheels and allow them to move up and down with road imperfections. If a ram sensor detects a bump in the road, it signals the computer. The computer can then activate the ram to move and follow the road surface. This principle can be used to increase ride smoothness tremendously.

Antilock brake systems can prevent wheel lock-up and loss of traction or directional stability. Wheel sensors monitor wheel rotation. If a tire and wheel slow down and begin to skid, the sensor and computer activate a hydraulic unit to limit hydraulic pressure to that wheel to prevent a skid.

Later textbook chapters will explain these and many other systems in detail. Study carefully and you will have a big advantage over other technicians trying to enter the field.

KNOW THESE TERMS

Electrical device, Electronic device, Electronic technician, System interaction, Interface, Sensor, Computer, Actuator, On-board diagnostics, Scan tool, Starting system, Charging system, Ignition system, Lighting system, Power lock system, Power seat system, Voice alert system, Automatic suspension damping, Active suspension, Antilock brake system.

REVIEW QUESTIONS – CHAPTER 1

1. Electrical and electronic devices are now being used in almost every system of a modern car. True or false?
2. Explain the difference between an electrical device and an electronic device.

3. All major vehicle systems, because of the computer, _____ or _____ which means they work together.
4. Studies show that electronics has peaked out and few new components will be used in future automobiles. Present electronic components will just be improved. True or false?
5. What is a vehicle sensor?
6. What is a computer?
7. What is an actuator?
8. In your own words, explain the basic operation of a computer system.
9. A sensor or input device serves as the _____, _____, and _____ of a computer network.
10. Another name for sensor is _____ _____.
11. Where are vehicle sensors located?
12. Another name for an automotive computer is _____ _____ _____.
13. How does an actuator do the work for a computer?
14. Explain the operation of the starting and charging systems.
15. With the engine running, voltage output from the alternator is approximately:
   a. 12 volts.
   b. 12.5 volts.
   c. 13 to 15 volts.
   d. 10 to 12 volts.
16. The _____ _____ is used to start combustion of the fuel in a gasoline engine.
17. Describe how electronics is now being used in fuel systems.
18. What is an active suspension system?
19. What is an antilock brake system?
20. Electronic fuel injection has almost totally replaced carburetion. True or false?

ASE CERTIFICATION–TYPE QUESTIONS

1. Technician A says electrical devices are not used on late-model vehicles. Technician B says electronic devices utilize moving parts for operation. Who is right?
   (A) A only.
   (B) B only.
   (C) Both A and B.
   (D) Neither A nor B.
2. All of the following are common automotive electronic components except:
   (A) vehicle sensors.
   (B) mechanical switches.
   (C) transistors.
   (D) diodes.
3. Technician A says an automotive computer system uses sensors to convert conditions to electrical signals. Technician B says an automotive computer system uses actuators to do work for the system. Who is right?
   (A) A only.
   (B) B only.
   (C) Both A and B.
   (D) Neither A nor B.

4. Technician A says an automobile's computer can be located under the dash. Technician B says an automobile's computer can be located in the engine compartment. Who is right?
   (A) A only.
   (B) B only.
   (C) Both A and B.
   (D) Neither A nor B.
5. Technician A says on-board diagnostics refers to the computer's ability to analyze the operation of its circuits and output data identifying problems. Technician B says the computer systems in all new cars have on-board diagnostic capabilities. Who is right?
   (A) A only.
   (B) B only.
   (C) Both A and B.
   (D) Neither A nor B.
6. Technician A says that during automotive starting system operation, electrical current flows from the ignition switch directly to the starting motor. Technician B says a small gear on the starting motor turns a large gear on the engine flywheel. Who is right?
   (A) A only.
   (B) B only.
   (C) Both A and B.
   (D) Neither A nor B.
7. Technician A says an automotive starting motor is normally located at the lower rear of the engine. Technician B says the starter solenoid is always mounted on the starting motor. Who is right?
   (A) A only.
   (B) B only.
   (C) Both A and B.
   (D) Neither A nor B.
8. Technician A says an automotive charging system's voltage regulator usually maintains an alternator output voltage between 15 to 18 volts. Technician B says the automotive charging system provides electricity for all electrical devices when the engine is running. Who is right?
   (A) A only.
   (B) B only.
   (C) Both A and B.
   (D) Neither A nor B.
9. All of the following are basic components in an automotive computer controlled suspension system except:
   (A) shock dampening actuators.
   (B) suspension control computer.
   (C) trigger rotor.
   (D) steering sensor.
10. A car's antilock brake system is malfunctioning. Technician A says this problem could be caused by a faulty hydraulic actuator. Technician B says this problem could be caused by a computer malfunction. Who is right?
    (A) A only.
    (B) B only.
    (C) Both A and B.
    (D) Neither A nor B.

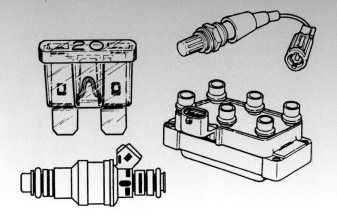

Chapter 2

Electrical Principles

After studying this chapter, you will be able to:
- *Explain the structure of the atom and how it relates to electricity.*
- *Describe the action of a magnetic field.*
- *Summarize how an electric current will produce magnetism.*
- *Define the laws of opposite and like charges.*
- *Explain how a magnetic field can be used to produce electricity.*
- *Describe the components of a simple electric circuit.*
- *Compare Conventional and Electron Theories of current flow.*
- *Define the term "voltage."*
- *Define the term "current."*
- *Define the term "resistance."*
- *Compare DC and AC current.*
- *Compare a simple water circuit with an electric circuit.*

Trying to fix an electronic system of a modern car without knowing the principles of electricity is like trying to "fight a forest fire with a squirt gun." You would NOT be properly equipped to get the job done, and you would get "burned."

By understanding the principles of electricity, you will be much better at problem solving or troubleshooting when working on electrical-electronic systems of a car. By knowing what electricity is and how it functions in nature, you will also have a much better grasp of more complex electronic components covered in later chapters.

This chapter will quickly review the most important aspects of electricity. You will learn about voltage, current, resistance, magnetism, a simple electric circuit, and the fundamental theories of electricity. Study carefully!

OUR ATOMIC STRUCTURE

To fully grasp electricity, you must first have a basic understanding of atoms and the atomic structure of matter.

Matter is a name for everything in the universe that occupies space and has mass (weight). Matter can be a solid, a liquid, or a gas. Only in a complete vacuum would space be void of matter. Basically, the smallest particle in matter is the atom. Look at Fig. 2-1.

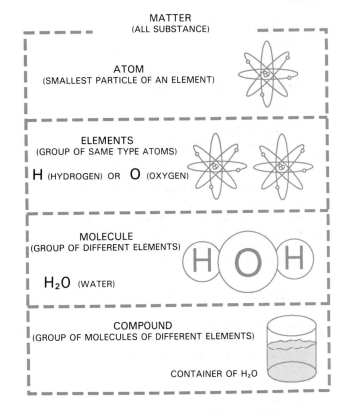

Fig. 2-1. Matter is composed of atoms. Atoms are basically smallest particles in matter and they produce electricity. Note other breakdown of matter.

Parts of matter

The *atom* is the "building block" of nature. Everything around you is made of microscopic particles called atoms. This book, air, the sun, even you are made of atoms. It takes the power of an electron microscope to see atoms.

An *element* is a group of one type of atom. For example, hydrogen is an element and it only contains atoms of hydrogen. There are over 100 elements in nature. They combine to form all types of matter.

A *molecule* is a group of different elements. Water (H_2O) is a molecule because it contains both atoms of hydrogen and atoms of oxygen. Each water molecule has two hydrogen atoms and one oxygen atom, hence H_2O. See Fig. 2-1.

A *compound* is a group of different molecules. A bucket of water would be classified as a compound. It would contain millions of molecules of water and an unimaginable number of atoms.

Parts of an atom

An atom consists of three basic parts:

1. ELECTRON (negatively charged particle that circles around center of atom).
2. PROTON (positively charged particle in the center of the atom).
3. NEUTRON (particle with no positive or negative charge in center of atom).

Fig. 2-2 shows the fundamental relationship of electrons, protons, and neutrons in an atom.

Our solar system can be used to visualize the action of an atom. The sun is the center of our solar system. The planets circle around the sun. Miraculous forces keep the planets spinning and flying at great speed around the sun, Fig. 2-3.

There is a balance of forces in our solar system, just as there is in an atom. Centrifugal force makes the planets or electrons try to fly out from the sun or *nucleus* (center). Natural attraction or gravity, however, has an equal force that keeps the planets or electrons circling in orbit.

Free electrons

Normally, an atom has a balance of forces. The number of electrons circling the center of the atom equal the number of protons. This makes the atom stable. However, it is possible for atoms to have extra electrons in their outer orbits, Fig. 2-4.

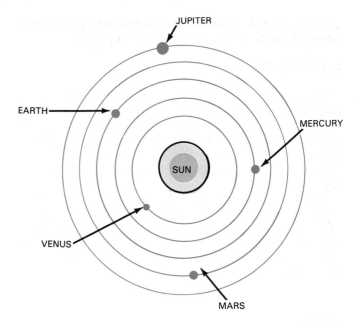

Fig. 2-3. Our solar system uses the same principles found in an atom. Planets circle sun at great speed. Centrifugal force trys to throw planets outward. Natural attraction holds planets in orbit. Unknown force keeps planets spinning and circling sun.

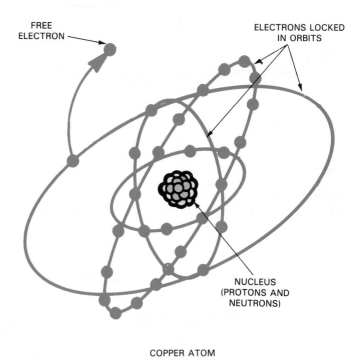

COPPER ATOM

Fig. 2-4. This atom of copper is good conductor of electricity because outer electron is not tightly bonded to atom. It can produce free electron that can move from atom to atom to produce electric current flow. (Chrysler Corporation)

Free electrons is a term referring to the extra electrons in some atoms that produce electricity. For example, air currents in the earth's atmosphere cause friction that can knock electrons free from atoms. This can cause a buildup of *ions* (like charges). With enough buildup of ions in the air, a bolt of lightning can arc through the air

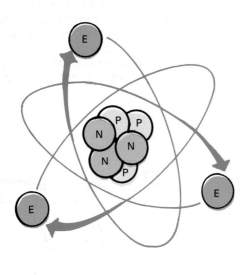

PROTON   NEUTRON   ELECTRON

Fig. 2-2. Nucleus of atom contains positively charged protons and neutrons with no charge. Negatively charged electrons fly around nucleus of atom.

to earth ground. In lightning, you are seeing a tremendous discharge of free electrons (electricity).

ELECTRICITY

Electricity can then be defined as the movement of free electrons from one place to another. Look at Fig. 2-5A.

If you have a *negative charge* (excess electrons) on one end of a wire and a *positive charge* (excess protons) on the other end, electrical flow or *discharge* will result. The electrons will flow through the wire to balance out the atomic forces.

Fig. 2-5B shows the basic principle of electrical flow. Imagine a single row of billiard balls. If you use the cue stick to hit the first pool ball, force will be transmitting through all of the balls and the last ball will fall off the table. This same principle applies to the movement of electrons.

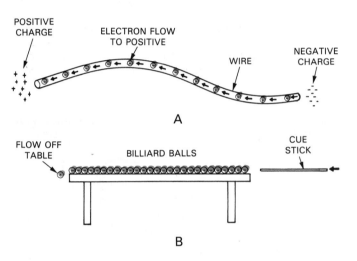

Fig. 2-5. A—If there is a negative charge on one end of wire and positive on other, electrons will try to flow to positive charge. B—Electron flow is like chain reaction of billard balls. When you hit first ball, forces transmit through all balls and last ball flows or falls off table.

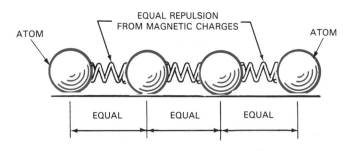

Fig. 2-6. Magnetic forces in atoms set up spring-like action that holds atoms apart. Comparatively, there is actually a large space between atoms. If matter has same charge, repulsion action becomes stronger.

Each atom is suspended in space and has equal repulsion. The magnetic repulsion acts like tiny "electrical springs" that hold the atoms away from each other. If you have several atoms with the same charge, the repulsion will become stronger and atomic forces will try to produce electricity, Fig. 2-6.

If there is enough *potential difference* (difference in positive and negative charges), an electron can enter the orbit in a new atom. This will upset the balance of forces in that atom. As a result, an electron will be forced to jump out of orbit in that atom and enter the orbit in an adjacent atom. This will cause a chain reaction and free electrons will continue to jump from atom to atom, as shown in Fig. 2-7. The result is electrical current flow.

Conductors and insulators

A *conductor* is a substance that allows the flow of free electrons. Wires would be the best example of conductors. They have unstable atoms that allow electrical flow from one point to another. Most metals are good conductors: silver, copper, aluminum, iron, etc.

An *insulator* is a substance that resists or stops the flow of electricy. The atoms in insulators are very stable and they do not allow easy electron movement. For instance, the insulation on wires is designed to prevent electrical flow out of the center conductor of the wire.

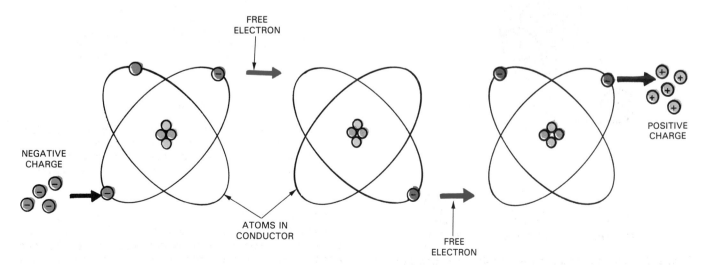

Fig. 2-7. Electricity is movement of free electron from orbit in one atom to orbit in next atom. This can occur very quickly and in vast numbers.

A few insulating substances would be air, glass, plastic, rubber, and porcelain.

Functions of electricity

Electricity or the movement of free electrons has three basic functions—to produce light, heat, and motion. Studied in later chapters, it is also used to produce artificial intelligence or memory using a computer.

For instance, electrons can be sent through a light bulb. The element in the bulb heats up and glows red hot. Some electrons shoot off of the bulb element and we see them as LIGHT reflecting off of other objects.

When free electrons flow through a resistance element (light bulb element for example), an "electrical friction" results. Just as rubbing your hands together produces heat, the electrons rubbing against the atoms in the bulb's resistance element produce HEAT.

Electricity is also used to produce movement of parts. As you will learn, electricity will produce magnetism. The magnetism is used inside electric motors, relays, solenoids, and other electrical devices to cause MOTION and to do work.

MAGNETISM

Before discussing the values of electricity, you should understand magnetism. It plays an important role in the production and use of electrical energy.

Magnetism is an atomic force that can attract or repel through space, air, or solid matter. No one can fully explain magnetism but it is based on how the forces in an atom can be balanced or unbalanced.

You are probably familiar with a permanent magnet. As shown in Fig. 2-8, it has North (positive) and South (negative) poles.

An invisible *magnetic field* or *flux* exists between the

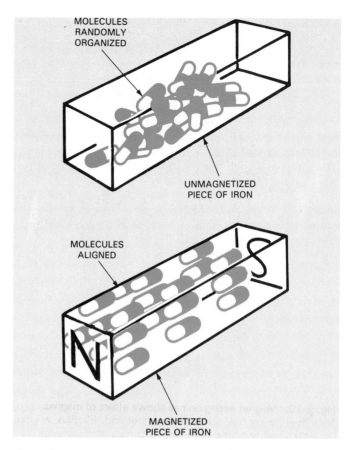

Fig. 2-9. The molecules in a magnet are aligned so that flux or field builds up. (Chrysler Corporation)

poles of a magnet. The magnetic field can be used to act upon *ferrous* (iron) substances. Even though the magnet is NOT in direct contact with the ferrous object, it can affect the other object.

When a piece of iron is magnetized, the molecules in the iron are aligned to produce north and south poles, Fig. 2-9. This makes a magnetic field develop around the magnet.

Fig. 2-10 illustrates how a permanent magnet acts on a piece of metal. Note how the magnetic field surrounds the magnet and the nail (metal). It seems as if the attractive force that holds the atoms of the nail together extend out to hold the nail to the magnet. If iron filings were placed on the tip of the nail, they too would cling to the nail because of the magnetic field.

A magnetic field has little or no effect on non-ferrous substances—plastic, glass, etc.

Like and unlike charges

All of the interaction of atoms, objects, even the planets just discussed are based upon another law of nature. This law states that LIKE charges REPEL and UNLIKE charges ATTRACT.

For example, try to touch the north poles of two magnets together. The two magnets will repel each other. If you push them together on a table top, they will actually slide apart. See Fig. 2-11A.

On the other hand, if you place unlike charges next to each other, they will attract. With a north and south

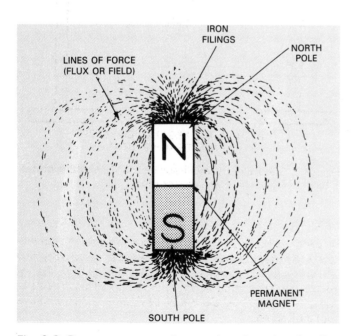

Fig. 2-8. Permanent magnet has north and south poles, like the earth. North pole has positive charge and south negative charge. If you sprinkle iron particles around magnet, you can see action of magnetic field. (Chrysler Corporation)

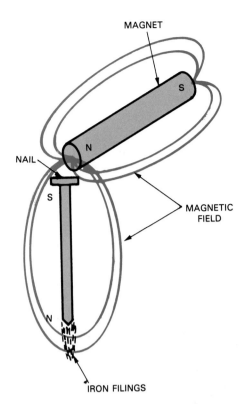

Fig. 2-10. Magnet acting on nail shows effect of magnetic flux. Note how flux or field surrounds magnet and nail. Flux will also make nail temporarily magnetic to hold iron particles.

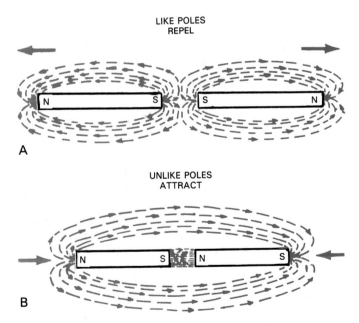

Fig. 2-11. Two bar magnets demonstrate action of like and unlike charges. A—If two like charges are brought together, they will repel each other. B—If two unlike charges are brought together, they will attract each other.

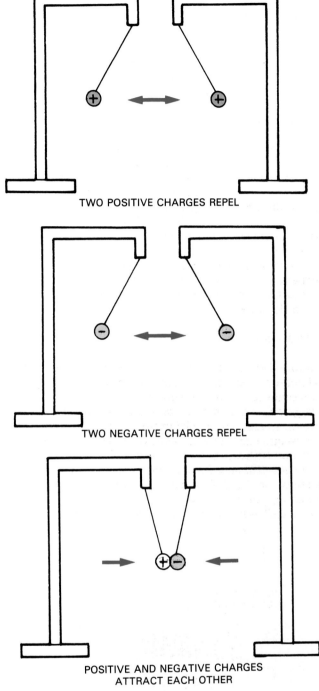

Fig. 2-12. Static charges on plastic balls will also show attraction and repulsion.

pole near each other, the two magnets will be pulled together with considerable force. Look at Fig. 2-11B.

Fig. 2-12 shows another example of the action of like and unlike charges. Two plastic balls are suspended from a string. If the two balls have the same statis charge they will repel and push each other away. If the two balls have different static charges, they will pull together. As you will learn later, this pushing and pulling force can be used in numerous electrical devices—motors, relays, solenoids, etc.

Electromagnetism

Electromagnetism is a branch of physics that deals with the interaction of electricity and magnetism. As you

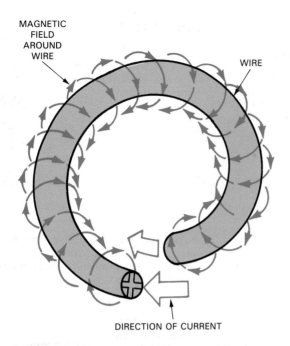

Fig. 2-13. Electric current through a wire sets up a weak magnetic field around the wire. (Sun Electric)

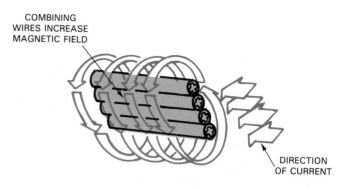

Fig. 2-15. If several current carrying wires are close together, magnetic field around them is strengthened. (Chrysler Corporation)

will learn, electricity can be used to produce magnetism and magnetic fields can be used to produce electricity.

As shown in Fig. 2-13, when electricity flows through a wire, an invisible magnetic field is set up around the wire. The magnetic field is very weak but it can be detected with electronic test equipment.

The flux or magnetic field sets up at right angles to the wire carrying the electric current. If you were to place a piece of cardboard around the wire and then sprinkle iron powder on the cardboard, you could see the effects of this flux. See Fig. 2-14.

If several current carrying wires are placed next to each other, the magnetic field is strengthened. This is illustrated in Fig. 2-15.

An *electromagnet* (electrically energized magnet) can be made by wrapping a wire around a piece of metal. The magnetic field or flux will be concentrated enough that the coil of wire will act as a strong magnet, Fig. 2-16. This principle, also covered in later chapters, is used in numerous electrical devices.

Induced electricity

Induced electricity, also called *induction,* results when a wire carrying electricity produces an electrical current in another wire. The magnetic flux around the current carrying wire induces a tiny electrical current in the second wire, Fig. 2-17.

Current can also be induced by passing a wire through a magnetic field. The flux will act upon the free electrons in the wire to produce electricity.

Studied later, the principle of electrical induction is used in alternators, meters, and other electrical-electronic components.

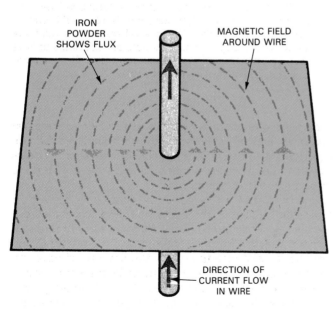

Fig. 2-14. Piece of cardboard around wire will show magnetic field produced by current. Sprinkle iron powder on cardboard and powder will align like field. (General Motors)

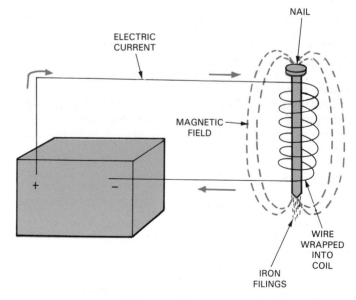

Fig. 2-16. Electromagnet can be made by wrapping wire around iron core. Current through wire will produce powerful magnetic field.

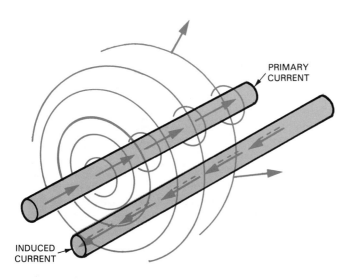

Fig. 2-17. Electric current can be induced in a wire by moving it through the magnetic field of a current carrying wire. Electrical induction can also be done by moving wire through flux of permanent magnet. (Ford Motor Co.)

SIMPLE ELECTRIC CIRCUIT

Now that you understand something about electrical principles, you are ready to review a basic electrical circuit.

A *simple electric circuit* consists of the basic components needed to utilize electrical energy. These components would include:
1. POWER SUPPLY (source of electrical energy—a battery for example).
2. CONDUCTOR (substance that will carry electrical current from power supply to load and from load back to the source—wires for example).
3. LOAD (a resistance device that will use the electrical energy—a light bulb or an electric motor for instance).

Fig. 2-18 shows a simple electric circuit. The battery (power supply) feeds electrical current into the wire (conductor). Electricity flows through the wire and light bulb element. The bulb element glows red hot and emits light. The light is the purpose for this circuit example. Electrical current returns to the battery negative through the return conductor.

Explained later, this simple circuit can be expanded to make much more complex electrical-electronic circuits. However, they all operate on the principles just discussed.

ELECTRICAL VALUES

In our previous coverage of electricity, we described electrical flow in general. However, there are three fundamental values that refer to the properties of electricity and a simple electrical circuit. These are:
1. VOLTAGE (electrical pressure).
2. CURRENT (electron flow).
3. RESISTANCE (opposition to current flow).

A water circuit can be used to introduce these electrical values. Look at Fig. 2-19.

Imagine two containers connected with a piece of

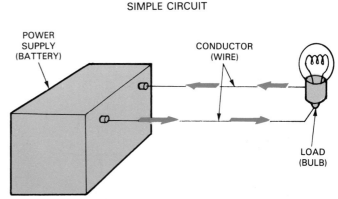

Fig. 2-18. Simple or basic electric circuit requires these basic parts. Battery or power source feeds current into circuit. Conductors carry electrons to and from load. Load utilizes electrical energy.

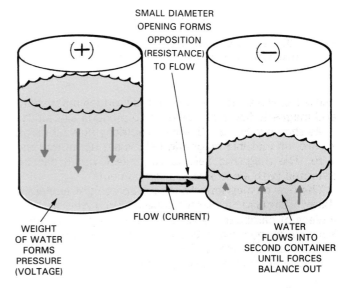

Fig. 2-19. Two containers connected by tubing will demonstrate electrical action. If left container is filled with water, water pressure or potential difference will result. This will force flow or current through tube. Tube acts as resistance to limit flow. Flow or current will stop when potential difference and water levels are same.

tubing. Fill one container with water and leave the other container empty. Water will flow through the tube and equalize the amount in the second container. This is similar to the electrical action of charges in atoms trying to balance out in a circuit.

The weight of the water in the first container would represent voltage or the pressure trying to balance out the forces. The flow through the tube would represent current or flow. The small diameter of the tubing would represent resistance to control the amount of flow. An electrical circuit can be thought of in the same way.

Another example is given in Fig. 2-20. A house garden hose shows the principles of voltage (water pressure), current (water flow), and resistance (water valve restriction).

A hydraulic circuit can also be used to demonstrate

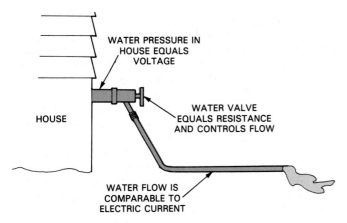

Fig. 2-20. Garden hose on house will also demonstrate electrical circuit principles. Water pressure would equal voltage and would produce current or flow. Water valve would equal resistance and would control flow. Higher voltage or pressure and lower resistance would increase current flow and vice versa.

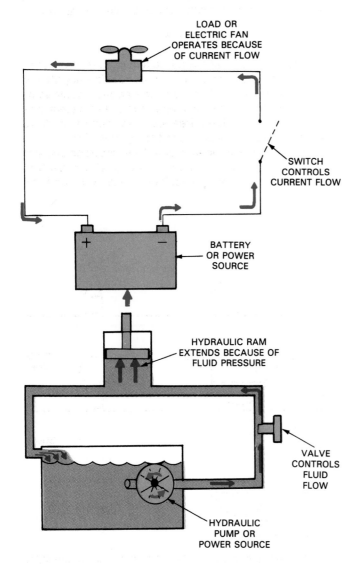

Fig. 2-21. Hydraulic circuit compared to electrical circuit. Hydraulic pump would be comparable to battery or power source. Switch would be equal to flow control valve. Load or motor and hydraulic ram would be purpose for circuits.

the action in an electrical circuit, Fig. 2-21. A hydraulic pump would be comparable to the battery or electrical power source. It produces the pressure for circuit operation.

The hydraulic hoses would equal the conductors or wires in the circuit. They allow flow between the power source and load device.

In the hydraulic circuit, a hydraulic ram would represent the load device and would be comparable to an electrical load (electric motor in this example), Fig. 2-21.

The control valve would be comparable to an electric switch. They both control flow through their circuits. If the valve (switch) is closed, it will stop flow and the circuit will NOT function.

Voltage (volts)

Voltage is the electrical force or pressure that pushes free electrons and causes current flow. Voltage can be abbreviated with the word volt and the letters V or E.

A HIGHER VOLTAGE will tend to increase current flow. A LOWER VOLTAGE will reduce current flow.

For example, if water pressure is higher, more water will squirt out of a garden hose, Fig. 2-20. In an electrical circuit, if the voltage applied is higher, more free electrons will flow through the circuit.

If a light bulb is in the circuit, higher voltage will force more electrons through the bulb element. The bulb will glow more brightly. If voltage applied is lower, the bulb will NOT glow as brightly. This applies to other circuits and loads as well.

Electromotive force, abbreviated EMF, is another name for voltage. It refers to how voltage has the power or force to cause electron movement through a conductor.

Current (amperage)

Current or *amperage* is the flow of electrons past a given point in a circuit. Abbreviated amps, I, or A, it is the result of voltage in a complete circuit.

Just as you can measure water flow out of garden hose into a bucket, you can measure electrical current in amps. Current flow will be HIGH if resistance is LOW or voltage is HIGH. Current will be REDUCED by HIGH resistance or a LOW supply voltage.

Electric current moves very quickly. It has been measured in scientific experiments and approaches the speed of light or 186,000 miles per second (300 000 kilometers per second). This is why electrical-electronic devices can sense and control automotive systems so effectively. They can react or send signals at almost the speed of light.

For current to flow, there must be an electrical power source, a complete conducting path, and a load. If the path or circuit is NOT *complete* (connected), current will NOT flow. If the power source or load is disconnected, this will also prevent current.

Resistance (Ohms)

Resistance is the opposition to free electron flow and it limits or controls current flow. Also called *Ohms* and abbreviated R or Ω, resistance is designed into all electrical circuits. The load (a light bulb for example) has an internal resistance that uses the energy of the current or electron flow.

Resistance would be comparable to the water valve on a garden hose. If the valve is opened fully, resistance would be low and flow would be high. If you partially shut the water valve, resistance would be higher and current would drop off. If you completely close the water valve, resistance would be MAXIMUM (infinite) and current flow would be completely stopped.

Note! Voltage, current, and resistance will be further discussed in the next chapter of this book.

Conventional and Electron Theories

There are two theories of how current flows through a circuit: Conventional Theory and Electron Theory.

The *Conventional Theory* says that electrons flow through a circuit from positive (+) to negative (−). Electrons leave the battery positive terminal. They flow through the circuit and then re-enter the battery negative terminal. This is the theory used in automotive electronics so that current leaves battery positive and then enters the circuit. See Fig. 2-22.

The *Electron Theory* says that electrons leave the negative (−) of the battery, flow through the circuit, and then re-enter the positive (+) terminal. The Electron Theory is just the opposite of the Conventional Theory. It is used in other fields of study, Fig. 2-22.

Actually, the Electron Theory is probably the most accurate. Electrons would naturally be attracted to the positive. However, it is more convenient to use the Conventional in automotives.

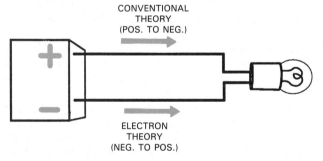

Fig. 2-22. Conventional Theory says current flows from positive to negative. Electron Theory is just the opposite.

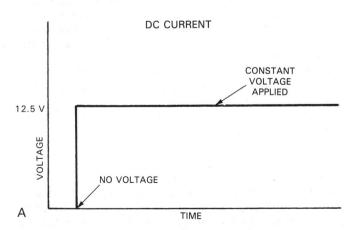

Fig. 2-23. Direct current only flows in one direction. Graph shows how voltage and direction stay the same.

DC and AC current

Direct current, abbreviated DC, is current flow in only one direction. As discussed previously, automotive circuits are primarily DC. Current flows smoothly through a circuit in only one direction from positive to negative (Conventional Theory). Look at Fig. 2-23.

Alternating current, abbreviated AC, flows in one direction, reverses, and then flows in the opposite direction. Its polarity cycles back and forth in the circuit. Most automotive circuits do NOT use AC current. However, as you will learn in later chapters, a charging system alternator has an internal AC current that is *rectified* (changed back into DC) before leaving the alternator. Some computer system sensors also produce an AC output.

Fig. 2-24 illustrates the action of AC. A *sine wave* is used to represent the action of the AC reversing current flow. Note how the curve goes up for flow in one direction and slopes down for the opposite direction.

In your home wiring, AC current cycles at 60 Hz (60 cycles per second). This is fast enough that it cannot be seen with the human eye. A lightbulb appears to be glowing constantly when it is actually turning on and off at 60 Hz.

SUMMARY

The atom is the smallest particle in matter. It is made up of electrons, protons, and neutrons. The negatively charged electrons circle around the center, nucleus of the atom. Some substances have free or extra electrons in their outer orbit. These free electrons can be made to move from atom to atom, producing electricity.

A conductor is a substance with free electrons and will allow electrical flow. An insulator does NOT have free electrons. The electrons are locked in their orbits and this resists electrical flow.

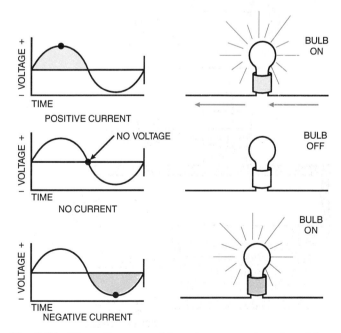

Fig. 2-24. Alternating current is not common in automobiles but is used in residential or home electrical systems. AC changes direction so quickly that it is not visible in a lightbulb with human eye. As you will learn in later chapters, some engine sensors produce an alternating type output.

A permanent magnet has an invisible magnetic field around it. This field will act upon ferrous objects.

Unlike charges (polarities) will attract each other. Like charges will repel each other. This principle is used to produce current flow, motion, and other functions.

An electromagnet can be made by wrapping wire around an iron core. Current flow through the wire will produce a magnetic field.

Current can be induced in a wire by passing the wire through a magnetic field. The field can be produced by a magnet or current-carrying wires.

A simple electric circuit consists of a power supply (battery), conductor (wires), and load (power using device).

Voltage is the pressure that moves free electrons through a conductor.

Current is the flow of free electrons past a given point. A high voltage or low resistance will increase current flow.

Resistance or ohms is the opposition to current flow. It is needed to limit current. The load device provides normal resistance to control current. High resistance reduces current and low resistance increases current.

An automobile electrical system primarily operates on direct or DC current that only flows in one direction. Alternating or AC current flows one way and then the other. It is found inside a charging system alternator and in the wiring to some sensors.

KNOW THESE TERMS

Matter, Atom, Element, Molecule, Compound, Electron, Proton, Neutron, Nucleus, Free electron, Electricity, Negative charge, Positive charge, Discharge, Potential difference, Conductor, Insulator, Magnetism, Magnetic field, Flux, Ferrous, Electromagnetism, Induction, Simple circuit, Power supply, Load, Voltage, Current, Resistance, Conventional Theory, Electron Theory, DC, AC, Sine wave.

REVIEW QUESTIONS—CHAPTER 2

1. Define the term "electricity."
2. A _____ is a substance that allows the flow of free electrons.
3. An _____ is a substance that resists or stops the flow of free electrons.
4. What are four functions of electricity.
5. Magnetism is an atomic force that can _____ or _____ through space, air, or solid matter.
6. Like charges attract and unlike charges repel. True or false?
7. Another name for a magnetic field is _____.
8. What is induction?
9. Explain the parts and action of a basic electric circuit.
10. Define the term "voltage."
11. Define the term "current."
12. Define the term "resistance."
13. If voltage increases, current flow will decrease. True or false?
14. If current increases, resistance would have been lowered or voltage increased. True or false?
15. Explain the difference between direct current and alternating current.

ASE CERTIFICATION–TYPE QUESTIONS

1. While discussing the theories of matter, Technician A says water is an atom. Technician B says hydrogen is a molecule. Who is right?
   - (A) A only.
   - (B) B only.
   - (C) Both A and B.
   - (D) Neither A nor B.
2. An atom consists of all of the following parts *except*:
   - (A) electrons.
   - (B) neutrons.
   - (C) molecules.
   - (D) protons.
3. Technician A says electricity is the movement of free atoms from one place to another. Technician B says electricity is the movement of free molecules from one place to another. Who is right?
   - (A) A only.
   - (B) B only.
   - (C) Both A and B.
   - (D) Neither A nor B.
4. Technician A says silver is a good electrical conductor. Technician B says iron is a good electrical conductor. Who is right?
   - (A) A only.
   - (B) B only.
   - (C) Both A and B.
   - (D) Neither A nor B.
5. Technician A says an insulator is a substance that resists the flow of electricity. Technician B says the atoms in an insulator are very stable and resist electron movement. Who is right?
   - (A) A only.
   - (B) B only.
   - (C) Both A and B.
   - (D) Neither A nor B.
6. Technician A says a load is a basic component of an electric circuit. Technician B says a "power supply" is a basic component of an electric circuit. Who is right?
   - (A) A only.
   - (B) B only.
   - (C) Both A and B.
   - (D) Neither A nor B.
7. The electrical pressure that causes current flow is known as:
   - (A) voltage.
   - (B) current.
   - (C) resistance.
   - (D) power.
8. Technician A says that as voltage increases, current flow increases. Technician B says that as voltage decreases, the number of free electrons flowing through a circuit decreases. Who is right?
   - (A) A only.
   - (B) B only.
   - (C) Both A and B.
   - (D) Neither A nor B.
9. Technician A says the Electron Theory of current flow states that electrons flow through a circuit from positive to negative. Technician B says the Conventional Theory of current flow states that electrons flow through a circuit from negative to positive. Who is right?
   - (A) A only.
   - (B) B only.
   - (C) Both A and B.
   - (D) Neither A nor B.
10. Technician A says DC voltage is not normally used in automotive circuits. Technician B says certain automotive computer sensors produce AC voltage. Who is right?
    - (A) A only.
    - (B) B only.
    - (C) Both A and B.
    - (D) Neither A nor B.

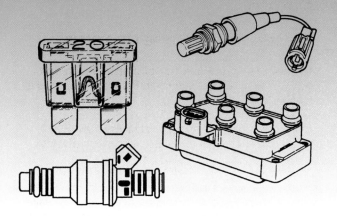

Chapter 3

Electrical Circuits, Ohm's Law

After studying this chapter, you will be able to:
* Draw a series circuit.
* Draw a parallel circuit.
* Draw a series-parallel circuit.
* Explain the operating characteristics of series and parallel circuits.
* Describe a frame ground or one-wire circuit.
* Recall Ohm's Law.
* Summarize the effects of voltage and resistance on current.
* Calculate an unknown circuit value using Ohm's Law.
* List the rules of series and parallel circuits as related to Ohm's Law.
* Recognize typical electrical-electronic symbols.

This chapter will continue your study of automotive electricity and electronics by detailing the arrangement and action of basic electrical circuits. As you will learn, even complex automotive circuits, which contain dozens of wires and components, simply consist of many basic circuits that are connected together. If you break a complex circuit down into its fundamental parts, it will be easy to analyze how the circuit should operate.

This chapter will start out by reviewing basic circuit types and how they function. The last half of the chapter discusses Ohm's Law. Even though the automotive technician does not frequently use Ohm's Law to make calculations, this law must be understood. It will help you tremendously when trying to troubleshoot circuit problems.

For example, if current is too high or low, you will automatically know what kind of problem might exist in the circuit by using the rules of Ohm's Law.

Note! Study this chapter carefully. It will prepare you to more fully comprehend later chapters in this textbook.

SERIES CIRCUIT

A *series circuit* has only one path for current flow. All of the current must flow through this path, or *leg*. One or more electrical *loads* (components) are wired into this single path. See Fig. 3-1.

Fig. 3-2 shows the basic action of a series circuit. If a switch is connected in series with three light bulbs, it will control all three bulbs. If the switch is *closed* (connected), the bulbs will operate. If the switch is *open*

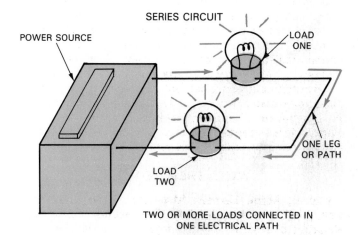

Fig. 3-1. Simple series circuits have one or more loads connected in single electrical path.

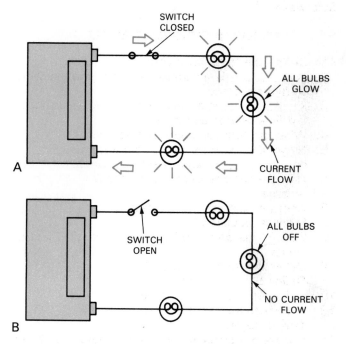

Fig. 3-2. Switch is wired in series with three light bulbs. A—Switch closed and all three bulbs glow. B—Switch open, and since in series, it blocks current flow to bulbs.

SERIES CHRISTMAS TREE LIGHTS

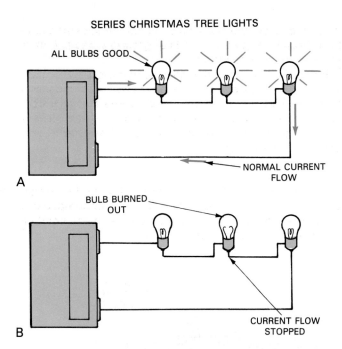

Fig. 3-3. Inexpensive Christmas tree lights can be wired in series. If one bulb burns out, all bulbs go out. A—Bulbs good. B—One bulb burned out.

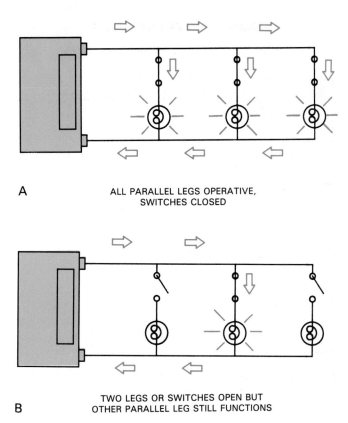

Fig. 3-5. In these circuits, switches and bulbs are parallel to each other. A—All switches are closed and all bulbs glow. B—Two switches are open to stop flow in their legs. However, since other leg is parallel and its switch is closed, bulb can still function.

(disconnected), all three bulbs will go out.

An inexpensive set of Christmas tree lights wired in series illustrates this fact. As shown in Fig. 3-3, if one of the series bulbs burns out, all other Christmas tree lights will go out. The burned element in the bulb would act as an open switch to stop current flow.

PARALLEL CIRCUIT

A *parallel circuit* has more than one path or leg for current flow. Illustrated in Fig. 3-4, two or more loads would require two separate circuits wired together.

Fig. 3-5 shows the basic operation of a parallel circuit. In A, the parallel legs are complete and all three function. In B, two of the switches are opened but the other

leg still operates. With the legs wired parallel, they can still function independently.

Again, Christmas tree lights wired in parallel demonstrate this principle, Fig. 3-6. If one light bulb burns out, it will not affect the operation of the other bulbs. For this reason, quality Christmas tree lights are wired parallel.

SERIES-PARALLEL CIRCUIT

A *series-parallel circuit* is a combination series circuit and parallel circuit. Some of the components are wired in series and others are in parallel, Fig. 3-7.

In Fig. 3-7A, the switch is closed and all light bulbs are glowing. Then, in Fig. 3-7B, the switch is opened. This *breaks* (opens) the circuit to two of the legs because the switch is in series with these legs. However, it does not stop the operation of the first leg because that leg is wired parallel.

In automotive circuits, a combination of these circuits is used to produce very complex networks. However, if you grasp these three basic circuits, you can troubleshoot any circuit by breaking it down into simpler, basic circuits like the ones just illustrated.

FRAME-GROUND CIRCUIT

A *frame-ground circuit,* also called a *one-wire circuit,* uses the metal structure of the car to return current to

PARALLEL CIRCUIT

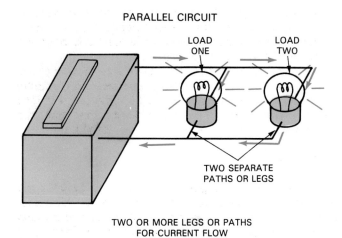

Fig. 3-4. Parallel circuit has more than one path for current flow. Two bulbs are wired parallel.

PARALLEL CHRISTMAS TREE LIGHTS

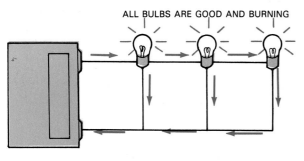

ALL BULBS ARE GOOD AND BURNING

OTHER PARALLEL BULBS STILL OPERATE

ONE BULB BURNED OUT

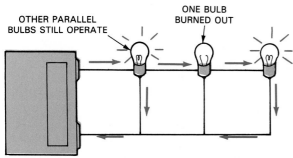

Fig. 3-6. Christmas tree lights in parallel will function even though bulbs burn out. There is still complete path around burned bulb.

SERIES-PARALLEL CIRCUIT

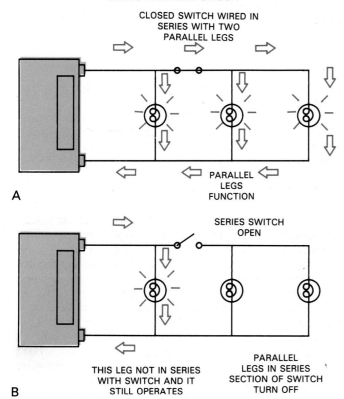

CLOSED SWITCH WIRED IN SERIES WITH TWO PARALLEL LEGS

PARALLEL LEGS FUNCTION

A

SERIES SWITCH OPEN

THIS LEG NOT IN SERIES WITH SWITCH AND IT STILL OPERATES

PARALLEL LEGS IN SERIES SECTION OF SWITCH TURN OFF

B

Fig. 3-7. Series-parallel circuit is combination series circuit and parallel circuit. In this example, bulbs are wired in parallel to each other. Switch is wired in series with two of the bulbs. A—Switch is closed and all legs receive current. B—Switch is open and current is blocked to two legs. However, since first leg is parallel to switch, it will work.

the *source* (car battery). This prevents the auto manufacturer from having to run yards of ground wire back from the electrical components.

Fig. 3-8 shows the principle of a frame-ground circuit. The negative battery cable is bolted to the car chassis or frame. This makes the car chassis serve as a large conductor to carry current. Current flows out the battery positive, to the load, into ground, through the frame, and back into the battery.

Hot and ground legs

The *hot leg,* also termed *hot wire,* refers to the section of the circuit that carries current to a load or component. It includes the part of the circuit between the positive source and the load. See Fig. 3-8.

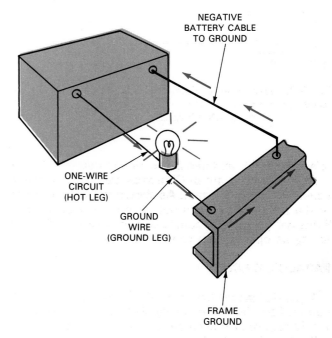

NEGATIVE BATTERY CABLE TO GROUND

ONE-WIRE CIRCUIT (HOT LEG)

GROUND WIRE (GROUND LEG)

FRAME GROUND

Fig. 3-8. Frame-ground circuit uses metal structure of car to complete ground side of circuit.

The *ground leg,* also called *ground wire,* is the section of the circuit after the load or electrical device, Fig. 3-9. It includes the circuit between the load and negative terminal of the battery or ground.

The term hot wire is used because this section of the circuit will activate a test light, produce an electrical short, etc. The ground side will NOT activate a test light because current will flow into ground rather than into a test light. This will be explained in detail later.

OHM'S LAW

Ohm's Law is a simple formula used to express the relationship between voltage, current, and resistance. Although you may not make many electrical calculations when on the job, you must comprehend this formula. It is invaluable when trying to diagnose electrical circuits because it will let you visualize possible problems more easily, Fig. 3-10.

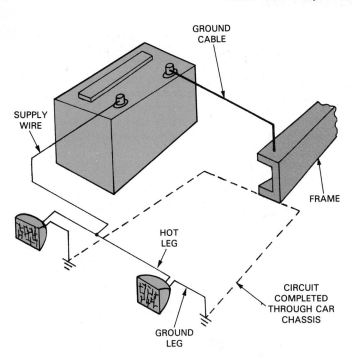

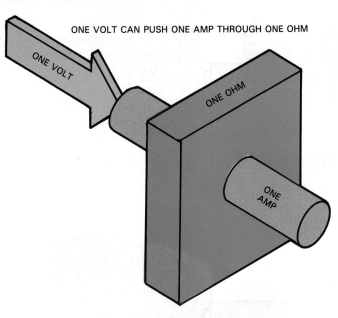

Fig. 3-11. Illustration shows how it takes one volt to push one amp through one ohm of resistance. This is why math can be used to calculate unknown value when two values are known.

Fig. 3-9. One-wire or frame-ground has battery connected to frame of car. Ground side of electrical component is also connected to frame or body structure of car. Current can then flow through metal parts of car and back to battery.

Change in circuit resistance

A change in circuit resistance will change current flow in a circuit. For instance, look at Fig. 3-12. If resistance is low, current will be high. If resistance is high, current will be low.

In auto electronics, most electrical problems are caused by a change in circuit resistance. A poor electrical connection, for example, will reduce current flow in the circuit. This might cause a light bulb to burn dimly (low current flow), or upset a signal from a computer system sensor.

For example, if a circuit has 12 V applied and a resistance of three ohms, Ohm's Law will let you calculate a current flow of four amps. However, if

Ohm's Law states three basic formulas:
1. Voltage equals current times resistance.

     volts = amps × ohms
2. Current equals voltage divided by resistance.

     amps = volts ÷ ohms
3. Resistance equals voltage divided by current.

     ohms = volts ÷ amps

As these formulas show, volts, amps, and resistance all interact to affect the operation of a circuit. Illustrated in Fig. 3-11, voltage pushes current through a resistance. If any one value changes, it will affect one or more of the others.

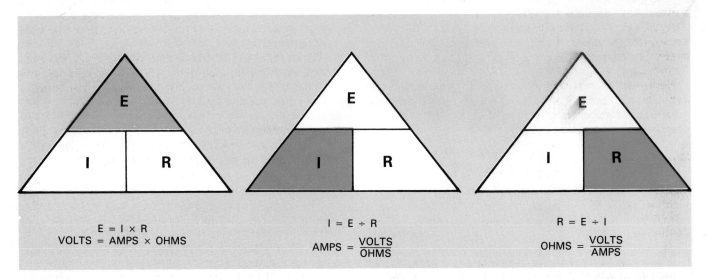

Fig. 3-10. Simple triangle diagram will help you remember Ohm's Law formulas. I and R are next to each other and would have to be multiplied to find E. E is over R and would have to be divided to find I. E is also over I and would have to be divided to find R.

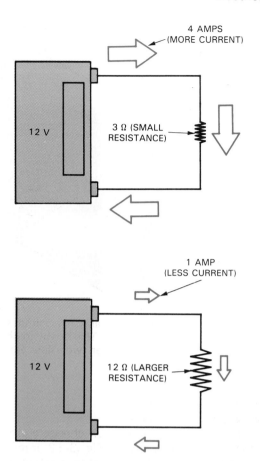

Fig. 3-12. Note how circuit with large resistance has less current than circuit with small resistance. More free electrons can flow through small resistance.

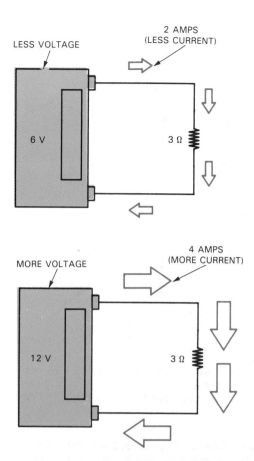

Fig. 3-13. In these circuits, different voltage values are connected to same resistance value. Note how current is higher with more electrical pressure or voltage.

resistance increases because of a bad connection to 12 ohms, current will drop to only one amp. See Fig. 3-12.

Change in circuit voltage

A change in circuit voltage will change current flow. Illustrated in Fig. 3-13, a higher voltage will increase current flow. A drop in voltage will decrease current.

Again, Ohm's Law and a simple circuit will demonstrate this principle. In Fig. 3-13A, an older six-volt battery is connected to a circuit with three ohms. Using Ohm's Law, you can find a current flow of two amps.

However, if a twelve-volt battery is connected to the same circuit, current will increase. Using Ohm's Law, current equals volts divided by ohms. Current would increase to four amps because the voltage applied doubled.

Change in circuit current

Any change in a circuit's current flow is a result of increased or decreased voltage or resistance. Current flow is dependent upon these two factors in a circuit.

If insufficient current flows in a circuit, the electrical or electronic components will not function properly. An electric motor might run too slowly or a bulb burn dimly. If two much current flows in a circuit, components or wires can overheat or burn up. As mentioned, a change in circuit resistance is the most common cause of circuit troubles.

Fig. 3-14 gives a chart summarizing how voltage and resistance alter current.

Series circuit rules

There are several rules that apply to a series circuit:
1. Current or amperage is the same everywhere in a series circuit. If you were to connect an ammeter to any point in a series circuit, your readings would be the same.
2. Total resistance, abbreviated R_t, is simply the sum of each resistance unit. Simply add all of the resistance values to get total resistance. The formula for total resistance in a series circuit is:
$$R_t = R_1 + R_2 + R_3.$$
3. The voltage drop across each resistance unit equals the voltage applied. If you measure how much voltage is used by all resistance elements, it will equal the supply voltage.

Fig. 3-15 shows a basic series circuit. Note how you would add the two resistances to get total resistance for the circuit. Then, the total resistance can be used with Ohm's Law to find current.

Fig. 3-16 shows another example of a series circuit. It has four resistance units in series. If you add them up, you get an R_t of 12 ohms. To get current, divide volts by ohms (12 divided by 12) and you get a current flow of one amp.

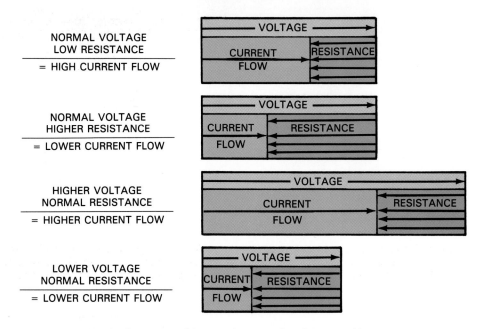

NORMAL VOLTAGE
LOW RESISTANCE
= HIGH CURRENT FLOW

NORMAL VOLTAGE
HIGHER RESISTANCE
= LOWER CURRENT FLOW

HIGHER VOLTAGE
NORMAL RESISTANCE
= HIGHER CURRENT FLOW

LOWER VOLTAGE
NORMAL RESISTANCE
= LOWER CURRENT FLOW

Fig. 3-14. Summary of how voltage and resistance affect current.

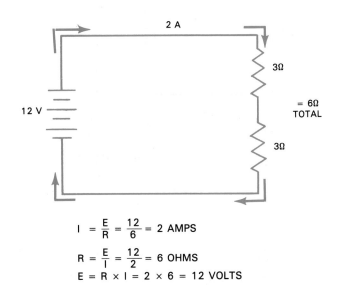

$$I = \frac{E}{R} = \frac{12}{6} = 2 \text{ AMPS}$$

$$R = \frac{E}{I} = \frac{12}{2} = 6 \text{ OHMS}$$

$$E = R \times I = 2 \times 6 = 12 \text{ VOLTS}$$

Fig. 3-15. In a series circuit, simply add up ohms values to get total resistance. Then, total resistance can be used to find current flow.

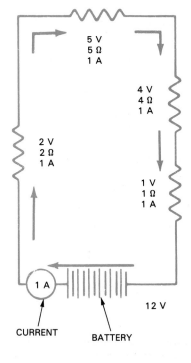

E_t = 12 VOLTS
R_t = 12 OHMS
I_t = 1 AMP

Fig. 3-16. Use Ohm's Law to check resistance and current in this series circuit. Add all resistance values to get R_t. Then, divide voltage by resistance to get amps.

Parallel circuit rules

As was described for series circuit, parallel circuits also have several rules that should be understood. These rules include:

1. Total current, abbreviated I_t or A_t, is the sum of all branch currents. If you have three branches carrying two amps each, then total circuit current would be six amps.
2. Total circuit resistance is LESS than any one branch. If you have two branches with four ohms each, the total resistance for the circuit would be two ohms.
3. Voltage applied to each branch is the same. If branches are parallel, they will receive the same supply voltage.

Fig. 3-17 illustrates how resistance controls current

in a parallel circuit. Note how current is lowest in the branches with the highest resistance. Also, total current would equal the sum of the currents in each leg.

This also shows the basic rule that CURRENT FOLLOWS THE PATH OF LEAST RESISTANCE! If one leg has a very low resistance, current can easily flow

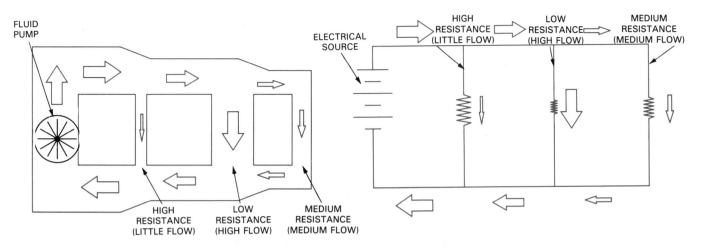

Fig. 3-17. Parallel circuit operation is more complex than series circuit. Note how hydraulic circuit can be used to show action of parallel legs with different resistance values. A high resistance would be comparable to a small hydraulic hose that allowed little flow. A low resistance would be comparable to a large hose that allowed more flow.

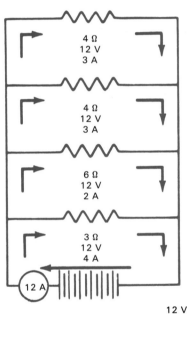

$$E_t = 12 \text{ V}$$
$$R_t = 1 \text{ }\Omega$$
$$I_t = 12 \text{ A}$$

Fig. 3-18. This parallel circuit shows how current is higher in low resistance legs. Also note how total resistance is lower than any one leg.

through that branch to reach ground.

Fig. 3-18 shows another parallel circuit. Note how the legs with the lower resistances allow more current flow and vice versa.

The formula for total resistance in a parallel circuit is:

$$R_t = \frac{R_1 \times R_2}{R_1 + R_2}$$

Fig. 3-19 shows the use of this formula with a parallel circuit. To find total circuit resistance, simply plug the circuit values into the formula. Multiply, add, and then divide them to arrive at R_t for a parallel circuit.

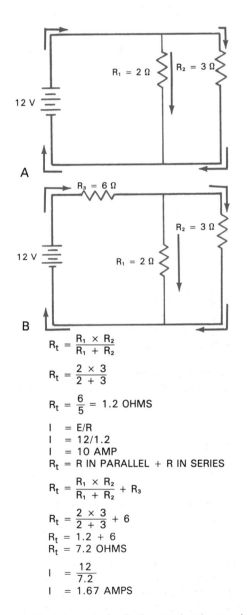

$$R_t = \frac{R_1 \times R_2}{R_1 + R_2}$$

$$R_t = \frac{2 \times 3}{2 + 3}$$

$$R_t = \frac{6}{5} = 1.2 \text{ OHMS}$$

$$I = E/R$$
$$I = 12/1.2$$
$$I = 10 \text{ AMP}$$
$$R_t = R \text{ IN PARALLEL } + R \text{ IN SERIES}$$

$$R_t = \frac{R_1 \times R_2}{R_1 + R_2} + R_3$$

$$R_t = \frac{2 \times 3}{2 + 3} + 6$$
$$R_t = 1.2 + 6$$
$$R_t = 7.2 \text{ OHMS}$$

$$I = \frac{12}{7.2}$$
$$I = 1.67 \text{ AMPS}$$

Fig. 3-19. Study formula for finding total resistance in a parallel circuit. Simply plug in values, multiply, add, and then divide. R_t can then be used to calculate I_t.

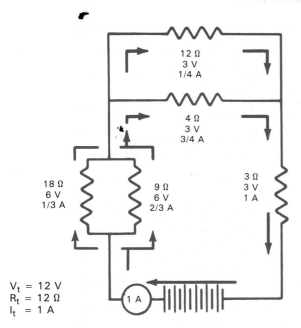

$V_t = 12\ V$
$R_t = 12\ \Omega$
$I_t = 1\ A$

Fig. 3-20. Here is series-parallel circuit. It is handled by working with each parallel and series section separately to arrive at R_t and I_t.

An even more complex series-parallel circuit is given in Fig. 3-20. When working with a series-parallel circuit, simply start out by working with the parallel sections of the circuit to arrive at R_t. Then add any series resistance to this value.

PREFIXES

Prefixes are used to quickly denote a multiplier or exponent of a value. They are used to give very large or very small electrical values. Fig. 3-21 gives a chart with common prefixes.

In automotives, current values in electronic circuits can be very small. In this case, a "milli" prefix might be used to show a tiny current draw—a milliamp would equal .001 (1×10^{-3}) amp.

Resistance values, of spark plug wire for instance, can be very large. In this case, resistance might be given in kilohms—a kilohm would equal 1,000 (1×10^{3}) ohms.

Also note the symbols or letters given in Fig. 3-21. They are sometimes used to denote a multiplier or exponent of an electrical-electronic value. A few examples include:

MULTIPLIER	EXPONENT FORM	PREFIX	SYMBOL
1 000 000 000 000	10^{12}	tera	T
1 000 000 000	10^{9}	giga	G
1 000 000	10^{6}	mega	M
1 000	10^{3}	kilo	k
10	10^{1}	deka	da
0.1	10^{-1}	deci	d
0.01	10^{-2}	centi	c
0.001	10^{-3}	milli	m
0.000 001	10^{-6}	micro	u
0.000 000 001	10^{-9}	nano	n
0.000 000 000 001	10^{-12}	pico	p

Fig. 3-21. Study values for each prefix. They are used to represent large or small electrical values.

1. 5 MΩ would equal 5,000,000 ohms. Pronounce it 5 megaohm.
2. 10 kΩ would equal 10,000 ohms. Pronounce it 10 kilohm.
3. 32 ma would equal .032 amp. Pronounce it 32 milliamp.
4. 12 uF would equal .000012 farad. Pronounce it 12 microfarad.

These symbols and exponents can sometimes be found in service manuals. Electronic specifications can be given in prefix form so you should memorize them, especially mega, kilo, milli, and micro. They are the most commonly used exponents found in automotive electronics.

ELECTRICAL POWER (WATT)

Electrical power is the work done by an electrical current, and its unit of measurement is the *watt.* Power equals voltage times current or it equals current squared times resistance.

The formulas for power (watts) are written:

$$P = E \times I$$
or
$$P = I^2 \times R$$

The watt is sometimes used in automotive electronics. Light bulbs, especially headlight bulbs, can have a watt rating. Car batteries, as studied in later chapters, can also have a watt rating to indicate their power potential.

ELECTRICAL-ELECTRONIC SYMBOLS

Electrical symbols and *electronic symbols* are used on wiring diagrams to denote circuit components and wiring connections. *Wiring diagrams* serve as "electrical road maps" that show how all wires connect to the components in a circuit. Symbols are used on wiring diagrams to save space and to simplify reading wiring diagrams.

Fig. 3-22 gives some of the most common symbols used in automotive wiring diagrams. Study them carefully. If you are to become a component technician, you must be able to recognize these symbols on sight.

An example of how an electrical circuit is drawn or converted into a wiring diagram is shown in Fig. 3-23. Note how the symbols are used in the diagram to replace the isometric drawing of the battery, fuse, switch, motor, and light bulb. It is much easier to look at the diagram and understand the relationship of the electrical components in the circuit. This is even more true with super-complex automotive electronic circuits.

Note! Electrical and electronic symbols are discussed further in following chapters. They are explained in Chapter 4 on electrical components, Chapter 5 on electronic components, and Chapter 6 on wiring diagrams.

Note that the symbols and diagrams themselves can vary in different service manuals. You should study different types to prepare for their use.

SUMMARY

A series circuit has one or more loads connected in the same path or leg. A parallel circuit has two separate paths or legs for current flow—one leg can operate independently

+	POSITIVE	⇉	CONNECTOR
−	NEGATIVE	→	MALE CONNECTOR
⏚	GROUND	⟩	FEMALE CONNECTOR
FUSE	FUSE	MULTIPLE CONNECTOR	MULTIPLE CONNECTOR
CIRCUIT BREAKER	CIRCUIT BREAKER	DENOTES WIRE CONTINUES ELSEWHERE	DENOTES WIRE CONTINUES ELSEWHERE
CAPACITOR	CAPACITOR	SPLICE	SPLICE
Ω	OHMS	SPLICE IDENTIFICATION	SPLICE IDENTIFICATION
RESISTOR	RESISTOR	THERMAL ELEMENT (BI-METAL STRIP)	THERMAL ELEMENT (BI-METAL STRIP)
VARIABLE RESISTOR	VARIABLE RESISTOR	"Y" WINDINGS	"Y" WINDINGS
COIL	COIL	DIGITAL READOUT	DIGITAL READOUT
STEP UP COIL	STEP UP COIL	SINGLE FILAMENT LAMP	SINGLE FILAMENT LAMP
OPEN CONTACT	OPEN CONTACT	DUAL FILAMENT LAMP	DUAL FILAMENT LAMP
CLOSED CONTACT	CLOSED CONTACT	L.E.D.-LIGHT EMITTING DIODE	L.E.D.-LIGHT EMITTING DIODE
CLOSED SWITCH	CLOSED SWITCH	THERMISTOR	THERMISTOR
OPEN SWITCH	OPEN SWITCH	GAUGE	GAUGE
TWO POLE SINGLE THROW SWITCH	TWO POLE SINGLE THROW SWITCH	TIMER	TIMER
PRESSURE SWITCH	PRESSURE SWITCH	MOTOR	MOTOR
SOLENOID SWITCH	SOLENOID SWITCH	ARMATURE AND BRUSHES	ARMATURE AND BRUSHES
DIODE OR RECTIFIER	DIODE OR RECTIFIER	DENOTES WIRE GOES THROUGH GROMMET	DENOTES WIRE GOES THROUGH GROMMET

Fig. 3-22. These are typical electrical-electronic symbols found on wiring diagrams. Look them over closely.

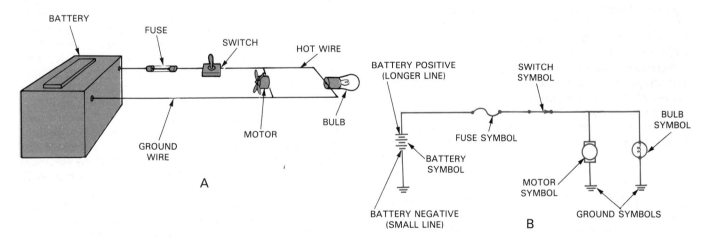

Fig. 3-23. Comparison of circuit illustration and wiring diagram. Both represent same components and electrical connections.

of the other. A series-parallel circuit has both series and parallel connections in one network.

Many automotive circuits are frame-ground or one-wire circuits. The car's metal structure is used to carry current back to the source. This reduces the amount of wire needed to complete the circuits.

The hot leg or hot wire carries current out to the load or electrical components. It will activate a test light or voltmeter when tested. The ground leg or ground wire is on the opposite side of the load. It carries current from the load back to the negative side of the source. The ground leg should not activate a test light.

Ohm's Law consists of a set of formulas for expressing the relationship between voltage, current, and resistance. If one electrical value is not known, Ohm's Law can be used to calculate the unknown value in a circuit.

Voltage equals current times resistance. Current equals volts divided by resistance. Resistance equals voltage divided by amps.

If circuit resistance increases, current will be reduced. If resistance drops, current increases. An increase in voltage will also increase current and a reduction of voltage will reduce current.

There are basic rules that apply to series circuits. Current is the same everywhere in a series circuit. Total resistance is the sum of all series resistances. The voltage drop across each series resistance equals the applied voltage source.

There are also basic rules that apply to a parallel circuit. Total circuit current flow is the sum of all branch currents. Total circuit resistance in a parallel circuit is less than any one branch resistance. The voltage applied to each branch is the same.

Prefixes are commonly used to express very large or very small electrical values. For example, a kilo equals 1000 units and milli equals .001 unit.

Electrical power is measured in watts. It is calculated by multiplying volts times amps or current squared times resistance.

Electrical symbols are used in place of actual components to simplify wiring diagrams. Wiring diagrams show how conductors connect to the electrical components or symbols in a circuit.

KNOW THESE TERMS

Series circuit, Parallel circuit, Open, Closed, Load, Path, Leg, Series-parallel circuit, Break, Frame-ground, One-wire, Hot wire, Ground leg, Ohm's Law, I_t, V_t, R_t, Prefix, Exponent, Milli, Mega, Micro, Kilo, Watt, Symbol, Wiring diagram.

REVIEW QUESTIONS—CHAPTER 3

1. A _____ _____ only has one path or leg for current flow.
2. What is a parallel circuit?
3. Why are many automotive circuits frame-ground or one-wire circuits?
4. _____ _____ is a formula used to express the relationship between voltage, current, and resistance.
5. If a circuit has a current flow of three amps and a resistance of five ohms, how much voltage is applied to the circuit?
6. If 25.4 amps is flowing in a circuit with 12.6 volts applied, what is the circuit resistance?
7. Calculate the total resistance and current for the following circuit.

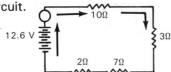

8. Find total resistance and current for this circuit.

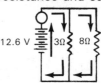

9. Explain three rules that apply to series circuits.
10. Explain three rules that apply to parallel circuits.

ASE CERTIFICATION–TYPE QUESTIONS

1. Technician A says a series circuit has only one path for current flow. Technician B says a series circuit can have only one load. Who is right?
   (A) A only. (C) Both A and B.
   (B) B only. (D) Neither A nor B.
2. Which of the following is not a common electrical circuit?
   (A) Parallel circuit.
   (B) Series-Parallel circuit.
   (C) Frame-ground circuit.
   (D) Series-ground circuit.
3. Technician A says the term *hot leg* refers to the section of the circuit after the load or electrical device. Technician B says the *hot leg* of a circuit is capable of producing an electrical short. Who is right?
   (A) A only. (C) Both A and B.
   (B) B only. (D) Neither A nor B.
4. Technician A says the ground leg of a circuit is capable of producing enough current to activate a test light. Technician B says the ground leg includes the circuit between the load and the negative terminal of the battery. Who is right?
   (A) A only. (C) Both A and B.
   (B) B only. (D) Neither A nor B.
5. A 12 volt electrical circuit has a resistance of 2 ohms. How much current is flowing through the circuit?
   (A) 4 amps. (C) 1 amp.
   (B) 6 amps. (D) 3 amps.
6. Technician A says that a change in circuit resistance will change current flow in the circuit. Technician B says a change in circuit voltage will change current flow in the circuit. Who is right?
   (A) A only. (C) Both A and B.
   (B) B only. (D) Neither A nor B.
7. Technician A says current is the same everywhere in a series circuit. Technician B says current is the same in each branch of a parallel circuit. Who is right?
   (A) A only. (C) Both A and B.
   (B) B only. (D) Neither A nor B.
8. One milliamp is equal to:
   (A) 1000 amps. (C) 0.001 amp.
   (B) 100 amps. (D) 10,000 amps.
9. 10,000 ohms can also be written as:
   (A) 10 kilohms. (C) 1 kilohm.
   (B) 1 megaohm. (D) 10 megaohms.
10. A particular 12-volt automotive circuit has a current flow of 3 amps. Technician A says the electrical power in this circuit is 36 watts. Technician B says the electrical power in this circuit is 4 watts. Who is right?
   (A) A only. (C) Both A and B.
   (B) B only. (D) Neither A nor B.

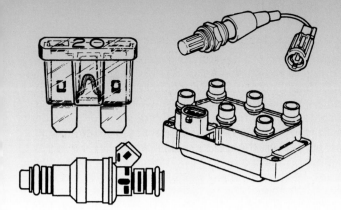

Chapter 4
Electrical Components

After studying this chapter, you will be able to:
- Explain the purpose of fundamental electrical components.
- Draw the symbols for common electrical devices.
- Describe ratings for electrical components.
- Explain how basic electrical components are used in automotive circuits.
- Describe special variations of basic electrical devices.
- More fully comprehend later textbook chapters that refer to the operation of electrical components.

This chapter will review the basic construction and operation of electrical components. *Electrical components* (resistors, condensers, relays, etc.) include devices used prior to the invention of electronic or solid state components (transistors, diodes, integrated circuits, etc.). Shown in Fig. 4-1, a modern car uses an array of electrical components.

Note! Study this chapter carefully. It will introduce many principles that apply to later study in other chapters.

RESISTORS

A *resistor* limits current flow or utilizes the electric current in a circuit. Resistors come in various shapes and sizes, depending on their function. For example, some older cars use a very large resistor or resistance wire to limit current to the ignition system. Resistors can also be microscopic units inside electronic circuit chips (integrated circuits).

Fixed resistors

A *fixed resistor* has one set ohms value that does not change. Fig. 4-2 shows two fixed resistors with their symbol and letter designation. Note that the symbol is

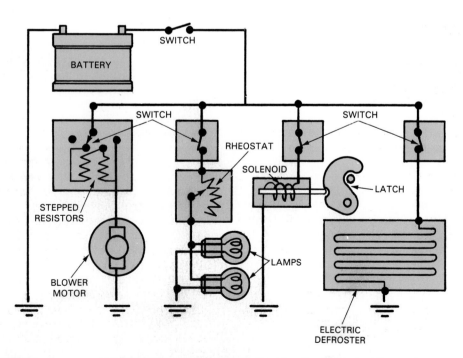

Fig. 4-1. As this illustration shows, conventional electrical components are still used to do many tasks in a car's electrical system. You will learn about these components in this and other chapters. (Ford)

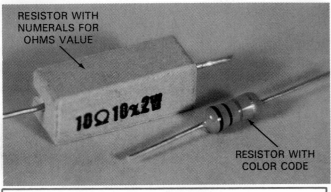

RESISTOR WITH
NUMERALS FOR
OHMS VALUE

RESISTOR WITH
COLOR CODE

FIXED RESISTOR	
SYMBOL	LETTER DESIGNATION
—⋀⋀⋀—	R

Fig. 4-2. Fixed resistor may be used to limit current flow in electric or electronic circuit. Note symbol and letter designation.

RESISTOR VALUES

COLOR	1st & 2nd BAND DIGITS	3rd BAND MULTIPLY BY	4th BAND TOLERANCE ± %
BLACK	0	1	—
BROWN	1	10	—
RED	2	100	—
ORANGE	3	1000	—
YELLOW	4	10000	—
GREEN	5	100000	—
BLUE	6	1000000	—
VIOLET	7	10000000	—
GRAY	8	100000000	—
WHITE	9	1000000000	—
GOLD	—	0.1	5
SILVER	—	0.01	10
NO COLOR	—	—	20

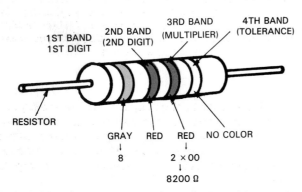

1ST BAND
1ST DIGIT

2ND BAND
(2ND DIGIT)

3RD BAND
(MULTIPLIER)

4TH BAND
(TOLERANCE)

RESISTOR

GRAY   RED   RED   NO COLOR
↓   ↓   ↓
8   2 × 00
↓
8200 Ω

Fig. 4-3. Note how bands around some resistors denote numbers that represent internal resistance of unit.

simply a zigzag line.

Some larger fixed resistors use a *color code* to denote the ohms or resistance value. This is illustrated in Fig. 4-3. Different color bands are placed around the resistor to represent the internal resistance. Color coded resistors can sometimes be found inside complex circuits, inside a radio for example. Resistors can also have the ohms value printed on them in number form.

Resistors also have a *watt rating* which gives the amount of power the resistor can handle without damage. When replacing a resistor, the watt rating must be the same or higher. If the watt rating is too low, the resistor will overheat and burn up in service, Fig. 4-4.

A *resistor tolerance* is a percent value representing how much the ohms value of the resistor can vary. If the tolerance is 5%, it means the resistor ohms value can be 5% above or below the stated specification, Fig. 4-4.

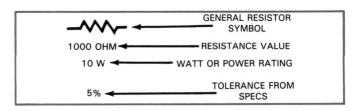

GENERAL RESISTOR SYMBOL

1000 OHM ← RESISTANCE VALUE

10 W ← WATT OR POWER RATING

5% ← TOLERANCE FROM SPECS

Fig. 4-4. Besides ohms value, resistor will also have watt rating and tolerance. Watt rating indicates how much load or power resistor can handle. Tolerance is how much resistor ohms can vary from specs.

Ballast resistors

A *ballast resistor* alters its own internal resistance as current flow changes. It acts as a current regulator. For instance, if current flow is low, the ballast resistor will have low resistance to maintain an average or desired current flow. However, if current rises, the ballast resistor will heat up and its internal resistance will increase. This will limit current flow to a normal level.

In the past, some ignition systems used a ballast resistor to maintain a constant supply current and voltage to the ignition coil. This is discussed in a later chapter.

Tapped resistors

A *tapped resistor* is designed to have two or more ohms values available by connecting to different taps or locations on the resistor. With one electrical connection, the resistance might be low. With another connection, the resistance might be higher to reduce current, Fig. 4-5.

One example of a tapped resistor would be in the car's heater blower circuit. In one switch position, the tapped or *stepped resistor,* has high resistance to produce a low fan or blower speed. When switched to high, the resistor has low resistance to increase current and blower rpm.

Variable resistors

A *variable resistor* has a range of internal resistance from low to high. By turning or sliding a knob, a contact moves along a resistor. This makes the resistance of the unit change since a different amount or length of resistor is connected inside the device. Fig. 4-6 shows one type

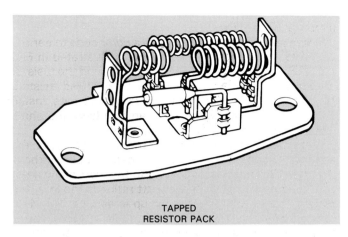

Fig. 4-5. Stepped resistor can have several fixed ohms values, depending upon which terminals are connected to circuit. This type resistor could be used to control various blower or fan speeds. (Ford)

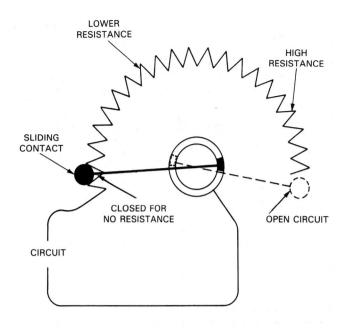

Fig. 4-7. Note action inside a variable resistor. In one position, sliding contact touches one end of resistor to produce high ohms. Then, it can be slid to touch opposite or low ohms end of resistor. (General Motors)

VARIABLE RESISTOR	
SYMBOLS	LETTER DESIGNATION
⌁	R V

Fig. 4-6. Variable resistors can be turned to produce infinite number of ohms values from high to low.

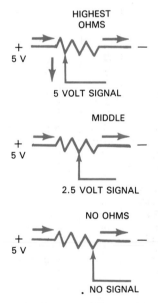

Fig. 4-8. Variable resistor can be used to produce different voltage signals for computer system. Note how voltage drop across resistor is highest when resistance is highest. As sliding contact is moved to reduce resistance, voltage also decreases. This will be detailed in a later chapter.

of variable resistor with its symbol.

A *rheostat* is a variable resistor with two electrical connections for its circuit. One terminal is wired to one end of the resistance unit. The other terminal is connected to the sliding contact. Turning the control knob moves the contact and alters the ohms value, Fig. 4-7.

A *potentiometer* is a variable resistor with three electrical connections. It has one connection at each end of the resistance unit and one for the sliding contact. Pictured in Fig. 4-8, this allows for more complex use of the variable resistance. For example, it can be used to produce a variable voltage drop or voltage signal.

Fig. 4-8 shows how a variable resistor can be used

to provide different voltage signals. As the sliding contact is moved along the resistance unit, the internal resistance and resulting voltage drop across the resistor changes. This is a good example of how a variable resistor might be used as a sensor for a computer system.

A variable resistor can be used as the volume control knob on a car radio for example. One can also be used

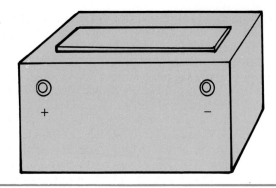

BATTERY	
SYMBOL	LETTER DESIGNATION
⊣⊢⊣⊢⊢	B

Fig. 4-9. Note battery symbol and letter designation.

to control the intermittent windshield wiper action. This is covered later in this text.

BATTERIES

A *battery* is a chemical-electrical device for storing and releasing electricity. In a car, a lead-acid battery is used because of its high current output. Discussed later, it is needed to operate the starting system. Fig. 4-9 shows the symbol and letter designation for a battery.

SWITCHES

A *switch* is used to connect or disconnect the power supply in a circuit. Illustrated in Fig. 4-10, there are various types of switches.

A *toggle switch* is hand-operated by flipping a small lever to one side. This either moves internal contacts into

or away from each other. Toggles might be used for fog lights or other dash-mounted controls.

A *push-button switch* has a spring-loaded button that, when pressed, makes or breaks an electrical connection across two contacts. One is shown in Fig. 4-11.

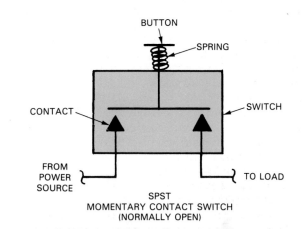

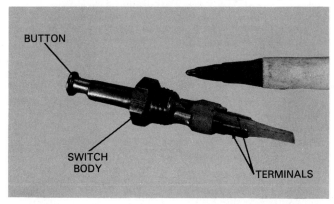

Fig. 4-11. This push button switch is normally open which means the circuit is disconnected unless button is pressed. (Ford and Universal Auto Supply)

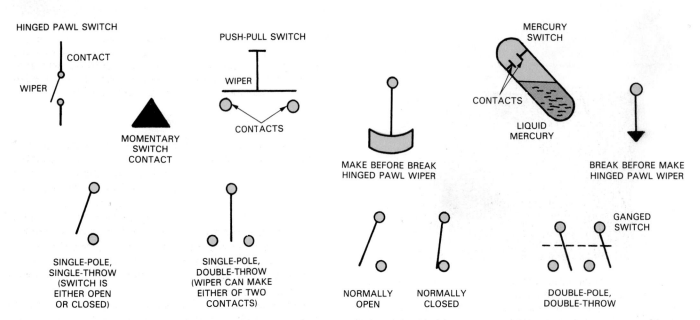

Fig. 4-10. Study symbols for different switch types. (Ford)

A *single-pole, single-throw switch* has one swinging arm that can make contact with one stationary contact. It is either opened or closed and has two external terminals, Fig. 4-10.

A *single-throw, double-pole switch* has one movable contact arm but two different stationary contacts. The wiper can make an electrical connection with either of the poles or stationary contacts, Fig. 4-10.

A *double-throw, double-pole switch* has two moving arms and two stationary contacts, Fig. 4-10.

A *normally open switch* is open or disconnected when at rest or when NOT activated. A spring-loaded push button switch would be an example of a normally open switch. Its symbol is given in Fig. 4-10.

A *normally closed switch* completes its internal connection when at rest or when NOT activated. Activating the switch opens the internal contacts to stop current flow. Its symbol is also shown in Fig. 4-10.

A *push-pull switch,* as implied, is pulled out or pushed in to activate the electrical contacts.

A *rotary switch* can select or make and break an electrical circuit. Turning the switch moves one or more moving contacts over stationary contacts.

A *thermal switch* is a temperature sensitive switch. It opens and closes with changes in temperature. A typical thermal switch is shown in Fig. 4-12. This type uses a *bi-metal strip* (two different metals bonded together).

When cold, the bi-metal strip is curved and the internal switch contacts are open. Then, when switch temperature increases, the two metals in the bi-metal arm will expand at different rates. This causes the arm to bend, closing the switch contacts. One example, a thermal switch, can be used to sense engine overheating and operate a dash warning light.

A *pressure switch* reacts to changes of internal pressure. Most have an internal diaphragm attached to an electrical contact. When pressure is low, the diaphragm is at rest and the contacts open. Then, when pressure is high enough, the diaphragm flexes to move the contacts closed. One type of pressure switch is pictured in Fig. 4-13.

One common application for a pressure switch is the engine oil light circuit.

A *mercury switch* uses liquid mercury, a good conductor, to open and close its switch contacts. It serves as a POSITION SWITCH that reacts to the location of a part. For example, a mercury switch can be used to activate the underhood light or the trunk light.

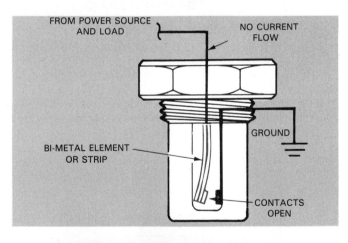

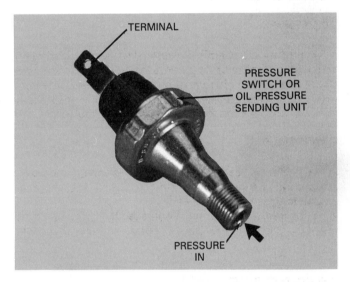

Fig. 4-13. This is one type of pressure switch. It is used to warn of low engine oil pressure. Low pressure allows diaphragm to close contacts in switch and activate dash light. Other pressure switches can also be found in a modern automobile. (Universal Auto Supply)

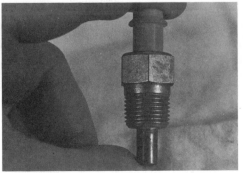

Fig. 4-12. Thermal switch or temperature switch uses bi-metal arm to react to heat. When cool, arm is bent so that contacts are open. Then, as unit heats up, bi-metal arm warps and closes points. This action could be used to operate engine temperature warning light for example. (Ford and Universal Auto Supply)

Fig. 4-14 illustrates the action of a mercury switch. When tilted in one position, the mercury is NOT touching the contacts and the switch is open. Then when tilted the other way (hood or trunk open), the mercury flows down over the contacts to close the switch.

There are dozens of other types of switches found in a modern automobile: ignition switch, dimmer switch, turn signal switch, stoplight switch, wiper switch, vacuum switch, inertia switch, etc. These more specialized types of switches will be explained in later chapters where they apply.

The symbols used in factory service manuals can vary. Refer to a symbol chart in the manual to find exact symbol used for each electrical or electronic component.

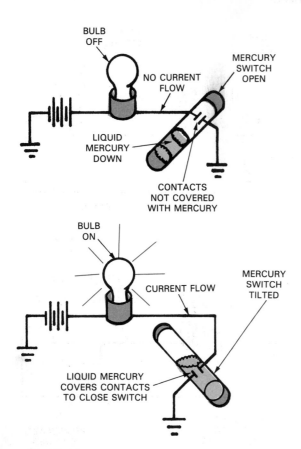

Fig. 4-14. Note action of mercury switch. In one position, liquid mercury is away from contacts and switch is open. Then when tilted the other way, mercury flows down over contacts to close switch. This type is commonly used to operate trunk and underhood lights.

CAPACITOR	
SYMBOL	LETTER DESIGNATION
—)|—	C

Fig. 4-15. Capacitors are used to store electricity and smooth out flow of DC current. Note symbol for capacitor.

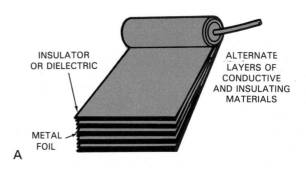

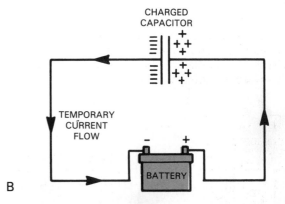

Fig. 4-16. A—Capacitor is made by wrapping two sheets of metal around insulator. B—DC current will flow in and charge capacitor. After charging, capacitor will block DC. (Chrysler)

CAPACITORS

A *capacitor,* also termed *condenser,* is a storage device for electrons or electricity. Basically, a capacitor is made by wrapping two conductor strips around an insulating strip. The insulating strip or dielectric keeps the two conductors from touching but allows them to be very close together. See Fig. 4-15.

A capacitor blocks DC or direct current. DC current cannot pass through a capacitor. A tiny amount of current enters the capacitor. This small current charges the capacitor and allows it to store electrical energy. Pictured in Fig. 4-16, a negative charge collects on one of the dielectrics (conductors). A positive charge collects on the other dielectric.

A capacitor will pass or conduct AC or alternating current. AC, since it flows one way and then the other, will charge a capacitor in one direction. Then, the capacitor will discharge back into the circuit when AC changes flow direction.

In a car, a capacitor is commonly used to block DC current and stop voltage fluctuations. For example, it can be called a *noise suppressor* when used to prevent static in a car radio or sound system. It can be connected into the wiring to absorb or counteract *voltage spikes* (rapid voltage changes) that would cause radio noise.

A capacitor or condensor was also used on older igni-

tion systems to absorb current to prevent arcing and burning of the contact points in the distributor. These topics will be discussed later.

A *variable capacitor* can be rotated to change its capacitance. Shown in Fig. 4-17, one type has movable conductor plates. If the conductor plates are moved down next to the other conductor plates, capacitance or electrical storage increases. Moving the plates away from each other would reduce capacitance. The tuning knob on some radios would be an example of a variable

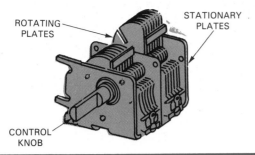

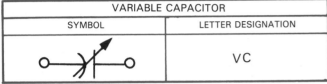

VARIABLE CAPACITOR	
SYMBOL	LETTER DESIGNATION
	VC

Fig. 4-17. Variable capacitor uses a stationary set of plates and a rotating set of plates. Turning knob moves one set of plates to alter capacitance. A variable capacitor may be used to tune in various stations on non-digital radios. (Kelvin Electronics)

capacitor application.

The size or electrical storage ability of a capacitor is rated in *farads.* A one farad capacitor connected to a one volt source will store 6.28×10^{18} electrons. A picofarad equals a trillionth of a farad. A microfarad equals a millionth of a farad.

When replacing a capacitor, you should install a new capacitor with an equal farad and voltage rating. This will assure that the circuit operates as it was designed.

FUSES

A *fuse* is used to protect a circuit from excess current flow damage. It is connected in series with the circuit, right after the source, so that all current must flow through the fuse. See Fig. 4-18.

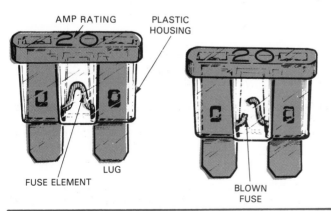

FUSE	
SYMBOL	LETTER DESIGNATION
	F

Fig. 4-18. Fuse protects circuit from excess amperage. It is wired in series at beginning of circuit. Note symbol. (Buick)

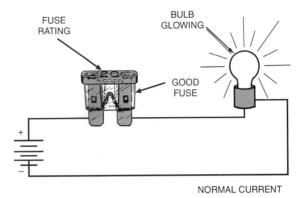

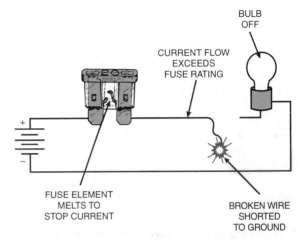

Fig. 4-19. Any problem that increases current flow too much will make fuse blow. Here wire has broken and shorted to ground. Resulting high current then burns fuse element in half to stop current and protect wiring.

Fig. 4-19 illustrates fuse action. When current flow is normal, current flows through the fuse element. If something goes wrong in the circuit to increase current flow too much, the element overheats and melts in half. The fuse "blows" to interrupt current. This breaks the circuit and protects the wires from overheating damage.

Without a fuse, an *"electrical fire"* could result from wires glowing red hot and catching their insulation on fire. A *short circuit* results when a hot wire touches ground and a tremendous amount of current flows through the circuit. This excess current can make wires glow red hot and burn up. A fuse is used to protect against shorts and electrical fires.

Note! Electrical problems, like shorts, will be explained in detail in Chapter 9, Electrical Tests, Circuit Problems.

Fuse types

There are three basic types of fuses: cartridge type, blade type, and in-line type. A *cartridge fuse* is a small cylinder with metal terminals on each end. It snaps into lugs in the fuse box.

A *blade fuse* has two male lugs sticking out for insertion into the female fuse box connectors.

An *in-line fuse* mounts in series in a small plastic fuse holder in one of the circuit wires. It does NOT install in the fuse box. An in-line fuse is sometimes needed when accessories (radio for example) are added to the car.

Fuse ratings

A *fuse rating* is given in amps. For example, 20 A printed on the fuse means that the fuse will handle 20 amperes of current without blowing. When replacing a fuse, always install a fuse with the same amp rating. In automotives, the voltage value is understood to be 12 V.

> DANGER! Never install a fuse with a higher amp rating. Even though this might keep the fuse from blowing, it can cause wires and electrical connections to overheat. You must correct the circuit problem and install the same fuse rating!

Fuse box (fuse panel)

A *fuse box* or *fuse panel* is a plastic housing with metal terminals for holding the car's fuses and other related electrical components (relays, flashers, etc.). Most fuse boxes mount under the dash of the car, Fig. 4-20.

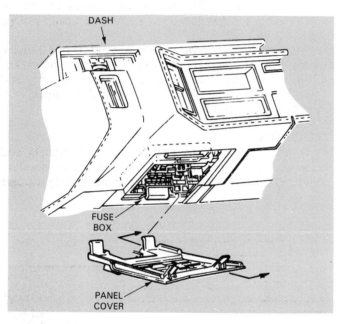

Fig. 4-20. Fuse panel or fuse box is normally located under dash. You may have to remove cover to gain access to fuses. (Pontiac)

Fuse panels will usually have the name of the circuit printed next to the fuse. Sometimes abbreviated, this will tell you which circuit is protected by each fuse. The amp rating may also be printed next to the fuse socket in case a fuse is removed. See Fig. 4-21.

Fuse link (fusible link)

A *fuse link* or *fusible link* is a small section of wire connected in series with the larger wire. It is designed to serve as a very large fuse. A fuse link is in Fig. 4-22.

Fuse links are normally located in the engine compartment where power feeds off of the battery or starter solenoid. They provide circuit protection before the fuse box in the passenger compartment. If a wire is shorted to ground before the fuse panel, the fuse link can overheat and burn in half. This will protect the rest of the wiring from major damage.

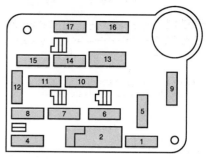

Fuse/CB/ Relay Location	Fuse Amp Rating	Description	
1	15A	• Turn signal lamps • Back-up lamps • Airbag module • Overdrive cancel • Brake shift solenoid	• Conv. top relay coil • Illum. entry module (shut-off)
2	30A	• Windshield wiper and washer systems	
4	10A	• Airbag module (aux. pwr.)	
5	15A	• Headlamp switch • Exterior lamps	• Cluster illum.
6	15A	• Clock • Speed control amp.	• Air conditioning clutch coil • Anti-theft module
7	10A	• ABS	
8	10A	• Chime for keys in ignition • Courtesy lamps • Engine compartment lamp • Glove compartment lamp	• Power mirrors • Radio • Instrument cluster • Clock • Trunk lamp • Anti-theft
9	15A	• Hazard warning • Stop lamps	• Brake shift interlock solenoid
10	15A	• Radio	
11	20A CB	• Deck lid release	• Door locks
12	10A	• Instrument panel • Illumination	lamps • Ashtray illum.
13	20A CB	• Power windows	
14	10A	• Low oil module • Low coolant module • Safety belt chime	• Cluster warning lamps • Cluster gauges
15	20A	• Flash-to-pass • Fog lamps • Anti-theft module	• Low beams • Ext. lamps
16	30A	• Air conditioning and heater blower motor	
17	20A	• Transmission shift module • Generator warn-	ing lights • Control module pwr. relay coil

Fig. 4-21. Each fuse has an amp rating. Note how service manual illustration gives amp value and circuit involved for each fuse.

> Note! When replacing a fuse link, use the recommended wire size. Do NOT use the same wire size as is used in the rest of the circuit or you will no longer have circuit protection.

Procedures for replacing a fuse link are explained in Chapter 6, Wiring, Wiring Repairs.

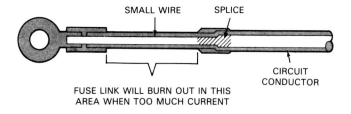

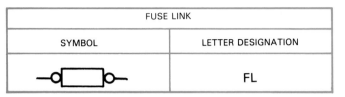

Fig. 4-22. Fuse link is simply a small wire connected to larger wire in circuit. Small wire or fuse link will burn in half if current draw becomes excessive. Fuse links are normally located in engine compartment where power feeds from battery to fuse box. (Ford)

FUSE LINK	
SYMBOL	LETTER DESIGNATION
—o▭o—	FL

 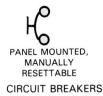

PANEL MOUNTED, SELF-RESETTING   PANEL MOUNTED, MANUALLY RESETTABLE   IN-LINE SELF-RESETTING

CIRCUIT BREAKERS

Fig. 4-24. Note symbol variations for a circuit breaker. (Ford)

CIRCUIT BREAKERS

A *circuit breaker* performs the same function as a fuse or fuse link; it protects a circuit from excess current damage. However, a circuit breaker is NOT ruined when activated. Most can sense a high current condition, disconnect the circuit temporarily, and then reset itself.

The circuit breaker will reconnect the circuit again after it cools down and if current draw returns to normal. This action is ideal for the headlight circuit which must not turn off permanently. See Fig. 4-23.

Fig. 4-24 shows the symbols for several types of circuit breakers. Note that a large symbol may indicate a circuit breaker with a higher amp rating. A button symbol on the circuit breaker symbol means that it must be reset manually (by hand). An in-line circuit breaker symbol may be enclosed in a box.

A circuit breaker contains a bi-metal strip (two metals bonded together). Under normal current flow, the bi-metal strip remains cool and straight. When a problem exists in the circuit, high current flow through the strip causes overheating. Then, different rates of thermal expansion makes the strip warp or bend. This opens the contacts in the breaker, Fig. 4-25.

A circuit breaker is normally located in the fuse panel, pictured in Fig. 4-26. Sometimes, however, circuit breakers are located elsewhere in the car. It simply plugs into the box.

A *circuit breaker rating* is given in amps. As with fuses, never install a circuit breaker with a higher amp rating. This could cause wire or component overheating, and possibly an electrical fire. Always install a breaker with the same current rating.

FLASHERS

A *flasher* is used to operate the turn signals and emergency flasher lights on a car. It is the component that makes and breaks circuit to make the light bulbs

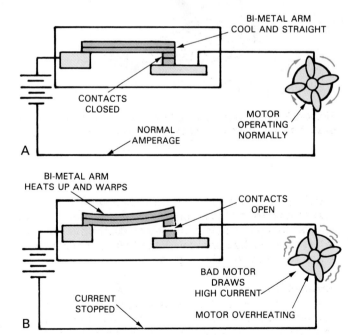

Fig. 4-25. Circuit breaker action. A—Circuit is functioning normally. Motor is in good condition and is drawing spec current. B—Motor has bad bearings. It is overheating and drawing too much amperage. As a result, circuit breaker arm overheats, bends, and opens circuit. After cooling, breaker will allow blower to operate until it again overheats and draws too much current.

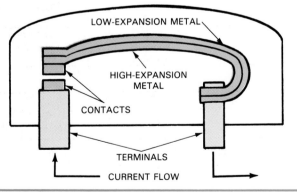

CIRCUIT BREAKER	
SYMBOL	LETTER DESIGNATION
—▭—	CB

Fig. 4-23. Circuit breaker acts as a fuse but it is not ruined when activated.

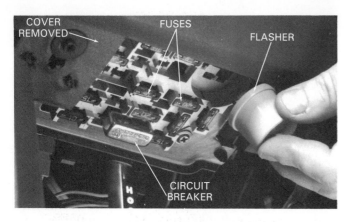

Fig. 4-26. Fuse panel may hold circuit breakers, fuses, and flasher units. Here technician is removing flasher unit that was bad and preventing turn signal operation.

flash on and off. Usually, one flasher is used for the turn signals and another for the emergency flasher lights.

A flasher is similar to a circuit breaker but it is designed to open and close the circuit at a constant rate, Fig. 4-27. It uses a bi-metal strip and a small heating element.

Current flow through the heating element warms and warps the bi-metal strip. This turns off the lights. Then, the strip cools and reconnects the circuit to flash the lights back on. This cycle is repeated to operate the turn signals or emergency lights. A clicking sound can be heard from a flasher as its points open and close.

Flashers can be located on the fuse panel, Fig. 4-26. They can also be wired in-line somewhere under the dash. Discussed in a later chapter, diagrams are available that show flasher locations.

LIGHT BULBS

Mentioned briefly in a previous chapter, a *light bulb* is a small resistance wire enclosed in an airtight glass enclosure. Current flow makes the element glow red hot, but since the element is not exposed to oxygen, it does not burn in half. It glows red hot and emits electrons we see as light.

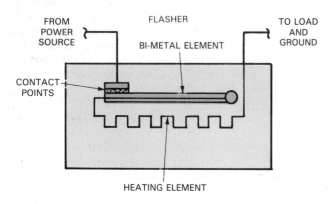

Fig. 4-27. Flasher uses small heating element to warm bi-metal arm. Current flow through contacts operates heating element. When arm warms, it bends and opens points. Then arm cools and reconnects heater and points. This action is repeated quickly and points click open and closed to make lights flash on and off. (Ford)

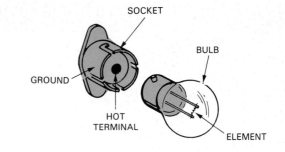

LIGHT BULB	
SYMBOL	LETTER DESIGNATION
	LT

Fig. 4-28. Note basic symbol for light bulb. Bulb installs in socket. (Fiat)

Fig. 4-28 shows the symbol for a light bulb. Explained in Chapter 17, there are numerous types of light bulbs.

COILS

A *coil,* also called *choke* or *inductor,* is an insulated wire wrapped in a spiral around an iron, ceramic, or air core. Used in complex electrical or electronic circuits, it resists the change or fluctuation of current and voltage. However, it gives little opposition to current flow as does a capacitor. Fig. 4-29 shows the symbols for fixed and variable coils.

In auto mechanics, coils are commonly used in electrical devices to provide a magnetic field. As you will learn, they are used in transformers, solenoids, motors, relays, and other components.

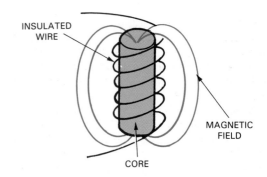

COIL	
FIXED COIL SYMBOL	VARIABLE COIL SYMBOL

Fig. 4-29. Coil, discussed in earlier chapter, is simply insulated wire wrapped around core. It can be used in numerous electrical devices.

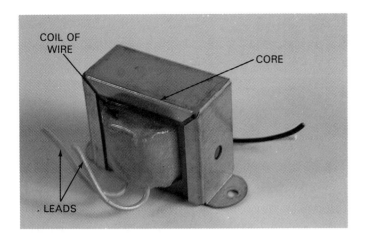

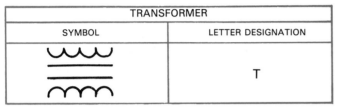

TRANSFORMER	
SYMBOL	LETTER DESIGNATION
ꖸꖸꖸ ⌒⌒⌒	T

Fig. 4-30. Transformer is two coils in one housing. It can be used to isolate two circuits, increase voltage, or decrease voltage.

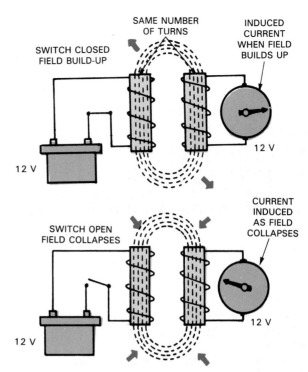

Fig. 4-31. Study how field around one coil can induce current and voltage in other coil when field builds or collapses. If number of turns are different, transformer can be used to increase or decrease voltage or current. (Ford)

TRANSFORMERS

A *transformer* uses two sets of coils to transform voltage and current to higher or lower levels, Fig. 4-30.

For example, an ignition system coil is used to transform battery voltage into "super high" voltage for firing the spark plugs. Other types of transformers are used to isolate different parts of a circuit, reduce voltage, or match the *impedance* (inductive resistance) of circuit sections.

Transformers are made by wrapping an insulated wire around a core, usually an iron core. Another set of windings is wrapped around a second or adjoining core. This is shown in Fig. 4-31.

If current flowing through one set of windings fluctuates (increases or decreases in strength), current is induced in the other set of windings. Current is NOT induced in the other windings if the current flow and the flux around the windings stays the same. This is illustrated in Fig. 4-31.

Turns ratio refers to the number of windings or wraps of wire in each transformer coil. If both windings have the same number of turns, the turn ratio would be one to one (1:1). The induced voltage in the second set of windings would be the same as in the input windings. This equal input and output would produce an *isolation transformer* (isolate one circuit from another).

A *step-up transformer* will increase output voltage higher than the input voltage. One example, a transformer might have a turns ratio of 1:2 (12 volts in would produce output of 24 volts).

A *step-down transformer* would reduce the output voltage compared to the input voltage. It might have a turns ratio of 2:1 (12 volts in would produce an output of only 6 volts).

When a transformer increases voltage, there is a loss of current. If a transformer reduces voltage, there is a current gain. Current can be sacrificed to gain voltage or voltage can be sacrificed to gain current.

RELAYS

A *relay* uses a small input current to control a larger current in a circuit. It uses a small coil to open and close a set of contact points. Look at Fig. 4-32.

For example, a car horn might use a relay. When you press the horn button on the steering wheel, a small control current flows to the horn relay. This closes the contacts in the relay and a larger current flows to and energizes the horn. This allows the wires running up the steering column to the horn button to be much smaller.

Relays can be located almost anywhere on a car. They are frequently located near the firewall or under the dash however. They are small devices housed in metal or plastic boxes, Fig. 4-33.

Fig. 4-34 shows the construction of a typical relay. Note that it uses a coil to produce a tiny electromagnet. When current flows through the coil, the magnetic field acts on the contact point arm. It pulls the arm down and closes the points. When current is disconnected from the coil, spring action opens the contact points.

A typical relay circuit is given in Fig. 4-35. A very small wire would run to the relay coil. A larger wire would connect to the power circuit and contact points. Note how a relay circuit is drawn in symbol form.

Fig. 4-36 shows a photo of actual relays in an engine compartment. You would need to refer to a service manual or wiring diagram to find out which circuit each

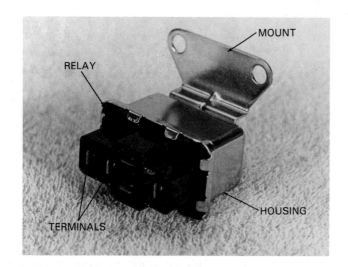

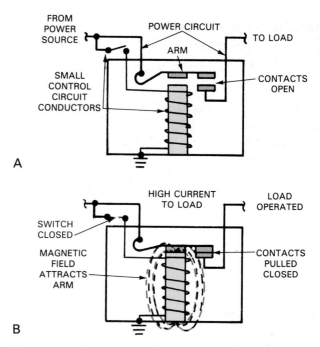

A

B

Fig. 4-34. Relay action. A—Control circuit is open and relay points are open. Load circuit is off. B—Control circuit is activated and magnetic field builds around coil. This attracts point arm and points are pulled closed. This turns main circuit on and larger current flows to load. (Ford)

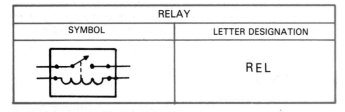

RELAY	
SYMBOL	LETTER DESIGNATION
	REL

Fig. 4-32. Relay serves as remote control switch. (Universal Auto Supply)

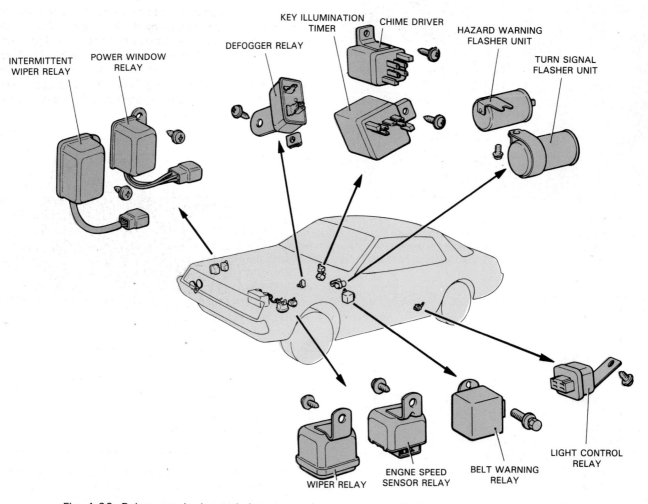

Fig. 4-33. Relays can be located almost anywhere in vehicle. Note ones used on this car. (Chrysler)

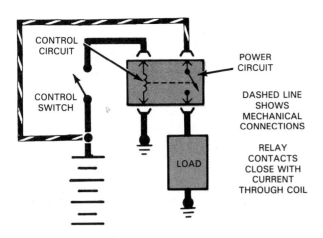

Fig. 4-35. This is an example of a basic diagram of a relay circuit. (Oldsmobile)

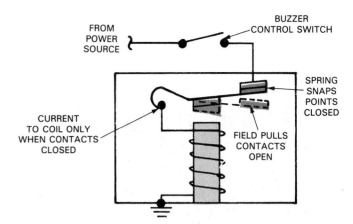

Fig. 4-37. Buzzer is similar to relay but coil current is fed through points. With points closed, field builds around coil and pulls points open. Then, field breaks down and points snap shut because of spring pressure. This is repeated quickly to produce a buzzing sound as the points snap open and closed.

SOLENOIDS

A *solenoid* is an electromagnet that moves a large metal plunger or core. The core movement can be used to close very large electrical contacts or move parts into engagement. See Fig. 4-38.

A solenoid is a device that uses electric current to produce motion. This motion might be used to lock a car door or close a set of electrical connections. Fig. 4-39 shows an example of one application of a solenoid. When current flows through the solenoid windings, the magnetic field pulls the core into the windings. Then, when current flow is broken, spring action can be used to push the core back out.

Fig. 4-36. These are relays found under hood of one make and model car. You would have to refer to shop manual to find out which circuit each controlled. (Saab)

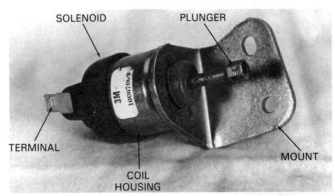

relay operated. Relay testing will be explained in a later chapter.

BUZZER

A *buzzer* is similar to a relay but its internal connections are different. This is illustrated in Fig. 4-37.

When the buzzer is energized, current flows through the normally closed contacts and into the coil. The coil's magnetic field then pulls down on the point arm and opens the points. This breaks the circuit to the coil and the flux collapses. Spring pressure then snaps the points back closed. This is repeated very quickly and the points open and close fast enough to make a buzzing sound.

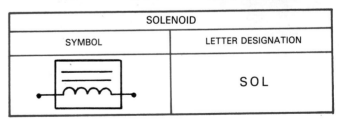

SOLENOID	
SYMBOL	LETTER DESIGNATION
	SOL

Fig. 4-38. Solenoid is also similar to a relay but it can handle much higher currents or it may be used to move other parts. This is an idle speed control solenoid with its symbol. (Universal Auto Supply)

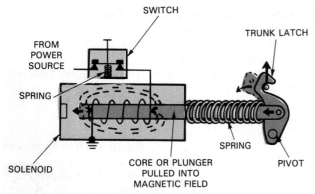

Fig. 4-39. This is an example of how a solenoid can convert electrical energy into motion or work. Magnetic field around coil pulls core or plunger into coil. This is being used to operate trunk latch in this example. (Ford)

In an automobile, a starter solenoid is used to complete the battery-to-starting motor circuit. It serves as a HUGE RELAY to connect this very high amperage circuit. Some starter solenoids also move the starter gear into engagement with the flywheel ring gear on the back of the engine.

Smaller solenoids can be used to control engine throttle position and engine speed. Studied later, solenoid action is also used to open and close gasoline injectors in an electronic fuel injection system.

Note! Solenoid applications will be explained in numerous other textbook chapters where they apply. Refer to the index for more information as needed.

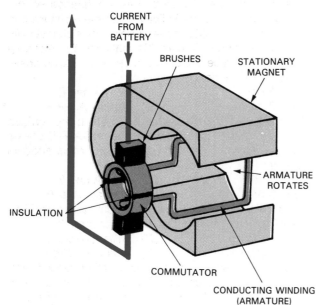

ELECTRIC MOTOR	
SYMBOL	MOTOR DESIGNATION
(M symbol)	M

Fig. 4-40. Motor uses magnetic fields to spin windings or armature. Motors are detailed in a later chapter. (Robert Bosch)

MOTORS

Electric motors use current and the resulting magnetic field to produce a powerful rotating action. A simple motor is illustrated in Fig. 4-40. Note its basic parts and how it could do work.

Detailed in the chapter on starting motors, a set of windings is wound around central core. This core is mounted on a shaft to form an *armature.* The shaft is mounted in bearings to allow the armature to rotate. Either stationary permanent magnets or stationary windings (electromagnets) are located around the center armature. A set of *brushes* is used to feed current into the commutator and armature.

When current flows into the armature, a strong magnetic field builds around the armature windings. This magnetic field pushes against or pulls into the magnetic field of the stationary magnetic field around the armature. As a result, a powerful turning force is produced. The *commutator* constantly reconnects the windings to keep the armature spinning in one direction.

OTHER ELECTRICAL COMPONENTS

More specialized electrical components will be introduced and detailed throughout this book. Refer to the text index to find where these components are discussed. Most of these more specialized electrical components will use the same principles described in this chapter.

SUMMARY

Even with the advent of electronics, conventional electrical components are still important to the operation of the modern automobile. As a consequence, it is critical for you to understand how electrical devices function.

A resistor limits or utilizes current flow in a circuit. A fixed resistor has only one ohms value. A variable resistor can be changed to have various ohms values. A tapped resistor can be connected differently to change its internal resistance.

A battery is a chemical-electrical device. It stores and can release electrical energy.

A switch will connect and disconnect power to and from a circuit. There are numerous switch designs. A normally-open switch is disconnected until activated. A normally-closed switch is connected until activated. A thermal switch reacts to changes in temperature and a pressure switch reacts to pressure. A mercury switch uses liquid mercury to react to a change in position.

A capacitor or condenser is a storage device for electricity. It is made by wrapping two small sheets of metal around an insulator or dielectric. A capacitor blocks DC but passes AC. It is commonly used to smooth current flow in a circuit, as to prevent radio noise.

Fuses are used to protect a circuit from a short and the resulting high current flow. Without a fuse, a short could cause enough current to burn up wires and components.

Fuses are mounted in a fuse panel or fuse box. The panel or box is normally located under the car dash. Circuit breakers and flashers can also mount on the fuse panel.

A fuse link, or fusible link, is a small section of wire connected to a much larger wire. The small wire will burn in half if current draw becomes too high. The fuse link protects the wiring before the fuse panel. Fuse links are normally located in the wiring harness in the engine compartment.

Circuit breakers are another form of circuit protection device. They can also stop current flow if amp draw becomes too high. However, most circuit breakers will automatically reset themselves after cooling down. This allows the circuit to again function if current draw is back to normal.

Flashers are devices for making and breaking a light circuit to produce an on-off light bulb action. They are used to operate the turn signals and emergency flasher lights. Flashers can be located on the fuse box or elsewhere under the dash.

A coil is simply an insulated wire wrapped around a core. A transformer uses two coils located close together. A transformer can isolate circuits, increase voltage, or decrease voltage.

A relay uses a small input current to control a larger circuit current. A horn might use a relay. Pushing the horn button activates a small current to the relay coil. Then, the relay points close to send a higher current flow to the horn. Smaller wires can then be ran up the steering column to the horn button.

A solenoid is an electromagnet used to move an iron plunger or core. It can be used to complete a very high amperage circuit, something like a relay. It can also be used to engage parts, to move the engine throttle linkage for example. Various types of solenoids are used in a modern automobile.

An electric motor uses magnetic forces to spin an armature (rotating windings). The spinning action can be used to do work.

KNOW THESE TERMS

Resistor, Fixed resistor, Color code, Resistor tolerance, Ballast resistor, Tapped resistor, Variable resistor, Rheostat, Potentiometer, Switch, Normally open, Normally closed, Thermal switch, Rotary switch, Pressure switch, Mercury switch, Capacitor, Noise suppressor, Variable capacitor, Farad, Fuse, Electrical fire, Short circuit, Fuse rating, Fuse box, Fuse link, Circuit breaker, Flasher, Coil, Transformer, Turns ratio, Isolation transformer, Step-up transformers, Step-down transformer, Relay, Buzzer, Solenoid, Motor.

REVIEW QUESTIONS—CHAPTER 4

1. A _____ is an electrical component that limits current flow in a circuit.
2. A _____ _____ might be used to control several set speeds for a blower motor in a heating and air conditioning system.
3. Explain the difference between a normally open and a normally closed switch.
4. How does a typical thermal switch operate?
5. Explain the application of a mercury switch.
6. A capacitor will block DC but pass AC. True or false?

7. How does a fuse protect a circuit?
8. How are fuses rated?
9. What could happen if you install a new fuse with a higher amp value?
   a. Circuit might not blow fuse and would function.
   b. Wires could overheat and burn up.
   c. It could still blow.
   d. All of the above are correct.
   e. None of the above are correct.
10. A _____ _____ is a small section of wire soldered to a larger wire for a circuit.
11. A _____ _____ does the same thing as a fuse but it is not ruined when activated by high current.
12. How does a flasher work?
13. This type transformer would decrease voltage but increase current.
    a. Isolation transformer.
    b. Step-up transformer.
    c. Step-down transformer.
    d. Impedence transformer.
14. Explain the basic purpose of a relay.
15. In your own words, how can a solenoid convert electricity into motion to do work?

ASE CERTIFICATION–TYPE QUESTIONS

1. Technician A says some resistors use a color code to denote their resistance value. Technician B says some resistors use printed numbers to denote their resistance value. Who is right?
   (A) A only.   (C) Both A and B.
   (B) B only.   (D) Neither A nor B.
2. A particular type of resistor has a tolerance of 3%. Technician A says this indicates that the resistor's current value can be 3% above or below its stated specification. Technician B says this indicates the resistor's ohm value can be 3% above or below its stated specification. Who is right?
   (A) A only.   (C) Both A and B.
   (B) B only.   (D) Neither A nor B.
3. Technician A says a ballast is used in the ignition system of late-model vehicles. Technician B says a ballast resistor alters its own internal resistance as current flow changes. Who is right?
   (A) A only.   (C) Both A and B.
   (B) B only.   (D) Neither A nor B.
4. Which of the following would be used in an automobile's heater blower circuit to control blower speed?
   (A) Fixed resistor.   (C) Ballast resistor.
   (B) Tapped resistor.   (D) Variable resistor.
5. Technician A says a rheostat is a ballast resistor with two electrical connections. Technician B says a potentiometer is a variable resistor with three electrical connections. Who is right?
   (A) A only.   (C) Both A and B.
   (B) B only.   (D) Neither A nor B.
6. Technician A says a capacitor blocks DC current and is commonly used as a noise suppressor for an automotive radio. Technician B says a capacitor has the ability to store electrical energy. Who is right?
   (A) A only.   (C) Both A and B.
   (B) B only.   (D) Neither A nor B.

7. Technician A says an in-line fuse normally mounts inside the car's fuse box. Technician B says an in-line fuse is often used when electrical accessories are added to a vehicle. Who is right?
   (A) A only.   (C) Both A and B.
   (B) B only.   (D) Neither A nor B.

8. Technician A says a 20 amp automotive fuse will handle 25 amps of current without blowing. Technician B says that a replacement fuse must have the same amp rating as the original. Who is right?
   (A) A only.   (C) Both A and B.
   (B) B only.   (D) Neither A nor B.

9. Technician A says a circuit breaker is designed to protect a circuit from high current. Technician B says a circuit breaker's rating is given in amps. Who is right?
   (A) A only.   (C) Both A and B.
   (B) B only.   (D) Neither A nor B.

10. A device that uses a small input current to control a larger current is known as a(n):
    (A) transformer.   (C) inductor.
    (B) relay.   (D) solenoid.

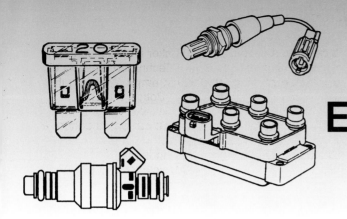

Chapter 5

Electronic Principles, Components, Digital Logic

After studying this chapter, you will be able to:
- *Explain the operation of semiconductor materials.*
- *Describe the action of common electronic components.*
- *Compare variations of electronic components.*
- *Summarize the operation of photonic devices.*
- *Explain pulses, waves, signals, and noise.*
- *Describe basic logic devices.*
- *Briefly explain the binary numbering system.*
- *Detail the construction and operation of integrated circuits.*

This chapter will continue your study of auto electronics by summarizing the construction, operation, and purpose of basic electronic components. You will learn about diodes, transistors, solar cells, logic devices, binary numbering, truth tables, and the dozens of other essential facts.

The terms *electronic* and *solid state* are used when referring to components that do NOT use moving parts. A relay, for example, uses a coil to move contact points to make or break a circuit. It is NOT solid state or electronic. As you will see, a transistor can do the same thing as a relay or switch without moving parts and in a fraction of the time and space. This is the fundamental advantage of electronic components.

Note! This is a very important chapter. It will prepare you to grasp later coverage of vehicle sensors, computers, actuators, and other components. Study everything thoroughly so that you will be ready for later chapters.

SEMICONDUCTORS

A *semiconductor* is a crystal material that can act as both a conductor or an insulator. Discussed earlier, a conductor will pass free electrons. An insulator will block free electrons. Depending on conditions, a semiconductor can act as either.

Semiconductors are made from sand, which is also called *silica* or *silicon.* This is a very abundant substance; only oxygen is more plentiful.

Basically to make semiconductor materials, silicon is melted and cooked at about 2600 °F (1 428 °C). Then the silicon is *doped* by adding other substances (phosphorus, boron, etc.). This causes the silicon to grow into very useful *crystals* (substances with symmetrical atomic structures).

P-type semiconductor

A *P-type semiconductor* is doped so that it has excess *holes* (protons), or spaces in atoms for free electrons. As a result, a P-type semiconductor is a more positive substance and it will attract electrons. Remember that ''P'' stands for POSITIVE.

N-type semiconductor

An *N-type semiconductor* is doped so that it has excess electrons in its atomic structure. Substances are added to the silicon so that there are free electrons that can move through the N-type semiconductor material. Remember that ''N'' stands for NEGATIVE.

Alone, both P-type and N-type silicon will conduct electricity. The resistance of either material is determined by the number of holes or free electrons that result from the doping process. Each material is not very useful by itself. However, if they are joined together, numerous useful devices can be manufactured.

DIODES

A *diode* is made by joining a small piece of N-type silicon with a small piece of P-type silicon. As shown in Fig. 5-1, a wire lead is attached to each end of the diode. The result is a device that will BLOCK current in one direction and PASS current in the other direction. A diode acts as an ''electrical check valve.''

Fig. 5-2 illustrates the symbol for a diode and shows how it can block or pass current.

Forward and reverse bias

When *forward biased,* a diode is connected so that it acts as a CONDUCTOR. The battery charge draws the

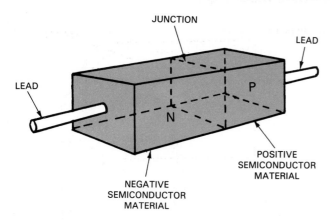

Fig. 5-1. Simplest semiconductor device is a diode. It is formed by joining chips of P and N materials.

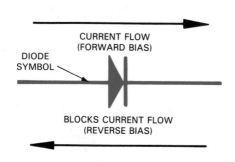

Fig. 5-2. Note diode symbol and direction of current. (Chrysler)

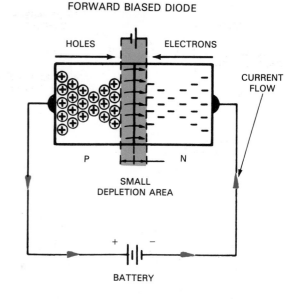

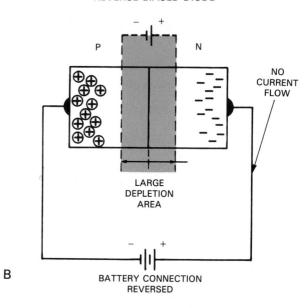

Fig. 5-3. Diode operation. A—Forward biased diode has small depletion area around P-N junction. Battery charge makes electrons flow across small depletion area. B—Reverse biased diode has large depletion area. Reverse polarity of battery pulls holes and electrons away from P-N junction. Junction acts as open switch to block current.

electrons and protons (holes) closer to the P-N junction. This reduces the size of the depletion area (area around N-P junction). As a result, electrons can flow across the depletion area and junction. A voltage of about 0.6 volts is needed to produce a forward bias current flow across a diode, Fig. 5-3A.

When *reverse biased,* a diode is wired so that it acts as an INSULATOR. The battery connections are reversed and the electrical charge pulls electrons and protons (holes) away from the P-N junction. This makes the depletion area larger and current cannot flow through the diode. The reverse biased diode can then block several volts, Fig. 5-3B.

The *reverse bias voltage* is a rating of the maximum voltage a diode can block without being damaged. If exceeded, the diode could be ruined.

Diode applications, rectification

A diode is commonly used to convert AC (alternating current) into DC (direct current). Illustrated in Fig. 5-4, if a diode is placed in a circuit with AC (reversing current flow), the diode will only pass current in one direction. No current will flow in the other direction.

Rectification refers to changing AC into DC. *Half-wave rectification* refers to changing only half of the AC sine wave into DC. *Full-wave rectification* refers to changing both the positive and negative halves of the AC sine wave into DC.

One diode in series with an AC source will only produce half-wave rectification. Fig. 5-5 shows how several diodes can be used to produce full-wave rectification.

Explained in later chapters, diodes are commonly used inside a car's alternator. The initial output of a charging system alternator is AC. The AC must be rectified into DC for use in the automobile's electrical system.

Zener diode

A *zener diode* is a special diode that serves as a voltage (pressure) relief valve. It will conduct current normally when forward biased. It will also block current when reverse biased. However, when a specific reverse bias voltage is reached, the zener diode will conduct current.

For instance, a zener diode might begin to conduct at 12 volts. This keeps the diode's voltage drop from going

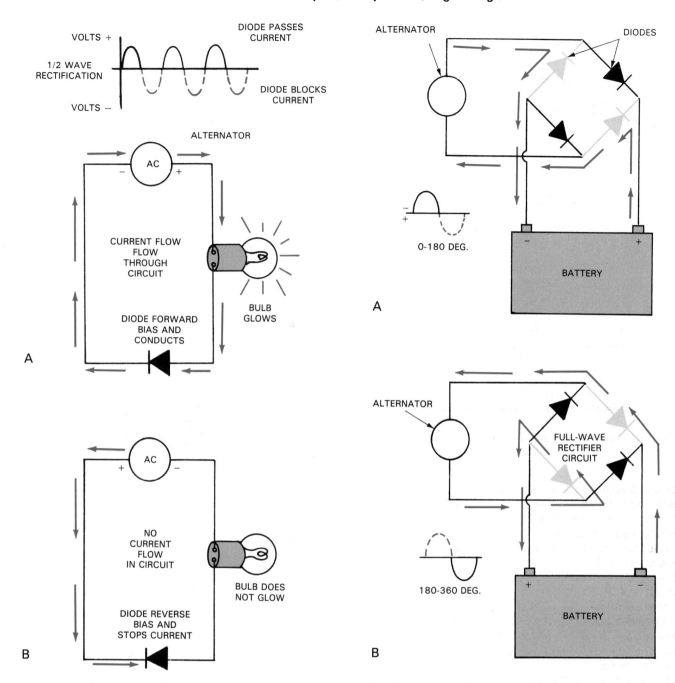

Fig. 5-4. If AC is fed into a diode, diode will only conduct current for half of sine wave. This will produce half-wave rectification. Bulb would only glow with diode forward bias.

Fig. 5-5. Several diodes wired as shown will produce full-wave rectification. Both halves of the AC sine wave will produce DC current.

above 12 volts and the zener diode acts as a voltage regulator. This can protect other electronic components from excess voltage and current damage, Fig. 5-6.

Note! Conventional diodes will be damaged if this reverse bias voltage is exceeded. Unlike a zener diode, the conventional diode will overheat and burn up.

TRANSISTORS

A *transistor* is a semiconductor device for switching or amplifying (increasing) current in a circuit. The letters "trans" mean transfer and letters "sistor" mean resistance for transfer of resistance. Therefore, a tran-

sistor transfers or changes from a resistor to a conductor with electrical stimulation. See Fig. 5-7.

A transistor is made by joining three semiconductor chips. An *NPN transistor* has two chips of N-type material and one chip of P-type material, Fig. 5-8. A *PNP transistor* has two P-chips and one N-chip bonded together, Fig. 5-8. Small wire leads are attached to each type material.

Base, emitter, collector

The *base* of a transistor is the "trigger" lead that changes the semiconductor material from an insulator to a conductor. Tiny current through the base turns a

57

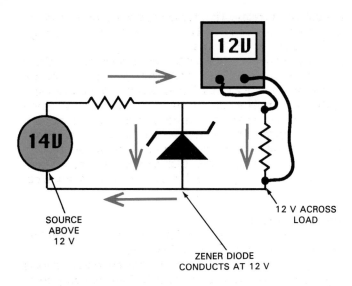

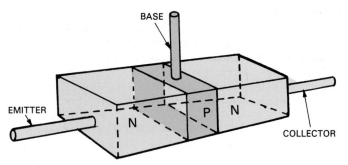

A—This is an NPN transistor.

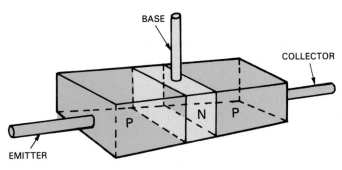

B—This is a PNP transistor.

Fig. 5-8. Note how semiconductor materials and leads are arranged in PNP and NPN transistors.

Fig. 5-6. Zener diode is commonly used as a voltage regulating device. When reverse bias, it will begin to conduct when specific voltage is reached. This will limit voltage drop across zener diode. Conventional diodes will burn up if reverse bias voltage is surpassed.

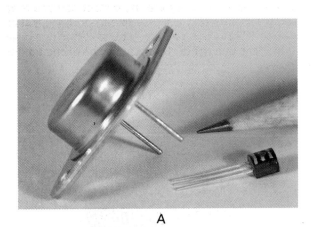

A

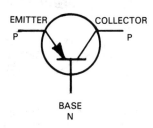

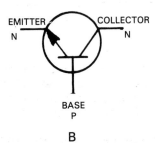

B

Fig. 5-7. A—Transistors can be used as solid state switches or current amplifiers. B—Transistor symbols.

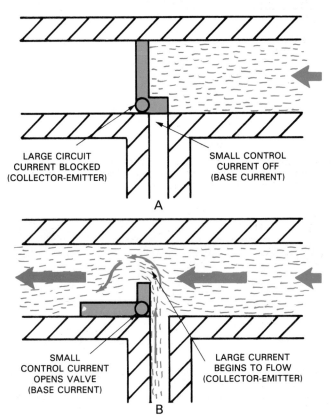

Fig. 5-9. Simple fluid circuit can be used to demonstrate action of a transistor. A—Fluid flow is blocked by valve. No current can flow to other side. B—Small amount of fluid has pushed flow valve open. Now much larger current can flow through larger section of circuit.

transistor on.

The *emitter* and *collector* are the high current load connections of a transistor. The circuit or load current flows through the emitter and collector leads.

Fig. 5-9 uses a simple hydraulic circuit to demonstrate the action of a transistor. A small control tube (base) can be used to open or close a main flow valve. When closed, the valve blocks fluid flow through the large tube (emitter-collector). Then, when a small pressure or current flows through the small control tube (base), the valve opens. This lets a large current flow through the large tubes (emitter-collector). This same principle is used in a transistor.

Transistor operation

Fig. 5-10 shows a simplified illustration of how a transistor operates. It also compares the action of a transistor to a relay for a horn circuit.

Battery voltage is connected to the transistor and to the relay. However, since the horn button switches are NOT activated, current does not flow through the transistor emitter-collector junction or the relay points. The horns do not sound.

Then, when the horn button switches are pushed, current flows through the base of the transistor and through

the coil of the relay. This turns the transistor on and the relay contacts close. High current can then flow through both circuits to the horns.

As you can see, a transistor and a relay can perform the same function. They both can use a small control current to operate a much larger circuit current. In a way, both have *amplified* (increased) a control current. Then much smaller wires can be used in the control circuit.

A transistor is much smaller than a relay and it does not have moving parts to wear out. A transistor can also turn on and off much faster than a relay. As a result, transistors are steadily replacing all types of mechanical contacts in the automobile.

Transistor types

There are numerous transistor types. You should be familiar with the most common ones.

A *signal transistor* is used to amplify low power signals or switch small currents on and off. These are very small transistors located in complex electronic circuits: computers, radios, amplifiers, etc.

A *power transistor* is used to control high current levels. It will commonly be used to turn power on and off to circuit loads. See Fig. 5-11.

For example, power transistors are used in radios to operate the speakers. They are the output devices that regulate the fluctuating current to make the speaker diaphragms vibrate and produce sound. Smaller signal transistors feed current to the base circuits of the power transistors.

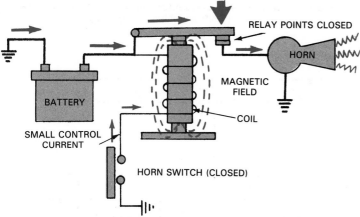

A—Horn button is pressed and small control current flows through relay windings. Magnetic field pulls on contact arm and closes points. Larger current then flows to and energizes horn.

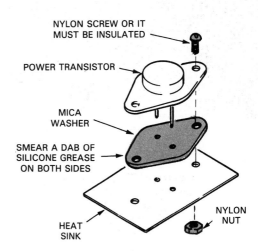

Fig. 5-11. This is power transistor. Note its shape and how it is usually mounted on heat sink. Heat sink dissipates heat to prevent transistor damage. Silicone grease and washer are used to help heat flow away from power transistor.

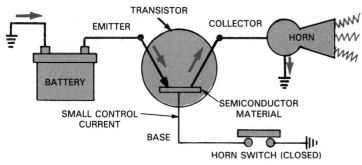

B—Horn button is wired to base of transistor. When pressed, tiny current flows to base of transistor. This changes emitter-collector junction into a conductor. Larger current then flows through main horn circuit.

Fig. 5-10. Relay, studied in previous chapter, is another excellent way to demonstrate action of transistor. Small control current or circuit is used to operate much larger circuit or horn current. (Echlin)

High frequency transistors are capable of turning on and off very quickly. The base region is made very thin and the chip is small so that it can react to changes in voltage easily. This type is also used in radios, for example.

A *field effect transistor,* abbreviated FET, is a very high impedance (resistance) device that needs almost no input current to turn on and off. Shown in Fig. 5-12, it

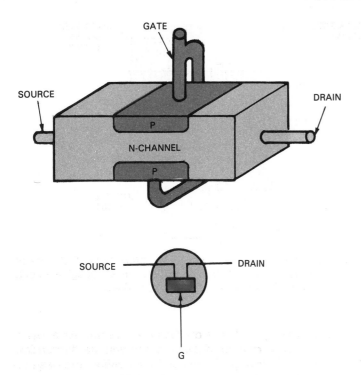

Fig. 5-12. Field effect transistor is good for controlling very weak electrical signals. Note its construction and symbol.

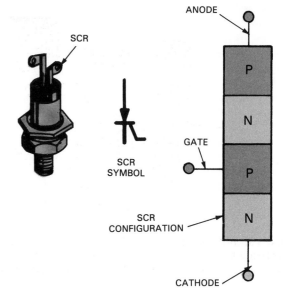

Fig. 5-13. Silicon controlled rectifier works like a transistor switch but cannot amplify current. (Robert Bosch)

uses a small channel surrounded by the opposite type semiconductor material. It works opposite to a conventional transistor.

The FET channel conducts current until a voltage is applied to the gate. With the gate energized, the channel resistance increases tremendously and current drain into the gate drops even more. A FET will operate with super small input or gate signals and might be used to amplify the small radio wave signals coming into a radio from the antenna.

There are dozens of other more specialized types of transistors. However, the ones just discussed should give you enough background to understand their operation.

THYRISTORS

A *thyristor,* like a transistor, has three leads—one lead triggers the unit to conduct current through the other two leads. It is a controllable diode that can only be used as a switch since it is either on or off. Unlike a transistor, it cannot be used to control different amounts of current or amplify different current levels.

A *silicon controlled rectifier* is a thyristor and a four layer semiconductor device. It is similar to a transistor but has a fourth layer of semiconductor material. As shown in Fig. 5-13, if the gate of the SCR is energized, the SCR begins to conduct through its anode-cathode leads.

Fig. 5-14 shows how a SCR could be used in a circuit. In this example, the SCR is used to operate a high current draw motor. When the motor switch is open, the SCR acts as an insulator and current cannot flow through the motor windings. However, with the switch closed, gate current activates the SCR and it changes to a con-

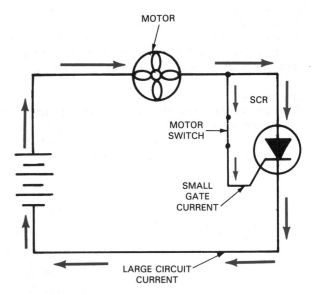

Fig. 5-14. Example of how SCR might be used as solid state switch. Switch can be closed to send small current to SCR. SCR then conducts larger current for operating motor.

ductor. Battery current can then flow through and operate the motor.

A *triac* is another type of thyristor but it is equivalent to two SCRs connected in parallel. It can switch both DC and AC current. Since a car uses DC, this type device is not common in automobiles. SCRs are more common and can be used in ignition system amplifiers and charging system voltage regulator circuits.

HALL-EFFECT CHIP

A *Hall-effect chip* is a semiconductor device that can produce a small signal voltage or current when acted upon by a magnetic field. This is illustrated in Fig. 5-15. In A, note how a small control current is used to ready

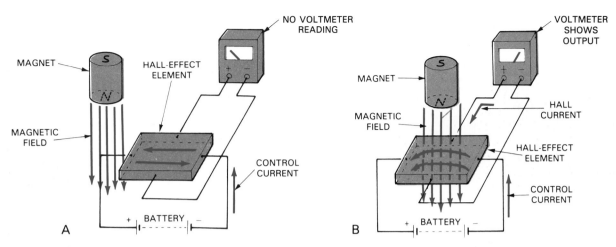

Fig. 5-15. Hall IC operation. A—Current from battery flows lengthwise through Hall-effect element. B—When Hall-effect element is exposed to a magnetic field, some current is diverted into separate circuit. Current then flows crosswise through element. This Hall current is used to signal electronic control box. (Kawasaki Motors Corp., U.S.A.)

the Hall-effect chip. Since it is NOT exposed to a magnetic field, current does NOT flow out of the device (to voltmeter). When a magnet is moved next to the Hall chip, the semiconductor material can then divert some current to the circuit (voltmeter in this example).

As you will learn in later chapters, a Hall-effect chip can be used as a vehicle sensor for measuring engine speed, crankshaft or camshaft position, etc.

Piezo crystal

A *piezo crystal* uses physical pressure to produce a small current output. Pictured in Fig. 5-16, a diaphragm can be linked to the piezo crystal to make a microphone. Sound waves make the diaphragm flex back and forth.

This presses and pulls on the piezo crystal. As a result, the piezo crystal produces a small voltage fluctuation. This small voltage signal can be amplified and used for various functions, like a pressure sensor.

PHOTONIC SEMICONDUCTORS

Photonic semiconductor is a classification of devices that can emit or detect light. This is a fast growing field of electronics that is now being found in automotive electronics.

Light emitting diodes

A *light emitting diode,* abbreviated LED, is a semiconductor that will emit light when electrically energized. It acts as a tiny light bulb and is commonly used as a small indicator light in various vehicle systems. Since an LED converts electricity directly into light, it is much more efficient than most other light sources.

Fig. 5-17 shows the basic construction and action of a light emitting diode. It is a N-P junction with special doped semiconductors. When connected to a power source, photons (electrons) are emitted from the

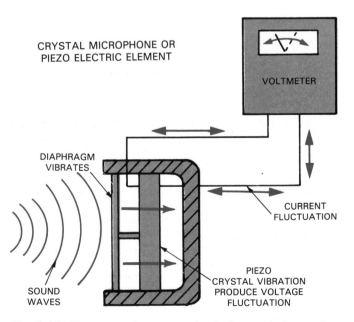

Fig. 5-16. Piezo crystal converts physical pressure into a tiny electrical output. This is ideal for making a microphone. Sound waves in air vibrate diaphragm and piezo crystal. Crystal generates voltage that corresponds to strength of sound waves. This voltage signal can be amplified to operate a speaker in a sound system for example.

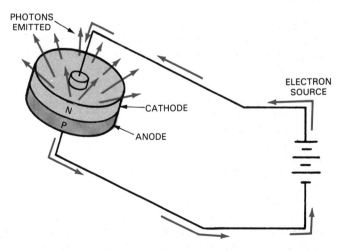

Fig. 5-17. LED is simply N-P junction. When current passes through special doped semiconductor materials, light is emitted.

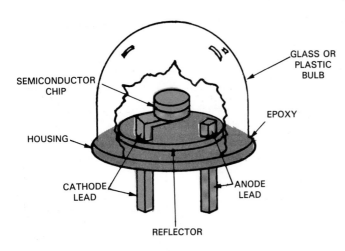

Fig. 5-18. Note construction of light emitting diode.

semiconductor substance. We see these photons as light.

A light emitting diode chip is housed in a glass or plastic bulb, Fig. 5-18. Tiny wire leads extend out the bottom of the housing and connect to the LED chip.

LEDs might be used as small indicator lights in the dash panel for the climate control system of a car. They are also used to produce a trouble code on the side of a few makes of car computers.

Photoresistors

A *photoresistor* is a semiconductor that acts as a resistor when in the dark but changes to a conductor when exposed to light. Fig. 5-19 demonstrates its operation.

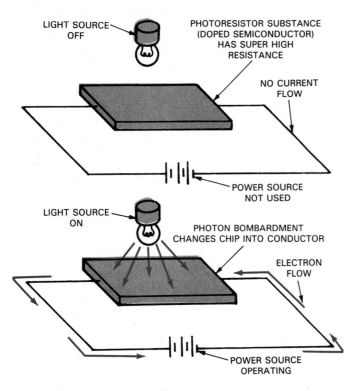

Fig. 5-19. Photoresistor will change resistance when exposed to different amounts of light.

If a battery is connected to the photoresistor with the light source off, no current flows through the device. When the light source turns on, the photoresistor changes to a conductor to allow current flow.

Fiber optics

Fiber optics is a field of electronics that uses light flowing through small strands of plastic or glass to send electrical information. Illustrated in Fig. 5-20, a light source can be turned on and off to send flashing light through the tiny strand of fiber optic material. The light will bounce off the inner wall of the strand and shoot out the other end of the fiber optic strand. A light detector can be used to sense the light signal. The signal can then be amplified into a larger current signal to operate other devices. One strand of fiber optic material can be used to send the same amount of electrical data as a large bundle of conventional metal wires. This subject will be discussed further in later chapters.

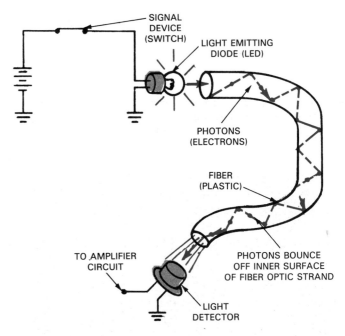

Fig. 5-20. Fiber optic material will carry light beam signals. Photons travel inside fiber optic strand. Detector can be used to transfer light pulses into another circuit.

Solar cells

A *solar cell* is another photonic device that will convert light directly into DC electricity, Fig. 5-21. It uses several layers of doped semiconductor material to pull photons or electrons out of light and feed them through small electrical leads.

Fig. 5-22 shows a solar cell connected to a digital voltmeter. Note how room light allows the solar cell to produce a small voltage. If many solar cells are connected together, a substantial source of electrical energy can be produced.

There are many potential applications for solar cells since they are almost free sources of electricity. They can be placed in the roof of a car to charge the battery or run a cooling fan for the interior of a parked car.

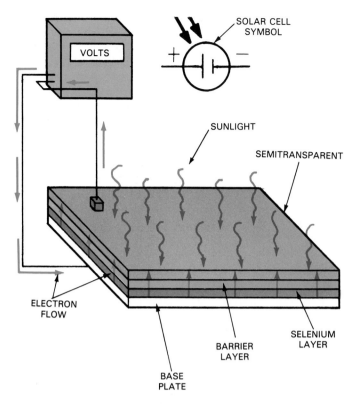

Fig. 5-21. Solar cell converts light into electrical current. Semiconductor surfaces trap light and feed electrons in light to output leads.

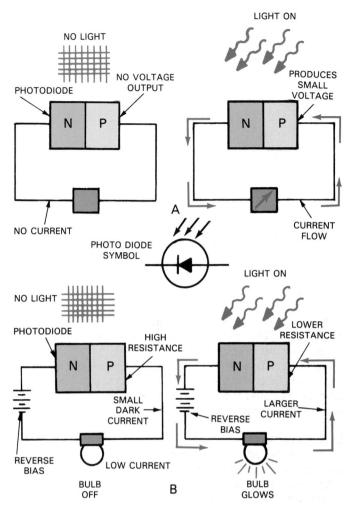

Fig. 5-23. Study action of photodiode. A—When in dark, photodiode has no voltage output. When exposed to light, photodiode produces small voltage. B—Reverse bias photodiode is being used to switch current on and off. Without light, it acts as insulator. With light, photodiode conducts current to light bulb.

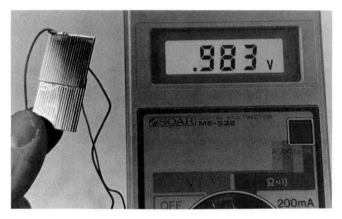

Fig. 5-22. Room light is making this solar cell develop almost one volt. (Union Electronic Distributors)

Photodiodes

A *photodiode* is a P-N junction device that is sensitive to light, as are all P-N junctions. This device will become a small source of current when excited by light. It can also be used to control current. Both applications are illustrated in Fig. 5-23.

Phototransistors

A *phototransistor* uses a small lens to direct light onto the P-N junction and perform a function similar to a photodiode. Shown in Fig. 5-24, when light strikes the phototransistor, the emitter-collector junction conducts current. When light is blocked, the emitter-collector junc-

tion changes to an insulator and blocks current.

A phototransistor might be used in an automatic headlight dimming system. It can be used as the sensor, in conjunction with a control circuit, to turn the headlights on and off by reacting to light conditions.

Liquid crystal displays

A *liquid crystal display* uses a fluid crystal material sandwiched between two sealed, glass plates. This device can be used to display numbers, letters, or other images by polarizing light.

The front glass of a liquid crystal display has a coating that forms the images (numbers for example). When electrical energized, the liquid crystal substance can arrange itself to either block light (appear dark) or reflect light (appear light or illuminated). This principle can be used to make images appear on the liquid crystal display. See Fig. 5-25.

Liquid crystal displays are commonly used in the instrument cluster of modern passenger cars. Miles per hour, tachometer graphics, odometer, and other displays

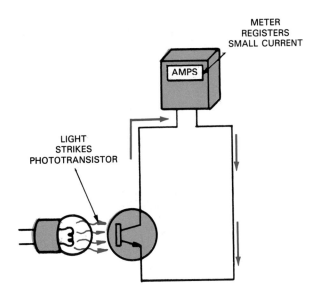

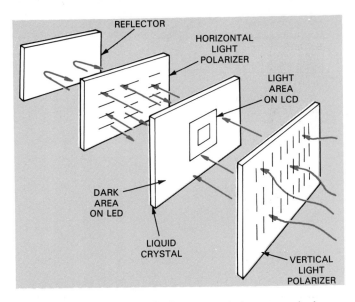

Fig. 5-25. Liquid crystal display uses polarizers to make image area light and nonimage area dark.

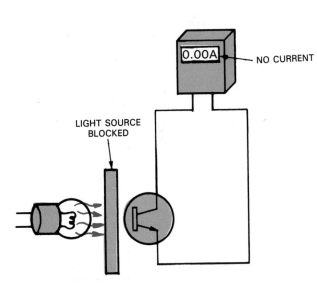

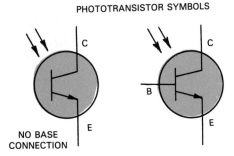

Fig. 5-24. Phototransistor also uses light to change semiconductor material from insulator to conductor. Transistor has small lens that directs light onto junction.

can be shown with liquid crystal devices. This will be explained further in Chapters 17 and 29.

Vacuum fluorescent displays

A *vacuum fluorescent display* generates light images by shooting electrons onto a phosphor material. Like a television picture tube, this makes the phosphor coating glow and emit light.

As in Fig. 5-26, the phosphor coating on each display segment is arranged into small bars. Energizing different sets of bars can form numbers from zero through nine. Energizing all of the outer bars and the center bar would produce an eight, for example. Words can also be formed. See Fig. 5-27.

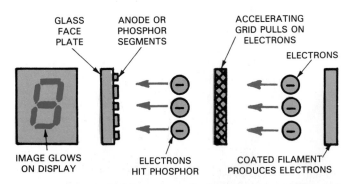

Fig. 5-26. Vacuum fluorescent display uses heated filament to produce electrons. Grid pulls electrons onto phosphor segments. Phosphor segments then glow to produce image on display. (Chrysler)

Fig. 5-27. Note how phosphor segments are visible on this display board. Illuminating different segments can be used to produce different numbers. (Union Electronic Distributors)

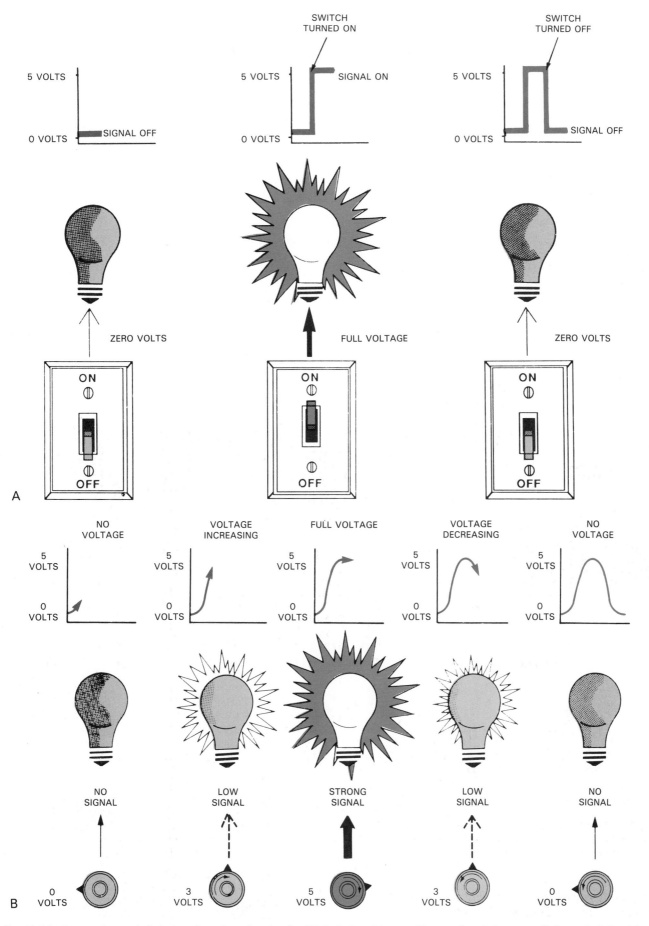

Fig. 5-28. Comparison of digital and analog signals. A—Digital signal is on-off type signal, just as a light switch is either on or off. Digital signal is represented by square wave. B—Analog signal is gradually changing voltage. Note how variable resistor can be used to produce analog signal. (Ford Motor Co.)

Vacuum fluorescent displays are normally brighter than liquid crystal displays. However, they are not as rugged and they consume more power.

PULSES, WAVES, SIGNALS, NOISE

Electronics is much more than just controlling DC current in a circuit or converting AC into DC. Just as a Morse Code can be used to send information or *data* over a telegraph network, various pulses, waves, and signals are used to send data in an auto computer system. This is how sensors "talk" to a computer.

A *pulse* is a sudden increase or decrease in voltage or current. A perfect *pulse* would have an almost instant increase or decrease in voltage or current. Fig. 5-28 illustrates a line representing several pulses. If all of the pulses are spaced evenly apart, the pulses could be used as a *clock pulse* to time when events will happen in electronic circuits.

A *wave* is a gradual increase or decrease (fluctuation) in voltage and current over a longer time span. The voltage changes from positive polarity to negative polarity. A wave is illustrated in Fig. 5-28.

A *square wave* has an almost instantaneous change in voltage. A *sine* or *analog wave* has a gradual change in voltage.

Fig. 5-29 explains the various parts of pulses and waves. Note how the lines represent voltages or on and off conditions.

Fig. 5-30 shows how the distance between waves represents frequency. *Frequency* is how fast or slow a pulse or wave changes from on or off or from positive to negative. *High frequency waves* would have rapid up and down swings and steep slopes. *Low frequency waves* would have a greater distance between humps and dips or rises and falls in voltage. The slopes of the waves would NOT be as steep.

An illustration of how wave or pulse voltage can vary is shown in Fig. 5-30. Note that the taller a wave or pulse, the higher its voltage and vise versa.

A *signal* is a specific arrangement of pulses or waves that carries electronic data or information. Just as a telegraph operator can send an SOS (help) signal by pressing the telegraph key in a certain pattern (3 dots, 3 dashes, 3 dots), signals are also used by automotive computers. In automotives, a signal might represent a condition (temperature, part location, rpm, etc.).

Noise refers to an UNWANTED VOLTAGE fluctuation in a circuit. Noise can enter a circuit from lightning, CB radios, from the ignition system, or charging system for example. Noise can upset the operation of an electronic circuit, Fig. 5-31. Capacitors or condensers are used to prevent noise in DC.

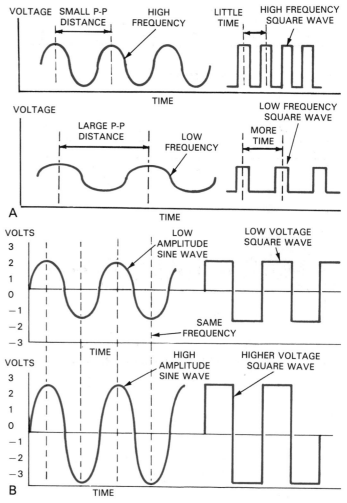

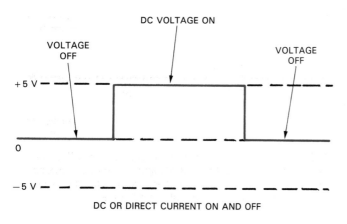

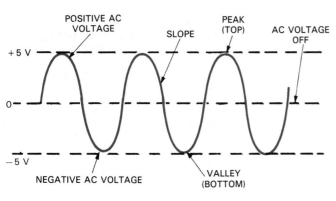

Fig. 5-29. Study basic parts of square wave and sine or analog wave.

Fig. 5-30. A—High frequency signal would have waves spaced closer together. Low frequency has peaks or waves farther apart. B—Note how height of wave or pulse denotes voltage. A tall wave would represent a higher voltage and vice versa.

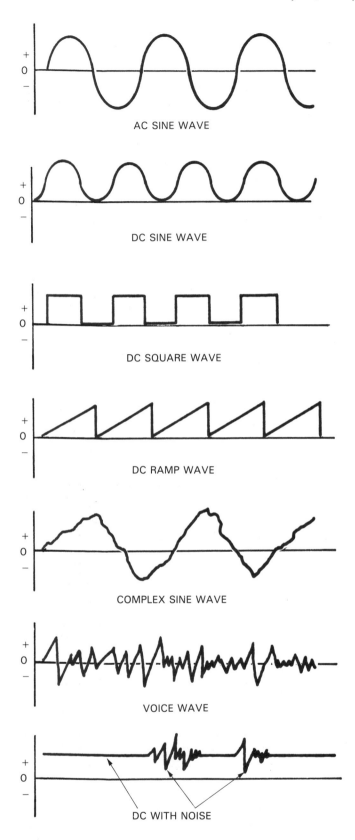

AC SINE WAVE

DC SINE WAVE

DC SQUARE WAVE

DC RAMP WAVE

COMPLEX SINE WAVE

VOICE WAVE

DC WITH NOISE

Fig. 5-31. Study these waveforms. Note that noise is unwanted voltage fluctuation.

Pulses, waves, signals, noise, and related topics will be discussed further in later chapters on sensors, computers, actuators, alternators, or where they apply.

DIGITAL ELECTRONICS

Digital electronics is a specialized field of study dealing with how a computer can have "artificial intelligence." A computer analyzes inputs or signals from sensors. It has memory. It can make logical decisions on how to control specific outputs using the inputs. Digital electronics explains how a computer can have this ability.

Binary numbering system

The *binary numbering system* only uses two numbers (zero and one) and is the key to digital electronics and computers. Zero (0) and one (1) can be arranged in different sequences to represent other numbers, letters, words, a computer input, or a computer output. Since electronic devices can be either on or off, the binary system is ideal. Remember "Bi" means two and this system only uses two numbers.

To use the binary system, a computer can turn switches (transistors for example) either on or off. Illustrated in Fig. 5-32, OFF would represent a zero (0) and ON would represent one (1) in the binary system.

Fig. 5-33 shows how the binary numbering system works. Note that a 0011 in binary would equal a 3 in

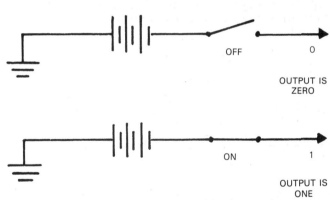

OFF   0

OUTPUT IS
ZERO

ON   1

OUTPUT IS
ONE

Fig. 5-32. Since electronic components can be on or off, binary numbering system is ideal for digital logic or computer circuits. Binary system only has two numbers, zero and one, which represent ON and OFF conditions.

DECIMAL NUMBER	BINARY NUMBER CODE 8 4 2 1	BINARY TO DECIMAL CONVERSION
0	0000	= 0+0 = 0
1	0001	= 0+1 = 1
2	0010	= 2+0 = 2
3	0011	= 2+1 = 3
4	0100	= 4+0 = 4
5	0101	= 4+1 = 5
6	0110	= 4+2 = 6
7	0111	= 4+2+1 = 7
8	1000	= 8+0 = 8

Fig. 5-33. Chart shows how binary numbers can be converted into decimal or base ten numbers. Note how right-hand binary number equals one and left-hand number equals eight. Study this chart.

NOT (INVERTER)

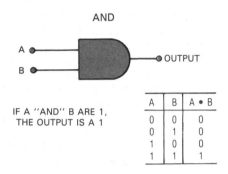

OUTPUT INVERTS INPUT

A	Ā
1	0
0	1

AND

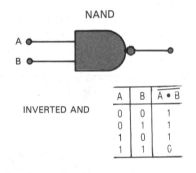

IF A "AND" B ARE 1,
THE OUTPUT IS A 1

A	B	A • B
0	0	0
0	1	0
1	0	0
1	1	1

NAND

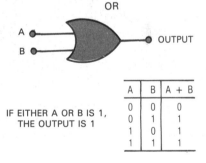

INVERTED AND

A	B	A̅ •̅ B̅
0	0	1
0	1	1
1	0	1
1	1	0

OR

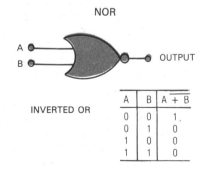

IF EITHER A OR B IS 1,
THE OUTPUT IS 1

A	B	A + B
0	0	0
0	1	1
1	0	1
1	1	1

NOR

OUTPUT

INVERTED OR

A	B	A̅ +̅ B̅
0	0	1
0	1	0
1	0	0
1	1	0

Fig. 5-34. These are the most common types of gates. A gate is an electronic circuit that will produce a specific output with specific inputs. Truth table shows what these outputs will be with conditions. (General Motors Corporation)

our decimal system. A 0110 in binary would equal a six in decimal. Binary code numbers could also be used to represent letters, words, and other outputs.

Note! In binary or computer language, a zero or a one would be called a *bit.* A pattern of four bits would be a *nibble.* A pattern of eight bits (zeros or ones) would be called a *byte,* pronounced "bite."

GATING CIRCUITS

A *gate* is an electronic circuit that produces a specific output for a given input. Just as a diode will pass current when forward biased (output lead would have voltage representing one) and block current when reverse biased (output would be zero or no voltage), gates have *programmed* (known or predetermined) outputs.

The most common gates include the following:
1. INVERTER. An *inverter gate,* also called a NOT GATE, will reverse its input. If the input has voltage applied (input is one), the output terminals will not have voltage (output is zero) or vice versa. An inverter can be used to make other gates, Fig. 5-34.
2. AND GATE. An *and gate* requires voltage (1) at both inputs to produce a voltage (1) at the output. As in Fig. 5-34, if pins A and B are both one (voltage applied or on), then the output will be one (on). If only A and NOT B has voltage, the output will be zero (off).
3. NAND GATE. A *nand gate* is an inverted AND gate. In Fig. 5-34, note the small circle on the output lead of the gate. The small circle represents an inverter and will reverse the normal output of the AND gate, producing a NAND gate.
4. OR GATE. An *or gate* will produce an output (one or on) if either input gate is energized (1). A or B input voltage (1) will result in voltage (1) at the output lead, Fig. 5-34.
5. NOR GATE. A *nor gate* is an inverted OR gate. Again, the output is inverted to produce the opposite output as an OR gate. See Fig. 5-34.

Truth tables

A *truth table* is a chart that shows what the output of a gate will be with different inputs. Truth tables for each basic gate are shown in Fig. 5-34. Study how they function!

For example, look at the truth table for an OR gate. The output will be ON (one) with A or B or both energized. Only when neither input is ON will the output be OFF (zero). A truth table graphically shows how a gate functions.

Gates are called logic devices because they make logical decisions (outputs) for specific inputs (facts). Illustrated in Fig. 5-35, it will require you to have several inputs (learning experiences) to develop good outputs (skills) as an automotive electronic technician.

Fig. 5-36 compares an AND gate and an OR gate with simple electrical circuits. Note that if two light switches are wired in parallel, either switch A or B will turn the light ON (output one). However, if the two light switches are wired in series, both A and B must be ON to activate the light bulb. Compare these circuits to the action of the gates and the truth tables.

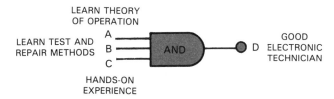

Fig. 5-35. Note how logic gate can be used to "think." For you to be good technician, you would need to have a yes, on, or one at each of these AND inputs. Then, your skill or output would be good, yes, or "on."

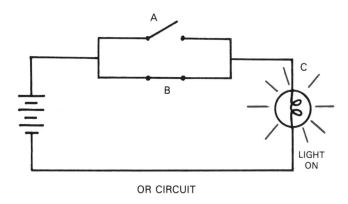

A	B	A OR B
0	0	0
0	1	1
1	0	1
1	1	1

A OR B ON = C ON

OR CIRCUIT

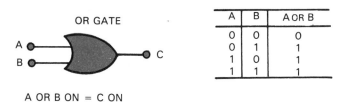

A	B	A AND B
0	0	0
0	1	0
1	0	0
1	1	1

AND CIRCUIT

Fig. 5-36. OR gate is like a circuit with two switches in parallel. A or B will produce an output. AND gate can be shown with circuit having two switches in series. A and B must be on to get output.

Using gates

Since one gate will produce a logical output from definite inputs, several gates can be wired together to make more complex outputs after reacting to more complex inputs. This is how a computer operates. Thousands of gates can be connected together to make a super complex circuit that can produce hundreds of outputs (decisions) from hundreds of inputs (facts).

Our brain works on the same principle. It is a massive chemical-electrical gate network. One example, if we touch a hot stove, our nervous system sends a tiny chemical-electrical pulse (input signal representing pain) up our arm, through our spinal cord, and into our brain. Our brain has "molecular gates" that analyze (add up) this input (pulse or signal) to produce an output. The output is another electrical-chemical signal that controls our reflex muscle action to pull back from the hot stove. Our brain has billions of cells and billions of these chemical-electrical gates and is much more *powerful* (intelligent) than any computer.

Note! This subject will be explained further in later chapters on automotive computers.

INTEGRATED CIRCUITS

An *integrated circuit* is an electronic circuit that has been reduced in size and placed on the surface of a tiny semiconductor chip. Abbreviated IC, it is a sophisticated electronic device containing extremely small components. In fact, a microscope is needed to see the components on an IC. Look at Fig. 5-37.

Fig. 5-37. Integrated circuit can contain hundreds of electronic components. Components have been reduced photographically and placed on small semiconductor chip.

To manufacture an integrated circuit, a doped silicon wafer is sliced into thin pieces, Fig. 5-38. Then, using photographic techniques of reduction, other semiconductor materials are deposited on the wafer to form electronic components and circuits. See Fig. 5-39.

Fig. 5-40 shows the basic construction of an integrated circuit. Note how different semiconductor substances are deposited in the silicone chip to produce resistors, diodes, and transistors. Metal conductors on the top of the chip connect these various electronic components to form the circuit. Wire leads are used to allow for input and output connections to the IC chip.

Fig. 5-41 shows a machine soldering an IC.

A cutaway of an IC is given in Fig. 5-42. Note that the small circuit chip is housed in a plastic body. Larger metal leads extend out of the body.

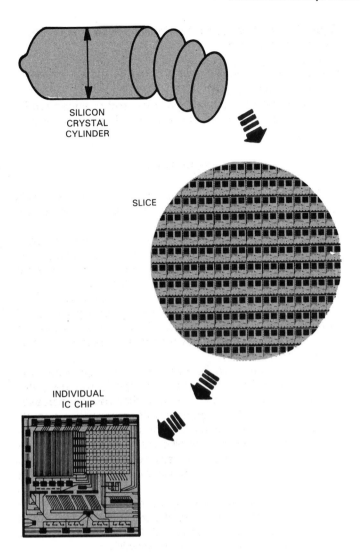

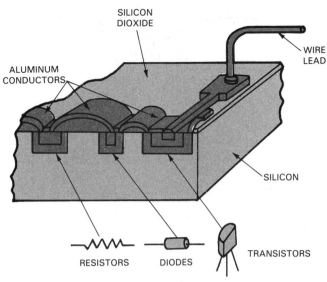

Fig. 5-40. Note how electronic components are formed on microscopic section of IC chip. Different semiconductor materials are deposited in silicon. Conductors are formed to connect various components.

Fig. 5-38. To make an integrated circuit, silicon cylinder is sliced into small wafers. Each slice can then be used to produce complex electronic circuit on surface of silicon. (Chrysler)

Fig. 5-41. This is photo showing precise equipment soldering leads onto IC circuit chip. Microscope would be needed to see circuit. (Delco Electronics)

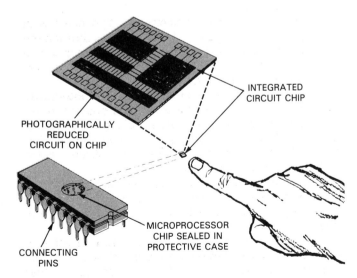

Fig. 5-39. Integrated circuit chip is tiny. It is housed inside plastic case. Pins extend out of case for connecting circuit chip to other circuits or components. (Ford)

Types of integrated circuits

There are many classifications of integrated circuits. The most general ones include:

A *digital* IC is an integrated circuit containing logic circuits. It might contain thousands of gates designed to analyze ON-OFF input signals or store signals. The logic circuits or gates can then produce preprogrammed outputs, Fig. 5-43.

An *analog* IC, also called a *linear* IC, contains complete amplifier circuits. The output will follow the input as signal strength (voltage) changes. A small input will result in a similar but stronger output. It operates similar

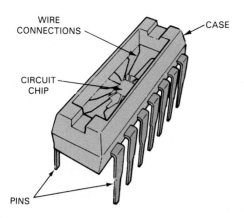

Fig. 5-42. Note how tiny chip installs inside plastic case. Tiny wires connect chip to metal pins. Pins then plug in or solder to other parts of circuit.

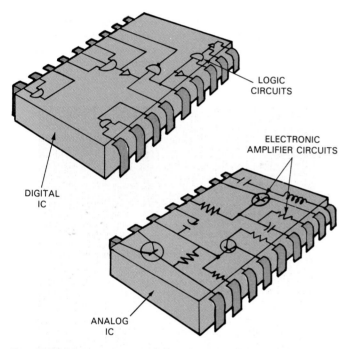

Fig. 5-43. These are two broad classifications of integrated circuits. Digital circuit uses gates to produce logic circuits for computers. Analog IC is small amplifier circuit for increasing output strength or altering output.

to a transistor amplifier. A typical analog or linear IC could be found in a modern car radio or computer. It would be used to amplify the radio signal, Fig. 5-43.

An *active* IC is a classification that includes integrated circuits that can change response to an external signal. Both analog and digital ICs would fall under this category.

A *passive* IC cannot change its output response from its original input. An example would be a *resistor pack IC* that contained several resistors. Even though the resistors would reduce the outputs compared to the inputs, it would not alter them otherwise.

A *DIP* is an integrated circuit with dual in-line pins (terminals). There is a row of pins on each side of the plastic case. This is a classification of the IC case and terminal arrangement. A DIP is the most common IC con-figuration and is used for logic circuits, amplifiers, resistor packs, etc.

A *SIP* is an integrated circuit with a single row of in-line pins or terminals. It is NOT as common as the DIP but is sometimes used as a voltage regulator circuit.

Note! Integrated circuit operation and replacement is discussed elsewhere in this textbook. Refer to the index as needed.

SUMMARY

Electronic devices do not use moving parts. Examples include diodes, transistors, solar cells, integrated circuits, etc.

A semiconductor is a substance that can change from an insulator to a conductor with external stimulation. A P-type semiconductor has more holes or a positive charge; N-type material has more electrons.

A diode is an electrical check valve. It will only pass current in one direction. It is made by joining two small pieces of N and P materials. When reverse biased, a diode acts as an insulator. When forward biased, it acts as a conductor.

A zener diode can be used as a voltage regulator. When a specific reverse bias voltage is reached, the zener diode conducts to prevent further voltage increase.

A transistor will switch or amplify current in a circuit. The base is usually the control for a transistor. When the base is energized with a small current, a much larger current can flow through the emitter-collector junction. There are several types of transistors: signal, power, high frequency, field effect, etc.

A thyristor is a diode that has three leads and functions like a transistor. A small gate current will switch a much higher circuit current. A thyristor can only do switching operations; it cannot amplify.

A hall-effect chip reacts to a magnetic field to produce a small signal current. A piezo crystal produces a small current when acted upon by pressure, sound waves for example.

An LED, or light emitting diode, is a small semiconductor that converts current into light.

Fiber optics is a field of electronics that deals with using light to transmit data. Light will travel through the small strands of glass or plastic. A light detector can be used to sense the light pulses or signals on the other end of the strand for operating other circuits.

Solar cells convert light directly into DC. Photodiodes and phototransistors also utilize light to produce current.

A liquid crystal display uses a fluid semiconductor sandwiched between two glass or plastic plates. Current can be used to polarize the semiconductor, making an image appear on the front.

A vacuum fluorescent display uses electrons to illuminate a phosphor material. Much like a TV picture tube, the phosphor coating glows to produce numbers or letters on the display.

A pulse is a sudden increase or decrease in voltage. A wave is a more gradual change in voltage. A signal is a specific arrangement of pulses or waves that represents data or information. Noise is an unwanted voltage fluctuation in a circuit.

The binary numbering system only uses two numbers:

zero (0) and one (1). Groups or specific arrangements of zeros and ones can be used to represent decimal numbers, letters, and other data.

Computers can use the binary system by using voltage to represent ON or ONE and no voltage to represent OFF or ZERO. Gates are switching circuits that will produce known outputs for specific inputs. Thousands of gates can be wired together to produce the ''brains'' of a computer.

A truth table is a chart that shows how a logic gate functions. It will give the outputs for all possible inputs.

An integrated circuit is an electronic circuit that has been reduced in size photographically. One small chip might contain hundreds of resistors, diodes, capacitors, and transistors.

KNOW THESE TERMS

Solid state, Semiconductor, Doped, Silicon, N, P, Diode, Reverse bias, Forward bias, Rectification, Half-wave, Full-wave, Zener diode, Transistor, Base, Emitter, Collector, Amplify, FET, Thyristor, SCR, Triac, Hall chip, Piezo crystal, Photonics, LED, Photoresistor, Fiber optics, Solar cell, Photodiode, Phototransistor, Vacuum fluorescent display, Liquid crystal display, Pulse, Wave, Signal, Noise, Binary system, Gate, Inverter, AND, NAND, OR, NOR, Truth table, IC, Digital IC, Analog IC, Active IC, Passive IC, DIP, SIP.

REVIEW QUESTIONS—CHAPTER 5

1. Semiconductors are made from _____, also called _____ or _____.
2. Explain the difference between P-type and N-type materials.
3. How does a diode function?
4. A zener diode is commonly used to:
   a. Amplify current.
   b. Amplify voltage.
   c. Regulate voltage.
   d. Rectify AC.
5. A _____ is a semiconductor device for switching or amplifying current in a circuit.
6. This type transistor might be used to drive the speakers in a car sound system.
   a. Power transistor.
   b. Signal transistor.
   c. Field effect transistor.
   d. High frequency transistor.
7. A _____ _____ _____, abbreviated _____, is a P-N junction semiconductor that will emit light when electrically energized.
8. How can fiber optic material be useful?
9. This device will convert light into electrical current.
   a. Phototransistor.
   b. Solar cell.
   c. Photodiode.
   d. None of the above.
   e. All of the above.
10. Explain the differences between pulses, waves, signals, and noise.
11. How can the binary numbering system be used by a computer to represent data?

12. Convert the following binary numbers into decimal numbers:
    a. 0010.
    b. 1010.
    c. 1110.
    d. 1111.
13. Explain the five basic types of gates.
14. A _____ _____ is a chart that shows the output of a gate for various inputs.
15. Describe six types of integrated circuits.

ASE CERTIFICATION—TYPE QUESTIONS

1. Technician A says a semiconductor can act like an insulator. Technician B says a semiconductor can be utilized as a conductor. Who is right?
   (A) A only.
   (B) B only.
   (C) Both A and B.
   (D) Neither A nor B.
2. When a diode is forward biased, it acts like a(n):
   (A) conductor.
   (B) insulator.
   (C) resistor.
   (D) transistor.
3. Technician A says a diode is commonly used to convert alternating current into direct current. Technician B says one diode in series with an AC source will produce full-wave rectification. Who is right?
   (A) A only.
   (B) B only.
   (C) Both A and B.
   (D) Neither A nor B.
4. Technician A says a transistor is a device used to amplify current in a circuit. Technician B says a transistor is a device used to rectify current in a circuit. Who is right?
   (A) A only.
   (B) B only.
   (C) Both A and B.
   (D) Neither A nor B.
5. All of the following are common types of transistors *except:*
   (A) power transistor.
   (B) Zener transistor.
   (C) signal transistor.
   (D) high frequency transistor.
6. Technician A says a thyristor is a controllable diode. Technician B says a thyristor can be used to control different amounts of current. Who is right?
   (A) A only.
   (B) B only.
   (C) Both A and B.
   (D) Neither A nor B.
7. All of the following are photronic semiconductors *except:*
   (A) light emitting diodes.
   (B) field effect transistors.
   (C) solar cells.
   (D) photoresistors.
8. Technician A says a square wave is a gradual increase or decrease in voltage and current over a certain time span. Technician B says an electronic "pulse" is a sudden increase or decrease in voltage or current. Who is right?
   (A) A only.
   (B) B only.
   (C) Both A and B.
   (D) Neither A nor B.
9. Technician A says that in computer language, a pattern of four bits is called a nibble. Technician B says a pattern of eight bits is called a byte. Who is right?
   (A) A only.
   (B) B only.
   (C) Both A and B.
   (D) Neither A nor B.
10. All of the following are classifications of integrated circuits *except:*
    (A) digital.
    (B) DIP.
    (C) FIP.
    (D) analog.

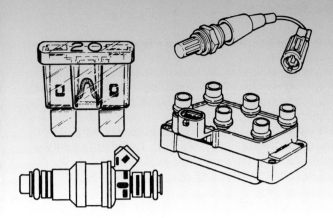

Chapter 6

Tools and Test Equipment

After studying this chapter, you will be able to:
- *Identify the most common tools used during electrical repairs.*
- *Compare analog and digital multimeters.*
- *Explain conventional and inductive meter pickups.*
- *Summarize the use of basic and advanced test equipment.*
- *Select the proper tool or tester for the job.*
- *Describe the equipment needed to troubleshoot computer systems.*
- *More fully comprehend later textbook chapters.*

To be a successful automobile electronic technician, you must be able to select and utilize specialized tools and equipment properly. The tools, testers, and other equipment used in electrical repair will allow you to grasp components; connect wires; measure current, voltage, or resistance; check ignition timing; read computer output data; etc. Without proper tools and equipment, it is impossible to work on late-model cars, which incorporate extensive "electronics."

This chapter will introduce the most common tools and equipment unique to the electronic technician. It is understood that you already have had previous training and are familiar with more general or basic tools.

Note! This chapter will only show and briefly explain specialized tools and equipment for this field of auto service. Other textbook chapters will detail how they are connected to a system and operated. Refer to the index for more information as needed.

SOLDERING TOOLS

Soldering tools are frequently used to join wires, terminals, and other components when making electrical repairs. Soldering provides the BEST METHOD of making a permanent electrical connection. It has the lowest resistance. It will resist corrosion and vibration and is a very rugged repair if done properly.

Solder

Solder is a mixture of lead and tin (60% lead and 40% tin, for example). It comes in roll form for easy application to a joint.

Rosin core solder contains a *flux* (cleaning agent), which is designed for use with electrical repairs. The flux is inside the solder.

Acid core solder has an internal acid flux and should NOT be used for electrical repairs. The acid can cause corrosion and electrical problems. See Fig. 6-1.

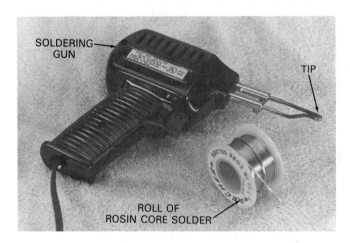

Fig. 6-1. Soldering gun and rosin core solder provide best method for making electrical repairs. Gun is used to heat joint. Then solder is melted onto joint to form connection.

Soldering guns and irons

There are two types of soldering tools used to heat the components (wires or terminals) and melt the solder to form an electrical connection: the soldering gun and the soldering iron. The most common soldering tool is the *soldering gun,* Fig. 6-1. It is ideal for automotive electrical repairs. A soldering gun has a high watt (power) rating and is trigger-operated. It only takes the tip a few seconds to heat up.

A *soldering iron* is also used to work with solder. However, it must be plugged into a wall outlet and heated up for several minutes before use. This makes it less convenient than a soldering gun with its trigger and fast heat-up.

Soldering aids

Soldering aids include various tools that can be helpful when soldering. A few include the following:

A *flux brush* can be used to apply a paste type flux to a joint. You can brush on extra flux to make the solder bond to the metal parts more easily. The flux will help

Fig. 6-2. These are a few tools that can be helpful when soldering. Brushes can be used to apply extra flux to a joint. Picks and small knives can be used to scrape parts clean or to position small components while soldering. (Easco-KD Tools)

clean the joint surfaces to make the solder bond better. Look at Fig. 6-2.

Soldering picks can be used to scrape off corrosion from components before soldering. They can also be used to help hold or pin down small components while soldering. Several are pictured in Fig. 6-2.

A *heat sink* is used to help prevent overheating of electronic components while soldering. It is simply a spring-loaded, clamp-on device. One is shown in Fig. 6-3A.

For example, a heat sink might be clamped onto the wires going to a transistor while soldering the leads to a circuit. This will prevent possibly overheating and damage to the sensitive transistor semiconductor materials.

A *desoldering bulb* is used to remove solder from a joint. The soldering gun is used to heat and melt the solder. Then, the bulb can be squeezed and released to

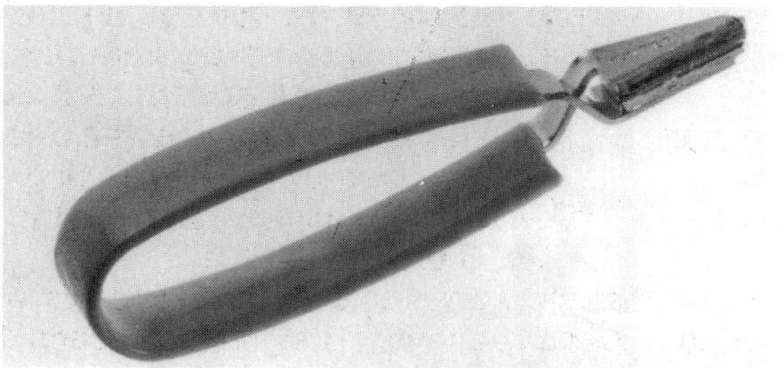

A

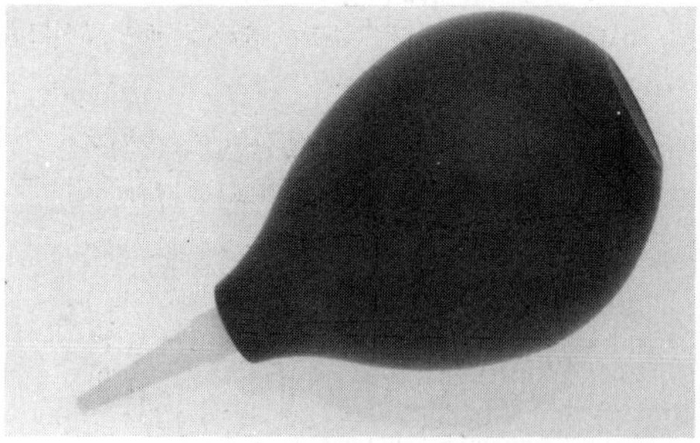

B

C

Fig. 6-3. A—Heat sink will help prevent overheating damage to electronic components while soldering. Heat will transfer into heat sink instead of electronic components. B—Desoldering bulb will suck molten solder off of joint for removing bad components. C—Sponges, soaked with water, will clean debris off of solder gun tip. (Easco-KD Tools)

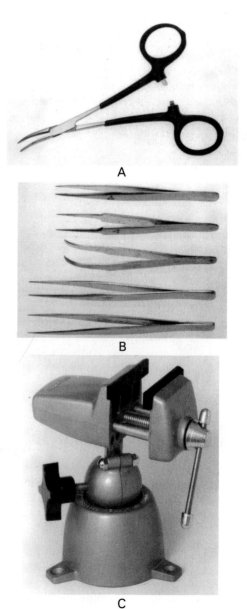

Fig. 6-4. A—Clamping tweezers will hold small components together while soldering. B—Various tweezers styles for positioning and holding tiny components. C—Small vise for holding parts while working. (Easco-KD Tools)

suck molten solder off of the joint. See Fig. 6-3B.

A *soldering sponge* is used to clean the soldering gun tip. When soaked with water, the tip can be rubbed lightly on the sponge to remove debris and ready the gun for making a clean joint. Refer to Fig. 6-3C.

Note! The procedures for soldering are explained in a later chapter.

Various *holding devices* may be needed when soldering components together. This frees your hands to use the soldering gun and solder. Fig. 6-4 shows a few holding devices that make soldering easier.

WIRE STRIPPING TOOLS, PLIERS

When making electrical repairs, the insulation must be *stripped* (insulation pulled off) to expose the metal conductor. Then, the wires can be soldered together or joined with crimp-on type electrical connectors.

All-purpose electrical pliers have special jaws for stripping insulation, forming crimp connectors, and cutting. These pliers have multi-purpose jaws and are one of the most handy tools for automotive electrical repairs. In Fig. 6-5A, note how these pliers have conventional pliers, different size holes for stripping, different size holes for cutting, and different shape jaws for crimping.

Wire stripping pliers have jaws for peeling off plastic or rubber insulation from wires. They do NOT have multiple jaws, Fig. 6-5B.

Lever stripping pliers use a lever action to force the insulation off of wires. You do NOT have to pull on the wire with your other hand. These are handy if you have to strip a large number of wires. Look at Fig. 6-5C.

Diagonal cutting pliers or *side cut pliers* are also used to cut wires and strip off insulation. They will cut off flush or in tight quarters. They will also make a clean cut on multi-strand wires. When used for stripping, care must be taken not to cut through or damage the wire conductor. See Fig. 6-6A.

Needle nose pliers are also used in electrical repair for grasping small components. They can also reach down into tight places easily, Fig. 6-6B.

Note! Steps for stripping wire, using crimp type connectors, and other electrical repairs are detailed later.

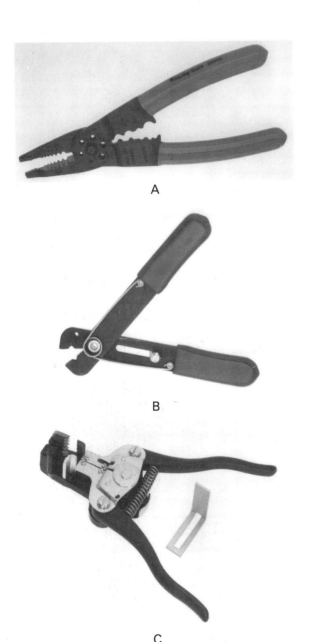

Fig. 6-5. Wire strippers. A—Multi-purpose electrical pliers will cut, strip, and crimp. They are the most handy for automotive applications. B—Wire strippers. C—Lever action wire strippers.

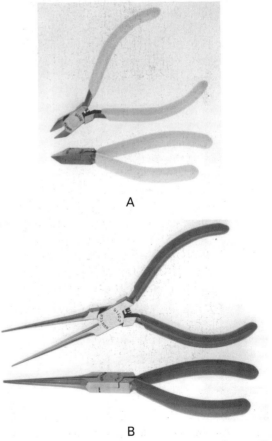

Fig. 6-6. A—Side cut pliers, or diagonal cutting pliers, will cut wires off flush with a surface. They can also be used to strip wires. B—Needle nose pliers will reach into tight places. They are also needed when twisting wires together.
(Easco-KD Tools)

SPECIAL SCREWDRIVERS

In electrical repair, special screwdrivers are needed for working with very small fasteners.

Fig. 6-7A shows an interchangeable screwdriver set. The screwdriver blades can be exchanged in the handle. This screwdriver is very small and is ideal for delicate electronic devices.

Fig. 6-7B shows clip or holding type screwdrivers. They will lock onto and hold small screws. This helps prevent dropping and loss of small screws.

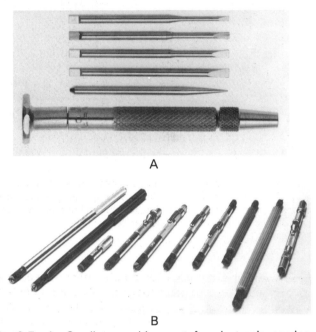

Fig. 6-7. A—Small screwdriver set for electronic service. Blades interchange in handle. B—Clip-type screwdrivers will lock into slot in screws for easy installation. (Easco-KD Tools)

OTHER TOOLS

Numerous other tools are used in electrical repair besides those just introduced. For instance, Fig. 6-8 shows several electrical service tools. Fig. 6-9 shows a mirror tool and pickup tool.

You must always think about tool selection while working. Try to find the best tool for the job. Using the right tool will make your repair work easier, more enjoyable, and more profitable.

ELECTRICAL TEST EQUIPMENT

Electrical test equipment is needed to check electrical-electronic circuits to find faults. This section of the

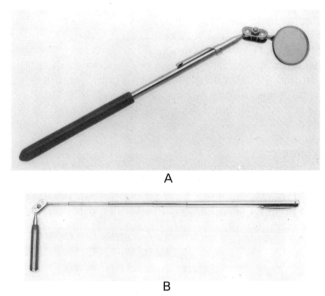

Fig. 6-9. A—Mirror probe will allow you to inspect hidden locations. B—Magnetic pick-up tool is handy if you drop small metal part or fastener in tight place.

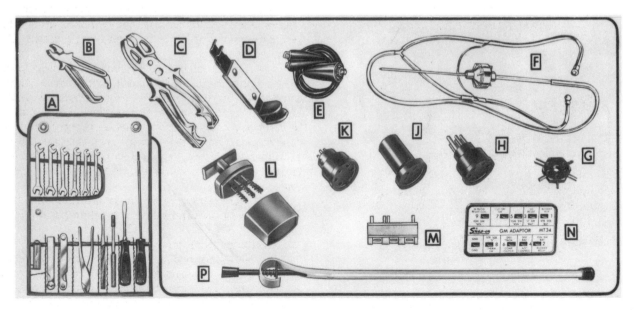

Fig. 6-8. A—Small electrical tool set. B—Plastic fuse puller. C—High tension wire pullers. D—Fuse puller. E—Remote starter switch. F—Stethoscope. G—Wire terminal tool or remover. H through K—Terminal adapters or checkers. L—Terminal or socket cleaning brush. M—Distributor test adapter. N—Electrical system test adapter. P—Pick-up tool. (Snap-On Tools)

chapter will introduce the most commonly used electrical test equipment.

Test lights

Test lights are frequently used to check a circuit for power or continuity. They provide the quickest method of checking for voltage or a complete circuit.

A *circuit-powered test light* is operated by the circuit voltage. An alligator clip is connected to any ground on the car. Then the pointed probe is touched to a circuit conductor. If the circuit has power, the test light bulb will glow. If the tester does NOT glow, something is preventing current flow in the circuit. Look at Fig. 6-10A.

A *self-powered test light* or *continuity light* uses a small battery to check a circuit for continuity (complete circuit path), Fig. 6-10B. The source of circuit voltage must be disconnected. Then the self-powered test light can be grounded and touched to the circuit. If the test light glows, the circuit is grounded or complete. This type is NOT used as much as the circuit-powered test light.

Warning! Some electronic circuits and components can be ruined by the current draw of a test light. Refer to a service manual if you are not sure about a testing procedure.

Multimeters

A *multimeter,* also called *volt-ohm-ammeter* or VOM, is used to measure exact electrical values. It combines a voltmeter, ohmmeter, and ammeter into one case. A VOM is an essential ''tool'' of the auto electronic technician.

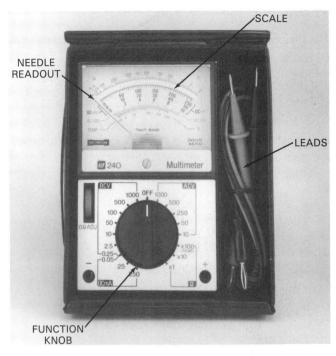

Fig. 6-11. Analog multimeter uses needle to show readings. This type meter is needed when reading might fluctuate or change. Needle movement will easily show changes in voltage, current, or resistance. (TIF)

An analog multimeter uses a conventional needle or pointer to show electrical readings. Besides constant readings, it will also detect changes in voltage, current, or resistance. The needle will wiggle or move up and down to show temporary or rapid changes in electrical values. An analog multimeter is shown in Fig. 6-11.

A *digital multimeter* uses a vacuum fluorescent or liquid crystal display to give a number readout. It does NOT use a swinging pointer to show the electrical value. A digital meter is suited more for constant readings. It draws less current and normally has higher internal resistance or impedance than an analog meter. One is pictured in Fig. 6-12.

An auto technician should have both an analog meter and a digital meter. As you will learn in later chapters, each is suited for specific testing procedures. A digital meter is recommended for testing many computer system devices. It will not draw as much current as an analog meter and is safer to use with delicate electronic components. However, an analog meter is also essential for reading trouble codes, finding intermittent problems, etc.

Note! The chapter, Basic Tests, Circuit Problems, will detail the use of multimeters and other testing devices.

Conventional and inductive pickups

A *conventional pickup* must be touched onto metal components in a circuit to take a reading. For example, to measure current with a conventional meter pickup, the wires must be disconnected and attached to the leads of the multimeter. Then the meter will show current draw through the circuit.

An *inductive pickup* does NOT have to be touched to

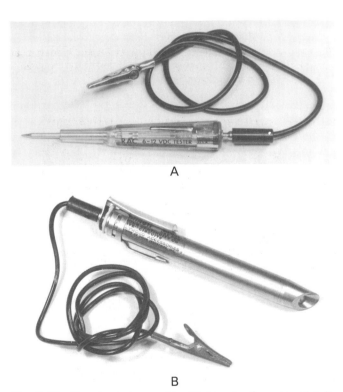

Fig. 6-10. Two basic types of test lights. A—Common circuit-powered test light uses circuit voltage to illuminate tester bulb. It will quickly show you if circuit has power or continuity. B—Self-powered test light has internal battery for illuminating tester bulb. If circuit is complete, tester bulb will glow.

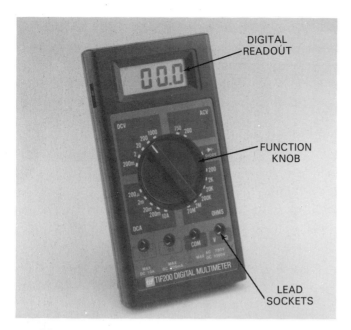

DIGITAL
READOUT

FUNCTION
KNOB

LEAD
SOCKETS

Fig. 6-12. Digital multimeter uses vacuum fluorescent display or liquid crystal display to give readings. This type meter is needed when testing some sensitive electronic components. It will draw less current than an analog meter and may prevent component damage.

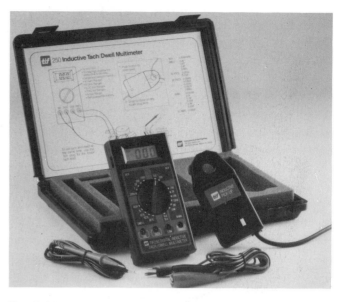

Fig. 6-14. Tach-dwell meter is commonly used in electrical-electronic repairs. Tach or tachometer will measure engine speed or rpm for various tests, adjustments, and repairs. Dwell meter can be used for contact point adjustment on older ignition systems and for checking computer signals to some carburetor solenoids. (TIF)

the metal components in a circuit. It will sense the magnetic field around a current carrying wire to make a measurement. For example, in auto mechanics, an inductive pickup might be used for measuring charging system or alternator current output. The inductive pickup is simply placed around the wire insulation to make an amperage reading.

Fig. 6-13 shows a clip-on multimeter. It is handy for making current readings. It will NOT make inductive DC voltage nor ohms readings however.

Fig. 6-14 pictures a multimeter with both conventional and an inductive pickup. This multimeter also has a tachometer for measuring engine rpm and dwell meter for ignition system and computer output measurements.

Insulation tester

An *insulation tester* is illustrated in Fig. 6-15. It will check the plastic or rubber insulation on wires for deterioration and *leakage* (current flowing out of insulation).

Fig. 6-13. Inductive meters do not have to be touched to the metal part or conductor. They simply clamp around the outside of wires. Since an automobile uses DC, only current is commonly measured with an inductive meter pick-up. (TIF)

Fig. 6-15. Insulation tester will check for leakage or breakdown of wire insulation. (TIF)

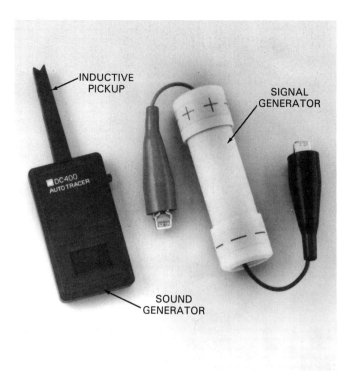

Fig. 6-16. Inductive wire tracer uses signal generator to produce fluctuating voltage in wiring. Then, pickup can be moved along next to wire. If conductor inside wire is broken or other problem is preventing current or signal flow, sound generator will change noise or stop making noise. (TIF)

Inductive wire tracer

An *inductive wire tracer* can be used to find internal breaks in wires and disconnected wires or terminals. One is pictured in Fig. 6-16.

A pulse generator is connected to the battery or to the circuit. It will produce a pulsing low voltage AC in the wiring. Then, the inductive probe can be moved along the wire.

The tester will make an audible beeping sound if the wire has continuity and is carrying the pulsing signal. When the tester moves past a break in a wire or poor connection, the signal will stop or change in tone. This shows you the location of the wiring problem.

Note! You might want to isolate the computer and other delicate electronic components when using an inductive wire tracer. This will assure they are not damaged while testing.

Temperature probe

A *temperature probe* can be used to make quick and accurate temperature measurements, Fig. 6-17. The probe is touched on the part or submerged in the fluid to be tested. Temperature measurements might be needed to check the operation of a temperature sensor or operating temperature of an engine (coolant).

BATTERY CHARGING, STARTING SYSTEM SERVICE TOOLS

This section of the chapter will review the most commonly used tools and equipment for servicing batteries,

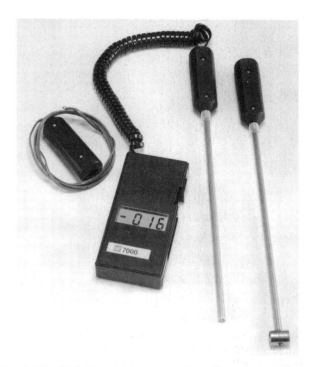

Fig. 6-17. Digital temperature probe will make quick and accurate temperature measurements. This might be needed to check action of temperature sensor or engine cooling system for example. (TIF)

the charging system, and the starting system. These tools are frequently used in electrical repair and are important if you are to become an auto electronic technician.

Battery service tools

There are many tools that fall into the category of battery service tools. The most common ones include the following:

Post or *terminal cleaning tools* are used to remove corrosion from the outer surface of battery posts or side terminals. Several types are pictured in Fig. 6-18.

Battery pliers are designed to grasp and remove battery cable ends. The jaws of the pliers are shaped to grasp the cable end without damage. See Fig. 6-18F and G.

Terminal adapters fit onto the posts or side terminals for charging the battery, Fig. 6-18H. One design fits on the posts to prevent post marring. Another type screws into the side terminals to allow hook-up of the charger leads.

Battery cable pullers clamp over battery cable ends. When tightened, they pull off the cable ends without loading or damaging the battery. This prevents loosening of the post in its case. Look at Fig. 6-18I through K.

A *battery strap* fits over the posts to form a handle for carrying a battery. One is shown in Fig. 6-18L.

A *battery tester* measures battery voltage as a means of checking battery condition. If battery voltage is low, it indicates a low charge or potential battery problem. A battery tester is needed on late model batteries with sealed vent caps. See Figs. 6-19 and 6-20.

A *hydrometer* will measure the specific gravity or density of battery acid. This reading can be used to determine the state of charge and general condition of a bat-

Fig. 6-18. Battery related service tools. A through E—Terminal cleaning tools. F—Battery cable end spreading pliers. G—Battery pliers. H—Side terminal adapters. I through K—Cable pullers. L—Battery carrying strap. M—Squeeze bulb for servicing battery water or electrolyte. N and O-Battery acid hydrometers. P—Battery service tool kit. Q—Battery water bottle. R—Dry charge filler. S—Battery carrying tool. (Snap-on Tools)

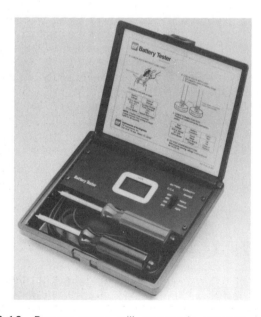

Fig. 6-19. Battery tester will accurately measure battery voltage to check charge and general condition of battery. It is needed for late model batteries with sealed vent caps. (TIF)

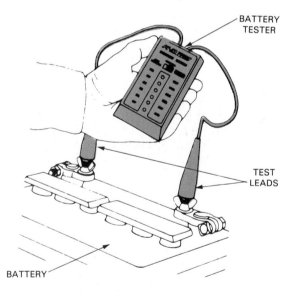

Fig. 6-20. This battery tester uses indicator light action to show condition of battery. (K-D Tools)

tery. Hydrometers are NOT as common as in the past because of sealed battery cases. See Fig. 6-18M and O.

Jumper cables are for starting a car with a "dead battery" (discharged battery). They connect from a good battery to the dead battery. The red jumper lead connects to each positive battery terminal. The black lead is connected to negative or ground, Fig. 6-21.

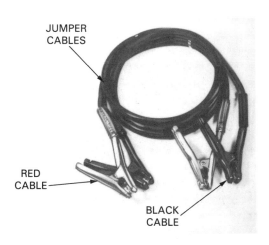

Fig. 6-21. Battery jumper cables can be connected between dead battery and charged battery for starting engine. (Snap-on Tools)

Load tester

A *load tester* is used to test batteries, the charging system, and the starting system. It can also be used to measure voltage current, and sometimes resistance in other circuits. Look at Fig. 6-22.

A load tester is commonly used to draw current out of the battery while measuring voltage. If voltage stays within specs with the spec current draw, the battery should be good. If not, a battery problem is indicated.

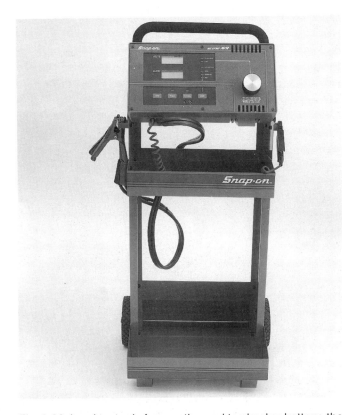

Fig. 6-22. Load tester is frequently used to check a battery, the charging system, and the starting system. Newer models have inductive amps pickup that clamps around battery cable. (Snap-on Tools)

A load tester can check the operation of the charging system by measuring current flow into the battery with the engine running. A load can be placed on the system to measure maximum alternator output.

A load tester is also used to check the condition of the starting system. Starter current draw can be measured and compared to specs.

Modern load testers usually have an inductive amps pickup. The amp lead is simply clamped around the outside of the battery cable. Older load testers require that the tester leads be connected in series with the cable to measure current.

Alternator bench tester

An *alternator bench tester* will check the output of an alternator off the car. The tester will spin the alternator rotor while measuring output. See Fig. 6-23.

A load tester will check alternator output on the car adequately. However, shops that rebuild alternators need the bench tester to check output before reinstalling the required alternator on the vehicle.

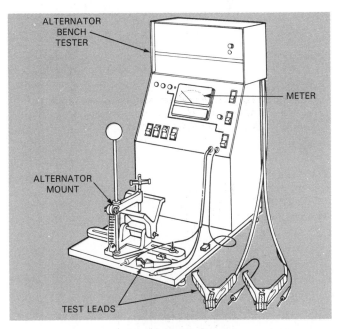

Fig. 6-23. Alternator bench tester will check operation of alternator off the car. This is handy if shop specializes in alternator service. (Champion Parts Rebuilders)

IGNITION SYSTEM TEST EQUIPMENT

Specialized tools and equipment are also needed to service a car's ignition system. This section of the chapter will introduce a few of these service tools.

Tach-dwell meter

A *tach-dwell meter* will measure engine speed, dwell (cam angle), and sometimes resistance. It is basically a tune-up test instrument but is also needed for electrically related service tasks. One is pictured in Fig. 6-24.

The tach or tachometer registers in RPM (revolutions per minute). It is needed when adjusting engine speed

Fig. 6-24. This is a conventional tach-dwell meter. It must be connected to metal components to take a reading.

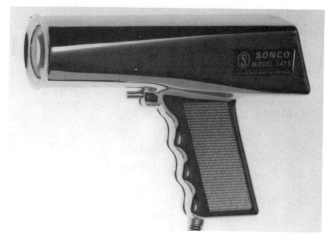

Fig. 6-26. Timing light is commonly used to set ignition timing on gasoline or spark ignition engine. It connects to battery and number one spark plug wire. It makes mark on crank damper visible with engine running. (Sonco)

settings and when doing other tests.

The dwell meter registers in degrees to show dwell (at rest) or off time. It is used to adjust older ignition system contact points and to check the signal going to some computer controlled carburetors.

A *photoelectric tachometer* can be used on diesels that do not have an electrical ignition system. It will read light flashes from reflective tape placed on the crankshaft damper. See Fig. 6-25.

Timing light

A *timing light* is a strobe light used to adjust ignition timing. It will flash on and off when connected to the ignition system secondary (number one spark plug wire). This will make the timing mark on the engine crankshaft damper or flywheel appear to stand still for comparing with marks on the engine. Refer to Fig. 6-26.

Note! Many new cars, with computer control, cannot have their ignition timing adjusted. Timing is permanently preset at the factory. However, a timing light can be used to make sure the computer system is controlling ignition timing properly.

Electronic ignition analyzer

An *electronic ignition analyzer* will check the condition of several ignition system components. Various designs are on the market and their capabilities vary.

Magnetic timing meter

A *magnetic timing meter* is needed on some car engines with provisions for a magnetic pickup. A magnetic probe from the tester slides into a holder on the front cover of the engine. The probe senses a notch in the crankshaft damper. This allows the meter to sense engine speed and crankshaft position information. See Fig. 6-27.

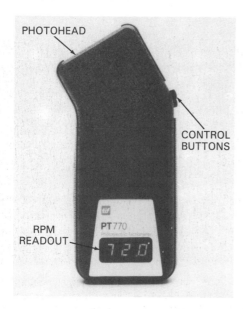

Fig. 6-25. Photoelectric tachometer reads light flashes from reflective tape on engine crankshaft damper. It converts these flashes into digital readout of engine speed. (TIF)

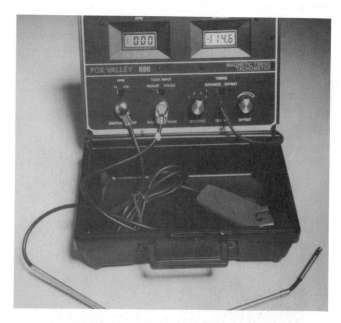

Fig. 6-27. This magnetic timing tachometer can be used on both gasoline and diesel engines. Some gasoline and diesel engines have a probe holder. The magnetic probe is installed in this holder to sense a notch in the crankshaft damper. This allows the tester to sense engine speed and piston position. (Fox Valley)

Vacuum tester

A *vacuum tester* will measure vacuum or suction and some have a hand-pump for producing vacuum, Fig. 6-28. A vacuum tester is used to test various vacuum devices: vacuum diaphragms, vacuum-solenoid switches, carburetor mixture solenoid, etc.

EXHAUST GAS ANALYZER

An *exhaust gas analyzer* will measure the chemical content in an engine's exhaust. This type tester is sometimes needed to find problems in the ignition system, computer system, and emission control systems. See Fig. 6-29.

DIESEL SERVICE TOOLS

A diesel engine does NOT use an electrical ignition system. However, it does use glow plugs to aid cold starting. Special tools are needed to do electrical tests on a diesel.

A *luminosity timing meter* is used to check or set injection timing on a diesel. A special probe installs in a glow plug hole. It will sense the light flash of combustion (burning fuel). The tester can use this signal to measure ignition (combustion or injection) timing. Look at Fig. 6-30.

A *glow plug harness tester* can be used, in conjunction with a multimeter, to test the diesel glow plugs and the operating condition of the diesel engine. The harness connects to the glow plugs. It can then be used to measure the internal resistance of each glow plug to find glow plug problems. Detailed later, it can also detect a "dead cylinder" because the temperature and resistance of a glow plug in a non-firing cylinder will be different than the others. See Fig. 6-31.

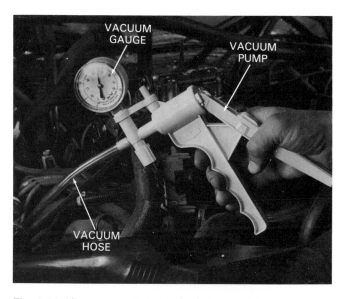

Fig. 6-28. Vacuum pump is useful for checking many vacuum devices. It will check operation of vacuum diaphragms, vacuum solenoid switches, etc. Pump can be used to apply vacuum to device. Gauge will show amount of vacuum applied for comparison to specs.   (Peerless)

Fig. 6-30. Luminosity diesel timer has probe that installs in diesel engine glow plug hole. Probe can then detect combustion flame for checking injection timing.   (OTC)

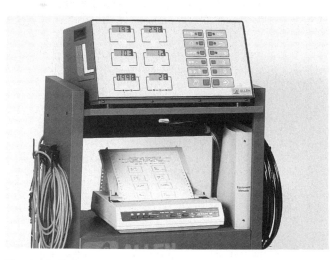

Fig. 6-29. Exhaust gas analyzer can be used to detect faulty electrical-electronic components. Analyzer measures chemical content in engine exhaust gases to determine efficiency of combustion.   (Allen Testproducts)

Fig. 6-31. Here technician is using a digital multimeter and a diesel glow plug harness to check engine operation. First, all glow plug resistances are measured cold. Then, engine is started and glow plugs are measured hot. All glow plug resistances should change about the same. If not, problem in cylinder with different ohms change is indicated.   (OTC)

SCAN TOOLS (SCANNERS)

A *scan tool,* or *scanner,* is needed to check the operation of vehicle sensors, actuators, wiring, and the computer itself. Various designs are on the market. They connect to a diagnostic terminal on the car. By measuring voltages or computer signals, the scanner can give the technician information about the condition of numerous components and circuits.

Fig. 6-32 shows a scan tool designed to be used on one make of car. When connected to the *diagnostic link* or test terminal, the tester will produce trouble code numbers. Each number represents a problem or condition. By comparing the scan tool output numbers to numbers in a service manual chart, the technician can find problems more easily.

The scan tool shown in Fig. 6-33 is designed to be used on a variety of vehicles. This tool is equipped with a removable *program cartridge,* which contains specific information about the vehicle to be scanned. Program cartridges are available for most domestic and import vehicles. New cartridges must be purchased as the on-board diagnostic systems are modified. Some scan tool manufacturers now offer generic storage cartridges that can be updated by downloading the up-to-date specifications to the scan tool from a computer.

OSCILLOSCOPE

An *oscilloscope* is a diagnostic tool that displays a line pattern, or trace, representing circuit voltages in relation to time. See Fig. 6-34. By comparing the scope pattern to a known good pattern, the technician can determine whether something is wrong in the circuit.

A scope is often used to check ignition system operating voltages. It can also be used to check the output signals from sensors and other electronic devices.

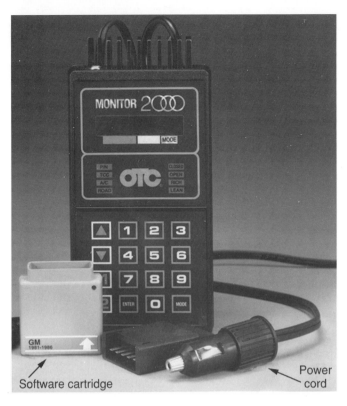

Fig. 6-33. This particular scan tool can be used on many different vehicles and systems. Note the removable program cartridge. (OTC)

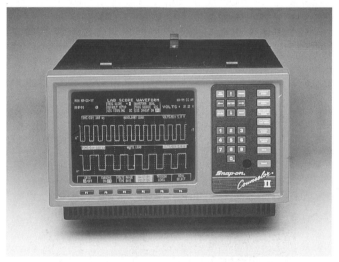

Fig. 6-34. An oscilloscope is a valuable diagnostic tool that displays voltage values in relation to time. (Snap-on Tools)

HAND-HELD SCOPE

A *hand-held scope* usually consists of an oscilloscope and a multimeter combined in one housing. It is a handy tool for advanced troubleshooting of electrical-electronic problems.

The hand-held scope can be used to perform voltage, current, and resistance measurements. It can also be used to show instantaneous voltage variations. See Fig. 6-35.

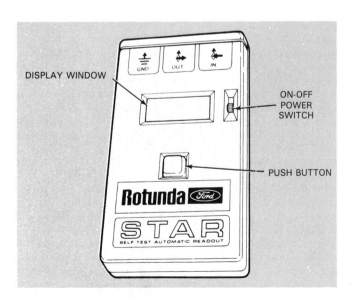

Fig. 6-32. This scan tool plugs into wiring harness connector on car. It can then read signals from computer for trouble codes. Numbers displayed on scan tool can be compared to chart in service manual to help find source of computer system problems. (Ford)

Fig. 6-35. This hand-held scope is designed for advanced testing of electronic components. (OTC)

ENGINE ANALYZER

An *engine analyzer* is a set of different testing instruments in one roll-around cabinet. It may include an oscilloscope, a tach-dwell meter, a VOM, an exhaust gas analyzer, and a scan tool. The analyzer can be connected to the various electrical systems of a car to do numerous tests. Refer to Fig. 6-36.

An *analyzer link* is a device that allows an engine analyzer to test an engine with a computer controlled distributorless ignition system. One is shown in Fig. 6-37. It has special wire connectors for hook-up with the multi-coil, computerized ignition.

Fig. 6-38 pictures another computerized engine analyzer addition. It has a powerful internal computer for analyzing inputs, giving detailed test procedures, and producing readouts of troubles in a car's on-board computer. Floppy discs are used to program the analyzer's computer for different makes and models of cars or for different testing programs. It has a remote control keypad for changing test functions while at the car.

With any computer tester, you must follow the

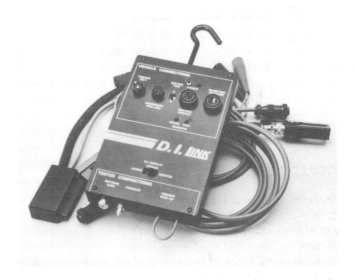

Fig. 6-37. Link may be needed to tie engine or computer analyzer to some late model distributorless ignitions. (Sun Electric)

Fig. 6-36. Engine or computer analyzer is several testers in one cabinet. Modern analyzers will automatically go through a series of different tests to help find source of engine and electrical-electronic problems. (Sun Electric)

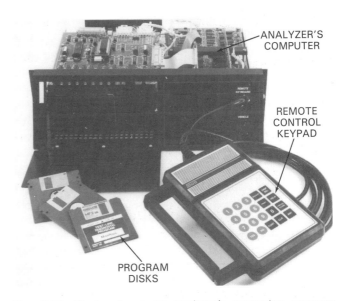

ANALYZER'S COMPUTER

REMOTE CONTROL KEYPAD

PROGRAM DISKS

Fig. 6-38. Photo shows an analyzer's computer, program disks, and remote keypad for working at car. Program disks allow analyzer to work on different makes and models of cars. (Sun Electric)

operating manual from the manufacturer. Procedures vary considerably.

SUMMARY

Today's cars are virtually impossible to fix without the right tools and equipment. This is especially true with electrical and electronic repairs. Modern cars, with their on-board computers, sensors, actuators, and other electrical devices, take the skill of a well-trained and well-equipped technician.

Soldering tools are needed to make wiring repairs. Solder provides the best method of joining wires and terminals. A soldering gun or iron is used to preheat the joint. Then, rosin core solder is melted on the joint. After cooling, this provides an excellent electrical connection.

Several soldering aids can make soldering easier. A flux brush can be used to apply extra flux to a joint. A heat sink is needed to prevent overheating of electronic components when soldering. A desoldering bulb will suck off solder from a joint after heating. A soldering sponge will help clean the tip of the soldering gun.

Stripping pliers are needed to pull insulation off wires. Care must be taken when stripping not to damage the conductor. Wire cutters are also needed to cut through the conductor.

A test light provides a quick way of checking a circuit for power or continuity. The alligator clip is grounded and then the test light tip is touched to the circuit.

A multimeter or VOM is used to measure voltage, current, and resistance. It is an essential tool of the auto electrical technician. An analog multimeter uses a conventional needle to show readings. It is good when readings might change or fluctuate. A digital multimeter uses vacuum fluorescent or liquid crystal displays to give readouts. It is better for steady state readings.

Many shop manuals warn against using a test light or analog meter to test some electronic circuits. They can draw too much current and damage delicate electronic components.

A conventional meter pickup must be touched on the metal conductors in a circuit. An inductive meter pickup simply has to be clamped around the outside of a wire and is used as an amps pickup.

An inductive wire tracer uses a signal generator to produce a weak AC signal in the car's wiring. The probe can then be used to find internal breaks or disconnected wires. The probe will stop making a signal or change its signal when the problem is found.

A temperature probe will make rapid temperature measurements. This might be needed for testing sensors or engine operating temperature.

Various battery service tools are needed. Post or terminal cleaners will remove corrosion without damage to the battery terminals. A battery tester will check state of charge and indicate battery condition by accurately measuring voltage. A hydrometer will check specific gravity to indicate the charge and condition of the battery.

Jumper cables are for starting a car with a dead battery. They can be connected from a good battery to the dead battery. This will allow the engine to crank and start.

A load tester is commonly used to check the operation of a battery, the charging system, and the starting system. It normally has an inductive amps pickup and conventional voltmeter. It has a device for loading the battery or charging system to check output.

A tach-dwell will measure engine speed, dwell, and sometimes resistance. It will measure RPM. It will also measure in degrees of dwell (off time) for adjusting ignition system contact points or for checking the signal to some computer controlled carburetors.

A timing light is for checking or adjusting ignition timing. It connects to the number one spark plug wire and to the battery. The light is then aimed on the engine timing marks with the engine running. The flashing strobe light will make the crank damper or flywheel timing mark appear to stand still for comparison with marks on the engine.

An exhaust gas analyzer will measure the chemical content in an engine's exhaust gases. This information can be used to find problems in the engine, computer system, fuel system, ignition system, and emission control systems.

A scan tool, or scanner, can be used to check the condition of the computer, sensors, actuators, and wiring. It will work with the car's on-board computer to produce trouble codes. These codes indicate what part or circuit might be at fault. Computer system testers vary with the manufacturer. Follow the equipment and service manual instructions when testing a computer system.

An oscilloscope is a diagnostic tool that displays a line pattern, or trace, representing circuit voltages in relation to time. A hand-held scope usually consists of an oscilloscope and a multimeter combined in one housing.

An engine analyzer is a group of test instruments in one cabinet. Modern engine analyzers have their own computer for doing complex tests on automobile on-board computer systems.

KNOW THESE TERMS

Rosen core solder, Acid core solder, Soldering gun, Soldering iron, Flux brush, Flux, Soldering pick, Heat sink, Desoldering bulb, Soldering sponge, Stripping pliers, Cutting pliers, Test light, Continuity light, Multimeter, VOM, Analog meter, Digital meter, Inductive pickup, Inductive wire tracer, Terminal cleaner, Terminal adaptors, Cable pullers, Battery strap, Battery tester, Jumper cables, Load tester, Tach-dwell meter, Photo-electric tach, Timing light, Distributor machine, Electronic ignition analyzer, Magnetic timing meter, Vacuum tester, Exhaust gas analyzer, Luminosity timing meter, Glow plug harness tester, Scan tool, Program cartridge, Oscilloscope, Hand-held scope, Engine analyzer.

REVIEW QUESTIONS—CHAPTER 6

1. _____ is a mixture of lead and tin and comes in a roll for easy application.
2. Why is a soldering gun with a trigger normally more convenient than a soldering iron?

3. This tool can be used to prevent overheating damage to electronic components while soldering.
   a. Soldering pick.
   b. Desoldering bulb.
   c. Heat sink.
   d. Heat sponge.
4. What are all-purpose electrical pliers?
5. How is a circuit-powered test light used?
6. A _____, also called a _____ or _____, is used to measure exact voltage, current, and resistance values.
7. When would an analog meter be better to use than a digital meter?
8. When would a digital meter be better than an analog meter?
9. Explain five battery related service tools.
10. Explain the use of a load tester.

ASE CERTIFICATION–TYPE QUESTIONS

1. An electrical repair needs to be performed on a circuit. Technician A says acid core solder can be used to repair this circuit. Technician B says rosin core solder can be used to repair this circuit. Who is right?
   (A) A only. (C) Both A and B.
   (B) B only. (D) Neither A nor B.
2. Technician A says using a soldering gun is a more efficient and quicker method of making electrical connections than using a soldering iron. Technician B says using a soldering iron is trigger-operated and should only be used with acid-core solder. Who is right?
   (A) A only. (C) Both A and B.
   (B) B only. (D) Neither A nor B.
3. All of the following tools are sometimes used when soldering *except:*
   (A) heat sink. (C) flux brush.
   (B) linear pick. (D) desoldering bulb.
4. The output voltage of an automobile's computer must be checked. Technician A says a digital meter can be used to check this voltage. Technician B says an analog meter can be used to check this voltage. Who is right?
   (A) A only. (C) Both A and B.
   (B) B only. (D) Neither A nor B.

5. Technician A says a load tester can be used to check the condition of a car's battery. Technician B says a load tester can be used to check the condition of a car's starting system. Who is right?
   (A) A only. (C) Both A and B.
   (B) B only. (D) Neither A nor B.
6. An automobile with computer control is brought into the shop for a tune-up. Technician A says a timing light can be used to make sure the computer is properly controlling ignition timing. Technician B says the vehicle's ignition timing may not be nonadjustable. Who is right?
   (A) A only. (C) Both A and B.
   (B) B only. (D) Neither A nor B.
7. Technician A says an oscilloscope can be used to check ignition system operating voltages. Technician B says an oscilloscope can be used to check output signals from computer system sensors. Who is right?
   (A) A only. (C) Both A and B.
   (B) B only. (D) Neither A nor B.
8. Technician A says a magnetic timing tachometer is equipped with a magnetic probe that slides into a holder on an engine's front cover. Technician B says some magnetic timing tachometers can be used on both gasoline and diesel engines. Who is right?
   (A) A only. (C) Both A and B.
   (B) B only. (D) Neither A nor B.
9. A diesel engine has a possible "dead cylinder." Technician A is going to use a magnetic timing meter to check this problem. Technician B is going to use a glow plug harness tester to check for a possible dead cylinder. Who is right?
   (A) A only. (C) Both A and B.
   (B) B only. (D) Neither A nor B.
10. Technician A says a scan tool can be used to check computer system actuator operation. Technician B says a scan tool can be used to check the operation of computer system sensors. Who is right?
    (A) A only. (C) Both A and B.
    (B) B only. (D) Neither A nor B.

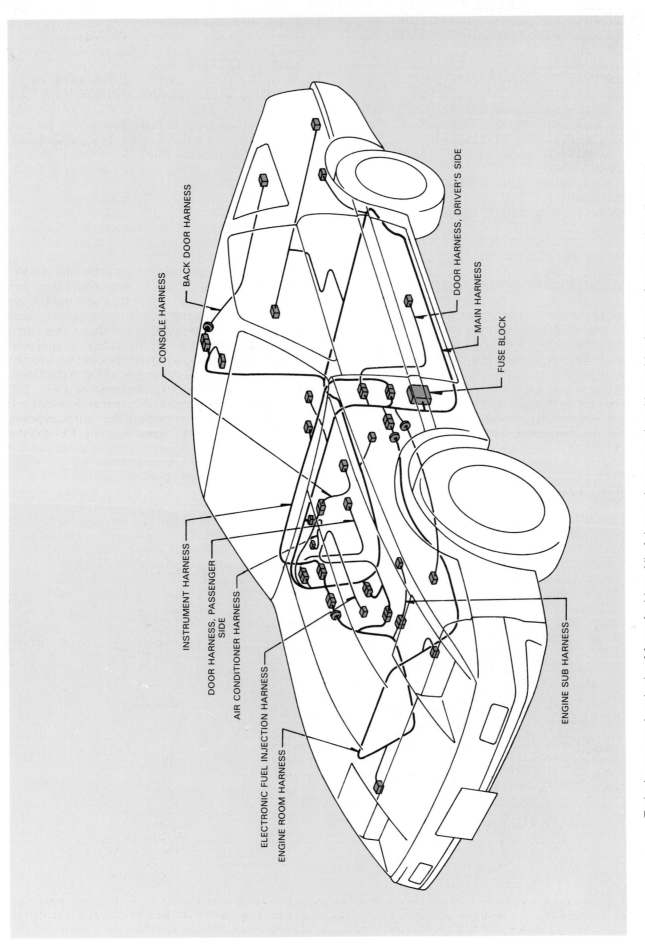

CONSOLE HARNESS

BACK DOOR HARNESS

DOOR HARNESS, DRIVER'S SIDE

MAIN HARNESS

FUSE BLOCK

INSTRUMENT HARNESS

DOOR HARNESS, PASSENGER SIDE

AIR CONDITIONER HARNESS

ELECTRONIC FUEL INJECTION HARNESS

ENGINE ROOM HARNESS

ENGINE SUB HARNESS

Today's cars use hundreds of feet of wiring. All of these wires are enclosed in a wiring harness for protection. For testing purposes, each section of a wiring harness is given its own name and/or code number. By sectioning harness into smaller parts, testing and repair is simplified. (Nissan)

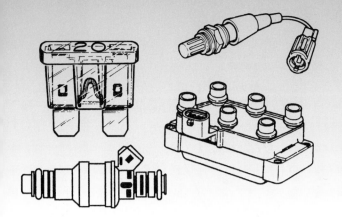

Chapter 7

Wiring, Wiring Repairs

After studying this chapter, you will be able to:
- *Summarize the importance of making proper wiring repairs on a modern car.*
- *Compare wire types and sizes.*
- *Explain wire color coding.*
- *Describe wire protection devices.*
- *Properly cut and strip wires.*
- *Solder wires and terminals.*
- *Use crimp type connectors.*
- *Explain connector types.*
- *Service automotive type connectors.*
- *Repair wires, connectors, and fusible links.*

A modern car can use well over a quarter mile of wires to link its vast number of electrical components. Hundreds of connectors can be used to join all of this wiring into workable circuits. The wires and connectors must also carry current under adverse conditions: heat, cold, vibration, moisture, etc. A problem with even one wire or connection can adversely affect the operation or performance of the car. This makes it essential that you fully understand wiring and how wiring is repaired, Fig. 7-1.

This chapter will summarize wiring specifications and explain wire types. It will introduce the various types of connectors used to fasten wires together. The chapter

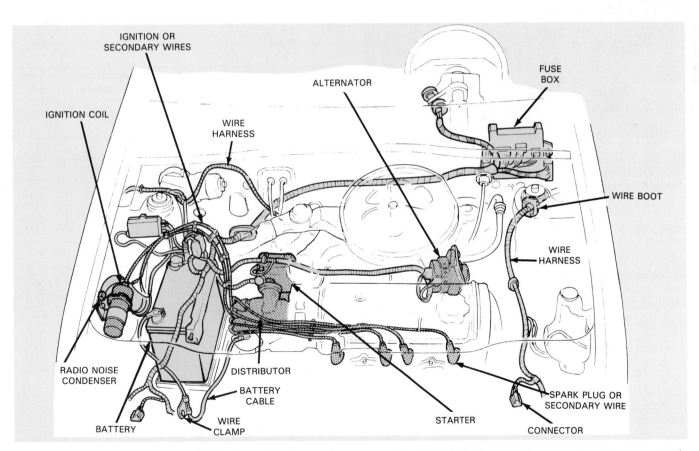

Fig. 7-1. A tremendous amount of wire is used in the modern automobile. With today's computers, sensors, actuators, and conventional electrical systems, an engine compartment can look like a ''bowl of spaghetti.'' As a consequence, it is important to know how to service wiring, connectors, and related components. (Honda)

will also describe how to solder and use crimp type connectors. It will introduce the basic skills needed to correct many electrical-electronic problems.

AUTOMOTIVE WIRING

Automotive wiring includes many types of conductors, from very small wires and printed circuit conductors to large battery cables. It is critical that you comprehend these classifications and understand their operation characteristics.

Solid and stranded wire

An electrical wire may have a solid metal conductor or a stranded wire conductor inside its insulation. Both types are pictured in Fig. 7-2.

A *solid wire* has only a single conductor in its insulation. This type is sometimes used inside components, a relay for example. Solid wire is a good conductor but it is not very flexible. The metal conductor can break with severe vibration or motion.

A *stranded wire* has numerous individual wires twisted together inside a single coating of insulation. Stranded wire is normally used to connect components because it can withstand vibration without breaking. Stranded copper wire is the most common type used in automotive wiring.

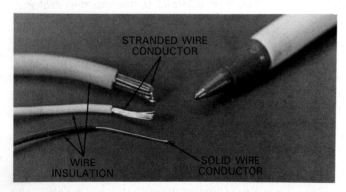

Fig. 7-2. Stranded wire is used in auto wiring because it can withstand movement and vibration without breaking. Solid wire can be found inside components, where there is no movement.

Wire size

Wire size is determined by the diameter of the conductor. It does NOT include the thickness or diameter of the insulation. Wire size limits how much current a wire can carry without overheating. If a small wire carries too much current, it can overheat and burn. Wire size must be matched to the circuit load or amperage draw. See Fig. 7-3.

In auto mechanics, wire size is rated by an AWG or American Wire Gauge system. Numbers are used to denote conductor diameters. A smaller number denotes a larger conductor diameter and vice versa. This system is designed for solid wires. However, stranded wire is also rated this way, with some variations depending upon the wire manufacturer.

For example, a 12 gauge wire is LARGER than a 13 gauge wire. Car wiring is usually between 8 and 20 gauge. Battery cable, since it must carry tremendous

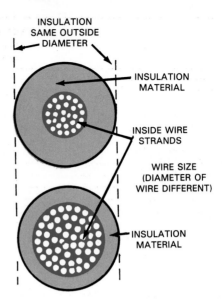

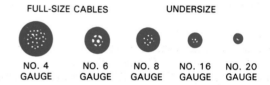

Fig. 7-3. Wire size is determined by the diameter of the conductor. It does not include insulation thickness. (Florida Dept. of Voc. Ed.)

AWG size (gauge)	Wire diameter (mils)		Cross-sectional area (circular mils)	Ohms per 1000 ft.
20	32.0	**Smallest**	1,020	10.1
18	40.3		1,620	6.39
16	50.8		2,580	4.02
14	64.1		4,110	2.52
12	80.8		6,530	1.59
10	101.9		10,380	.9988
8	128.5		16,510	.6281
6	162.0		26,240	.3952
4	204.3		41,740	.2485
2	257.6	**Largest**	66,360	.1563

Fig. 7-4. Chart shows wire gauge sizes, diameters, and resistances. Note how larger gauge number indicates a smaller conductor size and how smaller diameter wire increases resistance. This chart is for solid wire but is similar to stranded wire.

current, is very large, typically between 2 and 6 gauge.

Fig. 7-4 gives a chart showing the AWG ratings for wires. Note how the gauge size compares to diameter, cross-sectional area, and the resulting ohms or resistance.

A smaller diameter wire will have more resistance than a larger diameter wire. This is why smaller wire will overheat and burn if used to replace larger wire carrying too much current. The electrons moving through the

Metric wire size in mm²		AWG size in gauge size
.22	Smallest	24
.5		20
.8		18
1.0		16
2.0		14
3.0		12
5.0		10
8.0		8
13.0		6
19.0		4
32.0	Largest	2

Fig. 7-5. This chart compares gauge size with newer metric wire size.

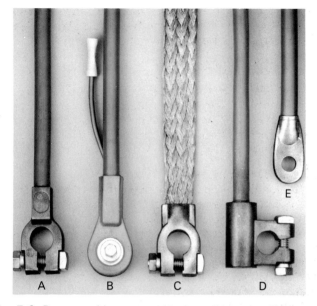

Fig. 7-6. Battery cables are very large and have small gauge number. A—Top post battery cable. B—Side terminal battery cable. C—Uninsulated ground cable. D—Top post cable with side mounted conductor. E—Starter or solenoid cable with eye. (Belden)

smaller wire will make so much "electrical friction" that tremendous heat is produced.

Fig. 7-5 shows a chart comparing AWG sizes and metric wire sizes. A *metric size wire* is given as the cross-sectional area of the wire in square millimeters (mm²).

Wire current carrying rules

There are several rules that apply to wires and their ability to carry current. These include:

1. Wire resistance INCREASES as conductor diameter DECREASES.
2. Resistance is dependent upon the material used in the conductor. For example, silver has LESS resistance than copper; copper has LESS resistance than aluminum.
3. Resistance INCREASES as the length of the wire INCREASES.
4. In most conductors, resistance INCREASES as temperature INCREASES.
5. EXCESS CURRENT will heat a conductor and can melt or burn its insulation.
6. Always replace a wire with the SAME wire gauge size. The conductor material must also be the same.
7. Some computer system wiring harnesses use special twisted wire to shield against any voltage that might induce into the wire. Follow service manual recommendations when replacing this type wire to prevent computer system problems.

Cables

Cables refer to the huge wires that carry battery current to the starting motor and return current to the battery from ground. This term also refers to shielded wire.

A *positive battery cable* connects the battery positive terminal to the car's electrical system. It usually connects to the starting motor solenoid. Then, smaller wires feed off the solenoid terminal to the fuse box and other devices.

A *negative battery cable* connects from the battery negative to ground. This cable usually bolts to the side of the engine block so a good connection is provided for the starting motor. The negative cable does NOT have to be insulated, Fig. 7-6.

A *starting motor cable* connects from an engine

compartment-mounted solenoid to the starting motor. Both ends of the cable have eye connectors, Fig. 7-6.

Primary and secondary wire

Primary wire refers to the wire used throughout most of the car. It is the smaller wire that carries battery voltage to the numerous electrical components in the vehicle. Another name for primary wiring is *body wiring*.

Secondary wire is the wire used to carry high voltage in the engine's ignition system, Fig. 7-7. Since it carries

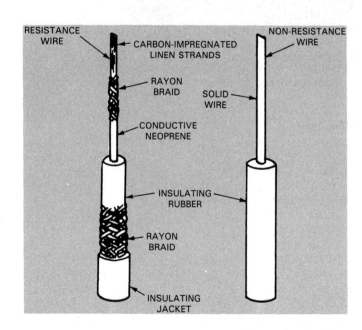

Fig. 7-7. Secondary wire or spark plug wire has tiny conductor but very thick insulation. Small current but high voltage flows through wire. Insulation prevents voltage leakage to ground. (AC Spark Plugs)

very little current, but high voltage, the conductor is relatively small and the insulation is very thick. This keeps high voltage from arcing through the insulation to ground. *Spark plug wires* are called secondary wires.

Secondary resistance wire or *TVRS* (Television-Radio Suppression) *wire* has a specific amount of resistance (ohms) per foot. Resistance is designed into the wire conductor to help prevent radio interference or static from the high voltage pulses going to the spark plugs.

Secondary wire non-resistance has a metal conductor with no extra resistance. This type wire is only used in high performance applications; such as off-road racing. It will cause static in nearby radios.

Secondary wire is discussed fully in the chapter on ignition systems.

Shielded wire

Shielded wire has the center conductor surrounded by an outer metal shield. Insulation separates the conductor and the braided metal shield. In this way, magnetic pulses cannot be induced into the center conductor and cause unwanted voltage pulses. See Fig. 7-8.

Also called *coax* or *coaxial cable,* this type wire is commonly used as antenna wire. The antenna lead must be protected from unwanted magnetic fields from the engine's ignition system, CB radios, and other sources. This prevents static from entering the cable and upsetting the reception of the radio.

Twisted shield wire uses multiple, insulated conductors wrapped around each other. This design also helps prevent unwanted magnetic fields from inducing into the wire. For instance, twisted shield type wire can be used to connect the computer and various sensors, especially those near the ignition system. This helps keep high voltage pulses from upsetting the tiny voltage signals going to the computer.

Printed circuit wiring

Printed circuit wiring has copper foil bonded on a plastic or fiber base to form compact conductors. This type wiring is used on the back of the instrument panel cluster and many electronic circuits. One example is pictured in Fig. 7-9.

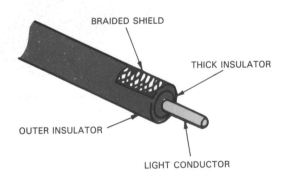

SHIELDED CABLE

Fig. 7-8. Shielded cable has metal shield around center conductor. This blocks out any magnetic fields that could induce current into wire. With low voltage and current levels in many circuits, this is important to assure proper operation. A radio antenna lead is shielded for example. (Chrysler)

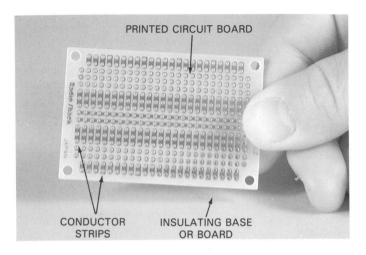

Fig. 7-9. Printed circuit wiring is made by depositing thin metal strips on plastic or fiber base material. Metal strips replace wires to save space and make for neat package. (Union Electronics)

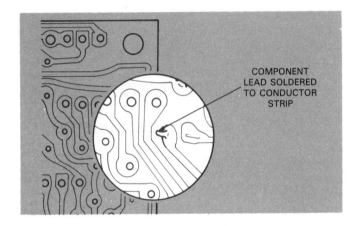

Fig. 7-10. Components have leads fed through holes in printed circuit conductor strips. Then leads are soldered to conductor strips. On instrument panel printed circuits, components snap or fasten to conductor strips. (Ford)

Fig. 7-10 shows how electronic components or wires can be soldered to a printed circuit board. Fig. 7-11 shows the back of an instrument cluster showing a printed circuit.

Aluminum wire

Aluminum wire uses an aluminum alloy conductor instead of the more common copper conductor. Aluminum is NOT as good a conductor as copper but it is lighter and cheaper. Aluminum wire must be larger in diameter to carry the same current as copper wire. Aluminum wire is also more brittle and is used in applications that keep the wire stationary. This prevents aluminum wire breakage.

Wire color codes

Color coding is used on the insulation of wires so that you can trace a wire from one location to another. Even if a wire travels through the car's firewall and is hidden, you can still find the other end of the wire by locating the identical color code markings.

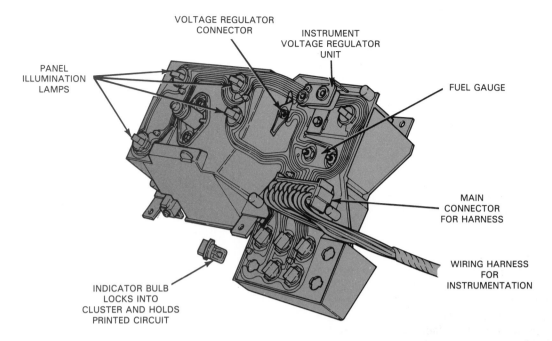

Fig. 7-11. Rear view of instrument cluster shows one application of printed circuit wiring. Components are not soldered to this type printed circuit. Nuts or snap fit lock components to printed circuit. (Ford)

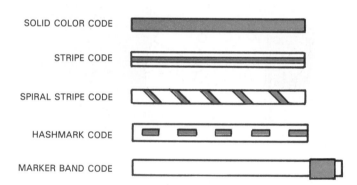

Fig. 7-12. Wire color codes allow you to follow a wire through a harness, even when wire is hidden from sight. Note examples of color code markings.

Fig. 7-12 gives a few examples of wire color codes. The wires can be solid color, have a stripe, bands, or hash marks. This makes it easy to tell one wire from another or to identify wires.

Using color codes and wiring diagrams is discussed in Chapter 8.

Wire protection devices

Wire protection devices include any device that protects a wire from damage: electrical tape, plastic tubing, retainers, clips, boots, straps, etc. These are shown in Fig. 7-13.

When working with wire, always replace all wire protection devices. They would NOT have been installed by the manufacturer if they were NOT needed. Failing to reinstall them could lead to wiring failures and comebacks.

Wiring harnesses

A *wiring harness* is a set of several wires enclosed or wrapped together with tape or in a plastic protection

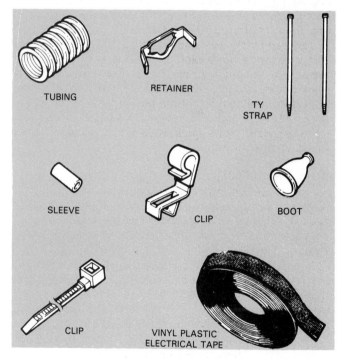

Fig. 7-13. Wire protection devices are needed to protect wires from damage with vehicle movement, vibration, heat, cold, etc. (Chrysler)

device. Wires or connectors branch out from the harness to connect to electrical components. A wiring harness protects the wiring and also makes for a neater appearance than dozens of individual wires running separately.

A wiring harness is usually named after its location in the car. For example, the harness feeding out to the sensors and other devices on an engine is termed an *engine wiring harness.* See Fig. 7-14.

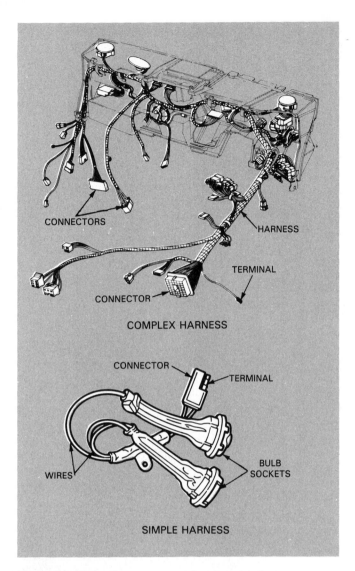

Fig. 7-14. Wiring harnesses can be very simple or very complex. Harness has several wires enclosed in tape or plastic enclosure. Special connectors allow wires to connect to other wires and other components. (Chrysler)

Connectors are plastic or rubber plug-together devices with metal terminals that fasten wires to components or other wires. Various designs are used in a modern car. Many have locking clips that hold the connectors together to assure a good electrical connection. Working with connectors is discussed shortly.

Note! If a large number of wires are damaged, by fire for instance, it is usually best to install a new section of wiring harness. The harness can be purchased from the car manufacturer or an auto selvage yard. This will normally save time and result in a better repair.

WIRING REPAIRS

Wiring repairs include many tasks that will return a circuit to normal operating condition. This might involve replacing a burned wire or connector, soldering a wire to a terminal, crimping a terminal over a wire, etc. This section of the chapter will summarize how to do these basic wiring repairs.

Cutting and stripping wire

Cutting wire can be done with side-cut pliers or the cutting jaws on multi-purpose electrical pliers. In any case, make sure you cut completely through the wire on the first try. If you cut partway through and then cut again, you can get uneven strands on the wire end. Look at Fig. 7-15.

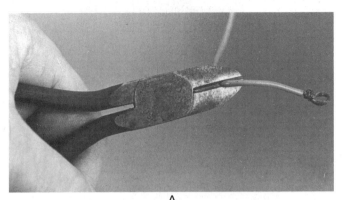

A

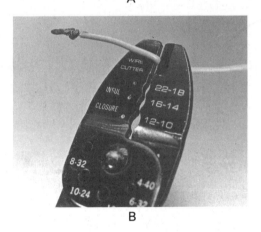

B

Fig. 7-15. When cutting wire, cut all the way through on the first try. This will ensure that strands are cut evenly and are not damaged. A—Using diagonal cutters to cut wire. B—Using all-purpose electrical pliers to cut wire.

If the wire is long enough, always make a new cut when joining the wire to another component. Even though the wire conductor may look fine, it may have missing strands or be weakened by movement or vibration. A new cut will expose new wire that has been protected inside the insulation.

Only strip wires with wire strippers. As shown in Fig. 7-16, select a stripping hole size that matches the specific wire size. Clamp the wire insulation in the stripping jaws. Then, use your hand to pull the wire through the jaws. This will cut and strip the insulation but will NOT damage the conductor.

Note! Cutting pliers can be used to strip off insulation but they are NOT recommended. Even if you are careful when cutting around the insulation, the conductor strands can be damaged and weakened. This can make the repair fail in service.

Remember the importance of good electrical connections, especially with today's computer circuits!

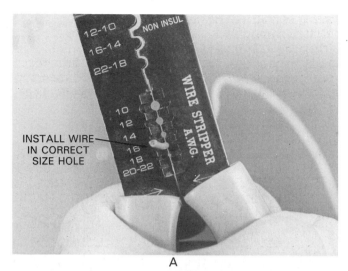

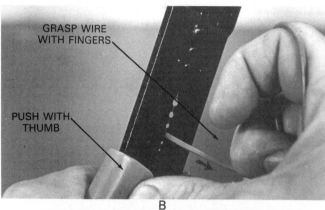

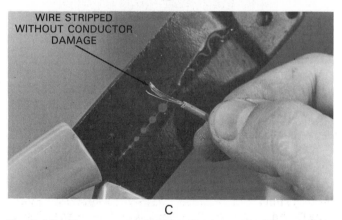

Fig. 7-16. Always use stripping pliers to peel off insulation. A—Insert wire into correct size stripping jaw. Jaw size must match wire size. B—Use thumb and fingers to pull wire through stripping jaws. C—After stripping, make sure none of the strands have been broken or damaged.

SOLDERING

Soldering involves using heat and solder to join electrical components or wires. Soldering is an essential skill and must be mastered before attempting even basic electrical repairs.

Discussed briefly in an earlier chapter, soldering is commonly done with an electric soldering gun or soldering iron. A pencil type soldering iron is shown in Fig. 7-17. It is good for small, intricate work. A soldering gun

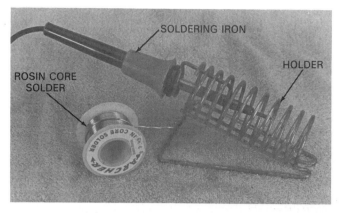

Fig. 7-17. Soldering is the best way to join wires and components. This small pencil type soldering iron is good for working with small components.

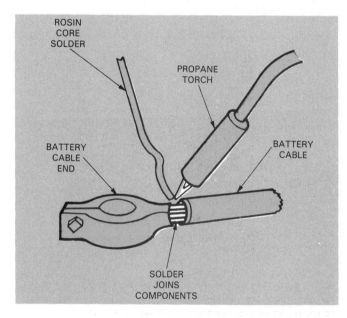

Fig. 7-18. In this illustration, a torch is being used to solder a new end on a battery cable. Soldering gun or iron may not provide enough heat for soldering something this large.

is better for most jobs because it heats up so quickly.

A torch, with its high heat output, can be used for soldering large cables. Fig. 7-18 shows a technician using a torch to solder on a new battery cable terminal.

Remember to only use ROSIN CORE SOLDER during electrical repairs. Do NOT use acid core solder because it can cause corrosion and increased resistance between connections when in service.

Tinning

Tinning is done to clean and prepare the surface of the soldering gun tip and/or the electrical components. It places a thin coating of solder on the tip or parts. This makes the solder joint easier to make and results in a better electrical connection. After tinning, heat can also transfer out of the soldering gun tip and into the parts to be soldered more easily.

To tin the soldering gun tip, heat the tip. If needed,

wipe debris from the trip on a water-soaked sponge. Then, melt some solder onto the tip. Make sure solder has adhered all the way around the tip, Fig. 7-19A.

If the soldering gun tip is pitted, use a file to form a clean, smooth surface. If badly pitted, replace the tip.

To tin the components, heat them with the soldering gun. Melt a thin layer of rosin core solder onto their surfaces. Then, when you heat them and they are in contact, the two tinned surfaces will melt and join easily.

Tinning components before soldering is not always necessary. It is only needed when the components fail to take solder readily.

Preheating components

Always preheat electrical components sufficiently before melting solder onto the joint. If you fail to preheat the parts, the solder will NOT bond to the parts properly. A poor electrical connection will result, Fig. 7-19B.

Preheat the components until the solder melts onto them. However, do NOT preheat the part so much that it melts wire insulation or damages plastic or electronic components.

Use a heat sink to protect any electronic components from heat damage. Diodes, transistors, integrated cir-cuits can all be ruined if overheated while soldering. Place the heat sink between the component and solder joint. Then heat can flow into the sink and not into the electronic components. See Fig. 7-20.

Warning! Never touch solder onto the soldering gun tip and allow it to drip onto the joint. The solder will NOT bond to the components securely. You must preheat the components!

Soldering components

After sufficient preheating, keep the soldering gun tip in contact with the joint. Move the rosin core solder into contact with BOTH the components and the gun tip. Do NOT melt the solder by only touching it on the tip. Touching both will assure enough heat that the solder bonds properly, Fig. 7-19C.

Make sure the solder flows onto both components. If the solder does not bond, brush on some extra paste type flux. Remove the heat and solder.

Do NOT wiggle or move the solder joint for a few seconds after soldering. This could weaken the solder joint. Allow the joint to cool before moving and inspecting it, Fig. 7-19D.

Fig. 7-21 shows how one auto manufacturer recom-

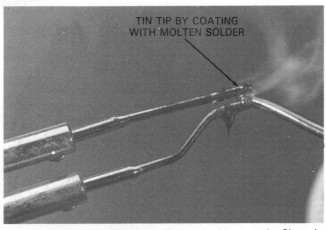

A—Tin soldering gun tip by melting layer of solder over tip. Clean tip on water-soaked sponge if needed.

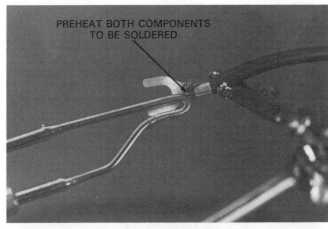

B—Preheat both components to be joined. Wire conductor and terminal are both being heated.

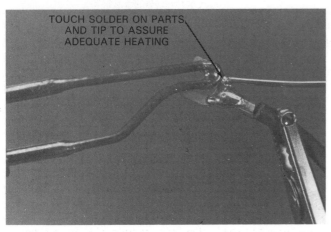

C—After preheating, move solder into contact with parts and tip. Solder should flow freely onto components.

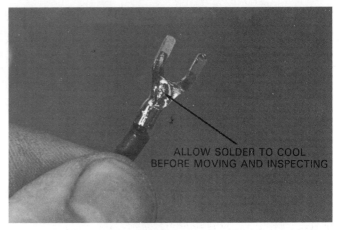

D—Allow solder to cool before moving joint. Make sure solder has bonded to components properly.

Fig. 7-19. Note basic steps for soldering. Study steps carefully!

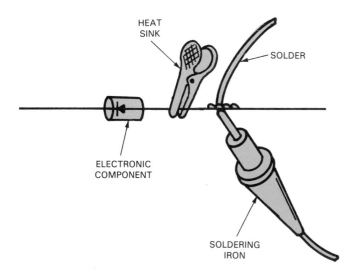

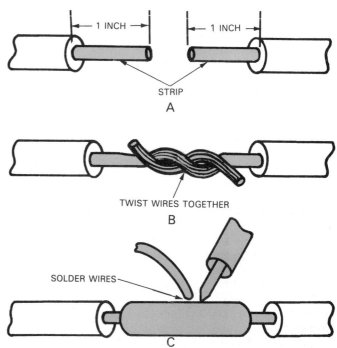

Fig. 7-20. If you are ever soldering new electronic components, use a heat sink as shown. This will reduce heat reaching electronic component and can prevent damage to semiconductor material.

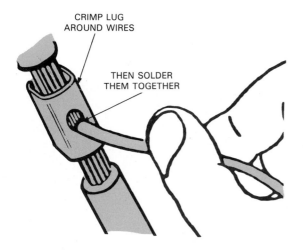

Fig. 7-22. Wires can also be joined as shown. A—Strip about one inch of insulation from both wires. B—Wrap or twist conductor ends together. C—Solder twisted ends and then tape them.

Fig. 7-21. The best way to join two wires is to first crimp metal lug over both wire ends. Then solder the wires and lug together into a single junction. Tape over the exposed conductor after checking joint. (General Motors)

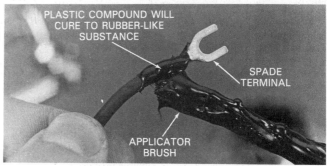

mends soldering or joining two wires together. A metal lug is crimped around the wires first. Then, solder is used to bond the wires and lug together. This makes for an excellent repair.

Fig. 7-22 shows how to solder two wires together without a crimp type lug. Strip the wires, leaving about one inch of conductor exposed. Twist the two wire conductors together. Then melt a layer of solder over the twisted wire ends.

Covering exposed conductors

Electrical tape is commonly used to cover and protect the soldered conductors. Use moderate pressure while wrapping the tape around the joint. Wrap the tape so that a neat, smooth, and tight layer of tape results.

Liquid electrical tape is a plastic type coating that can be applied over conductors, Fig. 7-23. It is coated on the components with a brush. It then dries to a plastic

Fig. 7-23. Liquid electrical tape is new product that can sometimes be used in place of conventional electrical tape. It is ideal when conductor must be sealed to keep out moisture. A—Liquid electrical tape container. B—Applying liquid electrical tape.

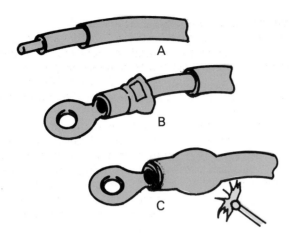

Fig. 7-24. Heat shrink tubing is another way of covering exposed conductor with insulation. A—Slide heat shrink over wire. B—Install terminal. C—Slide heat shrink down and heat it.

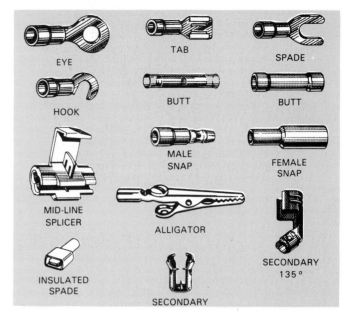

Fig. 7-26. These are most common types of single wire connectors and terminals. Study their names. (Belden)

or rubber-like substance that protects the conductor.

Liquid electrical tape is excellent when the joint must be protected from moisture. It will keep the joint dry while electrical tape can allow moisture entry.

Heat shrink tubing is another alternative to electrical tape. It is hollow plastic tubing, often termed "spaghetti," that reduces in diameter with heat, Fig. 7-24.

The heat shrink tube is slid over the joint. Then it is heated with a lighter, match, or heat gun. The heat makes the plastic tubing shrink down tightly around the wire to produce an insulating barrier over the conductor. See Fig. 7-25.

WIRE TERMINALS AND CONNECTORS

Various types of wire terminals and connectors can be found or used on the modern automobile. It is important for you to be able to identify, select, and properly install them.

Fig. 7-26 shows the most common types of single-wire connectors or terminals. Study their names.

Installing crimp connectors

Although not as good as a solder joint, crimp connectors can be used to make many electrical repairs. They provide a quick and easy way of joining wires or installing a terminal end on a wire.

To use a crimp connector, first strip the wire. Make sure the right amount of conductor is remaining. If the conductor is too short or too long, the crimp connector will not work properly.

After stripping, twist the conductor to hold the wire strands together. This will make the conductor feed into the crimp connector easily, Fig. 7-27.

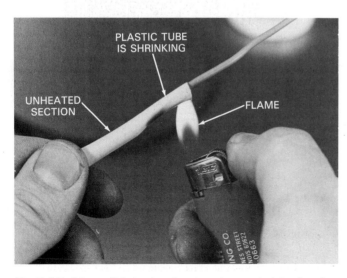

Fig. 7-25. After splicing two wires together, technician is using cigarette lighter to shrink plastic tightly around joint.

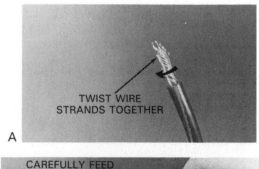

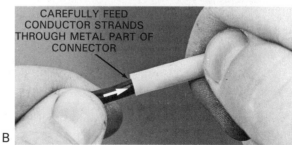

Fig. 7-27. A—Before inserting a standard wire into a terminal, twist the strands as shown. B—This will help all strands feed through the terminal.

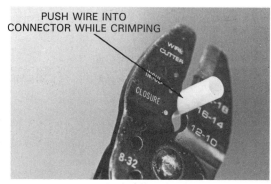

A—With wire properly inserted, crimp connector around wire conductor. Make sure you crimp the metal lug.

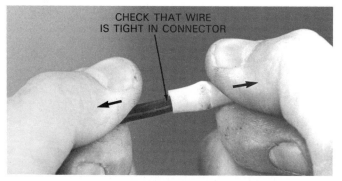

B—Pull on connector lightly to make sure it is secure.

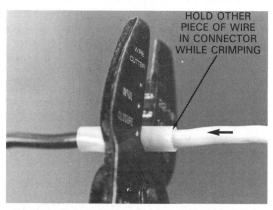

C—Install other wire and crimp other end of connector.

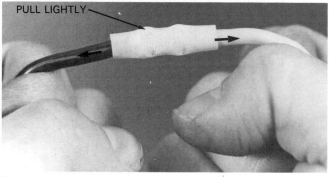

D—Again, check that connector is tight on wires.

Fig. 7-28. Steps for butt splicing wires with crimp connector.

Use crimping pliers to crush or form the metal part of the connector down around the wire conductor. Different size crimping jaws are normally provided so make sure you use the right ones, Fig. 7-28.

Note! A common mistake is to place the jaws over the plastic part of the connector and not over the metal lug inside the connector. This can compress only part of the metal lug and a weak connection will result. Make sure the jaws are positioned correctly over the metal lug before crimping.

After crimping, pull on the wire and connector lightly. Make sure the wire does not pull out of the connector. If it does, install a new connector and check it again.

Fig. 7-29 shows a technician installing a crimp type spade terminal. Again, make sure the conductor is properly installed into the terminal and position the jaws over the metal part of the terminal. Pull lightly on the terminal to check its installation.

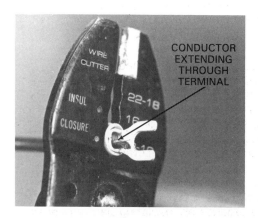

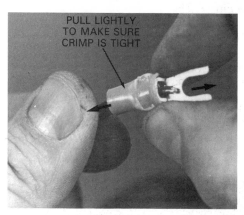

Fig. 7-29. Installing terminal on end of wire. A—Strip wire and insert conductor through terminal. Crimp connector down around conductor. B—Check installation by pulling lightly on terminal. If possible, you should also solder conductor to terminal.

Fig. 7-30 shows the action of the electrical pliers when forming a crimp connection.

Warning! If a wire were to pull out of a crimp connector, it could cause a short circuit. Make sure the connector is secure. Solder on a connector when possible.

Fig. 7-31 shows a variation of the conventional type crimp terminal. Note that it is designed to clamp down

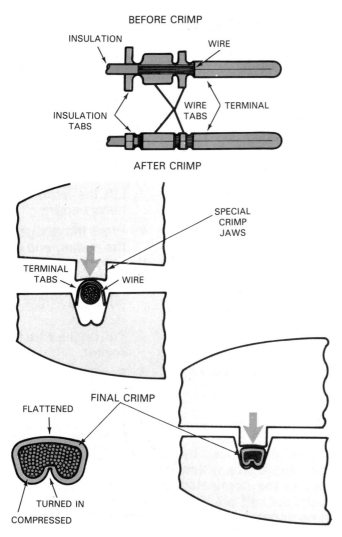

Fig. 7-30. Note how crimp is formed with this type terminal. (Ford)

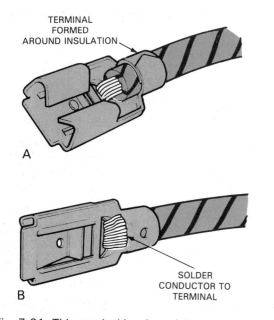

Fig. 7-31. This terminal is crimped down around wire insulation. Then, wire conductor must be soldered to terminal. (Lister Diesels)

over the insulation on the wire. Then, the conductor must be soldered to the metal terminal.

FACTORY CONNECTORS

Various types of connectors are installed on new cars at the factory. *Harness connectors* are multi-terminal connectors that join several wires and have a special locking feature. In most cases, the connector consists of a two-part plastic housing that snaps together to prevent the terminals from working free.

Disconnecting factory connectors

Most late-model electrical connectors require the use of special methods or special tools during disconnection. Many factory connectors have a plastic latch that holds the two halves of the connector together. You may have to squeeze or pry up on the latch to free the connector. Fig. 7-32 shows an example.

Note! Connector damage will result if you force a connector apart. Always obtain the right tool and use the proper methods when disconnecting harness connectors. If in doubt about how to release a connector, refer to the service manual.

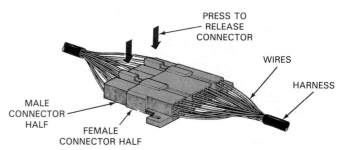

Fig. 7-32. Factory connectors can house several wires and terminals. Most have locking feature. You must release tabs before pulling connector apart. (Toyota)

Terminal replacement

Sometimes, it is necessary to replace a terminal inside a factory connector. Usually, the terminal has a small metal lug that locks inside the plastic connector. As shown in Fig. 7-33, a small screwdriver or special tool can be used to release and free the terminal lug. Then the wire and terminal will pull out of the plastic connector, Fig. 7-34.

When reinstalling a terminal in a factory connector, make sure the small metal lug is bent outward properly. It must stick out far enough to relock tightly inside the connector. Use a small screwdriver to bend the lug out if needed.

Fig. 7-35 shows the service manual procedures for repairing a special weather-pack type terminal. Always check in a shop manual for unusual procedures or connectors.

Fig. 7-36 shows a tool designed for releasing terminals inside of automotive connectors. It is slid inside the connector to release the locking device on the terminal.

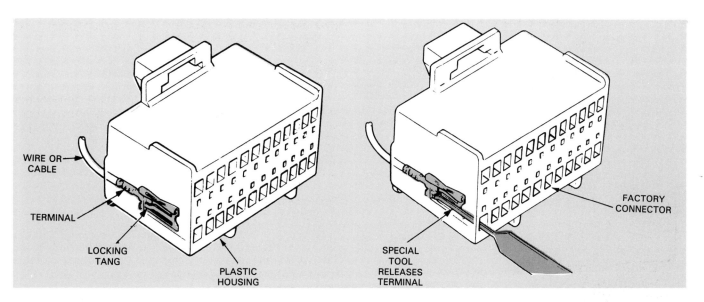

Fig. 7-33. Sometimes, terminals inside factory connectors can become damaged. Special tool or small screwdriver is needed to free terminal from connector. (Ford)

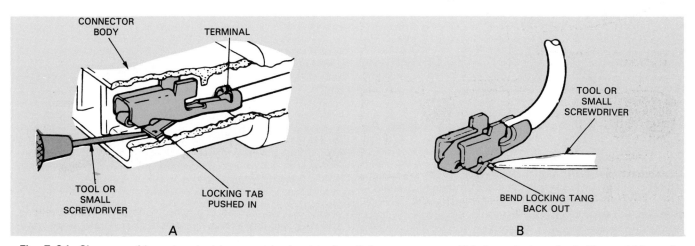

Fig. 7-34. Close-up of how terminal lug must be bent to free it from connector. This is typical method. (General Motors)

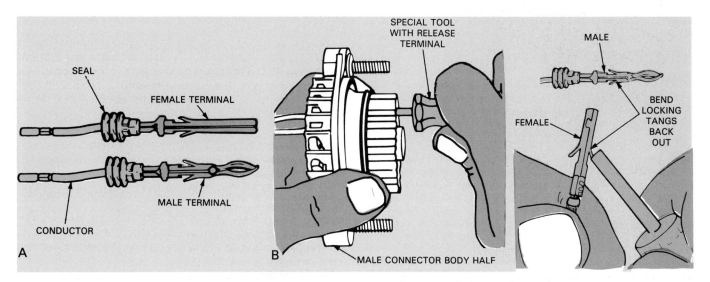

Fig. 7-35. Basic service manual steps for working with special waterproof connector. A—Types of terminals. B—Using special tool to release terminal from connector. C—Reforming tangs so terminals will lock back into connector. (General Motors)

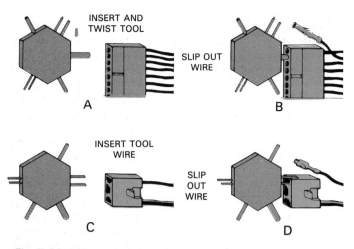

Fig. 7-36. This special tool is designed to release various types of terminals from their connector. It is handy. (Lisle Tools)

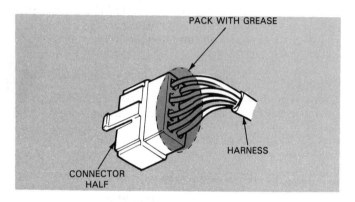

Fig. 7-37. Special grease is frequently used and recommended on terminals to prevent corrosion and bad connection. Grease can also be applied to outside of connector if there is a corrosion or moisture problem. (Honda)

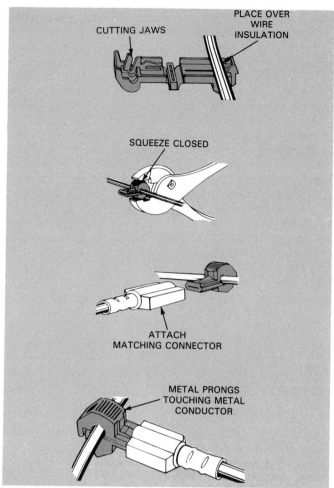

Fig. 7-38. This self-stripping connector makes it easy to splice into an existing wire. It snaps over wire and cuts through insulation to make contact with conductor. This type is commonly used when wiring up trailer lights for example. (G-P Parts)

Terminal grease

Before refastening connectors, it is usually recommended that you apply GREASE to the terminals. The special grease will help prevent corrosion. Sometimes, it is suggested that you pack the outer opening in the connector with grease. This will also keep moisture off of the terminals. Look at Fig. 7-37.

SELF-STRIPPING CONNECTOR

A *self-stripping connector* will cut through the wire insulation and lock onto the wire conductor automatically. This type connector is handy when you must connect to an existing wire in a harness. You can use this type connector to splice in a wire for an electrical accessory (trailer lights for instance) or to bypass a bad connection or wire, Fig. 7-38.

WIRING REPAIRS

This section of the chapter will summarize how to do basic wiring repairs. Other text chapters will detail how to do more specialized electrical tests and repairs. Refer to the index for more information.

Bypassing a connector

Bypassing a connector is done by using a new piece of wire to make an electrical path around the terminals in a connector. This might be needed if the connector is burned or damaged and a new one is not available. Refer to Fig. 7-39.

Cut off the affected wire leading into both sides of the connector. Then, butt splice a new piece of wire to join

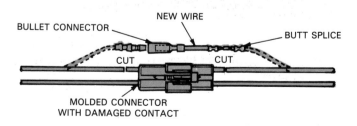

Fig. 7-39. When a connector is burned or damaged, it is sometimes easier to bypass bad connection with a new wire. Connector may not be readily available for example. Butt splice and solder new wire as shown. (Ford)

to two cut ends. Crimp connectors will work but solder the wires if possible.

Bypassing a connector can save time, especially if there are several wires in the connector. If they are good, all of the other wires and terminals can remain joined using the existing connector. Only the bad electrical connection is bypassed.

Bypassing a wire

Bypassing a wire can be done by using a new piece of wire to make an electrical connection around a bad section of a wiring harness. If tests find one wire to be broken or shorted inside a wiring harness, it might be easier to run a new wire in place of the bad one. Then the rest of the harness can remain intact. This is handy if the wire runs through a complex or hidden harness, one running under the dash, or through the firewall, for example. See Fig. 7-40.

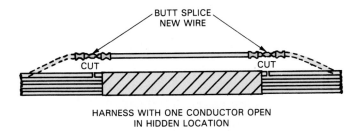

Fig. 7-40. If a wire is broken or shorted inside a complex wiring harness, bypassing wire may also be desirable. Simply cut bad wire on each end of harness where it is easily accessible. Then, run new wire to connect cut ends. (Ford)

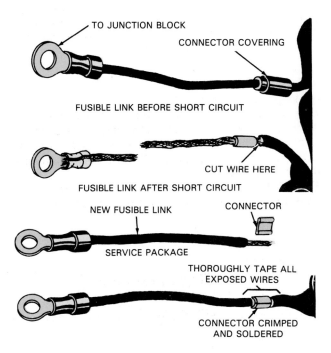

Fig. 7-41. When fuse link burns, several circuits in car may not function. Lights, starter, and other components may not work. Fuse link is usually near battery or starting motor. Cut off old link. Solder on new link or correct wire gauge size as a repair. (General Motors)

Fuse link service

Discussed in an earlier chapter, a *fuse link* protects the wiring before the fuse box. It will burn in half if a wire is shorted and draws excess current. This may "kill power" to several major circuits (starting, lighting, etc.).

Before replacing a fuse link, correct the short circuit problem (covered in Chapter 9). This will keep the new fuse link from burning. Disconnect the negative battery cable. Then, remove or cut off the burned fuse link. Remember that fuse links are usually in the engine compartment, near the battery or starting motor solenoid. Refer to Fig. 7-41.

Strip the end of the larger circuit wire. Obtain a factory fuse link or the correct gauge (size) replacement wire. It will be smaller gauge than the main circuit wiring. Use a metal connector to butt splice the link to the main circuit wire. Then, SOLDER the wires and connector together. Tape over the soldered connection. Reconnect the battery and check circuit operation.

Refer to the shop manual for added information concerning the specific make and model car. The manual will give special procedures and specifications for the fuse link wire.

Twisted cable service

Mentioned briefly, new cars can use shielded or twisted cable in some computer circuit wiring. It is

TWISTED/SHIELDED CABLE

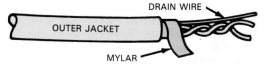

1. REMOVE OUTER JACKET.
2. UNWRAP ALUMINUM/MYLAR TAPE. DO NOT REMOVE MYLAR.

3. UNTWIST CONDUCTORS. STRIP INSULATION AS NECESSARY.

4. SPLICE WIRES USING SPLICE CLIPS AND ROSIN CORE SOLDER. WRAP EACH SPLICE TO INSULATE.
5. WRAP WITH MYLAR AND DRAIN (UNINSULATED) WIRE.

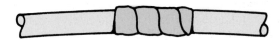

6. TAPE OVER WHOLE BUNDLE TO SECURE AS BEFORE.

Fig. 7-42. Note basic steps for repairing twisted-shielded wire for computer wiring harness. Solder and wrap each wire separately. Rewrap aluminum tape to form magnetic shield around conductors. Splice drain wire and wrap cable with electrical tape. (General Motors)

designed to prevent voltage from being induced into the wire and upsetting the operation of the computer. Many sensors operate on very low current and voltage levels and their signals can be affected by any induced voltage.

Fig. 7-42 shows a typical method for splicing and fixing twisted-shielded cable. Note that aluminum mylar tape is used inside the conventional plastic insulation.

To make a repair, solder each wire together. Wrap each with electrical tape. Rewrap the twisted section of the cable with aluminum tape. Splice and solder the outer wire. Wrap the outside of the cable with electrical tape.

SUMMARY

Today's car uses well over a mile of wire to connect its hundreds of electric-electronic components. As a result, it is critical that you have the basic skills needed to repair wiring problems.

Most automotive wires are stranded. This allows them to withstand vibration and movement better.

Wire size is commonly given as a gauge number. A smaller gauge number represents a larger diameter conductor. Car wiring is usually between 8 and 12 gauge. Battery cables are very large, between 2 and 6 gauge.

Wire resistance increases as conductor diameter decreases and as wire length increases. Resistance in aluminum wire is higher than in the more common copper wire. Wire resistance normally increases with temperature.

Primary wire refers to the wire that carries battery voltage throughout most of the car. Secondary wire is high voltage wire with thick insulation. Cable refers to larger wire, like battery cables. The term cable can also apply to special shielded or coaxial wire.

Printed circuit wire is metal strips deposited on a plastic or fiber base. It is commonly used on the back of an instrument cluster for instance.

Wire color codes are used so that you can trace wire from one location to the next, even when some of the wire is hidden from view. For example, color coding will let you follow a wire from the fuse box to where it might connect to another component in the engine compartment. The wire will have the same color markings on its insulation.

A wiring harness is a set of several wires enclosed in tape or a plastic protection device. Connectors branch out from the harness for linking to electrical components or other harness connectors.

Use wire strippers to remove insulation from wires. Avoid using cutters to strip wires.

Solder is the best way to join one wire to another or to join a wire to a terminal. Tin the soldering gun tip before starting. This will coat the tip with a thin layer of molten solder.

Preheat the components before applying the rosin core solder. Touch the solder on both the components and the soldering gun tip. This will assure that the solder bonds properly.

NEVER touch the solder directly on only the soldering gun tip and allow the solder to drip or run down onto the joint. This can result in a weak joint. Allow the solder joint to cool before moving it.

Electrical tape is commonly used to cover the metal joint after soldering. Liquid electrical tape is good when the joint must be protected from moisture. Heat shrink tubing will also cover and protect a soldered joint.

Crimp connectors provide a quick and easy method of joining wires or terminals to wires. Crimping pliers are used to form the metal part of the connector around the wire conductor. When possible, you should solder crimp connectors to assure a permanent electrical connection.

Factory connectors usually have a locking feature. Plastic clips lock the two parts of the connector together. This keeps the connectors from pulling apart with vibration. Use the correct procedure to release a connector to prevent damage.

A small screwdriver or special tool is needed to free metal terminals from inside a factory connector. Reform the lug on a terminal before reinstalling it in the connector.

Sometimes it is easier to bypass a bad connector or wire. It can be very time consuming to splice in a new connector having several wires. It can also be almost impossible to remove and replace a bad wire inside a complex wiring harness. Running a new wire around the bad terminal or wire can be more efficient.

When replacing a fuse link, use the correct replacement wire gauge size. Always solder the new link in place to prevent unwanted resistance.

KNOW THESE TERMS

Solid wire, Stranded wire, Wire size, Wire gauge, Metric wire size, Primary wire, Secondary wire, Battery cable, Secondary resistance wire, Shielded wire, Coax, Printed circuit wire, Aluminum wire, Copper wire, Wire color code, Wire protection devices, Wiring harness, Connector, Terminal, Splice, Strip, Solder, Tinning, Preheating, Rosin core solder, Acid core solder, Liquid electrical tape, Electrical tape, Heat shrink, Crimp connector, Factory connector.

REVIEW QUESTIONS—CHAPTER 7

1. Why is most automotive wire stranded?
2. Wire size is determined by the diameter of its _____.
3. A 10 gauge wire is smaller than a 12 gauge wire. True or false?
4. How is metric wire size given?
5. List seven rules for current in a wire.
6. Another name for primary wire is _____ _____.
7. What is shielded wire?
8. _____ _____ _____ has flat conductor strips mounted on a plastic or fiber base.
9. Aluminum wire is a better conductor than more common copper wire. True or false?
10. Why are wires color coded?
11. The following is NOT a wire protection device.
    a. Heat shrink tubing.
    b. Liquid electrical tape.
    c. Flux.
    d. Wiring harness.
12. Explain the procedure for installing a crimp connector.
13. In your own words, describe the proper way to solder a wire onto a terminal.

14. When is liquid electrical tape better to use than conventional electrical tape?

15. _____ a wire involves using a new piece of wire to make an electrical connection around a bad section of a wiring harness.

ASE CERTIFICATION–TYPE QUESTIONS

1. Technician A says stranded wire is normally used to connect an automobile's electronic components. Technician B says solid wire is generally more flexible than stranded wire. Who is right?
   (A) A only.   (C) Both A and B.
   (B) B only.   (D) Neither A nor B.

2. Technician A says automotive wiring is usually between 4 and 12 gauge. Technician B says automotive wire size must be matched to the circuit load. Who is right?
   (A) A only.   (C) Both A and B.
   (B) B only.   (D) Neither A nor B.

3. Technician A says wire resistance increases as conductor diameter decreases. Technician B says wire resistance increases as conductor length increases. Who is right?
   (A) A only.   (C) Both A and B.
   (B) B only.   (D) Neither A nor B.

4. Technician A says wire resistance is dependent on the type of material used for the conductor. Technician B says wire resistance is dependent on the temperature of the conductor. Who is right?
   (A) A only.   (C) Both A and B.
   (B) B only.   (D) Neither A nor B.

5. Technician A says secondary wire is used to carry high voltage in the engine's ignition system. Technician B says primary wire is used to carry battery voltage to various electrical components in the vehicle. Who is right?
   (A) A only.   (C) Both A and B.
   (B) B only.   (D) Neither A nor B.

6. Which of the following is the best tool to use when soldering large cable?
   (A) Pencil-type soldering iron.   (C) Propane torch.
   (B) Soldering gun.   (D) Soldering lug.

7. A wire has come loose from an automotive component. Technician A says the tip of the soldering gun should be tinned before the wire is soldered. Technician B says the wire and the component lead should be preheated before melting solder onto the joint. Who is right?
   (A) A only.   (C) Both A and B.
   (B) B only.   (D) Neither A nor B.

8. All of the following are common single wire connectors or terminals *except:*
   (A) insulated spade.   (C) male snap.
   (B) primary tab.   (D) eye.

9. A crimp connector must be replaced. Technician A twists the wire strands before inserting the wire into the connector. Technician B fastens the new connector to the wire by squeezing the connector's plastic cover. Who is right?
   (A) A only.   (C) Both A and B.
   (B) B only.   (D) Neither A nor B.

10. One of an automobile's fuse links is burned. Technician A says the circuit problem should be identified and corrected before the link is replaced. Technician B says the battery cable should be disconnected before the link is replaced. Who is right?
    (A) A only.   (C) Both A and B.
    (B) B only.   (D) Neither A nor B.

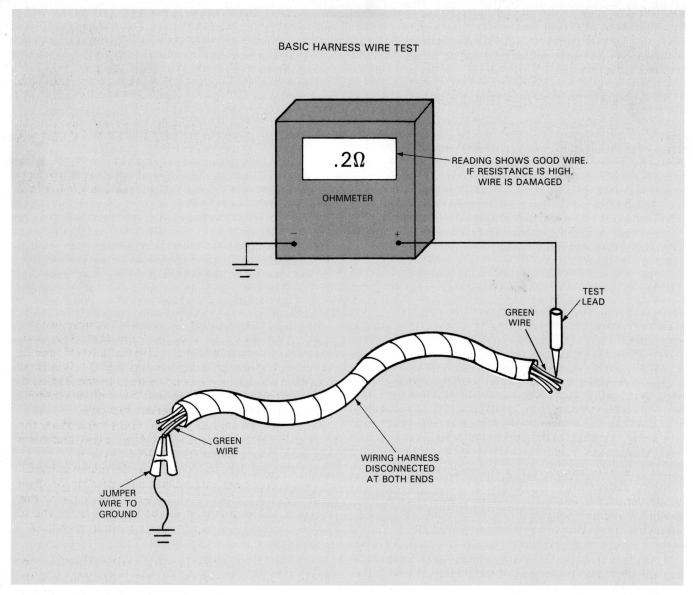

BASIC HARNESS WIRE TEST

.2Ω

OHMMETER

READING SHOWS GOOD WIRE.
IF RESISTANCE IS HIGH,
WIRE IS DAMAGED

TEST
LEAD

GREEN
WIRE

GREEN
WIRE

WIRING HARNESS
DISCONNECTED
AT BOTH ENDS

JUMPER
WIRE TO
GROUND

If you suspect a wire is broken inside harness, this is an easy way to test wire. Disconnect harness at both ends, ground suspected wire on one end. Then use ohmmeter to check resistance of wire. If high, wire would have to be bypassed or replaced.

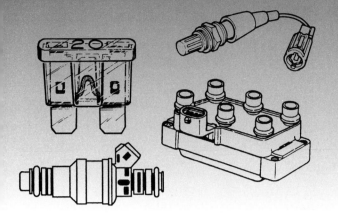

After studying this chapter, you will be able to:
- *Explain common abbreviations found in service manuals.*
- *Use different types of troubleshooting charts.*
- *Use alpha-numeric wiring code identification systems.*
- *Use component location charts and illustrations.*
- *Read electrical circuit diagrams.*
- *Locate specific components on wiring diagrams using a grid.*
- *Describe variations in wiring diagrams from different auto manufacturers.*
- *Use the information charts that accompany many wiring diagrams.*
- *Use connector illustrations when testing a circuit.*
- *Explain vacuum diagrams.*
- *Identify basic vacuum component symbols.*

If you look in a service manual for a late-model car, you will often find that over half the manual consists of wiring diagrams, electrical troubleshooting charts, and other information for fixing electrical problems. This proves that auto makers realize that their technicians need help with repairing electrical-electronic troubles.

This chapter will describe the most important aspects for the proper use of wiring diagrams, vacuum diagrams, troubleshooting charts, and other information in a service manual. Even an experienced technician must sometimes refer to an electrical diagram, specification for terminal voltage, wiring code chart, etc., when working. This chapter will help you become more proficient at using this valuable information.

USING SERVICE MANUALS

Service manuals contain detailed instructions, specifications, and illustrations to help with the repair of cars. Published by the auto manufacturers, they explain service methods for a specific make and model car.

Today's service manuals are written in very technical language. They use numerous abbreviations, terms common to only the specific manufacturer, and varying methods of testing. As a result, it can be time consuming if you are not fully prepared to use a manual properly.

Abbreviations

Abbreviations are used in service manuals to save space. They are letters that represent commonly used or very long technical terms. Abbreviations will also fit on a complex wiring diagram easily. Fig. 8-1 is a chart containing abbreviations recommended by the Society of Automotive Engineers. These and many other abbreviations are used in automotive service manuals.

Before using a service manual, you should study the chart giving abbreviations. Abbreviations vary and many refer to a unique name for a specific system.

For example, General Motors uses the abbreviation C^3I to mean computer controlled coil ignition or their distributorless ignition. If you are not familiar with this and other abbreviations, it will be impossible for you to fully understand the explanations given in a manual.

Illustrations

Service manual illustrations are used to show the construction, location, operation, etc., of various components. The illustrations can be very useful to the electronic technician.

When you are reading the manual, always refer to the illustrations when they are mentioned. Read the caption and study the photo or drawing. This will ensure that you fully comprehend the manual.

References

The *references* in a service manual require you turn to another page or area for additional information. For example, look at the diagnosis chart in Fig. 8-2.

The first line tells you to perform a ''Diagnostic Circuit Check.'' You would have to refer to the instructions for doing this test if not familiar with its procedures. Later in the same chart you are told to ''See Section 6C.'' You might need to refer to this section for more data.

Diagnosis charts

Diagnosis charts give logical steps for finding and correcting problems. Various types of charts can be found in service manuals.

Fig. 8-2 shows a typical diagnosis, or troubleshooting, chart. Simply find the appropriate condition in the left-hand column and then read across the chart to determine possible causes and corrections.

SAE-Recommended Abbreviations

Term	Abbreviation/	Term	Abbreviation/
Accelerator Pedal	AP	Inertia Fuel Shutoff	IFS
Air Cleaner	AC	Intake Air	IA
Air Conditioning	A/C	Intake Air Temperature	IAT
Automatic Transmission	A/T		
Automatic Transaxle	A/T	Knock Sensor	KS
		Malfunction Indicator Lamp	MIL
Barometric Pressure	BARO	Manifold Absolute Pressure	MAP
Battery Positive Voltage	B+	Manifold Differential Pressure	MDP
		Manifold Surface Temperature	MST
Camshaft Position	CMP	Manifold Vacuum Zone	MVZ
Carburetor	CARB	Mass Airflow	MAF
Charge Air Cooler	CAC	Mixture Control	MC
Closed Loop	CL	Multiport Fuel Injection	MFI
Closed Throttle Position	CTP		
Clutch Pedal Position	CPP	Nonvolatile Random Access Memory	NVRAM
Continuous Fuel Injection	CFI		
Continuous Trap Oxidizer	CTOX	On-Board Diagnostic	OBD
Crankshaft Position	CKP	Open Loop	OL
		Oxidation Catalytic Converter	OC
Data Link Connector	DLC	Oxygen Sensor	O2S
Diagnostic Test Mode	DTM		
Diagnostic Trouble Code	DTC	Park/Neutral Position	PNP
Direct Fuel Injection	DFI	Periodic Trap Oxidizer	PTOX
		Positive Crankcase Ventilation	PCV
Early Fuel Evaporation	EFE	Power Steering Pressure	PSP
EGR Temperature	EGRT	Powertrain Control Module	PCM
Electronically Erasable Programmable Read Only Memory	EEPROM	Programmable Read Only Memory	PROM
Electronic Ignition	EI	Pulsed Secondary Air Injection	PAIR
Engine Control	EC	Random Access Memory	RAM
Engine Control Module	ECM	Read Only Memory	ROM
Engine Coolant Level	ECL	Relay Module	RM
Engine Coolant Temperature	ECT		
Engine Modification	EM	Scan Tool	ST
Engine Speed	RPM	Secondary Air Injection	AIR
Erasable Programmable Read Only Memory	EPROM	Sequential Multiport Fuel Injection	SFI
Evaporative Emission	EVAP	Service Reminder Indicator	SRI
Exhaust Gas Recirculation	EGR	Smoke Puff Limiter	SPL
		Supercharger	SC
Fan Control	FC	Supercharger Bypass	SCB
Flash Electrically Erasable Programmable Read Only Memory	FEEPROM	System Readiness Test	SRT
Flash Erasable Programmable Read Only Memory	FEPROM	Thermal Vacuum Valve	TVV
Flexible Fuel	FF	Third Gear	3GR
Fourth Gear	4GR	Three Way + Oxidation Catalytic Converter	TWC+OC
Fuel Pump	FP	Three Way Catalytic Converter	TWC
Fuel Trim	FT	Throttle Body	TB
		Throttle Body Fuel Injection	TBI
Generator	GEN	Throttle Position	TP
Governor Control Module	GCM	Torque Converter Clutch	TCC
Ground	GND	Transmission Control Module	TCM
		Transmission Range	TR
Heated Oxygen Sensor	HO2S	Turbocharger	TC
Idle Air Control	IAC	Vehicle Speed Sensor	VSS
Idle Speed Control	ISC	Voltage Regulator	VR
Ignition Control	IC	Volume Airflow	VAF
Ignition Control Module	ICM	Warm Up Three Way Catalytic Converter	WU-TWC
Indirect Fuel Injection	IFI	Wide Open Throttle	WOT

Fig. 8-1. SAE-recommended automotive abbreviations. Although abbreviations will be the same in most manuals, you must be familiar with specialized terminology and abbreviations used by specific manufacturers.

TROUBLESHOOTING ENGINE PERFORMANCE PROBLEMS		
Condition	Possible cause	Correction
Engine misses on acceleration.	1. Dirty spark plug or improper gap.	1. Clean spark plugs and set gap.
	2. Dirt in fuel system.	2. Clean fuel system and replace fuel filter.
	3. Burned, warped, or pitted valves.	3. Install new valves.
	4. Faulty coil.	4. Test and, if necessary, replace coil.
Engine misses at high speed.	1. Dirty spark plug or improper gap.	1. Clean spark plugs and set gap.
	2. Faulty coil.	2. Test and, if necessary, replace coil.
	3. Dirty fuel injectors.	3. Clean injectors.
	4. Dirt or water in fuel system.	4. Clean system and replace fuel filter.
Engine will not start.	1. Weak battery.	1. Charge or replace battery as necessary.
	2. Corroded or loose battery connections.	2. Clean and tighten battery

Fig. 8-2. This troubleshooting chart lists possible causes and corrections for various engine performance problems.

Fig. 8-3 gives a tree diagnosis chart that fans out to give you a path to follow when troubleshooting. Simply start at the top and work your way down.

Fig. 8-4 illustrates how you may have to refer to other sections in the manual when using a tree type diagnosis chart. You may have to refer to a trouble code chart or to another troubleshooting chart. These cross-references actually produce a much more detailed diagnosis chart. Several charts can work together to make your troubleshooting path more complete.

Fig. 8-5 is an example of an illustrated diagnosis chart. It gives logical steps for troubleshooting. It also illustrates how to do the various tests.

Repair procedures

The *repair procedures* in a service manual are highly condensed instructions on how to remove, disconnect, repair, or replace components. An example is shown in Fig. 8-6. Note how the instructions ask you to refer to specific illustrations. The instructions also tell exactly what parts must be removed to get at parts.

If you have never done a specific repair or have not removed a specific component, the service manual procedures can save you time. They can give helpful hints for doing the repair properly.

Electrical specifications

Electrical specifications are exact measurements for a properly operating circuit or electrical component. They can be a voltage, current, or resistance value. Specs can also be a spark plug gap, rpm, alternator brush dimension, or measurement in degrees of rotation.

It is critical that you refer to specifications when needed. They will assure that a circuit or electrical component has an exact operating parameter.

An example of an electrical specification chart is in Fig. 8-7. Note the values given in this chart.

COMPONENT LOCATIONS

Component locations for electrical-electronic circuits can be given in illustrations, charts, or using a code on the wiring diagrams. For example, if you are not sure how to find a potentially faulty relay, you can refer to the service manual to find it.

Fig. 8-8 shows a service manual illustration giving locations for relays, amplifier circuits, and electronic control units. Note how this illustration would be very useful when doing many electrical repairs.

Fig. 8-9 shows another type of component location illustration. It is a diagram showing the top view of an engine compartment. It shows locations for harness connectors, special test points, sensors, and control devices (actuators). Again, abbreviations are used to save space.

A General Motors component location table is in Fig. 8-10. Note that many of the components are given as a letter-number code. For example, a C102A is a

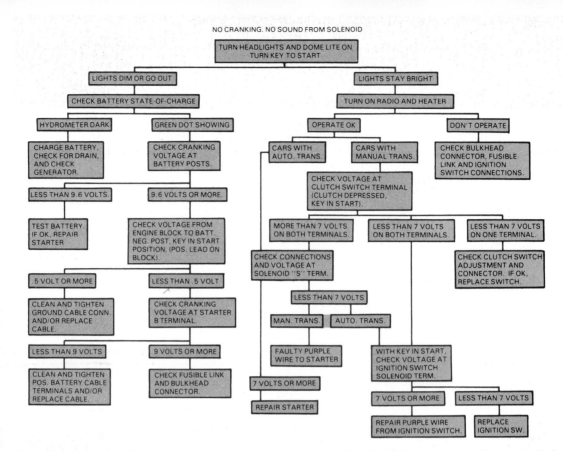

Fig. 8-3. This diagnosis chart is good because it gives exact electrical values that should be present during tests. It also guides you through logical sequence depending upon test results. (General Motors)

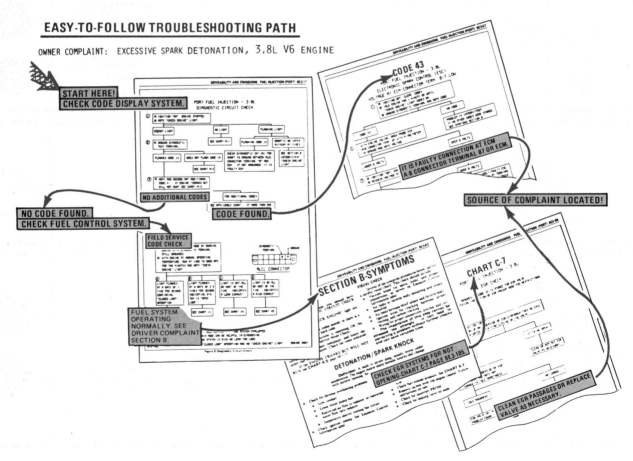

Fig. 8-4. With the complexity of today's electronics, it is important that you know how to use different manuals. Manual will usually have introductory information on using charts, instructions, and diagrams. Read this information before attempting to use manual.

Chart 3

PROBLEM: FUEL GAUGE AND COOLANT TEMPERATURE GAUGE BOTH MALFUNCTION (ALSO OIL PRESSURE GAUGE ON CHEROKEE, WAGONEER AND TRUCK

STEP   **SEQUENCE**   **RESULT**

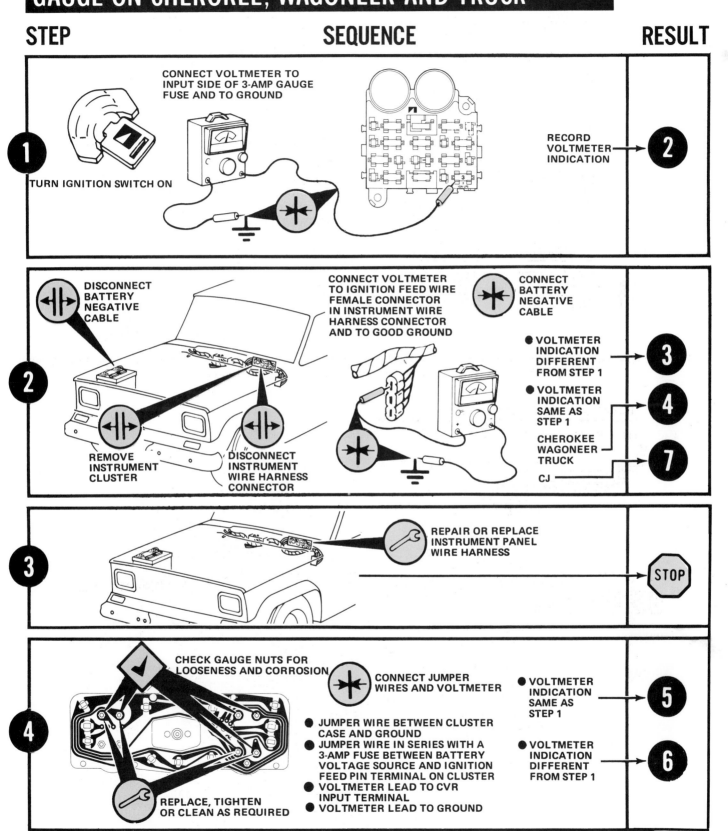

1 — TURN IGNITION SWITCH ON — CONNECT VOLTMETER TO INPUT SIDE OF 3-AMP GAUGE FUSE AND TO GROUND — RECORD VOLTMETER INDICATION → **2**

2 — DISCONNECT BATTERY NEGATIVE CABLE — REMOVE INSTRUMENT CLUSTER — DISCONNECT INSTRUMENT WIRE HARNESS CONNECTOR — CONNECT VOLTMETER TO IGNITION FEED WIRE FEMALE CONNECTOR IN INSTRUMENT WIRE HARNESS CONNECTOR AND TO GOOD GROUND — CONNECT BATTERY NEGATIVE CABLE
- VOLTMETER INDICATION DIFFERENT FROM STEP 1 → **3**
- VOLTMETER INDICATION SAME AS STEP 1 → **4**
- CHEROKEE WAGONEER TRUCK → **7**
- CJ → **7**

3 — REPAIR OR REPLACE INSTRUMENT PANEL WIRE HARNESS → **STOP**

4 — CHECK GAUGE NUTS FOR LOOSENESS AND CORROSION — REPLACE, TIGHTEN OR CLEAN AS REQUIRED — CONNECT JUMPER WIRES AND VOLTMETER
- JUMPER WIRE BETWEEN CLUSTER CASE AND GROUND
- JUMPER WIRE IN SERIES WITH A 3-AMP FUSE BETWEEN BATTERY VOLTAGE SOURCE AND IGNITION FEED PIN TERMINAL ON CLUSTER
- VOLTMETER LEAD TO CVR INPUT TERMINAL
- VOLTMETER LEAD TO GROUND
- VOLTMETER INDICATION SAME AS STEP 1 → **5**
- VOLTMETER INDICATION DIFFERENT FROM STEP 1 → **6**

Fig. 8-5. This is an illustrated diagnosis chart. It gives logical path and shows how to do various tests. It also gives specs. (Chrysler)

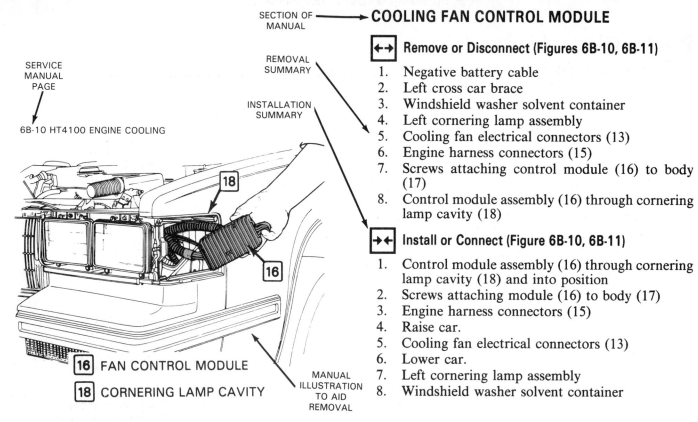

SECTION OF
MANUAL → **COOLING FAN CONTROL MODULE**

REMOVAL
SUMMARY

INSTALLATION
SUMMARY

←→ **Remove or Disconnect (Figures 6B-10, 6B-11)**

1. Negative battery cable
2. Left cross car brace
3. Windshield washer solvent container
4. Left cornering lamp assembly
5. Cooling fan electrical connectors (13)
6. Engine harness connectors (15)
7. Screws attaching control module (16) to body (17)
8. Control module assembly (16) through cornering lamp cavity (18)

→← **Install or Connect (Figure 6B-10, 6B-11)**

1. Control module assembly (16) through cornering lamp cavity (18) and into position
2. Screws attaching module (16) to body (17)
3. Engine harness connectors (15)
4. Raise car.
5. Cooling fan electrical connectors (13)
6. Lower car.
7. Left cornering lamp assembly
8. Windshield washer solvent container

16 FAN CONTROL MODULE

18 CORNERING LAMP CAVITY

MANUAL
ILLUSTRATION
TO AID
REMOVAL

Fig. 8-6. This is an example of service instructions given in manual. Always refer to illustrations as soon as they are called out in copy. Instructions are for specific make and model car. They can help if you have never done specific repair before. (Oldsmobile)

ELECTRICAL SPECIFICATIONS

			13 B E.G.I. Engine		13 B Turbocharged Engine
			M/T	A/T	M/T
Voltage		(V)	12, Negative ground		
Battery	Type and capacity (20—hour rate)		50D20L : 50AH 65D23L : 55AH (65D23L : Cold proof area)		
Ignition system	Distribution		Control Unit		
	Spark timing		Leading: 5°ATDC Trailing: 20°ATDC at idle		
	Spark advance		Control Unit		
	Spark plug	Type	Leading side ; SD-10A (NGK) S-29A (NIPPON DENSO) Trailing side ; SD-11A (NGK) S-31A (NIPPON DENSO)		
		Plug gap (mm (in))	2.0 (0.08)		
Alternator	Output	(V—A)	12—70		
	Regulated voltage	(V)	14.4 ~ 15.0 (with temperature—gradient characteristics)		
	Output test (at hot)	Voltage (V)	13.5		
		Current (A)	Min. 55		
		Speed (rpm)	2,500		
	Brush length	Standard (mm (in))	16.5 (0.650)		
		Wear limit (mm (in))	8.0 (0.315)		
Starter	Type		Coaxial reduction		
	Output	(KW)	1.2	2.0	1.2
	Output (No load)	Voltage (V)	11.0		
		Current (A)	Max. 90		
		Speed (rpm)	Min. 3,000		
	Brush length	Standard (mm (in))	17.5 (0.689)		
		Wear limit (mm (in))	10.0 (0.394)		

Fig. 8-7. Specifications are important when doing electrical repairs. You must compare known good voltage, current, or ohms value with electrical value actually present in vehicle system. Note specs given for this electrical system. (Toyota)

Body Electrical
– Relay, Amplifier and Control Unit Locations ——————

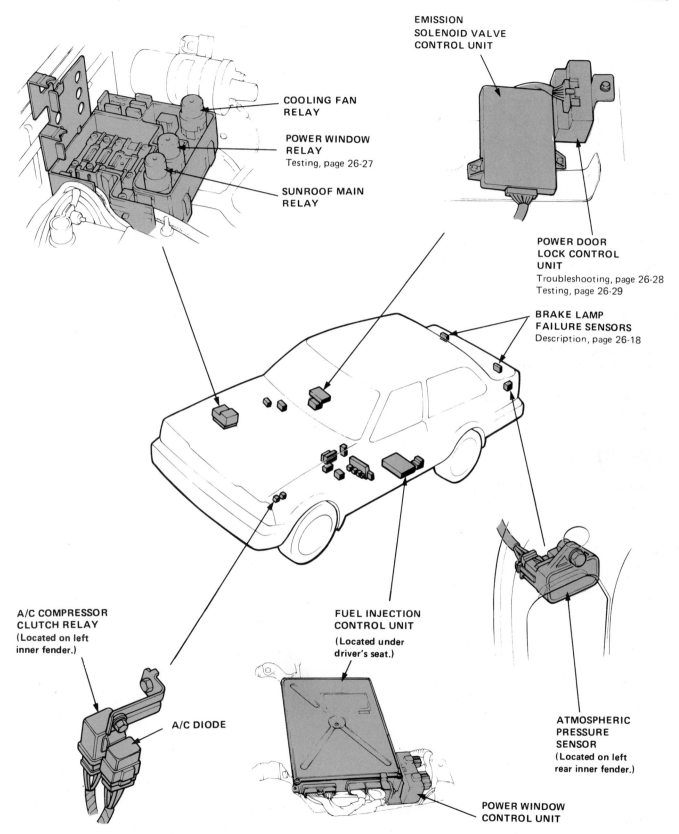

EMISSION
SOLENOID VALVE
CONTROL UNIT

COOLING FAN
RELAY

POWER WINDOW
RELAY
Testing, page 26-27

SUNROOF MAIN
RELAY

POWER DOOR
LOCK CONTROL
UNIT
Troubleshooting, page 26-28
Testing, page 26-29

BRAKE LAMP
FAILURE SENSORS
Description, page 26-18

A/C COMPRESSOR
CLUTCH RELAY
(Located on left
inner fender.)

A/C DIODE

FUEL INJECTION
CONTROL UNIT
(Located under
driver's seat.)

ATMOSPHERIC
PRESSURE
SENSOR
(Located on left
rear inner fender.)

POWER WINDOW
CONTROL UNIT

Fig. 8-8. Sometimes it can be difficult to find small electrical-electronic components. Most service manuals will have an illustration or chart giving component locations. This is one example. (Honda)

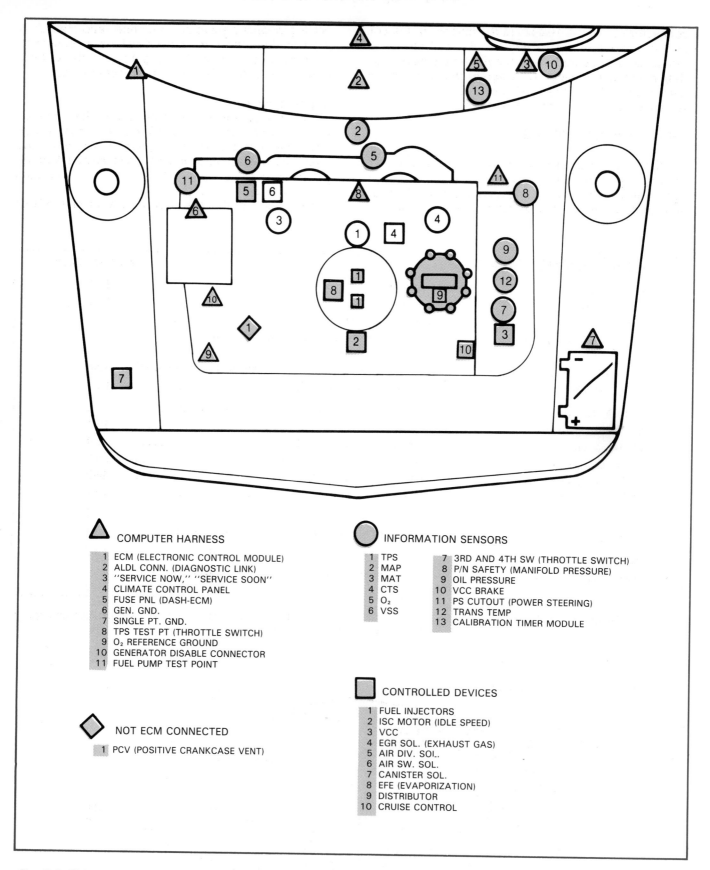

COMPUTER HARNESS

1 ECM (ELECTRONIC CONTROL MODULE)
2 ALDL CONN. (DIAGNOSTIC LINK)
3 "SERVICE NOW," "SERVICE SOON"
4 CLIMATE CONTROL PANEL
5 FUSE PNL (DASH-ECM)
6 GEN. GND.
7 SINGLE PT. GND.
8 TPS TEST PT (THROTTLE SWITCH)
9 O$_2$ REFERENCE GROUND
10 GENERATOR DISABLE CONNECTOR
11 FUEL PUMP TEST POINT

INFORMATION SENSORS

1 TPS
2 MAP
3 MAT
4 CTS
5 O$_2$
6 VSS
7 3RD AND 4TH SW (THROTTLE SWITCH)
8 P/N SAFETY (MANIFOLD PRESSURE)
9 OIL PRESSURE
10 VCC BRAKE
11 PS CUTOUT (POWER STEERING)
12 TRANS TEMP
13 CALIBRATION TIMER MODULE

NOT ECM CONNECTED

1 PCV (POSITIVE CRANKCASE VENT)

CONTROLLED DEVICES

1 FUEL INJECTORS
2 ISC MOTOR (IDLE SPEED)
3 VCC
4 EGR SOL. (EXHAUST GAS)
5 AIR DIV. SOL.
6 AIR SW. SOL.
7 CANISTER SOL.
8 EFE (EVAPORIZATION)
9 DISTRIBUTOR
10 CRUISE CONTROL

Fig. 8-9. This is a component location illustration for top view of an engine compartment. Study how it can be used to locate various sensors, actuators, etc. What is the general location of the oxygen sensor? (General Motors)

connector (C) with a 102 being the number of the connector on another wiring diagram. It has 7 cavities or terminals. It is located under the right-hand side of the dash near the fuse panel. The diagram showing this connector is at 10-1 in the service manual. What can you tell about C170 from the same chart?

USING WIRING DIAGRAMS

Wiring diagrams, also called *wiring schematics,* are drawings that show how the wires connect to each component in an electrical or electronic circuit. Symbols represent components and lines represent wires.

Wiring diagrams serve as "electrical road maps." A road map shows how streets and highways connect to each other and to cities. A wiring diagram shows how wires connect to each other and to components.

Body part names

Most wiring harnesses are named after their location on a car. They can also be referenced in the service manual by location. When using wiring diagrams, you should be aware of how wire locations may be denoted by body part names. Fig. 8-11 shows how body parts are typically called out.

The *left side* of a car is normally the driver's side or

COMPONENT LOCATION		Page-Figure
Blower Motor	Attached to RH cowl	45-1
Blower Resistors	On heater case	45-1
Blower Switch	Part of selector switch	84-1
Column Gearshift Switch	Base of steering column (automatic transmission)	
Console Gearshift Switch	Center console at shifter (manual transmission)	82-4
Fuse Block	Under lower RH side of I/P	10-1
C102A (7 cavities)	Under RH side of I/P near fuse block	10-1
C103 (6 cavities)	RH rear quarter extension wall	43-1
C104 (4 cavities)	Behind LH side of I/P	82-4
C110 (3 cavities)	Center I/P support brace	85-6
C170 (1 cavity)	Inside rear light harness	43-2
C175 (3 cavities)	At heater blower case	45-1
G108	Attached to RH tail panel	43-1
G111	RH front cowl, near heater blower case	45-1
S213	Rear lights harness, at end panel	43-2
S603	I/P harness between fuse block and steering column	15-1

Fig. 8-10. This example of a component location table gives written explanation of location and also service manual page or figure numbers for added data. (General Motors)

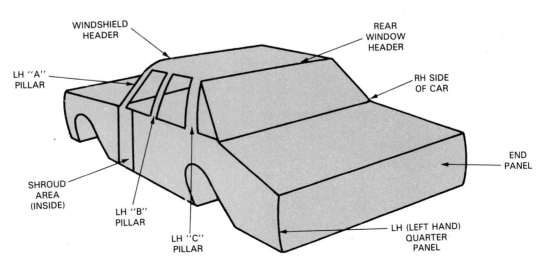

Fig. 8-11. Most wiring harnesses and components are called out by location in body structure of car. Remember that right and left of car are determined when sitting in a car, looking forward.

the side with the steering wheel. The left side may be abbreviated "LH" on a wiring diagram.

The *right side,* abbreviated "RH," is on the passenger side of the car. Right and left are determined as if you are sitting in the car looking forward.

Wire code identification system

Wire code identification system is a number-letter method for explaining the appearance, location, and gauge size of conductors on a wiring diagram. Wire code identification systems vary with the manufacturer. Refer to the service manual for specifics.

Fig. 8-12 gives two examples of wire code identification systems. One uses the gauge size number and the other the metric system of wire size. Both use color code abbreviations. One also uses a letter to denote the main circuit and section of the circuit. You would have to refer to other shop manual charts to find out what these abbreviations mean, Fig. 8-13.

Wiring Color Code Chart					
COLOR CODE	COLOR	STANDARD TRACER COLOR	COLOR CODE	COLOR	STANDARD TRACER CODE
BK	BLACK	WT	PK	PINK	BK OR WH
BR	BROWN	WT	RD	RED	WT
DB	DARK BLUE	WT	TN	TAN	WT
DG	DARK GREEN	WT	VT	VIOLET	WT
GY	GRAY	BK	WT	WHITE	BK
LB	LIGHT BLUE	BK	YL	YELLOW	BK
LG	LIGHT GREEN	BK	*	WITH TRACER	
OR	ORANGE	BK			

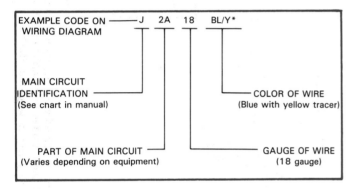

A—Example code using wire gauge size. First letter identifies main circuit which is explained by chart or diagram. Second alpha-numeric entry is specific section of main circuit. Third digit is gauge size of wire. Last entry is color code of wire insulation.

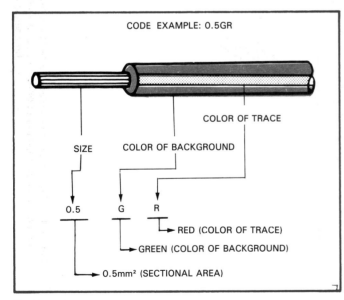

B—Example of metric wire identification system. First entry is size of wire conductor in square millimeters. Last two letters give color code for insulation.

Fig. 8-12. These are two common types of wire codes found in modern service manuals. (Chrysler and General Motors)

MAIN CIRCUIT IDENTIFICATION CODES

A1 Battery Circuit to Ammeter.
A2 Battery Circuit to Ammeter.
B Back Up Lamp Circuit.
C Air Conditioning and Heater Circuits.
D Emergency, Stop Lamp and Turn Signal Circuits.
E Instrument Panel Cluster, Switches and Illumination Circuits.
F Radio Speakers and Power Seat Circuits.
G Gauges and Warning Lamp Circuits.
H Horn Circuit.
J Ignition System Run Circuit.
J1 Ignition Switch Feed Circuit.
J3 Ignition Switch Start Circuit.
K Trailer Tow.

Fig. 8-13. Since codes vary, always refer to charts that explain abbreviations and codes. Note how these charts give color codes and circuit identification codes. Wiring diagram can have this type letter-number code. (General Motors)

Harness routing diagram

A *harness routing diagram* shows how major wiring is arranged and located in the car. One example is in Fig. 8-14. It shows how the main harnesses feed through the body of the vehicle. This diagram also uses a code system to identify the section of the harness.

Wiring splices

Wiring splices are where two or more wires are connected together. They are normally shown on a wiring diagram by a DOT where the wires connect. They can also be shown by just having the lines (wires) run together. Most wiring diagrams use the dot, however. Refer to Fig. 8-15.

Splice code charts can be used with the wiring diagram

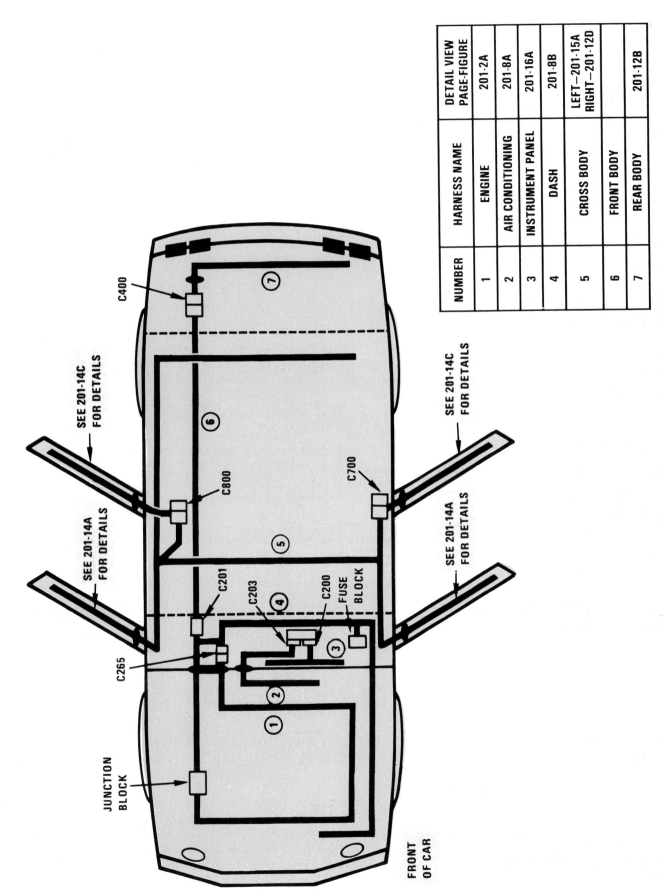

NUMBER	HARNESS NAME	DETAIL VIEW PAGE-FIGURE
1	ENGINE	201-2A
2	AIR CONDITIONING	201-8A
3	INSTRUMENT PANEL	201-16A
4	DASH	201-8B
5	CROSS BODY	LEFT – 201-15A RIGHT – 201-12D
6	FRONT BODY	
7	REAR BODY	201-12B

Fig. 8-14. Illustration gives main harness routing. This might be helpful when trying to find shorts or opens in harness wires. It shows location of main connectors for making electrical tests. Codes representing the harnesses and connectors will also be on some other detailed wiring diagrams. (Buick)

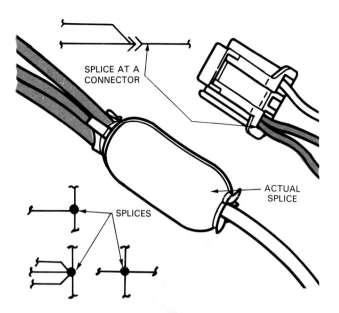

Fig. 8-15. Wire splices are usually denoted by dot over wires. However, note possible variation when wire is spliced at connector. (Ford)

to give added information about the circuit. Fig. 8-16 gives an example. A capital "S" denotes a splice with this type diagram.

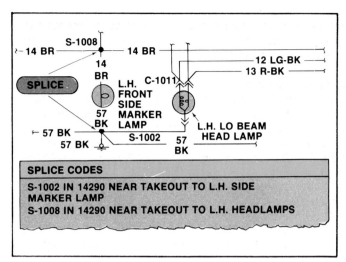

Fig. 8-16. Many wiring diagrams can have additional charts that give more information. Note how S-1008 is a splice and chart gives its exact location. (Ford)

Grounds

Grounds show where a circuit connects to the frame or chassis of the car. A *remote ground* has an extra wire running from the circuit to ground. A *chassis ground* uses the metal part of a component attached to ground.

In Fig. 8-17, note how the symbols for each type

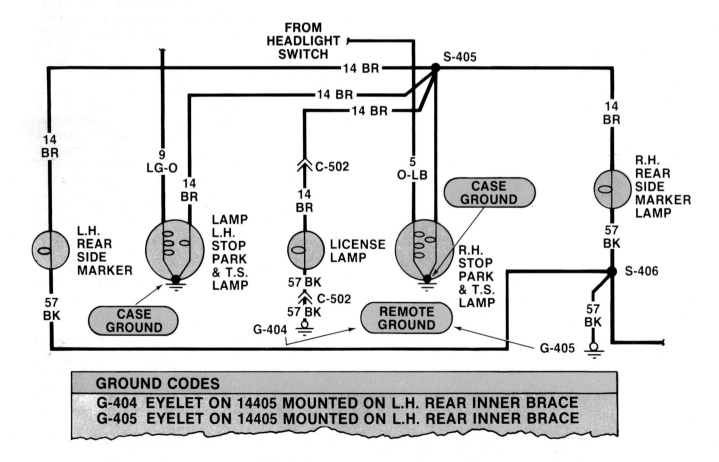

Fig. 8-17. Grounds are usually abbreviated as capital G. Note difference between remote ground and chassis or component ground. (Ford)

ground vary. Also note the chart that supplements the wiring diagram. A capital "G" can denote a ground on some schematics.

Alternate circuits

An *alternate circuit* is a possible circuit variation given on a wiring diagram. For example, a wiring diagram may show the electrical connections for a car with an automatic transmission and one with a manual transmission. This allows one diagram to serve as two diagrams, saving space in the service manual. See Fig. 8-18A.

Optional wiring

Optional wiring is wiring provided in a circuit that may not be in use, Fig. 8-18B. For example, wiring may be provided for trailer lights, even though the trailer package harness may not be installed on the vehicle.

Junction block

A *junction block* is a terminal that allows several wires to connect together. Terminals on the wires fasten to one or more terminals on the junction block. The junc-

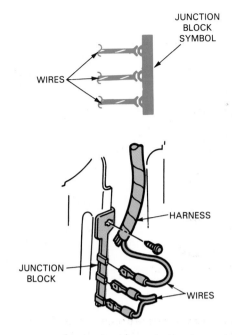

Fig. 8-19. Note junction block symbol and actual appearance.

tion block serves as a splice but the wires can easily be removed from the junction. Look at Fig. 8-19.

Connector diagrams

Connector diagrams can show the location of connectors and they can identify each terminal in a connector. They are very important when trying to diagnose problems. Connector diagrams show which connector terminals should be touched or tested when troubleshooting. A capital "C" can denote a connector.

Fig. 8-20 shows a diagram giving information on the location and destination of specific connectors. The illustration and the chart must be used together. For instance, C-401 is a connector shown in the illustration. The illustration shows the location of the connector. Then, the chart tells you the number of pins or terminals in the connector, and its destination (to the clock).

Fig. 8-21 is a detailed diagram of connectors for an ignition system module. It gives the location of each terminal and the color code of each wire running into the connectors. This would be needed when taking voltage or resistance measurements to check the wiring and other components.

An example of the abbreviations and their meanings for a connector are given in Fig. 8-22.

Connector electrical values

Connector electrical values are specifications given for voltage, current, and resistance for a known good circuit. Usually, an end view of the connector will be illustrated. The electrical value that should be present at each terminal in the connector will also be given. You can then use a multimeter to check the circuit for problems quickly and efficiently.

An example of a service manual page giving connector electrical values is in Fig. 8-23. Notice how it gives actual voltages and resistances for a good circuit. If any values are high or low, there is a circuit problem.

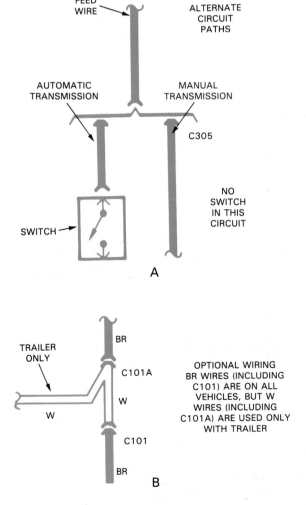

Fig. 8-18. A—Wiring diagrams commonly have alternate circuits. This allows one diagram to show all wire routing, even if car has one of two different options. B—Optional wiring may or may not be used. This shows example of trailer towing optional wiring.

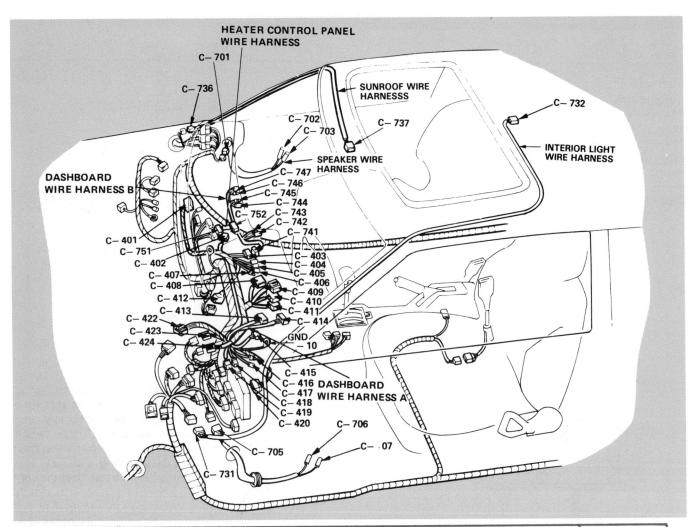

CONNECTOR, TERMINAL NUMBER	NUMBER OF PINS	LOCATION	DESTINATION	REMARKS
C401	6	Center dashboard	To clock	
C402	9	Behind right gauge panel	To hazard/rear defroster switch	
C403	3	Center dashboard	To dashboard wire harness B(C741)	
C404		Center dashboard	To cigarette lighter	
C405		Center dashboard	To cigarette lighter light	
C406		Center dashboard	To cigarette lighter light	
C407		Center dashboard	To cigarette lighter	
C408	5	Behind gauges	To speed sensor	
C409	14	Behind gauges	To safety indicator	
C410	10	Behind gauges	To A/T indicator	
C411	12	Behind gauges	To combination meter	
C412	4	Center dashboard	To heater wire harness (C216)	
C413	9	Behind right gauge panel	To headlight/sun roof switch	
C414	10	Behind warning light	To warning light	
C415	3	Left warning lights	To dash light brightness controller	
C416		Behind fuse box	To fuse box light	
C417		Behind fuse box	To fuse box light	
C418	2	Left kick panel	To key-on-warning chime	
C419	9	Under left dashboard	To headlight retract control unit	
C420	18	Behind fuse box	To fuse box	
C422	14	Behind fuse box	To side wire harness (C305)	
C423	18	Behind fuse box	To heater wire harness (C218)	
C424	10	Behind fuse box	To heater wire harness (C219)	(A/T only)
GND10		Under left dashboard	To body ground	

Fig. 8-20. With today's cars, finding the right connector can be challenging. Note how this illustration and chart give connector and ground locations, destinations, and identifying numbers. (Honda)

CONNECTOR DETAILS

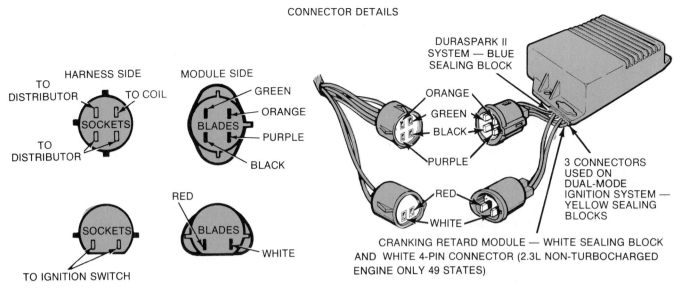

Fig. 8-21. Since you should avoid puncturing insulation when testing, connectors provide best place for taking electrical measurements. Manual will usually give end views of connectors. (Ford)

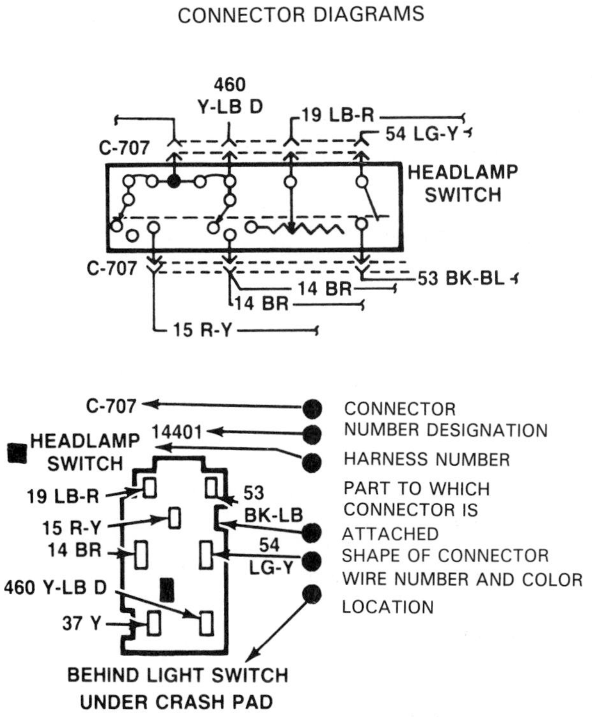

CONNECTOR DIAGRAMS

Fig. 8-22. Note abbreviations and codes used with this type connector diagram.

USING WIRING DIAGRAMS

Using wiring diagrams can be simple if you take the time to do the following:

1. Learn the abbreviations used in the specific service manual. Abbreviations can vary from one manual to another.
2. Study the color codes and how they are called out on the wiring diagram. This can also vary with the manufacturer.

3. Study the types of symbols used on the wiring diagram. Symbols can also vary.
4. Learn to use any charts that accompany the wiring diagrams. The charts can give essential information about circuit connections, grounds, connectors, etc.
5. Only study the affected section of the circuit diagram. Many diagrams have more information than you will need when troubleshooting a circuit.
6. Slowly trace the section of the circuit that you are working on. Use your finger or a pencil to slowly follow the wiring from one end to the other. This will let you note all connections and components that could be upsetting circuit operation.
7. Do not confuse overlapping wires with spliced wires. As mentioned, a splice usually has a dot on the wires. If the wires just cross over each other and do not make an electrical connection, a dot is NOT used.
8. As you read a wiring diagram, visualize the car you are working on. Make a mental image of the wire locations, where connectors are located, and the identity of components. This will help you when you begin working on the car.

Fig. 8-24 and 8-25 explain information given on a sample wiring diagram. Read through the explanations carefully and note how the diagram gives a large amount of data about the circuit.

Power distribution diagram

A *power distribution diagram* shows how battery current feeds to the main components or sections of the car's electrical system. It might be used if major systems are "dead." One is shown in Fig. 8-26.

Using this diagram, note how the battery cable is connected to the starter solenoid. Fuse links protect the circuitry before the fuse panel. Large wires feed off the solenoid terminal to the light switch, fuse panel or fuse block, generator (alternator), and elsewhere in the car.

If fuse link B were to blow, what circuits would and would not receive power? Power would not be fed to the light switch and fuse block. However, power would

INSTRUMENT PANEL (STANDARD CLUSTER)

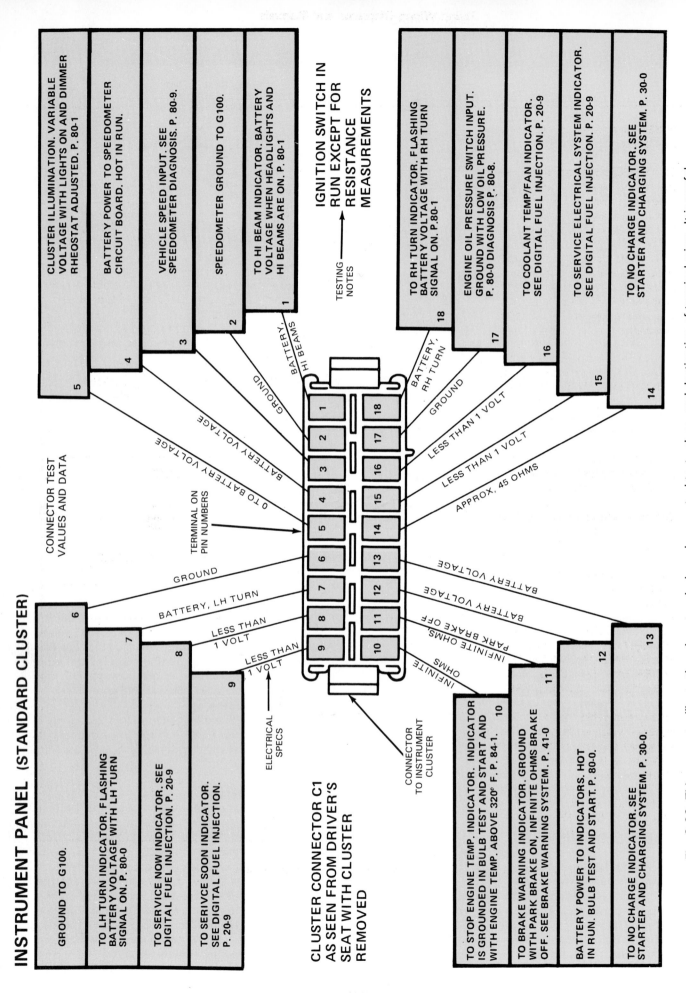

CONNECTOR TEST VALUES AND DATA

5 — CLUSTER ILLUMINATION. VARIABLE VOLTAGE WITH LIGHTS ON AND DIMMER RHEOSTAT ADJUSTED. P. 80-1

4 — BATTERY POWER TO SPEEDOMETER CIRCUIT BOARD. HOT IN RUN.

3 — VEHICLE SPEED INPUT. SEE SPEEDOMETER DIAGNOSIS. P. 80-9.

2 — SPEEDOMETER GROUND TO G100.

1 — TO HI BEAM INDICATOR. BATTERY VOLTAGE WHEN HEADLIGHTS AND HI BEAMS ARE ON. P. 80-1

IGNITION SWITCH IN RUN EXCEPT FOR RESISTANCE MEASUREMENTS

TESTING NOTES

18 — TO RH TURN INDICATOR. FLASHING BATTERY VOLTAGE WITH RH TURN SIGNAL ON. P.80-1

17 — ENGINE OIL PRESSURE SWITCH INPUT. GROUND WITH LOW OIL PRESSURE. P. 80-0 DIAGNOSIS P. 80-8.

16 — TO COOLANT TEMP/FAN INDICATOR. SEE DIGITAL FUEL INJECTION. P. 20-9

15 — TO SERVICE ELECTRICAL SYSTEM INDICATOR. SEE DIGITAL FUEL INJECTION. P. 20-9

14 — TO NO CHARGE INDICATOR. SEE STARTER AND CHARGING SYSTEM. P. 30-0

BATTERY, HI BEAMS

GROUND

0 TO BATTERY VOLTAGE

BATTERY VOLTAGE

TERMINAL ON PIN NUMBERS

BATTERY, RH TURN

GROUND

LESS THAN 1 VOLT

LESS THAN 1 VOLT

APPROX. 45 OHMS

BATTERY VOLTAGE

BATTERY VOLTAGE

INFINITE OHMS, PARK BRAKE OFF

INFINITE OHMS

GROUND

BATTERY, LH TURN

LESS THAN 1 VOLT

LESS THAN 1 VOLT

ELECTRICAL SPECS

CLUSTER CONNECTOR C1 AS SEEN FROM DRIVER'S SEAT WITH CLUSTER REMOVED

CONNECTOR TO INSTRUMENT CLUSTER

6 — GROUND TO G100.

7 — TO LH TURN INDICATOR. FLASHING BATTERY VOLTAGE WITH LH TURN SIGNAL ON. P. 80-0

8 — TO SERVICE NOW INDICATOR. SEE DIGITAL FUEL INJECTION. P. 20-9

9 — TO SERIVCE SOON INDICATOR. SEE DIGITAL FUEL INJECTION. P. 20-9

10 — TO STOP ENGINE TEMP. INDICATOR. INDICATOR IS GROUNDED IN BULB TEST AND START AND WITH ENGINE TEMP. ABOVE 320° F. P. 84-1.

11 — TO BRAKE WARNING INDICATOR. GROUND WITH PARK BRAKE ON, INFINITE OHMS BRAKE OFF. SEE BRAKE WARNING SYSTEM. P. 41-0

12 — BATTERY POWER TO INDICATORS. HOT IN RUN. BULB TEST AND START. P. 80-0.

13 — TO NO CHARGE INDICATOR. SEE STARTER AND CHARGING SYSTEM. P. 30-0.

Fig. 8-23. This connector illustration gives terminal numbers, actual test values, and destination of terminal wires. It is useful when trying to find faults in that section of wiring. (Cadillac)

FUSES Gives fuse amperage and fuse cavity.

Circuit identification code, circuit code, wire size, and color code. "A" shows it's a power feed, and it has 14-gauge black wire. You can follow the black wire to . . .

. . . a single connector. You see what the connector looks like, and notice that it has fusible link wire on the other side of the connector. The connector location is also indicated.

The fusible link wire, is a finer gauge with a lower melting point than the wires it's connected to. Here it's 20-gauge orange between the 14-gauge black and 14-gauge pink wires.

A splice symbol indicates the junction of the fusible link with the standard wire in the circuit.

The bulkhead connector symbol tells you the pink wire goes to cavity #31.

Circuit direction You are directed to page 47 for the rest of the A-3 circuit.

NOTE: THE CONNECTOR CAVITY MAY BE IDENTIFIED ON SOME DIAGRAMS WITH THE OLDER SYSTEM USING "S.C." (FOR SERVICE CONNECTOR).

This circuit code shows a tracer symbol (*) but not its color. Here you would look for a 14-gauge pink wire with a tracer which will be black or white.

Tracer color is indicated. Here tracer is/RD 12BK/RD*.

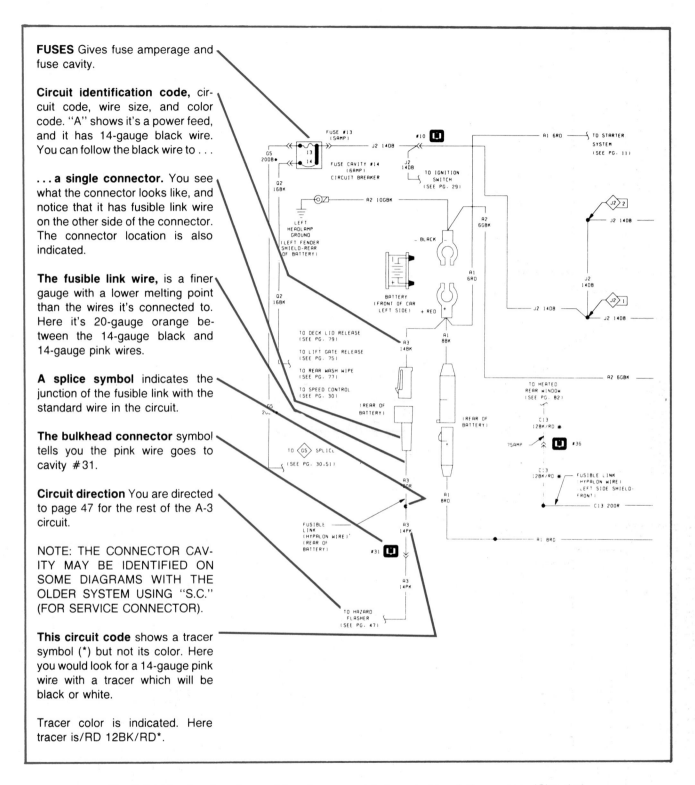

Fig. 8-24. Study what these wiring diagram symbols and abbreviations mean. (Chrysler)

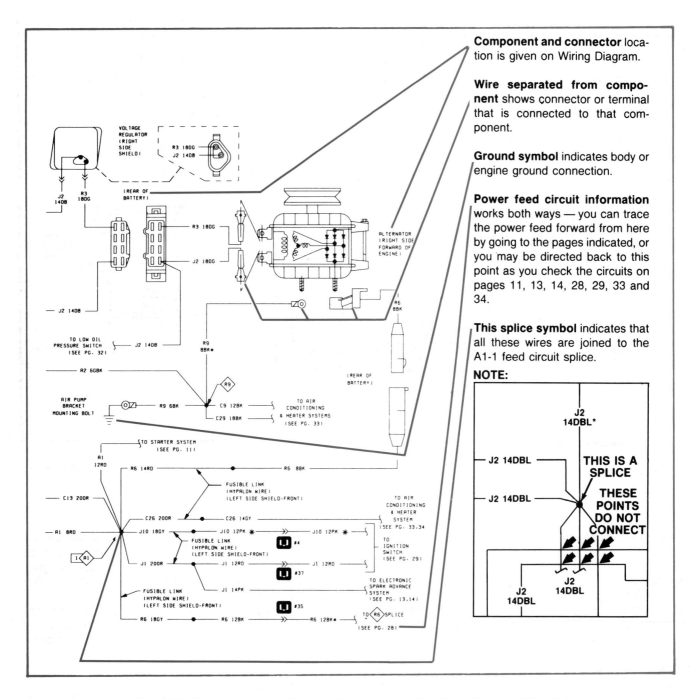

Fig. 8-25. Note examples of information given on this wiring diagram. (Chrysler)

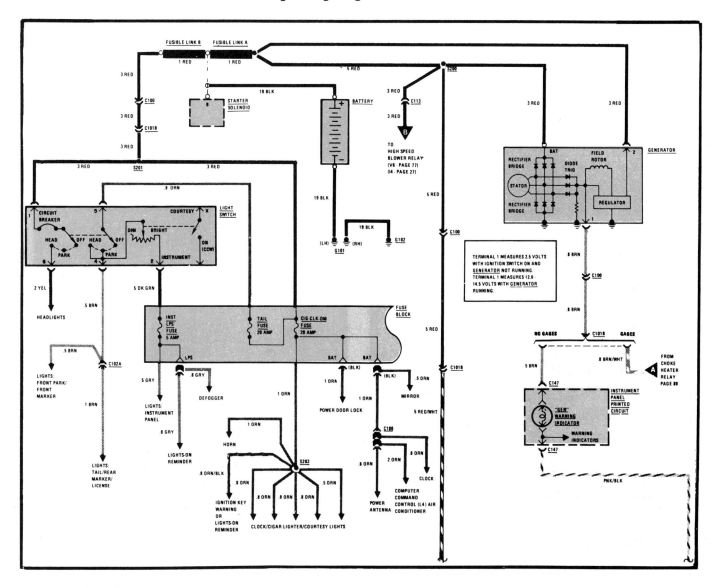

Fig. 8-26. A power distribution diagram is helpful when working on main wires that feed to light switch, fuse block, alternator, etc. Can you find the generator warning light? (General Motors)

still go to the alternator and to wire ''5 red'' which feeds somewhere else in the vehicle.

Diagram grid

A *wiring diagram grid* is used for quickly finding or locating components or connections on a wiring diagram. It is a number-letter system marked off around the outside of a wiring diagram. One is shown in Fig. 8-27.

To use the grid, the service manual might refer to 3C as the location of the ignition distributor. You would then align the intersection of 3 on one grid line with the C on the other grid line. This will produce a small area on the large wiring diagram and help you find the blower connector.

What components are located in the area 2C in the wiring diagram of Fig. 8-27?

Main wiring diagram

A *main wiring diagram* is a large diagram containing symbols for all major wiring and electrical-electronic

components on a car. Depending upon the manufacturer, the main diagram can vary. Different symbols can be used. The diagram may or may not have a location grid. The method of denoting color code and wire size can also vary. Always refer to the service manual.

Fig. 8-28 gives an example of a wiring diagram variation used by one auto maker. Only part of the complete diagram is shown. Note how the components are positioned horizontally, from left to right.

System wiring diagram

A *system wiring diagram* only contains the components and wires for a particular circuit. It contains a section of the main wiring diagram. A service manual might have an ignition system wiring diagram, fuel injection system wiring diagram, or computer control system wiring diagram, Fig. 8-29.

A system wiring diagram is useful when you have narrowed down a possible problem to a specific circuit. You can then analyze the circuit to locate the problem.

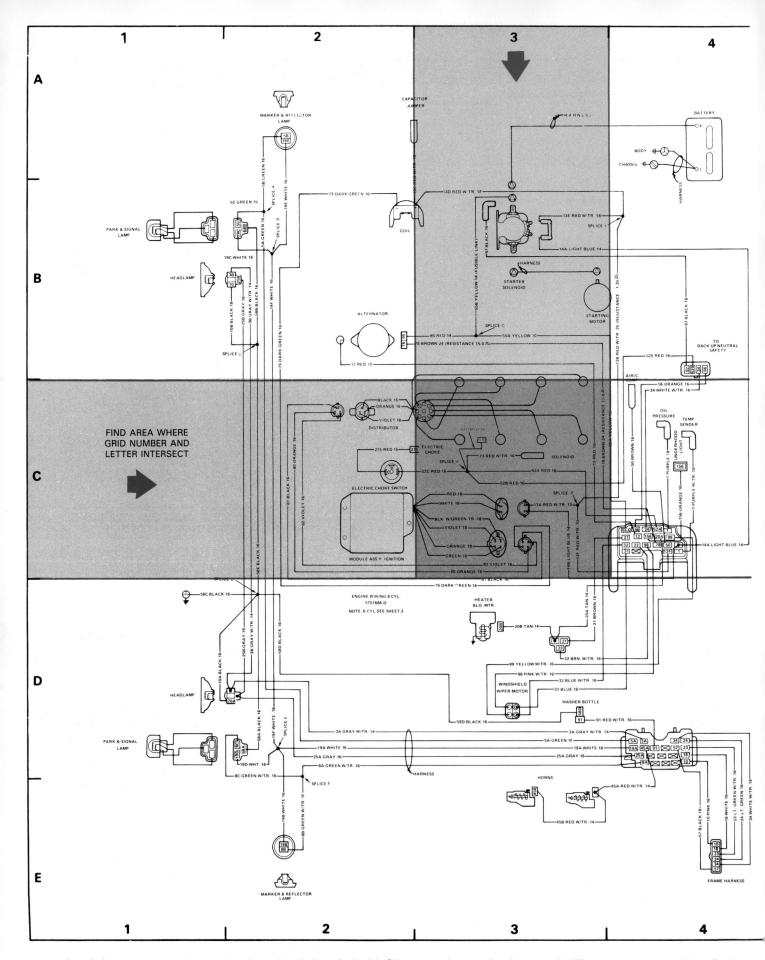

Fig. 8-27. This wiring diagram has very handy location grid. Chart can give number-letter code. Then you can use grid to find location on large diagram with component or connection. Note how you would look in grid area 3C. (Ford)

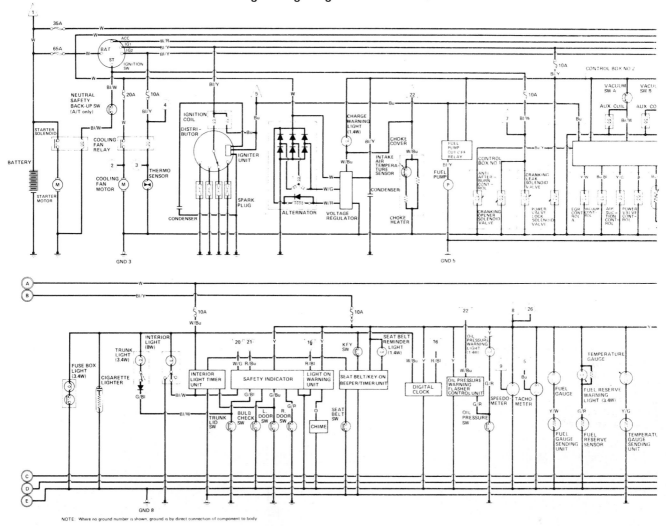

Fig. 8-28. This wiring diagram is organized from left to right. Note how battery is on left and wires feed out to other components. (Honda)

Block diagram

The *block diagram* uses simple boxes to show components and lines to show wires, hoses, or metal lines. It is simply used to illustrate how a system or circuit operates and how the components interact. One is given in Fig. 8-30.

By studying a block diagram, you can make a mental image of how the circuit functions. Then, you can think about the symptoms to help arrive at a possible solution of any circuit trouble.

VACUUM DIAGRAM

A *vacuum diagram* is like an electrical diagram, but it shows how vacuum hoses are connected to vacuum devices. As an electronic technician, you will need to know how to work with vacuum diagrams. Many vehicle components operate off of vacuum as' well as electrical energy.

Fig. 8-31 gives an example of a vacuum diagram. Note how it could be used to check the routing of the small vacuum hoses to each component. If even one vacuum hose is disconnected or connected improperly, engine and emission control system operation can be upset.

Some typical vacuum component symbols are shown in Fig. 8-32. Study them carefully.

TECHNICAL SERVICE BULLETINS

Technical service bulletins, or TSBs, help the technician stay up-to-date with recent technical changes, recalls, and other service-related information. Usually only a few pages long, these publications are mailed to the service manager, who passes them along to the technicians. Technical service bulletins are published by auto manufacturers and equipment suppliers.

COMPUTERIZED SERVICE DATA

Computerized service data is information stored or retrieved electronically using a personal computer. Information may be stored on a floppy disk, hard drive, CD-ROM, or computer network. A computer can find and retrieve this information quicker than a technician using a service manual. Modern repair shops are using more and more computerized service data.

A floppy disk is an inexpensive way to hold computer information. However, the storage capacity is limited. A

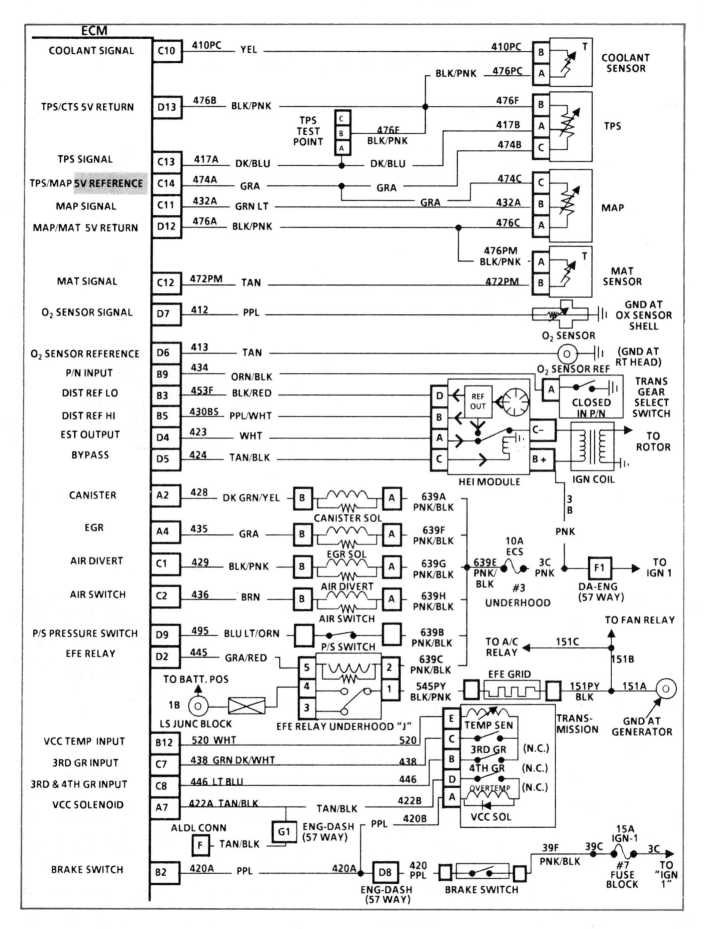

Fig. 8-29. This diagram only shows wiring for specific system relating to computer or electronic control module. Note codes.

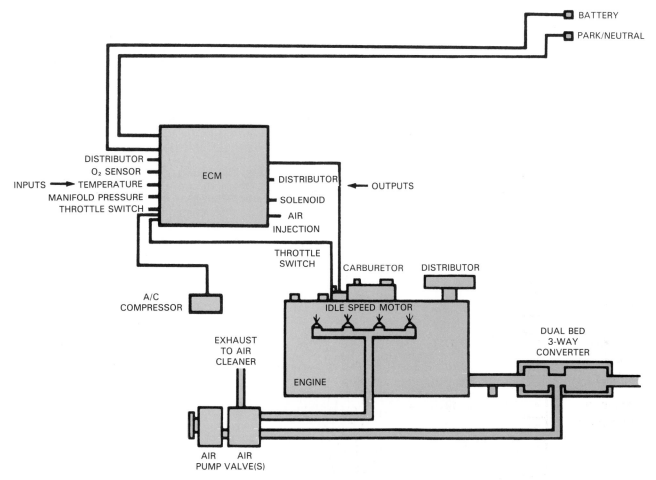

Fig. 8-30. This block diagram is for computer controlled emission control system. It uses basic block shapes to show how system operates.

CD-ROM, or *compact disc,* is a computer storage device with tremendous capacity for holding large amounts of data. One CD can hold the information from an entire set of service manuals.

Computer systems can be used to store a variety of service-related information, such as:

1. Repair procedures.
2. Repair illustrations.
3. Part prices.
4. Labor times.
5. Safety rules.
6. Troubleshooting charts.
7. Diagnostic trouble code charts.

ON-LINE SERVICES

Various *on-line services* allow the technician to access technical information using the Internet. The *Internet* is a electronic network that enables a computer to communicate with other computers via a telephone line. Several automotive-related sites have been established on the Internet to provide information on common vehicle troubles, manufacturers' recalls, new products, technician training, etc. These sites allow service facilities to find service information that is not available in the manuals or electronic media they have on hand. See Fig. 8-33.

TECHNICAL ASSISTANCE HOTLINES

A number of automobile and equipment manufacturers have established *technical assistance hotlines,* which allow technicians to speak directly to specially trained technical support personnel. These individuals have an extensive knowledge of the manufacturers' products and often have access to advanced troubleshooting and service information. They can help technicians solve difficult problems.

SUMMARY

To aid the technician, today's service manuals contain a large amount of information on finding and correcting electrical problems. You must know how to utilize this valuable information.

Abbreviations are commonly used throughout service manuals to save space. These abbreviations can vary with the auto manufacturer. You should become familiar with the terminology used in a specific service manual before trying to use the manual.

When reading a service manual, always refer to the illustrations as soon as they are mentioned. This will help you get full meaning from the manual. Also refer to references to obtain added information.

AIR	= AIR INJECTION REACTION SYSTEM		**EFE-DTVS**	= EFE-DISTRIBUTOR THERMAL VACUUM SWITCH
BP-EGR	= BACK PRESSURE EXHAUST GAS RECIRCULATION		**EFE-CV**	= EFE — CHECK VALVE
CC	= CATALYTIC CONVERTER		**EFE-TVS**	= EFE — THERMAL VACUUM SWITCH
CEAB-TVS	= COLD ENGINE AIR BLEED — TVS		**EGR/EFE-TVS**	= EXHAUST GAS RECIRC/EFE-TVS
CESS	= COLD ENGINE SENSOR SWITCH		**EGR/CP-TVS**	= EGR CANISTER PURGE TVS
CP-TVS	= CANISTER PURGE THERMAL VACUUM SWITCH		**EGR-DTVS**	= EGR DISTR. THERMAL VAC. SWITCH
CTVS	= CHOKE THERMAL VACUUM SWITCH		**EGR-TCV**	= EGR THERMAL CONTROL VALVE
CVB-VDV	= CHOKE VACUUM BREAK — VACUUM DELAY VALVE		**EGR-TVS**	= EGR THERMAL VACUUM SWITCH
DTVS	= DISTRIBUTOR THERMAL VACUUM SWITCH		**OS**	= OXYGEN SENSOR
DVDV	= DISTRIBUTOR VACUUM DELAY VALVE		**PCV**	= POSITIVE CRANKCASE VENTILATION
DVRV	= DISTRIBUTOR VACUUM REGULATING VALVE		**SAVM**	= SPARK ADVANCE VAC. MODULATOR
			SDV	= SPARK DELAY VALVE
			SRDV	= SPARK RETARD DELAY VALVE
ECM	= ELECTRONIC CONTROL MODULE		**TAC**	= THERMOSTATIC AIR CLEANER
EEC	= EVAPORATIVE EMISSION CONTROL		**VIS**	= VACUUM INPUT SWITCH
EFE	= EARLY FUEL EVAPORATION VALVE AND ACTUATOR		**VM**	= VACUUM MODULATOR
			VM-CV	= VACUUM MODULATOR CHECK VALVE

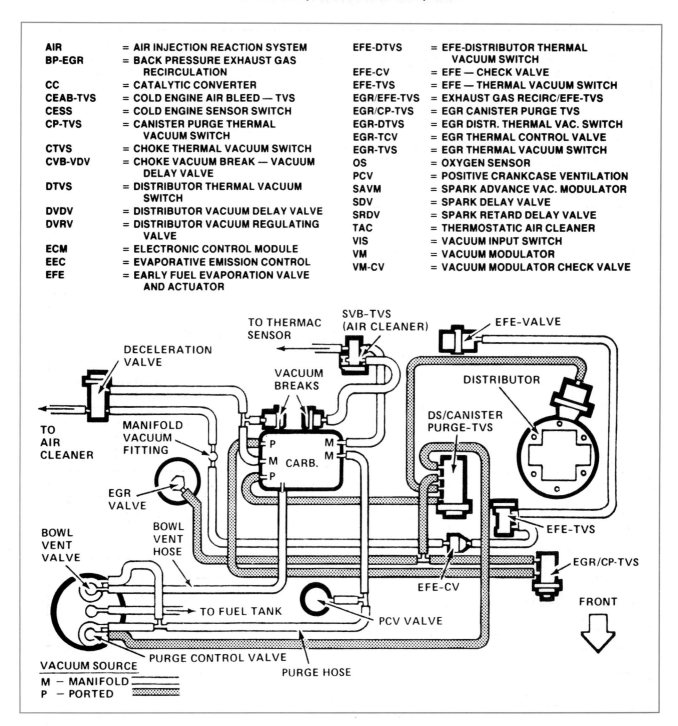

Fig. 8-31. Vacuum diagram is like wiring diagram. However, lines represent hoses and symbols represent vacuum devices. Also note abbreviations used by this auto maker. (General Motors)

Diagnosis charts give logical steps for finding problems. These charts can vary but all give help when a problem is difficult to locate.

Service manual specifications are exact measurements for a properly operating circuit or electrical component. For example, specs might say a circuit wire should have 2 ohms, if your test finds more or less ohms at that wire, you have found a wiring or component problem.

Wiring diagrams are like "road maps" that show how wires connect to the electrical-electronic components. You can study the wiring diagram to see what wires,

connections, and components might be causing electrical problems.

A wire code identification system is used to denote wire size, color code, and location of wires on a wiring diagram. One system uses the gauge system and another the metric wire size system. Both are in use today.

Wire splices are usually shown with a dot where the two wires connect. A remote ground has an extra wire running to ground. A chassis ground uses the metal part of the component to serve as the ground.

An alternate circuit is a possible circuit variation. One

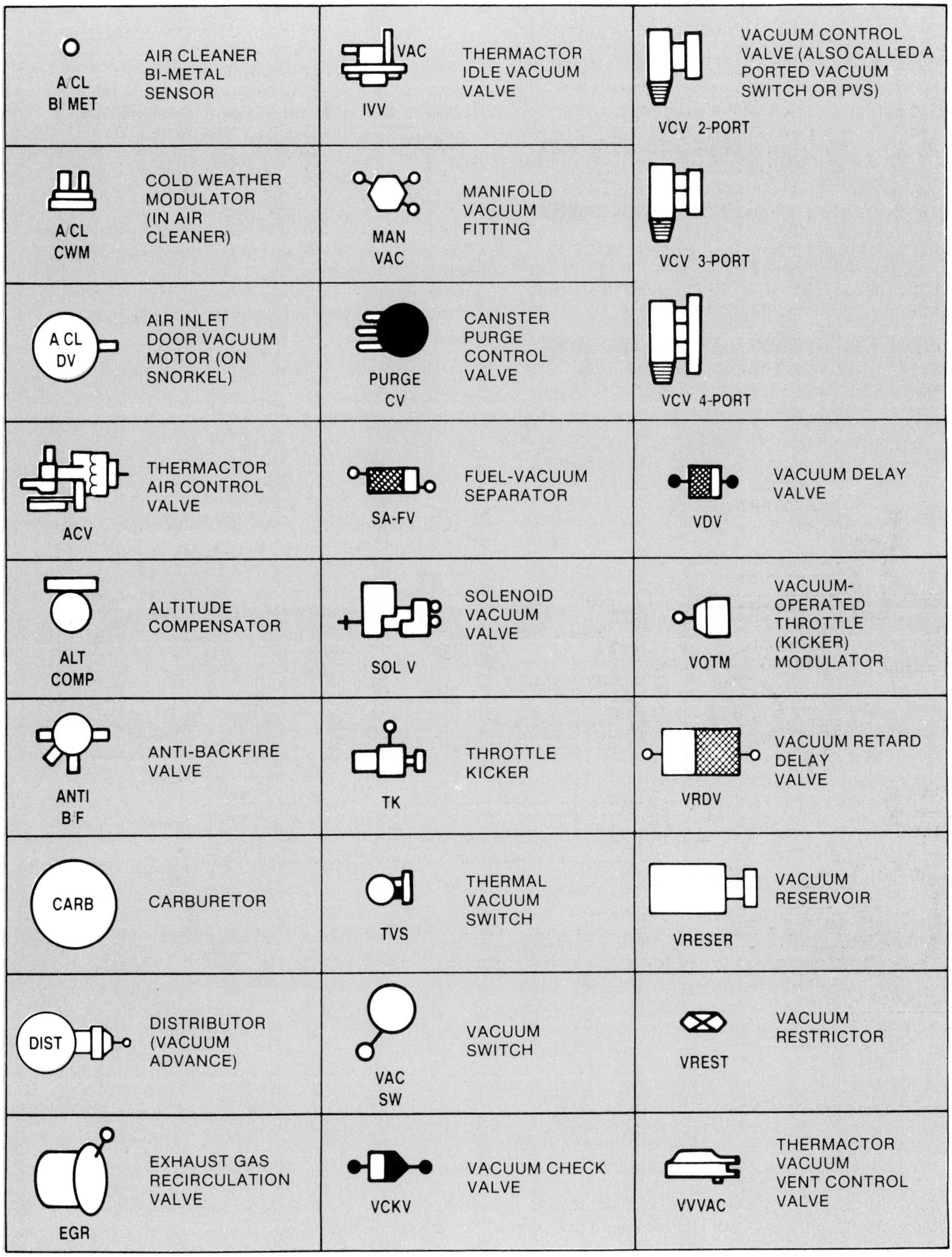

A/CL BI MET	AIR CLEANER BI-METAL SENSOR	THERMACTOR IDLE VACUUM VALVE (IVV)	VACUUM CONTROL VALVE (ALSO CALLED A PORTED VACUUM SWITCH OR PVS) (VCV 2-PORT)
A/CL CWM	COLD WEATHER MODULATOR (IN AIR CLEANER)	MANIFOLD VACUUM FITTING (MAN VAC)	(VCV 3-PORT)
A CL DV	AIR INLET DOOR VACUUM MOTOR (ON SNORKEL)	CANISTER PURGE CONTROL VALVE (PURGE CV)	(VCV 4-PORT)
ACV	THERMACTOR AIR CONTROL VALVE	FUEL-VACUUM SEPARATOR (SA-FV)	VACUUM DELAY VALVE (VDV)
ALT COMP	ALTITUDE COMPENSATOR	SOLENOID VACUUM VALVE (SOL V)	VACUUM-OPERATED THROTTLE (KICKER) MODULATOR (VOTM)
ANTI B/F	ANTI-BACKFIRE VALVE	THROTTLE KICKER (TK)	VACUUM RETARD DELAY VALVE (VRDV)
CARB	CARBURETOR	THERMAL VACUUM SWITCH (TVS)	VACUUM RESERVOIR (VRESER)
DIST	DISTRIBUTOR (VACUUM ADVANCE)	VACUUM SWITCH (VAC SW)	VACUUM RESTRICTOR (VREST)
EGR	EXHAUST GAS RECIRCULATION VALVE	VACUUM CHECK VALVE (VCKV)	THERMACTOR VACUUM VENT CONTROL VALVE (VVVAC)

Fig. 8-32. Here are some examples of vacuum device symbols. Study them. (Ford)

might be provided for a car with an automatic transmission and a different one for a manual transmission. Both can be given on the same wiring diagram. An optional circuit is one shown but may not be in use.

Connector diagrams can show connector locations and detail the terminals inside the connector. They are very useful when troubleshooting problems. Some connector diagrams give the voltage or resistance values that

131

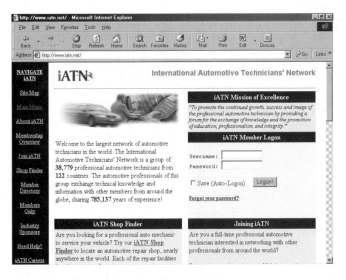

Fig. 8-33. Technical information is available on the Internet. Several Internet sites allow technicians to ask questions and share information about difficult problems. Many sites also provide listings of technical service bulletins.

should be present at each pin or terminal. You can then compare actual test values with the values that should be at each pin.

When using wiring diagrams, there are several rules to follow. Learn the specific abbreviations, color codes, and symbols used by the manufacturer. Learn to use any charts that supplement the diagrams. Only study the section of the circuit that might be causing the problem. Slowly trace each path of the affected circuit and note which wires, connections, and components might be at fault. As you read the diagram, mentally visualize the components and how they are actually wired on the car.

A power distribution diagram shows how battery current is fed to major components.

A diagram grid can be used for quickly finding the location of components or connections on a wiring diagram. A chart or explanation may show that a component is located at 3D, for example. You can then align the intersection of grid areas 3 and D to produce an imaginary box for finding the component.

A main wiring diagram shows all electrical components and wires. A system diagram only shows part of the main diagram. A block diagram uses squares to represent components and it is for visualizing system operation.

A vacuum diagram is similar to an electrical diagram. They both use symbols and lines to show how components connect.

Technical service bulletins help the technician stay up-to-date with recent technical changes, recalls, and other service-related information.

Computerized service data is information stored or retrieved electronically using a personal computer.

On-line services allow the technician to access technical information using the Internet. The Internet is a electronic network that enables a computer to communicate with other computers via a telephone line.

Technical assistance hotlines allow technicians to speak to specially trained support personnel.

KNOW THESE TERMS

Abbreviations, References, Diagnosis charts, Electrical specifications, Wiring diagrams, Wire code identification system, Harness routing diagram, Wire splice, Remote ground, Chassis ground, Alternate circuit, Optional circuit, Junction block, Connector diagram, Power distribution diagram, Diagram grid, Main wiring diagram, System wiring diagram, Block diagram, Vacuum diagram, Technical service bulletins, Computerized service data, CD-ROM, On-line services, Internet, Technical assistance hotlines.

REVIEW QUESTIONS—CHAPTER 8

1. What are service manual references?
2. _____ _____ give logical steps for finding and fixing problems.
3. What are some examples of electrical related specifications?
4. In America, the left side of a car would be the driver's side. True or false?
5. In your own words, explain the two common wire code identification and size systems.
6. A dot is over where two lines on a diagram intersect. What does this mean?
7. Explain the two types of grounds.
8. This allows several wires to make a common connection.
   a. Connector.
   b. Junction block.
   c. Terminal.
   d. Ground.
9. How can you use a connector diagram that gives electrical values?
10. List eight rules for using wiring diagrams.
11. Which of the following would you use to find out why major electrical circuits fail to have voltage?
    a. Main wiring diagram.
    b. Block diagram.
    c. Power distribution diagram.
    d. Schematic.
12. A vacuum diagram is used in much the same way as you use a wiring diagram. True or false?
Use Fig. 8-34 to answer questions 13 through 15.
13. What components are located in the grid area 1B?
14. What color wires connect to the ignition system pickup coil?
15. What is the grid location for the choke control relay?

ASE CERTIFICATION–TYPE QUESTIONS

1. Technician A says automobile manufacturers often use abbreviations in their service manuals to save space. Technician B says that all automobile manufacturers use the same abbreviations. Who is right?
   (A) A only.   (C) Both and B.
   (B) B only.   (D) Neither A nor B.
2. The SAE-recommended abbreviation for crankshaft position is:
   (A) CSP.   (C) CP.
   (B) CKP.   (D) CKPN.

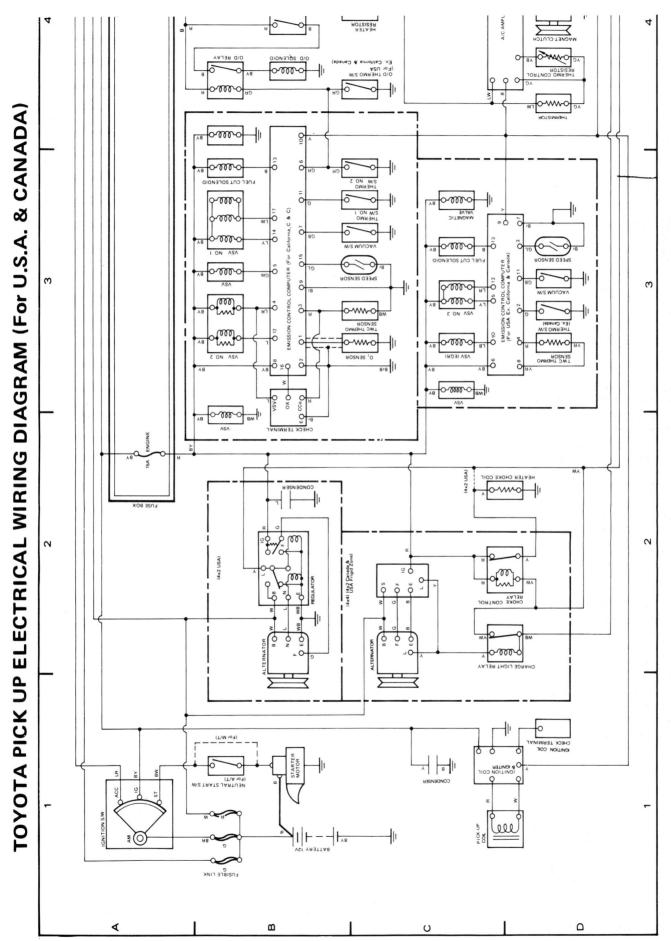

Fig. 8-34. Use this diagram to answer review questions 13 through 15.

3. Technician A says service manual illustrations may show the construction of various components. Technician B says that service manual references require you to look in different areas of the manual for additional information.
   (A) A only.
   (B) B only.
   (C) Both A and B.
   (D) Neither A nor B.

4. A car's computer system is malfunctioning. Technician A says a troubleshooting chart can be used to help diagnose the problem. Technician B says a tree-type diagnosis chart can be used to help locate the problem. Who is right?
   (A) A only.
   (B) B only.
   (C) Both A and B.
   (D) Neither A nor B.

5. Technician A says service manual electrical specifications are exact measurements for a properly operating electrical system. Technician B says a service manual electrical specification section may provide specs on starter motor brush dimensions. Who is right?
   (A) A only.
   (B) B only.
   (C) Both A and B.
   (D) Neither A nor B.

6. A car's fuel injection control unit is difficult to locate. Technician A checks a service manual's wiring diagram to help locate this component. Technician B checks a service manual's component location table to locate the car's fuel injection control unit. Who is right?
   (A) A only.
   (B) B only.
   (C) Both A and B.
   (D) Neither A nor B.

7. Technician A says the term "left side of the car" is sometimes abbreviated in an automotive wiring diagram as "LH." Technician B says the term "left side of the car" refers to the driver's side of the vehicle. Who is right?
   (A) A only.
   (B) B only.
   (C) Both A and B.
   (D) Neither A nor B.

8. Technician A says wire code identification systems provide information on the appearance, location, and size of wire in a given circuit. Technician B says service manual wire code identification systems vary from manufacturer to manufacturer. Who is right?
   (A) A only.
   (B) B only.
   (C) Both A and B.
   (D) Neither A nor B.

9. Technician A says wiring splices are normally designated on automotive service manual wiring diagrams by a "dot." Technician B says a capital G can be used on some schematics to designate ground. Who is right?
   (A) A only.
   (B) B only.
   (C) Both A and B.
   (D) Neither A nor B.

10. Technician A says technical assistance hotlines allow technicians to access the Internet. Technician B says the Internet is an electronic network that enables a computer to communicate with other computers via a telephone line. Who is right?
    (A) A only.
    (B) B only.
    (C) Both A and B.
    (D) Neither A nor B.

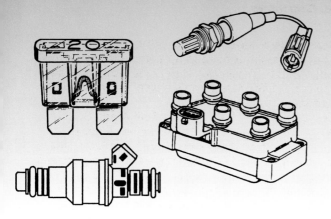

Chapter 9

Basic Electrical Tests, Circuit Problems

After studying this chapter, you will be able to:
- Use a systematic approach to find and correct electrical problems.
- Describe the symptoms and causes of an open circuit.
- Describe the symptoms and causes of a short circuit.
- Explain how shorts and opens have different effects on different circuit configurations.
- Use a jumper wire to check component operation.
- Use a test light or a multimeter to check for voltage in a circuit.
- Use a self-powered test light or an ohmmeter to check for continuity.
- Use a test light, compass, or inductive tester to find a short.
- Read the scales on an analog multimeter.
- Describe when to use a digital meter instead of an analog meter.
- Measure and use voltage drops to check resistances in a circuit.
- Test basic electrical and electronic components.

This is a very important chapter. It will introduce basic circuit problems, explain their causes, and summarize the tests needed to find and correct these malfunctions. Basic testing skills are essential to today's automotive technician. Knowing how to analyze circuit problems and use basic test instruments are "fundamental skills" that you must develop.

This chapter will lay the "groundwork" for many later chapters. It will give you the knowledge to completely understand later discussion of more specialized tests and repairs. Make sure you study and understand this chapter completely!

BASIC CIRCUIT PROBLEMS

Almost all electrical-electronic problems are actually basic circuit problems. A *basic circuit problem* is caused by something in the circuit that increases or decreases current, resistance, or voltage. For example, a broken wire could stop or decrease current flow or a charging system problem could increase output voltage and current flow.

Unfortunately, when a basic circuit problem occurs in a complex circuit, like a computer control system, it may NOT seem like a simple circuit problem. For example, a poor electrical connection in a feed wire to a sensor can cause a false signal returning to the computer. The computer, being "fooled" by the low sensor voltage, might then alter the operation of the fuel injection system, emission control systems, or ignition system. A technician could think that any of these systems or the computer itself is at fault. Several systems could appear to have a problem. In reality, it is simply a poor electrical connection in one wire that is causing all of the problem symptoms.

As you can see, it is important for an automotive technician to keep a "level head" when diagnosing electrical problems. If analyzed properly, problems can usually be found and corrected easily. If analyzed improperly, electrical problems can "drive you to the nut house!"

ELECTRICAL DIAGNOSIS AND REPAIR

Electrical diagnosis involves using a logical sequence of steps to find the source of a problem. The proper sequence for finding and fixing electrical problems can be remembered by the phrase: "Veronica never touches much voltage." This means:

VERONICA: *Verify* the symptoms and problem.
NEVER: *Narrow* down the problem sources.
TOUCHES: *Test* to find the cause.
MUCH: *Make* the repair.
VOLTAGE: *Verify* the repair.

To VERIFY THE SYMPTOMS AND PROBLEM, find out what the problem is causing. By checking out the symptoms, you will be sure that the customer has described the trouble accurately. Frequently, the car owner or service writer may not completely describe what is wrong with the car. Verifying the problem will give you added information when determining what to do next.

To NARROW DOWN THE PROBLEM SOURCES, use the symptoms to visually think of what is happening inside the circuit. Use your knowledge of the specific system and basic rules of electricity to analyze what might be wrong.

If not familiar with the circuit, use a diagram to trace

the circuit with the malfunction. For example, if the right headlight is not working but the left one is, you could narrow down the problem to the circuit feeding current to the right headlight. You have, through logical thought, narrowed down the source of the electrical problem to one section of the circuit.

If both headlights failed to function, then anything in the complete headlight circuit could be the cause. Further tests, probably at the power source to the circuit, would be needed to narrow down the cause.

To TEST THE CAUSE, determine what tests are needed to check the specific section of the electrical system. If one headlight does not work, you might check the bulb first. If the bulb is good, you might test for power to the bulb socket. Again, you must think of how the circuit operates to select the next most logical test.

When testing circuits, remember the following:

1. If only **one** component does NOT work, START YOUR TESTS at that component. Chances are the problem will be in the component or in the section of the circuit leading to the inoperative component.

2. If **more than one** component does not work, START YOUR TESTS at the power source for the circuit. A blown fuse, loose power feed wire, etc. could be preventing current flow into the whole circuit.

MAKE THE REPAIR after you have done tests to find the problem source. The repair might involve replacing a bad component, soldering a broken wire, or repairing a connector.

VERIFY THE REPAIR by making sure the circuit is operating normally. If needed, test drive the car to make sure road shock and vibration do not affect the repair. It would be very embarrassing if the problem was still present when returning the car to the customer.

What is the problem?

The most difficult aspect of making electrical repairs is finding the source of the problem. To find the source of electrical problems, you must ask yourself these kinds of questions:

1. What could be causing the specific symptoms? Mentally picture the parts in the circuit and how they function. Mentally trace through the circuit or use a wiring diagram to find out what wires, connections, and components are in the circuit leading to potential trouble sources.

2. How many components are affected? If several components are NOT functioning normally, you would know that something close to the power source should be at fault. If only one or two sections of the circuit are faulty, you would know to begin your tests at this section of the circuit.

3. Is the problem always present or is it *intermittent* (problem only occurs under some conditions)? If the trouble is intermittent, you would know that the conditions causing the problem would have to be simulated. For example, a loose electrical connection could open and close with vibration or movement. By wiggling wires in the circuit, you might simulate the driving conditions and make the problem occur.

4. Is the problem affected by heat or cold? If the problem only occurs on a hot day or with engine warmed to full operating temperature, you can arrive at a few

conclusions. Heat may be activating the problem. For example, electronic circuits (transistors in particular) are greatly affected by heat. In fact, too much heat can ruin an electronic component. This might tell you which component is at fault. It might also help you decide to use a heat gun to simulate the heat in an engine compartment.

5. Is the problem affected by moisture? If the trouble only occurs on a wet day, you again have more information to use when analyzing the source of a problem. Obviously, moisture cannot enter a sealed electronic circuit but it can enter and affect wire connections and components exposed to the environment. This type of thinking might help you.

No "shotgun approach"

NEVER use a "shotgun approach" when trying to find and correct electrical problems. The *shotgun approach* to problem solving involves using undesirable trial and error methods to fix problems.

By comparison, a shotgun hits a target by propelling numerous pellets or attempts at the target. Some hit the target but many others can miss. It would be better to aim a well thought out deduction (bullet) at correcting the fault or "hitting the target."

The untrained mechanic does NOT take the time to think about the symptoms and might not know how the circuit operates. Instead, he or she will fumble from component to component hoping that the next one will be causing the trouble. Common sense and logical thought are NOT used. This is a terrible, frustrating way to work on a car.

In the past, when electrical systems were very simple, a "shade tree" mechanic might have been able to get by using trial and error tests and part replacements. The older car did NOT have the large number of complex electronic circuits and components found on late model cars. Only a few tests or part replacements might find the fault.

Presently, a trial and error approach could take hours or DAYS to find a simple electrical problem. With today's on-board computers, vehicle sensors, actuators, and the interaction of major circuits, a systematic approach to problem diagnosis is essential!

Systematic approach to troubleshooting

A *systematic approach to troubleshooting* involves using the theory of system operation and logical deduction (thought) to find the source of the problem quickly. A well-planned procedure must be followed to find the source of a malfunction.

To troubleshoot properly, you must:

1. Narrow down the cause of the problem to one system if possible. This will let you concentrate on the components in that system or circuit.

2. Carefully analyze the *symptoms* (component NOT working, noise, blown fuse, or other condition). Try to determine what parts might be capable of causing the symptoms. Also, think of the parts that could NOT be causing the symptoms.

3. Determine where you should start your tests. If only one component is faulty, start testing at or near the component. If several components are affected, you

should start at the power source to that circuit.

4. Use proper testing methods to verify your assumption about what might be wrong in the circuit.

5. If your first assumption is NOT causing the trouble, proceed to the second most logical place to test.

6. If you have difficulty finding a problem, refer to the service manual troubleshooting charts and circuit diagrams. They will be for the specific vehicle and will give you ideas for finding the source of the problem.

7. Always think about the symptoms and problem while working. A new testing method, another potential problem source, etc. can "pop into your head." Visualize current flow through the circuit, each connection, and each component.

TYPES OF CIRCUIT PROBLEMS

There are only a few types of circuit problems: open circuit, high resistance problem, intermittent trouble, and short circuit. This section of the chapter will define these problems, list their causes, and explain how each can cause a different symptom depending upon the circuit configuration. It will also summarize tests to locate these troubles.

Open circuit

An *open circuit* has a complete break or disconnection. An open will stop current flow through that section of the circuit. See Fig. 9-1.

An open circuit can be caused by:
1. Broken wire conductor.
2. Blown fuse.
3. Burned switch contacts.
4. Burned or damaged connector terminals.
5. Failed electrical component.

When current is NOT reaching a component, find out which of these potential problems is present in the circuit, Fig. 9-2.

As shown in Fig. 9-3, the open can occur before the load, after the load, or in the load.

If the open occurs in series with a component, it will shut the component off. However, if the open occurs in a parallel leg, the opposite parallel leg will still function. Refer to Fig. 9-4.

High circuit resistance

High circuit resistance will reduce current flow, but it will not stop all current like an open. For example, a high resistance might make a bulb glow dimly or a motor turn too slowly, Fig. 9-5.

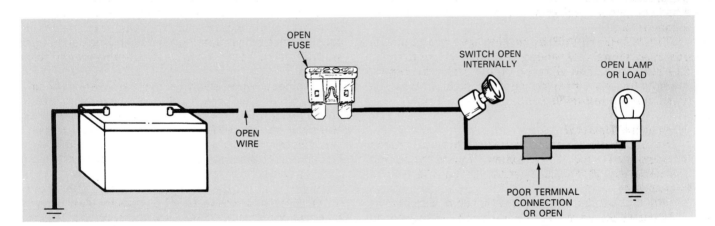

Fig. 9-1. These are some of the sources of opens or breaks in a circuit. In a series leg, everything after break would be "dead." (Chrysler)

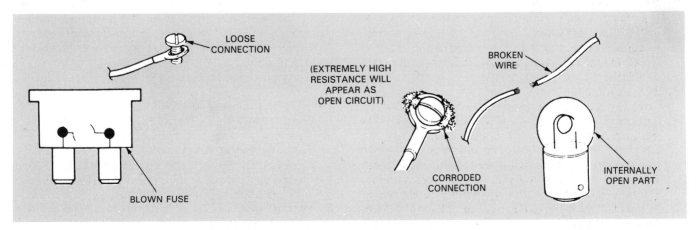

Fig. 9-2. When testing for an open, try to visualize how these troubles could stop current flow. (Chrysler)

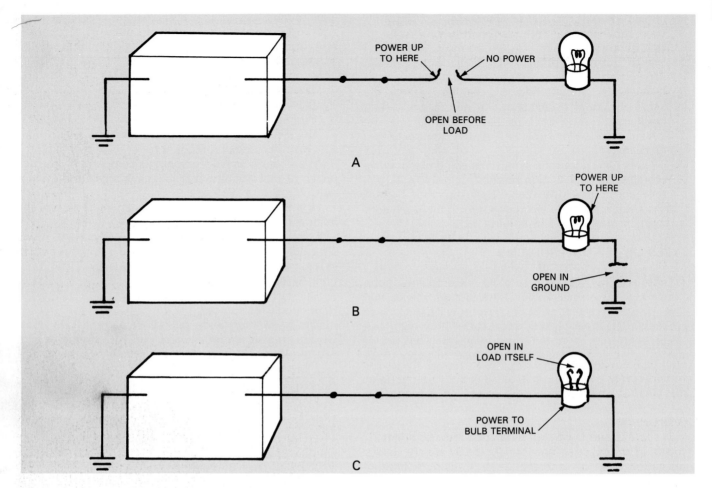

Fig. 9-3. A—With an open before the load, you would not get voltage to bulb socket. B—With open after bulb, bulb socket would not have return ground circuit path. C—Open in bulb itself is common example of open inside load.

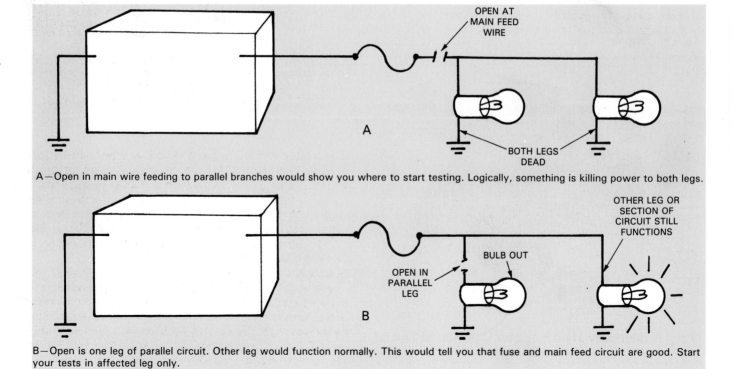

A—Open in main wire feeding to parallel branches would show you where to start testing. Logically, something is killing power to both legs.

B—Open is one leg of parallel circuit. Other leg would function normally. This would tell you that fuse and main feed circuit are good. Start your tests in affected leg only.

Fig. 9-4. Opens in parallel circuits cause different symptoms.

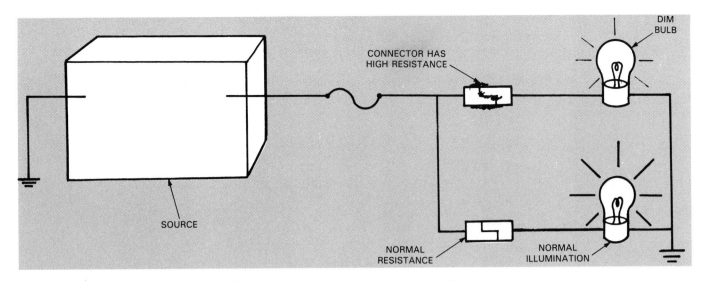

Fig. 9-5. A high circuit resistance is similar to an open but some current can still flow through circuit. One example, high ohms in connector would reduce current through one leg. Only the bulb in that leg would burn dimly.

High circuit resistance is usually caused by a poor electrical connection. A corroded or burned connector terminal is the most common cause. Faulty components can also have high internal ohms. See Figs. 9-6 and 9-7.

Short circuit

A *short circuit* is caused by a conductor accidentally touching ground or another conductor. There are several classifications of shorts, each causing different symptoms.

A *hot wire short to ground* will produce low circuit resistance and extremely high current flow. This will usually blow the fuse or kick out the circuit breaker. The fuse or circuit breaker will protect the circuit from excess current damage caused by the hot wire short, Fig. 9-8A.

A short in an unprotected section of a circuit can cause an "electrical fire." An *electrical fire* occurs when excess current overheats a conductor and melts its insulation.

Fig. 9-7. Here is an actual connector with a burned terminal. A poor connection between the terminals made the terminals act as "red hot" heating elements. This burned connector plastic and finally produced an open and dead circuit. (Nichols)

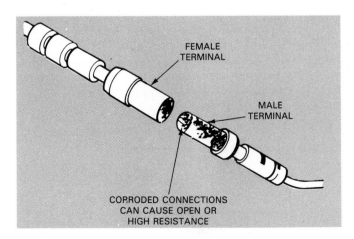

Fig. 9-6. With today's computer circuit, even the slightest increase in resistance between terminals in a connector can upset circuit operation. Some sensors produce less than one volt output, like an oxygen sensor. Any resistance in the circuit leading to the sensor could produce false signals for the computer.

The melted insulation can then allow other conductors to come into contact. As a result, several wires can begin to burn. This can all happen in a matter of seconds.

A *grounded circuit* is caused by a ground wire shorted to ground. This usually has no affect since the short is simply causing another ground connection, Fig. 9-8B.

Fig. 9-9 shows how a short in different locations in circuits can cause different symptoms.

Note how a short after a load does NOT blow the fuse. There is still a resistance unit (light bulb) between the power source and short to limit current flow. However, since the short is between two loads, it will shunt current away from the second load. The second load (bulb) will NOT function. The current will seek the path of least resistance through the short to ground, Fig. 9-9A.

Fig. 9-9B shows how a short before a switch can prevent a circuit from being shut off. The short before a

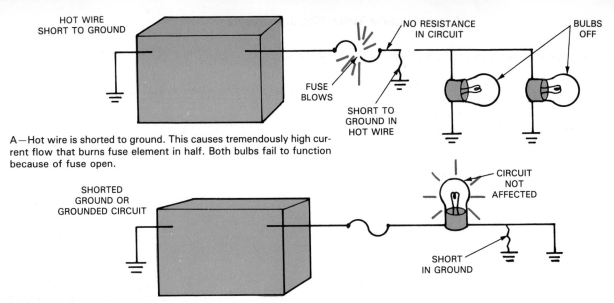

A—Hot wire is shorted to ground. This causes tremendously high current flow that burns fuse element in half. Both bulbs fail to function because of fuse open.

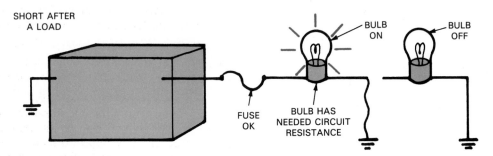

B—Ground wire is shorted to ground. This would not affect this circuit. A second path for ground is simply provided.

Fig. 9-8. Examples of short circuits.

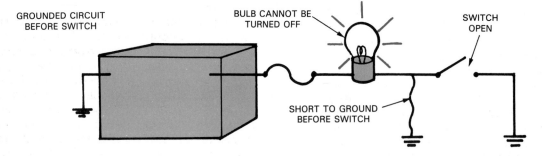

A—Short after a load. This short location would cut power to second bulb. However, first bulb would still work. Current flow would increase slightly because of less ohms in circuit. However, current flow may not increase enough to blow fuse with resistance of one bulb still in circuit.

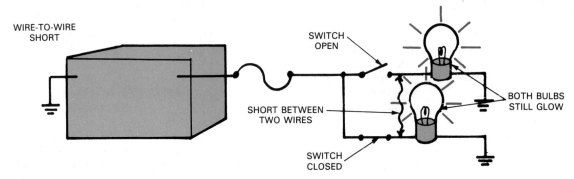

B—Short before a grounded switch. This would make load stay on all of the time, even with switch open. Current would bypass switch to ground.

C—Wire-to-wire short. This short would feed current across two legs. Even with one switch off, current would leak over to other leg. Only with both switches off would bulbs turn off.

Fig. 9-9. Location of short in a circuit will affect problem symptoms.

grounded switch would allow current flow, even with the switch off.

Fig. 9-9C shows an example of a wire-to-wire short. The conductors in two wires are touching because of damaged insulation. With this circuit, the short could make both loads (bulbs) function even with the switch to one turned off.

Shorts are caused by wire insulation damage. Something has cut or punctured the insulation, Fig. 9-10.

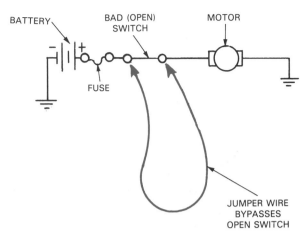

Fig. 9-11. Jumper wire provides easy way to bypass a component or to connect power directly to component or section of circuit. In this example, if bypassing switch makes motor run, switch is bad. (Ford)

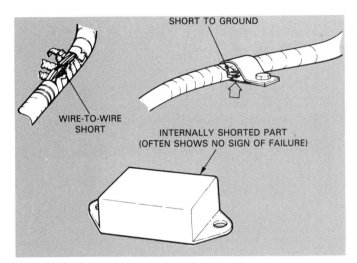

Fig. 9-10. These are the basic types of shorts: wire-to-wire short, short to ground, and short inside a component. (Chrysler)

Intermittent problems

Discussed briefly, an *intermittent problem* is one that only occurs under certain conditions. The problem may be present one time but may not show up later. This makes testing very difficult because there may not be a problem when you are checking out the trouble.

Many intermittent problems are caused by poor electrical connections. For example, two terminals in a connector may be loose. Most of the time the two terminals will make contact and the circuit will function. However, when the car hits a bump, the jolt can separate the loose terminals and the circuit can malfunction temporarily. An intermittent failure can result.

USING TESTING DEVICES

This section of the chapter will summarize the use of electrical testing devices. This will include using jumper wires, test lights, and multimeters. If you are to "survive" as an electrical-electronic technician, you must know the basics of using this equipment.

Using jumper wires

A *jumper wire* is a piece of wire with alligator clips on both ends. It is commonly used to bypass components or to apply voltage to a component or section of a circuit.

Fig. 9-11 shows a good example of how a jumper wire is used to check a switch. The jumper can be used to bypass the switch. Symptoms might point to an open switch; turning the switch on does NOT feed current to

the load (motor). If attaching the jumper around the switch turns the load (motor) on, then the switch is bad.

> DANGER! Never use a jumper wire to bypass a high resistance component, a fuse, or a circuit breaker. This could allow excess current flow and an "electrical fire."

A jumper can also be used to connect voltage directly to the load. If the load (motor for example) begins to work, something is wrong in the circuit leading to the load. If jumping directly to the load does not make it work, the load itself or the ground may be at fault.

Using a test light

A *test light* is a quick and easy way of checking a circuit for power or continuity (complete circuit path). Most have a sharp probe for touching conductors and an alligator clip for grounding. There are two types of test lights: circuit-powered and self-powered. A circuit-powered test light is more commonly used in auto repair.

A *circuit-powered test light* uses circuit voltage to illuminate the tester bulb. Fig. 9-12 shows how to use one to check for power. The alligator clip is connected to any good ground. Then the test probe can be touched on different points in the circuit. If the test light glows, the circuit is good up to that point. As soon as the test light fails to glow, you have found the problem area preventing circuit operation, Fig. 9-13.

Sharp test light probes can be used to puncture wire insulation to check for power. The probe can be pushed through the plastic insulation until it touches the wire conductor. This is handy when you cannot access a connector for your tests. The test light can also be inserted into the back of open connector so the probe touches one of the metal terminals in the connector. The connector could also be unplugged to check for voltage.

NOTE! Avoid using a test light probe to puncture the insulation on wires in a computer or sensor circuit. If the wire is to a sensor with a weak or low voltage signal, moisture could enter the hole in the insulation. This could upset the small signal going to the computer and a com-

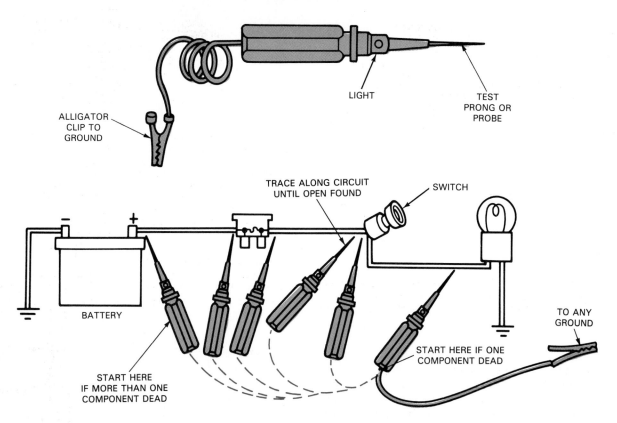

Fig. 9-12. Test light provides handy way to check for power or voltage in a circuit. With circuit-powered type, alligator clip is grounded. Then, test probe can be touched at different locations to find breaks in circuit. (Chrysler)

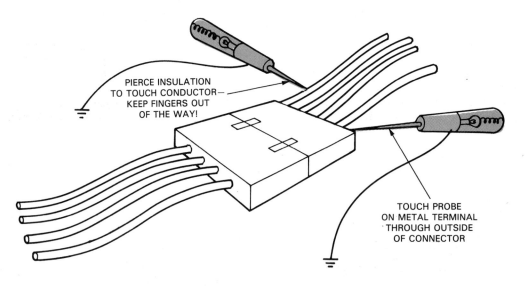

Fig. 9-13. Test light has sharp, pointed tip. It can be touched on terminal or pushed through wire insulation.

puter system malfunction could result.

A *self-powered test light* has an internal battery and the power source must be disconnected from the circuit while testing. Also called a *continuity tester,* it uses its own power source to check for a complete electrical path. Fig. 9-14 shows how a self-powered test light can be used to check continuity.

Using a test light to find shorts

Fig. 9-15 shows how a test light can be used to help find shorts. The test light is substituted for the fuse in

the affected circuit. As long as the short is present, the test light will glow. You can wiggle wires or disconnect components or wires until the test light goes out. When the test light does not glow, you have found the source of the short.

DANGER! Test light probes are very sharp. It is easy to jab the probe through your finger when penetrating wire insulation. Do not place fingers behind the probe when testing.

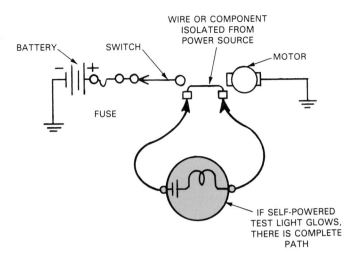

Fig. 9-14. Self-powered test light is not as commonly used as circuit-powered test light. Circuit power source must be disconnected. Then self-powered test light will check for continuity. (Ford)

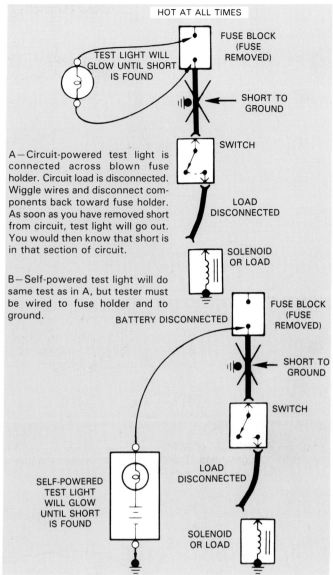

A—Circuit-powered test light is connected across blown fuse holder. Circuit load is disconnected. Wiggle wires and disconnect components back toward fuse holder. As soon as you have removed short from circuit, test light will go out. You would then know that short is in that section of circuit.

B—Self-powered test light will do same test as in A, but tester must be wired to fuse holder and to ground.

Fig. 9-15. Here is how you can use test lights to help find short circuits. (General Motors)

Using a compass to find a short

A circuit breaker and a compass can be used to find shorts. As shown in Fig. 9-16, the circuit breaker can be placed across the fuse holder that burns fuses. The short will make the breaker kick in and out. Current will flow through the circuit and then stop flowing as the breaker protects the circuit.

A compass can then be passed along next to the circuit wiring. The current flow and resulting magnetic field will act upon the compass needle before the short. When the compass needle stops deflecting, you have found the location of the short.

Using inductive circuit tracer

An *inductive circuit tracer* uses a signal generator and inductive pickup to find shorts. One is in Fig. 9-17.

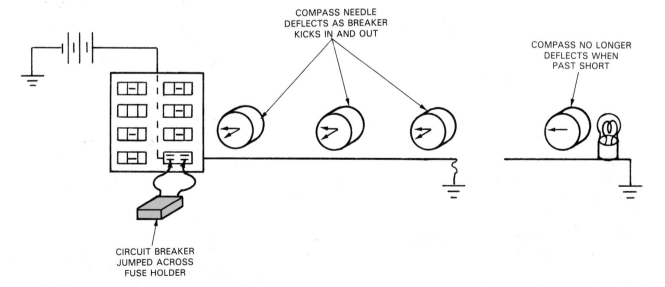

Fig. 9-16. Circuit breaker and compass can be used to find shorts. Circuit breaker will keep kicking in and out if there is short in circuit. Compass will stop deflecting when you have moved it past point of short.

Fig. 9-17. This is inductive circuit tracer. It uses same principle as compass described in Fig. 9-16. It senses changing magnetic field around wire to find shorts as well as opens. (TIF)

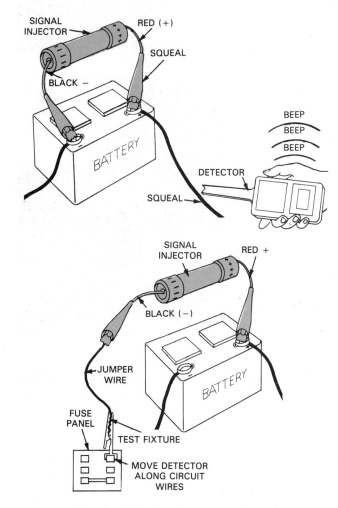

Fig. 9-18. Signal generator is connected across battery to produce fluctuating voltage in wiring. Connect signal generator across specific circuit to find shorts. Detector or pickup can then sense changing magnetic field for quickly finding shorts and opens. (TIF)

The *signal generator* or *signal injector* is connected to the car battery or to the battery and to the affected circuit. This will produce a weak fluctuating voltage in the wiring. See Figs. 9-18 and 9-19.

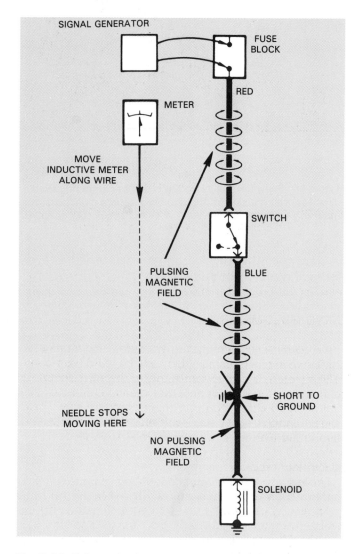

Fig. 9-19. Schematic shows how inductive tracer would work. Magnetic field would not be present beyond short or open. Tracer would change output tone or noise to signal the circuit problem. (Buick)

The *pickup* or *detector* can then be moved along the outside of the wiring. It will sense the fluctuating magnetic field around the outside of the wire. If you move the sensor over a short in the wire, it will change its audible tone or make a beeping sound, depending upon the particular tracer.

Wiggle wires

When looking for shorts or opens, you should wiggle or move the wires while testing, Fig. 9-20. This might move the conductor to produce the open or short. It might also correct the problem temporarily so that you can detect the trouble.

Always look for wire damage. Check for cut or

144

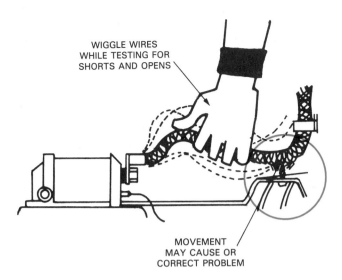

Fig. 9-20. With intermittent problems, wiggle and move wires. This could make problem occur. (Ford)

smashed wire insulation, loose connections, etc. Any of these could cause a malfunction.

USING MULTIMETERS

A *multimeter* is a voltmeter, ammeter, and ohmmeter combined in one housing. Also called a VOM (volt-ohm-milliammeter), it is an essential tool of the auto electronic technician. It will make accurate measurements of actual circuit values. You can them compare these test values to known good values. If high or low, you would then know if there is a problem in the circuit.

Multimeter types

There are two basic types of multimeters used in auto mechanics: analog meter and digital meter, Fig. 9-21.

An *analog multimeter* uses a conventional swinging needle to show test values. The needle swings from left to right. This action is needed to read gradual or small changes in voltage, current, or resistance. An analog meter is also good for finding intermittent problems since the needle will instantly react or move with a change in a test value.

A *digital multimeter* uses a vacuum fluorescent or liquid crystal display to give readings. Actual numbers are shown for the test values. This is handy for constant readings and when accuracy is important. However, since the digital readout can constantly change up or down slightly, it is difficult to detect slight or intermittent changes.

A high *impedence* (resistance) digital multimeter is recommended when testing most computer circuits. It will draw very little current and will not damage delicate computer circuits. An analog meter can draw more current and could burn up integrated circuits and other small electronic components.

Meter connections

Discussed in an earlier chapter, a *voltmeter* measures "electrical pressure," a potential difference, or voltage

A

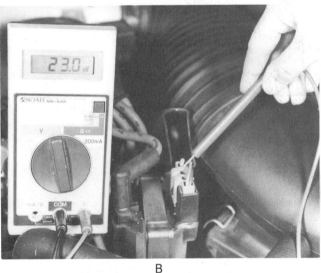

B

Fig. 9-21. Both analog and digital meters are needed by auto electronics specialist. Both have their advantages and disadvantages. A—Analog meter uses conventional needle to give readings. B—Digital meter uses number display for output readings.

(V or E). A voltmeter is connected PARALLEL with the circuit being tested. The circuit's power source must operate the voltmeter, Fig. 9-22A.

An *ammeter* measures current flow in amps (A or J). A conventional ammeter must be connected in SERIES with the circuit being tested. All circuit current must flow through the ammeter. However, inductive ammeters have a clip-on pickup that simply FITS OVER the wire

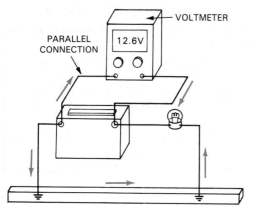

A—Voltmeter is normally connected in parallel with circuit. Then it can measure the "electrical pressure" in the circuit.

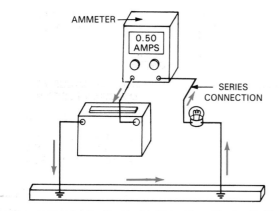

B—Conventional ammeter is wired in series with circuit. Then it can measure electron movement or current in circuit.

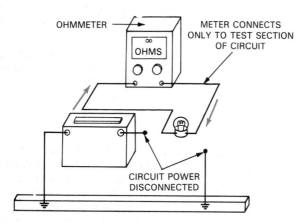

C—Ohmmeter must not be connected to circuit power. Power must be disconnected so that ohmmeter can use its battery power to measure resistance in ohms.

Fig. 9-22. These are the methods normally used to connect a voltmeter, ammeter, and ohmmeter to a circuit.

insulation. Then the pickup can sense and measure the magnetic field around the wire. The magnetic field is proportional to the current flow in the wire. See Figs. 9-22A and 9-23.

An *ohmmeter* measures the resistance to current flow in ohms (R or Ω). Power must be DISCONNECTED from the circuit. Then the ohmmeter can be connected to each

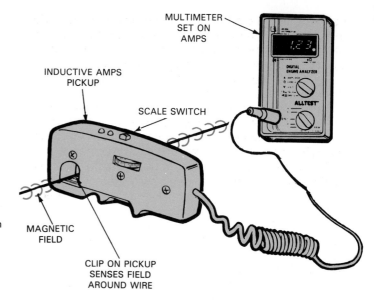

Fig. 9-23. Modern inductive ammeter is handy because you do not have to wire it in series. Clip the inductive pickup over the outside of the wire. Since the magnetic field around wire is proportional to current, meter will give amp reading. With a car's DC, you cannot use an inductive pickup to measure voltage. Only AC voltage can be read with inductive meter pickup.

end of a wire or component to check its internal resistance. This is shown in Fig. 9-22.

Meter controls

Most modern digital meters are partially automatic. Also called, *auto ranging,* they will automatically change to the correct scale. All you have to do is set the meter for volts, amps, or ohms, and the meter will adjust itself.

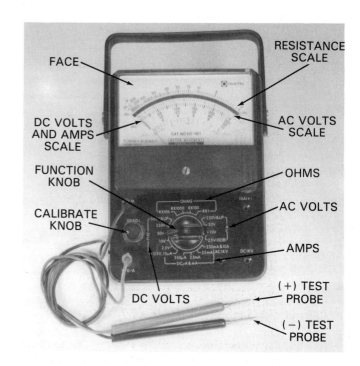

Fig. 9-24. Study basic parts of this analog multimeter.

For example, a digital meter might show a "K" when measuring a high resistance. This would mean that you must multiply the reading by three. If no other multiplier symbol is shown, the reading is full ohms.

Fig. 9-24 shows the parts of an analog meter. Note the knobs, leads, and face.

An *ohms calibrate knob* is used on many analog meters. It must be set before making resistance measurements. The calibrate knob will compensate for battery condition and provide accurate measurements.

To set the calibrate knob, touch or short the meter leads together. This will make the needle swing to the right or to zero ohms. Adjust the calibrate knob until the needle is exactly on zero.

The *function* or *range knob* is for selecting the desired test value. It can be switched to different voltage, current, and resistance values. For example, it can be switched to RX100 which means each ohms reading must be multiplied by 100. Various voltage and current settings are also provided.

Some meters also have different test lead sockets or holes. Each socket is for a different type and range of measurement. The value will usually be labeled next to the meter lead socket, Fig. 9-25.

Reading voltmeter scales

An analog meter will usually have several voltage scales. You must read the one that matches the range knob setting. Fig. 9-26 gives several examples of analog voltmeter readings. Note how the correct scale must be used depending upon the range switch position. Also study the abbreviations for the various voltage values.

For example, if the voltage range switch is set to 0-25 volts, you would use the 0-250 volts scale. However, you would ignore the extra zero after the scale reading. If set on 0-10 volts, you would read the scale with a maximum of 10 volts.

Reading ammeter scales

Fig. 9-27 illustrates how to read an analog ammeter scale. Just as with voltage, the range position switch setting will determine which amp scale to read.

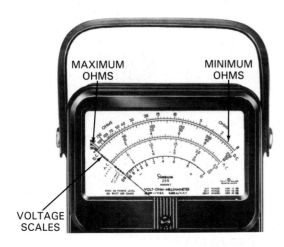

Fig. 9-25. It is important that you read meter face correctly. Ohms scale is usually on top. Voltage and current scales are below ohms scale. (Simpson)

READING AN ANALOG VOLTMETER

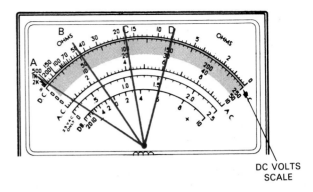

DC VOLTS SCALE

RANGE SWITCH POSITION	SCALE TO READ
5 V	0-5 (50)
25 V	0-25 (250)
50 V	0-5 (50)
250 V	0-25 (250)
500 V	0-5 (50)

ANSWERS

RANGE SWITCH POSITION		VOLTAGE VALUE AT INDICATOR POSITION			
	Scale	A	B	C	D
5 V	0-5	.1 V	1 V	2 V	3 V
25 V	0-25	.5 V	5 V	10 V	15 V
50 V	0-5	1 V	10 V	20 V	30 V

Abbreviation	Value	Symbol
1 MEGAVOLT	= 1 MILLION VOLTS (1,000,000 VOLTS)	(MV)
1 KILOVOLT	= 1 THOUSAND VOLTS (1,000 VOLTS)	(kV)
1 VOLT	= 1 VOLT	(V)
1 MILLIVOLT	= 1/1000 VOLT (.001 VOLT)	(mV)
1 MICROVOLT	= 1/1,000,000 VOLT (.000001 VOLT)	(μV)

Fig. 9-26. These are some examples of meter readings and voltage values. Try to read the needle readings for each range switch position before looking at the answers on the right of the chart.

Remember that automotive circuits operate on DC (direct or one-way current flow), NOT AC (alternating or reversing current flow). Also, most current values are very high and many analog multimeters are designed to measure very small current values, in fractions of an amp. You would need a specialized automotive type ammeter to make larger current measurements, as when testing a charging or starting system for instance.

Reading analog ohmmeter scale

Fig. 9-28 shows how to read an analog ohmmeter scale. The scale is read backwards. The highest resistance readings are on the left and the lowest are on the right. There is only one ohms scale. For higher readings, you must multiply the scale value by the range switch or knob position.

Voltage drop measurements

A *voltage drop measurement* is very useful because it determines the internal resistance of a wire or compo-

READING ANALOG AMMETER

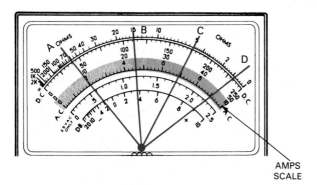

AMPS SCALE

1 AMPERE	= 1 AMPERE
1 MILLIAMPERE	= 1/1000 AMPERE OR .001 AMPERE
1 MICROAMPERE	= 1/1,000,000 or .000001 AMPERE

Range Switch Position	Scale Reads	Each Small Mark Equals
100 µA	0 to 100 µA	2 µA
10 mA	0 to 10 mA	.2 mA
100 mA	0 to 100 mA	2 mA
1000 mA	0 to 1000 mA	20 mA
10 A	0 to 10 A	.2 A

ANSWERS

Range Switch Position	Current Value At Indicator Position			
	A	B	C	D
100 µA	20 µA	46 µA	70 µA	92 µA
10 mA	2 mA	4.6 mA	7 mA	9.2 mA
100 mA	20 mA	46 mA	70 mA	92 mA
1000 mA	200 mA	460 mA	700 mA	920 mA
10 A	2 A	4.6 A	7A	9.2 A

Fig. 9-27. These are some examples of analog ammeter readings. Again, try to determine the readings for each range switch position before looking at answers.

READING AN ANALOG OHMMETER

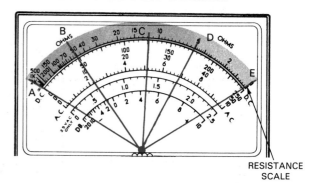

RESISTANCE SCALE

SCALE x 1	VALUE AS READ
SCALE x 10	MULTIPLY READING BY 10
SCALE x 1k	MULTIPLY READING BY 1000
SCALE x 100k	MULTIPLY READING BY 100,000

ANSWERS

Range Switch Position	Value in Ohms at Indicator Position				
	A	B	C	D	E
x 1	OPEN	50 Ω	12 Ω	5 Ω	SHORT
x 10	CIRCUIT	500 Ω	120 Ω	50 Ω	CIRCUIT
x 1K	∞	50 kΩ	12 Ω	5000 Ω	ZERO
x 100k	OHMS	5 MΩ	1.2 MΩ	500 kΩ	OHMS

Fig. 9-28. These are examples of ohmmeter readings. Note how you must use correct multiplier for each range switch position.

nent. Instead of disconnecting the power source and using an ohmmeter, you can check voltage drops. This is a much faster way of checking a circuit for high resistance.

If you suspect a switch of having a poor internal connection and high resistance, you can measure its voltage drop. As shown in Fig. 9-29, connect the voltmeter across the input and output leads of the switch. If the closed switch voltage drop reading is too high (over about one volt for most switches), then the switch has a poor internal connection. A good switch, when closed, will have little or no voltage drop.

Fig. 9-30 further illustrates the principle of voltage drop measurements. Note how the voltage drops would be equal if the load resistances are equal. The sum of all voltage drops also equals the supply voltage in a series circuit.

Fig. 9-31 shows how voltage drops vary with resistance. In this example, if a blower switch is set on low, a small amount of current will flow to the blower motor and the motor will run slowly. This would show up as a high voltage drop at the low speed (high ohms) ter-

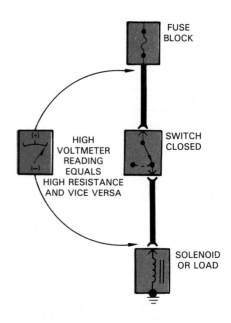

FUSE BLOCK

SWITCH CLOSED

HIGH VOLTMETER READING EQUALS HIGH RESISTANCE AND VICE VERSA

SOLENOID OR LOAD

Fig. 9-29. Voltage drop is very useful measurement. It will show resistance without disconnecting components as you would have to do with ohmmeter. If closed switch has high voltage drop, it would indicate high resistance problem.

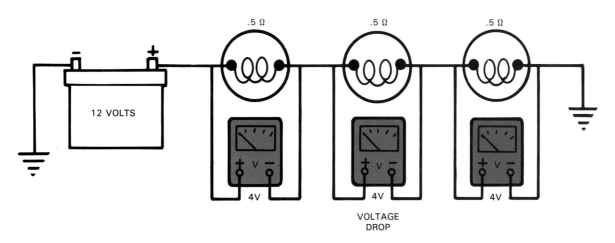

SINGLE CONTINUOUS
CURRENT PATH

TOTAL RESISTANCE = .5Ω + .5Ω + .5Ω = 1.5Ω
TOTAL VOLTAGE = 4V DROP + 4V DROP + 4V DROP = 12V

Fig. 9-30. Note how component resistance determines voltage drop. Sum of all component resistances in series circuit will equal total circuit resistance. Total circuit voltage drop will also equal voltage applied. (Chrysler)

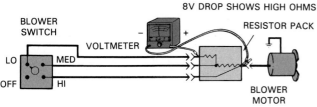

A—This leg of resistor pack is for low blower speeds so it shows high voltage drop and high resistance.

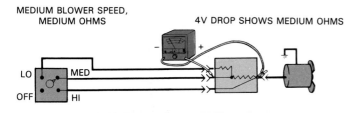

B—This leg of resistor pack is for medium blower speed. It has medium voltage drop and medium resistance.

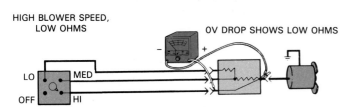

C—This leg of resistor pack is for high blower speed so resistance must be low to pass high current. Voltage drop would also be low.

Fig. 9-31. Examples of how voltage drops can be used to check internal resistances without disconnecting components from circuit. (Ford)

minal of the switch. With the switch on high or low resistance, more current could flow to the motor for higher blower rpm. Then the voltage drop would be zero because of no resistance across the resistor pack. This example shows the relationship of voltage, current, resistance, and voltage drop measurements.

Resistance measurements

Resistant measurements are commonly done when the circuit or component is disconnected or when very accurate ohms readings are needed. Fig. 9-32 illustrates some examples of resistance measurements.

Infinite resistance, shown with a ∞ symbol, means that there is not a complete circuit path. Something is preventing current flow through the tested circuit or component. There is NO CONTINUITY with an infinite resistance reading.

Zero resistance or no resistance means that there is a perfect electrical path between the two test points. This would show that there is continuity or zero ohms in the tested circuit or component.

Fig. 9-33 shows an example of using an ohmmeter to check a resistor pack. The wires from the switch and to the blower motor would have to be disconnected. Then, accurate ohms readings could be taken on the resistors in the pack. By comparing your readings to specs, you can determine the condition of the unit.

Amperage measurements

Mentioned briefly, amperage measurements are needed to check the condition of various components. Conventional ammeters are connected directly to the circuit conductors. Inductive ammeters are simply connected around the wire insulation.

Fig. 9-34 illustrates how an ammeter reading might be used to check the condition of a motor. Amp readings can be compared to known good readings. If current draw is high, it could point to a problem producing a drag

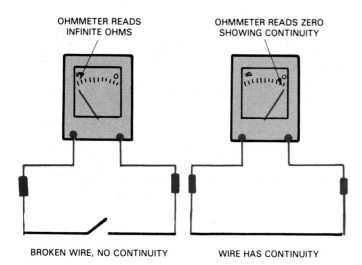

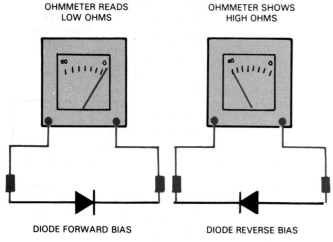

Fig. 9-32. These are some examples of resistance measurements. A—Conductor should have low ohms or continuity. B—Coil is simply a conductor wound in a spiral. It should have very low resistance and should not be shorted to ground. C—Ohmmeter should show high resistance when connected in one direction across diode. It should show low ohms in other direction. This would show that diode is functioning as one-way electrical check valve.

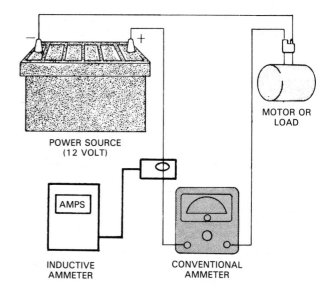

Fig. 9-33. Ohmmeter will also measure internal resistances but leads must be disconnected so other components do not affect readings. Compare this to Fig. 9-31. (Ford)

Fig. 9-34. Conventional ammeter must be wired in series. Inductive ammeter can be connected around wire. If current flow is too high, a low resistance or high voltage is indicated. If current is low, a high resistance or low supply voltage is indicated. (Ford)

on the motor (bad armature bearings for example) or a short in a winding. A low current measurement could point to a problem that is preventing normal current flow (burned motor brushes for instance, poor terminal connections, bad ground, etc.).

Voltage measurements

Voltage measurements to components are also useful in determining the condition of a circuit or components. By checking "electrical pressure," you can gather more information about the electrical problem.

For example, by simply measuring battery voltage, you can check the charge or condition of a car battery. A fully charged 12-volt battery should actually have 12.5 volts. If your voltmeter only reads 11 volts, the battery needs to be recharged or it has internal problems.

Another example, imagine that an engine will not start and there is no spark at the plug wires. You might measure voltage supplied to the ignition coil. If the voltage is low going to the coil, it may not be able to develop a good spark. Your tests might tell you that a high resistance or shunt to another conductor is preventing normal voltage supply to the ignition coil. This will be discussed in detail later.

RULES FOR USING MULTIMETERS

1. Make sure your test leads are connected properly. An incorrect connection could damage electronic components or the meter itself.
2. Set the meter to read a high enough value. If you have the meter set on 0 to 10 amps for example, and you try to measure 100 amps, it will burn up the meter or blow its fuse.
3. Use a digital meter when checking computer circuits. This will help prevent circuit damage that can be caused by an analog type meter.
4. Place the meter in a secure location. They are expensive and can be ruined if dropped. Also keep them away from moving or hot engine parts.
5. Keep the test leads away from hot or moving parts. They can get caught in engine fans, burned on hot exhaust manifolds, etc.
6. Use service manual specs for determining whether a circuit or component is faulty. Component and circuit resistance, voltage, and current values vary from model to model.
7. When using an analog meter with a needle, view straight at the face of the meter when reading values. If viewed at an angle, a parallax error and false readings can result.
8. If needed, zero or calibrate an analog meter ohmmeter before use to assure accuracy.
9. Use an analog type meter instead of a digital meter when trying to read small changes in voltage, current, or resistance. It is more difficult to detect slight changes with a digital readout.
10. To help find intermittent problems, wiggle wires and use a heat gun or freeze type spray on electronic components. This can help change the reading to indicate the problem.

BASIC COMPONENT TESTS

This section of the chapter will briefly explain how to test fundamental electrical and electronic components. This will help you later when studying about more specific tests.

Testing connectors

A *good connector* will have little or no resistance across its terminals. A *bad connector* will have resistance that will lower current flow through the connector. This reduced current can upset or stop the operation of the circuit on the other side of the connector.

A test light can be used to check for power on both sides of a connector. This test might be used when a circuit is completely dead, indicating power is not reaching a component or section of a circuit.

First check for power going into the connector, Fig. 9-35A. Then check for power on the other side of the connector. Make sure you check the same wire or terminal.

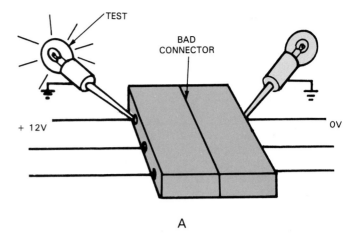

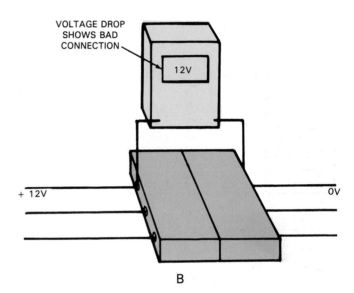

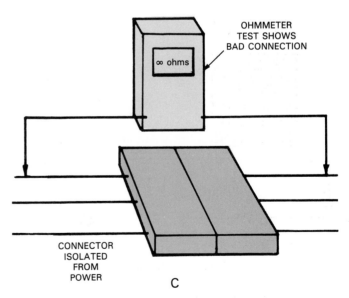

Fig. 9-35. Testing a connector. A—Test light will quickly check for power on both sides of connector. If test light only glows on one side, bad terminal connection is indicated. B—Voltmeter will check voltage drop across a connector; a high drop shows a high resistance problem. C—Ohmmeter will also check for high resistance or open in connector but connector must be isolated.

151

Unless it is a weatherpack type connector, you can touch the test probe on the terminals through the outside of the connector. If the test light does NOT glow on both sides of the connector, you have found a high resistance or poor electrical connection.

A voltage drop test can also be used to check a connector, Fig. 9-35B. A good connector will have little voltage drop. A high voltage drop would indicate poor terminal contact.

An ohmmeter can be used to check a connector if the power source is disconnected, as in Fig. 9-35C. An accurate reading of resistance may be needed in a computer network where even the slightest resistance could upset computer operation.

Testing resistors

Various types of resistors are used on the modern automobile. After a period of use, *bad resistors* can breakdown and change resistance. This can upset the operation of the circuit. An ohmmeter can be used to test actual resistance. A voltmeter can also be used to check its voltage drop. If not within specs, a new resistor would be needed, Fig. 9-36.

Detailed in later chapters, variable resistors are used as throttle sensors and other sensors in computer systems. Fixed resistors can be used in heater blower circuits, ignition feed circuits, and in many other systems.

Testing switches

A *good switch* should block current in one position and pass current freely in the other position. A switch can be tested with a test light, voltmeter, or ohmmeter. A *bad switch* will not turn on and off or it may have high resistance when on.

If still installed, a test light can be used to check for power in the two positions. A voltmeter can also be con-

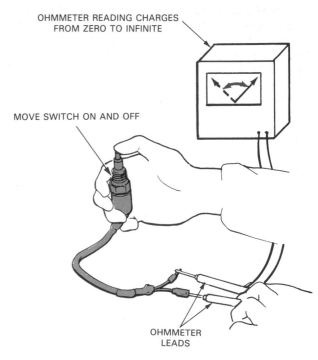

OHMMETER READING CHARGES FROM ZERO TO INFINITE

MOVE SWITCH ON AND OFF

OHMMETER LEADS

Fig. 9-37. A bad switch can be shorted closed or burned open. Resistance should be zero when closed and infinite when open. (Honda)

nected across the switch; it should show full voltage drop when off and little or no voltage drop when on.

An ohmmeter can be used if the switch is removed or isolated from the circuit. It should have zero resistance when on and infinite resistance when off, Fig. 9-37.

Testing fuses

When "hot" (supply voltage being fed to fuse), a fuse should have voltage on both sides of its metal ends. A *blown fuse* will only be hot on the feed side, Fig. 9-38.

A fuse can be quickly checked with a test light. The

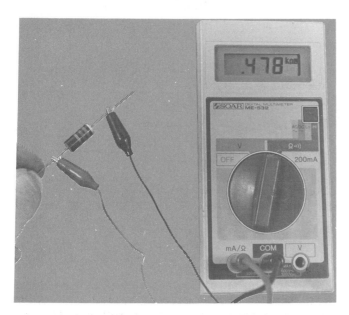

Fig. 9-36. Any resistor in vehicle must have ohms value within specs. After a period of service, resistor values can change enough to upset circuit operation. More specialized resistors, than the one shown, are used in autos. (Union Electronics)

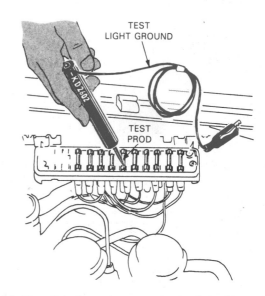

TEST LIGHT GROUND

TEST PROD

Fig. 9-38. Test light is easiest way to check for blown fuse. Blown fuse will light tester on feed side and will not light tester on output side.

test light should glow on both sides of the fuse. If the light only glows on the feed side, the fuse is blown. You would need to check for a possible short that has blown the fuse. However, sometimes fuses can fail after prolonged service, even if there is no short in the circuit.

A voltmeter can also be used to check a fuse but it is not as handy as a test light. If the meter is digital and makes an audible signal with a change in voltage, it will check the fuse without too much trouble. Again, voltage should be present on both sides of the fuse.

Testing variable resistors

A *good variable resistor* should exhibit a gradual change in resistance as you turn its shaft or move its slide. A *bad variable resistor* might be open (infinite resistance) or shorted (zero resistance). It may also be stuck with a specific ohms value that does not vary properly with movement.

An ohmmeter is the most accurate way of checking a variable resistor in most conditions. A service manual will usually give ohms specs for different variable resistor positions. If tests show different values, the variable resistor is bad, Fig. 9-39. Voltage drops will also check a variable resistor but specs are not given this way.

Testing a transducer switch

A *transducer switch* will change its internal resistance with a change in a condition. Some examples are temperature switches, position switch, pressure switches, etc. Sometimes, a *bad transducer switch* can fail and it will stay in the same position (on or off) with varying conditions.

One example, an ohmmeter is normally used to check a temperature switch because its leads can be disconnected easily, Fig. 9-40. Measure the units internal resistance when cold and hot (two conditions). You may have to remove the unit so that its temperature can be controlled on a hot plate or with a heat gun. A thermometer can be used to measure the temperature of the switch. If ohms values are NOT within specs for specific temperatures, the temperature switch has failed.

A quick way of checking a temperature switch is to bypass it. Use a jumper to connect the two leads that go to the temperature switch. This should make the temperature light glow or temperature gauge read fully hot or cold, depending upon gauge design.

Note! More information on testing sensors, pressure switches, etc. is given in Chapters 21 and 22. Refer to these chapters if needed.

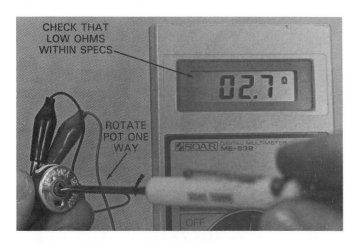

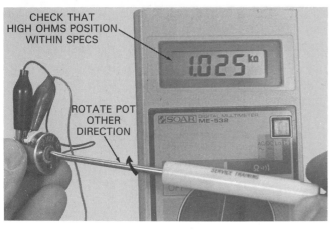

Fig. 9-39. Variable resistor or potentiometer should have specific ohms for specific positions. You must compare readings to those given in service manual. A—Variable resistor in low ohms position. B—Variable resistor in high ohms position. (Union Electronics)

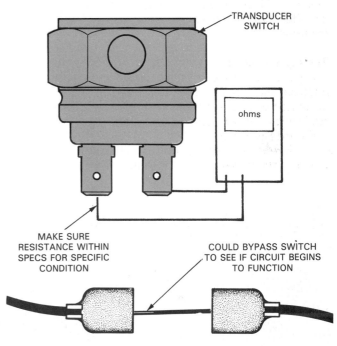

Fig. 9-40. Transducer switch can be open or shorted closed, or its resistance can be higher than normal. It is normally easy to remove wires and measure resistance of unit. Jumper wire can also be used to bypass transducer switch to see if circuit begins to function. (Renault)

Testing condensers (capacitors)

Discussed earlier, a *condenser* or *capacitor* is commonly used to absorb fluctuating voltage or current in a car's electrical system. It can be used to prevent interference in the radio caused by unsmooth DC current, switches opening and closing, etc. Condensers were also used in older contact point ignition systems to prevent contact point burning. A *bad condenser* can be shorted or open, Fig. 9-41.

> Warning! A condenser can store an electrical charge. You should always ground the lead on a condenser before testing it. A condenser cannot hurt you but it can startle you enough to make you jump and be injured. You also do not want a condenser to discharge into and damage your ohmmeter.

To test a condenser, diconnect and ground its lead. Use an analog ohmmeter on RX1 or RX100 range to measure its resistance. First, the ohmmeter should show low resistance as the condenser takes a charge from the ohmmeter batteries. Then, the ohmmeter reading should increase to infinite resistance. This shows that it is blocking DC current but storing voltage.

Condenser testers are also available. Follow their operating instructions.

Testing diodes

A *bad diode* can either have an internal open (PN junction burned and separated) or it can be shorted (PN junction burned and fused). An ohmmeter is normally used to check diodes. The diode should have infinite ohms in one direction or polarity and low ohms in the other. If not, the diode should be replaced.

Testing transistors

A *bad transistor* will no longer amplify its base signal. One of the internal PN junctions has been damaged. Special transistor testers are available but an ohmmeter can also be used to test transistors.

Note! In only a few instances are transistors tested and replaced in the automotive field. There are a few power transistors in various devices that frequently fail and can be checked and replaced in the field. Most transistors in complex circuits require the expertise of a specialized

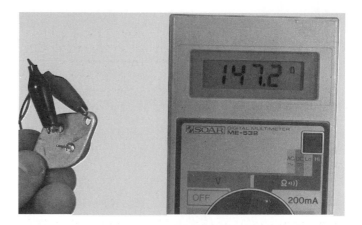

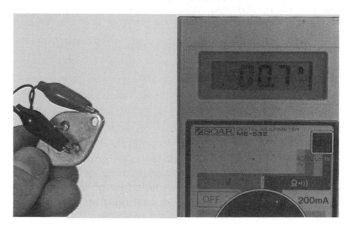

Fig. 9-42. Some day you may need to test a power transistor since they are usually easy to remove and replace in a circuit. First, you need to find the base of the transistor. The base will show the same ohms reading when kept as a common test point. Then, readings to emitter and collector can be checked. Usually, a bad transistor will be shorted (zero ohms) or opened (infinite ohms) from damage to PN junction.

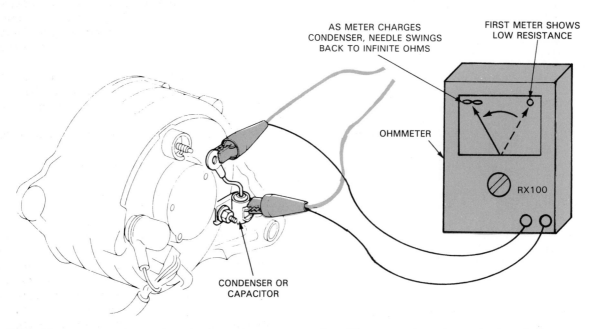

Fig. 9-41. Ohmmeter can be used to check condenser or capacitor. First, ground condenser lead to discharge any electricity in condenser. Connect test leads across condenser. Ohmmeter should charge condenser and meter reading should gradually increase to infinite resistance.

circuit technician.

To check a transistor with an ohmmeter, you must first find the base lead. To do this, connect an ohmmeter test lead to any of the transistor leads. You can tell the base because the ohmmeter will read the same when touching the other two transistor leads. The ohmmeter reading will vary when touching across the emitter-collector junction. See Fig. 9-42.

After finding the base, you must make four measurements. With one test lead on the base, measure resistance across the emitter and then the collector. Reverse the ohmmeter lead and check resistance to the emitter and collector again. In one direction, the ohms reading should be low (about 2 to 10 ohms). When reversed, the readings should be slightly higher (about 60 to 150 ohms). This would show that the transistor junctions are functioning normally.

A *bad transistor* will usually show infinite resistance or zero resistance across one or more of the junctions. This would tell you to replace the transistor.

Testing other components

The methods for testing other electrical and electronic components are discussed in later chapters. However, they require the same techniques just discussed. Fig. 9-43 shows how an ohmmeter and voltmeter can be used to test various components. If you use common sense, your knowledge of component operation, and recommended testing practices, you should have little trouble finding problems.

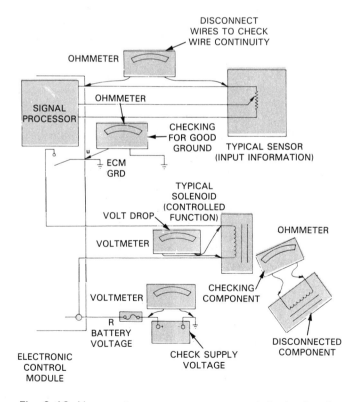

Fig. 9-43. You must use common sense and the basic rules given in this chapter when making electrical measurements. By thinking about the circuit and specific components, you should be able to use logical steps to find circuit problems. (Oldsmobile)

Electrical service chemicals

There are several chemicals that can be helpful when doing electrical tests and repairs.

Contact cleaner is a chemical for cleaning deposits off of contacts, switches, and other components. For example, if a variable resistor or volume control on a radio makes static or noise when adjusted, it may need cleaning. Spray contact cleaner into the device and rotate the knob back and forth. This will frequently clean off the variable resistor and wiping arm to correct the problem.

Freeze spray can be used to find intermittent problems in electronic components. Electronic components are very sensitive to temperature. If you spray the freeze solution on the component, it will lower its temperature instantly. This may make a change in the component's output and you can find an internal problem.

Electrical solvent can be used to clean oil and grease from components before soldering. It can also be used to clean off soldering flux.

SUMMARY

To be a competent automotive electronic technician, you must know how to correctly test and analyze circuit problems. This knowledge will allow you to use logical thought and a systematic approach to find and correct troubles.

Most circuit problems are caused by something very simple: a broken wire, loose terminal connection, burned transistor, etc. However, when this basic trouble is in a complex circuit, it can be very difficult to locate and repair. Correct techniques must be used to find electrical problems in a modern car.

You must first verify a problem. Observe the conditions to make sure the customer has described the symptoms properly. Then, narrow down the possible causes for the trouble. Use your knowledge of system operation and basic testing methods. After making the repair, recheck that the problem has been corrected before releasing the car to the customer.

If only one component does not work, start your tests at that component. If several components in the same circuit are not working, start your tests at the power source to the circuit.

When analyzing electrical problems, always think! Ask yourself these kinds of questions:
1. What could be causing the symptoms?
2. How many components are affected?
3. Is the problem constant or intermittent?
4. Is the problem affected by heat or cold?
5. Is the problem affected by moisture?

Carefully analyze the symptoms. Think of the components that could be causing the symptoms and those that could not. Select the most logical place to start your tests. If the first test does not find the trouble, use your second choice. Refer to a service manual troubleshooting chart if you have difficulty finding an electrical problem.

An open circuit has a complete break or disconnection. An open will stop current flow. An open can be caused by a broken wire, blown fuse, burned switch, bad connector, or failed component.

High circuit resistance will reduce current in a circuit. This problem might make a bulb glow dimly or make a motor run too slowly. Corroded connector terminals, burned relay contacts, burned motor brushes, and similar reasons can cause high circuit resistance.

A short circuit is caused by a conductor accidentally touching ground or another conductor. A hot wire short-to-ground can cause high current flow that can blow the circuit fuse. If not in a fused section of a circuit, a hot wire short-to-ground could burn wiring.

An intermittent problem only occurs under certain conditions. It is the most difficult type problem to find. You must try to simulate the conditions that cause the intermittent trouble.

Jumper wires can be used to bypass components or to jump voltage directly to a component or section of a circuit. For example, you could jump a switch in a dead circuit. If the circuit begins to work, the switch is bad.

A test light provides a quick way of checking for power in a circuit. The sharp probe can be touched on a conductor. If the tester bulb glows, you instantly know you have voltage in the circuit.

A voltmeter must be connected in parallel with the circuit. A conventional ammeter must be connected in series. An inductive ammeter can have its lead clipped over the outside of the wire. An ohmmeter must not be connected to a source of power. It uses internal batteries to measure circuit or component resistance.

When reading an analog meter with a needle, make sure you use the correct scale on the meter face. This will depend upon the range switch position. An auto ranging digital meter will automatically adjust for various measurement quantities.

Voltmeter drop measurements provide an easy way of checking for high resistance. You do not have to disconnect the power source and isolate the component, as with an ohmmeter. A high voltage drop indicates a high resistance. A low voltage drop indicates a low resistance.

KNOW THESE TERMS

Circuit problem, Electrical diagnosis, Shotgun troubleshooting, Systematic troubleshooting, Symptoms, Open, High resistance, Short, Hot wire short-to-ground, Electrical fire, Grounded circuit, Intermittent problem, Jumper wire, Self-powered test light, Circuit-powered test light, Continuity, Inductive circuit tracer, Multimeter, VOM, Analog meter, Digital meter, Voltmeter, Ammeter, Ohmmeter, Auto ranging, Ohms calibrate knob, Range knob, Voltage drops, Infinite resistance, Connector test, Resistor test, Switch test, Fuse test, Transducer test, Condenser test, Diode test, Transistor test, Contact cleaner, Freeze spray, Electrical solvent.

REVIEW QUESTIONS—CHAPTER 9

1. What is the meaning of the saying "Veronica never touches much voltage?"
2. If one component does not work, start your tests at the _____.
3. If more than one component does not work, start your tests at the _____ _____.
4. What are five questions you might ask yourself when trying to find a problem?
5. List seven ways of using a systematic approach to electrical troubleshooting.
6. An _____ is a break in a circuit and it will stop current flow.
7. What are some causes of no current flow in a circuit?
8. A high _____ _____ might make a bulb glow dimly or a motor run slowly.
9. Describe the term "electrical fire."
10. An _____ problem is one that only occurs under certain conditions.
11. How would you use a jumper wire to check a switch?
12. This is usually the quickest and easiest way to check a fuse.
    a. Voltmeter.
    b. Self-powered test light.
    c. Circuit-powered test light.
    d. Ohmmeter.
13. An _____ _____ _____ uses a signal generator and inductive pickup to find shorts and opens in wires.
14. This testing device should be used to check for voltage in a computer circuit.
    a. Test light.
    b. Inductive circuit tracer.
    c. Analog multimeter.
    d. Digital multimeter.
15. An ammeter must always be connected in series with the circuit. True or false?
16. How do you use an ohms calibrate knob on an analog meter?
17. An ohmmeter range switch is on RX100 and the needle is pointing at 25. What is the meter reading?
    a. 25M ohms.
    b. 2500 ohms.
    c. 25,000 ohms.
    d. 250K ohms.
18. In your own words, how can you use voltage drop measurements to determine circuit resistance?
19. A car keeps blowing its fuse to the lighting system. Technician A says that a larger amp fuse might correct the trouble quickly and easily.
    Technician B says that installing a larger fuse could cause a serious electrical fire.
    Who is correct?
    a. Technician A.
    b. Technician B.
    c. Both A and B.
    d. Neither A nor B.
20. List ten rules for using multimeters.

Use the circuit drawing in Fig. 9-45 to answer questions 21 through 25. The battery is 12 V (6 cells at 2.1 V each). The bulb burns very dimly with the switch on.
21. Would test A be needed with these symptoms or conditions?
22. What does test B tell you?

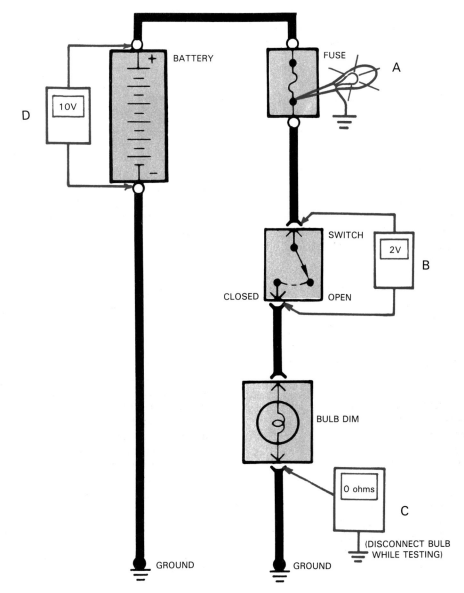

Fig. 9-45. Use this circuit illustration to answer review questions 21 through 25.

23. Test C would verify:
    a. That electricity is not leaking through the bulb socket.
    b. That the ground does not have low resistance.
    c. That the ground does not have high resistance.
    d. All of the above.
    e. None of the above.
24. What would you learn from test D?
25. How would you repair the circuit problem?

ASE CERTIFICATION–TYPE QUESTIONS

1. Technician A says a basic circuit problem is caused by something in the circuit that increases voltage. Technician B says a basic circuit problem is caused by something in the circuit that decreases resistance. Who is right?
   (A) A only.   (C) Both A and B.
   (B) B only.   (D) Neither A nor B.

2. An automobile is brought into the shop with an engine electrical problem. Technician A says the first step to electrical diagnosis is to verify the symptoms and the problem. Technician B says electrical diagnosis involves using a logical sequence of steps to find the source of the problem. Who is right?
   (A) A only.   (C) Both A and B.
   (B) B only.   (D) Neither A nor B.

3. More than one component in a particular automotive electrical circuit is not working. Technician A starts testing the circuit at the power source. Technician B starts testing the circuit at its load. Who is right?
   (A) A only.   (C) Both A and B.
   (B) B only.   (D) Neither A nor B.

4. There is an "open" in an automobile's headlight circuit. Technician A says this problem can be caused by a blown fuse. Technician B says the problem may be caused by burned switch contacts. Who is right?
   (A) A only.   (C) Both A and B.
   (B) B only.   (D) Neither A nor B.

5. Technician A says open will always stop current flow in a circuit. Technician B says high circuit resistance will normally reduce current flow in a circuit. Who is right?
   (A) A only.
   (B) B only.
   (C) Both A and B.
   (D) Neither A nor B.

6. Technician A says a "short circuit" can be caused by a conductor touching ground. Technician B says a "short circuit" can be caused by a conductor touching another conductor. Who is right?
   (A) A only.
   (B) B only.
   (C) Both A and B.
   (D) Neither A nor B.

7. Technician A says intermittent problems occur only under certain conditions. Technician B says intermittent problems are often caused by poor electrical connections. Who is right?
   (A) A only.
   (B) B only.
   (C) Both A and B.
   (D) Neither A nor B.

8. Technician A says an analog multimeter should be used to detect intermittent problems. Technician B says an analog multimeter should be used when testing computer system circuits. Who is right?
   (A) A only.
   (B) B only.
   (C) Both A and B.
   (D) Neither A nor B.

9. The current flow in an automotive taillight circuit needs to be checked. Technician A connects a conventional ammeter parallel with the circuit being tested. Technician B connects a conventional voltmeter in series with the circuit being tested. Who is right?
   (A) A only.
   (B) B only.
   (C) Both A and B.
   (D) Neither A nor B.

10. A particular diode has infinite ohms in both directions. Technician A says this indicates the diode is in good condition. Technician B says this indicates that the diode has an internal short. Who is right?
    (A) A only.
    (B) B only.
    (C) Both A and B.
    (D) Neither A nor B.

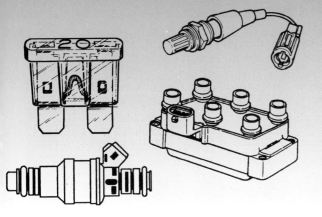

After studying this chapter, you will be able to:
- *List the types of accidents that can happen when doing electrical repairs.*
- *Summarize the dangers that are present on and around an automobile.*
- *Develop a safe work attitude.*
- *Describe general safety rules.*
- *Prevent shop accidents.*
- *Summarize what to do in case of an accident.*

This chapter will quickly review the most important ways of keeping a shop safe. You may have already had previous training in safety, but you should still review the information in this chapter. If you learn just ONE NEW safety technique, it could prevent a serious injury or even save a life.

An automotive electronic technician is exposed to many of the same dangers as an engine technician, front-end technician, or other specialized technician. All technicians must work around running engines, moving cars, cars on jack stands, batteries, electrical equipment, and other potentials for disaster.

The chapter will concentrate on safety that applies to the electronic technician. However, it will also review general safety that applies to everyone in the auto shop.

Remember! You can never know enough about safety!

ELECTRIC SHOCK

Electric shock results when current passes through the tissue of the human body. Your body tissue is actually a good conductor. To prove this, grasp the two test leads on an ohmmeter and it will register your body resistance.

An automobile electrical system operates on low voltage, usually around 13.5 volts with the engine running. This is normally NOT enough electrical pressure to cause electrocution and death. Twelve volts cannot produce enough current flow to damage flesh or upset your nervous system, Fig. 10-1.

A gasoline engine ignition system produces very high voltage—30,000 volts or more. However, this is a very short burst of voltage and current. It usually will not flow long enough to cause electrocution. If shocked by a car's ignition system, you can still be injured by the startle and jolt of pain from the high voltage. For example, if shocked by a spark plug wire, you could jump back and hit your head or fall. Look at Fig. 10-1.

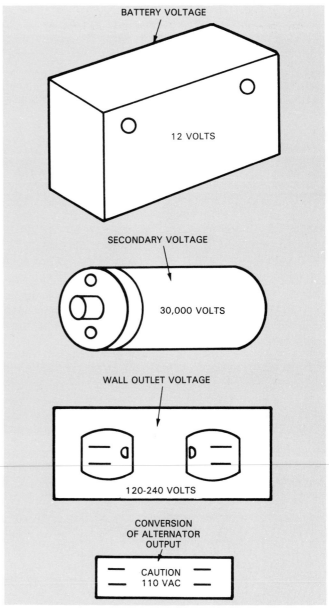

Fig. 10-1. These are the various sources of voltage in an auto shop. Low battery voltage will not cause electrocution. Ignition coil output will produce a startling shock but it is not commonly harmful. Some cars have converters that change alternator output to 110 volts AC, and it can be dangerous. Obviously, 120 or 240 volts in a wall outlet can be fatal.

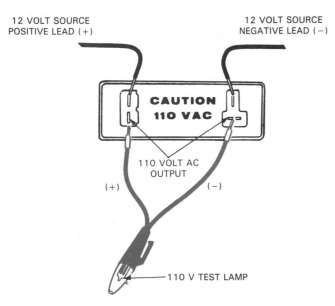

12 VOLT SOURCE POSITIVE LEAD (+)

12 VOLT SOURCE NEGATIVE LEAD (−)

CAUTION 110 VAC

110 VOLT AC OUTPUT

(+)   (−)

110 V TEST LAMP

Fig. 10-2. This is a service manual illustration showing how to use a special 110 volt test light to check AC converter. Do not come into contact with this stepped up voltage and do not use 12 volt test equipment or it can be damaged. (General Motors)

Note! Some cars are equipped with a circuit that converts alternator output into 110 volts AC for running accessory units: heated windshields, camping equipment, etc. This voltage can produce a current flow through your body that can cause electrocution. You do not want to come into contact with this 110 volt output, Fig. 10-2.

When in an auto shop, the most common cause of injury or death from electric shock is from wall outlets because of their 120/240 volt output. Technicians have been electrocuted by test equipment, electric drills, drop lights, and other power equipment.

To prevent electric shock, remember the following rules:

1. Always use the *ground prong* on equipment cords, Fig. 10-3. This round prong is the neutral to ground. If a short develops in the electrical equipment, current will flow through this connection to ground because of its low resistance. If you remove the ground prong, current will seek the next lowest resistance path to ground. This might be through your hands, body, and feet. Death can result!

2. Never use electrical equipment on a wet shop floor. The wet floor can complete the electrical connection from the floor (ground) to your body. You are then a much better conductor of electricity and a "candidate" for electrocution.

3. Keep electrical cords in good condition. If the insulation is cut or damaged, repair or replace the cord. Any exposed conductors in cords could be extremely dangerous.

4. Remember the danger of a broken lightbulb in a drop light. When a bulb is broken, "hot" conductors are exposed. If you touch the conductors in the broken bulb, you could be killed.

5. Never place a drop light where it could be splashed with coolant or other liquid. If splashed with a liquid, a hot bulb can break. Then, the exposed conductors can send current through the liquid. Someone standing in or touching the liquid (coolant for example) could then be electrocuted and die.

6. Respect wall outlet electricity. If you touch a high voltage, high current source, it will make your muscles reflex, contract, and tighten. This could make your hand automatically or involuntarily grasp the conductor even tighter. Even more current could flow through your hand and arm. If this current reaches the nerves running to your heart, your heart could stop beating and you could "meet your maker."

7. Some people are more susceptible to electric shock than others. Also, injury is dependent upon the path current takes through your body. One time current may harmlessly pass along the surface of your skin. However, the next time, the same current could cause death by passing to nerves that control your heart or breathing. Your body is a chemical-electrical machine; don't let a current source "short out your life."

8. Condensers can store electrical energy. Although they cannot be lethal, they can shock and scare you. This scare could cause other injuries as you jump back or fling your arms away from the shock. Discharge condensers by grounding their leads before handling them.

ELECTRICAL BURNS

Electrical burns are caused by the heat from electricity. Studied in earlier chapters, heat is the common output of electric current. The heat of a glowing lightbulb is one example. The heat from a soldering gun is another. Your eyes can also be burned by an electric arc.

For example, a technician was working under the dashboard of a car. The drop light she was using had a damaged cord. The damaged section of the cord was near her face when the wires shorted together. The resulting electric arc and flash caused severe eye burns and permanent eye damage.

In another example, a technician's finger was badly burned by a ring that was being worn while working on a

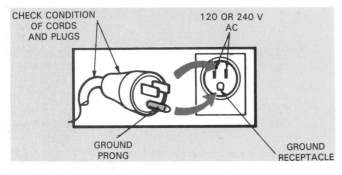

CHECK CONDITION OF CORDS AND PLUGS

120 OR 240 V AC

GROUND PRONG

GROUND RECEPTACLE

Fig. 10-3. Always make sure ground prong is not broken off plug. If power tool shorts out, current will pass through this ground connection. Without the ground, current can pass through your body if tool is shorted. (Ford)

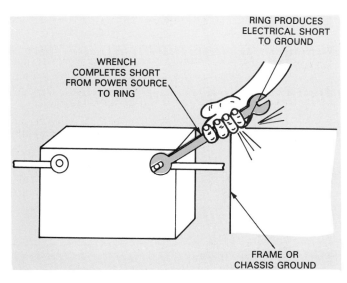

WRENCH COMPLETES SHORT FROM POWER SOURCE TO RING

RING PRODUCES ELECTRICAL SHORT TO GROUND

FRAME OR CHASSIS GROUND

Fig. 10-4. Here is one example of how jewelry can cause serious injury. Ring causes short circuit between car body and wrench. Huge current flows through ring. Ring becomes red hot, seriously burning technician's finger.

car battery. The technician was using a wrench to loosen a positive battery cable end. The ring came into contact with the car body and the wrench. A tremendous electrical short to ground resulted through the wrench and ring, Fig. 10-4.

Since the ring was a much smaller conductor than the wrench, it instantly became a heating element, conducting possibly a thousand or more amps. In a fraction of a second, the ring actually glowed "red hot" and the technician's finger sizzled from the glowing metal. The semi-molten ring could not be pulled off; so the technician ran screaming to the sink where the ring was dowsed with water and cooled.

To this day, the technician has a deep burn scar on his ring finger. Now he is smart enough to no longer wear a ring while working.

ELECTRICAL FIRES

Mentioned in earlier chapters, an *electrical fire* is the result of excess current heating and burning wire insulation. For instance, one wire may short to ground. It will then draw high current and begin to heat up. With more heat, the insulation can catch on fire. This can burn through the insulation on other wires. Then, a whole bundle of wires can start burning.

An electrical fire can happen in a few seconds and hundreds of dollars of damage can result or the whole car could burn up and be destroyed.

To prevent electrical fires, you must:
1. Disconnect the car battery when doing electrical repairs. When electrical wires are to be disconnected or electrical components removed, it is wise to disconnect the battery. Then, there is no possibility of wires shorting out and causing an electrical fire.
2. Make sure wires are not pinched under parts. It is

easy for a wire to drop down and get caught under other components. When you tighten fasteners, the part can smash down on the wire. The insulation can be split and the conductor could be grounded. When you reconnect the battery, a short and electrical fire could then result.
3. Never replace a bad wire with a wire of smaller diameter. A smaller size wire could overheat and begin to burn from current flow. Use a replacement wire of equal or larger size.
4. Do not use an extension cord that is too small for the load. If too small, an extension cord can overheat and burn. If you feel an extension cord getting warm, it is overloaded.
5. Do not connect too many cords into one wall outlet socket. This could make the wires in the shop wall overheat and burn.
6. Never replace a burned fuse with a fuse of a higher amp rating. The larger fuse will not limit normal current. The fuse may not blow or burn when needed, and an electrical fire may result from excess current in a circuit.

BATTERY DANGERS

Battery safety involves understanding the potential dangers of a car battery: chemical burns, facial cuts, loss of eyesight, and other injuries from battery explosions.

Battery explosions

Battery explosions can happen when a flame or spark ignites hydrogen gas that can hover over the top of a battery case. Hydrogen gas is produced when a lead-acid battery is being charged or discharged. *Hydrogen gas* is extremely flammable; our sun is burning hydrogen gas.

If only the hydrogen gas around the top of a battery ignites, it will sound like a large caliber gun going off. Only minor battery damage may result.

However, if the gas inside the case is ignited, a much more harmful battery explosion may result. Pressure can rapidly rise in the case until the case explodes. Chunks of battery case and a spray of *battery acid* can shoot out into the shop. If someone is near the battery, this can cause blindness and acid burns to the face and hands.

To prevent battery explosions, you must:
1. Keep sparks and flames away from batteries being recharged and from bad batteries that could be internally shorted and emitting large amounts of hydrogen gas.
2. Connect a battery charger to the battery BEFORE turning on or plugging in the battery charger. If the charger is on, a spark can jump to the battery as you connect the second charger lead. This could ignite any battery gas.
3. When connecting jumper cables between two batteries, make the last ground connection away from the battery. The black, ground jumper cable can be connected to any frame or chassis ground. Then, if there is a small spark, it will occur away from the battery.
4. When charging a battery, make sure the area is well ventilated. Also check that the battery is taking a charge and is not overheating.

Battery safety

There are several other rules you should follow when working with car batteries. These include:

1. Use a battery strap or carrier to remove and install car batteries. They are clumsy and heavy when trying to lift them in and out of a tight engine compartment. See Fig. 10-5.
2. Wear *eye protection* when working around a battery. The battery is full of acid that can cause serious eye damage. If you drop a battery, acid could squirt into your face, Fig. 10-6.
3. To protect the charging system alternator, disconnect the battery cables before charging a dead battery.
4. Never lay tools on top of a battery. They can short across the terminals, damaging the tools and battery. The battery could possibly explode! Acid can also corrode the tools.

GASOLINE DANGERS

Even in electrical repair, you will be working around gasoline—a tremendously flammable substance. You must remember several rules that apply to gasoline safety. These include:

1. NEVER use gasoline as a cleaning agent. Cleaning solvents are NOT as flammable as gasoline.
2. Keep sources of heat (soldering gun or torch for example) away from the engine's fuel system.
3. Wipe up gasoline spills right away. Do not spread "quick dry" (oil absorbent) on gasoline because the absorbent will become even more flammable.

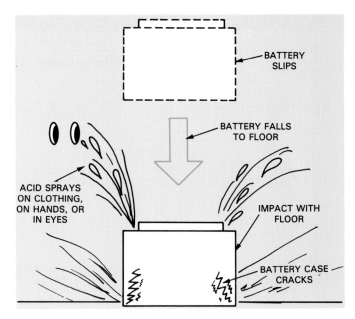

Fig. 10-6. If you drop a battery, acid can fly onto your hands or into your eyes. Wear eye protection, gloves, and use a carrier when moving a battery.

4. Disconnect the car battery when disconnecting a fuel line on an engine.
5. Wrap a rag around any fitting when disconnecting a fuel line. This will keep fuel from leaking or spraying out and possibly starting a fire when striking hot engine parts or electrical components that could produce a spark.
6. Store gasoline and other flammables in approved containers with a lid.

IN CASE OF FIRE

In the event of a fire in the shop, you should:

1. Shout to inform everyone in the shop of the fire.
2. Unless instructed otherwise, try to contain the fire if not too severe. Use the recommended type of fire extinguisher. Fig. 10-7 shows a chart summarizing fire extinguisher types.
3. If the fire is near a large quantity of gasoline or other flammables, get out of the shop. An explosion could engulf the shop in flames.
4. Call the fire department immediately if the fire cannot be extinguished.
5. Know the fire evacuation routes from the shop.
6. Try to prevent fires. Report any unsafe conditions to your instructor.

OTHER SHOP DANGERS

There are many other shop dangers besides those just discussed. For example, Fig. 10-8 shows some of the ways that you can be injured by a car itself.

Always think safety! Try to foresee anything that could inure you or others. In an auto shop, there are literally hundreds of different ways that you can be badly hurt or killed.

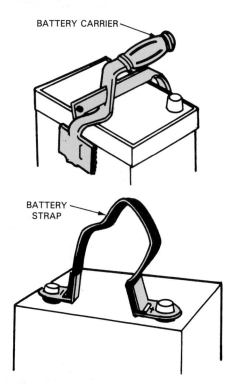

Fig. 10-5. Use a carrier or battery strap when installing or removing a car battery. (Florida Dept. of Voc. Ed.)

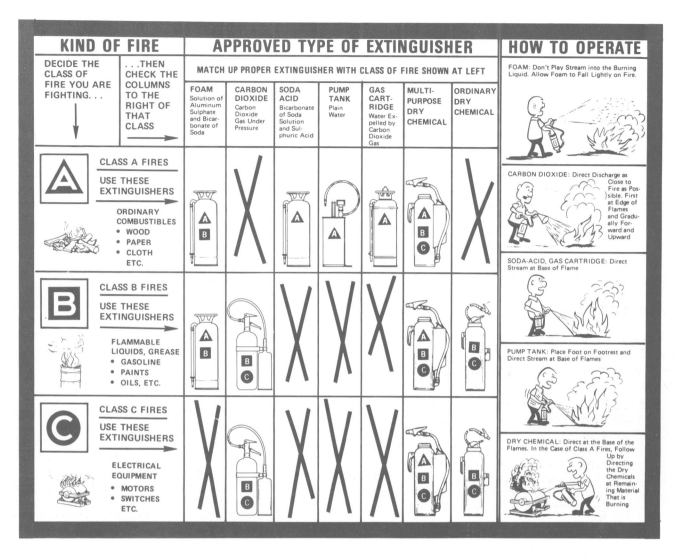

Fig. 10-7. Chart shows summary of fire extinguisher types and how they should be used. (Ford Motor Co.)

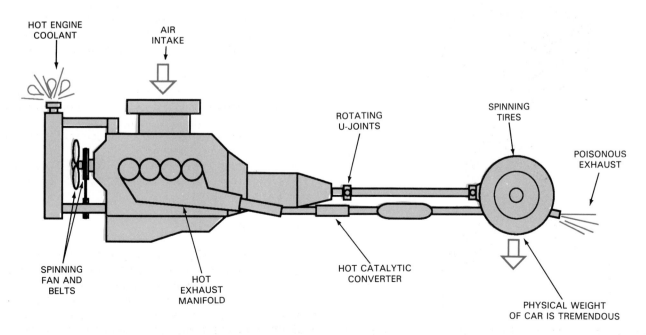

Fig. 10-8. These are some of the potential dangers on an automobile.

BASIC SAFETY RULES

Given are some basic safety rules that should be followed:

1. Wear eye protection when doing anything that could endanger your eyes! This would include operating power tools, working around a spinning engine fan, and carrying batteries. Look at Fig. 10-9.
2. Avoid anyone who does not take shop work seriously. Remember, a "clown" in an auto shop is "an accident just waiting to happen."
3. Keep your shop organized! Return all tools and equipment to their proper storage areas. Never leave tools, creepers, or parts on the floor.
4. Dress like a technician! Remove rings, bracelets, necklaces, watches, and other jewelry. They could cause electrical shorts or they could get caught in engine fans, belts, etc.—tearing off flesh, fingers, and ears. Roll up long sleeves and secure long hair; they can get caught in spinning parts.
6. Wear full face protection when grinding, welding, and during other operations where eye hazards are present, Fig. 10-9.
7. Work like a professional! When learning to be an automotive electronic technician, it is easy to get excited about your work. Avoid working too fast. You could overlook a repair procedure or safety rule and cause an accident.
8. Use the right tool for the job! There is usually a "best tool" for each repair task. Always ask yourself this question—is there another tool that will work better?
9. Keep equipment guards or shields in place! If a power tool has a guard, use it!
10. Lift with your legs, NOT with your back. When lifting, bend at your knees while keeping your back as straight at possible.

11. Use adequate lighting! A portable shop light increases working safety and also increases work speed and precision.
12. Ventilate your work area when needed! Turn on the shop *ventilation fan* or open shop doors any time fumes are present in the shop, Fig. 10-10.
13. Never stir up asbestos dust! *Asbestos* is a powerful CANCER-CAUSING AGENT. Do NOT use compressed air to blow asbestos dust off parts.
14. Jack up or raise a car slowly and safely! A car can weigh between one and two tons. Never work under a car unless it is supported by *jack stands.* It is NOT safe to work under a car held by a floor jack. Also, chock wheels when the car is on jack stands, Figs. 10-11 and 10-12.
15. Drive slowly when in the shop area! With other students and cars in the shop, it is very easy to have an accident.
16. Report unsafe conditions to your instructor! If you notice any type of hazard, inform your instructor right away.
17. Keep away from engine fans! The fan on a car engine is like a SPINNING KNIFE. It can inflict serious injuries. Also, if a part or tool is dropped

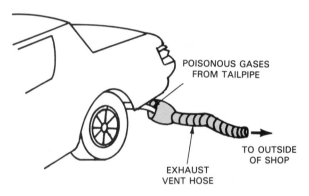

Fig. 10-10. Always install a shop vent hose over tailpipe of any car engine running in closed shop. This will prevent buildup of toxic fumes in shop.

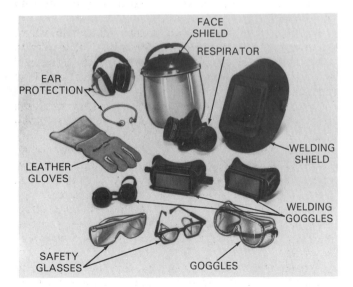

Fig. 10-9. Always use a protection device when needed. Remember to think of potential dangers and the action that must be taken to prevent injury.

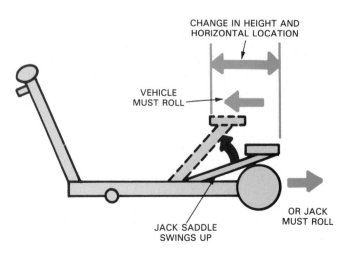

Fig. 10-11. When using a jack to raise a car, remember that either the jack or car must be able to roll. If not, jack saddle could slip and car could fall.

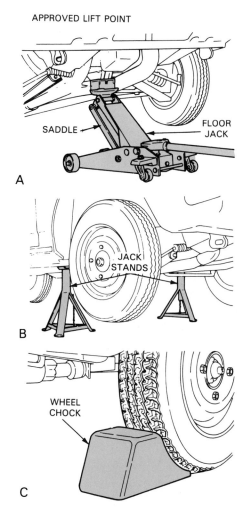

APPROVED LIFT POINT

SADDLE

FLOOR JACK

A

JACK STANDS

B

WHEEL CHOCK

C

Fig. 10-12. Secure a car properly before working under it. (Subaru) A—Make sure floor jack is on recommended lift point under car to prevent damage or slippage. B—After raising car, place jack stands under recommended points. Never work under a car unless it is on jack stands or on recommended lift. A floor jack could lower car and crush you. C—Once car is on jack stands, block wheels to keep car from rolling off stands.

into the fan, it can fly out and hit someone or damage the radiator.

18. Respect running engines! When a car engine is running, make sure the transmission or transaxle is in Park. Check that the emergency brake is set, and the wheels are blocked. If the transmission were knocked into gear, it could run over you or a friend.

19. No smoking! No one should smoke in an auto shop. Smoking is a serious fire hazard considering fuel lines, cleaning solvents, and other flammables may be exposed.

20. *Lead* absorbed through the skin and lungs can cause anemia, nerve damage, and brain disorders. Lead can be found in exhaust gases and gasoline of older cars. Avoid contact with lead!

21. *Chemical pneumonia* can result from inhaling oil mist. Dermatitis can result from too much skin contact with oil.

22. Obtain permission before using any new or unfamiliar power tool, lift, or other shop equipment! Your instructor or supervisor will need to give a demonstration.

23. ATTENTION! If an accident or injury ever occurs in the shop, notify your instructor or supervisor immediately. Use common sense on deciding to get a fire extinguisher or take other action.

SUMMARY

You can never know enough about safety! Always think safety when working. Try to detect unsafe conditions or procedures to prevent injuries.

Electric shock results when current passes through the tissue of the human body. Battery or charging system voltage will normally not produce enough current flow to cause a severe electric shock.

An engine ignition system produces very high voltage that can cause a painful shock. However, the current flow is so low that it is not normally a cause of electrocution. The painful shock can make you jump and become injured in other ways.

Some cars have a special circuit that changes alternator output to 110 volts. This is dangerous and could cause electrocution in some situations.

Wall outlet voltage can be 120 or 240 volts. This is the most common source of shop electrocution and death. Make sure the ground prong is on all electrical cords to help prevent electrocution.

Never use electrical equipment on a wet floor. Water and other fluids can make you a better conductor of electricity. A broken lightbulb is very dangerous since the bare conductors in the bulb are exposed. Never allow any fluid to spill on a hot lightbulb.

Discharge condensers or capacitors before handling them. They can store a charge and cause a startling shock if not grounded first.

Heat is a common output of electricity. An electric arc can burn your eyes. Current can also heat parts or jewelry to cause serious burns. Never wear jewelry of any kind while working.

Electrical fires result from excess current in wires. Disconnect the battery when doing electrical repairs to prevent shorts. Do not pinch wires under parts. Use equal or larger size replacement wire. Use the correct amp fuse replacement. Do not overload extension cords.

Car batteries can be very dangerous. They can emit hydrogen gas that is tremendously explosive. Keep sparks and flames away from batteries. Charge a battery in a well ventilated area. Wear eye protection when working around batteries. Use a battery strap or carrier when moving batteries. Disconnect the alternator when recharging a battery. Never place tools on a battery.

Gasoline poses a constant danger in an auto shop. Never solder or weld near gasoline, fuel hoses, or lines. Wipe up fuel spills right away. Store fuels in approved containers.

In case of a fire, inform everyone in the shop. Try to contain the fire if not too severe. Get out of the shop if told to do so by your supervisor or instructor. Call the fire department if needed. Know the shop's fire evacuation routes. Try to prevent fires!

Use common sense, an alert attitude, and basic safety procedures to keep your shop safe.

OTHER SAFETY RULES

Other more specialized safety rules are given in later chapters where they apply. This will help you remember and relate to these important rules more completely. Only the most general safety rules for the electronic technician have been discussed in this chapter.

KNOW THESE TERMS

Electric shock, Ground prong, Electrical burns, Electrical fire, Battery safety, Battery explosions, Hydrogen gas, Battery acid, Eye protection, Ventilation fan, Asbestos, Jack stands, Lead, Chemical pneumonia.

REVIEW QUESTIONS—CHAPTER 10

1. This is the most common cause of electrocution in an auto shop.
   a. Car batteries.
   b. Converters for 110 volts.
   c. Ignition voltage of 30,000 volts.
   d. 120-240 volt wall outlets.
2. Why is the ground prong on a cord so important?
3. What can happen if fluid spills on a hot drop light?
4. In your own words, how could a ring on your finger cause a bad burn when doing electrical repair?
5. What is an "electrical fire"?

ASE CERTIFICATION–TYPE QUESTIONS

1. Technician A says the voltage produced by an automotive ignition system is enough to cause a painful shock. Technician B says the current produced by an automotive ignition system usually does not flow long enough to cause electrocution. Who is right?
   (A) A only.   (C) Both A and B.
   (B) B only.   (D) Neither A nor B.
2. Technician A says some automobiles are equipped with a circuit that converts alternator output into 110 volts AC. Technician B says 110 volts AC can produce enough current to cause electrocution. Who is right?
   (A) A only.   (C) Both A and B.
   (B) B only.   (D) Neither A nor B.
3. While discussing how to prevent electrical fires, Technician A says you should disconnect the battery before performing electrical repairs on a car. Technician B says you should always replace a burned fuse with a fuse of a higher amp rating. Who is right?
   (A) A only.   (C) Both A and B.
   (B) B only.   (D) Neither A nor B.

4. Technician A says hydrogen gas is produced when a lead-acid battery is charged. Technician B says nitrogen gas is produced when a lead-acid battery is discharged. Who is right?
   (A) A only.   (C) Both A and B.
   (B) B only.   (D) Neither A nor B.
5. While discussing the rules to follow when working with an automotive battery, Technician A says you should never lay tools on top of a battery. Technician B says you should charge a battery in a well ventilated area. Who is right?
   (A) A only.   (C) Both A and B.
   (B) B only.   (D) Neither A nor B.
6. A battery must be removed from an automobile. Technician A says to wear eye protection when removing the battery from the car. Technician B says that a battery carrier should be used to lift the battery from the engine compartment. Who is right?
   (A) A only.   (C) Both A and B.
   (B) B only.   (D) Neither A nor B.
7. An automobile's battery needs charging. Technician A says you should plug a battery charger into the electrical outlet before connecting it to the battery. Technician B says you should disconnect the battery cables before connecting the battery charger to the car's battery. Who is right?
   (A) A only.   (C) Both A and B.
   (B) B only.   (D) Neither A nor B.
8. A fuel line needs to be disconnected from an EFI fuel system. Technician A says to wrap a shop rag around the fitting before removing the fuel line. Technician B says to disconnect the car's battery before removing this fuel line. Who is right?
   (A) A only.   (C) Both A and B.
   (B) B only.   (D) Neither A nor B.
9. All of the following are potential dangers when working on an automobile except:
   (A) hot exhaust manifold. (C) spinning engine fan.
   (B) hot ECR valve.   (D) rotating U-joints.
10. Technician A says it is acceptable to work under a car supported by a floor jack. Technician B says it is acceptable to work under a car supported by jack stands. Who is right?
    (A) A only.   (C) Both A and B.
    (B) B only.   (D) Neither A nor B.

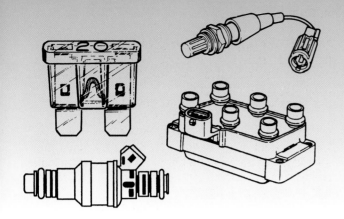

Chapter 11

Computers, Sensors, Actuators

After studying this chapter, you will be able to:
- Compare a computer system to the human nervous system.
- Describe the input, processing, and output sections of a basic computer system.
- Explain sensor classifications.
- Explain actuator classifications.
- Sketch a block diagram of a fundamental computer network.
- Summarize where computers, control modules, sensors, and actuators are typically located.
- Explain the basic parts of a computer.
- Summarize the flow of data through a computer.
- Explain how a computer uses sensor inputs to determine correct outputs for actuators.
- Describe the operation of vehicle sensors.
- Explain the operation of vehicle actuators.

Automotive computer systems are a "blessing" to the car owner because of the advantages and conveniences they provide. However, computers can be a "curse" to the poorly trained mechanic. Computer system devices can be found almost everywhere on a vehicle or from "bumper to bumper" (engine compartment to trunk). It is almost impossible to work on any system of a late model car that does not rely on computer control in some way. As a result, it takes a knowledgeable technician to work on today's vehicles—a technician who is trained in computers, sensors, and actuators.

This chapter will introduce the operating fundamentals of computer systems. Knowing how computers, sensors, and actuators work will help you develop the skills needed to properly diagnose and repair computer systems. If you can visualize the operation of an electronic system, you will be better prepared to analyze problems, select proper tests, and replace failed components.

Note! Several earlier chapters introduced information essential to the full understanding of this chapter. These chapters explained transistors, logic gates, integrated circuits, truth tables, the binary numbering system, etc. Make sure you comprehend these subjects before starting this chapter. Chapter 5 is especially important to the full understanding of computer systems.

CYBERNETICS

The term *cybernetics* refers to the study of how electrical-mechanical mechanisms can duplicate the actions of the human body. Comparing the human body to a computer system is an easy way to introduce this subject.

Just as your brain can communicate with and control the parts of your body, an automotive computer system can communicate with and control parts of a car.

Fig. 11-1 shows a chart that compares our nervous system with a computer system. Note how human senses can be related to vehicle sensors and human actions to computer actuators.

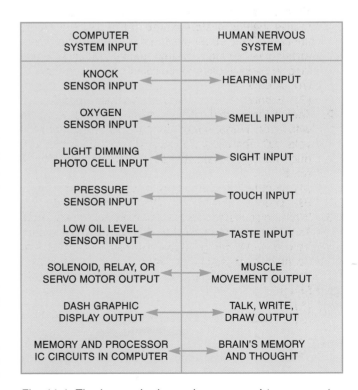

COMPUTER SYSTEM INPUT	HUMAN NERVOUS SYSTEM
KNOCK SENSOR INPUT	HEARING INPUT
OXYGEN SENSOR INPUT	SMELL INPUT
LIGHT DIMMING PHOTO CELL INPUT	SIGHT INPUT
PRESSURE SENSOR INPUT	TOUCH INPUT
LOW OIL LEVEL SENSOR INPUT	TASTE INPUT
SOLENOID, RELAY, OR SERVO MOTOR OUTPUT	MUSCLE MOVEMENT OUTPUT
DASH GRAPHIC DISPLAY OUTPUT	TALK, WRITE, DRAW OUTPUT
MEMORY AND PROCESSOR IC CIRCUITS IN COMPUTER	BRAIN'S MEMORY AND THOUGHT

Fig. 11-1. The human body can be compared to a computer system. Our human senses are comparable to the system's sensors, and our actions are comparable to the system's actuators.

Nervous system (input)

Your *nervous system* uses chemical-electrical signals to control body functions. For example, if you touch a hot stove, nerve cells in your finger "fire," sending a signal through a strand of nerve cells. The signal travels up your arm and into your brain. The strand of nerve cells forms a "wire" that connects your finger to your brain.

The nerve cells in the tip of your finger are comparable to an *input* sensor. They convert the heat of the hot stove into a signal.

The brain (processing)

Your brain is comparable to a "super powerful" computer. It can *process* inputs from the nervous system and determine what corrective actions should be taken. Its billions of cells are comparable to billions of logic gates.

In our example, the chemical-electrical signal of a hot stove would be sent into a specific area in the brain. The brain cells in that area are organized or programmed to analyze the inputs from your finger. Since the signal would tell the brain "my finger is being burned," the brain would take corrective action to protect your finger.

The brain makes decisions much like logic gates produce logical outputs depending upon its inputs. The billions of cells in the brain can be either CHARGED (on or one) or they may NOT be charged (off or zero). By connecting all of the brain cells into logic circuits, the brain can decide what to do with each situation.

The reflex action (output)

The finger burn signal would activate specific brain cells and a reflex output would be produced by the brain. The brain would send a signal back into the arm. This chemical-electrical output would stimulate the muscles in the arm to pull the finger from the hot stove.

The reflex action of your muscles would be comparable to an actuator or *output,* in a car's computer system. Depending upon sensor inputs, the computer will produce logical outputs to make the actuators make corrective actions.

HARDWARE AND SOFTWARE

The physical components in automotive computer systems are referred to as *hardware.* Hardware items include sensors, wiring harnesses, actuators, and electronic control units (computers).

The term *software* is used to refer to the programs that are stored in a computer. Software tells the computer what to do and when to do it. It also provides the computer with the information needed to interpret data and make decisions.

COMPUTER ADVANTAGES

Computers provide several advantages that increase driver comfort, safety, and convenience, including:
1. Computers can compensate for mechanical wear of components. Also, they do NOT have as many mechanical parts to wear and go out of calibration. Mechanical control systems wear and can no longer be accurate after a prolonged period of service.
2. Computers are very fast and can alter outputs in milliseconds (thousandths of a second). This lets a computer alter outputs almost instantly as input conditions change. Vehicle efficiency is improved.
3. Computers reduce fuel consumption by more precise control of fuel metering into the engine. Today's systems actually "sniff" the exhaust gases to find out if too much or too little fuel is entering the engine.
4. Computers can increase engine power by more accurate control of ignition timing, fuel injection, emission control system operation, etc.
5. Computers can reduce vehicle weight because they are lighter than mechanical control mechanisms. This improves fuel economy and acceleration.
6. Computers can help find system problems. Most computers have a self-test or self-diagnosis capability. They can produce an output code that tells the technician where a fault might be located.
7. Computers can increase driver convenience by better control of the passenger compartment environment and dash displays.
8. Computers can improve passenger safety by controlling the brake and suspension systems.
9. Computers can compensate and correct for component wear and failure to keep the car driveable.

The main disadvantage of a computer system is complexity. An untrained mechanic will have a very difficult time trying to fix a faulty computer system. However, as automakers standardize computer systems by using the same number and types of components and self-diagnostic systems, computer systems will become less confusing in the future.

COMPUTER ACTION

As mentioned, there are three stages of computer operation:
1. INPUT (vehicle sensors convert a condition into an electrical signal for the computer).
2. PROCESSING (computer uses sensor signals or inputs to determine what action should be taken to control vehicle operation).
3. OUTPUT (computer produces electrical output so actuators can perform physical actions to alter component operation for better efficiency).

Fig. 11-2 shows the three stages of computer operation. You must visualize this flow of electrical data.

Input classification (sensor categories)

An automobile uses several types of sensors to provide electrical data to the computer. The major sensor or input classifications include:
1. VARIABLE RESISTOR TYPE SENSOR (this type sensor changes its internal resistance with a change in a condition; its ohms value may change with temperature, pressure, etc.).
2. POTENTIOMETER TYPE SENSOR (like a variable resistor, it also varies resistance, and the resulting voltage signal with a change in a condition; this type is commonly used to sense part movement).
3. SWITCHING TYPE SENSOR (it opens or closes the sensor circuit to provide an electrical signal for the computer; it can sense almost any condition).
4. VOLTAGE GENERATOR TYPE SENSOR (this type sensor produces its own voltage output internally).
5. MAGNETIC TYPE SENSOR (it uses part movement

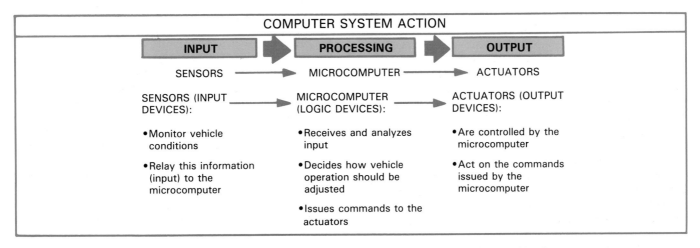

Fig. 11-2. These are the three stages of computer system operation. (Ford)

and induced current to produce a signal for the computer; this type is commonly used to sense speed or part rotation).

As you will learn later, there are dozens of specific names for vehicle sensors. However, they can all be classified into one of these five categories. Fig. 11-3A illustrates these input types.

Output classification (actuator categories)

A computer system also uses several types of actuators or outputs to control component or part operation. The major actuator or output classifications include:

1. SOLENOID TYPE OUTPUT (current through solenoid winding forms magnetic field that can move metal core and act upon other components).
2. RELAY TYPE OUTPUT (current flow from computer energizes relay to control larger current flow to another electrical component).
3. SERVO MOTOR TYPE OUTPUT (current is sent to small DC motor that can produce an output by turning and moving parts).

4. DISPLAY TYPE OUTPUT (current is sent to vacuum fluorescent or liquid crystal display to provide output data in car dash).
5. CONTROL MODULE OUTPUT (computer sends electrical signal to electronic control module; control module then amplifies or modifies signal to operate one of the previous four output devices).

Fig. 11-3B shows these types of outputs. Imagine how they could be used to control engine functions: idle speed, EGR valve action, etc.

Computer block diagram

A *computer block diagram* is a simple drawing that shows how the sensors, actuators, and computer interact. It uses basic squares or rectangles to show components and lines to show wires. A computer block diagram is handy when trying to find out what types of sensors are used and what conditions are controlled by a specific computer system.

Fig. 11-4 shows a block diagram for one computer control system. The computer or electronic control unit

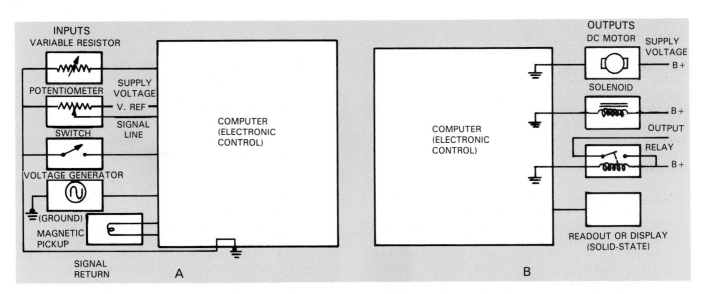

Fig. 11-3. Vehicle sensors and actuators can be categorized into groups. A—Note vehicle sensor categories. Resistor and switching sensors require a reference voltage to return signal to computer. B—Note actuator classifications. Computer will produce current output so actuators can alter operation of other components.

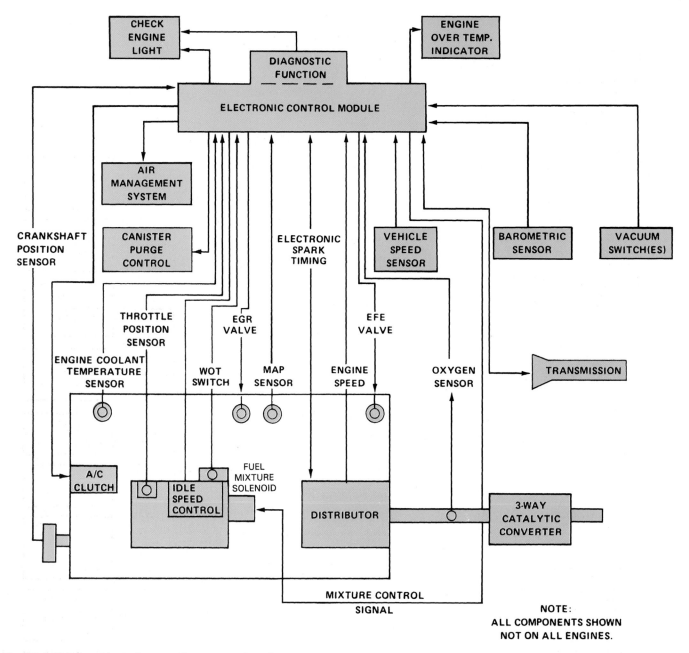

Fig. 11-4. This is a block diagram of one type of engine control computer system. Note conditions sensed and outputs controlled. (Oldsmobile)

is at the top. The engine is shown as a large box near the bottom. Study the various inputs and outputs.

Fig. 11-5 gives another block diagram illustrating computer action. The inputs are all on the left and the outputs are on the right. Note that this system uses a main computer or electronic control module and a second body computer.

COMPUTER LOCATIONS

Automotive computers are commonly located under the vehicle's dashboard, Fig. 11-6. This protects the delicate circuits and components in the computer from engine heat, vibration, and moisture. Computers can also be located in the engine compartment, in the trunk, under seats, etc.

When in the engine compartment, the computer is closer to most sensors and actuators. Less wiring and fewer connectors are needed to tie the system together. Control modules and power modules are often found in the engine compartment. The main computer is often mounted under the dash. See Fig. 11-7.

COMPUTER NAMES

The term *computer* refers to any electronic circuit configuration that can use multiple inputs to find outputs. Automobile manufacturers use many names for their computers, including:
1. Central processing unit (CPU).
2. Electronic control unit (ECU).
3. Electronic control module (ECM).

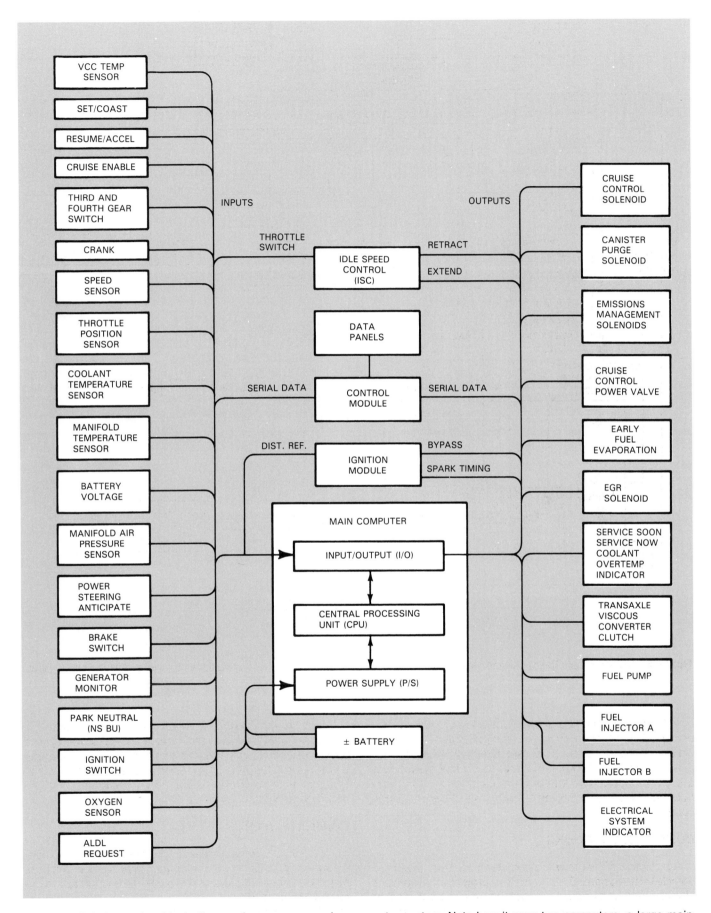

Fig. 11-5. This is another block diagram for a more complex computer system. Note how it uses two computers, a large main computer and a smaller control module. (Cadillac)

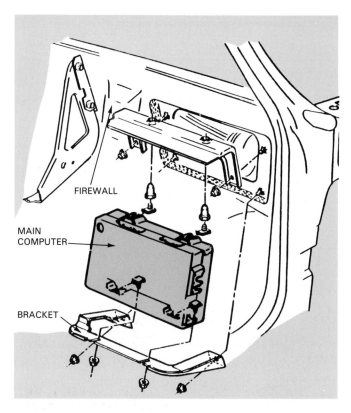

FIREWALL

MAIN COMPUTER

BRACKET

Fig. 11-6. The main computer normally mounts under car dash. This helps protect it from vibration, moisture, heat, and other conditions that could ruin it.   (General Motors)

4. Engine control module (ECM).
5. Electronic control assembly (ECA).
6. Power train control module (PCM).
7. Vehicle control module (VCM).
8. Microprocessor.
9. Logic module.

Keep these names in mind when reading service manuals. To prevent confusion, this textbook will use the term computer when referring to computers in general. When discussing a computer used to control one or more specific systems, the text will use the terms recommended by the Society of Automotive Engineers (J1930). Additionally, the term "module" will be used for an electronic circuit used to amplify and/or modify a single signal or control a single system, such as the module used to control the operation of the anti-lock brake (ABS) system. See Fig. 11-8.

COMPUTER TYPES

Several computers are often used in late-model vehicles. The number and types of computers will vary with the manufacturer. The most common types are:

1. VEHICLE CONTROL MODULE (powerful computer that processes data from sensors and other less powerful computers. It might coordinate engine, transmission, and anti-lock brake functions, for example).
2. ENGINE CONTROL MODULE (computer that uses sensor inputs to control engine operating conditions).
3. POWER TRAIN CONTROL MODULE (powerful

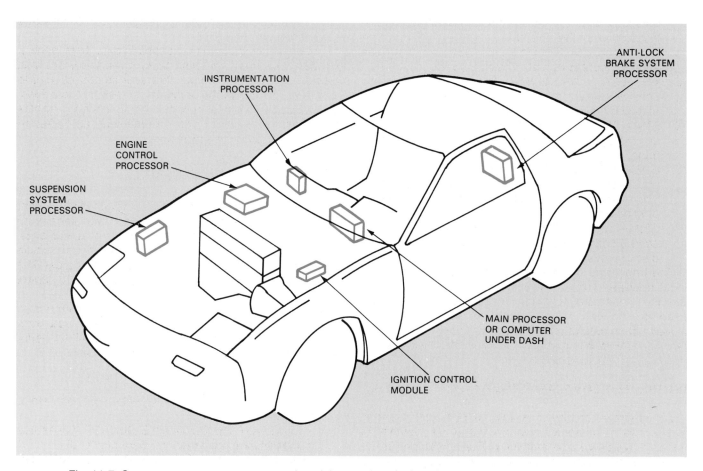

INSTRUMENTATION PROCESSOR

ANTI-LOCK BRAKE SYSTEM PROCESSOR

ENGINE CONTROL PROCESSOR

SUSPENSION SYSTEM PROCESSOR

MAIN PROCESSOR OR COMPUTER UNDER DASH

IGNITION CONTROL MODULE

Fig. 11-7. One or more computers or control modules can be used on the same car. Note potential locations.

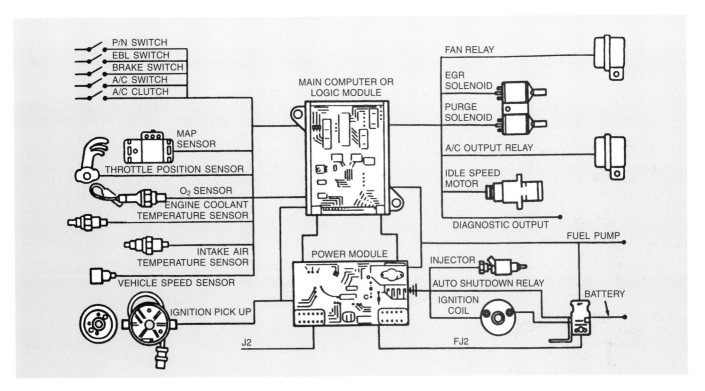

Fig. 11-8. Service manuals can call a computer by many other names—logic module, ECU, ECM, etc. To avoid confusion, the term computer will refer to the most powerful electronic control unit. The term module will mean a smaller computer that helps the main computer.   (Chrysler)

computer used to monitor and control engine, transmission, and other systems).

4. INSTRUMENTATION MODULE (computer that uses sensor inputs to operate dash displays).

5. ANTI-LOCK BRAKE MODULE (small module that uses wheel sensor inputs and other inputs to control anti-lock brake application).

6. IGNITION CONTROL MODULE (module that uses sensor inputs to control ignition timing, spark plug firing, or ignition coil pack operation).

7. SUSPENSION SYSTEM MODULE (module that uses suspension system, vehicle speed, and possibly steering sensor inputs to control ride stiffness or shock absorber action).

8. CLIMATE CONTROL MODULE (module used to control operation of heating, ventilation, and air conditioning systems).

The trend is to use a main computer to process most input data and control most outputs. In conjunction with the main computer, smaller computers (modules) are used for the brake system, ignition coils, suspension system, instrumentation, etc. Refer to an appropriate service manual to determine what types of computers are used on a specific vehicle.

INTEGRATED COMPUTER SYSTEM (MULTIPLEXING)

An *integrated computer system,* or *computer network,* is a series of computer systems that work together to improve overall vehicle efficiency. The computers in the network share common parts and wires. They exchange data from sensors to prevent duplication of parts and to reduce wiring. The term *multiplexing* is used to describe the interaction in vehicles.

A central computer uses feedback data from several smaller computer systems (braking, suspension, and traction control, for example) to better control all vehicle systems. This allows the computer to monitor more functions to better decide how to control braking, throttle action, ride stiffness, engine management, and differential action for optimum efficiency.

VEHICLE SENSOR OPERATION

A *vehicle sensor* is a transducer that changes a condition into an electrical signal. *Transduce* means to change from one medium to another. Just as our eyes, ears, nose, fingers, etc. can sense conditions, vehicle sensors can detect the operating conditions of a car. The computers use these "senses" (voltage signals) to control the actuators.

It is critical that you fully understand the operation of the most common types of vehicle sensors. If you know how sensors are supposed to operate, you will be better at finding a sensor that is NOT working properly.

Sensor types

The most common vehicle sensors that provide data to the main computer include:

1. INTAKE AIR TEMPERATURE SENSOR (measures temperature of air entering intake manifold).

2. ENGINE COOLANT TEMPERATURE SENSOR (measures temperature of engine coolant).

3. OXYGEN SENSOR (measures amount of oxygen in engine exhaust gases).
4. MANIFOLD ABSOLUTE PRESSURE SENSOR (measures pressure or vacuum inside engine intake manifold).
5. BAROMETRIC PRESSURE SENSOR (measures atmospheric pressure around engine).
6. THROTTLE POSITION SENSOR (measures opening angle of throttle valves on engine).
7. ENGINE SPEED SENSOR (measures engine rpm or ignition system operation).
8. CRANKSHAFT POSITION SENSOR (measures rotation or location of crankshaft and rpm).
9. AIRFLOW SENSOR (measures amount of air flowing into engine).
10. KNOCK SENSOR (detects engine pinging, preignition, or detonation).
11. TRANSAXLE/TRANSMISSION SENSOR (checks transaxle or transmission gear selection).
12. BRAKE SENSOR (detects application of brake pedal).
13. CAMSHAFT POSITION SENSOR (checks rotation or position of engine camshaft).
14. OIL LEVEL SENSOR (measures amount of oil in engine oil pan).
15. EGR POSITION SENSOR (measures position of exhaust gas recirculation valve).
16. IMPACT SENSOR (detects a collision or sudden deceleration of vehicle to shut OFF fuel pump and engine).

Depending upon the car, some or none of these sensors may be used. Older cars use none or just a few of these sensors. Newer cars might use almost all of these sensors.

Note! Many other sensors are used on a car besides the ones just listed. The anti-lock brake system, computer-controlled suspension and steering systems, climate control system, and other more specialized systems with their own control modules will use other sensors. These sensors will be described later. This chapter will concentrate on the sensors that feed data to the main computer.

Sensor locations

Vehicle sensors can be located almost anywhere on a car. Most are mounted on the engine, Fig. 11-9. Others can be on the transmission or transaxle, on the wheel hubs, on the suspension, or even in the trunk of the car (impact sensor). There can be sensors inside the fuel tank as well as inside the passenger compartment.

If in doubt, refer to the service manual for the specific automobile to find sensor types and locations. Refer to Fig. 11-10.

Active and passive sensors

An *active sensor,* also called *active transducer,* is one that generates its own voltage signal. Examples of active transducers would be the oxygen sensor, knock sensor, a photocell type sensor, and a magnetic pickup type sensor. They all generate a voltage internally.

A *passive sensor,* also termed a *passive transducer,* depends on an external source of voltage to return a signal to the computer. The internal resistance (ohms) of

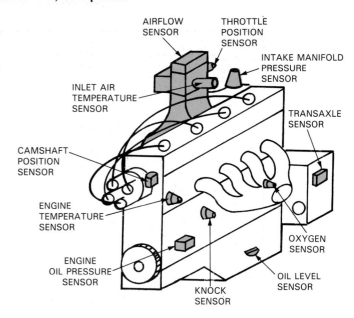

Fig. 11-9. Here are some of the many sensors that can be found on the engine and transaxle assemblies. Others can also be used elsewhere on car.

the transducer changes with a change in a condition, but it does not generate its own voltage signal. Examples of passive sensors include temperature sensors, throttle position sensors, switching type sensors, etc.

Sensor reference voltage

Sensor reference voltage is fed to passive sensors by the computer. A supply voltage is needed so that a change in sensor resistance can be read by the computer as a change in current and voltage. See Fig. 11-11.

The reference voltage, abbreviated Vref, is typically around 5 volts. The computer steps-down battery voltage so that a smooth, constant supply of DC voltage is present at the sensors.

Analog and digital signals

Mentioned earlier, the signal from the engine sensors can be either a *digital* or *analog* type voltage. The output from the computer can also be analog or digital.

Digital signals are instant on-off signals. An example of a sensor providing a digital signal is the crankshaft position sensor which shows engine rpm. Voltage output or resistance goes from maximum to minimum, like a switch to report rpm.

An *analog signal* progressively changes in strength. For example, sensor internal resistance may smoothly increase or decrease with temperature or part position. The sensor acts as a variable resistor.

Oxygen sensor

An *oxygen sensor,* also called an *exhaust gas sensor,* measures the oxygen content in the engine's exhaust system as a means of checking combustion efficiency. It often fits into the exhaust manifold or the exhaust pipe at a point before the catalytic converter. Look at Fig. 11-12.

Two or more oxygen sensors are used on late-model vehicles. One usually screws into a threaded hole or fitting

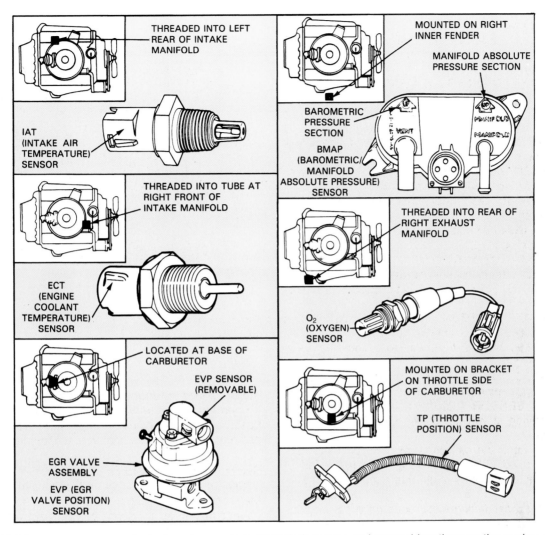

Fig. 11-10. These are some very typical engine sensors. Note their names and general locations on the engine.   (Ford)

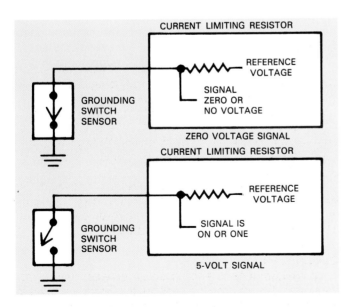

Fig. 11-11. A resistive type sensor, like this switching sensor, can be used to detect temperature change, part movement, pressure change, etc. It needs a supply or reference voltage so that a change in current will occur with a change in resistance or condition.

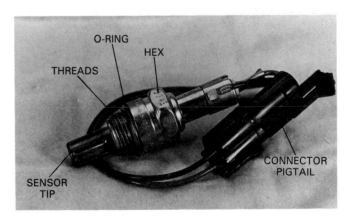

Fig. 11-12. The oxygen sensor is one of the most important sensors controlling engine operation.
(Universal Tire and Auto)

on the exhaust manifold or header pipe. The other is installed right after the catalytic converter. See Fig. 11-13.

Vehicles with OBD II use two oxygen sensors for each catalytic converter. Two oxygen sensors allow a more precise control of emissions.

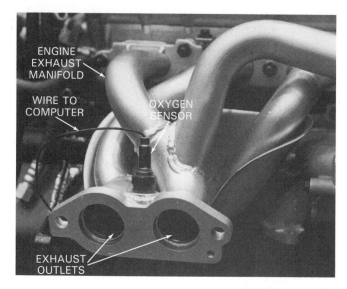

Fig. 11-13. Oxygen sensor is mounted so that its tip is exposed to the engine's exhaust gases. (AC-Delco)

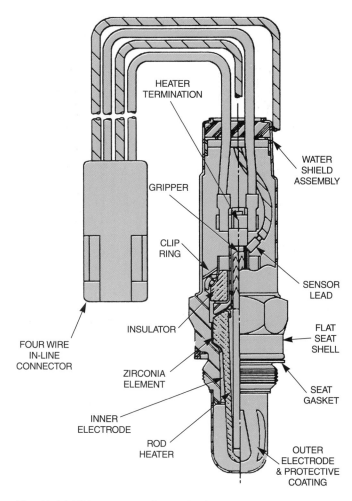

Fig. 11-14. This cutaway shows the internal parts of a heated zirconia oxygen sensor. Study its construction. (General Motors)

The voltage output (or resistance) of the oxygen sensor varies with changes in the oxygen content of the exhaust. For example, an increase in oxygen from a lean mixture makes the sensor output voltage decrease. A decrease in oxygen from a rich mixture causes the sensor output to increase.

In this way, the sensor supplies data on oxygen content to the computer. The computer can then alter the opening and closing of the injectors to adjust the air-fuel ratio for maximum efficiency.

Heated oxygen sensors

A heated oxygen sensor, abbreviated HO_2S, uses an electric heating element to quickly warm the sensor material to operating temperature. The heating element also stabilizes the temperature and operation of the sensor. The heating element allows the computer system to use the input sensor signals sooner.

Zirconia oxygen sensors

Most heated O_2 sensors are also called zirconia oxygen sensors because of their active materials. Zirconia and platinum are commonly used to produce the voltage output that represents oxygen in the exhaust gases. The platinum coating on the sensor surface causes any unburned fuel to ignite, which helps the sensor to maintain a high operating temperature. At an operating temperature of about 600°F (315°C), the oxygen sensor's element becomes a semiconductor and generates a small voltage. See Fig. 11-14.

The zirconia oxygen sensor has an inner cavity that is exposed to the atmosphere. Since the earth's atmosphere is comprised of approximately 21% oxygen, this percentage serves as a reference for the amount of oxygen in the exhaust gases. The outer surface of the oxygen sensor is exposed to the exhaust gases. The outer surface serves as the positive connection of the sensor circuit. The inner cavity of the sensor serves as the negative connection, or ground.

The difference between the oxygen content in the inner cavity and the oxygen content of the exhaust gases flowing over the sensor's outer surface causes the sensor to generate a voltage. The ECM compares the voltage produced by the sensor to a reference voltage of approximately 450 millivolts (.45 volts).

For example, if the engine's air-fuel mixture is too rich, there will be almost no oxygen in the exhaust gases. This creates a large difference in oxygen content between the sensor's surfaces and causes the sensor to generate a voltage of about 600 millivolts (.6 volts). This would inform the ECM to lean the mixture to reduce emissions. Refer to Fig. 11-15A.

With a lean air-fuel mixture going to the engine, there will be a smaller difference in oxygen content between the sensor's inner and outer surfaces. The sensor will generate a weaker voltage signal of about 300 millivolts (.3 volts), Fig. 11-15B. The ECM will then richen the fuel mixture and try to maintain a stoichiometric (chemically correct) air-fuel mixture. See Fig. 11-16.

Titania oxygen sensor

A titania oxygen sensor has the advantage of an almost instant oxygen content signal upon cold startup. There is no need to use a heating element to warm a titania sensor

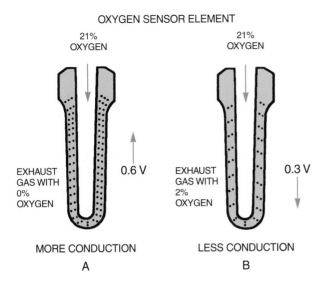

OXYGEN SENSOR ELEMENT

Fig. 11-15. Study the operation of a heated oxygen sensor. A—There is more voltage generated when the exhaust gas has a low oxygen content, indicating a rich mixture. B—There is less voltage generated when the exhaust has a relatively high oxygen content, indicating a lean mixture. (Chevrolet)

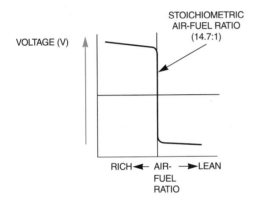

Fig. 11-16. A stoichiometric air-fuel ratio is chemically correct. This graph shows the relationship between oxygen sensor voltage and air-fuel ratio. (Honda)

to get it to operating temperature. This type of sensor uses a thick film of titania to detect the amount of oxygen present in the exhaust gases, Fig. 11-17.

The main difference between titania and zirconia oxygen sensors is how they produce their signal. A titania sensor varies its internal resistance to signal the ECM. The zirconia sensor actually generates its own voltage.

The titania sensor is also smaller than a zirconia sensor. It is manufactured as a sealed unit, which makes it less susceptible to outside contamination (engine oil leak dripping on outside of sensor, for example).

A constant 1-volt reference is often fed to the titania oxygen sensor's positive terminal from the ECM. If the sensor's output voltage is greater than the reference, the ECM knows that the engine air-fuel mixture is too rich. If the titania sensor's output is below reference, the ECM would know the mixture is too lean. In either case, the control module can adjust fuel injection pulse width accordingly.

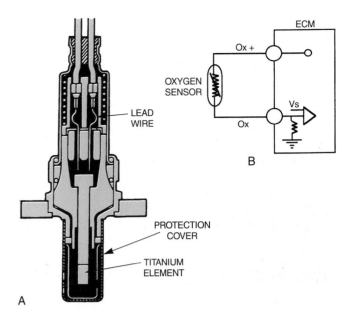

Fig. 11-17. A—A titania oxygen sensor heats up quickly and does not require an electric heating element. Its internal resistance changes with the engine exhaust's oxygen content. B—Basic circuit from the titania oxygen sensor to the ECM. (Snap-On Tool Corp.)

Open and closed loop

The terms open loop and closed loop refer to the operating mode of a computerized engine control system.

When an engine is cold, the computer operates *open loop* (no feedback from sensors). After the engine warms to operating temperature, the system changes to closed loop (uses feedback from sensors to control system) operation. See Fig. 11-18.

As mentioned, an oxygen sensor must heat up to several hundred degrees before it will function properly. This is the main reason computer systems have an open loop mode. The computer has preprogrammed information (injector pulse width, engine timing, idle speed motor rpm, etc.) that will keep the engine running satisfactorily while the oxygen sensor is warming up.

When the engine and oxygen sensor are cold, no information flows to the computer. The computer ignores any signals from the oxygen sensor. The "loop of information" is open.

After the sensor and engine are warm, the oxygen sensor, and other sensors, begin to feed data to the computer. This forms an "imaginary loop" (closed loop) as electrical data flow from the engine exhaust, to the oxygen sensor, to the computer, to the injectors, and back to the oxygen sensor. Normally, the computer system functions closed loop to analyze the fuel mixture provided to the engine. This lets the computer "doublecheck itself."

Intake air temperature sensor

An *intake air temperature sensor* measures the temperature of the air entering the engine. This sensor is usually located on the engine air inlet duct, Fig. 11-19, or the air cleaner.

Cold air is more dense than warm air, requiring a little more fuel. Warm air is NOT as dense as cold air, requiring a little less fuel. The intake air temperature sensor helps

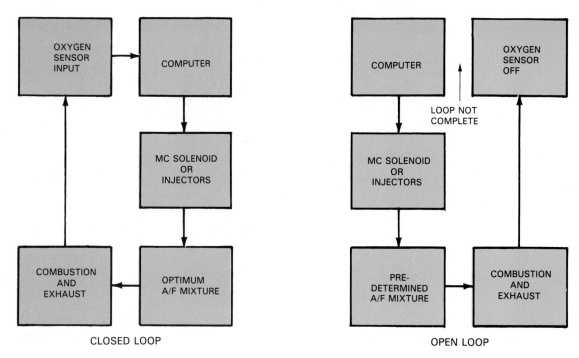

Fig. 11-18. Open loop refers to when computer system is not using oxygen sensor data. After warmup, the sensor produces an accurate voltage signal. Then the computer system goes closed loop and information forms a circle or loop as it travels through system. (Chrysler)

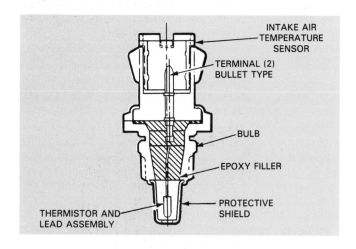

Fig. 11-19. This intake air temperature sensor mounts in air cleaner. It uses a thermistor to produce a different resistance for a different temperature. Thermistors were explained in Chapter 5.

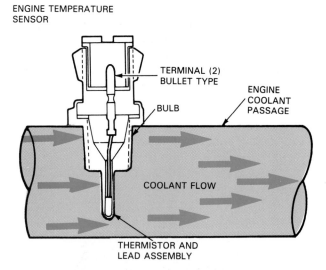

Fig. 11-20. Engine coolant temperature sensor also uses a thermistor to produce a signal for the computer. It mounts so that its tip touches engine coolant or antifreeze solution. (Ford)

the computer compensate for changes in outside air temperature and maintain an almost perfect air-fuel ratio.

Engine coolant temperature sensor

An *engine temperature sensor* monitors the operating temperature of the engine. It is mounted so that it is exposed to the engine coolant. See Fig. 11-20.

When the engine is cold, the sensor might provide a high current flow (low resistance). The computer would adjust for a richer air-fuel mixture for cold engine operation. When the engine warms, the sensor would supply information (high resistance, for example) so that the computer could make the mixture leaner.

Throttle position sensor

A *throttle position sensor* is a variable resistor, potentiometer, or multiposition switch connected to the throttle valve shaft. It provides data input on the power output of the engine.

When the driver presses on the accelerator pedal for more power, the throttle shaft and sensor are rotated. This changes the internal resistance of the sensor. The resistance change is proportional to angle change in degrees. The resulting change in current signals the computer to alter outputs to actuators as needed, Fig. 11-21.

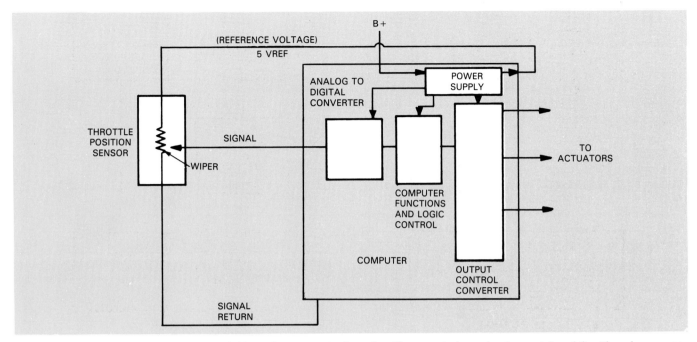

Fig. 11-21. Throttle position sensor is variable resistor or potentiometer. Movement of accelerator pedal and throttle valve moves resistor to produce signal. Computer must send out a reference voltage using voltage.   (Ford)

Two types of throttle position sensors are illustrated in Fig. 11-22.

A throttle position sensor is very important in determining computer outputs. Depending upon the make of car, it can affect air-fuel ratio, spark advance, emission control system operation, turbocharger boost, transaxle torque converter lockup, and air conditioner compressor engagement.

Flap airflow sensor

A *flap airflow sensor* measures the airflow into the engine, Fig. 11-23. This helps the computer determine how much fuel should be injected into the intake manifold. The airflow sensor usually mounts ahead of the throttle body assembly in the air inlet duct system.

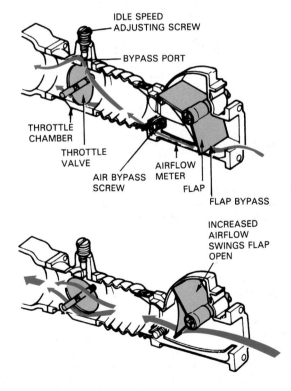

Fig. 11-23. Airflow sensor detects amount of air entering engine. This type uses a flap in air inlet to move variable resistor. This action converts airflow into flap movement and then into change of resistance. Computer would have to meter more fuel into engine as flap opens wider.   (Nissan)

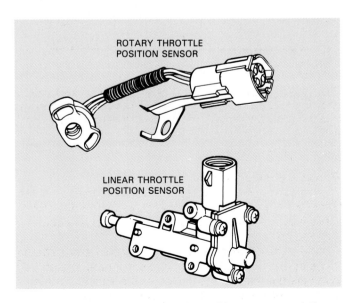

Fig. 11-22. These are two throttle position sensor variations. (Ford)

At idle, the sensor flap is nearly closed. Sensor resistance usually stays high. This tells the computer that the engine is idling and needs very little fuel.

As engine speed and airflow increase, air forces the flap to swing open. This normally moves the variable resistor to a low resistance position. The increased current flow now tells the computer that more air is flowing into the engine. The computer then increases injector pulse width as needed, Fig. 11-23.

Mass airflow sensor

A *mass airflow sensor* performs about the same function as a flap type sensor, but it sends more precise information to the computer. Look at Fig. 11-24.

Basically, the mass airflow sensor uses a small electrically energized, resistance wire or metal foil to detect airflow, Fig. 11-25. The wire's or foil's constant temperature of about 75°F drops as air flows over it. The greater the airflow, the lower its temperature. The control module measures the electrical power or current needed to keep the foil hot or at about 75°F. The power needed to heat the foil is proportional to airflow. More airflow requires more current and less airflow requires less current.

The power module on the mass airflow sensor converts this current value into a signal for the computer. It has memory tables that correspond to each power consumption value and can send out corresponding data to the main computer.

A mass airflow sensor, sometimes called a "hot wire" sensor, is desirable because it will automatically compensate for air temperature, atmospheric pressure, and humidity. All of these affect the engine's ideal air-fuel ratio. As a result, this type airflow sensor eliminates the need for an air temperature sensor, and the outside or barometric pressure sensor. By measuring air mass (weight) and NOT volume, as does a flap type sensor, the mass airflow sensor compensates for these changing air conditions.

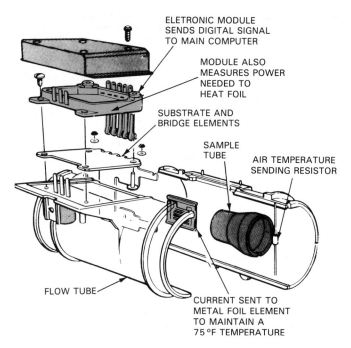

Fig. 11-25. Exploded view of mass airflow sensor shows basic parts. Note small electronic module that processes output from sensing element and compares signal to memory. Output is then sent from module to main computer. (General Motors)

Crankshaft and camshaft position sensors

A *crankshaft position sensor* usually mounts so that it can detect the rotation of a gear on the engine crankshaft. It can be at the front, side, or rear of the engine. Basically, the crankshaft position sensor is used to measure engine rpm for controlling fuel injection and ignition timing. It uses a magnetic type pickup that produces a fluctuating AC or digital type signal.

The *camshaft position sensor* is similar to the crankshaft sensor, but it monitors the rotation of the engine camshaft. The camshaft turns at one-half crank speed and this signal can be used to determine when the number one piston is at top dead center on its compression stroke. This is also used by the computer to initiate when a spark should occur at each spark plug. See Fig. 11-26.

Manifold absolute pressure sensor

A *manifold absolute pressure sensor* (MAP sensor) measures vacuum inside the engine intake manifold. A small vacuum hose usually connects this sensor to the engine, Fig. 11-27A.

Engine manifold pressure is a good way to indicate engine load. High pressure (low intake vacuum) occurs with a heavy load and high power output. The engine needs a rich fuel-air mixture and less spark advance. When manifold pressure is low (high intake vacuum), there is very little load. A lean mixture is sufficient and more spark advance can be used.

The MAP sensor basically changes resistance and the resulting current with changes in engine load. This data is used by the computer to alter the fuel mixture and other outputs.

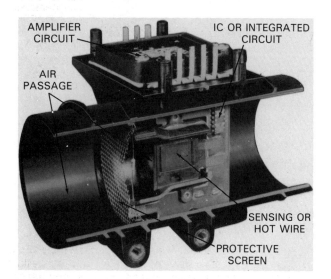

Fig. 11-24. This is a mass airflow sensor. It uses heated wire or foil to detect airflow. An air inlet temperature sensor is not needed with this type airflow sensor. (General Motors)

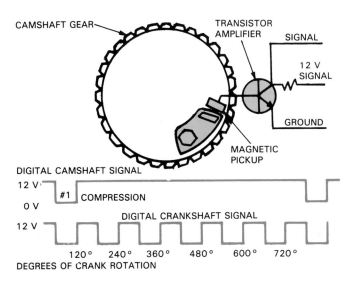

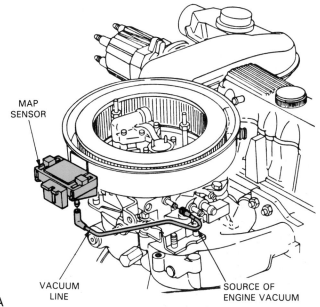

Fig. 11-26. Speed sensors can be on or near the crankshaft, camshaft, flywheel, and in the distributor. They are usually magnetic and produce a weak AC or alternating current signal. This AC can easily be converted into a digital signal once in the computer.

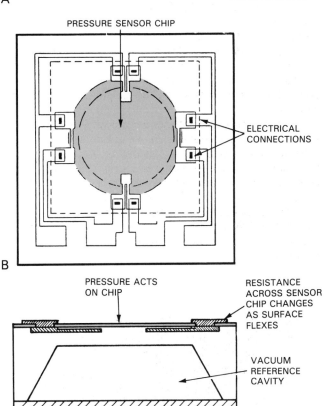

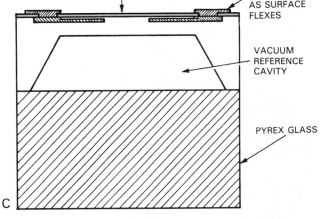

Fig. 11-27. A—This is a manifold absolute pressure sensor. It measures pressure or vacuum inside engine intake manifold which is an excellent indicator of load. B—This map sensor uses a piezoresistor chip that converts a change in pressure into a change in resistance. C—Side view of sensor shows vacuum reference cavity. Manifold pressure acts on top of sensor chip to flex it up and down. (General Motors)

There are three basic types of MAP sensors: strain gauge type, capacitive type, and transformer type.

A *strain gauge MAP sensor* has a small silicone chip mounted on a piece of pyrex glass. The chip is located so that it forms a reference chamber below its surface. The chip is thinner in the middle so that it can flex like a diaphragm. See Fig. 11-27B.

The silicone chip is doped with a semiconductor material that makes it a *piezoresistor.* Discussed in an earlier chapter, a piezoresistor changes internal resistance with pressure or "strain." As a result, the MAP sensor using the piezoresistor strain gauge can produce a signal for the computer. Manifold pressure flexes the silicone chip and produces a resistance and resulting current flow change that represents pressure. Look at Fig. 11-27C.

A *transformer type MAP sensor* uses a diaphragm or bellows to move a metal core in and out of a coil. The coil or transformer will then detect this core movement because it will affect the magnetic field around the coil. The current change can also be used as a signal representing intake manifold pressure. See Fig. 11-28.

A *capacitor capsule MAP sensor* uses two silicone chips mounted to form a sealed chamber. The chips form a variable capacitor. The capacitor can then be used to produce a varying signal for the computer that represents intake manifold pressure. Capacitors were explained in Chapter 4.

Knock sensor

A *knock sensor* can be installed on the engine to detect abnormal combustion (ping, preignition, or detonation). Its operation is illustrated in Fig. 11-29.

Many new cars, especially those with turbochargers, can suffer from engine knock. The sensor actually "listens" for the knocking of abnormal combustion. When it detects knock, an electrical signal allows the computer to retard the ignition timing or lower turbocharger boost enough to prevent engine damage.

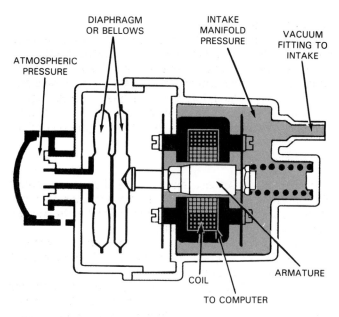

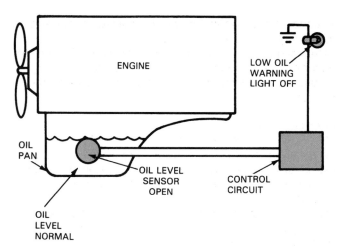

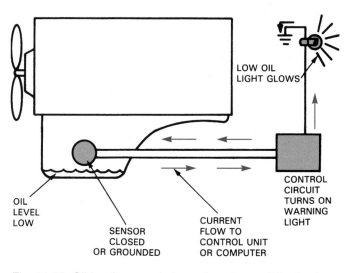

Fig. 11-28. This is a coil or transformer type MAP sensor. Pressure moves bellows, coils, and armature. This acts on magnetic field and produces an electrical signal.

Low oil level sensor

The *low oil level sensor* mounts in the engine oil pan to detect when oil is below a specific point. This allows the computer to activate a dash warning light or even "kill" the engine. Then, the driver is informed or protected from the potentially damaging condition. Fig. 11-30 illustrates the basic operation of an oil level sensor.

Vehicle speed sensor

The *vehicle speed sensor* produces a signal that represents how fast the car is moving. It can mount on the end of the speedometer cable at the transmission or transaxle or in the speedometer head in the dash. It produces a low

Fig. 11-30. Oil level sensor is in engine oil pan. It is simply a switching type sensor that signals when oil level is low. The computer can then activate dash light to warn driver.

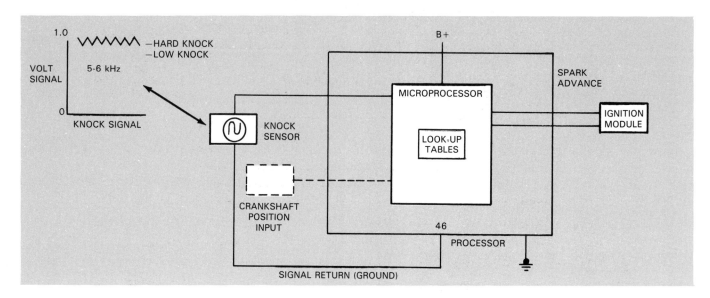

Fig. 11-29. Knock sensor actually "listens" for engine ping or spark knock. Abnormal combustion will make knock sensor generate weak voltage signal. Computer can use this signal to retard ignition timing, increase fuel mixture richness, or reduce turbocharger boost to stop the knocking or pinging.   (Ford)

frequency signal when the car is moving slowly and a higher frequency signal with more speed.

The computer can use the data from the vehicle speed sensor to control transmission/transaxle shift points, ignition timing, fuel injection, emission control system operation, etc.

Other sensors

Other sensors besides those just covered can be used in a computer control system. Some of them include sensors checking the operation of the suspension system, air conditioning system, brake system, and emission control systems.

Note! More information on these and other vehicle sensors is given in other locations in this textbook. Refer to the index as needed.

Circuit sensing

Circuit sensing involves using the computer itself instead of dedicated sensors to monitor component and circuit operation. The computer monitors current flow through various components and circuits. For example, some circuit sensing systems can monitor fuel injector operation (injector coil winding current), ignition coil action (current through ignition coil windings), and computer operation (current through computer circuits). The windings and the wires in the circuits serve as the sensors.

Multiple sensor inputs

The computer uses *multiple inputs* (inputs from more than one sensor) to determine the needed output. For example, the computer uses signals from the engine speed sensor to determine when to fire the fuel injectors. However, if a temperature sensor signals a cold engine, the computer would know to increase injector pulse width to enrich the fuel mixture for good cold engine operation.

ACTUATOR OPERATION

Mentioned earlier, *actuators* are the "hands and arms" of a computer. They allow it to do work and alter the operation of other components. This section of the chapter will summarize how actuators work.

When the computer turns on an actuator, it normally provides the actuator a GROUND CIRCUIT. Then, current can operate the actuator, Fig. 11-31.

Output drivers or *power transistors* in the computer control current flow through the actuators. When energized by the microprocessor in the computer, the drivers ground the actuator circuits. The actuators can then produce movement to affect vehicle operation.

Solenoid actuator operation

Fig. 11-32 gives a simplified illustration of how the computer can use a solenoid type actuator. In this example, input from the vehicle speed sensor enters the computer.

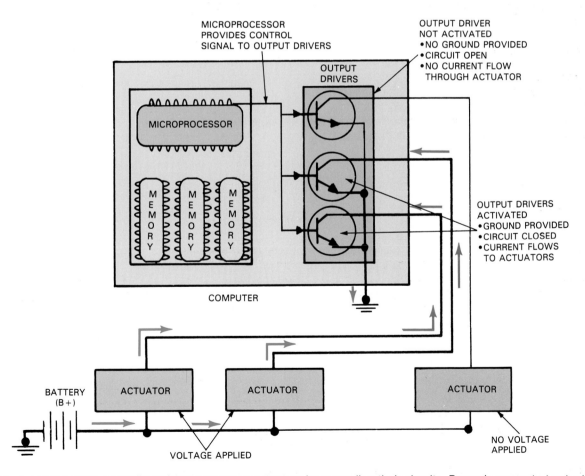

Fig. 11-31. A computer will normally activate outputs to actuators by grounding their circuits. Power is present at actuator at all times but there is not a complete circuit path. When drivers or power transistors are turned on, they will conduct current through ground to energize actuators. (Ford)

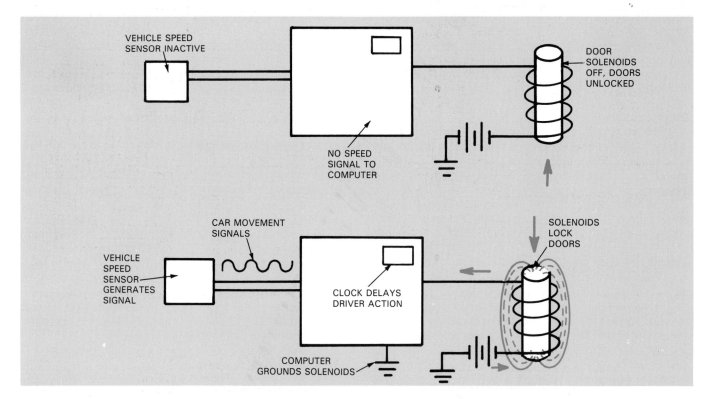

Fig. 11-32. Simple illustration of how sensor input can be used by computer to operate solenoid type actuator. When speed sensor produces a signal, computer can ground solenoid. The solenoid movement might be used to lock the doors of the car automatically.

When the computer detects vehicle travel or forward motion, it could use solenoid actuators to lock all of the car's doors.

The computer would ground the solenoid circuits and current would flow through the solenoid windings. This would produce a magnetic field in the windings. The magnetic field would pull on and move the plunger mounted in the solenoid windings. This plunger movement could be used to activate the door locks.

Fig. 11-33 shows a compound-wound solenoid type actuator. One set of windings is to initially pull the plunger in and the other is to hold the plunger in.

Fig. 11-34 shows how a solenoid can be used to operate a *vacuum switch.* When not energized, the vacuum switch would be closed and no vacuum would be applied to the vacuum circuit. When energized, the solenoid plunger would be pulled up. This would allow vacuum to be applied on the other side of the vacuum switch.

Solenoid type actuators can be used to do various tasks: operate EGR valve, control engine idle speed, etc.

Relay actuator operation

A *relay* can serve as a good actuator when a high current load must be controlled by the computer. The computer will simply ground the relay coil windings. Then, the relay coil field will pull the mechanical contacts closed and a large current will flow to the load.

Look at Fig. 11-35. It shows an example of how a computer can be used to control an electric motor using a relay.

Motor actuator operation

A *small DC motor* provides another way that a computer can act or produce an output. The computer can

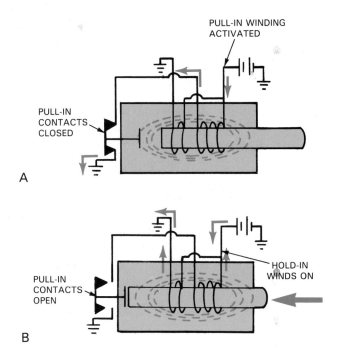

Fig. 11-33. Note operation of compound wound solenoid with pull-in and hold-in windings. A—Pull-in windings. B—Hold-in windings. (Ford)

ground the motor circuit and turn the motor on or off or reverse motor rotation as needed.

Sometimes the motor actuator is simply a reversible DC motor. The motor will turn a thread mechanism to produce

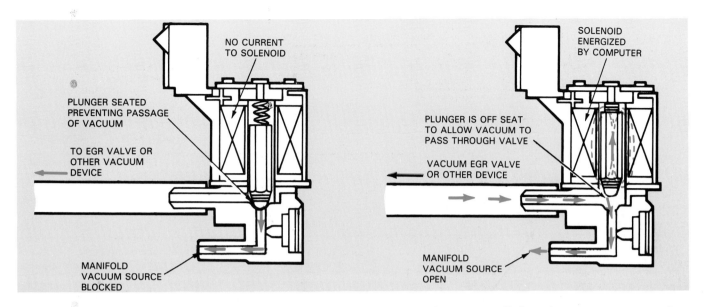

Fig. 11-34. Here is an example of how solenoid actuator can be used to control vacuum applied to other vacuum components.

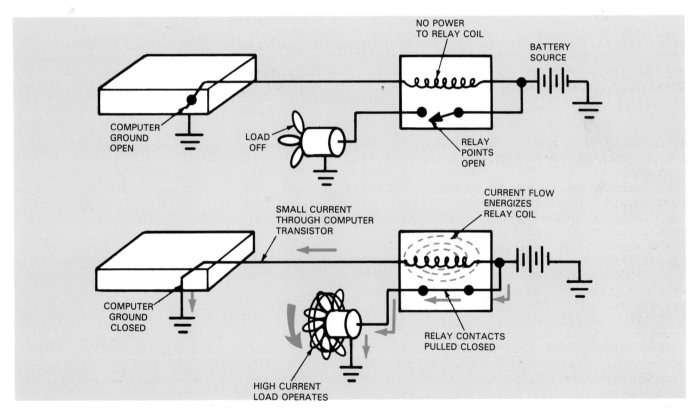

Fig. 11-35. A relay can also serve as an actuator to control a high current load. Small computer control current will close relay points. Then higher current will flow to load.

a controlled movement of a part. A good example would be an idle speed motor, Fig. 11-36.

A *servo motor,* also called a *stepper motor,* is a motor that can be stopped at specific points in its armature rotation. It allows the computer to make fine adjustments of output or movement, Fig. 11-37.

Fig. 11-38 shows how the computer can operate a

servo motor. Note that by grounding each winding, the motor armature will be attracted to and stop on specific windings.

Fig. 11-39 shows a thin-disc type servo motor. By energizing the coils, the motor can be made to spin or stop as needed. This provides a very precise output mechanism for the computer.

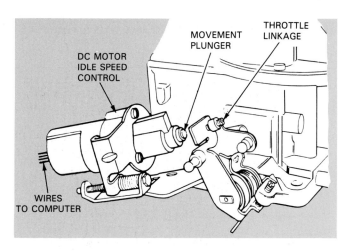

Fig. 11-36. Idle speed motor is excellent example of motor type actuator. Computer can make small motor run in either direction. Armature rotation turns screw mechanism that can open or close throttle to control idle speed accurately.

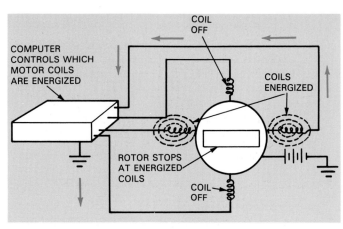

Fig. 11-38. Servo or stepper motor can be stopped in an exact position. Computer can energize specific coils so armature is attracted to and stopped next to coils.

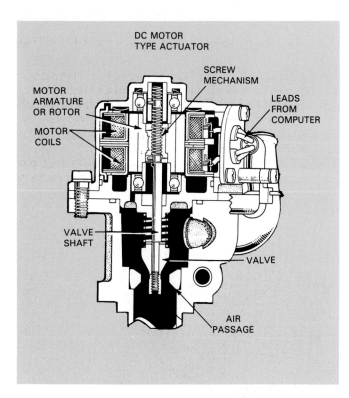

Fig. 11-37. Cutaway of this motor type actuator shows screw mechanism that causes part movement with motor armature rotation. This unit is used to control airflow into small idle air passage. Extra air bypassing throttle plates will increase engine idle speed.   (Toyota)

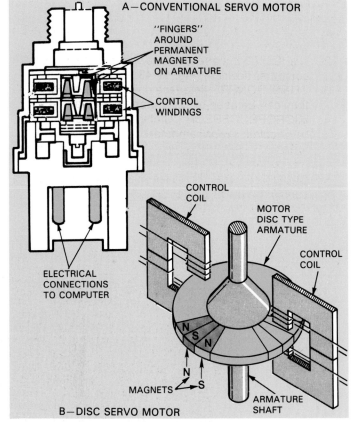

Fig. 11-39. Two possible variations of servo motors. A—Stepper motor with small fingers on armature. B—Disc type motor consumes little power.

Note that some actuator motors also serve as sensors for the computer. They can inform the computer as to their position. See Fig. 11-40.

COMPUTER OPERATION

A computer is often nicknamed a "black box." This is because it is enclosed in a box-shaped housing and contains mysterious circuits that can do complex operations. Few technicians have seen what is inside a computer.

Fig. 11-41 shows a photo of the inside of an automotive computer. Note that it uses printed circuit boards, integrated circuits, capacitors, resistors, power transistors, and many other basic electronic components. You learned about these components in Chapters 4 and 5 of this text.

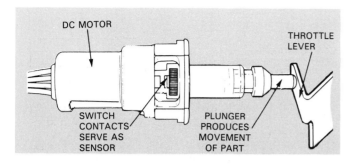

Fig. 11-40. This idle speed motor also contains contacts to send data back to computer.

If needed, review these chapters. You must comprehend the fundamentals before continuing.

Look at Fig. 11-42. It shows a line drawing of another make of computer. Note its basic components.

Parts of a computer

All computers can be divided into sections or parts.

Each section has a specific function. Basically, a computer can be divided into ten parts. These include:

1. VOLTAGE REGULATOR (supplies lower voltage for computer and sensors).
2. AMPLIFIERS (increase voltage and current for other computer devices), Fig. 11-43.
3. CONDITIONERS (interface units that alter signals so they can be used by computer and actuators).
4. MICROPROCESSOR (IC chip that makes decisions or calculations for computer).
5. MEMORY (IC chips that store data for microprocessor), Fig. 11-44.
6. CLOCK (IC that produces constant pulse rate to coordinate events in computer).

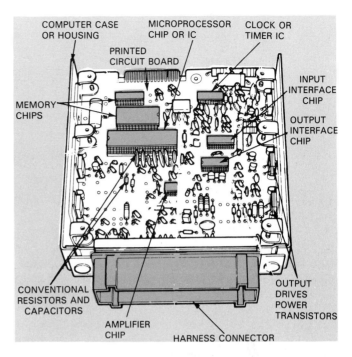

Fig. 11-42. Note names of basic parts in a computer.   (Ford)

7. OUTPUT DRIVERS (power transistors that step-up current to operate actuators or power modules).
8. CIRCUIT BOARDS (fiber boards with flat metal conductors that connect and hold computer components).
9. HARNESS CONNECTOR (multi-pin terminal for attaching to wiring harness of car).
10. COMPUTER HOUSING (metal enclosure that protects electronic components from induced currents and physical damage).

Fig. 11-41. Photo shows inside of computer or "black box." Note that it uses integrated circuits attached to printed circuit board. (Sun Electric Corp.)

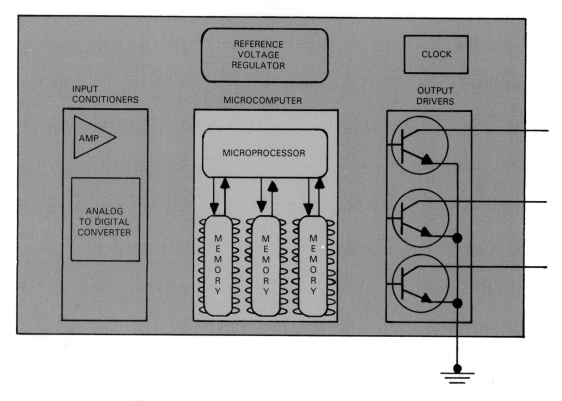

Fig. 11-43. These are the basic sections in a computer.

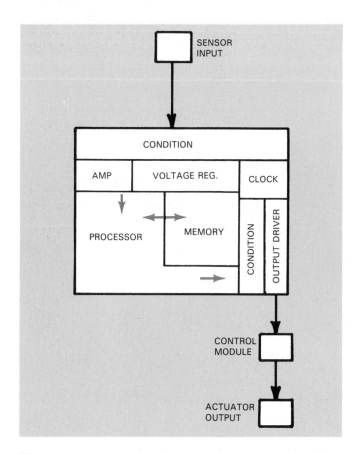

Fig. 11-44. A sensor signal usually cannot be used directly. It may need to be converted into digital signal, amplified, and timed for use in processor and memory IC chips. Output transistors can then be used to send current out to control modules or actuators.

Computer voltage regulator operation

A *computer voltage regulator* is needed to provide a reduced voltage for the electronic components in the computer and for some passive sensors. This voltage must be very *smooth DC voltage* that does NOT vary and that does NOT have small *spikes* (abrupt changes in voltage). See Fig. 11-45.

For example, a computer will frequently provide a *reference voltage* abbreviated Vref, to resistive or passive sensors. Then, a change in sensor resistance will result in a changing current flow to the computer.

Computer amplifier operation

A *computer amplifier* simply strengthens various signals when inside the computer. One might increase the voltage signal from the oxygen sensor which is less than one volt. Then, the signal is strong enough to be used by other components or circuits in the computer. Look at Fig. 11-45.

Computer conditioner (interface) operation

There are two basic types of conditioners in a computer: input conditioners and output conditioners. A conditioner can also be called *converter* or an *interface.*

An *input conditioner* alters the input signals from some sensors. They treat incoming data (voltage and current) for the computer so it can be utilized.

For instance, most vehicle sensors produce an *analog signal* (voltage signal gradually increases or decreases). An input conditioner is needed to convert this analog signal into a *digital signal* (voltage instantly changes from zero to one or from off to on depending on analog signal change). A digital signal is needed so that the microprocessor can handle and understand the data from the sensor.

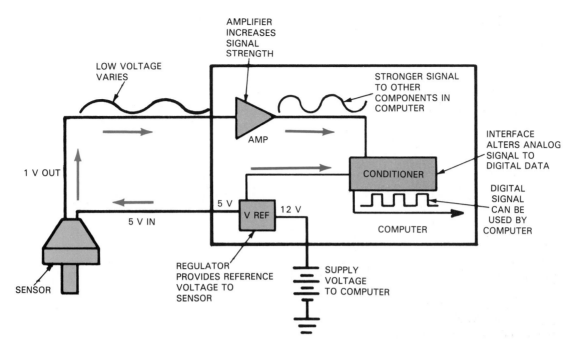

Fig. 11-45. A computer power supply or voltage regulator must send current to passive type sensors. Most sensors produce an analog signal. If weak, the analog signal is first amplified or increased in strength. A conditioner or interface converts the analog signal into a digital or binary signal. The digital signal can then be sent to the microprocessor chip in the computer.

An *output conditioner* is needed to change the digital signals back into analog signals. The output of the computer must usually be analog to operate the actuators and control modules, Fig. 11-44.

Sometimes the output from a computer is digital. As shown in Fig. 11-46, the signal sent to operate some fuel injectors is digital. It rapidly pulses on and off to precisely control how much fuel is injected into the engine for specific needs.

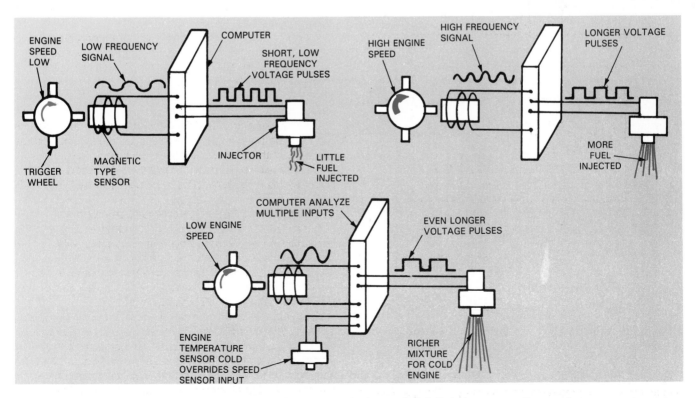

Fig. 11-46. Although most computer outputs are analog, some outputs are digital. Note how magnetic speed sensor sends analog signal into computer. In this example, computer must produce a digital output to open and close fuel injectors.

Buffer

A *buffer* is a computer device that can serve as a temporary storage area for the data. A buffer can also protect internal computer chips from improper data. For example, if data comes into the computer too quickly, the buffer can hold the data and then slowly feed data into other devices as needed.

Computer microprocessor operation

Microprocessor means SMALL (micro) COMPUTER (processor). A microprocessor is a small computer chip or integrated circuit capable of analyzing data and calculating what should be done. It is the "brain" of a computer, Fig. 11-47.

A microprocessor chip uses the binary number system to make decisions, comparisons, or calculations. Digital pulses from the conditioners or interfaces are fed into the microprocessor. Since these inputs are zero (off) or one (on) voltages, they can be used by the logic gates in the processor.

Fig. 11-48 illustrates how a basic circuit and computer logic gate or processor use information to produce a *programmed* (predetermined) output. In a starting motor circuit, both the ignition switch and neutral safety switch must be activated for starting. The gear shift must be in neutral (neutral safety switch closed or on) and the

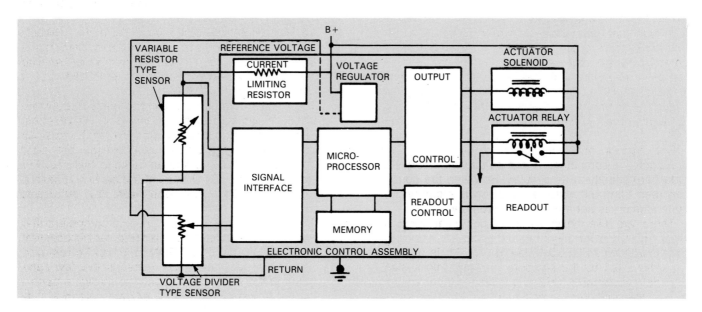

Fig. 11-47. Note block diagram for this computer system.

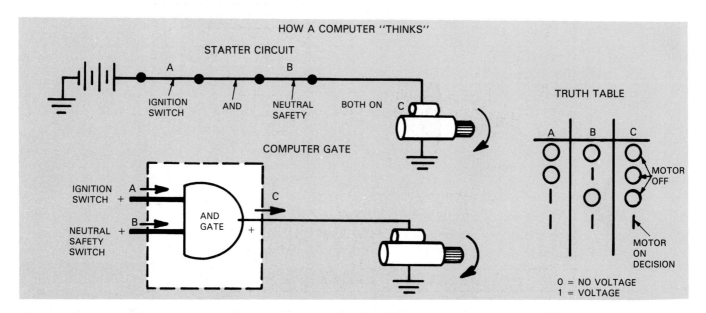

Fig. 11-48. Compare this starting system circuit with the computer gate circuit and truth table. It shows how a computer gate can make a decision. Two input conditions (A and B on or one) must be satisfied in both circuits for there to be an output to the starting motor. This same principle, only with thousands of gates and dozens of inputs and outputs, is used inside an automotive computer.

ignition switch must also be in the start position (closed or on). If both of these conditions are ONE (voltage through switch or on), then the starter can function.

Note how the truth table (explained in Chapter 5) shows the outputs for each input. As you can see, the computer gate was programmed only to allow engine starting IF both input conditions were satisfied (one or on). The computer gate MADE A DECISION based on the input data.

A microprocessor does exactly the same thing, only on a larger more complex scale. It might contain thousands of logic gates capable of making hundreds of output decisions based on dozens of inputs.

A microprocessor also uses data stored in memory chips. It compares input data and memory data to decide what the outputs should be for maximum efficiency.

Computer memory operation

A *computer memory* results from integrated circuits that are capable of storing data as voltage charges. The gates inside the memory chips will hold their information (on or off charges) until needed by the microprocessor. See Fig. 11-49.

A chip's *memory rating* is an indication of its ability to store information. Memory ratings are given in kilobytes (KB).

Both non-erasable and read-write memories are used in automotive computers. A *non-erasable memory* stores data permanently in its circuitry. However, the computer can read from and write to a read-write memory. Read-write memory is not a permanent memory.

There are five basic types of computer memories: RAM, ROM, PROM, EPROM, and KAM.

1. RANDOM ACCESS MEMORY (RAM) is a memory chip used by the computer to store information or data temporarily. This data is erased if battery power to the computer is lost. See Fig. 11-50.

2. READ ONLY MEMORY (ROM) stores permanent data that cannot be removed from memory. This memory chip contains calibration tables and look-up tables for the general make and model car. Refer to Fig. 11-51.

The calibration tables in ROM contain general data about the vehicle. The look-up tables in ROM have standard data about how the vehicle should perform under ideal conditions. For example, it might contain data about what the input should be from the oxygen sensor for specific conditions.

The microprocessor uses ROM to find out if the car is performing normally. It will compare input data from sensors to the data stored in ROM and then calculate any correction needed to improve performance. The microprocessor cannot write data into ROM.

3. PROGRAMMABLE READ ONLY MEMORY (PROM) is a memory chip containing permanent data that is more specific than the data stored in ROM. The microprocessor can read from the PROM, but it cannot write to the PROM.

The PROM contains specific information about the vehicle's engine (number of cylinders, valve sizes, compression ratio, fuel system type, etc.), transaxle (shift points, gear ratios, etc.), weight, tire size, optional accessories, and any unique features. For example, a car with a manual transaxle will have a different PROM than one with an automatic transaxle.

The PROM is the only part of some computers that is commonly serviced. During computer replacement on some vehicles, the PROM chip can be removed from the old computer and reused in the new computer. PROMs are also replaced to correct a performance problem. The PROM seldom fails, and it is

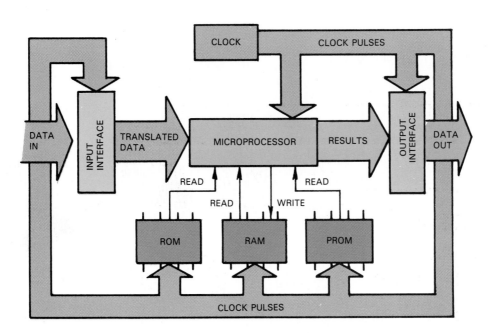

Fig. 11-49. Note flow of data in this flow or block diagram. Data comes in from sensors. Interface or conditioner changes input data into digital signal. Clock times when data moves from one place to another. Microprocessor can read from memory or write into memory. Microprocessor decides on outputs using logic gates. Results are sent from microprocessor to output interface or conditioner that changes binary data back into analog for actuators. (General Motors)

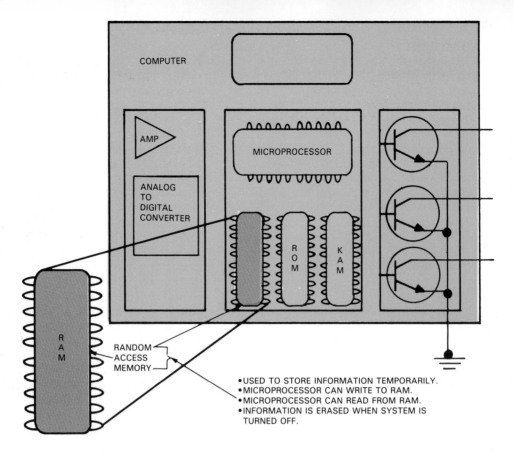

Fig. 11-50. Random access memory is temporary. Microprocessor can input into memory or pull from memory in RAM.   (Ford)

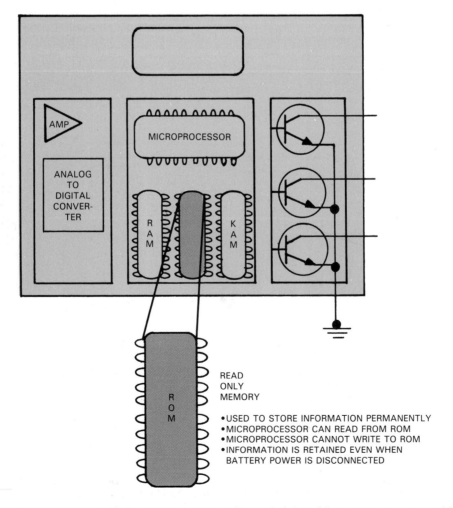

Fig. 11-51 . Read only memory is another IC that stores permanently needed data. Microprocessor can read from ROM but cannot write into ROM.   (Ford)

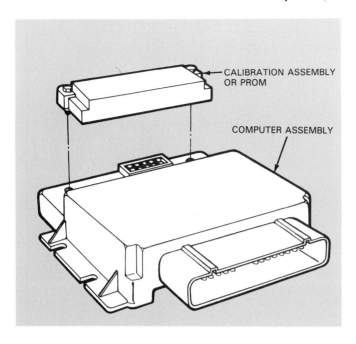

Fig. 11-52. PROM, also called a calibration unit, can be removed from most computers. It has data about specific options on car. (Ford)

programmed for the specific make and model car. Data is retained in the PROM even when the chip is removed from the computer. See Fig. 11-52.

4. ERASABLE PROGRAMMABLE READ ONLY MEMORY (EPROM) can be changed. However, in most cases, the changes can only be made by the manufacturer using special equipment. It is also responsible for storing semipermanent data, such as odometer or mileage readings in an electronic dash.

A variation of EPROM is electrically erasable programmable read only memory (EEPROM). EEPROM can be altered by the technician in the field. This allows the manufacturer to easily change operating parameters if a performance or driveability problem is discovered.

5. KEEP ALIVE MEMORY (KAM) is a memory chip that allows the computer to have an adaptive strategy. An adaptive strategy is needed as parts wear and components deteriorate.

The information stored in KAM allows the computer to maintain normal vehicle performance with abnormal inputs from sensors. It gives the computer the ability to also ignore false inputs to maintain good driveability. See Fig. 11-53.

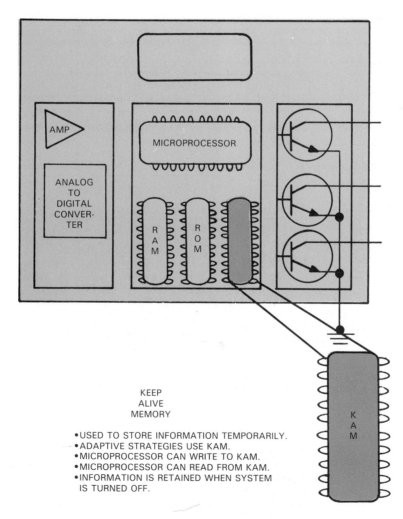

Fig. 11-53. Keep alive memory (KAM) is for altering outputs with changes in sensor inputs as parts wear or deteriorate. It helps keep car running acceptably with a worn or failed component. (Ford)

Note! Different computer designs will use different memory chips. Also, the names of these chips can vary. The ones discussed are typical.

Processor-memory bus

The term PROCESSOR-MEMORY bus refers to how these two sections of a computer communicate or exchange data. Just as a school bus transports people, a *data bus* allows the exchange of computer information.

Discussed in Chapter 5, digital integrated circuits use the binary (0 or 1) numbering system to produce artificial intelligence. By using a specific sequence of zeros and ones, the binary numbering system can represent any input condition or output. The computer's microprocessor and memory chips use this numbering system to *read* (remove) and *write* (input) data about how a car is functioning and should function.

When operating, data rapidly shuffles between the memory chips and the microprocessor chip. The microprocessor chip controls this flow of data. Sometimes it writes data about vehicle operation into memory or it may read out data about how the vehicle should operate.

Memory address

An *address* is a specific location in memory. One address might contain a calibration for the correct output of one sensor. Another address might temporarily store the present output value of the same sensor. As shown in Fig. 11-54, the memory address will store this type data as a binary number at specific pins or locations in the memory chips.

Data exchange

Fig. 11-55 shows how the microprocessor chip might read data out of memory. The microprocessor chip will send a signal (binary number) out to a certain memory

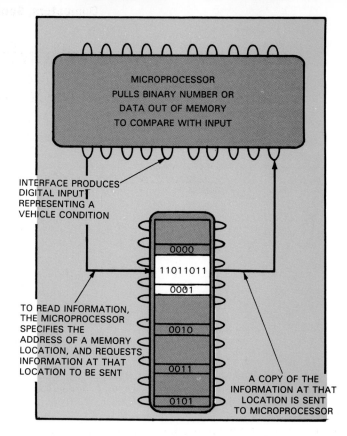

Fig. 11-55. Microprocessor will compare input binary number with known correct binary number in memory. Microprocessor can then determine what output is needed. (Ford)

chip pin. This will make the memory chip output a binary number answer for use by the microprocessor.

Fig. 11-56 illustrates how the exchange of binary numbers

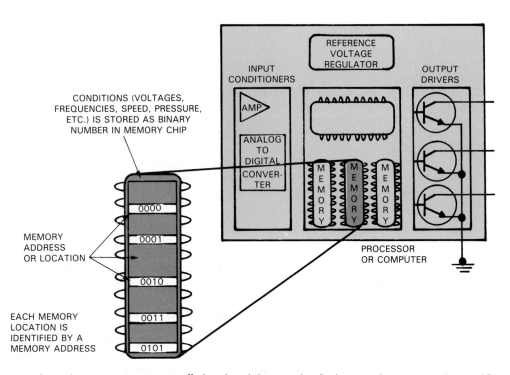

Fig. 11-54. Since computer gates can use an on or off signal and thousands of microscopic gates are in one IC, a computer can make complex decisions. It can store data as binary number or output binary number representing an output.

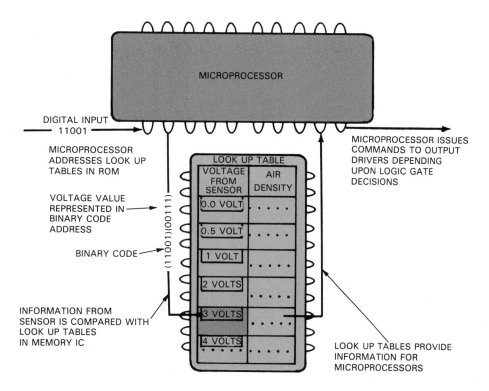

Fig. 11-56. Microprocessor will use binary number to represent a condition, like a voltage output from a sensor. If sensor voltage is low or binary number is incorrect, this would tell processor to alter output or enrich fuel mixture in this example. Microprocessor can "think" of correct output or make logical decision.

can be used to check the output of a sensor. Note how a binary number of 11001 might represent a sensor voltage signal of three volts. The microprocessor can read from memory to find out if this is the correct output from that sensor or to find out if a corrective action should be taken to improve performance.

MODES OF OPERATION

There are also specific modes of computer operation. One mode might be provided for engine starting, another for acceleration, deceleration, or cruising. These modes will be explained in later chapters. It will be easier to understand these modes if they are discussed for smaller, more specific systems.

COMPUTER CLASSIFICATIONS

Computers are often classified by the amount of data they can process. This data is measured in bits of information. A computer's *bit rating* is equal to the number of bits of digital information it can process.

SUMMARY

To review what you have just studied, we will trace the flow of data through a simplified computer system using one sensor and one actuator. Refer to Fig. 11-57.

The vehicle sensor detects a condition (temperature for example) and converts this condition into an analog voltage signal. In this sensor, the computer voltage regulator sends a reference voltage of about 5 volts through the sensor. As the sensor resistance changes, the voltage

signal returning to the computer changes in proportion to the condition change.

If the signal from the sensor is weak (like that from an oxygen sensor), an amplifier can be used in the computer to increase signal strength, Fig. 11-27.

The amplified analog signal is then sent into a conditioner, also called interface or converter. This device changes the analog signal into a digital or binary signal for use by the microprocessor and memory chips.

The binary signal concerning the sensor input then enters the microprocessor. The microprocessor can then determine whether to temporarily store this information in memory or to pull out memory data and compare it to the sensor input. The clock allows the microprocessor chip and memory chips to time or coordinate when data is read or written from one place to the next.

The memory chips serve as a specification chart or notepad that allows the microprocessor to compare input signals to known good signals. If an input signal from a sensor changes, the microprocessor can determine if an output needs to be changed to compensate for the new condition.

After calculating what should be done, the microprocessor will produce output signals. The signal is first sent to a conditioner or interface that changes the microprocessor's digital output into an analog output. A more constant DC or analog voltage is usually needed for the drivers. The drivers are power transistors that increase current so the actuators can be energized.

As a result, the actuators will move and respond to the input signals from the sensors. Since all this can take place in a fraction of a second, vehicle operation is very efficient.

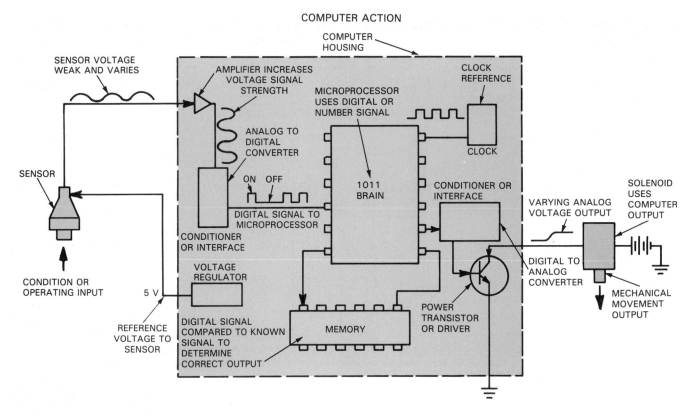

Fig. 11-57. Trace flow of data through this simplified computer system. Can you explain the purpose of each component?

KNOW THESE TERMS

Cybernetics, Nervous system, Hardware, Software, Input, Processing, Output, Variable resistor type sensor, Potentiometer type sensor, Switching type sensor, Voltage generator type sensor, Magnetic type sensor, Solenoid type output, Relay type output, Servo motor type output, Display type output, Control module output, Computer block diagram, Computer, Vehicle control module, Engine control module, Power train control module, Instrumentation module, Anti-lock brake module, Ignition control module, Suspension system module, Climate control module, Integrated computer system, Computer network, Multiplexing, Vehicle sensor, Transduce, Intake air temperature sensor, Engine coolant temperature sensor, Oxygen sensor, Manifold absolute pressure sensor, Barometric pressure sensor, Throttle position sensor, Engine speed sensor, Crankshaft position sensor, Airflow sensor, Knock sensor, Transaxle/transmission sensor, Brake sensor, Camshaft position sensor, Oil level sensor, EGR position sensor, Impact sensor, Active sensor, Passive sensor, Sensor reference voltage, Digital signals, Analog signal, Zirconia oxygen sensors, Titania oxygen sensor, Open loop, Flap airflow sensor, Mass airflow sensor, Strain gauge MAP sensor, Piezoresistor, Transformer type MAP sensor, Capacitor capsule MAP sensor, Vehicle speed sensor, Circuit sensing, Multiple inputs, Actuators, Output drivers, Power transistors, Vacuum switch, Relay, Small dc motor, Servo motor, Voltage regulator, Amplifiers, Conditioners, Microprocessor, Memory, Clock, Output drivers, Circuit boards, Harness connector, Computer housing, Smooth dc voltage, Spikes, Buffer, Programmed, Memory rating, Non-erasable memory, Random access memory, Read only memory, Programmable read only memory, Erasable programmable read only memory, Keep alive memory, Processor-memory bus, Data bus, Read, Write, Address, Bit rating.

REVIEW QUESTIONS—CHAPTER 11

1. The term _____ refers to the study of how electrical-mechanical mechanisms can duplicate the action of the human body.
2. Explain the three stages of computer operation.
3. What are the five sensor classifications?
4. What are the five actuator classifications?
5. A computer _____ _____ is a simple drawing that shows how computer components interact.
6. Usually, one computer and other control modules are used on late-model cars. True or false?
7. List some service manual names for a computer.
8. Describe seven types of computers.
9. List and explain 16 vehicle sensors.
10. Why do resistive sensors need a reference voltage?
11. How does an oxygen sensor work?
12. What is open loop and closed loop?
13. If a mass airflow sensor is used, which of these sensors would NOT be needed?
    a. Throttle position sensor.
    b. Intake air sensor.
    c. Oxygen sensor.
    d. Knock sensor.

14. A computer activates an actuator by grounding its circuit. True or false?
15. _____ _____ or _____ _____ are used to send current to the actuators.
16. List and explain the ten parts of a computer.
17. Vref from a computer is usually:
    a. Five volts.
    b. Twelve volts.
    c. Less than one volt.
    d. Six volts.
18. How does the microprocessor chip work?
19. Explain the four types of computer memory.
20. Sketch a basic computer system with one sensor and one actuator. Show the flow of data through the computer and write a summary of its operation.

ASE CERTIFICATION–TYPE QUESTIONS

1. Technician A says automotive computers can compensate for wear of mechanical components. Technician B says automotive computers can increase engine power. Who is right?
   (A) A only.   (C) Both A and B.
   (B) B only.   (D) Neither A nor B.
2. Each of the following is a stage of computer system operation *except:*
   (A) input.   (C) processing.
   (B) output.   (D) conversion.
3. Technician A says automotive computers are often located under the dashboard. Technician B says automotive computers can be located in the engine compartment. Who is right?
   (A) A only.   (C) Both A and B.
   (B) B only.   (D) Neither A nor B.
4. Technician A says a sensor changes a condition into an electrical signal. Technician B says an active sensor depends on an external voltage source to return a signal to the computer. Who is right?
   (A) A only.   (C) Both A and B.
   (B) B only.   (D) Neither A nor B.

5. Technician A says a zirconia oxygen sensor varies its resistance with changes in the oxygen content of the exhaust gases. Technician B says the voltage output of a titania oxygen sensor varies with changes in the oxygen content of the exhaust gases. Who is right?
   (A) A only.   (C) Both A and B.
   (B) B only.   (D) Neither A nor B.
6. Technician A says that output drivers provide a ground circuit for the computer actuators. Technician B says a solenoid-type actuator can be stopped at specific points in its armature rotation. Who is right?
   (A) A only.   (C) Both A and B.
   (B) B only.   (D) Neither A nor B.
7. The sections of the computer that alter signals so they can be used by the computer and the actuators are the:
   (A) output drivers. (C) microprocessors.
   (B) conditioners.   (D) amplifiers.
8. Technician A says a buffer can serve as a temporary storage area for computer data. Technician B says a buffer can protect internal computer chips from improper data. Who is right?
   (A) A only.   (C) Both A and B.
   (B) B only.   (D) Neither A nor B.
9. Technician A says RAM contains calibration tables and look-up tables for the general make and model vehicle. Technician B says ROM contains permanent data that cannot be removed from memory. Who is right?
   (A) A only.   (C) Both A and B.
   (B) B only.   (D) Neither A nor B.
10. Technician A says a PROM is a removable chip that can be replaced to correct a performance problem. Technician B says information in PROM is erased when battery power to the computer is lost. Who is right?
   (A) A only.   (C) Both A and B.
   (B) B only.   (D) Neither A nor B.

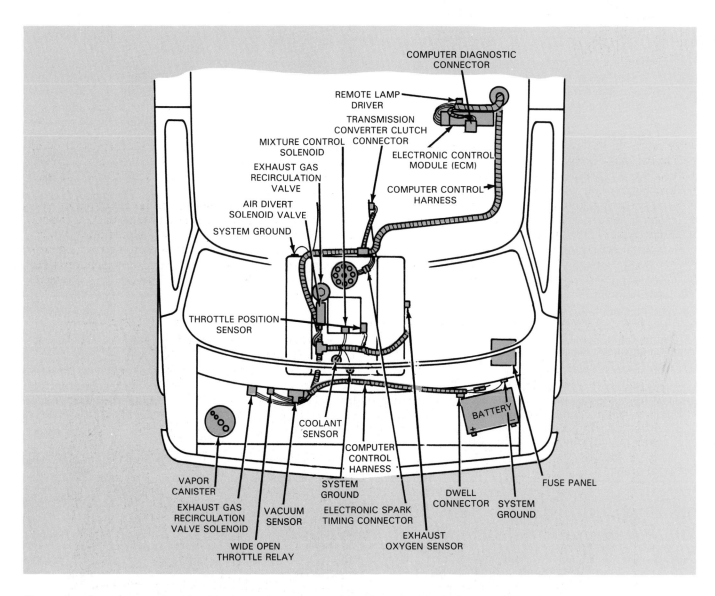

Illustration shows general location for electronic components in this car's electrical system. Hopefully, service manual will give similar illustration for specific car being repaired. (General Motors)

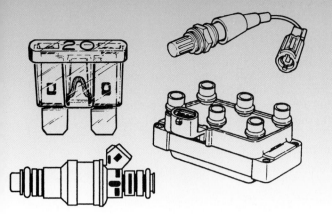

Chapter 12

Batteries

After studying this chapter, you will be able to:

- *Summarize the construction of an automotive battery.*
- *Explain the major parts of a car battery.*
- *Describe the operation of an auto battery.*
- *Give the voltage output from one or more battery cells.*
- *Compare battery terminal types.*
- *Explain typical battery ratings.*
- *Read a built-in hydrometer.*
- *Sketch the routing of battery cables.*
- *Summarize how a battery is mounted in a car.*

To be an automotive electrical technician, you must fully understand car batteries. A battery plays a very important role in an automobile's electrical system. See Fig. 12-1.

This chapter will briefly explain the construction and operation of a battery. It will also discuss battery cables, battery trays, battery ratings, and related information. By learning the principles of operation, you will be better qualified to service, troubleshoot, and test batteries.

Battery service is explained in Chapter 23 of this text.

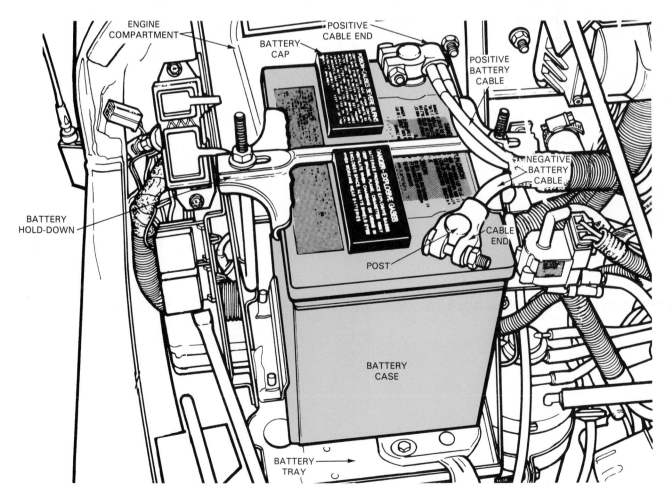

Fig. 12-1. Battery is vital part of a car's electrical system. The battery itself, as well as its cables, must be in good condition to ensure engine starting. (Chrysler)

199

BATTERY OPERATION

A *car battery* is a chemical-electrical device for storing and producing electrical current and voltage. *Chemical-electrical* means that the battery uses both chemical energy and electrical energy to operate.

An automotive battery produces DC (direct current). It has the potential to produce a tremendous amount of power or current for its size. A car battery is also very dependable. It will normally give several years of trouble-free service. An automotive battery is also called a *lead-acid battery* because these materials are used in its construction.

Battery discharge

Battery discharge refers to when current is flowing out of the battery. A discharge occurs when the battery is converting chemical energy into electrical energy. Battery current is being used to operate some electrical device. The battery is releasing stored energy, Fig. 12-2A.

Battery charging

Battery charging refers to when current is flowing back into the battery. An external voltage slightly higher than battery voltage must be applied to the battery terminals. This will cause current flow back through the battery.

Current flow into the battery restores the chemicals in the battery to reenergize the battery. Charging allows the battery to store chemical energy that can be converted back into electrical energy as needed, Fig. 12-2B.

Battery cell

A basic *battery cell* can be made by placing two dissimilar metal electrodes into an acid-filled container. Electrons will be pulled off of one electrode and attracted to the other and current can be produced, Fig. 12-3.

The parts of a basic battery cell include:
1. POSITIVE PLATE (usually made of a sheet of lead peroxide).

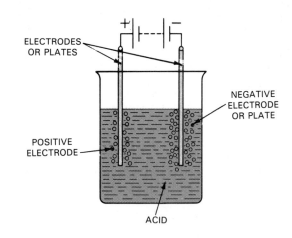

Fig. 12-3. A fundamental cell can be made by placing two unlike metal electrodes in a jar of sulfuric acid. Chemical action will make electrons flow between two electrodes.
(Robert Bosch)

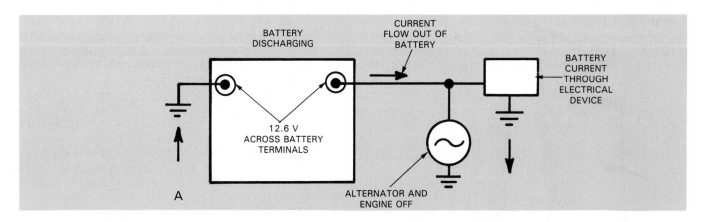

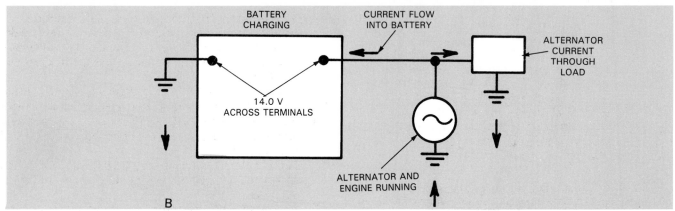

Fig. 12-2. A—When discharging, current flows out of battery and chemicals in battery are depleted. B—When being charged, external voltage must be slightly higher than battery voltage. Then current can flow back through battery to replenish chemicals.

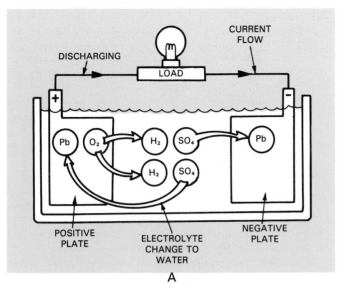

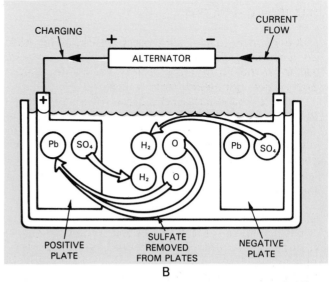

Fig. 12-4. Note basic chemical action inside battery. (Chrysler) A—Discharging changes battery acid into water. Pb or lead sulfate is formed on lead plates. With enough of this chemical change, the battery will finally become dead. B—Charging current reverses the chemical action that happened during discharge. Water is converted back into acid and lead sulfate is removed from plates.

2. NEGATIVE PLATE (usually made of a sheet of sponge lead).
3. ELECTROLYTE (sulfuric acid and water solution).
4. SEPARATOR (material that holds plates apart).

Fig. 12-4 illustrates the chemical action inside a battery cell when discharging and charging. When discharging, oxygen in the positive plate combines with hydrogen in the acid to form water. As the battery continues to discharge, the acid changes to water. The plates also become more similar (less dissimilar). With enough discharge, the acid will become weak and the plates will both contain lead sulfate. The battery will finally become "dead."

When charging, electrons are forced back into the battery from the alternator or from a battery charger. Electron flow through the plates reverses this chemical reaction. For current to flow back into the battery, the external voltage must be slightly HIGHER than the total cell voltage. See Fig. 12-4.

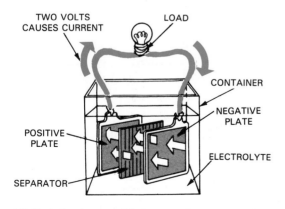

Fig. 12-5. A fundamental battery cell consists of a positive plate and negative plate held apart by a separator. These parts are submerged in container of sulfuric acid. One cell produces about 2 volts or 2.1 volts when load is not applied. (General Motors)

During charging, the sulfate on the plates is forced back into the acid or electrolyte. The water in the electrolyte is split into hydrogen and oxygen. This chemical action returns the lead peroxide to the positive plate and sponge lead to the negative plate. With enough recharging, the acid and plates are returned to their original state.

BATTERY VOLTAGE

Open circuit (no load) *cell voltage* is 2.1 volts, often rounded off to 2.0 volts, Fig. 12-5. Since the cells in an auto battery are connected in series, battery voltage depends upon the number of cells.

A *12-volt battery* has six cells that produce an open circuit voltage of 12.6 volts, called twelve volts in general terms. Modern autos use a 12 V battery and 12 V electrical system, Fig. 12-6.

A *6-volt battery* only has three cells with an open circuit voltage of 6.3 V. Older cars were designed to use 6 V batteries.

BATTERY FUNCTIONS

An auto battery has several important functions:
1. Operate the starting motor, ignition system, electronic fuel injection system, and other electrical devices for the engine during engine CRANKING and STARTING.
2. SUPPLY ALL ELECTRICAL POWER (radio, lights, etc.) for the car whenever the engine is NOT running.
3. HELP THE CHARGING SYSTEM provide electricity when current demands are above the output limit of the alternator.
4. Act as a capacitor (voltage stabilizer) that SMOOTHS CURRENT FLOW through the car's electrical systems.
5. STORE ENERGY (electricity) for extended periods.

To illustrate these functions, imagine the following sequence of events: You are sitting in your car with the

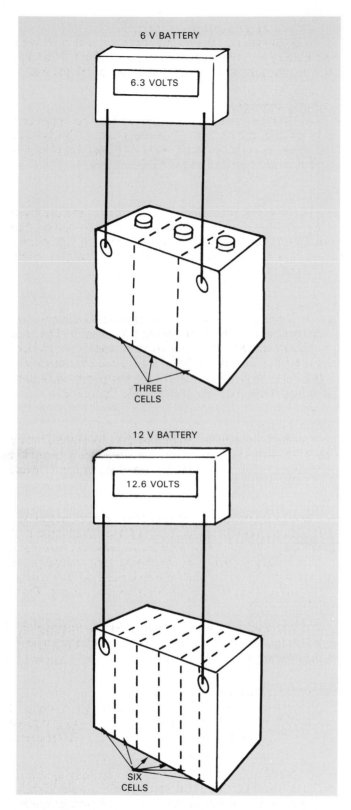

6 V BATTERY

6.3 VOLTS

THREE
CELLS

12 V BATTERY

12.6 VOLTS

SIX
CELLS

Fig. 12-6. Older batteries only had three cells to make six volts. Present day batteries have six cells and 12 volts.

radio ON, but the engine is OFF. The battery is supplying current to operate the radio and any dash indicator lights. It is slowly discharging.

When you start the engine, the battery provides a tremendous amount of current (well over 100 amps).

This energy operates the starting motor and essential engine systems. This drains more current out of the battery.

As soon as the engine starts, the charging system takes over. The alternator then recharges the battery and feeds current to other electrical devices.

If the load becomes too much for the charging system (engine idling slowly, all accessories ON for example), the battery may also feed current into the electrical system, even though the charging system is working.

BATTERY CONSTRUCTION

A car battery is built to withstand severe vibration, cold weather, engine heat, corrosive chemicals, high current discharge, and prolonged periods without use. An automotive battery must be well constructed.

Battery element construction

A *battery element,* mentioned briefly, is made up of positive plates, negative plates, straps, and separators. The element fits into a cell compartment in the battery case. A battery element is shown in Fig. 12-7.

Plate construction

The *battery plates* are made of a GRID (stiff mesh framework) coated with porous LEAD. Several battery plates are needed in each cell to provide enough battery power.

A lead strap connects several negative plates to form a *negative plate group.* Another lead strap connects the positive plates to make the *positive plate group.* Look at Fig. 12-8.

The chemically active material in the *negative plates* is sponge (porous) lead. The active material on the *positive plates* is lead peroxide. Calcium or antimony is normally added to the lead to increase battery performance and to decrease or lower *gasing* (acid fumes

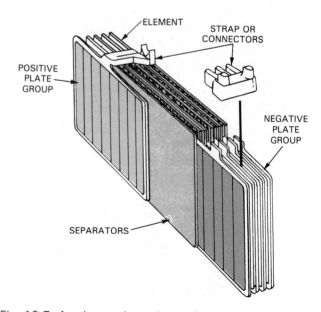

ELEMENT

STRAP OR
CONNECTORS

POSITIVE
PLATE
GROUP

NEGATIVE
PLATE
GROUP

SEPARATORS

Fig. 12-7. An element is made up of several positive plates, negative plates, and separators. Lead straps connect and form positive plate group and negative plate group. (General Motors)

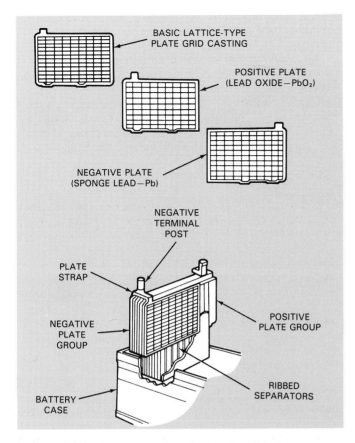

Fig. 12-8. Note how parts of an element install in battery case. Posts or terminals are made as part of straps. (Chrysler)

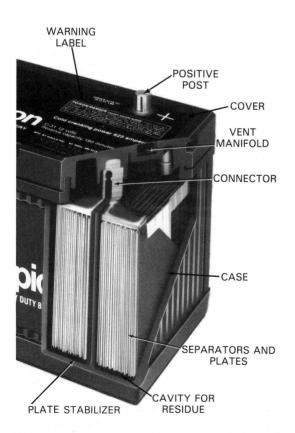

Fig. 12-9. Cutaway of battery shows internal parts. (Gould)

forming during chemical reaction).

Since the lead on the plates is porous, like a sponge, the battery acid easily penetrates into the lead. This helps the chemical reaction and the production of electricity.

Straps, connectors

Lead *battery straps* or *connectors* run the upper portion of the case to connect the plates. The battery terminals (posts or side terminals) are constructed as part of one end of each strap. See Fig. 12-8.

Separators

Separators fit between the battery plates to keep them from touching and shorting against each other. The separators are made of insulating material. They have openings which allow free circulation of the electrolyte around the plates. Look at Fig. 12-8.

Battery case

The *battery case* encloses the elements and acid solution. It is usually made of high quality plastic. The case must withstand extreme vibration, temperature change, and corrosive action of the battery acid. Dividers in the case form individual containers for each element. A container with its element, is one cell, Fig. 12-9.

Battery cover

The *battery cover* is bonded to the top of the battery case. It seals the top of the case. There is an opening above each battery cell for battery caps or a cell cover.

Battery cap

Battery caps snap into the holes or opening in the battery cover. They keep electrolyte from splashing out of the cover. Battery caps also serve as spark arrestors. *Spark arrestors* keep sparks or flames from igniting gases inside battery. Maintenance-free batteries have a large cover that is not removed during normal service. Refer to Fig. 12-10.

> DANGER! Hydrogen gas can collect at the top of batteries. If this gas is exposed to a flame or spark, it can explode.

Electrolyte (battery acid)

Electrolyte, often called battery acid, is a mixture of sulfuric acid and distilled water. Battery acid is poured into each cell until the plates are covered. Sulfuric acid is a very powerful corrosive substance.

> DANGER! Electrolyte must never come in contact with your skin or eyes. The sulfuric acid in the electrolyte can cause serious skin burns or even blindness.

Battery terminals

Battery terminals provide a means of connecting the battery plates to the car's electrical system. They are usually formed as part of the battery straps. Either two round posts or two side terminals can be used. Some large truck batteries use threaded posts, Fig. 12-11.

Battery posts are round metal terminals sticking out

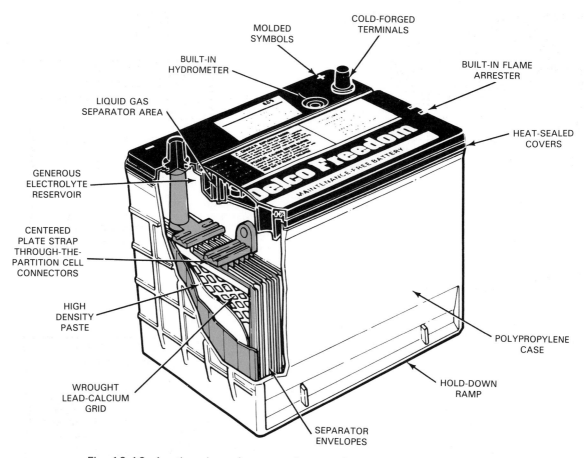

MOLDED SYMBOLS

COLD-FORGED TERMINALS

BUILT-IN HYDROMETER

BUILT-IN FLAME ARRESTER

LIQUID GAS SEPARATOR AREA

HEAT-SEALED COVERS

GENEROUS ELECTROLYTE RESERVOIR

CENTERED PLATE STRAP THROUGH-THE-PARTITION CELL CONNECTORS

HIGH DENSITY PASTE

POLYPROPYLENE CASE

WROUGHT LEAD-CALCIUM GRID

HOLD-DOWN RAMP

SEPARATOR ENVELOPES

Fig. 12-10. Another view of cutaway battery shows components. (Delco)

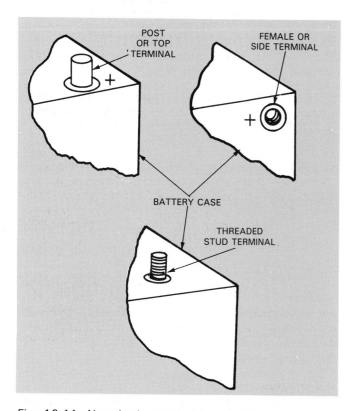

POST OR TOP TERMINAL

FEMALE OR SIDE TERMINAL

BATTERY CASE

THREADED STUD TERMINAL

Fig. 12-11. Note basic terminal types. Side terminals are becoming most common type because they resist corrosion very well.

of the top of the battery cover. They serve as male connections for female battery cable ends.

The *positive post* will be larger than the negative post. It may be marked with red paint and a positive (+) symbol. The *negative post* is smaller and may be black or green in color. It normally has a negative (−) symbol on or near it.

Side terminals are electrical connections on the side of the battery. They have female threads that accept a special bolt on the battery cable end. Side terminal polarity is identified by positive and negative symbols on the case.

Battery charge indicator (hydrometer)

A battery *charge indicator,* also called an *eye, test indicator,* or *hydrometer,* shows the general charge of the battery. One is pictured in Fig. 12-12.

The charge indicator changes color with changes in battery charge, Fig. 12-13. For example, the indicator may be green with the battery fully charged. It may turn black when discharged or yellow when the battery needs replacement, Fig. 12-14.

BATTERY CABLES

Battery cables are large conductors that connect the battery terminals to the electrical system of the car. Refer to Fig. 12-15.

The *positive cable* is normally red and fastens to the starter solenoid. The *negative battery cable* is usually

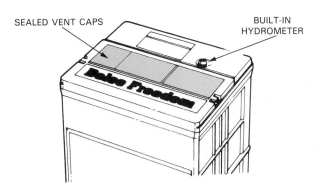

Fig. 12-12. This is a maintenance-free battery with a built-in hydrometer.

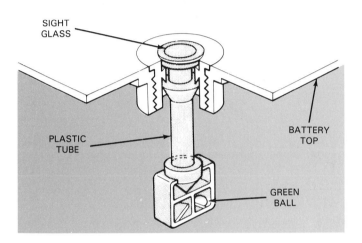

Fig. 12-13. Hydrometer or test indicator is mounted in battery cover. Small ball will float higher when acid strength and state of charge are high. (Chrysler)

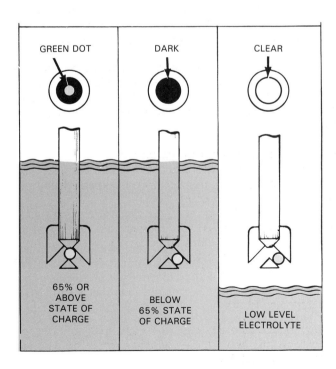

Fig. 12-14. Note operation of charge indicator. (General Motors)

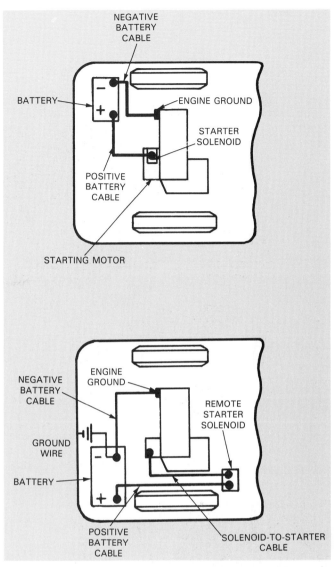

Fig. 12-15. Study how battery cable can be connected to vehicle's electrical system. Sometimes a junction box can be placed between positive terminals and solenoid.

black and connects to ground on the engine block.

Sometimes, the negative battery cable will have a *body ground wire* which assures that the vehicle body is grounded. If this wire does not make a good connection, a component grounded to the car body may NOT operate properly, Fig. 12-16.

Battery cable junction box

A *battery cable junction box* allows other wires to make electrical contact with the positive battery cable. One is shown in Fig. 12-17. It allows wires for the dash and other accessories to obtain a source of power. Sometimes, the starter solenoid can serve the same function.

Dual batteries

Dual batteries or two batteries can be used on some cars with diesel engines. A diesel engine's high compression ratio makes it difficult for the starting motor to crank the engine. Two batteries may be used to provide the

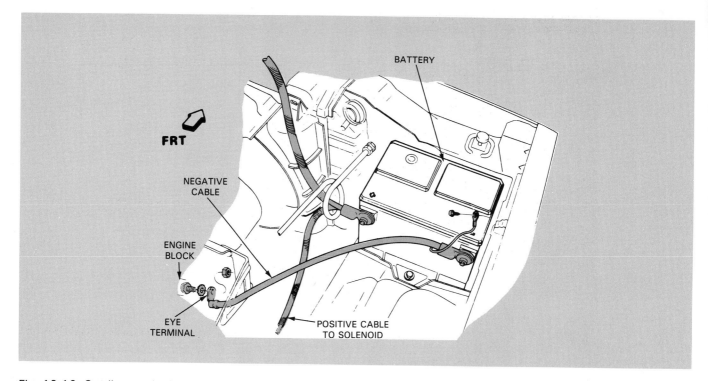

Fig. 12-16. Small ground wire assures that vehicle body is grounded. Engine block is mounted on rubber motor mounts and may not always be grounded to body properly. (Cadillac)

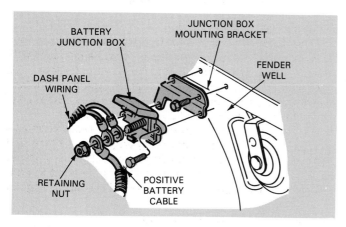

Fig. 12-17. Junction box may be used so that other wires can obtain power from positive battery cable. (GM Trucks)

high current for the starting motor on a diesel engine. The two batteries are wired in parallel so the output remains at 12 volts (actually 12.6 volts), Fig. 12-18.

When two batteries are connected in series, their output voltage DOUBLES. Keep this in mind when working with batteries. Two 12 V batteries in series produces 24 volts that could damage electrical devices.

BATTERY TRAY AND RETAINER

A *battery tray* and *retainer* hold the battery securely in place. They keep the battery from bouncing around during vehicle movement. It is important that the tray and retainer are in good condition and tight to prevent battery damage. See Fig. 12-19.

WET- AND DRY-CHARGED BATTERIES

There is no difference in the materials used in wet- and dry-charged batteries. The difference is in how the batteries are prepared for service during manufacture.

A *wet-charged battery* is filled with electrolyte and charged at the factory. The battery is then tested and placed in stock, ready for service.

A *dry-charged battery* contains fully charged elements but does NOT contain electrolyte. It leaves the factory in a dry state. Before use, the battery must be filled with electrolyte and charged. A dry-charged battery is commonly used because it has a much longer shelf life than a wet-charged battery.

Activation of a dry-charged battery is covered in a later chapter.

MAINTENANCE-FREE BATTERY

A *maintenance-free battery* is easily identified because it does NOT use removable filler caps. The top of the battery cells are covered with a large, snap-in cover. Small vent holes are in this cover.

Since calcium is used to make the battery plates, gassing and loss of electrolyte is reduced. Water does NOT have to be added to the electrolyte periodically.

The calcium in the plates reduces the production of battery gases. As a result, battery gas does not carry as much of the chemicals out of the battery. This increases battery service life and decreases service requirements.

New cars normally have maintenance-free batteries but aftermarket batteries can still be conventional with removable filler caps.

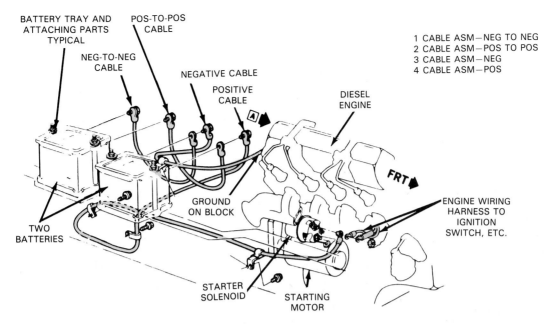

Fig. 12-18. Note use of two batteries connected in parallel to crank compression ignition or diesel engine. (GM Trucks)

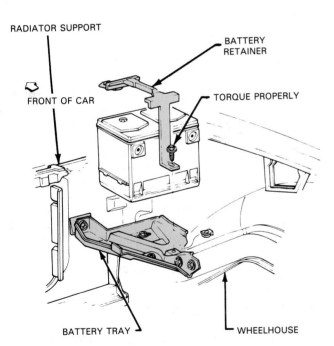

Fig. 12-19. Battery sits or rests on battery tray. Retainer holds battery down in tray during vehicle movement. Both must be in good condition and properly installed to protect battery from damage. (Cadillac)

BATTERY RATINGS

Battery ratings are set according to national test standards for battery performance. They let the technician and consumer compare the cranking power of one battery to another.

Two methods of rating lead-acid storage batteries are common. They were developed by the Society of Automotive Engineers (SAE) and the Battery Council International (BCI). These ratings are the cold cranking rating and reserve capacity rating.

Battery cold cranking rating

The *cold cranking rating* determines how much current (amps) the battery can deliver for 30 seconds at 0°F (−17.7°C) while maintaining terminal voltage of 7.2 volts or 1.2 volts per cell. This rating indicates the battery's ability to crank a specific engine (based on starter current draw) at a specified temperature.

For example, one auto manufacturer recommends a battery with 380 cold cranking amps for a small V-6 engine but a 450 cold cranking amp battery for a larger V-8 engine. A more powerful battery is needed to handle the heavier starter current draw of the larger engine.

Battery reserve capacity rating

The *reserve capacity rating* is the time needed to lower battery terminal voltage below 10.2 V (1.7 V per cell) at a discharge rate of 25 amps. This is with the battery fully charged and at 80°F (26.7°C).

Reserve capacity will appear on the battery as a time interval in minutes. For example, if a battery is rated at 90 minutes and the charging system fails, the driver has approximately 90 minutes (1 1/2 hours) of driving time under minimum electrical load before the battery goes completely dead.

A *watt rating* is another battery rating. It is the equivalent of the cold cranking rating. The watt rating measures how well the battery can crank an engine when at 0°F (−18°C).

BATTERY TEMPERATURE AND EFFICIENCY

As battery temperature drops, battery power is reduced. At low temperatures the chemical action inside the battery is slowed down. It will not produce as much current as when warm. This affects a battery's ability to start an engine in extremely cold weather, Fig. 12-20.

Also, when an engine is cold, the motor oil in the pan is very thick. The oil is difficult to pump through the engine and part friction is increased. This increases the amount of current needed to crank the engine with the starting motor. See Fig. 12-20.

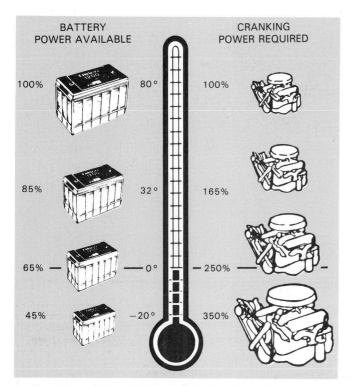

Fig. 12-20. Note how battery power is lower as temperature decreases. This is partially why engine cranks slowly in cold weather. (General Motors)

SUMMARY

Knowing how a battery is constructed and how it operates will help you analyze battery related problems.

A car battery is a chemical-electrical device for storing and producing electricity. When discharging, chemical energy is converted into electrical energy. When charging, current is forced into the battery to reverse the chemical action and reenergize the battery.

A battery cell is simply a container with two dissimilar electrodes surrounded by acid. The chemical reaction makes electrons flow between the electrodes.

One cell produces 2.1 volts. A twelve-volt battery has six cells that produces an open circuit voltage of 12.6 volts. Six-volt batteries are no longer used on modern automobiles.

A battery has several important functions. It must provide the current for cranking and starting the engine. It must serve as a capacitor to smooth alternator output current. It may also have to provide current when the electrical load is above the output of the alternator. The battery must also store energy for extended periods.

A battery element is made of positive plates, negative plates, straps, and separators. The negative plates are made of sponge (porous) lead. The positive plates are made of lead peroxide. Calcium or antimony may be added to the lead.

Straps connect the battery plates and also form the terminals. Separators keep the plates from shorting together.

The battery case houses the parts of the battery. A cover bonds to the case to form the top of the battery. Vent caps snap into an opening in the cover to allow venting and initial filling.

Hydrogen gas around the top of charging or discharging batteries is very explosive. Keep sparks and flames away from a battery to prevent a battery explosion.

Electrolyte is sulfuric acid. It must be handled with care to prevent chemical burns to the skin and eyes. Wear eye protection and gloves when working with batteries.

Battery posts are round terminals for connecting the battery to the electrical system of a car. Side terminals are female connections on the side of the battery. The positive terminal will be marked with a (+) sign. The negative terminal will be marked with a (−) sign.

A charge indicator or hydrometer is used in many new batteries. It will change color to indicate the condition of the battery.

Battery cables connect the two terminals to the vehicle electrical system. The positive cable usually connects to the starter solenoid. The negative cable usually connects to the side of the engine cylinder block.

The cold cranking rating determines how much current or amps the battery can deliver for 30 seconds at 0°F (−18°C) while maintaining a terminal voltage of 7.2 volts. The watt rating of a battery is the same as the cold cranking rating.

The reserve capacity rating is the time needed to lower battery terminal voltage below 10.2 volts at 25 amps current draw.

Battery temperature affects battery power. When cold, battery output current is reduced tremendously. If the engine is cold, the thickened oil also increases the current needed to crank the engine. This can make the engine difficult to start in cold weather.

KNOW THESE TERMS

Lead-acid battery, Discharge, Charging, Battery cell, Cell voltage, Battery voltage, Battery functions, Element, Plate, Plate group, Gassing, Straps, Separators, Battery case, Battery cover, Battery caps, Vents, Spark arrestors, Electrolyte, Sulfuric acid, Battery terminals, Posts, Side terminals, Positive terminal, Negative terminal, Charge indicator, Positive battery cable, Negative battery cable, Body ground wire, Cable junction box, Dual batteries, Battery tray, Wet-charged battery, Dry-charged battery, Maintenance-free battery, Cold cranking rating, Reserve capacity rating, Watt rating.

REVIEW QUESTIONS—CHAPTER 12

1. Open circuit battery cell voltage is ___2.1___ volts and a 12 V battery actually has an open circuit voltage of _____ volts.
   12.66

2. List the five functions of a car battery.
3. Explain the construction of battery plates.
4. Why are separators needed?
5. _____ or battery acid is a mixture of _____ _____ and distilled _____.
6. How can you tell a positive battery post from the negative post?

7. How does a charge indicator work?
8. From the battery, where do the two battery cables usually connect on the car?
9. Dual batteries for a diesel are normally connected in series. True or false?
10. Explain the cold cranking amp rating and the reserve capacity rating of a battery.

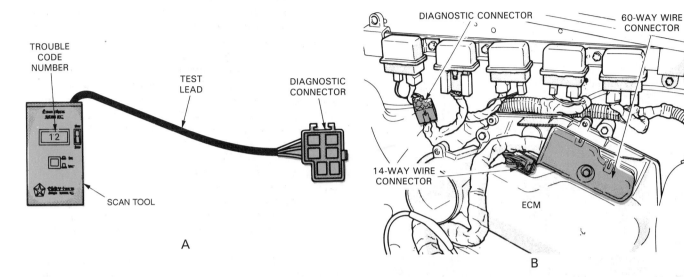

ALTERNATOR FAULT CODE CHART

Code	Type	Power Loss Lamp	Circuit	When Monitored By The Logic Module	When Put Into Memory	Actuation (ATM)) Test Code	Sensor Access Code
12	Indication	No	Battery Feed to the Logic Module	All the time when the ignition switch is on.	If the battery feed to the logic module has been disconnected within the last 50-100 engine starts.	None	None
16	Fault	Yes	Battery Voltage Sensing (Charging System)	All the time after one minute from when the engine starts.	If the battery sensing voltage drops below 4 volts for more than 20 seconds.	None	07
41	Fault	No	Alternator Field Control (Charging System)	All the time when the ignition switch is on.	If the field control fails to switch properly.	09	None
46	Fault	Yes	Battery Voltage Sensing (Charging System)	All the time when the engine is running.	If the battery sense voltage is more than 1 volt above the desired control voltage for more than 20 seconds.	None	None
47	Fault	No	Battery Voltage Sensing (Charging System)	Engine rpm above 1,500 rpm.	If the battery sense voltage is less than 1 volt below the desired control voltage for more than 20 seconds.	None	None
55	Indication	No			Indicates end of diagnostic mode.		
88	Indication	No			Indicates start of diagnostic mode. NOTE: This code must appear first in the diagnostic mode or fault codes will be inaccurate.		

C

Here is an example of how a scan tool can be used to perform tests relating to battery. It will also check charging voltage and other electrical values in computer system. Scanning is detailed in Chapter 21. A—One type of scan tool. B—Note location of this diagnostic connector for tapping into computer. C—Trouble code chart for battery voltage sensing. Battery temperature sensor can also be tested. (Chrysler)

ASE CERTIFICATION–TYPE QUESTIONS

1. Technician A says an automotive battery produces direct current. Technician B says an automotive battery is an electro-mechanical device. Who is right?
   - (A) A only.
   - (B) B only.
   - (C) Both A and B.
   - (D) Neither A nor B.

2. Technician A says battery discharge occurs when an automotive battery releases stored energy. Technician B says battery discharge occurs when an automotive battery converts chemical energy into electrical energy. Who is right?
   - (A) A only.
   - (B) B only.
   - (C) Both A and B.
   - (D) Neither A nor B.

3. Technician A says the cells of an automotive battery are made by placing two dissimilar metal electrodes in an acid-filled container. Technician B says the cells of an automotive battery are connected in series. Who is right?
   - (A) A only.
   - (B) B only.
   - (C) Both A and B.
   - (D) Neither A nor B.

4. Technician A says each cell in a 12 volt automotive battery produces 2.1 volts. Technician B says battery voltage depends on the number of cells. Who is right?
   - (A) A only.
   - (B) B only.
   - (C) Both A and B.
   - (D) Neither A nor B.

5. Technician A says an automotive battery helps the charging system provide electrical current when necessary. Technician B says an automotive battery acts as a "capacitor" for the car's electrical systems. Who is right?
   - (A) A only.
   - (B) B only.
   - (C) Both A and B.
   - (D) Neither A nor B.

6. During engine starting, an automotive battery provides:
   - (A) 10 amps.
   - (B) 50 amps.
   - (C) 75 amps.
   - (D) 100 amps or more.

7. Technician A says lead straps fit between the battery plates to keep them from touching and shorting against each other. Technician B says battery terminals are constructed as part of the battery plate separators. Who is right?
   - (A) A only.
   - (B) B only.
   - (C) Both A and B.
   - (D) Neither A nor B.

8. All of the following are basic parts of an automotive battery *except:*
   - (A) positive plate.
   - (B) separator.
   - (C) electrolyte.
   - (D) end frame.

9. Technician A says an automotive battery's charge indicator is called an "eye." Technician B says an automotive battery's charge indicator is called a "hydrometer." Who is right?
   - (A) A only.
   - (B) B only.
   - (C) Both A and B.
   - (D) Neither A nor B.

10. Technician A says an automotive battery's cold cranking rating is given in minutes. Technician B says an automotive battery's reserve capacity rating is given in amps. Who is right?
    - (A) A only.
    - (B) B only.
    - (C) Both A and B.
    - (D) Neither A nor B.

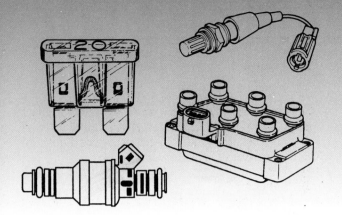

Chapter 13

Starting Systems

After studying this chapter, you will be able to:
• List the major parts of a starting system.
• Describe the operation of a starting system.
• Summarize the construction and operation of a starting motor.
• Explain the construction of a starter solenoid and relay.
• Describe the action of a starter drive mechanism.
• Compare field coil and permanent magnet type starting motors.
• Summarize the operation of a neutral safety switch.
• Sketch a basic starting circuit.

A *starting system* lets the driver use the ignition key switch to crank the engine until it "fires" and runs on its own power. Although it is a relatively simple system, it is a very important system.

This chapter will explain the operating principles and construction for major starting system components. This knowledge will help you in later discussions on how to diagnose, test, and repair starting systems. If you know how a starting system is supposed to work, you will be better at finding faults.

You should have studied Chapter 4 before studying this chapter. It covers basics (relays, solenoids, switches, etc.) that are essential for the full comprehension of this chapter.

MAJOR STARTING SYSTEM PARTS

The starting system uses a tremendous amount of battery power to operate a large dc motor. The starting motor has a small gear that meshes with a much larger gear on the engine flywheel. This allows the starter to rotate the flywheel and engine crankshaft. The engine goes through its four-stroke cycle. Fuel is pulled into the cylinders and ignited. The engine can then start and run on its own power.

As shown in Fig. 13-1, the major parts of a starting system include:
1. BATTERY (chemical-electrical device that sends high current to starting motor and other electrical components).
2. IGNITION SWITCH (start switch that completes circuit between battery and remainder of starting circuit).
3. NEUTRAL SAFETY SWITCH (switch on cars with

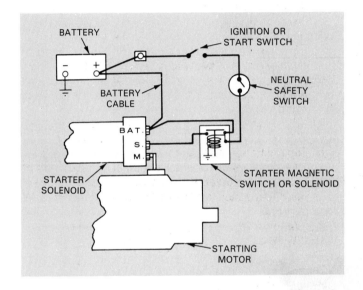

Fig. 13-1. This is a typical starting circuit. Note basic components and how they connect. (General Motors)

automatic transmissions or transaxles that prevents cranking unless shift lever is in neutral or park).
4. STARTER SOLENOID (high current, magnetic switch that connects high current to dc motor and may also engage starter gear with flywheel ring gear).
5. CRANKING MOTOR (starting motor on rear side of engine that rotates flywheel and crankshaft for engine starting).

As you turn the ignition key to the start position, the ignition switch connects the battery to the starter solenoid. If the neutral safety switch is closed, current flows to the starter solenoid.

The solenoid can then develop a magnetic field that attracts and closes the solenoid contacts. A high current then flows through the solenoid and into the starting motor. Solenoid plunger movement may also be used to push the starter gear into mesh with the flywheel ring gear.

The high torque of the starting motor spins the flywheel. As soon as the engine starts, the driver releases the key switch and the starting system is de-energized.

STARTING MOTOR OPERATION

The *starting motor,* also called *cranking motor,* changes the electrical energy from the battery into mechanical energy to spin the engine crankshaft. It is similar to other electric motors, but is super high torque.

As explained in an earlier chapter, all electric motors (wiper motors, fan motors, electric fuel pump motors, etc.) produce a spinning action through the interaction of magnetic fields inside the motor.

A *magnetic field* is made up of invisible lines of force. These lines of force flow between the poles of a permanent magnet or around the outside of a coil of wire that is carrying current.

Since like charges (fields) REPEL each other and unlike charges ATTRACT, magnetic fields can be used to produce motion. This principle is used inside a starting motor and other devices.

Basic starting motor

To construct a fundamental electric motor, start by bending a piece of wire into a loop. When current is passed through the *wire loop* or *winding,* a magnetic field forms around the wire. A magnet or *pole piece* would be needed to make the loop of wire move.

A magnetic field would be set up between the pole pieces, also called pole shoes. The attraction and repulsion could be used to spin the wire loop inside the stationary magnetic field, Fig. 13-2.

When current passes through the loop, the magnetic field around the loop and the field between the pole shoes act upon each other. The loop of wire is pushed and pulled away from the pole shoes, towards a vertical position.

Commutator and brushes

A commutator and several brushes are used to keep the electric motor spinning by controlling the current path

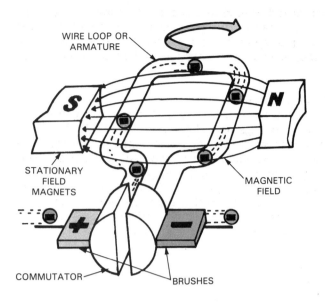

Fig. 13-2. Electric motor basically uses loop of wire inside stationary magnets. Attraction and repulsion between two can be used to make loop or armature rotate. (Ford)

through the windings (wire loops).

The *commutator* serves as a sliding electrical connection between the motor windings and the brushes. The commutator has *segments* (parts) insulated from each other. This is illustrated in Fig. 13-3.

The motor *brushes* ride on top of the commutator. They slide on the commutator to carry battery current to the spinning windings, Fig. 13-3.

As the winding rotates away from the pole piece, the commutator segments change the electrical connection between the brushes and windings. This reverses the magnetic field around the winding. Then the winding is

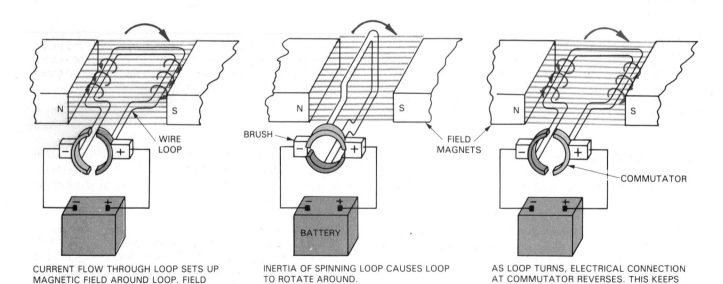

CURRENT FLOW THROUGH LOOP SETS UP MAGNETIC FIELD AROUND LOOP. FIELD PUSHES LOOP AWAY FROM PERMANENT MAGNETS.

INERTIA OF SPINNING LOOP CAUSES LOOP TO ROTATE AROUND.

AS LOOP TURNS, ELECTRICAL CONNECTION AT COMMUTATOR REVERSES. THIS KEEPS CURRENT FLOW IN LOOP SAME. AS A RESULT, LOOP CONTINUES TO SPIN UNDER POWER.

Fig. 13-3. Study basic action inside an electric motor. As loop or armature rotates, different electrical connections are made by brushes feeding current into commutator and loop of wire.

again pulled around and passes the other pole piece.

The constantly changing electrical connection at the windings keeps the motor spinning. A push-pull action is set up as each loop moves around inside the pole piece area.

Starter armature

The *starter armature* is a metal framework with several sets of windings (loops) wrapped around it. The commutator is also on one end of the armature. Several loops of wire or windings are needed to produce a strong enough motor to crank the engine.

Each set of windings is connected to a *segment* or part of the commutator. In this way, the brushes can electrically connect each segment and armature winding as the motor operates. See Fig. 13-4.

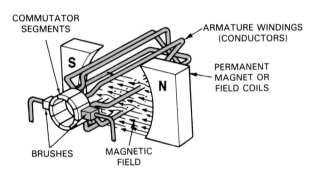

Fig. 13-4. Starting motor would not have enough power with only a single loop of wire. Each conductor in this illustration represents many wires wrapped around armature core. (Chrysler)

Starter field

The *starting motor field* is the stationary magnetic flux around the armature or wire loops. The stationary field makes the armature spin. Presently, there are two types of starting motor fields: field coils and field magnets.

Field coils

The *field coils* in a starting motor are insulated wires wrapped around iron cores. They are attached to the inside of the starting motor housing. When current flows through the field coils, a powerful magnetic field or flux forms. This magnetic field is used to rotate the armature. Four field coils are used in this type starting motor.

Permanent field magnets

Some new starting motors use only permanent magnets to produce the stationary field. Developed recently, these new magnets use iron, boron, and neodymium (rare element). The magnets develop an extremely strong flux for their small size. As a result, these permanent magnets can be used instead of the field coils. Windings are not needed, Fig. 13-5.

STARTER FRAMES

The *starter frames* or *starter housings* are the three main sections of the starting motor that hold the other components. Look at Fig. 13-6.

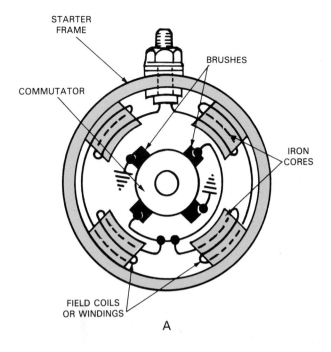

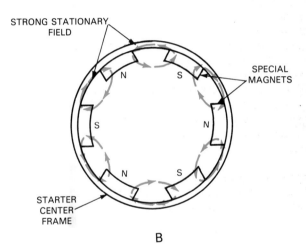

Fig. 13-5. A—This starter uses field coils wrapped around iron cores. Current flow through coils produces powerful magnetic field for action upon armature field. B—This new style starter does not need field coils. It uses special permanent magnets that are strong enough to rotate armature. (Ford and General Motors)

Center frame

The *center frame* or *field frame* is the large steel cylinder that holds the field coils and/or field magnets. The two end frames fasten to each end of the center frame. See Fig. 13-6.

Drive end frame

The *drive end frame* is the housing around the starting motor drive gear. When bolted to the engine, the drive end frame extends inside the clutch housing on the rear of the engine, Fig. 13-6.

The drive end frame contains a bushing for the armature shaft. The shaft spins inside this bushing. The drive end bushing helps keep the starter gear properly meshed with the flywheel ring gear, Fig. 13-7.

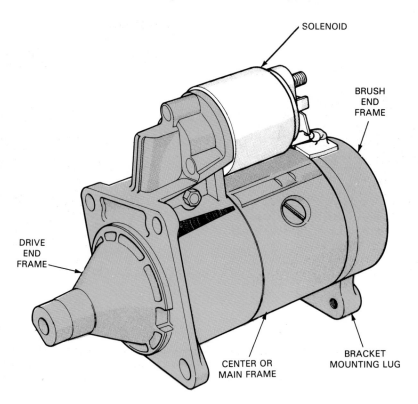

Fig. 13-6. Most starters have three major frames: center frame or field frame, drive end frame, and brush end frame. (Chrysler)

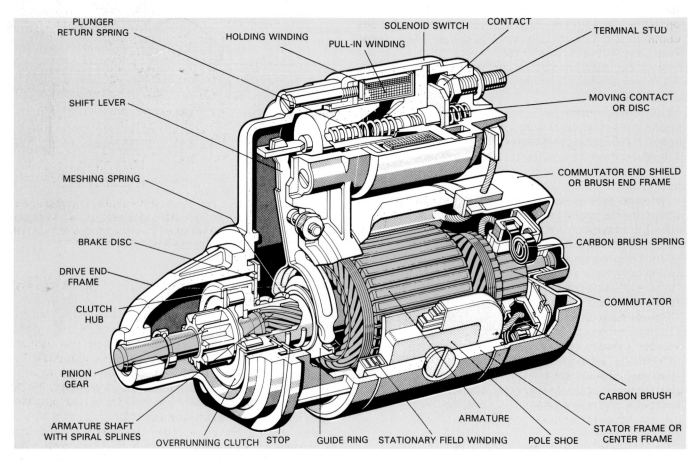

Fig. 13-7. Study parts of this starting motor carefully. Bushings or bearings in end frames support spinning armature. Brush springs hold brushes in contact with commutator. Overrunning clutch and pinion gear slide over end of splined armature shaft. (Robert Bosch)

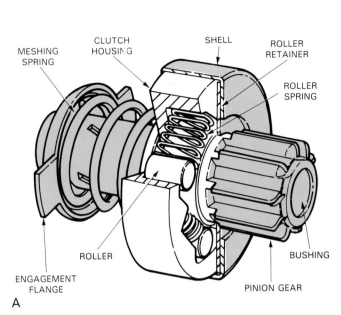

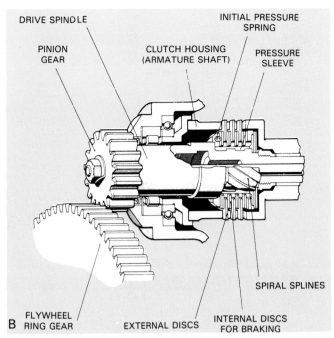

Fig. 13-8. Two variations of overrunning clutches with pinion gears. A—Spring-loaded rollers are mounted in ratchet type mechanism. They will let gear turn freely in one direction but make gear lock to housing in other direction. B—This pinion gear assembly uses overrunning clutch and clutch disc mechanism for braking gear after starting. (Ford and Robert Bosch)

Brush end frame

The *brush end frame* usually holds the brushes and springs around the armature commutator. It bolts to the end opposite the starter drive gear. Two long through-bolts commonly fit through the brush end frame and thread into holes in the drive end frame. This holds both end frames securely onto the center frame. Refer to Figs. 13-6 and 13-7.

Overrunning clutch

The *starter overrunning clutch* locks the pinion gear in one direction and releases it in the other. This allows the pinion gear to turn the flywheel ring gear for starting. It also lets the pinion gear freewheel when the engine begins to run.

Without the overrunning clutch, the starter could be driven by the engine flywheel. The flywheel gear could spin the starter too fast and cause armature damage. Look at Fig. 13-8.

Small spring-loaded rollers are located between the pinion gear collar and the clutch shell. The rollers wedge into the notches in the shell in one direction (driving direction). They slide back and release in the other direction (freewheeling direction). This is illustrated in Fig. 13-9.

Starter pinion gear

A *starter pinion gear* is the small gear on the overrunning clutch. It slides over the armature shaft. The pinion gear engages a large gear on the engine flywheel. It moves into and meshes with the flywheel ring gear anytime the starter is energized.

STARTING MOTOR CLASSIFICATIONS

There are two major classifications of starting motors: positive engagement and solenoid actuated. Both refer

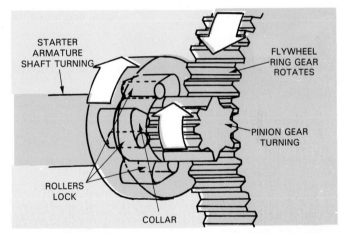

Fig. 13-9. Note action of overrunning clutch. It will lock and rotate flywheel ring gear for starting. However, when engine "fires," clutch will freewheel so that armature is not spun at high speed by flywheel. (Deere & Co.)

to the method used to move the pinion gear into mesh with the flywheel gear.

Positive engagement starter

The *positive engagement starter* uses the motor's magnetic field to pull down on a movable pole shoe. The *movable pole* shoe is attached to a lever arm or drive yoke. When the movable pole shoe is attracted by the starter field coils, the *lever arm* or *yoke* slides the pinion gear into engagement. See Fig. 13-10.

Fig. 13-11 shows a cutaway view of a positive engagement type starting motor. Note how a small pivot pin slides through the lever or yoke arm. Also note how a downward movement of the pole shoe would make the other end of the pivot arm move outward.

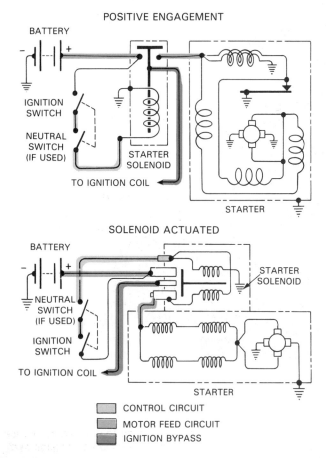

POSITIVE ENGAGEMENT

SOLENOID ACTUATED

CONTROL CIRCUIT
MOTOR FEED CIRCUIT
IGNITION BYPASS

Fig. 13-10. Study circuits for two types of starting motors. (Ford) A—Positive engagement starter has solenoid mounted away from motor. Movable pole shoe shifts pinion gear into ring gear. B—Solenoid-actuated starter uses solenoid to complete battery-to-motor circuit and to also engage pinion gear.

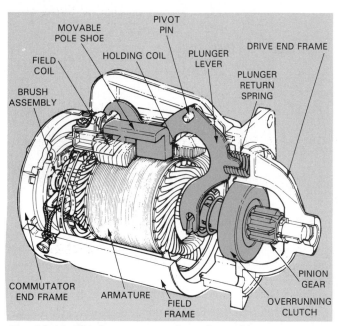

Fig. 13-11. This is a cutaway view of a positive engagement starting motor. Note movable pole shoe. It is mounted on lever attached to pinion gear assembly. When motor is energized, magnetic field pulls down on pole shoe. This moves shift lever out and forces pinion gear into mesh with ring gear. (Ford)

Solenoid-actuated starter

The *solenoid-actuated starter* uses solenoid plunger action to move the shift lever and pinion gear. The solenoid is mounted on top of the starting motor. This lets the starter use the plunger motion for pinion gear engagement and to close the motor circuit.

Fig. 13-12 illustrates a solenoid-actuated starting motor. Note how the solenoid plunger is attached to the yoke or shift lever. When current flows through the solenoid, the plunger is pulled in and the pinion gear is pushed out.

Internal motor circuits

Direct current electric motors have three common types of internal connections. These include the series, shunt, and compound.

Generally, *series wound* starting motors develop maximum torque at initial startup. Torque decreases as motor speed increases.

Shunt wound motors have less starting torque but more constant torque at varying speeds.

The *compound wound* motor has both series and shunt windings. It has good starting power with fairly constant operating speed.

Gear reduction starter

A *gear reduction starter* uses extra gears to increase the amount of torque at the pinion gear. This is another type of starting motor. The reduction gears lower the rpm of the pinion gear but increase turning force applied to the flywheel ring gear.

Fig. 13-13 illustrates a gear reduction starting motor using two bevel gears. A small gear on the armature turns a larger gear on the pinion gear shaft.

Fig. 13-14 shows a starting motor that uses a planetary gearset for reduction. The armature provides power to the planetary gearset. Another shaft, which turns at a lower speed, extends out of the gear set. Planetary gears provide a very compact and strong method of gear reduction to increase motor torque.

Figs. 13-15 through 13-17 show exploded views of starting motors. Compare their differences and similarities. Also study the part names and locations.

STARTER SOLENOIDS

Mentioned briefly, *starter solenoids* are similar in operation to relays. However, they use a larger plunger that slides back and forth to produce a magnetic switch and actuator. A *relay* uses a small contact on a flexible arm to control much smaller currents.

A solenoid for a positive engagement starter is different than one for a solenoid-actuated starter. These two types are pictured in Fig. 13-18.

When mounted on the starter, the solenoid must complete the battery-to-starter circuit and it must also engage the pinion gear. When away from the starter, the solenoid simply serves as a "high current relay" to energize the starting motor, Fig. 13-19.

A starter solenoid, depending on starter design, may have three functions:

1. Complete battery-to-starter circuit.

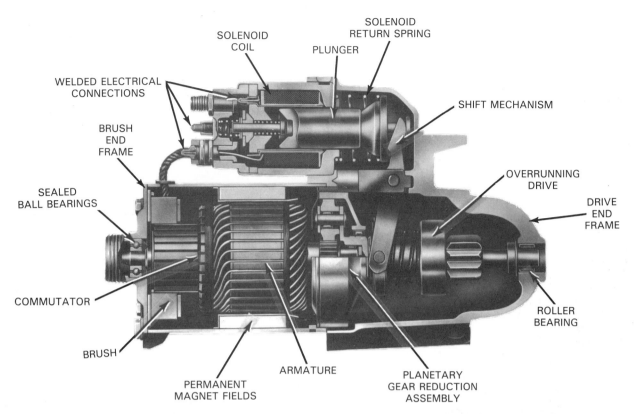

Fig. 13-12. This is a cutaway of a solenoid-actuated starting motor. Note how solenoid is mounted on top of motor. Plunger is connected to shift lever. Current flow to solenoid moves plunger. This energizes motor and moves pinion into engagement. (General Motors)

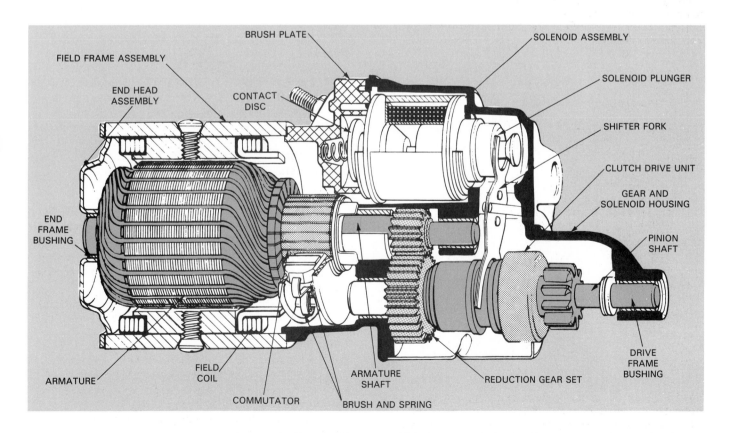

Fig. 13-13. Locate extra gears in this gear reduction starting motor. Pinion gear rpm is lower than armature rpm. Turning force, or torque, is higher at pinion gear however. Also note that armature commutator is near middle of starter housing. (Chrysler)

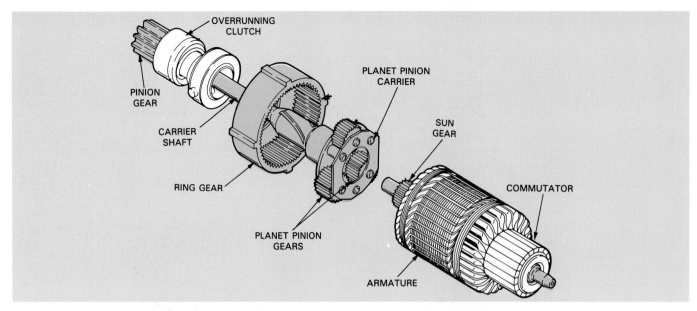

Fig. 13-14. This is a variation of the gear reduction starting motor. It uses a planetary gearset to produce the reduction. Planetary gears are very compact and strong for their size. (General Motors)

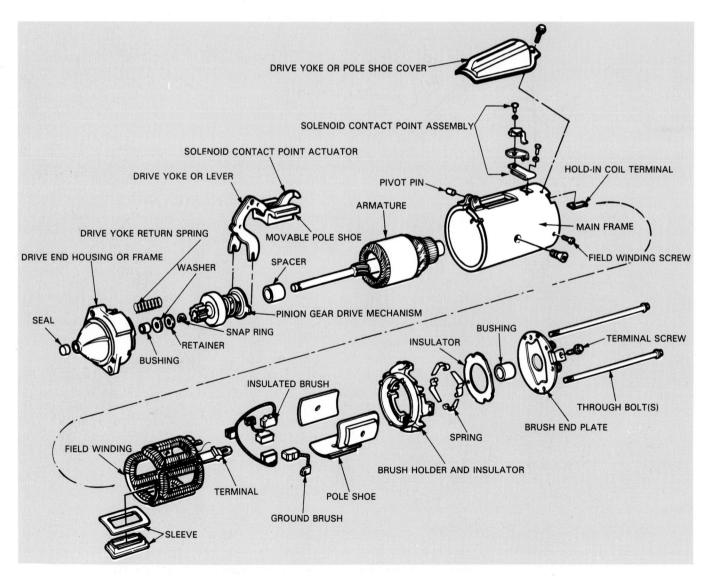

Fig. 13-15. Study parts in this exploded view of a positive engagement starter. (Ford)

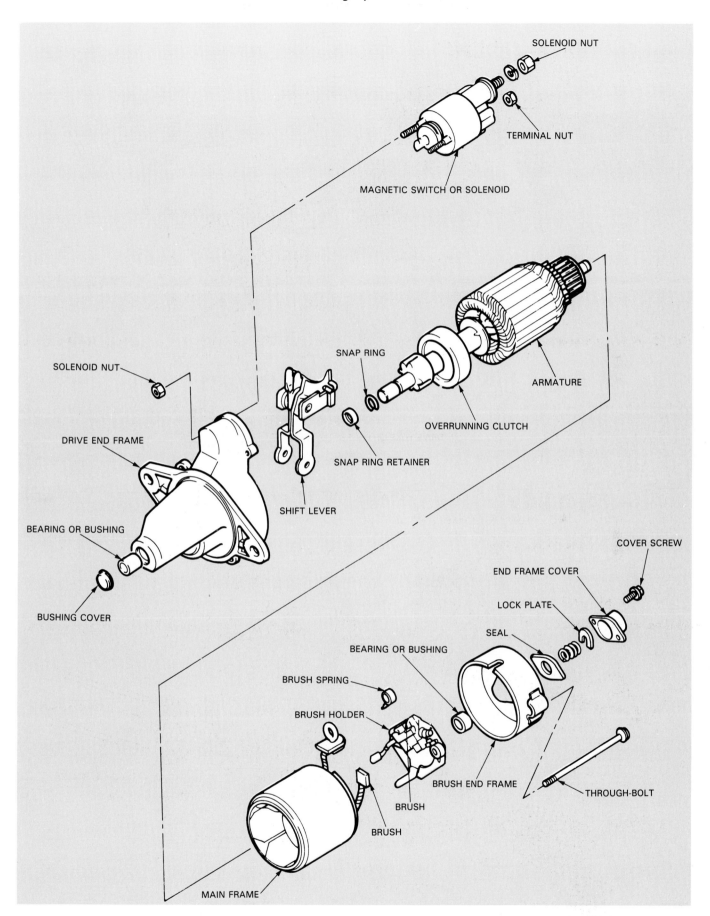

Fig. 13-16. Study the relationship of the parts in this solenoid-engaged starter. (Oldsmobile)

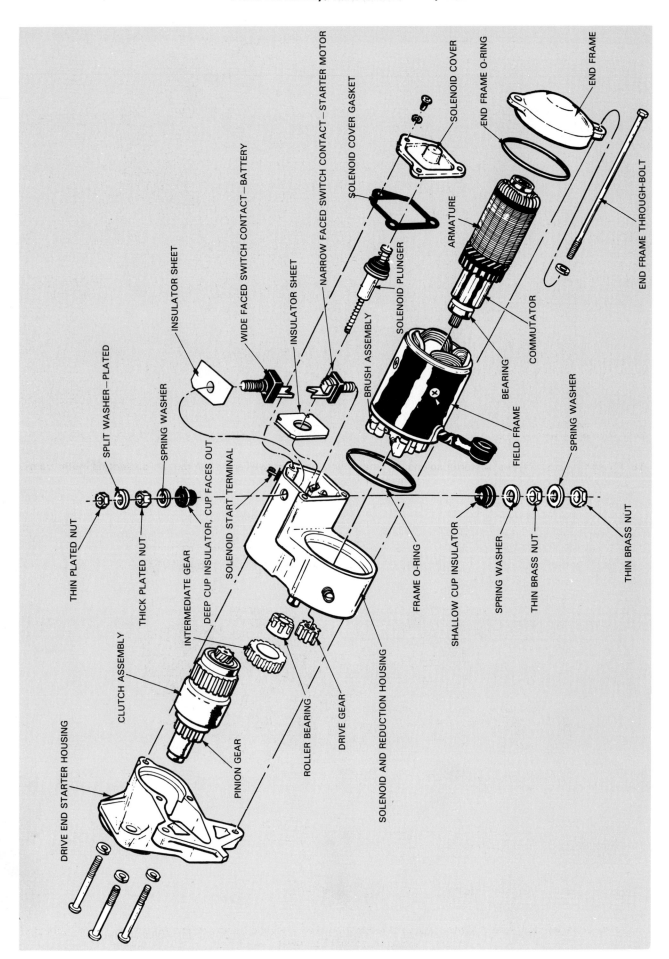

Fig. 13-17. Here is an exploded view of a gear reduction starting motor. Note its construction. (General Motors)

SOLENOID COVER

END FRAME O-RING

END FRAME

SOLENOID COVER GASKET

NARROW FACED SWITCH CONTACT—STARTER MOTOR

END FRAME THROUGH-BOLT

INSULATOR SHEET

WIDE FACED SWITCH CONTACT—BATTERY

ARMATURE

INSULATOR SHEET

SOLENOID PLUNGER

COMMUTATOR

BRUSH ASSEMBLY

BEARING

SPLIT WASHER—PLATED

INSULATOR SHEET

SPRING WASHER

FIELD FRAME

SPRING WASHER

DEEP CUP INSULATOR, CUP FACES OUT

SOLENOID START TERMINAL

SHALLOW CUP INSULATOR

SPRING WASHER

THIN PLATED NUT

THIN BRASS NUT

THICK PLATED NUT

FRAME O-RING

THIN BRASS NUT

INTERMEDIATE GEAR

CLUTCH ASSEMBLY

ROLLER BEARING

DRIVE GEAR

SOLENOID AND REDUCTION HOUSING

DRIVE END STARTER HOUSING

PINION GEAR

220

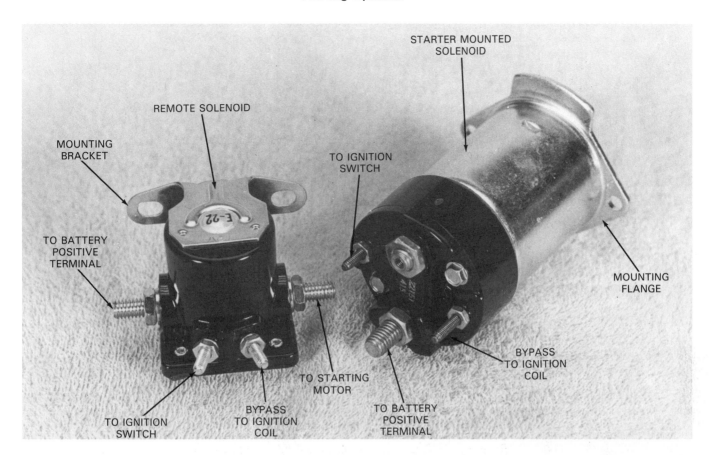

Fig. 13-18. Photo shows two types of starter solenoids. One mounts on fenderwell and other mounts on starting motor frame. (Universal Tire and Auto)

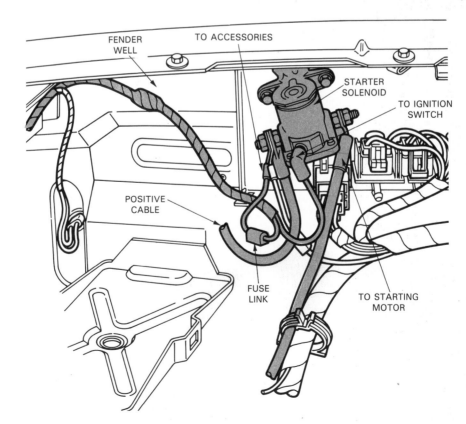

Fig. 13-19. With positive engagement starter, solenoid mounts on side of engine compartment. Note extra wires connected to battery side of solenoid terminal. (Ford)

2. Push starter pinion gear into mesh with flywheel gear.

3. Bypass resistance wire in ignition circuit (See Chapter on ignition systems).

Solenoid construction

The starter solenoid contains a set of *windings* to produce a field. A *metal plunger* mounts inside these windings to react to the magnetic field. A large *contact disc* is formed on one end of the plunger to complete the circuit. Two *terminal lugs* are positioned on the end of the solenoid so that they can touch the plunger contact disc. A *solenoid spring* holds the plunger in the normally open position. See Fig. 13-20.

A small terminal is on the outside of the solenoid. It connects to the ignition switch. A large terminal is for the positive battery cable. With a remote solenoid, a second large terminal is needed for the cable to the starting motor, Fig. 13-20.

Starter solenoid operation

When the ignition key is turned to the start position, a small current flows through the solenoid windings. This produces a magnetic field that pulls on the solenoid plunger. The plunger and disc are pulled into the coil windings.

The solenoid disc touches both of the terminals and completes the battery-to-starter circuit. About 150 to 200 amps then flow through the solenoid and to the starter. Current will vary with starter design and engine size.

When the ignition key is released, current is disconnected from the solenoid windings. The magnetic field collapses and the plunger is free to slide out of the windings. This opens the disc-to-terminal connection. The open connection stops current to the starter, and the motor shuts off.

Fig 13-21 shows the operation of a starter-mounted solenoid. When the key is first turned to start, battery current operates the solenoid. The solenoid plunger moves. Through lever action it begins to slide the pinion gear into mesh with the ring gear.

At the end of solenoid plunger travel, the contact disc touches the two terminals to activate the motor. The motor begins to spin and crank the engine.

STARTER RELAY

As you learned earlier, a *relay* is a device that opens or closes one circuit by responding to an electrical signal. Some starting systems use a relay between the ignition switch and the starter solenoid.

A *starter relay* uses a small current flow from the ignition switch to control a slightly larger current flow to the starter solenoid. This further reduces the load on the ignition key switch.

Starter relay operation

Look at Fig. 13-22. When the ignition switch is turned to start, current flows into the relay. This closes the relay contacts. The contacts complete the circuit to the solenoid windings and the starting system operates.

When the key is released, the relay opens. This stops the solenoid current to disengage the starting motor.

Fig. 13-23 shows a starter relay. Note the terminals and where they connect.

NEUTRAL SAFETY AND CLUTCH SWITCHES

A *neutral safety switch* prevents the engine from cranking unless the shift selector is in neutral or park. It stops the starting system from working when the transmission or transaxle is in gear. This provides a safety feature since injury could result if the engine were to crank and start while the car was in gear.

Cars with automatic transmissions or transaxles commonly have a neutral safety switch. The switch may be mounted on the shift lever mechanism or on the transmission/transaxle assembly.

A *clutch safety switch* can be used with cars using manual transmissions or transaxles to prevent engine

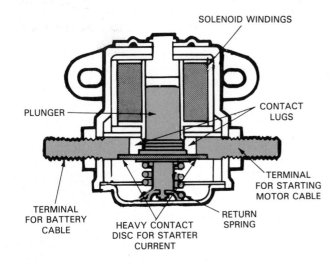

REMOTE SOLENOID

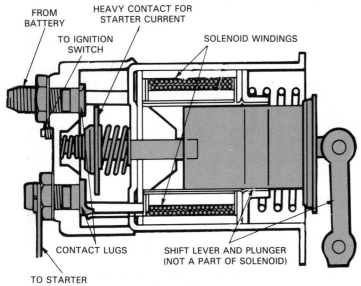

STARTER-MOUNTED SOLENOID

Fig. 13-20. Compare construction of two solenoids. Both use similar components but starter-mounted solenoid has separate or exposed plunger for moving shift lever. (Chrysler)

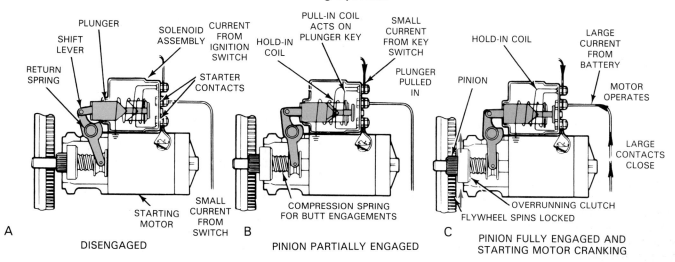

Fig. 13-21. Operation of starter-mounted solenoid. A—Current is fed to small terminal on solenoid from ignition switch. This forms magnetic field in solenoid and plunger is pulled into solenoid windings. B—The coil magnetic field attracts plunger and begins to move shift lever and pinion gear outward. C—As pinion gear is engaged with flywheel ring gear, large contact closes and connects battery to starting motor. Motor then begins to turn and rotate engine crankshaft for starting. (Robert Bosch)

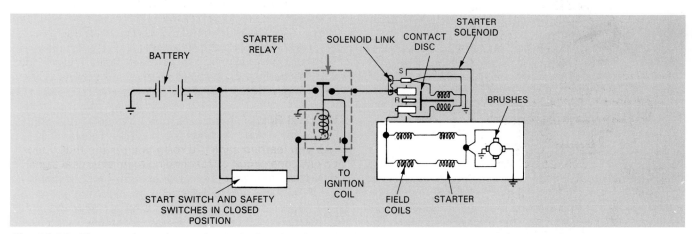

Fig. 13-22. Diagram shows how relay typically wires into starting motor circuit. Ignition switch sends small current to relay coil. Relay coil closes contacts and higher current is sent to starter solenoid. This closes solenoid contacts to feed even higher current into motor. (Ford)

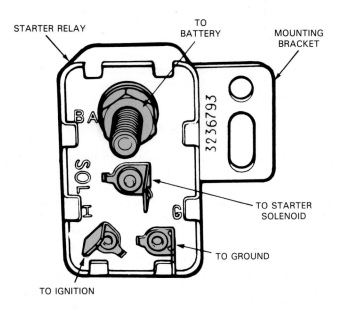

Fig. 13-23. Note terminals on this starter relay. (Renault)

cranking. The switch is only closed when the driver presses the clutch pedal down. This will prevent vehicle movement while cranking and provides an important safety feature.

A neutral safety switch and the clutch safety switch are usually wired in series with the starter solenoid or relay. They both block current flow unless they are closed.

Safety switch operation

A starting system circuit with a clutch safety switch is shown in Fig. 13-24. Note how the switch is wired into the circuit going to the starter solenoid. This is similar to a neutral safety switch.

When the clutch pedal is released, the safety switch is open (disconnected). This keeps current from activating the solenoid and starter when the ignition switch is turned to start.

When the clutch pedal is depressed, the safety switch is closed (connected). Current can then flow to the starter when the ignition key switch is turned.

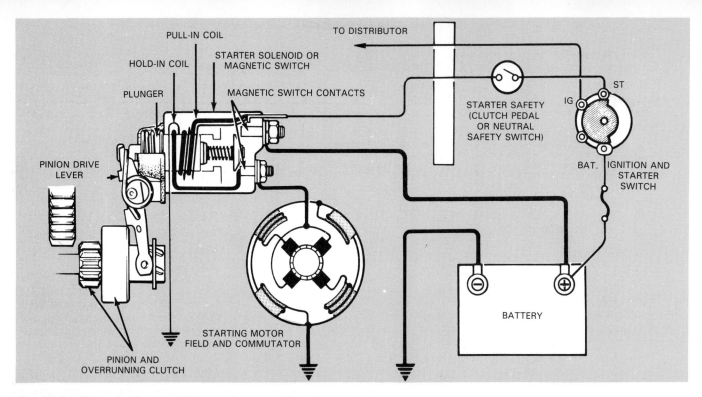

Fig. 13-24. Neutral safety switch is used to prevent engine cranking unless gear shift lever is in neutral or park with automatic transmissions or tranxaxles. Clutch pedal safety switch will prevent cranking unless clutch pedal is pressed down. This prevents vehicle movement during cranking. (Buick)

SUMMARY

The starting system uses battery energy and a powerful DC motor to crank the engine. The ignition switch sends current to a starter solenoid. The solenoid then closes high current contacts and battery power is connected directly to the starting motor. A small gear then engages a larger gear on the engine flywheel. This rotates the engine crankshaft until the engine "fires" and runs on its own power.

The starting motor consists of the following parts:
1. ARMATURE (set of rotating windings wrapped around a metal core).
2. COMMUTATOR (rotating contacts mounted on one end of the armature).
3. BRUSHES (sliding electrical contacts that ride on and send current into armature windings through commutator).
4. OVERRUNNING CLUTCH (one-way clutch that operates pinion gear).
5. PINION GEAR (small gear on end of armature shaft that turns flywheel ring gear).
6. FIELD COILS OR MAGNETS (stationary magnetic field around outside of armature).
7. STARTER FRAMES (outside housings that hold other parts of starter).

Some starters have the solenoid mounted on the frame; they are called solenoid-actuated starters. Other starters do NOT use a solenoid to engage the pinion gear; they are called positive engagement starters.

A solenoid-actuated starter uses solenoid plunger action to move a lever arm or yoke. The lever arm movement slides the pinion gear out and into mesh with ring gear. The positive engagement starter uses a moveable pole shoe. Magnetic attraction, caused by motor opera-

tion, pulls down on the pole shoe. The pole shoe moves a lever or yoke that engages the pinion gear.

Some starters use extra gears to increase output torque. These are called gear reduction starters.

A starter solenoid consists of:
1. SOLENOID WINDINGS (coil of wire that produces magnetic field to act upon solenoid plunger).
2. SOLENOID PLUNGER (metal core that is free to slide back and forth inside coil when attracted or released by magnetic field).
3. SOLENOID SPRING (spring that moves plunger to released or open position).
4. DISC CONTACT (round, metal ring on end of solenoid plunger that makes and breaks the connection between battery and starter).
5. HIGH CURRENT TERMINALS (large threaded lugs that make contact with disc and allow connection of conductors from battery and to starting motor).
6. IGNITION SWITCH TERMINAL (small terminal that allows wire from ignition switch to energize windings and activate solenoid).
7. SOLENOID HOUSING (plastic case that supports other components).

A starter relay is sometimes used to reduce the current flow through the ignition switch. The ignition switch will send current to the relay. Then, the relay contacts will close and send a slightly higher current to the starter solenoid. This closes the solenoid disc contact and an extremely high current is sent to the starter motor.

A neutral safety switch can be used on cars with automatic transmissions or transaxles. It prevents engine cranking unless the shift lever is in park or neutral.

A clutch safety switch can be used on cars with manual transmissions or transaxles. It will prevent engine cranking unless the clutch pedal is pressed down.

224

KNOW THESE TERMS

Starting system, Ignition switch, Starting motor, Pole piece, Commutator, Brushes, Armature, Field coils, Permanent field magnets, Center frame, Drive end frame, Brush end frame, Overrunning clutch, Starter pinion gear, Positive engagement starter, Moveable pole shoe, Solenoid-actuated starter, Shift lever, Yoke, Internal motor circuits, Gear reduction starter, Starter solenoid, Starter relay, Neutral safety switch, Clutch safety switch.

REVIEW QUESTIONS—CHAPTER 13

1. When you rotate the ignition key switch to the start position, current is first sent to the:
   a. Commutator.
   b. Armature.
   c. Field coils.
   d. Solenoid.
2. How does a motor produce a spinning motion?
3. Explain the operation of the commutator and brushes in a starting motor.
4. What are field coils?
5. Some starting motors do not use field coils; they use new magnets that are powerful enough to produce the stationary field. True or false?
6. Describe the three frame sections of a starting motor.
7. How does an overrunning clutch work?
8. In your own words, what is the difference between a positive engagement starter and a solenoid-actuated starter?
9. This type starter will produce a slightly slower cranking rpm but much higher cranking torque.
   a. Positive engagement starter.
   b. Gear reduction starter.
   c. Field coil starter.
   d. Permanent magnet starter.
10. A _____ _____ is similar in purpose to a relay but it controls a much higher current and can move other components.

ASE CERTIFICATION—TYPE QUESTIONS

1. Technician A says a neutral safety switch prevents an automotive engine from cranking unless the shift lever is in neutral or park. Technician B says a neutral safety switch is generally used on vehicles with manual transmissions and transaxles. Who is right?
   (A) A only.   (C) Both A and B.
   (B) B only.   (D) Neither A nor B.
2. Technician A says an automotive engine's starting motor engages and turns the engine's pinion ring gear. Technician B says an automotive engine's starting motor engages and turns the engine's flywheel and crankshaft. Who is right?
   (A) A only.   (C) Both A and B.
   (B) B only.   (D) Neither A nor B.
3. Technician A says a starting motor's commutator and brushes are used to control the current through the armature windings. Technician B says a starting motor's commutator is a sliding electrical connection between the motor windings and the brushes. Who is right?
   (A) A only.   (C) Both A and B.
   (B) B only.   (D) Neither A nor B.
4. Technician A says a starting motor armature is a metal framework with several sets of windings wrapped around it. Technician B says each set of armature windings is connected to a brush. Who is right?
   (A) A only.   (C) Both A and B.
   (B) B only.   (D) Neither A nor B.
5. Technician A says the field frame is one of the three main sections of an automotive starting motor. Technician B says the commutator end frame is one of the three main sections of an automotive starting motor. Who is right?
   (A) A only.   (C) Both A and B.
   (B) B only.   (D) Neither A nor B.
6. Technician A says a starting motor's overrunning clutch locks the pinion gear to the armature after the engine starts. Technician B says that without an overrunning clutch, the starter could be driven by the engine flywheel. Who is right?
   (A) A only.   (C) Both A and B.
   (B) B only.   (D) Neither A nor B.
7. While discussing automotive starting motor classifications, Technician A says a positive engagement starting motor utilizes a capacitor to activate the pinion gear. Technician B says a positive engagement starting motor utilizes a relay to activate the pinion gear. Who is right?
   (A) A only.   (C) Both A and B.
   (B) B only.   (D) Neither A nor B.
8. All of the following are basic parts of a positive engagement starting motor *except:*
   (A) Pole shoes.   (C) Rectifier end plate.
   (B) Field windings.   (D) Drive yoke.
9. Technician A says a gear reduction starter uses extra gears to decrease the amount of torque at the pinion gear. Technician B says that in a gear reduction starter, a large gear on the armature turns a smaller gear on the pinion gear shaft. Who is right?
   (A) A only.   (C) Both A and B.
   (B) B only.   (D) Neither A nor B.
10. Technician A says a starter solenoid can be mounted on the car's fenderwell. Technician B says a starter solenoid can be mounted on the starting motor's frame. Who is right?
    (A) A only.   (C) Both A and B.
    (B) B only.   (D) Neither A nor B.

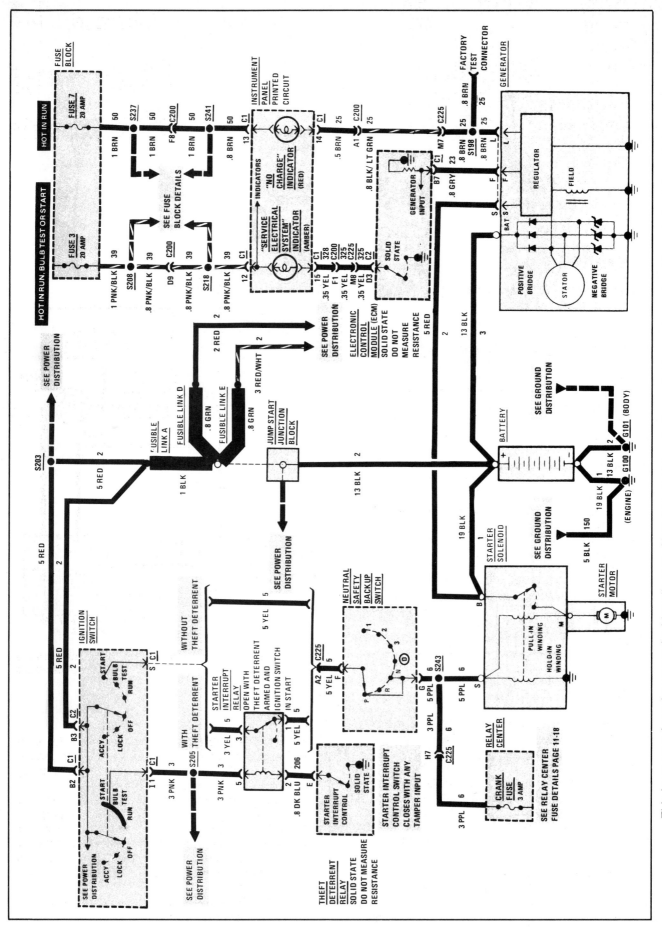

This is an actual service manual wiring diagram. Note how it shows battery, starting motor, solenoid, neutral safety switch, and anti-theft relay. (Cadillac)

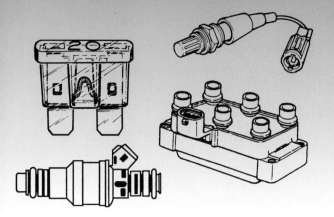

Chapter 14

Charging Systems

After studying this chapter, you will be able to:
• Sketch a basic charging circuit diagram.
• Explain the operation of a charging system.
• Identify the parts of an alternator.
• Explain the function of major alternator components.
• Summarize the construction of charging system parts.
• Describe voltage regulator variations.
• Explain AC rectification.
• Compare conventional and pulsed field regulation.
• Review DC generator operation.
• Explain the construction and operation of an alternator-mounted vacuum pump.

The *charging system* is the "heart" of the car's electrical system; it must "pump" current to all electrical-electronic components. It must do this anytime the engine is running. The charging system must re-energize the battery and provide for all of the electrical needs of the car. This makes the charging system very important to the study of automotive electricity and electronics.

This chapter will discuss the operation and construction of all major charging system components. It will also review charging system design variations. As a result, you will have a broad understanding of the charging systems used on all makes and models of cars.

Note! Several previous chapters explain principles essential for the full understanding of this chapter.

BASIC CHARGING CIRCUIT

A *basic charging circuit* uses the battery, alternator, voltage regulator, ignition switch, and indicator light. They work together to provide a source of electricity for the vehicle. A simple charging circuit is in Fig. 14-1.

When the engine is NOT running, the battery feeds current to the car's electrical system. When the engine is started, a belt spins the alternator. The alternator can then produce an electrical output. Current flows back to the battery and into other electrical circuits of the car.

Charging system components

The fundamental components of a charging system include:
1. ALTERNATOR (AC generator that uses engine

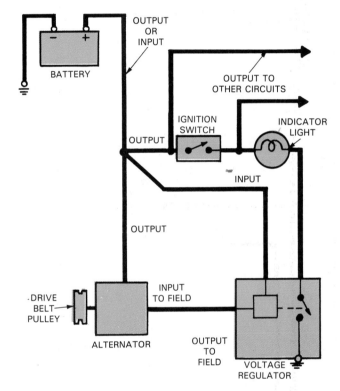

Fig. 14-1. This is a basic charging circuit. Note how alternator output is wired to battery and to electrical system of car. (Ford)

power to produce electricity).
2. VOLTAGE REGULATOR (electrical device for controlling output voltage and current of the alternator).
3. ALTERNATOR BELT (links engine crankshaft pulley with alternator pulley to drive alternator).
4. CHARGE INDICATOR (ammeter, voltmeter, or warning light to inform driver of charging system output).
5. CHARGING SYSTEM HARNESS (wiring that connects alternator, indicator light, and other components).
6. BATTERY (provides current to initially energize or excite alternator and also helps to stabilize alternator output).
7. IGNITION SWITCH (multi-position switch for feeding current to main electrical systems).

PURPOSE OF CHARGING SYSTEM

The *charging system* performs several important functions:

1. Recharges the battery after engine cranking or after the use of electrical accessories with the engine off.
2. Supplies all of the car's electricity when the engine is running.
3. Provides a voltage output that is slightly higher than battery voltage.
4. Changes output to meet different electrical loads.

ALTERNATOR OPERATION

An *alternator* is designed to change mechanical energy into electrical energy. It changes the spinning motion of the fan belt into electrical energy. The two main parts of a simplified alternator are the rotor and stator. This is illustrated in Fig. 14-2.

Rotor and stator operation

The *rotor* is a spinning magnetic field. It fits in the center of the alternator housing. The fan belt turns the rotor, making the field spin. See Fig. 14-3.

The *stator* is a stationary set of windings in the alternator. The stator surrounds the rotor. The stator serves as the output winding of the alternator, Fig. 14-3.

When the rotor spins, its strong magnetic field cuts

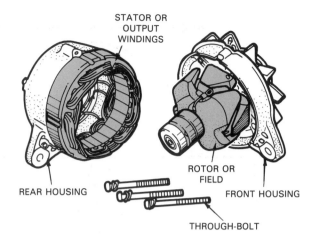

Fig. 14-3. Spinning rotor mounts inside stator. Stator produces high output current for alternator.

across the stator windings, Fig. 14-4. This induces current in the stator windings. If the stator windings are connected to a load (light bulb for example), the load would operate.

AC output

AC (alternating current) flows one way and then the other. The simple alternator in Fig. 14-2 has an AC output.

As the rotor turns into one stator winding, current is induced in one direction. Then, when the same rotor pole moves into the other stator winding, current reverses and flows out in the other direction. Look at Fig. 14-5.

Rectified AC current

An automobile electrical system is designed to use DC or direct current that only flows in ONE DIRECTION. It could NOT use alternating current as it comes out of the

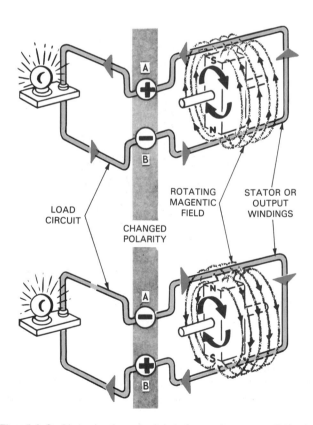

Fig. 14-2. Note basic principle of an alternator. Spinning magnetic field induces current into stationary windings. As north and south poles of spinning field cut across stationary windings, output current is generated. Spinning field would be rotor. Stationary windings would be stator. (Deere & Co.)

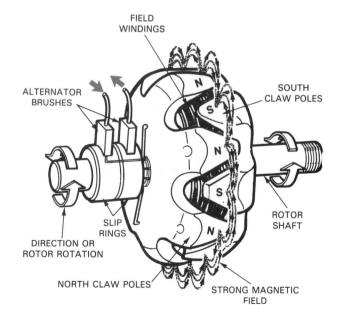

Fig. 14-4. Rotor has claw poles that surround its windings. This produces strong magnetic field for inducing current into stator. Note north and south poles of claws. (Delco)

228

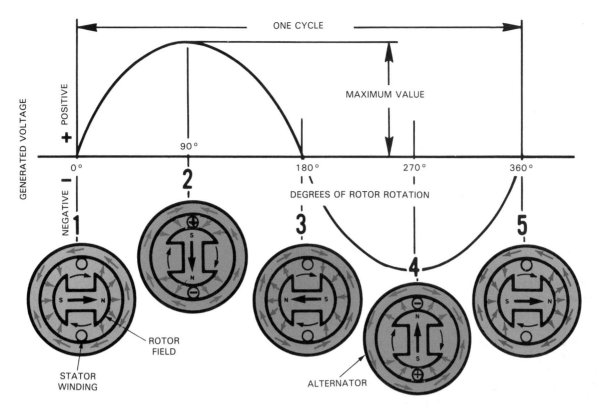

Fig. 14-5. As rotor turns inside stator, an AC or alternating current is produced. Sine wave represents reversing polarity or reversing current flow. (General Motors)

alternator stator.

Alternator current must be *rectified* (changed) into DC current before entering the electrical system, Fig. 14-6.

Diodes

Covered in an earlier chapter, a *diode* is an electronic device that allows current flow in only one direction, Fig. 14-7. It serves as an "electrical check valve."

When *forward bias,* the diode is connected to a voltage source so that current will pass through the diode. A for-

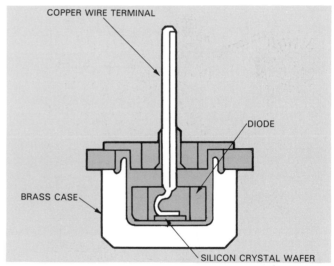

Fig. 14-7. Diode is one-way check valve for electricity. It is ideal for converting AC into DC. (Ford)

ward biased diode acts as a CONDUCTOR.

When *reverse bias,* the diode is connected to a voltage source so that current does NOT pass through. A reverse biased diode acts as an INSULATOR.

If a diode were placed on the stator output of our simple alternator, current would only flow out through the circuit in one direction.

Only one diode would NOT use all of the alternator's output. Also, it would result in pulsing DC, not smooth

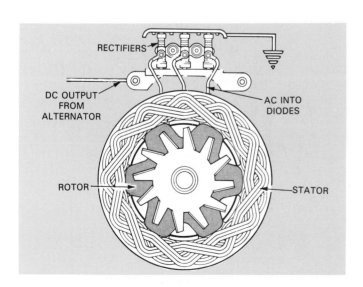

Fig. 14-6. A car's electrical system cannot use AC. Stator AC is fed into diodes that convert output to DC. (Chrysler)

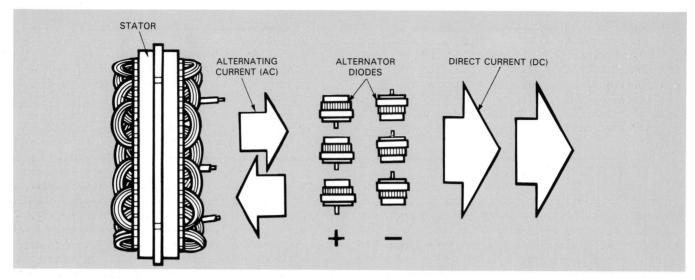

Fig. 14-8. One diode could not use all of the AC sine wave. Several diodes are needed to convert all of the AC into DC. (Chrysler)

current flow. A real alternator uses several diodes connected into a rectifier circuit. This produces more efficient DC output. See Fig. 14-8.

One diode would produce *half-wave rectification*

which means only half of the AC sine wave is used to produce DC. The other half of the wave or flow is blocked.

Fig. 14-9 shows how four diodes can be wired to produce full wave rectification.

Full-wave rectification means that both the positive and negative AC waves from the alternator stator are used to produce DC. Note how in Fig. 14-9A that current is flowing down through the resistor or load. In 14-9B, with stator current reversed, current still flows in the same direction through the load resistance. An alternator rectifier uses the same principle.

Fig. 14-10 illustrates a typical method of wiring the diodes inside an alternator. Note how the stator leads are connected to the diode circuit. The output from the diodes is connected to the terminals on the outside of the alternator.

Fig. 14-9. Study action of these diodes and how they convert AC into DC. A—Output from stator winding causes current to flow clockwise through stator section of circuit. Diodes block and pass current so that it flows through load resistance in clockwise direction. B—Now stator current has reversed because different claw pole passed stator winding. Current in stator circuit is counterclockwise. Diodes block and pass current so that it still flows clockwise through load resistance however. C—Pulsed DC sine wave.

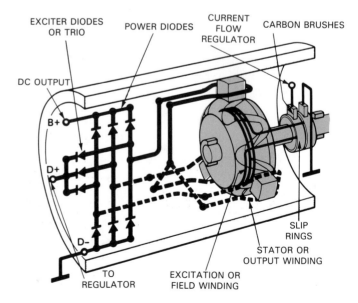

Fig. 14-10. Note how diodes, stator, field, and brushes are wired in this alternator. (Robert Bosch)

Heat sink

A *heat sink* can be used to protect the diodes from overheating damage. The diodes press-fit into the heat sink, Fig. 14-11. The heat sink is often made of aluminum because aluminum will transfer heat very quickly. The heat sink will allow the diodes to handle more current without overheating and failing. As you learned earlier, heat is very harmful to semiconductor materials.

ALTERNATOR CONSTRUCTION

The typical components of an alternator include:
1. *Rotor assembly* (field windings, claw poles, rotor shaft, and slip rings), Fig. 14-11.
2. *Stator assembly* (three stator windings or coils, stator core, and output wires).
3. *Brush assembly* (brush housing, brushes, brush springs, and brush wires).
4. *Rectifier assembly* (diodes, heat sink or diode plate, and electrical terminals), Fig. 14-11.
5. *Housing* (drive end frame, slip ring end frame, end frame bolts).
6. *Fan and pulley assembly* (fan, spacer, pulley, lock washer, and pulley nut).
7. *Integral regulator* (electronic voltage regulator mounted in or on rear of modern alternators). One is shown in Fig. 14-11.

Alternator rotor construction

An *alternator rotor* consists of field coil windings mounted on a shaft, Fig. 14-12. Two claw-shaped pole pieces surround the field windings to increase magnetic field strength. The rotor shaft is mounted on roller or needle bearings so the rotor can turn freely, Fig. 14-13.

The fingers on one of the pole pieces produces S (south) poles. The fingers on the other pole piece form N (north) poles. As the rotor spins inside the alternator, an alternating N-S-N-S polarity and AC current is produced. This pulls electrons one way and then the other to produce AC.

Alternator slip rings

Alternator slip rings are mounted on the rotor shaft to

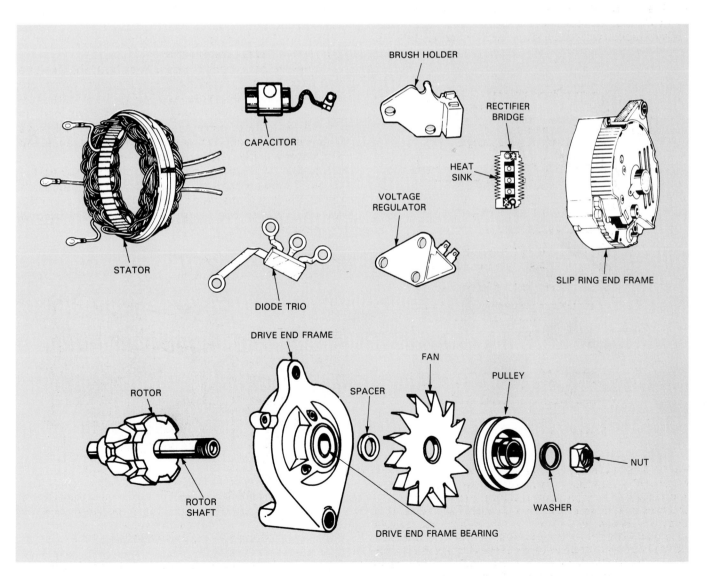

Fig. 14-11. Study exploded view of basic alternator. Note part names. (Florida Dept. of Voc. Ed.)

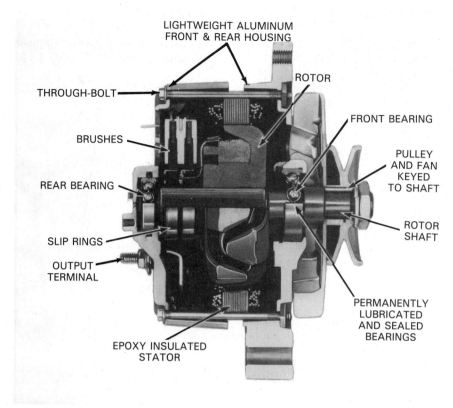

Fig. 14-12. Cutaway of actual alternator shows major parts. (Motorola)

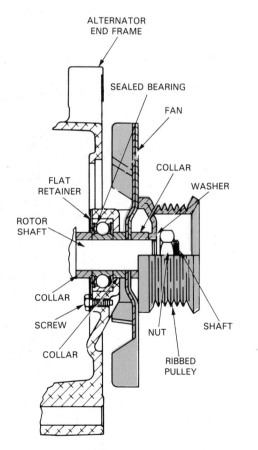

Fig. 14-13. Rotor shaft is mounted on anti-friction bearings. Pully uses belt to power rotor. Fan helps cool alternator. (General Motors)

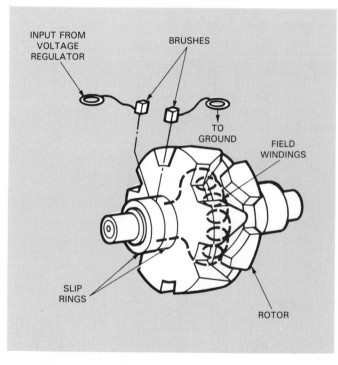

Fig. 14-14. Small brushes feed current into field windings. This excites field and produces magnetic field around rotor. (Ford)

feed a small current into the rotor windings, Fig. 14-14. Each end of the field coil connects to one of the slip rings. An external source of electricity is needed to excite the field and produce a magnetic field.

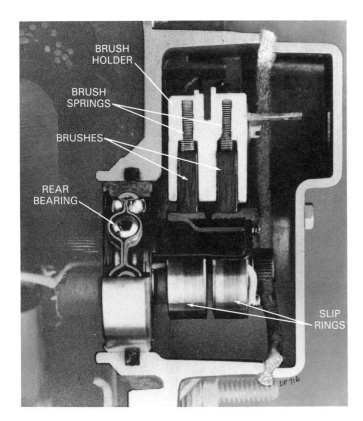

Fig. 14-15. Closeup shows how brushes are pushed into slip rings by small springs. (Motorola)

Alternator brushes

Alternator brushes ride on the slip rings to make a sliding electrical connection, Fig. 14-15. The brushes feed current into the slip rings and rotor windings.

Small *brush springs* push the brushes out and into contact with the slip rings. Since current flow into the rotor windings is low, the brushes are small compared to motor brushes. See Fig. 14-16.

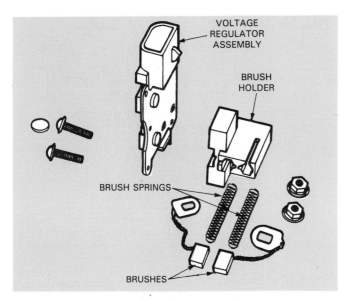

Fig. 14-16. Insulating brush holder holds springs and brushes in place over slip rings. (Ford)

A *brush holder* encloses the brush springs and brushes. It holds the brushes in alignment with the rotor slip rings. The brush holder is made of insulating material to prevent brush grounding, Fig. 14-16.

Stator construction

Mentioned briefly, the stator is a stationary set of windings mounted between the end frames, Fig. 14-17. The stator usually consists of three coils wrapped around

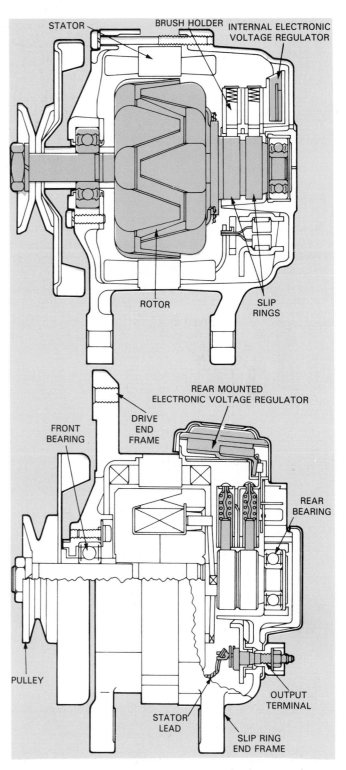

Fig. 14-17. Note internal and rear-mounted voltage regulators. Both are common on late model units.

an iron core. The iron core increases the field strength so that more current can be induced into the stator by the rotor field. The output of the stator is AC and is fed into the diodes that convert to DC.

A *Y-type stator* has the wire ends from the stator windings connected to a neutral junction. The circuit looks like the letter "Y." A Y-type stator provides good current output at low engine speeds, Fig. 14-18.

A *delta type stator* has the stator wires connected end to end. With no neutral junction, two circuit paths are formed between the diodes during each phase. A delta wound stator is used in high output alternators. One is illustrated in Fig. 14-18.

Alternator bearings

Needle or ball type *alternator bearings* are commonly used to produce a low friction surface for the rotor shaft. These bearings support the rotor and shaft as they spin inside the stator, Fig. 14-19.

The alternator bearings are normally packed with grease. The front bearing is frequently held in place with a small plate and screws. The rear bearing is usually press-fit into place.

Alternator fan

To provide cooling for the alternator, an *alternator fan* is mounted on the front of the rotor shaft. It is normally between the pulley and the front bearing.

As the rotor and shaft spin, the whirling fan helps draw air through and over the alternator. This cools the windings and diodes to prevent overheating damage. Refer to Fig. 14-19.

Alternator pulley and belt

An *alternator pulley* is secured to the front of the rotor shaft by a large nut, Fig. 14-19. It provides a means of spinning the rotor through the use of a belt.

An *alternator belt,* running off of the crank pulley, turns the alternator pulley and rotor. One of three types of belts may be used: V-belt, cogged V-belt, and ribbed belt.

VOLTAGE REGULATORS

A *voltage regulator* controls alternator output by changing the amount of current flowing through the rotor field windings. Any change in rotor winding current changes the field strength acting on the stator or output windings. In this way, the voltage regulator can maintain a preset charging voltage. See Fig. 14-20.

The voltage regulator keeps alternator output at a preset charging voltage of approximately 13 to 15 volts. Since this is HIGHER than battery voltage (12.6 volts) current flows back into the battery and recharges it.

Current also flows to the ignition system, electronic fuel injection system, on-board computer, radio, or any other device using electricity.

There are four basic types of voltage regulators:
1. Electronic voltage regulator mounted inside alternator.
2. Electronic voltage regulator mounted on rear of alternator, Fig. 14-21.
3. Electronic regulator mounted away from alternator in engine compartment.
4. Contact point type regulator mounted away from alternator in engine compartment.

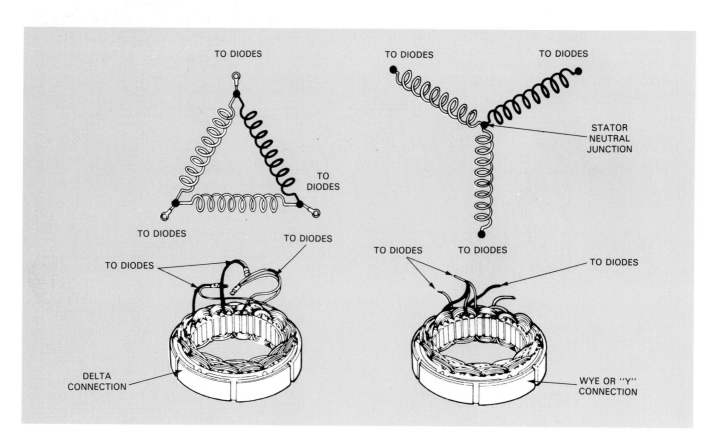

Fig. 14-18. These are the two types of stators. (Chrysler)

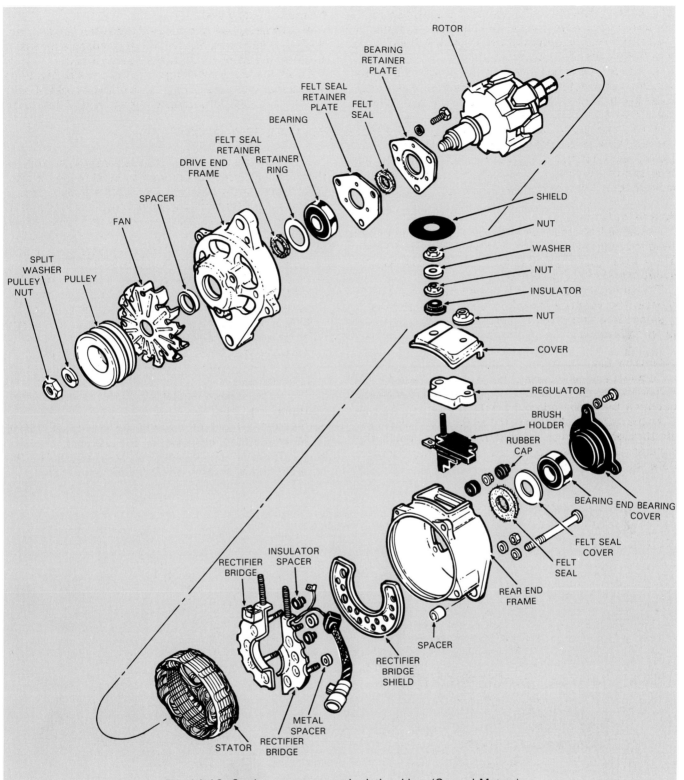

Fig. 14-19. Study part names and relationships. (General Motors)

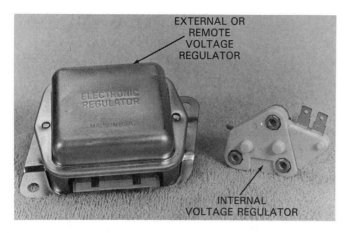

Fig. 14-20. Integral regulator mounts in or on alternator. It is the most common type. Older remote regulator mounts elsewhere in engine compartment.

Electronic voltage regulators

An *electronic voltage regulator* uses an electronic circuit (transistors, diodes, resistors, capacitors) to control rotor field strength and alternator output. A circuit diagram for an alternator and regulator is given in Fig. 14-22. Study it closely.

An electronic voltage regulator is a sealed unit and is not repairable. The electronic circuit must be sealed because it can be damaged by moisture, excessive heat, and vibration. Usually the circuit is surrounded by a rubber-like jell for protection.

An *integral voltage regulator* is an electronic regulator

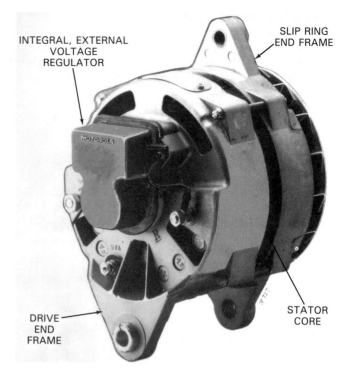

Fig. 14-21. This alternator has regulator mounted on rear end frame. (Motorola)

mounted inside or on the rear of the alternator. This is the most common type used on today's cars. It is very small, efficient, and dependable. Most use an IC (integrated circuit) to provide alternator regulation.

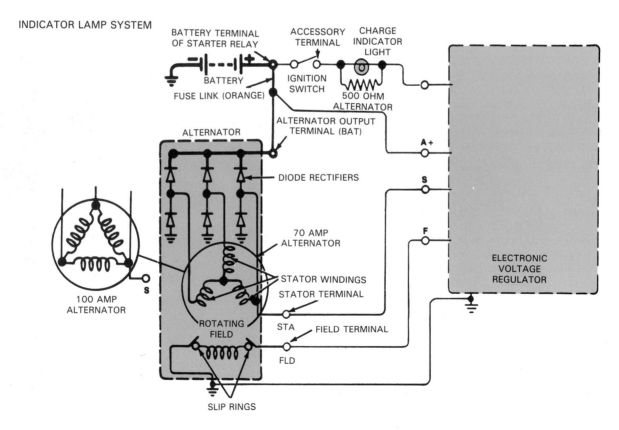

Fig. 14-22. Note wiring from regulator to alternator. (Ford)

236

Electronic voltage regulator operation

To increase alternator output, the electronic voltage regulator allows more current into the rotor windings, Fig. 14-22. This strengthens the magnetic field around the rotor. More current is then induced into the stator windings and out of the alternator.

To reduce alternator output, the electronic regulator places more resistance between the battery and the rotor windings. Field strength drops, and less current is induced in the stator windings.

Alternator rpm and electrical load determine whether the regulator increases or decreases charging output. If load is high or rotor speed is low (engine idling), the regulator will sense a drop in system voltage. The regulator then increases rotor field current until a preset output voltage is obtained. If load drops or rotor speed increases, the opposite occurs.

Fig. 14-23 shows another charging circuit diagram. Note that it also shows the circuit for the electronic voltage regulator. The transistor circuit reduces current flow to the rotor field when output is high. It increases current to the rotor when output is low.

An electronic voltage regulator must be replaced when it is not operating properly.

Temperature compensation

Some newer electronic regulators are *temperature compensating regulators.* This means the regulator changes alternator output as the outside temperature changes. In cold weather, alternator output voltage is increased. This helps recharge the battery more quickly. Cranking loads are higher in cold weather and battery drain is more severe. A temperature compensating regulator will decrease alternator output voltage in warm weather.

Diode trio

A *diode trio* can be used to feed current to the rotor field through the electronic regulator. As diagramed in Fig. 14-23, the stator coils are connected to each diode in the trio. This rectifies the current entering the voltage regulator and field or rotor windings.

Fig. 14-24 shows a cutaway of a late model alternator. Note the internal regulator.

Field circuit modulation

Field circuit modulation refers to how the voltage regulator can cycle the rotor field current on and off to control charging system output. See Fig. 14-25.

For example, if the battery is discharged, the regulator may cycle the field current on 90% of the time. This will increase output. If the electrical load is low, the regulator may cycle the field current off 90% of the time to decrease output. By controlling what percent of the time current is flowing through the rotor field, the modulating type regulator can control the alternator.

Alternator capacitor

An *alternator capacitor* or *condenser* can be used to prevent radio noise. It absorbs alternating current inside the AC generator. The capacitor can also protect the rectifying diodes from high voltage spikes and damage.

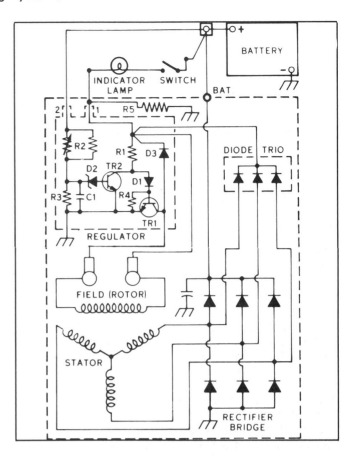

Fig. 14-23. This diagram shows alternator and regulator wiring. Note diode trio. (Oldsmobile)

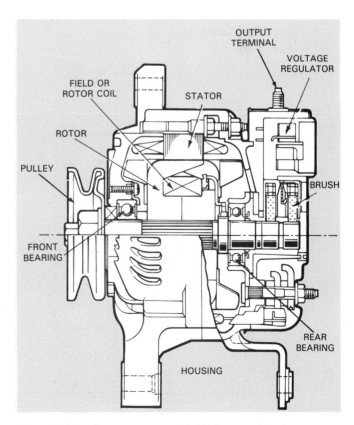

Fig. 14-24. Study cutaway of this late model alternator. (Buick)

237

Contact point voltage regulator

A *contact point voltage regulator* uses coils, set of points, and resistors to control alternator output. This is an older type of regulator that has been replaced by electronic or solid state regulators.

When alternator output is too high, high current flow through the voltage regulator coil pulls the movable contact down against the ground contact. This bypasses (stops) the current flowing to the alternator field, which causes the field current and the alternator output to decrease.

When charging output is too low, less current flows through the regulator coil. The spring on the movable contact then pulls the contact up. This connects the alternator field circuit to battery voltage. Current enters the alternator field and output increases. The coil points cycle at about 100 times per second to provide smooth regulation, Fig. 14-26.

The *field relay* coil simply disconnects power from the charging system when the ignition switch is OFF.

COMPUTER-CONTROLLED VOLTAGE REGULATION

In a *computer-controlled voltage regulation system,* the vehicle's on-board computer is used to regulate the alternator's output, eliminating the need for a conventional voltage regulator.

To accomplish this, the computer controls the duty cycle of the alternator's field windings. The *duty cycle* is the amount of time (given as a percentage) that current is fed to the windings. When the electrical load is heavy, the duty cycle is long. This causes the alternator to produce a high output. When the electrical load is light, the duty cycle is short and alternator output is low. A duty cycle of about 50% is normal in most systems.

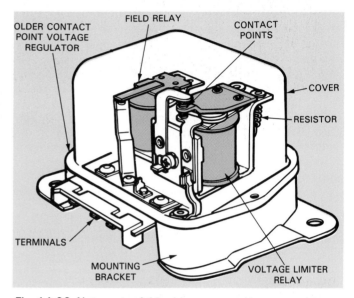

Fig. 14-26. Note parts of this older contact point type regulator. (Chrysler)

TYPES OF CHARGING SYSTEMS

There are two basic types of charging systems: AC generator (alternator) and DC generator types. The alternator type charging system has replaced the older DC generator. Keep in mind, however, an alternator is sometimes called a GENERATOR, meaning AC generator, Figs. 14-27 and 14-28.

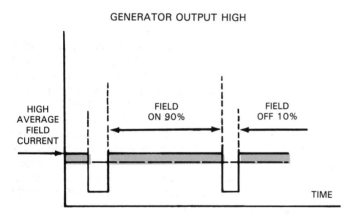

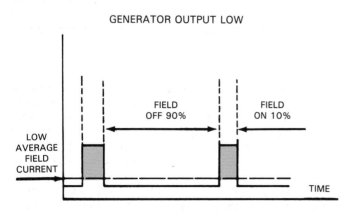

Fig. 14-25. Modulated alternator field is controlled by regulator. Amount of on versus off time determines alternator output. (General Motors)

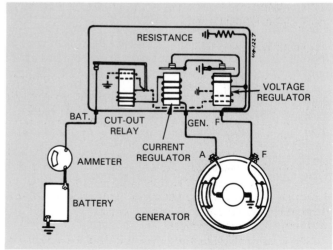

Fig. 14-27. Basic circuit for DC generator. (Motorola)

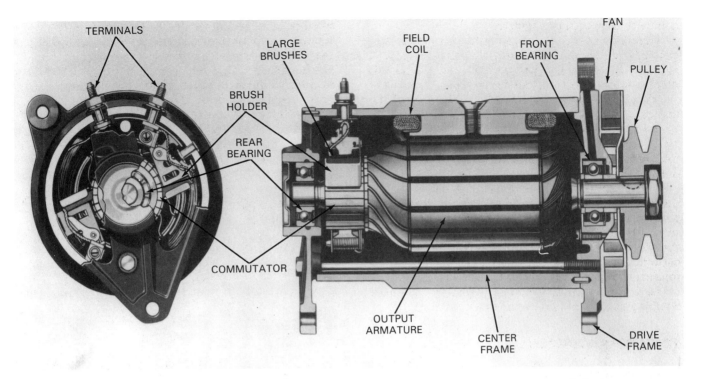

Fig. 14-28. Note parts of the old DC generator. It is similar to a starting motor. (Deere & Co.)

DC generator

The *DC generator* is made like an electric motor, Fig. 14-27. It has a stationary magnetic field. The output conductor (armature) spins inside this field. This induces current output from within the armature.

The DC generator was fine for producing electricity on early model cars. However, today's cars have more electrical components, requiring a higher current output. A DC generator would NOT be able to supply enough current for a modern car at idle speeds. DC generator efficiency is poor at low rpm.

Fig. 14-27 shows a DC generator circuit. Note how the contact point regulator could control output.

The *AC generator* (alternator) has replaced the DC generator because of its improved efficiency. It is smaller, lighter, and more dependable than a DC generator. The alternator will also produce more output at idle. This makes it ideal for late-model cars.

CHARGE INDICATORS

A *charge indicator* informs the driver about the operating condition or output of the charging system. There are three basic types of charging indicators:
1. Warning light (light bulb is ON or OFF to show alternator output).
2. Voltmeter (measures voltage output of alternator).
3. Ammeter (measures current output of alternator).

These indicators are mounted in the dash of the car. Normally, all cars have an indicator light. A voltmeter or ammeter may be added for more precise measurement of charging system action.

Some late model systems will turn on the charge indicator light if the output voltage is too LOW or too HIGH. Most older systems only warned of low charge voltage.

For more information on charge indicators, refer to the chapter on Lights and Instrumentation.

ALTERNATOR VACUUM PUMP

An *alternator vacuum pump* is a vane type pump mounted on the rear of the charging system AC generator. Alternator shaft rotation spins the pump vanes or blades. This produces a low pressure source for operating vacuum devices. See Fig. 14-29.

An alternator vacuum pump is commonly used with diesel engines. Diesels do NOT use throttle valves, and therefore, do not have their own source of vacuum for power brakes, vacuum diaphragms, etc. Either an alternator vacuum pump, a separate vacuum pump, or an electric motor-driven vacuum pump is needed to power the car's vacuum devices.

Fig. 14-30 shows an exploded view of a late model alternator. Can you find the vacuum pump, internal regulator, brush assembly, rotor, stator, and diode pack?

ALTERNATOR HIGH VOLTAGE

Alternator high voltage refers to when the alternator output is intentionally increased above the normal charging voltage of 13 to 15 volts. A common example is for a heated windshield, Fig. 14-31. Some heated windshield systems make the alternator produce up to 70 volts to send high current through the windshield heating element.

The *windshield heating element* is a film of conducting material bonded inside the glass. The film is so thin that is is invisible. This conducting material or film is usually a zinc and tin oxide substance bonded between two layers of glass.

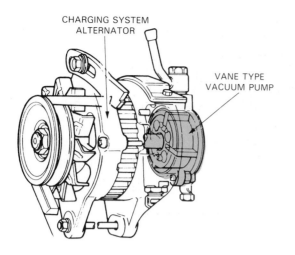

CHARGING SYSTEM
ALTERNATOR

VANE TYPE
VACUUM PUMP

Fig. 14-29. This alternator has a vane type vacuum pump in rear housing. It spins with rotor to produce vacuum for power brakes and other vacuum devices.

When the windshield heat is activated, a control module switches the alternator to *full field* (no regulation) and sends the resulting high voltage output only to the windshield. The rest of the car's electrical system is disconnected from the alternator and operates off of battery voltage.

With the alternator full fielded and no battery in the alternator's output circuit, output voltage increases to 30 to 70 volts to quickly heat the windshield film. The remainder of the electrical system must be disconnected from this high voltage to prevent component damage.

DANGER! This higher alternator output voltage (30 to 70 volts) is enough to cause serious electrical shock and injury. Use caution when working with this higher voltage.

You should refer to the service manual for the specific make and model of car to get more information. Systems vary with the auto manufacturer.

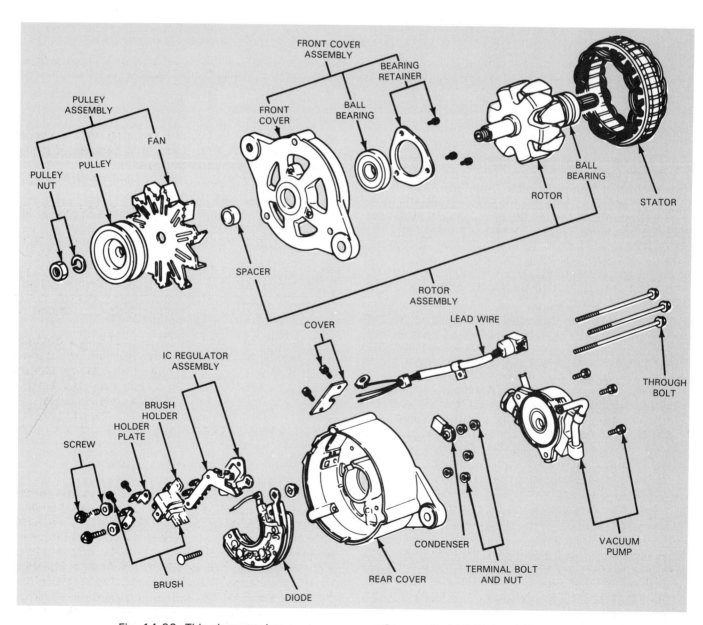

FRONT COVER
ASSEMBLY

BEARING
RETAINER

PULLEY
ASSEMBLY

FRONT
COVER

BALL
BEARING

FAN

PULLEY

PULLEY
NUT

BALL
BEARING

ROTOR

STATOR

SPACER

ROTOR
ASSEMBLY

COVER

LEAD WIRE

THROUGH
BOLT

IC REGULATOR
ASSEMBLY

BRUSH
HOLDER

HOLDER
PLATE

SCREW

BRUSH

DIODE

REAR COVER

CONDENSER

TERMINAL BOLT
AND NUT

VACUUM
PUMP

Fig. 14-30. This alternator has a vacuum pump. Can you find it? (General Motors)

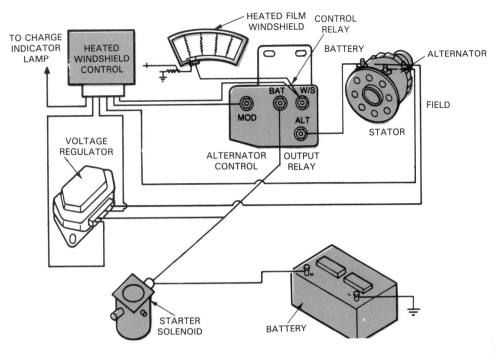

Fig. 14-31. Control module can isolate alternator from all but windshield heating film. It increases alternator output to 30 to 70 volts for quickly heating windshield. When activated, remainder of car's electrical system operates off of battery voltage. Relay responds to electrical signals from controller. (Ford)

SUMMARY

The charging system is the "heart" of a car's electrical system. It must "pump" current throughout the electrical system whenever the engine is running.

The alternator generates electricity using magnetic induction. The voltage regulator controls the output of the alternator.

A fan belt spins the alternator rotor when the engine is operating. The alternator rotor is a spinning magnetic field. The stator surrounds the rotor to serve as stationary, output windings for the alternator.

The alternator stator produces an AC or alternating current output. A set of diodes in the alternator convert this AC into DC so it can be used by the electrical system. A heat sink may be used to dissipate heat and protect the diodes from overheating damage.

Alternator brushes feed a small current into the rotor slip rings. The slip rings are wired to the rotor windings. The resulting magnetic field cuts across the windings in the stator. This induces current in the stator windings. Much more current is produced in the stator windings than is fed into the field or rotor windings.

The rotor shaft is mounted on anti-friction bearings. This lets the rotor spin freely in the alternator housing. A fan, mounted next to the drive pulley, circulates air through the inside of the alternator housing. This helps cool the alternator.

Late model voltage regulators are electronic. They maintain an alternator charging voltage of about 13 to 15 volts. Electronic regulators can be inside the alternator, on the back of the alternator, or elsewhere in the engine compartment.

Some late model voltage regulators are temperature compensating. They increase charging voltage in cold weather to speed battery recharging because of the increased cranking load in cold weather.

Some alternators use a diode trio to feed rectified current to the regulator and rotor field.

Some newer charging systems use a modulated field action to control alternator output.

An alternator capacitor can be used to prevent radio noise from the alternator AC. It can also help protect the diodes from high voltage spike damage.

Some alternators for diesel engines have a vacuum pump. The vacuum pump is mounted on the rear of the alternator housing. The pump provides a source of vacuum for various devices.

Some heating windshield circuits full field and isolate alternator output. Alternator output may be increased up to 70 volts to quickly warm a film inside the windshield glass. The other electrical devices operate off of battery voltage while the windshield is warming.

Use caution when working on a circuit carrying full fielded alternator output. The voltage is high enough to cause injury.

KNOW THESE TERMS

Charging system, Alternator, Voltage regulator, Alternator belt, Charge indicator, Charging system harness, Ignition switch, Rotor, Stator, AC, Rectified, Forward bias, Reverse bias, Full wave rectification, Heat sink, Brush assembly, Slip rings, Brush holder, Y-type stator, Delta-type stator, Alternator bearings, Alternator pulley, Charging voltage, Integral regulator, Diode trio, Alternator capacitor, Contact point regulator, Computer-controlled voltage regulation, DC generator, AC generator, Alternator vacuum pump.

REVIEW QUESTIONS—CHAPTER 14

1. List and explain the seven basic parts of a charging system.
2. An _____ is designed to change mechanical energy into electrical energy.
3. The _____ is the spinning magnetic field that fits in the center of the _____ windings.
4. How does an alternator produce full-wave rectification?
5. Why is a heat sink sometimes used in an alternator?
6. Why are the brushes in an alternator so small?
7. Describe the purpose of the alternator stator.
8. With the engine running, this voltage would be present in the car's electrical system and at the battery.
   a. 12.5 volts.
   b. 30 volts.
   c. 12 volts.
   d. 14 volts.
9. Explain the four types of voltage regulators and their locations.
10. How does a regulator control alternator output?
11. Why are some electronic voltage regulators temperature compensating?
12. _____ _____ _____ refers to how the regulator can cycle the rotor windings on and off to control charge voltage and current output.
13. Why is a capacitor sometimes used inside the alternator?
14. AC generators are no longer used because of their low output at engine idle speeds. True or false?
15. Some windshield heating systems can full field the alternator while isolating it from the battery and other electrical components. What output voltage can result?
   a. 30 to 70 volts.
   b. 13 to 15 volts.
   c. 50 to 150 volts.
   d. None of the above.

ASE CERTIFICATION—TYPE QUESTIONS

1. While discussing automotive charging systems, Technician A says the ignition switch is considered a component of the charging system. Technician B says the alternator belt is considered a component of the charging system. Who is right?
   (A) A only.
   (B) B only.
   (C) Both A and B.
   (D) Neither A nor B.
2. Technician A says a voltmeter is sometimes used as a charge indicator. Technician B says an ammeter is sometimes used as a charge indicator. Who is right?
   (A) A only.
   (B) B only.
   (C) Both A and B.
   (D) Neither A nor B.
3. Technician A says an automotive charging system's voltage output is equal to battery voltage. Technician B says a charging system's voltage output changes as the electrical load changes. Who is right?
   (A) A only.
   (B) B only.
   (C) Both A and B.
   (D) Neither A nor B.
4. Technician A says an alternator's stator is a stationary set of windings. Technician B says an alternator's stator is surrounded by the rotor. Who is right?
   (A) A only.
   (B) B only.
   (C) Both A and B.
   (D) Neither A nor B.
5. Technician A says an alternator's AC current flows in both directions. Technician B says an alternator's AC current must be rectified before it is used by the electrical system. Who is right?
   (A) A only.
   (B) B only.
   (C) Both A and B.
   (D) Neither A nor B.
6. Technician A says a forward biased diode acts as a conductor. Technician B says a diode acts as an electrical check valve, allowing current to flow in only one direction. Who is right?
   (A) A only.
   (B) B only.
   (C) Both A and B.
   (D) Neither A nor B.
7. Technician A says alternator slip rings are mounted on the stator shaft to feed current into the stator windings. Technician B says alternator brushes ride on the slip rings to make a sliding electrical connection. Who is right?
   (A) A only.
   (B) B only.
   (C) Both A and B.
   (D) Neither A nor B.
8. A voltage regulator controls alternator output by changing the amount of current flow through the:
   (A) stator windings.
   (B) output windings.
   (C) rotor field windings.
   (D) rectifier windings.
9. All of the following are basic components of a charging system's electronic voltage regulator *except:*
   (A) transistors.
   (B) resistors.
   (C) contact points.
   (D) diodes.
10. Technician A says an alternator capacitor helps prevent radio noise. Technician B says an alternator capacitor helps protect the rectifying diode from voltage spikes. Who is right?
   (A) A only.
   (B) B only.
   (C) Both A and B.
   (D) Neither A nor B.

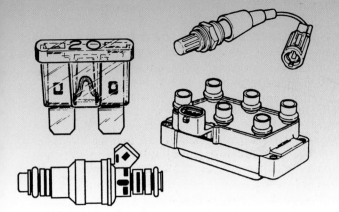

Chapter 15

Ignition Systems

After studying this chapter, you will be able to:
- Describe the basic principles of an ignition system.
- Compare the various types of ignition systems.
- Explain the construction and operation of major ignition system components.
- Explain the various methods of spark advance.
- Describe distributor types.
- Explain distributorless and direct ignition system variations.

In recent years, different types of ignition systems have been developed to enhance performance, increase efficiency, improve dependability, and reduce emissions. We have gone from the old contact point ignition system to "state of the art" distributorless ignitions in a relatively short period of time. New ignition systems use a crankshaft position sensor and an electronic control module (computer) to determine when to "fire" each spark plug. Mechanical advance weights, vacuum diaphragms, and other outdated parts are being replaced with more efficient electronic components and circuits.

This chapter explains modern electronic, distributorless, and direct ignition systems by comparing them to older, simpler contact point systems. This will give you a sound knowledge of all automotive ignition system types.

IGNITION SYSTEM FUNDAMENTALS

An *ignition system* must amplify battery or charging system voltage and deliver this high voltage to the spark plugs at the right time. Gasoline engines or spark ignition engines need an ignition system to initiate combustion on the power stroke. Diesels are compression ignition engines and do not need electronic ignition systems.

The basic parts of an ignition system are:
1. SPARK PLUG (provides air gap so electric arc can form inside engine combustion chamber to start burning of fuel charge), Fig. 15-1.

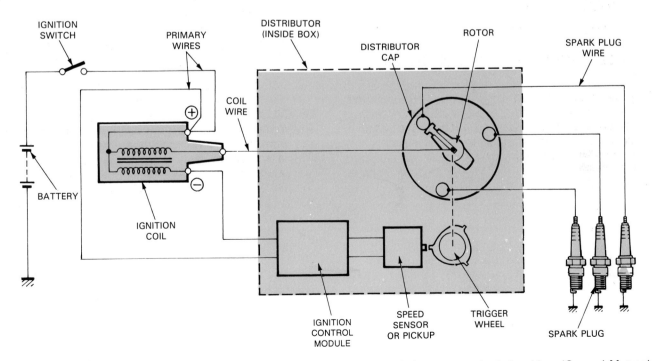

Fig. 15-1. These are the basic parts of an ignition system. Review their names and relationships. (General Motors)

2. SPARK PLUG WIRE (secondary lead with thick insulation that carries high voltage to spark plug).
3. DISTRIBUTOR CAP (insulated cap that transfers high voltage from rotor to spark plug wires).
4. ROTOR (spinning electrical connection that feeds high voltage to each cap terminal and plug wire).
5. DISTRIBUTOR (mechanism that sometimes controls ignition timing, operates rotor, senses engine speed, and helps operate ignition coil).
6. IGNITION CONTROL MODULE (electronic circuit used with speed sensor to make and break current to ignition coil).
7. SPEED SENSING DEVICE (pickup sensor detects speed to fire ignition coil properly).
8. IGNITION COIL (step-up transformer that increases battery voltage to 30,000 volts or more).
9. COIL WIRE (secondary wire that feeds high voltage to distributor cap or directly to spark plugs).
10. IGNITION SWITCH (key-operated switch that feeds battery voltage to ignition coil and some other ignition system components).
11. PRIMARY WIRES (small wires that feed low voltage to components in ignition system).

Ignition system operation

The basic operation of an ignition system is simple. When the driver turns the ignition key to start, current is fed to the ignition coil, Fig. 15-1. The current flow energizes the coil with a strong magnetic field. The starting motor turns the crankshaft, trying to make the engine "fire" and run. This causes the speed sensor to produce voltage signals that correspond to engine speed. The rotor is also turning inside the distributor cap.

The ignition control module allows battery current to flow through the ignition coil until it senses a signal from the speed sensor. It can then stop current flow through the ignition coil. This makes the ignition coil "fire" and feed high voltage into the coil wire

The high voltage enters the top of the distributor cap and flows into the rotor. The rotor feeds the high voltage to the correct spark plug wire. High voltage then flows through spark plug wire and into spark plug. High voltage makes spark jump gap to start combustion.

Combustion makes the engine start and the driver can then release the ignition key to run. This stops starting motor but still allows ignition system operation. When the driver turns the key off, current flow is shut off to the ignition coil and the engine stops running.

An actual ignition system is much more complex than the one just discussed. Cars have multiple cylinder engines and the timing of the sparks must vary with operating conditions.

Primary and secondary

The two main sections of an ignition system are the primary and secondary circuits.

The ignition system's *primary circuit* consists of all of the components and wires operating on low voltage (battery or alternator voltage). Small, conventional wires carry primary currents.

The ignition system's *secondary circuit* includes all parts carrying high voltage. It consists of the wires and parts between the coil output and the spark plug ground.

The secondary wiring must have THICK INSULATION to prevent *leakage* (arcing) of the high voltage. Ignition system *secondary operating voltage* ranges from 4000 to 30,000 volts, depending on system design.

SPARK PLUGS

The *spark plugs* use ignition coil high voltage to ignite the fuel mixture. Somewhere between 4000 and 10,000 volts are needed to make current jump the gap at the plug electrodes. This is much lower than the coil's output potential. Look at Fig. 15-2.

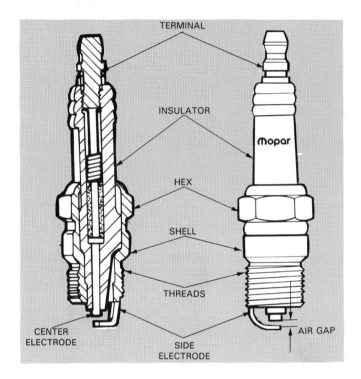

Fig. 15-2. Spark plug is simply used to produce electric arc inside engine combustion chamber. This starts fuel burning to force piston down on power stroke. (Chrysler)

The *spark plug center terminal* conducts electricity into the combustion chamber. The *spark plug side electrode* is grounded and causes the electricity to jump the gap and return to the battery through frame ground. This is shown in Fig. 15-3.

The *spark plug ceramic insulator* keeps the high voltage at the plug wire from shorting to ground. It makes sure current flows into the center electrode.

The *spark plug shell* supports the other parts of the plug and has threads for screwing into the engine cylinder head.

Fig. 15-4 shows a disassembled spark plug.

Spark plug sizes

Spark plug size generally refers to the size of the plug threads. It is a measurement of the diameter of the spark plug threads. The two most common spark plug sizes are 14 mm and 18 mm. The smaller 14 mm is replacing the larger 18 mm.

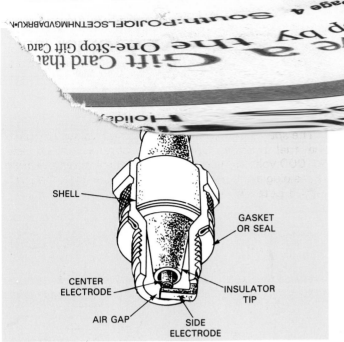

Fig. 15-3. Center electrode is enclosed in ceramic insulator. Insulator assures that current flows through electrode and jumps gap to side electrode. (Deere & Co.)

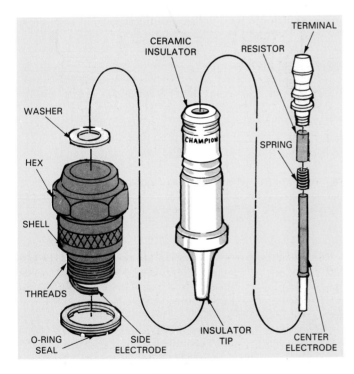

Fig. 15-4. Note parts of this disassembled spark plug. (Champion)

Non-resistor and resistor spark plugs

A *non-resistor spark plug* has a center electrode that is one piece of metal rod. The metal rod passes from the wire terminal down through the insulator to form the center electrode tip. Obviously, this type plug does NOT have internal resistance. A non-resistor plug is only used for off-road applications: racing for example. It will

...rence or static.

...*lug* has an internal resistor built into ...de. The resistor has about 10,000 ...tance is designed to reduce induced ...and to increase spark plug life (reduce ...Passenger cars should always use resistor ...spark plugs.

Fig. 15-5 shows how a resistor spark plug can prevent radio interference.

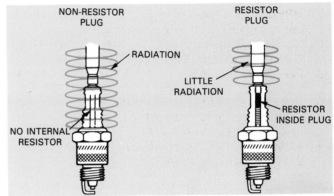

Fig. 15-5. Resistor spark plug helps prevent radiation of voltage that could upset operation of radios. (Champion)

Spark plug seats

The *spark plug seat* makes contact with the cylinder head to seal in the pressure of combustion. It must also allow heat to transfer out of the plug and into the head to prevent plug overheating and detonation. There are two types of seats: tapered seat and O-ring seat.

A *tapered seat* has an angle formed where the spark plug touches the cylinder head. When the plug is torqued, the tapered seat tightens down to make a good seal with the head. See Fig. 15-6.

An *O-ring seat* uses a separate metal O-ring and a flat seat to form a plug-to-head seal. A compressible metal seal fits around the plug threads. When tightened, the O-ring is partially compressed to conform to the head and plug surfaces, Fig. 15-6.

Spark plug reach

Spark plug reach is the distance between the end of the plug threads and the seat or sealing surface on the plug. Plug reach determines how far the plug extends through the cylinder head. See Fig. 15-6.

If spark plug reach is too long, the plug electrode may be struck by the piston at TDC. If reach is too short, the plug electrodes may not extend far enough into the chamber and combustion efficiency may be reduced.

Note! Never use the wrong plug reach or electrode design in a rotary engine. The wrong plug can easily be hit by the rotor seals. This will cause major damage to a rotary engine.

Spark plug heat range

Spark plug heat range is a rating of the operating temperature of the spark plug tip. Plug heat range is

245

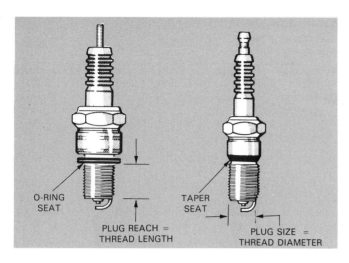

Fig. 15-6. These are two types of spark plug seats. Tapered seat is becoming more common on newer 14 mm spark plugs. (Mercedes Benz)

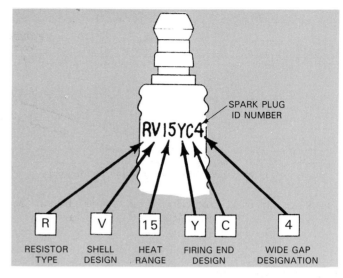

Fig. 15-8. This is one type of spark plug identification number. Note that R means resistor and the center number indicates the heat range of the plug. (Champion)

basically determined by the length and diameter of the insulator tip and the ability of the plug to transfer heat into the cooling system.

A *hot spark plug* has a long insulator tip and will tend to burn off deposits. This provides a self-cleaning action. Refer to Fig. 15-7.

A *cold spark plug* has a shorter insulator tip; its tip operates at a cooler temperature. A cold plug is used in engines operated at high speeds. The cooler tip will help prevent tip overheating and preignition, Fig. 15-7.

Auto manufacturers normally recommend a specific spark plug heat range for their engines. The heat range will normally be coded and given as a number on the plug insulator.

Generally, the larger the number on the plug, the hotter the spark plug tip will operate. For instance, a 52 plug would be hotter than a 42 or 32.

The only time you should deviate from plug heat range specs is when abnormal engine or driving conditions are encountered. For example, a hotter plug may be installed in an old, worn out, oil-burning engine. The hotter plug will help burn off oil deposits and prevent oil-fouling of

the plug.

Fig. 15-8 shows the alpha-numeric designation used by one spark plug manufacturer.

Spark plug gap

Spark plug gap is the distance or air space between the center and side electrodes. Normal gap specifications range from .030 to .080 inch (0.76 mm to 2.0 mm).

Smaller spark plug gaps are used on older cars equipped with contact point ignition systems. Larger spark plug gaps are now used with modern electronic ignition systems. The wide gap and higher voltage are needed to ignite today's lean fuel mixture efficiently.

SPARK PLUG WIRES

Spark plug wires carry coil voltage from the distributor cap side terminals to each spark plug. In more modern computer-coil (distributorless) ignitions, the spark plug wires carry coil voltage directly to the plugs. In late model direct systems, coils are mounted over the spark plugs and plug wires are NOT needed.

Spark plug wire boots protect the metal connectors from corrosion, oil, and moisture. Boots visually fit over both ends of the secondary wires. See Fig. 15-9.

Solid wire spark plug wires are used on racing engines and very old automobiles. The wire conductor is simply a stranded metal wire. Solid wires are no longer used because they cause *radio interference* (noise or static in speakers).

Resistance spark plug wires are now used because they contain internal resistance that prevents radio noise. They use carbon-impregnated strands of rayon braid. Also called *radio suppression wires,* they have about 10,000 ohms per foot. This avoids high voltage induced popping or cracking in the radio speakers. It can also prolong electrode life.

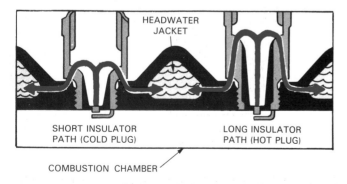

Fig. 15-7. Short insulator tip produces a colder running plug because more heat can transfer into head. Hotter plug results from longer insulator tip that cannot dissipate heat as well. (Champion)

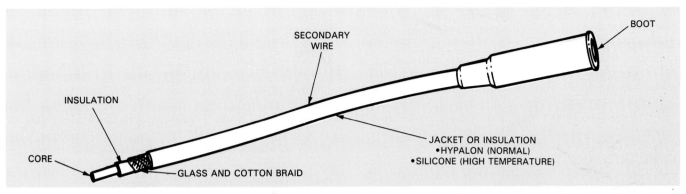

Fig. 15-9. Passenger car spark plug wires should be resistance or suppressor type. The wire conductor has internal resistance to help prevent voltage radiation into computer and radio systems. (Chrysler)

ENGINE FIRING ORDER

Engine firing order is the sequence that the arcs or sparks occur at the spark plugs. It is determined by the routing of the spark plug wires from the distributor cap to the plugs and direction of distributor rotation. It can also be determined by the electronic control unit in distributorless or direct ignition systems, Fig. 15-10.

Fig. 15-11 shows some common examples of engine firing orders. Note the location of the number one cylinders on each engine.

On V-type engines, the number one cylinder is usually offset slightly ahead of the cylinder on the opposite side of the engine. You can tell by looking at the engine from the side and sighting across the heads or valve covers. The side that is the farthest forward has the number one cylinder.

A four-cylinder engine may have one of two possible firing orders: 1-3-4-2 or 1-2-4-3. The cylinders would be numbered 1-2-3-4 starting at the front of the engine.

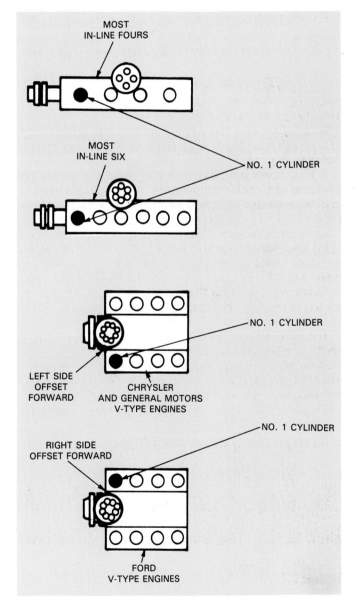

Fig. 15-11. These are typical examples of number one cylinder locations. When looking at an actual engine, you can usually locate side with number one cylinder by viewing from side of engine. Cylinder offset slightly forward normally has number one cylinder. (Chrysler)

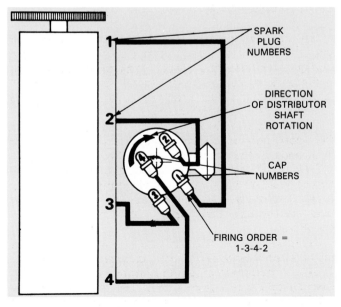

Fig. 15-10. Firing order is determined by direction of distributor rotation and routing of wires to spark plugs. (Chrysler)

In this way, you can tell which cylinders will fire in sequence. Firing orders and cylinder numbers for V-6 and V-8 engines vary.

Engine firing order is sometimes cast into the top of the intake manifold. When not on the manifold, the firing order can be found in a service manual.

Discussed in later chapters, the engine firing order is commonly used when installing spark plug wires and when doing other tune-up tasks.

IGNITION COIL

The *ignition coil* is a pulse-type transformer capable of producing the short burst of high voltage that starts combustion. The coil produces the low-current, high-voltage surge that jumps the rotor gap (if used), passes through the secondary resistance wires, and jumps the spark plug gap. See Fig. 15-12.

The ignition systems in older engines contain spark plugs with relatively small gaps. These systems operate at 4000 to 8000 volts. With today's wider spark plug gaps

and leaner fuel mixtures, more voltage is needed to make the electricity surge through all parts of the ignition system. Ignition systems in late model vehicles operate at about 15,000 volts, but operating voltages can vary from 4000 to 30,000 volts, depending on ignition system design.

If everything is in good condition, the ignition coil operates below its potential maximum output voltage. This keeps some voltage in reserve. The ignition coil's *open circuit voltage* (maximum voltage potential) ranges from 40,000 to 60,000 volts with modern designs.

Primary and secondary windings

The *primary windings* of the coil are several hundred turns of heavy wire, wrapped around or near the secondary windings. See Fig. 15-13.

The *secondary windings* are several thousand turns of very fine wire located inside or near the primary windings, Fig. 15-13.

Both windings are wrapped around an iron core and are housed inside the coil case.

Ignition coil operation

When battery current flows through the ignition coil primary windings, a strong magnetic field is produced. The action of the iron core helps concentrate and strengthen the field, Fig. 15-13.

When the current flowing through the coil is broken, the magnetic field collapses across the secondary windings. Since the secondary windings have more turns than the primary, 30,000 volts is induced into the secondary windings. High voltage shoots out of the top terminal and to a spark plug.

There are two common methods used to break current flow and fire the coil: mechanical breaker points or an electronic switching circuit. Electronic switching is found on late model cars and mechanical points are only found on older cars.

Ignition coil designs

With today's computer controlled ignition systems, ignition coils can be more complex than in the past. Depending on ignition system design, an engine can have one or more ignition coils. Some have one coil for all engine cylinders. A distributorless ignition system has one coil for every two cylinders. A direct ignition system has one coil for every engine cylinder.

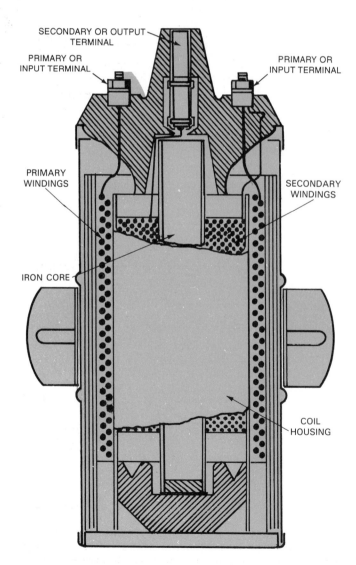

Fig. 15-12. Study construction of basic ignition coil. Primary windings surround secondary windings. Iron core is in center to concentrate magnetic fields. (Sun Electric)

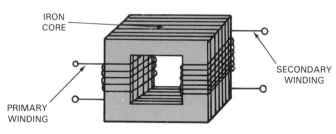

Fig. 15-13. Ignition coil is pulse type step-up transformer. It can make 12 volt input into 30,000 volt output. There is a loss of current because of the increase in voltage. Current is not critical in making an arc at the plugs. Current can be low but voltage must be high to provide enough ''electrical pressure'' to push an arc across the plug air gap.

A *coil pack* is several ignition coils combined into one assembly. As you will learn, this type of coil is used in distributorless ignition systems. No coil wire is needed. The spark plug wires connect from the ignition coil pack to the spark plugs. See Fig. 15-14.

Wasted spark ignition coil

A *wasted spark ignition coil* is wired so that it fires two spark plugs at the same time. Illustrated in Fig. 15-15, each end of the coil's secondary winding is connected to a spark plug wire. Then, when the primary magnetic field collapses across the secondary winding, a high-voltage, low-current surge is induced in both spark plug wires,

firing two spark plugs. Current flows through each spark plug gap with the opposite polarity. The engine ground connects the two spark plugs.

IGNITION SYSTEM SUPPLY VOLTAGE

The *ignition system supply voltage* is fed to the ignition system by the battery or alternator. The *battery* provides electricity when starting the engine. After the engine is running, the alternator supplies a slightly higher voltage to the battery and ignition system.

An ignition system *bypass circuit* is sometimes used to supply direct battery voltage to the ignition system during starting motor operation. See Fig. 15-16.

When the engine is being started, the ignition switch is in the start or fully clockwise position. This connects the battery to the starting motor and to the ignition

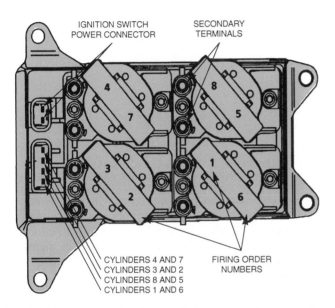

Fig. 15-14. Top view of coil pack. Note numbers for secondary wire connections and pins for primary wire connections. (Chevrolet)

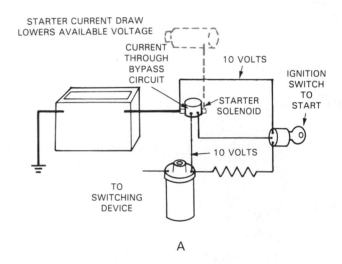

A

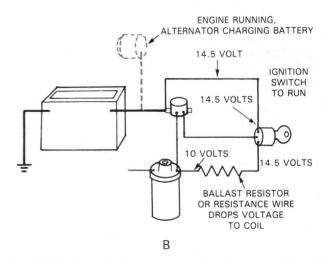

B

Fig. 15-16. Some ignition systems use resistance and bypass circuits to assure adequate input voltage to ignition system while cranking. A—Engine is cranking. Solenoid feeds full battery voltage to ignition coil. Voltage is lowered by draw of large starting motor. Input voltage is about 10 volts while cranking. B—Engine is now running. Charging system output is about 14 to 15 volts. Resistor can be used to lower this voltage to protect ignition coil from excess input current damage.

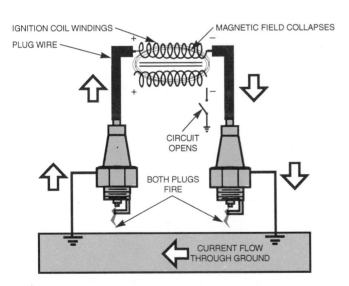

Fig. 15-15. Many coils fire two spark plugs at the same time. One spark plug starts combustion on the power stroke. The other spark plug produces a wasted spark, which occurs during the engine exhaust stroke. Note current flow through coil, plugs, and ground.

system. The electric motor spins the engine until the engine begins to run.

The starting motor draws high current and causes battery voltage to drop below 12.6 volts. The bypass circuit assures that there is still enough voltage and current for ignition operation and easy engine starting.

A *resistor circuit* may be used in the ignition system to limit supply voltage to the ignition system during alternator operation.

After the engine starts, the ignition key switch is released. A spring inside the switch causes it to return to the RUN POSITION.

Now, the alternator is functioning and supplying a higher voltage.

To protect the ignition from damage, the resistor circuit is between the switch and ignition coil to limit current flow, Fig. 15-16.

Either a special *resistance wire* (wire having internal resistance) or a *ballast resistor* (heat sensitive resistor that can regulate voltage) is used in the resistance circuit. The resistance circuit assures that a relatively steady voltage of approximately 9.5 to 10.5 volts is applied to the ignition system.

Note! Many electronic ignition systems do not use bypass or resistance circuits.

Coil wire

The *coil wire* carries high voltage from the high voltage (high tension) terminal of the ignition coil to the center terminal of the distributor cap. It is constructed like a very short spark plug wire.

With a unitized distributor or distributorless ignition, a coil wire is NOT needed.

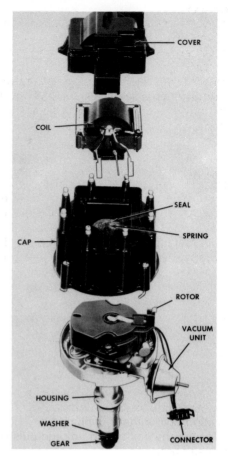

Fig. 15-17. Exploded view of common unitized distributor. ECU is inside distributor housing. (General Motors)

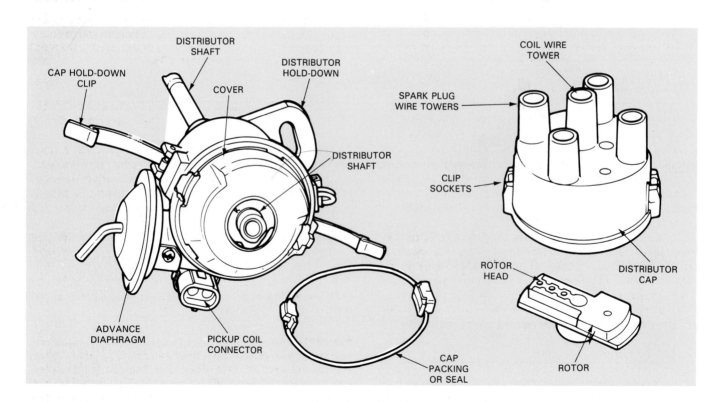

Fig. 15-18. Rotor mounts on distributor shaft. It spins and feeds high voltage to outside terminals in distributor cap. Seal helps keep moisture out of cap. (GM Trucks)

Distributor cap

The *distributor cap* is an insulating, plastic component that fits over the top of the distributor housing, Fig. 15-17. Its center terminal transfers voltage from the coil wire to the rotor.

The distributor cap also has outer or side terminals that send electric arcs to the spark plug wires. Metal terminals are molded into the plastic cap to make the electrical connections.

Rotor

The *distributor rotor* transfers voltage from the distributor cap center terminal to the distributor cap outer terminals and plug wires. The rotor is mounted on top of the distributor shaft. It is a spinning electrical switch that feeds voltage to each spark plug wire, Fig. 15-18.

A metal terminal on the rotor touches the distributor cap center terminal. The outer end of the rotor terminal ALMOST touches the outer cap terminals.

Voltage is high enough that it can jump the air space between the rotor and cap. About 3000 volts is used as the spark jumps this rotor-to-cap gap.

IGNITION DISTRIBUTORS

An *ignition distributor* has several functions:
1. It actuates the on/off cycles of current flow through the ignition coil primary windings.
2. It distributes the coil's high voltage pulses to each spark plug wire.
3. It must cause the spark to occur at each plug earlier in the compression stroke as engine speed increases and vice versa.
4. It changes spark timing with changes in engine load. As more load is placed on the engine, the spark timing must occur later in the compression stroke to prevent spark knock (abnormal combustion).
5. Sometimes, the bottom of the distributor shaft powers the engine oil pump.
6. Some distributors (unitized distributors) house the ignition coil and electronic switching circuit.

Fig. 15-17 shows a very common ignition distributor. It is called a *unitized ignition distributor* because the coil, pickup unit, and ignition control module are all housed inside the distributor.

The rotor fits on the distributor shaft. The cap fits over the distributor housing. See Fig. 15-18. A few distributors use a two-piece distributor cap.

The distributor mounts on the engine and is usually driven by the camshaft or sometimes an accessory shaft, Fig. 15-19. It may install in the cylinder block or on the cylinder head with some overhead camshaft engines. The distributor shaft is rotated at one-half engine rpm.

An exploded view of a distributor is given in Fig. 15-20. Study the part names and part relationships.

Distributor types

Distributors can be classified by the way they sense engine speed. Older distributors used mechanical contact points while the trend today is to do away with the distributor.

The basic distributor types are:

Fig. 15-19. Note how distributor is held in engine by forked clamp. Plug wires feed out from cap. Some distributors are mounted on end of cylinder head to be driven directly from end of camshaft. (Saab)

1. CONTACT POINT DISTRIBUTOR: It uses old fashioned mechanical breakers that are opened and closed by cam action.
2. MAGNETIC PICKUP DISTRIBUTOR: It uses a coil-magnet type sensor to detect rotation of a toothed wheel; the signal is sent to an ignition control module.
3. HALL EFFECT DISTRIBUTOR: Semiconductor sensor is used to detect rotation of trigger blades and the signal is sent to ignition control module.
4. PHOTODIODE DISTRIBUTOR: A photodiode is used to sense the light flashes produced by a light emitting diode and spinning trigger blades.

Each of these distributor types will be discussed briefly before learning about more modern ignition systems that do not use a distributor.

Magnetic pickup distributor

A *magnetic pickup distributor* is very common. It has a small sensing coil mounted inside the distributor housing. A *trigger wheel* is mounted on the upper end of the distributor shaft to induce current fluctuations in the pickup coil. The trigger wheel spins with the distributor shaft to produce a signal that corresponds to engine rpm.

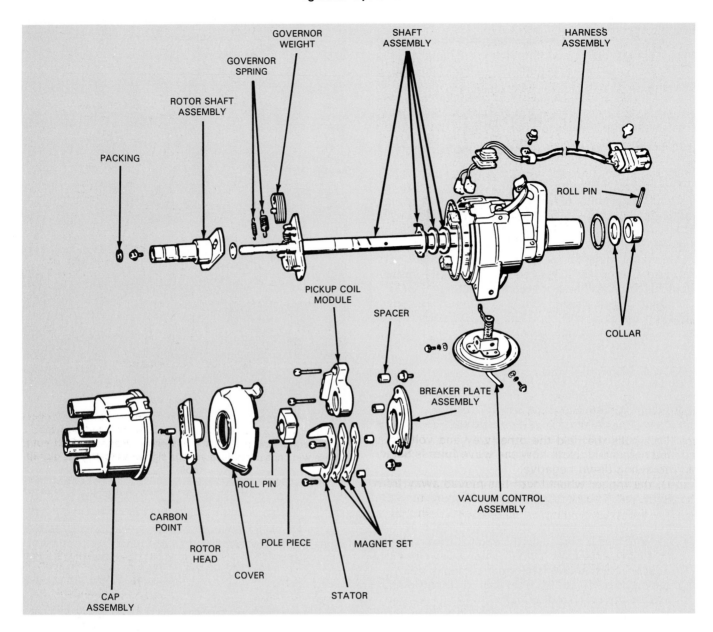

Fig. 15-20. Study parts of this distributor. (GM Trucks)

Other names for the trigger wheel are *reluctor* or *pole piece.* See Fig. 15-21.

Fig. 15-22 shows a photo of a common pickup coil. This type has teeth that correspond to teeth on the trigger wheel. As the two sets of teeth align and misalign, voltage and current are induced into the pickup coil leads.

An *air gap* is produced between the trigger wheel teeth and pickup coil assembly. This air gap must be small enough for good induction but not too small to allow the wheel to strike the pickup coil. Look at Fig. 15-23.

Magnetic pickup operation

Fig. 15-24 shows how a magnetic pickup coil operates.

In A, note how the tooth is beginning to move into the pickup coil. This affects the field around the permanent magnet. The field starts to cut across the coil windings and the voltage signal moves positive.

In B, the tooth has aligned with the pickup coil and

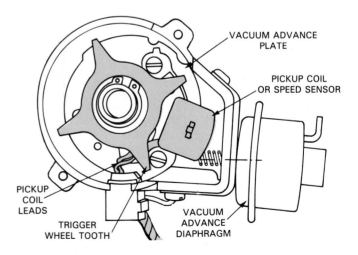

Fig. 15-21. Top view of distributor shows magnetic pickup coil and trigger wheel. Spinning trigger wheel induces small voltage in coil to signal and operate ECU. (Peugeot)

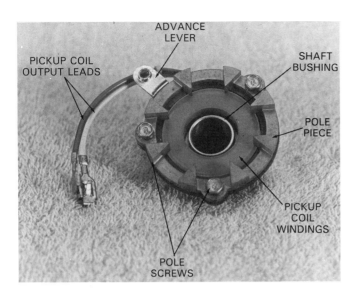

Fig. 15-22. This is a magnetic pickup coil out of a unitized distributor. Teeth on the pickup match teeth on the trigger wheel. A small AC voltage is generated and sent through small wires.

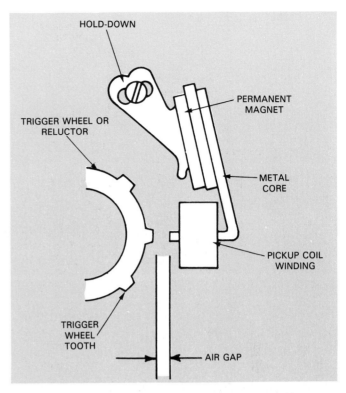

Fig. 15-23. Small air gap or space is formed between trigger wheel and pickup coil. Note how coil is mounted on permanent magnet and metal core assembly. Magnetic field cuts across windings to produce voltage signals as teeth pass pickup coil.

the field has moved back across the windings. This makes the voltage signal move back to zero.

In C, the tooth starts to move away from the pickup coil. This pulls the field the other way and voltage is induced negatively. Note how the wave form is beginning to swing down negative.

In D, the trigger wheel tooth has moved away from the pickup coil. This causes the induced voltage to return to zero. The cycle is repeated as the next tooth moves

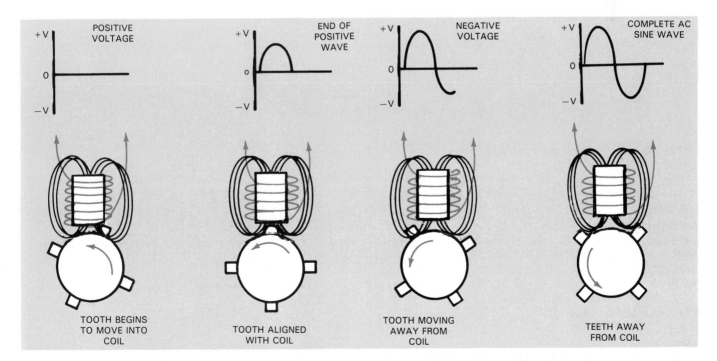

Fig. 15-24. Action of magnetic type speed sensor or distributor pickup coil. As trigger wheel passes pickup coil, it causes magnetic field to move across windings in pickup coil. This induces small current and voltage in pickup coil windings. Note how voltage moves positive when tooth moves into field and negative as it moves away from field. With wheel spinning, AC signal is generated by pickup coil.

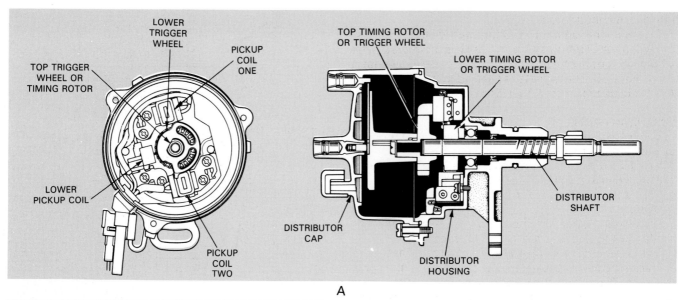

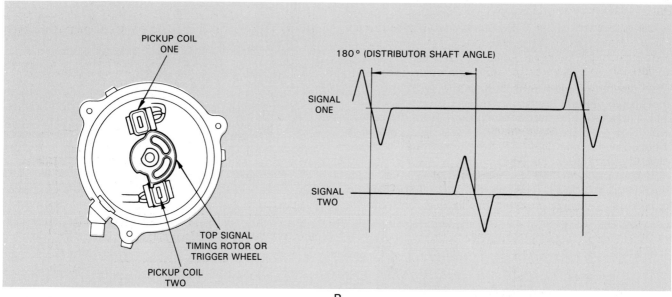

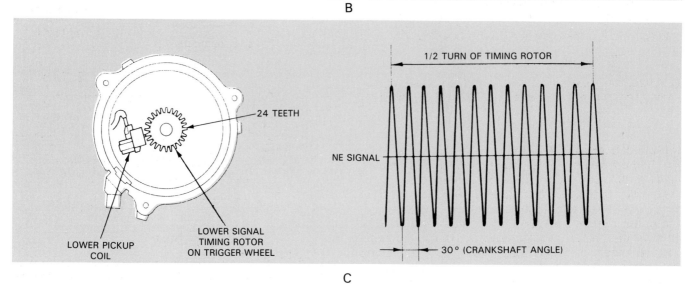

Fig. 15-25. This distributor has two trigger wheels mounted one below the other and three pickup coils. The top pickup coils are primarily for detecting crankshaft angle or rotation. The lower pickup is for crank angle and engine speed; its trigger wheel has 24 teeth for sending more precise data to electronic control unit. A—Distributor cutaway. B—Upper trigger wheel and pickup coils. C—Lower trigger and pickup coil. (Toyota)

into the magnetic field.

As the engine operates and the trigger wheel rotates, an AC or alternating voltage signal is produced. The voltage output from a magnetic pickup coil can vary from 3 to 8 volts AC. This signal is amplified by an ignition control module to operate the ignition or high voltage coil.

Dual pickup coils

Some distributors have dual pickup coils. The purpose of each can vary.

Fig. 15-25 shows a distributor that uses an engine speed pickup and a crank angle pickup. Two pickup coils are mounted one above the other in the distributor housing.

A *speed pickup coil* is used to sense engine rpm; it is similar to the pickup coils just discussed.

The *crank angle pickup coil* uses a trigger wheel with 24 teeth instead of the same number of teeth as engine cylinders. This allows the electronic control unit to detect exact crankshaft angle or rotation for more precise control of ignition timing and injection timing.

The distributor in Fig. 15-26 has a start pickup coil and a run pickup coil. Obviously, the *start pickup coil* is used to produce the engine speed signal when the engine is cranking. The *run pickup coil* is used to produce the speed signal after the engine is running.

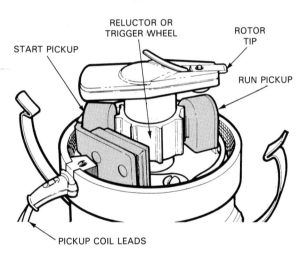

Fig. 15-26. This distributor has two pickup coils, one for engine starting and another for when engine is running. (Chrysler)

Hall-effect pickup operation

A *Hall-effect pickup*, as mentioned, is a semiconductor switch that reacts to the movement of a trigger wheel with blades. Another name for the trigger wheel blades are *vanes*. Look at Figs. 15-27 and 15-28.

In A, the vane or blade is rotated away from the Hall-effect device. The air gap is unobstructed. The magnetic field can then permeate (penetrate) the Hall-effect semiconductor layer. Hall voltage is maximum and the semiconductor switch is turned on. This turns off the ignition control module to fire the ignition coil and plug.

In B, the vane has moved inside the air gap. This blocks the magnetic field and the field is very weak. Hall voltage is minimum and the hall switch turns off. This signals

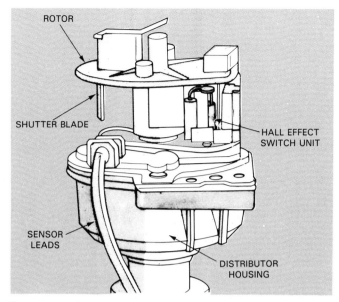

Fig. 15-27. A Hall-effect pickup is used in this model of distributor. Its operation is different than magnetic pickup. (Chrysler)

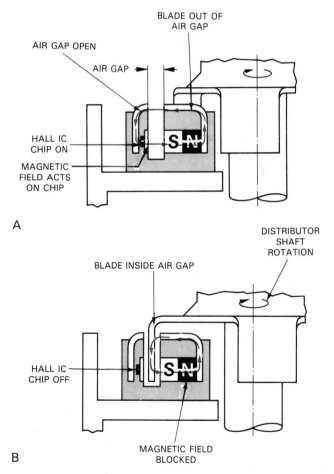

Fig. 15-28. Study operation of hall type pickup. A—Vane or blade is not inside hall pickup. Magnetic field can then saturate semiconductor material or chip. This turns on hall IC chip and signals the ECU. B—Vane or blade has rotated inside pickup. This prevents magnetic field from saturating semiconductor chip. Chip shuts off and ECU can then use this signal to operate ignition output coil. (Robert Bosch)

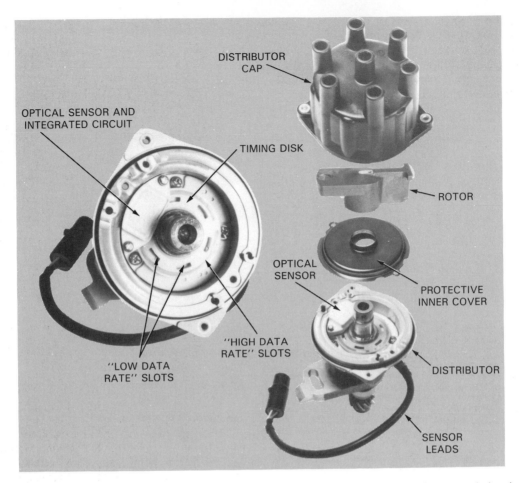

Fig. 15-29. Photo shows a distributor that uses a photodiode and a light emitting diode to produce speed signals. A slotted disk is mounted on shaft. As shaft and disk rotate, slots pass between light emitting diode and photocell type device. This makes photodiode produce voltage output that represents engine speed. (Chrysler)

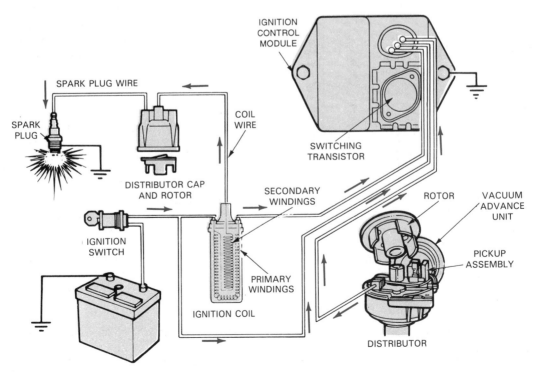

Fig. 15-30. Study how electronic control unit can use signals from speed sensor to operate ignition coil. Coil then sends high voltage out to spark plugs whenever ECU shuts off primary current. (Chrysler)

the control module to turn on and current is fed through the ignition coil to ready it for firing again.

Photodiode pickup operation

A distributor using a photodiode type speed sensor is pictured in Fig. 15-29. Also called an *optical sensor,* it can react to or ''see'' the flashing light from an LED (light emitting diode).

A *timing disk* or trigger wheel separates the LED and photodiode. As the timing disk rotates with engine operation, slots in the disk pass between the photodiode and LED. This allows a flashing light signal from the LED to hit the photodiode. The photodiode can then produce a voltage signal that corresponds to disk rotation and engine rpm. A small amplifier circuit increases the signal strength and sends the signal to an ignition control module.

ELECTRONIC IGNITION SYSTEM

An *electronic ignition system,* also called a *solid state* or *transistor ignition system,* uses an electronic control circuit and a distributor pickup coil to operate the ignition coil. Fig. 15-30 shows a typical circuit for an electronic ignition.

An electronic ignition is more dependable than a contact point type. There are no mechanical breakers to wear or burn. This helps avoid trouble with ignition timing and dwell.

An electronic ignition is also capable of producing much higher secondary voltages than a breaker point ignition. This is an advantage because wider spark plug gaps and higher voltages are needed to ignite lean air-fuel mixtures. Lean mixtures are now used for reduced exhaust emissions and fuel consumption.

Ignition control module

The *ignition control module* (ICM) is an "electronic switch" that turns the ignition coil primary current on and off. The ICM does the same thing as contact points but more efficiently.

An ignition control module is a network of transistors, resistors, capacitors, and other electronic components. The circuit is sealed in a plastic or metal housing.

The ICM can be located:
1. On the side of the distributor.
2. In the engine compartment, Fig. 15-30.
3. Inside the distributor, Fig. 15-31.
4. Under the car dash.

ICM operation

With the engine running, the trigger wheel spins inside the distributor. As the teeth pass the pickup, a change in the magnetic field causes a change in output voltage or current. This results in engine rpm electrical signals entering the ICM, Fig. 15-30.

The ICM increases these tiny pulses into ON/OFF current cycles for the ignition coil. When the ICM is ON, current flows through the primary windings of the ignition coil, developing a magnetic field. Then, when the trigger wheel and pickup turn the ICM OFF, the ignition coil field collapses and fires a spark plug.

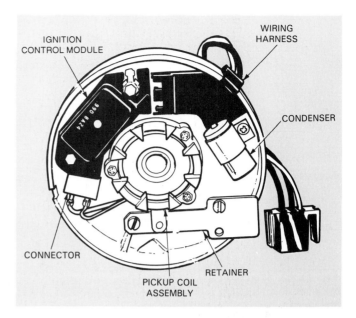

Fig. 15-31. Top view of this distributor shows pickup coil and ignition control module. ICM has electronic circuit that can amplify and modify small AC signal from pickup coil. (General Motors)

ICM dwell time (number of degrees circuit conducts current to ignition coil) is designed into the control module's electronic circuit. It is not adjustable.

CONTACT POINT IGNITION SYSTEMS

Although not produced for several years, thousands of older cars driving on city streets still have a contact point type ignition system. For this reason, you should still be familiar with this system's basic parts and operating principles. Many of the parts in a contact point system are similar to the components in present-day systems: spark plugs, secondary wires, ignition coil, etc.

The distributor for a contact point ignition contains the following:

Distributor cam

The *distributor cam* is the lobed part on the distributor shaft that opens the contact points, Fig. 15-32. The cam turns with the shaft at one-half engine speed. One lobe is normally provided for each spark plug.

Breaker points

The *contact points,* also called *breaker points,* serve as a spring-loaded electrical switch in the distributor, Fig. 15-32. Small screws hold the contact points on the distributor advance plate. A *rubbing block,* of fiber material, rides on the distributor cam. Wires from the condenser and ignition coil primary connect to the points.

Condenser

The *condenser* or capacitor prevents the contact points from arcing and burning, Fig. 15-32. It also provides a storage place for electricity as the points open. This electricity is fed back into the primary when the points reclose.

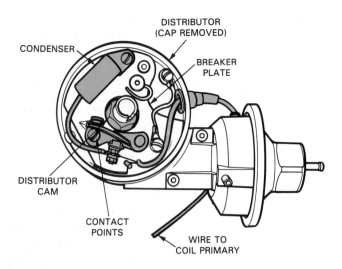

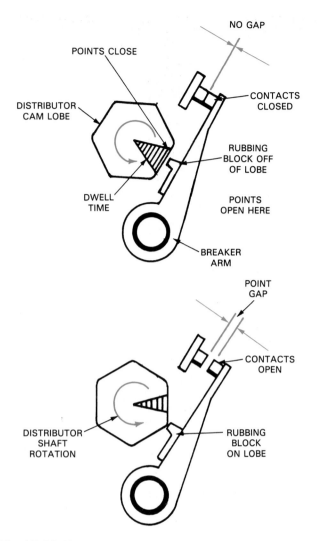

Fig. 15-32. This is an older contact point type distributor. Instead of using an ECU to make and break primary current to the ignition coil, the contacts open and close to fire the high voltage coil. Condenser helps limit point arcing and burning. (Ford)

Contact point system operation

With the engine running, the distributor shaft and distributor cam rotate. This causes the cam to open and close the points.

Since the points are wired to the primary windings of the ignition coil, the points make and break the ignition coil primary circuit. When the points are closed, a magnetic field builds in the coil. When the points open, the field collapses and voltage is sent to one of the spark plugs. This causes combustion.

With the distributor rotating at one-half engine rpm and with one cam lobe per engine cylinder, each spark plug fires once during a complete revolution of the distributor shaft and distributor cam.

Point dwell (cam angle)

Dwell or *cam angle* is the amount of time, given in degrees of distributor rotation, that the points remain closed between each opening. A dwell period is needed to assure that the coil has enough time to build up a strong magnetic field.

Without enough point dwell, a weak spark would be produced. With too much dwell, the *point gap* (distance between fully open points) would be too narrow. Point arcing and burning could result, Fig. 15-33.

IGNITION TIMING

Ignition timing, also called *spark timing,* refers to when the spark plugs fire in relation to the position of the engine pistons. Ignition timing must vary with engine speed, load, and temperature. See Fig. 15-34.

Timing advance occurs when the spark plugs fire sooner on the engine's compression strokes. The timing is set several degrees before TDC (top dead center). More timing advance is needed at higher engine speeds to give combustion enough time to develop pressure on the power stroke.

Timing retard occurs when the spark plugs fire later

Fig. 15-33. Note relationship between point closing and dwell. Every time contacts open, ignition coil fires. (Sun Electric Corporation)

on the compression strokes. It is the opposite of timing advance. Spark retard is needed at lower engine speeds and under high load conditions. Timing retard prevents the fuel from burning too much on the compression stroke, causing spark knock or ping (abnormal combustion).

There are three basic methods used to control ignition system spark timing:
1. *Distributor centrifugal advance* (controlled by engine speed).
2. *Distributor vacuum advance* (controlled by engine intake manifold vacuum and engine load).
3. *Electronic (computer) advance* (controlled by various engine sensors: engine rpm, temperature, intake manifold vacuum, throttle position, etc.).

Distributor centrifugal advance

The *distributor centrifugal advance* makes the ignition coil and spark plugs fire sooner as engine speed increases. It uses spring-loaded weights, centrifugal force, and lever action to rotate the distributor cam, or trigger wheel on the distributor shaft. By rotating the cam or trigger wheel against distributor shaft rotation, spark

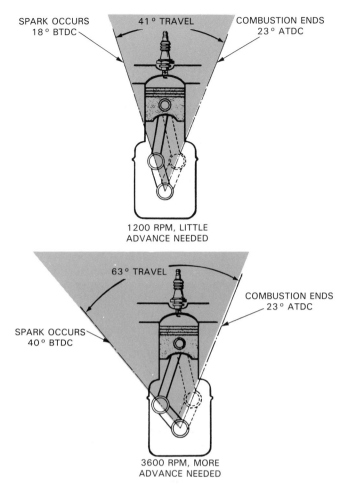

SPARK OCCURS
18° BTDC

41° TRAVEL

COMBUSTION ENDS
23° ATDC

1200 RPM, LITTLE
ADVANCE NEEDED

63° TRAVEL

COMBUSTION ENDS
23° ATDC

SPARK OCCURS
40° BTDC

3600 RPM, MORE
ADVANCE NEEDED

Fig. 15-34. Ignition timing must normally move more advanced as engine speed increases. This gives combustion more time to develop maximum cylinder pressure on power stroke. (Sun)

timing is advanced. See Fig. 15-35.

A distributor centrifugal advance mechanism basically consists of two advance weights, two springs, and an advance lever.

At low engine speeds, small springs hold the advance weights inward. There is not enough centrifugal force to push the weights outward. The timing stays at its normal initial setting (as long as vacuum advance is not functioning).

As engine speed increases, centrifugal force overcomes spring tension. The weights are thrown outward. The edge of the weights acts on the cam or trigger wheel lever. The lever is rotated on the distributor shaft. This also rotates the distributor cam or trigger wheel.

Since the cam or trigger wheel is turned against distributor shaft rotation, the points open sooner, or the trigger wheel and pickup coil turn off the ICM sooner. This causes the ignition coil to fire with the engine pistons not as far up in their cylinders.

As engine speed increases more, the weights fly out more and timing is advanced a greater amount. At a preset engine rpm, the lever strikes a stop and centrifugal advance reaches maximum.

Distributor vacuum advance

The *distributor vacuum advance* provides additional spark advance when engine load is low at part (medium) throttle positions. It is a method of matching ignition timing with engine load.

The vacuum advance mechanism increases FUEL ECONOMY because it helps maintain ideal spark advance at all times. Look at Fig. 15-36.

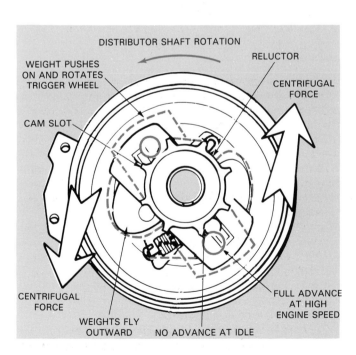

DISTRIBUTOR SHAFT ROTATION

WEIGHT PUSHES ON AND ROTATES TRIGGER WHEEL

RELUCTOR

CENTRIFUGAL FORCE

CAM SLOT

CENTRIFUGAL FORCE

WEIGHTS FLY OUTWARD

NO ADVANCE AT IDLE

FULL ADVANCE AT HIGH ENGINE SPEED

Fig. 15-35. Centrifugal advance uses spring-loaded weights to rotate trigger wheel on its shaft. Weights swing out more as engine speed increases. This allows weight action to advance ignition timing with increased engine rpm. (Chrysler)

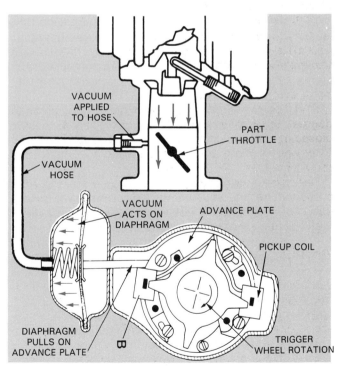

VACUUM APPLIED TO HOSE

PART THROTTLE

VACUUM HOSE

VACUUM ACTS ON DIAPHRAGM

ADVANCE PLATE

PICKUP COIL

DIAPHRAGM PULLS ON ADVANCE PLATE

TRIGGER WHEEL ROTATION

Fig. 15-36. Vacuum advance matches ignition timing with engine load and engine vacuum. Heavy load makes engine vacuum drop. Vacuum diaphragm reacts to vacuum to move advance plate and pickup coil or contact points. This too can be used to advance or retard timing. (General Motors)

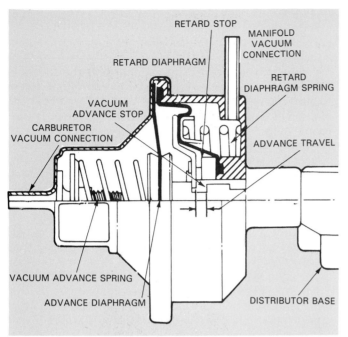

Fig. 15-37. This is a dual-diaphragm assembly. One diaphragm advances ignition timing and the other retards timing. This type was once used to help reduce exhaust emissions. (Ford)

A distributor vacuum advance mechanism consists of a vacuum diaphragm, link, movable distributor plate, and a vacuum supply hose.

At idle, the vacuum port to the distributor advance is usually covered. Look at Fig. 15-37. Vacuum (suction) is NOT applied to the vacuum diaphragm. Spark timing is NOT advanced.

At part throttle, the throttle valve uncovers the vacuum port and the port is exposed to engine vacuum. This causes the distributor diaphragm to be pulled toward the vacuum. The distributor plate (points or pickup coil) is rotated against distributor shaft rotation and spark timing is advanced.

During acceleration and full throttle, engine vacuum drops. Thus, vacuum is NOT applied to the distributor diaphragm and the vacuum advance does NOT operate. This prevents spark knock or ping.

Dual diaphragms

A *dual-diaphragm vacuum advance* mechanism contains two separate vacuum chambers: an advance chamber and a retard chamber. This type is used on some older distributors.

The *vacuum advance chamber* controls spark advance for cruise and part throttle engine operation. It performs the same functions as a single vacuum advance diaphragm.

The *vacuum retard chamber* is used to make the ignition spark occur later under certain driving conditions.

Usually, the advance diaphragm is connected to the ported vacuum source at the carburetor. The retard diaphragm may be connected directly to intake manifold vacuum. As a result, maximum retard is assured at idle and under deceleration.

Sometimes, a vacuum control switch is used in the distributor vacuum line to alter diaphragm action.

Vacuum delay valve

A *vacuum delay valve* restricts the flow of air to slow down the vacuum action on a vacuum device. The delay valve has a small orifice (opening) for vacuum. It may also have a check valve that only allows flow in one direction.

The vacuum delay valve keeps the vacuum advance from working too quickly, preventing possible knock or ping. The check valve allows free release of vacuum from the diaphragm when returning to the retard position.

Electronic spark advance

An *electronic spark advance* system uses engine sensors and a computer, or ECM, to control ignition timing. A distributor may be used, but it does NOT contain centrifugal or vacuum advance mechanisms.

The engine sensors check various engine operating conditions and send electrical data to the computer. The computer can then change ignition timing for maximum engine efficiency. Look at Fig. 15-38.

Sensors that can affect the ignition system include:
1. *Engine speed sensor* (reports engine rpm to computer).
2. *Crankshaft position sensor* (reports piston position).
3. *Intake vacuum sensor* (measures engine vacuum, an indicator of load).
4. *Inlet air temperature sensor* (check temperature of air entering engine).
5. *Engine coolant temperature sensor* (measures operating temperature of engine).
6. *Knock sensor* (allows computer to retard timing when engine pings or knocks).
7. *Throttle position sensor* (notes position of throttle).
8. *Vehicle speed sensor* (measures road speed of car).
9. *Transmission/Transaxle sensor* (detects gear selection).

The ECM may receive input signals (different current or voltage levels) from one or more of these sensors. It is programmed (preset) to adjust ignition timing to meet different engine conditions.

Electronic spark advance operation

One example of electronic spark advance, imagine a car traveling down the highway at 55 mph (88 km/h). The speed sensor would detect moderate engine rpm. The throttle position sensor would detect part throttle. The air inlet and coolant temperature sensors would report normal operating temperatures. The intake manifold pressure sensor would send high vacuum signals to the computer, Fig. 15-38.

The computer could then calculate that the engine would need maximum spark advance. The timing would occur several degrees before TDC on the compression stroke. This would assure that the engine attained high fuel economy on the highway.

If the driver began to pass a car, engine intake manifold vacuum would drop to a very low level. The vacuum sensor signal would be fed to the computer. The throttle position sensor would detect WOT (wide open throttle). Other sensor outputs would stay about the same. The computer could then retard ignition timing to prevent spark knock or ping.

Since computer systems vary, refer to a service manual for information on the operation of specific systems.

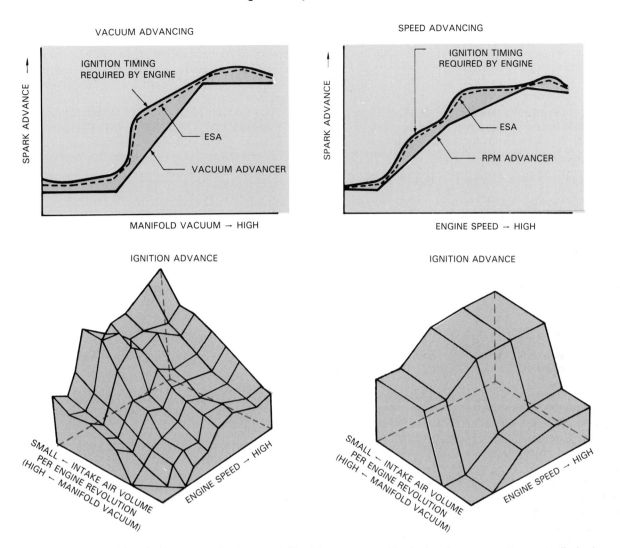

Fig. 15-38. Graphs show ignition timing curves for late model ignition system with electronic or computer-controlled advance.

Knock sensor circuit

The *knock sensor circuit* is used to retard ignition timing, and sometimes turbocharger boost pressure, during periods of engine knock, ping, or spark knock.

Discussed earlier, the *knock sensor* acts as a microphone mounted on the engine. It can "listen" for the sound of ping or knock. This sound will generate a signal in the knock sensor. This signal can be used by the engine control module and ignition system amplifier to retard ignition timing slightly. Retarded timing will make combustion occur later in the compression stroke and will normally stop pinging or knocking. See Fig. 15-39.

Ionization knock sensing systems

An *ionization knock sensing* system is sometimes used to detect knocking. In this type of system, the ECM prompts the ignition coil to send a low-voltage discharge across the spark plug gap immediately following combustion. The quality of combustion affects the resistance across the plug gap by varying the degree of ionization (the process by which atoms gain or lose electrons) in the gases between the plug electrodes. Consequently, the quality of combustion influences the strength of the discharge across the gap. The computer uses feedback

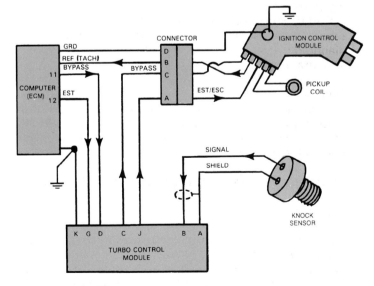

Fig. 15-39. This is a knock sensor circuit. Knock sensor will produce a signal if it "hears" engine pinging. Signal can then be used by electronic control circuits to retard ignition timing or reduce turbocharger boost pressure. Both changes will reduce knock tendencies. (General Motors)

from the discharge to determine if the spark advance or the turbocharger boost should be modified to reduce knocking. A conventional knock sensor is not needed in an ionization knock sensing system.

Electronic governor circuit

An *electronic governor circuit* can be used to limit maximum engine speed. It does this by operating a governor solenoid or by partially shutting off the ignition system. Fig. 15-40 shows an electronic governor circuit for an

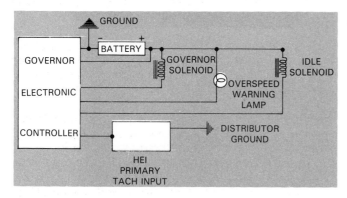

Fig. 15-40. This circuit is for an electronic governor system. It limits maximum engine speed, protecting the engine from high rpm damage. (GM Trucks)

engine used in a small truck. When the electronic controller circuit senses maximum engine speed from the speed sensor or tach input, it sends a control current to the governor solenoid. The solenoid action is used to close the throttle plates and limit air intake into the engine. Engine speed is then governed.

CRANKSHAFT TRIGGERED IGNITION

A *crankshaft triggered ignition* system places the pickup coil and trigger wheel (pulse ring) unit on the front of the engine. These parts are NOT located inside the distributor. See Fig. 15-41.

Pulse ring

A *pulse ring* is usually mounted on the crankshaft damper to provide engine speed information to the pickup unit, Fig. 15-42. It performs the same function as the trigger wheel in a distributor for an electronic ignition. The teeth on the pulse ring correspond to the number of engine cylinders. The pulse ring can also be on the rear or center of the crankshaft.

Crankshaft position sensor

The *crankshaft position sensor* is mounted next to the crank pulse ring and sends electrical pulses to the system computer, or ECM. It does the same thing as a distributor pickup. See Fig. 15-42.

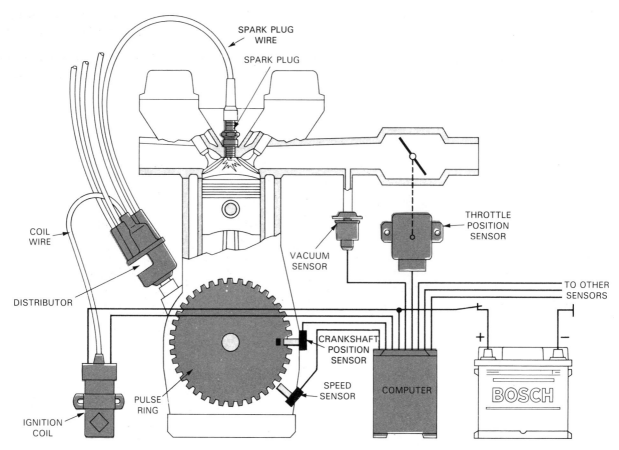

Fig. 15-41. This is a basic crankshaft triggered ignition system. Taking engine speed signals off of crankshaft is more accurate than distributor-mounted speed sensor because there is no play in distributor drive. This system still uses a distributor rotor and cap to send voltage to each spark plug wire. (Robert Bosch)

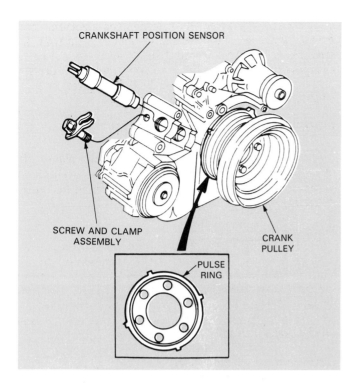

Fig. 15-42. Pulse ring replaces distributor trigger wheel with crank triggered ignition. It induces voltage in crank sensor for use by electronic control circuit. (Ford)

The distributor for a crankshaft triggered ignition is simply used to transfer high voltage to each spark plug wire. The rotor and cap are conventional.

The operation of a crank triggered ignition is similar to the other electronic systems already covered. A crank triggered ignition can maintain more precise ignition timing than a system with a distributor-mounted pickup coil. There is no backlash or play in the distributor drive gear, timing chain, or timing gears to upset ignition timing. Crank and piston position is "read" right off the crankshaft.

DISTRIBUTORLESS IGNITION

A *distributorless ignition,* also called a *computer-coil ignition,* uses multiple ignition coils, a coil control unit, engine sensors, and a computer to operate the spark plugs. A distributor is NOT needed, Fig. 15-43.

An *electronic coil module* consists of more than one ignition coil and a coil control unit that operates the coils. The module's control unit performs about the same function as the ICM in an electronic ignition. It must analyze data from engine sensors and the system computer, Fig. 15-44

A four-cylinder engine would need an electronic coil module with two ignition coils. A six-cylinder engine would need a module with three ignition coils.

The coils are wired so that they fire TWO SPARK PLUGS at once. One spark plug is on the power stroke. The other is on the exhaust stroke, and has no effect on engine operation.

A *camshaft position sensor* is commonly installed in place of the ignition distributor. It sends electrical pulses to the coil control unit, giving data on camshaft and valve position.

The *crankshaft position sensor,* as discussed, feeds pulses to the control unit which show engine speed and piston position, Fig. 15-44.

A *knock sensor* may be used to allow the system to retard timing if the engine begins to ping or knock.

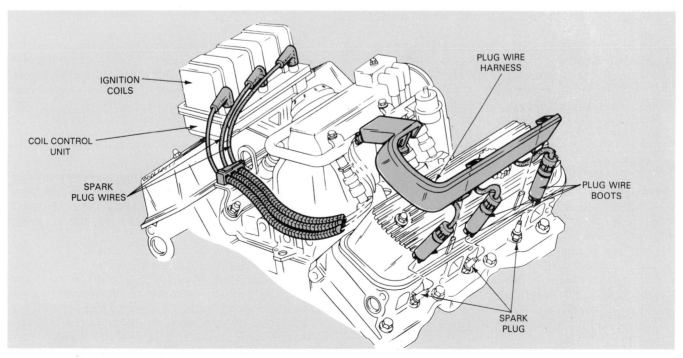

Fig. 15-43. Distributorless ignition system has multiple coils and coil control unit that replace distributor. Crank and cam sensors feed data to control unit. Each ignition coil fires two spark plug.   (Buick)

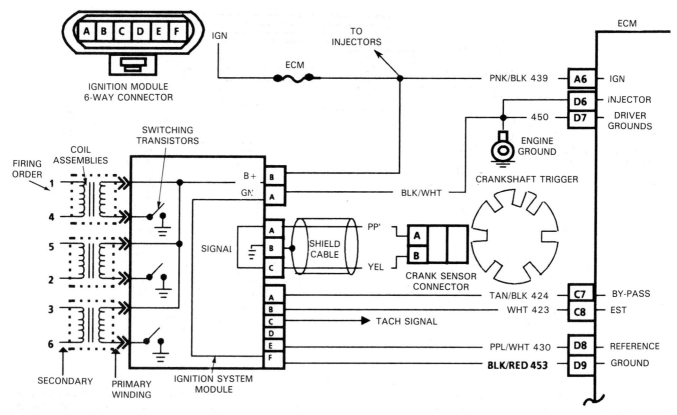

Fig. 15-44. Actual wiring diagram shows distributorless ignition system. Note crank sensor input, electronic control module connections, and three ignition coils. (General Motors)

Distributorless ignition operation

The on-board computer monitors engine operating conditions and controls ignition timing. Some sensor data is also fed to the electronic coil module, Fig. 15-45.

When the computer and sensors send correct electrical pulses to the coil module, the module fires one of the ignition coils.

Since each coil secondary output is wired to two spark plugs, both spark plugs fire. One produces the power stroke. The other spark plug arc does nothing because that cylinder is on the exhaust stroke. Burned gases are simply being pushed out of the cylinder.

When the next pulse ring tooth aligns with the crank sensor, the next ignition coil fires. Another two spark plugs arc for one more power stroke. This process is repeated over and over as the engine runs.

Advantages of a distributorless ignition

A distributorless ignition system has several possible advantages over ignition systems with a distributor. Some of these include:

1. No rotor or distributor cap to burn, crack, or fail.
2. All computer controlled advance. No mechanical weights to stick or wear. No vacuum advance diaphragm to rupture and leak.
3. Play in timing chain and distributor drive gear eliminated as a problem that could upset ignition timing. The crank sensor is not affected by slack in timing chain or gears.
4. More dependable because less moving parts to wear and malfunction.

5. Requires less maintenance. Ignition timing is usually NOT adjustable.

DIRECT IGNITION SYSTEM

A *direct ignition system* has ignition coils mounted on top of the spark plugs; spark plug wires are not needed. This type system has an individual coil for each spark plug. A four-cylinder engine would use four ignition coils. A direct ignition is very similar to a distributorless ignition, except for the lack of spark plug wires and the increased number of coils.

Fig. 15-46 illustrates one type of simplified, direct ignition system. Note its simplicity.

Sensor inputs allow the electronic control module to alter ignition timing with changes in operating conditions. The control unit can then make and break primary current into the correct ignition coil to make it produce high voltage.

Fig. 15-47 shows the coil for a direct ignition system. Note how the ignition coil is mounted over the spark plug. This eliminates the need for plug wires or conductor strips to the plugs. An electronic control unit and the sensors control when each coil fires its plug.

Note! Auto makers use many different terms to refer to their ignition systems. In one service manual for instance, the term direct ignition may be used to refer to a distributorless ignition that still uses spark plug wires. Keep this in mind when reading manuals.

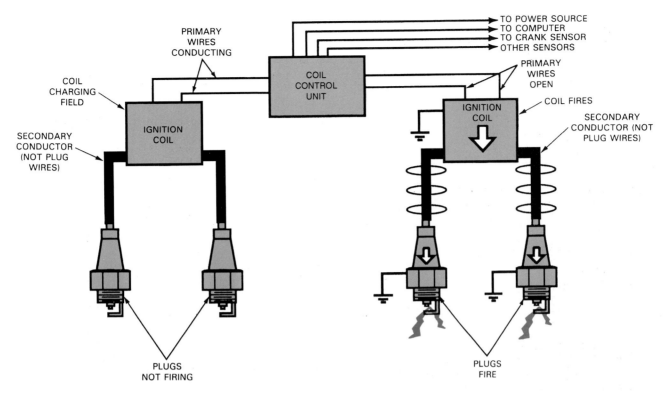

Fig. 15-45. Simplified illustration of distributorless ignition. Note how this system uses conductor strips instead of conventional spark plug wires. Coil control unit uses various sensor inputs to determine when to fire one of the ignition coils. When one coil fires, two spark plugs fire. One plug produces power stroke and other does nothing since that cylinder is on exhaust stroke.

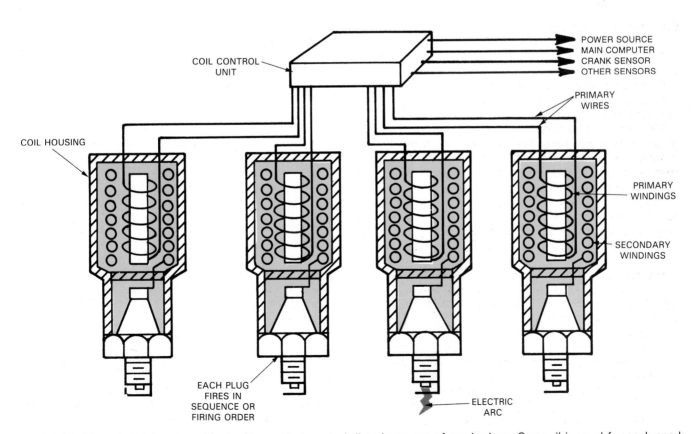

Fig. 15-46. Direct ignition system has ignition coils mounted directly on top of spark plugs. One coil is used for each spark plug. No plug wires or conductor strips are needed. Similar to distributorless ignition, electronic control circuit uses sensor and computer inputs to determine when to fire a plug and which spark plug to fire. Only one spark plug fires at once with this design.

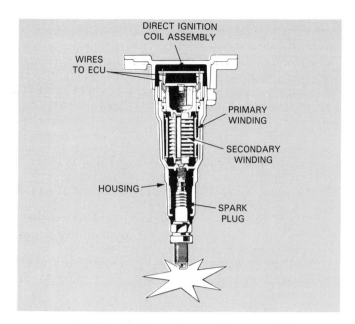

Fig. 15-47. Cutaway of an ignition coil for a direct ignition system. (Saab)

Ionic combustion sensing

An *ionic combustion sensing system* sends a low voltage across the spark plug gaps immediately after combustion. The computer monitors current flow across the ionized gas between the spark plug electrodes to determine combustion quality. The computer can then modify spark timing, turbocharger boost pressure, air-fuel ratio, and other variables to maintain maximum combustion efficiency, engine power, and fuel economy. This type of system is similar to the ionization knock sensing system discussed on page 261.

Dual spark plug ignition

A few high-performance engines have a *dual spark plug ignition system,* in which two spark plugs are used in each cylinder. One plug is located near the intake valve; the other is near the exhaust valve. Dual plugs help ensure better ignition and combustion of the air-fuel mixture.

With this design, one ignition coil may be used to fire both plugs at the same time, similar to the coil arrangement for a wasted spark distributorless ignition.

Multiple discharge ignition

A *multiple discharge ignition* fires the spark plugs more than once on each power stroke. By producing a series of sparks, it helps ensure more complete burning of fuel charge. This type ignition is commonly used on racing engines.

SUMMARY

In the past few years, design changes have been made to increase the efficiency and dependability of ignition systems. It is critical for automotive electronic technicians to be aware of the changes.

The ignition system must amplify battery or charging voltage and deliver this high voltage to the spark plugs.

Gasoline or spark ignition engines require an ignition system; diesels do not.

The spark plug places an air gap in the engine combustion chamber. When the ignition coil sends high voltage to the plug, an electric arc forms across this air gap. The arc is red hot and starts combustion on the engine's power stroke.

Some ignition systems use a distributor. The distributor can have various functions. It can sense engine speed and send signals to the electronic control unit. Sometimes, it can contain centrifugal and vacuum advance units for controlling ignition timing. The distributor will have a rotor and cap for sending high voltage to each spark plug wire.

Many late model ignition systems do not use a distributor. They use multiple ignition coils and a computer to feed high voltage to the plugs at the right time.

The primary section of an ignition system includes wires and components using low, battery voltage. The secondary section of the ignition system carries the high voltage output from the ignition coil.

Non-resistor spark plugs have a solid metal center electrode. They are not commonly used because they can cause radio interference. Resistor spark plugs contain a small resistor element that helps prevent radio noise. This type plug is normally recommended for passenger cars.

The spark plug seat makes contact with the cylinder head to form a leakproof seal. Spark plug heat range refers to the operating temperature of the plug tip. A hot plug has a longer insulator tip and will help burn off oil deposits. A cold plug has a shorter insulator tip and is good for high speed engine operation.

Spark plug gap is the distance between the side and center electrodes. Newer cars use a wider gap to help ignite lean air-fuel charges.

Spark plug wires can also be resistor or non-resistor. A non-resistor wire has a stranded metal core and is not for passenger cars. A resistor wire has a carbon-impregnated core and will prevent radio noise.

Engine firing order refers to the sequence in which the spark plugs fire. This information is needed when installing new plug wires or when doing tune-up type tasks.

The ignition coil is a step-up transformer. It increases battery or charging system voltage to 30,000 volts or more. This high voltage is needed by the spark plugs.

A coil wire is used in some ignition systems to carry coil voltage to the distributor cap center terminal. The rotor transfers this voltage to each cap outer terminal. The plug wires connect to the distributor cap outer terminals.

A unitized distributor contains all major ignition system parts: pickup coil, trigger wheel, ignition coil, ignition control module, etc.

The older contact point distributor contains mechanical breakers. They are used to make and break the ignition coil primary current to fire the coil. A condenser prevents point arcing and burning. Centrifugal and vacuum advance are commonly used with older contact points.

The magnetic pickup coil distributor is very common. It uses a small coil and permanent magnet to sense the rotation of the distributor shaft-mounted trigger wheel. A small voltage is induced in the pickup coil as the teeth pass the coil windings. This AC signal can be amplified by the ignition control module to operate the high voltage ignition coil.

A hall effect distributor contains a semiconductor type speed sensor. The hall sensor switches on and off as vanes or blades pass inside the sensor. This can also be used by the ICM to fire the ignition coil.

A photodiode distributor uses an LED and photodiode to produce an engine speed signal. The photodiode produces a voltage signal when energized by the LED light source. Since a slotted wheel passes between the LED and photodiode, a speed (alternating voltage) signal is produced for the ignition control module.

Ignition timing refers to when the spark plug fires in relation to the engine piston positions. Timing advance means the plugs fire sooner, while the pistons are further down in their cylinders. Timing retard means the plugs fire later, while the pistons are further up on their compression stroke.

Distributor centrifugal advance uses spring-loaded weights and lever action to rotate the cam on the distributor shaft. The cam rotates against the direction of distributor rotation. This lets the centrifugal weights advance timing with engine speed.

The vacuum advance uses a vacuum diaphragm to advance timing with low engine loads and retard timing with high load. Engine manifold vacuum controls the operation of the vacuum advance.

Electronic or computer controlled ignition timing is replacing vacuum and centrifugal advance. Inputs from various sensors allow the computer to accurately match ignition advance with engine operating conditions.

A crankshaft triggered ignition system has the speed sensor or pickup down next to the crankshaft. A pulse ring on the crankshaft replaces the distributor trigger wheel. This provides more accurate control of ignition timing because play in the distributor drive gear, timing chain, etc. is eliminated.

A distributorless ignition uses multiple ignition coils and a computer to control the ignition system. One ignition coil is usually provided for every two spark plugs. When a coil fires, one plug produces the power stroke and the other does nothing. An electronic coil module is used in conjunction with the computer to operate the ignition coils.

A direct ignition system is similar to a distributorless ignition except the coils are mounted on top of the spark plugs. One ignition coil is needed for each spark plug. This eliminates the need for spark plug wires. A computer and coil control unit operate this type ignition system.

KNOW THESE TERMS

Ignition system, Spark plug, Spark plug wire, Distributor cap, Rotor, Distributor, Ignition control module, Speed sensor, Ignition coil, Coil wire, Ignition switch, Primary wires, Secondary wires, Spark plug size, Non-resistor plug, Resistor plug, Spark plug seat, Spark plug reach, Spark plug heat range, Hot plug, Cold plug, Spark plug gap, Resistance plug wire, Non-resistance plug wire, Firing order, Ignition supply voltage, Resistance wire, Ballast resistor, Unitized ignition, Magnetic pickup coil, Trigger wheel, Reluctor, Pole piece, Hall effect pickup, Optical sensor, LED, Timing disk, Electronic ignition system, ICM, ICM dwell time, Distributor cam, Breaker points, Condenser, Cam angle, Dwell, Timing advance, Timing retard, Centrifugal advance, Vacuum advance, Electronic advance, Dual vacuum diaphragms, Vacuum delay valve, Knock sensor, Ionization knock sensing, Electronic governor, Crank triggered ignition, Pulse ring, Crankshaft position sensor, Distributorless ignition, Direct ignition system, Ionic combustion sensing.

REVIEW QUESTIONS—CHAPTER 15

1. Ignition systems have remained about the same for the last 20 years. True or false?
2. What is the basic function of an ignition system?
3. The _____ _____ feed low voltage to components in the ignition system.
4. The ignition coil is a _____ transformer that increases battery voltage to _____ volts or more.
5. What is the difference between the primary and secondary sections of an ignition system?
6. What is the most common spark plug size?
7. Non-resistor spark plugs are normally recommended for passenger cars. True or false?
8. A car enters the shop with oil-fouled spark plugs. Tests show that the engine has worn rings but the customer cannot afford an engine rebuild.
   Technician A says to install colder plugs to help prevent plug fouling.
   Technician B says to install hotter plugs to help prevent plug fouling.
   Who is correct?
   a. Technician A.
   b. Technician B.
   c. Both A and B.
   d. Neither A nor B.
9. Spark plug gaps can range from _____ to _____ inch.
10. A resistance spark plug wire has about _____ ohms per foot to help reduce _____ _____.
11. How can you quickly tell which is the number one cylinder on most V-type engines?
12. How does an ignition coil operate?
13. The distributor _____ transfers high voltage from the cap center terminal to the cap outer terminals and _____ _____ _____.
14. What are six possible functions of an ignition distributor?
15. Describe the four types of distributors.
16. A magnetic pickup coil uses a spinning _____ _____ to induce current and generate a speed signal of about _____ to _____ volts AC.
17. What is the purpose of the ignition system ECU?
18. Explain the three ways of controlling ignition timing.
19. How does a knock sensor circuit operate?
20. Explain the difference between a distributorless ignition and a direct ignition system.

ASE CERTIFICATION—TYPE QUESTIONS

1. Technician A says a modern automotive ignition coil is a step-up transformer that increases battery voltage to 30,000 volts or more. Technician B says a

distributor cap transfers high voltage from the rotor to the spark plug wires. Who is right?

(A) A only.
(B) B only.
(C) Both A and B.
(D) Neither A nor B.

2. Technician A says an automotive engine's primary wires carry high voltage to the spark plugs. Technician B says an engine's coil wire is a secondary wire. Who is right?

(A) A only.
(B) B only.
(C) Both A and B.
(D) Neither A nor B.

3. While discussing the basic components of a modern automotive ignition system, Technician A says an ignition control module controls current to the ignition coil. Technician B says an ignition control module is a speed sensing device. Who is right?

(A) A only.
(B) B only.
(C) Both A and B.
(D) Neither A nor B.

4. Technician A says an automotive ignition system's primary circuit operates on battery voltage. Technician B says an automotive ignition system's secondary circuit consists of the wires and parts between the coil output and the spark plug ground. Who is right?

(A) A only.
(B) B only.
(C) Both A and B.
(D) Neither A nor B.

5. Technician A says the lower the number on the spark plug, the hotter the spark plug tip will operate. Technician B says a cool plug should be installed in a worn, oil-burning engine. Who is right?

(A) A only.
(B) B only.
(C) Both A and B.
(D) Neither A nor B.

6. Technician A says spark plug gap specifications normally range from .030" to .080". Technician B says spark plugs used in electronic ignition systems require smaller gaps. Who is right?

(A) A only.
(B) B only.
(C) Both A and B.
(D) Neither A nor B.

7. A car equipped with a four-cylinder engine is in the shop for a tune-up. Technician A says this engine's firing order may be 1-3-4-2. Technician B says this engine's firing order may be 1-2-4-3. Who is right?

(A) A only.
(B) B only.
(C) Both A and B.
(D) Neither A nor B.

8. Technician A says a distributorless ignition system has one ignition coil for each engine cylinder. Technician B says a wasted spark ignition coil fires two spark plugs at once. Who is right?

(A) A only.
(B) B only.
(C) Both A and B.
(D) Neither A nor B.

9. Which of the following is not a common type of distributor?

(A) Hall-effect distributor.
(B) Magnetic pickup distributor.
(C) Photodiode distributor.
(D) Piezo sensor distributor.

10. Technician A says timing is generally not adjustable in a distributorless ignition system. Technician B says direct ignition systems do not contain spark plug wires. Who is right?

(A) A only.
(B) B only.
(C) Both A and B.
(D) Neither A nor B.

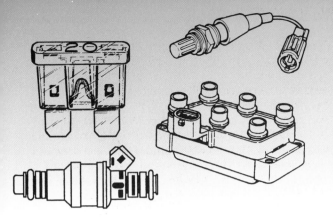

Fuel and Emission Control Systems Electronics

After studying this chapter, you will be able to:
- *Sketch a block diagram for a computerized fuel system.*
- *Summarize the overall operation of a modern computerized fuel system.*
- *Explain the construction and operation of electrical-electronic components in a fuel system.*
- *Review how the oxygen sensor produces open and closed loop fuel system operation.*
- *Summarize the modes of fuel system operation.*
- *Describe how a computer alters idle speed and fuel mixture ratios.*
- *Explain the use of electronics in diesel fuel systems.*
- *Describe the control and operation of electric fuel pumps.*
- *Review the use of electronics in emission control systems.*

In previous chapters, you learned about computers, sensors, and actuators. Today's fuel systems use dozens of sensors, several actuators, and one or more computers. The computer system allows for much more precise control of how much fuel is metered into the engine. This precise fuel metering increases fuel economy and engine power while reducing harmful exhaust emissions. As an electronic technician, you must be able to understand fuel system electronics.

This chapter will continue to "build" upon what you have learned previously. It will briefly review the construction, operation, and design of electrical-electronic fuel system parts. As a result, you will be much more familiar with these parts when trying to do electrical-electronic repairs.

Note! You should have studied Chapter 11 before starting this chapter.

FUEL SYSTEM TYPES

There are several types of fuel systems as concerned with electronics. The most common classifications include:
1. ELECTRONIC GASOLINE INJECTION (sensors and a computer are used to control solenoid-operated injectors).
2. ELECTRONIC CARBURETION (sensors and computer are used to operate mixture control solenoid in carburetor).
3. ELECTRONIC DIESEL INJECTION (sensors and computer are used to control solenoids on injection pump that affect fuel metering).

Within these three classifications are many variations. However, if you understand the electronic principles of a typical example, you will be able to relate this information to all fuel system design variations.

ELECTRONIC GASOLINE INJECTION

Electronic gasoline injection is the most common type of modern fuel system. It has replaced the computer-controlled carburetor in all late-model vehicles. Electronic gasoline injection, also called *electronic fuel injection* (EFI), can more closely control fuel entry into the cylinders than carburetion. Electronic diesel systems are becoming more common, but are few in number compared to EFI.

Single and multi-point injection
The *point* (location) of fuel injection is one way to classify a gasoline injection system.

A *single-point injection system,* also called *throttle body injection* (TBI), has the injector nozzle(s) in a throttle body assembly on top of the engine. Fuel is sprayed into the top center of the intake manifold.

A *multi-point injection system,* also called *multiport injection,* has one fuel injector in the intake manifold port (air-fuel runner or passage) going to each cylinder. Gasoline is sprayed into each intake port, toward each engine intake valve. Hence, the term multi-point (more than one location) fuel injection is used.

Both single-point and multi-point injection systems have been used on cars. Multi-point is more common and has replaced single-point on all new models.

Gasoline injection timing
The *timing* of a gasoline injection system refers to when fuel is sprayed into the engine intake manifold. There are three basic classifications of gasoline injection

timing: intermittent, timed, and continuous.

An *intermittent* gasoline injection system opens and closes the injector valves independently of the engine intake valves. This type may spray fuel into the engine when the valves are open or when they are closed. Another name for an intermittent injection system is MODULATED injection system.

A *timed,* also called *sequential,* injection system squirts fuel into the engine right before or as the intake valves open. It is timed to the opening of the engine intake valves. This type is becoming the most popular because it improves engine efficiency.

A *continuous* gasoline injection system sprays fuel into the intake manifold all of the time. Anytime the engine is running, some fuel is forced out of the injector nozzles and into the engine. The air-fuel ratio is controlled by increasing or decreasing fuel pressure at the injectors.

Injector opening relationship

Simultaneous injection means all of the injectors open at the same time. The injectors are pulsed ON and OFF together.

Sequential injection has the injectors open one after the other. One opens and then another.

Group injection has several, but not all, injectors opening at the same time. For example, a V-6 engine might have three injectors open at once and then the other three open next.

FUEL SYSTEM SUB-SYSTEMS

A fuel system can be divided in sub-systems or sections. A breakdown that applies to all types of fuel systems would be:
1. FUEL SUPPLY SYSTEM (pumps, lines, and filters that feed clean fuel to the fuel metering system).
2. AIR SUPPLY SYSTEM (filters, ducts, valves that control how much clean air enters engine).
3. FUEL METERING SYSTEM (parts that meter correct amount of fuel into air entering engine).

The exact components that would be included in each

of these sub-systems would vary with fuel system type and exact design.

FUEL SYSTEM DIAGRAMS AND SCHEMATICS

Service manuals will have various types of diagrams and schematics for computer-controlled fuel systems. Some are very simple to read; others are very complex. It is important that you understand the advantages of the common types of diagrams and schematics.

Fuel system block diagrams

A *fuel system block diagram* is a simplified way of showing how major components interact. One is shown in Fig. 16-1 for a typical fuel injection system. Note how this injection system can be broken down in sub-systems:
1. FUEL SUPPLY SYSTEM (parts that pressurize and feed fuel through system).
2. FUEL METERING SYSTEM (parts that control how much fuel enters engine with different conditions).
3. FUEL CONTROL SYSTEM (computer related components that operate injectors or actuators and use sensor inputs).
4. DETECTING SYSTEM (sensors that monitor operating conditions and send this electrical data to control system or computer).

There are obviously many other ways to sub-divide a fuel system. Fig. 16-2 shows another block diagram for a fuel injection system. It uses blocks that represent more specific components. Note how the electronic control unit receives inputs and produces outputs. This would make it comparable to the control system in the previous illustration.

Another block diagram is given in Fig. 16-3. It has the sensors on the left and actuators (injectors) on the right. The computer or ECU (electronic control unit) is in the center, processing data and producing control signals.

Block diagrams for fuel systems are frequently given in service manuals. They provide a very quick way of seeing which sensors and actuators affect fuel system

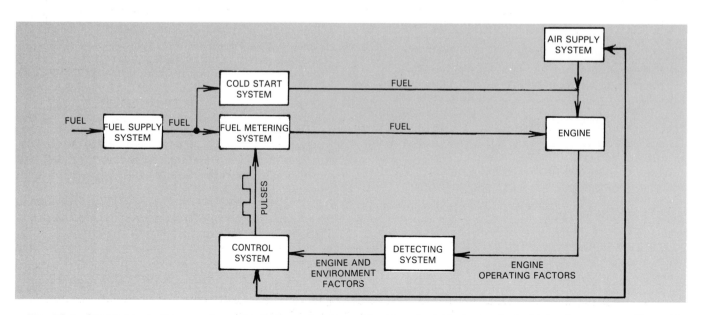

Fig. 16-1. Simple block diagram shows basic flow of data and fuel in a typical electronic fuel injection system. (Renault)

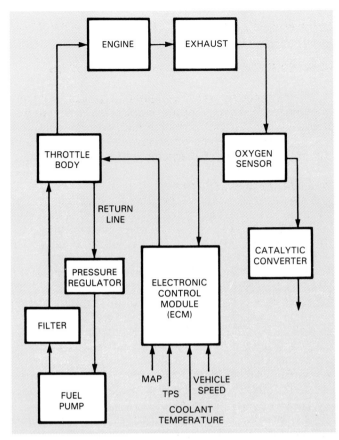

Fig. 16-2. This fuel control system diagram is slightly more detailed than the one in the previous illustration. (General Motors)

operation. This information can be useful when trying to find the source of trouble.

Conventional fuel system diagrams

A *fuel system diagram* uses simple drawings and lines to show the interconnection of components. It is more detailed and informative than a block diagram. Components are drawn to show their general shape and all major parts are given.

An example of a fuel injection system diagram is in Fig. 16-4. Note how wires (lines) feed into and away from the ECU. Both symbols and graphic representations of components are utilized.

Remember, however, that a diagram does NOT usually show the exact electrical wiring. Like a block diagram, it informs you of how components interact.

Service manuals will often have diagrams for their specific fuel system. They can be very helpful when trying to visualize the operation of the system.

Fuel system schematics

A *fuel system schematic* is a very detailed circuit drawing using symbols to represent components and lines to represent wires. It is more accurate than a block diagram and a system diagram. See Figs. 16-5 and 16-6.

The schematic is useful when trying to trace wires from component to component. It will show wire connectors, color codes, grounds, and other details of the fuel system.

An *input schematic* for a fuel injection system shows the sensors that feed data to the computer. In Fig. 16-5, note the vane airflow meter, throttle position sensor, EGO (exhaust gas oxygen) sensor, and other sensors. This type schematic might be handy if a trouble code indicated a problem in one of the sensor circuits. You could then trace the wire color codes and note any connectors in the affected circuit.

An *output schematic* for a fuel injection system shows the actuators controlled by the ECU or computer. One

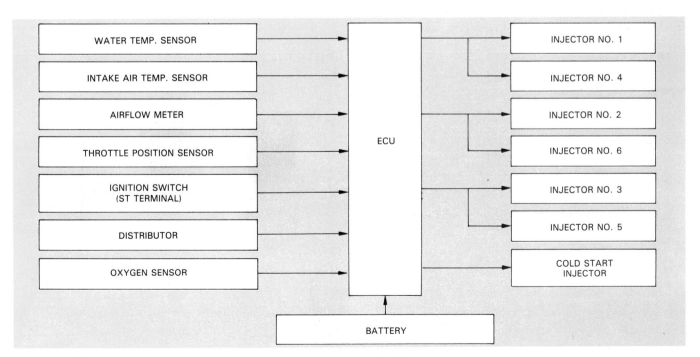

Fig. 16-3. Block diagram shows sensors on left and actuators on right. It would be helpful in determining which sensors affect fuel system operation when troubleshooting.

271

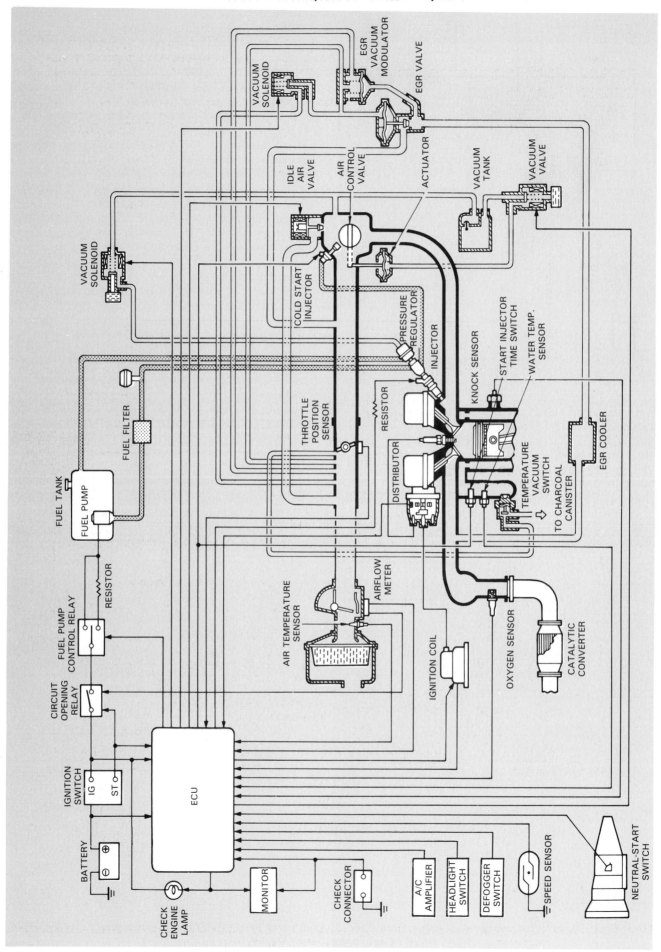

Fig. 16-4. This is a much more detailed diagram of an EFI system. Study the components carefully. (Toyota)

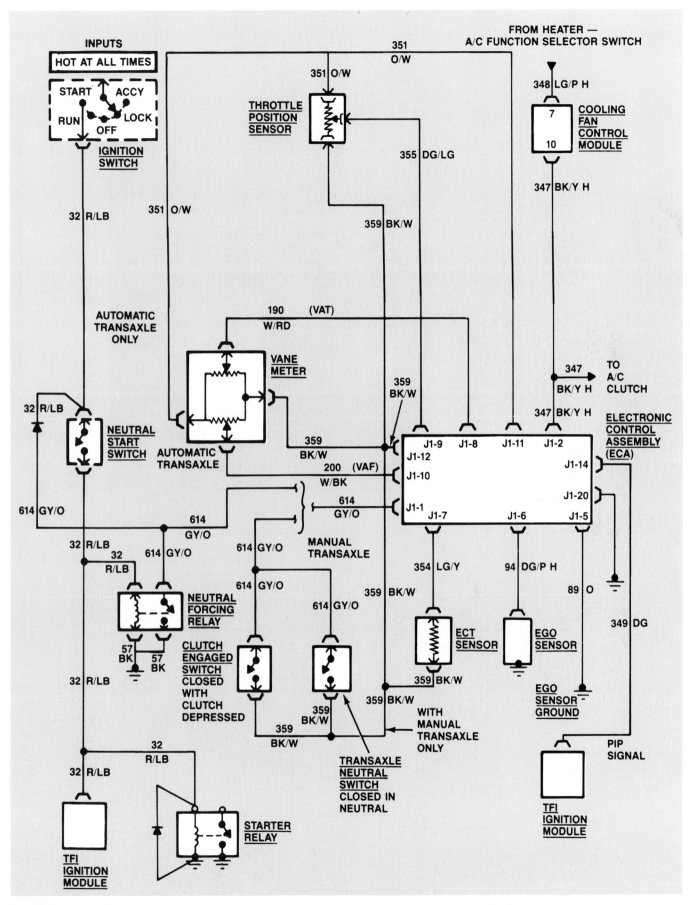

Fig. 16-5. Input schematic for computerized fuel system shows sensors that input data to ECU. Since it shows wire color codes, connectors, etc., it would be very handy when diagnosing problems. (Ford)

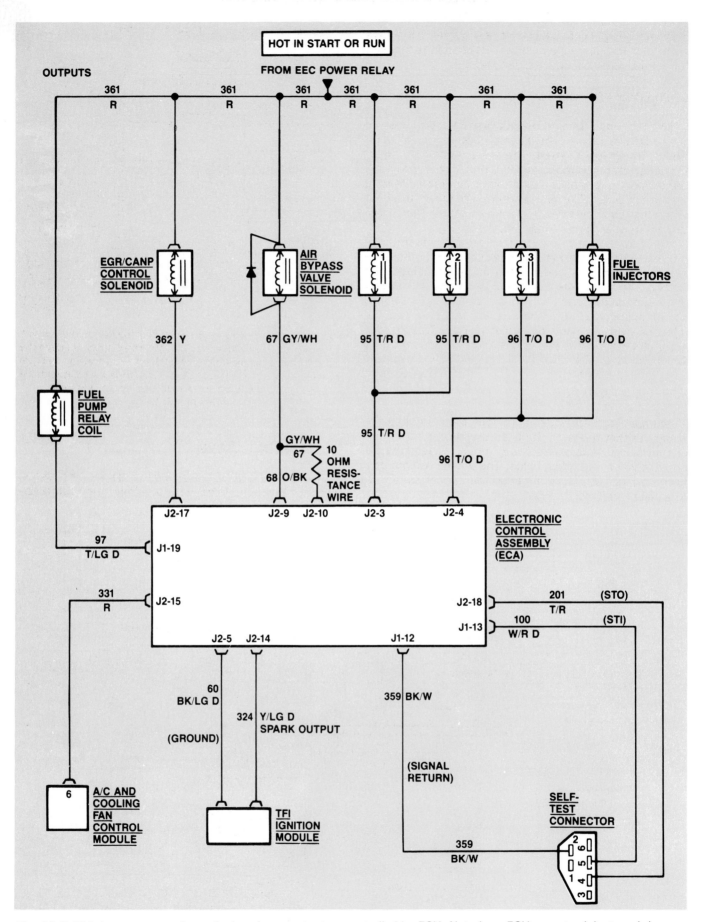

Fig. 16-6. This is an output schematic that shows actuators controlled by ECU. Note how ECU operates injector, air bypass valve, fuel pump relay, and emission control system solenoid. (Ford)

is shown in Fig. 16-6. Like an input schematic, it shows wire color codes, connectors, and other things that can be helpful when diagnosing problems.

OPEN LOOP AND CLOSED LOOP

When in *open loop,* the electronic injection system does NOT use engine exhaust gas content as a main control of the air-fuel mixture. The system operates on information stored in the computer. With the engine cold, the exhaust gas sensor cannot accurately provide data for the computer. The computer is set to ignore this data when the engine is cold. The system would then function in an open loop mode, Fig. 16-7.

When in a *closed loop* mode, the EFI system uses information from the exhaust gas sensor and other sensors to control the air-fuel mixture. A complete loop (circle) is formed in theory as data flows from the sensor to the computer, and back to the exhaust gas sensor. Under most operating conditions, an electronic gasoline injection system functions in closed loop. This lets the computer double-check the fuel mixture it is providing for the engine, Fig. 16-7.

FUEL BACK-UP MODE

The *fuel back-up mode* is provided by a circuit in the computer that operates the injectors in case of a component failure. Also called *limp-in mode,* it keeps the car drivable when a part has failed. The engine will not perform normally but will still run so the car can be driven to a repair facility. See Fig. 16-8.

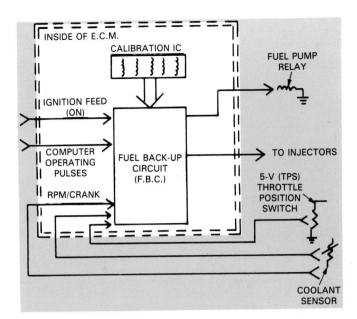

Fig. 16-8. Some computers have a fuel back-up circuit. It will take over to operate injectors if some sensors fail. It keeps the car drivable. Coolant sensor, throttle position sensor, and rpm sensor still send data to computer. These are very dependable sensors compared to oxygen sensor, for example. (General Motors)

GASOLINE INJECTORS

Gasoline injectors, as discussed earlier, are simply solenoid-operated fuel valves. They are computer-

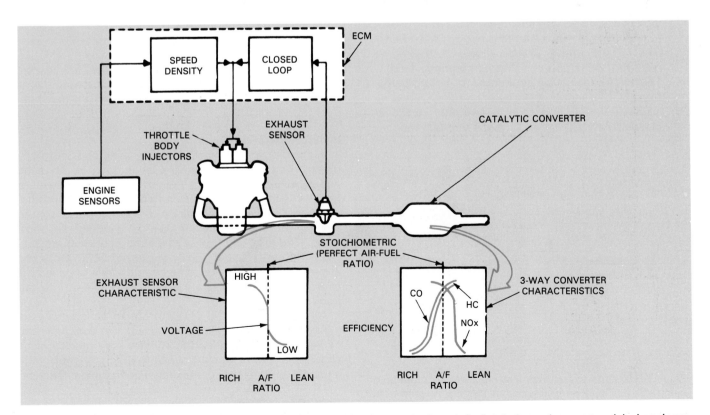

Fig. 16-7. Exhaust or oxygen sensor ''sniffs'' exhaust gases to check whether air-fuel ratio is too lean or too rich. Imaginary loop is produced as data flows through system. (General Motors)

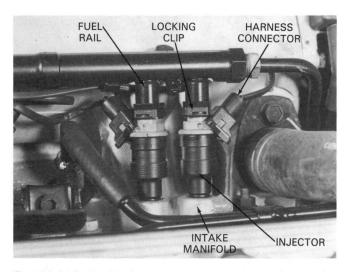

Fig. 16-9. Photo shows injectors mounted in engine intake manifold. Note wires that come from ECU. Fuel rail feeds constant fuel pressure into injectors.

controlled actuators that respond to voltage outputs from the computer or ECU.

Fig. 16-9 shows a photo of injectors on a late model engine. Note how they install in the intake manifold and have a fuel rail that feeds them fuel. A wiring harness connects them to the ECU.

Shown in Fig. 16-10, the basic parts of a gasoline injector are:

1. FUEL INLET (opening for connection to fuel rail so fuel can enter injector from fuel pump).
2. INJECTOR FILTER (small screen that blocks and traps debris before it can enter injector).
3. COIL WINDINGS (solenoid windings that produce magnetic field when carrying current from ECU).
4. ARMATURE (metal plunger that is attracted and pulled up by action of solenoid magnetic field).
5. TERMINAL (electrical connector for wiring harness from ECU).
6. NEEDLE VALVE (tip of armature that opens and closes to control spray of fuel from injector).

7. NOZZLE (opening that produces cone shaped spray pattern for good atomization during fuel injection into intake manifold of engine).
8. INJECTOR BODY (housing that encloses other parts of injector).

Fig. 16-11 shows a cutaway for a throttle body injector. Note its similarities and difference from the multipoint injector in Fig. 16-10.

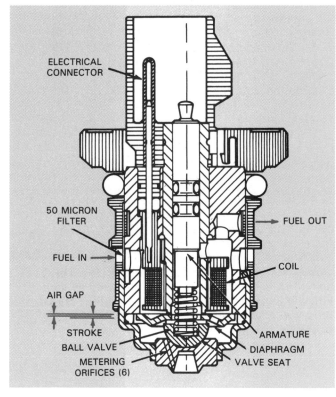

Fig. 16-11. Cutaway shows single-point electronic injector. Its operation is similar to multi-point electronic injector. Note differences in construction, however. (Ford)

Injector operation

Injector operation is simple. The injector is normally closed. The armature spring pushes down to hold the needle valve closed. Even though there is fuel pressure inside the injector, no fuel can pass out of the nozzle.

When the computer sends a current pulse to the injector terminal, the coil or solenoid windings are energized. The resulting flux or magnetic field then attracts the armature. This pulls up on the armature, overcoming armature spring tension. The needle valve is pulled off of its seat and a short spray of fuel is forced into the intake manifold.

As soon as the ECU cuts current to an injector, the spring snaps the needle valve closed. The computer can cycle or open and close the injector very quickly. This allows the electronic control unit to precisely control the engine's air-fuel ratio for maximum power and efficiency.

Cold start injector

A *cold start injector* is an additional fuel injector valve sometimes used to supply extra gasoline for cold engine

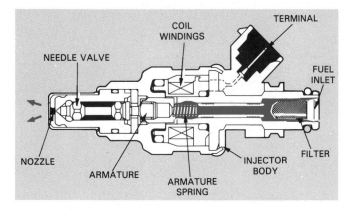

Fig. 16-10. Cutaway shows internal parts of multi-point, electronic fuel injector. Coil windings produce magnetic field that pulls up on armature. This opens needle valve so fuel can spray into engine. Spring closes needle valve when ECU current shuts off. (Toyota)

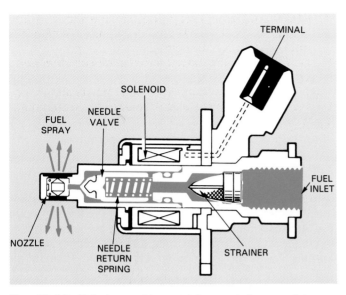

Fig. 16-12. This is a cold start injector. It is extra injector mounted in intake manifold. (Toyota)

starting. The engine temperature sensor, a thermo-time switch, or the system computer can be used to operate the cold start injector. It is constructed like a conventional, solenoid type injector, Fig. 16-12.

When the sensor detects a cold engine, the switch closes to energize the cold start injector, Fig. 16-13. The cold start injector and the other injectors all spray fuel into the intake manifold. Like a carburetor choke, this provides a very rich mixture to sustain cold engine operation.

When the engine warms, the temperture sensor can

signal the ECU or open the injector circuit directly. This will shut off the cold start injector to prevent engine flooding.

INJECTOR PULSE WIDTH

The *injector pulse width* is the amount of time voltage is applied to keep an injector open. The computer controls the injector pulse width.

Under full acceleration, the computer would sense a wide open throttle, high intake manifold pressure, and high inlet airflow. The computer would then increase injector pulse width to richen the mixture for more power.

Under low load conditions, the computer would shorten the injector pulse width. With the injectors closed a larger percentage of time, the air-fuel mixture would be leaner for better fuel economy.

Fig. 16-14 illustrates how the computer can alter injector pulse width as operating conditions change. In this example, six conditions can lengthen or shorten pulse width to change the air-fuel ratio.

For example, more air quantity or volume, a lower engine temperature, a lower air temperature, rapid acceleration, a lean air-fuel ratio (lean oxygen sensor signal), and low manifold pressure would all increase injector pulse width. More fuel would be needed to satisfy these operating conditions. With the opposite conditions, a shorter pulse width and leaner mixture would be needed.

A graph showing the operating conditions of another fuel injection system is given in Fig. 16-15. The top line on the graph represents the engine air-fuel ratio. Note what sensor conditions increase graph height and fuel richness.

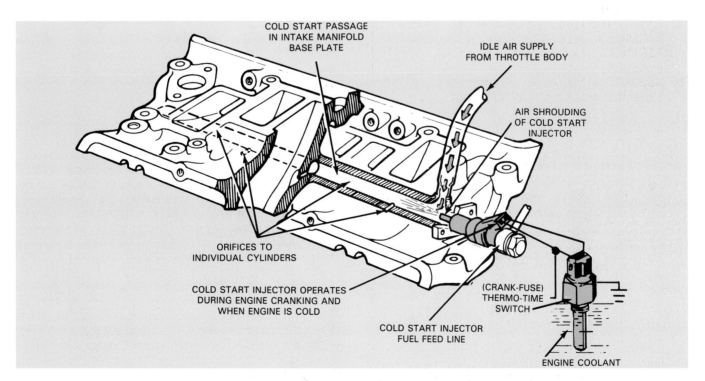

Fig. 16-13. Temperature sensor can operate cold start injector directly or through ECU. Cold start injector is only energized when temperature is below specific level. This richens mixture to aid cold engine operation. (General Motors)

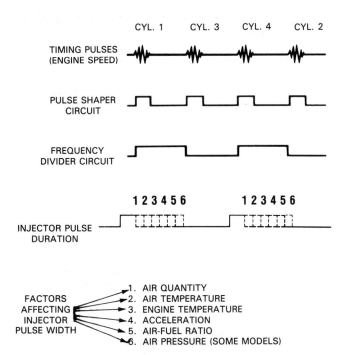

Fig. 16-14. Study how different conditions or inputs can be used to alter how long injectors are pulsed open. For example, if throttle position sensor signals a wide open throttle condition or acceleration, computer would then hold injectors open a little longer to provide more engine power. A cold engine temperature sensor would also "tell the computer" to increase injector pulse width to richen mixture. (Renault)

When the engine is first started cold, the mixture is extremely rich because of cold start injection action. It quickly leans out as the engine warms and the cold start injector is shut off.

Also note how the mixture goes richer right after idle. This is comparable to a carburetor accelerator pump that squirts raw fuel into air inlet as the throttle is moved open. The mixture also goes rich at full throttle when the throttle position switch signals the computer.

AIR-ASSISTED FUEL INJECTION

In *air-assisted fuel injection systems,* fresh air is admitted into the base of the fuel injectors to help improve fuel atomization. Air lines run from the air cleaner housing to each injector. When engine speed reaches approximately 1500 rpm, the computer opens a solenoid air valve, allowing air to be pulled into the injectors, Fig. 16-16. Calibrated orifices regulate airflow through the injectors.

IDLE AIR CONTROL VALVE

In the past, a thermostatic air valve was commonly used to help control idle speed; however, this type of valve was not very dependable. Consequently, late model vehicles rely on an *idle air control valve* to help control idle speed, Fig. 16-17. A vehicle's computer uses signals from the coolant temperature sensor and the air temperature sensor to determine optimum idle speed. It

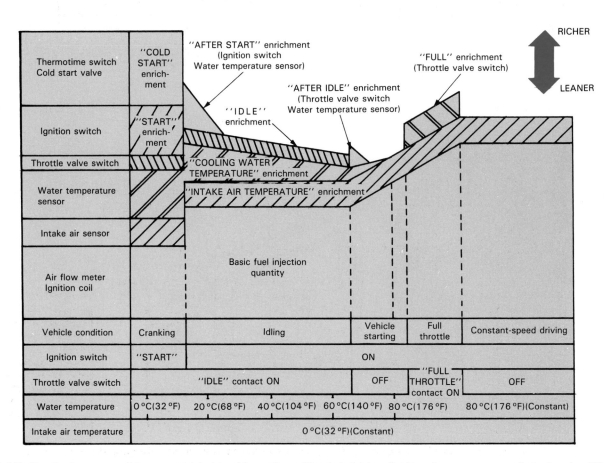

Fig. 16-15. Graph shows conditions or sensors and how they affect air-fuel ratio. Top line represents air-fuel ratio. (Nissan)

can then prompt the idle air control valve to open or close, increasing or decreasing idle speed. See Figure 16-18.

When open, the idle air control valve allows more air to enter the intake manifold, Fig. 16-19. This tends to increase engine idle rpm. When closed, the valve decreases bypass air and reduces idle speed. The idle air control valve can be used to control both slow and fast idle speeds.

IDLE SPEED SOLENOID

An *idle speed solenoid* also alters engine idle speed, but it moves the throttle valves open and closed. It performs

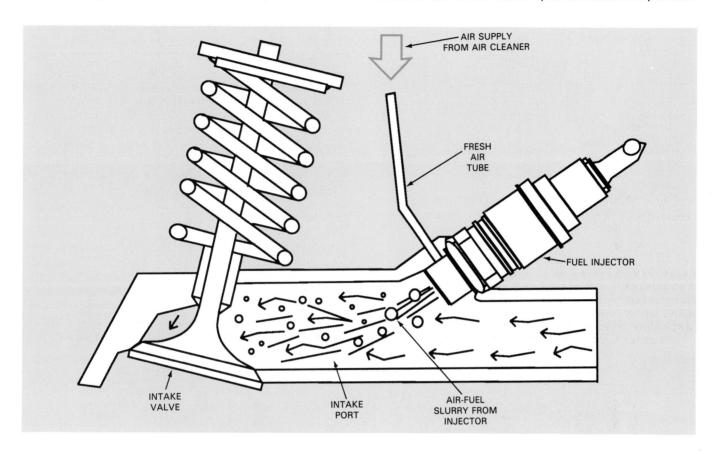

Fig. 16-16. Air-assisted fuel injector. Note the air tube, which is connected to the air cleaner. During injection, air and fuel are mixed inside the injector to improve atomization.

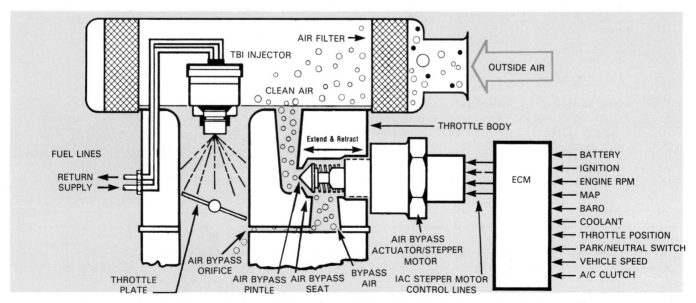

Fig. 16-17. TBI has injector in throttle body assembly. Air bypass valve can be used to control engine idle speed. As air is bypassed around throttle plates, engine speed increases.

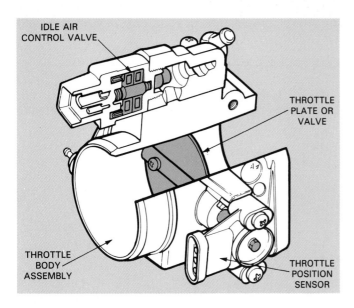

Fig. 16-18. Cutaway of throttle body for multi-point injection system shows air bypass valve. Also note throttle position sensor. (General Motors)

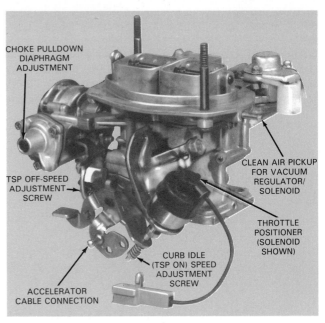

A

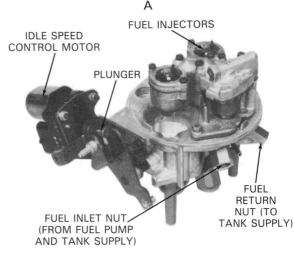

B

Fig. 16-20. Idle speed solenoid and motor are other means of controlling engine idle speed. A—Carburetor with idle speed solenoid. B—TBI unit with idle speed motor. (Ford and General Motors)

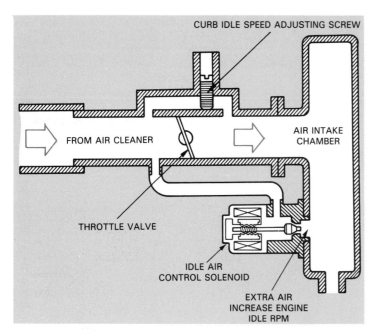

Fig. 16-19. Idle air control solenoid opens and closes small passage around throttle valves. This provides computer one way of quickly adjusting engine idle rpm. (Toyota)

the same function as the idle air control valve. Look at Fig. 16-20.

An idle speed solenoid is frequently used on carburetors. When current is fed to the solenoid, its plunger will extend. The plunger contacts the throttle lever and the throttle is held partially open to increase idle rpm.

When shut off, the solenoid plunger retracts and the engine returns to curb idle. The solenoid is frequently shut off when the engine is shut off. This helps prevent engine *dieseling* or *run-on* (engine continues to run with ignition key off).

IDLE SPEED MOTOR

An *idle speed motor* is a servo motor that does the same thing as the idle speed solenoid. The small motor operates a thread mechanism that can extend or retract a plunger. The plunger action can be used to act upon the throttle. The computer controls the idle speed motor and resulting engine idle speed.

ELECTRIC CHOKE

An *electric choke* is used on a carburetor to control choke opening right after cold engine starting. When cold, a spring closes the carburetor choke. After engine start-up, current is fed to the electric choke. The current heats a small element in the choke mechanism. The

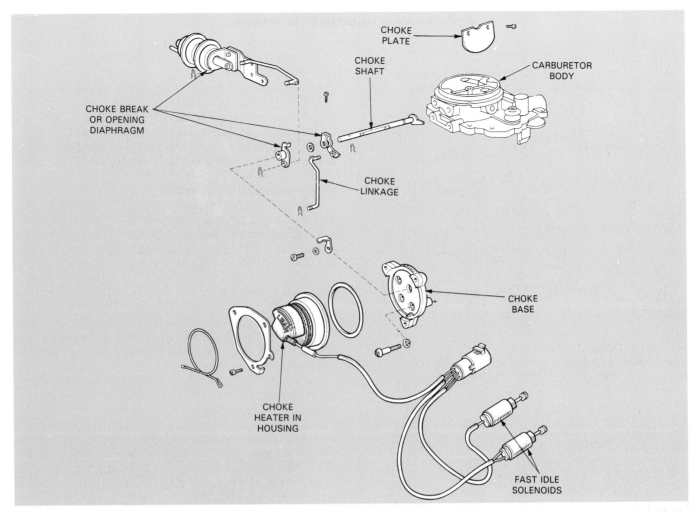

Fig. 16-21. Electric choke contains small heating element. Current heats element to warm thermostatic spring. This helps spring open choke quickly and consistently. (Toyota)

heat warms a thermostatic spring in the choke housing to assure proper choke opening. Look at Fig. 16-21.

SOLENOID BOWL VENT

A *solenoid bowl vent* is used to control when the carburetor fuel bowl is vented or open at the top. The solenoid operates a small valve that can open or close the bowl vent. On late model carburetors, the bowl is usually vented to a vapor canister. See Fig. 16-22.

When the engine is shut off, the vent opens. This allows any fuel fumes to flow to the vapor or charcoal canister for storage. Upon engine restarting, the vent usually closes and the vapors are drawn out of the canister and back into the engine for burning.

FUEL SHUT-OFF SOLENOID

A *fuel shut-off solenoid* is used on some carburetors to block the idle passage when needed. For example, the solenoid can block the idle passage during deceleration or when the engine is shut off. This prevents fuel from being drawn out of or dripping from the idle passage. Fuel economy and exhaust emissions are improved.

Fig. 16-23 shows a fuel shut-off solenoid. Study how it can open and close the idle port in the carburetor.

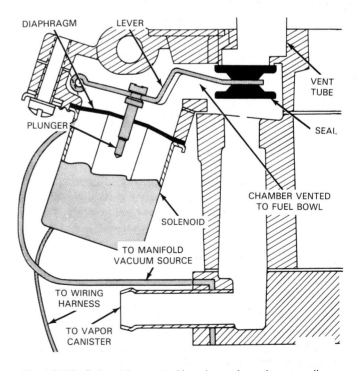

Fig. 16-22. Solenoid-operated bowl vent in carburetor allows ECU to control flow of vapors to charcoal canister or out of canister for burning in engine.

281

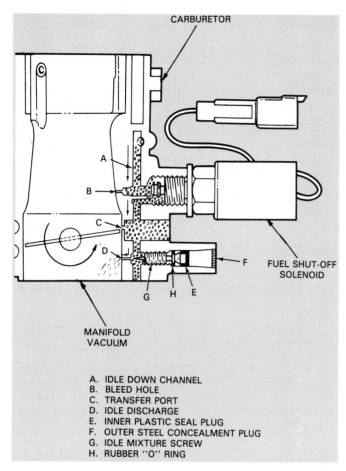

A. IDLE DOWN CHANNEL
B. BLEED HOLE
C. TRANSFER PORT
D. IDLE DISCHARGE
E. INNER PLASTIC SEAL PLUG
F. OUTER STEEL CONCEALMENT PLUG
G. IDLE MIXTURE SCREW
H. RUBBER "O" RING

Fig. 16-23. Fuel shut-off solenoid on this carburetor can block idle passage. This can keep fuel from being pulled through idle passage during deceleration or when engine is shut off. (Ford)

COMPUTER-CONTROLLED CARBURETORS

A *computer-controlled carburetor* normally has a solenoid-operated valve to respond to commands from the computer, or electronic control unit. Like EFI, the system uses various sensors to send information to the computer. The computer then calculates how rich or lean to set the carburetor's air-fuel mixture. See Fig. 16-24.

Electro-mechanical carburetor

An *electro-mechanical carburetor* is controlled by both electrical and mechanical devices. This type is used with a computer control system. It has electrical components (sensors and actuators) for interfacing with the computer and conventional mechanical parts as well.

Mixture control solenoid

A *mixture control solenoid* in the computer-controlled carburetor, responds to electrical signals (or dwell signals) from the computer to alter the air-fuel ratio. The signals trigger the solenoid to open and close air and fuel passages in the carburetor.

The electronic control unit (ECU) is capable of receiving information sent to it by sensors located in various places on the automobile. It can process this information and then electronically control the carburetor's mixture control solenoid, Fig. 16-25.

For example, the ECU will receive reports from the oxygen sensor in the exhaust system about the amount of oxygen in the exhaust gas. The ECU, which can do very complicated calculations in a fraction of a second, compares this signal with the information stored in its memory. If the oxygen makeup of the exhaust gas is not correct, the memory sends a signal to other parts of the

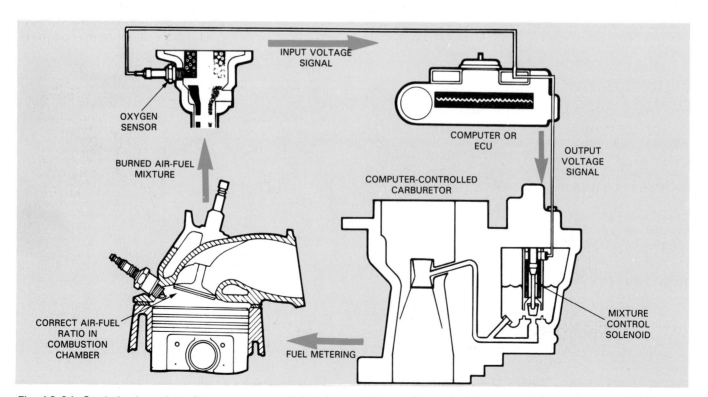

Fig. 16-24. Study basic action of computer-controlled carburetor system. Oxygen sensor checks to determine if air-fuel ratio is too rich or lean. Then, computer can use this data to cycle mixture control solenoid to adjust fuel metering. (Chrysler)

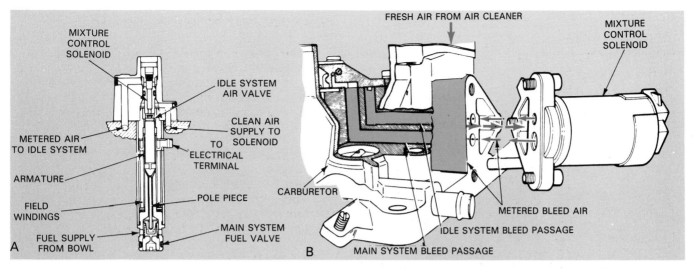

Fig. 16-25. Mixture control solenoid can be used to open and close both air and fuel passages in carburetor. A—Cutaway of one type mixture control solenoid. B—Another mixture control solenoid and how it controls flow inside carburetor passages. (Chrysler and Ford)

ECU. A control signal will then be sent out to the carburetor's mixture solenoid which is energized to adjust the air-fuel mixture to produce the correct oxygen content in the exhaust gas.

Computer-controlled carburetor operation

In a computer-controlled carburetor, the air-fuel ratio is maintained by CYCLING the mixture solenoid ON and OFF several times a second. Fig. 16-26 shows how the control signals from the computer can be used to meter different amounts of fuel out of the carburetor.

When the computer sends a rich command to the solenoid, the signal voltage to the mixture solenoid is usually OFF more than it is ON. This causes the solenoid to stay open more. Typically, the idle air bleed valve and

main metering rod move up to increase fuel flow.

During a lean signal from the computer, the signal usually has more ON time. This causes less fuel to pass through the solenoid valve. The mixture becomes leaner. The idle air bleed valve and main metering rod move down to restrict fuel flow.

COMPUTER-CONTROLLED DIESEL INJECTION

A *computer-controlled diesel injection system* uses an ECU to control solenoids on the injection pump. Sensors feed data to the ECU and then the ECU can alter injection pump operation for better efficiency.

In the past, diesel injection systems were mechanical. Only mechanical devices in the injection pump controlled

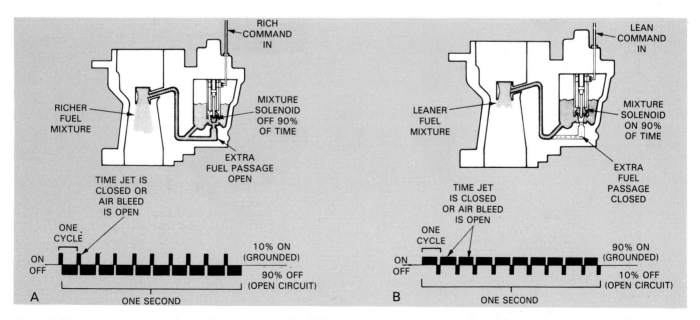

Fig. 16-26. Note mixture control solenoid action. A—ECU produces a signal that is OFF 90 percent of the time. This causes mixture control solenoid to stay open more and richen fuel mixture for more power. B—ECU produces signal that is ON 90 percent of the time. This causes mixture solenoid to stay closed more to lean mixture for less power but more fuel economy. (Chrysler)

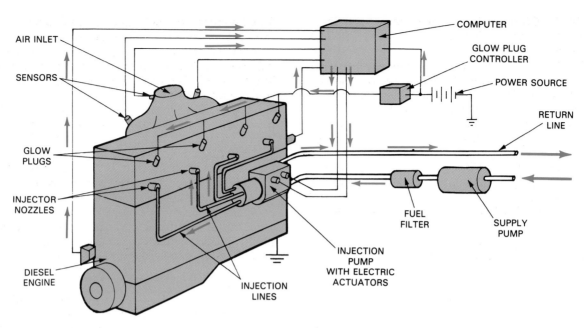

Fig. 16-27. Study basic parts used in electronic diesel injection system.

the fuel metering system. Now electronics is being used with the high pressure diesel injection pump.

Fig. 16-27 shows a simplified illustration of diesel system using a computer. Note how sensors feed data into the computer or ECU. Then output signals can be sent to the injection pump actuators or solenoids. Actuators are typically used to control fuel metering and injection timing.

A *fuel shutoff solenoid* can be used to block fuel entry into the pumping plungers of an injection pump. This action is used to shut a diesel engine off. Stopping fuel flow is the only way to keep a diesl from running.

Glow plug system

A diesel *glow plug system* is used to electrically warm the combustion chambers to aid cold engine starting. The fundamental parts of a glow plug system are shown in Fig. 16-28 and they include:

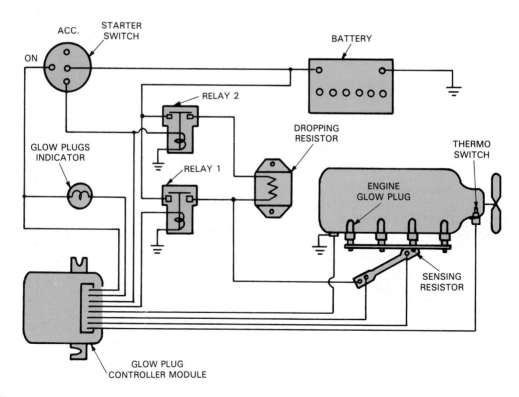

Fig. 16-28. Glow plugs are turned on and off by action of temperature sensor, electronic controller, and relays. Glow plugs are only energized for short period of time when engine is cold. (General Motors)

1. GLOW PLUGS (electric heating elements that install in cylinder head; their tips extend into combustion chambers).
2. THERMO SWITCH (engine temperature sensor that signals control module of cold or warm engine).
3. GLOW PLUG CONTROL MODULE (electronic circuit that uses sensor input to turn glow plugs on or off).
4. GLOW PLUG RELAY (device for interfacing controller with glow plugs; it makes and breaks high current circuit to glow plugs).
5. GLOW PLUG INDICATOR (light that shows driver when glow plugs are energized and engine should not be cranked).
6. GLOW PLUG HARNESS (wiring that connects parts of system).

A diesel engine relies on the heat of compression or compressed air to ignite and burn its fuel. Spark plugs are not used. As a result, a diesel engine can be difficult to start in cold weather. The heat of compression alone may not be enough to heat the air adequately to ignite the fuel.

Glow plugs are used to help heat the air in the diesel pre-chambers to aid starting. Then, when fuel is injected into the combustion chambers on the compression stroke, the air is hot enough to make the fuel start burning. The glow plugs need a few seconds to heat up. A dash indicator light informs the driver of when the engine can be cranked.

After engine start-up, the controller deactivates the relay and glow plugs. Combustion will quickly develop enough heat to sustain diesel engine operation. The thermal sensor only activates the controller and plug when below a specific temperature.

ELECTRIC FUEL PUMPS

An *electric fuel pump* is commonly used to force fuel from the fuel tank to the engine. One or more electric fuel pumps can be found in modern fuel systems. One might be inside the fuel tank. Another can be between the tank and engine.

Electric fuel pumps have replaced older mechanical fuel pumps. An electric fuel pump provides instant fuel pressure upon engine cranking. It is also located near the tank and away from engine heat that could cause *vapor*

lock (overheated fuel boils and air bubbles prevent normal fuel movement through lines).

An electric fuel pump is typically a small DC motor that spins an impeller or pumping mechanism. One is shown in Fig. 16-29. The motor can actually be submerged in fuel during operation.

Fig. 16-30 illustrates an in-tank fuel pump. Note how it is constructed as part of the sending unit for the fuel gauge circuit. A "sock" type strainer is on the inlet of the in-tank pump to keep out debris.

A less common solenoid type electric fuel pump is in Fig. 16-31. Instead of a motor that spins an armature, it uses a solenoid to move a plunger up and down. The solenoid attracts the plunger with its magnetic field. Once pulled into the field, the solenoid current is broken and a spring pushes the plunger back up. This reciprocating action can be used to pump fuel.

Inertia switch

An *inertia switch* is used to disable the electric fuel pump after an auto accident. It is a normally closed switch that opens after an impact or sudden change in inertia. Since the switch is wired into the fuel pump circuit, it can prevent the fuel pump from running after a collision. This is a good safety feature that can prevent a serious fire!

Fig. 16-32 shows a basic diagram for an inertia switch. Note how it is wired in series with the two elec-

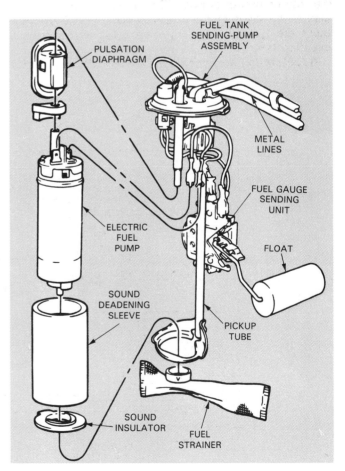

Fig. 16-30. Note construction of this in-tank electric pump and fuel sending unit. (General Motors)

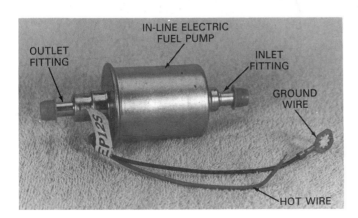

Fig. 16-29. This is an in-line electric fuel pump. (Universal Tire and Auto)

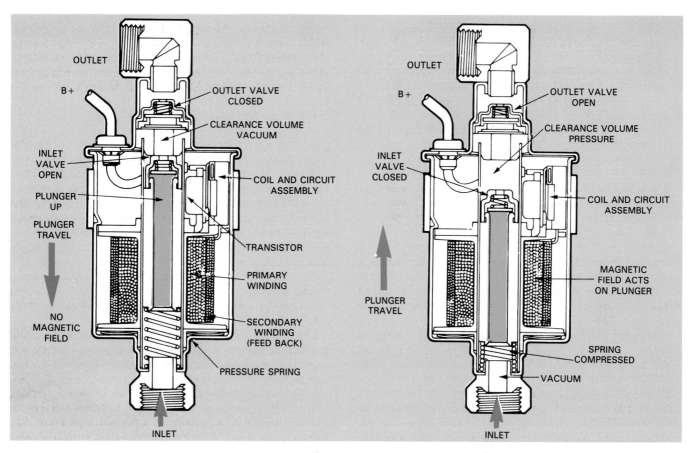

Fig. 16-31. Solenoid electric fuel pump produces back and forth pumping action.

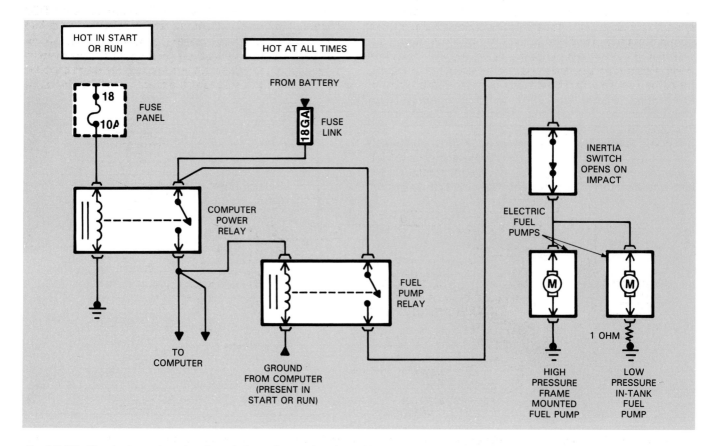

Fig. 16-32. Circuit shows how inertia switch can be used to shut off electric fuel pumps after auto accident or severe impact. (Ford)

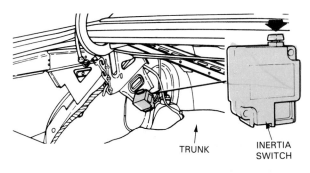

Fig. 16-33. Inertia switch, or impact switch, can be in trunk as shown or elsewhere in car. After an impact, pressing button will reset switch so electric pumps will again operate.

tric fuel pumps. It is located between the fuel pump relay or ECU and the fuel pumps.

The inertia switch is frequently located inside the car's trunk, Fig. 16-33. After an accident, the inertia switch must normally be reset. You must push the reset button on the inertia switch so the fuel pump will again operate.

THROTTLE-BY-WIRE SYSTEMS

Throttle-by-wire systems move the engine throttle valves electronically instead of using conventional mechanical linkage from the accelerator pedal. An accelerator pedal sensor feeds data that corresponds to pedal depression to the computer. The computer then sends a signal to an actuator that controls the engine throttle valve. The computer can regulate acceleration, cruise consistency, and deceleration to improve fuel economy, reduce exhaust emissions, and prevent abrupt speed changes that could affect drive train service life.

Some throttle-by-wire systems allow the driver to choose between sport and comfort modes. In the sport mode, the computer provides rapid throttle response for more aggressive driving. In the comfort mode, throttle response is reduced by the computer. The engine does not accelerate as quickly when the accelerator is pushed down abruptly. Throttle-by-wire systems are found on both gasoline- and diesel-powered vehicles.

EMISSION CONTROL ELECTRONICS

Emission control systems are used to reduce the amount of harmful substances emitted into the atmosphere by the automobile. Electronic devices are now used to help improve these systems. A few electronically-controlled emission systems will be briefly explained. Remember that the fuel systems electronics already discussed also reduce vehicle emissions.

Computer-controlled catalytic converter

A *computer-controlled catalytic converter system* uses the ECU to operate the air injection system that helps the catalytic converter burn engine exhaust pollutants. One is pictured in Fig. 16-34.

The ECU or ECM uses sensor inputs to determine the operating conditions of the engine. It can then produce output signals for solenoid-vacuum actuators that operate the air injection system.

The *air injection system* uses a belt driven air pump, control valves, and connecting lines to force outside air into the catalytic converter or in the exhaust manifold. The extra oxygen in the air promotes burning or oxidation in the exhaust system.

Electronically-controlled EGR

An *electronically-controlled EGR system* uses the ECU to control EGR valve opening and closing. A simplified illustration of a typical system is given in Fig. 16-35.

EGR stands for exhaust gas recirculation. This system directs burned exhaust gases back into the engine intake manifold. The burned gases are then pulled into the com-

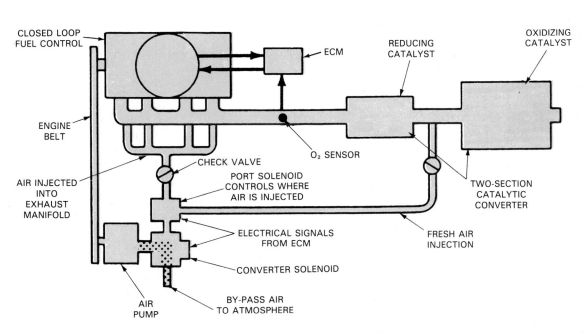

Fig. 16-34. ECM or computer is used to operate air injection solenoid. This allows computer to direct air to exhaust manifold or to center of catalytic converter. Extra air makes fuel burn while in exhaust system.

bustion chambers with the fresh air-fuel charge. The burned gases are *inert* (do not burn) and help reduce combustion flame temperatures to prevent NOx or one form of exhaust pollution.

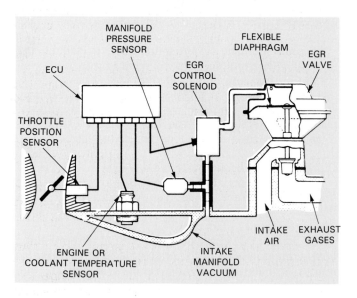

Fig. 16-35. ECU is used to operate EGR or exhaust gas recirculation system. Sensors report conditions to ECU. ECU then produces output for EGR solenoid. Solenoid controls whether vacuum is applied to EGR diagram. Vacuum will lift EGR valve open and allow burned exhaust gases to enter engine intake manifold. This lowers combustion temperatures to reduce NOx or one form of emission.

The ECU helps provide a more precise control over EGR valve action. It uses the throttle position sensor, engine temperature sensor, manifold pressure sensor, and sometimes other sensors to know when to open or close the EGR valve.

Electronic evaporative emissions control

Electronic evaporative emission control refers to how the ECU can operate a vapor storage canister valve. The *vapor canister* is a container filled with activated charcoal for storing fuel vapors from the fuel system. The *canister purge valve* regulates flow of these vapors or fumes back into the engine intake manifold for burning. This keeps toxic, unburned fuel vapors from entering the atmosphere.

Fig. 16-36 shows a diagram that includes a canister purge solenoid. Also note the solenoids used to operate the EGR valve and air injection system.

With the evaporative emissions system, any fumes from the fuel tank, carburetor if used, and lines are routed into the charcoal canister. The charcoal absorbs and stores these fumes while the engine is off. When the engine is started, the purge solenoid is energized and intake manifold vacuum is applied to the canister. This pulls the vapors back out of the charcoal and into the engine intake manifold for combustion.

ELECTRONIC TURBOCHARGER CONTROL

An *electronic turbocharger control system* uses a solenoid to control the vacuum applied to the turbo wastegate. The *wastegate* is a vacuum diaphragm device that can open or close an exhaust passage to control turbo speed and boost pressure. The ECU uses sen-

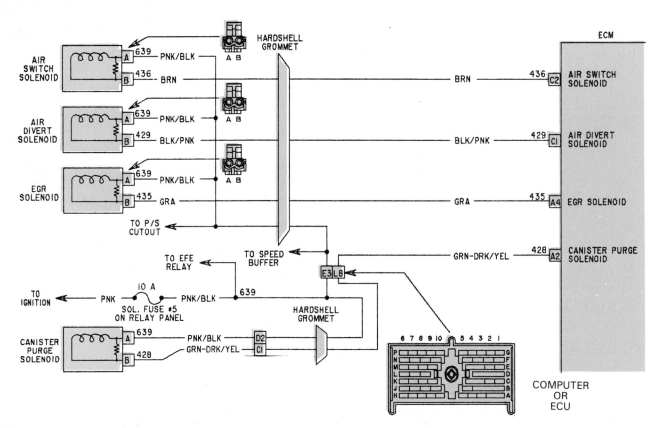

Fig. 16-36. Circuit diagram shows various solenoids that affect emission control systems. ECU feeds current to operate solenoids.

sor inputs to know when to increase or decrease boost pressure. See Fig. 16-37.

Discussed under knock sensors, the ECU might have the wastegate solenoid reduce boost pressure if the engine begins to ping or knock. A lower boost pressure will reduce combustion pressures and knocking tendencies.

SUMMARY

Today's fuel systems use dozens of electrical-electronic devices to improve fuel economy, engine power, and lower emissions.

Gasoline injection is the most common type of modern fuel system. A multi-point injection system has one injector for each engine cylinder. Solenoid-operated injectors are controlled by signals from the computer. Single-point injection only has one or two injectors mounted at the air inlet of the engine intake manifold.

A computer-controlled carburetor uses a mixture control solenoid. It can react to signals from the computer to open and close fuel and air passages. This action can be used to control how much fuel is metered into the engine for different conditions.

The fuel supply system consists of the parts that force fuel from the tank to the fuel metering section of the fuel system. The air supply system includes the filters, ducts, and valves that control airflow into the engine. The fuel metering system consists of the parts that control how much fuel enters the engine.

When a fuel system is open loop, it operates off of stored memory in the computer. When in closed loop, the oxygen sensor detects the engine air-fuel ratio by sensing the amount of oxygen in the exhaust gases. Under normal conditions, the fuel system operates in closed loop.

A solenoid fuel injector uses a coil to open and close the needle valve. When energized by the computer, the coil magnetic field attracts the armature and needle valve. This pulls the needle valve open and fuel sprays out of the nozzle. A spring pushes the injector needle valve closed when no signal is sent to the coil windings.

A cold start injector can be used to richen the engine fuel mixture for cold starting. It is an extra injector mounted in the engine intake manifold. A temperature sensor controls when the cold start injector is energized.

Injector pulse width refers to the amount of time that the injector is open. It is the time that voltage is applied to the injector by the ECU. A long injector pulse width would richen the air-fuel mixture.

An idle air solenoid can be used to alter engine idle speed. When open, it bypasses air around the throttle plates. This extra air increases engine idle rpm.

An idle speed solenoid can be used to control the engine idle speed by moving the throttle plates. It has a small plunger that can be moved out to hold the throttle lever off of curb idle.

An idle speed motor is a small servo motor that operates a gear mechanism. Motor operation and the gears are used to move a plunger. Since the plunger contacts the throttle lever, motor position controls the engine idle speed.

Late model diesel fuel systems can use electronics to increase efficiency. Engine sensors report to the computer concerning operating conditions. The computer can then energize solenoids or servo motors on the injection pump to control fuel metering.

Glow plugs are used to aid starting of a cold diesel engine. The glow plugs are electric heating elements in the engine prechambers. They warm the air in the chambers so the fuel will begin to burn and start combustion more easily.

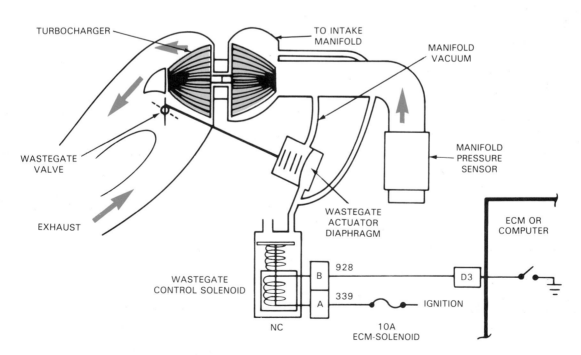

Fig. 16-37. This turbocharging system is controlled by the ECU. It uses manifold pressure sensor to limit boost pressure in intake manifold. When boost is high enough, pressure sensor signals computer. Computer then sends current to solenoid. Solenoid releases vacuum source to wastegate actuator and wastegate valve opens to prevent further increase in turbo boost. Too much manifold boost could cause detonation or knock and engine damage. (General Motors)

KNOW THESE TERMS

Electronic injection, EFI, Throttle body injection, Multiport injection, Timed injection, Sequential injection, Intermittent injection, Continuous injection, Group injection, Fuel supply system, Air supply system, Fuel metering system, Block diagram, Schematic, Open loop, Closed loop, Fuel back-up mode, Needle valve, Nozzle, Cold start injector, Injector pulse width, Air-assisted fuel injection, Idle air control valve, Idle speed solenoid, Idle speed motor, Electric choke, Solenoid bowl vent, Fuel shut-off solenoid, Electro-mechanical carburetor, Mixture control solenoid, Computer-controlled diesel injection, Glow plug system, Electric fuel pump, Inertia switch, Throttle-by-wire systems, Computer-controlled catalytic converter system, Electronically-controlled EGR, Electronic evaporative emissions control, Electronic turbocharger control, Wastegate.

REVIEW QUESTIONS—CHAPTER 16

1. This is the most common type of fuel system.
   a. Electronic carburetion.
   b. Electronic diesel injection.
   c. Throttle body injection.
   d. Multi-point injection.
2. Explain the difference between single-point and multi-point fuel injection.
3. This is the most efficient and popular classification of EFI used on late model cars.
   a. Timed injection.
   b. Continuous injection.
   c. Intermittent injection.
   d. Group injection.
4. Describe the three major sub-systems of a fuel system.
5. This type drawing would show how all of the sensors connect to the ECU.
   a. Block diagram.
   b. Input schematic.
   c. Output schematic.
   d. Fuel system diagram.
6. The _____ _____ _____ is provided by an extra computer circuit that operates the injectors after a component failure.
7. Explain the eight major parts of an electronic fuel injector.
8. How does a cold start injector function?
9. The _____ _____ _____ is the amount of time that voltage is applied to an electronic injector by the computer.
10. How does a computer-controlled carburetor system work?

ASE CERTIFICATION—TYPE QUESTIONS

1. Technician A says an electronic carburetion system uses intake manifold vacuum to operate the carburetor's mixture control solenoid. Technician B says electronic gasoline injection uses sensors and a computer to control solenoids on the injection pump. Who is right?
   (A) A only.
   (B) B only.
   (C) Both A and B.
   (D) Neither A nor B.

2. Technician A says a single-point injection system's injector is normally located in the intake manifold. Technician B says a single-point injection system is sometimes called a throttle body injection system. Who is right?
   (A) A only.
   (B) B only.
   (C) Both A and B.
   (D) Neither A nor B.
3. An automobile equipped with a "sequential" gasoline injection system is brought into the shop with a fuel system problem. Technician A says this type of injection system is timed to the opening of the engine's intake valves. Technician B says this type of injection system controls the air-fuel ratio by increasing or decreasing fuel pressure at the injectors. Who is right?
   (A) A only.
   (B) B only.
   (C) Both A and B.
   (D) Neither A nor B.
4. Which of the following is not a sub-system of an automotive fuel system?
   (A) Air supply system.
   (B) Fuel metering system.
   (C) Fuel supply system.
   (D) Air detecting system.
5. Technician A says an input schematic for a fuel injection system shows the sensors that feed data to the computer. Technician B says an input schematic for a fuel injection system shows wire color codes and connectors. Who is right?
   (A) A only.
   (B) B only.
   (C) Both A and B.
   (D) Neither A nor B.
6. Technician A says when an automotive computer system is in the open loop mode, the EFI system operates on information stored in the computer. Technician B says when an automotive computer system is in the closed loop mode, the EFI system uses information from the exhaust gas sensor, as well as information from other sensors, to help control the air-fuel mixture. Who is right?
   (A) A only.
   (B) B only.
   (C) Both A and B.
   (D) Neither A nor B.
7. Each of the following is a basic part of a gasoline injector except:
   (A) armature.
   (B) needle valve.
   (C) air bypass.
   (D) coil windings.
8. While discussing the operation of a gasoline injector, Technician A says injector pulse width is controlled by the automobile's computer system. Technician B says injector pulse width changes as operating conditions change. Who is right?
   (A) A only.
   (B) B only.
   (C) Both A and B.
   (D) Neither A nor B.
9. Technician A says an electric fuel pump provides instant pressure. Technician B says an electric fuel pump is generally a small AC motor. Who is right?
   (A) A only.
   (B) B only.
   (C) Both A and B.
   (D) Neither A nor B.
10. Technician A says an electronically-controlled EGR system directs burned exhaust gases back into the engine's exhaust manifold. Technician B says an electronically-controlled EGR system helps increase combustion flame temperatures. Who is right?
    (A) A only.
    (B) B only.
    (C) Both A and B.
    (D) Neither A nor B.

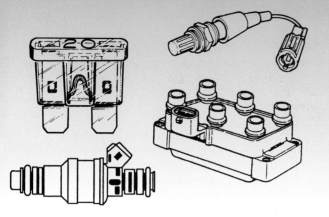

Chapter 17

Lighting Systems, Instrumentation

After studying this chapter, you will be able to:
- *Sketch the wiring diagrams for the major lighting circuits.*
- *Explain the operation of a typical headlamp switch.*
- *Compare headlight bulb designs.*
- *Summarize lamp delay and auto-dimming systems.*
- *Explain brake, back-up, and turnlight circuit operation.*
- *Describe the various types of switches used in light and instrumentation systems.*
- *Sketch the circuits for basic gauge systems.*
- *Describe low fuel and fuel consumption indicator systems.*
- *Summarize instrument cluster construction.*
- *Compare conventional and digital instrumentation systems.*
- *Explain instrumentation computer operation.*
- *Summarize the operation of a CRT display.*
- *Describe the operation of a voice alert system.*

Lighting and instrumentation systems on today's cars can be "super complex." They can use their own computer and power supply to operate digital displays and even a television type picture tube. The number of wires and electronic devices in and under the dash can be "mind boggling."

This chapter will summarize the typical lighting and instrumentation systems found on late-model vehicles. It will give you the background for using factory service manuals. A service manual is needed to fully understand specific light and instrumentation systems. Because there is so much variation from one system to another, the manual is needed to explain the design and circuitry of the specific system being serviced.

Note! Several previous textbook chapters were to prepare you to comprehend the information presented in this chapter. Unless you are an experienced technician, you should have studied these previous chapters before beginning this chapter.

LIGHTING SYSTEMS

Lighting systems include any circuit or system that produces illumination (light). Within the lighting system would be the headlight system, brake light system, turnlight system, back-up light system, interior light system, and instrumentation lights.

Headlight system

The *headlight system* typically consists of the battery, headlamp related wiring, fuse panel, light switch, dimmer switch, headlamps, taillights, marker lights, and instrument lights. If the headlamps are concealed, the system also has either a vacuum or electric motor mechanism to operate the doors (flaps) over the headlamps.

Headlight switch

The *headlight switch* is a multi-function switch for controlling the headlamps and other lights. A typical schematic for a headlight circuit is in Fig. 17-1.

Power is fed into the headlight switch from the fuse panel. Mechanical contacts in the headlight switch control current flow out of the switch. Contacts may be provided for low and high beams.

A *combination headlight switch* may also contain devices for dimming the instrument panel, activating the headlight dimmer system, or controlling the autolamp shut-off system. A combination headlamp switch is in Fig. 17-2.

The headlight switch is usually mounted in the dash. It is fairly large. Some headlight switches also have a vacuum switching valve. The vacuum valve can be used to operate concealed headlamps that use engine vacuum to power the headlight doors.

A *rheostat* (variable resistor) can be included in some headlight switches for dimming the instrument lamps. The rheostat can also be a separate unit in the dash. It can be turned to high resistance for dimming the dash lights or vice versa.

Dimmer switch

A *dimmer switch* is used to change from low to high or high to low headlight beams. Newer cars have the dimmer switch on the steering column. It is made part of the turn signal switch. Older cars have the dimmer switch on the floor for foot operation.

Shown in Fig. 17-1, the dimmer switch simply connects voltage to individual high beam bulbs (four headlamps) or to a second set of filaments in the headlamps (only two headlamps).

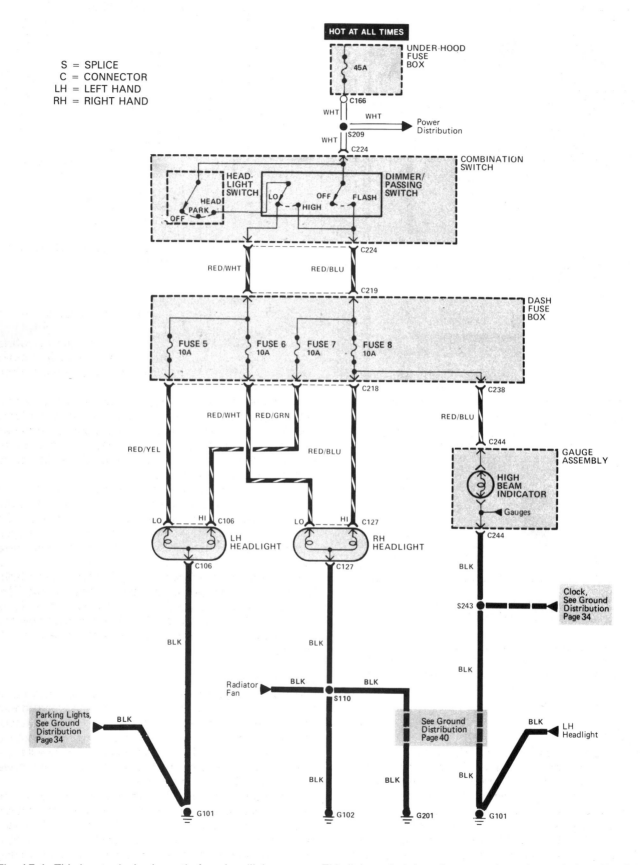

Fig. 17-1. This is a typical schematic for a headlight system. This light switch has dimmer and passing switches. No. 2 bulbs are used with dual elements for low and high beams. (General Motors)

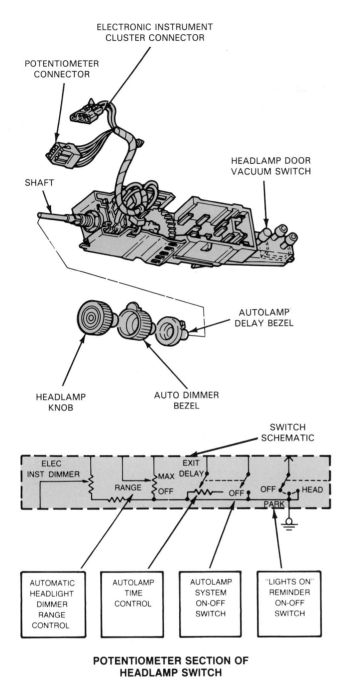

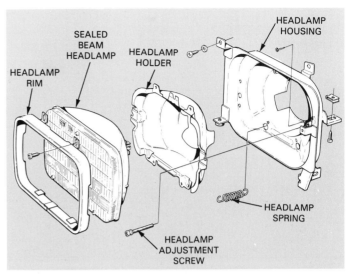

Fig. 17-3. Note parts of conventional headlamp bulb assembly. (Saab)

POTENTIOMETER SECTION OF
HEADLAMP SWITCH

Fig. 17-2. A rheostat is frequently used in a dash-mounted headlight switch. Note various functions performed by this switch. It also has vacuum switching valves for headlamp doors. (Ford)

Headlight bulbs

The *headlamp bulbs* are used to illuminate the road by heating a resistance filament. When current flows through the element or filament, the element glows white hot as electrons are emitted. The reflector and lens direct this light forward. See Fig. 17-3.

There are several headlamp bulb designs:

1. SEALED HOUSING HEADLAMP (conventional bulb with one or two filaments inside a vacuum-sealed, glass housing).
2. SEALED HALOGEN HEADLAMP (small halogen bulb

is enclosed inside a conventional, vacuum-sealed glass bulb), Fig. 17-4.

3. HALOGEN INSERT BULB (small halogen miniature bulb installs in large unsealed outer housing; outer bulb housing or reflector can be glass, or more often lightweight plastic).

There are two different types of conventional sealed beam bulbs: number 1 and number 2. A number 1 lamp has only one lighting element. The number 2 lamp has two lighting elements (high and low beam). Vehicles with only two headlamps use two number 2 headlamps to provide high and low beams.

Many late model cars use halogen headlamps. A *halogen headlamp* contains a small, inner halogen bulb. A halogen headlamp increases light output by about 25 percent with no increase in current draw. The halogen bulb is also whiter than a conventional bulb, which also increases lighting ability or *illuminance.*

The trend is toward using the small halogen insert bulb. It is enclosed in a large bulb housing made of plastic. This makes most of the headlamp assembly out of light-weight, shatterproof plastic. Fig. 17-4B shows how the halogen bulb element locks into its plastic reflector-bulb assembly.

Retractable headlamps

Retractable headlamps use a vacuum or electric motor setup to swing the headlamps or headlamp doors (covers) up and down in the car body. When retracted, the car body has a more aerodynamic shape to increase fuel economy, Fig. 17-5. Sometimes, the headlamps move open or just the covers over the bulbs can move while the bulbs remain stationary.

If vacuum operated, vacuum hoses run up to the headlamp vacuum motors. The *vacuum motors* are large diaphragms that convert vacuum into motion. When supplied vacuum by the headlamp switch, the diaphragm contracts and pulls the headlamps closed or open. Spring tension commonly moves the headlamps or doors in one direction. A manual control knob is sometimes provided

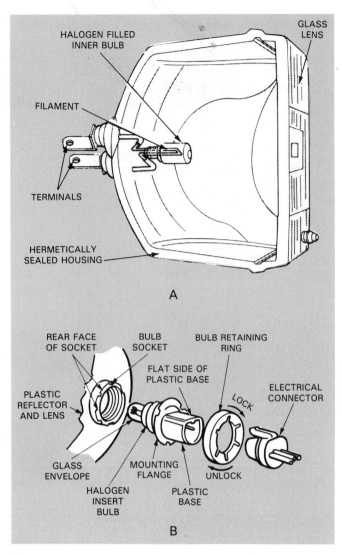

Fig. 17-4. Halogen headlamps will usually produce more light output with equal or less power consumption. A—Sealed housing has bulb element enclosed in small halogen gas-filled mini bulb. B—Halogen bulb insert can be installed in unsealed plastic reflector housing. This makes bulbs very light and resistant to breakage. (Chrysler and Ford)

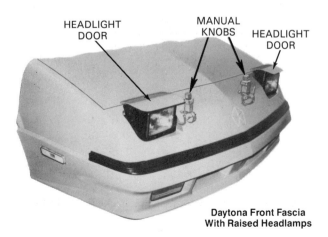

Daytona Front Fascia
With Raised Headlamps

Fig. 17-5. This car uses retractable headlights. Small knobs are used for manually raising doors in case of system failure. (Chrysler)

for raising the headlamp doors in an emergency or after a part failure.

When small electric motors are used to power the headlamp doors, they are usually connected to a small gear mechanism. The gear mechanism converts motor rotation into motion for opening or closing the headlamp doors.

Fig. 17-6 shows a complete wiring diagram for an exterior lighting system. Note that it uses small electric motors to open the headlamp doors. The ignition switch feeds current to headlight motor relays. The relays then connect a higher current to the headlamp motor doors.

Autolamp system

An *autolamp system* uses a light sensor, control circuit, switch, and relay to automatically control headlamp operation. Some systems turn the headlights on at dark or dim the headlights when the headlights from oncoming traffic hit a light sensor. Others can keep the interior and/or headlights on temporarily while the driver locks the car. Exact features of autolamp systems vary.

A diagram for one make of autolamp system is given in Fig. 17-7. The *light sensor* is used to control headlight operation. It can be located in the front of the car, near the grille. It can also be located in the rear view mirror or on the dash. The sensor sends a signal to an electronic controller. Depending upon circuit design, the controller can then turn on the headlights or dim them as needed. A relay is frequently used between the controller and headlamp circuit.

Refer to a service manual for the specific make and model car. It will give a more detailed explanation for the exact type system.

TURN, EMERGENCY, STOPLIGHTS

The turn, emergency, and stoplight systems are normally considered separate circuits. However, they commonly use some of the same wiring, electrical connections, and light bulbs.

The lights in these systems are small incandescent bulbs. They can contain either one or two elements. This was explained in an earlier chapter.

Turnlight system

The *turnlight system* basically consists of a fuse, turnlight switch, flasher unit, turnlight bulbs, indicator bulbs, and related wiring. When the steering column mounted switch is activated, it causes the right or left side turnlamps to flash. Turn indicator lights in the instrument panel or fenders also flash.

Fig. 17-8 shows a turn signal and hazard light circuit.

Some turn signal switches mount in the center of the steering column, under the steering wheel. Another type termed a *multi-function switch,* controls the turnlights and other systems, Fig. 17-9. This switch can also function as a horn and dimmer switch.

The *turn signal flasher* automatically opens and closes the turn signal circuit, causing the bulbs to flash ON and OFF. Discussed earlier, the flasher unit contains a temperature sensitive bimetallic strip and a heating element. The bimetal strip is connected to a set of contact points and to the fuse panel, Fig. 17-8.

When current flows through the turn signal flasher, the bimetallic strip is heated and bends. This opens the con-

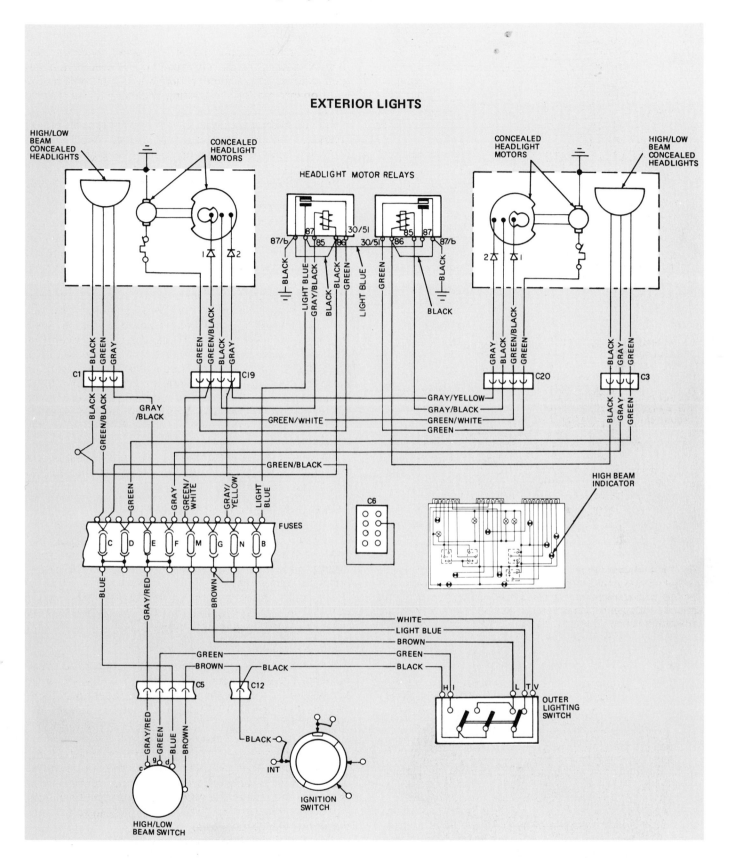

Fig. 17-6. Schematic shows complete exterior light system. Study use of electric motors to operate concealed headlamps. (Fiat)

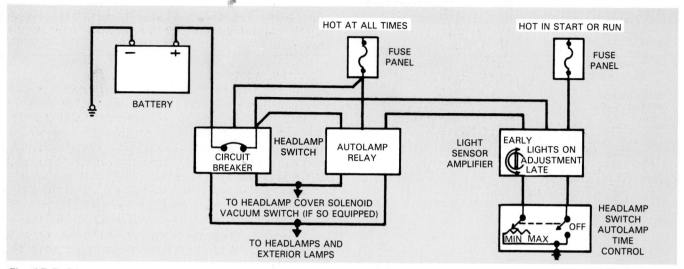

Fig. 17-7. Diagram shows autolamp system. Adjustment knob is for setting time delay for keeping lights on while exiting car. System designs vary. (Ford)

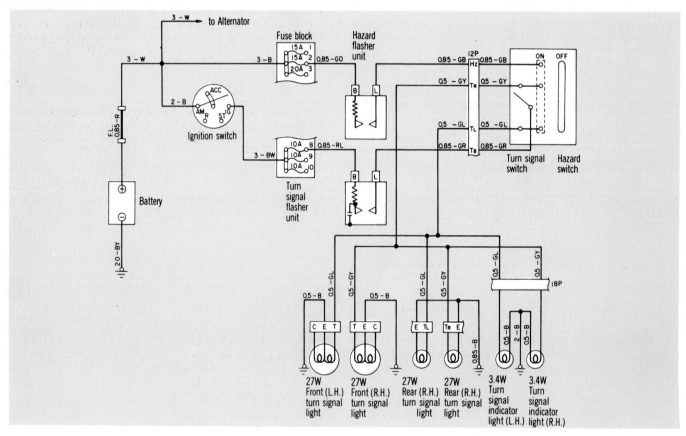

Fig. 17-8. Study this turn signal and hazard warning light circuit. Find the two flasher units and note how they are wired into circuit. (Chrysler)

tact points and breaks the circuit. As the bimetal strip cools, it closes the points and again completes the circuit. This heating and cooling cycle takes place in about a second. As a result, the turnlights flash as the points open and close.

The turn signal flasher is frequently mounted on the fuse panel. However, on a few cars, it may be located somewhere else under the dash. A shop manual will give flasher locations.

Emergency flasher system

The *emergency flasher system,* also termed *hazard warning system,* consists of a switch, flasher unit, the four turn signal lamps, and related wiring. The emergency light switch is normally mounted on the steering column. It is usually a push-pull switch, Fig. 17-9.

When the switch is closed, current flows through the emergency flasher, Fig. 17-8. Like a turn signal flasher, the emergency flasher opens and closes the circuit to

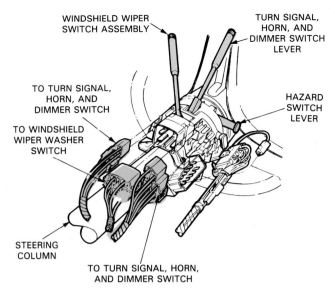

WINDSHIELD WIPER
SWITCH ASSEMBLY

TURN SIGNAL,
HORN, AND
DIMMER SWITCH
LEVER

TO TURN SIGNAL,
HORN, AND
DIMMER SWITCH

TO WINDSHIELD
WIPER WASHER
SWITCH

HAZARD
SWITCH
LEVER

STEERING
COLUMN

TO TURN SIGNAL, HORN,
AND DIMMER SWITCH

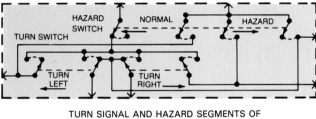

TURN SIGNAL AND HAZARD SEGMENTS OF
MULTI-FUNCTION SWITCH

Fig. 17-9. New cars commonly use multifunction switch on steering column for turn signals, windshield wipers, high and low beams, hazard warning, etc. Note schematic of internal connections in switch. (Ford)

the lights. This causes all four turn signals to flash. Oncoming traffic is warned of a possible emergency or hazard.

Stoplight system

The *stoplight system* or *brake light system* is commonly made up of a fuse, brake light switch, two rear lamps, and related wiring. The brake light switch is normally mounted on or near the brake pedal. A schematic of a brake light system is given in Fig. 17-10. When the brake pedal is pressed, it closes the switch and turns on the rear brake lights. See Fig. 17-11.

Older brake systems and some trucks can use a hydraulic switch to turn on the brake lights. The hydraulic pressure switch is usually connected at the master cylinder with a T-fitting, but it can also be connected to a brake line. Brake pressure closes the switch and activates the brake lights.

Brake warning light

A *brake warning light* is used to inform the driver of a problem in the hydraulic brake system. It is operated by a pressure sensitive switch in the brake lines. An unequal pressure on one side of the brake system will shift and activate the switch to turn on the dash warning lamp.

Backup light system

A *backup light system* typically has a fuse, gear shift or transmission/transaxle mounted switch, two backup lamps, and wiring to connect these components.

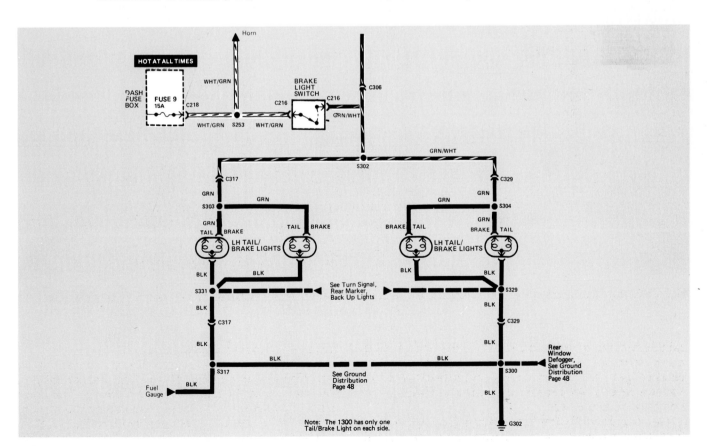

Fig. 17-10. Brake light circuit is simple. Brake light switch simply connects fuse box supplied voltage to brake light elements in taillights. (General Motors)

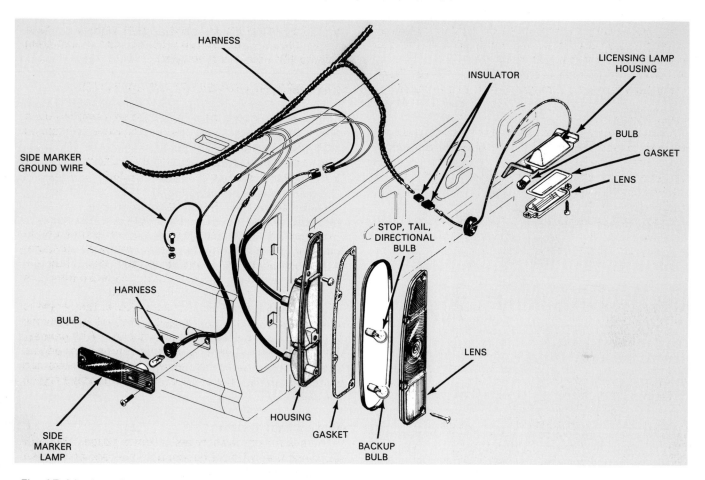

Fig. 17-11. Long harness carries current to taillights, side marker lights, and license plate light. Connectors are provided for easy service of lamp housing and for testing. (Chrysler)

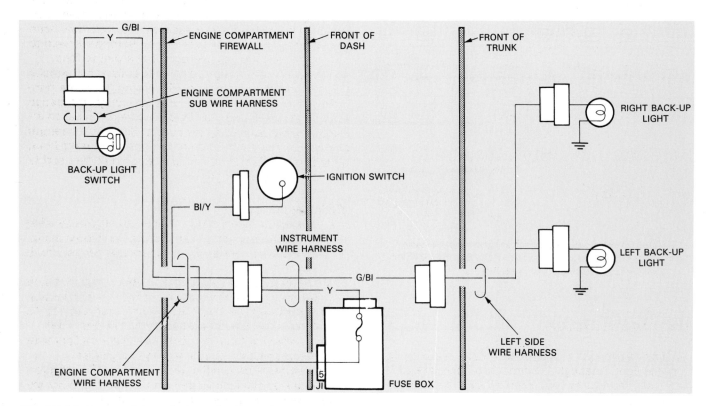

Fig. 17-12. Backup light switch can be located on bottom of steering column, on shift mechanism, or on transmission/trans-axle. This diagram uses large dividers to show component locations. (Honda)

The *backup lamp switch* closes the light circuit when the transmission is shifted into reverse. This illuminates the area behind the car.

A backup light circuit is shown in Fig. 17-12. Trace current flow from the ignition switch to the bulbs.

Interior light system

The *interior light system* uses a dash switch and door switches to operate small lights inside the passenger compartment. The headlight switch commonly activates the interior lights when turned fully clockwise. Additional switches can be located in the dash, on the dome light, etc. See Fig. 17-13.

Interior light systems are simple. However, their circuit designs can vary. Again, refer to the shop manual for a diagram of the exact circuit design.

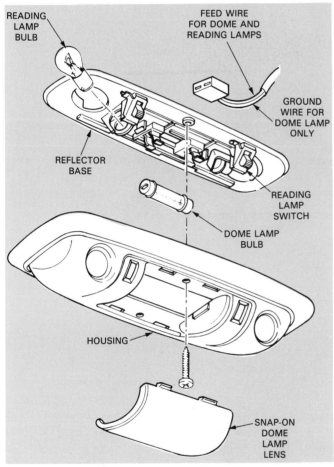

Fig. 17-13. Interior lights usually have a snap on or screw on lens. Switches are frequently used for turning on just one of the interior lights. (Chrysler)

LIGHT FAILURE SYSTEM

A *light failure system* turns on a dash warning light if a brake light, headlight, or other light burns out. This is a safety feature to help keep all of the car's lights working properly.

Basically, a control circuit is used to measure the amount of current flowing through each of the light cir-

cuits. If a bulb burns out, less current draw will result in that circuit. The electronic control circuit can then activate the dash warning light.

LIGHT AND INSTRUMENTATION SWITCHES

Fig. 17-14 shows the most common switches used in the light and instrumentation circuits. Note their names and typical locations.

Basic switch types were explained in Chapter 4. Refer to this chapter for information if needed.

INSTRUMENTATION GAUGES

Gauges are used to show an actual value for a condition. Gauges are commonly used to show oil pressure, engine temperature, charging voltage, etc. They are better than indicator or "idiot lights" because they give warning before potential engine damage.

For example, when an idiot light glows, the engine is already dangerously overheated. If the oil light comes on, oil pressure is already dangerously low. With gauges, the driver can detect a slight increase in engine temperature or slight drop in oil pressure. Repairs can be made before a severe failure or before possible engine damage.

Gauge types

There are two basic types of dash gauges: bimetal gauge and magnetic coil gauge. Both are used on modern passenger cars. Look at Fig. 17-15.

The *bimetal gauge* uses two types of metal bonded to form a single strip. The heat expansion characteristics of each piece of metal are different. Since the two are bonded together, they warp or bend when heated. Current flow through the strip causes heat to warp and bend the bimetal strip. This movement or warpage is used to swing the indicator needle across the gauge face.

A *magnetic coil gauge* uses small coils and magnetic fields to rotate the gauge needle. Using the same principles as an electric motor, current through the gauge coils produces a magnetic field. The field is used to attract an armature holding the needle. Since field strength and needle movement are proportional to current flow, a variable resistor or current input can also be used to operate this type gauge.

Temperature gauge

A *temperature gauge circuit* uses an engine sending unit to operate the gauge in the dash. As shown in Fig. 17-16, the basic parts of a temperature gauge circuit include:

1. *Temperature sending unit* (variable resistance unit that changes its ohms value as the engine heats up).
2. *Temperature gauge* (mechanism that deflects a pointer or needle in proportion to current flow).
3. *Instrument voltage regulator* (small device for maintaining constant supply voltage to gauges).

The temperature sending unit is usually a thermistor; its internal resistance changes with temperature. For example, when cold, the sending unit might have high resistance. Then, only a small current can flow through the temperature gauge. The gauge needle would stay at

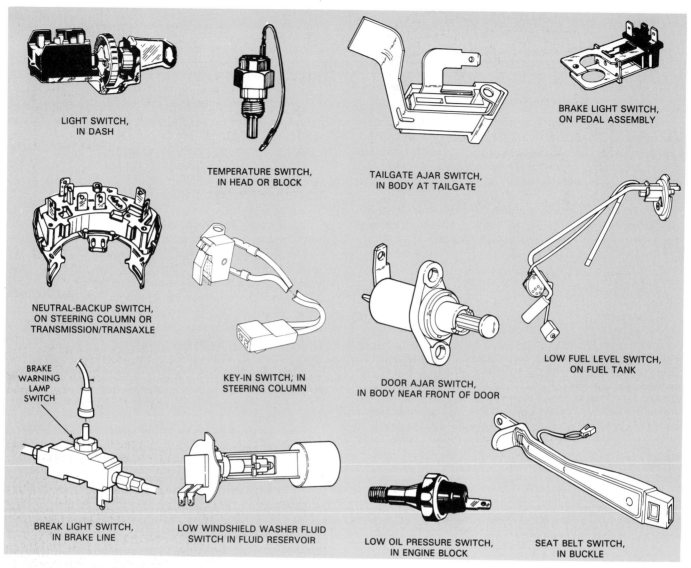

LIGHT SWITCH,
IN DASH

TEMPERATURE SWITCH,
IN HEAD OR BLOCK

TAILGATE AJAR SWITCH,
IN BODY AT TAILGATE

BRAKE LIGHT SWITCH,
ON PEDAL ASSEMBLY

NEUTRAL-BACKUP SWITCH,
ON STEERING COLUMN OR
TRANSMISSION/TRANSAXLE

KEY-IN SWITCH; IN
STEERING COLUMN

DOOR AJAR SWITCH,
IN BODY NEAR FRONT OF DOOR

LOW FUEL LEVEL SWITCH,
ON FUEL TANK

BRAKE
WARNING
LAMP
SWITCH

BREAK LIGHT SWITCH,
IN BRAKE LINE

LOW WINDSHIELD WASHER FLUID
SWITCH IN FLUID RESERVOIR

LOW OIL PRESSURE SWITCH,
IN ENGINE BLOCK

SEAT BELT SWITCH,
IN BUCKLE

Fig. 17-14. Study various switches used in light and instrumentation systems. (GP Parts and Chrysler)

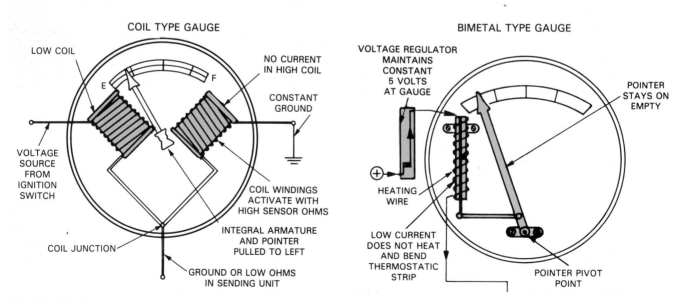

COIL TYPE GAUGE

LOW COIL

NO CURRENT
IN HIGH COIL

E   F

CONSTANT
GROUND

VOLTAGE
SOURCE
FROM
IGNITION
SWITCH

COIL WINDINGS
ACTIVATE WITH
HIGH SENSOR OHMS

INTEGRAL ARMATURE
AND POINTER
PULLED TO LEFT

COIL JUNCTION

GROUND OR LOW OHMS
IN SENDING UNIT

BIMETAL TYPE GAUGE

VOLTAGE REGULATOR
MAINTAINS
CONSTANT
5 VOLTS
AT GAUGE

POINTER
STAYS ON
EMPTY

HEATING
WIRE

LOW CURRENT
DOES NOT HEAT
AND BEND
THERMOSTATIC
STRIP

POINTER PIVOT
POINT

Fig. 17-15. These are the two basic types of gauges. A—Magnetic or coil type gauge uses magnetic field to deflect needle. High sending unit ohms would cause current flow in right coil. B—Bimetal gauge uses warpage of strip to deflect needle. Current flow heats and bends bimetal strip to swing needle to right.

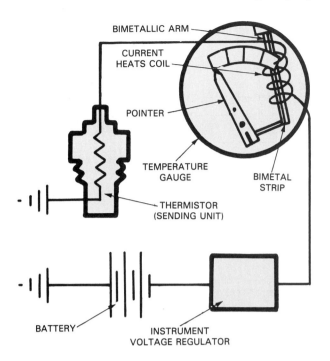

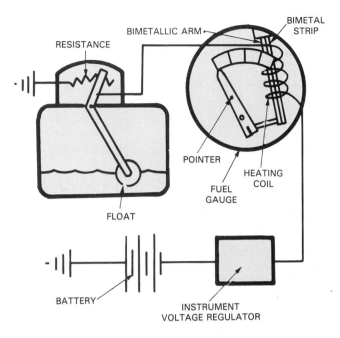

Fig. 17-16. Basic temperature gauge circuit uses sending unit to control current flow through gauge. Cold engine might make sending unit have high resistance. Low current flow would then allow bimetal strip to remain straight. As engine warms, resistance in sending unit drops. This would allow increased current flow to heat and bend bimetal strip, moving needle to right. (Chrysler)

Fig. 17-17. Fuel gauge circuit uses tank sending unit. Float rises and falls as fuel is added or used. Float moves variable resistor to control current flow to fuel gauge. Low fuel level would produce high resistance and low current flow. Needle would stay near empty. (Chrysler)

rest or on cold.

As the engine warms, the sending unit resistance drops. This will allow more current flow to the gauge. The increased current deflects the needle to the right to indicate more engine heat.

Fuel gauge

A basic *fuel gauge circuit* uses a variable resistor to operate either a bimetal or magnetic type indicator assembly. A basic circuit is shown in Fig. 17-17.

The *tank sending unit* is a float and arm that operates a variable resistor. When the tank is empty of fuel, the float would be down and the variable resistance would be high. This would allow little current flow through the fuel gauge. The bimetal arm would stay cool and the needle would show low or empty.

When the fuel tank is filled, the float will rise to the top of the tank. This will slide the wiper to the low resistance position on the variable resistor. More current will then flow through the fuel gauge circuit. The bimetal arm will then heat up and warp to move the needle to full.

Fig. 17-18 shows the outside of a fuel tank sending unit. It is frequently held in the tank with a lock ring. Note the fuel gauge terminal and ground wire.

Fuel consumption indicator

A *fuel consumption indicator* uses the vehicle speed sensor, fuel flow sensor or tank sending unit, engine control computer, and possibly other inputs to show average fuel consumption and miles-to-empty displays. The input data from the sensors is fed into an instrumentation computer. The computer can then drive the instrument

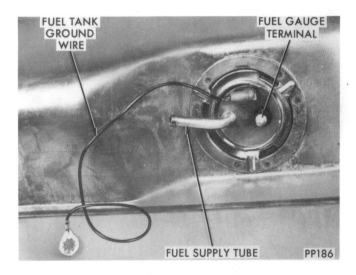

Fig. 17-18. Fuel tank sending unit is frequently held in tank by lock ring. Note terminals for fuel gauge wire and ground. (Chrysler)

panel cluster.

A diagram for a fuel consumption indicator or trip monitor is shown in Fig. 17-19. Note how the vehicle speed sensor, engine control module, and fuel gauge sending unit feed data into the body or instrumentation computer. The body computer then outputs control signals to the cluster.

Fuel consumption indicator circuits vary. However, most use the vehicle speed sensor and a fuel sensor as main input devices. Again, refer to the shop manual for more specific information.

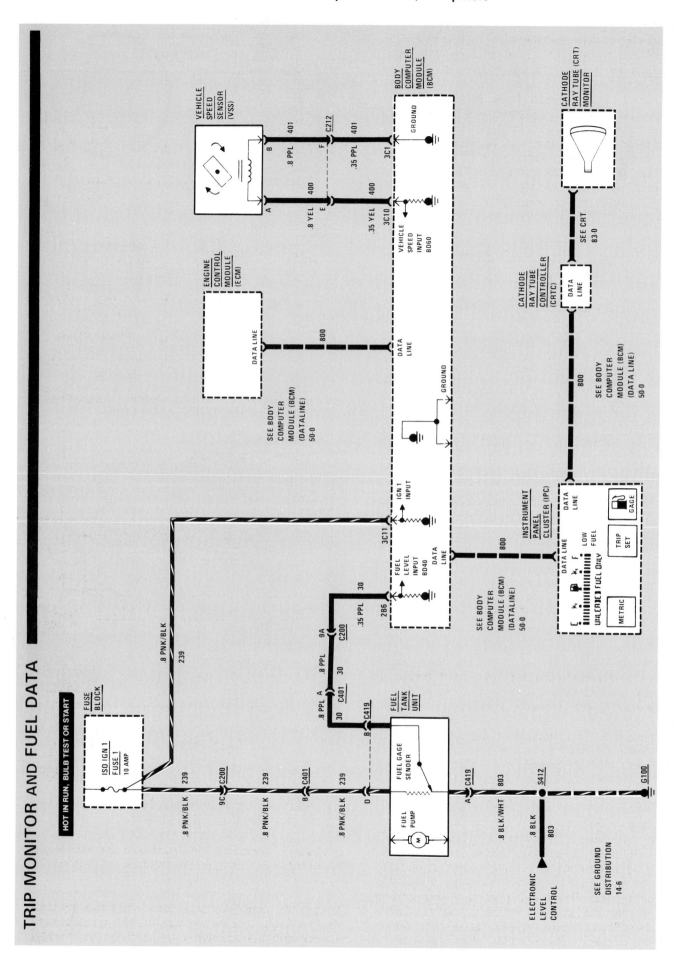

Fig. 17-19. Vehicle speed sensor and current signal from fuel tank sending unit are used by computer to output display for fuel economy display, miles-to-empty display, etc. (General Motors)

Low fuel warning light

Some fuel gauge circuits have a low fuel warning light. The *low fuel warning light circuit* can use either a control circuit or extra thermistor mounted on the fuel tank sending unit.

If a control circuit is used, it simply detects when sending unit current is at a specific level. This triggers the circuit to illuminate the low fuel light. See Fig. 17-20.

With a thermistor, the unit heats up when fuel is low. Without cool liquid fuel around the thermistor, current flow heats the thermistor and lowers its internal resistance. This lowered resistance can be used to turn on the low fuel indicator lamp.

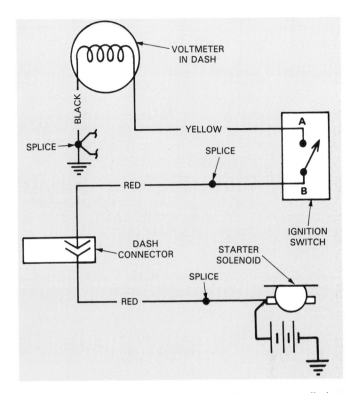

Fig. 17-21. This voltmeter simply reads voltage applied to ignition switch. (Chrysler)

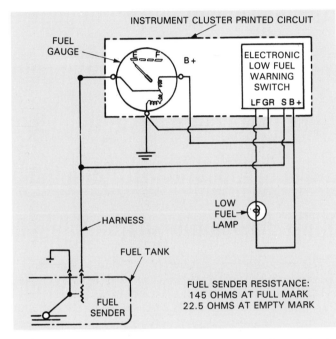

Fig. 17-20. This low fuel warning system uses electronic circuit to turn dash light on when current to gauge is low enough. Low current triggers circuit to complete electrical path to low fuel indicator bulb in dash. (Ford)

Voltmeter circuit

A *voltmeter* is used to check the output of the charging system. A small voltmeter gauge or a digital display are in the dash. This informs the driver about the condition of the charging system.

A basic circuit for a voltmeter indicator is in Fig. 17-21. When the charging system is in good condition, the voltmeter should register around 13 to 15 volts. If the gauge shows only battery voltage (12.6 volts), a problem is indicated.

Oil pressure gauge

The *oil pressure gauge circuit* uses a variable resistance sending unit to operate a needle type gauge. The sending unit installs in the engine so that its tip is exposed to an engine oil gallery. See Fig. 17-22.

High oil pressure flexes a diaphragm in the sending unit. Diaphragm movement is used to move the variable resistor. Sending unit resistance may decrease as engine oil pressure increases. This will allow higher current flow

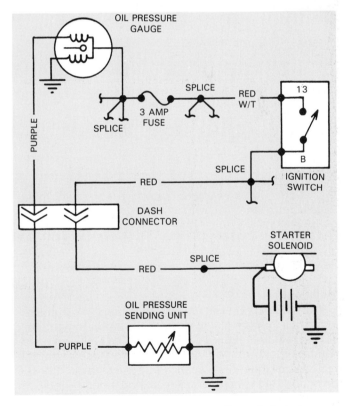

Fig. 17-22. Oil pressure gauge uses sending unit that changes resistance with change in oil pressure. (Chrysler)

through the pressure gauge to deflect the indicator needle to high. Low oil pressure allows the diaphragm to relax and the variable resistor slides to the high resistance position. This reduces current flow to the oil pressure gauge and moves the needle to the left.

Low oil level indicator

A *low oil level indicator circuit* uses a sensor in the side of the engine oil pan to operate an indicator light. When there is enough oil in the pan, the sensor could have high resistance. No current would flow through the circuit and the indicator light remains off. If oil level drops too low, the sensor resistance drops to turn on the dash light.

A *timing circuit* is commonly used in the low oil level indicator system. It is needed to prevent the indicator light from flashing on and off as the oil splashes around inside the oil pan. As shown in Fig. 17-23, it serves as a buffer between the sensor and dash lamp.

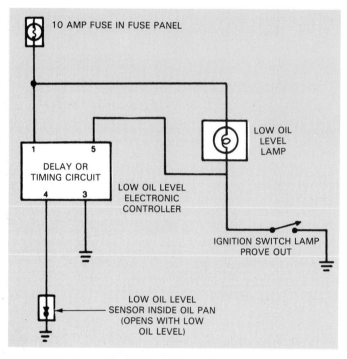

Fig. 17-23. Low oil level circuit uses float type switch in pan to detect dangerously low oil level conditions. Timing circuit delays operation of warning light until low oil level condition has existed for short period of time. This keeps dash light from flickering. (Ford)

Tachometer

The *tachometer* uses the pulsing voltage or current going to the ignition coil to operate the indicator showing engine rpm (revolutions per minute). The ignition system electronic control unit shuts current off each time the ignition coil must fire a spark plug. The tach circuit uses this on/off signal to operate an analog (needle) or digital (number display) tachometer in the dash, Fig. 17-24.

INSTRUMENT CLUSTER CONSTRUCTION

The *instrument cluster* houses most of the dash gauges, speedometer, and indicator lights. It is usually made of plastic and is held in the dash with screws. A typical instrument cluster is in Fig. 17-25.

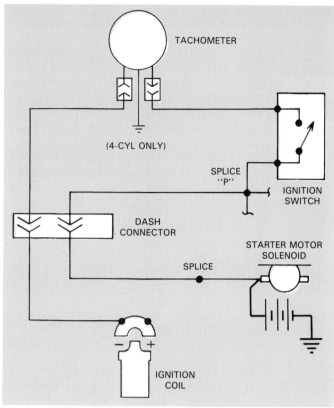

Fig. 17-24. This conventional tachometer picks up engine speed signal off of ignition coil.

The basic parts of an instrument cluster include:
1. *Visor or lens* (clear plastic cover over front of cluster assembly).
2. *Panel or face* (plate that fits in front of gauges and has writing, scales, and numbers for gauges and indicator lights).
3. *Instrument housing* (rear plastic enclosure that holds gauges, speedometer head, indicator bulbs, printed circuit, and other devices).
4. *Printed circuit* (plastic sheet with metal conductor strips that electrically connect components in instrument cluster).
5. *Voltage regulator* (small device for maintaining constant supply voltage to gauges in cluster).
6. *Gauges and indicators* (devices for showing or informing driver of vehicle operating conditions).

Obviously, the construction of a digital instrument cluster would be different than a conventional analog cluster. This will be discussed shortly.

Fig. 17-26 shows the rear of an instrument cluster. Note how the indicator bulbs install through the printed circuit and lock into the housing. A service manual will give an illustration like this one so that you can determine the location of each indicator bulb for replacement.

Instrument panel wiring

The *instrument panel wiring* connects power to all of the dash-mounted devices. An example is shown in Fig. 17-27. Note how the harness connects to the various components. Again, the service manual will usually illustrate the dash wiring harness. It can be very complex and the manual will identify the connectors.

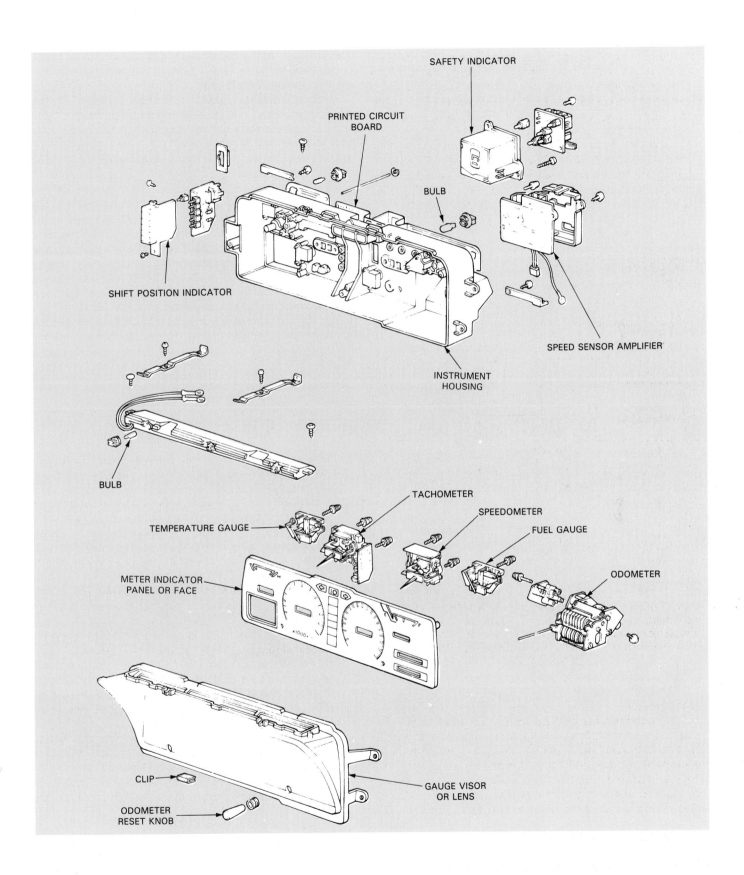

Fig. 17-25. Note parts in this instrument cluster. (Honda)

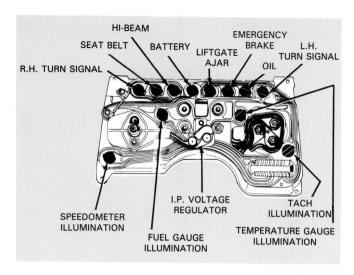

Fig. 17-26. Rear view of instrument cluster shows how indicator bulbs fit into housing. Printed circuit sheet fits between bulb sockets and housing to connect components electrically. (Ford)

Speedometer

The *speedometer* shows vehicle speed as miles-per-hour or kilometers-per-hour. There are two basic types of speedometers: conventional cable-driven speedometer and electronic speedometer.

A *cable-driven speedometer* has a cable linking the transmission or transaxle with the speedometer head. The speedo cable can also be linked to another cable driving the speed control unit.

The *speedometer cable* is a flexible, stranded metal, wire cable with a drive gear on one end. The flexible drive cable is inside a stationary cable housing. The inner cable gear meshes with a small drive gear in the transmission or transaxle. When the car is moving, the gears spin the speedometer cable.

The *speedometer head* uses the rotation of the speedometer cable to produce needle movement in the dash. Basically, the cable spins a small magnet in the speedometer head. The resulting magnetic force is used to deflect the needle or pointer to show mph or km/h.

An *electronic speedometer* does NOT use a speedometer cable: it uses integrated circuit chips to react to electrical signals from the vehicle speed sensor. Specific electronic speedometer circuits vary.

Fig. 17-28 shows an electronic, analog (deflecting needle) type "speedo" head that uses a small stepper motor. The speed sensor sends a pulsing signal that is

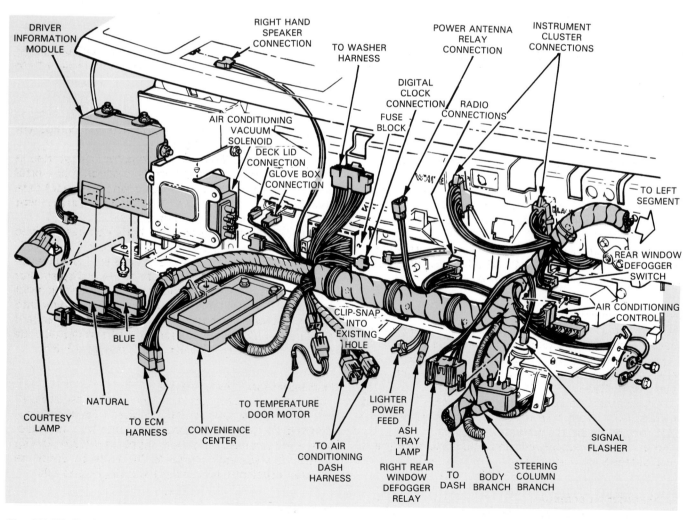

Fig. 17-27. Dash or instrument panel wiring harness can be complex. Service manual illustration will identify connectors and other units. (General Motors)

Fig. 17-28. This is an electronic-analog speedometer head. Vehicle speed sensor sends signal to integrated circuit on speedo head. IC and other circuit components can then be used to run small stepper motor. Motor spins speedometer head to drive indicating needle and odometer. (Chrysler)

proportional to car speed. The ICs can then use this frequency to power the stepper motor and deflect the speedometer needle proportionally. The stepper motor also drives the odometer.

A *digital speedometer* is a numerical display to show vehicle speed. Typically, it also uses input signals from the vehicle speed sensor. One or two computers are then used to drive the display.

Fig. 17-29 shows a service manual diagram for a conventional instrument cluster. Study the various components and electrical connections.

Digital instrument clusters

A *digital instrument cluster* does NOT use analog or needle type gauges; it uses computer-driven number or graphic displays. The trend is to use digital displays in new cars. They are easy to read, lightweight, and dependable. See Fig. 17-30.

An actual vacuum fluorescent digital cluster is pictured in Fig. 17-31. Note how it has its own integrated circuits that drive the displays.

Note! Vacuum fluorescent and liquid crystal displays were detailed in Chapter 5.

Instrumentation computer

The *instrumentation computer,* sometimes called body computer, reacts to signals from vehicle sensors and other on-board computers to operate the digital display.

Its construction and design is similar to the computers discussed in previous chapters.

An instrumentation or body computer is illustrated in Fig. 17-33. Its integrated circuits produce a powerful processor that can handle a large quantity of input data and then rapidly send out control data for the instrument displays and sometimes other devices.

A block diagram of a how the body computer drives the vacuum fluorescent display is shown in Fig. 17-32.

Fig. 17-34 gives an example of how the instrumentation computer processes data to show a display. For instance, the fuel sending unit produces an analog input signal. The converter changes the analog signal into binary. A binary output is then sent to the instrument cluster. The ICs on the cluster can use this digital code to drive the various displays. Look at Fig. 17-35.

Instrumentation power supply

An *instrumentation power supply* can be used to provide a constant, unfluctuating voltage for the digital displays, ICs, and other related devices. One manufacturer's instrumentation power supply is pictured in Fig. 17-36. It steps up voltage to 60 volts to drive the displays efficiently and make them bright enough.

CRT display

A CRT or *cathode ray tube* is a television type picture tube that can be used to produce instrumentation type

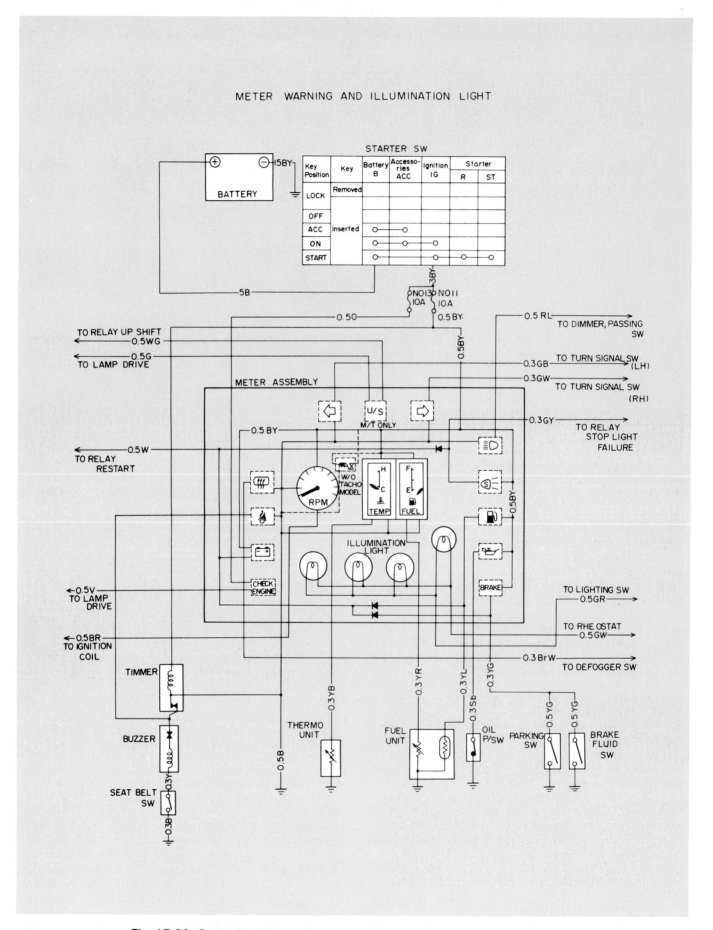

Fig. 17-29. Study this diagram for an analog instrument cluster. (General Motors)

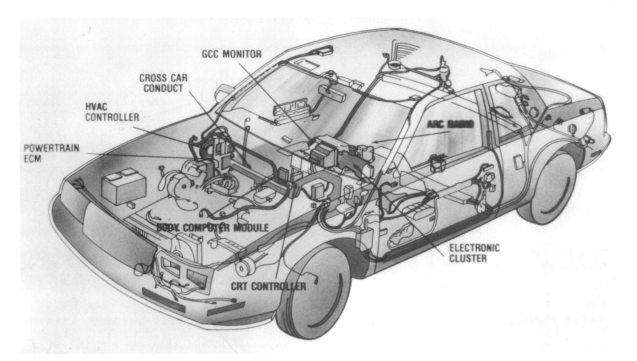

Fig. 17-30. Note various control units used on this late model car. It has digital instrumentation and cathode ray tube display. (General Motors)

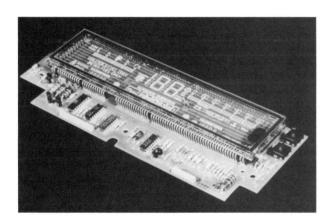

Fig. 17-31. Vacuum fluorescent instrument cluster has integrated circuits that drive displays and indicator lights using data from body computer. (General Motors)

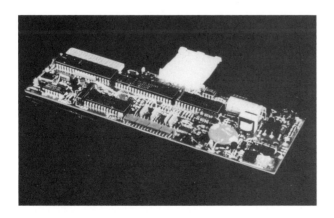

Fig. 17-32. This processor or computer is used to analyze signals for vehicle sensors and from other electronic control units. It can then send signals to the digital instrument cluster.

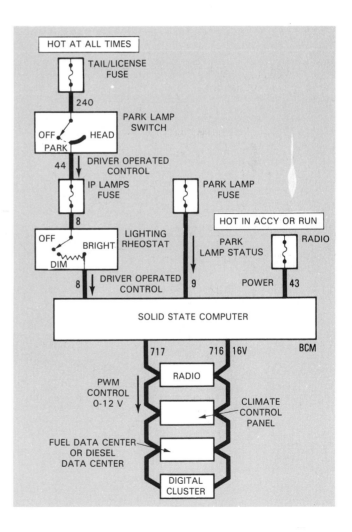

Fig. 17-33. Simple diagram shows how body or instrumentation computer is fed power and outputs to other components.

309

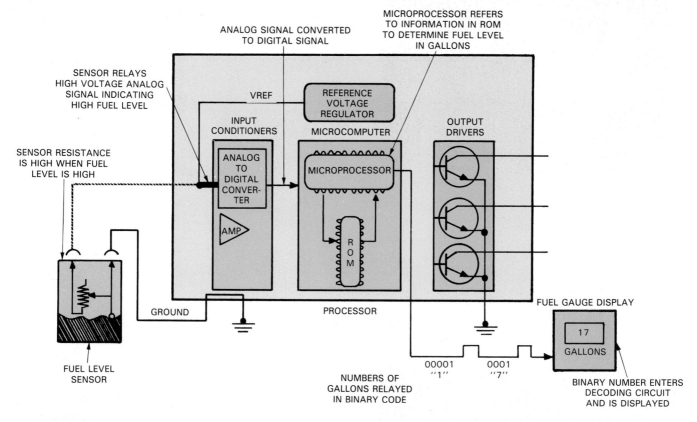

Fig. 17-34. This is an example of how computer generates signal for digital instrumentation. Fuel level sending unit outputs an analog current signal by moving variable resistor. Converter feeds altered signal into microprocessor. Microprocessor generates digital signal for instrument cluster. Circuit in or on instrument cluster can then illuminate correct segments in digital display to show amount of fuel in tank. (Ford)

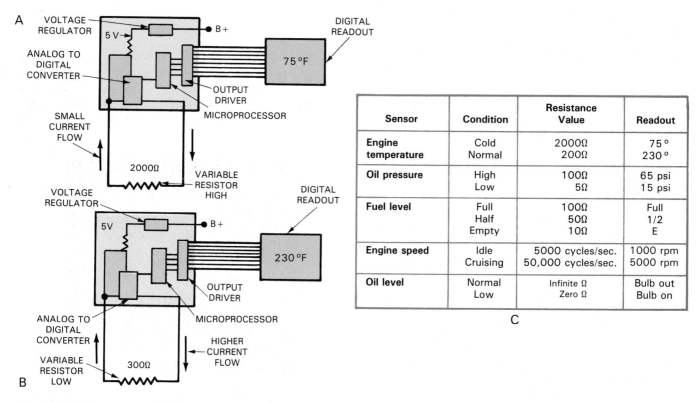

Sensor	Condition	Resistance Value	Readout
Engine temperature	Cold Normal	2000Ω 200Ω	75° 230°
Oil pressure	High Low	100Ω 5Ω	65 psi 15 psi
Fuel level	Full Half Empty	100Ω 50Ω 10Ω	Full 1/2 E
Engine speed	Idle Cruising	5000 cycles/sec. 50,000 cycles/sec.	1000 rpm 5000 rpm
Oil level	Normal Low	Infinite Ω Zero Ω	Bulb out Bulb on

Fig. 17-35. Most sensors for instrumentation are variable resistors. Study example of how different sensor values can be used by instrumentaiton computer to generate display. For instance, change in resistance and resulting change in current flow is proportional to change in condition. A—Cold engine. B—Warm engine. C—Sensor chart.

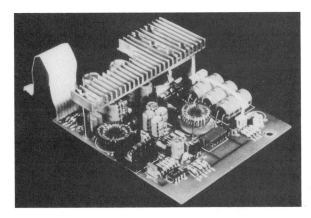

Fig. 17-36. Instead of small voltage regulator used with conventional gauges, some digital displays and CRT displays require a larger power supply. This power supply circuit steps up voltage to 60 volts for illuminating displays more efficiently. (General Motors)

Fig. 17-37. This experimental car has two display screens in dash. CRT displays are becoming more common. They provide an excellent way to show vehicle operating conditions, troubles, etc. (Buick)

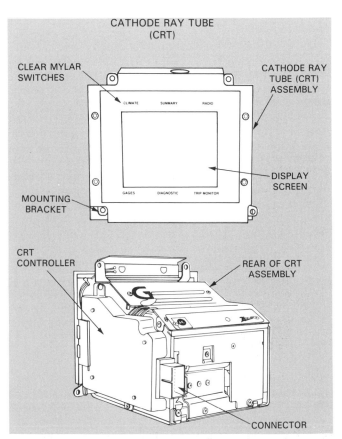

Fig. 17-38. This CRT has control switches on surface of screen. Invisible conductors feed out from mylar switches. Pressing surface of screen closes switch to activate new readout. CRT is like small television set. (AC-Delco and Zenith)

CRT controller

A CRT *controller* is used as an interface between the main computer and the cathode ray tube display. It processes the data from the body computer to drive the electron beam gun in the CRT. One is shown in Fig. 17-39. The CRT controller mounts under the dash. It is

Fig. 17-39. CRT controller uses input signals from other components to drive electron beam inside CRT. Control circuit operates electron beam similar to circuits inside TV set. (General Motors)

displays, Fig. 17-37. Several car manufacturers are now using, or will soon be using, a CRT display.

A CRT used by one manufacturer is shown in Fig. 17-38. It has invisible mylar switches on its surface. Transparent conductors feed away from these surface switches. Pressing on the surface of the CRT will activate these switches for selecting a new CRT display or output.

The CRT works like a television set. An electron beam gun "shoots" electrons at the inner face of the screen. A phosphor coating on the screen glows when hit by the electron beam. The beam is rapidly deflected or scanned across the screen. By cycling the beam ON and OFF, images are formed on the CRT face.

In the future, a CRT could be used as a rear view mirror. A video type camera could be located at the rear of the car. The camera could drive the CRT for easy, wide angle viewing behind the car.

similar in construction to other computers or electronic control circuits.

Fig. 17-40 shows a diagram for a display system using a CRT. Study how the CRT controller is connected between the body computer and the cathode ray tube.

Voice alert system

A *voice alert system* uses an electronic circuit to drive a speaker for verbally explaining conditions to the driver. A diagram for one voice alert system is in Fig. 17-41.

Various sensors, usually switch type sensors, input to the instrumentation computer. The computer can then determine if something is wrong. For example, if a car door is not shut, that door switch will be open or not grounded. If the transaxle is shifted into drive, the computer might then output to the electronic voice alert circuit. The voice circuit will then drive the speaker to say "Your door is ajar!" This same principle is used for many other situations.

In Fig. 17-41, study how the alert system can warn the driver of a burned out bulb, low brake fluid, worn brake pads, trunk ajar, and many other conditions.

SUMMARY

In recent years, lighting and instrumentation systems have become rather complex. Digital displays, cathode ray tubes, and voice alert systems have all added to the knowledge needed by the auto electronic technician.

The headlamp switch is a multi-function switch for controlling the headlights, parking lights, and some other lamps. It frequently has a variable resistor for dimming the instrument panel lights. Sometimes, a vacuum switch is combined in the light switch for operating concealed headlamp doors.

There are several types of headlamp bulbs. The conventional sealed beam bulb can have one or two filaments. A sealed halogen bulb has a small inner halogen bulb element inside a conventional bulb housing. A halogen insert bulb is a removable, miniature bulb that installs in an unsealed plastic housing reflector.

An autolamp system uses a photocell or light sensor to automatically turn on or dim the headlights as needed.

Turn and emergency lights use a flasher unit. It has a bimetal strip that makes and breaks the light circuit to make the bulbs flash.

The stop light system uses a brake light switch. This switch is usually mounted on or next to the brake pedal. A few systems use a hydraulic or pressure type switch. When the brakes are applied, the brake switch connects voltage to the brake lamps.

A brake warning light is used to warn of a brake system failure. If pressure drops in one section of the brake system, it activates a switch that turns on a brake light in the dash. This should not be confused with a low brake fluid warning light operated by a float type switch in the master cylinder.

There are two types of dash gauges: bimetal gauge and magnetic gauge. The bimetal gauges uses a strip made of two dissimilar metals. Current flow through the strip generates heat. The heat warps the strip and this motion is used to move the gauge needle. The magnetic gauge uses current flow to generate a magnetic field around small coils. The magnetic field is used to attract

DISPLAY-ON-ENTRY

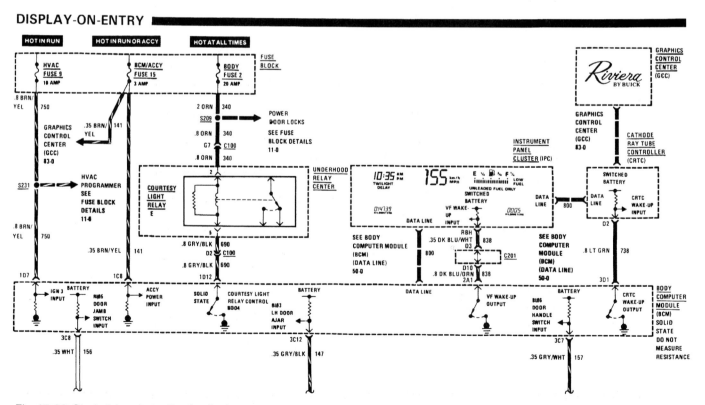

Fig. 17-39. Study this schematic of a display-on-entry system. Locate CRT, CRT controller, body computer, and instrument cluster. (Buick)

and deflect the gauge needle.

Sending units are used to operate dash gauges. Most sending units are variable resistance devices. They convert a condition change (temperature, pressure, etc.) into a current flow change. This altered current flow is used to power the gauges.

The instrument cluster houses the gauges or digital displays and indicator lights. A printed circuit sheet on the back of the instrument cluster electrically connects all of the components. A small voltage regulator can be used to feed a constant, reduced voltage to the gauges.

An electronic speedometer uses input signals from the vehicle speed sensor. It has integrated circuits that power a stepper motor. The motor then turns the speedo head and indicator. A digital speedometer uses a computer to react to signals from the speed sensor. The body computer sends output signals to the instrumentation ICs and they drive the displays.

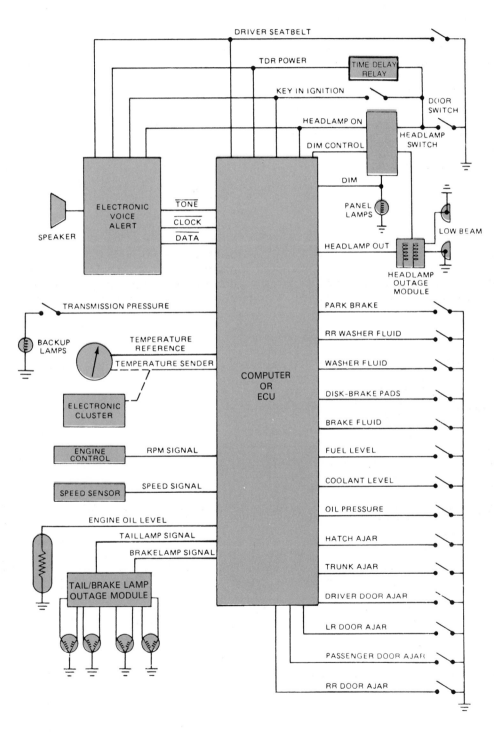

Fig. 17-41. Circuit diagram shows major parts of typical voice alert system. On right, various switches feed data into electronic control circuit. On left, various sensors and light out module feed signals into ECU. If a condition is not satisfied, electronic control circuit outputs signal to voice alert circuit. It can then generate simulated voice signal for operating speaker so car can ''talk'' to driver. (Chrysler)

A CRT or cathode ray tube can be used to show dash displays. It can have surface switches that allow the driver to call up various readings. The CRT is like a television picture tube. An electronic controller is used to operate the CRT. It responds to inputs from the body computer and then outputs a signal to drive the CRT display.

KNOW THESE TERMS

Headlight switch, Rheostat, Dimmer switch, No. 1 bulb, No. 2 bulb, Halogen bulb, Halogen bulb insert, Vacuum motor, Autolamp system, Light sensor, Turn signal flasher, Brake light switch, Backup light switch, Light failure system, Bimetal gauge, Magnetic coil gauge, Sending unit, Instrument voltage regulator, Fuel gauge circuit, Fuel sending unit, Low fuel warning circuit, Fuel consumption indicator, Oil pressure sending unit, Low oil level indicator, Timing circuit, Instrument cluster, Cluster printed circuit, Electronic speedometer, Digital speedometer, Digital cluster, Instrumentation computer, Body computer, Instrumentation power supply, CRT, CRT controller, Voice alert system.

REVIEW QUESTIONS—CHAPTER 17

1. Many headlight switches contain a _____ for dimming the instrument lights.
2. What are two dimmer switch locations?
3. Explain a halogen insert type headlamp.
4. A halogen bulb increases light intensity about _____ percent without an increase in _____.
5. Describe two common methods to power retractable headlamps or headlamp doors.
6. How does an autolamp system function?
7. Explain the operation of a flasher unit.
8. This system uses an electronic control circuit to measure how much current is flowing through each light bulb.
   a. Light dimming system.
   b. CRT system.
   c. Light failure system.
   d. Autolamp system.
9. What are the two types of gauges?
10. A temperature _____ _____ is a variable resistor that sends current to the dash gauge.
11. How does a conventional fuel gauge operate?
12. Why is a timing circuit sometimes used in a low oil level indicator?
13. Explain the six major parts of an instrument cluster.
14. An electronic speedometer uses the _____ _____ _____ to power the speedo head instead of a conventional standard, metal _____.
15. The _____ _____, also called _____ _____, reacts to signals from sensor and other computers to drive the digital displays and CRT if used.

ASE CERTIFICATION—TYPE QUESTIONS

1. Technician A says some retractable headlight doors are vacuum operated. Technician B says some retractable headlight doors are electrically operated. Who is right?
   (A) A only. (C) Both A and B.
   (B) B only. (D) Neither A nor B.
2. While discussing the operation of automotive headlight switches, Technician A says a rheostat is used in certain headlight switches for dimming the instrument panel lamps. Technician B says a rheostat is used in certain headlight switches to control voltage to the high beam bulbs. Who is right?
   (A) A only. (C) Both A and B.
   (B) B only. (D) Neither A nor B.
3. Technician A says vehicles equipped with only two conventional sealed beam headlights use "number 1" headlamps. Technician B says all sealed beam headlamps have two filaments. Who is right?
   (A) A only. (C) Both A and B.
   (B) B only. (D) Neither A nor B.
4. Technician A says a halogen headlamp draws 45 percent more current than a conventional sealed beam headlamp. Technician B says a halogen headlamp increases light output by approximately 25 percent. Who is right?
   (A) A only. (C) Both A and B.
   (B) B only. (D) Neither A nor B.
5. The component used to cause the turnlight bulbs to flash on and off is the:
   (A) blinker. (C) controller.
   (B) flasher. (D) turn relay.
6. Technician A says an automotive brake light switch is normally located on or near the brake pedal. Technician B says the pressure switch used to trigger the brake warning light is usually located in the brake lines. Who is right?
   (A) A only. (C) Both A and B.
   (B) B only. (D) Neither A nor B.
7. Technician A says that bimetal dash gauges are used on modern passenger cars. Technician B says that magnetic coil dash gauges are used on modern passenger cars. Who is right?
   (A) A only. (C) Both A and B.
   (B) B only. (D) Neither A nor B.
8. While discussing the operation of an electronic speedometer, Technician A says this type of speedometer uses a conventional speedometer cable. Technician B says this type of speedometer reacts to electrical signals from the vehicle speed sensor. Who is right?
   (A) A only. (C) Both A and B.
   (B) B only. (D) Neither A nor B.
9. Technician A says an automotive instrumentation computer receives information from vehicle sensors to operate the digital dash displays. Technician B says an instrumentation computer receives information from other computers to operate the digital dash displays. Who is right?
   (A) A only. (C) Both A and B.
   (B) B only. (D) Neither A nor B.
10. Technician A says switching sensors are normally used to activate a voice alert system. Technician B says a voice alert system uses an electronic circuit to drive a speaker. Who is right?
    (A) A only. (C) Both A and B.
    (B) B only. (D) Neither A nor B.

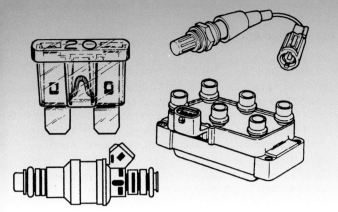

Chapter 18

Wiper and Horn Systems

After studying this chapter, you will be able to:
* *Explain the major parts of a windshield wiper system.*
* *Describe how a windshield wiper system operates.*
* *Summarize the operation and parts of a typical windshield washer system.*
* *Compare variations in wiper-washer systems.*
* *Sketch a basic wiper-washer circuit.*
* *Explain the operation of a horn circuit.*
* *Describe the construction of a horn.*
* *Sketch a basic horn circuit.*
* *Summarize a typical theft deterrent system.*

Windshield wiper, washer, and horn systems have not changed too much over the years and most cars have similar systems. This makes the study of windshield wiper and horn systems fairly simple.

This chapter will describe the general construction and operation of typical windshield wiper, windshield washer, and horn systems. The chapter will also review a typical theft deterrent system. This will give you the knowledge needed to be able to refer to and use a service manual when servicing these systems.

WINDSHIELD WIPER SYSTEM

A *windshield wiper system* uses an electric motor and linkage setup to power the wiper blades. The major parts of a windshield wiper system include the parts shown in Fig. 18-1.

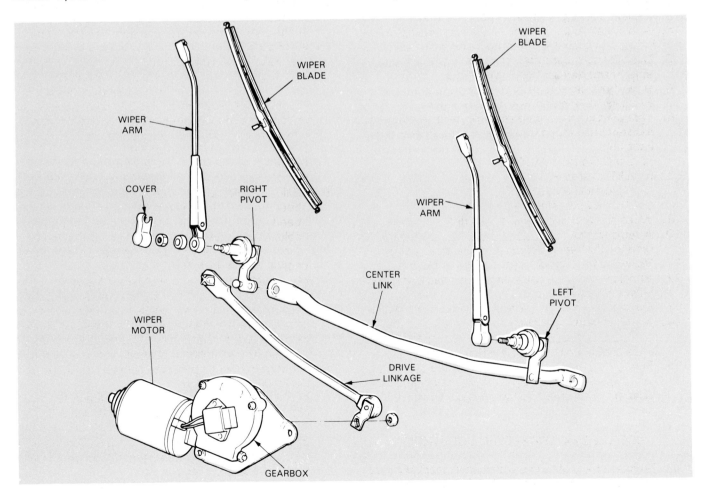

Fig. 18-1. Study the basic parts of this windshield wiper system.   (Nissan)

1. WIPER MOTOR (small DC motor for producing power to move wiper linkage and arms).
2. WIPER GEARBOX (housing and set of gears that change motor armature rotation into a back and forth motion).
3. DRIVE ARM (linkage that transfers reciprocating motion from gearbox to wiper pivot).
4. WIPER PIVOT (lever arms that transfer motion from linkage to wiper arms).
5. CENTER LINK (arm that connects two wiper pivots).
6. WIPER ARM (metal framework that holds and supports wiper blade).
7. WIPER BLADE (synthetic rubber blade that squeegees water off of windshield glass).

Wiper operation

When the driver closes the wiper switch, current flows to the wiper motor. The motor armature spins and turns the worm gear on the end of the armature shaft. The worm gear engages and turns a larger output gear. This produces a gear reduction and increases turning force.

A drive arm or shaft is connected to the gearbox output gear. Since its connection point is to one side of the gear axis, a back and forth motion is produced as the gear revolves, Fig. 18-2.

The drive arm connects to and drives the wiper linkage. The linkage connects to the wiper pivots. The pivots attach to and move the wiper arms across the windshield. The wiper arms support the rubber blades as they slide over the glass.

Wiper motor construction

An exploded view of a typical wiper motor is shown in Fig. 18-3. Study the part relationships.

The wiper motor is a small DC motor using permanent magnets as the field. Small brushes feed current into the armature. The worm gear is usually machined on the end of the armature shaft, and it is metal. Sealed bearings or bushings support and allow rotation of the armature.

The output gears are frequently made of plastic.

The wiper motor gearbox bolts to one end of the motor or it can enclose most of the motor. The gearbox housing holds the output gear into mesh with the worm gear. Sometimes, several gears are used to further increase gear reduction. Heavy grease is normally used to lubricate the gearbox.

Rubber grommets are commonly used where the motor assembly bolts to the car. They allow for slight motor movement on its mount during wiper operation. They also reduce the transfer of noise into the passenger compartment. See Fig. 18-3.

Note that this wiper motor assembly uses a printed circuit board to provide the delayed wiping action.

A *park switch* is normally located on the gearbox assembly. When the driver turns off the wipers, the park switch causes the gear mechanism to lower the blades to the bottom of the windshield. It does this by engaging a *park switch actuator,* Fig. 18-3.

WINDSHIELD WASHER SYSTEM

A *windshield washer system* uses a small electric, mechanical, or manual pump to force solution onto the windshield. Modern systems use either an electric motor or mechanical type pump. Older cars use a manual bellows type pump.

The parts of a typical washer system are shown in Fig. 18-4 and they include:
1. WASHER FLUID RESERVOIR (plastic container for holding washer solution and sometimes electric pump assembly).
2. WASHER PUMP (rotary or reciprocating pump mounted in reservoir or on wiper motor assembly).
3. WASHER HOSE (small rubber hose for carrying fluid from reservoir to windshield).
4. WASHER NOZZLES (small metal or plastic spray outlets for directing fluid across windshield).
5. WASHER SWITCH (switch that activates electric or mechanical pump to force fluid through system).

The trend is to use a small electric pump in the bottom of the fluid reservoir. A filter is installed on the inlet to the pump to keep out debris. A second strainer is over the fill opening on the reservoir to also keep debris out of the system, Fig. 18-5.

Fig. 18-6 shows a rear window wiper and washer system. Note how a long hose runs from the engine compartment to the rear glass. A check valve is used in the hose to keep fluid from draining out of the lines when not in use.

Some rear window washer systems have a separate reservoir mounted in the rear of the car. It is similar in operation to the windshield washer setup discussed earlier.

Washer pump construction

The *electric motor washer pump* is usually an impeller type pump. The small DC motor spins an impeller or fanlike blade. The resulting centrifugal force throws the fluid outward and pressurizes it. This makes the fluid flow through the system.

A cutaway view of an electric motor washer pump is in Fig. 18-7. Study its construction.

A *mechanical washer pump* uses the reciprocating

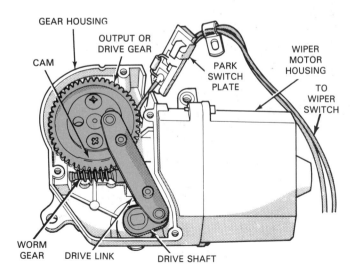

Fig. 18-2. Wiper motor has worm gear on armature shaft. Worm gear turns larger output gear to produce gear reduction. Drive link is pinned to output gear. It is pushed back and forth as gear revolves. Drive shaft transfers motion to wiper linkage. (Chrysler)

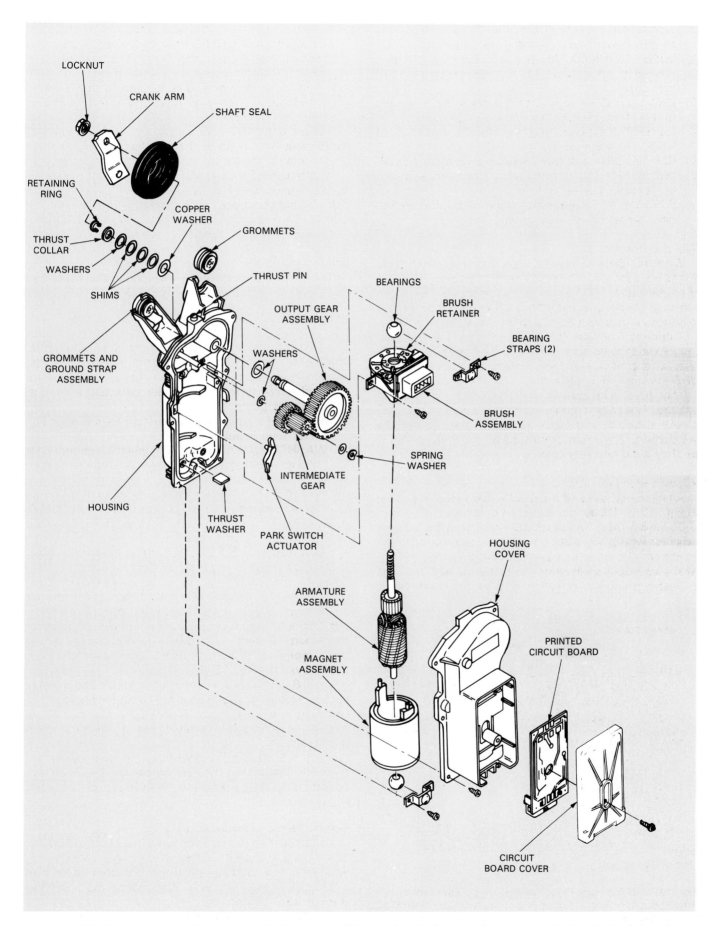

Fig. 18-3. Exploded view shows parts of wiper motor. Note park switch, reduction gears, and printed circuit board. (General Motors)

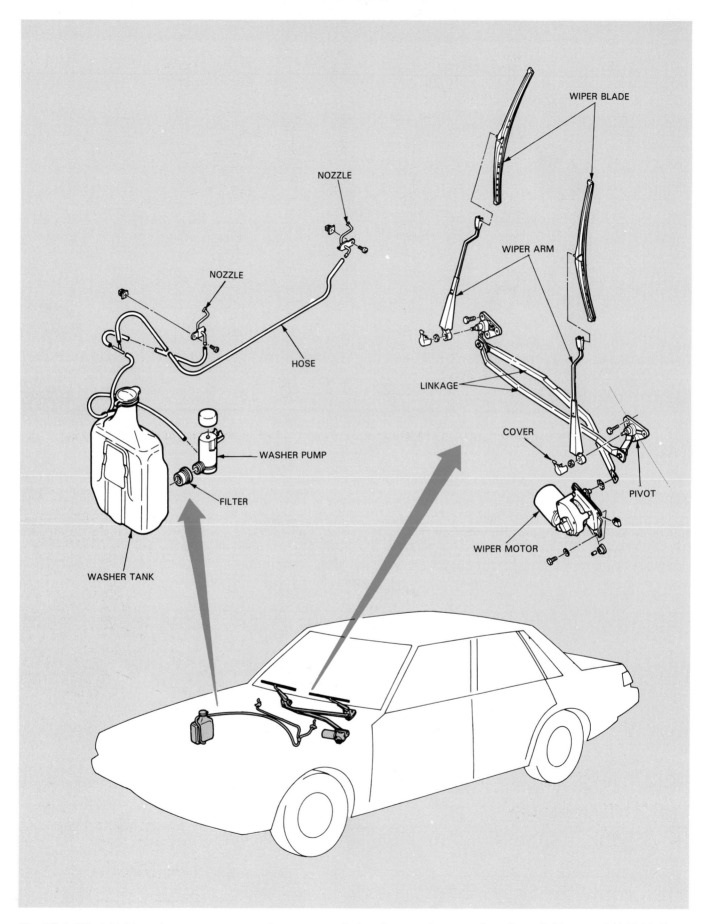

Fig. 18-4. Windshield washer system commonly uses a small electric pump in reservoir to force fluid onto windshield. Note other components. (Nissan)

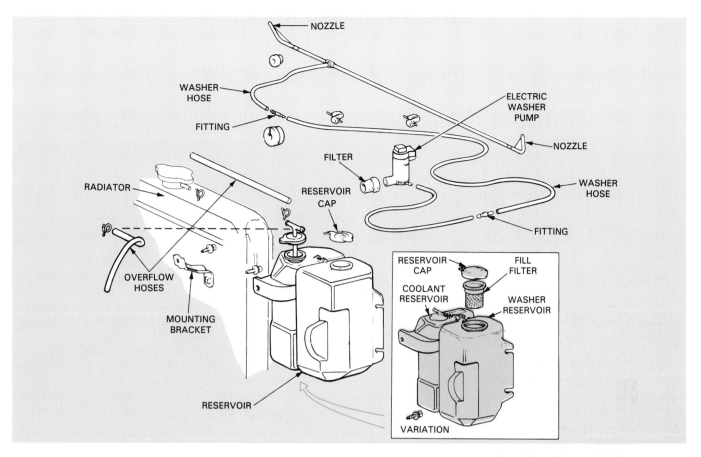

Fig. 18-5. Filters are usually provided at inlet to washer pump and over fill hole in top of reservoir. (Toyota)

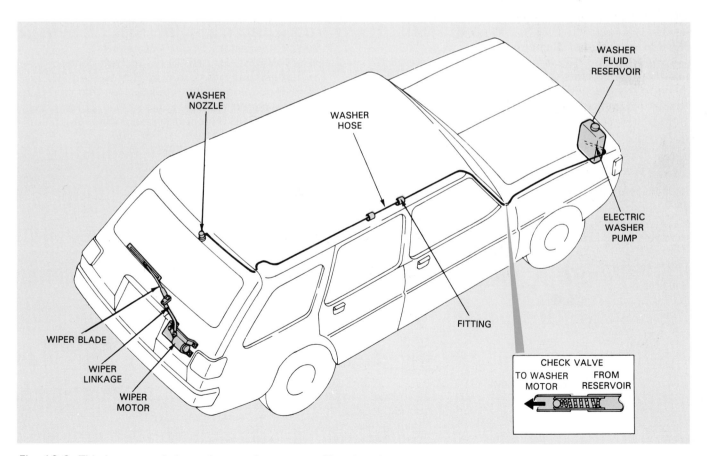

Fig. 18-6. This is a rear window wiper-washer system. Note long hose that runs from reservoir to rear nozzle. Check valve keeps fluid from draining out of long hose when not in use. (Chrysler)

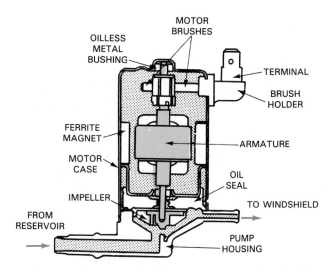

Fig. 18-7. Cutaway shows internal components of typical electric washer motor pump. Armature spins impeller. Impeller blade then forces fluid out of reservoir and through system.

motion provided by the wiper motor. This type pump is mounted on the wiper motor so that cam action in the gearbox acts on the pump mechanism. A back and forth motion is produced to move the pump's diaphragm in and out. Check valves in the pump use this motion to force fluid through the hoses and nozzles.

Two views of a mechanical or reciprocating type washer pump are illustrated in Fig. 18-8. Note the action of the diaphragm and check valves. It is an older, less common type of washer pump.

Wiper-washer circuit diagram

A *wiper-washer circuit diagram* shows how all of the electrical components connect. It may be needed when trying to troubleshoot electrical problems in the wiper-washer system.

Fig. 18-9 is a typical example of a wiper-washer circuit. Study how the switches and other components are wired into the circuit.

Pulse wiper action

Most new cars have a pulse or delay wiper feature. It commonly uses a variable resistor to control the delay action. The variable resistor controls how fast a capacitor is electrically charged.

For example, when the variable resistor knob is turned to high resistance (long delay), the current through the circuit is reduced, Fig. 18-9. This requires more time for the circuit capacitor to charge up. After the delay, the capacitor charges enough to fire the electronic control circuit or a relay. Then, the wiper motor turns on and the wipers move across the windshield one time.

If the control knob is turned to the lower resistance position (less delay), more current can flow to the capacitor. Less time is needed to charge the capacitor and fire the electronic control circuit or a relay. Less delay is provided between each wiper sweep.

A *programmable windshield wiper system* allows the driver to select the exact interval between wiper blade movements. To program most systems for intermittent wiper operation, the driver simply holds the wiper button in for the amount of time desired between wiper movements.

HORN SYSTEM

The *horn system* uses a coil-operated diaphragm to produce sound waves and an audible sound. The horn system is simple; it consists of:

1. FUSE or CIRCUIT BREAKER (electrical safety device that protects horn circuit from shorts).
2. HORN WIRING HARNESS (wires that connect fuse to harness and horns to horn button switch).
3. HORNS (diaphragm-operated devices that vibrate to produce sound waves).
4. HORN SWITCH (steering wheel or steering column-

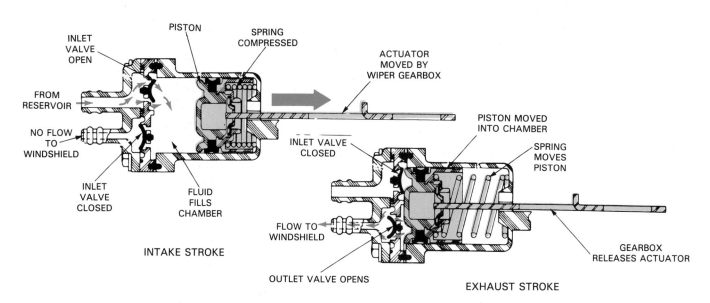

Fig. 18-8. Note action of less common mechanical washer pump. It uses action of wiper motor to move actuator. Actuator then flexes diaphram to produce pumping action. Spring is used to produce pumping force. Motor action simply compresses spring and fills chamber with fluid. (General Motors)

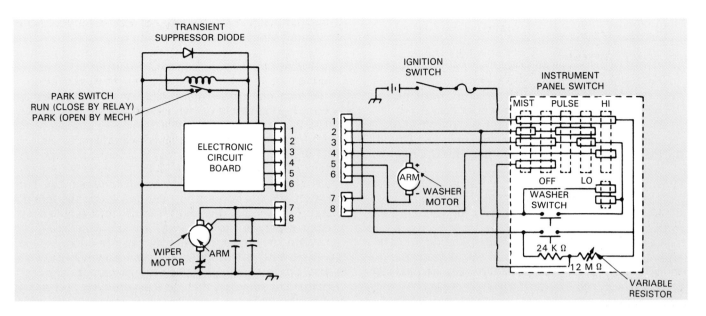

Fig. 18-9. This is a circuit drawing for a typical wiper-washer system with an intermittent wiper feature. Variable resistor can be used to control length of each pause before each wiper sweep. Variable resistor controls how fast capacitor charges up before firing electronic circuit that actuates wipers. (General Motors)

mounted switch for completing horn circuit).

Fig. 18-10 shows a basic horn system. Note how power is fed to the horns by the fuse. Power is present at the horns and in the harness whenever the ignition switch is turned on. The horns switch grounds the circuit to activate the horns.

When the driver presses the horn button, the wire leading from the horns is grounded. This causes current to flow through the fuse and horns. The resistance in the horn coils limits how much current flows into ground.

When the driver releases the horn button, a spring pushes the switch back open. This breaks or disconnects the ground circuit. No current can then flow through the horns and they stop sounding.

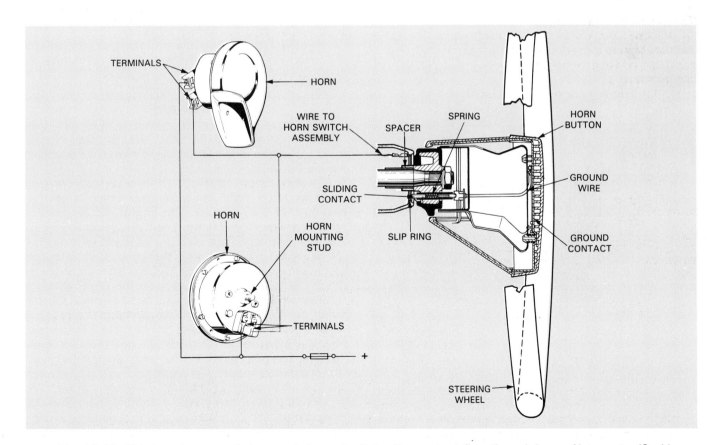

Fig. 18-10. This horn button switch grounds horn circuit to allow current flow through horns. Note parts. (Saab)

Horn construction

A cutaway view of a typical horn is given in Fig. 18-11. It is made up of the following parts:

1. HORN COIL (set of windings that produce magnetic field when energized by current flow).
2. CONTACTS (breaker points that open and close to control current flow through horn coil).
3. DIAPHRAGM (flexible membrane in horn that moves back and forth to produce air waves and sound).
4. PLUNGER (metal core that is attracted by magnetic field of coil windings).
5. WIRE TERMINAL (connector for making electrical connection with wiring harness).
6. OUTLET (opening in horn housing for directing sound to front of car).

When the driver presses the horn button, current flow enters the wire terminal and horn coil. A magnetic field forms around the coil. The field attracts and pulls the plunger into the coil. Since the plunger is attached to the diaphragm, the diaphragm is flexed back toward the coil.

With enough movement, the edge of the plunger touches one of the contact point arms. This pushes the contacts open and interrupts the current flow through the coil. Without current, the magnetic field collapses and the diaphragm snaps or flexes back into its normal position.

Once the diaphragm and plunger move back, the contacts reclose. This reenergizes the coil and the diaphragm

is again pulled back toward the coil. The process is repeated rapidly and the diaphragm vibrates back and forth in the horn housing. The resulting vibration set up in the surrounding air can be heared as a "honking" sound.

A *tone adjustment screw* is normally provided for changing the sound of the horn. Shown in Fig. 18-11, it can be turned to affect the action of the contact points and frequency of the diaphragm vibration.

Horn relay

A *horn relay* is sometimes used between the horn switch and the horns. It is used to reduce the amount of current flowing through the horn switch. A horn circuit using a relay is shown in Fig. 18-12.

When the driver presses the horn switch, a small current flow enters the horn relay. This energizes the small coil in the relay to close the relay contacts. Then, a larger current flows through the closed relay points and to the horns.

THEFT DETERRENT SYSTEM

Some *theft deterrent systems* use the horn circuit to warn if someone is tampering with the car. It is also illustrated in Fig. 18-12.

A *theft control module* is used to detect if someone is trying to get into and start the car. It can send out a current signal to a theft deterrent relay.

The *theft deterrent relay,* when energized, sends current to the horn relay. As a result, the horns sound if someone is trying to steal the car. Also note in the diagram that the theft deterrent relay can also be used to turn on the headlights. This can also help scare off a potential thief.

Remember that theft deterrent systems can vary with the car model and make. Refer to the shop manual for accurate wiring diagrams and descriptions.

SUMMARY

The windshield wiper system uses a small electric motor, gearbox, and linkage setup to move the wipers across the windshield glass.

The wiper motor is a small DC motor with a worm gear on its armature shaft. The worm gear turns a larger output gear in the gearbox. The wiper motor gearbox mounts on the wiper motor. It contains gears and shafts that change rotating motion into a back and forth motion.

The wiper linkage transfers the wiper gearbox motion to the wiper arms and wiper blades. The wiper pivots direct the motion of the linkage to the wiper arms.

Most windshield washer systems use a small electric pump to force fluid through the system. The pump is often mounted in the bottom of the washer fluid reservoir. Rubber hose carries the solution to the windshield nozzles. The nozzles direct the spray across the glass.

A few cars use a mechanical, reciprocating type windshield washer pump. It mounts on the wiper motor. The wiper motor gearbox moves an actuator arm. The arm motion then acts on a diaphragm to produce a pumping action. Check valves control flow through this type of pump.

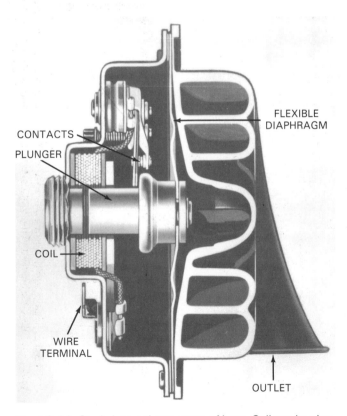

CONTACTS
PLUNGER
COIL
WIRE TERMINAL
FLEXIBLE DIAPHRAGM
OUTLET

Fig. 18-11. Study internal structrure of horn. Coil can be electrically energized to attract plunger magnetically. Plunger and diaphragm are then pulled toward coil. With enough movement, edge of plunger opens contact points. This breaks current flow through coil and diaphragm snaps back away from coil. This back and forth motion happens fast enough to make honking sound. (Deere & Co.)

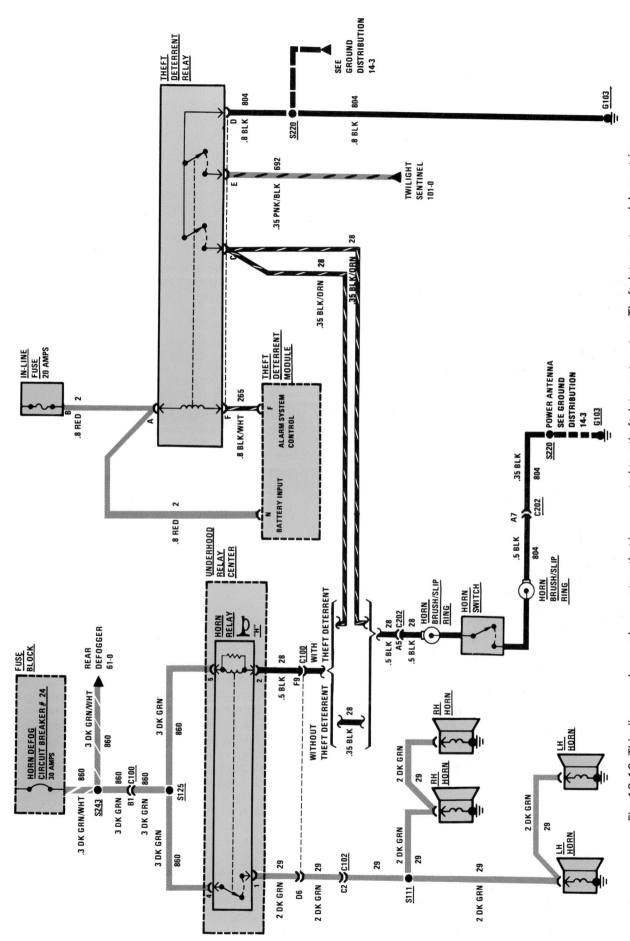

Fig. 18-12. This diagram shows a horn system that is connected to a theft deterrent system. Theft deterrent module can trigger deterrent relay if triggered. This will cause relay to activate horns through horn relay. Deterrent relay also turns on headlights of car. (Cadillac)

323

A pulse wiper action is usually provided by a variable resistor knob on the steering column or dash. When the resistor is set for high ohms, only a small current can flow into a circuit capacitor. It then takes more time for the capacitor to charge up and fire a control circuit or relay. This provides more wiper action delay. Turning the variable resistor to low ohms allows for more rapid capacitor charging and less delay.

The horn system uses a steering wheel or steering column switch to energize the horns. The horn uses a coil and contacts to move a diaphragm back and forth. A horn relay is sometimes used between the horn switch and horns. Some theft deterrent systems use a control unit to sound the horns if someone tampers with the car.

KNOW THESE TERMS

Wiper motor, Wiper gearbox, Drive arm, Wiper pivot, Wiper arm, Wiper blade, Park switch, Washer fluid reservoir, Washer pump, Washer hose, Washer nozzles, Washer switch, Electric washer pump, Mechanical washer pump, Wiper variable resistor, Programmable windshield wiper system, Horn system, Horn switch, Horn coil, Horn contacts, Horn diaphragm, Horn plunger, Tone adjustment screw, Horn relay, Theft control module, Theft control relay.

REVIEW QUESTIONS—CHAPTER 18

1. How does the wiper motor move the wiper blades across the windshield?
2. List and explain the seven major parts of a windshield wiper system.
3. A _____ _____ is used to make the wiper motor gearbox lower the wipers to the bottom of the windshield when not in use.
4. List and explain the five major parts of a windshield washer system.
5. The mechanical washer pump is the most common type used on present-day automobiles. True or false?
6. Where are most washer pumps located?
   a. On the wiper motor.
   b. In-line with the washer hose.
   c. In the bottom of the reservoir.
   d. On top of the reservoir.
7. Explain the operation of a typical wiper delay or pulse wiper system.
8. Most horn circuits feed voltage to the horns through a solenoid. True or false?
9. How does a horn operate?
10. Describe a theft deterrent system that uses the horns to scare off potential thieves.

ASE CERTIFICATION–TYPE QUESTIONS

1. All of the following are considered basic wiper system components *except:*
   (A) wiper motor. (C) washer pump.
   (B) drive arm. (D) wiper gearbox.
2. Technician A says a wiper motor worm gear is normally made of plastic and bolted to the armature shaft. Technician B says a wiper motor worm gear meshes with the output gear. Who is right?
   (A) A only. (C) Both A and B.
   (B) B only. (D) Neither A nor B.
3. The wiper system component that transfers motion from the gearbox to the wiper pivot is the:
   (A) drive arm. (C) drive link.
   (B) center link. (D) output gear.
4. Technician A says an impeller-type windshield washer pump is often located in the fluid reservoir. Technician B says a mechanical washer pump is mounted on the wiper motor. Who is right?
   (A) A only. (C) Both A and B.
   (B) B only. (D) Neither A nor B.
5. The wiper delay feature on modern automobiles is usually controlled by a:
   (A) transistor. (C) variable resistor.
   (B) diode. (D) relay.
6. Technician A says some automobiles use a fuse to protect the horn circuit from shorts. Technician B says some automobiles use a circuit breaker to protect the horn circuit from shorts. Who is right?
   (A) A only. (C) Both A and B.
   (B) B only. (D) Neither A nor B.
7. Technician A says when an automotive horn button is pressed, the wire leading from the horn touches a positive terminal. Technician B says power is normally present in the horn's wiring harness, even when the ignition switch is in the "off" position. Who is right?
   (A) A only. (C) Both A and B.
   (B) B only. (D) Neither A nor B.
8. All of the following are basic parts of an automotive horn *except:*
   (A) horn coil. (C) flexible diaphragm.
   (B) bridge rectifier. (D) plunger.
9. Technician A says turning a horn's tone adjustment screw affects the action of the contact points. Technician B says turning a tone adjustment screw changes the frequency of diaphragm vibration. Who is right?
   (A) A only. (C) Both A and B.
   (B) B only. (D) Neither A nor B.
10. A relay is sometimes used in an automotive horn circuit to reduce the amount of power flowing through the:
   (A) horn contacts. (C) wire terminals.
   (B) horn switch. (D) windings.

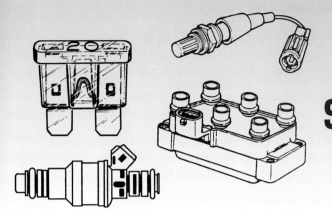

Chapter 19

Seat, Window, Lock, Mirror, and Sound Systems

After studying this chapter, you will be able to:
- *Summarize the parts of a power window system.*
- *Explain how power windows operate.*
- *Describe a power door lock system.*
- *Summarize the operation of power seats.*
- *Explain how memory seat positions are attained.*
- *Summarize the operation of a keyless entry system.*
- *Describe the construction and operation of an electric rear view mirror system.*
- *Explain the operation of a radio.*
- *List and describe the major parts of a sound system.*
- *Compare AM and FM signals.*
- *Explain tape player operation.*
- *Summarize compact disc operation.*

Today, cars are commonly ordered with a wide array of options. These include power seats, power windows, power rear view mirrors, power antennas, and exotic sound systems. To be a competent electronic technician, you must be able to understand how these systems operate and are constructed. This chapter will summarize the principles of these optional systems. It will prepare you for later chapters that cover diagnosis and repair.

POWER WINDOWS

A *power window* uses a small DC motor to move the window glass up and down. Fig. 19-1 shows the basic layout of a typical system. The major parts of a power window system include:

1. WINDOW SWITCH (spring-loaded, normally-off switch that controls current flow to window motors).
2. WINDOW MOTOR (reversible electric motor that drives gearbox).
3. WINDOW MOTOR GEARBOX (gear mechanism mounted on window motor for increasing torque applied to window regulator gear).
4. WINDOW REGULATOR (gear and lever mechanism for sliding window up and down in its track). Look at Fig. 19-2. It shows a window regulator.
5. WINDOW MOTOR HARNESS (wiring that connects switches to window motors).

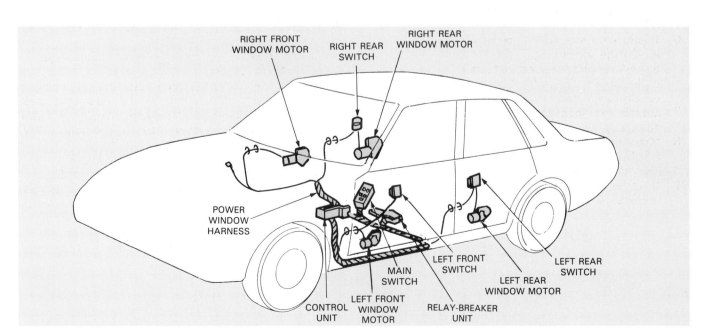

Fig. 19-1. Power window system uses small, reversible, electric motors in each door. Switches control current flow to motors. This system also uses a control unit and circuit breakers. (Subaru)

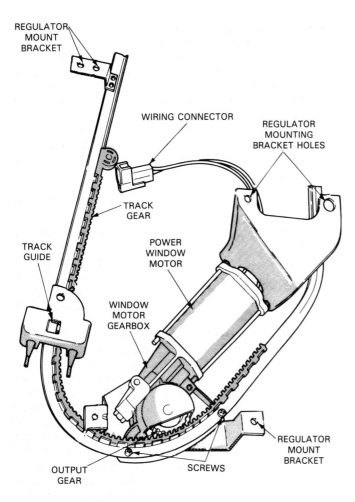

REGULATOR MOUNT BRACKET

WIRING CONNECTOR

REGULATOR MOUNTING BRACKET HOLES

TRACK GEAR

TRACK GUIDE

POWER WINDOW MOTOR

WINDOW MOTOR GEARBOX

OUTPUT GEAR

SCREWS

REGULATOR MOUNT BRACKET

Fig. 19-2. Power window has electric motor and motor gearbox that drive window regulator. Gearbox produces gear reduction for increasing torque. Small output gear can then act upon regulator track gear to move window up or down. (Chrysler)

6. BREAKER POINTS (small points in window motors that protect motor from damage if switch is held too long after full glass travel).

The window switches are normally fed current whenever the ignition switch is on. A fuse or circuit breaker protects the power window circuit from shorts and excess current draw.

When the driver presses a window switch, current flows to one of the window motors. The motor armature spins a worm gear. The worm gear then acts on a larger gear in the motor gearbox. A small output gear transfers this high torque to a large toothed gear or track on the window regulator. See Fig. 19-2.

If the window switch is pushed the other way, current flow through the window motor is reversed. This causes the armature to spin the other way and the window moves in the opposite direction.

POWER DOOR LOCKS

Power door locks use switches to activate solenoids inside each door to move the latch mechanisms. Designs vary but the principles of most systems are similar. Fig. 19-3 shows a power door lock mechanism.

The fundamental parts of a door lock system are:
1. LOCK SWITCHES (key-operated and interior switches that send current to door actuators).
2. ACTUATORS (solenoids or motors that convert current flow into motion for acting upon door linkage and latches).
3. LATCH ASSEMBLY (mechanical mechanism that reacts to linkage rod movement to lock or unlock door).
4. LINKAGE RODS (small steel rods that transfer motion from actuator, or manual lever to latch mechanism).
5. LOCK HARNESS (wiring that connects power to switches and to actuators or solenoids).

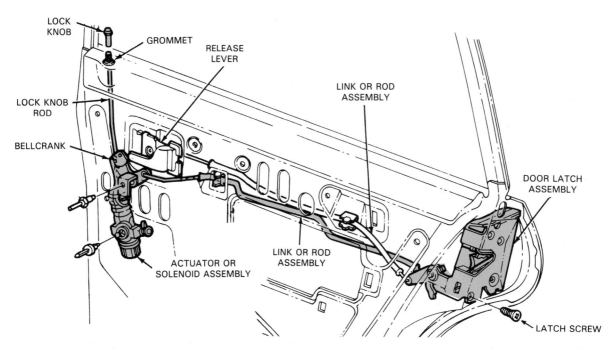

LOCK KNOB

GROMMET

RELEASE LEVER

LINK OR ROD ASSEMBLY

LOCK KNOB ROD

BELLCRANK

ACTUATOR OR SOLENOID ASSEMBLY

LINK OR ROD ASSEMBLY

DOOR LATCH ASSEMBLY

LATCH SCREW

Fig. 19-3. Internal view of door shows solenoid for activating door locks. Current flow from switch can be reversed to make plunger move in or out to lock or unlock doors. (Ford)

6. KEY ACTIVATED SWITCH (sometimes used in door, key activated to energize solenoids and unlock or lock doors).

When the driver activates the door key, current flows through the switch and to the door actuators. The actuators are usually small solenoids. Current flows through the small coils in the solenoids. This forms a magnetic field in the solenoids that attracts their metal plungers. The plungers are pulled into the field and movement is produced. Since the plungers are connected to the door linkage rods, the lock mechanisms on the door latches are locked or unlocked.

Keyless entry system

A *keyless entry system* uses an input keypad to send electrical data to a small processor or computer. The keypad is mounted in the door and usually has five numbers. Pressing the numbers in the correct sequence will send a valid code to the processor for unlocking the doors. If the wrong number sequence is used, the processor will ignore the electrical signals from the keypad and keep the doors locked. The processor sends current to the door solenoids only when the keypad is pressed in the right sequence.

Fig. 19-4 shows a typical keyless entry system. Note that it also has an actuator or solenoid for the trunk latch. Pressing an extra number after the unlock code will usually make the processor energize the trunk latch release solenoid.

POWER SEATS

A *power seat* uses small electric motors to drive a seat transmission that repositions the seat on its track. An exploded view of a power seat is given in Fig. 19-5. Note the parts and part relationships.

The major parts of a power seat system are:
1. POWER SEAT SWITCHES (switches on seat or door panel that control current flow to seat motors).
2. SEAT MOTORS (small, reversible DC motors that provide power to move seats into different positions).
3. SEAT DRIVE CABLES (steel cables that transfer motion from seat motors to seat transmission).
4. SEAT TRANSMISSION (gearbox that changes rotating motion from motors and cables into linear motion for the seats).
5. SEAT TRACK (metal guides that allow seat to move on the base of the floor mount assembly).

Several switches are normally provided to operate the power seat motors. One may provide for back and forth movement on the tracks by energizing the correct motor. Another switch can raise and lower the seat by energizing a different motor. Another switch or another position in a multi-position switch can energize a seat tilting motor.

Power seat designs vary. Some have a lumbar adjustment that pushes out on the lower back of the seat to serve as a pillow. It uses motor and lever action.

Some seat systems have a seat memory feature that will return the seat to a previously programmed position. The system is connected to a *seat memory module* which is a small computer that can "remember" previous seat positions. *Seat position sensors* feed data to the module. The module can store the sensor input. The module can then send current to each motor to reposition the seat properly. Refer to a service manual for more specific information on the particular seat memory system.

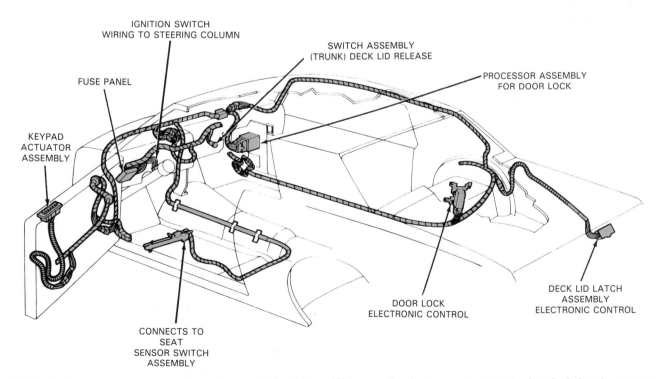

Fig. 19-4. Keyless entry system has keypad on outside of door. When number buttons are pressed, electrical signals are sent to processor. If correct number sequence is pressed, processor will send current to door solenoids to unlock doors. Keypad and processor can also be used to unlock trunk and other doors. (Ford)

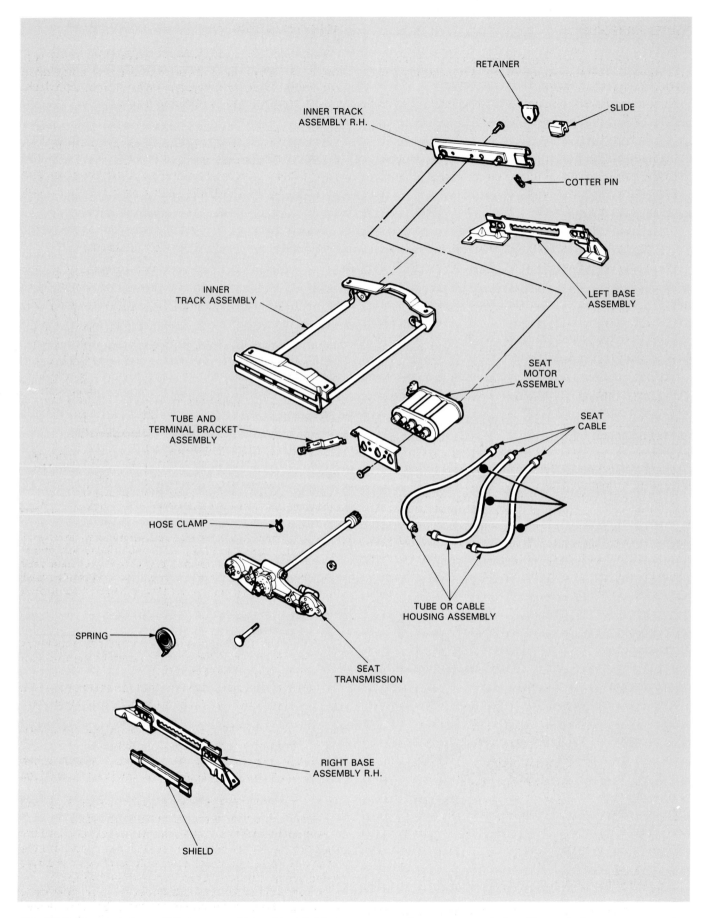

Fig. 19-5. Power seats use DC motors to drive cables. Cables are connected to seat transmission. Transmission converts rotating motion of motors into motion for moving seat into various positions. (Ford)

POWER MIRRORS

Power mirrors use tiny electric motors to pivot the rear view mirrors. A multi-position switch activates the small motors inside the mirrors.

A phantom view of a power rear view mirror is shown in Fig. 19-6. Study its construction.

The basic parts of a power rear view mirror system include:

1. MIRROR SWITCH (multi-position switch that can send current to either mirror motor and reverse current flow through motors).
2. VERTICAL CONTROL MOTOR (small, reversible, DC motor that actuates up and down swivel of rear view mirror glass).
3. HORIZONTAL CONTROL MOTOR (small, reversible, DC motor that actuates side to side swivel of mirror glass).
4. GEAR REDUCTION (small gear and screw mechanisms that increase output torque and convert motor rotation into linear action).
5. MIRROR (reflective coated glass that is attached to swivel base and to output plungers of mirror motors).
6. MIRROR HOUSING (metal or plastic housing that encloses parts of rear view mirror).
7. POWER MIRROR HARNESS (wiring that connects switch to mirror motors).

The power mirror switch is usually a ''joy stick'' or four-position type switch. It can be moved up and down and from side to side. The contacts in the switch connect and disconnect to control current flow to the mirror motors to correspond to switch movement.

For example, if the power mirror switch is pushed up, current flows to the vertical control motor. It could make the motor armature spin in a direction that would unscrew its plunger, Fig. 19-6. The plunger might push on the bottom of the mirror glass to raise the angle of rear sight. The same is true if the switch is pushed down or left and right.

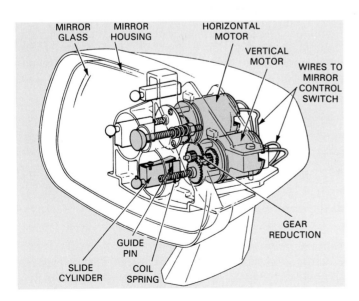

Fig. 19-6. Power rear view mirror commonly uses two, tiny electric motors to rotate gear and screw mechanism. Screws can be turned to tilt mirror glass into various angles. (Chrysler)

SOUND SYSTEMS

A car *sound system* commonly uses a radio to power one or more speakers. New cars also come equipped with more exotic sound systems with stereo, tape deck, power booster, and multiple speakers.

Radio system

The fundamental parts of a ratio system are illustrated in Fig. 19-7 and they include:

1. ANTENNA (metal shaft or wire in window glass that picks up electromagnetic waves sent from radio station).

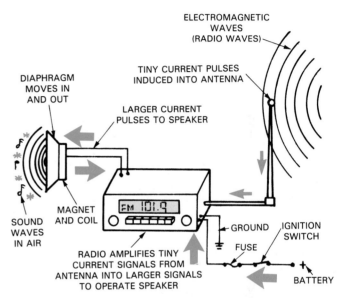

Fig. 19-7. Radio station broadcasts an electromagnetic signal. Antenna can pick up these signals through electromagnetic induction. Voltage signal flows through coaxial antenna cable and into radio. Radio circuitry can process and amply broadcast signal. Stronger current signals are then sent out to drive speakers.

2. ANTENNA CABLE (coaxial cable that protects weak electrical signal induced into system by electromagetic radio waves), Fig. 19-8.
3. RADIO (receiver-amplifier that strengthens weak radio wave signals and electronically processes them to drive speakers).
4. SPEAKER WIRES (small gauge wires that carry pulsing current signals to speaker coils).
5. SPEAKERS (coil-operated diaphragms that move back and forth to cause vibrations in air to produce sound).
6. RADIO POWER SUPPLY CIRCUIT (wiring, fuse, and other parts that feed DC current to radio).

A modern *radio* contains complex electronic circuits that receive and amplify the radio signal to operate the speakers. It also contains a *tuner* that allows the driver to adjust to different radio frequencies (stations).

An *antenna* picks up the broadcast signal and feeds it through the antenna lead to the radio. Some antennas are a very fine piece of wire in the windshield glass. Other antennas are a metal mast (rod) mounted in the car body.

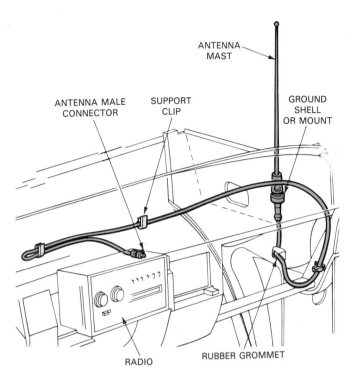

Fig. 19-8. Conventional mast type antenna bolts to car body. Coaxial antenna cable is used to protect weak signal as it flows into radio. Male plug on cable slides into female socket on back of radio. (Chrysler)

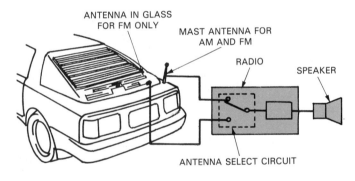

Fig. 19-9. This car uses both a mast antenna and wire type antenna in glass. Radio has internal circuit that will switch to the antenna receiving the strongest signal. Sometimes mast will have better reception and other times wire will have better signal strength. (Toyota)

See Figs. 19-8 and 19-9.

A *power antenna* uses a small electric motor and gear mechanism to raise and lower the antenna mast. Fig. 19-10 shows power antenna construction.

A *speaker* uses a permanent magnet and a coil of wire mounted on a flexible diaphragm to convert electricity into motion and sound, Fig. 19-11. When current passes through the coil of wire, the resulting magnetic field pulls the coil and diaphragm toward the permanent magnet. Rapid movement of the speaker diaphragm causes pressure waves in the air. We hear these pressure waves as sound.

The speakers may be mounted in the doors, dash, behind the rear seat, or inside the passenger seats. AM radios normally have only one speaker in the top of the dash. FM stereo radios have two, four, six, or more speakers. See Fig. 19-12.

AM and FM radio

There are two types of radio signals: AM (amplitude modulating) and FM (frequency modulating), Fig. 19-13.

An *AM radio* is designed to pick up a radio signal that varies in amplitude (strength). It operates on a frequency of 530 to 1610 kilohertz (kHz) which gives it a longer broadcasting range than FM.

An *FM radio* is designed to receive a radio signal that varies in frequency (fluctuating speed). The FM band is a higher frequency, from 88 to 108 megahertz (MHz). Since the FM radio wave is not reflected off the ionosphere (upper atmosphere), it has a relatively short broadcasting range (approximately 35 miles or 56 kilometers). FM radio is capable of producing stereo (stereophonic or multi-dimensional) sound. A *stereo* uses at least two speakers and has different sounds coming from each speaker.

Tape player

A *tape player* may be incorporated into the radio. A cassette tape player uses a small tape cartridge.

An *audio tape* is coated with iron oxide so that it can be magnetically charged for producing sound, music, and voice simulation. The tape player has *tape heads* that convert the magnetic charges on the tape into voltage signals as the tape slides over the heads.

A small drive motor rotates the tape and moves the tape over the player heads. The electronic circuitry in the radio-tape player can amplify the weak voltage signals from the tape player heads to drive the speakers.

Power booster

A *power booster* is simply an electronic amplifier. It increases the current output of the radio or tape player for driving the speakers more efficiently. The power output of a radio alone may not be enough to power several speakers. The power transistors can be overdriven if the volume is turned to high and sound distortion can result. The power transistors in a radio may not be able to handle the current needed with the volume set high or with high wattage (power) speakers.

A power booster can be connected between the radio and speakers. It contains more powerful transistors to drive speakers without distortion. Distortion results when the speaker output is not a good reproduction of the original input. See Fig. 19-14.

Sound systems vary considerably with the make and model car. Refer to the service manual for a more detailed description.

Compact disc player

A *compact disc* uses a special plastic surface to store data for producing high quality sound reproduction. The *compact disc player*, also called a *disc changer,* is used to rotate and read the digital data on the compact disc.

The compact disc is manufactured so that it has reflective and nonreflective cells on its surface. This is similar

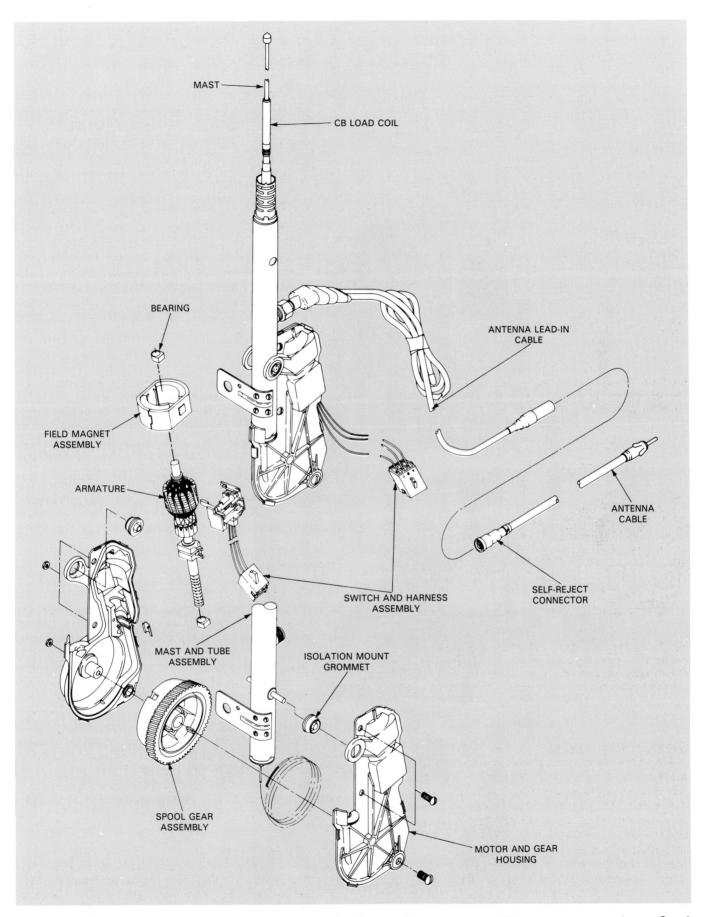

MAST

CB LOAD COIL

BEARING

ANTENNA LEAD-IN
CABLE

FIELD MAGNET
ASSEMBLY

ARMATURE

ANTENNA
CABLE

SWITCH AND HARNESS
ASSEMBLY

SELF-REJECT
CONNECTOR

MAST AND TUBE
ASSEMBLY

ISOLATION MOUNT
GROMMET

SPOOL GEAR
ASSEMBLY

MOTOR AND GEAR
HOUSING

Fig. 19-10. Note construction of typical power antenna. Small motor drives worm gear. Worm gear turns spool gear. Spool gear can move antenna up and down. (General Motors)

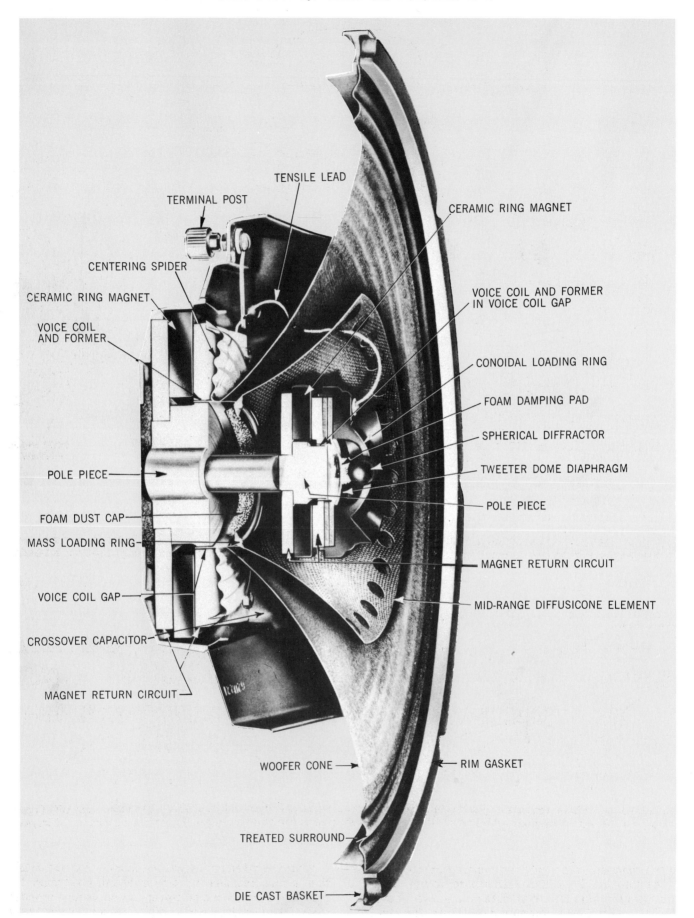

TENSILE LEAD

TERMINAL POST

CERAMIC RING MAGNET

CENTERING SPIDER

VOICE COIL AND FORMER
IN VOICE COIL GAP

CERAMIC RING MAGNET

VOICE COIL
AND FORMER

CONOIDAL LOADING RING

FOAM DAMPING PAD

SPHERICAL DIFFRACTOR

POLE PIECE

TWEETER DOME DIAPHRAGM

POLE PIECE

FOAM DUST CAP

MASS LOADING RING

MAGNET RETURN CIRCUIT

VOICE COIL GAP

MID-RANGE DIFFUSICONE ELEMENT

CROSSOVER CAPACITOR

MAGNET RETURN CIRCUIT

WOOFER CONE

RIM GASKET

TREATED SURROUND

DIE CAST BASKET

Fig. 19-11. Study construction of a typical speaker. It uses coil to produce magnetic field. Field attracts metal plunger to move diaphragm in and out. Diaphragm causes vibrations in surrounding air that we hear as sound. (Universal Sound)

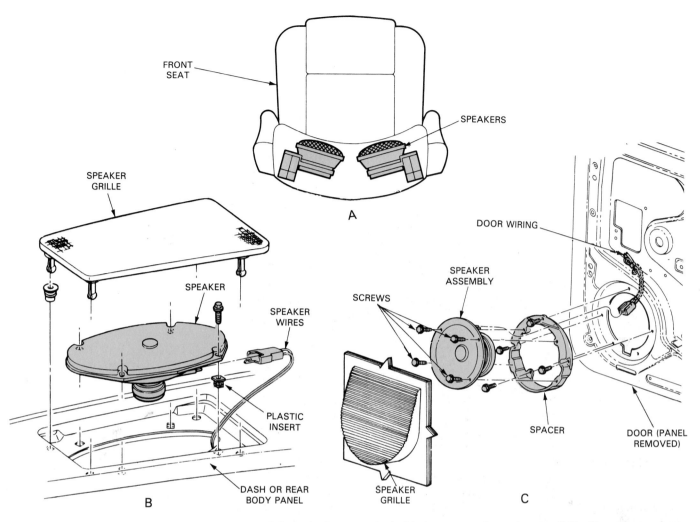

Fig. 19-12. Speakers can be mounted on top of dash, in door panels, behind rear seat, in seats, etc. Grille fits over speakers for appearance and speaker protection. A—Seat speakers. B—Dash or rear speaker type mounting. C—Door speaker. (General Motors)

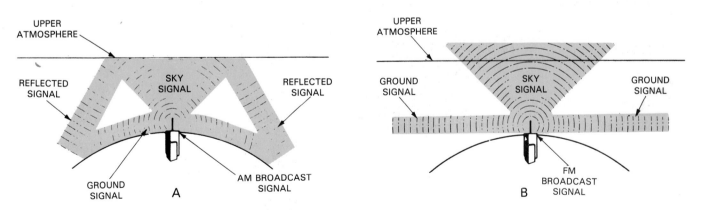

Fig. 19-13. A—AM reception is long distance because broadcast signal follows curvature of earth and also bounces off of upper atmosphere. B—FM signal does not travel as far. It does not follow earth curvature or bounce off upper atmosphere. (Chrysler)

to the magnetic tape that has charged bands.

The compact disc player uses a motor to turn the disc and a laser to read the digital data on the disc. The electronic circuitry in the compact disc player changes the digital data into analog outputs for driving the stereo speakers.

A compact disc can reproduce sound more accurately than a tape because the data is digital. Integrated circuits in the compact disc player can accurately process the input disc data and a digital-to-analog converter outputs a fluctuating voltage for operating the speakers.

Sometimes, a motor head or a changer for the com-

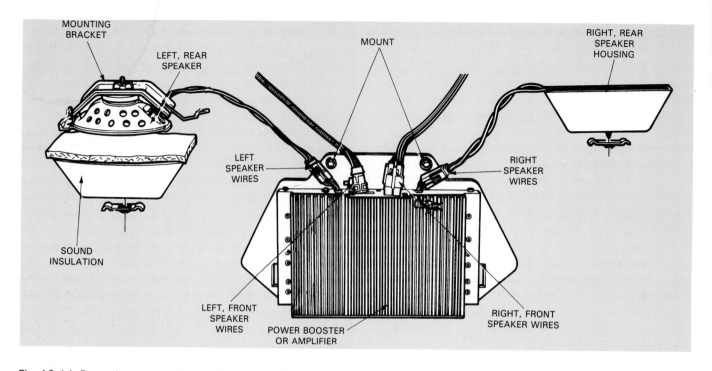

Fig. 19-14. Power booster can be used between radio or tape player and speakers. It simply strengthens current pulses to speakers and helps reduce distortion. (General Motors)

pact disc is mounted in the trunk of the car. Some can automatically play several compact discs like a record changer. The control head for the compact disc system is mounted in the car dash or it can be hand-held.

SUMMARY

Modern cars are frequently ordered with numerous options and most are electrically powered. As an electronic technician, you must comprehend the operating principles of these devices.

Power windows use small electric motors to turn a gearbox. The gearbox transfers motion to the window regulator. The window regulator slides the window glass up and down as motor direction is reversed. Small points are commonly used in the window motors to protect the motors from overheating damage.

Power door locks use solenoids to activate the door latches. A key or interior switch can energize the solenoids to unlock or lock the doors. Many trunk lock systems use the same principle.

A keyless entry system has a keypad that is connected to a small processor. The keys on the keypad must be pressed in a specific sequence for the processor to energize the door lock solenoids.

Power seats use DC motors under the front seats. The motors drive a seat transmission that changes rotating motion into back and forth, up and down, or tilting motion for seat adjustment. The seat moves on tracks. Multi-position switches control seat motor direction.

A seat memory system uses position sensors and a small computer. The sensors feed data to the computer. Then, the computer can use its memory to store previous seat positions for each driver of the car.

Power mirrors use tiny, reversible electric motors to aim the rear view mirrors. A joy or four-position toggle switch is usually used to feed current to the mirror motors. One motor provides for vertical mirror adjustment and the other horizontal mirror adjustment. A gear and screw mechanism changes motor rotation into linear movement for tilting the mirrors.

A radio system uses an antenna and coaxial cable to feed electromagnetic radio waves into the system. The antenna can be a post or wire type in the window glass. The radio processes and amplifies the radio broadcast signal. The amplified signal is then sent out to the speakers. The speakers change the electrical pulses into motion for acting upon the surrounding air. We hear these air vibrations as sound.

An audio tape is magnetically charged in a pattern that represents sound. The tape player heads are able to sense and change these magnetic charges into voltage signals. The radio amplifier is used to strengthen these voltage signals enough to drive the speakers.

A power booster can be used to amplify the radio output signals for multiple speakers. When several high wattage speakers are used or when increased volume is desired without distortion, a booster can be wired between the radio and speakers.

Distortion is when the input signal (radio wave signal, signal from tape, etc.) is not the same as the output signal fed to the speakers. It is usually due to overdriving the power transistors in the radio or tape player.

KNOW THESE TERMS

Window switch, Window motor, Window regulator, Window motor gearbox, Window motor points, Door lock switches, Door lock actuator, Door latch, Door linkage rods, Keyless entry system, Power seat switches, Seat motors, Seat drive cables, Seat transmission,

Seat track, Seat memory module, Seat position sensors, Mirror switch, Vertical mirror motor, Horizontal mirror motor, Antenna, Antenna cable, Radio, Speaker wires, Speakers, Grille, AM, FM, Tape player, Audio tape, Tape heads, Compact disc, Power booster.

REVIEW QUESTIONS—CHAPTER 19

1. List and explain the six major parts of a power window system.
2. If the driver holds the power window switch down too long, what will usually happen?
   a. Strip motor gearbox.
   b. Open motor contact points.
   c. Damage window regulator.
   d. Nothing.
3. How does a power door lock system operate?
4. Describe a typical keyless entry system.
5. List and explain the five major parts of a power seat system.
6. How does a seat memory system function?
7. List and describe the seven major parts of a power mirror system.
8. List and explain the six major parts of a radio system.
9. This signal varies in frequency.
   a. Seat memory sensor signal.
   b. AM radio signal.
   c. FM radio signal.
   d. All of the above.
   e. None of the above.
10. How does an audio tape and compact disc player work?

ASE CERTIFICATION—TYPE QUESTIONS

1. Technician A says an automobile's power window system uses reversible electric motors to move the glass up and down. Technician B says breaker points are used to protect a power window system's motors from an overload. Who is right?
   (A) A only.   (C) Both A and B.
   (B) B only.   (D) Neither A nor B.
2. Technician A says window regulators are used in an automotive power window system to slide each window up and down in its track. Technician B says window regulators are used in an automotive power window system to regulate current flow to each window switch. Who is right?
   (A) A only.   (C) Both A and B.
   (B) B only.   (D) Neither A nor B.

3. Technician A says relays are normally used in a power door lock system to operate the latch mechanisms. Technician B says solenoids are normally used in a power door lock system to send current to the door actuators. Who is right?
   (A) A only.   (C) Both A and B.
   (B) B only.   (D) Neither A nor B.
4. Technician A says a "keypad" is normally a basic component of a keyless entry system. Technician B says a "processor" is normally a basic component of a keyless entry system. Who is right?
   (A) A only.   (C) Both A and B.
   (B) B only.   (D) Neither A nor B.
5. All of the following are basic components of an automotive power seat system except:
   (A) seat transmission.   (C) seat drive cables.
   (B) seat regulator.   (D) seat track.
6. Technician A says an automotive power mirror system's horizontal control motor operates the up-and-down movement of the mirror glass. Technician B says an automotive power mirror system's gear reduction decreases output torque. Who is right?
   (A) A only.   (C) Both A and B.
   (B) B only.   (D) Neither A nor B.
7. Technician A says some automotive radio antennas are located in the windshield glass. Technician B says some automotive radio antennas are located in the automobile's body. Who is right?
   (A) A only.   (C) Both A and B.
   (B) B only.   (D) Neither A nor B.
8. Technician A says an AM radio has a longer broadcasting range than an FM radio. Technician B says FM radio signals vary in frequency. Who is right?
   (A) A only.   (C) Both A and B.
   (B) B only.   (D) Neither A nor B.
9. Technician A says audio tape is coated with iron oxide. Technician B says a tape player's heads convert magnetic charges to voltage signals. Who is right?
   (A) A only.   (C) Both A and B.
   (B) B only.   (D) Neither A nor B.
10. Technician A says a compact disc has reflective and nonreflective cells on its surface. Technician B says a compact disc player's circuitry changes the analog data produced by the disc into digital outputs for driving the speakers. Who is right?
   (A) A only.   (C) Both A and B.
   (B) B only.   (D) Neither A nor B.

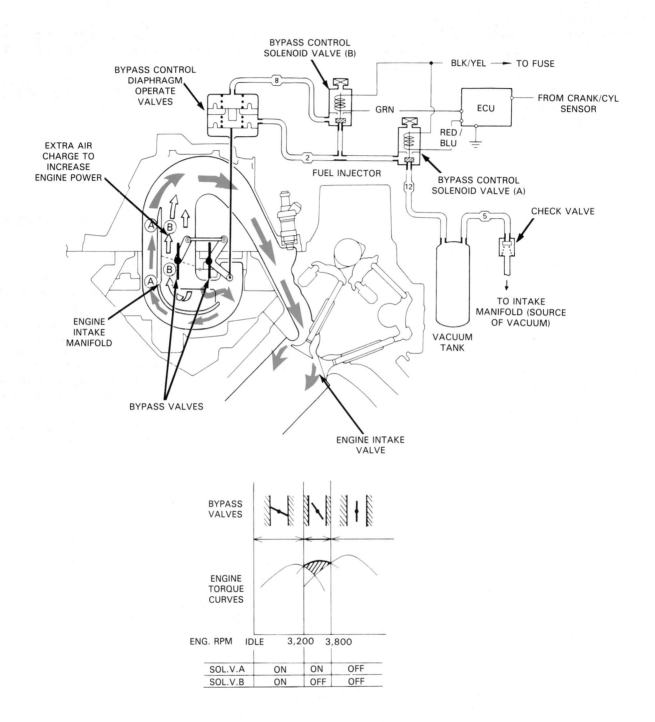

BYPASS CONTROL
SOLENOID VALVE (B)

BYPASS CONTROL
DIAPHRAGM
OPERATE
VALVES

BLK/YEL — TO FUSE

FROM CRANK/CYL
SENSOR

ECU

GRN

RED /
BLU

EXTRA AIR
CHARGE TO
INCREASE
ENGINE POWER

FUEL INJECTOR

BYPASS CONTROL
SOLENOID VALVE (A)

CHECK VALVE

ENGINE
INTAKE
MANIFOLD

TO INTAKE
MANIFOLD (SOURCE
OF VACUUM)

VACUUM
TANK

BYPASS VALVES

ENGINE INTAKE
VALVE

BYPASS
VALVES

ENGINE
TORQUE
CURVES

ENG. RPM	IDLE	3,200	3,800
SOL.V.A	ON	ON	OFF
SOL.V.B	ON	OFF	OFF

An electronic control unit is used to operate bypass valves in this engine intake manifold. Crank angle sensor sends signal to computer showing engine speed. This allows ECU to keep bypass valves closed at lower engine rpm. The closed valves increase air velocity to increase fuel economy and combustion efficiency. At a preset engine rpm, computer energizes solenoids to provide vacuum to diaphragm which opens bypass valves. As the extra valves open, it increases engine power output. (Honda)

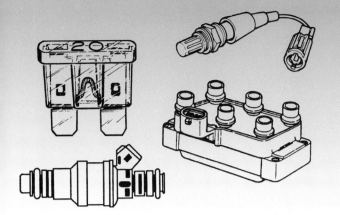

Chapter 20

Other Electronic Systems

After studying this chapter, you will be able to:
• Explain the major parts of an anti-lock brake system.
• Summarize the operation of anti-lock brakes.
• Describe an electronic ride height control system.
• Explain an electronic shock absorber system.
• Summarize the parts and operation of an electronic climate control system.
• Explain the operation of a typical cruise control system.
• Describe the action and parts of an air bag system.
• Summarize the operation of an electronically controlled automatic transaxle.

This chapter will discuss anti-lock brakes, electronically controlled suspension systems, electronic climate control, and other systems not covered in previous chapters. As you will learn, electronics is being used almost everywhere on the modern car.

ANTI-LOCK BRAKE SYSTEM (ABS)

An *anti-lock brake system*, abbreviated *ABS*, uses wheel speed sensors, a computer, and an electro-hydraulic unit to prevent tire skid during hard braking. If a tire locks up and skids on the road surface, braking distance can increase and steering control can be lost. The anti-lock brake system improves driver and passenger safety by reducing stopping distances and increasing directional stability under panic stop conditions. Look at Fig. 20-1.

Fig. 20-2 shows the advantages of having ABS. With this example, one side of the road is very slippery and

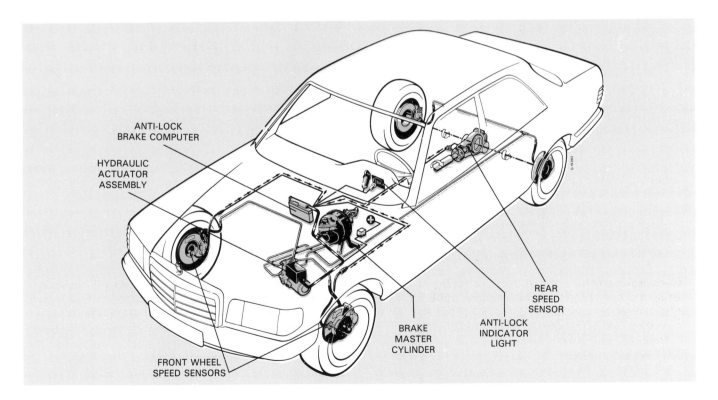

Fig. 20-1. ABS or anti-skid braking systems use these basic components. Wheel speed sensors send electrical signals to computer. Computer can then use hydraulic actuator to reduce brake fluid pressure to any wheel that slows down too much and is ready to skid. (Mercedes Benz)

337

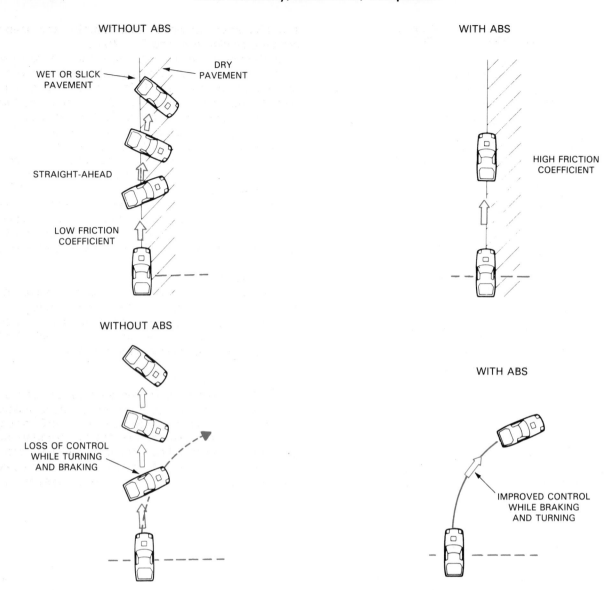

Fig. 20-2. Without ABS, tires can lock up and lose adhesion with road. This can cause a loss of control during hard braking or when braking and trying to steer. Even if one side of road is slick, brakes will be cycled so that none of the tires skid. Maximum braking results when tires are just about ready to skid; traction is reduced if tires lock up.

the other side is dry. This poses a problem if a panic stop is required. Without ABS, the car would tend to skid to the right because of higher tire adhesion on the right. With ABS, the car would still travel straight ahead with hard braking. The brake units would be cycled to prevent tire skid and a loss of control. Also note how the car can be steered while braking with ABS.

ABS components

Shown in Fig. 20-1, the major parts of an anti-lock braking system include:

1. WHEEL SPEED SENSORS (magnetic pickups for detecting rolling or rotating speed of each tire and wheel assembly).
2. SENSOR ROTOR (toothed wheel that rotates at same rpm as wheel and tire).
3. ELECTRONIC CONTROL UNIT (small computer or processor that uses sensor inputs to control hydraulic actuator).

4. HYDRAULIC ACTUATOR (solenoid-operated valve and electric pump mechanism for controlling how much hydraulic pressure is applied to each wheel brake cylinder).
5. INDICATOR LIGHT (dash light that informs driver of problem in ABS system).

Wheel speed sensors

The *wheel speed sensors* produce an AC type signal that corresponds to wheel and tire speed. These signals are fed into the anti-lock brake system computer.

Look at Fig. 20-3. It shows how one wheel speed sensor mounts in the car's steering knuckle assembly. The sensor tip is located next to the sensor rotor. Only a small air gap separates the sensor tip from the teeth on the sensor rotor. In this example, the sensor rotor is mounted on the back of the brake disc. A hex bolt and O-rings secure the sensor in the steering knuckle.

Wheel speed sensors can also mount on the axle shaft

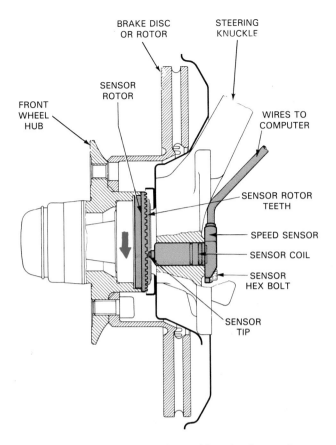

Fig. 20-3. Cutaway shows how this wheel speed sensor mounts in steering knuckle. Sensor tip is next to spinning sensor rotor. Teeth pass next to sensor tip. (Mercedes Benz)

and drive shaft. However, their function and operation are very similar. Refer to Fig. 20-4.

As the tire and wheel rotates, the sensor rotor spins next to the wheel speed sensor. As each tooth passes the sensor, the magnetic field around the sensor is affected. This induces a weak AC or alternating current signal in the wheel sensor coil. The frequency of this AC signal is dependent upon tire and wheel speed. The AC signal is used by the anti-lock brake system computer to check for tire skid. A rapid decrease in sensor AC signal frequency would indicate that a tire is starting to lock up and skid.

Note! The operation of a wheel speed sensor is similar to a crankshaft sensor and a magnetic pickup coil in an ignition system. Refer to the discussion of these sensors for more information on coil and trigger wheel operation.

ABS computer

The *ABS computer* uses wheel speed sensor inputs to control the operation of the hydraulic actuator. It is constructed and operates like the other computers or electronic control units discussed in this book. A photo of an ABS control module is in Fig. 20-5.

ABS hydraulic actuator

The *ABS hydraulic actuator* regulates the amount of fluid pressure applied to each wheel brake assembly during hard braking. It is controlled by the ABS computer. In an integrated system, the master cylinder-booster assembly is an integral part of the hydraulic actuator. In a non-integrated system, the hydraulic actuator does not contain the master cylinder-booster assembly. The

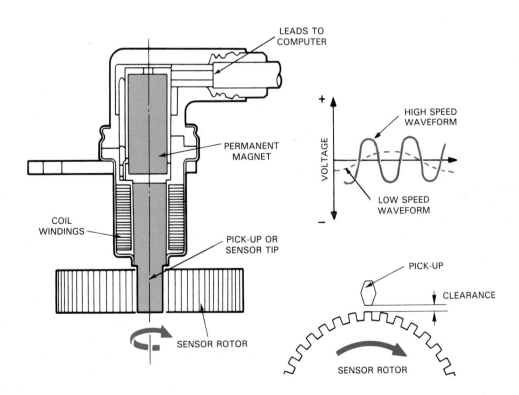

Fig. 20-4. Wheel speed sensor is simply a coil mounted around core. When teeth of sensor rotor pass sensor coil, an alternating voltage is induced into sensor coil and output wires to computer.

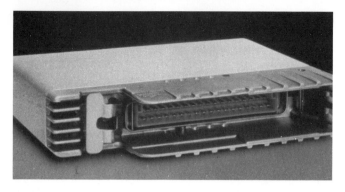

Fig. 20-5. This is an electronic control unit or computer for one ABS system. (General Motors)

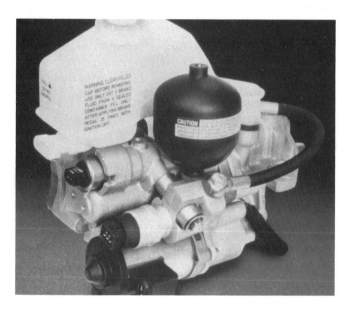

Fig. 20-6. Hydraulic actuator has solenoid-operated valves that can reduce pressure to each wheel brake assembly. It is frequently mounted on brake master cylinder assembly. (General Motors)

hydraulic actuator normally mounts in the engine compartment, Fig. 20-6.

An exploded view of an ABS hydraulic actuator is given in Fig. 20-7. Its major parts include:

1. FLUID RESERVOIR (container for holding extra supply of brake fluid).
2. SOLENOID VALVE BLOCK (coil-operated valves that control brake fluid flow to the wheel brake cylinders; they are contained in valve block assembly).
3. ACCUMULATOR (chamber for storing fluid under high pressure).
4. HYDRAULIC PUMP AND MOTOR (high pressure pump operated by small electric motor; they provide brake fluid pressure for system).
5. PRESSURE SWITCH (monitors system pressure and controls operation of electric motor for hydraulic pump).
6. MASTER CYLINDER-BOOSTER ASSEMBLY (conventional master cylinder with power assist for operating brakes under normal conditions).

ABS systems and hydraulic actuators vary with the specific make and model car. Another type hydraulic actuator

is illustrated in Fig. 20-8. It also uses a small electric motor to drive the high pressure pump. Note that it only has three solenoid valves. Two operate the front brakes and the other operates both rear brakes. The computer energizes the pump and valves using the relays mounted on the unit.

ABS operation

Refer to Fig. 20-9 as the operation of a typical ABS is summarized.

Under normal braking, the ABS system is not used. The master cylinder reacts to brake pedal movement. It sends fluid pressure out to each wheel cylinder normally. A proportioning valve is commonly used to reduce pressure to the rear brakes.

If the brakes are applied in a panic stop and one wheel begins to stop rotating, the ABS system activates. The wheel sensor on the slowing wheel would instantly send a slower AC pulsing signal to the computer. The computer would detect that this wheel is slowing down more than the others and is getting ready to slide or skid. The computer would then send an electrical current output to the correct solenoid on the hydraulic actuator assembly.

When current is sent to the solenoid, the solenoid closes a valve to limit the pressure to the brake unit with the slowing wheel. The computer will quickly cycle the current to the solenoid on and off to artifically "pump the brakes" to keep the tire from skidding and losing traction. It does this several times a second. When ABS takes over, the brake pedal will usually rise and vibrate slightly. This is due to the pressure entering the system from the accumulator and from the cycling of the solenoid valves. This is usually normal and will stop when the ABS system is no longer functioning.

If hydraulic pressure in the system drops below a specific point, the pressure switch closes and energizes the electric motor. This drives the pump to build pressure back up. Once pressure is normal, the pressure switch opens and the motor and pump shut off.

If an ABS component malfunctions, the computer will detect an abnormal condition. It will then light an ABS warning light in the dash and deactivate the ABS. The brake system will still function normally, but without the anti-lock feature.

ELECTRONIC HEIGHT CONTROL

An *electronic height control system* uses a height sensor to control the operation of a small electric air compressor. This type system is used on the rear of the car to compensate for loads placed in the trunk or when passengers fill the back seat. The basic parts of a typical electronic height control system are shown in Fig. 20-10. These parts include:

1. HEIGHT SENSOR (lever-operated switch that reacts to changes in car body height and suspension movement).
2. COMPRESSOR ASSEMBLY (electric motor-powered air pump that produces pressure for system).
3. PRESSURE LINES (air hoses that connect compressor with air shock absorbers).
4. AIR SHOCKS (air-filled shock absorbers that can act

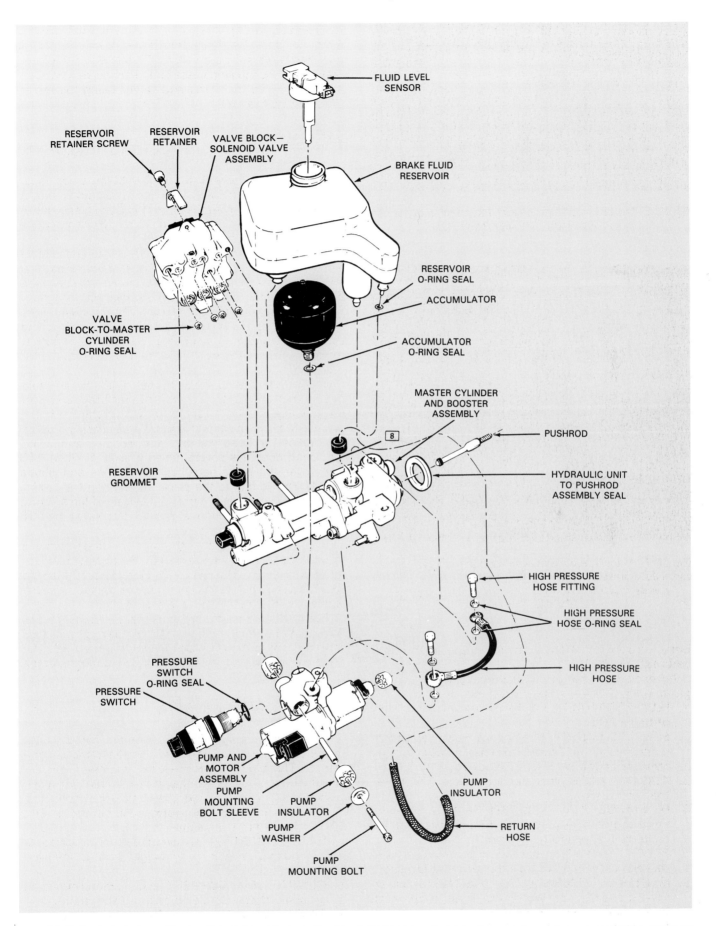

Fig. 20-7. Exploded view of hydraulic actuator shows valve block that holds solenoid valves, motor and pump assembly, pressure switch, and master cylinder assembly. (Cadillac)

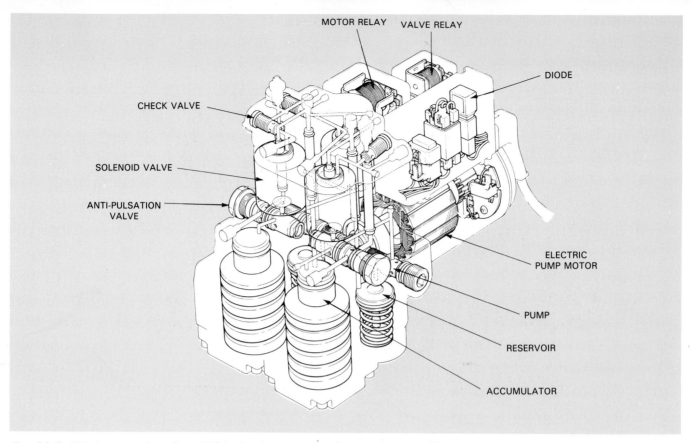

Fig. 20-8. This is a variation of an ABS hydraulic actuator. It also uses motor-driven pump to pressurize system and solenoid-operated valves to control pressure to each wheel brake assembly.

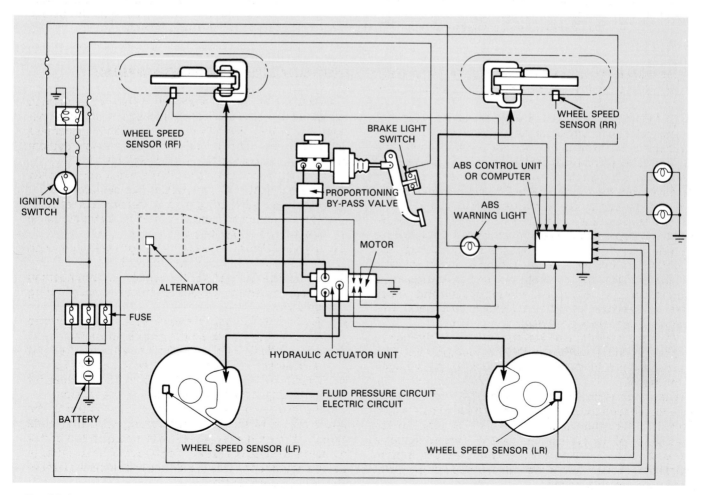

Fig. 20-9. Diagram shows arrangement of typical anti-lock brake system. Note how sensors feed data to computer. Computer can then operate hydraulic actuator when needed.

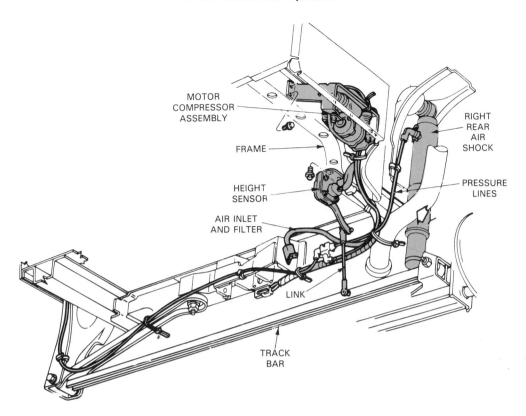

Fig. 20-10. Electronic height control system commonly uses an electric motor-driven compressor, height sensor, and air shocks to automatically maintain correct ride height. Sensor link moves sensor arm up and down with changes in ride height. Sensor can then turn on compressor or activate pressure release solenoid as needed. (Chrysler)

on suspension system to alter ride height of car).
5. SENSOR LINK (linkage rods that connect height sensor to suspension system).
6. SOLENOID VALVE (solenoid-operated air valve that can release air pressure from the system).

When the car body is at a normal or riding height, the electronic height control system is off. Air pressure in the shocks is adequate to keep the car body the correct distance from the road surface. The height sensor does not feed current to the compressor or solenoid.

If the trunk is loaded with heavy luggage for example, it will compress the rear air shocks. This will make the ride height too low. When the car is started, the height sensor will be activated by the action of the sensor link and the sensor switch closes to energize the compressor. The compressor motor turns on and pumps more air pressure into the rear shock absorbers. This extends the shocks and raises the car body.

When the specific ride height is reached, the height sensor switch opens to turn OFF the compressor. This restores the previous ride height, even with extra weight in the trunk.

When the weight is removed from the trunk, the car body would tend to rise. The height sensor switch is then moved in the other direction by the link. This closes another set of contacts in the switch. This energizes a pressure release solenoid valve. Air pressure is then expelled from the rear shocks until the body drops down to the correct ride height.

ELECTRONIC SHOCK ABSORBER SYSTEM

An *electronic shock absorber system* uses various vehicle sensors, a computer, and shock absorber actuators to control ride stiffness. It is designed to increase comfort and safety by matching suspension system action to driving conditions. See Fig. 20-11.

Although exact designs vary, the major components of a typical electronic shock absorber system are:
1. STEERING SENSOR (detects steering wheel rotational direction and speed to feed data about vehicle direction to computer).
2. BRAKE SENSOR (usually brake light switch is used to report when brakes are applied).
3. ACCELERATION SENSOR (usually throttle position sensor is used to detect when car is accelerating rapidly).
4. MODE SWITCH (dash switch that allows driver to input desired shock action or ride stiffness).
5. ELECTRONIC CONTROL UNIT (small computer that uses sensor inputs to control shock actuators).
6. SHOCK ACTUATORS (solenoid-operated valves for controlling fluid flow inside shock absorbers).

If the car is being driven on curving country roads, the driver might switch to a stiff setting with the mode switch. The computer would then energize the shock actuators to close or restrict the shock valves to increase dampening action. This would make the car ride more stiffly but corner better.

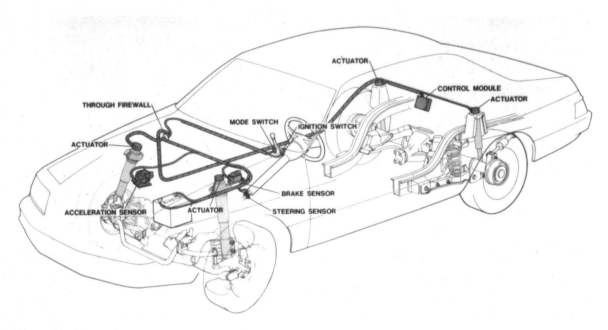

Fig. 20-11. Study parts in this electronic shock absorber or suspension control system. (Ford)

If driving on rough highways, the mode switch might be set to soft. The computer would then energize the shock actuators to open the valves more. This would soften the ride by allowing easier shock movement.

Under hard braking, the brake sensor would send a signal to the computer. The computer could then stiffen the shocks to prevent the front of the car from diving.

With rapid turning or cornering, the steering sensor could also signal the computer. The computer could then stiffen the shocks to prevent excess body roll or lean in turns. Look at Fig. 20-12.

Fig. 20-13 shows one type of shock actuator. Note how it uses a solenoid and small DC motor to act upon the shock absorber piston rod. The shock piston rod can be moved up or down to control fluid flow resistance and shock stiffness or dampening.

Some cars use air type shocks or air bags instead of hydraulic shock absorbers. The operation of this type system is similar.

One type of steering sensor is in Fig. 20-14. Note that it uses light emitting diodes, a slotted disc, and photo transistors. The slotted disc is connected to the steering shaft. It rotates with the steering wheel. As the disc openings pass between the LEDs and the photo tran-

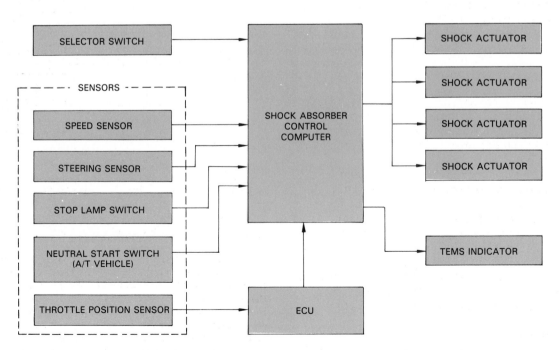

Fig. 20-12. Block diagram shows how various sensors feed electrical data to computer. Computer can then energize shock actuators to control ride stiffness and shock action. (Toyota)

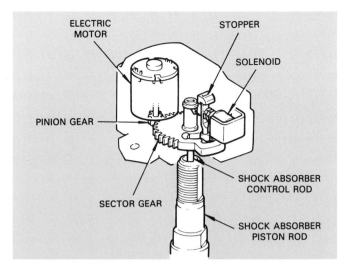

Fig. 20-13. This shock actuator uses small electric motor and solenoid to move shock piston rod in and out. Piston rod movement alters shock dampening action.

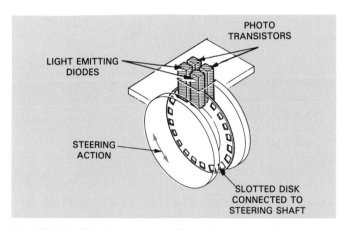

Fig. 20-14. This is one type of steering sensor. It uses two light emitting diodes and two photo transistors. Slotted disc rotates with steering wheel and steering shaft. As holes pass between LEDs and photo transistors, photo transistors are energized and produce electrical signals that represent steering action.

sistors, a signal is produced. The photo transistors produce a small voltage signal as they react to the light flashes from the disc rotation and LEDs. The computer uses this signal to detect steering direction and to control the shock system.

One type of electronic shock absorber system uses a *sonar* (soundwave) type sensor to detect actual road conditions. The sensor mounts at the front of the car.

The *sonar sensor* produces sound waves that bounce off the road and are deflected back into the sensor. The sensor action detects the time needed for the waves to bounce back into the sensor. If there is a dip in the road, the sensor can signal a different distance and signal the shock or suspension system computer. The computer can then adjust shock action for the road surface.

Active suspension system

An *active suspension system* uses hydraulic rams instead of conventional suspension system springs and shock absorbers. The hydraulic rams support the weight of the car and also react to the road surface and different driving conditions. An active suspension system is similar to an electronic shock absorber system but is more complex. See Fig. 20-15.

The active suspension system can theoretically eliminate most body movement as the car travels over small dips and bumps in the road. It can prevent body roll or even tilt the car body against a turn to improve handling. It can also prevent nose dive on braking and body squat on acceleration.

Basically, pressure sensors on each hydraulic ram are used as the main control for the system. They react to suspension system movement and send signals to the computer. The computer can then extend or retract each ram to match the road surface.

For example, if one side of the car travels over a bump in the road, the pressure sensors can instantly detect a rise in pressure inside the ram as the tire and wheel push up on the suspension and hydraulic ram. Instead of making the car body rise with spring action, the computer can release enough ram pressure to allow the suspension to move up over the bump without body movement.

Then, as the tire travels back down over the bump, the sensor detects a pressure drop in the ram and the computer can increase ram pressure so the tire follows the road surface.

An hydraulic pump provides pressure to operate the suspension system rams. Look at Fig. 20-15.

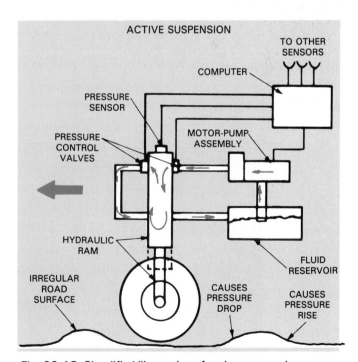

Fig. 20-15. Simplified illustration of active suspension system shows major components. Pressure sensor on hydraulic ram reacts to up and down movement of ram and resulting pressure changes. If pressure in ram rises from going over bump, sensor signals computer. Computer can quickly react to release ram pressure so suspension moves up with bump. As wheel travels down other side of bump, sensors make computer increase ram pressure so suspension travels back down to original road surface.

ELECTRONIC CLIMATE CONTROL

An *electronic climate control system* uses a computer or processor, sensors, and actuators to maintain a preset passenger compartment temperature. See Fig. 20-16. Although specific designs vary, you should understand the construction and operation of typical components.

The basic parts of an electronic climate control system include:

1. CONTROL PANEL (dash panel containing switches for programming processor).
2. DIGITAL DISPLAY (usually vacuum fluorescent display that shows temperature readouts).
3. POWER SUPPLY (electronic circuit that provides constant DC voltage to computer, and sometimes display or other components).
4. VACUUM ACTUATOR (actuator that uses computer signals to control vacuum supply to various vacuum diaphragms).
5. CONTROL MODULE (small electronic circuit that is sometimes used to control blower motor and air conditioning compressor clutch).
6. VACUUM DIAPHRAGMS (flexible vacuum-operated chambers that serve as output devices for moving airflow control doors).

ELECTRONIC CRUISE CONTROL SYSTEM

A modern *electronic cruise control system* uses a computer, sensors, and a throttle actuator to maintain vehicle speed when highway driving. The major parts of a typical system are in Fig. 20-17. These parts include:

1. POWER SWITCHES (feed current to computer to activate and ready system for operation).
2. CONTROL SWITCH (signals computer to maintain present vehicle speed when activated).
3. VEHICLE SPEED SENSOR (feeds pulsing signal into computer that represents velocity of car in mph or km/h).
4. CRUISE COMPUTER (uses input signals to control outputs to throttle actuator).

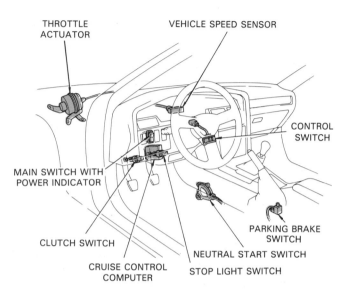

Fig. 20-17. Note basic parts of electronic cruise control system.

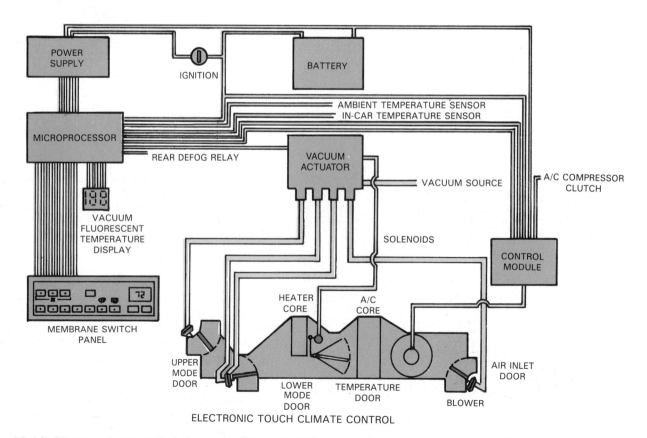

Fig. 20-16. Diagram shows typical electronic climate control system. Study part relationships. (General Motors)

5. THROTTLE ACTUATOR (physically moves engine throttle lever to control engine power and resulting vehicle speed).
6. BRAKE LIGHT SWITCH (stop light switch that signals computer to shut off cruise control when brakes are applied).
7. CLUTCH SWITCH (signals computer to deactivate cruise control when clutch pedal is depressed).
8. NEUTRAL SAFETY SWITCH (signals computer to shut off cruise when shift lever is moved out of drive to prevent engine racing.

When set on cruise using the power and control switches, the vehicle speed sensor feeds an AC type signal into the computer. The computer circuits use this signal to move throttle actuator back and forth to maintain same vehicle speed or sensor frequency.

For example, if the car starts to go up a hill, the vehicle speed will start to drop. The computer will detect a slower frequency signal from the speed sensor. It can then move the throttle actuator for more engine power to keep the car traveling at the preset speed. The opposite occurs if the car starts down a hill.

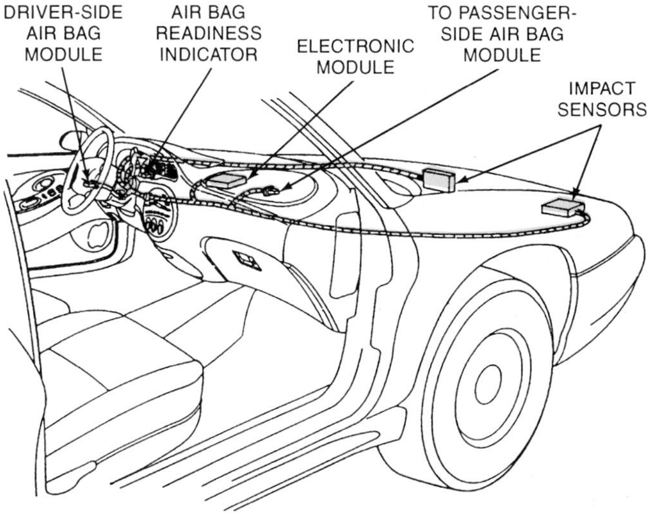

AIR BAG SYSTEMS

An *air bag system* uses an inflatable nylon bag to help protect the driver and, in most cases, the front passengers during a frontal collision. See Figs. 20-18 and 20-19. The typical air bag system consists of the following basic components:

1. IMPACT SENSORS (normally open inertia switches that close when vehicle is involved in a severe frontal collision, Fig. 20-20).
2. SAFING SENSOR (fail-safe sensor located in passenger compartment that helps prevent accidental or unnecessary air bag deployment).
3. ELECTRONIC MODULE (computer that controls air bag deployment, monitors system operation, and contains a backup power source).
4. AIR BAG MODULE (unit mounted in center of steering wheel that contains the igniter, gas-generating material, and air bag).

Fig. 20-19. Air bag is inside steering wheel. If safing sensor and one or more impact sensors are activated by front end collision, electronic module deploys air bag to protect driver from injury. (Ford)

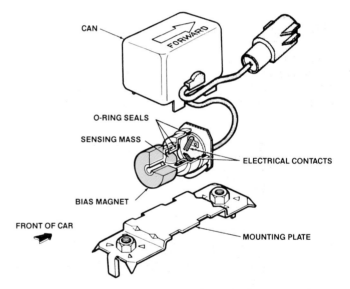

Fig. 20-20. Typical air bag impact sensor. When vehicle is involved in a severe frontal collision, sensing mass breaks away from bias magnet and strikes electrical contacts. This causes electrical contacts to close, activating air bag system. Note that sensing mass and electrical contacts are often gold plated to improve conductivity. (Ford)

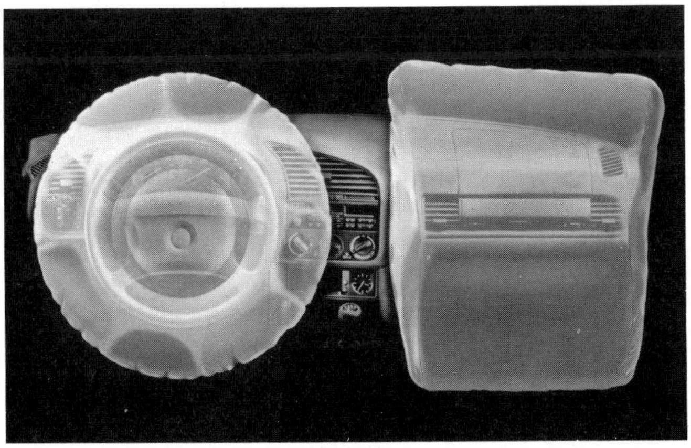

When a vehicle is involved in a frontal collision that is severe enough to cause the safing sensor and at least one impact sensor to close, the electronic module triggers the igniter in the air bag module. The igniter produces heat, which activates the gas-generating material. The resulting gas fills the air bag in about 50 milliseconds. This is fast enough to prevent the driver (and passengers) from striking the steering wheel or the dashboard during the collision. After deployment, the air bag will deflate rapidly through large vents in the back of the unit.

Fig. 20-18. Deployed driver- and passenger-side air bags. These units protect driver and front passengers during frontal collisions. (BMW)

Warn your customers that seat belts must be worn in vehicles equipped with air bag systems. The bag deploys at over 200 mph and may cause unnecessary injury if occupants are not wearing seat belts.

In vehicles equipped with passenger-side air bags, children and small adults should ride in the back seat whenever possible. The force of air bag deployment can seriously injure these individuals.

AUTOMATIC ROLLOVER-PROTECTION SYSTEMS

Because convertibles provide relatively little occupant protection in the event of a rollover, a few manufacturers are installing automatic rollover-protection systems in their convertible vehicles. An *automatic rollover-protection system* deploys a roll bar or reinforced headrests when a rollover is likely. See Fig. 20-21. A *tilt sensor*, or *roll sensor*, which is a device used to detect abnormal vehicle *attitude* (position in relation to a reference plan), is generally used to trigger the rollover-protection system. Some vehicles, however, use the air bag sensors to trigger the system. Two spring-loaded mechanisms are often used to force the roll bar (or headrests) up into a locked position.

ELECTRONIC TRANSMISSION/TRANSAXLE CONTROL SYSTEMS

In many late-model vehicles, the transmission or transaxle is controlled electronically. *Electronically controlled transmissions* (and transaxles) use a control unit, sensors, and solenoids to control shift points and torque converter (fluid clutch) lockup. Electronic control provides more efficient transmission operation, improving performance and increasing fuel economy.

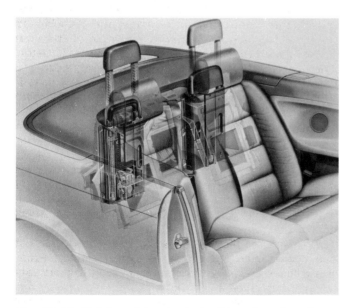

Fig. 20-21. Reinforced headrests in this automatic rollover-protection system extend 10 in. above conventional headrests to protect occupants in the event of a rollover. When activated, reinforced headrests are deployed in 3/10 of a second. (BMW)

A diagram of an electronically controlled transaxle is shown in Fig. 20-22. Note how various sensors feed data to the electronic control unit (ECU). The ECU can then activate the shift solenoids and torque convertor lockup solenoid as necessary. As the solenoids are turned on and off, they open and close fluid passages to operate the transaxle.

ELECTRONIC FOUR-WHEEL STEERING SYSTEMS

Electronic four-wheel steering systems use two rack-and-pinion gearboxes that are driven by electric motors to turn all four wheels. The front gearbox is controlled by rotating the steering wheel. The rear gearbox is controlled by an electronic control unit (ECU). Electronic four-wheel steering systems accurately control rear-wheel turning angles to improve vehicle handling.

Steering angle sensors, which are located at the gearboxes, provide the basic input signals to the ECU. In response to these signals and the vehicle speed sensor signal, the ECU directs the rear steering motor to turn the rear wheels.

In many designs, a sensor in the steering column provides the ECU with the same information sent by the steering angle sensors. As a result, a fail-safe system is produced. The two circuits continuously check on each other to prevent the failure of the electronic steering system. Also, a mechanical link to the front rack-and-pinion gearbox prevents a loss of directional control if the electronic system fails.

Electronic four-wheel steering systems reduce the number of components needed in a four-wheel power steering system. Also, hydraulic steering components, which tend to develop leaks, are not used in these systems.

SUMMARY

Anti-lock brake systems use wheel speed sensors as the main input devices. The wheel speed sensors produce a lower frequency signal if a wheel begins to slow down and skid. The computer can use this slower signal to activate an hydraulic actuator. The hydraulic actuator can cycle a valve to reduce pressure to that brake assembly. This keeps the tire and wheel from locking up and skidding.

An electronic height control system uses a height sensor, usually mounted on the rear axle assembly. The sensor is linked to the suspension system. If weight is added to the rear of the car, the springs and suspension are compressed lower to the ground. The height sensor then signals the air compressor. The air compressor turns on to raise the rear of the car. It forces more air into the air shocks or air bags to maintain the correct ride height. The height sensor activates a solenoid valve to release pressure and lower the car when weight is removed.

An electronic shock absorber system uses a steering sensor, brake sensor, acceleration sensor, and sometimes other sensors to feed data to a computer. The computer can analyze this data to operate shock absorber actuators. This allows the driver to switch to stiff shock action for handling or to softer shock action for cruising. The system will also react to rapid cornering, braking, and acceleration by automatically stiffening shock action. It helps prevent squat, sway, and dive.

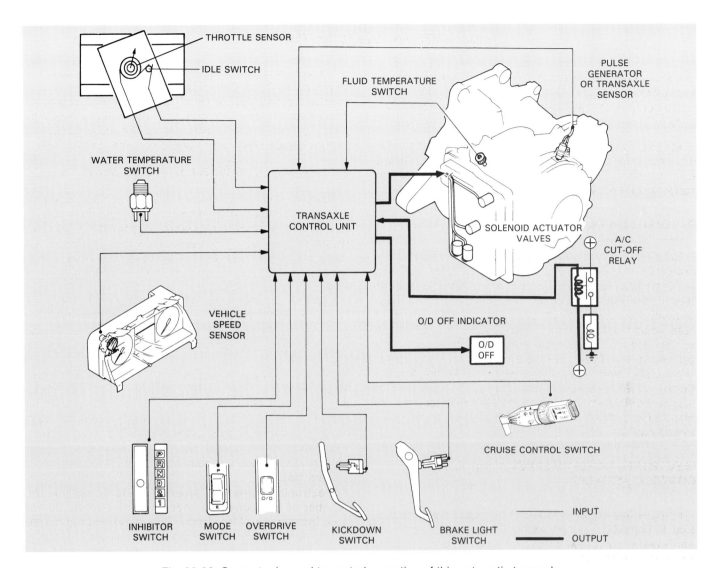

Fig. 20-22. Computer is used to control operation of this automatic transaxle.

Active suspension uses hydraulic rams in place of shock absorbers and suspension system springs. The rams support the weight of the car and allow for suspension action. Basically, pressure sensors on the rams signal the computer when the tire hits a bump (increased ram pressure) or hole (decreased ram pressure) in the road surface. The computer can instantly react to a pressure change to signal the ram actuators. It can make the actuators move up or down to follow the road surface. This helps prevent road imperfections from causing as much body movement. Vehicle ride is improved considerably. Active suspension can also react to prevent body sway in corners, body squat on acceleration, and body dive when braking. An hydraulic pump provides pressure for ram operation.

Electronic climate control systems use a small computer to monitor and control system operation. A control panel allows the driver to program temperature, etc., into the system. A digital readout is commonly used to show temperature, mode, etc. The computer can then use a temperature sensor to operate the system. A power supply may be used to send clean, DC current to the computer and readouts. A vacuum actuator serves as an interface between the computer and vacuum diaphragms. The vacuum diaphragms are used to move the control doors for feeding airflow through the vents.

Electronic cruise control uses sensors, a computer, switches, and a throttle actuator to maintain a preset vehicle speed. The speed sensor produces a signal frequency that corresponds to vehicle speed. If the speed or frequency rises or falls with the angle of the road surface, the computer activates the throttle actuator. The throttle actuator moves the engine throttle valve to increase or decrease engine power and cruising speed. Brake, clutch, and neutral switches are commonly used to disable the system.

An air bag system uses an inflatable balloon of tough nylon to protect the driver and in some cases, the front passengers during a head-on collision. Several impact sensors are located in the front of the car. If one or more impact sensors and the safing sensor are energized, the computer triggers a gas-generating material. This material fills the air bag with nitrogen gas in a fraction of a second.

Automatic rollover-protection systems are used in a few convertibles to protect the occupants in the event of a rollover. These systems deploy reinforced headrests or a roll bar when a rollover is likely.

The transmission or transaxle in many late-model vehicles is controlled electronically. These units use sensors, an electronic control unit, and solenoids to improve shifting efficiency.

Electronic four-wheel steering systems use steering gearboxes that are driven by electric motors to turn all four wheels. These systems eliminate the need for leak-prone hydraulic steering components.

KNOW THESE TERMS

Anti-lock brakes, Wheel speed sensors, Hydraulic actuator, Sensor rotor, ABS, Accumulator, Solenoid valve block, Hydraulic pump and motor, ABS pressure switch, Height sensor, Compressor assembly, Air shocks, Height sensor link, Electronic shock absorber system, Steering sensor, Brake sensor, Acceleration sensor, Shock mode switch, Shock actuators, Sonar sensor, Active suspension system, Electronic climate control, Power supply, Vacuum actuator, Vacuum diaphragms, Electronic cruise control, Vehicle speed sensor, Throttle actuator, Air bag system, Automatic rollover-protection system, Electronically controlled transmissions, Electronic four-wheel steering system.

REVIEW QUESTIONS—CHAPTER 20

1. How do anti-lock brakes improve safety?
2. Explain the five major parts of ABS.
3. How does ABS prevent tire skid?
4. A customer complains of pedal rise and pedal vibration during hard braking. The car has ABS. Technician A says that this is normal with many ABS systems. It indicates that the hydraulic actuator is cycling pressure to the brake assemblies. Technician B says that the car must be taken for a test drive to fully analyze the symptoms. Who is correct?
   a. Technician A.
   b. Technician B.
   c. Both A and B.
   d. Neither A nor B.
5. Explain the operation of an electronic height control system.
6. List and describe the six major parts of a typical electronic shock absorber system.
7. An _____ _____ _____ uses hydraulic rams in place of conventional suspension system springs and shock absorbers.
8. Why is a power supply sometimes needed with an electronic climate control system?
9. In your own words, how does an air bag system function?
10. How can a computer and solenoids control transaxle shift points?

ASE CERTIFICATION—TYPE QUESTIONS

1. When discussing the operation of an automotive anti-lock brake system, Technician A says an ABS reduces a vehicle's stopping distance during panic stop conditions. Technician B says an ABS improves the directional stability of the vehicle during panic stop conditions. Who is right?
   (A) A only.   (C) Both A and B.
   (B) B only.   (D) Neither A nor B.

2. Technician A says some wheel speed sensors are mounted on the vehicle's steering knuckle assemblies. Technician B says some wheel speed sensors are mounted on the vehicle's axle shafts. Who is right?
   (A) A only.   (C) Both A and B.
   (B) B only.   (D) Neither A nor B.

3. Technician A says an ABS computer uses wheel speed sensor inputs to control the operation of the system's sensor rotors. Technician B says an ABS computer uses wheel speed sensor inputs to control the operation of the system's hydraulic actuator. Who is right?
   (A) A only.   (C) Both A and B.
   (B) B only.   (D) Neither A nor B.

4. Technician A says an ABS hydraulic actuator regulates the amount of fluid pressure applied to each wheel brake assembly. Technician B says the master cylinder-booster assembly is an integral part of some actuators. Who is right?
   (A) A only.   (C) Both A and B.
   (B) B only.   (D) Neither A nor B.

5. Technician A says a "fluid reservoir" is a basic part of an anti-lock brake system's hydraulic actuator. Technician B says a "pressure switch" is a basic part of an anti-lock brake system's hydraulic actuator. Who is right?
   (A) A only.   (C) Both A and B.
   (B) B only.   (D) Neither A nor B.

6. Technician A says an electronic shock absorber system's shock actuators are solenoid-operated. Technician B says the brake light switch often serves as a brake sensor in an electronic shock absorber system. Who is right?
   (A) A only.   (C) Both A and B.
   (B) B only.   (D) Neither A nor B.

7. Technician A says an active suspension system uses pneumatic shock absorbers and hydraulic rams to match suspension action to driving conditions. Technician B says a hydraulic pump is used to operate an active suspension system's rams. Who is right?
   (A) A only.   (C) Both A and B.
   (B) B only.   (D) Neither A nor B.

8. Each of the following is a basic component of an electronic climate control system except:
   (A) vacuum actuator.   (C) pressure solenoids.
   (B) control module.   (D) vacuum diaphragms.

9. Technician A says an electronic cruise control system's vehicle speed sensor feeds AC output signals to the throttle actuator. Technician B says an electronic cruise control system's throttle actuator moves the engine throttle lever to control vehicle speed. Who is right?
   (A) A only.   (C) Both A and B.
   (B) B only.   (D) Neither A nor B.

10. Technician A says an air bag system's impact sensors are normally closed switches that open during a severe frontal impact. Technician B says an automotive air bag system's safing sensor is normally located in the passenger compartment. Who is right?
    (A) A only.   (C) Both A and B.
    (B) B only.   (D) Neither A nor B.

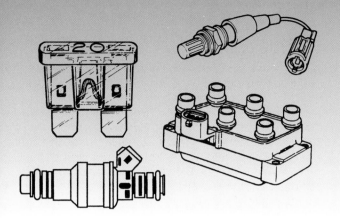

On-Board Diagnostics, Scan Tools

After studying this chapter, you will be able to:
- *Discuss the purpose and operation of on-board diagnostic systems.*
- *Explain the use of scan tools to simplify reading of trouble codes.*
- *Compare OBD I and OBD II system capabilities and procedures.*
- *Locate the data link connector on most makes and models of cars.*
- *Activate on-board diagnostics and read trouble codes with and without a scan tool.*
- *Use a trouble code chart in a service manual or code conversion by a scan tool.*
- *Erase diagnostic trouble codes.*

On-board diagnostics refers to a vehicle computer's ability to analyze the operation of its circuits and to output data identifying any problems found. All new cars and light trucks have this self-test feature. It is critical that you know how to use this vital troubleshooting aid.

This chapter will summarize recent changes in on-board diagnostic capabilities and explain the fundamental use of scan tools. It will prepare you for other text chapters on troubleshooting and servicing vehicle systems.

ON-BOARD DIAGNOSTIC SYSTEMS

Modern automotive computer systems are designed to detect problems and indicate where they might be located. The computer is programmed to detect abnormal operating conditions and store a code representing the problem location. It actually scans its input and output circuits to detect an incorrect voltage, resistance, or current.

Today's on-board diagnostics will check the operation of almost every electrical-electronic part in every major vehicle system. A vehicle's engine control module can detect engine misfiring and air-fuel mixture problems. It monitors the operation of the fuel injectors, ignition coils, fuel pump, emissions system parts, and other major components that affect vehicle performance and emissions control. You can scan for problems in the engine and its support systems, the transmission, the suspension system, the anti-lock brake system, and other vehicle systems. This has greatly simplified the troubleshooting of complex automotive systems.

If the on-board computer finds any abnormal values, it will store a trouble code and light a malfunction indicator light on the instrument panel. This will inform the driver and the technician that something is wrong and must be fixed.

Since some vehicles have six or more computers, on-board diagnostics can be a time saver when trying to narrow down possible problems. The computers can interact with dozens of sensors and actuators and, in some cases, with each other. No longer can the untrained mechanic hope to repair modern vehicles. It takes the skill of a well-trained technician versed in on-board diagnostics to troubleshoot and repair today's vehicles.

Early on-board diagnostic systems

Most early on-board diagnostic systems could only check a limited number of items. Although these systems were able to detect a problem in the circuit, they were unable to determine what type of problem the circuit, sensor, or system had. Technicians who were unfamiliar with a particular manufacturer's line of vehicles found it difficult to accurately diagnose problems caused by a computer system failure.

Also, there was little or no standardization among these early systems. A wide range of connectors and methods were used to retrieve stored trouble codes. This was confusing for tool manufacturers and made it necessary for the shop or technician to purchase a variety of harness adapters, program cartridges, and service literature. Even the names of the systems and their components were different, making part identification difficult.

Early diagnostic systems are often referred to as *on-board diagnostics generation one* or *OBD I*. See Fig. 21-1. There are millions of vehicles on the road that use OBD I systems.

On-board diagnostics II (OBD II)

A poorly tuned or malfunctioning automobile is a serious source of air pollution. It can produce several times the normal amount of emissions. For this reason, the California Air Resources Board (CARB), along with the Environmental Protection Agency (EPA), recommended and passed regulations that require on-board diagnostic systems to detect problems *before* they could result in the production of harmful exhaust emissions. These regulations also require auto manufacturers to standardize the performance monitoring systems on their cars and light trucks.

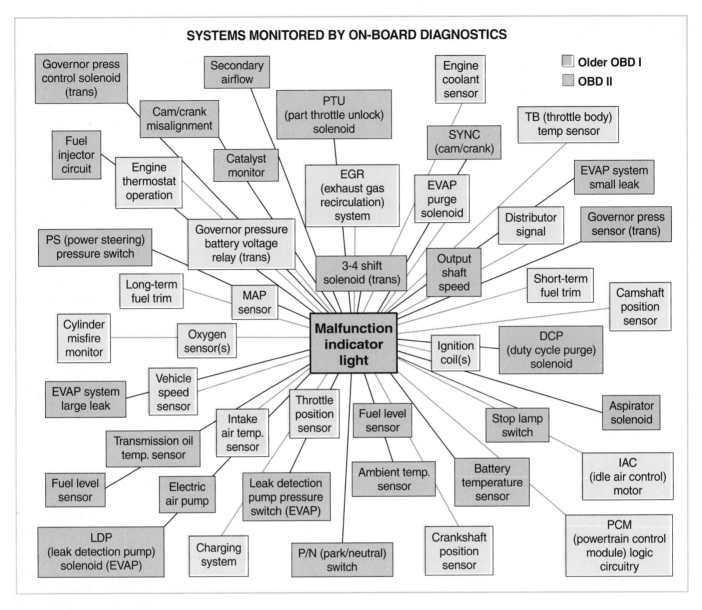

Fig. 21-1. Compare OBD I diagnostic system's capabilities with OBD II system's abilities.

As mentioned, OBD I diagnostic systems simply stored a code and illuminated a dash light once a sensor or circuit stopped working completely. The new standard requires on-board diagnostic systems to go a step further by monitoring how efficiently each part of the system is operating. *On-board diagnostics generation two*, abbreviated *OBD II*, is designed to more efficiently monitor the condition of hardware and software that affect emissions. OBD II diagnostics detect part deterioration (changes in performance), not just complete part failure. For example, if a sensor become lazy or remains in the low end of its normal operating range, this potential problem is stored as a trouble code in the computer memory for retrieval at a later date. Refer to Fig. 21-1. OBD II is designed to keep the vehicle running efficiently for at least 100,000 miles (160 000 km).

The on-board computers used in OBD II systems have greater processing speed, more memory, and more complex programming than computers used in OBD I systems.

New vehicles now monitor more functions and can warn the driver and technician of more possible problems that affect driveability and emissions.

The OBD II diagnostic system can produce *over 500* engine performance-related trouble codes. It checks the operating parameters of switches, sensors, actuators, in-system components, their related wiring, and the computer itself.

For example, with OBD II, engine misfire (engine not completely burning the fuel mixture) and fuel system malfunctions will cause the malfunction indicator light in the dash to flash on and off. This is to warn that the misfire or poor mixture could damage the catalytic converter. This warns the driver that the vehicle could be damaged and should be serviced immediately.

OBD II also standardized data link connections, trouble codes, sensor and output device terminology, and scan tool capabilities. In the past, one manufacturer required over a dozen different connectors for the ECMs used in their vehicles. This made it very expensive for the small repair shop to purchase all of the necessary adapters. To solve this problem, the federal government and the Society of Automotive Engineers (SAE) have set standards for all auto makers to use.

Malfunction indicator light (MIL)

If an unusual condition or electrical value is detected by the on-board diagnostic system, the computer will turn on an amber-colored indicator light in the dash instrument panel or driver information center. In OBD II systems, this light is referred to as a *malfunction indicator light (MIL)*. OBD I systems use a red- or amber-colored *check engine light*, *service engine soon light*, or other lights with a similar name. Some vehicles use the silhouette of an engine as its MIL light.

The malfunction indicator light will notify the driver that the vehicle needs service. If the MIL has a *continuous glow*, the trouble is not critical but should be repaired. If the MIL light comes on and then goes out, this means that the problem may be intermittent. However, a *flashing* MIL in an OBD II equipped vehicle means that the trouble could damage the catalytic converter and is, therefore, considered critical. The MIL will flash on and off every second conditions that could damage the catalytic converter exist. Whenever the MIL is illuminated, drivers should be advised to bring the vehicle in for service as soon as possible. The technician can then use a scan tool to retrieve information about the problem.

A *trouble code chart* in the service manual will state what each number code represents. Most scan tools have the capability to perform trouble code conversion. *Trouble code conversion* means the scan tool is programmed to automatically convert the number code into abbreviated words that explain the potential problem. The technician can then use the service manual to further isolate the problem.

Diagnostic trouble codes

Diagnostic trouble codes (DTC) are digital signals produced and stored by the computer when an operating parameter is exceeded. An *operating parameter* is an acceptable minimum and maximum value. The parameter might be an acceptable voltage range from the oxygen sensor, a resistance range for a temperature sensor, current draw from a fuel injector coil winding, or an operational state from a monitored device. In any case, the computer "knows" the operating parameters for most inputs and outputs. This information is stored in its permanent memory chips.

Computer system problems

Common problems that can affect vehicle performance and cause the computer system to set a code and light the MIL in the dash are shown in Fig. 21-2. These problems include:

1. LOOSE ELECTRICAL CONNECTION (input signal from a sensor not reaching the computer properly or an actuator not responding to the computer's output).
2. CORRODED ELECTRICAL CONNECTION (high resistance in a wiring connector, upsetting sensor input or actuator output).

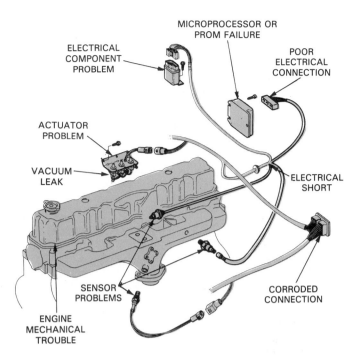

Fig. 21-2. Always remember that about 80% of all performance problems are *not* caused by the computer, its sensor, and its actuators. Most problems are the result of conventional problems, like loose wires, broken wires, vacuum leaks, mechanical problems, etc.

3. FAILED SENSOR (opened or shorted sensor or other sensor malfunction preventing normal computer system operation).
4. FAILED ACTUATOR (solenoid, servo motor, relay, or display shorted, open, or does not react to computer signals).
5. LEAKING VACUUM HOSE (vacuum leak or poor operation of engine or vacuum-operated actuator that reduces engine or system performance).
6. ELECTRICAL SHORT (wires touching ground or each other to cause a current increase or incorrect current path).
7. IGNITION SYSTEM PROBLEMS (open spark plug wires, fouled spark plugs, weak ignition coil voltage, bad crankshaft sensor, etc. For example, a spark plug misfire causing unburned fuel to enter the exhaust can trick the oxygen sensor into trying to create a leaner mixture. The misfire upsets computer system operation and can be detected in OBD II systems by variations in the crankshaft sensor signal).
8. FUEL SYSTEM PROBLEMS (leaking or clogged injectors, bad pressure regulator, faulty electric fuel pump or other problems).
9. EMISSION SYSTEM PROBLEMS (problems with the catalytic converter, EGR valve, vapor storage system, etc. Many emission components are monitored electronically and will set a trouble code if a malfunction occurs).
10. ENGINE PROBLEMS (mechanical problem that cannot be compensated for by the computer modifying system operation. Engine misfire due to mechanical wear will also trip a trouble code on OBD II systems).

11. COMPUTER MALFUNCTION (an incorrect PROM, wrong internal programming, internal failure of integrated circuit, or failure of other components can disable the computer and alter the operation of related systems).

12. WEAK OR LAZY COMPONENT (sensor, actuator, or computer is not outputting normal operating values. In some cases, a sensor's current, voltage, or resistance values are within specs, but the component is sending signals to the ECM at a reduced rate of speed. A lazy sensor can trick the computer system into compensating for an artificial lean or rich condition; it may trip codes on OBD II-equipped vehicles).

13. TRANSMISSION PROBLEMS (electronically controlled transmissions are monitored and will trip trouble codes if there is a mechanical problem. Transmission problems include a bad vehicle speed sensor, a faulty shift sensor or solenoid, or faulty wiring).

14. ANTI-LOCK BRAKE SYSTEM PROBLEMS (modern anti-lock brakes are monitored by an on-board computer. Anti-lock brake system problems include bad wheel speed sensors, faulty wiring, or a malfunctioning hydraulic unit).

15. AIR CONDITIONING (today's air conditioning systems are also monitored electronically for operational state, leaks, and high pressure. Typical problems include faulty pressure and temperature sensors).

16. AIR BAG PROBLEMS (problems with the air bag system, such as faulty impact sensors, a malfunctioning arming sensor, or a damaged air bag module, will trip trouble codes).

17. OTHER SYSTEM FAULTS (most other vehicle systems have some monitored functions that will trip a trouble code).

Most computer system problems are conventional (loose electrical connection, mechanical problem, etc.). Only about 20% of all performance problems are caused by an actual fault in the computer or one of its sensors. For this reason, always check for the most common problems before testing more complex computer-controlled components.

SCANNING COMPUTER PROBLEMS

A *scan tool* is an electronic test instrument designed to retrieve trouble codes from the computer's memory and to display the codes as a number and words explaining the problem. Also called a *diagnostic readout tool*, the scan tool makes it easier to read diagnostic trouble codes. In some cases, it is the only way to access the computer's diagnostic system. Refer to Fig. 21-3.

A scan tool is by far the most common way to use on-board diagnostics. It will save time and effort. A scan tool is now the most important tool of the automobile technician, Fig. 21-4.

To use the scan tool, read the operating instructions for the specific type of scan tool. Operating procedures vary. Some scan tools have buttons to control functions. Others have a rotary knob that lets you scroll down through scan tool functions.

Scan tool program cartridges

Most scan tools come equipped with several *program cartridges.* These removable cartridges house one or more computer chips that contain specific information about the vehicle to be scanned, Fig. 21-5.

One type of scan tool cartridge is a *vehicle program cartridge.* This type of program cartridge provides data for one or more vehicle manufacturers (GM, Ford, Chrysler, Asian, European, etc.). Scan tool cartridges must match the model year (vehicle manufacturing date). Program cartridges are also available for certain systems, such as anti-lock brakes, automatic transmissions, etc. New cartridges must be purchased as the on-board diagnostic systems are modified. Some scan tool manufacturers now offer generic storage cartridges that can be updated by downloading the up-to-date specifications to the scan tool from a computer.

Avoid touching the cartridge or the scan tool terminals. Static electricity can destroy the delicate electronics in the unit. See Fig. 21-6.

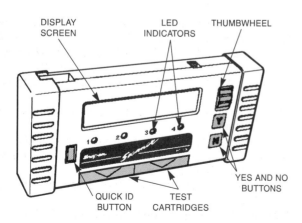

Fig. 21-3. A scan tool is the most important tool of the automotive technician. It will tell you where problems are located. (Snap-On Tools)

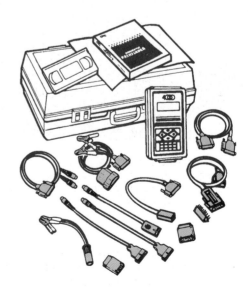

Fig. 21-4. Scan tool designs vary. Always read the owner's manual that comes with the tool. (OTC)

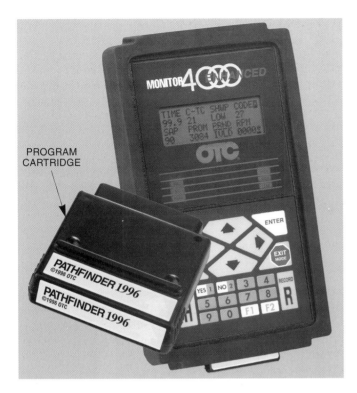

PROGRAM CARTRIDGE

Fig. 21-5. Scan tool cartridges store information for troubleshooting a specific make, model, and year of vehicle. Troubleshooting cartridges sometimes give added instructions for helping to solve the problem.   (OTC)

Fig. 21-6. When installing a scan tool cartridge, do not touch the metal terminals. Static electricity could damage the cartridge's internal chips or electronic components. (Snap-On Tools)

Many scan tools also come with a *troubleshooting cartridge,* which can give additional information on how to verify the source of various trouble codes. This is a handy device that can help guide you to the most common sources of trouble. Look at Fig. 21-7. However, the

Fig. 21-7. Install the correct cartridge into the scan tool. Make sure it is fully seated.   (Snap-On Tools)

troubleshooting cartridge must be used in conjunction with the vehicle cartridge. This makes it necessary to have a scan tool that can access two cartridges at the same time.

Many scan tools will hold two cartridges, one for the vehicle being tested and another for added convenience. However, most scan tools can access the information from one cartridge at a time. A few scan tools can access both cartridges at the same time. This capability allows for the use of the troubleshooting cartridge discussed earlier. Install the right cartridge(s) into the scan tool. Slide the cartridge straight into the tool to prevent damage.

Data link connector

The *data link connector (DLC)* is a multi-pin terminal used to link the scan tool to the computer. In the past, this connector was identified by a variety of names, including *diagnostic connector* and *assembly line diagnostic link (ALDL).*

OBD I diagnostic connectors came in various shapes and sizes, and were equipped with a varying number of pins or terminals. With OBD II, the DLC is a *standardized* 16-pin connector. The female half of the connector is on the vehicle, and the male half is on the scan tool cable. See Fig. 21-8.

Some of the most common locations for the diagnostic connector include:
1. Under the dash, within arm's reach when sitting in the driver's seat, Figures 21-8A and 21-8B. This is the standard OBD II location.
2. Near the firewall in the engine compartment, Fig. 21-8C.
3. Near or on the side of the fuse box, Fig. 21-8D.
4. Near the inner fender panel in the engine compartment, Fig. 21-8E.
5. Under the center console, Fig. 21-8F.

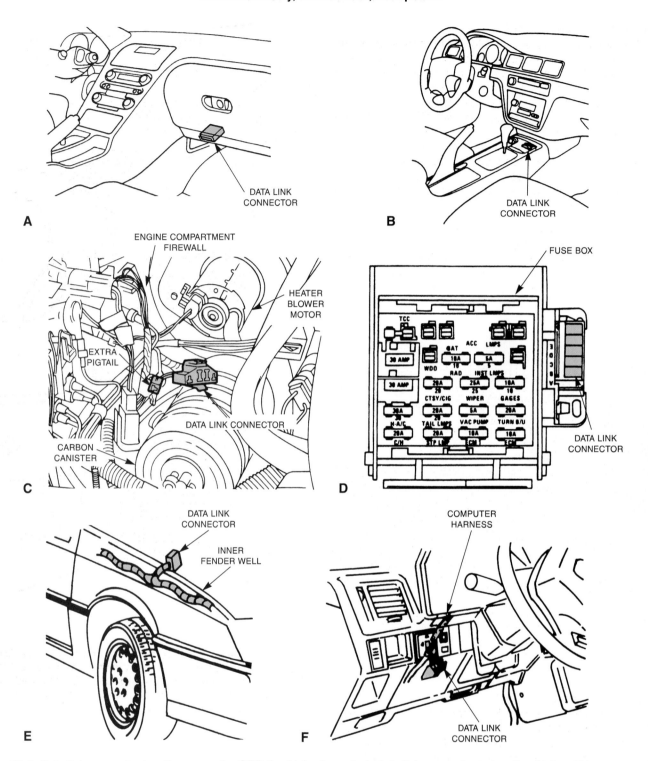

Fig. 21-8. Data link connector locations vary. A—OBD II vehicles have their data link connector below the dash, within easy reach of the driver's seat. B—OBD II connector is sometimes located in the center console. C—Some diagnostic connectors are on the firewall, near the back of engine. D—Some early General Motors connectors may be under the right side of the dash or next to fuse box. E—Early Chrysler diagnostic connectors may be located in the engine compartment. F—Other data link connectors may be located under the dash, in or behind the glove box, under the center console, etc. Refer to the service manual if needed. (General Motors, Ford, and Snap-On Tools)

With OBD II diagnostic systems, you should be able to connect a scan tool to the vehicle's data link connector with one hand while sitting in the driver's seat or kneeling outside the vehicle.

Some OBD I vehicles are equipped with a 16-pin, OBD II–style data link connector. Do not assume that a vehicle equipped with a 16-pin data link connector is OBD II compliant.

Connecting the scan tool

The scan tool cable should slide easily into the vehicle's data link connector. If not, something is wrong. Never force the two together or you could damage the pins on the tool cable or the data link connector. You may have to use an *adapter* so the scan tool connector will fit the vehicle's DLC or communicate with different pin configurations, Fig. 21-9.

If not powered through the DLC, connect the scan tool to battery power. In most cases, you can use a cigarette lighter adapter to connect power to the scan tool. See Fig. 21-10. You can also use alligator clips to connect the tool to the battery.

> WARNING! Make sure you are connecting the scan tool to the vehicle properly. Some technicians have mistakenly connected scan tools to the wrong connector (tach connector, for example), which can damage the scan tool.

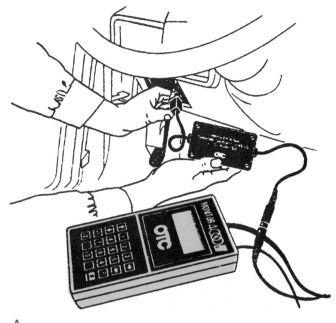

A

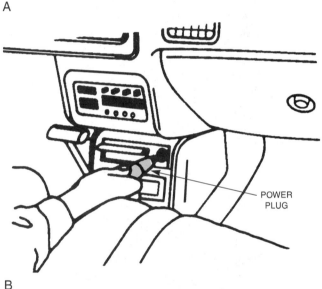

B

Fig. 21-10. A—Connect the scan tool cable to the vehicle's data link connector. Make sure the pins match up. Do not force the connector together. B—Scan tools can be powered by a cigarette lighter plug. In some cases, the tool must be connected directly to the battery. (OTC)

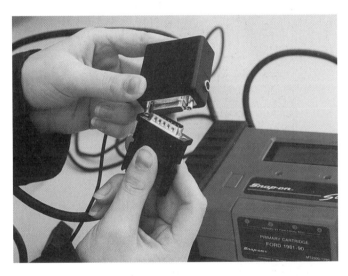

Fig. 21-9. An adapter is sometimes needed between the scan tool cable and the vehicle's data link connector. (Snap-On Tools)

Using scan tools

Modern scan tools will give *prompts,* or step-by-step instructions in their display windows. The prompts tell you how to input specific vehicle information and run diagnostic tests. See Fig. 21-11. Scan tool instructions are procedures and specifications programmed into the cartridge.

First, the scan tool may ask you to input VIN information from the plate on the top of the dash. You may be asked to input specific numbers and letters from the VIN. Refer to Fig. 21-12.

The VIN data lets the scan tool know which engine, transmission, and options are installed on the vehicle. With some makes, however, the on-board computer will contain this data and will automatically download it into the scan tool. Then, you will be able to select the information that you would like the scan tool to give you. Some of the information you can request includes:

1. STORED DIAGNOSTIC TROUBLE CODES (gives trouble code number).
2. FAULT DESCRIPTION (explains what each stored diagnostic code means. This information is given with the trouble code number on most scan tools).
3. DATASTREAM INFORMATION (displays the operating values of all monitored circuits and sensors).
4. RUN TESTS (performs sensor and actuator tests).
5. OXYGEN SENSOR MONITORING (performs detailed tests of the O_2 sensor signal).
6. FAILURE RECORD (lists the number of times a particular trouble code has occurred by keystarts or warm-ups).

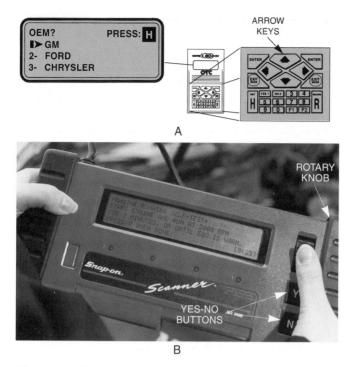

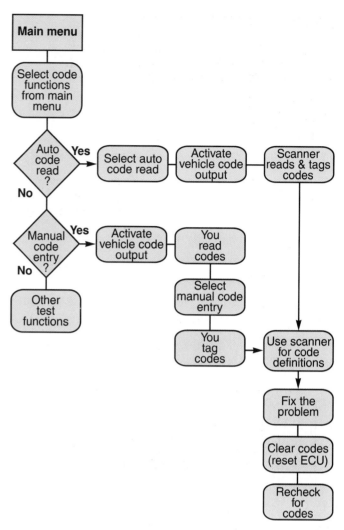

Fig. 21-11. Controls on scan tool will vary by manufacturer. A—This scan tool uses a keypad and arrow keys for inputting requested information about the vehicle and desired tests. B—This scan tool has an easy-to-use rotary knob and yes-no buttons for inputting requested data.
(OTC and Snap-On Tools)

Fig. 21-12. The scan tool may ask you to input VIN information. This lets the tool know how the vehicle is equipped—engine type, fuel system type, computer configuration, etc. (Snap-On Tools)

Fig. 21-13. Flowchart showing basic steps for using a scan tool. (Snap-On Tools)

7. FREEZE FRAME (takes a snapshot of sensor and actuator values when a problem occurs).
8. TROUBLESHOOTING (provides help and instructions for diagnosing faults).

Fig. 21-13 gives the general sequence for using a scan tool. You can ask the scan tool to give more information on a trouble code, and the tool will display words that give sensor resistance values, common problems, and other useful information. Figs. 21-14 and 21-15 show some examples of scan tool troubleshooting tips.

Most technicians will check the ECM for stored diagnostic trouble codes before performing tests on specific components. This is a quick way to go right to any hard failure, so it can be repaired first.

As stated earlier, some scan tools are able to take a snapshot, or *freeze frame,* of sensor and actuator values when a problem occurs. The tool records the values from all monitored components so they can be further evaluated. This helps you locate and correct intermittent problems more easily.

Always correct the cause of the *lowest number* diagnostic trouble code first. Sometimes fixing the cause of the lowest code will clear other codes because of component interaction. If not, you can use other scan tool features to find and solve more complex problems.

A trouble code does *not* mean that a certain component is bad. It simply indicates that a possible problem has been detected in that particular device or circuit.

Most ECMs count the number of times a trouble code has occurred. This information is stored in a *failure record,* or *failure recorder,* that also indicates the number of keystarts since the last time the trouble code occurred. The failure recorder in OBD II systems counts the number

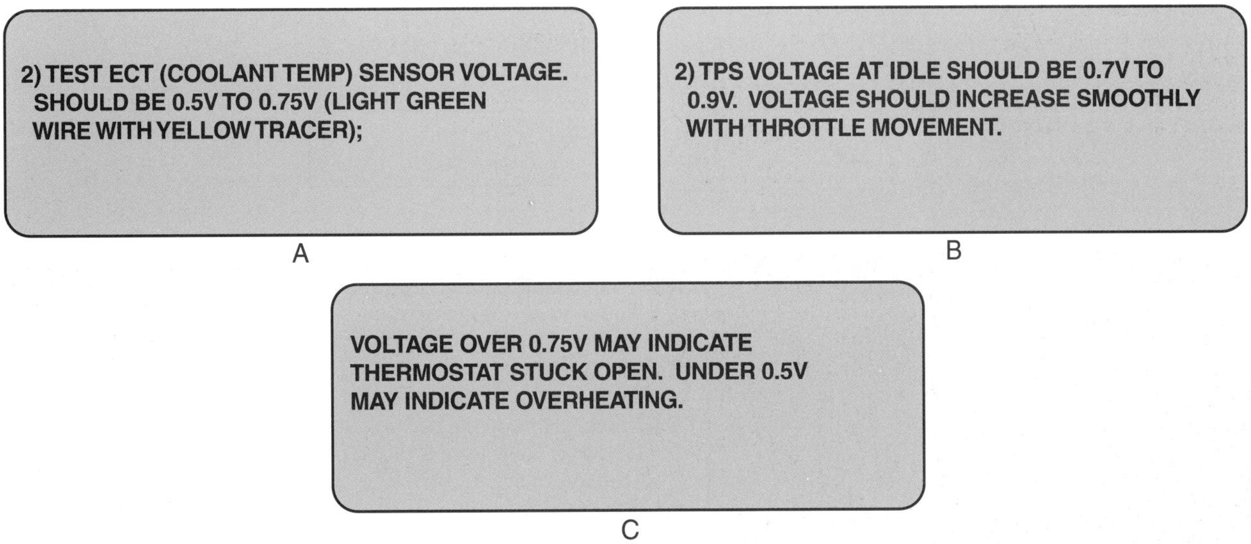

> **2) TEST ECT (COOLANT TEMP) SENSOR VOLTAGE. SHOULD BE 0.5V TO 0.75V (LIGHT GREEN WIRE WITH YELLOW TRACER);**

A

> **2) TPS VOLTAGE AT IDLE SHOULD BE 0.7V TO 0.9V. VOLTAGE SHOULD INCREASE SMOOTHLY WITH THROTTLE MOVEMENT.**

B

> **VOLTAGE OVER 0.75V MAY INDICATE THERMOSTAT STUCK OPEN. UNDER 0.5V MAY INDICATE OVERHEATING.**

C

Fig. 21-14. Here are examples of how scan tools will give specifications and tips for finding the source of a problem. A—The scan tool is showing normal sensor voltage and which wire to probe when measuring actual voltage. B—This scan tool is giving more information for testing throttle position sensor. C—Scan tools can also give hints on how engine overheating or overcooling can fool the computer into signaling a problem with the engine coolant temperature sensor.

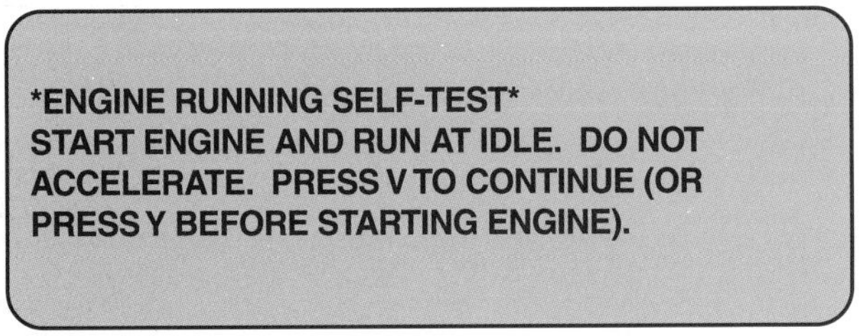

> ***ENGINE RUNNING SELF-TEST***
> **START ENGINE AND RUN AT IDLE. DO NOT ACCELERATE. PRESS V TO CONTINUE (OR PRESS Y BEFORE STARTING ENGINE).**

Fig. 21-15. A key-on/engine-on test is sometimes needed to further diagnose problems. You must allow the engine to reach operating temperature first so all sensors are operating normally.

of times the engine reached operating temperature, rather than keystarts, since the last time the code was set. If one code has occurred more frequently than the others, investigate this code first. In many cases, the lowest number code and the most frequently stored code are the same.

Diagnostic trouble code identification

As mentioned, early on-board diagnostic systems were not standardized. Often, technicians would have to refer to the service manual to find out what a particular code number meant. OBD I and earlier codes were different for each manufacturer.

To simplify troubleshooting, OBD II requires all auto manufacturers to use a set of *standardized alpha-numeric trouble codes*. Each trouble code identifies the same problem in all vehicles, regardless of the manufacturer.

OBD II codes contain a letter and a four-digit number. The letter in all OBD II codes indicates the *general function* of the affected system (power train, chassis, etc.).

The first digit of the number indicates whether the code is a standard trouble code or a nonuniform code. *Standard trouble codes,* or SAE codes, are indicated by the number 0. *Nonuniform codes* (nonstandard OBD II codes that are

assigned by the auto manufacturers) have the number 1 after the system letter. The second number in the OBD II code indicates the *specific function* of the system where the fault is located, such as fuel, computer, etc.

The code's last two digits refer to the specific *fault designation*. It pinpoints exactly which component or circuit of the system might be at fault, as well as the type of problem. Regardless of the type of vehicle being serviced, the core trouble code numbers will be the same. The scan tool must explain the code and, in some cases, may describe how to fix the problem.

Fig. 21-16 gives a breakdown of the OBD II diagnostic code. Study it carefully. Fig. 21-17 shows the display window of a scan tool that has found a stored trouble code.

Failure types

Computer system failures can be grouped into two general types: hard failures and soft failures. A *hard failure* is a problem that is always present in a computer system. An example of a hard failure is a disconnected wire or another problem that would cause a general circuit failure. A hard failure does not come and go with varying conditions. After the computer memory is cleared, any hard failures will usually reset as soon as the engine is started or the affected system is energized.

A *soft failure,* or *intermittent failure,* is a problem that only occurs when certain conditions are present. It might be present one minute and gone the next. Soft failures will usually be stored in memory for 30-50 key starts or engine warm-ups. An example of a soft failure is a loose terminal that connects and disconnects as the vehicle travels over bumps in the road. Low-input, high-input, and improper range failures are usually classified as soft failures.

Computer system failure types can be further broken down into four general categories:

1. A *general circuit failure* means the circuit or component has a fixed value, no output, or an output that is out of specifications. This is the most severe fault,

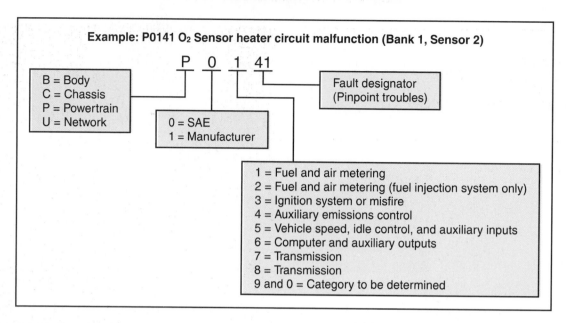

Example: P0141 O$_2$ Sensor heater circuit malfunction (Bank 1, Sensor 2)

P 0 1 41

B = Body
C = Chassis
P = Powertrain
U = Network

0 = SAE
1 = Manufacturer

Fault designator
(Pinpoint troubles)

1 = Fuel and air metering
2 = Fuel and air metering (fuel injection system only)
3 = Ignition system or misfire
4 = Auxiliary emissions control
5 = Vehicle speed, idle control, and auxiliary inputs
6 = Computer and auxiliary outputs
7 = Transmission
8 = Transmission
9 and 0 = Category to be determined

Fig. 21-16. OBD II trouble codes are alpha-numeric. Note what each part of trouble code means. The first part of the code tells you which system might be having problems. The last part of the number gives the specific problem circuit or component.

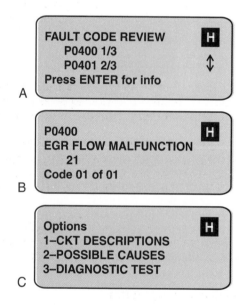

A—

FAULT CODE REVIEW   H
  P0400 1/3
  P0401 2/3   ↕
Press ENTER for info

B—

P0400   H
EGR FLOW MALFUNCTION
      21
Code 01 of 01

C—

Options   H
1–CKT DESCRIPTIONS
2–POSSIBLE CAUSES
3–DIAGNOSTIC TEST

Fig. 21-17. This is an example of what you might see on the display of most scan tools. A—The scan tool will give you the trouble code numbers and a description of each fault. B—If you request information on the stored trouble codes, the tool will explain what each code means. C—Options will allow you to use the scan tool to get detailed descriptions of each code, list possible causes, or perform diagnostics tests.   (OTC)

but it is the easiest to locate. It is caused by disconnected wires, high-resistance connections, shorts, or a component constantly operating out of parameter.

2. A *low-input failure* is one that produces a voltage, current, or signal frequency below normal operating parameters. A weak or abnormally low signal is being sent to the on-board computer. This type of failure is often caused by high circuit resistance, a poor electrical connection, a contaminated or failed sensor, or a similar problem.

3. A *high-input failure* results when the signal reaching the on-board computer has more voltage, more current, or a higher frequency than normal. This type of failure is often caused by a faulty sensor or a mechanical fault that is "fooling" the computer system.

4. An *improper range/performance failure* occurs when a sensor or actuator is producing values slightly lower or higher than normal. The circuit is still functioning, but not as well as it should under normal conditions. This type of failure can be caused by a contaminated sensor, a partial sensor failure, a poor electrical connection, and similar problems. Improper range/performance failures were not detected in OBD I systems and were often difficult to find. OBD II systems can detect improper range/performance failures.

Diagnostic scan values

Diagnostic scan values, or *datastream values*, produced by the vehicle's computer give electrical operating values of sensors, actuators, and circuits. These values can be read on a scan tool's digital display and compared to known normal values in the service manual. Diagnostic scan values give additional troubleshooting information when trying to locate a problem.

Engine-off/key-on diagnostics

In order to access the ECM data on most vehicles, it is necessary to turn the ignition key on. *Engine-off/key-on diagnostics* are performed by triggering the ECM's on-board diagnostic system with the ignition key in the *on* position but *without* the engine running. This allows you to access any stored trouble codes in the computer's memory chips. Engine-off/key-on diagnostics are usually performed *before* engine-on/key-on diagnostics. Look at Fig. 21-18.

REVIEW CODES
** KEY ON, ENGINE OFF CODES-FIX FIRST **
54 AIR CHARGE TEMP SIGNAL HIGH--CKT OPEN
** CONTINUOUS MEMORY CODES-FIX LAST **

A

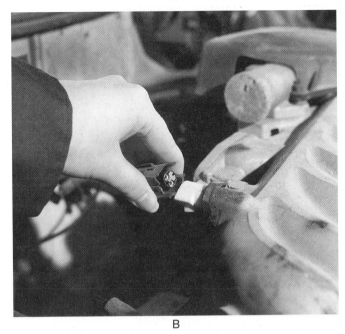

B

Fig. 21-18. Most technicians check for stored trouble codes first. A—This scan tool readout shows a problem with the intake air temperature sensor. B—You would then know to check that sensor and its wiring for problems. (Snap-On Tools)

Fig. 21-19. The wiggle test involves moving wires and connectors while scanning for trouble codes. If wiggling a wire trips a code, you found the location of the problem.

If you anticipate working in the engine-off/key-on diagnostic mode for over 30 minutes, connect a battery charger to the vehicle. This will prevent the extended current draw from draining the battery and upsetting the operation of the computer while in the diagnostic mode. False trouble codes could result from a partially drained battery.

Wiggle test

Many computer system failures, especially intermittent failures, are caused by loose, dirty, or corroded connections. These can be found by performing a wiggle, or "flex," test.

To perform a *wiggle test,* connect a scan tool to the vehicle and choose the appropriate test options. Refer to the instructions provided with the scan tool. Place the vehicle in the engine-off/key-on diagnostic mode. Flex wires and wiggle harness connectors while scanning for problems. If wiggling a wire or connector produces a new diagnostic trouble code, check the wire or electrical connection more closely. It may be loose, corroded, or damaged, Fig. 21-19.

Some technicians perform a wiggle test while the engine is running. If engine operation changes suddenly

(stalls or idles high, for example) when a connector or wire is flexed, the problem is located at or near that point. Be careful when performing a wiggle test on a running vehicle.

You might also want to use a heat gun to heat potentially faulty components during a wiggle test. For example, electronic amplifiers and modules tend to malfunction when hot. This could help find an intermittent problem.

WARNING! Exercise care when using a heat gun. The heat generated by the gun can easily melt most plastics and damage electronic components.

Engine-on/key-on diagnostics

Engine-on/key-on diagnostics are performed with the engine running at full operating temperature. These tests check the condition of the sensors, actuators, computer, and wiring while they are operating under normal conditions.

Switch diagnostic test

A *switch diagnostic test* involves activating various switches while using a scan tool. The scan tool will tell you which switch to move and will monitor its operation. The scan tool will quickly indicate if the switch is working normally, Fig. 21-20.

For example, you might be told to shift the transmission shift lever through the gears, press on the brake pedal, and turn the air conditioning on and off. As each step is performed, the scan tool will indicate if the affected switch is *OK* and whether or not the ECM is reading the switch input. Refer to the service manual for details of the switch diagnostic.

TEST IN PROGRESS. CYLINDER ID = 6 CYL.
TO TEST BRAKE SWITCH AND POWER STEERING
SWITCH: PRESS AND RELEASE BRAKE PEDAL
TURN STEERING WHEEL 180° AND RELEASE.

Fig. 21-20. Most scan tools will also perform switch and actu-ator tests. This is sometimes done automatically. You will be prompted to close different switches to make sure each one is working. The scan tool may also be able to perform additional actuator tests.   (Snap-On Tools)

Actuator diagnostic tests

An *actuator diagnostic test* uses the scan tool to order the vehicle's computer to energize specific output devices with the engine on or off. This will let you find out if the actuators are working. Most actuator diagnostic tests are considered intrusive tests, since engine or vehicle opera-tion will be drastically affected while the device is being tested. Actuator diagnostic tests might:
1. Fire or prevent the firing of the ignition coil.
2. Open and close the fuel injectors.
3. Cycle the idle speed motor or solenoid.
4. Energize the digital EGR valve solenoids.

You can then watch or listen to make sure these actua-tors are working. With OBD II, the scan tool will give read-outs showing whether there is trouble with any actuators.

Not all vehicle manufacturers provide switch and actu-ator diagnostic tests. Refer to the service manual or scan operating manual for details.

Scanning during a test drive

With a modern scan tool, you can also check for prob-lems while driving the vehicle to simulate the conditions present when the trouble happens, Fig. 21-21. For example, if the problem occurs only while driving at a spe-cific speed when the engine is cold, you can scan under these conditions. Start the cold engine and drive at the specified speed while scanning for problems. You can then take a snapshot, or freeze frame, (if the scan tool has this feature) when the problems occurs.

ENERGIZING OBD I SYSTEMS WITHOUT A SCAN TOOL

If you do not have a scan tool and are working on an OBD I–equipped vehicle, there are several ways to acti-vate the computer's on-board diagnostics and to retrieve trouble codes, Fig. 21-22. The most common methods include:
1. Using a jumper wire to ground one of the data link connector terminals and then reading the flashing code on the dash-mounted check engine light, Fig. 21-23.
2. Connecting an analog voltmeter to vehicle ground and to one terminal on the data link connector while jumping from the pigtail (extra wire) to the data link connector. The code is produced by the meter's needle movement.
3. Turning the ignition key on and off several times within a few seconds and reading the flashing code on the dash-mounted check engine light. See Figure 21-23.
4. Pushing two dash-mounted climate control buttons at the same time and reading the dash display, Fig. 21-24.

Fig. 21-21. Scan tools are sometimes used while test driving vehicles. This will allow you to check engine and vehicle operating parameters while duplicating the conditions when the problem occurred.   (OTC)

ENERGIZING SELF-DIAGNOSIS (TROUBLE CODES)

The three major automakers use different procedures to make their car's on-board computer spit out trouble codes. The computer can actually detect if a sensor or actuator has failed or if a bad electrical connection has developed. This will help you know where to test for possible computer system problems.

The following is a summary of typical methods used to make an on-board computer produce these codes:

General Motors Corporation Trouble Codes

1. Locate diagnostic connector. It is usually under dash near fuse panel or steering column.
2. Use a jumper wire or paper clip to short across designated terminals in connector.
3. Watch engine light flash on and off in a Morse-type code. Count number of flashes between each pause and note them. Three flashes, a pause, and two flashes would equal code 32.
4. Refer to trouble code chart in service manual for an explanation of code number.
5. Test suspected component or circuit with a digital VOM. Compare your test readings to factory specs.
6. Note that some GM cars require you to press two climate control buttons on dash at same time to enter self-diagnosis. Then, trouble code number will appear in dash. You would then need to find the same number in service manual trouble code chart.

Ford Motor Company Trouble Codes

1. Locate diagnostic connector. It is usually in engine compartment on firewall, fender well, or near engine intake manifold.
2. Connect an analog or needle-type VOM to designated terminals in diagnostic connector.
3. Use a jumper wire to connect extra pigtail near connector to service-manual-designated terminal in connector.
4. Observe needle fluctuations on voltmeter as you did when watching engine light for a GM car. Count needle movements between each pause. Two needle movements, a pause, and then six needle movements would equal code 26.
5. Refer to service manual trouble code chart to find out what number code means.
6. Use conventional testing methods and your VOM to pinpoint cause for problem.

Chrysler Corporation Trouble Codes

1. Chrysler provides a diagnostic connector in engine compartment on late-model cars. However, connector is NOT needed to energize self-diagnosis. It is provided so a scanner-tester can be connected to system.
2. To trip trouble codes, simply turn ignition key on and off three times within five seconds. Turn key on, off, on, off, and then leave it ON.
3. Observe engine light flashing on and off. Count number of flashes between each pause. Three flashes, a pause, and then one flash would equal a trouble code of 31.
4. Refer to the service manual trouble code chart to find out which component or circuit is indicated by the trouble code.
5. Use conventional VOM tests to find the source of the trouble. Test the sensor or actuator and the wiring between the device and the computer.

Note! Computer self-diagnosis systems and procedures can vary from the methods just described. Always refer to a factory service manual when in doubt!

Fig. 21-22. Study the basic methods for reading computer trouble codes without a scan tool. (TIF Instruments)

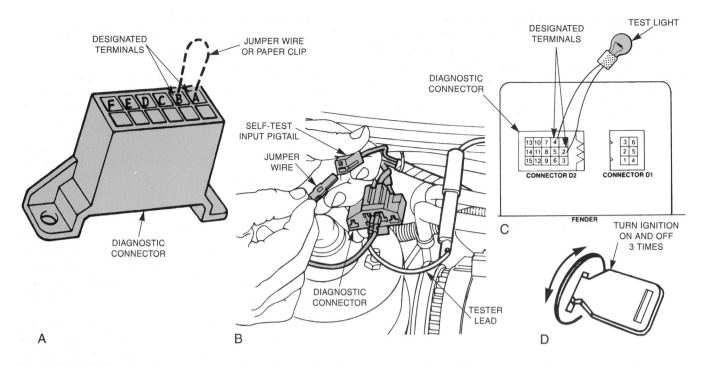

Fig. 21-23. OBD I systems have various methods to energize the computer on-board diagnostics. A—Use a jumper wire or paper clip to ground specified terminals in most GM connectors. B—Jump from the extra pigtail to a specified terminal in many Ford connectors. C—Connect a test light across specified terminals in this connector. D—Turning the ignition key on, off, on, off, and then on within five seconds will energize on-board diagnostics with most Chrysler cars. (Chrysler, General Motors, and Ford)

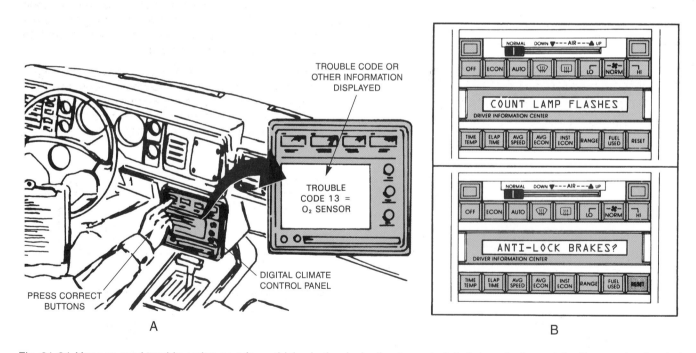

Fig. 21-24. You can read trouble codes on a few vehicles in the dash climate control digital readout panel A—By pressing two buttons at same time, the readout will give you any stored trouble code numbers. B—Some systems will actually describe each trouble code. (Ford and General Motors)

Always refer to the service manual for detailed instructions. Procedures vary from model to model as well as from year to year. These methods will not work on vehicles equipped with OBD II.

Some older vehicles with on-board computers do *not* have on-board diagnostics. You must use conventional testing methods to pinpoint problems on these vehicles.

Reading trouble codes without a scan tool

Reading trouble codes manually involves noting the computer output after the on-board diagnostics have been energized. There are several different ways that trouble codes can be read on older vehicles. The most typical methods include:

1. Observing the check engine light as it flashes on and off.
2. Noting an analog voltmeter's needle as it deflects back and forth.
3. Watching a test light connected to the data link connector flash on and off.
4. Observing the LED display on the side of the ECM.
5. Reading the digital display in a climate control panel or driver's information center.

The check engine light indicates each code as it blinks on and off with long and short pauses between each flash. Some codes are single-digit numbers and others are two-digit numbers. The number of flashes between each pause designates a single-digit code or one-half of a two-digit code, Fig. 21-25. With a single-digit code, count the number of pulses and this equals the code number. After a pause, the next code number would be given.

Reading a two-digit code is a bit more involved. If, for example, the check engine light blinks twice, pauses momentarily, and then blinks two more times, the trouble code would be 22 (2 pause 2). If the light flashes once, pauses, and flashes three more times, the trouble code would be 13 (1 pause 3). When there are multiple two-digit codes, there will be a relatively long pause between codes.

An analog voltmeter code is read by counting the number of needle deflections between each pause. This is similar to the dash light flashes. However, the computer usually produces 5 volt pulses for the test meter.

An example of a two-digit code would be if the needle deflected once, paused, and then deflected four more times. The first digit would be one and the second would be four. This would be a trouble code 14. A few digital test meters have a bar graph that will show trouble code pulses. Look at Fig. 21-26. However, most digital meters cannot read trouble codes. A test light code is read by noting the flashes of the tester bulb.

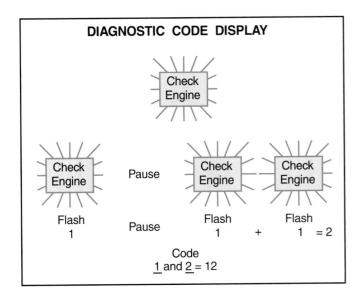

Fig. 21-25. A dash indicator light will normally glow if the computer detects a potential fault. This tells the driver and technician something is wrong. After entering the computer's diagnostic mode, the dash light may flash on and off to produce a number code. Note how this code is read. (General Motors)

WARNING! Use only a high-impedance (10 megohms or higher) test light or multimeter when testing computer circuits. A high current draw from a conventional test light could shorten electronic circuit life or even destroy delicate integrated circuits.

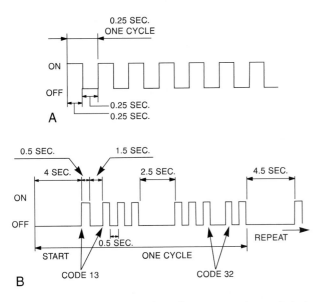

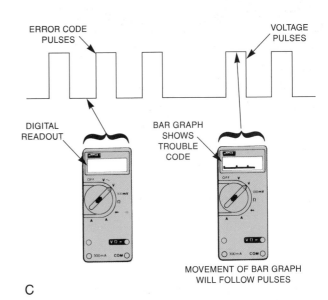

Fig. 21-26. Another method of reading a computer code is by noting light flashes or pulses. A—If the computer system is normal, pulses or flashes will occur two times per second. B—However, if a malfunction is present, the pulses and pauses denote any stored trouble codes. C—This digital VOM has a bar graph for reading coded voltage pulses. (Fluke)

An LED trouble code is produced by indicator lights on the side of the computer. This is a less common method to display computer trouble codes.

Dash digital codes are read like scan tool codes. These codes are retrieved after pressing two dash buttons, usually climate control buttons, at the same time. The climate control or temperature readout will then show any trouble codes.

Trouble code charts

A *trouble code chart* in the service manual will explain what each trouble code number means, Fig. 21-27. It will indicate which section or circuit of the computer system might have faults. This will help you know where to start further tests on specific components.

Study the other service manual trouble code charts given in Figs. 21-28 to 21-30.

Fig. 21-31 shows how one auto manufacturer allows you to check dash display functions, a form of actuator test, by pressing buttons on the dash.

ERASING TROUBLE CODES

Erasing trouble codes, also termed clearing diagnostic codes, removes the stored codes from computer memory after system repairs have been made. In most cases, codes will be automatically erased after 30-50 engine starts or warm-ups. However, codes should be erased to prevent a possible misdiagnosis by the next technician who works on the vehicle. There are various methods

DTC No.	DTC detecting condition	Trouble area
P0171	When the air fuel ratio feedback is stable after engine warming up, the fuel trim is considerably in error on the RICH side.	• Air intake (hose loose) • Fuel line pressure • Injector blockage • Heated oxygen sensor malfunction • Mass airflow meter • Engine coolant temp. sensor
P0172	When the air fuel ratio feedback is stable after engine warming up, the fuel trim is considerably in error on the LEAN side.	• Fuel line pressure • Injector leak, blockage • Heated oxygen sensor malfunction • Mass airflow meter • Engine coolant temp. sensor

Fig. 21-27. This is a trouble code chart for one type of vehicle. Study how different code numbers show possible problems and causes.   (General Motors)

Code No.	Item	Check Engine Lamp On (O) Off (X)	Diagnosis	Trouble Area
—	Normal condition	X	—	—
11	ECU power supply	X	Power cut, however temporary, to ECU	O Electrical system
12	RPM signal	O	No Ne or G signal to ECU while engine is cranked	O Distributor circuit O Crank position, starter signal circuit O Distributor O ECU
13	RPM signal	O	No Ne signal to ECU within several seconds after engine reaches 1,000 rpm	O Distributor circuit O Crank position, starter signal circuit O Distributor O ECU
14	Ignition signal	O	No signal from ignitor six times in succession	O Igniter circuit O Igniter O Ignition coil O ECU
21	Oxygen sensor signal	O	Open or short in oxygen sensor signal	O Oxygen sensor circuit O Oxygen sensor O ECU
22	Water thermo sensor signal	O	Open or short circuit in coolant temperature sensor signal	O Water thermo sensor circuit O Water thermo sensor O ECU
23	Intake air thermo sensor signal	X	Intake air thermo signal is open or short-circuited	O Intake air thermo sensor circuit O Intake air thermo sensor O ECU
31	Air flow meter signal	O	Open circuit in Vc when idle contacts are closed	O Air flow meter circuit O Air flow meter O ECU

Fig. 21-28. Study explanations given on this type of trouble code chart. (Toyota)

BCM DIAGNOSTIC CODES

CODE	CIRCUIT AFFECTED
▼ F10	OUTSIDE TEMP SENSOR CKT
▼ F11	A/C HIGH SIDE TEMP SENSOR CKT
▼ F12	A/C LOW SIDE TEMP SENSOR CKT
▼ F13	IN-CAR TEMP SENSOR CKT
▼ F30	CCP TO BCM DATA CKT
▼ F31	FDC TO BCM DATA CKT
▼ F32	ECM-BCM DATA CKT'S
▼ F40	AIR MIX DOOR PROBLEM
▼ F41	COOLING FANS PROBLEM
☑ F46	LOW REFRIGERANT WARNING
☑ F47	LOW REFRIGERANT CONDITION
☑ F48	LOW REFRIGERANT PRESSURE
▼ F49	HIGH TEMP CLUTCH DISENGAGE
▼ F51	BCM PROM ERROR

☑ TURNS ON "SERVICE AIR COND" LIGHT

▼ DOES NOT TURN ON ANY LIGHT

COMMENTS:

F11 TURNS ON COOLING FANS WHEN
  A/C CLUTCH IS ENGAGED
F12 DISENGAGES A/C CLUTCH
F32 TURNS ON COOLING FANS
F30 TURNS ON FT. DEFOG AT 75° F
F41 TURNS ON "COOLANT TEMP/FANS"
  LIGHT WHEN FANS SHOULD BE ON
F47 & F48 SWITCHES FROM "AUTO"
  TO "ECON"

Fig. 21-29. Body computer trouble code chart lists problems relating to climate control system. A separate trouble code chart would be provided for main on-board computer network. (Cadillac)

used to erase trouble codes from the computer:

1. Use a scan tool to remove stored diagnostic codes from the on-board computer. This is the best way to remove old codes after repairs. In OBD II systems, the ECM may retain stored codes for several days without battery power. See Fig. 21-32.
2. Disconnect the battery ground cable or strap. This will also erase the digital clock memory, all radio presets, and any adaptive strategy information from the computer.
3. Unplug the fuse to the ECM. This will also erase all other information stored in the computer's temporary memory.

WARNING! Some auto manufacturers warn against unplugging or plugging in the computer harness connector with the ignition key on or the engine running. This could cause a voltage spike that could damage the computer.

After erasing trouble codes, re-energize the on-board diagnostics and check for diagnostic trouble codes. If no trouble codes are displayed, you have corrected the problem.

SUMMARY

On-board diagnostics refers to a vehicle computer's ability to analyze the operation of its circuits and output data showing any problems.

A scan tool is used to communicate with the vehicle's computers to retrieve trouble codes, display circuit and sensor electrical values, run tests, and give helpful hints for finding problem sources.

OBD I and earlier on-board diagnostic systems could only check a limited number of items. On-Board Diagnostics II, abbreviated OBD II, is designed to more efficiently monitor the condition of hardware and software that affect emissions. New vehicle diagnostics detect part deterioration and not just complete part failure. If an unusual condition or electrical value is detected, the computer will turn on a malfunction indicator light (MIL) in the dash instrument panel or driver information center.

Diagnostic trouble codes (DTCs) are digital signals produced by the computer when an operating parameter is exceeded. Most scan tools come equipped with different program cartridges. A scan tool cartridge contains information about the specific make of vehicle to be scanned.

The data link connector (DLC) is a multi-pin terminal for reading computer trouble codes or scanning problems. A scan tool snapshot or freeze frame is an instantaneous readout of operating parameters at the time of a malfunction.

OBD II diagnostic trouble codes contain a letter and a four-digit number. The letter in all OBD II codes indicates the general function of the affected system. The first digit of the number in OBD II codes indicates whether the code is a standard trouble code or a nonuniform code. The second digit of the number in the OBD II code indicates the specific function of the system where the fault is located. The last two digits in the OBD II code refer to the specific fault designation.

A wiggle test is done by moving wires and harness connectors while scanning to find soft failures.

If you do not have a scan tool or are working on an older computer-controlled vehicle, there are several other ways to activate computer on-board diagnostics to pull out trouble codes.

KNOW THESE TERMS

On-board diagnostics, On-board diagnostics generation one (OBD I), On-board diagnostics generation two (OBD II), Malfunction indicator light (MIL), Check engine light, Service engine soon light, Trouble code chart, Trouble code conversion, Diagnostic trouble codes (DTC), Operating parameter, Scan tool, Program cartridges, Troubleshooting cartridge, Data link connector (DLC), Diagnostic connector, Assembly line diagnostic link (ALDL), Adapter, Prompts, Freeze frame, Failure record,

DFI DIAGNOSTIC TESTING CONDITIONS

(1)	TESTING REQUIREMENTS (2)				FAILURE REQUIREMENTS (3)		(4)	(5)
TROUBLE CODE	VEHICLE SPEED (MPH)	THROTTLE ANGLE	THROTTLE SWITCH	ENGINE SPEED (RPM)	ADDITIONAL REQUIREMENTS	FAILURE CONDITION	TIME (SEC)	FAILSOFT ACTION	DISABLED FUNCTIONS
12					CRANKING	NO REFERENCE PULSES	2.1	N	N
13		>6° <29°	OPEN	>800	COOLANT >80°C	0₂ VOLTAGE = >.275 AND <.630	30	N	B,D,G
14					MANIFOLD AIR <105°C	COOLANT >142°C		1	B
15					MANIFOLD AIR >5°C	COOLANT <−35°C		1	B
16				>800	NOT CRANKING	FUEL PUMP VOLTAGE <10 OR >16	5	N	A→F
18				>800		CRANK SIG. = 0 V SINCE IGNITION ON		N	N
19				= 0	NOT CRANKING & COOLANT LIGHT ON	FUEL PUMP VOLTAGE >11	3	N	N
20				>24		FUEL PUMP VOLTAGE <2	3	N	N
21				>25 <1000		THROTTLE ANGLE >80	1.5	2	E
22				>600		THROTTLE ANGLE <−5	1.5	2	N
23-A				>304	NOT CRANKING & NOT IN BYPASS	EST SIGNAL GROUNDED		N	N
23-B				>304	NOT CRANKING & IN BYPASS	EST SIGNAL NOT GROUNDED		3	N
23-C					NOT IN BYPASS & EST GROUNDED	RPM DROPS TO 0		3	N
24			OPEN	>1400	4TH GEAR, BRAKE OFF, DRIVE & MAP <85 kPa	VEHICLE SPEED = 0 MPH	3	N	E,F

Fig. 21-30. Note requirements and conditions given in this trouble code chart. (Cadillac)

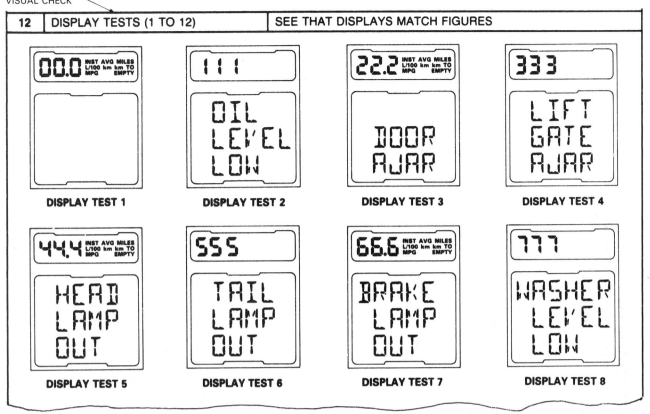

Fig. 21-31. This service manual illustration shows how you can check operation of dash display quickly and easily. By pressing two dash buttons, computer will cycle through all display outputs and show any trouble code numbers. This self-actuation test will quickly determine whether all dash displays are working properly. (Ford)

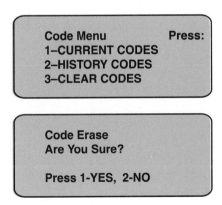

Fig. 21-32. Scan tool is fastest and easiest way to erase stored trouble codes. With most scanners, move to erase code and press yes. (OTC)

Standardized alpha-numeric trouble codes, Standard trouble codes, Nonuniform codes, Fault designation, Hard failure, Soft failure, General circuit failure, Low-input failure, High-input failure, Improper range/performance failure, Datastream values, Engine-off/key-on diagnostics, Wiggle test, Engine-on/key-on diagnostics, Switch diagnostic test, Actuator diagnostic test.

REVIEW QUESTIONS—CHAPTER 21

1. Define on-board diagnostics.
2. What are the advantages of OBD II systems?
3. If an unusual condition or electrical value is detected by an OBD II system, it will turn on the _____ _____ _____.
4. List and summarize 17 types of problems that can affect computer system operation.
5. Only about _____ of all performance problems are caused by the computer, sensors, and actuators.
6. List five locations for the data link connector.
7. Summarize the OBD II alpha-numeric diagnostic code.
8. A _____ _____ is always present and a _____ _____ is intermittent.
9. Name the four general categories of computer system failures.
10. _____ values give the electrical operating values of sensors, actuators, and circuits.
11. Describe the procedure for performing a wiggle test.
12. A(n) _____ _____ _____ involves using a scan tool to operate specific output devices.
13. Explain several ways to read trouble codes without a scan tool.
14. What are trouble code charts?

15. A(n) _____ multimeter should be used when checking computer circuits.
    a. analog
    b. low-capacitance
    c. high-impedance
    d. None of the above.

ASE CERTIFICATION–TYPE QUESTIONS

1. Technician A says an automotive computer can scan its input and output circuits to detect incorrect voltage problems. Technician B says an automotive computer can scan its input and output circuits to detect an incorrect resistance problem. Who is right?
   (A) A only.   (C) Both A and B.
   (B) B only.   (D) Neither A nor B.

2. Technician A says if an automotive computer system detects an abnormal condition, the car's malfunction indicator light will normally be activated. Technician B says if an automotive computer system detects an abnormal condition, it will store a diagnostic trouble code. Who is right?
   (A) A only.   (C) Both A and B.
   (B) B only.   (D) Neither A nor B.

3. Technician A says a faulty actuator can affect the operation of an automotive computer system. Technician B says a leaking vacuum hose can affect the operation of an automotive computer system. Who is right?
   (A) A only.   (C) Both A and B.
   (B) B only.   (D) Neither A nor B.

4. Which of the following is a possible location for an automotive computer system's data link connector?
   (A) Under right side of dash.
   (B) Near the firewall in the engine compartment.
   (C) Under the center console.
   (D) All of the above.

5. When a trouble code number is looked up in a service manual, the trouble code chart says oxygen sensor. Technician A says to test the sensor and its circuit. Technician B says to replace the oxygen sensor. Who is right?
   (A) A only.   (C) Both A and B.
   (B) B only.   (D) Neither A nor B.

6. A wiggle test is being performed on an automotive computer system. Technician A performs this test with the engine and the ignition key off. Technician B performs this test with the engine off and the ignition key on. Who is right?
   (A) A only.   (C) Both A and B.
   (B) B only.   (D) Neither A nor B.

7. All of the following can normally be performed during an automotive computer system actuator self-test except:
   (A) open and close injectors.
   (B) fire the ignition coil.
   (C) operate the reed valve.
   (D) activate the idle speed motor.

8. Technician A says on certain models of automobiles, you can activate the computer's self-diagnostics by pushing two dash climate control buttons at the same time. Technician B says on certain models of automobiles, you can activate the computer's self-diagnostics by turning the ignition key on and off within a few seconds. Who is right?
   (A) A only.   (C) Both A and B.
   (B) B only.   (D) Neither A nor B.

9. Which of the following test instruments can be used to read automotive computer system trouble codes?
   (A) Test light.   (C) Scan tool.
   (B) Voltmeter.   (D) All of the above.

10. Trouble codes need to be erased from an OBD II computer system. Technician A wants to accomplish this by unplugging the ECM fuse. Technician B wants to accomplish this by using the shop's scan tool. Who is right?
    (A) A only.   (C) Both A and B.
    (B) B only.   (D) Neither A nor B.

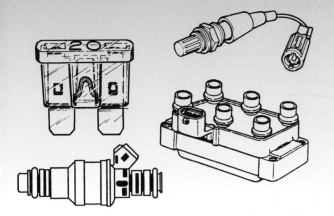

Chapter 22

Sensor, Actuator, Computer Service

After studying this chapter, you will be able to:
- *Explain the preliminary inspections that should be done when troubleshooting computer system malfunctions.*
- *Describe why remembering basic tests and problems is important to working on cars with computer controls.*
- *Use a breakout box to make electrical measurements and tests.*
- *Test various voltage generating sensors.*
- *Test variable resistance and switching type sensors. Use specialized sensor testers.*
- *Service an oxygen sensor.*
- *Adjust a throttle position sensor.*
- *Properly remove and replace various sensors.*
- *Test servo motors, solenoids, injectors, electric fuel pumps, and other types of actuators.*
- *Remove and replace a computer PROM.*
- *Measure computer reference voltage output to sensors with a VOM and computer signals to a mixture control solenoid with a dwell meter.*
- *Remove and replace a computer.*

In previous chapters, you learned how sensors, actuators, computers, and other electronic components operate. You also learned how to use computer self-diagnosis, scanners, and analyzers to help find electronic problems.

This chapter will concentrate on how to do specific tests on computer system components. Most sensors and actuators can be checked with a high impedance digital VOM. The wiring leading from the computer, to these devices, can also be checked for opens and shorts. This chapter will help you develop the skills needed to verify WHERE PROBLEMS ARE after reading trouble codes and using scanners or analyzers. Remember that trouble codes only indicate the area of a trouble, NOT what part is at fault. It is, therefore, imperative that you know how to do pinpoint tests on individual components.

PRELIMINARY INSPECTION

A *preliminary inspection* involves looking for signs of obvious trouble: loose wires, leaking vacuum hoses, part damage, etc. For example, if the trouble code says there is something wrong in the engine coolant temperature sensor circuit, you could check the sensor resistance and the wiring going to that sensor.

When there is a malfunction in a system, always remember the cause is usually something basic. It is easy for the untrained technician to instantly think "computer problems" when an engine misses, runs rough, fails to start properly, or exhibits some other performance problem.

Cipet principle

The abbreviation *cipet* refers to an easy way to remember a logical way to find performance problems. Cipet stands for:

1. COMPRESSION—do any of the cylinders have low compression?
2. IGNITION—is the ignition system operating properly?
3. POWER—is each cylinder producing equal and sufficient power?
4. EXHAUST—what is the chemical content of the engine exhaust?
5. TIMING—is the timing set and is it advancing properly?

If you use conventional methods to answer these questions, you will find the source of most engine performance problems. Studies have shown that 80% of all engine performance problems are caused by something other than the computer system electronics. Only 20% of all performance problems are due to the computer, sensors, or actuators themselves.

You must find out if the engine is in good mechanical condition, if the ignition is firing the plugs normally, if timing is correct, if the fuel system is up to specs, etc.

For example, even extremely DIRTY ENGINE OIL can trigger a computer trouble code. Contaminated oil fumes can be drawn into the engine intake manifold from the crankcase. The PCV system is designed to remove these fumes from the lower engine area and burn them in the engine. If these fumes are excessively strong, the oxygen sensor could be fooled into signaling a rich fuel mixture. The computer would then lean the fuel mixture to compensate for the crankcase fumes. An oxygen sensor trouble code could be produced and engine performance problems could result.

As this points out, it is critical that you check or troubleshoot conventional or BASIC PROBLEMS FIRST. Start checking for computer or electronic problems only after all basic system troubles have been eliminated.

Kiss principle

Kiss is another abbreviation that could help you find the source of performance problems on a computer-controlled car. *Kiss* stands for "keep it simple stupid!" This means that you should start your troubleshooting with the simple checks and tests. Then, as the simpler, more common problems are eliminated, you can move to more complex tests of sensors and actuators. The kiss principle will help you become a more competent auto electronic technician.

SENSOR SERVICE

Sensor service involves testing and sometimes replacing computer system sensors. Since sensor designs vary and some can be damaged by incorrect testing methods, it is important for you to know the most common ways of checking sensor values.

Basically, a VOM is used to measure the actual sensor output. Then, this output (voltage, resistance, or current) can be compared to factory specs. If the test value is too high or too low, you would know the sensor is faulty and must be replaced.

The number and types of sensors will vary with the specific make and model car. Refer to the car's service manual for exact sensor types and locations. Sometimes, the manual will show what sensors are used and where they are located, Fig. 22-1.

The shop manual will also have a wiring diagram for the computer system. The diagram will show the color codes of wires and number of connectors that are used to feed data from the sensor back to the computer. This can be very helpful when working on a computer system that you have never worked on before, Fig. 22-2.

Poor electrical connections

Poor electrical connections are the most common cause of electrical related problems in a computer system. Discussed in previous chapters, a wiggle test will help find bad connections and intermittent problems. Always check electrical connections when diagnosing sensors and other electronic components, Fig. 22-3.

Vacuum leaks

Vacuum leaks are frequently caused by deteriorated, broken, or loose vacuum hoses. Some vacuum leaks can

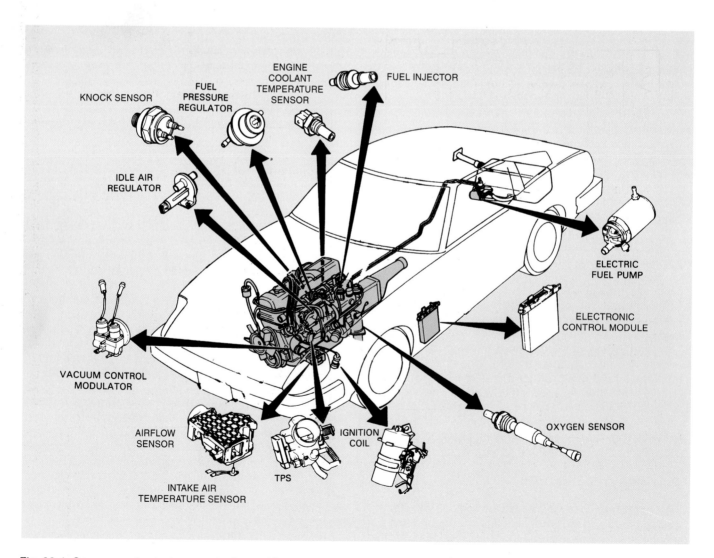

Fig. 22-1. Sensors and actuators can be located in various places on a car. The service manual will give exact locations and list what sensors and actuators are utilized.   (Nissan)

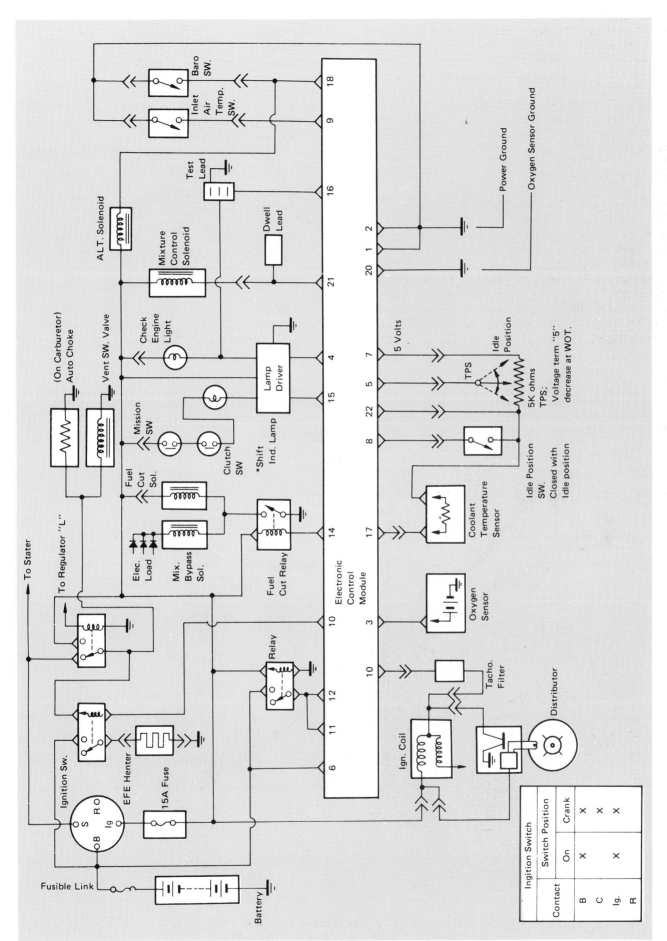

Fig. 22-2. The manual will also provide diagrams for the specific computer network. This will allow you to trace wires and find connectors for testing sensors and their wiring. (General Motors)

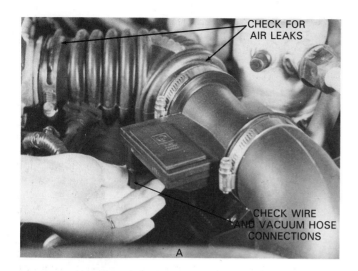
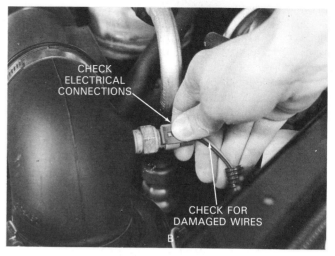

Fig. 22-3. A preliminary inspection will help find some problems. Check that wiring connectors are tight and vacuum hoses are secure. Also look for air leaks after the airflow sensor.

upset the operation of a computer system and cause a wide range of symptoms. Also, several engine sensors and vacuum actuators (vacuum switches) rely on engine vacuum for operation.

Always check for vacuum leaks when they could be causing a performance problem. For example, if the trouble code indicates a problem with the MAP (manifold absolute pressure) sensor, always check any vacuum lines leading to the sensor. If leaking, the sensor cannot function normally, Fig. 22-4.

Air leaks, after an airflow sensor, can also cause problems. The sensor cannot measure the air being drawn into the engine through the leak and an incorrect air-fuel mixture will result.

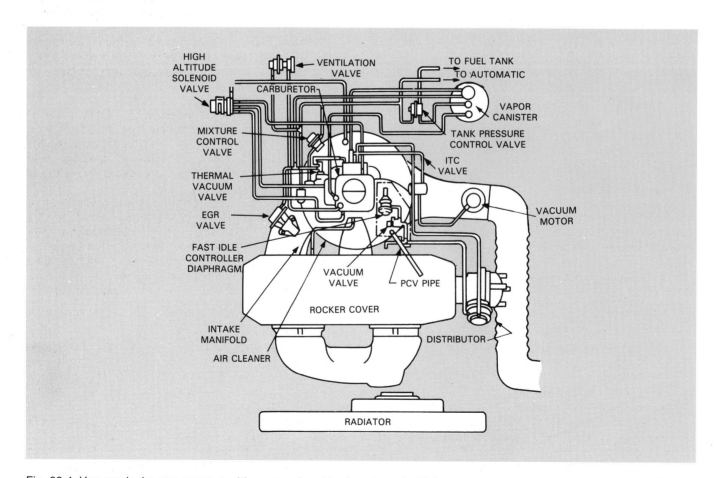

Fig. 22-4. Vacuum leaks can cause a wide range of problems, many of which can appear to be computer related. A vacuum gauge-pump may be needed during problem diagnosis. This is one example from a service manual. (Oldsmobile)

Breakout box

A *breakout box* can be connected to the computer wiring harness so electrical values can be measured more easily. The service manual will explain when a breakout box might be useful. It will also describe how to use the recommended type of breakout box. See Fig. 22-5.

Using a breakout box is similar to taking electrical measurements and an ECU terminal. You can touch your digital meter onto specific box terminals and compare the test values with specs. With a breakout box, you can touch your meter onto the box instead of inside the small ECU connector terminals.

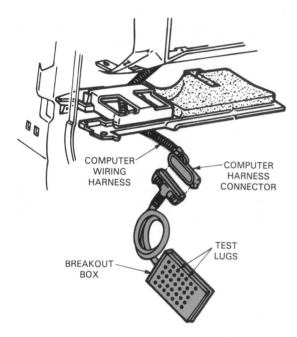

Fig. 22-5. Breakout box plugs into computer harness connector. Then, meter can be touched onto breakout box lug to more easily read electrical values in system.   (Cadillac)

SENSOR PROBLEMS, TESTING, REPLACEMENT

Sensors and their circuits can sometimes cause computer system malfunctions. As with other electronic components, sensors and sensor circuits can develop opens, shorts, or abnormal resistance or voltage values. When your tests find a problem, the sensor should be replaced or the circuit repaired.

Detailed in earlier chapters, sensors can produce signals for the computer in several ways:

1. VOLTAGE GENERATING SENSOR (oxygen sensor and some speed sensors produce an internal voltage during operation).
2. SWITCHING TYPE SENSORS (sensor simply acts as either a conductor or an insulator to switch on and off with condition changes; a brake switch and neutral safety switch would be examples).
3. VARIABLE RESISTANCE SENSORS (sensor ohms changes with condition to signal computer by altering current flow back to computer).

Each type of sensor needs a slightly different testing method. A voltage generating sensor requires a digital meter to read the small or weak voltage output. An ohmmeter and voltmeter are commonly used to check switching and variable resistance type sensors.

Electrical component damage

Semiconductor devices, such as transistors and integrated circuits, are very easy to damage. They can be damaged by static electricity, voltage spikes, heat, and impact shocks. Here are some things to remember when working with semiconductor devices and their wiring:

1. Arc welding can damage the on-board computers. If welding on the vehicle is necessary, remove all of the on-board computers. If this is not possible or too time-consuming, unplug their connectors and make sure the welder's lead is securely grounded.
2. Never disconnect the battery cables while the engine is running. In the past, some technicians would do this to see if the alternator was working. This can destroy or weaken electronic circuits, causing failure in a short period of time.
3. Do not disconnect or connect wiring, especially the computer wiring, with the ignition key on. This can cause a current surge that can damage the computer.
4. Make sure you do not reverse the battery cable connections. This can destroy electronic components.
5. Wear an anti-static wrist strap whenever you handle static-sensitive components (removable PROM chips for example) to protect them from damage.
6. Only use high impedance test lights and meters when checking electronic circuits or their wiring. A conventional test light or meter will draw too much current and destroy electrical components.
7. Do not disconnect a scan tool from the data link connector while the ignition key is on. This could create a voltage spike that can damage the computer.

Reference voltage

A *reference voltage* of typically FIVE VOLTS is fed to switching and variable resistance type sensors. Then, when conditions and sensor resistance change, the amount of current flowing back to the computer also changes. The reference voltage is needed so that a signal returns to the computer.

If you disconnect the reference voltage wire from a resistive sensor, an ohmmeter can be used to check the sensor. However, the voltage drop across the sensor can also be used to check resistive type sensors with the reference wire still connected to the sensor. You must use a service manual and your own judgment to determine which testing method should be used under the circumstances.

Engine speed sensor service

A *bad engine speed sensor* will sometimes keep an engine from running by disabling the ignition system. The engine speed sensor can be mounted in the distributor (pickup coil) or on the engine (crank position sensor) so that it can detect crankshaft rotation.

Most speed sensors are magnetic and produce a weak voltage signal. You can use a VOM or scope to check the speed sensor. An ohmmeter can also be used to measure the internal resistance of the sensor coil windings.

An ohmmeter will produce a static (nonrunning) test of a speed sensor. Disconnect the sensor wires, and

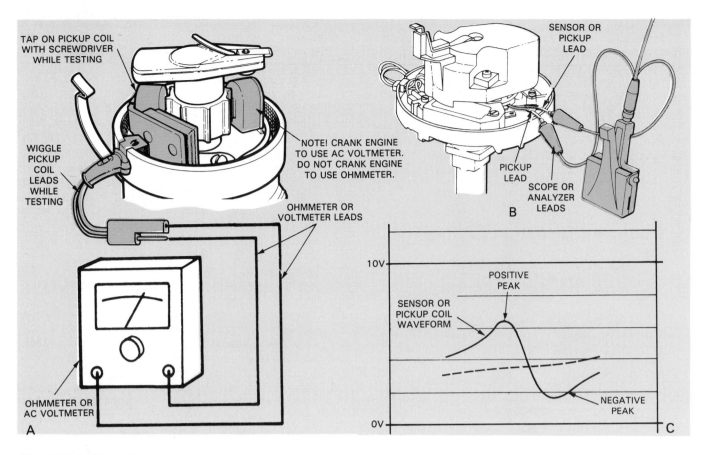

Fig. 22-6. A—Magnetic speed sensor or pickup coil can be tested with an ohmmeter. Coil windings should have spec resistance. Wiggle wires while testing to check for internal breaks in wires. B—AC voltmeter or a scope can also be used to measure small voltage output of magnetic sensor while cranking engine. C—Scope pattern.   (Chrysler and Sun)

measure the internal resistance of the sensor coil, Fig. 22-6A. Resistance specs will vary from about 250 to 1500 ohms so refer to the manual for an accurate value.

To use a digital VOM, set the meter on AC volts and connect the test leads to the sensor wires, Fig. 22-6B. Crank the engine and read the meter. Typically, a good sensor will produce an AC voltage output of about 1.5 to 3 volts. Again, check specs before condemning a speed sensor.

An oscilloscope can also be used to measure the voltage output from most speed sensors. As shown in Fig. 22-6C, connect engine analyzer leads to the pickup coil. Crank the engine and read the AC voltage output waveform on the scope screen.

A faulty speed sensor will have high resistance, low resistance, a low or no voltage output. Fig. 22-7 shows the location of some speed sensors. Replace the sensor if not within factory specs.

A nonmagnetic feeler gauge may be needed to adjust some distributor-mounted pickup coils or speed sensors. The gap between the sensor and its trigger wheel must be correct. However, most speed sensors lock in place and do not require adjustment. Fig. 22-8 shows how to adjust one type of speed sensor.

Vehicle speed sensor service

A *bad vehicle speed sensor* will usually reduce engine performance and fuel economy but will not normally keep the engine from running. It provides data for precise control of fuel metering, ignition timing, transmission/ transaxle shift points, etc. A bad vehicle speed sensor might also affect transmission torque converter lockup.

A vehicle speed sensor is tested in much the same way as an engine speed sensor. Sensor resistance or voltage output is usually measured and compared to specs.

Oxygen (O₂) sensor service

A *bad oxygen* or *O₂ sensor* will primarily upset the fuel injection system or the computerized carburetor system. The voltage signal from the sensor represents air-fuel ratio. If the oxygen sensor produces a false output (incorrect voltage), the computer cannot precisely control how much fuel is metered into the engine. A rich mixture or lean misfire condition could result.

O₂ sensor contamination

Normally, oxygen sensors are designed to last about 50,000 miles (81 000 km). However, its life can be shortened by contamination, blocked outside air, shorts, and poor electrical connections.

Oxygen sensor contamination can be caused by:
1. LEADED FUEL. Leaded fuel is the most common cause of oxygen sensor contamination. Lead coats the ceramic element and the sensor cannot produce enough voltage output for computer.
2. SILICONE. Sources are anti-freeze, volatile RTV silicone sealers, waterproofing sprays, and gasoline additives. Silicone forms a glassy coating.

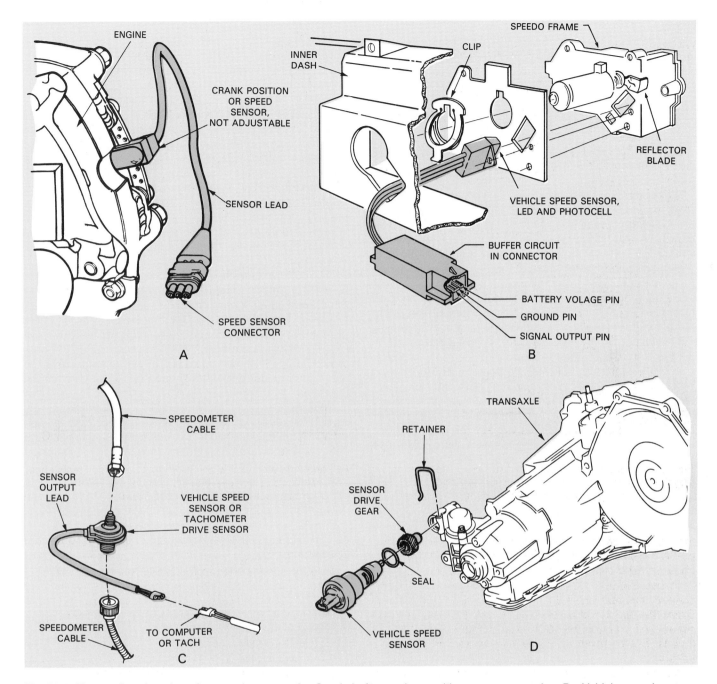

Fig. 22-7. Note various locations for speed sensors. A—Crankshaft speed or position sensor on engine. B—Vehicle speed sensor in speedometer head. C—Vehicle speed sensor in speedometer cable. D—Vehicle speed sensor on automatic transaxle. (General Motors and Chrysler)

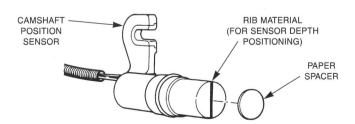

Fig. 22-8. This camshaft speed sensor uses a paper spacer to aid in adjustment. Mounting screw is loosened and spacer is placed between sensor tip and trigger wheel tooth on camshaft. After sensor is reinstalled and mounting screws are tightened, spacer is removed. (Chrysler)

3. CARBON. Carbon contamination results from rich fuel mixtures. Carbon in fuel coats the sensor.

Carbon and moderate lead contamination can sometimes be reversed. Run the engine at high speeds with a large vacuum hose (PCV hose for example) removed and with only unleaded fuel in the tank. This will sometimes burn off light lead and most carbon deposits. The sensor may start working normally again.

O_2 sensor inspection

Also, check that the outside of the sensor and its electrical connection are free of oil, dirt, undercoating, and other deposits. If outside air cannot circulate through the oxygen sensor, the sensor will not function.

An oxygen sensor only generates a tiny voltage (an average of about .5 volts). A poor electrical connection can prevent this small voltage from reaching the computer. Always check the sensor's electrical connections.

O_2 sensor testing

Discussed earlier, most computer systems will now produce a trouble code indicating when the output from the oxygen sensor is NOT within normal parameters. This would tell you to do further tests on the oxygen sensor and its circuit.

Many computer systems have a limp-in mode. If the oxygen sensor or some other sensor fails and produces an incorrect output, the system will go into this emergency limp-in mode. A predetermined oxygen sensor voltage (.5 volts for example) or other output will be simulated by the computer and used to keep the engine running well enough to drive in for repairs.

Remember from the previous chapter that some analyzers will read oxygen sensor voltage when connected to the computer system. This allows you to check O_2 sensor output without removing the wires to the sensor. This is also true for some other sensors.

A digital voltmeter can also be used to test the output of an oxygen sensor. Warm the engine to full operating temperature to shift the computer system into closed loop. The sensor must be hot (about 600°F or 315°C) to operate properly. You may have to warm the engine at fast idle for up to 15 minutes with some cars. Note that a few systems can drop out of closed loop at idle.

Warning! Only use a high impedance, digital meter to measure oxygen sensor voltage. A conventional analog or low resistance meter can draw too much current and damage the O_2 sensor.

Unplug the sensor leads and connect a digital voltmeter to the oxygen sensor, as shown in Fig. 22-9.

O_2 sensor output voltage

Oxygen sensor output voltage should cycle up and down from about .4 volts (400 mV) to .7 volts (700 mV), Fig. 22-10. A .4 volt or low reading would show a lean air-fuel ratio condition and a .7 volt or high reading would show a richer condition. A high or low reading does not always mean the O_2 sensor is bad. Another problem (leaking or clogged fuel injector for example) could make the sensor read high or low, Fig. 22-11.

A quick test to see if the oxygen sensor reacts to a change in air-fuel mixture is to pull off a large vacuum hose, like the PCV valve. This extra air should make the oxygen sensor try to enrich the fuel mixture and compensate for the air leak (lean condition). The output voltage should then go DOWN (to about .3 or .4 volts) to signal a need for more fuel to adjust for the vacuum leak or extra air.

When the engine throttle is snapped open and closed, O_2 sensor output should also cycle up and down to show the change in air-fuel mixture.

If you block the air inlet at the air cleaner or inject propane gas into the air inlet (creating a rich mixture), the oxygen sensor voltage should INCREASE (go up to about .8 to .9 volts). It should try to signal the computer that too much fuel, or not enough air, is entering the combustion chambers.

If the oxygen sensor voltage does not change properly as you simulate rich and lean air-fuel ratios, the oxygen sensor is faulty. You might try running the engine at high speeds, with a large vacuum hose removed, to clean off light lead or carbon contamination.

A faulty oxygen sensor will usually be locked at one voltage output level and will not cycle voltage up and down normally. It also may not produce enough voltage.

Fig. 22-12 shows a specialized oxygen sensor tester. It can also be used to check voltage output and sensor condition.

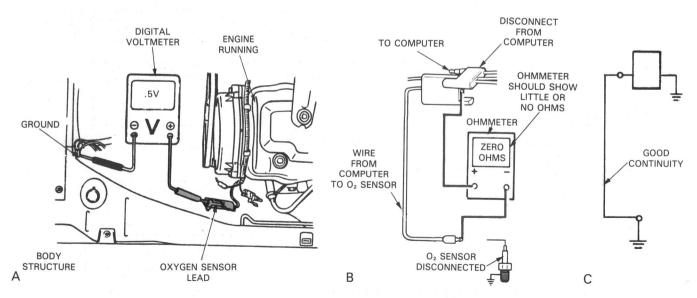

Fig. 22-9. Oxygen sensor is common trouble point. It can be tested with a digital voltmeter. A—Connect digital voltmeter to oxygen sensor and to ground. With engine running and warmed, sensor voltage should be around one-half volt. B—If sensor checks good, also check wiring leading to sensor. Wiring should have good continuity between computer and sensor connector. C—Continuity good between computer and sensor.   (General Motors and Ford)

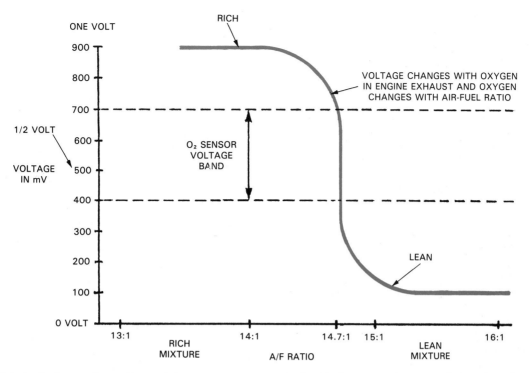

Fig. 22-10. Note typical operating voltages for an oxygen sensor. As throttle is snapped open and closed to alter fuel metering, oxygen sensor voltage should swing up and down to signal computer or fuel mixture change.

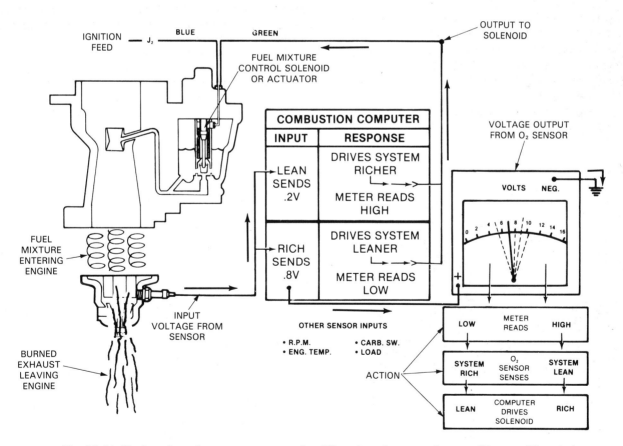

Fig. 22-11. Study action of oxygen sensor under different engine operating conditions. (Chrysler)

379

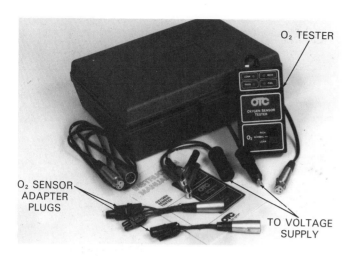

Fig. 22-12. This oxygen sensor tester can make trouble-shooting easier. Note connectors for different car makes and models. (OTC)

Reading oxygen sensor

To *read an oxygen sensor,* inspect the color of the sensor's tip, Fig. 22-13:

1. A LIGHT GRAY TIP is a normal color for an oxygen sensor.
2. A WHITE SENSOR TIP might indicate a lean mixture or silicone contamination. Sensor MUST usually be replaced.
3. A TAN SENSOR TIP could be lead contamination. It can sometimes be cleaned away by briefly running the engine lean on unleaded fuel.
4. A BLACK SENSOR TIP normally indicates a rich mixture and carbon contamination which can sometimes be cleaned after correcting the cause.

Note that some manufacturers recommend OXYGEN SENSOR REPLACEMENT after only 12,000 miles (19 308 km) when the sensor is removed. Therefore, the O_2 sensor is normally replaced with a new one when unscrewed from the exhaust system. Reading an oxygen sensor can indicate fuel system problems, silicone contamination, leaded fuel in the tank, and other troubles.

Testing O_2 sensor circuit

If the oxygen sensor has normal voltage, you should check the circuit leading to the sensor. Measure the resistance of the wires leading to the oxygen sensor. You can use long test leads, as in Fig. 22-9B. You can also ground one end of the sensor wire and check it for continuity at the other end, Fig. 22-9C.

Oxygen sensor replacement

Disconnect the negative battery cable. Then, separate the sensor from the wiring harness by unplugging the connector. Never pull on the wires themselves as damage may result.

The oxygen sensor may have a permanently attached pigtail. Never attempt to remove it. Use a wrench to unscrew the sensor. Inspect its condition. Some sensors may be difficult to remove at temperatures below 120°F. Use care to avoid thread damage.

Follow these rules when replacing an oxygen sensor:

1. Do NOT touch the sensor element with anything (water, solvents, etc.).
2. Coat sensor threads before installation with anti-seize compound to prevent seizure and damage.
3. Do NOT use silicone based sealers on or around exhaust system components. Only use low volatile silicone sealers sparingly on engine components. The PCV system can draw silicone fumes into engine intake manifold and over O_2 sensor.
4. Hand start sensor to prevent cross threading.
5. Do NOT overtighten the O_2 sensor. It could be damaged.
6. Make sure outside vents are clear so that air can circulate through the sensor.
7. Make sure wiring is reconnected securely to sensor.
8. If sensor checks out good, check continuity of wiring between sensor and computer.
9. Check oxygen sensor output and fuel system operation after installing sensor.
10. Repair any engine oil leaks that might contaminate new oxygen sensor right away.

Fig. 22-13. Reading an oxygen sensor involves removing and inspecting color and condition of sensor. This is similar to reading spark plugs and may help you find other problems with engine and computer system. When sensor is removed and been in service for awhile, it is wise to install a new sensor. Use thread anti-seize compound on sensor threads. (Universal Tire and Auto)

Manifold absolute pressure sensor service

A *bad manifold absolute pressure sensor* can affect the air-fuel ratio when the engine accelerates and decelerates. It serves the same basic function as a power valve in a carburetor. It senses engine vacuum to signal when more fuel is needed under a load or when gaining speed. It might also have some effect on ignition timing and a few other computer outputs.

To test a manifold absolute pressure sensor, measure sensor circuit voltage or sensor resistance while applying vacuum to the unit. As shown in Fig. 22-14, a vacuum pump is attached to the sensor's vacuum fitting. Apply specified vacuum levels while measuring the output of the MAP sensor.

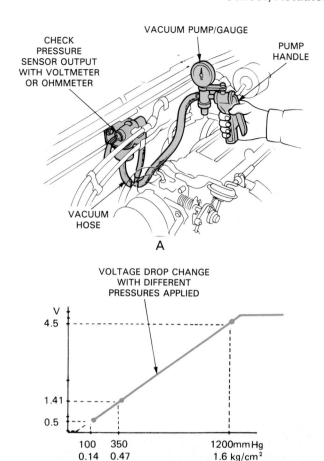

Fig. 22-14. Manifold absolute pressure sensor is tested by applying vacuum to the unit while measuring voltage or resistance. A—Test connection. B—One example of specs. (Honda)

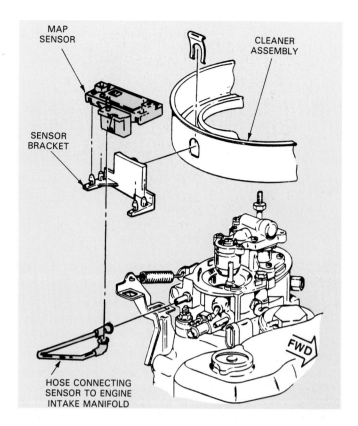

Fig. 22-15. Always check vacuum line running to MAP sensor closely. Any leaks can upset its operation. (General Motors)

Some manuals instruct you to measure sensor voltage at a specified test terminal. Others might have you disconnect the wires from the sensor and compare ohmmeter readings to specs.

In any case, sensor values must be within limits at the various vacuum levels. If testing at the test terminal, check the wiring harness before condemning the sensor. A poor connection or short could upset a reference voltage flowing to the sensor.

If problems are indicated, measure the voltage going to the sensor. Make sure any reference voltage is up to specs (usually about 5 volts). If needed, check harness resistance. Replace the sensor or repair the wiring as needed, Fig. 22-15.

Jumper wires are often used when testing a MAP sensor. Connect the jumpers between the sensor's terminals and the wiring harness. This allows you to measure actual sensor circuit voltage with the unit operating. See Fig. 22-16.

Throttle position sensor service

A *bad throttle position sensor* (TPS) can also affect fuel metering, ignition timing, and other computer outputs. It can also trip several trouble codes on some systems and can be a frequent cause of problems. Many throttle position switches use contact points or variable resistors that

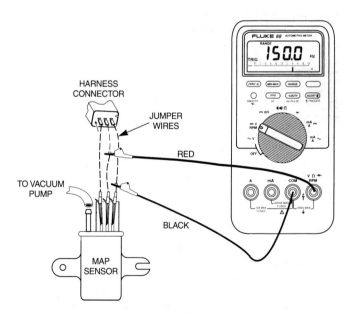

Fig. 22-16. Small jumper wires are often used when measuring sensor circuit values. Make sure you do not short two jumper wires together or to ground. This test is used to measure the frequency signal in hertz from a manifold absolute pressure sensor. (Fluke)

can wear and fail after prolonged operation.

A throttle position sensor is comparable to a carburetor accelerator pump and metering rod. It signals the computer when the gas pedal is depressed to different positions for acceleration, deceleration, idle, cruise, and full

381

power. It can cause a wide range of performance problems. If shorted, it might make the fuel mixture too rich. If open, it can make the mixture too lean.

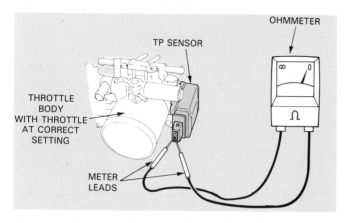

Fig. 22-17. Throttle position sensor is usually tested by measuring resistance or voltage across sensor terminals at specific throttle openings. If not within specs, adjust or replace the unit. (Toyota)

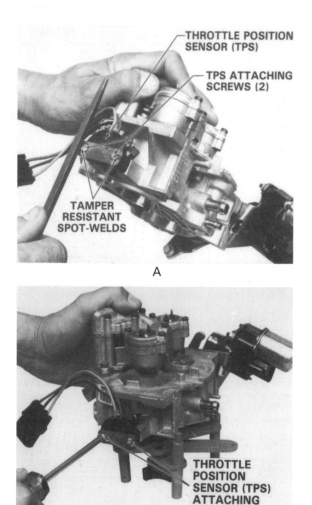

Fig. 22-18. A—To replace a TPS, you must normally file or drill out stakes that lock screws in place. B—Then screws and sensor can be removed. (Buick)

The throttle position sensor can sometimes be tested at a special tester terminal in the wiring harness. Some manuals say you should measure voltage drops across the sensor at specified throttle positions. A reference voltage is fed to the sensor by the computer. The sensor change in resistance changes the voltage across the resistance.

Many manuals also recommend checking the resistance of the throttle position sensor at different throttle openings. The manual might have you measure ohms at

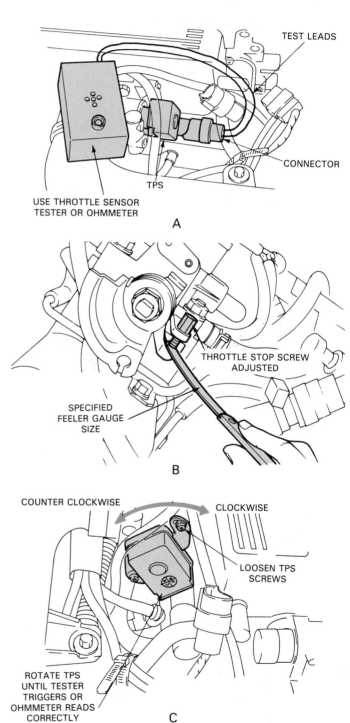

Fig. 22-19. Here is how a tester can be used to adjust one type of TPS. A—Connect tester to sensor connector. B—Open throttle recommended amount. C—Rotate sensor until tester is triggered; then tighten hold-down screws. (Mazda)

idle, half throttle, and full throttle, Fig. 22-17. If resistance is within specs, check the wiring leading to the TPS.

Throttle position sensor removal

To remove many throttle position sensors, you must file or grind off stakes (small welds) on the sensor screws, Fig. 22-18. You might also have to drill into the screws from the bottom of the throttle body assembly. This will let you turn and remove the screws and TPS. Refer to the service manual for details.

Throttle position sensor adjustment

Some throttle position sensors must be adjusted; some cannot be adjusted. Many are mounted so that they can be rotated on the carburetor or throttle body. Either a special tester or an ohmmeter is commonly used to adjust a throttle position sensor, Fig. 22-19.

Basically, you must measure sensor resistance or note tester output with the throttle at specific positions. You may have to insert a feeler gauge under the throttle lever or have the throttle plates at curb idle, for example. With the throttle plates at the correct angle, the TPS should trigger the tester or show a specified ohms value. If an adjustment is needed and possible, loosen the sensor mounting screws. Rotate the TPS until the correct ohms reading is obtained. Then, tighten the mounting screws and recheck the meter reading.

Idle switch service

A *bad idle switch* can fail to signal the computer when the engine is at curb idle. It can affect idle fuel mixture and ignition timing slightly.

An ohmmeter is commonly recommended to test the idle switch. Generally, the switch should open and close as the throttle lever is moved opened and closed. If not, the switch has failed and must be replaced, Fig. 22-20.

Engine coolant temperature sensor service

A *bad engine coolant temperature sensor* can also affect air-fuel ratio and ignition timing by not accurately informing the computer of the engine operating temperature. The engine coolant temperature sensor serves a similar function to a carburetor choke; it richens the mixture when cold and leans the mixture when hot. If opened, the coolant temperature sensor might affect cold engine driveability. If shorted, it might affect warm engine driveability.

An ohmmeter is commonly used to measure coolant temperature sensor resistance when cold and when hot. The service manual will give a chart giving ohms readings for specific temperatures, Fig. 22-21.

TEMPERATURE TO RESISTANCE VALUES FOR TEMPERATURE SENSOR (Approximate)		
Deg. F	**Deg. C**	**Ohms**
210	100	185
160	70	450
100	38	1,800
70	20	3,400
40	-4	7,500
20	-7	13,500
0	-18	25,000
-40	-40	100,700

A

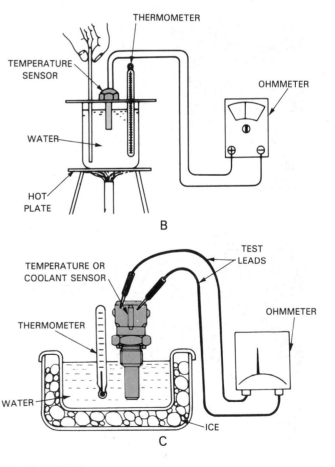

B

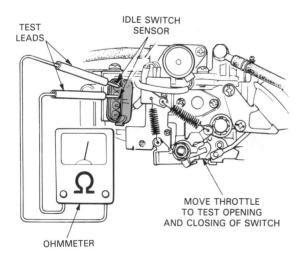

C

Fig. 22-20. Various switching type sensors can be tested for opening and closing action with ohmmeter. Here ohmmeter is being used to test carburetor micro-switch sensor. (General Motors)

Fig. 22-21. Engine temperature or coolant temperature sensor testing is normally done with ohmmeter. A—One example of sensor ohms for specified temperatures. B—Heating sensor while testing action. C—Cooling sensor to check action.

You can test the sensor while still in the engine by checking ohms when the engine is cold and after it warms. However, a more precise method is to submerse the sensor in water and heat it on a hot plate. This will let you compare thermometer readings and resistance readings with exact specs.

Fig. 22-22 shows another way to test a thermal switch or sensor. This unit controls a cold start injector. A battery and test light are connected to the sensor. With an increase in temperature, the sensor may switch off and the test light will go out. The exact temperature and action of the switching sensor can vary with the manufacturer.

Note that temperature sensor operation and ratings can vary. When purchasing a new temperature sensor, or any sensor, make sure you have the RIGHT ONE. For example, Fig. 22-23 shows how similar temperature sensors can have different operating temperatures. If you install the wrong one, it will upset the operation of the computer system.

When replacing a coolant temperature sensor, use a deep socket or six-point wrench to unscrew the old unit. Double-check that you have the correct replacement sensor. You might want to coat the sensor threads with approved sealer. Then, hand start and tighten the sensor in the engine. Do not overtighten the coolant sensor, or it could bottom out in the engine and be ruined.

Thermal-vacuum switch service

A *bad thermal-vacuum switch* will fail to control vacuum to another device and can cause a wide range of symptoms depending upon its function. Fig. 22-24 shows how to test a thermal-vacuum switch. The sensor is heated in water while applying vacuum to the inlet fitting. The unit should pass or block vacuum with a change in

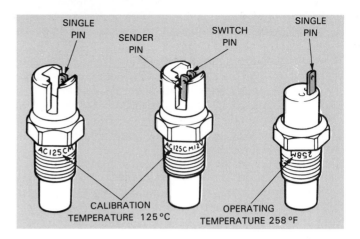

Fig. 22-23. Make sure you always have the correct replacement sensor. For example, note how these temperature sensors have different operating temperatures. If you install the wrong one, computer system may not function properly. (Pontiac)

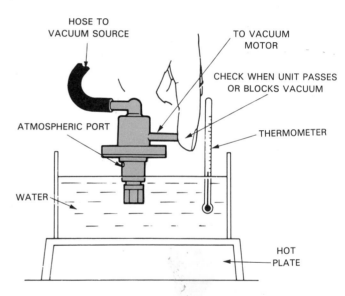

Fig. 22-24. Vacuum source is being applied to thermal vacuum switch. As temperature changes, switch should block or pass vacuum. (General Motors)

temperature. The service manual will explain specific temperatures and switch points.

Intake air temperature sensor service

A *bad intake air temperature sensor* will usually not have a pronounced effect on vehicle operation. It normally allows the computer system to make fine adjustments of air-fuel ratio and timing with changes in outside air temperature. If the sensor fails, it will normally trigger a self-diagnosis code and you would know to test the sensor and its circuit.

An ohmmeter is commonly recommended for checking an air temperature sensor. As with an engine coolant temperature sensor, the unit is frequently a thermistor that changes internal resistance with temperature. The sensor should have spec ohms for certain temperatures. If not, replace the sensor. Look at Fig. 22-25.

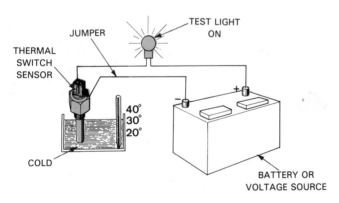

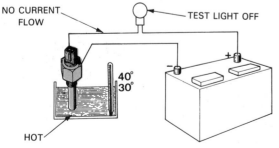

Fig. 22-22. Connecting voltage source and test light to sensor is another testing method for thermal sensor. As temperature or conditions change, test light should turn on or off. This sensor operates cold start injector. (Peugeot)

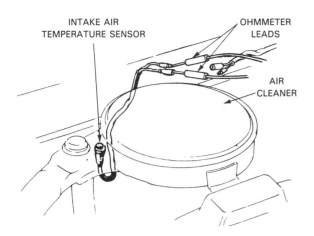

Fig. 22-25. Intake air temperature sensor is usually a thermistor. Use ohmmeter to compare resistance for specific temperature. (Honda)

Airflow sensor service

A *bad airflow sensor* will normally cause the system to go into limp-in mode, as will several other sensors. If shorted or opened, the computer will begin to operate on preprogrammed values. The car will perform poorly and get lower fuel economy.

Since there are various types of airflow sensors, you must refer to the shop manual for exact procedures. Many manufacturers have you use an ohmmeter to check the airflow sensor when it is a variable resistance type, Fig. 22-26. Others have integrated circuits on the sensor and special testing methods are required to prevent potential sensor damage. Specific terminals on the sensor must be touched to make readings, Fig. 22-27.

If faulty, you must usually remove and replace the airflow sensor. During replacement, make sure that you have the correct unit. Also, tighten all fittings carefully. An AIR LEAK after the airflow sensor will upset its operation, and can trigger trouble codes, Fig. 22-28.

Fuel sending unit service

A *bad fuel sending unit* can open, short, or develop high or low resistance and cause the fuel gauge to read improperly. It can also upset the operation of the trip computer

system. This sensor is simply a variable resistor operated by a float. The float follows the fuel level in the tank so that resistance changes proportionately with the fuel level.

Many manufacturers give ohm values for specific float arm positions, Fig. 22-29. Your ohmmeter must read closed.

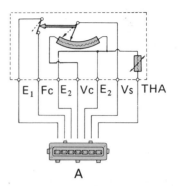

A

Between terminals	Resistance	Temperature
$E_2 - V_S$	$20 - 400\ \Omega$	–
$E_2 - V_C$	$200 - 400\ \Omega$	–
$E_2 - THA$	$10 - 20\ K\Omega$ $4 - 7\ K\Omega$ $2 - 3\ K\Omega$ $0.9 - 1.3\ K\Omega$ $0.4 - 0.7\ K\Omega$	$-20°C\ (\ 4°F)$ $0°C\ (\ 32°F)$ $20°C\ (\ 68°F)$ $40°C\ (104°F)$ $60°C\ (140°F)$
$E_1 - FC$	Infinity	–

B

Fig. 22-27. A—Note internal diagram of one type airflow sensor. When testing airflow meter, refer to the service manual. It will tell you which terminals to touch with meter and what test results should be. Some airflow sensors have internal integrated circuits that could be damaged by an improper testing method. B—Specs for just one airflow sensor. (Toyota)

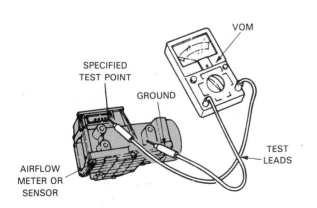

Fig. 22-26. Depending upon airflow sensor type, different testing methods are required. This type requires ohmmeter to check internal resistance change as flap is opened and closed.

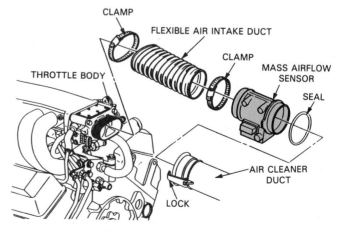

Fig. 22-28. When replacing airflow sensor, make sure there are no air leaks to upset operation.

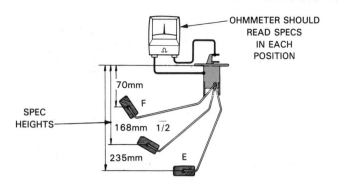

Fig. 22-29. Fuel sending unit or sensor should have specific resistance for specific float arm positions. (Toyota)

within specs for each float arm position. Special testers are also available for checking the gauge circuit.

The fuel sending unit is normally held in the fuel tank by a large locking ring. Rotating the lock ring will free the sender from the tank.

DANGER! Make sure the fuel tank is almost empty before removing the sending unit or gallons of gasoline or diesel fuel can pour out of the tank.

Water-in-fuel sensor

A *bad water-in-fuel sensor* can improperly illuminate the dash light or it may not warn when water is in the diesel fuel. Many diesel fuel systems use this sensor to protect from internal corrosion caused by water contamination. Fig. 22-30 shows how one automaker recommends testing the water-in-fuel sensor.

Knock sensor service

A *bad knock sensor* can upset ignition timing and affect turbocharger boost pressure. It is used to detect abnormal

combustion or ping. When it "hears" pinging or knocking, it will retard ignition timing or lower turbo boost with the turbo wastegate. Many computers will store a trouble code if there is a potential problem with the knock sensor.

To check a knock sensor, tap on the engine right next to the knock sensor. This will simulate pinging or knocking and should make the computer retard the ignition timing. The light taps should make the engine speed drop slightly. You might need to prop open the throttle to increase engine speed slightly so timing is advanced and will retard.

If tapping next to the sensor has no effect on timing and engine speed, you can check it with a VOM. Refer to the manual for recommendations. Remember to check the wiring leading to the knock sensor before removing or replacing the sensor!

Diesel metering valve sensor

A *bad diesel metering valve sensor* can effect how much fuel the diesel injection pump injects into the cylinders. This can upset the diesel's air-fuel ratio and reduce performance and fuel economy. This sensor is only used on late model diesels with computer control.

A digital voltmeter or an ohmmeter can be used to check the metering valve sensor. As in Fig. 22-31, sensor voltage output or resistance must be within specs. If not, replace the sensor.

ACTUATOR SERVICE

Actuator service involves testing solenoids, servo motors, displays, and other output devices for possible electrical and mechanical problems. Like sensors, if an actuator fails to function properly, the computer cannot control the vehicle system.

Idle speed motor service

A *bad idle speed motor* may not be able to maintain the correct engine idle speed. Engine idle speed may be too low or too high for conditions. The servo motor could have shorted windings, opened windings, bad internal bearings,

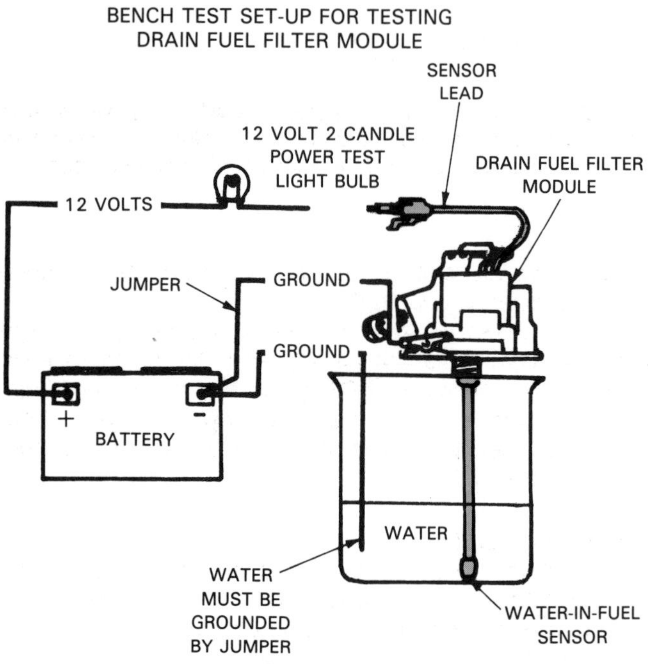

Fig. 22-30. Note how you can test this water-in-fuel detector. (Ford)

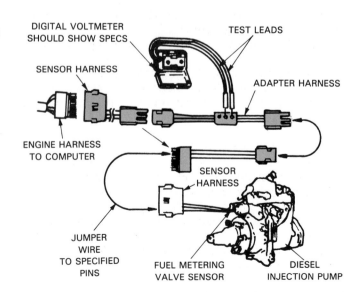

Fig. 22-31. Digital voltmeter is needed to check the conditions of this metering valve sensor in diesel injection pump. (Ford)

or other problems that upsets its operation.

Fig. 22-32 shows a common way to check the operation of the idle speed motor. Battery voltage is jumped to specific terminals on the servo motor. This should make the idle speed motor plunger retract and extend as the connections are reversed. A faulty motor will usually not function.

If the idle speed motor works when jumped to battery voltage, check the wiring leading to the motor. The wiring harness could have an open or short. A computer or relay problem could also prevent motor operation.

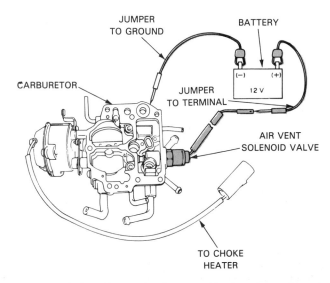

Fig. 22-33. Solenoid can also be tested by jumping voltage to windings. This should activate solenoid plunger movement.

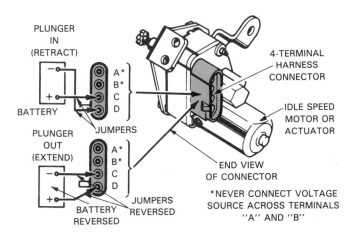

Fig. 22-32. This actuator is an idle speed motor. To test it remove the wires to the unit and jump a battery to the recommended terminals. Motor should run and reverse direction as jumpers are reversed. (General Motors)

Idle air control valve service

A *bad idle air control valve* will upset engine idle speed like a bad idle speed motor. It uses solenoid action to open and close an air passage bypassing the throttle plates. In this way, it can increase or decrease engine idle rpm. If failed, engine rpm will be constant and may not increase with a cold engine or decrease as the engine warms to operating temperature.

To check the idle air control valve, jump battery voltage to the windings. This should trigger the solenoid and change engine speed. If the engine speed does not change, check the output voltage to the idle air control valve before removing the unit. An ohmmeter may also be recommended to check the windings.

Air vent solenoid service

A *bad air vent solenoid* can affect the operation of a computer-controlled emission system and other systems depending upon its function. It usually controls fuel bowl venting to a charcoal canister. Again, voltage can be jumped to an air vent solenoid, or any solenoid, to check operation. See Fig. 22-33.

Fig. 22-34 shows how to test another solenoid actuator that controls vacuum to emission control devices.

Mixture solenoid service

A *bad mixture control solenoid* will throw off the computer-controlled carburetor's fuel mixture. The mix-

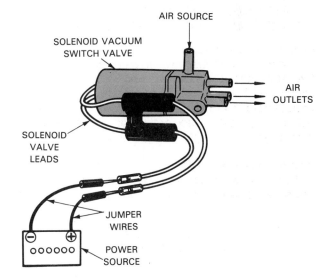

Fig. 22-34. This solenoid actuator is used to control vacuum applied to various components. When voltage is jumped to solenoid, different air passages should open or close.

ture can be too lean or too rich and engine performance and fuel economy can suffer.

Fig. 22-35 shows a typical way of checking a mixture control solenoid. Vacuum is applied to the solenoid while connecting and disconnecting voltage to the windings. With voltage applied, the unit should usually hold vacuum. When voltage is disconnected, vacuum should then be released.

Glow plug service

A *bad glow plug* will not heat up and the diesel engine will be difficult to start when cold. Usually, the glow plug will burn open and will not be able to conduct electricity. Use an ohmmeter to measure glow plug resistance. This can be done with the glow plug still in the cylinder head or with it removed, Fig. 22-36. Replace the glow plug if its resistance is not within specs.

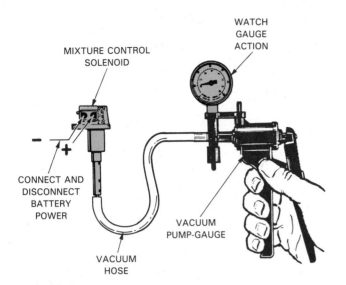

Fig. 22-35. Carburetor mixture control solenoid is tested by applying vacuum to unit while energizing solenoid. When voltage is applied, unit should hold vacuum. When voltage is disconnected, unit should release or pass vacuum. (General Motors)

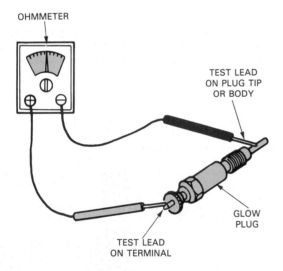

Fig. 22-36. A glow plug is simply a resistive heating element. Use an ohmmeter to measure resistance with the plug in or out of the engine. A bad glow plug will usually be open and have infinite ohms. You can also use an ammeter to measure current flow into each glow plug. An inductive ammeter can be slipped over wires and nothing has to be disconnected for testing. No current flow usually means a bad glow plug. (General Motors)

You may also need to check the circuit feeding current to the glow plugs. The glow plug controller for example might not be feeding current to the glow plugs.

An ammeter can also be used to measure current flow into the glow plugs. This is an easy way to check their operation because you can simply clip the inductive pickup over the wires. Nothing has to be disconnected.

Servicing other actuators

The service of other actuators is similar to those just discussed. A solenoid for a door latch is constructed like

a solenoid in a fuel injector or other solenoid type actuator. Servo motor actuators are also similar to other motors, as in fuel pumps. Remember to refer to the service manual for testing and replacement details.

COMPUTER SERVICE

Computer service usually involves a few tests, and computer replacement if needed. The computer is usually one of the last components to be tested and suspected. Only after all other potential sources of trouble have been eliminated is the computer suspected of being the problem source. It is sometimes possible for an integrated circuit, transistor, or other electronic part in the computer to fail and upset system operation, Fig. 22-37.

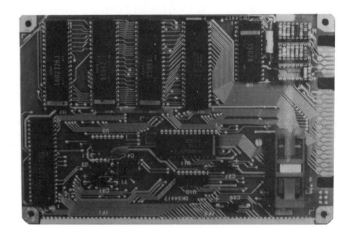

Fig. 22-37. Computers are quite dependable. However, they can sometimes fail to operate properly because of problems with integrated circuits, transistors, and other electronic components. Make sure other problems, radiation interference, sensors, wiring, etc., are not the trouble before replacing a computer. (Buick)

Measuring computer output

A *computer output* can be a reference voltage to a sensor, current flow or supply voltage to operate an actuator, or dwell signal to open and close a mixture control solenoid or injector.

Use a voltmeter to make sure the correct reference voltage is being sent to a sensor. Most computers produce a reference voltage of about 5 volts. If not correct, check the wiring before condemning the computer. You can also measure voltage to make sure the correct voltage output is being fed to operate actuators.

An oscilloscope can also be used to check the computer output signal. In addition to checking reference voltage, you can measure and observe pulses going to the fuel injectors, solenoids, and servo motors. See Fig. 22-38.

Again, always refer to the service manual for exact procedures for testing a computer system. One wrong electrical connection can "fry" delicate electronic components.

Saving memory

Saving memory can be done by connecting a small battery (such as a 9 volt battery) across the two battery

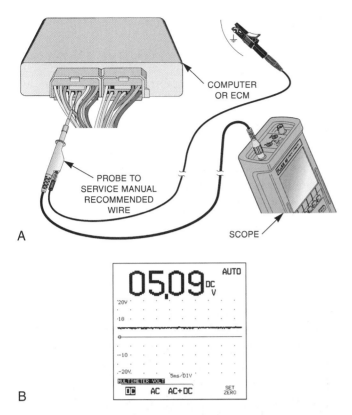

A

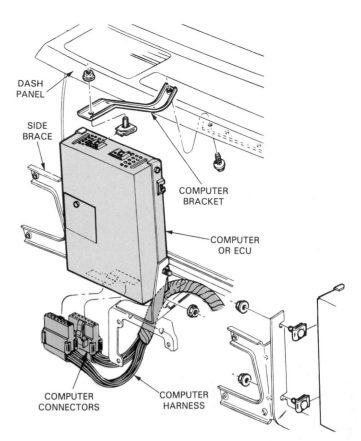

B

Fig. 22-38. A—A scope will also check reference voltage going to sensors and the control pulses from the ECM to the actuators. Compare readings and waveforms to service manual specifications. B—Reference voltages should meet specifications and the waveforms should reflect smooth dc voltage. (Fluke)

Fig. 22-39. To replace a computer, unplug harness connectors but make sure key is off. Unbolt brackets and lift unit out from under dash or other location. (General Motors)

cables BEFORE the vehicle's battery is disconnected. The small battery cannot produce enough current to cause an electrical fire or operate the starting system, but it will provide enough power to keep the clock, stereo, and computer from losing the information stored in their memories. When using a memory saver, turn off all accessories (radio, blower, etc.). The current drain from these devices, combined with even the smallest voltage drop, could cause electronic devices (computer, clock, radio, etc.) to lose their preprogrammed data.

Computer replacement

When removing a computer, the ignition key should be off and car battery disconnected. This will prevent any voltage spike from possibly damaging components when the ECU harness connectors are pulled apart. As shown in Fig. 22-39, unplug the computer connectors and unbolt the brackets holding the computer in place.

Identification information is usually stamped or printed on the computer. This is shown in Fig. 22-40. Use this data and the year, make, and model of car to order the correct replacement computer. The vehicle VIN (vehicle identification number) may sometimes be helpful.

PROM service

Most computers use the old *PROM* (memory chip) during computer replacement. The PROM seldom fails and stores data for the specific make and model car. You must commonly remove the old PROM and install it in the new computer.

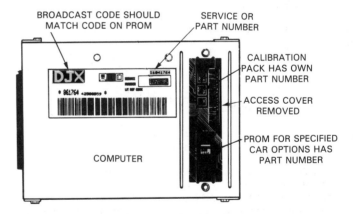

Fig. 22-40. When ordering a new computer, make sure you are getting the right one. Identification numbers will normally be printed on computer and should match PROM number.

Illustrated in Fig. 22-41, remove the cover over the PROM. Then, use a PROM tool to grasp and pull the PROM out of its socket. Avoid touching the PROM with your fingers because the body oils on your hand could affect PROM operation.

Before installing the old PROM in the new computer, check that the PROM pins (terminals) are straight. Bend them straight if needed. Also, check the reference mark on the PROM. A PROM usually has an indentation or other marking to show how to reinstall the unit. Make sure that the PROM has the correct part number for the car.

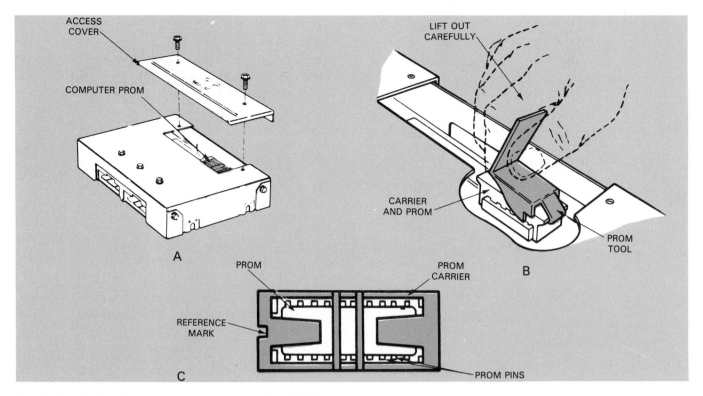

Fig. 22-41. Most main computers have a removable PROM or memory type integrated circuit. This chip is calibrated for the exact car. It must usually be removed and reused in new computer. A—Remove access cover to PROM. Screws normally hold cover in place. B—Use a PROM tool to grasp and pull carrier and chip out of its socket. Avoid touching PROM with your hands. C—PROM is frequently enclosed in carrier. Carrier protects PROM pins during replacement.

To install the PROM, place the PROM pins into the socket with the reference mark correctly positioned. Then, use a blunt tool, like a wooden dowel, to press the PROM down into the computer. Press on each corner to make sure the PROM pins are fully seated in their sockets.

Some PROMs use a *carrier* which is a plastic part that surrounds the outside of the integrated circuit chip. If used, you must use a blunt tool to push the PROM so that its top is flush with the top of the carrier, Fig. 22-42. This will ready the PROM for installation into the computer. Install the carrier and PROM in the computer with the reference mark pointing properly. First press down on the carrier only. Then, press down on the center of the PROM with a blunt tool. Press on the corners until the PROM is fully seated in the ECU, Fig. 22-42.

Install the PROM access cover and then install computer into its mounts. Connect the connectors to the computer. Reconnect the car battery, turn on the ignition, and activate self-diagnostics. Make sure no trouble codes are set as a check of the computer and PROM. A code might be set if the PROM is not fully seated or a pin is bent over, for example.

NOTE! If you install a PROM backwards, it will usually require replacement because of damage.

Computer adjustments

A few computers or electronic control units have provisions for various adjustments. Most often, a screw might be located on the side of the computer. Turning the screw will change an operating parameter. This might be base ignition timing, cruise control sensitivity, and other functions. Keep this in mind and refer to a service manual when in doubt. See Fig. 22-43.

Updated PROMs

An *updated PROM* is a modified integrated circuit produced by the auto manufacturers to correct a driveability problem or improve a vehicle's performance. The old PROM is simply removed from the computer and replaced with the updated PROM.

Updated PROMs are produced to correct problems like surging, extended cranking periods, excessive emissions, cold and hot start problem, and unusual driveability problems that cannot be isolated to one system. If you are faced with a problem and cannot find the cause, you should check with the local dealership to find out if there are any updated PROMs for the vehicle that address the problem.

Due to the popularity of aftermarket chips, or so-called "hot PROM" performance chips (PROM chips that enhance engine performance, and in many cases, increase exhaust emissions), federal regulations require the computers in all new vehicles to be equipped with fixed PROMs. With the frequent number of updated PROMs released in the past, electrically erasable PROMs, or EEPROMs, are now used. EEPROM programming is covered in the next section.

EEPROMs can be reprogrammed to correct driveability problems or improve performance. EEPROMs are permanently fixed to the circuit board, which makes the installation of a hot PROM almost impossible.

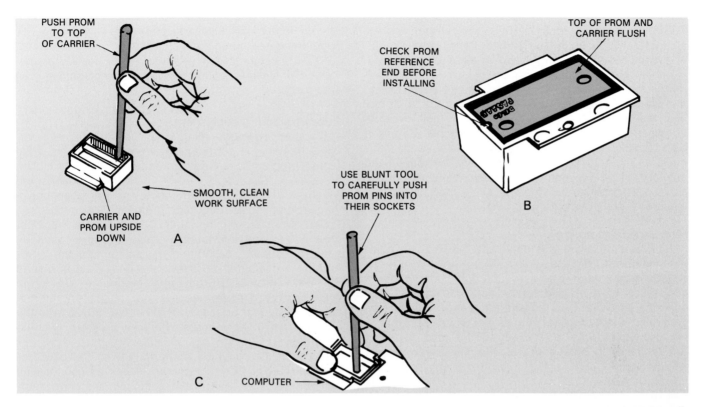

Fig. 22-42. Most PROMs use a PROM carrier which is a plastic case around IC chip. A—Before installing chip in new computer, use a blunt tool to push top of chip flush with top of carrier. Pins should be sticking up and straight. B—Make sure reference mark on PROM is positioned correctly before installation. If you install PROM backwards, it will normally be ruined. PROM and carrier are flush on top. C—Touching only carrier, position PROM pins into socket in computer. Use blunt tool or small wooden dowel to carefully push PROM into its socket. Push lightly on each corner until fully seated. Do not press too hard.   (General Motors)

EEPROM programming using computerized equipment

Most newer computers use Electrically Erasable Programmable Read Only Memory (EEPROM) or Flash Erasable Programmable Read Only Memory (FEPROM) chips that are permanently soldered to the circuit board. These chips must be programmed using electronic equipment. They can also be reprogrammed in order to correct driveability and performance problems.

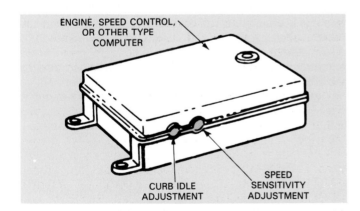

Fig. 22-43. A few computers have provisions for making adjustments. There may be small screws or tiny levers that can be moved or turned to change a computer output—base ignition timing, speed control trigger points, etc.   (Chrysler)

EEPROMs are programmed using a method referred to as flash programming. *Flash programming* may be performed by downloading the vehicle's information through a computer, a computerized diagnostic analyzer, or a scan tool. Actual programming details vary between manufacturers, but the basic procedure begins by placing the computer in the programming mode. One of three methods is used to program the computer:

1. Direct programming using a service computer or computerized analyzer.
2. Indirect programming using a scan tool and a computer or computerized analyzer.
3. Remote programming with the computer off the vehicle.

Direct programming

Direct programming is the fastest and simplest method. The new information is downloaded by attaching a shop recalibration device (usually a computer or computerized analyzer) directly to the data link connector. The erasure and programming is done by accessing the programming menu and following the instructions as prompted by the computer. Then, the vehicle's operating information and parameters are entered into the vehicle's computer through the connector.

Indirect programming

To perform *indirect programming,* the proper scan tool must be available to connect to the programming computer and to the vehicle, as well as to reset some computer-controlled vehicle systems after programming. The programming computer may resemble the personal computer (PC) used in the home, or it may be a computerized analyzer like the one used for direct programming.

In this type of programming, the vehicle information is downloaded from the PC or computerized analyzer into the scan tool. It is then downloaded from the scan tool into the vehicle's computer. The scan tool menu is accessed using the keypad. Most scan tools will use a high-capacity generic program cartridge to store the information. Some newer scan tools have sufficient fixed memory to hold the information and, therefore, do not use a separate program cartridge. In either case, follow the manufacturer's procedure as prompted.

Remote programming

Remote programming is done with the vehicle's computer removed from the vehicle. This procedure is used when changes need to be made through a direct modem connection to a manufacturer's database computer. It can also be done in cases where direct or indirect programming is not practical or possible. Since special connectors and tools are required for this type of programming, this procedure is done only at new vehicle dealerships.

EEPROM programming procedure

To begin programming the EEPROM-equipped computer, make sure the battery is fully charged. Recharge the battery if necessary. Do not charge the battery during the programming procedure, as damage to the computer will result. Connect the service computer or scan tool to the computer data link connector. Make any other vehicle connections as needed before proceeding with the programming sequence.

> CAUTION! Do not disconnect the scan tool or service computer from the data link connector during the programming sequence. Doing so will damage the vehicle's computer.

To start the programming sequence, the analyzer or scan tool prompt may ask you to enter the engine type, vehicle type, and vehicle identification number (VIN), in a specific sequence. Once the vehicle information is entered, go to the programming software and follow the directions as prompted.

Depending on the manufacturer, it may be necessary to turn the ignition switch on or off during the connection and programming procedure. Double-check any instructions on ignition switch position before making any connections or beginning computer erasure and programming. The next step is to determine the type of programming that is needed.

Programming a new computer

If a new computer is being installed, only program that computer. In many cases, other on-board computers can be accessed and programmed using the data link connector. While most computers have internal circuitry that protects them from accidental programming, be careful not to program the wrong computer. Do not attempt to program a new computer with information from the old computer or a computer from another vehicle. Any attempt to do this will set a failed programming sequence code in the new computer's memory.

NOTE! In some cases, an erasure may need to be performed on a new computer before initial programming can take place.

Reprogramming computers

If you are reprogramming a vehicle's computer, determine the date the current programming was downloaded or the program's calibration number. If the information installed is the latest version, no further actions are required. If the latest information has not been downloaded, proceed with the reprogramming sequence.

Before reprogramming most computers, you must first erase the existing information. After this step is complete, select the updated calibration information from the reprogramming computer or scan tool menu. Then download the new information into the computer. On some systems, the erasure step is not necessary as the service computer or scan tool will erase or overwrite the old information as it loads the new program into the computer.

NOTE! If the computer does not accept the new program or cannot be programmed, check all connections first. Ensure that the correct computer is being reprogrammed with the correct information and that all procedures are being followed. If the computer still cannot be programmed, it may need to be replaced.

Allow sufficient time for the programming to take place. Monitor the computer or scan tool to determine when the programming sequence is complete. Do not touch any connections until you are sure that the programming sequence is complete. After programming is completed, turn the ignition switch to the position called for and disconnect the computer or scan tool. Then, use a scan tool to check the computer and control system operation. While doing this, make sure that you have installed the proper program into the computer by checking the program calibration number.

Computer learn procedures

Once the computer is connected and programmed, when necessary, it must adjust to, or "learn," the vehicle's sensor inputs and to control output actuators. The computer must receive inputs to formulate adaptive strategy to set some of its output parameters. This is usually done by driving the vehicle for a few minutes to allow the computer to learn the sensors and output actuators, and to adjust system operation according to the EEPROM programming. In a few cases, sensors or actuators may have to be manually adjusted using a scan tool.

SUMMARY

Always start service of a computer system with an inspection. Most problems are caused by conventional causes. Avoid thinking "computer problem" when the engine or another system fails to work properly. Remember the basics!

Most sensors fall into one of three categories: voltage generating, switching, and variable resistance. You can normally use a digital VOM to measure sensor resistance or voltage output. If not within spec limits, something is wrong with the sensor or its wiring.

Many resistance or switching sensors are fed a reference voltage (about 5 volts) by the computer. This allows a current signal to flow back to the computer.

Each sensor can be compared to some part of a carburetor or to a general purpose. By using this logic, you can help narrow down possible problem sensors.

Do not use a low impedance meter or test light to check computer system components. The current draw through the meter or light could be high enough to damage some electronic components.

Actuator service involves testing the system solenoids, servo motors, and displays. They can develop opens, shorts, and other problems.

The computer is one of the last components to suspect. If it must be replaced, you must normally reuse the old PROM. Use proper techniques when replacing a PROM to avoid damage.

KNOW THESE TERMS

Preliminary inspection, Cipet, Kiss, Sensor service, Poor electrical connections, Vacuum leak, Breakout box, Voltage generating sensor, Switching type sensors, Variable resistance sensors, Reference voltage, Oxygen sensor contamination, Leaded fuel, Silicone, Carbon, Oxygen sensor output voltage , Read an oxygen sensor, Actuator service, Computer service, Computer output, Saving memory, PROM, Carrier, Updated PROM, Flash programming, Direct programming, Indirect programming, Remote programming.

REVIEW QUESTIONS—CHAPTER 22

1. A _____ _____ involves looking for signs of obvious trouble: loose wires, leaking vacuum hoses, part damage, etc.
2. Extremely dirty engine oil can sometimes trigger a trouble code. True or false?
3. With new cars, the computer system is the cause of most driveability problems. True or false
4. How is a VOM used to do a basic test on any type of sensor?
5. A _____ _____ can be connected to the computer harness so that electrical values can be measured more easily.
6. A bad _____ _____ sensor can keep the engine from running because it triggers the ignition system.
7. A bad vehicle speed sensor will usually keep the engine from running. True or false?
8. Typically, how do you test a coolant temperature sensor?
9. Explain one way to see if an idle speed motor is functioning.
10. In your own words, describe a few ways to find out if multi-point fuel injectors are working.
11. Explain the procedure for checking a glow plug.

12. The computer is usually one of the _____ components to be tested.
13. A computer output can be a _____ _____ to a sensor, or _____ flow to a(n) _____.
14. How can you save computer memory while still disconnecting the car battery for safety?
15. In your own words, how do you replace an on-board computer?

ASE CERTIFICATION–TYPE QUESTIONS

1. An automobile is brought into the shop with a engine coolant temperature sensor circuit problem. Technician A checks the wires going to this particular sensor. Technician B performs a resistance test on the engine coolant temperature sensor. Who is right?
   (A) A only.
   (B) B only.
   (C) Both A and B.
   (D) Neither A nor B.
2. An automobile's engine is misfiring. Technician A first checks the computer and its sensor network. Technician B first checks the engine for any mechanical or ignition system problems. Who is right?
   (A) A only.
   (B) B only.
   (C) Both A and B.
   (D) Neither A nor B.
3. While discussing computer system problems, Technician A says poor electrical connections are the most common causes of electrical-related problems. Technician B says that vacuum leaks can upset computer system operation. Who is right?
   (A) A only.
   (B) B only.
   (C) Both A and B.
   (D) Neither A nor B.
4. A variable resistance type sensor must be tested. Technician A disconnects the reference voltage wire and measures the sensor's resistance. Technician B measures the voltage drop across the sensor without disconnecting the reference voltage wire. Who is right?
   (A) A only.
   (B) B only.
   (C) Both A and B.
   (D) Neither A nor B.
5. An engine's oxygen sensor is believed to be malfunctioning. Technician A checks the sensor's output voltage with an analog voltmeter. Technician B checks the sensor's output voltage with a high impedance digital VOM. Who is right?
   (A) A only.
   (B) B only.
   (C) Both A and B.
   (D) Neither A nor B.
6. An automobile computer system triggers a trouble code indicating a MAP sensor circuit problem. After performing a preliminary inspection, Technician A checks sensor circuit voltage while applying vacuum to the sensor. Technician B checks sensor resistance while applying vacuum to the unit. Who is right?
   (A) A only.
   (B) B only.
   (C) Both A and B.
   (D) Neither A nor B.
7. Which of the following is *least likely* to cause a severe engine performance problem?
   (A) Faulty manifold absolute pressure sensor.
   (B) Defective throttle position sensor.
   (C) Bad intake air temperature sensor.
   (D) Faulty coolant temperature sensor.

8. Technician A says a defective knock sensor can affect ignition timing. Technician B says a defective knock sensor can affect turbocharger boost pressure. Who is right?
   (A) A only.
   (B) B only.
   (C) Both A and B.
   (D) Neither A nor B.

9. A vehicle's idle air control valve is believed to be faulty. Technician A applies battery voltage to the valve's windings and watches for changes in engine speed. Technician B checks the output voltage to the idle air control valve. Who is right?
   (A) A only.
   (B) B only.
   (C) Both A and B.
   (D) Neither A nor B.

10. An automobile computer's output signals must be checked. Technician A says a voltmeter can be used to check the computer's output signals. Technician B says an oscilloscope can be used to check the computer's output. Who is right?
   (A) A only.
   (B) B only.
   (C) Both A and B.
   (D) Neither A nor B.

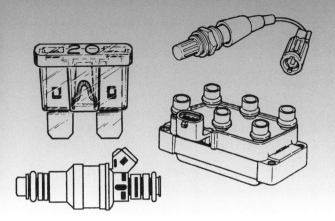

Chapter 23

Battery and Starting System Service

After studying this chapter, you will be able to:
- *Troubleshoot battery problems.*
- *Test and service a battery.*
- *Use a load tester.*
- *Test battery cables.*
- *Troubleshoot starting system problems.*
- *Test a starting system.*
- *Remove and replace a starting motor.*
- *Rebuild a starting motor.*
- *Test and replace a starter solenoid.*
- *Use jumper cables and a battery charger.*

In previous chapters, you learned the principles of battery and starting system operation. This chapter will continue your study of auto electricity-electronics by summarizing how to locate and correct problems with batteries and starting systems. See Fig. 23-1.

To avoid repetition, it is understood that you studied previous chapters that detailed how to do basic tests of motors, relays, coils, circuits, wiring, etc. This chapter will concentrate on the more specific tasks done to test, service, and repair problems with batteries, starters, and related parts.

BATTERY SERVICE

A *discharged* or *"dead"* battery is a very common problem. The engine will not crank or will crank slowly for starting. Even though the headlights and horn may work, there is not enough "juice" or electrical power in the battery to rotate the starting motor armature. A starter draws a tremendous amount of current.

Since a slow or no crank trouble is common, it is important to know how to inspect, test, and service car batteries in detail.

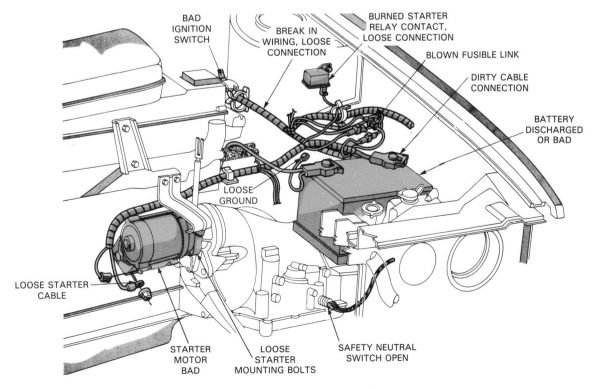

Fig. 23-1. These are some common types of troubles that you will find in a starting system. (Chrysler)

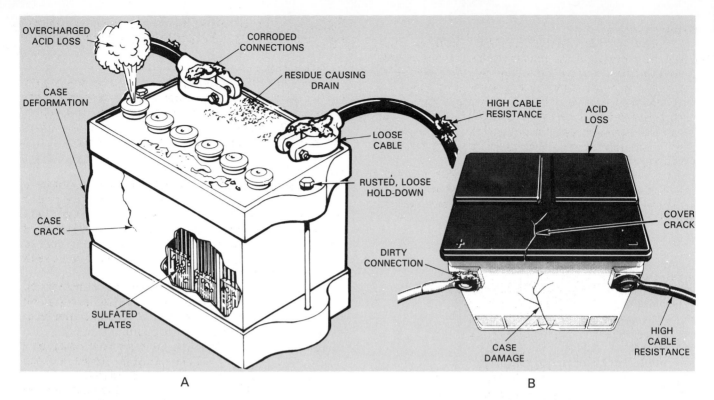

Fig. 23-2. When inspecting a battery, look for these troubles. A—Top post battery. B—Side post battery.
(Florida Dept. of Voc. Ed. and Sun Electric)

Inspect battery

Inspect the battery and cables whenever the hood is opened! As shown in Fig. 23-2, look for:
1. Dirt buildup on the battery case top.
2. Case damage.
3. Loose or corroded connections.
4. Rusted or missing battery hold-down.
5. Any other trouble that could upset battery operation.
   If any problems are found, correct them.

Battery leakage test

A *battery leakage test* determines if current is discharging across the top of a dirty battery case. A dirty battery can discharge when not in use. This can shorten battery life and cause starting problems.

To do a battery leakage test, set a voltmeter on a low setting. Touch the probes on the battery as shown in Fig. 23-3. If the meter registers voltage, current is leaking out of the battery cells and you need to clean the battery top.

Remember to wipe any residue off of the test probes to prevent their corrosion.

Parasitic loads

A *parasitic load* includes any current draw present when all electrical-electronic devices are shut off. This load would include anything that requires a small current when the engine and ignition key are turned off. On-board computers and the dash clock need a small amount of current to retain memory. This results in a parasitic load on the battery.

If a vehicle sits unused for prolonged periods, the parasitic load can drain the battery enough to prevent starting. A battery must be in good condition to withstand prolonged parasitic load.

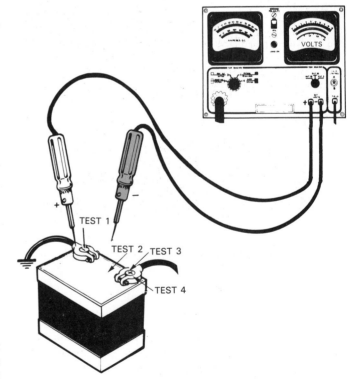

Fig. 23-3. Touch voltmeter in these four locations to check for trouble. 1—Voltage drop over .5 V across post and terminal while cranking would indicate bad connection. 2—Voltage reading across top of battery would require top cleaning. 3—Total battery voltage will indicate state of charge. If below 12.4, low charge might be indicated. 4—Below 9.4 volts across both connections at once when cranking would indicate possible battery or starting system troubles.

Battery terminal test

A *battery terminal test* checks for a poor electrical connection between the battery cables and terminals. A voltmeter is used to measure voltage drop across the cables and terminals with the engine cranking, Fig. 23-4.

Touch the negative meter lead to the battery cable end. Touch the positive meter lead to the battery post. Disable the ignition system or injection system so the engine will not start. Then, crank the engine while watching the voltmeter reading.

If the voltmeter shows over about .5 volt, there is a high resistance or bad connection at the cable. This would tell you to clean the battery connections. A clean, good electrical connection would have less than .5 volt drop while cranking.

TO POST

TO CABLE

Fig. 23-4. This technician is cranking engine while checking voltage drop across battery connection. If above about .5 volts, clean connection.

BATTERY MAINTENANCE

If a battery is NOT maintained properly, its service life will be reduced. Battery maintenance should be done periodically—during tune-ups, grease jobs, or anytime symptoms indicate battery problems.

Battery maintenance typically includes:
1. Checking electrolyte level or indicator eye.
2. Cleaning battery terminal connections.
3. Cleaning battery top.
4. Checking battery hold-down and tray.
5. Inspecting for physical damage to case and terminals.

Wear EYE PROTECTION when working around bat-teries. Batteries contain acid that could cause blindness. Even the film buildup on a battery can contain acid.

Cleaning battery case

If the top of the battery is dirty, wash it down with baking soda and water or soap and water. This will neutralize and remove the acid-dirt mixture on the battery. If NOT a maintenance-free battery, do not let debris fall into the filler openings. Look at Fig. 23-5.

Cleaning battery terminals

To clean the battery terminals, remove the battery cables, Fig. 23-5. Use a six-point wrench if the bolt or nut is extremely tight. Use pliers only on a spring type cable end or when the fastener head is badly corroded and rounded off. Be careful not to damage the post or side terminal with excess side force. Spread it open with pliers if stuck to the post.

To clean post type terminals, use a post cleaning tool. Use the female end to clean the post. Use the male end on the terminal. Rotate the tool to remove a thin layer of oxidized metal on the connections.

To clean side terminals, use a small wire brush or a side post cleaning tool. Polish both the cable end and the mating surface on the battery terminal.

Do NOT use a knife or scraper to clean battery terminals. This removes too much metal and can ruin the terminal connection.

When reinstalling the cables, coat the terminals with petroleum jelly or white grease. This will help keep acid fumes from corroding them again. Tighten the fasteners just enough to secure the connection. Overtightening can strip the cable bolt threads or split the soft lead terminal.

Checking battery electrolyte

Unlike an older style battery, a maintenance-free battery does NOT need periodic electrolyte service under normal conditions. It is designed to operate for long periods without loss of electrolyte. Older batteries with removable vent caps, however, must have their electrolyte level checked. Refer to Fig. 23-6.

DANGER! The invisible HYDROGEN GAS produced by the chemical reaction in a battery is explosive. Keep all sparks and flames away from a battery. Batteries can EXPLODE if the gas is ignited!

Many old style batteries must have their vent caps removed when checking the electrolyte. The electrolyte should just cover the top of the battery plates and separators. Most batteries have a *fill ring* (electrolyte level indicator) inside the filler cap opening. The electrolyte should be even with the fill ring.

If the electrolyte is low, fill the cells to the correct level with DISTILLED WATER (purified water). Distilled water does NOT contain many of the impurities found in tap water. Water taken directly out of a water faucet can reduce battery life. Contaminants can collect in the battery and the cell plates can SHORT OUT, ruining the battery.

Battery overcharging

If water must be added to the battery at frequent intervals, the charging system may be overcharging the

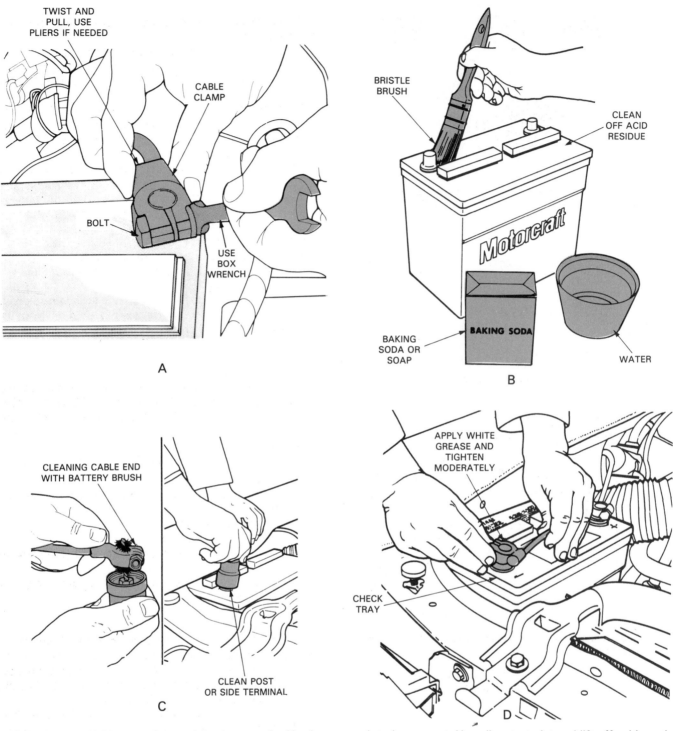

Fig. 23-5. Note basic steps for servicing battery. A—Use box wrench to loosen nut. Use pliers to twist and lift off cable end. B—Wash battery top with soap and water or baking soda and water. C—Clean post and cable end with special brush. Side post brush is also available. D—Apply white grease to post and reinstall cable end. Do not overtighten and break terminal! (Ford and Chrysler)

battery. A faulty charging system can force excessive current into the battery. Battery gasing can then remove water from the battery.

CHECKING BATTERY CHARGE

When you measure *battery charge,* you check the condition of the battery electrolyte and battery plates. For example, if someone leaves their lights ON without the engine running, the battery will run down (discharge). Current flow out of the battery will steadily reduce available battery power. There are several ways to measure battery charge, Fig. 23-6.

Several modern batteries use a *charge indicator eye* that shows battery charge. You simply look at the eye in the battery cover to determine battery charge.

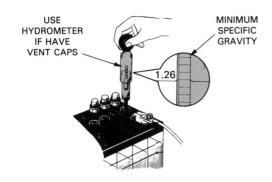

A—Hydrometer will check older batteries with vent caps. Draw acid into tester. Specific gravity reading should be 1.26.

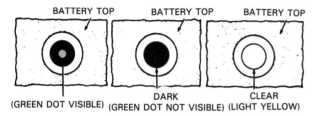

B—If provided, check eye in battery top to check charge.

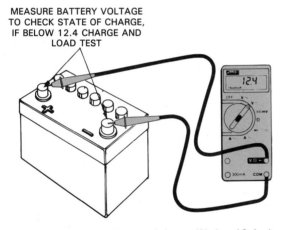

C—Accurate voltmeter will check state of charge. If below 12.4, charge battery and load test.

Fig. 23-6. Methods of checking state of charge.
(Toyota, GM, and Fluke)

Hydrometer

A *hydrometer* measures the specific gravity (weight or density) of a liquid. A *battery hydrometer* measures the specific gravity or the state of the charge for the battery electrolyte, Fig. 23-6.

Water has a specific gravity standard of ONE (1.000). Fully charged electrolyte has a specific gravity of between 1.265 and 1.299. The larger number denotes that electrolyte is more dense or heavier than water.

As a battery becomes discharged, its electrolyte has a larger percentage of water. Thus, a discharged battery's electrolyte will have a lower specific gravity than a fully charged battery. This rise and drop in specific gravity can show battery charge.

There are several types of hydrometers: float, ball, and the needle types.

To use a *float type hydrometer,* squeeze the hydrometer bulb. Immerse the end of the hydrometer tube in the electrolyte. Then release the bulb. This will fill the hydrometer with electrolyte.

Compare the numbers on the hydrometer float with the top of the electrolyte. Hold the hydrometer even with your line of sight. Wear safety glasses and do NOT drip acid on anything.

The *ball type battery hydrometer* is gaining popularity because you do not have to use a temperature correction chart. The balls change temperature when submersed in the electrolyte. This allows for any temperature offset.

To use the ball type hydrometer, draw electrolyte into the hydrometer with the rubber bulb. Then note the number of balls floating in the electrolyte. A chart with the hydrometer will say whether the battery is fully charged or discharged.

A *needle type hydrometer* uses the same principle as the ball type. When battery acid is sucked into the hydrometer, the electrolyte causes the plastic needle to register specific gravity.

Hydrometer readings

A *fully charged battery* should have a hydrometer reading of at least 1.265 or higher. If BELOW 1.265, the battery needs RECHARGING or it may be defective.

Discharged battery

A *discharged battery* could be caused by:

1. Defective battery.
2. Charging system problem, loose alternator belt for example.
3. Starting system problem.
4. Poor cable connections.
5. Engine performance problem requiring excessive cranking time.
6. Electrical problem drawing current out of battery with ignition key OFF.

Defective battery

A *defective battery* can be found with a hydrometer by checking the electrolyte in every cell. If the specific gravity in any cell VARIES EXCESSIVELY from other cells (25 to 50 points), the battery is usually ruined. The cells with the low readings may be shorted.

When all of the cells have an equal gravity, even if all of them are low, the battery can usually be recharged.

With maintenance-free batteries, the hydrometer is not commonly used. A voltmeter, ammeter, or load tester covered later, is needed to quickly determine battery condition.

BATTERY VOLTAGE TEST

A *battery voltage test* is done by measuring total battery voltage with an accurate voltmeter or special tester. It will determine general state of charge and battery condition quickly.

Connect the meter across the battery terminals. Turn on the car's headlights or heater blower to provide a light load. Read the meter. Refer to Fig. 23-6.

A well charged battery should have over 12 volts. If the meter reads about 11.5 volts, the battery may not be charged adequately or it may be defective.

A battery voltage test is used on maintenance-free batteries. These batteries do NOT have filler caps that can be easily removed for testing with a hydrometer.

Cell voltage test

A *cell voltage test* will let you know if the battery is defective or just discharged. Just like a hydrometer cell test, if one or more cells is lower (voltage less) than the others, the battery must usually be replaced.

Note! Some manufacturers recommend battery fast charging during this test. Refer to a service manual for details.

If cell voltages are low, but equal, recharging will usually restore the battery. If cell voltage readings vary more than .2 volts, the battery is BAD.

DANGER! Make sure you do NOT drip battery acid on the car or your skin when using a hydrometer or cell voltage tester. The acid will eat the car's paint or burn your skin.

JUMP STARTING

In emergency situations, it may be necessary to *jump start* the car by connecting another battery to the discharged battery. The two batteries are connected POSITIVE to POSITIVE and NEGATIVE to NEGATIVE.

Connect the red jumper cable to the positive terminal of both batteries. Then, connect the black jumper cable to any ground on both vehicles. See Fig. 23-7.

WARNING! Do NOT short the jumper cables together or connect them backwards. This could cause serious damage to the charging system or computer.

BATTERY CHARGERS

When tests show that the battery is discharged, a battery charger may be used to re-energize the battery. The *battery charger* will force current back into the battery to restore the charge on the battery plates and in the electrolyte. It contains a step-down transformer that changes wall outlet voltage (around 120 volts) to slightly above battery voltage (14 to 15 volts).

There are two basic types of battery chargers: slow charger and fast charger.

Slow (trickle) charger

A *slow charger* or *trickle charger* feeds low current into the battery, Fig. 23-8. Charging time is long (about 12

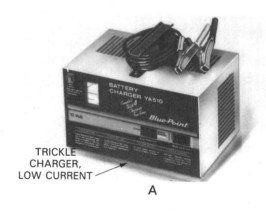

TRICKLE CHARGER, LOW CURRENT

A

BOOST CHARGER, HIGH CURRENT

B

TO FRAME GROUND AWAY FROM DEAD BATTERY TO NEGATIVE

CABLE TO POSITIVE TERMINALS

DEAD BATTERY

Fig. 23-7. When jump starting car, connect jumper cables as shown. Last connection should be away from batteries to prevent possible explosion. (Volvo)

Fig. 23-8. A—Trickle charger is fine if you can charge battery all day or overnight. B—Fast charger is needed when repair time is limited. (Snap-On Tools)

hours at 10 amps). However, the chemical action inside the battery is improved. The active materials are plated back on the battery plates better. When repair time allows, use a slow charger.

Fast (boost) charger

A *fast charger* or *boost charger,* forces a high current flow into the battery for rapid recharging. It is commonly used in auto shops. When the customer needs the car, time may NOT allow the use of a slow charger.

Fast charging will usually allow engine starting in a matter of minutes. See Fig. 23-8.

Charging a battery

DANGER! Before connecting a battery charger to a battery, make sure the charger is turned OFF. Also, check that the work area is well ventilated. If a spark ignites any battery gas, the battery could EXPLODE. Wear eye protection!

To use a battery charger, connect the RED charger lead to the positive terminal of the battery. Connect the BLACK charger lead to the negative terminal of the battery. With side terminal batteries, use adapters.

Make sure you do NOT reverse the charger connections or the charging system in the car could be damaged. Set the charger controls and turn on the power.

When fast charging, do NOT exceed a charge rate of about 35 amps. Also, battery temperature must NOT exceed around 125 °F (52 °C). Exceeding either could damage the battery, Figs. 23-9 and 23-10.

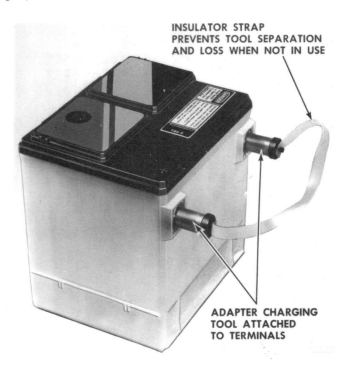

INSULATOR STRAP PREVENTS TOOL SEPARATION AND LOSS WHEN NOT IN USE

ADAPTER CHARGING TOOL ATTACHED TO TERMINALS

Fig. 23-10. Note adapter for charging side post battery. (General Motors)

BATTERY LOAD TEST

A *battery load test* or *battery capacity test* is one of the BEST methods of checking battery condition. It tests the battery under full current load. See Fig. 23-11.

The hydrometer and voltage tests were GENERAL INDICATORS of battery condition. The battery load test, however, actually measures the current output and performance of the battery. It is one of the most common and informative battery tests used in modern automotive garages. See Fig. 23-12.

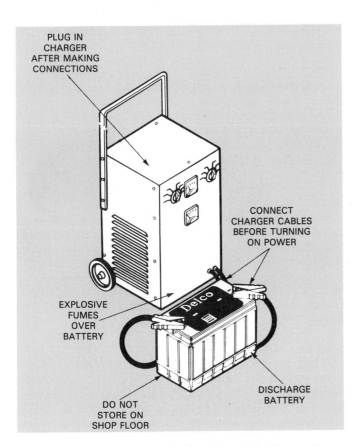

PLUG IN CHARGER AFTER MAKING CONNECTIONS

CONNECT CHARGER CABLES BEFORE TURNING ON POWER

EXPLOSIVE FUMES OVER BATTERY

DISCHARGE BATTERY

DO NOT STORE ON SHOP FLOOR

Fig. 23-9. Connect charger leads to battery before turning on power. (General Motors)

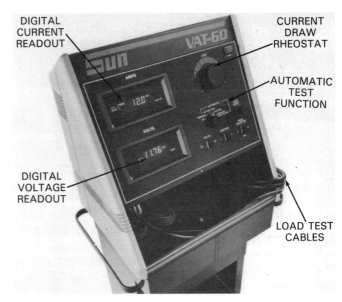

DIGITAL CURRENT READOUT

CURRENT DRAW RHEOSTAT

AUTOMATIC TEST FUNCTION

DIGITAL VOLTAGE READOUT

LOAD TEST CABLES

Fig. 23-11. Load tester provides quick and accurate way of testing battery condition. (Sun Electric Corp.)

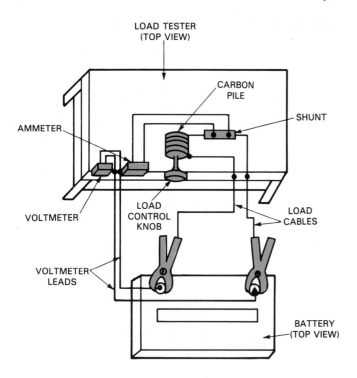

Fig. 23-12. Study operation of basic load tester. It allows high current to flow out of battery to check maximum output or power of battery. When current draw is set to specs, voltage must stay above about 9.4 volts or battery is bad.

Connecting load tester

Connect the load tester to the battery terminals. If the tester is an *inductive type* (clip-on ammeter lead senses field around outside of cables), use the connections shown in Fig. 23-13. If the tester is NOT inductive, you must connect the ammeter in series.

Control settings and exact procedures vary. Follow the directions provided with the testing equipment.

Double-check battery charge

Before a load test, make sure the battery is adequately charged. Use a hydrometer, digital voltmeter, or the load tester itself.

To check battery charge with the load tester, adjust the load control to draw 50 amps for ten seconds to remove any surface charge. Then, check no-load battery voltage, also called open circuit voltage (OCV).

A FULLY CHARGED BATTERY should have an OCV of 12.4 volts (plus or minus a few tenths due to meter error) or higher. If battery voltage is BELOW 12.4 volts, charge the battery before load testing.

Determine battery load

Before load testing a battery, calculate how much current draw should be applied to the battery. If the amp-hour rating is given, load the battery to THREE TIMES its amp-hour rating. For example, if the battery is rated at 80 amp-hours, test the battery at 240 amps (80 x 3 = 240).

Many batteries are now rated in SAE cold cranking amps, instead of amp-hours. To determine the load test for these batteries, DIVIDE the cold crank rating BY TWO. For instance, a battery with 500 cold cranking

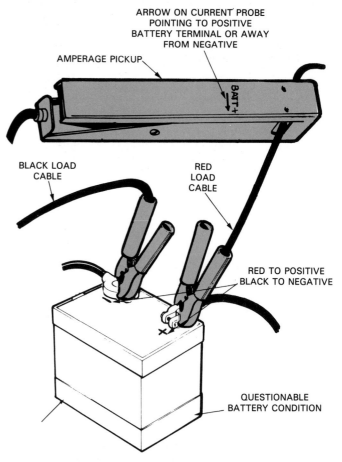

Fig. 23-13. Most modern load testers are inductive. The amps probe simply clips over battery cable. Large load cables connect to battery terminals.

amps should be loaded to 250 amps (500 ÷ 2 = 250). This will give test current.

The *watt* is another battery performance rating. Fig. 23-14 gives a chart which compares battery ratings.

A load conversion chart will normally be provided with the load testing equipment. Refer to this material when in doubt.

Loading the battery

After checking battery charge and finding the amp load value, test battery output. Double-check that the tester is connected properly. Then, turn the load control knob until the ammeter reads the correct load for your battery.

Hold the load for 15 seconds. Then, read the VOLT-METER while the load is applied. Then, turn the load control completely OFF so the battery will NOT be discharged.

Load test results

If the voltmeter reads 9.5 volts or MORE at room temperature, the battery power is acceptable. Six volt batteries should maintain 4.8 volts. These voltages are based on a battery temperature above 70°F (21°C).

A cold battery may show a lower voltage. You might need a *temperature compensation chart*, like the one in Fig. 23-14. It allows for any reduced battery performance caued by a low temperature.

BATTERY RATINGS			LOAD TEST AMPS
Cold Cranking Current	Amp-Hour (Approx.)	Watts	
200	35-40	1800	100 amps
250	41-48	2100	125 amps
300	49-62	2500	150 amps
350	63-70	2900	175 amps
400	71-76	3250	200 amps
450	77-86	3600	225 amps
500	87-92	3900	250 amps
550	93-110	4200	275 amps

Temperature °C	Temperature °F	Minimum Voltage
21° or Greater	70° or Greater	9.6
16° to 20°	60° to 69°	9.5
10° to 15°	50° to 59°	9.4
4° to 9°	40° to 49°	9.3
-1 to 4°	30° to 39°	9.1
-7 to -1°	20° to 29°	8.9
-12 to -7°	10° to 19°	8.7
-18 to -12°	0° to 9°	8.5

Fig. 23-14. A—Note chart that gives amount of current that should be applied to battery for different battery ratings. B—Note chart for correcting test voltages for battery temperature. (Cadillac and Marquette)

If the voltmeter reads below 9.5 volts at room temperature, battery power is POOR. This would show that the battery is NOT producing enough current to properly run the starting motor. Before replacing the battery, however, a quick charge test should be completed.

Quick (3 minute) charge test

A *quick charge test,* also termed *3 minute charge test,* will determine if the battery is sulfated (plates ruined). If the battery load test results are poor, fast charge the battery. Charge it for 3 minutes at 30 to 40 amps. Test the voltage while charging. If the voltage goes ABOVE 15.5 volts (12-volt battery) or 7.8 volts (6-volt battery), the battery plates are sulfated and ruined. A new battery should be installed.

OTHER BATTERY-RELATED PROBLEMS

If the battery passes all of its tests but the battery does NOT perform properly (starting motor does not crank for example), the following are a few problems to check:

1. Defective charging system.
2. Battery drain (a light or other accessory staying ON).
3. Loose alternator belt.
4. Corroded, loose, or defective battery cables.
5. Defective starting system.

ACTIVATING DRY CHARGED BATTERY

Before installing a new, dry charged battery, it must be *activated* (readied for service). Put on safety glasses and rubber gloves. Remove the cell caps or covers. Pour electrolyte into each cell, Fig. 23-15. Pour in enough electrolyte to just cover the plates and separators.

Replace the caps. Charge the battery as recommended by the manufacturer. After charging, recheck the electrolyte level and install the battery.

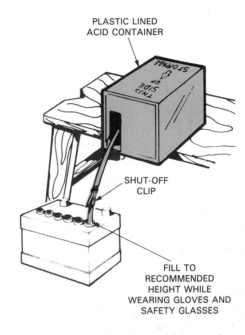

Fig. 23-15. When filling dry charged battery, be careful not to spill acid. Wear eye and hand protection. (Florida Dept. of Voc. Ed.)

REMOVING AND REPLACING BATTERY

To remove a battery, first disconnect the battery cables. Then loosen the battery hold-down. Using a battery strap or lifting tool, lift the battery carefully out of the car.

DANGER! Always wear safety glasses when carrying a battery. If you were to drop a battery, acid could squirt out of the vent caps or broken case and into your face and eyes.

To install a battery, gently place the battery into its clean tray or box. Check that the battery fits properly. The box must not cut through and rupture the plastic case. Secure the hold-down and install the cables.

The replacement battery should have a power rating EQUAL to factory recommendations. If an undersize battery (lower watt rating) is installed, battery performance and service life will be reduced.

Battery drain test

A *battery drain test* checks for an abnormal current draw with the ignition key off. When a battery goes dead overnight, check for a current drain. There could be a short or other problem discharging the battery.

A battery can be discharged if an electrical accessory remains ON when the ignition switch is shut OFF. A shorted closed trunklight switch could cause a dead battery, for instance. This could make the light stay on and slowly drain the battery.

To do a battery current drain test, make the ammeter connections shown in Fig. 23-16. Pull the fuse for the dash clock. Close the doors and trunk. Then read the ammeter. If everything is OFF (good condition), the ammeter should read zero. However, an ammeter reading would point to a drain and a problem.

To help pinpoint a drain, pull fuses one at a time. When the ammeter reads zero, the problem is in the circuit on that fuse, Fig. 23-17.

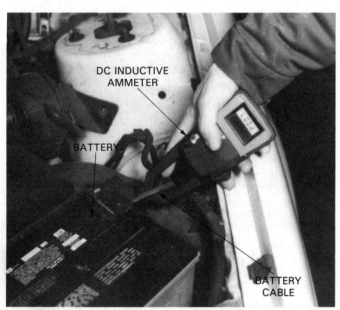

Fig. 23-16. Mechanic is using inductive ammeter to check for current drain out of battery with everything shut off. (TIF Instruments)

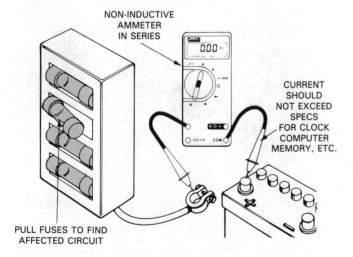

Fig. 23-17. Conventional ammeter is connected in series to measure current drain. Remember to account for small current that always flows to clock and on-board computers. Pull fuses to isolate circuit. (Fluke)

STARTING SYSTEM DIAGNOSIS

A starting system is easy to repair compared to the car's other electrical systems. It only has about five major components that cause problems.

Common starting system problems

A *slow cranking problem* is evident when the engine crankshaft rotates at lower than normal speed. It is usually caused by the same kind of problems producing a no-crank problem.

A *no-crank problem* occurs when the engine crankshaft does NOT rotate properly when the ignition key is turned. The most common causes are a dead battery, poor electrical connection, or faulty system component.

A *buzzing* or *clicking sound* from the solenoid, without cranking, is commonly due to a discharged battery or poor battery cable connections. Low current flow is causing the solenoid plunger to rapidly kick in and out, making a clattering sound.

A *single click sound,* without cranking, may point to a bad starting motor, burned solenoid contacts, dead battery, or engine mechanical problems. The click is usually the solenoid closing or the pinion gear contacting the flywheel gear.

A *humming sound,* after momentary engine cranking, may be due to a bad starter overrunning clutch or pinion gear unit. Pinion gear wear can make the gear disengage from the flywheel gear too soon. This can let the motor armature spin rapidly, with a resulting humming sound. Worn flywheel ring gear teeth can also cause this condition.

A *metallic grinding noise* may be caused by broken or worn flywheel teeth or pinion gear teeth wear. The grinding may be the gears clashing over each other.

Normal *cranking, without starting,* is usually NOT caused by the starting system. There may be trouble in the fuel or ignition systems. With a diesel engine, check engine cranking speed. If cranking rpm is low, the diesel may NOT start.

Sometimes the starting solenoid feeds current to the ignition system after engine starting. If the engine *starts and then DIES* (stops running) as the ignition key is released, check voltage from the solenoid to the ignition system. You could have an open wire or connection in the solenoid circuit. A defective ignition switch or wiring problem could also be at fault.

Starting headlight test

A *starting headlight test* will quickly indicate the causes of trouble in a starting system. Turn the headlights ON and try to start the engine. Note any sounds and watch the brightness of the headlights.

No cranking with *no headlights* points to a dead battery or open in the electrical system. The battery connections may be bad. The fusible link may be blown. A main feed wire to the fuse box could also be broken or disconnected.

If the *lights go out* when cranking, the battery may be weak. The starting motor may be shorted. The engine could also be dragging from mechanical problems. Dimming headlights indicate heavy current draw or poor current supply from the battery.

404

If the *lights stay bright*, without proper cranking, there may be a high resistance or open in the starting circuit. The problem could be in the ignition switch, wiring, solenoid, starter cable connections, or relay.

Depending upon what the headlights and starter do when testing, you can decide what further tests are needed.

CHECK THE BATTERY FIRST

A *dead* or *discharged battery* is one of the MOST COMMON reasons the starting system fails to crank the engine properly. A starting motor draws several times the amount of current as any other electrical component. A discharged or poorly connected battery can operate the lights but may NOT have enough power to operate the starting motor.

If needed, load test the battery as described earlier. Make sure the battery is good and fully charged. A starting motor will NOT function without a fully charged and well connected battery.

STARTER CURRENT DRAW TEST

A *starter current draw test* measures the number of amps used by the starting system. It will quickly tell you about the condition of the starting motor and related parts. If current draw is higher or lower than specs, there is a problem.

To do a starter current draw test, connect meters to measure battery voltage and current flow out of the battery. A load tester or engine analyzer may also be used, Figs. 23-18 and 23-19.

To keep the engine from starting during the test, disconnect the coil supply wire or ground the coil wire. With a diesel engine, disable the injection system. You may have to unhook the fuel shut-off solenoid. Check a shop manual for details.

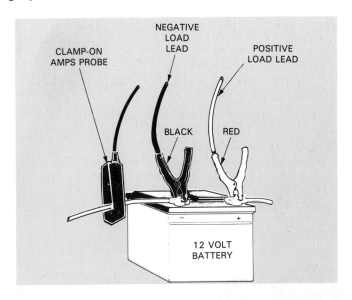

Fig. 23-19. These are typical connections for testing starting system with a modern load tester. (Sun)

WARNING! Do NOT crank the engine for more than 15 to 30 seconds or starter damage may result. If cranked too long, the starter could overheat and melt solder connections. Allow the starter to cool a few minutes if more cranking time is needed.

Crank the engine and note the voltage and current readings. If NOT within specs, something is wrong in the starting system or engine. Further tests would be needed. Fig. 23-20 gives the average current draw values for various engine sizes.

ENGINE DISPLACEMENT	12-VOLT SYSTEM MAX. CURRENT
Most 4-6 Cylinders	125-175 Amps Max.
Under 300 C.I.D.	150-200 Amps Max.
300 C.I.D. or Over	175-250 Amps Max.

CRANKING CIRCUIT TROUBLESHOOTING CHART		
Cranking Voltage	Cranking Amps	Possible Problem
Voltage Within Specs	Current Within Specs	System OK
Voltage OK	Current Low Engine Cranks Slowly	Starter Circuit Connections Faulty
Voltage Low	Current Low Engine Cranks Slowly	Battery Low
Voltage Low	Current High	Starter Motor Faulty

```
CRANKING/PINPOINT TESTS    HOLD
                                          210
0   100   200   300   400   500   RPM
ENGINE      210   RPM
CURRENT    -170   AMPS
BATTERY    10.2   VOLTS
DIST RES   1.16   VOLTS
DWELL      13.7   DEG. (22.9%)
TIMING      0.0   DEG      TEST
HC           ↑    PPM      DATA
VACUUM      1.3   "HG      SAVE D

                                          4.5
0    5    10    15    20    25    "HG

            ENGINE KILL

8 CYL      TEMP 72° C
```

Fig. 23-18. Note display given by advanced analyzer during cranking pinpoint tests. It gives cranking speed, current draw, battery volts, etc. This would provide quick, convenient test results. (Sun Electric)

Fig. 23-20. Chart shows typical values for checking operation of starting system during current draw test. Engine size affects current draw because of increased engine torque resistance. Check service manual specs when in doubt. Some starters are more efficient than others. (Marquette)

STARTING SYSTEM VOLTAGE DROP TESTS

Voltage drop tests will quickly locate a part with higher than normal resistance. They provide an easy way of checking circuit condition. You do NOT have to disconnect wires and components to check internal resistances (voltage drops).

Insulated circuit resistance test

An *insulated circuit resistance test* checks all parts between the battery positive and the starting motor for excess resistance. Touch your voltmeter probes on the battery positive terminal and the starting motor input terminal, Fig. 23-21.

Disable the ignition or injection system. Then crank the engine. The voltmeter should not read over about .2 to .5 volts. If voltage drop is HIGHER, something has excessive resistance. There may be a loose electrical connection, burned or pitted solenoid contact, or other problem. Test each part individually.

Starter ground circuit test

A *starter ground circuit test* checks the circuit between the starting motor ground and the negative battery terminal. Touch the voltmeter prods on the battery negative terminal and the starter end frame or engine block. Crank the engine and note the meter reading. Look at Fig. 23-22.

If HIGHER than around .2 to .5 volts, check the voltage drop across the negative battery cable. The engine may NOT be grounded properly. Clean, tighten, or replace the cable if needed. Also make sure the cable-to-engine bolt and starter bolts are tight.

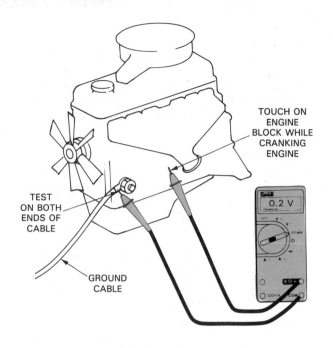

Fig. 23-22. Test for checking ground connection on block. Do not forget this connection when diagnosing problems. (Fluke)

BATTERY CABLE PROBLEMS

Mentioned briefly, a *battery cable problem* can produce symptoms similar to a dead battery, bad solenoid, or weak starting motor. If cables do NOT allow enough current flow, starter will turn slowly or not at all.

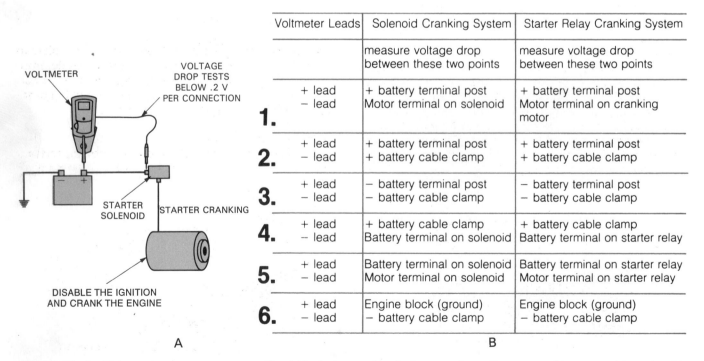

	Voltmeter Leads	Solenoid Cranking System	Starter Relay Cranking System
		measure voltage drop between these two points	measure voltage drop between these two points
1.	+ lead − lead	+ battery terminal post Motor terminal on solenoid	+ battery terminal post Motor terminal on cranking motor
2.	+ lead − lead	+ battery terminal post + battery cable clamp	+ battery terminal post + battery cable clamp
3.	+ lead − lead	− battery terminal post − battery cable clamp	− battery terminal post − battery cable clamp
4.	+ lead − lead	+ battery cable clamp Battery terminal on solenoid	+ battery cable clamp Battery terminal on starter relay
5.	+ lead − lead	Battery terminal on solenoid Motor terminal on solenoid	Battery terminal on starter relay Motor terminal on starter relay
6.	+ lead − lead	Engine block (ground) − battery cable clamp	Engine block (ground) − battery cable clamp

A

B

Fig. 23-21. A—Voltage drop measurements will quickly find poor electrical connections. Note tests of battery cable, solenoid, and solenoid-to-starter cable. B—Chart summarizes voltmeter test locations for two major types of starting systems. Voltage drops should not be over .2 to .5 volts. (TIF and Florida Dept. of Voc. Ed.)

Testing battery cables

To test the battery or starter cables, connect a voltmeter to each cable and perform a voltage drop test. If any cable shows a high voltage drop during cranking, clean and tighten its connections. Then retest the cable. If still high (above .2 to .3 volts), replace or repair the cable.

Replacing battery cables

When replacing battery cables, make sure the new cables are the same as the old ones. Compare cable length and diameter. Cables with lead terminals are BETTER than ones with steel ends. The soft lead will more easily conform to the shape of the battery terminal.

CAUTION! NEVER remove starting system parts without disconnecting the battery first. The engine could be cranked over or an electrical fire could result if wires are shorted.

When tightening the ends of battery or starter cables, only snug down the fasteners. Many of the threaded studs, bolts, and nuts are made of soft metals. They can strip and break easily.

STARTER SOLENOID SERVICE

A *faulty starter solenoid* can cause many symptoms: click with no cranking, no cranking with no click, or slow cranking. With some circuits, it can also keep the engine or starting motor from shutting off (feeds current to ignition system).

Usually, the large disc-shaped contact in the solenoid will burn and pit. The disc can develop high resistance that blocks current flow to the starter.

An open or shorted solenoid winding can keep the contact disc from closing. No click will occur and the engine will not crank.

Testing starter solenoid

To test the solenoid, connect a voltmeter as shown in Fig. 23-23. This will measure the voltage drop and resistance of the solenoid lugs or nuts and contacts. Crank the engine and note the voltmeter reading. If above .2 to .3 volts, replace the solenoid. However, make sure the nuts holding the cables are tight. They can loosen and cause high resistance. You must remove the cable to tighten the inner nut, Fig. 23-24.

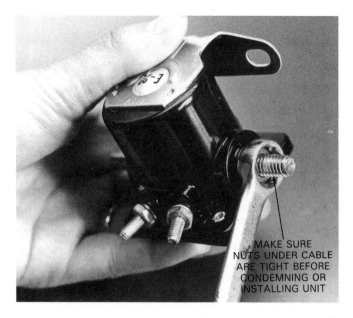

Fig. 23-24. Before condemning a solenoid after it shows high voltage drop, make sure inner nuts are tight. Tightening outer nuts will not assure good connection if inner nuts are loose. (Nichols)

MAKE SURE NUTS UNDER CABLE ARE TIGHT BEFORE CONDEMNING OR INSTALLING UNIT

Replacing starter solenoid

To replace a solenoid mounted away from the starter, simply remove the cables and wires. Unbolt the solenoid from the fenderwell and install the new one.

If the solenoid is starter mounted, the starter must be removed from the engine. Then, the solenoid is unscrewed from the starting motor and replaced.

The procedures for removing, assembling, and installing a starter are covered later.

IGNITION SWITCH SERVICE

A *faulty ignition switch* can keep the starter solenoid from energizing. It can also keep the solenoid from de-energizing. The contacts in the ignition switch can wear or burn causing either an open (no cranking problem) or short (engine cranks all the time).

Testing ignition switch

To test an ignition switch no crank problem, touch a test light to the starter solenoid START(S) terminal. If

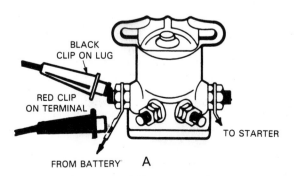

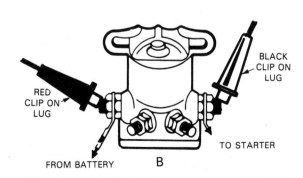

BLACK CLIP ON LUG
RED CLIP ON TERMINAL
TO STARTER
FROM BATTERY   A

RED CLIP ON LUG
BLACK CLIP ON LUG
TO STARTER
FROM BATTERY   B

Fig. 23-23. Voltage drop test will quickly check condition of solenoid and its electrical connections. A—Check solenoid lug-to-cable connection for high resistance. B—Checking condition of disc contact and terminals in solenoid. (Marquette)

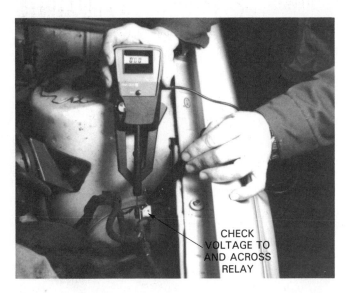

CHECK
VOLTAGE TO
AND ACROSS
RELAY

Fig. 23-25. Some starter circuits use a relay. Check voltage to and out of relay if engine will not crank. (TIF Instruments)

the ignition switch is good, the test light will glow when the key is turned to start the engine. The test light should go out when the key is released.

If the test light on the solenoid DOES NOT GLOW, either a wire in the ignition switch circuit is open or the ignition switch is defective. Test the wires coming out of the ignition switch to eliminate the possibility of a bad wire or connection.

If the test light touched to the start terminal on the solenoid glows in both the start and run position, the ignition switch is probably shorted. The engine would crank all the time.

More ignition switch service information

Again, these are simplified tests. You will need to use your own judgment and a service manual to perform more detailed tests.

STARTER RELAY SERVICE

A *faulty starter relay* can keep the starter solenoid from working. This will prevent engine cranking. The winding or the contact points in the relay could be bad.

To test a starter relay, use a test light or VOM to check for voltage going INTO and coming OUT of the relay terminals, Fig. 23-25. Refer to a wiring diagram for test points if needed. Replace the relay if needed.

If voltage is NOT reaching the relay, test at the ignition switch. The problem may be in the switch or wiring to the relay.

NEUTRAL SAFETY SWITCH SERVICE

A *misadjusted* or *bad neutral safety switch* can also keep the engine from cranking when the key is turned to start. If the neutral safety switch is open, current cannot flow from the ignition switch to the starter solenoid.

Checking neutral safety switch action

Before testing the switch, move the transmission gear

shift lever into various positions while trying to start the engine. The switch may close, letting the starter operate. If the starter begins to work, the neutral safety switch may only need adjustment. This switch can be located on the top of the steering column near the firewall, on the transmission, or on the floor shift mechanism.

Adjusting neutral safety switch

To adjust a neutral safety switch, loosen the fasteners holding the switch. With the switch loosened, place the shift selector into park (P). Then, while holding the ignition switch to START, slide the neutral switch on its mount until the engine cranks. Without moving the switch, tighten its hold-down screws. This should make the engine start only with the shift lever in park or neutral. Check operation after adjustment.

Testing neutral safety switch

To test a neutral safety switch, touch a 12-volt test light on the switch output wire connection while moving the transmission shift lever. The light should glow as the shift lever is slid into PARK and NEUTRAL. The test light should NOT glow when the transmission is in all other positions.

If not working properly, check the mechanism that operates the neutral safety switch. There should be a prong or other device that actuates the neutral safety switch. If the problem is in the switch, remove, replace, and adjust it.

STARTER SERVICE

A *faulty starting motor* can cause a wide range of symptoms: slow cranking, no cranking, overheating of starter cables, and abnormal noises while cranking. If the battery, cables, solenoid, and other starting system parts are good but the engine does not crank properly, the starter may be bad.

A current draw test and other tests would indicate when the starter motor should be removed for further inspection and testing.

Starting motor rebuild

A *starting motor rebuild* typically involves:

1. Removal and disassembly of starting motor, Figs. 23-26 and 23-27.
2. Cleaning and inspection for part wear or damage.
3. Replacement of brushes, bushings, and any other worn or damaged parts.
4. Polishing and sometimes turning (machining) of commutator.
5. Lubrication, reassembly, testing, and installation of starting motor.

Many shops do NOT rebuild starting motors. They purchase and install a new or factory-rebuilt unit. The cost of labor may be too high to make in-shop rebuilding economical. Also, the factory rebuilt unit will have a limited warranty.

Note! When the starter must be repaired, you may only need to disassemble some of the starter. For example, a worn pinion gear assembly can make the gear retract. The clutch will freewheel without proper engine cranking. The pinion gear assembly can be replaced by simply

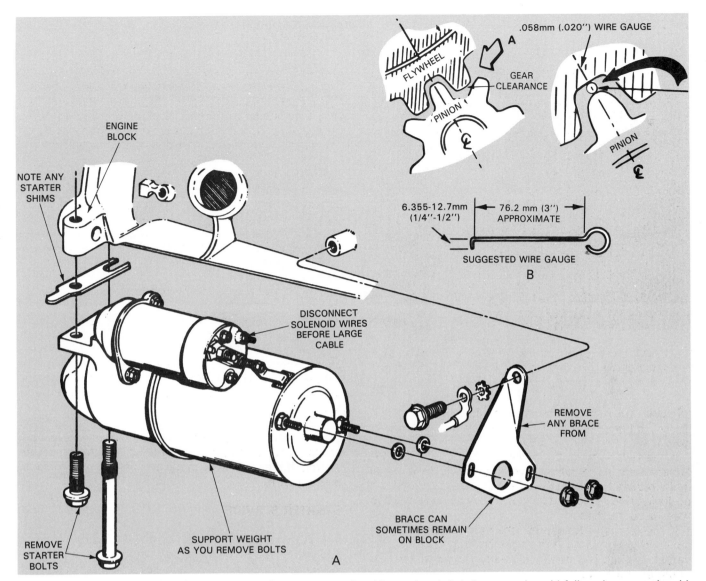

Fig. 23-26. A—When removing starter from engine, support it with one hand. It is heavy and could fall or damage solenoid wires. Note location of any shims. Allow starter to drop down partially to remove solenoid wires if needed. B—Checking gear mesh for shimming motor. (General Motors)

removing the drive end frame and a C-lock. The brushes and other end of the motor can remain together. Keep this in mind during starter service.

Starting motor removal

Before deciding to remove the starting motor, inspect it closely for problems. Check that the starter-to-engine bolts are tight. Loose starter bolts can upset motor operation by causing a poor ground or incorrect pinion gear meshing. Make sure all wires on the motor and solenoid are tight.

To remove the starting motor, first DISCONNECT THE BATTERY. Then, disconnect the battery cable and solenoid wires (starter mounted solenoid type) and any braces on the motor. Unscrew the bolts while holding up on the motor. Refer to Fig. 23-26.

CAUTION! Be careful not to drop the starting motor when removing it. The motor is heavy enough to cause injury if it falls.

Starter shims may be used to adjust the space

between the pinion gear and the flywheel ring gear. Shims hold the starter pinion gear farther away from or closer to the ring gear, Fig. 23-26.

During starter removal, ALWAYS check for shims. They must be installed in the same place during reassembly. If NOT replaced, the pinion and flywheel gears may not mesh properly. A grinding noise can result.

Some late model engines place the starting motor under the engine intake manifold. You must remove the manifold to service the starting motor. Usually, only a few easy-to-reach bolts secure the engine intake manifold.

Starter disassembly

If the starter has a solenoid, remove the small fasteners that hold it in place. Pull the solenoid off the motor. You may need to rotate the solenoid slightly.

Fig. 23-27 gives a typical sequence for starter disassembly.

Remove the through-bolts after PUNCH-MARKING the end frames. Tap off the end frames with a plastic hammer while noting the position of all internal parts. See Fig. 23-28.

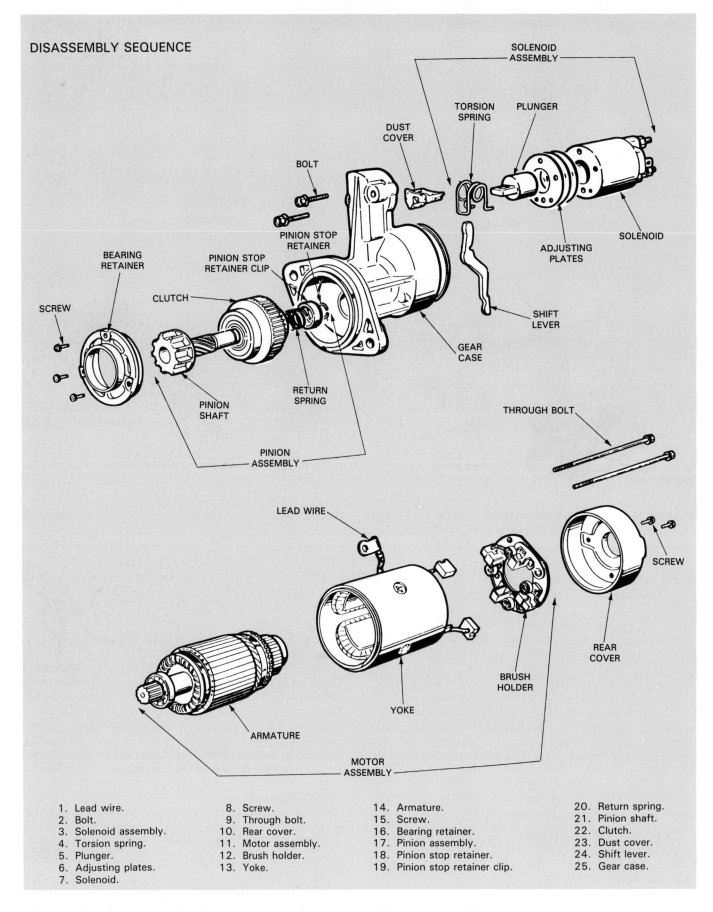

DISASSEMBLY SEQUENCE

1. Lead wire.
2. Bolt.
3. Solenoid assembly.
4. Torsion spring.
5. Plunger.
6. Adjusting plates.
7. Solenoid.
8. Screw.
9. Through bolt.
10. Rear cover.
11. Motor assembly.
12. Brush holder.
13. Yoke.
14. Armature.
15. Screw.
16. Bearing retainer.
17. Pinion assembly.
18. Pinion stop retainer.
19. Pinion stop retainer clip.
20. Return spring.
21. Pinion shaft.
22. Clutch.
23. Dust cover.
24. Shift lever.
25. Gear case.

Fig. 23-27. This service manual illustration gives numbers that show sequence for part removal during starter rebuild. Study sequence. (Oldsmobile)

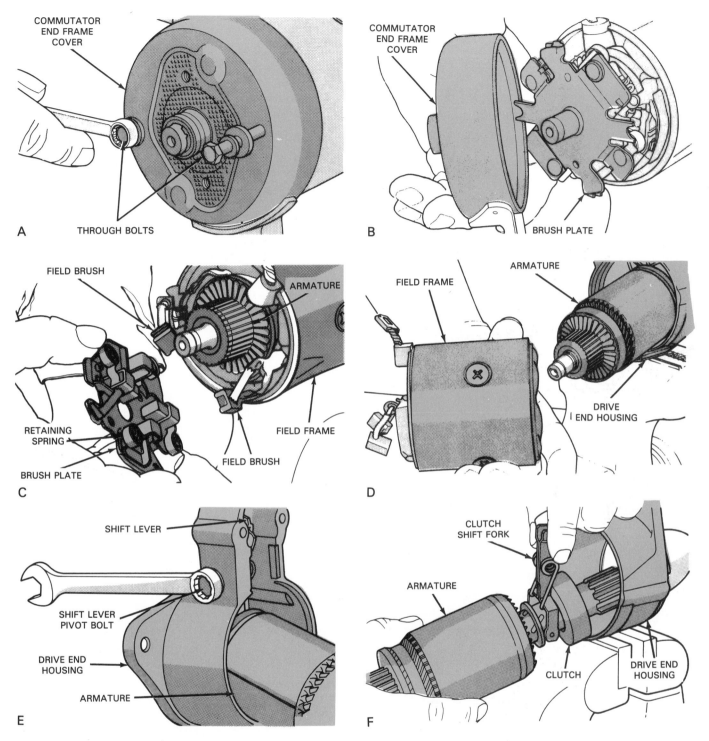

Fig. 23-28. Basic steps for starter disassembly: A—Remove through-bolts. Scribe mark parts for realignment. B—Remove end cover. C—If needed, remove brush assembly. Sometimes, armature will slide out other end and brush stays in main frame. D—Remove armature. E—Disassemble shift lever assembly. F—Remove clutch and pinion gear from armature. (Chrysler)

Slide the armature out of the field frame after removing the end frames, Fig. 23-28. Remove the C-clip holding the pinion gear on the armature shaft. Then slide the pinion gear off.

Place all of the parts in an organized pattern on your workbench. This will help if you forget how to put something together. If needed, also refer to a service manual for added details.

Cleaning and inspecting motor components

First, blow all of the parts clean with compressed air. Wear eye protection. Look at Fig. 23-29.

Then, wipe the armature, field windings, brushes, and overrunning clutch with a clean, dry cloth. These parts should NOT be cleaned using solvent. The solvent can damage the wire insulation; soak into the brushes; or wash lubricant out of the pinion gear clutch.

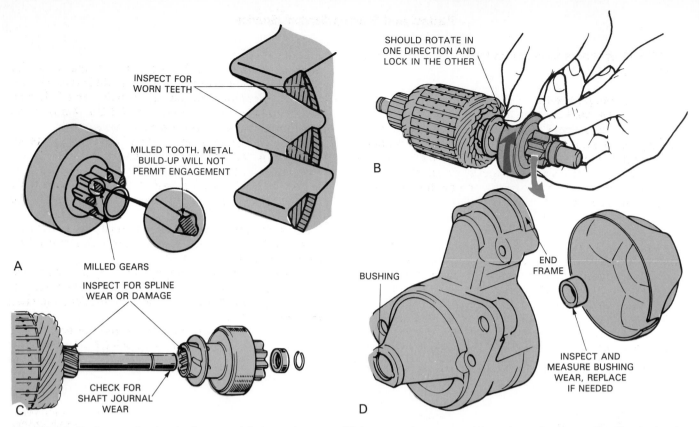

Fig. 23-29. Basic part checks. A—Inspect pinion gear for wear. Slightest tooth wear would require replacement. B—Check clutch action. It should lock one way and freewheel in other. It is usually replaced. C—Inspect splines in pinion assembly and on armature shaft. D—Measure bushing wear and replace them if worn.

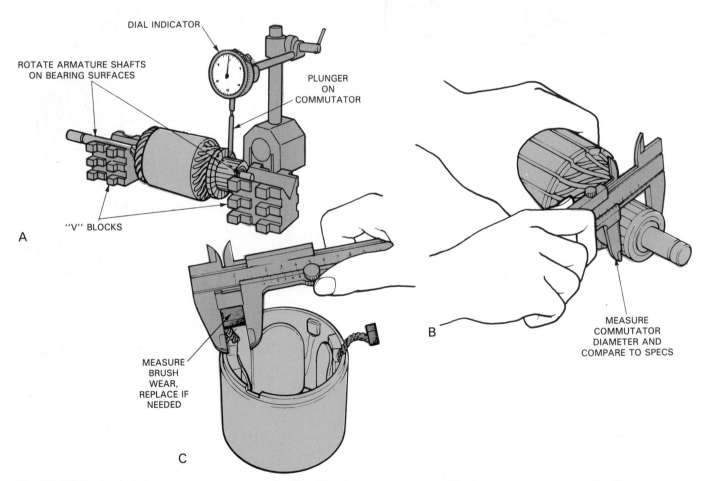

Fig. 23-30. Basic starting motor measurements. A—Checking for armature runout. Replace or turn as needed. B—Measure comutator diameter. Replace if diameter is too small. C—Measure brush wear and compare to specs.

With all of the parts clean and dry, inspect them for wear, Fig. 23-30.

Starter bushing service

Worn starter bushings can let the armature drag or rub on the field pole shoes. This can cause serious starter damage. Look inside the field shoes to check for rubbing. Also, insert the end of the armature shaft into the bushings. If the shaft wiggles excessively in the bushings, replace them. Press out the old bushings and press in new ones.

Starter brush service

Check for *worn starter brushes* which can reduce starter torque or cause excessive starter current draw. Some manufacturers recommend a minimum height for the brushes. If worn shorter than specs, the brushes must be replaced. See Fig. 23-30.

The brush wire leads are usually soldered in place. If so, a soldering gun and rosin core (not acid core) solder must be used to replace the brushes. Also, check the brush holder for shorts to ground, as in Fig. 23-31.

Armature service

Inspect the armature for wear or damage. Look for signs of burning or overheating on the windings and commutator. If the armature has been rubbing on a field pole shoe, the shaft may be bent, Fig. 23-30. Also, check the ends of the shaft for wear or burrs.

To check for an *armature short circuit,* mount the armature on a *growler* (armature tester), Fig. 23-31.

After reading the instructions for the growler, turn on the power. Hold a thin strip of metal or hacksaw blade next to the armature while rotating the armature in the growler.

With a shorted armature, the metal strip or hacksaw blade will VIBRATE when passed next to the shorted leg of the windings.

To check *armature continuity,* do an *open circuit test.* You can sometimes use a growler (type with meter) or an ohmmeter, Fig. 23-31. Follow the directions provided with the growler.

When using an ohmmeter, touch the meter prods to each commutator segment, Fig. 23-31. If the meter reads infinite resistance on any segment, that segment

A—Use ohmmeter to check for grounds and opens in coils.

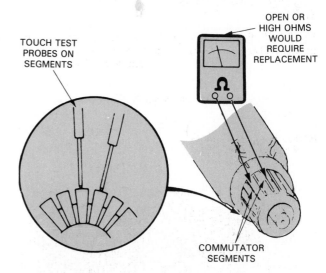

B—Use ohmmeter to check for opens in commutator.

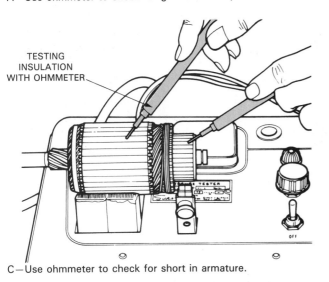

C—Use ohmmeter to check for short in armature.

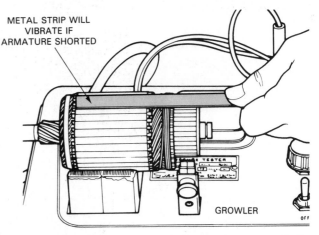

D—Growler is being used to check for shorts. Metal strip will vibrate when moved next to shorted winding.

Fig. 23-31. Basic starter electrical tests. (GM and Toyota)

winding is open. The armature must be replaced.

You should also check for an *armature ground* (short from winding to shaft or core), Fig. 23-31.

Touch the ohmmeter prods on the armature coil core and the commutator segments. Repeat this test on the commutator segments and armature shaft. If there is continuity (low resistance), then the armature is grounded and must be replaced.

If the windings are in good condition, the commutator should be cleaned using very fine sandpaper; do not use emery cloth.

If the commutator is badly worn, it should be turned (machined) on a lathe. Then, the mica (insulation) between each commutator segment must usually be undercut. A special tool or a hacksaw blade can be used to cut the mica lower than the surface of the segments. Refer to Fig. 23-32.

Also check the armature shaft. If there are any burrs at the lock ring groove, file them off.

Field coil service

Inspect the field windings inside the starter frame. Look for signs of physical damage or burning.

To test for *open field coils,* use a test light (battery powered type) or an ohmmeter. Touch the test prods to wires or brushes that connect to the field windings. This connection may vary with some starters so check in a manual, Fig. 23-31.

If the test light *glows* or the ohmmeter reads zero, the field windings are NOT open. When the test light does NOT glow or the meter reads infinite (maximum)

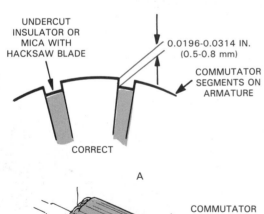

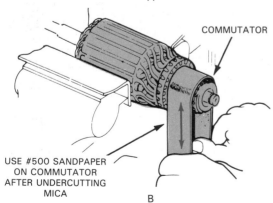

Fig. 23-32. A—Mica or insulation on commutator should be recessed below surface of metal. Use hacksaw blade to undercut if needed. B—Polish commutator clean and smooth with #500 sandpaper, not emery cloth.

resistance, the field windings are open (broken) and must be replaced.

To test for *grounded field coils* (winding shorted to frame or other starter component), touch the test light or ohmmeter prods across the field coil and ground. The light should NOT glow or the meter should read infinite resistance. If the starter has a shunt winding, disconnect it before making the test. If a winding is grounded, it must be replaced.

Overrunning clutch (pinion gear) service

Normally, the overrunning clutch or pinion gear assembly is replaced anytime the starting motor is disassembled. The pinion gear is subjected to extreme wear and tear when engaged and disengaged from the engine flywheel. It is usually wise to replace the pinion gear during starter service.

If the pinion gear is to be used over, check the ends of the gear teeth for wear. Also, check the action of the overrunning clutch. It should let the gear turn freely in one direction but lock the gear in the other direction.

Starter reassembly

Reassemble the starter using the reverse order of disassembly. Lubricate the armature shaft bushings, pinion gear splines, and other parts as recommended by the manufacturer. See Fig. 23-33.

> WARNING! Do NOT use too much oil or grease to lubricate the bushings and other parts of a starting motor. If lubricant gets on the brushes and commutator, starter service life and starter power will be reduced.

The only difficult part of starter reassembly can be brush installation. With many starters, the brushes can be locked out of the way using the brush springs. The springs are wedged on the sides of the brushes. This will hold the brushes up so you can slide the armature and commutator into place. Then, the brushes may be snapped into place on the commutator, Fig. 23-33.

After reassembly, test the starter before installing it on the engine. Pictured in Fig. 23-34, connect the starter to a battery using jumper cables. Connect the positive cable first and then the negative cable. Hold or clamp the starter securely because it will kick (lurch) and rotate when energized.

Make sure the motor spins at the correct speed and that the pinion gear moves into the correct position.

Starter *pinion gear clearance* is the distance between the pinion and the drive end frame with the pinion engaged. Always check pinion gear clearance during a starter bench test. With the starter energized, check the clearance.

If pinion gear clearance is NOT within specs, bend the shift lever or replace worn parts. Check in a service manual for exact specs and procedures.

Installing starting motor

Install the starter in the reverse order of removal. Make sure that any spacer shims are replaced between the motor and the engine block. If these shims are left out, the pinion gear may not mesh with the flywheel gear properly.

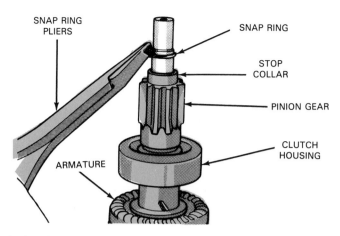

A—Install new pinion gear onto shaft. Install snap ring into shaft groove.

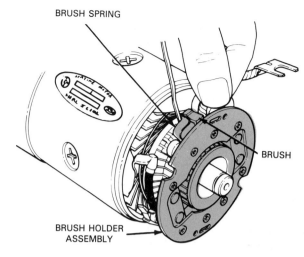

B—Lock brushes up out of the way if needed with brush springs. Wedge springs onto sides of brushes to hold them open. This is not needed if brushes come out of frame as an assembly.

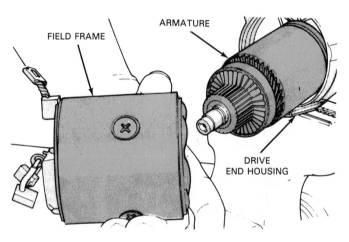

C—Install armature into center frame. Install brushes onto commutator.

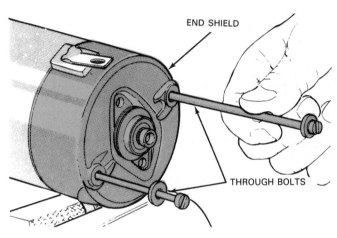

D—Align parts and install through-bolts.

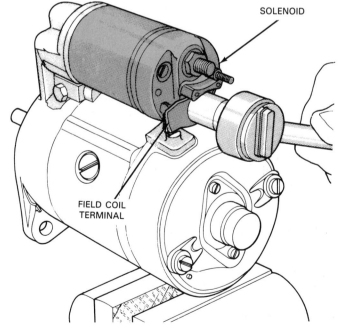

E—Install starter solenoid if mounted on motor.

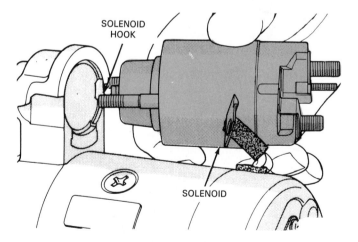

F—Secure solenoid connections and make sure inner nuts are snug.

Fig. 23-33. Basic steps for starter assembly. (Chrysler and General Motors)

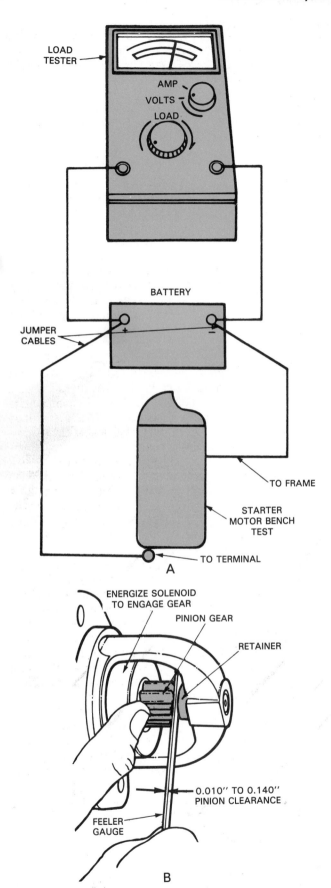

Fig. 23-34. Make these checks before installing starting motor after rebuild. A—Connect battery to starter and measure current draw. B—Energize solenoid and make sure pinion gear is engaging properly. Compare clearance to specs. (Ford and GM)

If the starter has a solenoid on it, connect the wires on the solenoid before bolting the starter to the engine. Tighten the starter bolts to the recommended torque. Replace any bracket or shields and reconnect the battery. Crank the engine several times to check starting motor operation.

SUMMARY

Cars normally use 12 volt batteries that actually have an open circuit voltage of 12.6 volts. A maintenance-free battery has a sealed top and usually a charge indicator eye.

When troubleshooting and repairing a battery charging system or a starting system, remember that these systems interact. One example: a dead battery can be caused by the battery itself, a faulty alternator, regulator, or shorted starting motor.

A car battery should be properly maintained to assure dependable engine starting. Inspect the battery for problems whenever you are working under the hood.

A battery terminal test measures the voltage drop across the battery terminals. A higher than .5 volt drop would indicate corroded connections and high resistance.

Jump start a car by connecting the jumper cables positive to positive and negative to negative. The negative cables should be connected to any ground (negative) away from the batteries.

Make sure a battery charger is shut off before connecting the cables to the battery. A spark could make the battery explode!

A load test is the best way to check battery condition. After connecting the load tester, turn the load control knob until the ammeter reads the output specs for the specific battery. Hold the load for 15 seconds while reading the voltmeter. The voltmeter should stay above 9.5 volts at room temperature if the battery is good. A lower voltage reading would indicate a bad battery.

A starter current draw test will check the general condition of the starting motor. Measure current flow out of the battery with the engine cranking. If current draw is too high, it may be due to a bad starter. A low current draw would indicate a high resistance in the circuit or motor.

Voltage drop tests will help find high resistance in cable connections and components. If a voltage drop is too high (over about .2 to .5 volt) when cranking, a poor electrical connection is indicated.

A faulty starter solenoid can cause numerous symptoms, no cranking, clicking, slow cranking. The large contact in the solenoid can burn and not make a good electrical connection. The solenoid coil windings can also fail.

A voltmeter can be used to check for power to and out of the solenoid. A voltage drop test will check for burned contacts and loose connections.

The ignition switch feeds current to the starter solenoid. If the contacts in the ignition switch burn, it can prevent cranking. Use a test light to check for voltage out of the ignition switch when needed. Replace it if defective.

A starter relay is used in some cranking circuits. It is

energized by the ignition switch to feed current to the solenoid. If its coil or contacts fail, it can prevent normal cranking.

A starter rebuild involves complete disassembly, cleaning, and reassembly. All worn or bad parts are replaced. This is a time consuming process. Therefore, most mechanics install factory rebuilt starters.

Always replace any starter shims. They space the pinion gear the right distance from the flywheel ring gear. If not replaced, abnormal cranking noise can result from improper gear meshing.

KNOW THESE TERMS

Discharged, Battery leakage, Battery terminal test, Battery maintenance, Hydrogen gas, Distilled water, Charge indicator eye, Hydrometer, Jump start, Cell voltage test, Battery charger, Slow charge, Fast charge, Battery voltage test, Battery load test, Inductive pickup, Battery load, Temperature compensation chart, Battery drain test, Starting headlight test, Starter current draw test, Starting system voltage drop tests, Neutral safety switch adjustment, Starting motor rebuild, Starter shims, Growler, Pinion gear clearance, Starter bench test, Parasitic load.

REVIEW QUESTIONS—CHAPTER 23

1. List four checks that should be made during battery inspection.
2. A _____ _____ _____ determines if current is draining across the top of a dirty battery top.
3. How do you do a battery terminal test?
4. Why should you make your last jumper cable connection on the frame, away from the dead battery?
5. In your own words, how do you complete a battery load test?
6. Name five conditions that can appear to be a bad battery.
7. Describe four starting system problem symptoms.
8. What information would a starter current draw test give you?
9. How do you adjust a neutral safety switch?
10. In your own words, summarize the steps for rebuilding a starting motor.

ASE CERTIFICATION—TYPE QUESTIONS

1. A car is brought into the shop with battery problems. Technician A inspects the condition of the battery cables. Technician B checks the condition of the battery case. Who is right?
   (A) A only.   (C) Both A and B.
   (B) B only.   (D) Neither A nor B.

2. Current is believed to be discharging across the top of an automotive battery. Technician A performs a battery leakage test. Technician B performs a battery draw test. Who is right?
   (A) A only.   (C) Both A and B.
   (B) B only.   (D) Neither A nor B.

3. During a battery terminal test, the voltage reading should not exceed:
   (A) 1 volt.   (C) .25 volt.
   (B) .5 volt.   (D) 6 volts.

4. An automotive battery's side terminals need cleaning. Technician A uses a wire brush to clean the terminals. Technician B uses a scraper to clean the battery terminals. Who is right?
   (A) A only.   (C) Both A and B.
   (B) B only.   (D) Neither A nor B.

5. A battery must be charged. Technician A says the battery charger should be turned off before connecting it to the battery. Technician B says the charging rate should never exceed 10 amps. Who is right?
   (A) A only.   (C) Both A and B.
   (B) B only.   (D) Neither A nor B.

6. A load test must be performed on a 700 cold cranking amp automotive battery. Technician A says no-load battery voltage should be checked before performing the test. Technician B says the load tester should be set to draw 350 amps before performing the test. Who is right?
   (A) A only.   (C) Both A and B.
   (B) B only.   (D) Neither A nor B.

7. An automobile has a no-crank problem. Technician A says a starting headlight test can be used to determine the cause of trouble. Technician B says a dead or discharged battery is a common cause of a no-crank problem. Who is right?
   (A) A only.   (C) Both A and B.
   (B) B only.   (D) Neither A nor B.

8. When performing a starter current draw test, the engine should never be cranked for more than:
   (A) 5 seconds.   (C) 60 seconds.
   (B) 30 seconds.   (D) 90 seconds.

9. Technician A says a defective neutral safety switch can cause a no-crank problem. Technician B says a defective starter relay can cause a no-crank problem. Who is right?
   (A) A only.   (C) Both A and B.
   (B) B only.   (D) Neither A nor B.

10. A starter motor must be tested for open field coils. Technician A uses a battery powered test light to check the field coils. Technician B uses an ohmmeter to test the starter's field coils. Who is right?
   (A) A only.   (C) Both A and B.
   (B) B only.   (D) Neither A nor B.

FUSES
① EFI (15A) in the main fuse box
② No.4 (15A)
③ 7.5A near the under-dash fuse box
④ No.3 (10A)
⑤ HAZARD on the battery positive terminal
⑥ No.9 (20A)

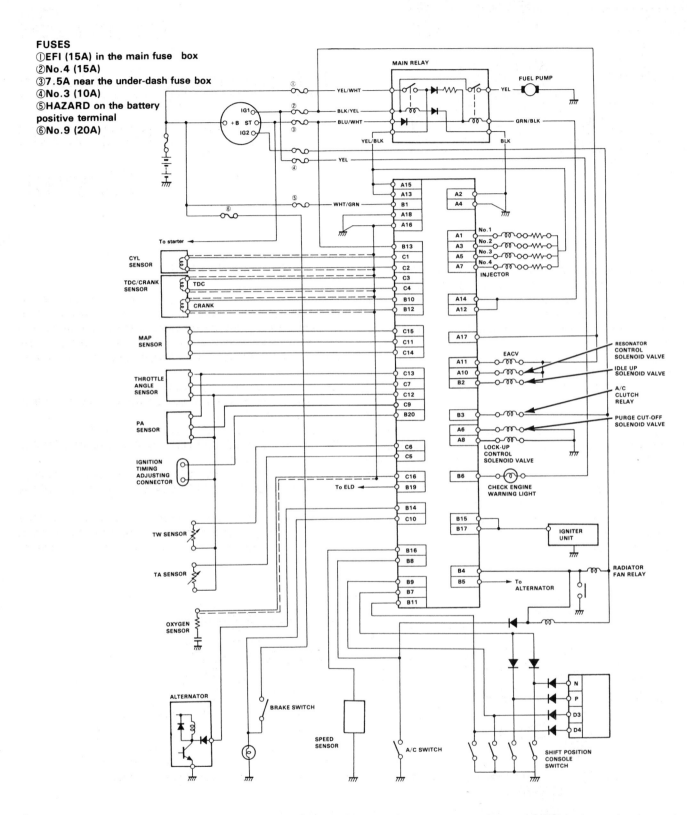

Study wiring diagram for computer control system. Can you find the charging system alternator? What pin number is used to feed power to the computer? (Honda)

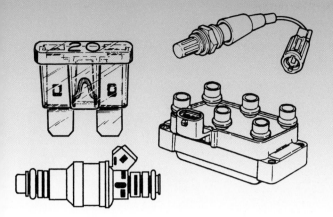

Chapter 24

Charging System Diagnosis and Repair

After studying this chapter, you will be able to:
- *Troubleshoot problems in a charging system.*
- *Test the voltage output of a charging system with a VOM and a load tester.*
- *Bypass the regulator to isolate a charging system problem.*
- *Remove and replace an alternator.*
- *Remove and replace a voltage regulator.*
- *Rebuild an alternator.*

In Chapter 14, you learned the operating principles of a charging system. This knowledge will help when diagnosing problems because you will know how each charging system part is supposed to operate. As you study this chapter, you will learn the most common methods used to find the source of alternator and voltage regulator troubles. You will also learn how to fix these problems. This should give you enough background or knowledge to use a service manual to work on any type of charging system.

CHARGING SYSTEM DIAGNOSIS

Even though a charging system only has two major parts (alternator and regulator), be careful when troubleshooting. Sometimes, another system fault (bad starting motor, battery, or wiring) will appear to be caused by problems in the charging system, Fig. 24-1.

Charging problem symptoms

There are four types of symptoms caused by charging system problems:
1. DEAD BATTERY (slow or no cranking).
2. OVERCHARGED BATTERY (water must be added to battery frequently).
3. ABNORMAL NOISES (grinding, squealing, buzzing).
4. INDICATOR SHOWS PROBLEM (light glows all the time).

Verify these problems by starting or trying to start the engine. It is possible that the symptoms have been mistaken by the service writer or customer. For exam-

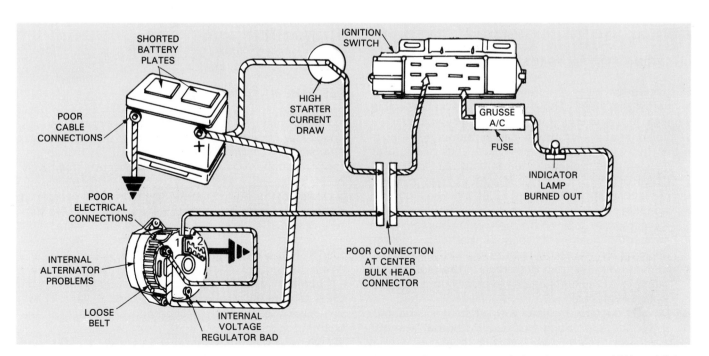

Fig. 24-1. Note some of the problems that can affect or appear to affect operation of charging system. (Oldsmobile)

ple, a problem described as a no-charge condition may really be a shorted starting motor, battery drain, or other trouble.

Visual inspection

Open the hood and visually inspect the parts of the charging system. Check for obvious troubles.

Check for battery problems: loose battery cables, discharged battery, corroded terminals, low water level, or case damage.

Check for alternator belt problems. Make sure the belt is adjusted properly. A loose belt may squeal or flap up and down.

Also inspect the condition of the alternator belt. Check for cracks, glazing (hard, shiny surface), grease or oil contamination, and deterioration.

If needed, adjust alternator belt tension. Loosen the alternator mounting and adjusting bolts. Then pry on a strong surface of the end frame. Pull only hard enough to produce proper tension. Tighten the adjusting bolt while holding the pry bar. Tighten the other mounting bolt or bolts. Recheck tension.

> WARNING! Only tighten an alternator belt enough to prevent belt slippage or flap. Overtightening is a COMMON MISTAKE that quickly ruins alternator bearings!

Check for wiring problems in the charging system. Check for loose electrical connections, corroded connections, shorted wires (missing insulation), and other problems.

In particular, check the connections on the back of the alternator and regulator (type mounted away from alternator). WIGGLE THE WIRES while running the engine. If the indicator light goes out or dash gauge begins to read properly when a wire is moved, the problem is in that area of the wiring.

Listen closely for abnormal noises in the alternator or regulator (contact point type). If needed, use a stethoscope to listen to the alternator, Fig. 24-2. Try to detect any other unusual sounds.

CHARGING SYSTEM PRECAUTIONS

Observe the following precautions when working on a charging system. They will help prevent possible damage to the charging and other electrical systems.

1. Disconnect the battery cables before connecting a battery charger to the battery. A voltage surge or high charge voltage can damage ELECTRONIC COMPONENTS in the alternator, regulator, computer system, fuel injection, or emission control systems.
2. Never reverse polarity! If battery or jumper cables are connected backwards, serious electrical damage could occur. Reversing polarity can blow the diodes in the alternator, ruin the circuit in the regulator or burn electronic components in other computer controlled systems.
3. Do NOT operate alternator with output disconnected. If the alternator is operated with the output wire off, alternator voltage can increase to above normal levels. Do not run the engine and alternator with the

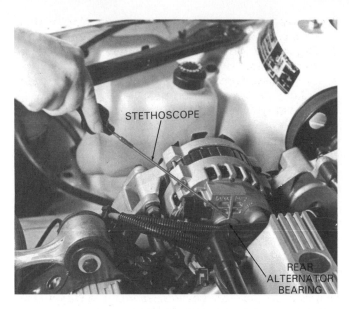

Fig. 24-2. Stethoscope will help check for worn, dry alternator bearings during initial inspection. Loud grinding noise indicates trouble. Another trick, ferrous rod or screwdriver will be attracted to and stick to rear of alternator if it is producing output or magnetic field.

battery disconnected. Alternator or other circuit damage could result.

4. Never short or ground any charging system terminal unless instructed to do so by a shop manual. Some circuits can be grounded or shorted without damage; others will be seriously damaged. Check in a service manual when in doubt.
5. Do NOT attempt to polarize an alternator. Older DC generator systems had to be polarized (voltage connected to generator field) after repairs. This must NOT be done with an alternator.

> 6. DANGER! Some heated film windshield systems make the alternator full-field and produce over 100 volts AC. This could be enough voltage and current to cause electrocution and death. Use caution when working on these systems!

TEST THE BATTERY FIRST

When analyzing problems in the charging system, check the condition of the battery first. Even though charging system problems often show up as a dead battery, you must NOT forget that the battery itself may be at fault.

Measure the battery state-of-charge and perform a battery load test. Then, you will be sure that the battery is not affecting your charging system tests.

CHARGING SYSTEM TESTS

Charging system tests should be done when symptoms point to low alternator voltage and current. These will quickly determine the operating condition of the charging system.

1. *Charging system output test* (measure of current and voltage output of charging system under a load.)

2. *Regulator voltage test* (measure charging system voltage under low output—low load conditions).
3. *Regulator bypass test* (connect full battery voltage to alternator field, leaving regulator out of circuit).
4. *Circuit resistance tests* (measure resistance in insulated and ground circuits of system).

Charging system tests are frequently performed in two ways: using a LOAD TESTER (same tester used to check battery and starting system in earlier chapter) or by using a common VOM or multimeter.

VOLTMETER TEST OF CHARGING OUTPUT

A voltmeter can be used to test the output of a charging system when a load tester is not available. It will measure charging system voltage with an accessory load. The voltage reading will be an indicator of current output and charging system condition. If charging system output voltage is NOT above battery voltage with an accessory load, the battery cannot be recharged and a problem exists. See Fig. 24-3.

The four basic steps for testing a charging system with a voltmeter are:

1. *Base voltage* (measure battery voltage with engine OFF).
2. *No-load voltage* (measure voltage at battery with engine running, electrical accessories OFF).
3. *Load voltage* (measure voltage at battery with engine running, all electrical accessories ON).
4. *Calculate charge voltage* (load voltage must be higher than base voltage for battery charging, no-load voltage must be within specs).

Voltmeter base reading

To test the charging system with a voltmeter, connect the meter probes across the terminals of the battery.

Fig. 24-3. Good VOM can be used to check operation of charging system. It is simply connected to battery posts or cables. Readings are then taken with engine OFF and running.

Take a *base reading* (battery voltage with engine off). This will compensate for any variation in the condition of the battery and accuracy of your meter. The base reading should be around 12.6 volts with a good, fully charged battery, Fig. 24-4.

Voltmeter no-load reading

Start and fast idle the engine at about 1500 rpm with all electrical accessories OFF. This is called the *no-load test* because it measures charging system voltage without a current draw. The voltmeter reading should increase over the base reading, but NOT OVER about

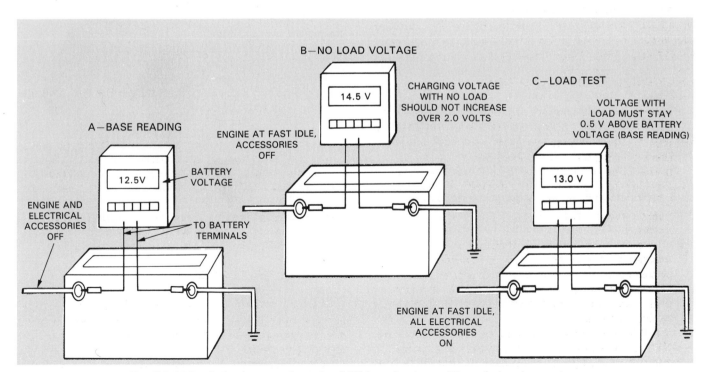

Fig. 24-4. Study basic steps for using VOM to check condition of charging system.

two (2) volts.

For example, if your base reading was 12.7 volts, then your no-load reading should be approximately 13 to 15 volts maximum.

If the no-load voltage increased MORE THAN 2 to 3 volts, then the alternator is overcharging the battery. Either the voltage regulator or wiring is bad.

If the no-load reading was BETWEEN .5 and 2 volts higher than the base reading, then this part of the test is good.

If the no-load voltage did NOT INCREASE above your base reading, then the charging system is NOT working. Either the alternator, regulator, or wiring could be faulty. Then, you need to perform a regulator bypass test discussed shortly.

Voltmeter load test

If the system passed the no-load test, you should also complete a load test. Start the engine and run it at about 2000 rpm.

TURN ON ALL ELECTRICAL ACCESSORIES (headlights, wipers, blower motor, air conditioning) to load the charging system. This will check the charging system output under high current draw conditions, Fig. 24-4.

The voltmeter must read at least .5 volts HIGHER than your base battery reading.

The LOAD TEST shows that the charging system is providing current for all of the electrical units and still has enough current to recharge the battery.

If the load voltage is NOT .5 volts above battery or base voltage, bypass the regulator to help find out which component (alternator or regulator) is faulty.

LOAD TESTER CHECK OF CHARGING SYSTEM

A load tester provides the most accurate method of checking a charging system. It will measure both system current and voltage.

There are several different makes of charging system testers. The operating procedures for each may vary. With any type tester, it is important to understand general test procedures. Then you can relate general test methods to any make or model of equipment.

Charging system output test

A *charging system output test* measures system current and voltage under maximum load (current output). To check output with a load tester, connect the tester leads as described by the manufacturer.

With modern testers, two large leads or cables fasten to the battery terminals. The inductive (clip-on) amps pickup fits around the insulation on the negative battery cable.

Procedures differ with noninductive testers. Check the operating directions when in doubt.

1. With the load tester controls set properly, turn the ignition key switch to RUN. Note (write down) this ammeter reading.
2. Start the engine. Adjust the idle speed to the test specs (about 2000 rpm).
3. Adjust the load control on the tester until the ammeter reads specified current output, but do NOT let voltage drop below specs (about 12 volts). Note (write down) this ammeter reading.

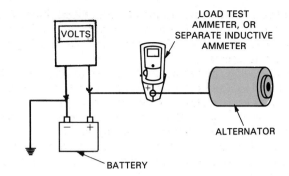

Fig. 24-5. Modern inductive DC ammeter or load tester will measure actual current output of alternator for more accurate test of charging system. (TIF)

4. Rotate load control to OFF. Evaluate your test readings.

Charging output test results

To calculate charging system output, add your two ammeter readings (current with ignition switch at run plus current with engine running). This will give you total charging system output in amps. Compare this figure to service manuals. See Fig. 24-5.

Current output specs for charging systems will depend on the size (rating) of the alternator. For instance, a car with few electrical accessories may have an alternator rated at only 35 amps. A larger, luxury car, with many accessories (air conditioning, speed control, power windows), might have an alternator with a much higher rating—40 to 80 amps. Always check in a service manual to obtain exact values.

If the charging system output current tested low, complete regulator voltage and regulator bypass tests. They will let you determine whether the alternator, regulator, or circuit wiring is at fault.

Regulator voltage test

Even if the previous output test was within 10 percent of specs, perform a regulator voltage test.

A *regulator voltage test* will check the calibration of the voltage regulator and detect a high or low voltage setting. See Fig. 24-6.

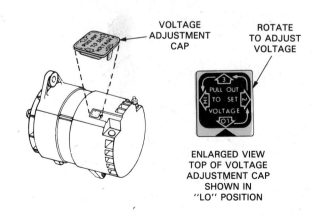

Fig. 24-6. If voltage regulator tests bad, it must usually be replaced. However, a few electronic units and most contact point types can be adjusted. (General Motors)

Set the meter selector to the correct test position. With the load control OFF, run the engine at 2000 rpm or specified test speed. Note the voltmeter reading and compare to specs.

Most voltage regulators are designed to operate in the 13.5 to 14.5 volt range. This range is stated for normal temperatures with the battery fully charged.

If the meter reading is steady and within recommended values, then the regulator setting is OK.

If the volt reading is steady, but too high or too low, then the regulator may need adjustment or, more often, replacement.

If the reading is not steady, then there may be a bad wiring connection, alternator problem, or a defective regulator.

Regulator bypass test

When a charging system fails either the output or regulator tests, a regulator bypass test should be done.

A *regulator bypass test* is a quick and easy way of finding out if the alternator, the regulator, or the circuit is faulty.

Procedures for a regulator bypass test are similar to the output test already explained. However, the regulator is taken out of the circuit.

Direct battery voltage (unregulated voltage) is used to excite the rotor field. This should make the alternator produce maximum output.

Depending upon system design, there are several ways to bypass the voltage regulator. One involves shorting a test tab to ground on the rear of the alternator, Fig. 24-7. Another requires a jumper wire to connect battery voltage to the field, Fig. 24-8.

Follow manufacturer's directions to avoid damage. You must NOT short or connect voltage to the wrong wire or the diodes or regulator may be ruined.

Regulator bypass test results

If charging voltage and current INCREASE to normal levels when the regulator is bypassed, you usually have

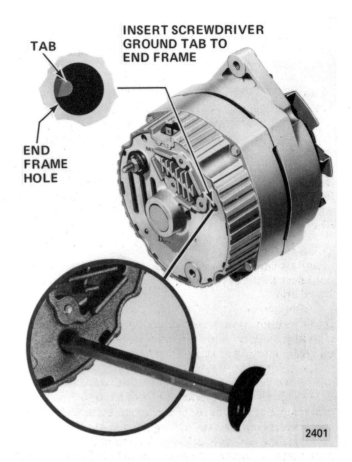

Fig. 24-7. Note how to full field alternator with this design. Grounding tab will make alternator produce maximum output. Never stick screwdriver or other tool into back of alternator unless you are sure that it is an acceptable procedure. (Chevrolet)

a BAD REGULATOR.

If system output REMAINS THE SAME when the regulator is bypassed, then you normally have a BAD

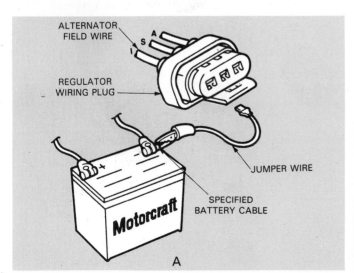

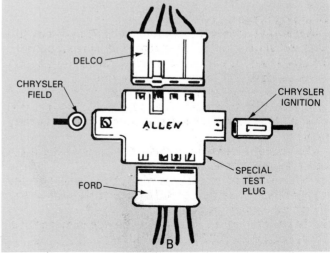

Fig. 24-8. A—This charging system alternator is full fielded by connecting jumper wire between battery and wire disconnected from remote voltage regulator. Check service manual for directions since procedures vary. B—This special adapter can be used to quickly full field several types of charging systems. (Ford and Allen)

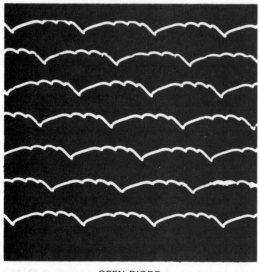

NORMAL ALTERNATOR

ALTERNATOR.

Fig. 24-9 shows how an oscilloscope will show bad alternator diodes. Fig. 24-10 shows an oscilloscope test of alternator windings. Also see Fig. 24-11.

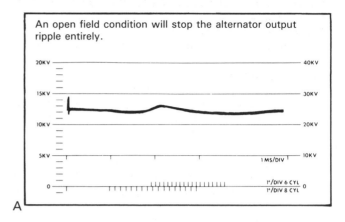

A

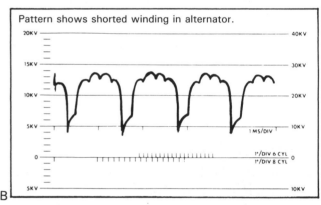

B

Fig. 24-10. A—Scope pattern shows open field. B—Scope pattern shows a shorted winding. (Allen)

OPEN DIODE

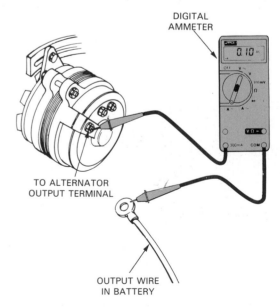

Fig. 24-11. Digital multimeter is being used to check for diode leakage. Connect meter in series with output lead and output terminal. Leakage current should be less than about 500 microamps. (Fluke)

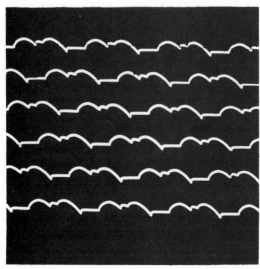

SHORTED DIODE

Fig. 24-9. Note scope waveforms showing condition of alternator diodes. (Sun)

Circuit resistance tests

Circuit resistance tests are used to locate wiring problems in a charging system: loose connection, corroded terminal, partially burned wire, or other similar types of troubles. Resistance tests should be performed when symptoms point to problems other than the alternator or regulator.

There are two common circuit resistance tests: insulated resistance test and ground circuit resistance test.

Insulated circuit test

To do an *insulated circuit resistance test* on a charging system, connect the tester as described by the manufacturer. The voltmeter is typically connected across the alternator output terminal and positive battery terminal. See Fig. 24-12.

With the vehicle running at a fast idle, turn the load control to obtain a 20 amp current flow at 15 volts or less. All lights and accessories should be OFF. Read the voltmeter.

If the circuit is in good condition, the voltmeter should NOT read over about .7 volt (.1 volt per electrical connection).

If the voltage drop is higher than .7 volt, circuit resistance is high. A poor connection exists in that section of the circuit.

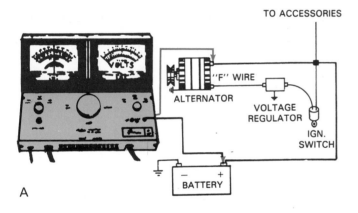

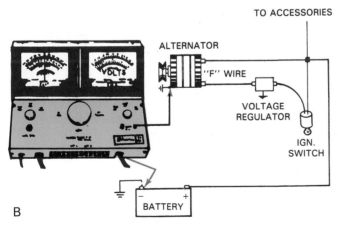

Fig. 24-12. Voltage drop or resistance tests will find problems in wiring. A—Connections for insulated circuit resistance test. B—Connections for ground circuit resistance test. Voltage reading above .1 V per connection indicates resistance problems. (Snap-On Tools)

Ground circuit test

A *ground circuit resistance test* is similar. However, the voltmeter is placed across the negative battery terminal and alternator housing.

The voltmeter should NOT read over .1 volt per electrical connection. If the voltmeter reading is higher, look for loose connections, burned plug sockets, or similar problems.

OTHER TESTER FUNCTIONS

Charging system testers, depending on make and model, may have other test modes (positions). They may be switched to check the alternator stator, diodes, or regulator for example. Read the tester instructions closely to learn about these tests.

CHARGING SYSTEM COMPONENT SERVICE

Now that you have learned how to test a charging system, you are ready to learn how to remove, repair, and replace each part.

ALTERNATOR SERVICE

A bad alternator will show up during your tests as a low voltage and current output problem. Even when the regulator is bypassed and full voltage is applied to the alternator field, charging voltage and current will NOT be up to specs.

Alternator removal

Before unbolting the alternator, DISCONNECT THE BATTERY to prevent damage to parts if wires are shorted. Most alternators are held to the front of the engine with two bolts. Loosen the bolts and remove the belt. Then remove the alternator.

When removing the wires from the back of the alternator, note their location and whether special insulating washers are used. If you make a mistake attaching the wires to the alternator, system damage can occur. Refer to Fig. 24-13.

Alternator disassembly

To disassemble an alternator, first scribe marks on the outside of the housing, Fig. 24-14. This will let you assemble the housing correctly, Fig. 24-15. When clamping the alternator in a vise, be careful not to damage the housing or bend the fan.

Use the directions in a shop manual to disassemble an alternator. An Allen wrench may be needed to hold the shaft while removing the pulley and shaft nut. Use a puller, if needed, to remove the pulley, Fig. 24-16.

Remove the alternator through-bolts. Tap the drive end frame with a plastic or lead mallet. Slide the end frame from the rotor shaft. As you remove the remaining alternator parts, watch how everything fits together.

Depending upon the type of repair, you may have to either completely or partially disassemble the alternator. For example, to replace worn alternator bearings, you would NOT have to remove the diodes, built-in regulator, or other unrelated parts. However, if alternator output was low, you may need to completely disassemble the

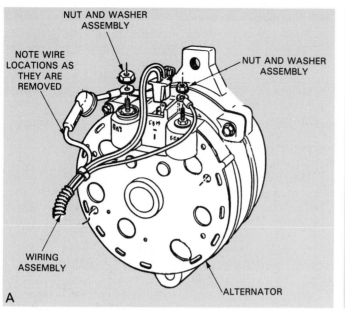

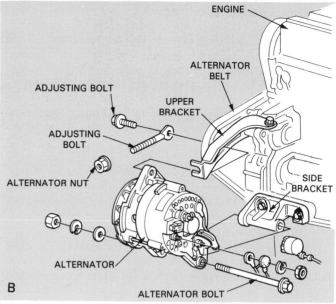

Fig. 24-13. A—When removing wires from back of alternator, note their locations. Also make sure battery is disconnected first. B—To remove alternator, you must normally remove two or three bolts from alternator brackets. Brackets can normally stay on engine. (Ford and Toyota)

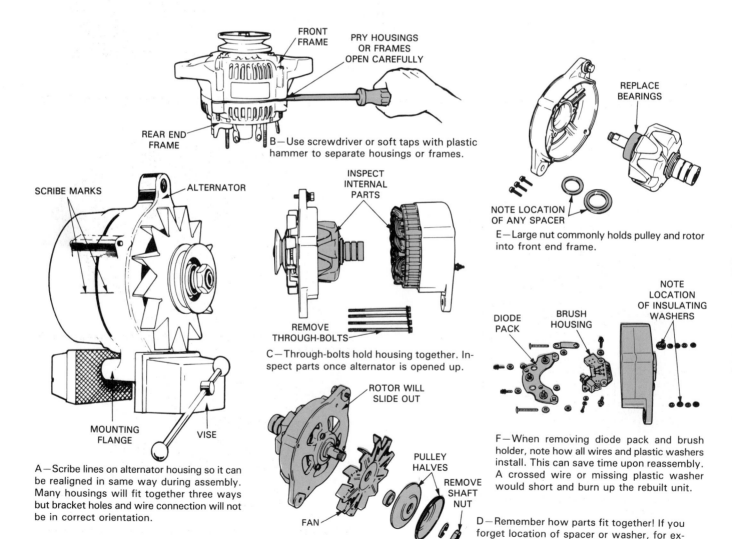

B—Use screwdriver or soft taps with plastic hammer to separate housings or frames.

C—Through-bolts hold housing together. Inspect parts once alternator is opened up.

E—Large nut commonly holds pulley and rotor into front end frame.

F—When removing diode pack and brush holder, note how all wires and plastic washers install. This can save time upon reassembly. A crossed wire or missing plastic washer would short and burn up the rebuilt unit.

A—Scribe lines on alternator housing so it can be realigned in same way during assembly. Many housings will fit together three ways but bracket holes and wire connection will not be in correct orientation.

D—Remember how parts fit together! If you forget location of spacer or washer, for example, problems can result upon reassembly.

Fig. 24-14. Study major steps for alternator disassembly. (Florida Voc. Ed., GM, and Subaru)

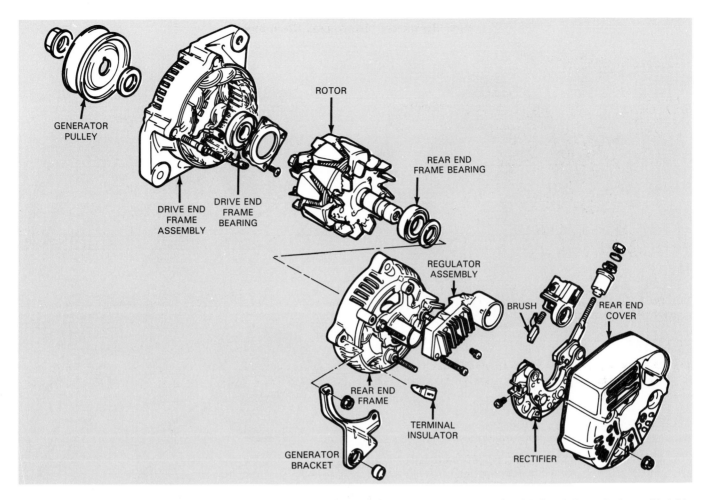

Fig. 24-15. This is a typical example of sequence for part removal during an alternator rebuild. Read through them. (Buick)

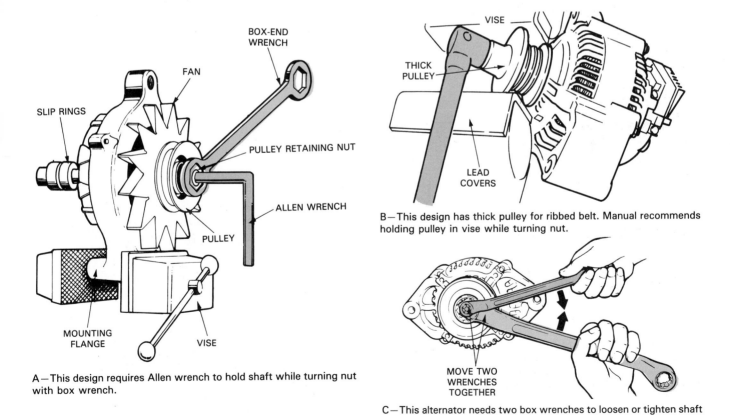

A—This design requires Allen wrench to hold shaft while turning nut with box wrench.

B—This design has thick pulley for ribbed belt. Manual recommends holding pulley in vise while turning nut.

C—This alternator needs two box wrenches to loosen or tighten shaft nut.

Fig. 24-16. There are several methods for removing rotor shaft nut depending upon design.

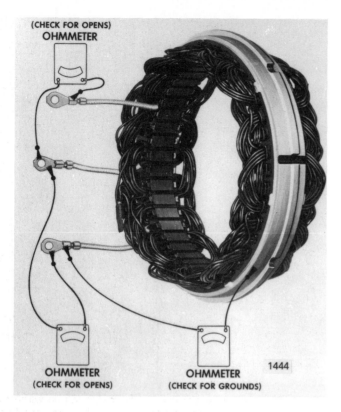

Fig. 24-17. Ohmmeter can be used to check condition of stator windings. (Pontiac)

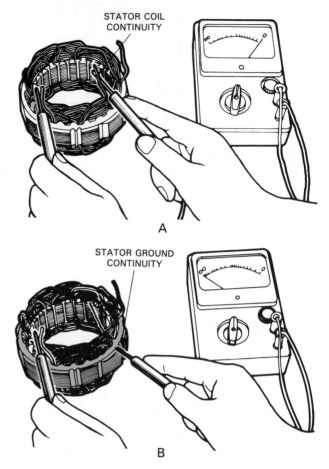

Fig. 24-18. A—Measuring stator coil continuity should show complete circuit path or low ohms. B—Stator coil ground test should show no continuity or high ohms. (Chrysler)

alternator for a major rebuild.

Keep all of your parts organized and clean. If you get grease on the brushes, replace them. Grease or oil will ruin the brushes.

Do NOT soak the rotor, stator, diode pack, regulator, or other electrical components in solvent. Solvent could ruin these components.

Alternator stator service

A *bad alternator stator* can have shorted or open windings. Inspect the stator windings for signs of burning (darkened windings with a burned insulation smell). An open winding is usually detected using an ohmmeter.

To test a stator for open or grounded windings, connect an ohmmeter to the stator leads, as in Figs. 24-17 and 24-18.

Alternator rotor service

A *bad alternator rotor* can have a bent shaft, scored slip rings, open windings, or shorted windings. Visually inspect the rotor closely. Make sure the rotor is in good condition before assembling the alternator. There are several tests designed to check an alternator rotor.

A *rotor winding short-to-ground test* measures resistance between the rotor shaft and windings, Fig. 24-19. The ohmmeter should read infinite (maximum) resistance to show no short to ground.

A *rotor winding open circuit test* measures the resistance between the two slip rings. The meter should read low resistance (about 2 to 4 ohms). This would show that the windings are NOT broken, Fig. 24-20.

A *rotor current test* checks the windings for internal

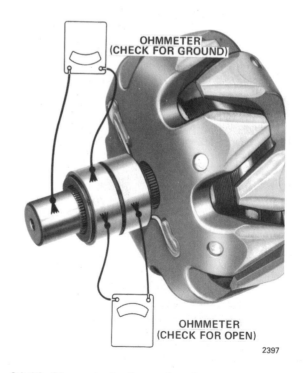

Fig. 24-19. Ohmmeter is also used to check condition of rotor windings. (Pontiac)

428

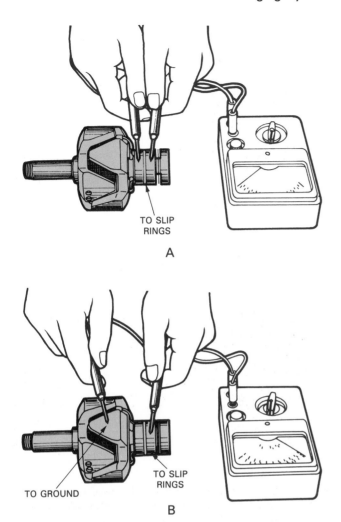

Fig. 24-20. A—When ohmmeter is across both slip rings, ohmmeter should show continuity or low ohms. B—When connected to a slip ring and to rotor body, resistance should be infinite or high. (Chrysler)

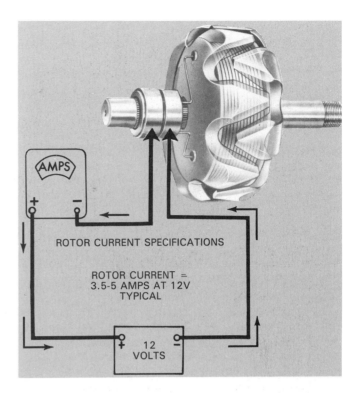

Fig. 24-21. Note how battery and ammeter can be wired to test rotor windings under a current load. This is better test than with ohmmeter. Fuse or circuit breaker should also be wired into circuit in case rotor is shorted. (Oldsmobile)

shorts. It is recommended by some manufacturers. Connect a 12 V battery and ammeter to the slip rings. Measure current flow through the rotor and compare it to specs. Typical rotor current should be around 3 to 6 amps, Fig. 24-21.

Replace the alternator rotor if it fails any of these three tests.

Alternator diode service

Bad alternator diodes reduce output current and voltage. They are a very frequent cause for alternator failure. It is important to check the condition of diodes when rebuilding an alternator.

There are various methods used to test alternator diodes: ohmmeter, test light, scope, or special diode tester. However, the ohmmeter is the most common.

When using an ohmmeter or test light, the diodes must normally be unsoldered and isolated from each other. Some special diode testers, however, will check the condition of the diodes with all of the diodes still connected to each other. An oscilloscope will also detect failed diodes because smooth DC output will NOT be generated.

Ohmmeter test of diodes

To use an ohmmeter to test the diodes, connect the ohmmeter to each diode in one direction and then the other. The meter should read HIGH RESISTANCE in one direction and LOW RESISTANCE in the other. This will show you that the diode is functioning as an ''electrical check valve.'' The test should be performed on each diode, Fig. 24-22.

A *bad diode* can either be shorted or opened. An *open diode* will have a high (infinite) resistance in both directions. A *shorted diode* will have a low (almost zero) resistance in both directions. In either case, the diode must be replaced, Fig. 24-23.

If you had to unsolder the diodes, they will have to be resoldered during installation. After pressing in the new diode or obtaining a new diode pack, use a soldering gun and rosin core solder to attach the diode leads. Heat the wires quickly to avoid overheating the diodes. Excess heat can ruin a diode.

Fig. 24-24 shows how one manual illustrates a test of a diode trio. Fig. 24-25 illustrates one test for an internal voltage regulator. Remember that test procedures may vary with the particular component design.

Alternator bearing service

Worn or *dry alternator bearings* produce a rumbling or grinding noise during operation. They can also become loose enough to upset alternator output by allowing too much rotor shaft movement. When rebuilding an alternator, it is common practice to replace the alternator bearings.

The front alternator bearing, also called the drive end

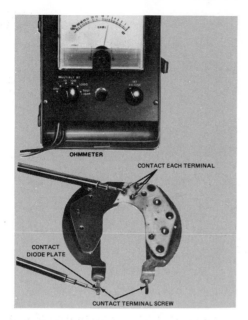

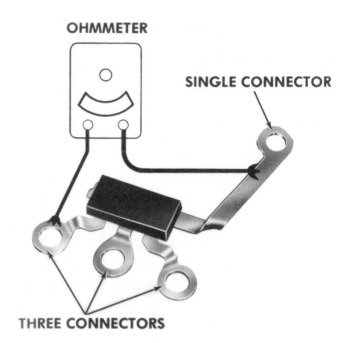

Fig. 24-22. With each diode disconnected or isolated from each other, ohmmeter should show high ohms in one direction and low ohms in other. If not, bad diode is indicated. (Ford)

Fig. 24-24. Ohmmeter should also be used to check diode trio if used. Again, use the manual to test trio properly. (Oldsmobile)

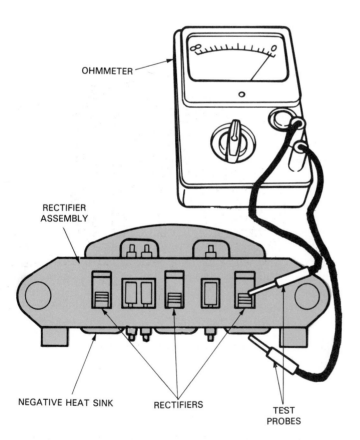

Fig. 24-23. How you connect ohmmeter to test diodes can vary with alternator design so refer to service manual. (Chrysler)

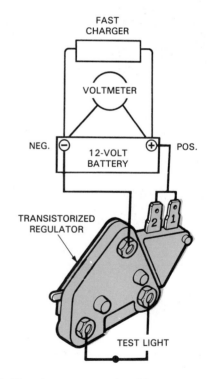

Fig. 24-25. Here is one example of how a specific type of internal voltage regulator can be bench tested. Voltmeter should read between about 13.5 and 15.5 volts if regulator is good. (General Motors)

bearing, is usually held in place with a cover plate and small screws. To replace the bearing, remove the screws and plate. Then lift out the old bearing.

The rear alternator bearing, also termed the diode or slip ring end bearing, is normally pressed into the rear

end housing. It may be pressed or carefully driven out of the alternator housing for replacement.

If the bearings are relatively new and you do not replace them, make sure you put a moderate amount of grease into the rear bearing. The front bearing is usually

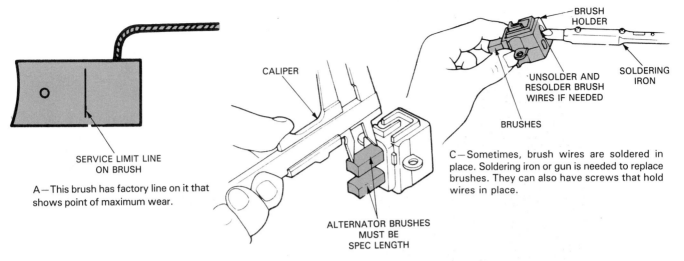

SERVICE LIMIT LINE
ON BRUSH

A—This brush has factory line on it that
shows point of maximum wear.

CALIPER

ALTERNATOR BRUSHES
MUST BE
SPEC LENGTH

B—Calipers can also be used to measure brush length for comparing
to specs.

BRUSH
HOLDER

SOLDERING
IRON

UNSOLDER AND
RESOLDER BRUSH
WIRES IF NEEDED

BRUSHES

C—Sometimes, brush wires are soldered in
place. Soldering iron or gun is needed to replace
brushes. They can also have screws that hold
wires in place.

Fig. 24-26. Always check brushes carefully during alternator repairs. If worn too short or covered with oil or grease, replace
them. (Chrysler, Toyota, Subaru)

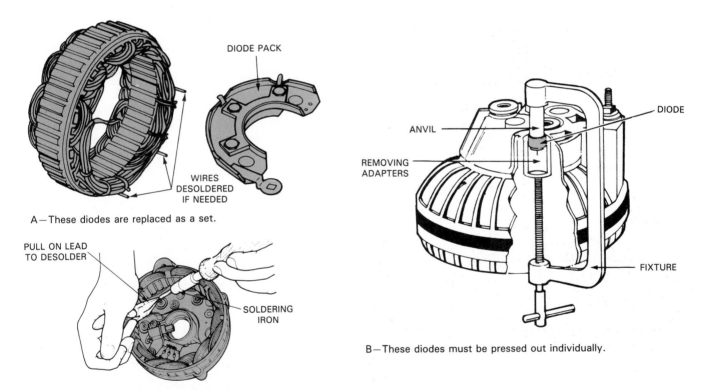

DIODE PACK

WIRES
DESOLDERED
IF NEEDED

A—These diodes are replaced as a set.

PULL ON LEAD
TO DESOLDER

SOLDERING
IRON

C—Wires can be soldered to diode pack. Use needle nose pliers to grasp
wires as they are desoldered. This will help prevent too much heat from
entering and ruining good diodes.

DIODE

ANVIL

REMOVING
ADAPTERS

FIXTURE

B—These diodes must be pressed out individually.

Fig. 24-27. Diodes are sometimes replaced as a set or they can be replaced individually. (General Motors and Chrysler)

sealed and cannot be greased.

To check the action of the front bearing, rotate it with
your finger while feeling for roughness or dryness.
Replace the bearing if there is any sign of failure.

Alternator brush service

Worn brushes can affect the output voltage and
current of an alternator, Fig. 24-26. As the brushes

wear, spring tension and brush pressure on the slip rings
will be reduced.

Inspect the brushes and measure their length. When
the brushes are worn beyond specs or soaked in oil or
grease, replace them.

Alternator reassembly

After you have inspected and tested the components

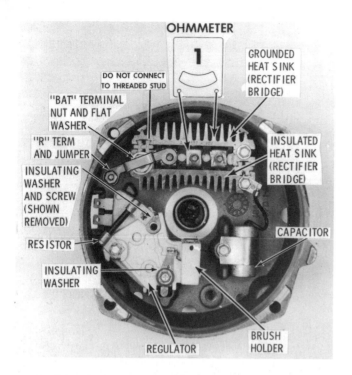

Fig. 24-28. When working on alternator, make sure all components are reinstalled in correct locations.

rear of the end frame, you sometimes need to use a piece of mechanic's wire or small Allen wrench to install the brushes. Push the brush spring and brush up into place. Then slide your wire or Allen wrench into a hole in the rear end frame of the alternator. Push the next spring and brush into place. Slide the wire the rest of the way through the hole, Fig. 24-29.

The wire or Allen wrench will hold the brushes out of the way as you slide the rotor into the housing.

Fit the front end frame into position and check the alignment pins or marks. Install and tighten the through-bolts.

Pull out the piece of wire or Allen wrench. You should hear the brushes CLICK into place on the slip rings, Fig. 24-30. If you fail to remove the piece of wire, severe part damage will result.

Finally, install any spacer, the fan, front pulley, lock washer, and nut. Torque the pulley nut to specs. Then, spin the rotor shaft and pulley to check for free movement. The rotor should spin freely without making unusual noises.

Test the alternator output on a *bench tester* (unit for off-car output test of alternator) if one is available. See Fig. 24-31.

of an alternator, you are ready for reassembly. Since alternator construction varies, refer to a service manual describing the particular style unit. In general, assemble the alternator in reverse order of disassembly.

Install all of the components in the rear or slip ring end frame: electronic regulator, diode pack, rear bearing, terminals, and nuts. See Figs. 24-27 and 24-28.

When the brushes are NOT mounted on the outside,

Alternator installation

With the battery still disconnected, fit the alternator onto the front of the engine. If needed, install the wires on the back of the alternator first. Hand start the bolts and screw them in without tightening.

Check the condition of the alternator belt. Replace it if needed. Slip the belt over the engine fan and alternator pulley. Make sure the belt is aligned properly on each pulley. Adjust belt tension and tighten bolts. Reconnect the battery.

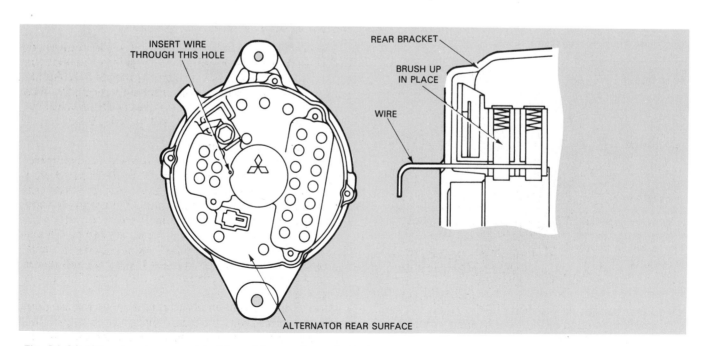

Fig. 24-29. When brushes mount inside end frame, piece of wire is commonly used to hold brushes out of way while installing rotor. Use a small screwdriver or bent piece of rod to push rear brush and spring up into brush holder. Then, slip wire through brush holder to lock brush in place. Repeat on other brush. Remember to remove piece of wire before installing alternator or severe damage will occur.

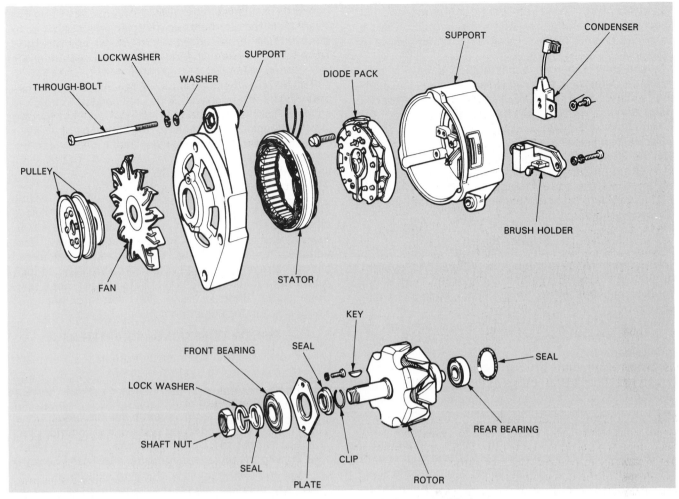

Fig. 24-30. Study exploded view of typical alternator. (Fiat)

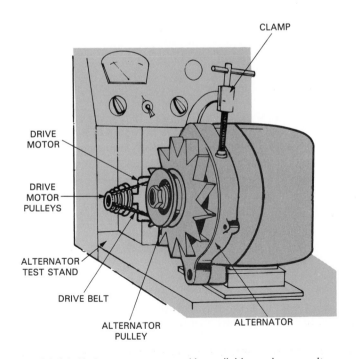

Fig. 24-31. If alternator test stand is available, make sure alternator output is acceptable before installation on car. (Florida Dept. of Voc. Ed.)

REGULATOR SERVICE

When a regulator fails a voltage test, either adjustment or replacement is required. A regulator cannot be repaired. However, if the regulator setting is only slightly high or low, you can sometimes adjust a regulator. This is true for most contact type regulators and a few electronic regulators. Refer back to Fig. 24-25.

Electronic regulator service

If faulty, it is a simple task to replace an electronic regulator. An electronic regulator may be located on a fenderwell, on the back of the alternator, or inside the alternator. Obtain the correct replacement regulator and install it. Then recheck charging system output.

A few types of electronic voltage regulators are adjustable. They can have a small adjusting screw inside a hole in the outer case. Turning the screw will lower or raise the voltage setting of the regulator. Check in a shop manual for details.

Normally, the engine is idled with a voltmeter connected to measure no-load charging voltage. The regulator screw is rotated until the voltmeter reads within specs.

Point type regulator service

Discussed in the previous chapter, point type

regulators were used on early alternator and DC generator type charging systems. The regulator, due to point wear and pitting, was a common cause of problems.

If you ever work on a car equipped with a point regulator, refer back to an early service manual. Circuits and regulator operation vary. You would need a specific manual covering the exact type regulator circuit. It will tell you how to file, test, and adjust the regulator points.

Basically, a point type regulator is adjusted as follows. Idle the engine while measuring no-load voltage. You must either turn an adjusting screw or bend an adjusting tab to obtain the correct output.

If the regulator cannot be adjusted to obtain the proper voltage, replace it.

SUMMARY

When analyzing problems in a charging system, remember that battery, starting system, and wiring troubles can appear to be problems in the charging system.

Charging system problems will cause a dead battery, overcharged battery, abnormal noises, cranking troubles, and indicator activation.

Visual inspection of the charging system will sometimes find the trouble. A loose alternator belt, disconnected wire, bad battery cable can all affect or seem to affect the charging system.

When working on a charging system, disconnect the battery. Do not reverse polarity when connecting a jumper battery or charger. Do not start the engine with battery cables removed. Never short or ground the alternator output terminals accidentally. Be careful when working on cars that full field the alternator and produce over 100 volts AC.

There are four tests commonly done on the charging system: output test, regulator voltage test, regulator bypass test, and circuit resistance test. One or more of these tests may be needed to find the source of trouble.

A voltmeter will help you find the source of alternator problems if used properly. However, a load tester is better because you can measure actual current output at maximum load.

Many mechanics do NOT rebuild alternators. They install factory rebuilt units to save time and to get a guarantee on the alternator. However, if only some parts are bad (bearings, brushes, diodes), many mechanics will open up and replace components in an alternator.

A bad alternator will show up as a low voltage, low current output during your tests. The low output will not be corrected when you full field or take the regulator out of the circuit.

Before removing the alternator, disconnect the battery to prevent a possible short and "electrical fire." remove the two or three bolts that hold the alternator to the engine. Disconnect the wires from the back of the alternator while noting their location or how they connect.

Scribe mark the alternator housing before disassembly. This will let you realign parts properly when reassembling. Remove the through-bolts and separate the housing. Inspect and measure all critical parts. Install new parts as needed. Most mechanics replace the bearings and brushes during a rebuild. Also test the diodes and

windings if needed (low output). Frequently, only the bearings in the alternator need replacement and a complete rebuild is not necessary. Perform any electrical tests needed while following the detailed instructions in the service manual.

Reassemble the alternator in reverse order of disassembly. A piece of wire is usually needed to hold the small brushes out of the way when you slide the rotor into the housing. Remember to pull this piece of wire out or severe alternator damage can result.

KNOW THESE TERMS

Battery problems, Alternator belt problems, Wiring problems, Alternator noises, Reverse polarity, Full-fielded alternator, Charging output test, Regulator voltage test, Regulator bypass test, Circuit resistance test, Base voltage, No-load voltage, Load voltage, Calculated charge voltage, Charging system circuit resistance test, Alternator rebuild, Stator test, Rotor tests, Diode test, Open diode, Shorted diode, Dry alternator bearings, Voltage regulator adjustment.

REVIEW QUESTIONS—CHAPTER 24

1. Explain the four common symptoms that can result from a charging system problem.
2. What charging system checks are made during a visual inspection?
3. Describe six charging system service precautions.
4. When testing a charging system, it is common practice to test the condition of the _____ first.
5. Explain the four steps for using a VOM to check the general operation of a charging system.
6. Two technicians have used a voltmeter to test the operation of a charging system. The loaded voltage reading was five volts above the base reading.
   Technician A says that this shows a good charging voltage.
   Technician B says the voltage regulator might be bad.
   Who is correct?
   a. Technician A.
   b. Technician B.
   c. Both A and B.
   d. Neither A nor B.
7. In your own words, how do you use a load tester to check the performance of a charging system?
8. A _____ _____ _____ will help find out if a charging problem is caused by the alternator or the regulator.
9. _____ _____ _____ are used to help find wiring problems in a charging system.
10. Summarize alternator disassembly.
11. During a typical rotor current test, current should be about _____ to _____ amps.
12. An _____ diode will have high resistance in both directions; a _____ diode will have low resistance in both directions.
13. During an alternator rebuild, the bearings do NOT normally have to be replaced. True or false?
14. Explain how alternator brushes are usually held in place during rotor installation.
15. An alternator belt should NOT be tightened as much as other belts. True or false?

ASE CERTIFICATION-TYPE QUESTIONS

1. An automobile is brought into the shop with an apparent charging system problem. Technician A says a faulty battery is sometimes mistaken for a charging system problem. Technician B says a faulty starting motor is sometimes mistaken for a charging system problem. Who is right?
   - (A) A only.
   - (B) B only.
   - (C) Both A and B.
   - (D) Neither A nor B.

2. While troubleshooting an automobile's charging system, Technician A disconnects the alternator output wire with the engine running to check voltage regulator operation. While troubleshooting a car's charging system, Technician B disconnects the battery with the engine running to check voltage regulator operation. Who is right?
   - (A) A only.
   - (B) B only.
   - (C) Both A and B.
   - (D) Neither A nor B.

3. A car's charging system output is tested at the battery with a voltmeter. The voltage readings indicate that the battery's "base voltage" is higher than the "load voltage." Technician A says this test indicates that the battery is faulty. Technician B says this test indicates a charging system problem. Who is right?
   - (A) A only.
   - (B) B only.
   - (C) Both A and B.
   - (D) Neither A nor B.

4. A load tester is used to perform a charging system output test on a particular automobile. Technician A connects the inductive amps pickup to the positive battery cable. Technician B checks the tester's ammeter reading with the ignition switch in the "run" position and again with the engine running. Who is right?
   - (A) A only.
   - (B) B only.
   - (C) Both A and B.
   - (D) Neither A nor B.

5. While performing a regulator bypass test on a particular automobile, charging current increased to normal levels. Technician A says the results of this test indicate a faulty regulator. Technician B says the results of this test indicate that the alternator is not operating properly. Who is right?
   - (A) A only.
   - (B) B only.
   - (C) Both A and B.
   - (D) Neither A nor B.

6. There is a problem with an automobile's charging system other than the alternator or regulator. Technician A is going to perform an insulated circuit resistance test on this charging system. Technician B is going to perform a ground circuit resistance test on this charging system. Who is right?
   - (A) A only.
   - (B) B only.
   - (C) Both A and B.
   - (D) Neither A nor B.

7. An alternator's stator is believed to be faulty. Technician A says the stator should be checked for open windings. Technician B says the stator should be checked for grounded windings. Who is right?
   - (A) A only.
   - (B) B only.
   - (C) Both A and B.
   - (D) Neither A nor B.

8. An alternator's diodes are believed to be faulty. Technician A uses an ohmmeter to check the diodes. Technician B uses an oscilloscope to check the diodes. Who is right?
   - (A) A only.
   - (B) B only.
   - (C) Both A and B.
   - (D) Neither A nor B.

8. An alternator's slip ring end bearing needs replacement. Technician A says to remove this bearing by loosening the bearing's cover plate. Technician B says to carefully drive the bearing from the alternator housing. Who is right?
   - (A) A only.
   - (B) B only.
   - (C) Both A and B.
   - (D) Neither A nor B.

10. An automobile's electronic voltage regulator has failed a voltage test. Technician A replaces the voltage regulator. Before replacing the regulator, Technician B looks in a service manual to see if this type of voltage regulator is adjustable. Who is right?
   - (A) A only.
   - (B) B only.
   - (C) Both A and B.
   - (D) Neither A nor B.

The automotive technician must be able to troubleshoot and repair today's complex ignition systems. This late-model engine is equipped with a distributorless ignition system, which uses multiple ignition coils to fire the spark plugs.   (Buick)

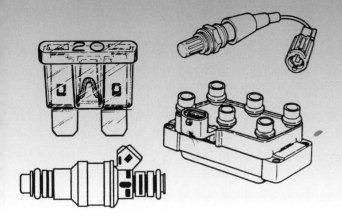

Chapter 25

Ignition System Diagnosis and Repair

After studying this chapter, you will be able to:
- Troubleshoot problems in an ignition system.
- Describe the symptoms that are produced by typical part failures.
- Summarize tests used to pinpoint ignition system troubles.
- Gap and replace spark plugs.
- Adjust contact point and pickup coil air gaps.
- Adjust ignition timing, when possible.
- Service a distributor.
- Analyze problems in a computer-controlled or distributorless ignition system.

Partial failure of an ignition system part might reduce engine performance; complete failure of a part could keep the engine from running. Since this is the most important system for gasoline engine operation, many problems are easily noticed by the driver: engine miss, engine cranks but won't start, poor fuel economy, engine spark knock, etc. Since you already learned the function of major ignition system parts in an earlier chapter, you are now prepared to learn diagnosis and repair. This chapter will continue your study by summarizing the most important service tasks done on modern ignition systems. It will prepare you to use service manual specs to do competent ignition system repair work.

TROUBLESHOOTING IGNITION PROBLEMS

Ignition system troubleshooting involves using logical thought and tests to find the source of a malfunction. Troubleshooting an ignition system is simple if you can make a "mental picture" of how a good system should operate. You should be able to visualize current flow through every part of the ignition system. If you cannot, refer back to Chapter 15.

Ignition system inspection

To start diagnosis, inspect the overall condition of the ignition system with and without the engine running. Look for obvious problems: loose primary connections, spark plug wire pulled off, deteriorated secondary wire insulation, cracked distributor cap or other trouble. Also look over other engine systems. Try to find anything that could upset engine operation, Figs. 25-1 through 25-3.

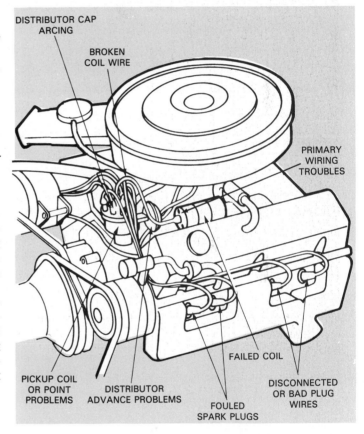

Fig. 25-1. Note some basic troubles that can be found in an ignition system. (Florida Dept. of Voc. Ed.)

Scanning for ignition system problems

With late model vehicles, especially those equipped with OBD II diagnostic systems, you can connect a scan tool to the vehicle computer to find many ignition-related problems. The scan tool can detect troubles in the following ignition system circuits and components:
1. Crankshaft position sensor.
2. Crankshaft speed sensor.
3. Camshaft position sensor.
4. Knock sensor.
5. Ignition coil(s) primary circuit.
6. Ignition coil(s) secondary circuit.
7. Timing reference signal.

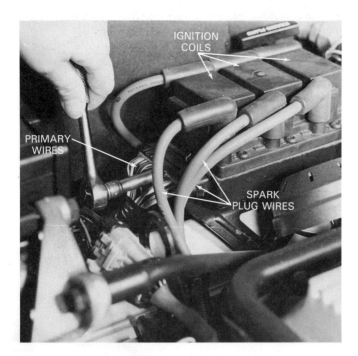

Fig. 25-2. Loose electrical connections can cause problems in ignition as in other electrical systems. Technician is securing loose connector to coil module on distributorless ignition system.

Fig. 25-3. Even with computer control, always check for conventional problems, like disconnected or loose wires. Loose or disconnected spark plug wire is common trouble!

Start your pinpoint tests at the component or circuit indicated on the scan tool readout. You might test the component first and then its circuit. This will depend on the specific circumstances of the symptoms and vehicle design.

If your scan tool readout indicates a *misfire* condition, the engine has failed to ignite and burn its air-fuel mixture properly. This increases exhaust emissions, lowers engine power, and increases fuel consumption. Misfire can be caused by problems in the ignition system, the fuel injection system, the emission control system, or the engine itself. Additional tests and the use of more specific scan tool data would be needed to pinpoint the problem causing the misfire condition.

If you are working on a vehicle without on-board diagnostics or a vehicle equipped with an early self-diagnostic system, you will have to use basic testing methods to check problem sources.

Engine cranks, will not start

When an engine cranks, or turns with the starting motor, but will NOT start and run, you should check for SPARK AND FUEL. This will narrow down the cause to either the ignition system or the fuel system. The basic steps are:

1. To check for spark (ignition system operation), pull a plug wire. Insert a small screwdriver or a spark tester into the plug wire. Hold the screwdriver next to ground (about 1/8 inch away from ground) or clip the spark tester to ground. Crank the engine and a hot electric arc should jump to ground, Fig. 25-4. If you have a good spark, check for fuel supply to the engine. If you do NOT have spark, perform further tests on the ignition system.

2. To check for fuel, inspect the inlet of the carburetor or throttle body injector. Fuel should squirt out of a carburetor when you move the throttle linkage opened and closed. Fuel should squirt out of a TBI when the engine is cranked. With multi-point injection, you would need to install a pressure gauge and do other tests.

Performing these two tests will help isolate the reason that an engine does not start. Remember—if an engine fails to start but cranks, check for spark first and then for fuel!

> DANGER! Unlike older ignition systems, some late model ignition systems can produce enough wattage to cause serious electrical shock. Electronic, crank triggered systems can easily produce 40,000 volts at 100 watts. As a result, enough current could pass into your body to cause serious injury or death. Use caution when working around late model ignition systems!

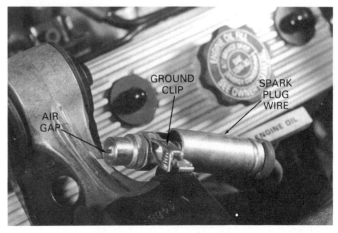

Fig. 25-4. Spark test will check whether ignition system is producing "hot arc" to fire plugs. This spark tester produces wide gap for checking spark intensity. You can also hold secondary wire next to ground. If you have spark and engine will not run, check for fuel!

Spark intensity test

A *spark intensity test,* also called a *spark test,* measures the brightness and length of the electric arc (spark) produced by the ignition system. It provides a quick and easy way of checking the general condition of the ignition system.

The spark test is commonly used when an engine cranks, but will NOT start. The test will help tell you whether the trouble is in the fuel system (no fuel problem) or in the ignition system (no spark problem). It may also be used to check the spark plug wires, distributor cap, and other secondary components.

A *spark tester* is a device with a very large air gap for checking ignition system output voltage. It is like a spark plug with a wide gap and a ground wire, Fig. 25-4.

You can make a spark tester out of an old spark plug. Cut off a section of the side electrode to widen the gap. Drill a hole in the plug shell. Then, use a screw to attach a small jumper wire to the shell.

Remove one of the secondary wires from a spark plug. Insert the spark tester into the wire. Ground it on the engine. Crank or start the engine. Observe the spark at the tester air gap, Fig. 25-4.

> WARNING! Only run the engine for a short period of time with a spark plug wire off. Unburned fuel from the dead cylinder could foul and ruin the catalytic converter.

Spark test results

A *strong spark* (wide, bright, snapping electric arc) shows that ignition system voltage is good. The engine no-start problem might be due to fouled spark plugs, fuel system problem, or engine trouble. A strong spark indicates that the ignition coil, pickup coil, ignition control module, and other ignition system parts are functioning.

Note however, it is possible to have a good spark when there are still problems in the ignition system. For example, if the gear on the bottom of the distributor partially spins (gear pin shears off), sparks could be produced but would be out of time with the engine. The engine would not start even though the spark plugs were firing. Keep this in mind during diagnosis.

With a *weak spark* or *no spark,* something is wrong in the ignition system. If the spark is weak at all of the spark plug wires, the problem is common to all of the cylinders (bad ignition coil, rotor, coil wire). Other tests (covered shortly) would be needed to pinpoint the trouble.

Check for dead cylinder

A *dead cylinder* is a cylinder (combustion chamber) that is NOT burning fuel on the power stroke. It could be due to ignition system troubles or problems in the engine, fuel, or another system. A very rough idle and a puffing noise in the engine exhaust may indicate a dead cylinder.

To check for a dead cylinder, pull off one spark plug wire at a time. With the wire off, engine rpm and idle smoothness should DECREASE.

If idle smoothness and rpm stay the same with the plug wire off, that cylinder is DEAD. It is NOT producing power. You would need to check for spark at the wire, spark plug condition, and, possibly, low compression.

Evaluating the symptoms

After checking the system, you must evaluate the symptoms and narrow down the possible causes. Use your knowledge of system operation, a service manual, troubleshooting chart, basic testing methods, and common sense to locate the trouble.

Fig. 25-5 shows how an engine analyzer will produce a printout to help troubleshoot a dead cylinder.

Engine analyzers

An *engine analyzer* contains several types of test equipment (oscilloscope, dwell meter, tachometer, VOM) housed in one large, roll-around cabinet. It is often used to check the operation of an ignition system. See Figs. 25-6 and 25-7.

CYLINDER BALANCE TEST

*Low Compression - Valve/Rings/Head
     Gasket Problem-
    Repair Cylinder **Number 3**

Test RPM- 1422

Cylinder-				
	1st	2nd	3rd	4th
Cranking amps-	168	163	**111**	159
Percent RPM drop-	18.2	18.2	**3.8**	18.3

Fig. 25-5. Modern engine analyzers will do automatic power balance test, similar to pulling a plug wire, to help check operation of ignition system, fuel system, and engine itself. Instantaneous cranking amps reading for each cylinder indicates compression pressure in each cylinder. Starting motor current draw is proportionate to compression stroke pressure. If compression indication is acceptable and cylinder shows low rpm drop with cylinder shorted, there may be a problem with ignition system.

IGNITION SECONDARY ANALYSIS

* Defective Plug Wire - Replace Wire
    Cylinder **Number 4**

* Fouled Plug/Shorted Wire - Replace
    Parts Cylinder **Number 2**

Cylinder-	1st	2nd	3rd	4th
Load KV-	19	7	8	**44**
Average KV-	6	3	7	**43**
Firing Time-	1.7	3.0	1.8	**0.2**

Fig. 25-6. This is printout showing ignition secondary or high voltages. Note that printout shows that cylinder four has higher than normal ohms, indicating open plug wire or wide plug gap. Cylinder two has low ohms, indicating shorted wire insulation or fouled plug.

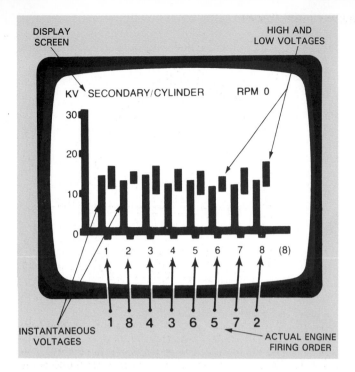

Fig. 25-7. This is an example of a bar type scope output. Secondary voltages are given as bar graph on analyzer display. Handy shorter lines indicate average secondary voltages. (All-Test)

An *oscilloscope* or *"scope,"* detailed in Chapter 21, will precisely measure the operating voltages of an ignition system, Fig. 25-8. It uses a television type picture tube to show voltage changes in relation to degrees of distributor or crankshaft rotation. The technician can compare the scope test patterns with known good patterns to determine the condition of the system.

Electronic ignition tester

An *electronic ignition tester* is a handy instrument

Fig. 25-8. Technician is using engine analyzer to diagnose problems in ignition system. Refer to Chapter 29 for more information on analyzers. (Sun Electric)

which speeds ignition system diagnosis by indicating specific problems. The ignition tester is connected to the ignition circuit or to a special test plug provided on the side of the engine compartment. Indicator lights then show whether problems exist.

Scanners will also show some problems in an ignition system on late model cars. They indicate problem locations, will fire the ignition coil, etc.

SPARK PLUG AND COIL WIRE SERVICE

A *faulty spark plug wire* or *coil wire* can either have a burned or broken conductor or it could have deteriorated, leaking insulation, Fig. 25-9.

Most spark plug wires have a resistance conductor that

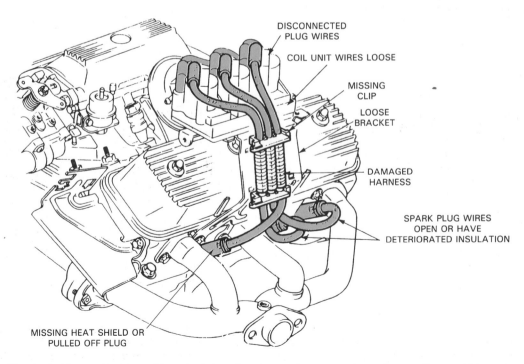

Fig. 25-9. Note types of trouble to look for when inspecting secondary wires. (General Motors)

440

is easily separated. If the conductor is broken, voltage and current cannot reach the spark plug.

If the spark plug insulation is faulty, sparks may leak through the insulation to ground or to another wire, instead of reaching the spark plugs.

Secondary wire removal

To remove spark plug wires, make sure they are numbered to simplify installation. Remove each wire from its plug and the distributor cap or coil module. Refer to Fig. 25-10.

Secondary wire resistance test

A *secondary wire resistance test* will check the condition of a spark plug or coil wire conductor. It should be used to check for a bad wire when an oscilloscope (Chapter 21) is NOT available.

To do a wire resistance test, connect an ohmmeter across each end of the spark plug or coil wire, as in Fig. 25-11. The meter will read wire internal resistance in ohms. Compare your reading to specs.

Typically, spark plug wire resistance should NOT be over approximately 5000 ohms per inch or 100K (100,000) ohms total. Since specs vary, always check in a service manual for an exact value. A bad spark plug wire will often have almost infinite (maximum) resistance.

Secondary wire insulation test

A *secondary wire insulation test* checks for sparks arcing through the insulation to ground. An ohmmeter test will NOT detect bad insulation.

To check spark plug and coil wire insulation, place fender covers over the sides of the car hood to block out light. Start the engine. Inspect each wire.

A special test light or grounded screwdriver can be moved next to the wire insulation. If sparks jump through the insulation and onto the tool, the wire is bad.

Spark plug wire leakage is a condition where electric arcs pass through the wire insulation. This problem requires wire replacement.

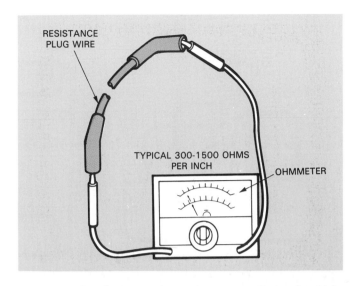

Fig. 25-11. Spark plug and coil wire commonly develop high resistance that prevents spark plugs from firing. Use ohmmeter to measure wire internal resistance. Bad wire will usually have almost infinite resistance. If over about 5,000 ohms per inch, replace wire.   (Ford)

Replacing spark plug wires

Installing new spark plug wires is simple, especially if one wire at a time is replaced, Fig. 25-12. Compare old wire length with the length of the new wire. Keep wire lengths equal. Make sure the wire is fully secure on the plug and in the distributor or coil module.

Spark plug wire replacement is more complicated if all of the wires are removed at once. Then, you must use the engine firing order and cylinder numbers to route each wire correctly. Refer to Fig. 25-13.

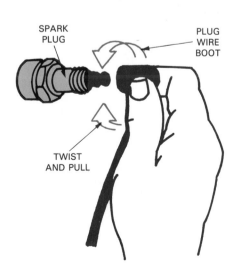

Fig. 25-10. When removing plug wire, twist and pull at same time. Grasp boot, not the wire itself. Special plug wire pliers are available for grasping boot.   (Florida Dept. of Voc. Ed.)

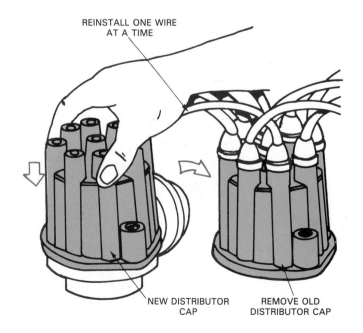

Fig. 25-12. When replacing spark plug wires or distributor cap, remove and install one wire at a time. This will help you prevent getting wires mixed up in cap or in computer coil module. (Florida Dept. of Voc. Ed.)

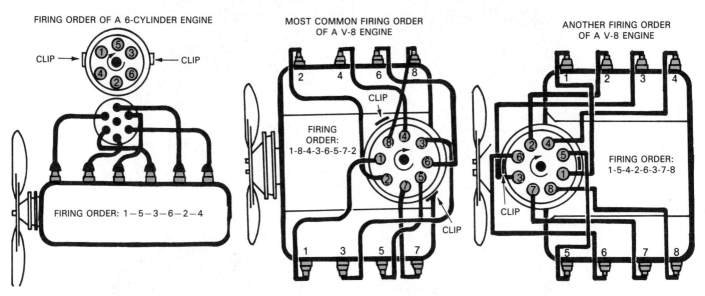

Fig. 25-13. Service manual will give firing order and wire routing to specific terminal in distributor cap or coil assembly. Note variations for different engines.

SERVICING SPARK PLUGS

Bad spark plugs can cause a wide range of problems: missing, lack of power, poor fuel economy, hard starting. After prolonged use, the spark plug tip can become coated with ash, oil, and other substances. Also, the plug electrodes can burn and widen the gap. This can make it more difficult for the ignition system to produce an arc between the electrodes.

To test the spark plugs, use an oscilloscope. Bad plugs will show up on the scope waveforms (patterns). If a scope is NOT available, remove the plugs and inspect their condition. Refer to Fig. 25-14.

Spark plug removal

To remove spark plugs, first check that the spark plug wires are numbered or located correctly in their clips.

Fig. 25-14. After removing plug, read it by inspecting insulator closely for abnormal condition.

Grasping the spark plug wire boot, pull the wire off. Twist the boot back and forth if stuck.

> WARNING! NEVER remove a spark plug wire by pulling on the wire. Always grasp and pull on the boot. If you pull on the wire, you can break the conductor in the wire.

Blow any rocks and dirt away from around the spark plug holes with compressed air. You can also loosen the plugs and crank the engine. Compression pressure will blow away debris. This will prevent dirt and pebbles from falling into the engine cylinders when the plugs are removed.

Using a spark plug socket, extension, and ratchet, as needed, unscrew each spark plug. As you remove each plug, lay it in order on the fender cover or workbench. Do not mix up the plugs. After all of the plugs are out, inspect them to diagnose the condition of the engine.

Reading spark plugs

To *read spark plugs,* closely inspect and analyze the condition of each spark plug tip and insulator. This will give you information on the condition of the engine, fuel system, and ignition system.

For example, a properly burning plug should have a BROWN to GRAYISH-TAN color.

A BLACK or WET PLUG indicates that the plug is NOT firing or that there is an engine problem (worn piston rings and cylinders, leaking valve stem seals, low engine compression, or rich fuel mixture) in that cylinder.

Study the spark plugs in Fig. 25-15 very carefully. Learn to read the condition of used spark plugs. They can provide valuable information when troubleshooting problems.

Cleaning spark plugs

Spark plugs may be cleaned using a *spark plug cleaner* (air powered device that blasts plug tip with abrasive).

Some manufacturers do NOT recommend spark plug cleaning. Blasting can roughen the insulator and lead to fouling, misfiring, and loss of performance.

Be very careful that abrasive (sand) does NOT wedge

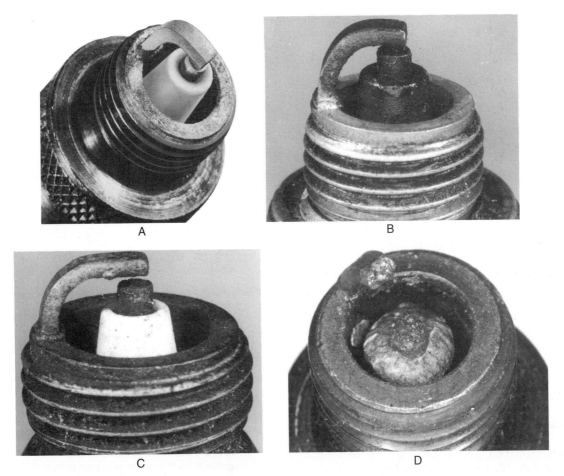

Fig. 25-15. Study spark plug conditions. A—Normal burning plug. B—Oil fouled plug indicates engine mechanical problem like leaking rings or valve seals. C—Crusted deposits on plug show overheating. Cooling system problems or too hot of a plug are indicated. D—Melted electrodes indicate detonation from severe overheating, too much turbocharger boost, etc.

up inside the insulator. The sand could fall into the cylinder and cause cylinder scoring. Most shops install new plugs rather than taking the time to clean used plugs.

Gapping spark plugs

Obtain the correct replacement plug (heat range and reach) recommended by the manufacturer. Then, set *spark plug gap* by spacing the side electrode the correct distance from the center electrode. If the new spark plugs have been dropped or mishandled, the gap may NOT be within specs.

A *wire feeler gauge* should be used to measure spark plug gap. Slide the feeler gauge between the electrodes, Fig. 25-16. If needed, bend the side electrode until the

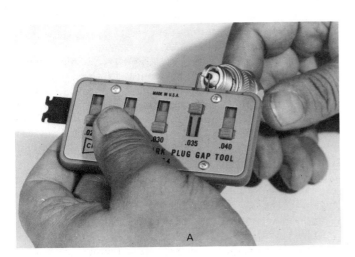

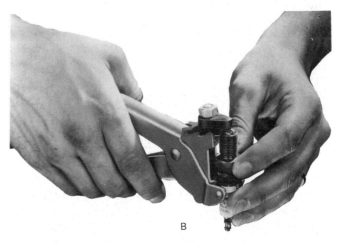

Fig. 25-16. A—Spark plug gap should be measured with wire feeler gauge, not flat feeler gauge. Bend side electrode to regap if needed. Gauge should drag lightly when pulled through electrodes. B—This is a plier type spark plug gapping tool. Gauge fits in plug gap and pliers quickly bend side electrode for setting. (Champion and Lisle)

feeler gauge fits snugly. The gauge should drag lightly as it is pulled in and out of the gap.

Spark plug gaps vary from approximately .030 inch (0.76 mm) on contact point ignitions to over .080 inch (2.03 mm) on electronic systems.

Installing spark plugs

Spark plugs set to the correct gap are ready for installation. Use your fingers, a spark plug socket, or a short piece of vacuum hose to START the plugs in their holes, Fig. 25-17. Do NOT use the ratchet because the plug and cylinder head threads could be crossthreaded and damaged.

With the spark plugs threaded into the head a few turns by hand, spin them in the rest of the way with your ratchet, Fig. 25-18.

Tighten the spark plugs to specs. Some automakers give a spark plug torque. Others recommend bottoming the plugs on the seat and then turning an additional one-quarter to one-half turn. Refer to a service manual for exact procedures.

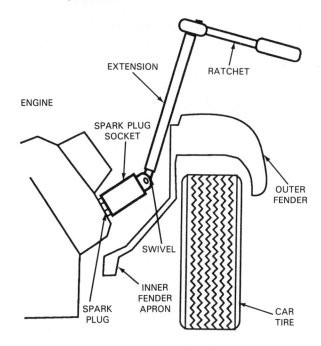

Fig. 25-18. Swivel type spark plug socket and long extension will sometimes help with spark plug installation and removal.

Fig. 25-17. Tool can be used in place of fingers to unscrew or start spark plug in head.

DISTRIBUTOR SERVICE

A *distributor* is very critical to the proper operation of an ignition system. It may have to detect engine speed, alter ignition timing, and distribute high voltage to each spark plug wire. If any part of the distributor is faulty, engine performance can be reduced.

Distributor cap and rotor problems

A *bad distributor cap* or *rotor* can cause engine missing, *backfiring* (popping noise in induction system), other engine performance problems, or the engine may not start, Fig. 25-19.

A common trouble arises when a *carbon trace* (small line of carbon-like substance that conducts electricity) forms on the distributor cap or rotor. The carbon trace will short coil voltage to ground or to a wrong terminal lug in the distributor cap. A carbon trace can cause the spark plugs to fire poorly, out of sequence, or not at all.

When problems point to possible distributor cap or rotor troubles, remove and inspect them. Using a drop light, check the inside of the cap for cracks and carbon traces. A carbon trace is black, making it difficult to see on a black colored distributor cap.

If a crack or carbon trace is found, replace the cap or rotor. Also check the rotor tip for excessive burning, damage, or looseness. Make sure the rotor fits snugly on the distributor shaft.

Distributor cap and rotor replacement

Distributor caps may be secured by either screws or spring type metal clips. Normally, turn the screws counterclockwise for removal. With clips, pry on the top of the spring clips, being careful not to crack the cap. The clip should pop free. Wiggle and pull upward to remove the cap from the distributor body.

Rotors may be held by screws or they may be force-fit around the distributor shaft. Pulling by hand will usually free a press-fit rotor. However, if stuck, carefully pry under the rotor.

With some ignition systems, the ignition coil is housed inside the distributor cap. In this case, the coil must be taken out of the old cap and installed in the new one.

When installing a rotor, line up the rotor on the distributor shaft properly. With a press-fit rotor, a tab inside the rotor fits into a groove or slot in the shaft. With a screw-held rotor, the rotor may have round and/or square dowels that fit into holes in the distributor.

When installing a distributor cap, a notch or tab on the cap must line up with a tab or notch on the distributor housing. This assures that the cap is installed correctly. Before securing the spring clips or screws, push down and twist the cap. Make sure it will NOT wiggle on the distributor.

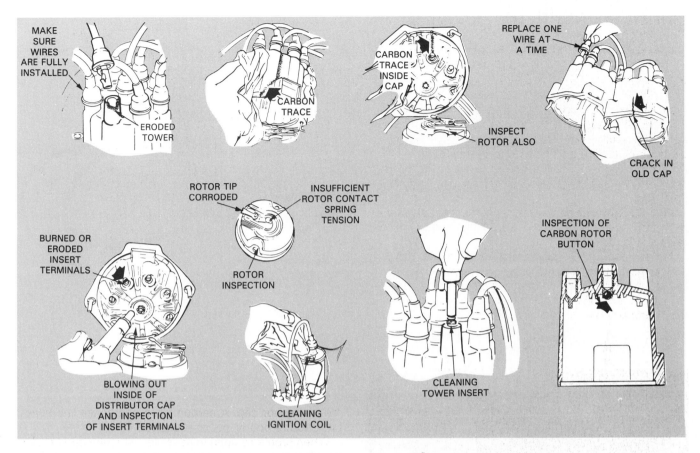

Fig. 25-19. Note steps for servicing and inspecting distributor cap.   (General Motors)

WARNING! If a distributor cap is NOT installed correctly, rotor and distributor damage can result. The whirling rotor can smash into the sides of the distributor cap.

ELECTRONIC DISTRIBUTOR SERVICE

Most electronic type distributors use a pickup coil to sense trigger wheel (distributor shaft) rotation and engine speed. The pickup coil sends small electrical pulses to the ignition control module.

If the distributor fails to produce these tiny electrical signals properly, the complete ignition system can stop functioning. It is important to know how to perform several basic tests on electronic ignition distributors.

Pickup coil problems

A *bad pickup coil* can produce a wide range of problems: engine stalling, engine missing, no-start troubles, engine looses power at specific speeds. If the tiny windings in the pickup coil break, they can cause intermittent problems that only occur under certain conditions.

Also, because of vacuum advance movement, the tiny wire leads going to the pickup coil can break internally. The wires may look fine but the conductor could be separated inside the insulation.

Pickup coil resistance

A *pickup coil ohmmeter test* compares actual pickup coil resistance with specs. If pickup coil resistance is too high or low, the unit is bad.

Connect an ohmmeter across the pickup coil output leads, Fig. 25-20. Observe the meter reading. WIGGLE THE WIRES to the pickup coil while watching the meter. This will help locate a break in the leads to the pickup.

Also, lightly tap on the coil with the handle of a screwdriver. This could uncover any break in the coil windings, Fig. 25-21.

Pickup coil resistance will usually vary between 250 and 1500 ohms. Check a service manual for exact specs. If the meter reading changes when the wire leads are moved or when the coil is tapped, replace the pickup.

Pickup coil AC voltage output

A low-reading AC VOLTMETER may be a better way to test a pickup coil. With the engine cranking, a small AC voltage (around 1 to 1.5 volts) should be produced by the pickup coil. Refer to specs for exact voltage values. The VOM is simply connected to the pickup leads. When the engine is cranked, an AC voltage signal should be produced if the unit is working, Fig. 25-22.

Pickup coil replacement

A distributor pickup coil can usually be replaced simply by removing the distributor cap, rotor, and the screws on the advance plate. Sometimes the pickup coil is mounted around the distributor shaft. Since procedures vary, find detailed directions for the particular distributor in a service manual, Fig. 25-23.

The *pickup coil air gap is* the space between the pickup coil and a trigger wheel tooth. With some designs, it must

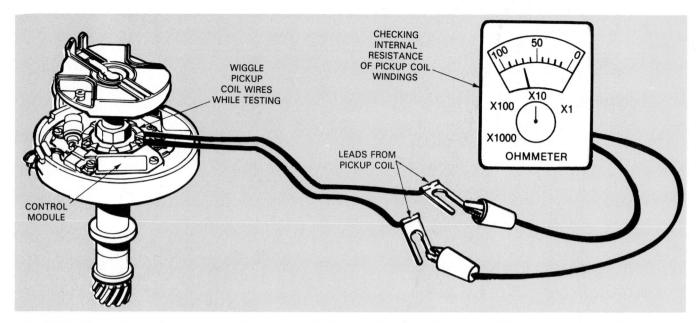

Fig. 25-20. Ohmmeter can be used to check pickup coil. Resistance should be within specs. Wiggle pickup wires while measuring resistance to check for internal breaks in wires.   (Florida Dept. of Voc. Ed.)

Fig. 25-21. Service manual will illustrate which wires on distributor go to pickup coil, so cap removal may not always be needed when testing pickup coil.   (Peerless Instrument)

be set after installing the pickup coil. To obtain an accurate reading, slide a NON-MAGNETIC FEELER GAUGE (plastic or brass gauge) between the pickup coil and trigger wheel. One of the trigger wheel teeth must point at the pickup coil. Move the pickup coil in or out until the correct size gauge fits in the gap. Tighten the pickup screws and double-check the air gap, Fig. 25-24.

Contact point and condenser problems

Bad contact points (points having burned, pitted, misaligned contacts or worn rubbing block) cause a wide range of engine performance problems: high speed

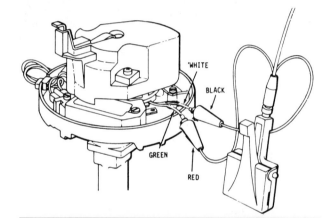

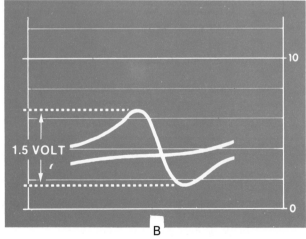

Fig. 25-22. An AC voltmeter on an engine analyzer will also check operation of ignition system pickup coil. A—Voltmeter leads connect to pickup coil leads. Engine is cranked. B—Scope waveform is set to read very low voltage. Note waveform shows 1.5 volts peak to peak. This is typical output for good pickup coil. AC voltmeter should also show spec voltage when testing.   (Sun Electric Corp.)

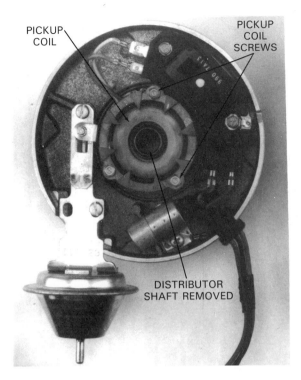

Fig. 25-23. Most pickup coils are simply held in by screws and they come out easily. However, this unitized distributor has pickup coil mounted around distributor shaft. You must remove distributor from engine, distributor drive gear, shaft, and then pickup coil. (General Motors)

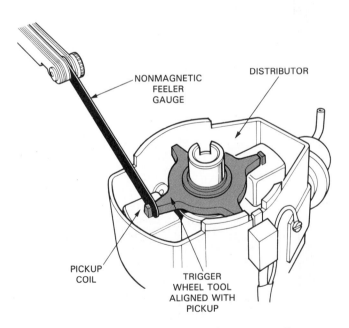

Fig. 25-24. Some pickup coils provide for air gap adjustment. Use a nonmagnetic flat feeler gauge. This will prevent sensor magnet from attracting gauge and upsetting feel or drag as blade is slid inside gap. (Renault)

missing, no-start problem, and many other ignition related troubles, Fig. 25-25.

A *faulty condenser* could be *leaking* (allow some DC current to flow to ground), be *shorted* (direct electrical

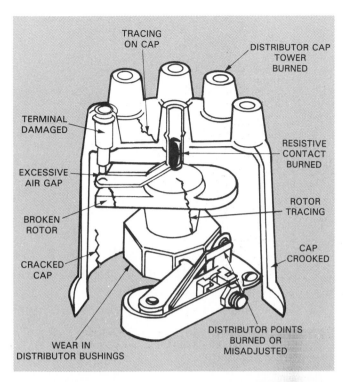

Fig. 25-25. Study types of problems that can develop in an older contact point distributor. Some of these also relate to modern pickup coil distributors. (Florida Dept. of Voc. Ed.)

connection to ground), or be *opened* (broken lead wire to condenser foils)!

If leaking or open, a condenser will cause POINT ARCING and BURNING. If the condenser is shorted, primary current will flow to ground and the engine will NOT start.

Fig. 25-26 summarizes common distributor problems.

Testing distributor points

Many technicians visually inspect the surfaces of the contact points to determine their condition. If burned and pitted or if the rubbing block is worn, the points are replaced. If the points look good, point resistance should be measured. Many dwell-tachometers have a scale for measuring point resistance.

Crank the engine until the points are closed. Connect the meter to the primary point lead and to ground. If the ohms reading is too high (out of scale markings) the points are burned and must be replaced.

Testing distributor condenser

Most technicians simply replace a condenser anytime symptoms point to a condenser problem. However, an ohmmeter can be used to test a condenser.

The ohmmeter is connected to the condenser (capacitor). The meter should register slightly and then return to infinity (maximum resistance). Any continuous reading other than infinity means that the condenser is leaking and must be replaced.

Removing points and condenser

Normally, the distributor points and condenser are held in place by small screws. To prevent dropping the screws, use a magnetic or clip-type screwdriver that firmly holds

447

DEFECT	WILL CAUSE	CORRECTION
Too much side play of distributor shaft OR Distributor shaft binds when rotated	Changes in contact point dwell AND Changes in ignition timing	Replace the shaft and bushings. Replace the distributor housing if necessary.
Binding or looseness of breaker plate	Incorrect timing advance Change in contact point dwell	Replace the breaker plate assembly and/or the nylon guides.
Cam lobe wear	Change in contact point dwell	Replace the cam.
Lack of lubrication	Rapid wear of the shaft and bushings Rapid wear of the rubbing block and cam	Lubricate at the oilers. Lubricate the cam with cam lubricant.
Too much lubrication	Burning of contact points	Replace the distributor seal and/or clean the breaker plate assembly and cam.
Defective electrical leads	Ignition short, or open circuit	Replace the condenser and/or coil lead. Tighten the connections.
Dirty, pitted, or burned points	Engine missing, skipping, or hard to start	Replace the contact points.
Bad pickup coil	No start	Replace.
Broken pickup coil wires	No start, engine miss or surge, stalling	Replace or repair wires.
Bad electronic control unit	Missing, no start, stalling	Replace.
Bad condenser	No start, burned points	Replace.

Fig. 25-26. Chart shows how distributor defects cause specific symptoms. Also note ways of correcting problems.

the screws. If you drop one of the screws into the distributor (under advance plate), the distributor may have to be removed from the engine. Use a small wrench to disconnect the primary wires from the points.

Lubricate distributor and rubbing block

Wipe the distributor cam and breaker plate clean before installing the new parts. If recommended, apply a small amount of oil to lubrication points on the distributor (wick in center of shaft, cam wick, or oil hole in side of distributor housing). Do NOT apply too much oil because it could get on the points.

To prolong service life, place a small amount of grease on the side of the breaker arm rubbing block. This will reduce friction between the cam and fiber block.

Installing points and condenser

Place the new points into position in the distributor. Install the point screws and primary wires. If the distributor has a window (square metal plate) in the distributor cap, fully tighten the point hold-down screws. If the distributor does NOT have a window, only partially tighten the screws so the points can be adjusted.

Distributor point adjustment

Distributor points can be adjusted using either a *feeler gauge* (blade of metal ground to precision thickness) or a *dwell meter* (meter that electrically measures point setting in degrees of distributor rotation).

Gapping distributor points

To use a feeler gauge to gap (set) distributor points, crank the engine until the points are FULLY OPEN. The point rubbing block should be on top of a distributor cam lobe. This is illustrated in Fig. 25-27.

Distributor point gap is the recommended distance between the contacts in the fully open position. Look up

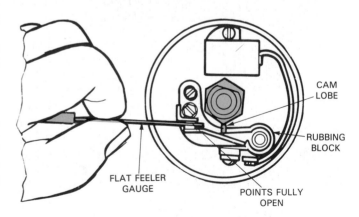

Fig. 25-27. When gapping or adjusting distributor points, points must be fully opened. Rubbing block on points must ride on one of the shaft cam lobes. Slide spec size feeler between points. A slight drag will result when points are adjusted correctly. (Chrysler)

this spec in the service manual. It may also be given on the emission sticker in the engine compartment.

Typical point gap settings average around .015 in. (0.38 mm) for eight-cylinder engines to .025 in. (0.53 mm) for six and four-cylinder engines.

With the distributor points open, slide the specified thickness feeler gauge between the points. Adjust the points so that there is a slight drag on the blade. Use a screwdriver or Allen wrench, depending upon design, to open or close the points. If needed, tighten the hold-down screws and recheck the gap.

CAUTION! Make sure your feeler gauge is clean before inserting it in the points. Oil or grease will reduce the service life of the points.

Dwell meter point adjustment

To use a dwell meter to adjust distributor points, connect the meter to the ignition. Follow the directions provided with the meter.

Typically, connect the red meter lead to the distributor side of the coil (wire going to contact points). Connect the black meter lead to ground (any metal part on engine). If an opening is provided in the distributor cap, the points should be set with the engine running. Install the distributor cap and rotor. Start the engine.

With the meter controls set properly, adjust the points using an Allen wrench or special screwdriver type tool. Turn the point adjustment screw until the dwell meter reads within specs, Fig. 25-28.

If the distributor cap does NOT have an adjustment window, set the points with the cap removed. Instead of starting the engine, ground the coil wire (connect output end on engine). Crank the engine with the starting motor. This will simulate engine operation and allow point adjustment with the dwell meter, Fig. 25-29.

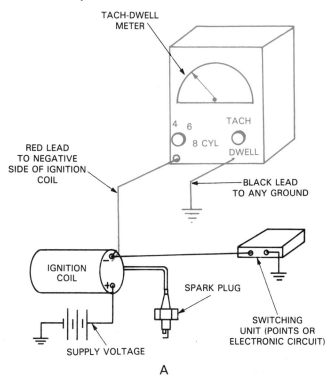

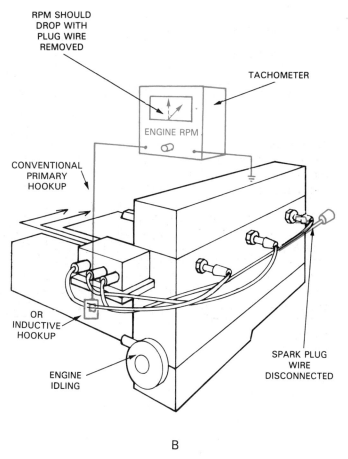

Fig. 25-28. The points in this distributor have a screw that is turned with hex driver for adjustment. Point hold-down screws are fully tightened during adjustment. (Peerless Instrument)

Fig. 25-29. A—Tach-dwell meter is connected to older ignition system to detect opening and closing of ignition control module circuit or points. B—With modern distributorless ignitions, refer to service manual for instructions for connecting tach-dwell meter. Inductive, clip-on tachs are available. (TIF)

449

Dwell specifications

Dwell specifications vary with the number of cylinders in the engine and the type of ignition system used (point, electronic, or computerized). An 8-cylinder engine with contact points will usually require 30° of dwell. An engine with fewer cylinders will normally require more dwell time, Fig. 25-30.

An electronic or computer-controlled system can have a different amount of dwell time to energize the ignition coil(s). Always obtain exact dwell values from a service manual.

Fixed and variable dwell

Dwell specifications for modern electronic or computer-controlled ignition systems can vary with system design. There are a few terms you should understand concerning ignition dwell.

Fixed dwell means that the dwell time should remain the same at all engine speeds. Fixed dwell is found on contact point ignition systems and older electronic systems. If the dwell varies when it should not, the distributor shaft or bushing may be worn or the ignition control module may be faulty.

Variable dwell means the engine control module alters ignition coil dwell time with changes in engine speed. This is common in late-model vehicles. At low engine speeds, the control module can use a short dwell period to build an adequate magnetic field around the coil windings for good spark. However, at higher engine speeds, the module increases dwell time to make sure the coil(s) fires the spark plugs properly. If a system fails to alter dwell when it should, the engine control module is faulty and should be replaced.

Current-limiting dwell means the engine control module sends a large amount of current through the ignition coil windings until a strong magnetic field develops around the windings. Once the module senses a *saturated ignition coil* (coil's magnetic field is fully formed), it reduces the amount of current sent through the coil windings. Only a small primary current is needed to maintain the strong magnetic field in the coil. At high engine speeds, the current-limiting feature may not be needed. Full control-module current output may be required to fully charge the ignition coil to ready it to fire the spark plugs at high engine rpm.

Dwell variation problem

Dwell variation (changes in dwell meter reading) indicates distributor wear problems with contact points. Dwell should remain constant as engine speed is increased or decreased.

Generally, if dwell varies more than about three degrees, the distributor should be rebuilt or replaced. The distributor shaft, bushings, or advance plate could be worn and loose, allowing a change in dwell.

As dwell increases, point gap decreases. As dwell decreases, point gap increases. Also, any change in point gap or dwell will change ignition timing. The points should always be adjusted BEFORE the ignition timing.

Note! With electronic ignitions, dwell changes with engine speed can be normal.

CYLINDER BALANCE TEST

Discussed earlier, a *cylinder balance test* will check that each engine cylinder is producing equal combustion power. It provides a quick way of finding problems in parts that affect the burning of the fuel mixture in each cylinder. Since you just learned about connecting a tachometer to an ignition system, we will review a cylinder balance test as related to ignition system troubleshooting.

With the tach connected to the engine, you can either pull one spark plug wire off or use an engine analyzer to electronically short out the spark plug. When this is done, engine rpm should drop slightly. This rpm drop shows that the cylinder is no longer helping to spin the engine crankshaft, Fig. 25-31A.

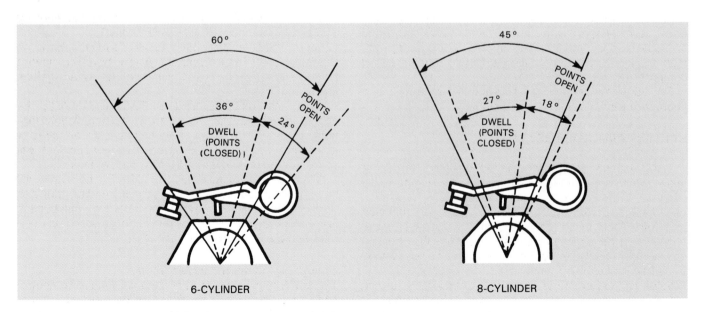

Fig. 25-30. Dwell is another way to adjust points. Dwell meter will measure how long points are closed electrically. Because of less lobes, a 6-cylinder engine will have more dwell than an 8-cylinder. Refer to specs for an exact value.
(Florida Dept. of Voc. Ed.)

A—Tach shows rpm drop when cylinder is shorted out.

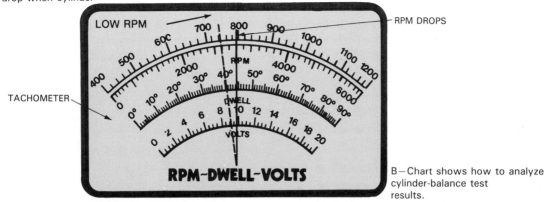

B—Chart shows how to analyze cylinder-balance test results.

CYLINDER BALANCE TEST RESULTS	SCOPE KV	PROBLEMS
1. One or more cylinders dead (no RPM drop)	High (above 5 kV)	Suspect an open spark plug wire or bad distributor cap
2. One or more cylinders dead (no RPM drop)	Low (below 5 kV)	Suspect a fouled spark plug or bad cylinder
3. One or more cylinders low	Low	Check compression
4. One or more cylinders low	High	Check for vacuum leak
5. Two adjacent cylinders dead or low	Low	Suspect a blown headgasket; check the radiator for signs of bubbling in the coolant
6. Four cylinders low. (All four cylinders use the same intake manifold passageway)	High	Suspect unbalanced carburetor or intake manifold leak

Fig. 25-31. Cylinder balance test will quickly check which cylinders are making good power or are firing properly. This test can be done with a conventional tachometer or with sophisticated engine analyzer. Basically, a plug wire is opened by removing it from the distributor or by using buttons on analyzer that automatically prevent coil from firing for specific spark plug. When a cylinder is shorted and no spark is reaching one plug, engine rpm should drop a specific amount. If rpm does not drop, something is wrong in that cylinder.

For example, if only one cylinder shows little or no rpm drop, then that cylinder has problems. Its spark plug could be fouled, plug wire burned opened, distributor cap cracked, etc. There could also be engine problems (low compression from burned valve, bad rings, etc.).

Fig. 25-31B gives a chart showing what might cause improper cylinder balance test results.

IGNITION TIMING ADJUSTMENT

Initial ignition timing, also called *base timing,* is the spark timing set by the technician with the engine idling (no centrifugal, vacuum, or electronic advance). It must be adjusted anytime the distributor has been removed and reinstalled in an engine. During a tune-up, initial timing must be checked and then adjusted if not within specs. Many computer controlled ignitions do not provide a method for adjusting base timing.

Initial ignition timing is commonly changed by turning the distributor housing in the engine. This makes the pickup coil and ignition control module or breaker points fire the ignition coil sooner or later.

Turning the distributor housing against distributor shaft rotation ADVANCES THE TIMING. Turning the housing with shaft rotation RETARDS THE TIMING.

Some computer controlled ignition systems have no provision for timing adjustment. A few, however, have a tiny screw or lever on the computer for small ignition timing changes.

When the ignition timing is TOO ADVANCED, the engine may suffer from spark knock or ping. A light tapping sound may result when the engine is accelerating or is under a load. The *ping* (abnormal combustion) will sound like a small hammer tapping on the engine.

When ignition timing is TOO RETARDED the engine will have poor fuel economy, power, and will be very sluggish during acceleration. If extremely retarded, combustion flames blowing out of the opened exhaust valve can overheat and crack the exhaust manifolds.

Energizing computer base timing

Base timing is the ignition timing without computer-controlled advance. Base timing is checked by disconnecting a wire connector in the computer wiring harness or by jumping across specific pins on a diagnostic connector. The connector may be in the engine compartment (sometimes next to the distributor) or in the passenger compartment. Refer to a manual if in doubt.

When in the base timing mode, you can use a conventional timing light to measure ignition timing. If timing is not correct, it can sometimes be adjusted by rotating the distributor or by moving the mounting for the engine speed sensor or the crankshaft position sensor.

In most late model vehicles, ignition timing cannot be adjusted. If timing is incorrect on these vehicles, the ECM or another component affecting timing must be replaced. Refer to the service manual for more information on specific vehicle.

A dual trace scope is sometimes needed to check ignition timing. One scope lead is connected to the ignition coil primary; another lead is connected to the crankshaft position sensor. The two waveforms can be compared to measure timing advance or retard. This is discussed in Chapter 29, Advanced Diagnostics.

Measuring ignition timing

A *timing light is* used to measure ignition timing. Shown in Fig. 25-32, a timing light normally has three leads. The two small leads connect to the battery. The larger lead usually connects to the NUMBER ONE spark plug wire.

Depending upon the type of timing light, the large lead may clip around the plug wire (inductive type), Fig. 25-33. It may also need to be connected directly to the metal terminal of the plug wire (conventional type). Some engines require a magnetic pickup lead on the timing light, Fig. 25-34.

When the engine is running, the timing light will flash ON and OFF like a strobe light. This action can be used to make a moving object appear stationary.

Before measuring engine timing, disconnect and plug the vacuum advance hose going to the distributor if needed. This will prevent the vacuum advance from functioning and upsetting your readings. With *electronic advance, you* may need to disconnect a wire or use a scanner to place computer system at base timing.

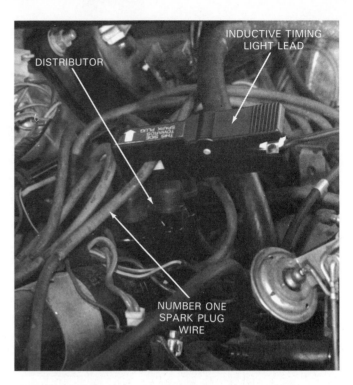

Fig. 25-33. This is an inductive timing light pickup lead. It simply slips over outside of plug wire to trigger the light. Some lights do not have inductive pickup and they must be wired in series with spark plug wire. (Peerless Instrument)

Start the engine and shine the timing light on the timing marks. The timing marks may be on the front cover and harmonic balancer of the engine. The timing marks may also be on the engine flywheel, Fig. 25-35.

The flashing timing light will make the mark or marks on the harmonic balancer or flywheel appear to stand still. This will let you set timing properly, Fig. 25-36.

A few engines require an *average timing* method where timing light is connected to coil wire or to two different plug wires to get an average timing reading, Fig. 25-34.

Ignition timing specs

Ignition timing is very critical to the performance of an engine. If the ignition timing is off even 2 or 3 degrees, engine fuel economy and power can drop considerably. Always obtain the exact timing specs from the engine emission control sticker or a service manual.

DISTRIBUTOR ADVANCE SERVICE

Both electronic and contact point type distributors can use similar advance mechanisms. A faulty advance mechanism will reduce engine performance and fuel economy.

Testing centrifugal advance (in-car)

A timing light can be used to test the general operation of a distributor centrifugal advance. Connect the timing light. Remove the vacuum hose going to the distributor. Start and idle the engine.

While aiming the timing light on the engine timing marks, slowly increase engine speed to approximately

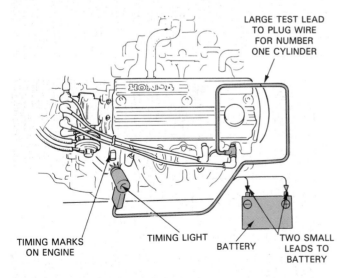

Fig. 25-32. This is common way of connecting a timing light to cars with conventional ignition system. Large lead connects to number one spark plug wire. Two small leads from timing light connect to battery. Timing light is then aimed at engine timing marks with engine idling. (Honda)

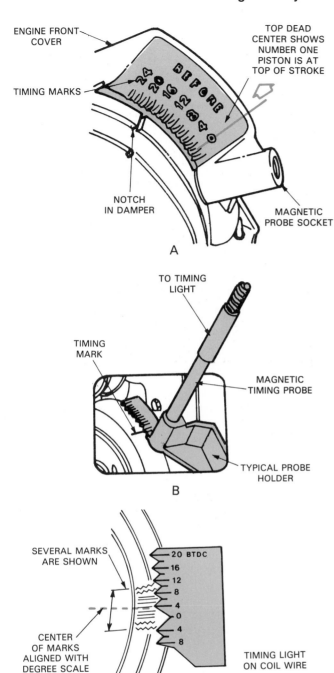

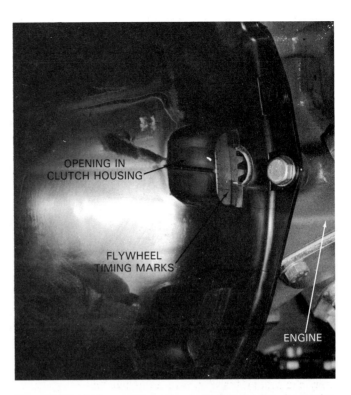

Fig. 25-35. A few engines have timing marks on engine flywheel, instead of at front on crankshaft damper. (Saab)

Fig. 25-34. A—When reading timing light, compare mark on spinning damper with stationary marks on degree scale. B—Some engines need magnetic probe to read timing. C—Average timing method is done by connecting timing light to coil wire. Center area of marks is then used to check timing. (Chrysler and Snap-On)

3500 rpm. Note the movement of the timing mark. See Fig. 25-37.

If the centrifugal advance is working, the mark should steadily move more advanced with the increase in speed.

If the timing mark jumps around or DOES NOT MOVE smoothly, the centrifugal advance is faulty. It may be worn, rusted, have weak springs, or other mechanical problems.

Fig. 25-36. When using timing light, you may have to find correct angle to aim timing light onto timing marks. Hoses and other parts may be in the way. Keep light away from spinning fans and belts! (Saab and Peerless Instrument)

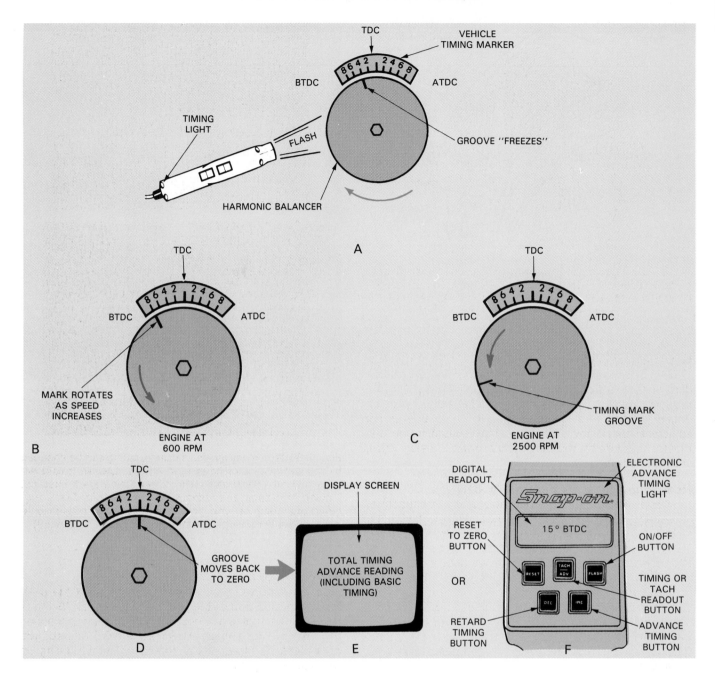

Fig. 25-37. Timing light with advance feature and most timing lights on engine analyzers can be used to check ignition advance. A—Timing light freezes mark on balancer or flywheel. B—At low engine rpm, timing should not be very advanced. C—As engine rpm increases, centrifugal or electronic advance should move timing mark more BTDC and out of view. D—With electronic advance timing light, mark can be moved back to zero and into view with timing light controls. E—Advance is then read off timing light or analyzer screen. F—Timing light controls. (Snap-On and All-Test)

Testing vacuum advance (in-car)

To test the distributor vacuum advance, connect a timing light. Remove the vacuum advance hose from the distributor. Start the engine and increase engine speed to approximately 1500 rpm. Note the location of the timing marks. Then, reconnect the vacuum hose on the distributor diaphragm, Fig. 25-37.

As soon as vacuum is reconnected, engine speed should increase and the timing marks should swing more advanced.

If vacuum advance is NOT working, check vacuum diaphragm and supply vacuum to distributor.

Testing vacuum advance diaphragm

To check the vacuum advance diaphragm, apply a vacuum to the unit using a hand-vacuum pump. When suction is applied to the diaphragm, the advance plate in the distributor should swing around. When vacuum is released, the advance plate should snap back and click into its normal position, Fig. 25-38.

If the ADVANCE DIAPHRAGM LEAKS and will not hold vacuum, it must be replaced. If the advance mechanism is stuck, check components for binding, rust, or other problems.

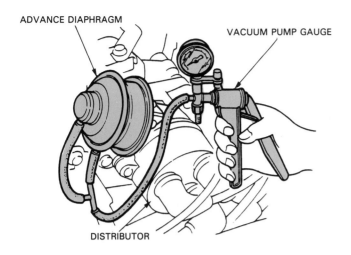

Fig. 25-38. When a vacuum advance is used, use a vacuum pump to activate diaphragm while measuring timing change. Timing should advance a specific amount as spec vacuum values are applied.   (Honda)

Checking advance supply vacuum

To check the supply vacuum going to the distributor, disconnect the diaphragm vacuum hose. Connect it to a vacuum gauge. Measure the amount of vacuum with the engine running at a specified rpm. If the vacuum is not sufficient, check any part controlling vacuum to the distributor (carburetor, thermal vacuum switch, delay valve, vacuum hose).

Measuring distributor advance (in-car)

Special timing lights are available that are capable of measuring exact distributor advance with the distributor installed in the engine. The timing light has a DEGREE METER built into the back of its case. The meter will register exact centrifugal or vacuum advance quickly and accurately, Fig. 25-37. Most large engine analyzers also have this feature.

A *distributor tester* may also be used to check distributor operation. The distributor is removed and mounted in the tester. The tester will check all distributor functions (pickup coil output, point dwell, centrifugal and vacuum advance).

Changing ignition timing

With a conventional, adjustable system, adjust the ignition timing if the timing marks are not lined up correctly. Loosen the distributor hold-down bolt.

A *distributor wrench* (long, special shaped wrench for reaching under distributor housing) is handy. Only loosen the distributor bolt enough to allow distributor rotation. Do NOT remove the bolt, Fig. 25-39.

With the distributor hold-down loosened, again shine the timing light on the engine timing marks. Turn the distributor one way or the other until the correct timing marks line up. Tighten the hold-down and double-check the timing. Reconnect the distributor vacuum hose and disconnect the timing light.

> DANGER! Keep your hands and the timing light leads away from the engine fan and belts. The spinning fan and belts can damage the light or cause serious injury!

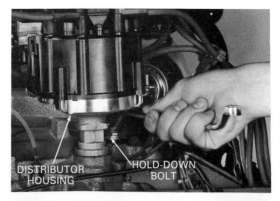

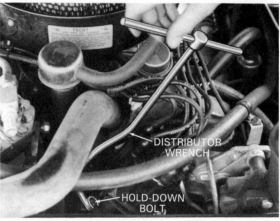

Fig. 25-39. With many ignition systems, timing can be changed by rotating distributor housing in engine. Loosen hold-down bolts and turn distributor until correct timing mark lines up. Tighten hold-down and recheck with timing light. Crank triggered and computer-coil ignition may not have conventional provisions for timing adjustment.   (Peerless Instrument)

Removing ignition distributor

Before removing a distributor, carefully mark the position of the rotor and distributor housing, Fig. 25-40. Place marks on the engine and housing with a scribe or marking pen. Then, if the engine crankshaft is NOT rotated, you will be able to install the distributor by simply lining up your marks, Fig. 25-41.

To remove the distributor, remove the distributor cap, rotor, primary wires, and distributor hold-down bolt. Pull the distributor upward while rotating it back and forth. If stuck, use a slide hammer puller with a two-prong fork.

Rebuilding a distributor

A *distributor rebuild* involves disassembly, cleaning, inspection, worn part replacement, and reassembly. Depending upon distributor type, exact procedures vary. Always refer to a shop manual for detailed directions and specifications, Fig. 25-42.

Mark the distributor gear and shaft. Drive the roll pin from the drive gear. Remove the gear and pull the distributor shaft out of the distributor housing. Remove the pickup coil or points, breaker or pickup coil plate, centrifugal weights, vacuum advance diaphragm, and any other part requiring service.

Look over all of the distributor parts closely, Fig. 25-43. Inspect the distributor shaft where it rides in the bushings.

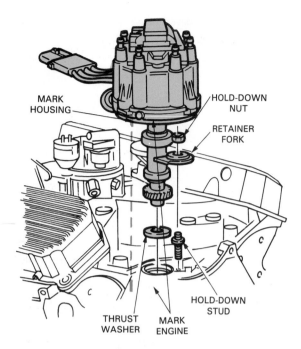

Fig. 25-40. When removing distributor from engine, mark distributor housing and engine for proper installation. If engine crankshaft will not be rotated during repairs, you should also mark location of rotor. (Buick)

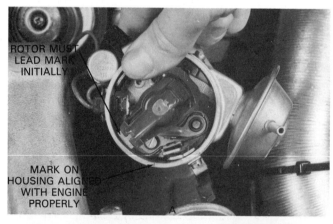

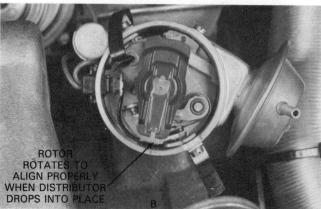

Fig. 25-41. A—When installing distributor, line up the mark on engine with mark on the distributor housing. You must also position rotor ahead of mark on housing. Rotor will turn as distributor gear meshes with drive gear on camshaft. B—Note how rotor now lines up with mark on housing. (Saab)

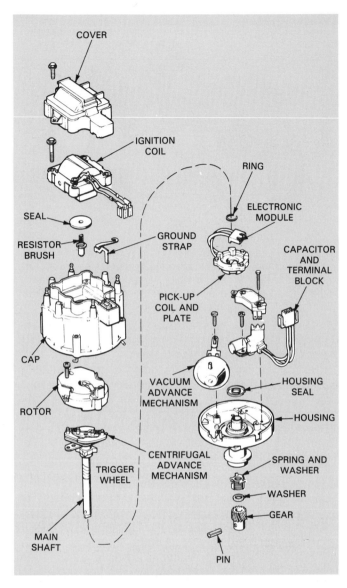

Fig. 25-42. Study relationship of parts in this distributor. (General Motors)

If worn, replace the shaft. Apply vacuum to the advance diaphragm. If it leaks or fails to retract, replace the vacuum diaphragm.

Most technicians replace the distributor bushings, small breaker plate bushings, centrifugal advance springs, advance diaphragm, and any other parts found to be worn.

Installing a distributor

If you made reference marks and the engine crankshaft was NOT turned, install the distributor as it was removed. Align the rotor and housing with the marks on the engine.

Double-check the position of the rotor after installation because the rotor will turn as the distributor gear meshes with its drive gear.

To install a distributor when the engine crankshaft has been rotated, remove the number one spark plug. Bump (crank) the engine until you can feel air blowing out of the spark plug hole. As soon as air blows out, slowly turn the crankshaft until the engine timing marks are on TDC.

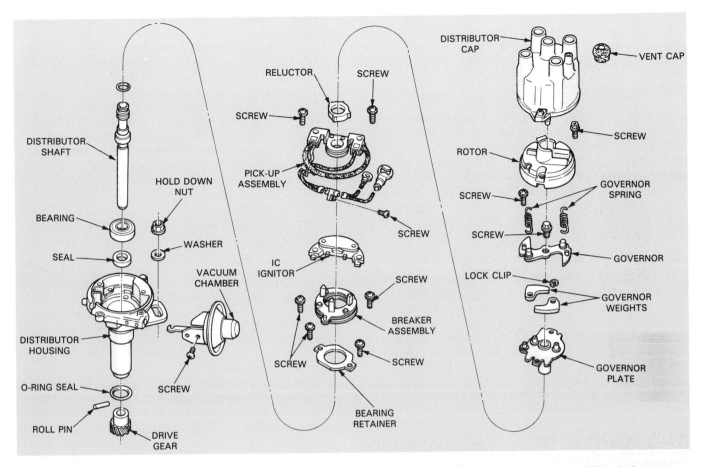

Fig. 25-43. The service manual will give illustration of specific type of distributor being serviced. (Chrysler)

With the crankshaft in this position, the distributor rotor should point at the NUMBER ONE SPARK PLUG WIRE. Fit the distributor into the engine so that the rotor points at number one distributor cap tower or plug wire.

Also, make sure the distributor housing is installed properly. The advance unit should be pointing as it was before removal.

IGNITION RESISTANCE CIRCUIT TESTING

Quite often, when a resistance wire or ballast resistor is open (infinite resistance), the engine will crank and start but then stall when the key is released to the run position. The ignition coil receives voltage when starting because of the by-pass circuit. It does not receive electricity in the run position because of the open circuit in the resistance wire or ballast resistor. This is a common symptom of problems in the resistance circuit of an ignition system.

Ballast resistor testing

A ballast resistor test may be needed when the voltage to the ignition coil in the RUN position is below or above specs. The resistance value of the unit may have changed, upsetting the voltage going to the coil.

An ohmmeter is connected across the resistor to measure internal resistance, Fig. 25-44. If the meter reading is NOT within specs, the resistor must be replaced.

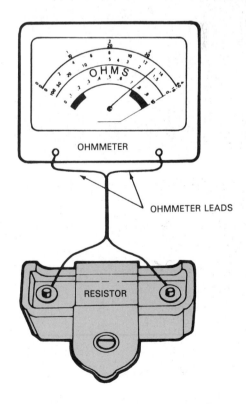

Fig. 25-44. Ohmmeter can be used to check ballast resistor or resistance wire between ignition switch and ignition coil. The ohms reading must be within specs. You would make this test if voltage to coil tested low or high.

Resistance wire testing

A resistance wire performs the same basic function as a ballast resistor. It limits the voltage going to the coil to prevent coil overheating and possible damage.

IGNITION COIL SERVICE

A *faulty ignition coil* may result in a weak spark, intermittent spark, or no spark at all. The engine may miss, stop running when the coil heats up, or cause a no-start problem. The windings inside the coil can break and produce a resistance or open in the coil circuit.

A coil may only act up when hot, after being exposed to engine heat. The heat can make the coil windings expand and open, with a resulting loss of high voltage output to the spark plugs.

Testing an ignition coil

A coil test may be needed when the ignition system fails the spark test but proper supply voltage was found. Since coil designs are different, testing procedures vary.

Generally, an ohmmeter is used to measure the internal resistance of the coil windings, Fig. 25-45. The meter is connected to the terminals of the coil. An infinite or out-of-specs reading would indicate a faulty ignition coil.

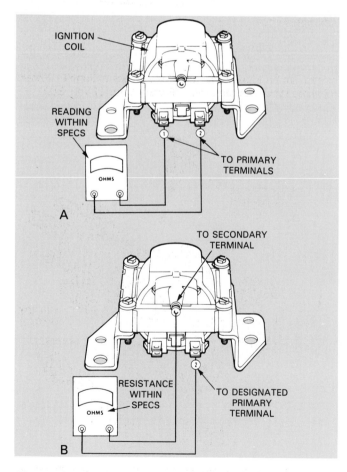

Fig. 25-45. If spark is weak, you may need to test ignition coil. A—Measure resistance of primary windings. Resistance should be low, approximately one ohm. B—Measure resistance between primary and secondary. Resistance should be higher ohms, but not infinite. (Echlin)

A spark intensity test also checks ignition coil output quickly.

A *bad coil pack* may only affect or kill two cylinders. In many cases, only one coil in the coil pack is faulty. The other coils in the assembly may be working normally. If you find misfiring or two dead cylinders that correspond to one coil in a coil pack, suspect the coil pack.

When testing a coil pack, check the windings of the coil with the spark problem. If, for example, the #2 cylinder is not firing, the coil for that cylinder should be checked first. Normally, a bad coil pack winding will show infinite resistance, or open.

Replacing an ignition coil

When the ignition coil is mounted on the engine, coil replacement involves removing the wires and bolts securing the old coil. Then, bolt on the new coil.

Be careful not to connect the coil in *reverse polarity* (primary wires accidentally connected backwards). This would reduce secondary voltage output.

When the coil is mounted inside the distributor cap (unitized type ignition), the distributor cap must be disassembled to install the new coil.

Ignition switch service

A *bad ignition switch* can cause several problems. The engine may NOT crank or start. The engine may NOT shut off when the ignition key is turned off. The starter may not disengage when the ignition key is returned to RUN. These types of problems point to a defective ignition switch.

Testing an ignition switch

A test light is an easy way to check the action of an ignition switch. When a test light is touched to the start terminal on the back of the switch, the light should only glow when the key has been turned to START. It should NOT glow when the key is released to the RUN position.

In the RUN position, the test light should glow when touched on the RUN terminal of the switch.

With the ignition key in the OFF position, neither switch terminal (start or run) should light the test light.

Replacing ignition switch

The ignition switch may be located in the dash or on the steering column.

If dash mounted, the *tumbler* (lock mechanism) must be removed from the switch. Normally, a small piece of wire is inserted into a hole in the front of the switch and the key is turned. This will release the tumbler from the switch so the tumbler can be pulled free. Then, unplug the wires and remove the old switch, Fig. 25-46.

If steering column mounted, the ignition switch is separate from the tumbler. It is normally about halfway down and on top of the steering column. Remove the fasteners holding the column to the dash. This will let the column drop down so you can replace the ignition switch, Fig. 25-47.

IGNITION SUPPLY VOLTAGE TEST

An *ignition supply voltage test* measures the amount of voltage going to the positive terminal of the ignition coil. It checks the circuit between the battery feed wire and the

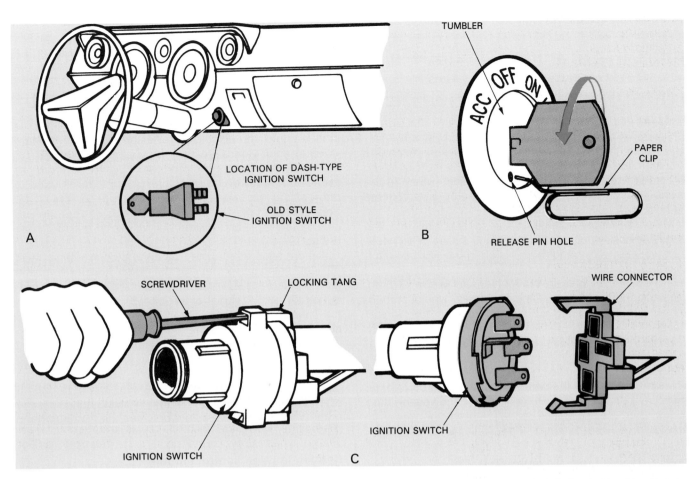

Fig. 25-46. A—Servicing older style ignition switch. B—Small piece of wire can be slipped into small hole in face of tumbler. Rotate key and slide out tumbler. C—Unscrew face nut and disconnect wires for switch removal.   (Florida Dept. of Voc. Ed.)

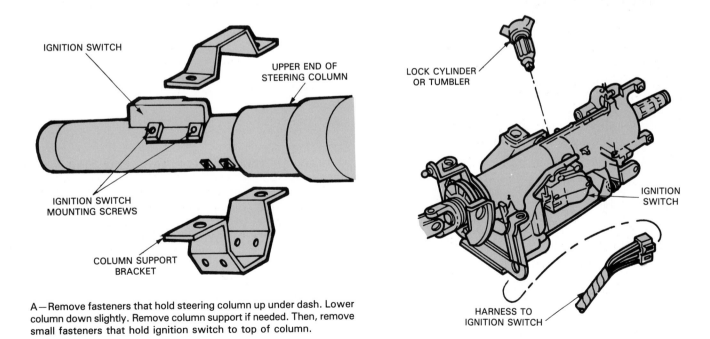

A—Remove fasteners that hold steering column up under dash. Lower column down slightly. Remove column support if needed. Then, remove small fasteners that hold ignition switch to top of column.

B—Remove wiring harness and small rod that activates ignition switch. Adjust ignition switch during installation. Hold key to start and slide switch until starting motor activates and tighten it down.

Fig. 25-47. Servicing steering column mounted ignition switch.   (Florida Dept. of Voc. Ed.)

coil. A supply voltage test will help locate troubles in the:
1. Ignition switch.
2. Bypass circuit.
3. Resistance circuit.
4. Electrical connections and primary wires.

If the ignition system fails a spark test, for example, a supply voltage test may help locate the source of the problem, Fig. 25-48.

Before using a voltmeter, connect a test light to the battery side of the coil. The light should glow with the engine cranking and with the ignition switch in the RUN position. If it does NOT glow, there is an open somewhere in the primary supply circuit. Perform voltage drop tests until the point of high resistance is found.

Measure supply voltage to the ignition coil with the engine cranking to check the bypass circuit. Also, measure voltage with the ignition switch in the RUN position to check the resistance circuit if used.

If the voltage going to the ignition coil is low or high, measure the resistance of the resistance wire. Compare the ohmmeter reading to specs. Replace the wire if needed.

Some service manuals recommend the use of a voltmeter to check the ignition system resistance wire. With the wire intact and the ignition key ON, measure the voltage drop across the wire. If the voltage drop is high, then the resistance of the wire is high. If the voltage drop is low, then the resistance is low. Replace the wire if its voltage drop is not within acceptable limits.

IGNITION CONTROL MODULE SERVICE

A *faulty ignition control module* will produce a wide range of problems: engine stalls when hot, engine cranks but fails to start, engine misses at high or low speeds.

Quite often, an ignition control module problem will show up after a period of engine operation. Engine heat will soak into the control module, raising its temperature. The heat will upset the operation of the electronic components in the unit.

Ignition control module testing

Many shop manuals list the ignition control module (ICM) as one of the last components to test. If all of the other components are in good working order, then the problem might be in the control module.

If a specialized tester is available, it may be used to quickly determine the condition of the control module. The wires going to the module are unplugged. The tester is plugged into the circuit. The tester will then indicate whether an ICM fault exists.

Fig. 25-49 shows a trick for checking the operation of the ICM. A screwdriver or soldering gun can be used to induce current into the wires going to the ICM. This should make the ICM fire the high voltage ignition coil. Note that a bad pickup coil will keep the ICM from firing.

A more accurate test can be done by connecting small 1.5 volt flashlight battery to the wires leading from the pickup coil to the ICM. Since a pickup coil commonly produces an output signal of about 1.5 volts peak-to-peak, the small battery can be used to replace the pickup coil output and help isolate the problem, Fig. 25-50.

When the small battery is connected and disconnected from the ICM wires, the ICM should fire the coil and high voltage should jump out of the coil wire or one of the spark plug wires. Make sure the ignition key is turned on when testing. Before condemning the ICM, make sure the primary wires and connectors between the distributor and ICM are not blocking current flow into the ICM.

Heating ignition control module

The microscopic components (transistors, diodes, capacitors, resistors and IC's) inside ignition control modules are very sensitive to high temperatures.

When testing the ignition control module, many technicians use a heat gun or heat lamp to warm the module. This will simulate the temperature in the engine compartment after the engine has been running. The heat may make the ignition control module act up and allow you to find an erratic problem, Fig. 25-51.

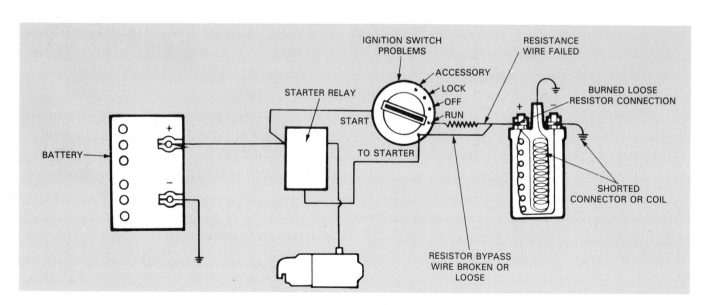

Fig. 25-48. Study types of problems that can keep ignition system from working in primary or low voltage supply system. (Florida Dept. of Voc. Ed.)

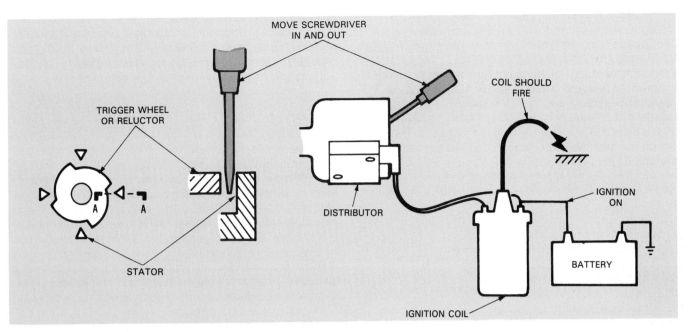

Fig. 25-49. Screwdriver or soldering gun can be used to fire pickup coil and electronic control circuit. Screwdriver can be moved past pickup coil. Resulting change in magnetic field should make control module fire coil. Soldering gun produces fluctuating magnetic field. When side of gun is placed next to pickup coil, ignition coil should fire rapidly. Do not touch hot tip on parts!

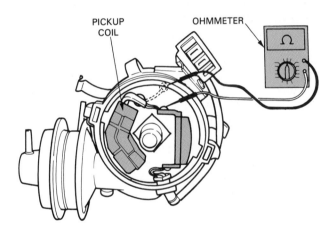

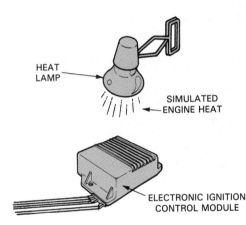

Fig. 25-51. When checking intermittent problem, use heat lamp or gun to warm ignition control module. Heat may separate internal connection in circuit and cause problems. (Ford)

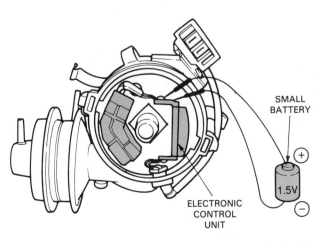

Fig. 25-50. Small flashlight battery can be used to fire ignition control module. If ignition begins working or firing with battery trigger, pickup coil may be bad. If system still fails to fire, check ICM, ignition coil, and wiring.

WARNING! Do not apply too much heat to an ignition control module or it may be ruined. Only heat the module to a temperature equal to its normal operating temperature.

Replacing an ignition control module

Replacement of an ignition control module is a simple task. If the module is mounted in the engine compartment or under the dash, carefully unplug the wiring harness. Unbolt the old unit and install the new unit.

If the ignition control module is mounted inside the distributor, remove the distributor cap and control module screws. Before installing the new module, check in a service manual for specific instructions.

In many cases, the bottom of the ignition control module must be coated with a SPECIAL GREASE (silicone grease, dielectric heat transfer compound, or heat sink compound). The grease or gel helps heat transfer into the distributor, protecting the ignition control module from overheating and circuit damage. See Fig. 25-52.

Always make sure you have the correct ignition control module. A new control module may look identical to the old one but may have internal circuit differences. Even the same year and make car can require different ignition control modules.

COMPUTERIZED IGNITION SYSTEM SERVICE

Many of the components of a computer controlled ignition system are similar to those of electronic or contact point ignition systems. This makes testing about the same for many parts (spark plugs, secondary wires, ignition coil). However, the computerized ignition has engine sensors and a computer which add to the complexity of the system.

Computer self-diagnosis mode

Most computerized systems have a check engine light in the dash that glows when a problem exists. The computer

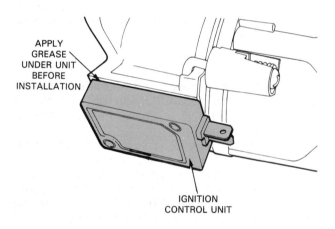

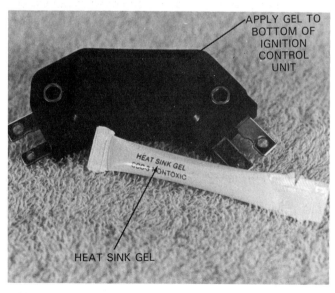

Fig. 25-52. When replacing an ignition control module, apply approved silicone grease or gel to bottom of device. This will allow the module to dissipate heat properly.

can be activated to produce a number code. The code can be compared to information in the car's service manual to pinpoint the source of a problem. This makes testing and repairing a computerized system much easier.

> WARNING! A computerized ignition system can be seriously damaged if the wrong wire is shorted to ground or if a meter is connected improperly. Always follow manufacturer's testing procedures.

Computer ignition testers

Most auto makers provide specialized testing equipment for their computerized ignition systems. Like an ignition control module tester, the computer system tester plugs into the wiring harness. It will then measure internal resistances and voltages in the system to determine where a problem is located.

Refer to the index for more information on servicing computer-controlled ignition systems. The sensors, actuators, and computer can tie to several other systems.

DIRECT IGNITION SYSTEM SERVICE

The procedures for servicing a direct ignition system are similar to those described for other types of ignition systems. The main difference is that you must test the ignition coil of the affected cylinder. For example, if the #1 spark plug is not firing, tests should be performed on the #1 ignition coil. Typical direct ignition system tests are shown in Fig. 25-53.

A direct ignition coil is tested like other ignition coils. Measure both primary and secondary winding resistance. Also make sure you are getting primary voltage to the coil.

SUMMARY

Ignition system problems can cause a wide range of symptoms. You must use logical thought and basic electrical tests to find the source of the trouble.

If an engine cranks, but will not start, check for spark and for fuel. This will help narrow down the cause of the problem to either the ignition system or the fuel system. Then you will know where to test further.

Check for spark at one of the spark plug wires while cranking the engine. A hot spark should jump a small gap formed between the wire and ground. Check for fuel in the carburetor while moving the throttle linkage or in the TBI while cranking the engine. With multi-point injection, a pressure gauge would be needed to check for fuel pressure.

A bad spark plug wire or coil wire can cause engine missing and other symptoms. An ohmmeter can be used to measure wire internal resistance. A bad spark plug wire will normally have a very high resistance.

To check for deteriorated secondary wire insulation, look for small sparks jumping off of the wires to ground. Darken the engine compartment so you can see any arcing and leaking.

When replacing spark plug wires, replace them one at a time. This will make replacement easier since you do not have to trace from the distributor or coil module to each spark plug in firing order.

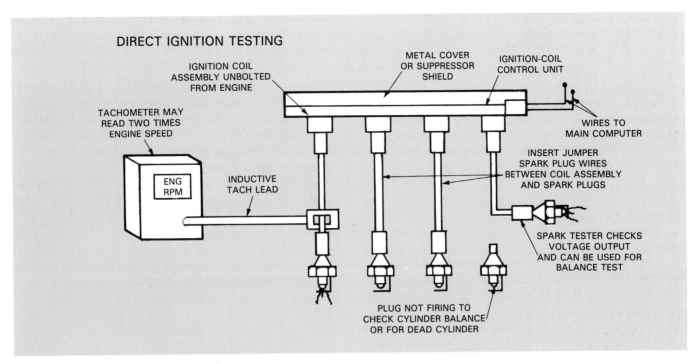

DIRECT IGNITION TESTING

Fig. 25-53. Study how to perform tests on direct ignition system. Coil module assembly can be unbolted and removed from engine. Then, spark plug wires can be used to jump from coil assembly to spark plugs. This will let you connect inductive tachometer to engine. You can also use spark tester to check high voltage output and to short out each plug to make sure each cylinder is firing. Scope or timing light can also be connected to engine with this setup.

A spark plug socket, extension, and ratchet are normally used to remove and install spark plugs.

You should read spark plugs as they are removed. Inspect the plug tip to determine the condition of the engine, fuel system, and to check plug firing. A properly burning plug should have a brown to grayish-tan color.

A wire feeler gauge should be used to gap the spark plugs. Insert the specified size feeler into the plug gap. It should touch both electrodes and drag slightly. Bend the side electrode opened or closed as needed.

When installing spark plugs, start the plugs by hand. Then use the ratchet and socket to snug them down. Overtightening is a common problem that can damage the threads in the cylinder head.

A carbon trace can form inside a distributor cap and upset engine operation. The trace can conduct the high voltage to ground or to the wrong lug inside the cap. This can keep one or more of the spark plugs from firing. A cracked distributor cap can do the same thing.

A bad distributor pickup coil can also cause a wide range of symptoms. An ohmmeter can be used to check pickup coil condition. Resistance should be within specs. An AC voltmeter will also check pickup coil condition. With the engine cranking, a magnetic pickup coil should produce about 1.5 volts.

Older contact points can be adjusted with a flat feeler gauge. Crank the engine until the points are fully open. The point rubbing block must be on top of one of the distributor cam lobes. Insert the right size feeler into the point gap. Move the adjustable contact until the gap is correct. Some points should be adjusted with the engine running while using a dwell meter. A window is provided so that a hex wrench can be used to set the points.

A tach-dwell meter connects to the distributor side of the ignition coil and to ground. This can vary with modern electronic or computerized ignition systems. Refer to a service manual if in doubt.

When a distributor is used, you can usually adjust initial ignition timing. A timing light is connected to the number one spark plug wire and to the car battery. This will make the light flash every time the number one plug fires. By shining the timing light on the engine timing marks, you can check and adjust ignition timing.

To change ignition timing, you can often rotate the distributor housing in the engine. With computerized ignitions, you may not be able to change base timing.

When removing a distributor, you should mark the location of the housing and rotor. Then, if the engine crankshaft is not turned, the distributor is reinstalled with the same orientation.

KNOW THESE TERMS

Engine miss, Dead cylinder, Spark test, Oscilloscope, Electronic ignition tester, Reading spark plugs, Spark plug gap, Secondary wire resistance, Backfiring, Carbon trace, Pickup coil air gap, Shorted condenser, Dwell meter, Distributor point gap, Dwell variation, Initial ignition timing, Timing light, Distributor wrench, Reverse polarity, Tumbler.

REVIEW QUESTIONS—CHAPTER 25

1. What should you do if an engine cranks but will NOT start?
2. What is the purpose of a spark intensity test?

3. A _____ _____ will NOT produce combustion power.

4. How do you read spark plugs?

5. How do you gap spark plugs?

6. A _____ _____ can conduct electricity to the wrong distributor cap lug or to ground.

7. In your own words, how do you adjust older distributor contact points?

8. How does a timing light connect to an early model ignition system?

9. You cannot adjust ignition timing on some late model cars. True or false?

10. In your own words, how do you remove and replace a distributor?

11. If the engine is cranked with the distributor removed, what must be done?

12. What are two ways to check an ignition coil?

13. How can you use a battery to check an ignition control module?

14. With a unitized distributor, special _____ or _____ should be applied to the bottom of the ignition control module to help transfer heat.

15. How can computer self-diagnosis help find problems in an ignition system?

ASE CERTIFICATION–TYPE QUESTIONS

1. An automotive engine cranks but will not start and run. Technician A inspects the condition of the engine's ignition system. Technician B checks the operation of the engine's fuel system. Who is right?
   (A) A only.
   (B) B only.
   (C) Both A and B.
   (D) Neither A nor B.

2. A spark intensity test is performed on an automobile's ignition system. The test results indicate that the spark is weak at all the engine cylinders. Technician A removes the distributor cap and checks for a defective rotor. Technician B tests the operation of the ignition coil. Who is right?
   (A) A only.
   (B) B only.
   (C) Both A and B.
   (D) Neither A nor B.

3. A resistance test is performed on the secondary wires of an engine's ignition system. All of the spark plug wires in this ignition system have infinite resistance. Technician A says these test results indicate that the spark plug wires in this system are in good condition. Technician B says these test results indicate that the plug wires in this ignition system are bad. Who is right?
   (A) A only.
   (B) B only.
   (C) Both A and B.
   (D) Neither A nor B.

4. The tips and insulators of an engine's spark plugs are black. Technician A checks the compression of each engine cylinder. Technician B inspects the condition of the engine's valve stem seals. Who is right?
   (A) A only.
   (B) B only.
   (C) Both A and B.
   (D) Neither A nor B.

5. The pickup coil in an engine's distributor is believed to be malfunctioning. Technician A checks the resistance of this pickup coil with an ohmmeter. Technician B uses a low-reading DC voltmeter to test the operation of this pickup coil. Who is right?
   (A) A only.
   (B) B only.
   (C) Both A and B.
   (D) Neither A nor B.

6. A certain automobile engine is equipped with a contact point distributor. When engine speed is increased, the distributor's point dwell increases six degrees. Technician A says the distributor shaft or bushings could be worn. Technician B says the advance plate could be loose. Who is right?
   (A) A only.
   (B) B only.
   (C) Both A and B.
   (D) Neither A nor B.

7. A cylinder balance test is performed on an automotive engine. When the engine's "number 2" cylinder's spark plug wire is removed, the tachometer shows no variation in engine rpm. Technician A checks the compression in this cylinder. Technician B inspects the distributor cap for cracks. Who is right?
   (A) A only.
   (B) B only.
   (C) Both A and B.
   (D) Neither A nor B.

8. An automobile engine cranks and starts but stalls when the ignition key is released to the "run" position. Technician A inspects the distributor's centrifugal advance mechanism. Technician B uses an ohmmeter to check the resistance of the ignition system's ballast resistor. Who is right?
   (A) A only.
   (B) B only.
   (C) Both A and B.
   (D) Neither A nor B.

9. An automotive engine's ignition system fails to produce a spark. Technician A believes the problem could be caused by a faulty ignition coil. Technician B believes the problem could be caused by improper coil supply voltage. Who is right?
   (A) A only.
   (B) B only.
   (C) Both A and B.
   (D) Neither A nor B.

10. When an automobile engine reaches full operating temperature, it stalls. Technician A says the problem could be the ignition control module. Technician B says the problem could be the ignition coil. Who is right?
    (A) A only.
    (B) B only.
    (C) Both A and B.
    (D) Neither A nor B.

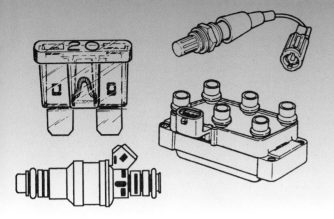

Fuel and Emission Control Systems Electronics Service

After studying this chapter, you will be able to:
* *Test electrical/electronic components found on late model fuel and emission control systems.*
* *Use a fuel system wiring diagram.*
* *Explain new OBD II monitoring features used on late model fuel injection and emission control systems.*
* *Describe the IM 240 emissions testing program.*
* *Cite safety rules that should be followed when testing fuel and emission control systems.*

Government studies have shown that emissions from passenger vehicles have dropped over 90% in the last 15 years. This reflects well on the automotive industry, which has done its share in reducing air pollution. Design improvements in the fuel and emission control systems have contributed greatly to this decrease in motor vehicle emissions. See Fig. 26-1.

This chapter describes the most common symptoms, tests, and adjustments for the major parts of gasoline injection and emission control systems. It is very important that you, as an automotive technician, be able to diagnose and repair fuel and emission control systems. By keeping these systems in good working order, you are protecting THE AIR WE BREATHE!

FUEL SYSTEM ELECTRONICS SERVICE

Today's fuel injection systems are primarily controlled electronically. Electric fuel pumps pressurize the system. Sensors feed data back to the electronic control module so it can fire the injector solenoids at just the right time and for the correct duration. This helps keep the correct amount of fuel metering into each cylinder for maximum efficiency. It is critical that the electronic technician know how to diagnose and test modern fuel system electronic components.

Inspecting injection system

A general inspection of the engine and related components will sometimes uncover gasoline injection system troubles. Look at Fig. 26-2. Check the condition of all hoses, wires, and other injection system components. Look for fuel leaks, vacuum leaks, kinked lines, loose electrical connections, and other problems. Thoroughly check the components most likely to cause the particular symptoms. See Fig. 26-3.

With an EFI system, you may need to disconnect and check the terminals of the wiring harness. Inspect the terminals for rust, corrosion, and burning. High resistance at the terminal connections is a frequent cause of problems.

> Warning! Do not disconnect an EFI harness terminal when the ignition switch is in the *on* position. This can damage the control module. Refer to a service manual for details. You may be instructed to disconnect the negative battery terminal during EFI service.

Fuel system on-board diagnostics

Most electronic fuel injection systems have on-board diagnostic abilities, which means the vehicle's control module can detect possible faults, such as a bad component, and produce a *trouble code* pinpointing the problem. Specific systems vary, depending on make, model, and year.

When a *malfunction indicator light* (MIL) in the dashboard glows, it indicates that something is wrong. The technician can then use service manual procedures to

Fig. 26-1. Emissions from all sources have been reduced over the past few years. However, we must all do our part to reduce pollution even more by keeping cars and trucks running at maximum efficiency. (Petroleum Institute)

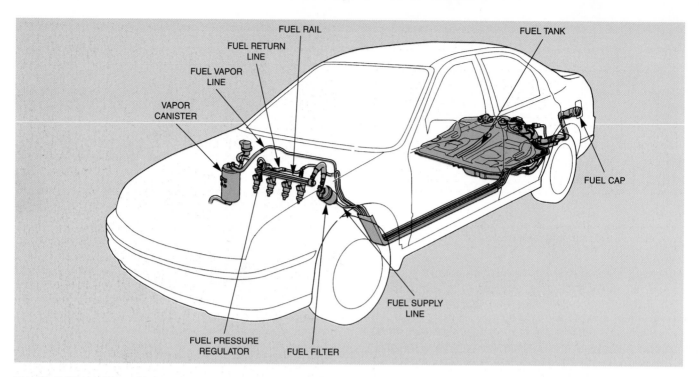

Fig. 26-2. When diagnosing fuel system problems, there are only a few electrical-electronic parts that could be at fault—electric fuel pump, injectors, sensors, and computer. However, there are many mechanical parts that could prevent normal operation—damaged fuel lines, fuel cap, pressure regulator, vapor return line, etc. (Honda)

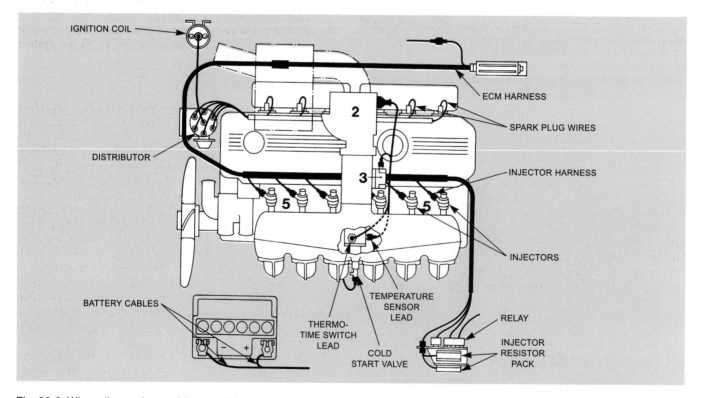

Fig. 26-3. When diagnosing problems in EFI systems, check electrical connections closely. One loose or disconnected wire could upset system operation.

activate the self-diagnostic mode or to connect a scan tool to the system.

Some older diagnostic systems display the trouble codes as *numbers* in a digital display located on the dash panel. See Fig. 26-4. Other systems produce an *on-off* type code by flashing the check engine light. In some systems, the diagnostic codes must be retrieved with an analog meter that is connected to a specified circuit test

SELF-DIAGNOSIS TROUBLE
CODE INDICATES TROUBLE

A

Programmed ECM trouble codes	
Code	**Circuit affected**
12	No tack signal.
13	Oxygen sensor not ready.
14	Shorted coolant sensor circuit.
15	Open coolant sensor circuit.
16	Generator output voltage out of range.
17	Crank signal circuit high.
18	Open crank signal circuit.
19	Fuel pump circuit high.
20	Open fuel pump circuit.
21	Shorted TPS circuit.
22	Open TPS circuit.
23	EST/by-pass circuit shorted or open.
24	Speed sensor failure.

B

Fig. 26-4. Modern EFI systems have a self-diagnostic mode. When a trouble light flashes, technician knows system should be checked. After activating computer, computer will show a number code in dash. A—Dash number indicates trouble. B—Partial list of trouble code from one service manual. (Cadillac)

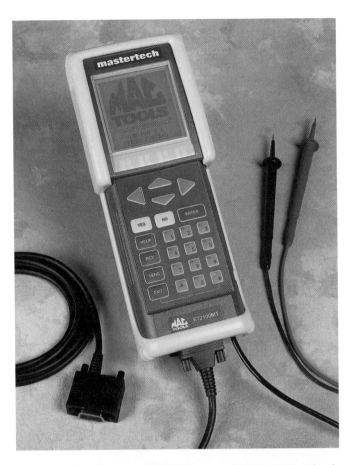

Fig. 26-5. With late model vehicles, scan tool is used to check for trouble codes that indicate fuel or emission system circuit failures.

point. In all cases, the code numbers must be compared to a chart in the service manual to pinpoint the faulty section or component.

A *scan tool* will find and display many trouble codes related to an electronic fuel injection system, Fig. 26-5. It is connected to a test connector on the vehicle.

Modern scan tools will automatically convert the trouble code number into an explanation of potential problems. The scan tool will tell you which sensors, injectors, and other monitored components are not operating normally. The scan tool may also indicate what might be wrong with the component. This will save considerable time when troubleshooting.

Always retrieve trouble codes before attempting other diagnostic procedures. This may help you find the source of the problem more quickly.

OBD II fuel system monitoring

Vehicles equipped with OBD II systems can set trouble codes that pinpoint injector problems. For example, if the scan tool readout shows a problem with the number three injector, you know to test this injector and its supply circuit for problems. With late model vehicles, the scan tool will also help you find common problems with system sensors and other actuators. You would then perform pinpoint tests to validate the scan tool readout.

Fuel system monitoring involves checking whether a stoichiometric, or theoretically perfect, fuel mixture is being fed to the engine. Primarily, the feedback from the upstream oxygen sensor (located before catalytic converter) is used to determine fuel mixture content. If the oxygen sensor detects abnormal combustion resulting from a poor fuel mixture, it trips a trouble code.

Before a trouble code is tripped, however, the control module will try to adjust the fuel mixture as needed. It will alter the temporary fuel trim or injector pulse width to compensate for abnormal combustion by-products. *Short term fuel trim* refers to the temporary adjustment of injector pulse width to correct the fuel mixture. *Long term fuel trim* is a permanent adjustment of injector pulse width to compensate for altered operating parameters. The control module uses fuel trim data to determine if the vehicle will pass an emission test.

Minor fuel trim adjustments are normal with part wear. However, if the control module determines the vehicle might fail an emission test from fuel trim data, it will trip a trouble code to warn the driver and technician.

Injector noid light test

A *noid light* is a special test light that is used to check electronic fuel injector feed circuits, Fig. 26-6A. Different noid lights are made to fit wiring harnesses from each auto manufacturer. Usually the make of vehicle the noid light will fit is printed on the tool.

A

B

Fig. 26-6. A—Noid lights are designed to check for normal current pulse being sent to each injector. Correct noid light must be used to prevent wiring connector damage. B—To use a noid test light, disconnect harness from injector. To avoid damage, release locking mechanism on connector. Do not force it off. Install noid light into injector connector. Start engine. Noid light should flash on and off showing electrical pulses for injector. If not, check wiring, connections, and control unit. (OTC)

To use a noid light, disconnect the wiring harness from the fuel injector. Make sure you release the connector properly to prevent part damage. Most harness connectors use a positive lock to keep the wiring from vibrating loose. Fit the correct noid light into the injector harness connector, Fig. 26-6B.

Start the engine and check the light. If the noid light flashes, you know that power is reaching the injector from the control module. If the noid light does *not* flash, something is keeping current from reaching the injector. You could have an open in the wiring, a bad connection, open injector resistors, or control module troubles.

Repeat the noid light test on any injector that is not operating. Your stethoscope will quickly tell you which injector is "dead" and not clicking.

Refer to a wiring diagram when solving complex fuel injection electrical problems. The diagram will show all electrical connections and components that can upset the function of the injection system.

Caution! Some EFI multi-point systems use dropping resistors before the injectors. The resistors lower the supply voltage to the injectors. Do *not* connect direct battery voltage to this type of injector or coil damage may occur.

EFI testers

Early EFI systems may not have on-board diagnostics. An EFI tester can sometimes be used to locate system troubles in these systems. The tester, also called an EFI analyzer, is connected to the wiring harness of the system. See Fig. 26-7.

An *EFI tester* uses indicator lights and, in some cases, a digital meter (volt-ohmmeter-ammeter) to check system operation. The technician refers to the instructions provided with the tester and uses indicator light action to make various tests.

EFI testers are usually vehicle specific. Most testers are only designed to test one make of vehicle. They are often used in large new car dealerships.

An *injector balance test* involves the use of a fuel injector tester to measure the amount of fuel flowing through each injector. This is a common test performed on modern multi-point, electronic fuel injection systems. It will tell you if any injectors are clogged or not opening fully.

Instead of the control module, the tester feeds current to the injector coil to make it open for a controlled time span.

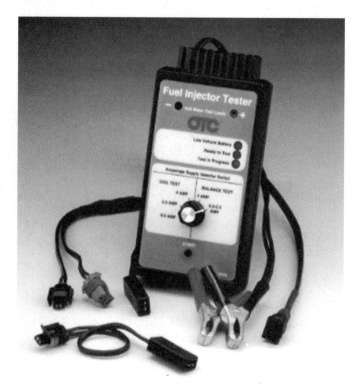

Fig. 26-7. This is an injector flow balance tester. It can find clogged or partially failed fuel injectors. (OTC)

To perform an injector balance test, connect a pressure gauge to the test fitting on the fuel rail. Make sure all fittings are tight and not leaking. Close off the valve for measuring fuel volume if provided on the fuel gauge assembly. Connect the balance tester to the injector in question. See Fig. 26-8.

Turn the ignition key on to pressurize the system. Then, turn the ignition key back off. Press the injector balance tester button while watching the pressure gauge drop. Record your pressure drop reading. Repeat this test on the other fuel injectors. This will allow you to measure how much fuel each injector is feeding into the engine when energized.

If one of the injectors shows a relatively low pressure drop, it is not injecting as much fuel as the others. That injector could be clogged or worn. If an injector shows a relatively high pressure drop, it could be sticking open and not closing properly.

INJECTOR PROBLEMS

A *bad injector* can cause a wide range of problems: rough idle, hard starting, poor fuel economy, engine miss. It is very important that each fuel injector provide the correct fuel spray pattern.

A *leaking injector* richens the fuel mixture by allowing extra fuel to drip from the closed injector valve. The injector valve may be worn or dirty, or the return spring may be weak or broken.

A *dirty injector* can also restrict fuel flow and make the air-fuel ratio too lean. If foreign matter collects in the valve, a poor spray pattern and inadequate fuel delivery can result.

An *inoperative injector* normally has shorted or opened coil windings. Current is reaching the injector, but since the coil is bad, a magnetic field cannot form and open the injector valve.

A *continuous injector* that does not use a solenoid will usually operate, but it may have other problems. It may have a poor spray pattern or weak spring (incorrect opening pressure).

SERVICING EFI MULTI-POINT INJECTORS

To quickly make sure an EFI injector is opening and closing, place a *stethoscope* (listening device) against the injector. A clicking sound means the injector is opening and closing. If you do *not* hear a clicking sound, the injector is not working. The injector solenoid, wiring harness, or control module control circuit may be bad. Repeat this check on each injector.

With the engine off, you can check the condition of the coils on the inoperative injector. Use an ohmmeter to measure the resistance across the injector coil and to check for shorts to ground. If the coil is open (infinite resistance) or shorted (zero resistance to ground), replace the injector. Special injector coil testers are also available.

If the injector tests good, you may need to check the wiring going to that injector. Following the service manual instructions, check the supply voltage to the inoperative injector. You may also need to measure the resistance in the circuit between the injector solenoid and the control module. A high resistance would indicate a frayed wire, broken wire, or poor electrical connection.

Fig. 26-9 shows how to use an injector tester. It fires each injector for a specific time span. Then, you can read the pressure gauge to make sure each injector is flowing the right amount of fuel (correct or same pressure drop).

Replacing multi-point injectors

A multi-point fuel injector is easy to replace. After bleeding off fuel system pressure, simply remove the hose from the injector and fuel rail. Unplug the electrical connection and remove any fasteners holding the injector. Pull the injector out of the engine. In some cases, the fuel rail and the injectors must be removed as an assembly.

Inspect the boot and other rubber parts closely. Some manufacturers suggest that you replace the boot, seals, and hose if the injector is removed for service.

Install the new or serviced injector in the reverse order of removal. Refer to a shop manual for details.

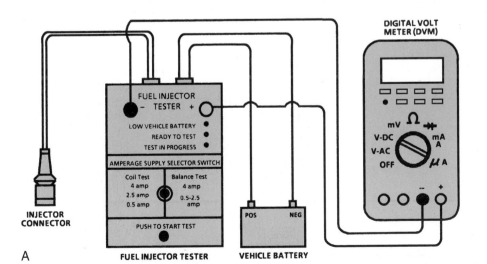

Fig. 26-8. This is setup for doing injector coil or winding test. Engine and injectors must be a prescribed temperature during test. A—Connect tester to injector and to battery. Connect voltmeter to tester. Trigger tester to fire injector and take the lowest voltage reading produced. B—Compare voltage readings for each injector. They must all be within specs. Note how injector number 5 failed the coil test. (Chevrolet)

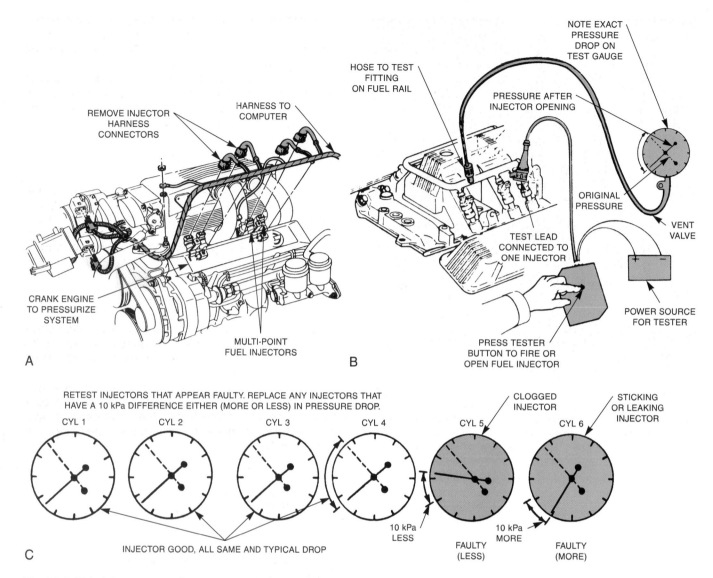

Fig. 26-9. This injector tester fires each injector for a specific time span. Then, you can read the pressure gauge to make sure each injector is flowing the right amount of fuel. Each injector should show same or correct pressure drop. If pressure drop is too low, not enough fuel is flowing through clogged or faulty injector. If pressure drop is too high, injector may be leaking or sticking open. (Chevrolet)

TESTING IDLE SPEED CONTROL MOTOR

A *bad idle speed control motor* may not be able to maintain the correct engine idle speed. Engine idle speed may be too low or too high for conditions. The servo motor could have shorted windings, open windings, bad internal parts, or other problems.

To check an idle speed motor, jump battery voltage to specific terminals on the servo motor. This should make the idle speed motor plunger retract and extend as the connections are reversed. A faulty motor will usually not function.

If the idle speed motor works when jumped to battery voltage, check wiring leading to motor. The wiring harness could have an open or a short. A control module or relay problem could also prevent motor operation.

Idle air control valve service

A *bad idle air control valve* will upset engine idle speed like a bad idle speed motor. It uses solenoid action to open and close an air passage bypassing the throttle plates. In this way, it can increase or decrease engine idle rpm. If the idle air control valve fails, engine rpm will be constant and may not increase with a cold engine or decrease as the engine warms to operating temperature.

To check the idle air control valve, jump battery voltage to the windings. This should trigger the solenoid and change engine speed. If the engine speed does not change, check for blockage in the passage at the idle air control valve before replacing the unit. An ohmmeter may also be recommended to check the windings.

Idle motor tester

An *idle air control motor tester* energizes the solenoid or servo motor to check its affect on engine idle speed. See Fig. 26-10. Disconnect the wiring going to the idle air motor. Connect the tester harness to the motor.

As you press the up arrow on the tester, engine idle

Fig. 26-10. Idle air control motor tester will quickly determine if motor is capable of altering engine idle speed. Install tool on idle air control motor connector and idle engine. Pushing buttons should let you increase and decrease engine idle speed. If not, check for passage restrictions or failed motor.

speed should increase. As you press the down arrow, engine idle speed should decrease. If engine idle speed does not change, you may have a bad idle air control motor, clogged passage, or bad vacuum leak.

If the tester shows a functioning idle air control motor, check that the control module is sending the right amount of voltage to the motor. You could have an open in the wiring or a control module problem. Refer to Fig. 26-11.

FUEL SYSTEM WIRING DIAGRAMS

When you have difficulty finding and correcting fuel system problems, refer to the service manual wiring diagrams. They will show all the components in the circuit that could be causing the symptoms, Fig. 26-12. The service manual will also give detailed directions for finding problems.

FUEL TANK SENDING UNIT SERVICE

A *faulty fuel tank sending unit* can cause inaccurate fuel gauge readings. Usually, the variable resistor in the sending unit fails. However, the fuel gauge or the gauge circuit may be at fault.

Before condemning the sending unit, test the fuel gauge. Fig. 26-13 shows a fuel gauge tester. It is connected to the wire going to the fuel tank sending unit. When the tester is set on *full*, for example, the fuel gauge should read *full*.

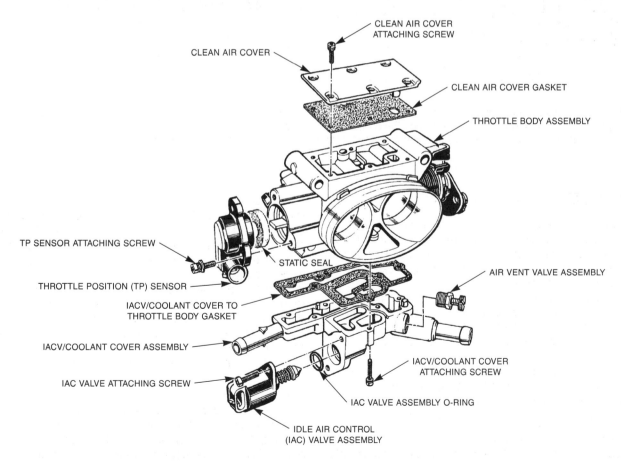

Fig. 26-11. Note how throttle position sensor and idle air control valve assembly mount in this throttle body.   (Chevrolet)

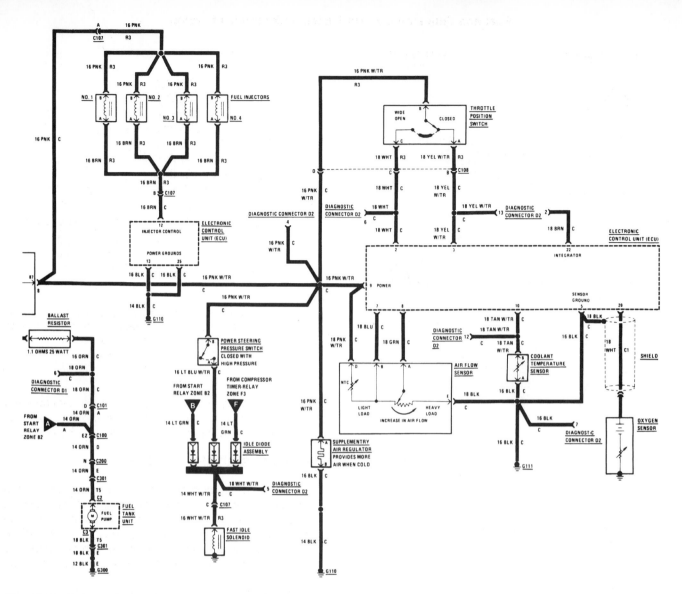

Fig. 26-12. Always refer to wiring diagram of fuel injection system when in doubt. It will give wire color codes, show wiring routing, and help you trace to problem source.   (Renault)

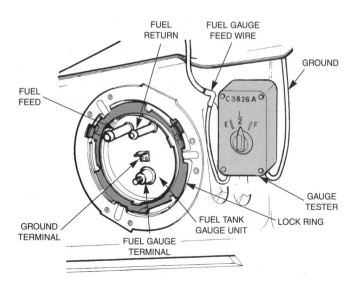

Fig. 26-13. Special tester will quickly check condition of fuel gauge and circuit. If circuit and gauge are working well, problem may be in tank sending unit. Note how sending unit is held in fuel tank by lock ring.   (Chrysler)

If the gauge does not function, either the gauge or the gauge circuit is faulty. If the fuel gauge begins to work with the tester in place, the tank sending unit is bad.

If your tests indicate an inoperative tank sending unit, the unit must be removed for further testing. After draining the fuel tank, unscrew the cam lock holding the sending unit in the tank. If you do not have a special cam tool, use a drift punch and light hammer blows to rotate the lock tabs. Lift the unit out of the tank.

With the sending unit removed, measure its resistance with an ohmmeter, Fig. 26-14. If the resistance is not within the factory specifications, install a new sending unit.

Also, check the float for leakage. Shake the float next to your ear. If you can hear liquid splashing, replace the float. If the tank unit resistance is correct, check the tank ground. A poor ground could prevent operation.

FUEL PUMP SERVICE

Fuel pump problems include low fuel pressure, inadequate fuel flow, abnormal pump noise, fuel leakage from the pump. Both mechanical and electric fuel pumps can fail after prolonged operation.

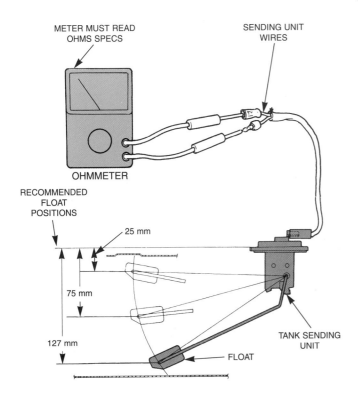

Fig. 26-14. Ohmmeter can be used to check condition of tank sending unit. Ohms should be within specs with float in prescribed positions. (Honda)

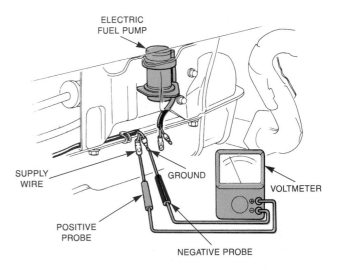

Fig. 26-15. Before condemning an electric fuel pump, make sure circuit is in good condition. Measure amount of voltage being supplied to pump and compare to specs. If voltage is low, repair circuit. (Honda)

Low fuel pump pressure can be caused by worn pump bearings, high resistance in the electric pump circuit, leaking check valves, or physical wear of moving parts. Low fuel pump pressure can make the engine starve for fuel at higher engine speeds.

High fuel pump pressure, which is more frequent with electric pumps, indicates an inoperative pressure relief valve. If the relief valve fails to open, both pressure and volume can be above normal. A faulty fuel pressure regulator can also cause high fuel pressure. This can produce a rich fuel mixture or even flood the engine.

Most electric fuel pumps make some noise (buzz or whirl sound) when running. Only when the pump noise is abnormally loud should an electric fuel pump be considered faulty. A clogged tank strainer can also cause excessive pump noise. Pump speed can increase because fuel is not entering the pump properly.

Electric fuel pump circuit tests

Many electric fuel pump problems are caused by electrical circuit problems. Broken wires, bad relays, shorts, blown fuses, computer malfunctions, and other troubles can affect electric fuel pump operation.

If an electric fuel pump does not pass its pressure or volume tests, measure the amount of voltage being fed to the pump motor. Look at Fig. 26-15. If supply voltage is low, there is a problem in the electrical circuit to the pump.

When circuit problems must be found, use the service manual and your knowledge of basic electrical testing procedures. Generally, test the circuit at various points until the source of the trouble is found.

There are only a few components and connections that could upset pump operation. Make sure to check the electric fuel pump relay if power is not reaching the pump.

FUEL PUMP SHUTOFF CIRCUITS

An *inertia switch* can be used to block current flow to the electrical fuel pump after a severe impact or collision. It is a safety device that can prevent a serious fire after an auto accident. The inertia switch is usually located in the trunk or near the electric fuel pump. After a collision, you must press a button on the inertia switch before the electric pump will function again.

An *oil pressure switch* can be used to shut off the electric fuel pump if engine oil pressure drops too low. Its circuit is designed to protect the engine from major mechanical damage caused by insufficient lubrication.

EMISSION MAINTENANCE REMINDER

The *emission maintenance reminder* is a circuit that automatically turns on a dash light to indicate the need for emission control system service. Some vehicles use a mechanical flag that is located inside the speedometer cluster.

After the prescribed adjustments and repairs are done, you must deactivate the emission maintenance light. There are numerous methods to turn this light off. You might have to remove the speedometer cluster in order to move a small lever hidden in the dash, jump across a specific connector, etc. Since there are so many variations, refer to the service manual for specific instructions. It will give the exact location and methods for deactivating the emission maintenance reminder light.

EMISSION CONTROL SYSTEM ELECTRONICS SERVICE

Computer-controlled emission control systems can cause a wide range of problems. The computer may control the EGR valve, the evaporative emission purge valve, and other components. A defect in any of these parts affects the operation of the computer system and can increase emissions.

OBD II computers have the ability to monitor many functions that affect emissions. Most OBD II systems will monitor catalytic converter efficiency, engine misfire, O_2 sensor output, EGR valve action, fuel injection system performance, air injection system operation, and evaporative emissions system operation.

If any problems are detected, the ECM will turn on the malfunction indicator light (MIL) to warn the driver and technician of a problem. If the problem could damage the catalytic converter, the ECM flashes the MIL once per second while the problem is occurring.

OBD II evaporative emissions system monitoring

Evaporative emissions system monitoring checks components for leakage and restrictions that could increase emissions. The computer energizes the solenoid valves to seal the system. This allows the computer to detect leaks or blockages in hoses and components. If the system does not pressurize and depressurize normally, the computer sets a trouble code to warn of an evaporative emissions system problem.

OBD II EGR monitoring

EGR monitoring is done when the computer turns the EGR off while checking O_2 sensor readings. Changes in EGR valve opening and closing affect the air-fuel mixture and resulting O_2 sensor readings. If changes in the EGR valve do not affect O_2 sensor readings normally, a trouble code is produced.

Air injection system monitoring

Air injection system monitoring uses data from the rear O_2 sensor to determine if the right amount of air (oxygen) is being injected into the engine's exhaust stream. A low amount of air (oxygen) would trip a trouble code.

OBD II oxygen sensor monitoring

Oxygen sensor monitoring is done to keep the normally closed loop mode of operation efficient. It usually checks the upstream oxygen sensor for abnormal voltage, slow response times, and similar problems. It also checks the downstream oxygen sensor for normal voltage output. If operating values are not within specified parameters, a trouble code is produced.

Note that oxygen sensors in OBD II systems are heated to speed warm-up. Quicker oxygen sensor warm-up allows the computer system to go from open loop (startup or cold mode) to closed loop (full operating temperature mode) in less time. In closed loop, the computer system makes its own adjustments based on feedback information for sensors.

The oxygen sensor heater monitor checks the action of the heating element in the sensor. It does this by rapidly turning the heating element on and off while checking its response. If the computer detects an abnormal heater response, it trips a trouble code.

Catalyst monitor

OBD II systems use at least two oxygen sensors—one before the catalytic converter and one after it. The *catalyst monitor,* also called the rear oxygen sensor or the secondary oxygen sensor, is located after the catalytic converter. It checks the oxygen content of the exhaust gases after exiting the catalytic converter to determine if the catalyst elements are working.

If the signal from the catalyst monitor becomes too similar to the engine-mounted oxygen sensor signal(s), the catalytic converter is not cleaning the exhaust gases as it should. The ECM would then turn on the malfunction indicator light to warn the driver and technician of a possible catalytic converter failure.

Scanning emission systems

Emission system scanning involves using a scan tool to check the condition of monitored parts of the various emission control systems.

Modern vehicles have elaborate on-board diagnostic systems that will find troubles in almost all emission-related components.

Explained in detail in Chapter 22, a scan tool will help you troubleshoot late-model vehicles quickly and easily. Connect the scan tool to the vehicle's diagnostic connector. If needed, install the correct scan tool cartridge for the specific make vehicle and connect power to the tool. First check for stored trouble codes and retrieve any scan tool information that might help fix the problem. The scan tool readout will tell you where the faults are located.

For example, if the scan tool says there is a constant low voltage signal from the catalyst monitor, you would know where to start your tests but would not know exactly what is wrong. A trouble code from the catalyst monitor could be due to the sensor itself, its wiring, or a defective catalytic converter. Keep this in mind when scanning a vehicle's computer system. Think about how the system is supposed to operate and determine whether other components could cause the abnormal sensor signal.

INSPECTING EMISSION CONTROL SYSTEMS

Using information from the scan tool, you must find the source of the problem. Start out by inspecting all engine vacuum hoses and wires. A leaking vacuum hose or disconnected wire could trip a trouble code and upset the operation of the engine and emission control systems.

A section of vacuum hose can be used as a listening device. Place one end of the hose next to your ear. Move the other end of the hose around the engine compartment, along vacuum hoses and connections. When the hose nears a vacuum leak, you will be able to hear a loud hissing sound. You can also remove the metal probe from your stethoscope instead of using a piece of vacuum hose.

Look for evidence of disconnected wires, oil leaks onto the oxygen sensor, extremely dirty engine oil, and blowby, all of which could trip a trouble code. Also, inspect the air cleaner for clogging. Check that the air pump belt is properly adjusted. Try to locate any obvious problems. If nothing is found during your inspection, each system should be checked and tested.

EMISSIONS TESTING PROGRAMS

Many states have some form of *emissions testing program.* These programs, often referred to as *inspection and maintenance programs,* generally involve taking exhaust gas readings as a vehicle's engine operates at idle and at a set rpm. They may also involve checking the vehicle for the presence of a catalytic converter and a fuel inlet restrictor.

Exact test procedures vary from state to state. However, the federal government has passed laws that require stricter emission testing of vehicles in areas with air pollution problems. These tests are referred to as IM 240.

For detailed information on using an exhaust gas analyzer, refer to Chapter 29, Advanced Diagnostics.

IM 240

The *IM 240* emissions test requires that the vehicle be operated on a dynamometer at speeds of up to 55 mph (89 kmh) for 240 seconds while exhaust gas emissions are measured. Two additional tests—the evaporative emissions system purge test and the evaporative emissions system pressure test—are required in some areas.

The EPA estimates that approximately 25% of the vehicles tested will fail their emission tests. Repair costs to customers to try to pass the emission tests is capped at a fixed amount in most areas, usually between $100 and $500. If the capped repair amount is spent and the vehicle still does not pass, the owner will receive a waiver on further testing for a specified period of time. The emission testing facilities provide a printout of the emission fail records to help technicians repair the problem(s).

VACUUM SOLENOID SERVICE

Various vacuum solenoids are used to interface emission system electronics with the devices that operate off engine vacuum. They can be used in almost all emission control systems.

When trying to find problems, you should refer to a *vacuum hose diagram,* which shows the routing of all vacuum hoses. Just as a wiring diagram helps you trace circuit problems, a vacuum hose diagram will give useful information on finding incorrectly routed hoses, leaking or restricted hoses, and bad vacuum components.

When troubleshooting vacuum solenoids, check for hard, brittle hoses that can leak and prevent normal operation of parts, Fig. 26-16. Next, check for voltage going to the vacuum solenoid. Connect a voltmeter to the solenoid terminals and start the engine. Make sure you are getting voltage to the unit when needed, Fig. 26-17.

You may also need to check that the solenoid valve opens and blocks vacuum as designed. Connect a vacuum gauge or hand pump to the vacuum connections on the unit. When the solenoid is energized and de-energized, it should switch vacuum on and off.

You can also connect a remote source of voltage to a vacuum solenoid to check its operation. When voltage is connected to the solenoid, it would switch vacuum on or off.

EVAPORATIVE EMISSIONS CONTROL SYSTEM SERVICE

A faulty evaporative emissions control system can cause fuel odors, fuel leakage, fuel tank collapse (vacuum buildup), excess pressure in the fuel tank, or rough engine idle. These problems usually stem from a

Fig. 26-16. Solenoid-vacuum valves are common source of trouble in emission control systems. Use voltmeter to check for voltage to solenoid. If you are not getting control voltage, trace back through wiring to ECM. (Fluke)

Fig. 26-17. Vacuum pump-gauge assembly will check that solenoid is turning vacuum source on and off as designed.

defective fuel tank pressure-vacuum cap, leaking charcoal canister valves, deteriorated hoses, or incorrect hose routing.

Evaporative emissions system purge test

The *evaporative emissions system purge test* measures the flow of fuel vapors into the engine. It is performed during the IM 240 test. A flow meter transducer is installed into the system purge line between the charcoal canister and the engine intake manifold fitting. A personnel computer connects to the flow transducer to analyze data. The computer can then detect if there is adequate purge flow to remove fumes from the canister to burn them in the engine.

Evaporative emissions system pressure test

An *evaporative emissions system pressure test* checks the system for leaks into the atmosphere. It is performed during the IM 240 test. Pressure test equipment is connected to the evaporative emission system's vapor vent line. A computer then meters low pressure nitrogen into the system (evaporative emission system, fuel lines, fuel tank, filler neck, etc.).

When about 0.5 psi (3.4 kPa) pressure is reached, the computer closes off the system and checks for a pressure drop for two minutes. If pressure remains above recommendations, the evaporative emission system passes the pressure test. If pressure drops too much, repairs would be needed to fix the leakage.

Evaporative emissions control system maintenance and repair

Maintenance on an evaporative emissions control system typically involves cleaning or replacing the filter in the charcoal canister. Service intervals for the canister filter vary. However, if the vehicle is operated on dusty roads, clean or replace the filter more often.

Also inspect the condition of the fuel tank filler cap. Make sure the cap is installed properly and the seals are in good condition. Special testers are available for checking the opening of the pressure and vacuum valves in the cap. The cap should be tested when excessive pressure or vacuum problems are noticed.

All hoses in the evaporative emissions system should also be inspected for signs of deterioration (hardening, softening, cracking). When replacing a hose, make sure you use special fuel-resistant hose. Vacuum hose can be quickly ruined by fuel vapors.

Use a hand vacuum pump to test the charcoal canister vacuum purge solenoids for diaphragm leakage. If a diaphragm will not hold a vacuum, it is ruptured and must be replaced. You can also use the vacuum gauge to check for a vacuum supply to any canister vacuum solenoid. See Fig. 26-17.

EGR SYSTEM ELECTRONIC SERVICE

EGR system malfunctions can cause engine stalling at idle, rough idle, detonation, and poor fuel economy. If the EGR valve sticks open, it will cause a lean air-fuel mixture. The engine will run rough at idle or stall. If the EGR fails to open or the exhaust passage is clogged, higher combustion temperatures can cause abnormal combustion (detonation) and knocking.

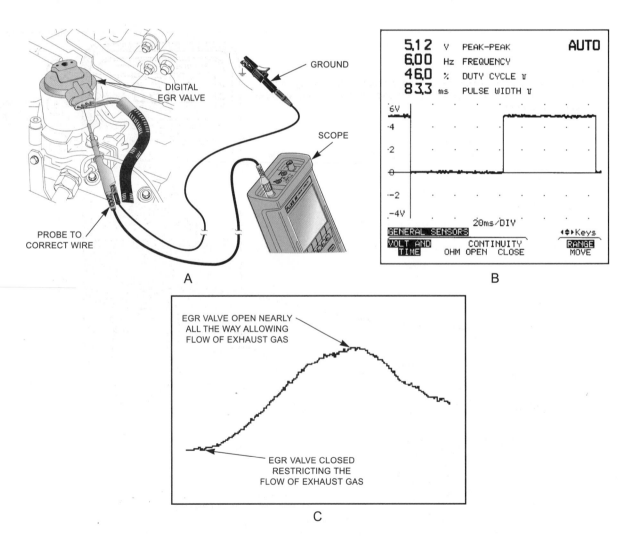

Fig. 26-18. Small scope can be used to check digital EGR valves and their ECM control circuit. A—Connect scope to ground and probe through connector. Service manual wiring diagram will tell you which wires to probe. B—Scope should show normal signal going to EGR valve from ECM. C—Scope can also be connected to read signal from EGR sensor. (Fluke)

Caution! It is fairly common for small rocks to fly into the engine compartments of four-wheel-drive vehicles during off-road driving. If the right size, these small rocks may become lodged in the EGR valve and cause it to stick open. The engine will have a low idle, run rough, or stall. This may or may not trip a trouble code.

EGR system testing (electronic type)

Most problems with late-model electronic, or digital, EGR valves will trip a trouble code. Your scan tool will then isolate most problems quickly and easily. EGR valves that provide electrical data to a computer control system require special testing procedures. Refer to a shop manual covering the specific system. Component damage could result from using an incorrect testing method.

To pinpoint test a digital EGR valve, connect a scope to the wires going to the valve. The scope's waveform will measure the voltage applied to the EGR from the ECM and it will also check the condition of the EGR windings. See Fig. 26-18. If you do not have voltage to the EGR, check for a bad electrical connection. You could also have an ECM problem in the control circuit to the EGR valve.

OXYGEN SENSOR SERVICE

A bad primary oxygen sensor will affect engine performance and emissions. If it does not work properly, fuel metering will be too lean or rich. A bad secondary oxygen sensor may not detect an inoperative catalytic converter.

A lazy O_2 sensor will not alter its output signal fast enough to maintain an efficient air-fuel ratio. The sensor will be slow to change its voltage or resistance with a change in exhaust content.

A dead O_2 sensor has little or no resistance or voltage output change. Even when the exhaust content changes, the signal remains almost constant.

Most O_2 sensor problems will trip a trouble code with OBD II systems. However, there are times when several components will be close to, but not out of, their operating parameters. This can reduce efficiency while not tripping a trouble code. Even if the scanner shows a problem with the O_2 sensor, pinpoint tests will also be needed to verify the source of the trouble.

If the scan tool readout shows O_2 sensor circuit voltage is abnormal, you might want to measure actual O_2 sensor output voltage or resistance with a multimeter. This is shown in Fig. 26-19.

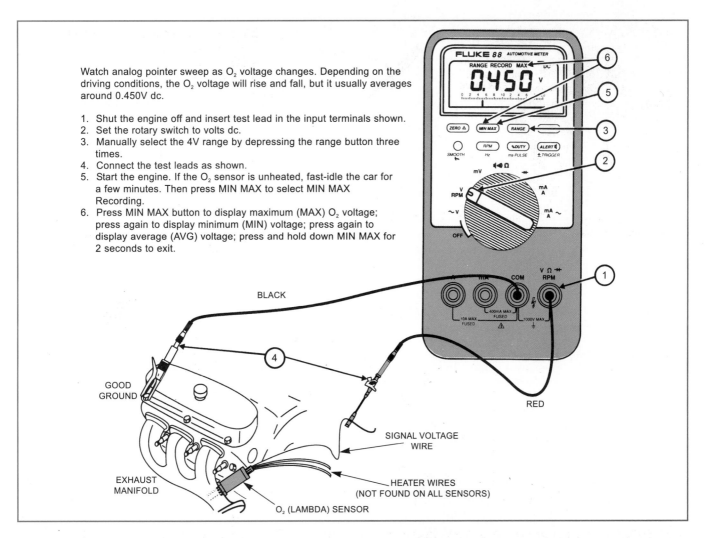

Watch analog pointer sweep as O_2 voltage changes. Depending on the driving conditions, the O_2 voltage will rise and fall, but it usually averages around 0.450V dc.

1. Shut the engine off and insert test lead in the input terminals shown.
2. Set the rotary switch to volts dc.
3. Manually select the 4V range by depressing the range button three times.
4. Connect the test leads as shown.
5. Start the engine. If the O_2 sensor is unheated, fast-idle the car for a few minutes. Then press MIN MAX to select MIN MAX Recording.
6. Press MIN MAX button to display maximum (MAX) O_2 voltage; press again to display minimum (MIN) voltage; press again to display average (AVG) voltage; press and hold down MIN MAX for 2 seconds to exit.

Fig. 26-19. If scanner shows possible problem with oxygen sensor, you might want to use multimeter to check actual output. Read through detailed procedures. (Fluke)

Oxygen sensors should be replaced at periodic intervals. After prolonged service, they become coated or fouled with exhaust by-products. As this happens, fuel economy and emissions will be adversely affected. If gas mileage is 10 to 15 percent lower than normal, suspect the oxygen sensor of slow response. One- and two-wire sensors should be replaced at about 60,000 miles. Heated three-wire oxygen sensors should be replaced at about 100,000 miles. For detailed information on oxygen sensor service, refer to Chapter 22.

Oxygen sensor signal generator

An oxygen sensor signal generator is a tool used to send a false 200 to 700 mV signal to the computer for testing purposes. You can then alter air-fuel ratio (simulate vacuum leak for example) and perform other testing functions. Since the computer thinks it is closed loop, you can do tests without the computer tripping a trouble code or trying to compensate for your intentional modifications of engine operating conditions.

SUMMARY

Government studies have shown that emissions from passenger vehicles have dropped over 90% in the last 15 years.

Today's fuel injection systems are primarily controlled electronically. Most electronic fuel injection systems have on-board diagnostic abilities which means the vehicle's computer can detect and record possible faults. With late model on-board diagnostic (OBD II) systems, the vehicle's computer will record a large number of potential problems in its memory.

A scan tool will find and display many problems related to an electronic fuel injection system. A noid light is a special test light for checking electronic fuel injector feed circuit. An EFI tester uses indicator lights and sometimes a digital meter (volt-ohmmeter-ammeter) to check system operation.

To quickly make sure an injector is opening and closing, place a stethoscope (listening device) against the injector. To check an idle speed motor, jump battery voltage to specific terminals on the servo motor.

Low fuel pump pressure can be caused by a worn dragging pump bearings, high resistance in electric pump circuit, leaking check valves, or physical wear of moving parts. After a collision, you must press a button on the inertia switch before the electric pump will function again.

Most OBD II systems will monitor catalytic converter efficiency, engine misfire, O_2 sensor output, EGR valve action, fuel injection system performance, air injection system operation, and fuel evaporative system functioning.

The Federal Government has passed laws that require stricter emission testing of vehicles in areas with air pollution problems. Called the I/M 240 Test, this type emission test has the vehicle go up to speeds of 55 mph (89 kmh) on a dynamometer for 240 seconds while measuring exhaust gas emissions.

All hoses in the evaporation system should also be inspected for signs of deterioration (hardening, softening, cracking).

If the scan tool readout shows O_2 sensor voltage is abnormal, you might want to measure actual O_2 sensor output voltage or resistance with a multimeter. Oxygen sensor output voltage should cycle up and down from about .4 volts (400 mV) to .7 volts (700 mV). Do NOT touch the oxygen sensor element with anything (water, solvents, etc.). Oxygen sensors should be replaced at periodic intervals.

KNOW THESE TERMS

Trouble code, Malfunction indicator light, Scan tool, Fuel system monitoring, Short term fuel trim, Long term fuel trim, Noid light, EFI tester, Injector balance test, Leaking injector, Dirty injector, Stethoscope, Idle air control motor tester, Inertia switch, Oil pressure switch, Emission maintenance reminder, Emission system scanning, Emissions testing program, Inspection and maintenance programs, IM 240, Vacuum hose diagram, Evaporative emissions system purge test, Evaporative emissions system pressure test.

REVIEW QUESTIONS - CHAPTER 26

1. Government studies have shown the _____ from passenger vehicles have dropped over 90% in the last 15 years.
2. Today's fuel injection systems are primarily controlled electronically. True or false?
3. Why should you usually scan for trouble codes when starting problem diagnosis?
4. What is the main purpose of the upstream or first oxygen sensor?
5. Describe minor fuel trim.
6. How could you check the action of an idle speed motor with jumper wires?
7. List some common electric fuel pump circuit problems.
8. Summarize OBD II evaporative system monitoring.
9. How does OBD II air injection system monitoring work?
10. Explain the IM 240 test.

ASE CERTIFICATION–TYPE QUESTIONS

1. Technician A says short term fuel trim is the temporary adjustment of injector pulse width. Technician B says minor fuel trim adjustment is normal with part wear. Who is right?
   (A) A only.   (C) Both A and B.
   (B) B only.   (D) Neither A nor B.
2. An engine is running roughly at idle. The scan tool shows a problem with a fuel injector. Technician A checks the operation of the injector by listening to it with a stethoscope and does not hear it opening and closing. Technician B suggests testing the injector circuit with a noid light before replacing the injector. Who is right?
   (A) A only.   (C) Both A and B.
   (B) B only.   (D) Neither A nor B.
3. A customer complains of inaccurate fuel gauge readings. Technician A says the fuel tank sending unit could be at fault. Technician B says the fuel gauge circuit could be at fault. Who is right?
   (A) A only.   (C) Both A and B.
   (B) B only.   (D) Neither A nor B.

4. Low fuel system pressure can be caused by all of the following *except:*
   - (A) worn fuel pump bearings.
   - (B) a pressure relief valve that fails to open.
   - (C) high resistance in the fuel pump circuit.
   - (D) leaking check valves.

5. Multimeter tests show that no voltage is reaching the electric fuel pump when the key is turned on and the engine is cranked for starting. Technician A says to check the inertia switch. Technician B says to check engine oil pressure or the low oil pressure switch circuit. Who is right?
   - (A) A only.
   - (B) B only.
   - (C) Both A and B.
   - (D) Neither A nor B.

6. During OBD II EGR monitoring, the computer turns the EGR valve off while checking:
   - (A) engine coolant temperature.
   - (B) oxygen sensor voltage.
   - (C) exhaust gas temperature.
   - (D) manifold pressure.

7. Technician A says a catalyst monitor is located after the catalytic converter. Technician B says the signal from the catalyst monitor should be similar to that from the primary oxygen sensor. Who is right?
   - (A) A only.
   - (B) B only.
   - (C) Both A and B.
   - (D) Neither A nor B.

8. Technician A says that EGR system malfunctions can cause engine stalling at idle, rough engine idling, detonation (knock), and poor fuel economy. Technician B says that if the EGR valve sticks open, it will act as a large vacuum leak, causing a lean air-fuel mixture. The engine will run rough at idle or stall. Who is right?
   - (A) A only.
   - (B) B only.
   - (C) Both A and B.
   - (D) Neither A nor B.

9. Technician A says a lazy O_2 sensor will have little or no voltage output or its resistance will not change. Technician B says that a lazy O_2 sensor will not alter its output signal fast enough to maintain an efficient air-fuel ratio. Who is right?
   - (A) A only.
   - (B) B only.
   - (C) Both A and B.
   - (D) Neither A nor B.

10. Technician A says if the scan tool readout shows O_2 sensor voltage is abnormal, you might want to measure actual O_2 sensor output voltage or resistance with a multimeter. Technician B says that you should also check the wiring leading to and from the O_2 sensor. Who is right?
    - (A) A only.
    - (B) B only.
    - (C) Both A and B.
    - (D) Neither A nor B.

This vehicle is equipped with flush-mounted, aerodynamic composite headlamps. Insert-type halogen bulbs are used in this system.   (Buick)

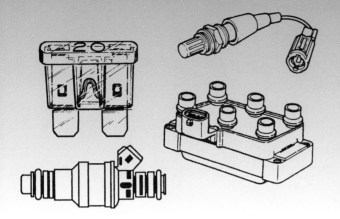

Chapter 27

Lighting System Diagnosis and Repair

After studying this chapter, you will be able to:
- Troubleshoot common lighting system problems.
- Perform basic tests on a lighting system.
- Remove and replace headlight and other bulbs.
- Aim headlights.
- Test and service light switches.
- Test and service lightbulb sockets.
- Test and replace flasher units.
- Replace a turn light switch.
- Test instrument and warning light sending units.
- Test gauges.
- Remove and replace a dash cluster.

This chapter will summarize the most important information for working on a car's lighting system. As an electrical-electronic technician, you will be required to do considerable work on a car's headlights, turnlights, instrumentation, and other lighting circuits.

As you will learn, most of the repairs on a lighting system are fairly simple. Only when you begin to diagnose and repair digital instrumentation does the work become extremely mentally challenging.

LIGHTING SYSTEM DIAGNOSIS

Lighting system diagnosis is easy if you use logical thought. Try to visualize all of the major parts of the circuit when thinking about the trouble. Then select the most likely problem source. This will save you time and effort. See Fig. 27-1.

One bulb out

If only one bulb is out, you would know that only a small portion of the circuit is affected. The bulb might be burned out, the socket connections corroded, or the socket feed-wire might be disconnected.

Start by removing the bulb. Inspect its elements. See if they are burned in half. Also, look inside the socket to see if there is corrosion on the small contacts. Replace the bulb or clean the inside of the socket if needed.

All bulbs out

If all of the bulbs in a circuit are out, you should go to the source of power. You could have a blown fuse, bad circuit breaker, relay, or similar trouble. Normally, several bulbs will NOT burn out all at once. There could be a disconnected terminal, broken wire, or bad switch. Use the basic testing methods you learned in earlier chapters to find the cause of the lack of power.

If none of the lights work, you might also suspect a burned fusible link. The small section of wire link can burn if there is a serious short in the main feed circuit. Discussed earlier, the fuse link is usually located in the engine compartment near the battery or starting motor.

Lights flicker

When lights flicker, or go on and off, you could have a loose electrical connection or a circuit breaker kicking in and out. If only one light flickers, suspect a problem near the bulb (loose bulb in socket, broken wire, loose connector, etc.). If all lights in a circuit flicker, then suspect the circuit breaker or something in the feed section of the circuit.

Try to find out if the lights only flicker under certain conditions. For example, if they only flicker when hitting a bump in the road, a loose connection would be indicated. A circuit breaker is seldom affected by road shock. If the lights only flicker with the high beams on, you would know that the problem is common to the high beam section of the circuit. There could be a short in the high beam wiring, in the dimmer switch high side, etc.

Lights dim

When lights are dim, there is a high resistance in the circuit or a low voltage supply. Again, if all lights in a circuit are dim, the problem is at the beginning, or source, of the circuit. If only one light is dim, start your tests at or near that bulb.

The most common cause of high resistance and dim bulbs is a corroded plug terminal or socket. Moisture and salt can enter the connector or socket, causing corrosion at the metal terminals. This can cause a high resistance that reduces current flow to the bulb.

Voltage drop tests will help find a high resistance. A test light can also be used to find areas of high resistance. It will be dim when connected after the area of high resistance and bright when connected before the area of high resistance.

HEADLIGHT SERVICE

Headlight service primarily involves headlamp replacement, headlamp aiming, and wiring related repairs. Today's cars use both conventional sealed beam bulbs and more modern halogen insert bulbs, Fig. 27-2.

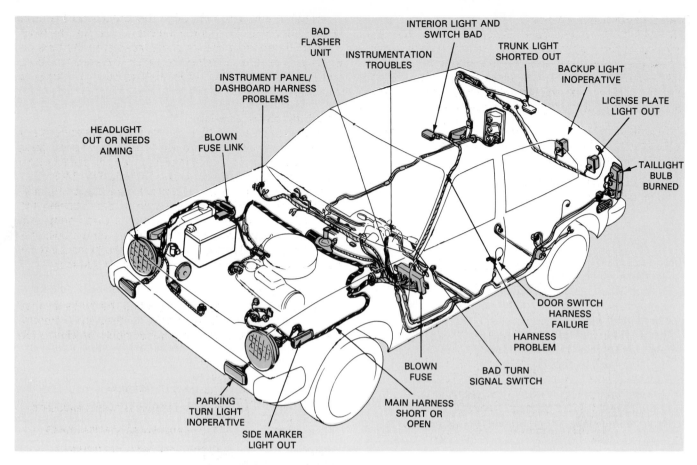

Fig. 27-1. Note types of problems that can happen in lighting system of car. (Honda)

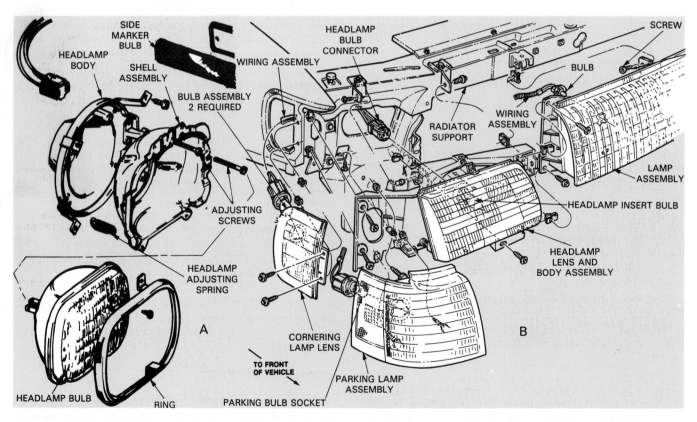

Fig. 27-2. Illustration shows headlamps, parking lamps, and side marker lamps. A—Conventional headlamps. B—Insert type headlamps.

Sealed beam replacement

To replace a *sealed beam bulb,* you must normally remove a cover or shroud that fits around the bulb. Then, remove the screws that hold the *trim ring* and bulb in its shell. Make sure you do not accidentally turn or try to remove the headlight adjustment screws. Pull the lamp out and unplug it without pulling on the wires.

Warning! Do not pull on the wires when unplugging a headlamp. This could ruin the connector and cause a time-consuming repair.

Fig. 27-3 shows the major steps for replacing a conventional headlamp.

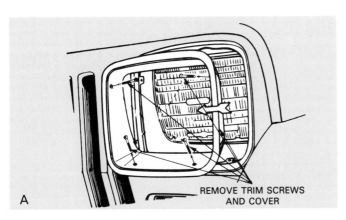

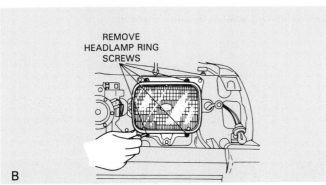

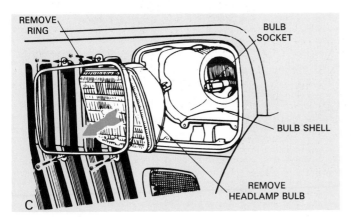

Fig. 27-3. Study basic steps for replacement of conventional sealed headlamp. A—Remove screws and cover. B—Remove trim ring screws and ring. Do not turn adjustment screws. C—Lift out lamp and carefully unplug harness connector. Do not pull on wires, only grasp plastic part of connector while wiggling and pulling.

To install the new bulb, align the prongs on the bulb with its connector. Then force the connector over the lamp prongs. Fit the lamp into its shell. Make sure the tabs on the bulb fit securely into the notches in the shell lip. Then, screw on the trim ring while making sure the lamp is seated in its shell.

Insert headlamp service

To replace an *insert type headlamp,* you must normally remove the insert from the rear of its plastic or glass housing. Access to the rear of the lamp is usually provided in the car's body structure. Refer to Fig. 27-2.

Make sure you have the correct insert bulb replacement. When handling the new bulb, avoid touching the bulb with your fingers. Handle it with a clean shop rag. This will prevent body oil from depositing on the bulb surface. The oil could reduce bulb service life by causing different rates of heat expansion on the bulb surface.

Headlamp aiming

Headlamp aiming involves adjusting the bulbs so they are pointing at a specified height and direction in front of the car. Improperly aimed headlamps could be aiming too

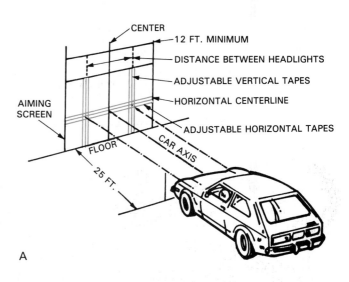

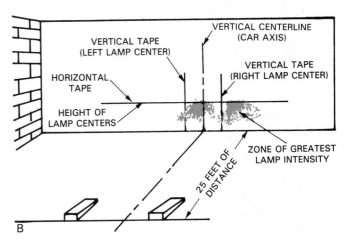

Fig. 27-4. Marking wall for aiming headlights. A—Typical distances for car and wall lines. B—Service manual description for markings. (Florida Dept. of Voc. Ed. and Chrysler)

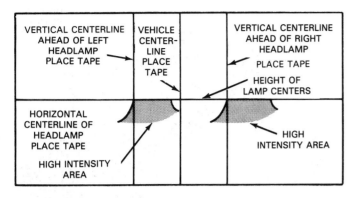

Fig. 27-5. This is a low beam pattern on wall recommended by one auto manufacturer.

low, too high, or to one side of the road. This would decrease visibility and reduce safety. Many vehicle safety inspections check headlight aiming.

There are several methods for aiming headlights. One involves drawing lines on a wall and marking a specific distance from the wall on the shop floor. The headlamps should strike the lines on the wall when parked over the floor markings. Some shops have one stall set up with lines for quick and easy headlamp aiming. See Figs. 27-4 and 27-5.

Most shops, however, use *headlamp aimers* which are devices for adjusting headlamp direction without a marked wall. Aimers can vary in design. One type is shown in Fig. 27-6.

With this design, the aimers are first adjusted for the

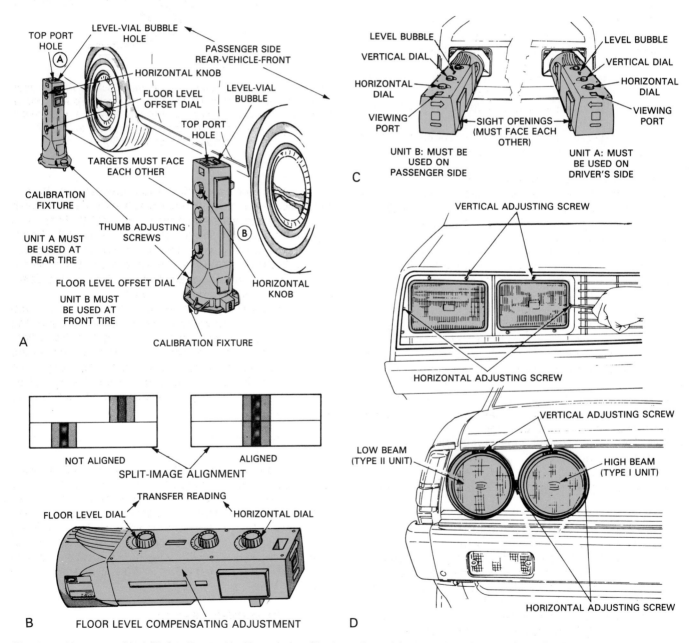

Fig. 27-6. Note use of headlight aimers. A—Aimers must first be adjusted for any slope in shop floor. B—These aimers use split image for adjustment. C—Mount aimers on headlights using suction cups. Internal leveling floats allow for up and down adjustment. Sight glass between two aimers allows for left and right adjustment. D—Note screws for up and down or left and right adjustment of headlights.

slope of the floor using leveling bubble devices. Then, suction cups are used to mount the aimers on the front of the headlamps. Alignment marks in the aimers will then tell you if and how to adjust the screws on the headlamp shells.

A *vertical aiming screw* on the top or bottom of the headlamp shell lets you move the light beam up or down. Turning it in or clockwise raises the beam.

A *horizontal aiming screw* to one side of the headlamp lets you move the light beam right or left. See Fig. 27-6D.

After turning the aiming screws, recheck the reading on the headlamp aimers or how the lamps show on the marked wall. Readjust the screws if needed.

Fig. 27-5 shows a low beam pattern recommended by one automaker. Always check the headlamps on both high and low beam and adjust them as recommended by the manufacturer.

If the aiming screws are difficult to rotate, spray them with rust penetrant. This could help prevent the screw heads or threads from stripping, requiring time-consuming screw replacement.

Note! A timesaving trick is to aim a car's headlights accurately with aimers. Then use the same car to mark a line on the shop floor and areas or circles on the wall where light intensity is greatest for high and low beams. You can then use the floor line and marks or circles on the wall to quickly align other car headlights.

Dimmer switch diagnosis and repair

A *bad dimmer switch* can be shorted or open on one or both sides. Frequently, only the low side or the high side will fail. This will make either the low beams or high beams not function properly.

An open dimmer switch will prevent current flow to the headlamp elements. A shorted dimmer will kick out the fuse or circuit breaker and the lights may flash on and off.

Fig. 27-7 shows how to use a test light to check one type of dimmer switch. First check that power is being fed to the switch when the light switch is on. If not, the light switch or feed circuit is open. Then check that power is switched back and forth to the high and low output wires as the switch is moved. If power is NOT switched, replace the dimmer switch.

Also check that the plug to the dimmer switch is not burned or loose. If the plastic connector shows signs of overheating, repair or replace the connector or its terminals. This is also true for other switch connectors.

Use the same procedure for a steering column-mounted dimmer switch. You may need to refer to a service manual to get wire color codes for probing the correct wires.

Headlamp switch diagnosis and repair

A *bad headlamp switch* can also be shorted or open preventing both headlights from working. The mechanical contacts in the switch can burn and develop high resistance or can mechanically short out. High resistance or an open is the most common problem.

Again, a test light is a quick way of checking the operation of a headlight switch. Simply check that power is switched to the various output wires as the switch knob is moved. Also check that power is being fed to the switch. If the switch is working, check any relay between the headlight switch and the bulbs.

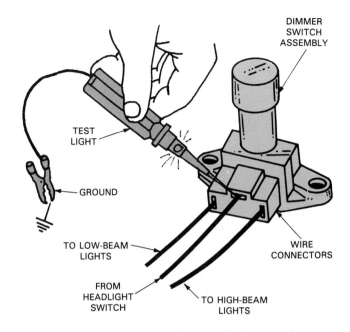

Fig. 27-7. Test light is being used to check action of older floor mounted dimmer switch. When switch is pushed down, power should be switched from one output wire to next. If not, switch is bad. Make sure power is being fed to switch. (Florida Dept. of Voc. Ed.)

Procedures for headlamp switch removal vary. With a conventional switch, you must reach up under the dash and unplug the wiring connector, Fig. 27-8. Then, you might have to push a small button on the side of the headlight switch while pulling on the switch knob. This will release the knob plunger and it will pull out. Unscrew the nut on the front of the switch and pull it out of the dash. Install the new switch in reverse order.

If the light switch mounts on the steering column, you must normally remove the plastic cover around the column. If you still need more room to get at the switch, remove the two nuts that hold the column up against the dash. This will allow the steering column to drop down and provide more clearance around the switch. See Fig. 27-9.

Refer to the factory service manual for testing information.

FOG LAMP SERVICE

Fog lamp problems include burned bulbs, switch problems, and sometimes wiring troubles. The fog lamps are usually operated by a separate fog lamp switch. This makes the circuit simple and relatively easy to diagnose.

Use basic testing methods to find problems in a fog lamp circuit. Normally the bulbs simply burn out and require replacement. Occasionally, the fog lamp switch fails and requires replacement. Fig. 27-10 shows an exploded view of a fog lamp assembly.

BULB AND SOCKET SERVICE

Numerous smaller bulbs and sockets are used throughout the car. If you know how to test and clean one, you can relate this information to other types.

If a bulb fails to work, first remove and inspect it for a

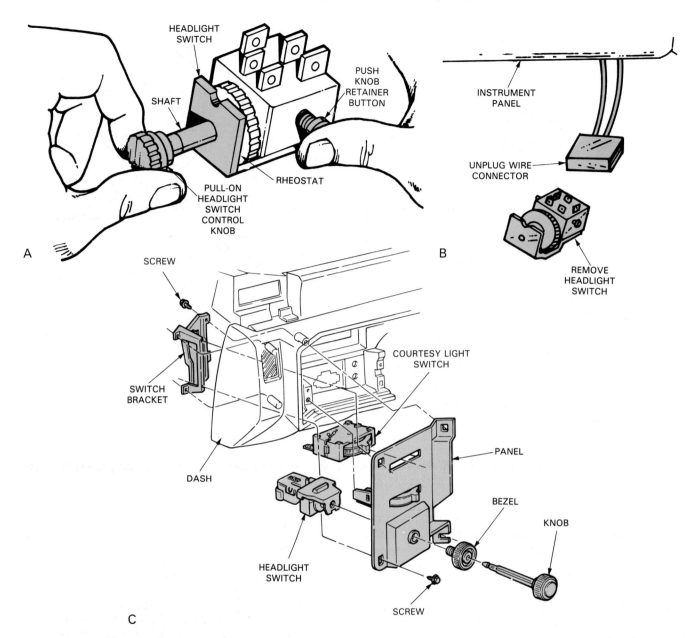

Fig. 27-8. A—Many conventional headlamp switches have a small release button for removing knob. Push button and pull on knob for removal. B—Unplug harness connector and remove retaining nut before lifting switch out of dash. C—Exploded view shows late model light switch.

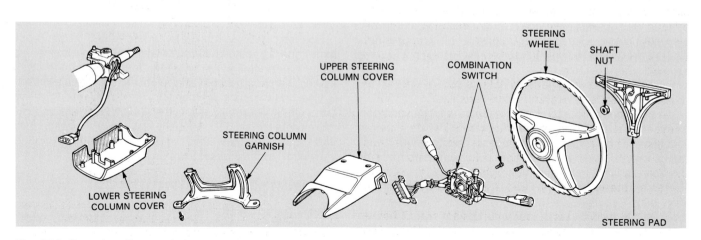

Fig. 27-9. Some headlamp switches are part of a combination switch on steering column. Removal of cover will allow access to switch. Service manual would be needed for testing. (Toyota)

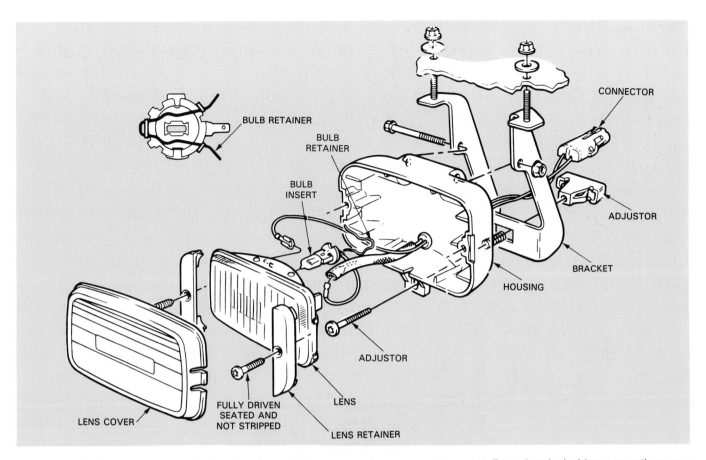

Fig. 27-10. Fog lamp circuits are simple. Usually, bulb burns out and requires replacement. Poor electrical wiring connections can also develop.   (General Motors)

burned element. The tiny wire element will often be burned in half if the bulb is blown. Also inspect the metal contacts on the bulb. If badly worn down, they may not make good contact inside the socket. Broken index lugs on the side of the bulb can also prevent a good electrical contact. See Fig. 27-11A.

Use a test light or VOM to check for power to the socket if the new bulb does NOT correct the problem. If you do NOT have power in the socket, trace for power back through the wiring, Fig. 27-11B.

When cleaning a socket, shut the circuit off. This will prevent a possible short that could blow the fuse for the circuit. Scrape off the metal contact with a small screwdriver or wire brush. Electrical contact cleaning spray will also help clean out a corroded socket. Use compressed air to blow debris out of the socket. Make sure it works properly after cleaning.

Fig. 27-12 shows several variations for getting at or removing bulbs and sockets. Some are easy to remove; some are more difficult to remove because of their location.

You should also learn the part numbers for a few bulbs. The most common automotive bulb is the 1157 that has two elements and staggered socket lugs. It is commonly used for parking, turn, and stop light bulbs. One element serves as the parking light and the other as the turn or stop light.

The 1046 bulb is the second most common. It has a single element and evenly positioned socket lugs. The 1046 is used for single purpose applications: back-up lights for example.

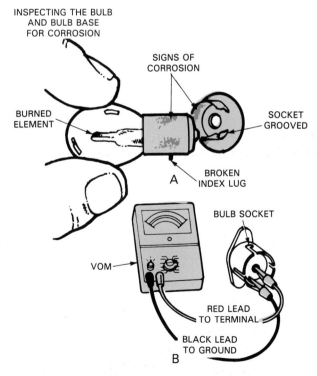

Fig. 27-11. Note bulb and socket service. A—Inspect bulb element for burning. Also inspect metal contacts for wear. Inside of socket could also be corroded or damaged. B—If bulb looks good or new bulb will not work, check for power to socket and repair as needed.   (Florida Dept. of Voc. Ed. and Fiat)

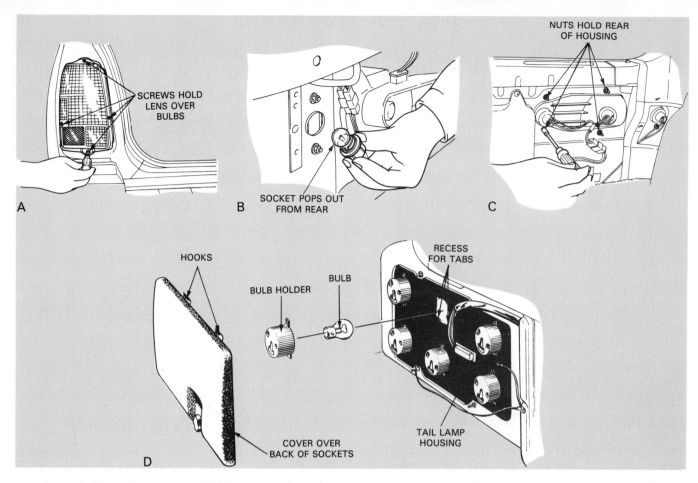

Fig. 27-12. Study methods for service of various bulb mountings. A—Removal of lens screws and lens will gain access to bulbs. B—Removal of socket from rear gains access to bulb. C—Removal of small nuts will allow access to bulbs. D—Removal of inside cover will give access to bulbs. (VW and Subaru)

FLASHER SERVICE

A *bad flasher* will keep the emergency flasher lights or the turn lights from working. One flasher normally operates the turn lights and another the emergency lights. The flashers can be located in the wiring under the dash or on the fuse box, Fig. 27-13.

A service manual will usually give a chart showing

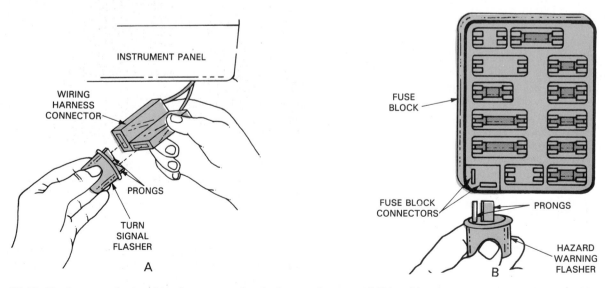

Fig. 27-13. Flashers can be in wiring harness under dash or on fuse panel. If in wiring harness, you may have to refer to manual for location. They can be hidden in dash and hard to find if not clicking or working. Make sure you get correct replacement flasher. (Florida Dept. of Voc. Ed.)

flasher location. A bad flasher will NOT make a clicking sound and can be hard to find without a location chart.

Only suspect the flasher when both turn signals fail to work. If only the right or left side fails to work, there is probably a burned bulb. One burned bulb will reduce current enough so that the flasher cannot kick in and out. However, also remember that one bulb on both sides can sometimes burn out.

Make sure you get the correct replacement flasher. They have different current ratings. If you get the wrong flasher, the bulbs may flash too slowly or blink off and on very rapidly.

TURN SIGNAL SWITCH SERVICE

A *bad turn signal switch* can be open or shorted on one or both sides. Many late model cars use a *combination switch* that combines the turn signal switch with the headlamp, washer-wiper, and other switches. This can make diagnosis more challenging.

A service manual will usually give a diagram showing the function of each terminal on a turn signal or combination switch. This may be in the form of a wiring diagram or a pictorial drawing, Fig. 27-14.

Most later model turn signal switches are mounted on the top or side of the steering column. They can be tested or replaced by removing the cover around the column. Most older turn signal switches are mounted under the steering wheel. You must use a wheel puller to remove the steering wheel to gain access to the switch. See Figs. 27-15 and 27-16.

BRAKE LIGHT SWITCH SERVICE

A *bad brake light switch* will normally fail to close and complete its circuit. The internal contacts burn and develop high resistance. Most brake light switches are

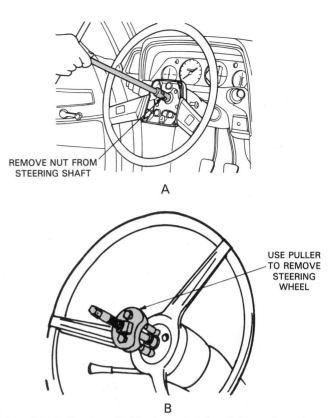

REMOVE NUT FROM STEERING SHAFT

A

USE PULLER TO REMOVE STEERING WHEEL

B

Fig. 27-15. Service of older turn signal switch requires steering wheel removal. A—Use breaker bar to remove large nut from steering column shaft. B—Use wheel puller for removing steering wheel. Wear safety glasses!   (Subaru and Chrysler)

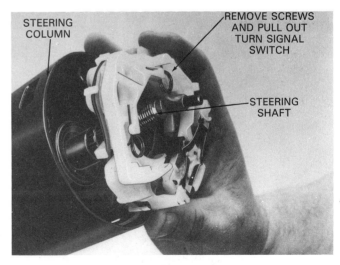

STEERING COLUMN

REMOVE SCREWS AND PULL OUT TURN SIGNAL SWITCH

STEERING SHAFT

Fig. 27-16. When replacing this type turn signal switch, you must usually cut off old connector so wires will pull out of column. Then wires for new switch can be fed down through column.   (Chrysler)

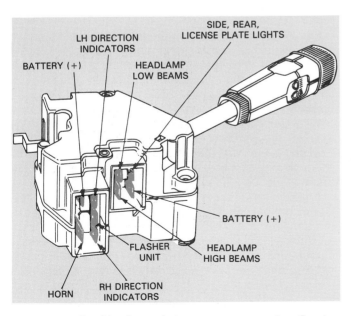

SIDE, REAR, LICENSE PLATE LIGHTS

LH DIRECTION INDICATORS

BATTERY (+)

HEADLAMP LOW BEAMS

BATTERY (+)

FLASHER UNIT

HEADLAMP HIGH BEAMS

HORN

RH DIRECTION INDICATORS

Fig. 27-14. Combination switches are very complex. Service manual would be needed to test probe output from switch. This is an example of one type of combination switch with manual explanation.   (Chrysler)

mounted on the brake pedal and work off of mechanical action. A few are hydraulically operated and mount on the master cylinder or on a brake line.

Use a test light or VOM to check the switch while operating the brake pedal. If it does not work, replace it. Also check for power entering the switch, Fig. 27-17.

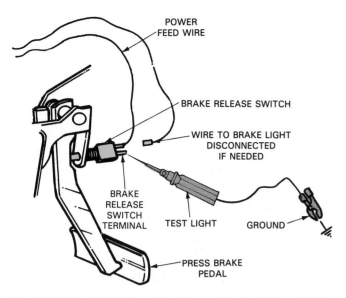

Fig. 27-17. Test light will quickly tell you if brake light switch is working or if power is being fed to switch. (Florida Dept. of Voc. Ed.)

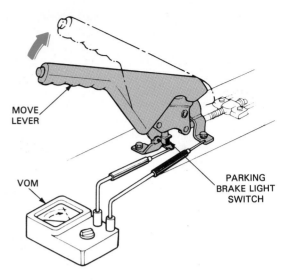

Fig. 27-19. Other switches, like this emergency brake switch, are tested in the same way. Either VOM or test light is used to check for opening and closing as switch is activated. (Honda)

SERVICING OTHER LIGHT SWITCHES

Numerous other light switches are used in a car: interior light switches, back-up light switch, emergency brake light switch, trunk light switch, etc. They are all tested in basically the same way.

Fig. 27-18 shows typical interior light switches in the door jambs. Most simply pop out of the jambs and can be tested. If the switches are working, double-check the bulbs and bulb sockets before testing for wiring troubles.

Fig. 27-19 shows how to test a parking brake light switch. Simply check for power out of the switch as the lever is engaged. If needed, refer to the wiring diagram for the specific light circuit. This will help you locate connectors and other components that may be affecting circuit operation, Fig. 27-20.

Scanners can also be used to quickly check various switches on some late model cars.

INSTRUMENTATION SERVICE

Instrumentation problems include bad sending units, failed gauges, faulty electronic control circuits, burned bulbs, bad displays, and a wide array of other troubles. In the past, fixing basic gauges was not too difficult. With today's digital dashes and computer navigation systems, repair can be challenging.

Fig. 27-21 shows a circuit diagram for a typical gauge circuit. Note how the sending units feed current to the dash gauges. When gauges or indicator lights fail to work properly, check the sending units first. They are one of the most common reasons that gauges fail to register properly.

With conventional gauges, you can simply ground the wire to the sending unit to check gauge operation. Grounding the wire should make the gauge read maximum or minimum, depending upon design. This is illustrated in Fig. 27-22.

A *gauge tester* is a more accurate and safe way to test late model gauges. The tester is connected to the lead at the sending unit. Then, the tester is set to the correct resistance. This should make the gauge read a specific output. For example, if connected to the fuel gauge sending unit wire, a one-half tester setting should make the gauge read one-half full. This also applies to testers for temperature and oil pressure gauges.

If the gauge begins to function when the lead is grounded or connected to the tester, suspect a bad sending unit. You could then use an ohmmeter to check sending unit action. See Fig. 27-23.

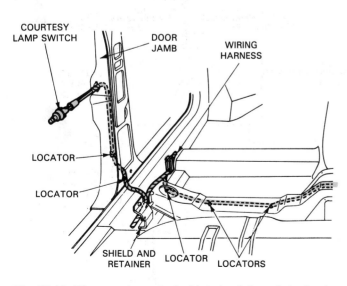

Fig. 27-18. Diagram shows typical interior light switch circuit. Switches normally will pop out of door jambs for testing or replacement. (Ford)

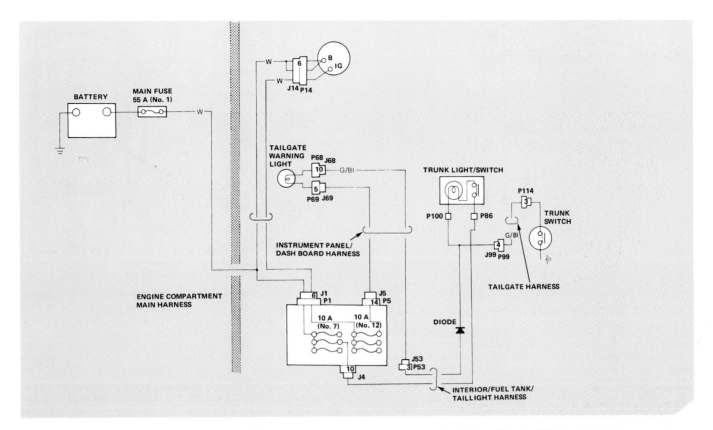

Fig. 27-20. Remember to refer to service manual wiring diagram for help with hard to find problems. This trunk light diagram shows how power is fed to light. If trunk light switch sticks closed, it will discharge battery because light will stay on all the time. (Honda)

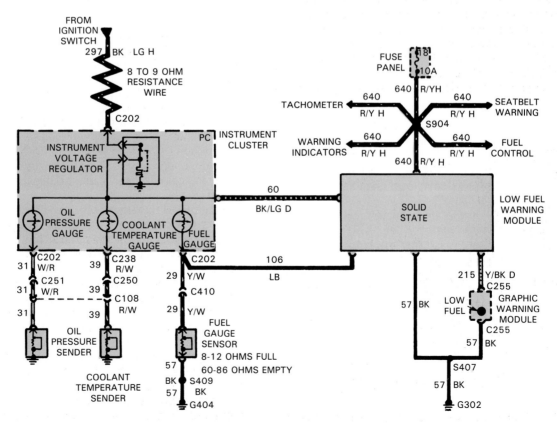

Fig. 27-21. This is a typical diagram for dash gauges. Note how sending units feed current to gauges. Solid state circuit operates low fuel warning display. If a gauge or indicator fails to work, check at sending units first. (Ford)

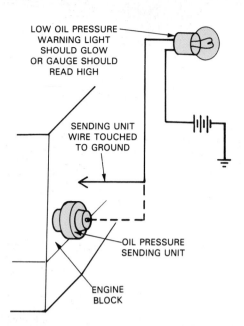

Fig. 27-22. With most gauges, you can simply ground wire to sending unit to check gauge operation. Grounding should make gauge needle swing to max or sometimes to minimum. With computer controlled graphics, check manual before grounding sending unit wire. In any case, do not ground wire for over a second or two to prevent gauge damage.

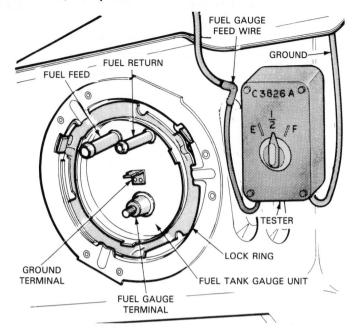

Fig. 27-23. The safest way to check gauges is with a gauge tester. It will simulate sending unit resistance and provide a controlled current to gauge. It is connected to sending unit wire and to ground. Variable resistor in tester will allow you to check gauge accuracy. (Chrysler)

If the sending unit checks good and grounding the unit lead does not power the gauge, you need to test at the gauge itself. This will determine whether the gauge itself or wiring to the gauge is at fault. Normally, the gauge cluster must be removed from the dash for testing.

Fig. 27-24 shows the basic steps for removing a gauge cluster. Also see Fig. 27-25.

A service manual is usually needed to test dash gauges. It will give test points, electrical values, and other essential information, Fig. 27-26. This is especially true with digital clusters because the wrong testing method can damage components.

If a digital cluster is found to be bad, usually a complete circuit board or large section of the cluster must be replaced. If the customer has limited funds, you might try to purchase used dash cluster parts from a salvage yard. This could save the customer considerable money and make you look like a "hero."

When replacing a digital dash cluster, many units have a removable *odometer memory chip* that electronically stores the mileage on the car. You would have to remove the old odometer chip and install it in the new or used cluster. This would maintain the correct mileage reading for the car. See Figs. 27-27 and 27-28.

Handle an odometer memory chip as you would a computer PROM discussed in Chapter 22. Keep your fingers off the chip and do not bend its pins.

DASH VOLTAGE LIMITER SERVICE

A *faulty dash voltage limiter,* also called *dash voltage regulator,* can make all of the gauges inoperative or inaccurate. It feeds a lower voltage to the gauges so they do NOT show fluctuations in their readings with changes in charging system voltage. Whenever all of the gauges show problems, suspect the dash voltage regulator, Fig. 27-29.

The dash voltage regulator is usually mounted on the back of the instrumentation cluster. You must remove the cluster to test and replace the regulator.

Use a voltmeter to measure the voltage on each side of the dash voltage regulator. It should show battery or alternator voltage on one side and a reduced voltage of about 6 volts on the other. If not, replace the unit. Check the service manual for additional information on testing and replacement.

SUMMARY

Use logical thought when troubleshooting a lighting system. Visualize the circuit and how it should function. This will help you select best inspecting-testing location.

If only one of several bulbs is out, you would know that only a small section of the circuit is affected. If all bulbs are out, you would know that the feed section of the circuit is at fault.

A burned fuse link can prevent all of the lights from working. It is usually located near the battery or starting motor in the engine compartment.

Flickering lights can be caused by a short and circuit breaker action. It can also be caused by a loose electrical connection.

Dim lights are caused by a high resistance in the circuit. A connector or socket could be corroded. A wire could be loose in a connector. Look for these kinds of problems.

When replacing a sealed beam headlamp, do NOT pull on the wires when disconnecting the connector. This

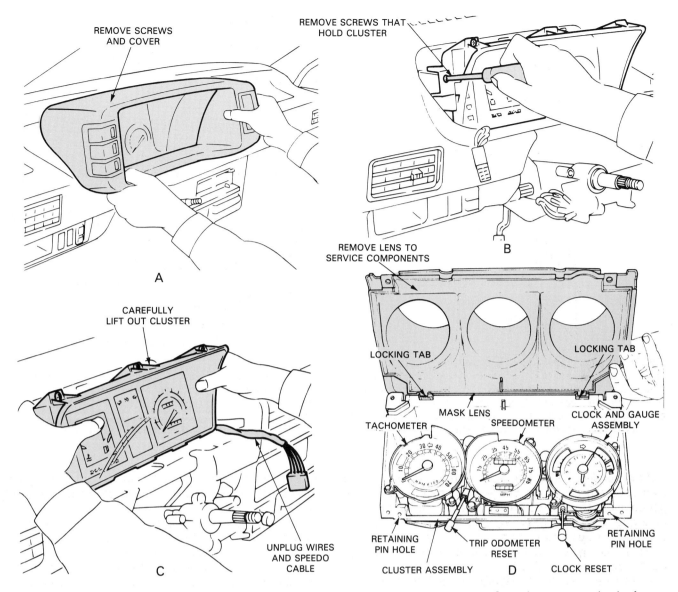

Fig. 27-24. Note basic steps for dash cluster removal. A—Remove screws holding dash cover. Sometimes nuts on back of cover must be removed. B—Then remove hex screws that hold cluster into dash. C—Pull cluster forward and remove wires and speedometer cable. D—With cluster out, you can remove lens to gain access to internal components. (General Motors)

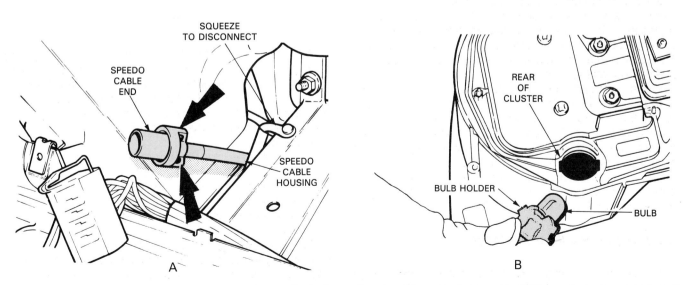

Fig. 27-25. A—When removing cluster, you will usually have to disconnect speedometer cable. With most designs, you must squeeze on the cable end to free it from the cluster. With some older designs, you must unscrew a nut. B—Most indicator bulbs are partially rotated to free them from back of cluster. (Ford)

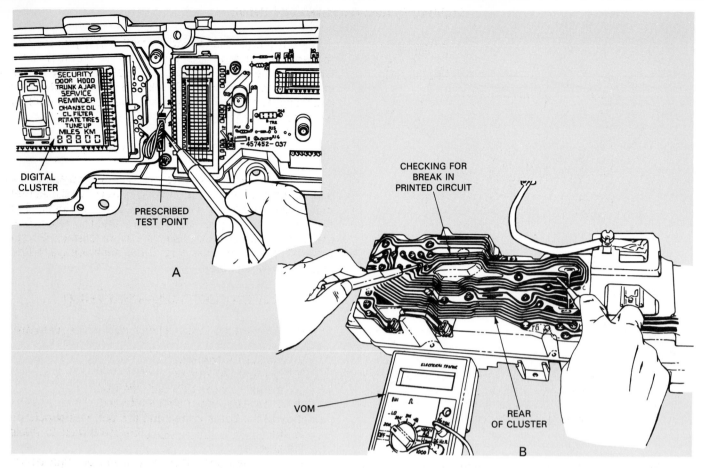

Fig. 27-26. Testing a late model dash cluster requires the data in a factory service manual. It will give you the specs and test points to prevent component damage. A—Technician is prodding to check voltages to cluster. B—Technician is testing printed circuit on back of cluster.

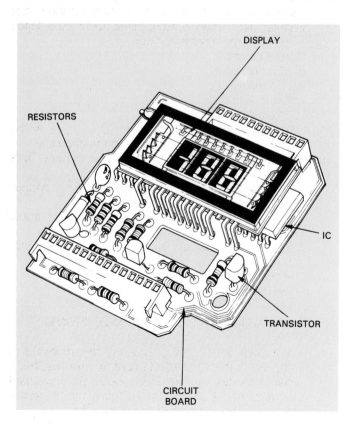

Fig. 27-27. Replacement is normally needed when digital display fails. New ones can be expensive so check salvage yard first. (Oldsmobile)

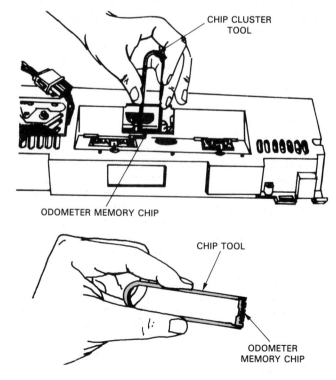

Fig. 27-28. When changing dash clusters, you must make sure mileage on car remains the same. It is a federal offense to alter the odometer reading on a car. Here technician is switching odometer chip or IC from old cluster to new cluster. Chip permanently stores car's mileage. (Chrysler)

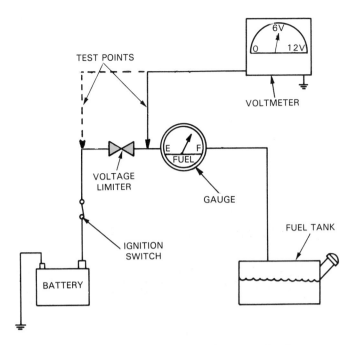

Fig. 27-29. Voltage limiter is often used to control voltage supplied to gauges. It maintains about 6 volts to gauges. Voltmeter can be used to measure voltage on each side of limiter to check its condition.

could damage the wiring or connector. Pull on the connector itself. Make sure the bulb is fully seated in its shell.

When replacing an insert type headlamp, avoid touching the bulb with your fingers. Oil on your hands could reduce bulb life. Handle it with a clean shop rag.

Headlamp aiming can be done two ways. You can mark lines on a wall and on the floor at specific distances. You can also use headlight aimers. Both methods are accurate if done properly.

Screws are provided for vertical and horizontal adjustment of the headlights. Check them on both high and low beam settings.

Light switches are all tested in about the same way. Use a test light or VOM to make sure the switch opens and closes the circuit when activated. The test light should glow on the output side of the circuit with the switch on and it should not glow when the switch is turned off.

A shorted switch will allow the test light to glow in both positions. An open switch will not turn the test light on in either position when on the output wire.

You would need a service manual to test a headlamp switch since most have several functions. With some headlamp switches, you must push a button on the back of the switch to free the knob plunger.

When replacing a burned bulb, check the condition inside the bulb socket. If it is corroded, clean it with electrical contact cleaning spray. Be careful not to short the socket while working. Turn circuit switch off.

One burned bulb can keep a flasher unit from working. Always check for a burned bulb before condemning a flasher unit. Flashers can be hard to find when under the dash. Most manuals give a flasher location chart. Make sure you purchase the correct replacement flasher. Current or amp ratings vary.

When a gauge fails to read correctly, start your tests at the sending unit on the engine or at the fuel tank. Grounding the lead to the unit will usually make the gauge needle swing to the right. Check in a service manual for directions before grounding digital dash sending units to avoid part damage.

KNOW THESE TERMS

Trim ring, Headlamp aiming, Headlamp aimers, Vertical aiming screw, Horizontal aiming screw, Bad dimmer switch, Bad headlamp switch, Fog lamp problems, Bad flasher, Bad turn signal switch, Combination switch, Bad brake light switch, Instrumentation problems, Gauge tester, Odometer memory chip, Faulty dash voltage limiter, Dash voltage regulator.

REVIEW QUESTIONS—CHAPTER 27

1. If only one bulb in a circuit is out, you would know that:
   a. the bulb is burned.
   b. feed current is open.
   c. a small portion of circuit affected.
   d. a large portion of circuit affected.
2. If all of the bulbs in a circuit are out, you should go to the _____ _____ _____ for the circuit to make initial tests.
3. A car's headlights flash only when on high beam. The problem is NOT affected by bumps in the road and other driving conditions. They even flash when the car is parked. Technician A says there could be a short in the high beam wiring kicking out the circuit breaker. Technician B says there could be a loose wire causing the lights to flash.
   Who is correct?
   a. Technician A.
   b. Technician B.
   c. Both A and B.
   d. Neither A nor B.
4. When lights are dim, there is a _____ _____ in the circuit or a _____ _____ supply to the circuit.
5. Why should you avoid touching the surface of a headlamp insert bulb?
6. When replacing a headlamp, pull on the harness, NOT the connector. True or false?
7. Sketch a headlight aiming wall on a separate sheet of paper.
8. Explain how you would use headlight aimers to adjust headlights.
9. Describe 1157 and 1046 bulbs.
10. What is an odometer chip?

ASE CERTIFICATION–TYPE QUESTIONS

1. A customer brings his/her car into the shop with a complaint that both headlights are not working. Technician A checks the fuse in the headlight circuit and then tests the circuit for shorts. Technician B checks the fuse in the headlight circuit and then tests the operation of the headlight switch. Who is right?
   (A) A only.   (C) Both A and B.
   (B) B only.   (D) Neither A nor B.

2. An automobile's right taillight is dim. Technician A checks the circuit breaker in the taillight circuit. Technician B inspects the condition of this particular taillight's socket. Who is right?
   (A) A only.
   (B) B only.
   (C) Both A and B.
   (D) Neither A nor B.

3. One of an automobile's headlights is aimed too low. Technician A turns the headlamp's horizontal aiming screw clockwise to raise the beam. Technician B turns the headlamps vertical aiming screw counterclockwise to raise the beam. Who is right?
   (A) A only.
   (B) B only.
   (C) Both A and B.
   (D) Neither A nor B.

4. A vehicle is suspected of having a defective headlamp switch. Technician A makes sure that power is being fed to the switch. Technician B makes sure that power is switched to various output wires as the switch knob is moved. Who is right?
   (A) A only.
   (B) B only.
   (C) Both A and B.
   (D) Neither A nor B.

5. An automobile's left turn signal bulb has been replaced, but the turn signal is still not working. Technician A uses a test light to check the condition of the bulb. Technician B uses a test light to check for power at the bulb socket. Who is right?
   (A) A only.
   (B) B only.
   (C) Both A and B.
   (D) Neither A nor B.

6. An automobile's emergency light flasher is believed to be bad. Technician A looks for the flasher in the wiring under the dash. Technician B looks for the flasher on the car's fuse box. Who is right?
   (A) A only.
   (B) B only.
   (C) Both A and B.
   (D) Neither A nor B.

7. A late model car's turn signal switch is "shorted" on both sides and must be replaced. Technician A is going to use a wheel puller to remove the steering wheel in order to gain access to the turn signal switch. Technician B is going to gain access to this switch by removing the cover around the steering column. Who is right?
   (A) A only.
   (B) B only.
   (C) Both A and B.
   (D) Neither A nor B.

8. An automobile's brake light switch needs testing. Technician A operates the brake pedal and tests the switch with a VOM. Technician B operates the brake pedal and checks the brake light switch with a test light. Who is right?
   (A) A only.
   (B) B only.
   (C) Both A and B.
   (D) Neither A nor B.

9. The oil pressure gauge on an automobile's instrumentation panel is not working properly. Technician A says the problem could be the gauge sending unit. Technician B says the problem could be the gauge itself. Who is right?
   (A) A only.
   (B) B only.
   (C) Both A and B.
   (D) Neither A nor B.

10. A particular automobile has a 12 volt electrical system. This car's dash voltage regulator has been tested and the test results show that there are 13.5 volts on both sides of the regulator. Technician A says these voltage readings indicate that the regulator is operating properly. Technician B replaces the dash voltage regulator. Who is right?
    (A) A only.
    (B) B only.
    (C) Both A and B.
    (D) Neither A nor B.

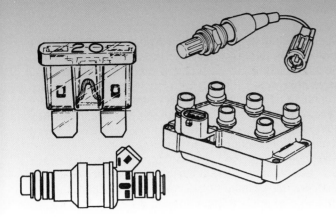

After studying this chapter, you will be able to:

- *Diagnose and repair a wiper circuit.*
- *Service a windshield washer system.*
- *Repair inoperative horns.*
- *Diagnose and repair power windows.*
- *Service power door locks.*
- *Adjust a radio antenna trimmer screw.*
- *Replace a radio and its speakers.*
- *Use condensers to correct some types of radio noise.*
- *Remove and replace a door panel.*
- *Clean a tape player head.*
- *Describe basic tests for antilock brake systems.*
- *Service a rear window defogger circuit.*
- *Test and service a blower motor and its circuit.*
- *Describe speed control service.*

This chapter will summarize the most common tests and repairs used to correct problems in the *accessory system* of a car. This would include the washer-wiper system, radio, tape player, power windows, power door locks, anti-lock brakes, and other systems.

WIPER-WASHER SYSTEM TESTING AND REPAIR

The *wiper-washer system* is a relatively simple system that is not very difficult to diagnose and repair. You must think of how the system works and compare symptoms to possible causes. Fig. 28-1 gives a typical wiring diagram. Note how it could help you determine possible causes for malfunctions.

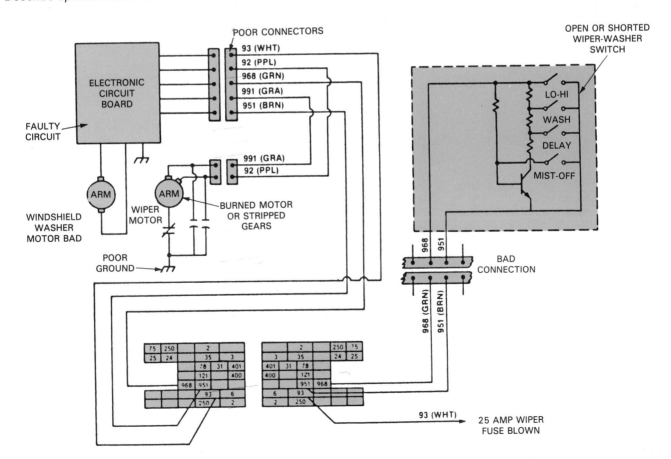

Fig. 28-1. Note types of problems that you can find in a wiper system.   (General Motors)

Wiper malfunctions

When the windshield wipers will NOT WORK, start your tests at the wiper motor if easily accessible. Check for

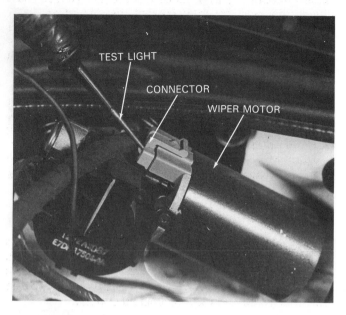

Fig. 28-2. If easily accessible, check for power to wiper motor first if wipers do not work. Turn on ignition key and wiper switch. If you are getting power to motor, motor may be bad.

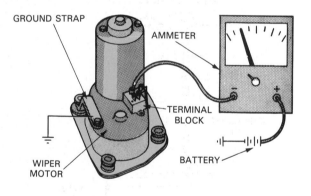

Fig. 28-3. If wiper fuse keeps blowing, check motor current draw. If excessive, replace the motor. If not excessive, check for shorted wiring. Manual will give current specs.   (Chrysler)

power reaching the motor, Fig. 28-2. If voltage is NOT reaching the motor, then test at the wiper switch. If you have power at the motor, then the motor or gearbox may be at fault.

If you can hear the wiper motor running (humming), but the wiper arms do NOT move, check the motor gearbox and wiper linkage arms. A stripped gear or disconnected arm may be preventing wiper action.

If voltage is reaching the motor, you can also check motor resistance or current draw, Fig. 28-3. A shorted or open wiper motor may be the problem. You could use a jumper wire to apply battery voltage directly to the motor. This would provide another way of checking motor operation while isolating the supply circuit.

A poor electrical ground is another cause of inoperative wipers. The poor ground could keep the wipers from working or it can keep them from *parking* (moving to full down position). Check the motor ground with a jumper wire if needed.

If the wiper motor checks bad, removal can be from the engine compartment side of the firewall or from under the dash. Several hex screws normally hold the wiper motor in place. After unscrewing the motor, you can remove a clip that holds the wiper crank arm to the wiper linkage. See Fig. 28-4.

Mentioned briefly, if the wiper motor can be heard running but the wiper arms do not move, the plastic gears in the gearbox can be stripped. These gears can usually be purchased and installed so the whole motor does NOT require replacement. By removing a cover plate, the plastic gears can be easily replaced. Make sure you pack the gearbox with heavy grease during gear replacement.

Also check for a disconnected wiper linkage arm. If one of the arms becomes disconnected, motion will not transfer from the motor to one or both of the wiper blades. It is easy for one of the clips to fall off, disconnecting the wiper linkage.

Windshield washer service

An *inoperative windshield washer* is usually caused by one of the following:
1. Clogged washer or fluid hose nozzle.
2. Disconnected washer hose.
3. Clogged washer system filter or strainer.
4. Burned or open washer motor.
5. Ruptured diaphragm with old style units.

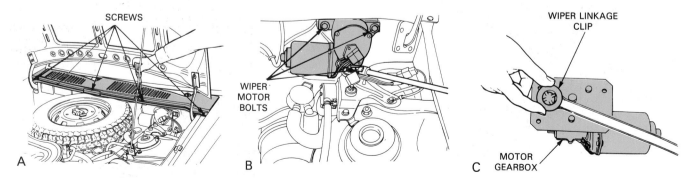

Fig. 28-4. Note steps for wiper motor removal and installation. A—Sometimes you must remove cowl panel to gain access to wiper motor. Motor can also be under dash in passenger compartment. B—Small hex screws normally hold wiper motor in place. Rubber grommets insulate body from wiper motor noise. C—Clips normally secure wiper arms to motor and to each other.

To begin diagnosis, check for these kinds of troubles. If you think the nozzles are clogged, disconnect the hose. If water squirts out with the hose off, use a small piece of wire to clean out the nozzles, Fig. 28-5.

If fluid does NOT flow out with the hose removed from the nozzle, suspect the washer motor. With an electric washer motor, test for voltage to the motor. The switch could be bad. If you have voltage to the motor but the motor will NOT run, the washer motor is probably bad. See Fig. 28-6.

If voltage is not reaching the washer motor, check for voltage leaving the washer switch. The switch could be open and need replacement. The wiring between the switch and washer motor could also be open. Replace the switch or repair wiring as needed.

HORN SERVICE

An *inoperative horn system* can be caused by an open horn switch, open wire, loose connection, faulty horn, or similar trouble. Fig. 28-7 shows a typical horn circuit. Note the components that could prevent horn operation.

If the horns fail to shut off or blow all of the time, check the horn button or switch. It can stick closed and prevent the horns from shutting off. If a horn relay is used, it could also keep the horns from sounding or from shutting off.

A test light is commonly used to check how power is acting at the horn. If the test light goes on and off as the horn button is pressed, the horn is probably bad. Check the horn ground, however, before condemning the horn. If voltage is not reaching the horn, check the horn button and for breaks in the wiring leading to the horn. See Fig. 28-8.

POWER WINDOW SERVICE

Power window problems are normally caused by a bad window switch, bad window motor, or wiring trouble. If all of the windows fail to work, check the fuse or circuit breaker. If only one window will NOT work, check its switch or probe for power reaching the motor.

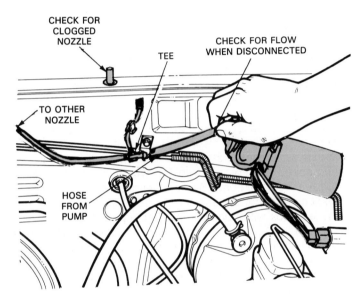

Fig. 28-5. If windshield washers do not work, check for blocked nozzles. Remove hose before nozzles. If fluid squirts out hose, nozzles must be cleaned out with piece of wire and compressed air. (Ford)

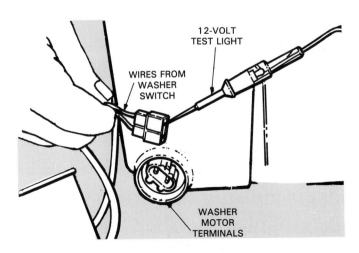

Fig. 28-6. If washer system is not blocked, check for power to washer pump with test light or VOM. If you do not get power, washer switch or wiring may be open. If you get power, the washer motor is probably bad.

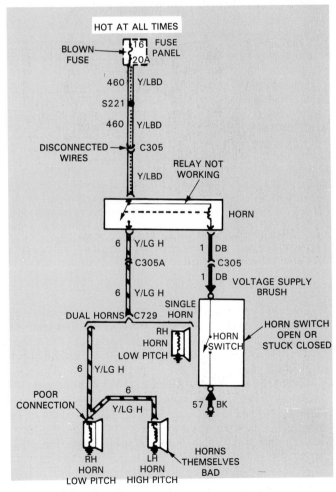

Fig. 28-7. This is a typical horn circuit. Note the kinds of troubles that can occur in system. (Ford)

499

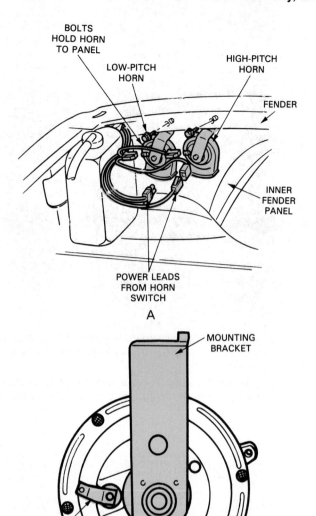

Fig. 28-8. A—Horns are usually bolted inside front fender. Check for power to horn before suspecting horn. B—Adjusting screw is set at factory but may require adjustment if it has been tampered with by someone. (Pontiac)

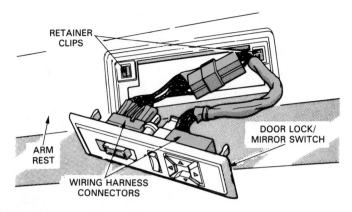

Fig. 28-9. If power windows do not work and fuse is good, the easiest place to start your tests might be at main switch assembly. You can pop it out to check for feed power to switch, for power to motors when switches are pressed, etc. If the switch is passing current, you would need to remove door panel to check window motor. (Chrysler)

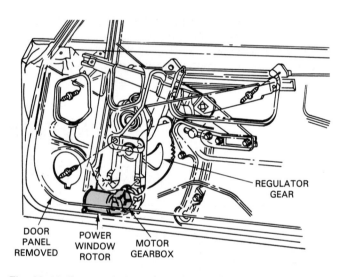

Fig. 28-10. Power window motor bolts inside door. Sometimes drilling holes over mounting bolts simplifies motor R & R. Bolts can be hard to reach without drilled holes.

POWER DOOR LOCK SERVICE

Power door lock problems commonly result from bad switches, disconnected wires, or failed lock solenoids (motors). As with power windows, if ALL locks do NOT work, the power source for the circuit is open. If only one lock is NOT operative, check its switch and then the solenoid or motor.

Fig. 28-13 shows one circuit for a typical four-door lock network. Note how power flows through the circuit.

Fig. 28-14 shows how a door lock motor mounts in the door. If the switch is working, test for power directly at the door lock solenoid or motor. Replace the solenoid or motor if needed.

Fig. 28-15 shows the major steps for door panel removal.

Note: A common electrical problem results when the wires leading from the car body into the door break internally. When the door has been opened and closed

The power window switches are usually in the doors but they can also be in the console. Removal of the switch will let you probe for power to the switch and out of the switch. This can help you isolate the problem to a location before or after the switch, Fig. 28-9.

If power is leaving the window switch and entering the inside of the door, you would need to remove the door panel for further tests, Fig. 28-10. Check for power at the window motor. If you have power at the motor, the motor may be bad. If the motor runs but the window does NOT move, the plastic gears in the motor gearbox may be stripped, Fig. 28-11. Like a wiper motor, you can usually replace the gears to salvage the window motor. If the motor itself is bad, a new or used motor would have to be installed. Fig. 28-12 shows a power window system.

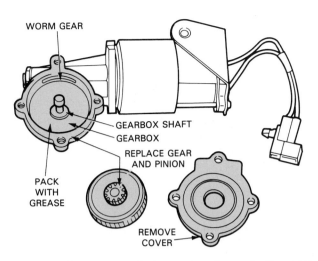

Fig. 28-11. Most power window motors have plastic gears in gearbox. They can strip and prevent window movement. Plastic gears can normally be removed and replaced to repair window motor assembly. (Chrysler)

thousands of times, the metal in the wires can fatigue and break. This can keep the power door locks, power windows, power rear view mirror, etc., from working normally. Frequently, these components will only work when the door is moved or is in a certain position. You would need to open the wiring harness between the door and body to probe for and fix the broken wires.

POWER SEAT SERVICE

If both front power seats fail to function, check the common section of the circuit. Inspect the fuse, circuit breaker, wire connections, or any other component affecting both seats.

If only one of the seats is inoperative, test its control switch and wiring between the switch and motors. When the seat only fails in one mode (up and down for example), check the motor and transmission (gear mechanism) providing that action.

If you have difficulty repairing a power seat, read the information in a service manual. It will give directions for servicing the particular type unit.

DOOR PANEL REMOVAL

Door panel removal can be needed when servicing power windows, seat control switches, door latches, and radio speakers.

Basically, you must remove the window crank handle. A screw or inner clip may secure the handle. You may also

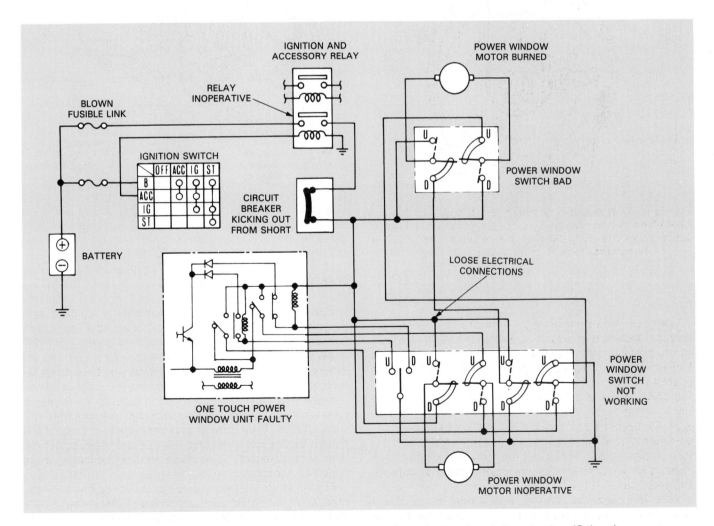

Fig. 28-12. Study wiring diagram and possible troubles for typical power window circuit. (Subaru)

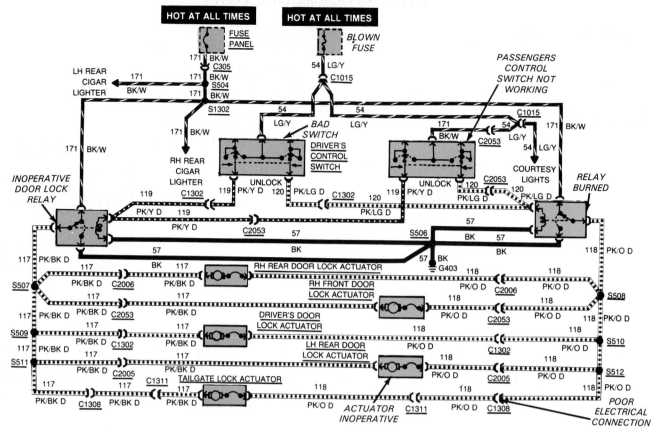

Fig. 28-13. Note typical power door lock circuit and its potential problems.   (Ford)

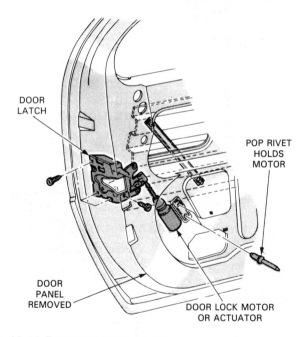

Fig. 28-14. Power door lock actuator can be held by screws or rivets. Make sure wiring to solenoid is complete before condemning solenoid.   (Chrysler)

have to remove the armrest, rear view mirror knob, lock knob, etc.

With all hardware and screws through the panel removed, you must carefully pop out several metal or plastic clips holding the door panel to the door. You can use a wide gasket scraper or special tool to remove the clips without door panel damage.

RADIO SERVICE

Radio problems can be internal and NOT serviceable in the field or they can be external which can often be fixed in the field. Internal radio problems require the experience of a specialized electronic radio technician. The radio must be removed and sent to the specialty shop for repairs. External problems, like bad speakers, broken wires, antenna troubles, etc., can usually be repaired by the automobile technician, Fig. 28-16.

Use the information in a service manual to diagnose radio problems. You may have external problems: blown fuse, open antenna lead, bad speakers, or other problems keeping the radio from functioning properly. Do NOT condemn the radio until all other problem sources have been eliminated.

An *antenna trimmer screw* tunes the radio circuit to the antenna resistance. It might need to be adjusted when the radio has been removed for repairs or after antenna replacement. After reconnecting the radio to the antenna, speakers, and power supply in the car, set the tuner to a weak station. Then, turn the trimmer screw until the weak station comes in the loudest and clearest. See Fig. 28-17.

If the radio is totally dead, do NOT forget to check the fuse. Many radios have two feed wires. A *switched feed* (ignition switch controls power to radio) is used for the main radio circuit. An *unswitched feed* (wire always hot) is used to keep the station memory and clock (if equipped) alive.

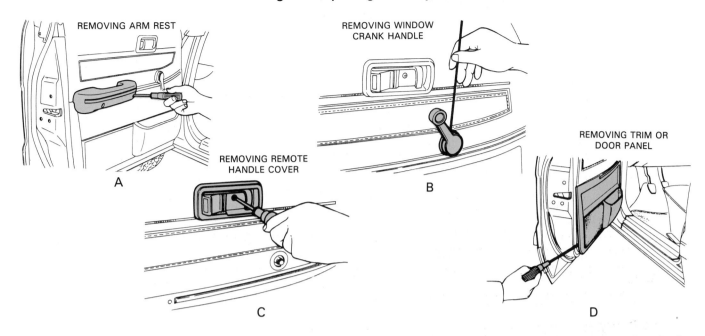

Fig. 28-15. Study typical steps for door panel removal. A—Remove screws holding arm rest if needed. They can be under plastic, pop-out plugs. B—Remove window crank handle. It can be held by C-clip from rear, requiring tool to reach behind and pull out clip. Screw can also be in center of crank handle under glued-on cover. C—Remove screws and other components: lock cover, door lock knob, rear view mirror knob, etc. D—Use screwdriver, gasket scraper, or special tool to pop out clips holding door panel to door. Be careful not to tear panel. (Subaru)

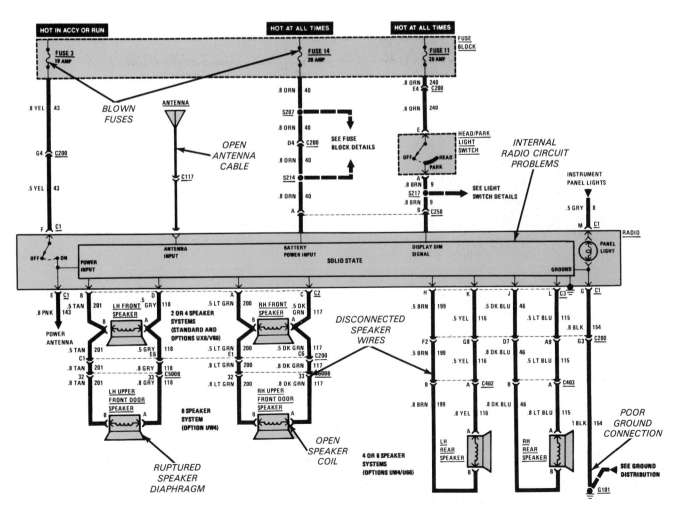

Fig. 28-16. Study problems that could develop in radio circuit. (Oldsmobile)

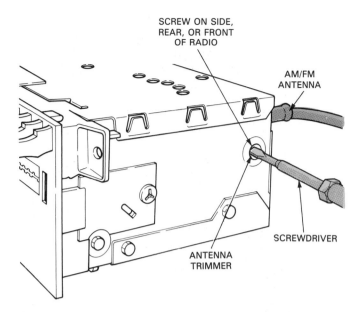

Fig. 28-17. Antenna trimmer screw tunes radio circuitry to resistance or capacitance of antenna. Set radio to a weak station. Then, turn trimmer screw for the best reception. (Chrysler)

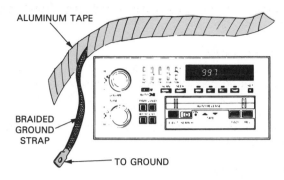

Fig. 28-18. A poor ground is common reason for some types of radio interference. Here aluminum tape and ground strap have been used to reduce radio static. (Buick)

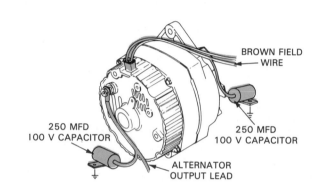

Fig. 28-19. Capacitors can be located at various points in car wiring to prevent noise from alternator, ignition system, etc., from entering radio circuitry. Capacitors or condensers smooth out current flow for radio power supply. (Buick)

Just because the clock works does not mean that power is being fed to the radio internal circuitry. Always check for a blown fuse or disconnected wire with a dead radio.

Radio noise

Radio noise is undesired interference or static (popping, clicking, or crackling) obstructing the normal sound of the radio station. Radio noise is commonly caused by a bad antenna, open or shorted noise suppressor (capacitor), bad spark plug wire, radio troubles, or other problems. If the stations are too far away, noise will interfere with the signal.

Generally, study the sound of the radio noise to determine its source. For example, a low frequency clicking, that changes with engine speed, may be from the ignition system (open spark plug wire). A higher pitched, whirring sound that also changes with engine speed could be from the electrical system (bad capacitor allows alternator whine). See Fig. 28-18.

One of the first parts to check with radio noise is the antenna. Plug a known GOOD ANTENNA into the radio. Ground the antenna base and note any changes in radio output. If the noise is eliminated, the old antenna is faulty. If the noise remains the same, then check the noise suppressors, Fig. 28-19.

Noise suppressors are capacitors that absorb voltage fluctuations in the car's electrical system. They result in smoother DC current entering the radio, which reduces radio noise.

Noise suppressors can be located at the alternator, voltage regulator, ignition coil, distributor, and heater blower motor. All of these components can produce voltage fluctuations and noise. Refer to a service manual for exact suppressor locations.

A clip-on capacitor can be used to test noise suppressors. Connect the test capacitor across or in place of the

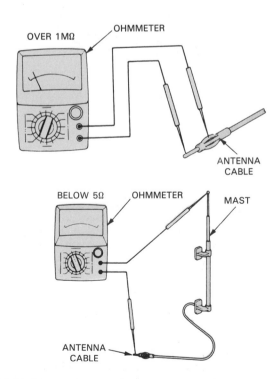

Fig. 28-20. Note two tests of radio antenna. A—Ohmmeter is being used to test for short in cable. Resistance should be very high. B—Ohmmeter is being used to check continuity in center wire of cable. Resistance should be very low. (Toyota)

suppressor. If the radio static is reduced, install a new suppressing capacitor.

Antenna service

Servicing an antenna is relatively simple. If plugging in a test antenna improves reception, the antenna or cable needs replacement. You can also use an ohmmeter to check an antenna cable, Fig. 28-20.

Refer to a service manual for detailed procedures for service. Methods can vary with antenna designs.

Speaker service

A *faulty speaker* will distort the sound of the radio or may not work at all. The speaker may rattle, especially when the volume is adjusted to a higher output level. A broken coil winding or terminal-to-coil wire can make the speaker totally inoperable.

Speakers are normally NOT repairable and should be replaced when defective, Fig. 28-21. However, terminal-to-coil wires can sometimes be soldered when broken.

Fig. 28-22 shows the importance of keeping speaker polarity correct.

Tape player service

As with radios, internal problems with a tape player often require a specialized electronic technician. However, you can perform some repairs, such as removing broken tape or cleaning the tape head. Refer to

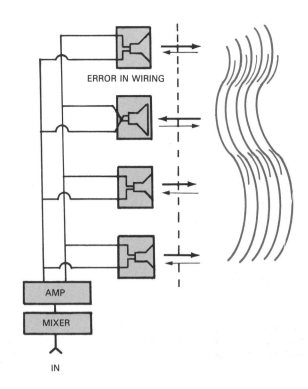

INCORRECT

BASS CANCELLATION, PHASE
DISTORTION AND LOSS OF
ACOUSTIC POWER

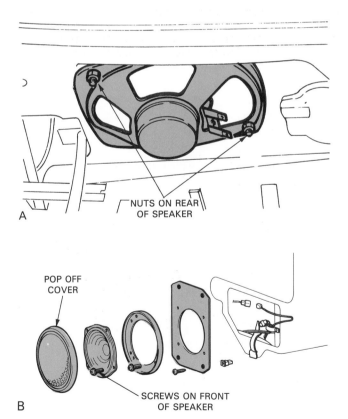

Fig. 28-21. Speakers can be held in place in several ways. A—On this rear-mounted speaker, nuts hold speaker and are accessible from trunk. B—This door-mounted speaker has screws that hold it in place. Cover pops off speaker. Sometimes, however, door panel must be removed to get at speaker screws.   (Chrysler)

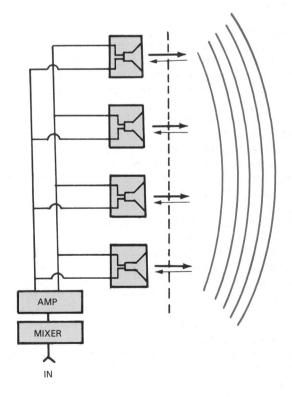

CORRECT

ALL SPEAKERS TOGETHER!
STRONG, COHERENT WAVEFRONT

Fig. 28-22. Note how reversing polarity of speakers can adversely affect sound quality in radio or stereo system.

a shop manual for diagnosis and service procedures. See Figs. 28-23 and 28-24.

ANTILOCK BRAKE SYSTEM SERVICE

If the antilock brake system has self-diagnosis, you can energize the computer and it will produce trouble codes. The trouble codes will be in number form and will represent possible problem areas in the system. You can compare the number code to a service manual chart to find out what parts might be faulty. See Fig. 28-25.

Refer to the textbook index for more information on self-diagnosis and trouble codes.

A *breakout box* plugs into the computer wiring harness to allow for easy electrical measurements with some antilock brake systems. Shown in Fig. 28-26, the breakout box plugs into a connector and has a breadboard-type surface for touching the meter test probes. You can compare actual internal voltages and resistances to service manual recommended good values.

Wheel speed sensor service

A *bad wheel speed sensor* will normally be opened and will not produce a wheel rpm signal for the computer. You can usually test the sensors at the breakout box or you can check them at each wheel. If they check bad at the breakout box, make sure you check the wiring to the sensor before condemning the sensor.

The wheel speed sensors normally bolt to the steering knuckle or brake backing plate. Removing one or two bolts will normally free the sensor, Fig. 28-27.

The trigger wheel for the wheel speed sensor is normally trouble free. Normally, it is only serviced when making suspension or drive train repairs, Fig. 28-28.

ABS hydraulic unit service

The *ABS hydraulic unit* normally contains an electric pump and two or more switches that help operate the system.

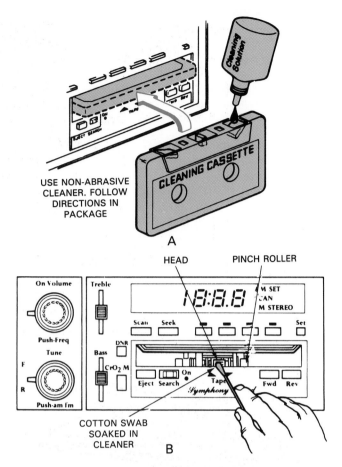

Fig. 28-24. Here are two methods for cleaning tape player heads. A—Use solution and special cleaning tape. B—Place solution on cotton swab and rub over head.   (Cadillac)

To check the general operation of the hydraulic unit, block the vehicle's wheels to keep it from rolling. Release the parking brake, place the shift lever in neutral, and start the engine. Press down firmly on the brake pedal

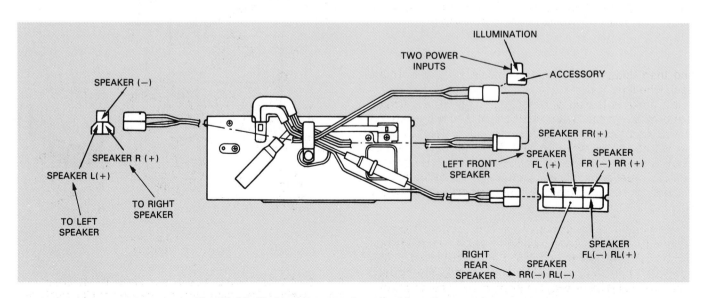

Fig. 28-23. Study wire connections for this radio-tape player.

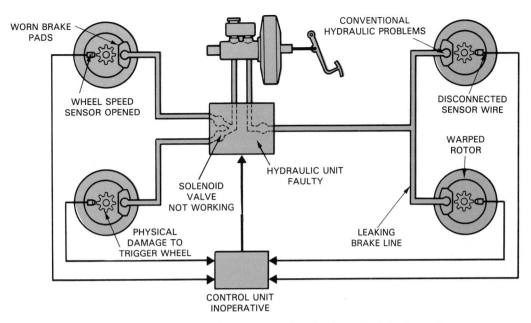

Fig. 28-25. Note problems that can develop in antilock brake system.

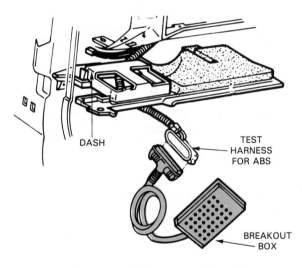

Fig. 28-26. Breakout box will let you easily probe voltages in this ABS system. (General Motors)

and then release it. Raise the vehicle and try to rotate each wheel by hand.

If a brake is locked or dragging, check for a mechanical problem in the brake mechanism. If the mechanism is working properly, the problem may be caused by sticking valves in the hydraulic unit. This can be verified by using a scanner to detect trouble codes. Follow service manual procedures when working on a hydraulic unit since it is critical to brake system operation and safety. See Fig. 28-29.

Danger! Always release hydraulic pressure before working on an ABS hydraulic unit. An accumulator can maintain high pressure that can cause injury. To relieve pressure, you can normally pump the break pedal several times with the ignition key off until brake pedal feel changes. Refer to a manual for details.

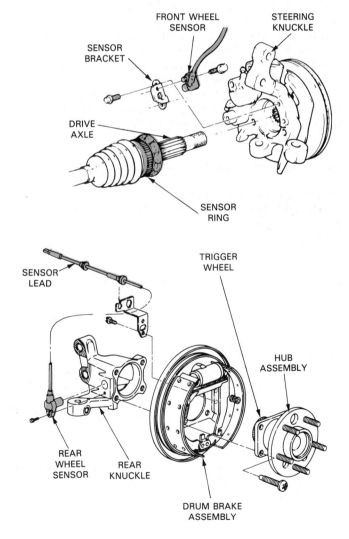

Fig. 28-27. Wheel speed sensors are tested like other similar speed sensors. Remember that conventional brake problems can also upset system operation.

Fig. 28-28. Trigger wheel for ABS is trouble free unless damaged by road debris or in an accident. Always inspect them. (GM)

The switches and motor on the hydraulic unit are tested like any other switch or motor. Compare your measurements to specs to determine if part replacement is needed.

Servicing other ABS components

The computer, relays, and other components in the ABS system are serviced in a conventional manner. When you have difficulty solving a problem, refer to a factory troubleshooting chart and a wiring diagram. They will help you visualize the circuit and select the most logical place to start your tests. Some systems have self-diagnosis that will output trouble codes.

A diagram for one type of ABS is given in Fig. 28-30. Note how the wheel speed sensors feed data into the

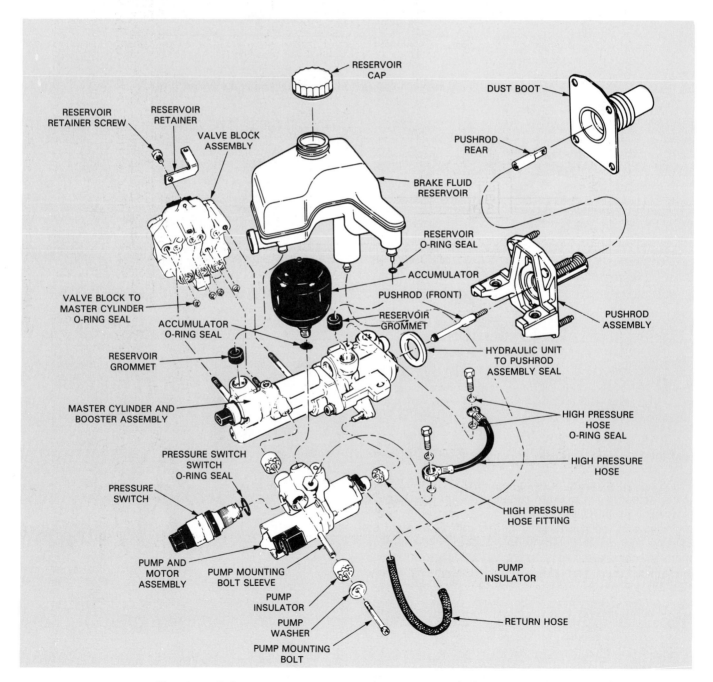

Fig. 28-29. Refer to service manual when working on an ABS hydraulic unit.

508

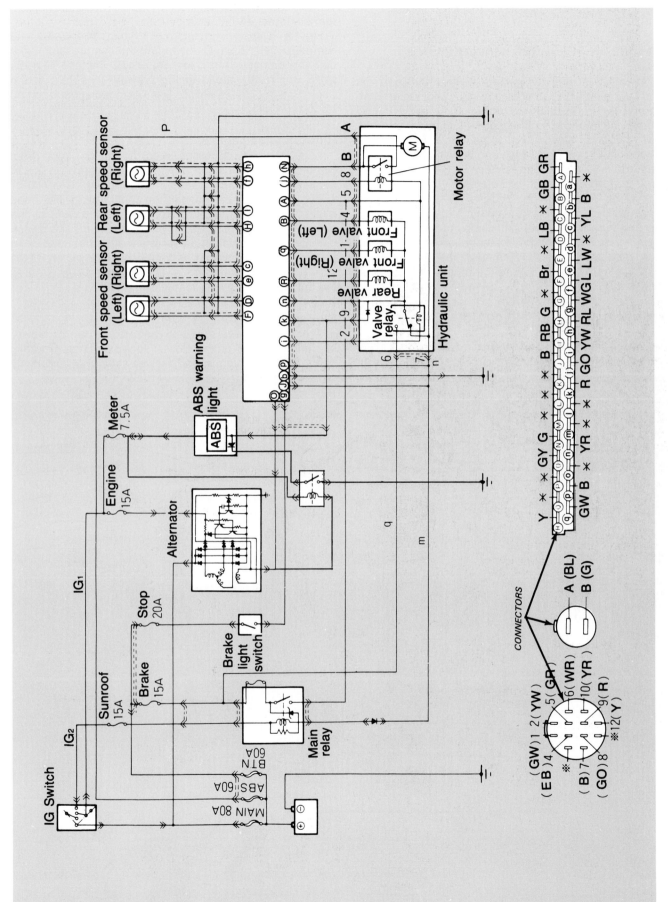

Fig. 28-30. Study diagram for this ABS.

computer. Also note how the hydraulic unit is wired to the computer.

REAR WINDOW DEFOGGER SERVICE

An *inoperative rear window defogger circuit* can be caused by a blown fuse, bad switch, open heating grid, or wiring problem. First, check for power at the rear window grid. If you have power to the grid, then suspect the grid itself. If you do not have power, something in the feed circuit is open. Check at the switch and work your way back.

If the grid is formed on the surface of the glass, it can become torn and open. An ohmmeter will let you check the grid wires for opens, Fig. 28-31A.

Some service manuals recommend using a special repair material to fix breaks in the surface-mounted defogger grid, Fig. 28-31B. The conductive material is painted onto the glass to reconnect the broken grid. Then, a heat gun is used to cure the repair material. See Fig. 28-31C.

HEATER, AIR CONDITIONING CIRCUIT REPAIRS

The circuits for the heater blower and air conditioning systems vary considerably from car to car. Therefore, you should refer to a factory service manual for a description and diagrams of the exact system.

Fig. 28-32 shows a diagram of a typical heater, AC, and rear defogger circuit. Can you find the compressor clutch coil, the defogger relay, and the blower motor? With the skills you have gained in the previous chapters of the book, you should be able to use basic techniques to find troubles in almost any electrical circuit.

Blower switch service

A *bad blower switch* can keep the fan or blower from working. A multi-position switch can also prevent one or more of the blower speeds from working. The blower switch is normally mounted in the control head. The head might have to be removed from the dash to get at the back of the switch for testing or replacement. The switch can also be in the dash away from the control head.

Test the blower switch as you would any switch. Make sure you have power to the switch and that power is being fed through each set of contacts.

Blower resistor pack service

A *bad blower resistor pack* will prevent fan or blower operation on one of the slower speed settings. If totally open, only the high speed blower setting will normally

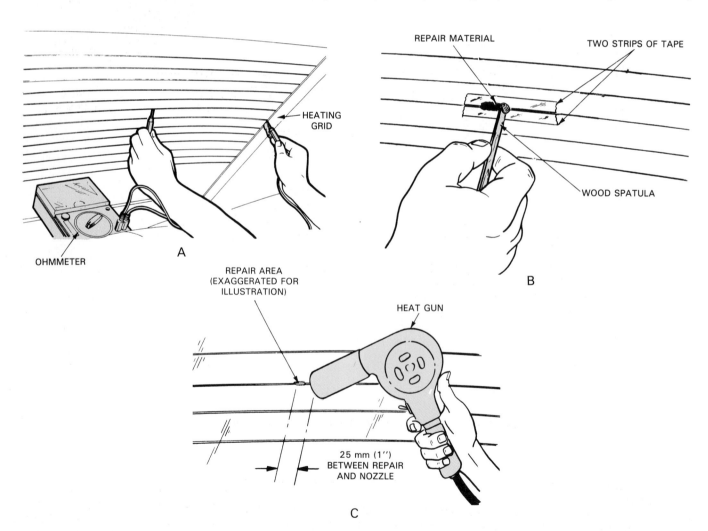

Fig. 28-31. A—Some rear window defoggers are mounted on surface of glass. They can be tested easily with ohmmeter. B—Repair material is being applied to broken section of conductor. C—Heat gun is being used to cure repair material.   (Chrysler)

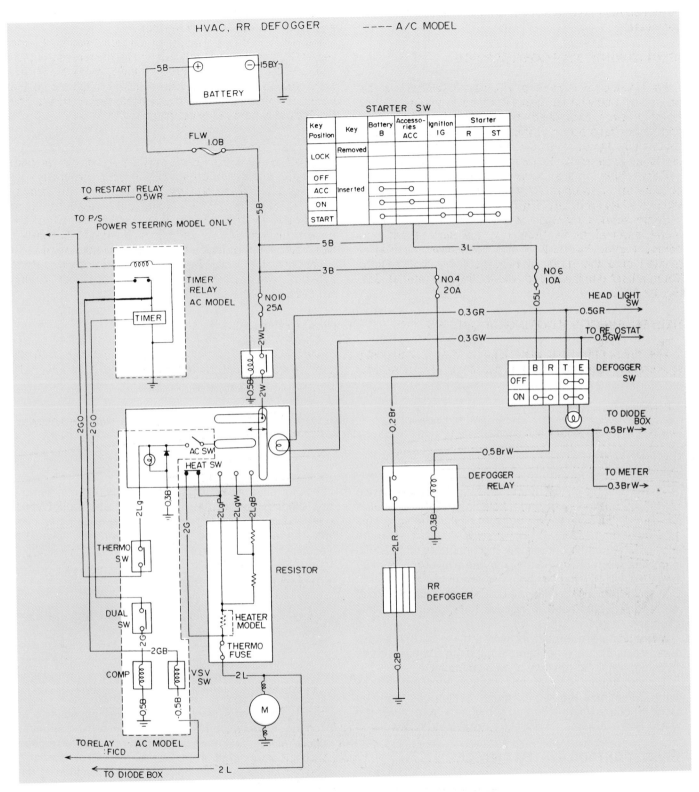

Fig. 28-32. Study this circuit for heater and air conditioning system.

operate. This is because the switch is bypassing the resistor pack.

The resistor pack is usually located on the firewall near the blower motor. Fig. 28-33 shows some basic tests for checking the resistor pack and blower motor. Refer to the manual for details.

Blower motor service

A *bad blower motor* can have dry, noisy bearings or it could have open or shorted windings that prevent operation. Dry blower bearings is a common problem. The dry bearings will make a squeaking or chirping type sound, especially at low blower speeds.

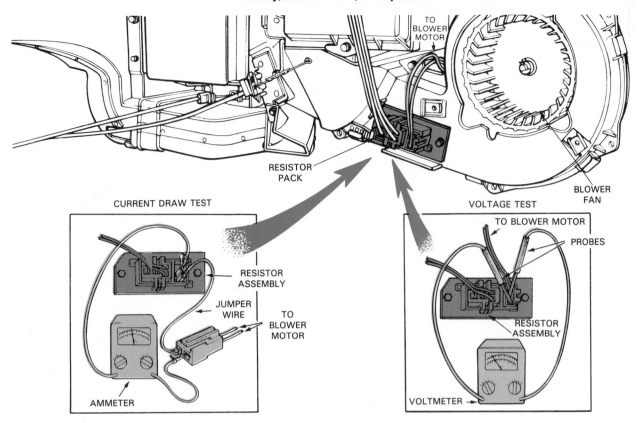

Fig. 28-33. Note tests recommended for one type resistor assembly and blower motor. Others are similar.   (Ford)

A dry bearing in the blower motor can sometimes be corrected by drilling a small hole in the blower at the bearing. Then, squirt a few drops of oil into the hole. This may quiet the bearing. Do not inject too much oil into the blower or you can contaminate the brushes and produce a burned oil smell. In most cases, the blower motor must be REPLACED when the bearings are noisy.

A loose fan on the blower motor can also cause a loud noise. You would have to remove the blower to fix this problem.

When installing the blower motor, make sure it is centered on its mount. If not centered, the fan could rub on its housing, requiring removal and adjustment.

Blower motor removal and replacement procedures vary. Sometimes the blower motor comes out from the engine compartment side and sometimes from under the dash. Refer to a shop manual for exact instructions.

SPEED CONTROL SYSTEM SERVICE

Speed control system designs vary and so do testing and repair methods. Fig. 28-34 shows a drawing of a basic speed or cruise control system. Note the types of troubles that can develop.

If the system fails to engage, check the fuse and main switch. They could be open and preventing current from entering the system. A brake release switch stuck in the closed position could also prevent cruise engagement. Again, use a system diagram and basic electrical testing techniques to find the trouble.

If the system will not hold a steady speed or it wanders,

check for physical binding at the engine vacuum servo. A dry, binding speedometer cable can also upset speed control system operation. A broken speedometer cable will render the cruise control inoperative. Check all vacuum lines for signs of leakage.

AIR BAG SYSTEM SERVICE

DANGER! To prevent injury, consult the proper service manual before attempting to troubleshoot or service an air bag system. Improper service procedures may cause unintentional air bag deployment. Always disable the air bag before servicing any component on or near the system.

Air bag systems have self-diagnostic capabilities and produce trouble codes when a system malfunction occurs. A scan tool must be used to retrieve these codes.

Most components in an air bag system cannot be repaired. When a faulty component is identified, it must generally be replaced. Similarly, many manufacturers recommend replacing all air bag components after air bag deployment. Reusing impact sensors or other components can cause unprovoked system activation.

When an air bag is deployed, it releases a powder that may irritate the eyes, skin, and respiratory system. Always wear protective gloves, eye protection, and a respirator when servicing a deployed bag. Before removing a deployed air bag, cover the vent holes in the back of the bag to prevent additional powder from escaping. Blow the powder from the air conditioning vents by operating the

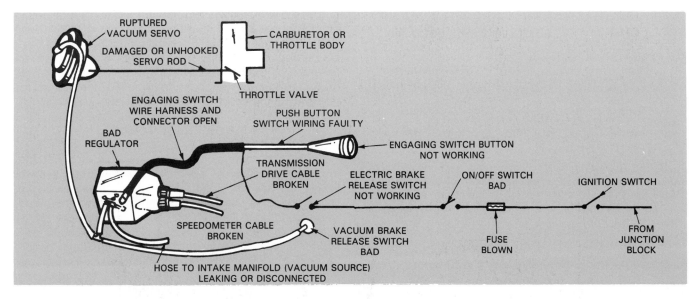

Fig. 28-34. Study types of problems that can develop in speed control system. (Florida Dept. of Voc. Ed.)

fan on the high setting. After turning off the fan, use a vacuum cleaner to remove the powder from the dash, seats, carpet, and other surfaces. After vacuuming, wipe the interior surfaces with a damp cloth.

Be careful when handling replacement parts. If an air bag module or impact sensor is accidentally dropped, it must be replaced. When carrying a "live" inflator module, point the metal inflator housing toward the shop floor. This will help to prevent injury if the bag accidentally deploys.

When replacing impact sensors, make sure the arrows on the sensors point toward the front of the vehicle. Some sensor and inflator module connections are secured with locking pins to ensure tightness. All pins and other fasteners must be reinstalled properly.

ELECTRONICALLY CONTROLLED TRANSMISSION SERVICE

WARNING! Before attempting to service an electronically controlled transmission, always consult an appropriate service manual. Improper service procedures may damage control system components.

When electronically controlled transmission problems are suspected, make sure the engine and the engine control system are operating properly. An electronically controlled transmission will not shift correctly if the engine is not operating properly. Similarly, many of the sensors that send inputs to the engine control computer also provide inputs to the transmission control unit. It is important to note that in some vehicles, the engine and the transmission are controlled by the same computer.

If the engine and the engine control system are operating correctly, check the power supply to the transmission control unit. Also check the ground to the control unit and inspect all connectors. A faulty ground or a corroded connection can cause a variety of problems.

Most electronically controlled transmissions have self-diagnostic capabilities. Trouble codes are produced by the control unit when a system malfunction is detected. A scan tool is used to retrieve these trouble codes from the control unit.

The transmission must often be isolated from its control system to determine whether the problem is in the solenoids, the control system, or the transmission itself. This is accomplished by using a scan tool or remote switches to control the solenoids. If the solenoids are working properly, they should click when triggered with the scan tool or the switches.

If the solenoids do not respond when activated with the scan tool or the remote switches, the connections to the solenoids should be inspected. If necessary, the resistance of each solenoid can be checked with an ohmmeter. Solenoids that do not meet the manufacturer's specifications must be replaced.

Some manufacturers recommend activating the solenoids while road testing the vehicle. If the transmission is working properly, it will shift into the desired gear when the appropriate solenoids are activated, Fig. 28-35. If the solenoids work properly but the transmission does not shift correctly, the transmission may need mechanical repairs.

If the transmission shifts correctly when the solenoids are activated manually but does not shift properly when governed by the control unit, the control system should be checked for problems. Use a digital voltmeter to measure the voltages to and from the control unit. If your measurements are not within the manufacturer's specifications, refer to the service manual for appropriate repair procedures.

OTHER SYSTEM SERVICE

Diagnosing and repairing other electrical-electronic systems is similar. If you know how to work on one system, you should be able to transfer this knowledge to other systems as well. Always remember to stick to the basics and to use logical thought when analyzing problems.

Remember that a factory service manual is one of the best sources of information when working on complex

GEAR	SOLENOID 1	SOLENOID 2
First	On	On
Second	Off	On
Third	Off	Off
Fourth	On	Off

Fig. 28-35. Solenoid operating combinations for one particular electronically controlled transaxle. When servicing an electronic transaxle or transmission, consult an appropriate manual for specific solenoid operating combinations.

electrical-electronic circuits. It will give the correct diagrams, test points, electrical values, and other data needed to do competent work.

SUMMARY

The wiper-washer system is fairly easy to fix. Problems are usually in the switch or motor assembly. Sometimes the plastic gears in the motor strip off and must be replaced. It is also possible for the linkage arms to become disconnected. A poor motor ground can sometimes keep the wiper blades from parking.

When the windshield washers will not work, check for internal clogging. The nozzles could be stopped up or the screen in the reservoir could be plugged. Also check for loose or disconnected washer hoses.

Most washer pumps are operated by a small DC motor. Check for power to the motor. If you do not get power to the feed wire, check the washer switch and wiring. If you get power, the washer motor is probably bad.

Inoperative horns are usually caused by a bad horn switch, loose wire, or a shorted or open horn. Use a test light or VOM to check these components.

Power windows can be inoperative for several reasons. First check the fuse for the system if all windows are inoperative. If only one of the power windows will not work, check at the switch. If power is leaving the switch, the motor itself may be at fault.

Internal radio problems will require radio removal so that it can be sent to a specialist. External problems can be fixed in the field. Always check for power reaching the radio. Check for an open in the antenna. Adjust the antenna trimmer screw if stations are weak or if you replace the antenna. Radio noise can sometimes be corrected by installing condensers to prevent spikes in the DC supply voltage.

A bad speaker can rattle. It must be removed and replaced. Make sure the rattling is not caused by a loose mounting.

Antilock brake system service is straightforward if you refer to a service manual. The manual will detail system operation, specs, and give diagrams and troubleshooting charts. Most systems have self-diagnosis and the trouble codes will help you find problems.

A bad blower switch can prevent the fan from working on slower speeds; so can the resistor pack. Check them with a test light or VOM. Dry blower bearings can make a squeaking or chirping sound. The blower may be removed on the engine compartment side of the firewall or out from under the dash. Again, check the manual for the specific car.

KNOW THESE TERMS

Accessory system, Wiper-washer system, Parking, Inoperative windshield washer, Inoperative horn system, Power window problems, Power door lock problems, Radio problems, Antenna trimmer screw, Switched feed, Unswitched feed, Radio noise, Noise suppressors, Faulty speaker, Breakout box, Bad wheel speed sensor, ABS hydraulic unit, Inoperative rear window defogger circuit, Bad blower switch, Bad blower resistor pack, Bad blower motor.

REVIEW QUESTIONS—CHAPTER 28

1. If windshield wipers do NOT work, where is one of the most common places to start your tests?
2. If you can hear the wiper motor running, but the arms do NOT move, what might be the problem?
   a. Stripped motor gears.
   b. Poor ground.
   c. Open winding.
   d. All of the above.
3. List five causes for inoperative windshield washers.
4. A horn constantly sounds and will NOT shut off. Technician A says the horn button could be stuck closed. Technician B says a horn relay could be burned closed. Who is correct?
   a. Technician A.
   b. Technician B.
   c. Both A and B.
   d. Neither A nor B.
5. All power windows in a car do not work. Technician A says the main control switch could be at fault. Technician B says the power feed to the main circuit must be open. Who is correct?
   a. Technician A.
   b. Technician B.
   c. Both A and B.
   d. Neither A nor B.
6. If a power window motor runs but its output gear does NOT turn, you can sometimes purchase and replace the _____ _____ inside the unit.
7. List some external radio problems that can sometimes be fixed in the field.
8. How and when do you adjust an antenna trimmer screw?
9. _____ _____ are capacitors that absorb voltage fluctuations in the car's electrical system. The result is smoother _____ _____ entering the radio and quieter operation.
10. How do you find problems in an antilock brake system?

ASE CERTIFICATION–TYPE QUESTIONS

1. An automobile's windshield wiper motor "runs", but the wiper arms do not move. Technician A inspects the condition of the wiper motor gearbox. Technician B checks the wiper linkage arms. Who is right?
   (A) A only.   (C) Both A and B.
   (B) B only.   (D) Neither A nor B.

2. A customer brings his/her car to the shop complaining that the car's windshield washer is not working. Technician A checks for an "open" washer motor. Technician B checks to see if the washer system's fluid hose nozzle is clogged. Who is right?
   (A) A only.   (C) Both A and B.
   (B) B only.   (D) Neither A nor B.

3. A car's horn system is not working. Technician A uses a test light to check for power at the horn. Technician B checks the horn's ground circuit. Who is right?
   (A) A only.   (C) Both A and B.
   (B) B only.   (D) Neither A nor B.

4. A customer complains that his/her car's right-front power window is not working. Technician A first checks the switch at this power window. Technician B first checks the power window system's fuse at the automobile's fuse panel. Who is right?
   (A) A only.   (C) Both A and B.
   (B) B only.   (D) Neither A nor B.

5. An automobile's left rear power door lock is inoperative. Technician A says the power door lock's switch could be causing the problem. Technician B says the power door lock's actuator could be causing the problem. Who is right?
   (A) A only.   (C) Both A and B.
   (B) B only.   (D) Neither A nor B.

6. Radio noise is coming from a car's stereo system. Technician A checks the condition of the vehicle's spark plug wires. Technician B inspects the condition of the radio antenna. Who is right?
   (A) A only.   (C) Both A and B.
   (B) B only.   (D) Neither A nor B.

7. The left front wheel on a car equipped with an antilock brake system is not sending a wheel rpm signal to the ABS control unit. Technician A checks for a damaged trigger wheel. Technician B checks the wheel for an open wheel speed sensor. Who is right?
   (A) A only.   (C) Both A and B.
   (B) B only.   (D) Neither A nor B.

8. The blower motor in an automobile's heating system will not work on the low setting. Technician A checks the motor for open or shorted windings. Technician B checks the condition of the blower resistor pack. Who is right?
   (A) A only.   (C) Both A and B.
   (B) B only.   (D) Neither A nor B.

9. An automobile's speed control system will not engage. Technician A checks the system for a blown fuse. Technician B checks to see if the system's brake release switch is working properly. Who is right?
   (A) A only.   (C) Both A and B.
   (B) B only.   (D) Neither A nor B.

10. A car's electronically controlled transmission is not shifting properly. Technician A uses a scan tool to check the operating conditions of the system's solenoids. Technician B checks the car's engine for any operating malfunctions. Who is right?
    (A) A only.   (C) Both A and B.
    (B) B only.   (D) Neither A nor B.

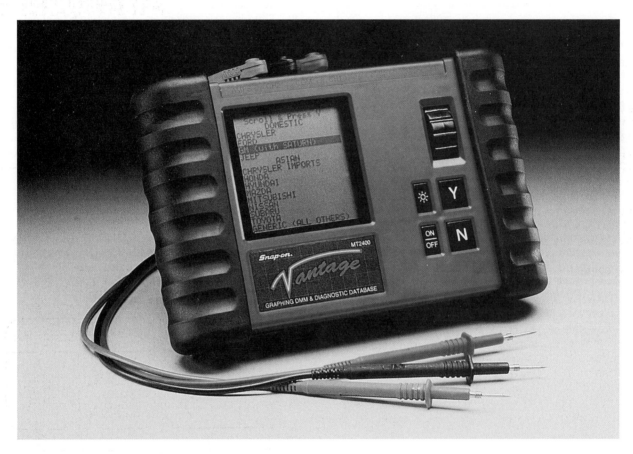

With today's complex, computer-controlled vehicles, hand-held scopes are becoming a necessary "tool." This unit will record dual waveforms, perform flight record functions, and provide information and tips on testing procedures. (Snap-on Tools)

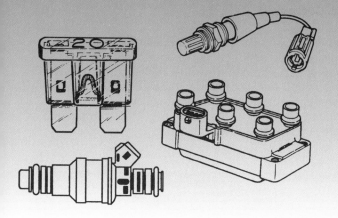

Chapter 29

Advanced Diagnostics, Analyzers

After studying this chapter, you will be able to:

- *Use advanced methods to troubleshoot problems caused by electrical-electronic devices.*
- *Use a scan tool to find problems not tripping trouble codes by using datastream values.*
- *Use a break-out box to measure circuit values.*
- *Explain the principles of an oscilloscope.*
- *Summarize how to use an engine analyzer and hand-held scope.*
- *Summarize how to use waveforms to analyze the operation of sensors, actuators, ECU outputs, and other electrical-electronic devices.*
- *Evaluate ignition system waveforms.*
- *Use an exhaust gas analyzer to find problems caused by the computer system.*

Earlier chapters explained how to diagnose problems using a scan tool, a multimeter, and specialized testing devices. If these basic methods fail to pinpoint the source of the problem, you may need to use more complex diagnostic methods to find and fix the trouble.

This chapter summarizes advanced methods for troubleshooting difficult-to-locate problems. It also introduces the operating principles of vehicle analyzers, with emphasis on using the oscilloscope and the exhaust gas analyzer.

STRATEGY-BASED DIAGNOSTICS

Strategy-based diagnostics involves using a consistent, logical procedure to narrow down the possible problem sources. Basically, you verify the complaint, make preliminary checks, read service bulletins about the vehicle, and perform service manual–recommended checks.

If the scan tool shows a trouble code, you should test everything related to that circuit. Pinpoint tests would be needed to determine whether the wiring or an electronic part is at fault. If no hard trouble codes are present, refer to the service manual. It will give specific instructions and specifications for finding the soft failure. Fig. 29-1 gives a chart showing the basic flow as you use strategy-based diagnosis.

When diagnosing problems, evaluate the symptoms. Use your knowledge of system operation to determine which part could be malfunctioning and causing the symptoms.

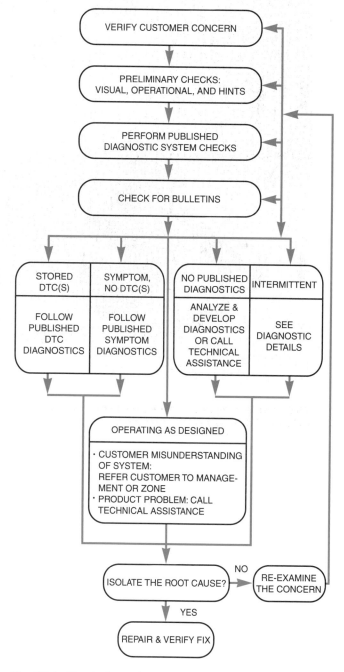

Fig. 29-1. Chart shows basic steps for strategy-based diagnostics. Read through chart carefully.   (Oldsmobile)

For example, if an engine misses only when cold, think of which parts affect cold engine operation. You should think of the coolant temperature sensor, the intake air temperature sensor, and the cold start injector. These components are monitored and/or controlled by the ECM, which enriches the air-fuel mixture when the engine is cold.

Fig. 29-2 is a chart that summarizes various factors and the parts that might be affected or act up under various conditions. Note how you can perform basic service procedures to help find part problems.

ADVANCED DIAGNOSTICS

At one time or another, every technician encounters a problem that seems impossible to fix. He or she might replace a part that seems bad, only to find the same annoying symptoms when the repair is complete. The part must be removed and further diagnosis completed until the real "culprit" is found. This is when advanced diagnostic techniques come in handy.

By learning a few advanced "tricks of the trade" (using datastream values, a breakout box, an exhaust gas analyzer, and an oscilloscope), even the most difficult problems can be located and corrected with minimum frustration.

Scan tool snap-shot

A scan tool *snap-shot* is an instantaneous reading of operating parameters. It is often taken when a problem is

hard to find or when intermittent troubles are present. For example, if a car only acts up when driving at a specific highway speed, you can drive the vehicle at the trouble-causing speed and scan under these conditions. When the symptom occurs (engine misses), you can press a tool button to capture the operating values while the problem is happening. See Fig. 29-3.

Fig. 29-3. Scan tool is being used with add-on board to take snap-shot of operating parameters while test driving vehicle.   (OTC)

	Variable factor	Influential part	Target condition	Service procedure
1	Mixture ratio	Pressure regulator	Made lean	Remove vacuum hose and apply vacuum.
			Made rich	Remove vacuum hose and apply pressure.
2	Ignition timing	Crankshaft position sensor	Advanced	Rotate distributor clockwise.
			Retarded	Rotate distributor counterclockwise.
3	Mixture ratio feedback control	Oxygen sensor	Suspended	Disconnect oxygen sensor harness connector.
		ECM	Operation check	Perform on-board diagnostic system (On-board Diagnostic Test Mode II) at 2000 rpm.
4	Idle speed	IAC valve-AAC valve	Raised	Turn idle adjusting screw counterclockwise.
			Lowered	Turn idle adjusting screw clockwise.
5	Electrical connection (Electric continuity)	Harness connectors and wires	Poor electrical connection or improper wiring	Tap or wiggle.
				Race engine rapidly. See if the torque reaction of the engine unit causes electric breaks.
6	Temperature	ECM	Cooled	Cool with an icing spray or similar device.
			Warmed	Heat with a hair drier. **[WARNING: Do not overheat the unit.]**
7	Moisture	Electric parts	Damp	Wet. **[WARNING: Do not directly pour water on components. Use a mist sprayer.]**
8	Electric loads	Load switches	Loaded	Turn on headlamps, air conditioning, rear defogger, etc.
9	Closed throttle position switch condition	ECM	ON-OFF switching	Rotate throttle position sensor body.
10	Ignition spark position	Timing light	Spark power check	Try to flash timing light for each cylinder using ignition coil adapter (SST).

Fig. 29-2. Compare variable factors to influential parts, conditions, and service procedures. This will give you a general idea of how to analyze difficult problems.   (Nissan)

You then return to the shop to look for any operating parameter that is almost out-of-specs. The operating parameter may not be tripping a trouble code, but it may be affecting vehicle operation. Sometimes, two electrical values can be almost out of specs. Since both values are near their extremes, they do not trip a code. Combined, however, they have an adverse effect on vehicle performance.

You would have to go through all operating values and mark any that are near their extreme. By using this information, you can often make further conclusions about what is causing the problem. You might have two sensors ready to fail, a poor electrical connection in combination with a mechanical failure, etc.

Scan tool datastream values

Scan tool datastream values are "live" electrical values measured with the vehicle running or driving. They almost eliminate the need for a breakout box or pinpoint

For Cold Key On, Cold Idle and Hot Idle: Vehicle in PARK, A/C turned OFF, no power steering load, all ACC.'s OFF, Brake Pedal Released. For 55 MPH Cruise: Vehicle in Drive 4, A/C turned ON and no power steering load, compare data after driving for approximately 1 mile.						
Scan Tool Parameter	**Display Units**	**Data List**	**Cold Key ON**	**Cold Idle**	**Hot Idle**	**55 MPH Cruise**
Engine Speed	RPM	ENG 1	0	Within 80 RPM of Desired Idle	Within 80 RPM of Desired Idle	1730
Desired Idle	RPM	ENG 1	0	700 to 1200	550 to 675	720
MAF	gms-sec	ENG 1	0.0	9.8 to 11.0	5.0 to 6.0	20 to 28
TP Sensor	V/°	ENG 1	0.63 / 1.7	.60 mV / 0.8°	.60 mV / 0.8°	1.06 / 11.0
ECT	°C	ENG 1	80° C	−20° C to 50° C	90° C to 110° C	90° C to 110° C
IAT	°C	ENG 1	80° C	−20° C to 50° C	0° C to 90° C	0° C to 90° C
MAP	kPa/V	ENG 1	97 / 4.63	30 to 50 kPa 1.50 v @ 38 kPa	30 to 50 kPa 1.50 v @ 38 kPa	64 / 2.88
BARO	kPa/V	ENG 1	97 / 4.65	85 to 103 kPa	85 to 103 kPa	98 / 4.69
TP Angle	%/°	ENG 1	0% / 0.0°	0% / 0.0°	0% / 0.0°	11% / 8.6°
Engine Load	%	ENG 1	0%	1 to 5%	1 to 5%	13%
Engine Speed	RPM	ENG 1	0	Within 80 RPM of Desired Idle	Within 80 RPM of Desired Idle	1730
IAC Position	counts	ENG 1	160	Varies	30 to 80	100
Inj. PWM Bank 1	ms	ENG 1	0.0	3.75 to 4.50	3.20 to 3.75	5.1 ms
Inj. PWM Bank 2	ms	ENG 1	0.0	3.75 to 4.50	3.20 to 3.75	5.2 ms
HO2S Bn 1 Sen. 1	mV	ENG 1	67	Varies	Varies	Varies
HO2S Bn 2 Sen. 1	mV	ENG 1	111	Varies	Varies	Varies
Rich to Lean Status Bn 1 Sen. 1	Lean/Rich	ENG 1	Lean	Varies	Varies	Varies
Rich to Lean Status Bn 2 Sen. 1	Lean/Rich	ENG 1	Lean	Varies	Varies	Varies
HO2S Bn 1 Sen. 2	mV	ENG 1	45	Varies	Varies	Varies
HO2S Bn 1 Sen. 3	mV	ENG 1	156	Varies	600 mV or more	600 mV or more
Rich to Lean Status Bn 1 Sen. 2	Lean/Rich	ENG 1	Lean	Varies	Varies	Varies
Rich to Lean Status Bn 1 Sen. 3	Lean/Rich	ENG 1	Lean	Varies	Varies	Varies
Fuel Trim Cell	Number	ENG 1	0	16	16	5
Fuel Trim Learn	Disabled/ Enabled	ENG 1	Disabled	Disabled	Enabled	Enabled
Shrt Term FT Bn 1	%	ENG 1	0% / 128	−2.0 to 2.0	−3.0 to 3.0	−6.0 to 6.0

Fig. 29-4. Scan tool datastream values can be helpful when you have performance problems that do not set trouble codes. Datastream values will be electrical values detected by ECM. If pinpoint test values with VOM do not match datastream values, suspect wiring or ECM problems. If two or more values are almost out of specs, this can also steer you in right direction for testing. (Oldsmobile)

measurements of electrical values. You can read the scan tool screen to see weak values or values that are almost out of specs.

For example, if you have a performance problem and no trouble codes are set, look at datastream values. Values that are almost out of specifications may signal a problem area. Datastream values give added information for finding troublesome problems.

Quite often, you will have two or more datastream values almost out of specs that are causing the performance problem. Fig. 29-4 gives a few datastream values that can be read by a scan tool.

Using personal computers

Personal computers are being used more and more by the technician. They can store and quickly retrieve a huge amount of data. CD-ROMS contain "encyclopedic volumes" of service information. They can also access outside sources of service information via modem and the Internet. The computer can be a valuable tool when doing advanced diagnostic work. Look at Fig. 29-5.

Fig. 29-6 shows a technician using a specialized computer analyzer that communicates with the vehicle manufacturer by modem. The analyzer can retrieve the latest service information, which is very helpful when trying to find difficult problems. Vehicle manufacturer's keep records and can send out "electronic service bulletins" covering common but troublesome repair tasks.

Performing the OBD II drive cycle

The *OBD II drive cycle* is designed to tell the technician whether the OBD II system is operating properly. It involves attaching a scan tool to the vehicle and driving the vehicle for a specified period of time. The drive cycle will include periods of acceleration, cruising, and deceleration.

The drive cycle is normally performed when the battery or ECM has been disconnected, or after diagnostic trouble codes have been erased. Additionally, some states require the drive cycle to be performed before an emissions test.

Carefully study the drive cycle procedure and scan tool operation before starting the drive cycle. You should be

Fig. 29-6. This technician is using large cabinet type analyzer to communicate with vehicle manufacture. This allows reference to latest repair information via modem.   (GM)

reasonably sure that you can complete the drive cycle. If the drive cycle has to be aborted for any reason, the engine must be allowed to cool, which can cause a considerable delay.

The drive cycle is different for each vehicle, so check the service manual for specific instructions. To begin the drive cycle, check that the coolant temperature is low enough to allow the ECM to start in the open loop mode. On most engines, coolant temperature should be below 120°F (49°C). Be sure to allow for variations in coolant temperature sensor calibration. In warm climates, the cool down period can take as long as six hours. If possible, allow the vehicle to sit overnight before starting the drive cycle.

Attach the scan tool and set the tool to record the ECM status as the engine operates. Some scan tools have a dedicated drive cycle option. A typical drive cycle will cover engine warm-up, idling, accelerating, decelerating, and cruising, in a specific order. This order must be followed as outlined in the service manual. Some scan tools will prompt the technician throughout the drive cycle. After ensuring that the engine temperature is low enough to start the drive cycle, start the vehicle and complete the drive cycle sequence as outlined in the service manual.

A typical drive cycle will take from 8-15 minutes to complete, depending on the manufacturer. Some drive cycles require the technician to turn the air conditioning on and off at certain times, to decelerate without braking, and to decelerate with the manual transmission clutch engaged or released, depending on the portion of the cycle being performed. Some state air quality programs eliminate the warm-up portion of the drive cycle, as it is impractical to allow the vehicle to cool off before testing.

Performing the drive cycle with the vehicle on a chassis dynamometer will allow the scan tool to gather readings in the shortest possible time. If the vehicle is driven on the road, it may be impossible to complete the drive cycle exactly as designed. Therefore, some scan tools can be paused when the drive cycle must be delayed. However, if the engine is shut off for any reason, the drive cycle must be restarted from the beginning.

Fig. 29-5. Scan tool stored data is being used in conjunction with personal computer to analyze problem.   (OTC)

The scan tool will indicate when the drive cycle is complete, *not* whether the vehicle passed or failed. Any malfunctions will be stored as trouble codes in the scan tool. Check for stored trouble codes and make further diagnostic checks and repairs as needed. After repairs are complete, repeat the drive cycle to ensure that the vehicle is repaired. See Fig. 29-7.

Checking computer terminal values

Computer terminal values are tested at the metal pins of the ECM. A digital VOM can be used to read terminal voltage and resistance values. These readings can then be compared to known good values. Often, the readings are taken with one or more wiring harnesses connected to the ECM. This often saves you from having to unplug connectors to make electrical measurements.

Fig. 29-8 shows a service manual illustration of ECM terminal voltages for a specific vehicle. Note how the pin numbers correspond to certain circuits and electrical values.

Caution! Never connect a low-impedance (resistance) analog meter or test light to a computer system unless instructed to do so by the service manual. A low-impedance meter or tester could draw enough current to damage delicate electronic devices.

Using a breakout box

A *breakout box* allows you to test electrical values at specific pins on an ECM or in the system the ECM controls. It is one of the last tools used in diagnostics, as it is time consuming, Fig. 29-9. It is also used to locate problems in systems that do not have self-diagnostic capabilities.

The breakout box is connected in place of the ECM in the wiring harness. Then, a multimeter is used to touch specific terminals on the breakout box. The measured circuit values are compared to the manufacturer's specifications. If the measured values are not within specifications, you usually have a defective component or a wiring problem. If the values are within specifications, the problem is in the ECM itself.

Isolating electromagnetic interference

Electromagnetic interference (EMI), or radiation interference, occurs when an induced voltage enters another system's wiring. Sources of EMI can include loose, misrouted, or unshielded spark plug wires; police and CB radios; and aftermarket accessories.

In the past, electromagnetic interference was limited to noise in the radio speakers. In late-model vehicles, EMI can cause a computer-controlled system to malfunction.

For example, induced voltage from a loose spark plug wire could enter a sensor wire. This unwanted voltage then enters the computer as false data. Numerous computer malfunctions or false outputs can result.

To isolate the source of electromagnetic interference, try turning off or disabling circuits or devices. If, for example, removing the drive belt from the alternator corrects the problem, suspect problems inside the alternator. If the problem only occurs with the heated windshield turned on, check components within the heated windshield circuit.

A small transistor radio can be used to find induced voltage sources. Turn the radio on and set it on the AM band, but do not tune it to a station. If the shop is equipped with fluorescent lights, turn them off or test the vehicle outside, away from power lines and any other sources of EMI.

Move the radio around the engine compartment and under the dash with the engine running. If EMI noise (static) is present, a popping or cracking noise will be produced by the transistor radio. You can also use a car antenna cable and the car radio as a "noise sniffer." See Fig. 29-10.

To correct an EMI problem, you must stop the source of the interference (replace leaking spark plug wire, use suppressing condenser, etc.) or shield the affected system's wiring from the interference (reroute the sensor wire, or wrap the wire with foil-type tape, for example).

Typical OBD II Drive Cycle

Diagnostic Time Schedule for I/M Readiness	
Vehicle Drive Status	**What Is Monitored?**
Cold Start, coolant temperature less than 50° C (122° F)	—
Idle 2.5 minutes in Drive (Auto) Neutral (Man), A/C and rear defogger ON	HO2S Heater, Misfire, Secondary Air, Fuel Trim, EVAP Purge
A/C off, accelerate to 90 km/h (55 mph), 1/2 throttle	Misfire, Fuel Trim Purge
3 minutes of Steady State – Cruise at 90 km/h (55 mph)	Misfire, EGR, Secondary Air, Fuel Trim, HO2S, EVAP Purge
Clutch engaged (Man), no braking, decelerate to 32 km/h (20 mph)	EGR, Fuel Trim, EVAP Purge
Accelerate to 90-97 km/h (55-60 mph), 3/4 throttle	Misfire, Fuel Trim, EVAP Purge
5 minutes of Steady State Cruise at 90-97 km/h (55-60 mph)	Catalyst Monitor, Misfire, EGR, Fuel Trim, HO2S, EVAP Purge
Decelerate, no breaking. End of Drive Cycle	EGR, EVAP Purge
Total time of OBD II Drive Cycle 12 minutes	—

Fig. 29-7. Chart shows OBD II drive cycle.   (GM)

ECM TERMINAL VOLTAGE
5.0L (V.I.N. H)

THIS ECM VOLTAGE CHART IS FOR USE WITH A DIGITAL VOLTMETER TO FURTHER AID IN DIAGNOSIS. THESE VOLTAGES WERE DERIVED FROM A KNOWN GOOD CAR. THE VOLTAGES YOU GET MAY VARY DUE TO LOW BATTERY CHARGE OR OTHER REASONS, BUT THEY SHOULD BE VERY CLOSE.

THE FOLLOWING CONDITIONS MUST BE MET BEFORE TESTING:
- ENGINE AT OPERATING TEMPERATURE •
- CLOSED LOOP •
- ENGINE IDLING (FOR "ENGINE RUN" COLUMN) •
- TEST TERMINAL NOT GROUNDED •
- SCANNER NOT INSTALLED •

Left connector (terminals 22–12 / 1–11)

Voltage Key "ON"	Voltage Engine Run	Voltage Circuit Open	Description	Term	Term	Description	Voltage Key "ON"	Voltage Engine Run	Voltage Circuit Open
0	0	0	SENSOR RETURN	22	1	BARO SENSOR SIGNAL DECREASES WITH ALTITUDE	4.75	4.75	*.5
5	5	5	5V REFERENCE	21	2	TPS SENSOR SIGNAL	*1.0 †5.0	*1.0	5.0
.5-.65	3–5	*.5	VACUUM SENSOR OUTPUT	20	3	COOLANT TEMP. SENSOR SIGNAL	*2.5	*2.5	5.0
12	4-7 (VAR)	*.5	PWM EGR SOLENOID	19	4	AIR CONTROL SOLENOID	12.5	*1.0	*.5
12	5–10 (var.)	*.5	M/C SOLENOID	18	5	DIAGNOSTIC TEST TERM	5	5	5
*.5	*.5	12	3RD GEAR SWITCH	17	6	A/C W.O.T. CUTOUT (5.7L)	12	14	*.5
**10	**11	10	VSS SIGNAL	16	7	COOLANT TEMP. SENSOR RETURN	0	0	0
			NOT USED	15	8	NOT USED			
*.5	*.5	1.7	OXYGEN SENSOR – LO	14	9	OXYGEN SENSOR – HI	.3–.45	.1–.9 (var.)	.3–.45
*.5	*.5	*1.0	DIST REF PULSE – LO	13	10	DIST. REF. PULSE – HI	*.5	1–2 (var.)	*.5
*.5	1–2 (var.)	*.5	EST	12	11	IGN. MODULE BY-PASS	*.5	3.7	*.5

Right connector (terminals J–A / K–U)

Voltage Key "ON"	Voltage Engine Run	Voltage Circuit Open	Description	Term	Term	Description	Voltage Key "ON"	Voltage Engine Run	Voltage Circuit Open
			NOT USED	J	K	NOT USED			
*.5 P/N 12 D/R	*.5 P/N 14 D/R	12	PARK/NEUTRAL SWITCH	H	L	ESC (5.0L)	7-10	7-10	*.5
10	*.5	*.5	"CHECK ENGINE" LAMP	G	M	NOT USED			
			NOT USED	F	N	4TH GEAR SWITCH IF USED	*.5	*.5	12
12	*1.0	*.5	THROTTLE KICKER	E	P	TRANS CONVERTER CLUTCH SOLENOID	12	14	*.5
			NOT USED	D	R	TROUBLE CODE MEMORY POWER	12	14	*.5
12	14	*.5	IGN 1 POWER	C	S	NOT USED			
12	14	*.5	AIR SWITCHING SOLENOID	B	T	NOT USED			
0	0	0	GROUND (TO ENGINE)	A	U	GROUND (TO ENGINE)	0	0	0

* = Value Shown or Less Than that Value
† = Wide Open Throttle
(var.) = variable
P/N = Park or Neutral
D/R = Drive or Reverse
** = If Less than 1V Rotate Drive Wheel to Verify.

Fig. 29-8. Service manual will usually give ECM terminal values for specific vehicle. This will tell you the electrical values that should be present at each terminal at the computer connector. (GM)

Fig. 29-9. Breakout box is one of the last tools used to find hidden performance problems. It is connected to wiring harness in computer system. Then, VOM can be connected to test terminals on breakout box to measure actual operating voltage, resistance, and current values. They can be compared to known good ones or to datastream values to arrive at source of trouble.

Digital pyrometer testing

A *digital pyrometer* is an electronic device for measuring temperature. Measuring actual temperature can help you verify scan tool readouts and find hard-to-locate problems. It is handy for advanced diagnosis of various systems and components. A digital pyrometer can be used to check:

1. Engine operating temperature.
2. Exhaust temperature.
3. Coolant temperature.
4. Sensor temperature.
5. Ambient temperature.
6. Air conditioning outlet temperature.

You can test a temperature sensor while it is still in the engine by checking pyrometer readings against sensor resistance when the engine is cold and after it warms. Touch the pyrometer's probe to the sensor to get a reading of its operating temperature. This will let you compare sensor temperature and resistance readings with manual specifications.

Finding temperature-related performance problems

When an engine performance problem only occurs at a specific temperature, suspect electronic parts. Electronic circuits, especially ignition control modules, can be affected by temperature extremes.

To check a component for problems affected by temperature, use a heat gun to warm the component or a can of freeze spray to cool the unit. If the problem occurs with the temperature change, the unit is at fault and should be replaced. See Fig. 29-11.

Caution! Do not apply too much heat to an electronic module. Excessive heat can damage components. Only match the engine operating temperature of about 200°F. (93°C). Use a digital thermometer to monitor the temperature when heating the unit.

Using a dynamometer

A *dynamometer*, often referred to as a *dyno*, is used to measure an engine's power output and performance. By loading the engine, the dynamometer can check engine acceleration, maximum power output, and on-the-road performance characteristics. Fig. 29-12 shows a chassis dynamometer.

If you are having trouble finding a driveability problem, you might perform diagnostic tests while operating the

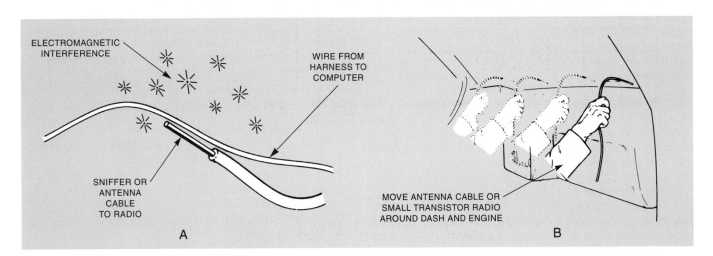

Fig. 29-10. A—Radiation interference can be caused by ignition secondary voltage, leaking diode in alternator, and other sources of voltage spikes or magnetic field. B—A cheap transistor radio or an extra antenna cable connected to vehicle's radio will "listen" or "sniff" for source of interference. Radiation can upset operation of computer sensor signals and car radio. (GM)

Fig. 29-11. With intermittent engine problems affected by heat or period of engine operation, suspect electronic control circuits in ECM. Cold spray directed onto ECM may cause or solve engine performance problem. If it does, replace ECM.

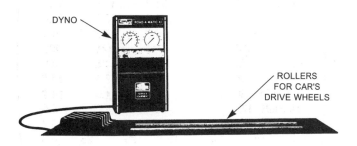

Fig. 29-12. Chassis dynamometer will measure engine power output under road conditions. It will also load engine while doing other tests.   (Sun Electric Corp.)

vehicle on a dynamometer. This will let you simulate any condition that causes the problem.

For example, you could connect a five-gas exhaust analyzer to the tailpipe and operate the vehicle under load. You can also shift the vehicle through each gear, accelerate to the speed at which the problem occurs, walk around the vehicle to listen for abnormal noises, or connect listening devices—all while simulating driving conditions.

ENGINE ANALYZER (COMPUTER ANALYZER)

An *engine analyzer*, also called a *vehicle analyzer* or computer analyzer, consists of a group of test instruments that includes a scope, a tach-dwell meter, a VOM, an exhaust gas analyzer, and, sometimes, a scan tool. These tools are mounted in a large, roll-around cabinet. The operation of each instrument is often controlled by a computer that interfaces all the testing devices. See Fig. 29-13.

When connected to the vehicle, the analyzer will help you check the condition of the engine and its support systems. An engine analyzer will help find problems when a scan tool does not show a trouble code or an out-of-parameter operating value.

Fig. 29-13. Analyzer can do a number of different tests and measurements. It is like having a VOM, tach-dwell, exhaust analyzer, timing light, and other testers connected at once for problem isolation.

For example, if an engine misfire is being diagnosed, the analyzer will help find which parts are defective. It will pinpoint fouled spark plugs, open plug wires, rich or lean fuel mixtures, inoperative fuel injectors, and other problems, even before removing and inspecting parts.

Modems

Some analyzers can transmit data over telephone lines for comparison to information stored in a larger mainframe computer by using a modem. A *modem* is an electronic device that allows computer data or signals to be sent or received over telephone lines.

Data can be sent back and forth between modems. This allows the technician to access information that could be used to troubleshoot difficult problems. Most dealerships have modem-equipped computer analyzers. The analyzer is plugged into the vehicle's data link connector and the information is sent by modem to the mainframe computer.

A *mainframe computer* is a very large computer that can store tremendous amounts of data. It can also do multiple tasks or transfer information to several computer analyzers at the same time.

The auto or equipment manufacturer's mainframe computer can have information about common problems, both hard and soft codes, stored in memory for each vehicle. Steps for finding problems, common faults, specific voltages, and other electrical values for each model can also be stored in mainframe memory.

Engine analyzer differences

There are a number of different makes of analyzers on the market. The controls and meter faces may be organized differently, but the basic test equipment and operation of each are almost the same.

Most analyzers will check:
1. Battery, charging, and starting systems.
2. Ignition system.
3. Engine condition.
4. Fuel system.
5. Emission control systems.
6. Sensor and ECM signals.

Analyzer test equipment

Typically, an electronic analyzer will contain several pieces of test equipment, including:

1. OSCILLOSCOPE (high speed meter that uses a liquid crystal display or a television picture tube).
2. VOLTMETER, AMMETER, AND OHMMETER (meters used to measure electrical values).
3. TACHOMETER (meter used to measure engine speed in rpms. It is commonly used for fuel injection, ignition timing, and other adjustments).
4. DWELL METER (instrument that measures ignition module or contact point conduction time in degrees of distributor rotation. It will detect point misadjustment and other problems).
5. TIMING LIGHT (strobe light for ignition timing adjustment. Most analyzer timing lights have a degree meter for measuring distributor advance).
6. VACUUM GAUGE (gauge used to measure vacuum when checking the operation of the engine operation and various vacuum-operated devices).
7. VACUUM PUMP (pump capable of producing a supply vacuum for operating and testing vacuum devices).
8. CYLINDER POWER BALANCE TESTER (unit for electrically shorting out one or more fuel injectors or spark plugs. It will determine if a cylinder is firing properly and producing power).
9. EXHAUST GAS ANALYZER (measures the chemical content and amount of pollution in the vehicle's exhaust).
10. SCAN TOOL (often incorporated into analyzers for retrieving trouble codes and circuit operating values).
11. DIGITAL DISPLAY (displays operating values for various components in numeric form. Modern analyzers have a screen that displays digital readings of various test values, such as engine rpm, charging system voltage, exhaust gas content, etc.). See Fig. 29-14.
12. PRINTER (prints information about ignition timing, dwell, engine speed, emission levels, and other values on paper. If repairs are needed, the technician can show the customer the improper readings on the printout. If the vehicle is in good condition, the printout can serve as a record if later repairs are needed). See Fig. 29-15.

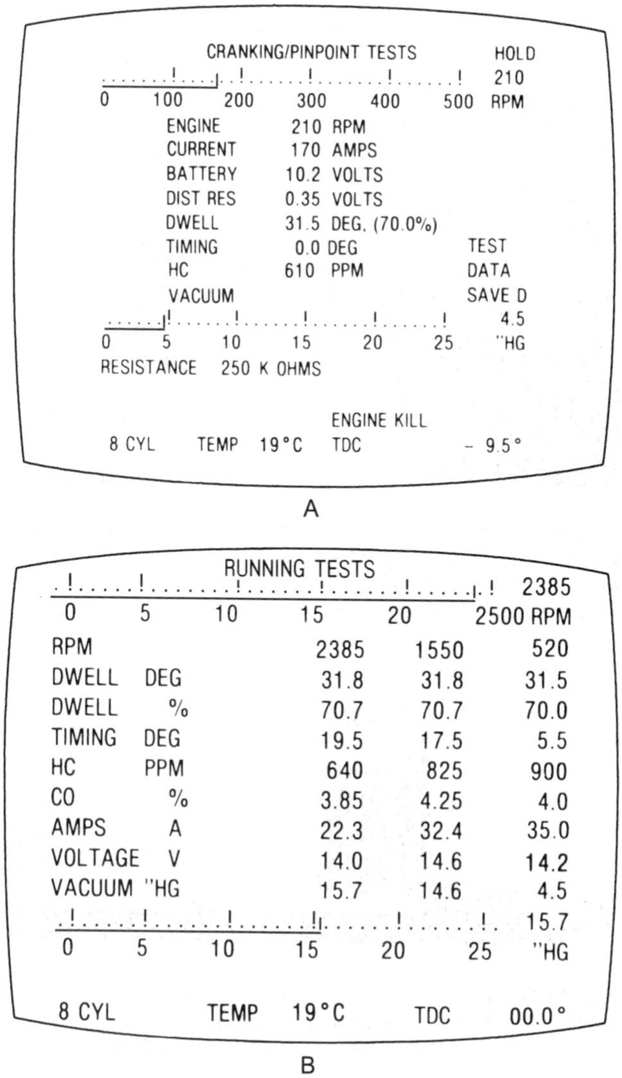

ANALYZER CONNECTIONS

Analyzer connections differ with each type and model. Nevertheless, most have the same general test connections. Modern analyzers will give you directions for connecting the test leads to the vehicle, Fig. 29-16.

Test leads should be connected as described in the user's manual. Special leads and hoses may be provided for measuring starting current, charging voltage, engine vacuum, fuel pump pressure, sensor signals, and exhaust gas content. These tests are generally the same as those covered in other chapters using hand-held instruments.

Fig. 29-17 shows how to connect an analyzer to conventional and unitized ignition coils. An adapter may be needed to connect the analyzer to a distributorless ignition system, Fig. 29-18A. You must install secondary

Fig. 29-14. Many modern analyzers are capable of producing a digital or number display on extra screen. A—Digital display for cranking tests. B—Digital display for running tests. Study readout capabilities. (Snap-on Tools)

jumper wires on some direct ignition systems so the inductive test leads can be clamped around them to read voltages, Fig. 29-18B.

USING AN ANALYZER

To use an analyzer, plug the electrical cord into a wall outlet. Set the controls and connect the test leads to the vehicle. If needed, read the operating manual for the analyzer.

Caution! Before starting the engine, make sure all leads are away from hot or moving parts. The analyzer leads are very expensive and can be easily damaged by contact with a hot exhaust manifold or a spinning fan blade or pulley.

Set the parking brake and start the engine. Many analyzer manufacturers recommend increasing engine idle speed to around 1500 rpm during scope tests.

Closely inspect each pattern. Check each section of the

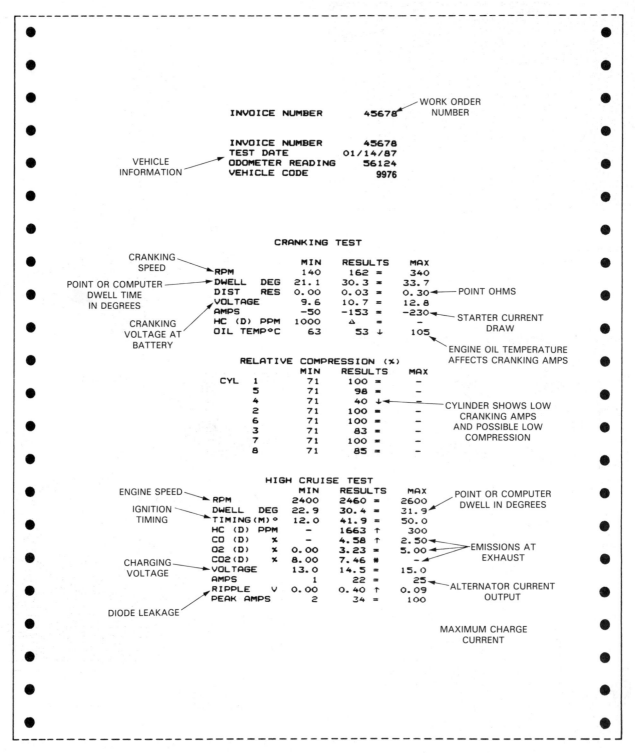

Fig. 29-15. Printer will type test results on paper for customer or evaluation. (Snap-on Tools)

waveform carefully. Look for any sign of variation from a normal pattern. Voltages should be within specifications, and the spark lines should be clean and almost straight. Dwell times must be correct.

Ignition coil output test

A scope *ignition coil output test* measures the maximum available voltage produced by the ignition coil. A spark plug only requires about 5-20 kV for operation.

However, the ignition coil should have a higher reserve voltage. Without this extra voltage, the spark plugs could misfire under load or at high engine speeds when voltage requirements are greater.

To perform the coil output test, set the analyzer controls and display to the highest kV range. Run the engine at 1000-1500 rpm. Using insulated pliers, disconnect a spark plug wire. Hold the end of the wire away from ground while watching the scope screen.

Fig. 29-16. Most late model scopes will give detailed instructions for making connections to vehicle and for doing each test. This simplifies analyzer operation considerably. (Snap-on Tools)

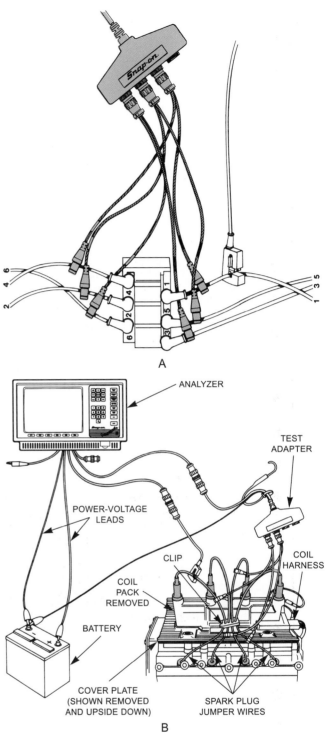

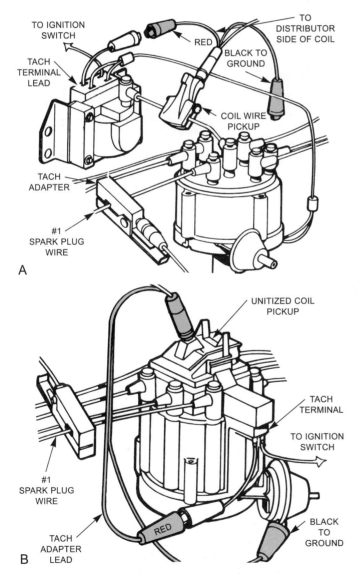

Fig. 29-17. Connecting analyzer to ignition systems. A—System in which coil is separate from distributor. B—System with unitized coil.

Fig. 29-18. Operating manual illustration for connecting an analyzer to distributorless and integrated direct ignition systems. A—Separate inductive leads are needed for each wire on this distributorless ignition system. B—Note jumper spark plug wires between coil pack and spark plugs. (Snap-on Tool Corp.)

With a coil pack, you will have to test each coil's output voltage separately. Just because one coil passed its tests does not mean the others will. By using the coil pack firing order and the secondary pattern, you can tell which coil should be tested.

With the spark plug wire removed, a tall firing line should stand out from the others. Look over to the scope scale on the side of the screen. Read the voltage even with the top of the spike. This value should equal the capacity of the ignition coil.

> Caution! A few electronic ignitions may be damaged by disconnecting spark plug wires while the engine is running. Be sure to check manufacturer's directions.

With older electronic ignitions, coil output voltage should range between 30,000-45,000 volts. However, some electronic ignition coils are able to produce up to 100,000 volts.

> Warning! Even though ignition coil or coil pack current is too low to normally cause electrocution, the high voltage could injure you or cause a potentially deadly heart attack.

If the ignition coil voltage is below specifications, do not condemn the coil until completing further tests. Low coil output could be due to low primary supply voltage, leaking secondary wires, or similar problems. Eliminate these as sources of the problem before replacing the ignition coil.

Load test

A *load test,* or *acceleration test,* measures the spark plug firing voltages when engine speed is rapidly increased. When an engine is accelerated, higher voltage is needed to fire the spark plugs. While a defective component may not produce an abnormal scope pattern at idle, it may not operate properly under load.

To perform a load test, set the scope on parade and idle the engine between 1000-1200 rpm. While watching the firing lines on the scope, quickly open the injection throttle valve (or carburetor throttle plate) and release it. The firing voltage should increase, but it must not exceed certain limits.

The highest firing line should not be more than 75% of actual coil output. Typically, voltage should *not* exceed 15 kV in a contact point ignition or 20 kV in an electronic ignition. The upward movement of the firing lines during the load test should be the same. If any of the firing lines are high or low, a defect is present.

Cylinder balance test

A *cylinder balance test,* also called a *power balance test,* measures the power output from each of the engine's cylinders. As each cylinder is shorted, the tachometer should indicate an rpm drop. During a cylinder balance test, all cylinders should have the same percentage of rpm drop (within 5%). If a shorted cylinder does not produce an adequate amount of rpm drop, the cylinder is not firing properly.

> Caution! Never short a cylinder in a vehicle with a catalytic converter for more than 15 seconds; converter damage could result.

If the rpm drop in one or more cylinders is below normal, a problem common to those cylinders is indicated. The cylinders could have low compression (burned valve, blown head gasket, worn piston rings), a lean

mixture (vacuum leak, faulty fuel injector, computer malfunction), or other problems.

Cranking balance test

A *cranking balance test* is done to check the engine's mechanical condition. It can be used to isolate a cylinder with low compression due to a burned valve, worn piston rings, or other problems. The analyzer will show how much current is drawn by the starter motor as each cylinder goes through its compression stroke. High current draw means high compression stroke pressure. Low current draw (low display line) means that cylinder has low compression. Look at Fig. 29-19.

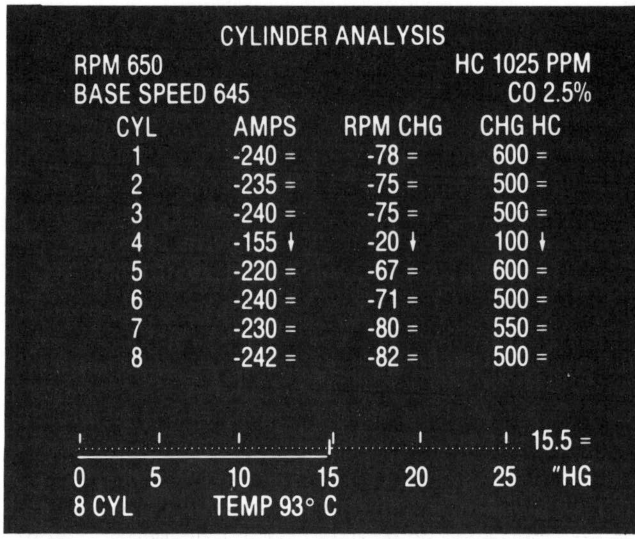

Fig. 29-19. Cylinder analysis can be used to check general engine compression. If any cylinder does not load starting motor as much as others, it has a lower compression pressure and mechanical leak.   (Snap-on Tools)

OTHER ANALYZER TESTS

An analyzer is usually capable of performing other tests besides those discussed in this chapter. These include starter cranking amps, charging voltage, and exhaust gas analysis. Such tests are almost identical to those done with individual instruments explained in other chapters.

OSCILLOSCOPE

An *oscilloscope,* often called a *scope,* is a piece of test equipment that displays voltages in relation to time. When connected to circuit voltage, the scope produces a line on a cathode ray tube or a liquid crystal screen. The line illustrates the various voltages present in the circuit over short periods of time.

By comparing the scope pattern (line shape) to a known good pattern, the technician can determine whether something is wrong in the circuit. An oscilloscope is usually a major component of an analyzer. However, it may be mounted by itself on a small, roll-around cart, or it may be part of a hand-held scan tool or multimeter.

Reading the scope screen

The *scope screen* can give instructions, display voltages as a trace, or give other values as digital displays. The oscilloscope's ability to draw a *trace,* or pattern of circuit voltages, for very short time spans makes it very useful for testing ignition and computer system performance. You should learn to recognize good scope patterns. Then, you can easily detect scope patterns that indicate problems.

Voltage is shown on the scope screen along the vertical (up and down) axis, or scale. Voltage values are given on the right and left borders of the screen.

With the controls set on kV, the numbers on the screen represent kilovolts. One kV equals 1000 volts; 5 kV equals 5000 volts; etc. If a line on the scope screen extends from zero to 7 kV, the scope is reading 7000 volts.

If the scope is set to read 0-10 volts for checking the ECM and its sensors, a line five divisions tall would indicate 5 volts. Similarly, a waveform five divisions tall would be a reading of 5 volts peak-to-peak (from the top of the positive trace to the bottom of the negative trace).

Voltage is the most commonly used value on a scope screen. As voltage increases, the white trace line on the scope moves up. As voltage drops, the trace line moves down a proportionate amount.

Scope time is given on the horizontal scale of the scope screen in degrees, milliseconds, or duty cycle.

Different scales may be given on the bottom of the screen for four-, six-, or eight-cylinder engines. These scales are calibrated in degrees of distributor rotation. Degrees may also be given as a percentage, for quick reference to any number of cylinders.

The scope screen may also have a milliseconds scale for measuring actual time. This makes it possible to measure how long each spark plug fires in milliseconds. A certain amount of time is needed to properly ignite and burn the air-fuel mixture.

Scope sweep rate

Scope sweep rate is the frequency or time division shown on the screen during each test. The sweep rate adjustment affects the horizontal, or time, measurement. The scope sweep rate must be set to match the waveform frequency to be analyzed. Sweep rate is commonly given in milliseconds (ms).

A *low scope sweep rate* will compress the waveform, and too much information will be shown at once. A *high sweep rate* will expand the waveform, and only a small section of the complete duty cycle will be displayed.

Trial and error adjustment of sweep rate is commonly used. The sweep rate knob, or sweep knob, (time/division) on the scope is turned until the desired waveform is displayed on the screen. Compare the waveform pattern on the scope to a known good pattern.

IGNITION SYSTEM PATTERNS

A vehicle's ignition system is designed to produce wide fluctuations in voltage. When an ignition system is functioning properly, these voltages are within specifications.

A component with higher-than-normal resistance (open spark plug wire, for example) would be indicated on the scope as higher-than-normal voltage trace. The high resistance would produce a high voltage drop. A shorted component (fouled spark plug) would have low resistance and would produce lower-than-normal voltage trace.

An oscilloscope's controls allow it to display either the primary (low voltage) pattern or the secondary (high voltage) pattern of the ignition system. The scope patterns are similar, but important differences should be understood.

To introduce the basic sections of a scope pattern, the primary and secondary patterns for *one cylinder* will be explained. More complex patterns for specialized tests will be covered later in this chapter.

Primary scope pattern

The *primary scope pattern* shows the low voltage, or primary voltage, changes in an ignition system. A primary scope pattern is shown in Fig. 29-20.

The primary ignition pattern has three sections: firing, intermediate, and dwell. Note how the voltages change in each section of the pattern.

The ignition secondary circuit cannot work properly unless the primary circuit is in good condition. A problem in the primary circuit will usually affect the secondary circuit. For this reason, the secondary circuit pattern is *checked more often* than the primary pattern.

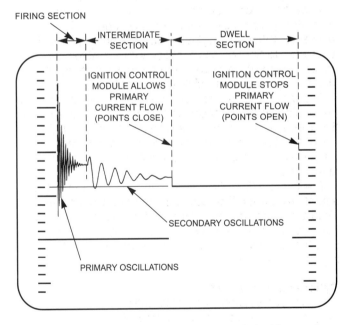

Fig. 29-20. Typical primary waveform for basic ignition system. Study parts or sections of trace.   (FMC)

Secondary scope pattern

The *secondary scope patterns* show the high voltages needed to fire the spark plugs. Fig. 29-21 illustrates the secondary pattern for one cylinder.

Secondary firing section

The secondary pattern starts on the left with the firing section. The *firing section* will pinpoint problems with the spark plugs, the plug wires, the distributor rotor, and the distributor cap, Fig. 29-21.

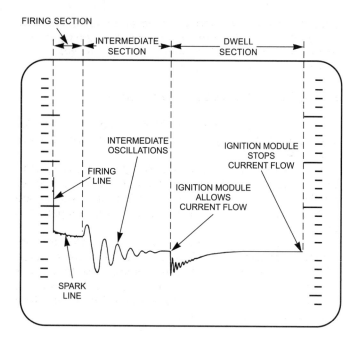

Fig. 29-21. Secondary waveform for one cylinder in basic ignition. Firing line is voltage needed to fire spark plug. Spark line is voltage needed to maintain arc at plug. Intermediate oscillations shows coil and condenser action. Dwell is amount of time primary current flows through ignition coil to build magnetic field. (FMC)

The *firing line* is the tall spike or line representing the amount of voltage needed to cause the electric arc to jump across the spark plug gap. It is normally the peak voltage in the ignition system, Fig. 29-21.

The *spark line* shows the voltage used to maintain the arc across the spark plug electrodes, Fig. 29-21. Once the spark is started, less voltage is needed to maintain the arc. The spark line should be almost straight, clean, and about one-fourth as high as the firing line.

Secondary intermediate section

The secondary pattern's *intermediate section,* or *coil oscillations section,* shows voltage fluctuations after the spark plug stops firing. Typically, the voltage should swing up and down four times (four waves) at low engine speeds. This section of the pattern will indicate problems with the ignition coil or coil pack. See Fig. 29-21.

The voltage oscillations will disappear at the end of the intermediate section as the ignition amplifier begins to conduct or the breaker points close.

Secondary dwell section

The secondary pattern's *dwell section* starts when the ignition module conducts primary current through the ignition coil. In a contact point system, it is the time when the points are closed. The ignition coil is building up a magnetic field during the dwell section.

The dwell section will indicate problems such as a faulty ignition module, burned contact points, or a leaking condenser. Contact point dwell (related to point gap) can be read by measuring the length of the dwell section along the bottom scale of the scope screen.

An electronic ignition can have different dwell periods

from cylinder to cylinder. However, if the dwell varies in a contact-point type ignition, it indicates distributor wear or damage.

The scope pattern for an electronic ignition will vary from the pattern of a contact point–type ignition. The firing and intermediate sections are similar, but the dwell sections differ. Instead of mechanical contact points, an ignition module operates the ignition coil. The circuit design inside the module determines the shape of the dwell section. If you are not familiar with electronic ignition waveforms, they can be easily misinterpreted.

SCOPE TEST PATTERNS

There are five scope test patterns commonly used by the technician when checking ignition system operation: primary superimposed, secondary superimposed, parade (display), raster (stacked), and expanded display (cylinder select).

As you will learn, each of these patterns is capable of showing certain types of problems.

Primary superimposed pattern

The *primary superimposed pattern* shows the low voltages in the primary system—the ignition module or the condenser, coil primary windings, and points.

Superimposed means that the patterns for all the cylinders are placed on top of one another. This makes the trace line thicker than the single cylinder pattern discussed earlier.

Sometimes, an experienced technician will inspect the primary superimposed pattern before going to the more informative secondary pattern. Look at Fig. 29-22A.

Secondary superimposed pattern

The *secondary superimposed pattern* places all the cylinder waveforms on top of each other, but it also shows the high voltages produced by the ignition coil. It is one of the most commonly used scope patterns. The superimposed secondary waveform allows you to quickly check the operating condition of all cylinders.

For example, if one spark plug is not firing properly, the waveform for that cylinder (spark plug) will not align with the others. The abnormal trace will stand out because the firing voltage is higher or lower than normal.

The secondary superimposed pattern is used to check for general problems in the ignition system. If one of the waveforms is out of place, the other scope patterns may be used to find exactly which component is causing the problem.

Parade pattern

The *parade pattern*, also called the *display pattern*, lines up the waveform for each cylinder side-by-side across the screen. The number one cylinder is on the left. The other cylinders are displayed in firing order going to the right, Fig. 29-22B.

The parade pattern takes the superimposed waveforms and separates each along a horizontal axis. This makes the parade pattern useful for comparing firing voltages of each spark plug. If one or more firing lines are too tall or short, a problem is present in those cylinders.

During normal operating conditions, secondary voltages will vary from 5-12 kV for contact point–type igni-

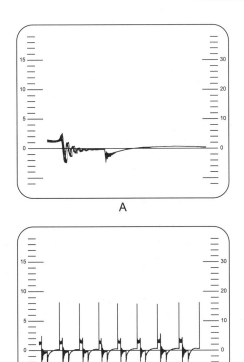

Fig. 29-22. Two common scope test patterns. A—Superimposed has all patterns on top of each other. Any variation shows problem. B—Parade has cylinder patterns side-by-side in firing order. Number one cylinder is on right. This often is used to find high circuit resistance which will cause higher or taller trace. (FMC)

tions and from 7-25 kV for electronic ignitions. The electronic ignition normally produces higher voltages because of the wider spark plug gaps needed to ignite lean fuel mixtures.

A *tall firing line* on the parade pattern indicates high resistance in the ignition secondary caused by an open spark plug wire, a wide spark plug gap, a burned distributor cap side terminal, or a burned secondary connection in a distributorless ignition. High resistance requires higher voltage output from the ignition coil.

A *short firing line* indicates low resistance in the ignition secondary, which may be an indication of leaking spark plug wire insulation, oil-fouled spark plugs, carbon tracking on the distributor cap or coil pack, or similar problems. Not as much voltage would be needed.

Raster pattern

In a *raster pattern*, or *stacked pattern*, the voltage waveforms are placed one above the other. The bottom waveform is the number one cylinder. The other cylinders are arranged in firing order from the bottom up.

The raster pattern is normally used to check timing or dwell variations between cylinders.

EXPANDED DISPLAY

Some oscilloscopes have a control that allows one cylinder waveform to be displayed above the parade pattern. This arrangement is called an *expanded display,* or *cylinder select.* If a problem is located in one trace, that trace can be expanded (enlarged and moved up on screen) for closer inspection.

READING OSCILLOSCOPE PATTERNS

To read a scope pattern, inspect the waveform for abnormal shapes (high or low voltages, incorrect dwell or time periods).

Since there are so many variations of electronic ignition waveforms, refer to the scope operating manual or another reference. Locate an illustration of a good scope pattern for the particular ignition system and compare it to the test pattern.

Fig. 29-23 shows electronic ignition waveforms from several manufacturers. They can be used as a guide when troubleshooting. Fig. 29-24 shows the true spark and the waste spark that occur when one ignition coil in a coil pack fires two spark plugs at once. Fig. 29-25 gives several faulty scope patterns.

COMPUTER SYSTEM SCOPE TESTS

An oscilloscope will help you find computer system problems. When the scan tool does not find anything and you still have performance problems, you may need to check sensor and ECM signals with a scope.

Analyzing square and sine wave signals

When analyzing a square wave, there are several things you should check. They include:
1. The *base line* is the reference line, or zero volts.
2. The *rising edge,* or *leading edge,* is where the square wave goes from zero to high voltage.
3. The *on-time,* or *high-time,* is the part where the square wave stays at maximum voltage.
4. The *trailing edge,* or *falling edge,* is the drop in voltage back to zero.
5. The *off-time,* or *low-time,* is where the square wave stays on the base line.
6. The *amplitude,* or *peak-to-peak voltage,* of a square wave is determined by the horizontal distance from the base line to the high-time.

You can inspect these sections of the waveform to determine if there is a problem. Some common problems that can affect a square wave include:
1. Low or high resistance in the circuit or its components.
2. Faulty electronic circuit.
3. Circuit contaminated by moisture.

When analyzing sine waves, check the following:
1. Analog peak-to-peak voltage. (Is the waveform voltage strong from top to bottom?)
2. Analog wave shape. (Is the trace normal for a known good component?)
3. Analog wave frequency. (Is the distance between waves normal?)
4. Analog wave smoothness. (Is there unwanted hair or static on sine wave?)

Distributor pickup coil scope testing

An oscilloscope can also be used to check the output signal of a distributor pickup coil. It will not only measure

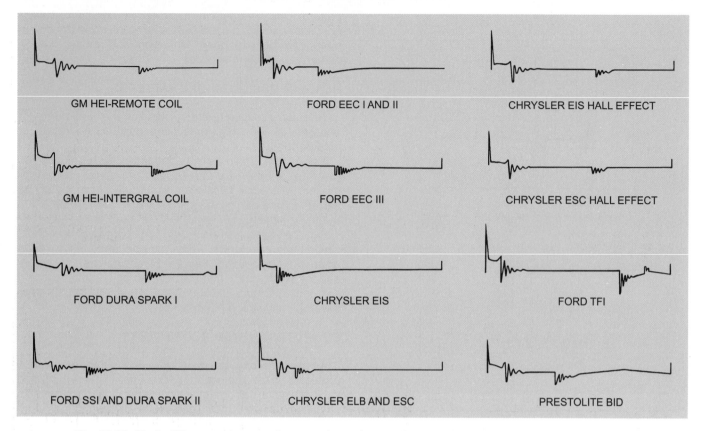

Fig. 29-23. Study differences in secondary waveforms from various auto manufacturers.   (Snap-on Tools)

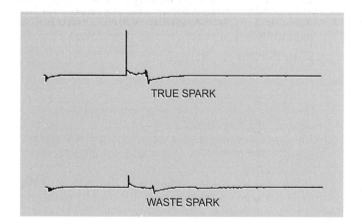

Fig. 29-24. Note differences between true spark and waste spark when one coil fires two spark plugs at same time. True spark starts air-fuel mixture burning. Waste spark does nothing since cylinder is on exhaust stroke.   (Snap-on Tools)

voltage, but it will also show the shape of the signal leaving the pickup coil.

Magnetic sensor testing

A *magnetic sensor test* is done by measuring the output voltage from the sensor with the engine cranking. With a magnetic sensor, connect the scope primary leads to the pickup coil. Set the selector to primary and the primary height control to 40v. Adjust the pattern length to minimum.

With the engine cranking, an ac (alternating current) signal about 1.5v peak-to-peak should be generated, Fig. 29-26.

Hall-effect sensor testing

A *Hall-effect sensor test* is best done by checking the sensor's output waveform with an oscilloscope. Without disconnecting the circuit reference voltage, probe the output wire at the sensor connector. The service manual will give pin numbers for probing. See Fig. 29-27.

A Hall-effect sensor waveform should switch rapidly, have vertical sides, and have the specified voltage output (typically about 4-5 volts peak-to-peak). The top of the square wave should reach reference voltage and the bottom should almost reach ground, or zero. Signal frequency should change with engine cranking speed or engine rpm. Hall-effect pickups can be found in distributors and some crankshaft position sensors. Since specifications vary for Hall-effect sensors, refer to the service manual for that vehicle. See Fig. 29-28.

Optical sensor testing

An optical sensor can also be tested with an oscilloscope. You can probe the output wires from the sensor and compare the waveform to specifications.

A *optical pickup test* measures the output generated by the photo diodes as they are energized by the LEDs. It is also easily done with a hand-held scope probing into the sensor's electrical connector. Again, refer to the service manual to find the connector pin numbers for the optical pickup's output wire. Optical sensors are used in

Advanced Diagnostics, Analyzers

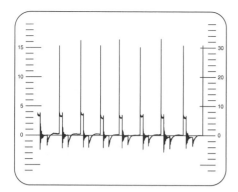

All firing lines fairly even but too high. Look for problems common to all cylinders such as: worn spark plug electrodes, excessive rotor gap, coil high-tension wire broken or not seated fully, late timing, excessively lean air-fuel mixture, or air leaks in intake manifold

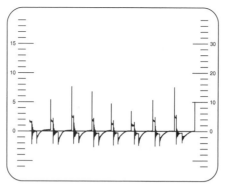

Uneven firing lines. Can be caused by worn electrodes, a cocked or worn distributor cap, fuel mixture variations, vacuum leaks, or uneven compression.

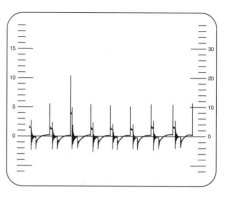

Consistently high firing line in one or more cylinders. Caused by a broken spark plug wire, a wide spark plug gap, or a vacuum leak.

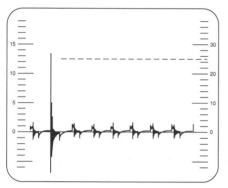

Maximum available voltage during coil test should be within the manufacturer's specifications. Disconnect plug wire to check maximum coil output.

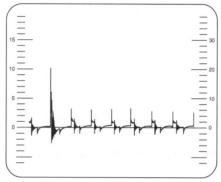

With plug wire removed for coil output test, a short intermittent, or missing lower spike indicates faulty insulation. This is usually caused by a defective spark plug wire, distributor cap, rotor, coil wire, or coil tower.

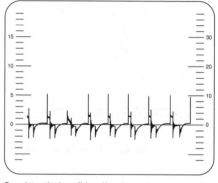

Consistently low firing line in one or more cylinders. Caused by fouled plug, shorted wire, low compression (valve not closing), or rich mixture.

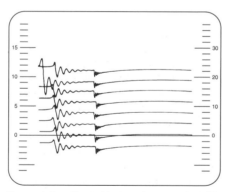

No spark line. Caused by complete open in cable or connector

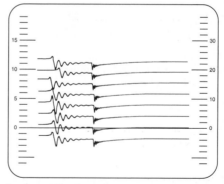

Long spark line. Caused by a shorted spark plug or partially grounded plug wire.

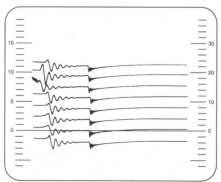

Sloped spark line, usually with hash. Caused by fouled spark plug.

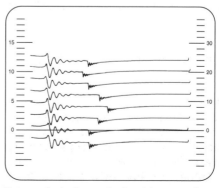

Poor vertical alignment of point-open spikes. Caused by worn or defective distributor shaft, bushings, cam lobes or breaker plate.

Fig. 29-25. Examples of bad scope patterns. Study shape of trace and problems for each.   (FMC)

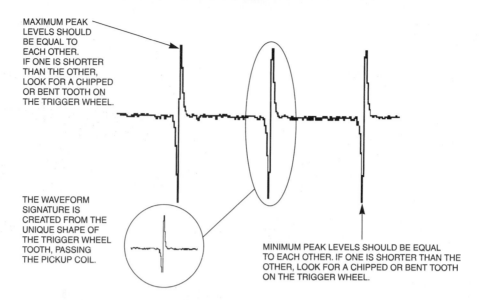

MAXIMUM PEAK LEVELS SHOULD BE EQUAL TO EACH OTHER. IF ONE IS SHORTER THAN THE OTHER, LOOK FOR A CHIPPED OR BENT TOOTH ON THE TRIGGER WHEEL.

THE WAVEFORM SIGNATURE IS CREATED FROM THE UNIQUE SHAPE OF THE TRIGGER WHEEL TOOTH, PASSING THE PICKUP COIL.

MINIMUM PEAK LEVELS SHOULD BE EQUAL TO EACH OTHER. IF ONE IS SHORTER THAN THE OTHER, LOOK FOR A CHIPPED OR BENT TOOTH ON THE TRIGGER WHEEL.

Fig. 29-26. Typical waveform from a magnetic distributor pickup. (Fluke)

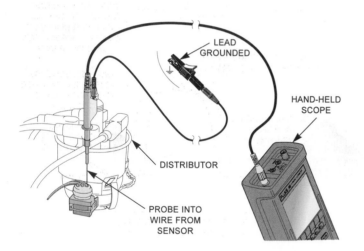

LEAD GROUNDED

HAND-HELD SCOPE

DISTRIBUTOR

PROBE INTO WIRE FROM SENSOR

Fig. 29-27. Scope being used to check signal from a Hall effect sensor. (Fluke)

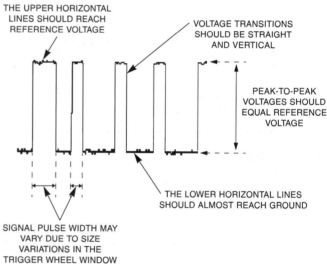

THE UPPER HORIZONTAL LINES SHOULD REACH REFERENCE VOLTAGE

VOLTAGE TRANSITIONS SHOULD BE STRAIGHT AND VERTICAL

PEAK-TO-PEAK VOLTAGES SHOULD EQUAL REFERENCE VOLTAGE

THE LOWER HORIZONTAL LINES SHOULD ALMOST REACH GROUND

SIGNAL PULSE WIDTH MAY VARY DUE TO SIZE VARIATIONS IN THE TRIGGER WHEEL WINDOW

Fig. 29-29. Typical waveform generated by an optical sensor. If the shutter blade widths vary, the pulse width will also vary. (Fluke)

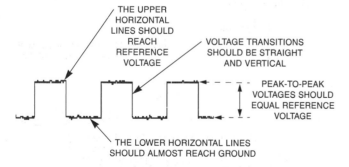

THE UPPER HORIZONTAL LINES SHOULD REACH REFERENCE VOLTAGE

VOLTAGE TRANSITIONS SHOULD BE STRAIGHT AND VERTICAL

PEAK-TO-PEAK VOLTAGES SHOULD EQUAL REFERENCE VOLTAGE

THE LOWER HORIZONTAL LINES SHOULD ALMOST REACH GROUND

Fig. 29-28. Hall-effect sensor signal. Frequency of the signal should increase as engine speed increases. (Fluke)

a few distributor designs and are never used in crankshaft sensors.

An optical sensor's waveform should have straight sides and adequate voltage output. The upper horizontal line on the waveform should almost reach reference voltage. The bottom horizontal line should almost reach ground, or zero. See Fig. 29-29.

Remember that optical sensors are susceptible to dirt. An oil mist or a film of dirt can prevent light transfer from the LEDs to the photo diodes. Again, refer to the manufacturer's service information for specific information.

Crankshaft position sensor testing

Fig. 29-30A shows how to use a hand-held scope to test a crankshaft position sensor. You can use the needle probe on the scope lead to check for an output signal without disconnecting wires. This scope will show both ac output and a trace for voltage signal variations. Note that this testing method would also work on engine block-mounted magnetic crankshaft position sensors.

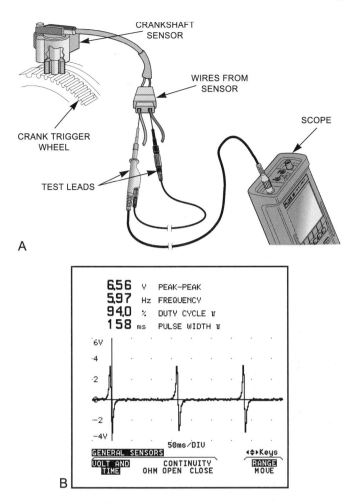

Fig. 29-30. Scope test of crankshaft position sensor is similar to magnetic sensor. A—Connect scope to sensor terminals as specified. B—Note the resulting display from the sensor. (Fluke)

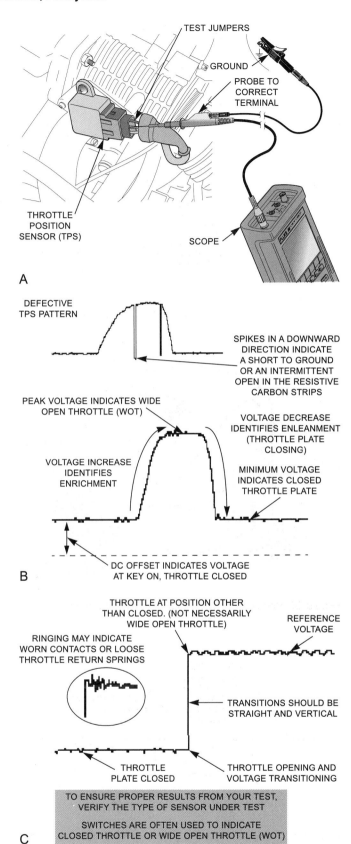

29-31. Throttle position sensor can also be checked with a scope. A—Probe through wires or use jumpers so power can be connected to sensor. B—Potentiometer or variable resistor type TPS should produce smooth curve as throttle is moved opened and closed. Spikes indicate sensor problem. C—Switching-type TPS should produce good square wave without ringing. (Fluke)

Some electrical connectors are sealed and do not allow easy probing. You may need to install a test connector or jumper wires between the two halves of the connector to probe sensor voltages.

When reading the sensor waveform, make sure the peak voltage levels are equal to each other. If one is short or missing, inspect the trigger wheel for a broken tooth. Peak-to-peak voltage levels should be within specifications. See Fig. 29-30B.

As with any sensor, reference voltages, wiring, and other criteria will vary. If in doubt, always refer to the service manual for the vehicle being tested to get accurate electrical values.

Throttle position sensor testing

To scope test a throttle position sensor (TPS), connect the test leads to the sensor output wire and to ground. Voltage should still be fed to the sensor from the ECM. Move the throttle opened and closed. The TPS waveform should show a smooth curve, without any spikes. See Fig. 29-31.

Manifold absolute pressure sensor testing

A scope can also be used to test the operation of both analog and digital manifold absolute pressure sensors. Accelerate the engine and note the changes in airflow signals going to the ECM. Compare the amplitude and shape of the waveform to known good patterns. This is shown in Fig. 29-32.

Mass airflow sensor testing

To test analog or digital mass airflow sensors using a scope, probe the connector as recommended in the service manual. Compare your scope readings to factory specifications and known good readings. See Fig. 29-33.

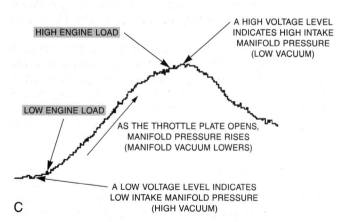

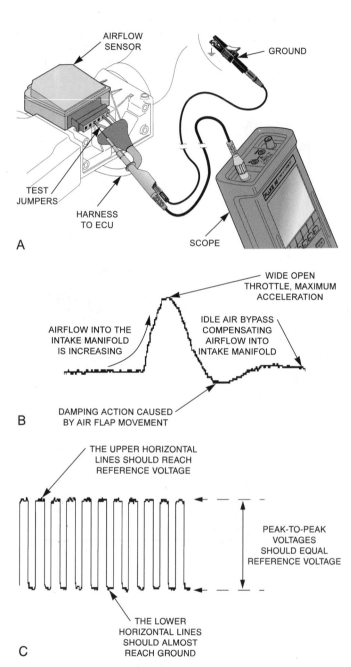

Fig. 29-32. Manifold absolute pressure sensor can also be checked with scope. A—Here scope is probing through connector to test MAP sensor. Other lead is grounded. B—With digital MAP, signal frequency should increase with engine speed. C—With analog MAP, amplitude should increase with engine speed. (Fluke)

Fig. 29-33. Note basic method for testing analog and digital airflow meters. A—Jumpers are being used to allow power to remain connected to sensor. Probe service manual recommended pins or wires. B—As flow increases, analog airflow meter should produce more voltage. C—With digital airflow meter, signal frequency usually increases with engine speed and airflow. (Fluke)

Knock sensor testing

To test a knock sensor with a scope, connect the scope test leads to the sensor. Then tap lightly on the engine next to the sensor with a small hammer or a wrench. See Fig. 29-34A. This should make the sensor produce a signal that is similar to the one shown in Fig. 29-34B.

Another way to check a knock sensor and the ECM is to measure ignition timing while tapping on the engine next to the sensor. The ECM should retard ignition timing when you tap on the engine.

Alternator diode testing

Most analyzers are capable of checking alternator diode condition. The scope will display the alternator's voltage output. If the alternator diodes are good, the pattern should be wavy but almost even.

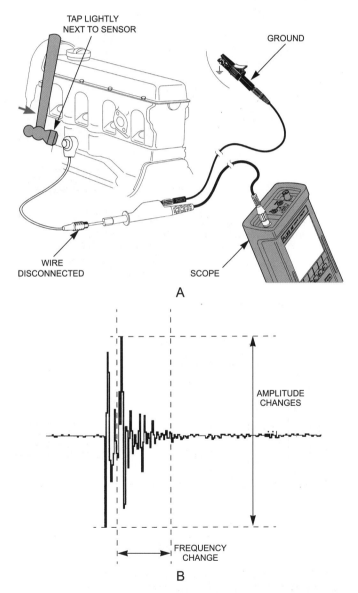

Fig. 29-34. Knock sensor signal can also be analyzed with scope. A—Connect scope lead to knock sensor and other lead to ground. Tap on engine with small hammer or wrench to produce output signal. B—Knock sensor should produce normal frequency and amplitude signal when engine is tapped on. (Fluke)

Electronic fuel injector testing

Oscilloscopes can also be used to check injector operation in an electronic fuel injection system. Refer to equipment and service manual instructions for details. Fig. 29-35 shows typical waveforms for good and defective fuel injectors.

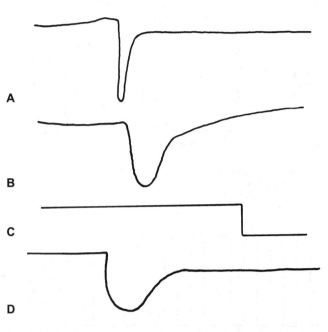

Fig. 29-35. These are waveforms for electronic injectors. A—Normal injector pattern. B—Stuck injector. C—Open injector. D—Partially shorted injector. (Snap-on Tool Corp.)

Oxygen sensor testing

An oscilloscope can be used to check the signal produced by an oxygen sensor. See Fig. 29-36. By comparing actual voltage (zirconia sensor) or resistance (titania sensor) levels to scan tool values, you can determine whether the sensor, the wiring, or the ECM is at fault.

If you are using a dual trace scope, you can compare the voltage signals from the front oxygen sensor (primary sensor) and the rear oxygen sensor (catalyst monitor). If the signals from the sensors are similar, the catalytic converter may not be working properly. Fig. 29-37.

Fig. 29-38 shows some of the on-board diagnostic tests run on the oxygen sensors in OBD II vehicles.

ECM scope testing

An oscilloscope can be used to check the output pulses leaving an electronic control module. You can measure and observe the pulses going to fuel injectors, solenoids, and servo motors. You can also check the reference voltage being sent to sensors, Fig. 29-39.

Since ECM testing varies and is complex, always refer to the service manual for detailed instructions. You must compare your test waveform or voltage to known correct values. If the ECM fails to produce a good pulse or reference voltage, it should be replaced.

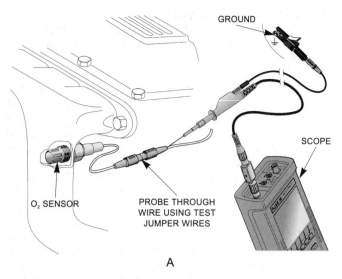

A

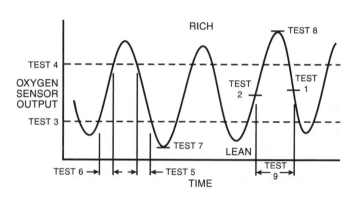

FRONT O₂ SIGNAL

CATALYST MONITOR

Fig. 29-37. With dual trace scope, you can compare signals from front and rear oxygen sensors in OBD II systems. Generally, if waveform from second O₂ sensor is too similar to front sensor, catalytic converter is dead and should be replaced. (Oldsmobile)

B

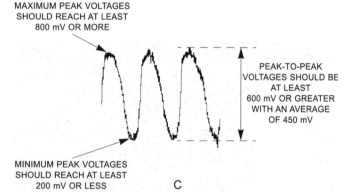

MAXIMUM PEAK VOLTAGES SHOULD REACH AT LEAST 800 mV OR MORE

PEAK-TO-PEAK VOLTAGES SHOULD BE AT LEAST 600 mV OR GREATER WITH AN AVERAGE OF 450 mV

MINIMUM PEAK VOLTAGES SHOULD REACH AT LEAST 200 mV OR LESS

C

Fig. 29-36. Oscilloscope can also be used to check output signal from oxygen sensor when trouble is hard to find. A—Ground one lead and probe through connector. After probing through connector or wiring, seal hole with liquid electrical tape to prevent corrosion. B—Signal output should vary up and down as shown. Also note digital readout on this scope face. C—This is typical waveform for zirconia-type O₂ sensor. (Fluke)

Fig. 29-38. Drawing shows nine sensor tests available on OBD II—equipped vehicles. (OTC)

When the problem occurs, press the storage button on the scope. The scope will then store a picture of the sensor output for analysis.

EXHAUST GAS ANALYZER

An *exhaust gas analyzer* is a test instrument that measures the chemical content of the engine's exhaust gases. See Fig. 29-40.

With the engine running, the exhaust analyzer will sample, analyze, and indicate the amount of pollutants and other gases in the exhaust. The technician can use this information to determine the condition of the engine and other systems affecting emissions. An exhaust gas analyzer is an excellent diagnostic tool that will indicate excessive emissions caused by:

1. Fuel metering problems.
2. Engine mechanical problems.
3. Vacuum leaks.
4. Ignition system problems.
5. PCV troubles.
6. Clogged air filter.
7. Faulty air injection system.
8. Evaporative emissions control system problems.
9. Computer control system troubles.
10. Catalytic converter condition.

Flight record test

A *flight record test* stores the sensor waveform in the scope's memory when a problem occurs. For example, when trying to check an intermittent problem, connect the hand-held scope to the sensor and test drive the vehicle.

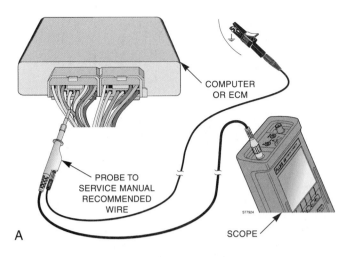

A

B

Fig. 29-39. A—A scope will also check reference voltage going to sensors and the control pulses from the ECM to the actuators. Compare readings and waveforms to service manual specifications. B—Reference voltages should meet specifications and the waveforms should reflect smooth dc voltage. (Fluke)

Types of exhaust gas analyzers

There are three different kinds of exhaust gas analyzers: two-gas analyzers, four-gas analyzers, and five-gas analyzers.

The *two-gas exhaust analyzer* can measure the amount of hydrocarbons (HC) and carbon monoxide (CO) in a vehicle's exhaust system. A common analyzer, it has been used for a number of years. However, the two-gas analyzer cannot accurately analyze the exhaust gases from newer engines. Therefore, it is being replaced by the four-gas analyzer.

The *four-gas exhaust analyzer* measures the quantity of hydrocarbons (HC), carbon monoxide (CO), carbon dioxide (CO_2), and oxygen (O_2), in an engine's exhaust. Most state air quality agencies use the four-gas analyzer.

Although carbon dioxide and oxygen are not toxic emissions, they provide useful data about the engine's operating efficiency. Late-model engines are so efficient that a four-gas exhaust analyzer is needed to accurately evaluate the makeup of the exhaust gases. It provides extra information for diagnosing problems and making adjustments.

The *five-gas exhaust analyzer* will measure hydrocarbons, carbon monoxide, carbon dioxide, oxygen, and oxides of nitrogen. It is the most modern and informative type of exhaust gas analyzer. Oxides of nitrogen are a toxic pollutant that should be measured, if possible, as a means of diagnosis. See Fig. 29-41.

Using an exhaust gas analyzer

To use an exhaust gas analyzer, plug the machine in and allow it to warm up as described by the manufacturer. After warm-up, zero and calibrate the analyzer. Exhaust gas analyzer *calibration* involves zeroing the meter scales

Fig. 29-40. Exhaust gas analyzer measures chemical content of engine exhaust. It will tell if vehicle is emitting too much air pollution, indicating system problems.   (OTC)

Fig. 29-41. Exhaust gas analyzer can be used as last resort to help find source of electronic problems.   (OTC)

while sampling clean air (no exhaust gases present in room) with the analyzer. Newer analyzers sample a *calibration gas* (mixture of several gases) to adjust the meter readings for accuracy. The gas is automatically metered while the meter scales are calibrated. In most cases, any calibration adjustment is done automatically by the analyzer when commanded by the technician. Older analyzers may have to be manually adjusted.

Warning! Never inhale exhaust gas analyzer calibration gas. The gas contains emission gases that can be harmful to your health.

Before testing the vehicle, take it on a thorough road test. This allows the vehicle to reach the proper operating temperature. Never test a vehicle with a cold engine, as inaccurate readings will result. To begin the test, install the probe in the vehicle's tailpipe. If working in an enclosed shop, slide the probe though a hole in the shop's vent hose. Since exact procedures vary, always follow the operating instructions for the particular exhaust analyzer. This will ensure accurate measurements.

Warning! When using an exhaust analyzer, do *not* let engine exhaust fumes escape into an enclosed shop area. Engine exhaust can kill. Use the shop exhaust ventilation system to trap and remove the toxic fumes, Fig. 29-42.

Most analyzers measure hydrocarbons and carbon monoxide at idle and approximately 2500 rpm. If you have a five-gas analyzer, it will also measure oxygen, oxides of nitrogen, and carbon dioxide. Compare the analyzer readings with specifications.

When testing some electronic fuel injection systems without a load, only idle readings on the exhaust analyzer will be accurate. A dynamometer must be used to load the engine to simulate actual driving conditions.

Exhaust gas analyzer readings

Before testing the vehicle, take it on a thorough road test. This allows the vehicle to reach the proper operating temperature. Never test a vehicle with a cold engine, as inaccurate readings will result. Although most states provide emission specifications in parts per million and percentage, some states give emission specifications in grams per mile. When this is the case, the vehicle must be operated on a chassis dyno so that the amount of emissions produced per mile driven can be calculated.

Hydrocarbon readings

An exhaust gas analyzer measures hydrocarbons (HC) in parts per million (PPM) by volume. For example, an analyzer reading of 10 PPM means there are 10 parts of hydrocarbons for every million parts of exhaust gas.

A vehicle that is 10-15 years old, for example, will have a relatively high hydrocarbon specification, such as 900 PPM. A newer vehicle, having stricter emission requirements, could have a 220 PPM hydrocarbon specification. If a vehicle's hydrocarbon reading is higher than the standard permits, the vehicle's hydrocarbon emissions (unburned fuel) are excessive.

Always refer to the emission control sticker in the engine compartment or a service manual for emission level specifications. Values vary year by year.

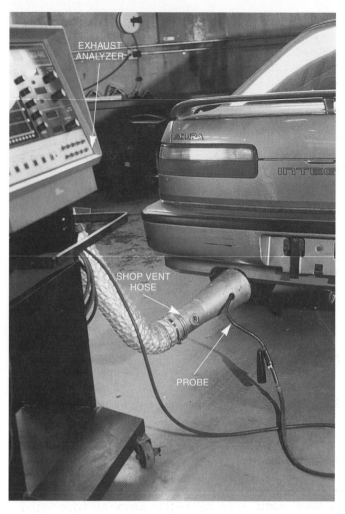

Fig. 29-42. Note how exhaust analyzer is installed in vehicle tailpipe. Adapter on vent hose prevents toxic vapors from entering shop. Warm and calibrate meters before placing test probe in tailpipe. Following equipment instructions, read meters and compare to specs for year of vehicle.

A rotten egg smell from the exhaust is often an indication of the presence of unburned fuel and, therefore, excessive hydrocarbons. Higher-than-normal HC readings can be caused by one or more of the following conditions:

1. Fuel system malfunction (leaking fuel injector, faulty pressure regulator, improper fuel pressure, or carburetor problems).
2. Improper ignition timing (distributor, computer, or adjustment problem).
3. Engine problems (blowby, worn rings, blown head gasket).
4. Faulty emission control system (bad PCV, catalytic converter, EGR valve, evaporative control system).
5. Ignition system troubles (fouled spark plug, cracked distributor cap, open spark plug wire).
6. Computer control system problems (defective input sensor, output actuator, or ECM).

Carbon monoxide readings

An exhaust analyzer measures carbon monoxide (CO) in percentage by volume. For instance, a 1.2% analyzer reading would mean that 1.2% of the engine exhaust is made up of carbon monoxide. The other 98.8% consists of other substances. High carbon monoxide is caused by an incomplete burning of fuel or a lack of air (oxygen) during the combustion process.

If the exhaust analyzer reading is higher than specifications, the engine is producing too much carbon monoxide. You would need to locate and correct the cause of the problem.

The exhaust analyzer's carbon monoxide reading is related to the air-fuel ratio. A *high* carbon monoxide reading would indicate an over-rich mixture (too much fuel compared to air). If a high carbon monoxide reading is accompanied by a high HC reading, the problem is related to something that will make the engine run rich. A *low* carbon monoxide reading would indicate a lean air-fuel mixture (too much air compared to fuel). Typical causes of high carbon monoxide readings are:

1. Fuel system problems (sticking or leaking injector, leaking fuel pressure regulator, high float setting, clogged carburetor air bleed, restricted air cleaner, choke out of adjustment, defective input sensor, computer control problem).
2. Emission control system troubles (almost any emission control system problem can upset the carbon monoxide readings).
3. Incorrect ignition timing (timing too far advanced or improper vacuum going to the vacuum advance unit).

Oxides of nitrogen readings

A five-gas analyzer can measure oxides of nitrogen, while a four-gas analyzer cannot. Since oxides of nitrogen are toxic, some state air quality agencies have made exhaust emission measurements with a five-gas analyzer mandatory.

Typical causes of high NOx emissions include:

1. High combustion chamber temperatures—excessively high engine compression ratio, carbon deposits in the combustion chambers, low cooling system, blocked water jackets, etc.
2. EGR system problems—burned gases are not being injected into the intake manifold and combustion flame temperature is too high.

Carbon dioxide readings

Four- and five-gas exhaust analyzers measure carbon dioxide (CO_2) in percent by volume. Typically, CO_2 readings should be above 8%. CO_2 readings provide more data for checking and adjusting the air-fuel ratio.

Carbon dioxide is a by-product of combustion. It is produced when one carbon molecule combines with two oxygen molecules in the combustion chamber. Carbon dioxide is not toxic at low levels. When you breathe, for example, you exhale carbon dioxide.

Normally, oxygen and carbon dioxide levels are compared when evaluating the content of the engine exhaust. For example, if the percent of carbon dioxide exceeds the percent of oxygen, the air-fuel ratio is on the rich side of a stoichiometric (chemically correct) mixture. It is also a good indicator of possible dilution of the exhaust gas sample through an exhaust leak.

Oxygen readings

Four- and five-gas exhaust analyzers measure oxygen (O_2) in percentage by volume. Typically, oxygen readings should be between 1% and 7%. Oxygen is needed for the catalytic converter to burn HC and CO emissions. Without oxygen in the engine exhaust, exhaust emissions can pass through the converter and out the vehicle's tailpipe.

There are two systems that add oxygen to the engine exhaust: the air injection system and the pulse air system. As air is added to the exhaust, CO and HC emissions decrease. As a result, oxygen readings can be used to check the operation of the fuel injection system, air injection system, catalytic converter, and computer.

The oxygen level in the engine exhaust sample is an accurate indicator of a vehicle's air-fuel mixture. It is also a good indicator of a possible exhaust leak, which can dilute the exhaust gas sample. When an engine is running lean, oxygen increases proportionately with the air-fuel ratio. As the air-fuel mixture becomes lean enough to cause a *lean misfire* (engine miss), oxygen readings rise dramatically. This provides a very accurate method of measuring lean and efficient air-fuel ratios.

If you find any exhaust gas analyzer reading to be abnormally high or low, use your knowledge of system operation to pinpoint the trouble. By knowing which emissions are affected by which engine problem or emission system trouble, you can narrow down the source of the problem to specific components. You would then need to test each component or circuit to verify your conclusions.

Warning! An engine with a defective thermostat can fail an emission test. If the engine operating temperature is too high, it can affect engine combustion efficiency and the operation of the computer control systems, which will try to compensate for the overheating engine. If the engine cannot reach the proper operating temperature, the computer will not be able to go into closed loop mode. Keep these basic system malfunctions in mind when diagnosing problems.

SUMMARY

Strategy-based diagnosis involves using a consistent, logical procedure to narrow down possible problem sources. Basically, you verify the complaint, make preliminary checks, read service bulletins about the vehicle, and perform service manual–recommended checks.

At one time or another, every technician encounters a problem that seems impossible to fix. By learning a few advanced "tricks of the trade", even the most difficult problems can be located and corrected with minimum frustration.

A scan tool snap-shot is an instantaneous reading of operating parameters. It is often taken when a problem is hard to find or when intermittent troubles are present. Scan tool datastream values are "live" electrical values measured with the vehicle running or driving. They almost eliminate the need for a breakout box or pinpoint measurements of electrical values. A digital VOM can be used to read computer terminal voltage and resistance values. These readings can then be compared to known good values.

Personal computers are being used more and more by the electronic technician. The computer can be a valuable tool when doing advanced diagnostic work.

The OBD II drive cycle is designed to tell the technician whether the OBD II system is operating properly. The drive cycle is normally performed when the battery or ECM has been disconnected or after diagnostic trouble codes have been erased. Additionally, some states require that the drive cycle be performed before an emissions test. The drive cycle is different for each vehicle, so check the service manual for specific instructions.

A breakout box allows the technician to test electrical values at specific pins on an ECM or in the system the ECM controls. It is one of the last tools used in diagnostics, as it is time-consuming.

Electromagnetic interference (EMI), or radiation interference, occurs when an induced voltage enters another system's wiring. Sources of EMI can include loose, misrouted, or unshielded spark plug wires; police and CB radios; and aftermarket accessories.

A digital pyrometer is an electronic device that measures temperature. Measuring actual temperature can help you verify scan tool readouts and find hard-to-locate problems.

When an engine performance problem only occurs at a specific temperature, suspect electronic parts. To check a component for problems affected by temperature, use a heat gun to warm the component or a can of freeze spray to cool the unit. If the problem occurs with the temperature change, the unit is at fault and should be replaced.

A dynamometer is used to measure an engine's power output and performance. By loading the engine, the dynamometer can check acceleration, maximum power output, and on-the-road performance characteristics.

An engine analyzer, also called a vehicle analyzer or computer analyzer, consists of a group of test instruments that includes a scope, a tach-dwell meter, a VOM, an exhaust gas analyzer, and, sometimes, a scan tool. These tools are mounted in a large, roll-around cabinet. Some analyzers can transmit data over telephone lines for comparison to information stored in a large mainframe computer. Analyzer connections differ with each type and model. Test leads should be connected as described in the user's manual.

A scope ignition coil output test measures the maximum available voltage produced by the ignition coil. A load test, or acceleration test, measures the spark plug firing voltages when engine speed is rapidly increased. A cylinder balance test, also called a power balance test, measures the power output from each of the engine's cylinders. A cranking balance test is done to check the engine's mechanical condition.

An oscilloscope, often called a scope, displays voltages in relation to time. By comparing the scope pattern to a known good pattern, the technician can determine whether something is wrong in the circuit. Scope voltage is shown along the vertical axis of the screen. Time is given on the horizontal axis of the screen.

An oscilloscope is often used to diagnose ignition system problems. The scope's controls allow it to display both primary and secondary ignition system patterns. The primary scope pattern shows the low voltage changes in an ignition system. The secondary pattern shows the high voltages needed to fire the spark plugs.

There are five scope test patterns commonly used by the technician when checking ignition system operation: primary superimposed, secondary superimposed, parade (display), raster (stacked), and expanded display (cylinder select).

An oscilloscope can also be used to find computer system problems. When the scan tool does not find anything and you still have performance problems, you may need to check sensor and ECM signals with a scope.

An exhaust gas analyzer measures the chemical content of the engine's exhaust gases. With the engine running, the exhaust analyzer will sample, analyze, and indicate the amount of pollutants and other gases in the exhaust. The technician can use this information to determine the condition of the engine and other systems affecting emissions.

There are three different types of exhaust gas analyzers: two-gas analyzers, four-gas analyzers, and five-gas analyzers. The two-gas exhaust analyzer can measure the amount of hydrocarbons and carbon monoxide in a vehicle's exhaust system. The four-gas exhaust analyzer measures the quantity of hydrocarbons, carbon monoxide, carbon dioxide, and oxygen in an engine's exhaust. The five-gas exhaust analyzer will measure hydrocarbons, carbon monoxide, carbon dioxide, oxygen, and oxides of nitrogen. It is the most modern and informative type of exhaust gas analyzer.

KNOW THESE TERMS

Strategy-based diagnostics, Snap-shot, OBD II drive cycle, Scan tool datastream values, Breakout box, Electromagnetic interference (EMI), Digital pyrometer, Dynamometer, Engine analyzer, Modem, Mainframe computer, Ignition coil output test, Load test, Acceleration test, Cylinder balance test, Power balance test, Cranking balance test, Oscilloscope, Scope screen, Trace, Scope time, Scope sweep rate, Primary scope pattern, Secondary scope patterns, Firing section, Firing line, Spark line, Intermediate section, Coil oscillations section, Dwell section, Primary superimposed pattern, Superimposed, Secondary superimposed pattern, Parade pattern, Display pattern, Tall firing line, Short firing line, Raster pattern, Stacked pattern, Expanded display, Cylinder select., Base line, Rising edge, Leading edge, On-time, High-time, Trailing edge, Falling edge, Off-time, Low-time, Amplitude, Peak-to-peak voltage, Magnetic sensor test, Hall-effect sensor test, Optical pickup test, Flight record test, Exhaust gas analyzer, Calibration, Calibration gas.

REVIEW QUESTIONS

1. _____-_____ diagnosis involves using a consistent, logical procedure for narrowing down the possible problem sources.
2. Explain a scan tool snap-shot.
3. How can you use scan tool datastream values?
4. A(n) _____ _____ allows you to pinpoint test electrical values at specific pins on the ECM or in the computer system. It is one of the last tools used during problem diagnosis and can be time-consuming.
5. _____ _____ results from induced voltage into wires and can cause a computer to malfunction.

6. List six things you can check with a digital pyrometer.
7. When might a dynamometer come in handy during advanced diagnostics?
8. What is a vehicle analyzer?
9. List and explain ten test instruments found in a vehicle analyzer.
10. Secondary _____ scope pattern is used to check for general ignition system problems.

ASE CERTIFICATION–TYPE QUESTIONS

1. An engine misses when cold. Technician A says all parts that affect cold engine operation should be checked until the problem is found. Technician B says the coolant temperature sensor should be replaced. Who is right?
   - (A) A only.
   - (B) B only.
   - (C) Both A and B.
   - (D) Neither A nor B.

2. The OBD II drive cycle must be performed before an emissions test. Technician A says the drive cycle generally takes between 20 and 30 minutes to complete. Technician B says you should allow the engine to reach normal operating temperature before starting the drive cycle. Who is right?
   - (A) A only.
   - (B) B only.
   - (C) Both A and B.
   - (D) Neither A nor B.

3. Technician A says freeze spray can be used when checking electronic parts for temperature-related performance problems. Technician B says a heat gun and a digital thermometer can be used when checking electronic components for temperature-related performance problems. Who is right?
   - (A) A only.
   - (B) B only.
   - (C) Both A and B.
   - (D) Neither A nor B.

4. An engine analyzer can be used to check each of the following *except:*
   - (A) charging system operation.
   - (B) engine condition.
   - (C) sensor signals.
   - (D) oil pressure.

5. Technician A says a cylinder balance test can be used to check cylinders for low compression. Technician B says a cranking balance test can be used to check cylinders for low compression. Who is right?
   - (A) A only.
   - (B) B only.
   - (C) Both A and B.
   - (D) Neither A nor B.

6. Scope sweep rate is commonly given in:
   - (A) seconds.
   - (B) milliseconds.
   - (C) microseconds.
   - (D) nanoseconds.

7. An oscilloscope is being used to check for ignition system problems. Technician A says the secondary scope pattern is generally used to check system operation. Technician B says the primary scope pattern is generally used to check system operation. Who is right?
   - (A) A only.
   - (B) B only.
   - (C) Both A and B.
   - (D) Neither A nor B.

8. Technician A says the intermediate section of the secondary pattern shows voltage fluctuations after the plug stops firing. Technician B says voltage in the intermediate section should swing up and down six times at low engine speeds. Who is right?
   - (A) A only.
   - (B) B only.
   - (C) Both A and B.
   - (D) Neither A nor B.

9. A four-gas exhaust analyzer can be used to measure each of the following *except:*
   - (A) hydrocarbons.
   - (B) oxides of nitrogen.
   - (C) carbon monoxide.
   - (D) oxygen.

10. An exhaust gas analyzer reveals a high carbon monoxide reading. Technician A says a leaking fuel injector could be causing the problem. Technician B says a defective input sensor could be causing the problem. Who is right?
   - (A) A only.
   - (B) B only.
   - (C) Both A and B.
   - (D) Neither A nor B.

Working as an apprentice is a good way to gain the experience required for ASE certification. This apprentice works under the supervision of a certified technician. (Fluke)

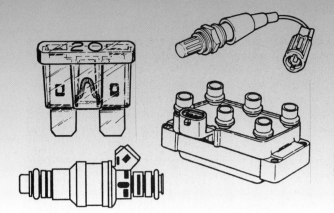

Chapter 30

ASE Electrical System Certification

After studying this chapter, you will be able to:
- *Summarize the ASE testing program.*
- *Explain the Electrical/Electronic Systems Test content.*
- *Describe why ASE certification can be helpful to the technician and to the shop owner.*
- *Summarize methods of taking an ASE test successfully.*

This chapter will quickly review the ASE (NIASE) testing program. It will explain the test available in electrical service and give hints on how to pass it.

Remember! Always try to learn more about auto electronics. Electronic systems are changing at a rapid pace. If you do NOT continue to study and read technical publications, you will fall behind in your knowledge. Your ability to diagnose and repair electrical-electronic systems will suffer.

With the precision and complexity of today's cars, the mechanic should be called the "technician." The term "technician" implies a higher degree of skill. No longer can the "shade tree mechanic" survive with modern computer controlled automobile designs.

ASE (NIASE)

ASE stands for "Automotive Service Excellence." It was shortened from NIASE, which is an abbreviation for "National Institute for Automotive Service Excellence." ASE is a nonprofit, nonaffiliated (no ties to industry) organization formed to help ensure the highest standards in automotive service.

ASE directs an organized program of self-improvement under the guidance of a 40-member board of directors. These members represent all aspects of the automotive industry—educators, shop owners, consumer groups, government agencies, aftermarket parts companies, and auto manufacturers. This broad group of experts guides the ASE testing program and helps it stay in touch with the needs of the industry.

VOLUNTARY CERTIFICATION

ASE tests are voluntary. They do not have to be taken and they do not license technicians.

Some countries have made technician certification a requirement. In the U.S.A., however, technicians take the tests for personal benefit and to show their employers and customers that they are fully qualified to work on a specific assembly or system. See Fig. 30-1.

According to ASE statistics, over 500,000 technicians have taken certification tests and passed them. Thousands of these technicians have been retested and recertified after five years to maintain their credentials.

Fig. 30-1. This technician has passed the ASE Electrical/Electronic Systems Test. He is a certified technician, as is evident by the patch on his shirt sleeve.

TEST CATEGORIES

In automotive technology, there are eight test categories: Engine Repair, Engine Performance, Automatic Transmission/Transaxle, Manual Drive Train and Axles, Suspension and Steering, Brakes, Electrical/Electronic Systems, and Heating and Air Conditioning.

You can take any one or all of these tests. However, only four tests (200 questions maximum) can be taken at one testing session.

There are also seven tests in heavy-duty truck repair

and five tests in collision repair and refinishing.

Fig. 30-2 gives a breakdown of what each automotive service test involves. Study what they cover!

ASE Electrical/Electronic Systems Test

The *ASE Electrical/Electronic Systems Test* is used to evaluate how well you can correct electrical, electronic, and computer system problems. It primarily covers the diagnosis and repair of electrical systems and does NOT cover theory of operation

To prepare for the test, you should study both the theory and service chapters in this book, however. A knowledge of theory, or how things work, is needed to properly diagnose problems. If you know how something

---

Specifications for the Automobile Tests Content Area/Number of Questions

A1 Engine Repair 60
A. General Engine Diagnosis 17
B. Cylinder Head and Valve Train Diagnosis and Repair 14
C. Engine Block Diagnosis and Repair 14
D. Lubrication and Cooling Systems
 Diagnosis and Repair 8
E. Fuel, Electrical, Ignition, and Exhaust
 Systems Inspection and Service 7

A2 Automatic Transmission/Transaxle 50
A. General Transmission/Transaxle Diagnosis 25
 1. Mechanical/Hydraulic Systems (11)
 2. Electronic Systems (14)
B. Transmission/Transaxle Maintenance and Adjustment 4
C. In-Vehicle Transmission/Transaxle Repair 8
D. Off-Vehicle Transmission/Transaxle Repair 13
 1. Removal, Disassembly, and Assembly (4)
 2. Gear Train, Shafts, Bushings, Oil Pump and Case (5)
 3. Friction and Reaction Units (4)

A3 Manual Drive Train and Axles 40
A. Clutch Diagnosis and Repair 6
B. Transmission Diagnosis and Repair 6
C. Transaxle Diagnosis and Repair 8
D. Drive Shaft, Half Shaft and Universal Joint/Constant Velocity (CV)
 Joint Diagnosis and Repair (Front and Rear Wheel Drive) 6
E. Rear Axle Diagnosis and Repair 7
 1. Ring and Pinion Gears (3)
 2. Differential Case Assembly (2)
 3. Limited Slip Differential (1)
 4. Axle Shafts (1)
F. Four-Wheel Drive/All-Wheel Drive
 Component Diagnosis and Repair 7

A4 Suspension and Steering 40
A. Steering Systems Diagnosis and Repair 10
 1. Steering Columns and Manual Steering Gears (3)
 2. Power-Assisted Steering Units (4)
 3. Steering Linkage (3)
B. Suspension Systems Diagnosis and Repair 11
 1. Front Suspensions (6)
 2. Rear Suspensions (5)
C. Related Suspension and Steering Service 2
D. Wheel Alignment Diagnosis, Adjustment, and Repair 12
E. Wheel and Tire Diagnosis and Repair 5

A5 Brakes 50
A. Hydraulic System Diagnosis and Repair 14
 1. Master Cylinder (4)
 2. Lines and Hoses (3)
 3. Valves and Switches (3)
 4. Bleeding, Flushing, and Leak Testing (4)
B. Drum Brake Diagnosis and Repair 6
C. Disc Brake Diagnosis and Repair 12
D. Power Assist Units Diagnosis and Repair 4
E. Miscellaneous Systems Diagnosis and Repair 7
F. Antilock Brake System (ABS) Diagnosis and Repair 7

A6 Electrical/Electronic Systems 50
A. General Electrical/Electronic System Diagnosis 13
B. Battery Diagnosis and Service 4
C. Starting System Diagnosis and Repair 5
D. Charging System Diagnosis and Repair 5
E. Lighting Systems Diagnosis and Repair 6
 1. Headlights, Parking Lights, Taillights, Dash Lights,
 and Courtesy Lights (3)
 2. Stoplights, Turn Signals, Hazard Lights,
 and Back-up Lights (3)
F. Gauges, Warning Devices, and Driver
 Information Systems Diagnosis and Repair 6
G. Horn and Wiper/Washer Diagnosis and Repair 3
H. Accessories Diagnosis and Repair 8

A7 Heating and Air Conditioning 50
A. A/C System Diagnosis and Repair 12
B. Refrigeration System Component Diagnosis and Repair 10
 1. Compressor and Clutch (5)
 2. Evaporator, Condenser, and Related
 Components (5)
C. Heating and Engine Cooling Systems Diagnosis and Repair 5
D. Operating Systems and Related Controls Diagnosis and Repair 16
 1. Electrical (8)
 2. Vacuum/Mechanical (4)
 3. Automatic and Semi-Automatic Heating,
 Ventilating and A/C Systems (4)
E. Refrigerant Recovery, Recycling and Handling 7

A8 Engine Performance 65
A. General Engine Diagnosis 11
B. Ignition System Diagnosis and Repair 11
C. Fuel, Air Induction, and Exhaust Systems Diagnosis and Repair 12
D. Emissions Control Systems Diagnosis and Repair
 (including OBDII) 9
 1. Positive Crankcase Ventilation (1)
 2. Exhaust Gas Recirculation (3)
 3. Secondary Air Injection (AIR) and Catalytic Converter (2)
 4. Evaporative Emissions Controls (3)
E. Computerized Engine Controls
 Diagnosis and Repair (including OBDII) 18
F. Engine Electrical Systems Diagnosis and Repair 4
 1. Battery (1)
 2. Starting System (1)
 3. Charging System (2)

Fig. 30-2. ASE certification test categories for automobiles. If you pass one test and fulfill the experience requirements, you will be certified as an ASE Automobile Technician. If you pass all eight tests and fulfill the experience requirements, you will be certified as a Master Automobile Technician. (ASE)

is supposed to work, you will be better at finding causes when something doesn't work!

WHO CAN TAKE ASE TESTS?

To take ASE certification tests and receive certification, you must either have two years of on-the-job experience or one year of approved educational credit and one year of work experience.

However, you may take the tests even if you do NOT have the required two years experience. You will be sent a score for the test, but NOT certification credentials. After you have gained the mandatory experience, you can notify ASE and they will mail you a certificate.

You will be granted credit for formal training by one, or a combination, of the following types of schooling:

1. High school training for three full years in automotives may be substituted for one year of work experience.
2. Post-high school training for two years in a public or private facility can be substituted for one year of work experience.
3. Two months of short training courses can be substituted for one month of work experience.
4. Three years of an apprenticeship program, where you work under an experienced technician as a form of training, can be substituted for both years of work experience.

To have schooling substituted for work experience, you must send a copy of your transcript (list of courses taken), a statement of training, or certificate to verify your training or apprenticeship. Each should give your length of training and subject area. This should accompany your registration form and fee payment.

TEST LOCATIONS AND DATES

ASE administers tests twice a year in over 700 locations across the country. The test sites are usually community colleges or high schools. Tests are given in May and November of each year. Contact ASE for more specific dates and locations for the tests.

TEST RESULTS

The results of your test will be mailed to your home. Only YOU will find out how you did on the tests. You can then inform your employer if you like.

Test scores will be mailed out a few weeks after you have completed the test. If you pass a test, you can consider taking more tests. If you fail, you will know that more study is needed before retaking the test.

TEST TAKING TECHNIQUES

The Electrical/Electronic Systems Test has 50 multiple-choice questions. You must carefully read each question and evaluate it. Then, read through the possible correct

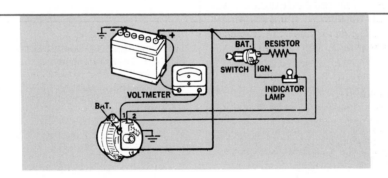

1. The meter in the setup shown above is used to check:
   (A) Charging circuit output voltage.
   (B) Indicator lamp operating voltage.
   (C) Charging circuit voltage drop.
   (D) Ignition switch voltage drop.

2. Turn signals on a vehicle with a two-prong flasher work OK in one direction but not in the other. The bulbs are OK. Which of these is the most likely cause?
   (A) A bad flasher.
   (B) A bad voltage regulator.
   (C) A blown turn signal fuse.
   (D) A poor ground on the problem side.

3. The alternator output current is 0 amps.
   Technician A says that an open diode could be the cause.
   Technician B says that an open rotor winding could be the cause.
   Who is right?
   (A) A only.   (B) B only.   (C) Both A and B.   (D) Neither A nor B.

Fig. 30-3. Try to answer these sample ASE questions. Ask your instructor for the answers if needed.   (ASE)

answers. You must then select the MOST CORRECT response. One answer will be more correct than the others. Sometimes more than one response is correct. Fig. 30-3 gives three example questions. Try to answer them before reading the caption.

You will NOT be required to recall exact specifications unless they are general and apply to most makes and models of cars. For example, charging system voltages or readings are typically the same for a properly operating system, and so are many sensor resistance and voltage specifications. This type of general or typical information might be needed to answer some questions.

These are a few tips that might help you pass ASE certification tests:

1. Read the statements or questions slowly. You might want to read through them twice to make sure you fully understand the question.
2. Analyze the statement or question. Look for hints that make some of the possible answers wrong.
3. Analyze the question as if you were the technician trying to fix the car. Think of all possible situations and use common sense to pick the most correct response.
4. When two technicians give statements concerning a problem, try to decide if either one is incorrect. If both are valid statements about a situation, mark both technicians correct. If only one is correct or neither is correct, mark the answer accordingly. This is one of the most difficult types of questions.
5. If the statement only gives limited information, make sure you do not pick one answer as correct because it may be a more common condition. If the statement does not let you conclude one answer is better than another, both answers are equally correct.
6. Your first thought about which answer is correct is usually the correct response. If you think about a question too much, you will usually read something into the question that is not there. Read the question carefully and make a decision.
7. Do not waste time on a question. Make sure you have time to answer all of the questions on the test.
8. Visualize how you would perform a test or repair when trying to answer a question. This will help you solve the problem more accurately.

BENEFITS OF ASE CERTIFICATION

When you pass an ASE test, you will be given a shoulder patch for your work uniform. The patch has the Blue Seal insignia with either the words ''Automotive Technician'' (passed test in one area or more) or ''Master Auto Technician'' (passed all tests).

The patch will serve as good public relations, showing everyone that you are well trained to work on today's complex vehicles. It will also tell employers that you are someone special who has taken extra effort to prove your value as a technician. It should lead to more rapid advancement and more income as customers indicate their preferences for a certified technician.

MORE INFORMATION

For more information on ASE certification tests, write for a registration booklet from:

ASE Registration Booklet
101 Blue Seal Drive, S.E.
Leesburg, VA 20175

The bulletin will give test locations, testing dates, costs, sample questions, and other useful information.

SUMMARY

ASE stands for Automotive Service Excellence. Previously called NIASE (National Institute for Automotive Service Excellence), this is a non-profit organization. It is not affiliated directly with any industry or organization.

The ASE tests are voluntary. They will help show your employer and customers that you are fully competent to work on their electrical systems.

When taking the test, read the questions and statements slowly. Mentally drop the incorrect responses. Try to imagine you are really working on a car when reading the question. Usually, your first idea of the right answer or answers is correct. If you think too much about an answer, you might pick the second most correct response. Do not waste too much time on any question or you may not have time to answer all of the questions.

Write to ASE for a registration booklet. It will give test dates, locations, costs, etc.

KNOW THESE TERMS

ASE, NIASE, nonaffiliated, Electrical/Electronic Systems Test, Test taking techniques, Shoulder patch, Registration booklet.

REVIEW QUESTIONS—CHAPTER 30

1. How many questions are there on the electrical test?
2. ASE tests are mandatory in some states. True or false?
3. How many tests and questions can be taken at one time?
   a. Five tests and 250 questions.
   b. Four tests and 200 questions.
   c. Three tests and 150 questions.
   d. All of the tests and no limit on questions.
4. Who can take ASE tests?
5. Explain eight hints for taking ASE tests.

ASE CERTIFICATION–TYPE QUESTIONS

1. Technician A says ASE is under the guidance of a 30-member board of directors. Technician B says the ASE board of directors is made up of members from all aspects of the automotive industry. Who is right?
   (A) A only.   (C) Both A and B.
   (B) B only.   (D) Neither A nor B.
2. Technician A says ASE certification is a requirement in some countries. Technician B says ASE certification is voluntary in the United States. Who is right?
   (A) A only.   (C) Both A and B.
   (B) B only.   (D) Neither A nor B.
3. Technician A says "Manual Drive Train and Axles" is one of the ASE test categories. Technician B says "Heating and Air Conditioning" is one of the ASE test categories. Who is right?
   (A) A only.   (C) Both A and B.
   (B) B only.   (D) Neither A nor B.

4. While discussing ASE testing procedures, Technician A says only two tests can be taken at each testing session. Technician B says five tests can be taken at each testing session. Who is right?
   (A) A only.   (C) Both A and B.
   (B) B only.   (D) Neither A nor B.

5. Technician A says the ASE Electrical/Electronic Systems Test mainly covers electrical theory. Technician B says the ASE Electrical/Electronic Systems Test contains questions on charging system diagnosis and repair. Who is right?
   (A) A only.   (C) Both A and B.
   (B) B only.   (D) Neither A nor B.

6. Technician A says that to take the ASE tests, an individual must have formal training in automotive technology. Technician B says anyone can take the ASE tests. Who is right?
   (A) A only.   (C) Both A and B.
   (B) B only.   (D) Neither A nor B.

7. Technician A says that an individual must have two years of on-the-job experience in order to receive certification. Technician B says that in some cases, one year of approved training can be substituted for one year of work experience. Who is right?
   (A) A only.   (C) Both A and B.
   (B) B only.   (D) Neither A nor B.

8. Two technicians are discussing the months in which the ASE certification tests are given. Technician A says ASE tests are given in May. Technician B says ASE tests are given in November. Who is right?
   (A) A only.   (C) Both A and B.
   (B) B only.   (D) Neither A nor B.

9. Technician A says ASE tests results are mailed to the test taker's employer. Technician B says ASE test results are mailed to the test taker's home. Who is right?
   (A) A only.   (C) Both A and B.
   (B) B only.   (D) Neither A nor B.

10. Technician A says the ASE tests contain short-answer questions. Technician B says the ASE tests contain multiple-choice questions. Who is right?
    (A) A only.   (C) Both A and B.
    (B) B only.   (D) Neither A nor B.

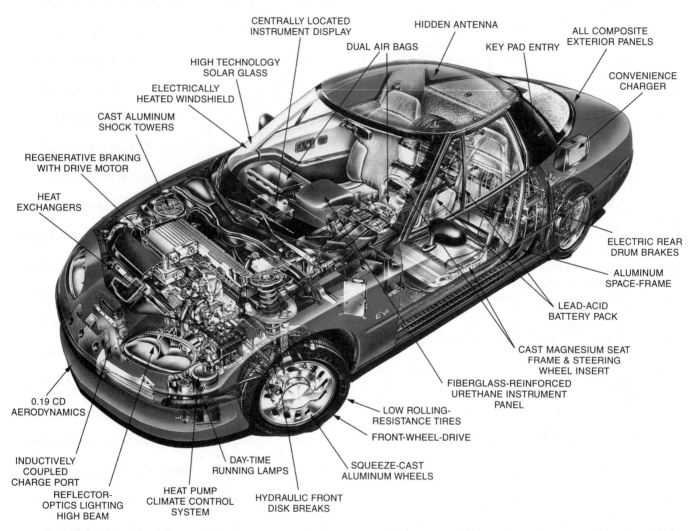

CENTRALLY LOCATED
INSTRUMENT DISPLAY

HIDDEN ANTENNA

ALL COMPOSITE
EXTERIOR PANELS

DUAL AIR BAGS

KEY PAD ENTRY

HIGH TECHNOLOGY
SOLAR GLASS

CONVENIENCE
CHARGER

ELECTRICALLY
HEATED WINDSHIELD

CAST ALUMINUM
SHOCK TOWERS

REGENERATIVE BRAKING
WITH DRIVE MOTOR

HEAT
EXCHANGERS

ELECTRIC REAR
DRUM BRAKES

ALUMINUM
SPACE-FRAME

LEAD-ACID
BATTERY PACK

CAST MAGNESIUM SEAT
FRAME & STEERING
WHEEL INSERT

FIBERGLASS-REINFORCED
URETHANE INSTRUMENT
PANEL

0.19 CD
AERODYNAMICS

LOW ROLLING-
RESISTANCE TIRES

FRONT-WHEEL-DRIVE

INDUCTIVELY
COUPLED
CHARGE PORT

REFLECTOR-
OPTICS LIGHTING
HIGH BEAM

DAY-TIME
RUNNING LAMPS

SQUEEZE-CAST
ALUMINUM WHEELS

HEAT PUMP
CLIMATE CONTROL
SYSTEM

HYDRAULIC FRONT
DISK BREAKS

Cutaway view of an electric vehicle. This vehicle can travel approximately 80 miles on a single charge and can be recharged in approximately three hours. The demand for technicians skilled in servicing this type of vehicle is likely to increase in the future.   (GM)

OBD II Diagnostic Trouble Codes

The following are the generic SAE codes (core codes) generated by OBD II diagnostic systems. Manufacturer-specific codes (codes that begin with a P1 alpha-numeric designator) should be looked up in the service manual.

P01XX Fuel and Air Metering

Note: For systems with a single O_2 sensor, use codes for Bank 1, Sensor 1. Bank 1 contains cylinder #1. Sensor 1 is the O_2 sensor closest to the engine.

P0100 Mass or Volume Air Flow Circuit Malfunction

P0101 Mass or Volume Air Flow Circuit Range/Performance Problem

P0102 Mass or Volume Air Flow Circuit Low Input

P0103 Mass or Volume Air Flow Circuit High Input

P0104 Mass or Volume Air Flow Circuit Intermittent

P0105 Manifold Absolute Pressure/Barometric Pressure Circuit Malfunction

P0106 Manifold Absolute Pressure/Barometric Pressure Circuit Range/Performance Problem

P0107 Manifold Absolute Pressure/Barometric Pressure Circuit Low Input

P0108 Manifold Absolute Pressure/Barometric Pressure Circuit High Input

P0109 Manifold Absolute Pressure/Barometric Pressure Circuit Intermittent

P0110 Intake Air Temperature Circuit Malfunction

P0111 Intake Air Temperature Circuit Range/Performance Problem

P0112 Intake Air Temperature Circuit Low Input

P0113 Intake Air Temperature Circuit High Input

P0114 Intake Air Temperature Circuit Intermittent

P0115 Engine Coolant Temperature Circuit Malfunction

P0116 Engine Coolant Temperature Circuit Range/Performance Problem

P0117 Engine Coolant Temperature Circuit Low Input

P0118 Engine Coolant Temperature Circuit High Input

P0119 Engine Coolant Temperature Circuit Intermittent

P0120 Throttle/Pedal Position Sensor/Switch A Circuit Malfunction

P0121 Throttle/Pedal Position Sensor/Switch A Circuit Range/Performance Problem

P0122 Throttle/Pedal Position Sensor/Switch A Circuit Low Input

P0123 Throttle/Pedal Position Sensor/Switch A Circuit High Input

P0124 Throttle/Pedal Position Sensor/Switch A Circuit Intermittent

P0125 Insufficient Coolant Temperature for Closed Loop Fuel Control

P0126 Insufficient Coolant Temperature for Stable Operation

P0130 Oxygen Sensor Circuit Malfunction—Bank 1, Sensor 1

P0131 Oxygen Sensor Circuit Low Voltage—Bank 1, Sensor 1

P0132 Oxygen Sensor Circuit High Voltage—Bank 1, Sensor 1

P0133 Oxygen Sensor Circuit Slow Response—Bank 1, Sensor 1

P0134 Oxygen Sensor Circuit No Activity Detected—Bank 1, Sensor 1

P0135 Oxygen Sensor Heater Circuit Malfunction—Bank 1, Sensor 2

P0136 Oxygen Sensor Circuit Malfunction—Bank 1, Sensor 2

P0137 Oxygen Sensor Circuit Low Voltage—Bank 1, Sensor 2

P0138 Oxygen Sensor Circuit High Voltage—Bank 1, Sensor 2

P0139 Oxygen Sensor Circuit Slow Response—Bank 1, Sensor 2

P0140 Oxygen Sensor Circuit No Activity Detected—Bank 1, Sensor 2

P0141 Oxygen Sensor Heater Circuit Malfunction—Bank 1, Sensor 2

P0142 Oxygen Sensor Circuit Malfunction—Bank 1, Sensor 3

P0143 Oxygen Sensor Circuit Low Voltage—Bank 1, Sensor 3

P0144 Oxygen Sensor Circuit High Voltage—Bank 1, Sensor 3

P0145 Oxygen Sensor Circuit Slow Response—Bank 1, Sensor 3

P0146 Oxygen Sensor Circuit No Activity Detected—Bank 1, Sensor 3

P0147 Oxygen Sensor Heater Circuit Malfunction—Bank 1, Sensor 3

P0150 Oxygen Sensor Circuit Malfunction—Bank 2, Sensor 1

P0151 Oxygen Sensor Circuit Low Voltage—Bank 2, Sensor 1

P0152 Oxygen Sensor Circuit High Voltage—Bank 2, Sensor 1

P0153 Oxygen Sensor Circuit Slow Response—Bank 2, Sensor 1

P0154 Oxygen Sensor Circuit No Activity Detected—Bank 2, Sensor 1

P0155 Oxygen Sensor Heater Circuit Malfunction—Bank 2, Sensor 1

P0156 Oxygen Sensor Circuit Malfunction—Bank 2, Sensor 1

P0157 Oxygen Sensor Circuit Low Voltage—Bank 2, Sensor 2

P0158 Oxygen Sensor Circuit High Voltage—Bank 2, Sensor 2

P0159 Oxygen Sensor Circuit Slow Response—Bank 2, Sensor 2

P0160 Oxygen Sensor Circuit No Activity Detected—Bank 2, Sensor 1

P0161 Oxygen Sensor Heater Circuit Malfunction—Bank 2, Sensor 2

P0162 Oxygen Sensor Circuit Malfunction—Bank 2, Sensor 2

P0163 Oxygen Sensor Circuit Low Voltage—Bank 2, Sensor 3

P0164 Oxygen Sensor Circuit High Voltage—Bank 2, Sensor 3

P0165 Oxygen Sensor Circuit Slow Response—Bank 2, Sensor 3
P0166 Oxygen Sensor Circuit No Activity Detected—Bank 2, Sensor 3
P0167 Oxygen Sensor Heater Circuit Malfunction—Bank 2, Sensor 3
P0170 Fuel Trim Malfunction—Bank 1
P0171 System too Lean—Bank 1
P0172 System too Rich—Bank 1
P0173 Fuel Trim Malfunction—Bank 1
P0174 System too Lean—Bank 2
P0175 System too Rich—Bank 2
P0176 Fuel Composition Sensor Circuit Malfunction
P0177 Fuel Composition Sensor Circuit Range/Performance
P0178 Fuel Composition Sensor Circuit Low Input
P0179 Fuel Composition Sensor Circuit High Input
P0180 Fuel Temperature Sensor A Circuit Malfunction
P0181 Fuel Temperature Sensor A Circuit Range/Performance
P0182 Fuel Temperature Sensor A Circuit Low Input

P0183 Fuel Temperature Sensor A Circuit High Input
P0184 Fuel Temperature Sensor A Circuit Intermittent
P0185 Fuel Temperature Sensor B Circuit Malfunction
P0186 Fuel Temperature Sensor B Circuit Range/Performance
P0187 Fuel Temperature Sensor B Circuit Low Input
P0188 Fuel Temperature Sensor B Circuit High Input
P0189 Fuel Temperature Sensor B Circuit Intermittent
P0190 Fuel Rail Pressure Sensor Circuit Malfunction
P0191 Fuel Rail Pressure Sensor Circuit Range/Performance
P0192 Fuel Rail Pressure Sensor Circuit Low Input
P0193 Fuel Rail Pressure Sensor Circuit High Input
P0194 Fuel Rail Pressure Sensor Circuit Intermittent
P0195 Engine Oil Temperature Sensor Malfunction
P0196 Engine Oil Temperature Sensor Range/Performance
P0197 Engine Oil Temperature Sensor Low
P0198 Engine Oil Temperature Sensor High
P0199 Engine Oil Temperature Sensor Intermittent

P02XX Fuel and Air Metering

P0200 Injector Circuit Malfunction
P0201 Injector Circuit Malfunction—Cylinder 1
P0202 Injector Circuit Malfunction—Cylinder 2
P0203 Injector Circuit Malfunction—Cylinder 3
P0204 Injector Circuit Malfunction—Cylinder 4
P0205 Injector Circuit Malfunction—Cylinder 5
P0206 Injector Circuit Malfunction—Cylinder 6
P0207 Injector Circuit Malfunction—Cylinder 7
P0208 Injector Circuit Malfunction—Cylinder 8
P0209 Injector Circuit Malfunction—Cylinder 9
P0210 Injector Circuit Malfunction—Cylinder 10
P0211 Injector Circuit Malfunction—Cylinder 11
P0212 Injector Circuit Malfunction—Cylinder 12
P0213 Cold Start Injector 1 Malfunction
P0214 Cold Start Injector 2 Malfunction
P0215 Engine Shutoff Solenoid Malfunction
P0216 Injection Timing Control Circuit Malfunction
P0217 Engine Over Temperature Condition
P0218 Transmission Over Temperature Condition
P0219 Engine Overspeed Condition
P0220 Throttle/Pedal Position Sensor/Switch B Circuit Malfunction
P0221 Throttle/Pedal Position Sensor/Switch B Circuit Range/Performance Problem
P0222 Throttle/Pedal Position Sensor/Switch B Circuit Low Input
P0223 Throttle/Pedal Position Sensor/Switch B Circuit High Input
P0224 Throttle/Pedal Position Sensor/Switch B Circuit Intermittent
P0225 Throttle/Pedal Position Sensor/Switch C Circuit Malfunction
P0226 Throttle/Pedal Position Sensor/Switch C Circuit Range/Performance Problem
P0227 Throttle/Pedal Position Sensor/Switch C Circuit Low Input
P0228 Throttle/Pedal Position Sensor/Switch C Circuit High Input
P0229 Throttle/Pedal Position Sensor/Switch C Circuit Intermittent

P0230 Fuel Pump Primary Circuit Malfunction
P0231 Fuel Pump Secondary Circuit Low
P0232 Fuel Pump Secondary Circuit High
P0233 Fuel Pump Secondary Circuit Intermittent
P0235 Turbocharger Boost Sensor A Circuit Malfunction
P0236 Turbocharger Boost Sensor A Circuit Range/Performance
P0237 Turbocharger Boost Sensor A Circuit Low
P0238 Turbocharger Boost Sensor A Circuit High
P0239 Turbocharger Boost Sensor B Circuit Malfunction
P0240 Turbocharger Boost Sensor B Circuit Range/Performance
P0241 Turbocharger Boost Sensor B Circuit Low
P0242 Turbocharger Boost Sensor B Circuit High
P0243 Turbocharger Wastegate Solenoid A Malfunction
P0244 Turbocharger Wastegate Solenoid A Range/Performance
P0245 Turbocharger Wastegate Solenoid A Low
P0246 Turbocharger Wastegate Solenoid A High
P0247 Turbocharger Wastegate Solenoid B Malfunction
P0248 Turbocharger Wastegate Solenoid B Range/Performance
P0249 Turbocharger Wastegate Solenoid B Low
P0250 Turbocharger Wastegate Solenoid B High
P0251 Injection Pump A Rotor/Cam Malfunction
P0252 Injection Pump A Rotor/Cam Range/Performance
P0253 Injection Pump A Rotor/Cam Low
P0254 Injection Pump A Rotor/Cam High
P0255 Injection Pump A Rotor/Cam Intermittent
P0256 Injection Pump B Rotor/Cam Malfunction
P0257 Injection Pump B Rotor/Cam Range/Performance
P0258 Injection Pump B Rotor/Cam Low
P0259 Injection Pump B Rotor/Cam High
P0260 Injection Pump B Rotor/Cam Intermittent
P0261 Cylinder 1 Injector Circuit Low
P0262 Cylinder 1 Injector Circuit High

Tables

P0263 Cylinder 1 Contribution/Balance Fault
P0264 Cylinder 2 Injector Circuit Low
P0265 Cylinder 2 Injector Circuit High
P0266 Cylinder 2 Contribution/Balance Fault
P0267 Cylinder 3 Injector Circuit Low
P0268 Cylinder 3 Injector Circuit High
P0269 Cylinder 3 Contribution/ Balance Fault
P0270 Cylinder 4 Injector Circuit Low
P0271 Cylinder 4 Injector Circuit High
P0272 Cylinder 4 Contribution/Balance Fault
P0273 Cylinder 5 Injector Circuit Low
P0274 Cylinder 5 Injector Circuit High
P0275 Cylinder 5 Contribution/Balance Fault
P0276 Cylinder 6 Injector Circuit Low
P0277 Cylinder 6 Injector Circuit High
P0278 Cylinder 6 Contribution/Balance Fault
P0279 Cylinder 7 Injector Circuit Low

P0280 Cylinder 7 Injector Circuit High
P0281 Cylinder 7 Contribution/Balance Fault
P0282 Cylinder 8 Injector Circuit Low
P0283 Cylinder 8 Injector Circuit High
P0284 Cylinder 8 Contribution/Balance Fault
P0285 Cylinder 9 Injector Circuit Low
P0286 Cylinder 9 Injector Circuit High
P0287 Cylinder 9 Contribution/Balance Fault
P0288 Cylinder 10 Injector Circuit Low
P0289 Cylinder 10 Injector Circuit High
P0290 Cylinder 10 Contribution/Balance Fault
P0291 Cylinder 11 Injector Circuit Low
P0292 Cylinder 11 Injector Circuit High
P0293 Cylinder 11 Contribution/Balance Fault
P0294 Cylinder 12 Injector Circuit Low
P0295 Cylinder 12 Injector Circuit High
P0296 Cylinder 12 Contribution/Balance Fault

P03XX Ignition System or Misfire

Note: Bank 1 contains cylinder #1.

P0300 Random/Multiple Cylinder Misfire Detected
P0301 Cylinder 1 Misfire Detected
P0302 Cylinder 2 Misfire Detected
P0303 Cylinder 3 Misfire Detected
P0304 Cylinder 4 Misfire Detected
P0305 Cylinder 5 Misfire Detected
P0306 Cylinder 6 Misfire Detected
P0307 Cylinder 7 Misfire Detected
P0308 Cylinder 8 Misfire Detected
P0309 Cylinder 9 Misfire Detected
P0310 Cylinder 10 Misfire Detected
P0311 Cylinder 11 Misfire Detected
P0312 Cylinder 12 Misfire Detected
P0320 Ignition/Distributor Engine Speed Input Circuit Malfunction
P0321 Ignition/Distributor Engine Speed Input Circuit Range/Performance
P0322 Ignition/Distributor Engine Speed Input Circuit No Signal
P0323 Ignition/Distributor Engine Speed Input Circuit Intermittent
P0325 Knock Sensor 1 Circuit Malfunction—Bank 1 or Single Sensor
P0326 Knock Sensor 1 Circuit Range/Performance—Bank 1 or Single Sensor
P0327 Knock Sensor 1 Circuit Low Input—Bank 1 or Single Sensor
P0328 Knock Sensor 1 Circuit High Input—Bank 1 or Single Sensor
P0329 Knock Sensor 1 Circuit Input Intermittent—Bank 1 or Single Sensor
P0330 Knock Sensor 2 Circuit Malfunction—Bank 2
P0331 Knock Sensor 2 Circuit Range/Performance—Bank 2
P0332 Knock Sensor 2 Circuit Low Input—Bank 2
P0333 Knock Sensor 2 Circuit High Input—Bank 2
P0334 Knock Sensor 2 Circuit Input Intermittent—Bank 2
P0335 Crankshaft Position Sensor A Circuit Malfunction
P0336 Crankshaft Position Sensor A Circuit Range/Performance
P0337 Crankshaft Position Sensor A Circuit Low Input
P0338 Crankshaft Position Sensor A Circuit High Input

P0339 Crankshaft Position Sensor A Circuit Intermittent
P0340 Camshaft Position Sensor Circuit Malfunction
P0341 Camshaft Position Sensor Circuit Range/Performance
P0342 Camshaft Position Sensor Circuit Low Input
P0343 Camshaft Position Sensor Circuit High Input
P0344 Camshaft Position Sensor Circuit Intermittent
P0350 Ignition Coil Primary/Secondary Circuit Malfunction
P0351 Ignition Coil A Primary/Secondary Circuit Malfunction
P0352 Ignition Coil B Primary/Secondary Circuit Malfunction
P0353 Ignition Coil C Primary/Secondary Circuit Malfunction
P0354 Ignition Coil D Primary/Secondary Circuit Malfunction
P0355 Ignition Coil E Primary/Secondary Circuit Malfunction
P0356 Ignition Coil F Primary/Secondary Circuit Malfunction
P0357 Ignition Coil G Primary/Secondary Circuit Malfunction
P0358 Ignition Coil H Primary/Secondary Circuit Malfunction
P0359 Ignition Coil I Primary/Secondary Circuit Malfunction
P0360 Ignition Coil J Primary/Secondary Circuit Malfunction
P0361 Ignition Coil K Primary/Secondary Circuit Malfunction
P0362 Ignition Coil L Primary/Secondary Circuit Malfunction
P0370 Timing Reference High Resolution Signal A Malfunction
P0371 Timing Reference High Resolution Signal A Too Many Pulse
P0372 Timing Reference High Resolution Signal A Malfunction
P0373 Timing Reference High Resolution Signal Intermittent/Erratic Pulses
P0374 Timing Reference High Resolution Signal A No Pulse

P0375 Timing Reference High Resolution Signal B Malfunction

P0376 Timing Reference High Resolution Signal B Too Many Pulses

P0377 Timing Reference High Resolution Signal B Too Few Pulses

P0378 Timing Reference High Resolution Signal B Intermittent/Erratic Pulses

P0379 Timing Reference High Resolution Signal B No Pulse

P0380 Glow Plug/Heater Circuit Malfunction

P0381 Glow Plug/Heater Indicator Circuit Malfunction

P0385 Crankshaft Position Sensor B Circuit Malfunction

P0386 Crankshaft Position Sensor B Circuit Range/Performance

P0387 Crankshaft Position Sensor B Circuit Low Input

P0388 Crankshaft Position Sensor B Circuit High Input

P0389 Crankshaft Position Sensor B Circuit Intermittent

P04XX Auxiliary Emission Controls

Note: Bank 1 contains cylinder #1.

P0400 Exhaust Gas Recirculation Flow Malfunction

P0401 Exhaust Gas Recirculation Flow Insufficient Detected

P0402 Exhaust Gas Recirculation Flow Excessive Detected

P0403 Exhaust Gas Recirculation Circuit Malfunction

P0404 Exhaust Gas Recirculation Circuit Range/Performance

P0405 Exhaust Gas Recirculation Sensor A Circuit Low

P0406 Exhaust Gas Recirculation Sensor A Circuit High

P0407 Exhaust Gas Recirculation Sensor B Circuit Low

P0408 Exhaust Gas Recirculation Sensor B Circuit High

P0410 Secondary Air Injection System Malfunction

P0411 Secondary Air Injection System Incorrect Flow Detected

P0412 Secondary Air Injection System Switching Valve A Circuit Malfunction

P0413 Secondary Air Injection System Switching Valve A Circuit Open

P0414 Secondary Air Injection System Switching Valve A Circuit Shorted

P0415 Secondary Air Injection System Switching Valve B Circuit Malfunction

P0416 Secondary Air Injection System Switching Valve B Circuit Open

P0417 Secondary Air Injection System Switching Valve B Circuit Shorted

P0420 Catalyst System Efficiency Below Threshold—Bank 1

P0421 Warm Up Catalyst Efficiency Below Threshold—Bank 1

P0422 Main Catalyst Efficiency Below Threshold—Bank 1

P0423 Heated Catalyst Efficiency Below Threshold—Bank 1

P0424 Heated Catalyst Temperature Below Threshold—Bank 1

P0430 Catalyst System Efficiency Below Threshold—Bank 2

P0431 Warm Up Catalyst Efficiency Below Threshold—Bank 2

P0432 Main Catalyst Efficiency Below Threshold—Bank 2

P0433 Heated Catalyst Efficiency Below Threshold—Bank 2

P0434 Heated Catalyst Temperature Below Threshold—Bank 2

P0440 Evaporative Emission Control System Malfunction

P0441 Evaporative Emission Control System Incorrect Purge Flow

P0442 Evaporative Emission Control System Leak Detected (small leak)

P0443 Evaporative Emission Control System Purge Control Valve Circuit Malfunction

P0444 Evaporative Emission Control System Purge Control Valve Circuit Open

P0445 Evaporative Emission Control System Purge Control Valve Circuit Shorted

P0450 Evaporative Emission Control System Pressure Sensor Malfunction

P0451 Evaporative Emission Control System Pressure Sensor Range/Performance

P0452 Evaporative Emission Control System Pressure Sensor Low Input

P0453 Evaporative Emission Control System Pressure Sensor High Input

P0454 Evaporative Emission Control System Pressure Sensor Intermittent

P0455 Evaporative Emission Control System Leak Detected (gross leak)

P0460 Fuel Level Sensor Circuit Malfunction

P0461 Fuel Level Sensor Circuit Range/Performance

P0462 Fuel Level Sensor Circuit Low Input

P0463 Fuel Level Sensor Circuit High Input

P0464 Fuel Level Sensor Circuit Intermittent

P0465 Purge Flow Sensor Circuit Malfunction

P0466 Purge Flow Sensor Circuit Range/Performance

P0467 Purge Flow Sensor Circuit Low Input

P0468 Purge Flow Sensor Circuit High Input

P0469 Purge Flow Sensor Circuit Intermittent

P0470 Exhaust Pressure Sensor Malfunction

P0471 Exhaust Pressure Sensor Range/Performance

P0472 Exhaust Pressure Sensor Low

P0473 Exhaust Pressure Sensor High

P0474 Exhaust Pressure Sensor Intermittent

P0475 Exhaust Pressure Control Valve Malfunction

P0476 Exhaust Pressure Control Valve Range/Performance

P0477 Exhaust Pressure Control Valve Low

P0478 Exhaust Pressure Control Valve High

P0479 Exhaust Pressure Control Valve Intermittent

Tables

P05XX Vehicle Speed, Idle Control, and Auxiliary Inputs

P0500 Vehicle Speed Sensor Malfunction
P0501 Vehicle Speed Sensor Range/Performance
P0502 Vehicle Speed Sensor Circuit Low Input
P0503 Vehicle Speed Sensor Intermittent/Erratic/High
P0505 Idle Control System Malfunction
P0506 Idle Control System RPM Lower Than Expected
P0507 Idle Control System RPM Higher Than Expected
P0510 Closed Throttle Position Switch Malfunction
P0530 A/C Refrigerant Pressure Sensor Circuit Malfunction
P0531 A/C Refrigerant Pressure Sensor Circuit Range/Performance
P0532 A/C Refrigerant Pressure Sensor Circuit Low Input
P0533 A/C Refrigerant Pressure Sensor Circuit High Input
P0534 Air Conditioner Refrigerant Charge Loss
P0550 Power Steering Pressure Sensor Circuit Malfunction
P0551 Power Steering Pressure Sensor Circuit Range/Performance

P0552 Power Steering Pressure Sensor Circuit Low Input
P0553 Power Steering Pressure Sensor Circuit High Input
P0554 Power Steering Pressure Sensor Circuit Intermittent
P0560 System Voltage Malfunction
P0561 System Voltage Unstable
P0562 System Voltage Low
P0563 System Voltage High
P0565 Cruise Control On Signal Malfunction
P0566 Cruise Control Off Signal Malfunction
P0567 Cruise Control Resume Signal Malfunction
P0568 Cruise Control Set Signal Malfunction
P0569 Cruise Control Coast Signal Malfunction
P0570 Cruise Control Acceleration Signal Malfunction
P0571 Cruise Control/Brake Switch A Circuit Malfunction
P0572 Cruise Control/Brake Switch A Circuit Low
P0573 Cruise Control/Brake Switch A Circuit High
P0574 through **P0580** Reserved for Cruise Control System Codes

P06XX Computer and Auxiliary Outputs

P0600 Serial Communication Link Modification
P0601 Internal Control Module Memory Check Sum Error
P0602 Control Module Programming Error
P0603 Internal Control Module Keep Alive Memory (KAM) Error

P0604 Internal Control Module Random Access Memory (RAM) Error
P0605 Internal Control Module Read Only Memory (ROM) Error
P0606 PCM Processor Fault

P07XX Transmission

P0700 Transmission Control System Malfunction
P0701 Transmission Control System Range/Performance
P0702 Transmission Control System Electrical
P0703 Torque Converter/Brake Switch B Circuit Malfunction
P0704 Clutch Switch Input Circuit Malfunction
P0705 Transmission Range Sensor Circuit Malfunction (PRNDL Input)
P0706 Transmission Range Sensor Circuit Range/Performance
P0707 Transmission Range Sensor Circuit Low Input
P0708 Transmission Range Sensor Circuit High Input
P0709 Transmission Range Sensor Circuit Intermittent
P0710 Transmission Fluid Temperature Sensor Circuit Malfunction
P0711 Transmission Fluid Temperature Sensor Circuit Range/Performance
P0712 Transmission Fluid Temperature Sensor Low Input
P0713 Transmission Fluid Temperature Sensor Circuit High Input
P0714 Transmission Fluid Temperature Sensor Circuit Intermittent
P0715 Input/Turbine Speed Sensor Circuit Malfunction
P0716 Input/Turbine Speed Sensor Circuit Range/Performance
P0717 Input/Turbine Speed Sensor Circuit No Signal

P0718 Input/Turbine Speed Sensor Circuit Intermittent
P0719 Torque Converter/Brake Switch B Circuit Low
P0720 Output Speed Sensor Circuit Malfunction
P0721 Output Speed Sensor Circuit Range/Performance
P0722 Output Speed Sensor Circuit No Signal
P0723 Output Speed Sensor Circuit Intermittent
P0724 Torque Converter/Brake Switch B Circuit High
P0725 Engine Speed Input Circuit Malfunction
P0726 Engine Speed Input Circuit Range/Performance
P0727 Engine Speed Input Circuit No Signal
P0728 Engine Speed Input Circuit Intermittent
P0730 Incorrect Gear Ratio
P0731 Gear 1 Incorrect Ratio
P0732 Gear 2 Incorrect Ratio
P0733 Gear 3 Incorrect Ratio
P0734 Gear 4 Incorrect Ratio
P0735 Gear 5 Incorrect Ratio
P0736 Reverse Incorrect Ratio
P0740 Torque Converter Clutch Circuit Malfunction
P0741 Torque Converter Clutch Circuit Performance or Stuck Off
P0742 Torque Converter Clutch Circuit Stuck On
P0743 Torque Converter Clutch Circuit Electrical
P0744 Torque Converter Clutch Circuit Intermittent
P0745 Pressure Control Solenoid Malfunction
P0746 Pressure Control Solenoid Performance or Stuck Off

P0747 Pressure Control Solenoid Stuck On
P0748 Pressure Control Solenoid Electrical
P0749 Pressure Control Solenoid Intermittent
P0750 Shift Solenoid A Malfunction
P0751 Shift Solenoid A Performance or Stuck Off
P0752 Shift Solenoid A Stuck On
P0753 Shift Solenoid A Electrical
P0754 Shift Solenoid A Intermittent
P0755 Shift Solenoid B Malfunction
P0756 Shift Solenoid B Performance or Stuck Off
P0757 Shift Solenoid B Stuck On
P0758 Shift Solenoid B Electrical
P0759 Shift Solenoid B Intermittent
P0760 Shift Solenoid C Malfunction
P0761 Shift Solenoid C Performance or Stuck Off
P0762 Shift Solenoid C Stuck On
P0763 Shift Solenoid C Electrical
P0764 Shift Solenoid C Intermittent
P0765 Shift Solenoid D Malfunction
P0766 Shift Solenoid D Performance or Stuck Off

P0767 Shift Solenoid D Stuck On
P0768 Shift Solenoid D Electrical
P0769 Shift Solenoid D Intermittent
P0770 Shift Solenoid E Malfunction
P0771 Shift Solenoid E Performance or Stuck Off
P0772 Shift Solenoid E Stuck On
P0773 Shift Solenoid E Electrical
P0774 Shift Solenoid E Intermittent
P0780 Shift Malfunction
P0781 1-2 Shift Malfunction
P0782 2-3 Shift Malfunction
P0783 3-4 Shift Malfunction
P0784 4-5 Shift Malfunction
P0785 Shift/Timing Solenoid Malfunction
P0786 Shift/Timing Solenoid Range/Performance
P0787 Shift/Timing Solenoid Low
P0788 Shift/Timing Solenoid High
P0789 Shift/Timing Solenoid Intermittent
P0790 Normal/Performance Switch Circuit Malfunction

Tables

	TYPICAL ELECTRICAL/ELECTRONIC SYMBOLS		
+	POSITIVE		CONNECTOR
−	NEGATIVE		MALE CONNECTOR
	GROUND		FEMALE CONNECTOR
	FUSE		MULTIPLE CONNECTOR
	CIRCUIT BREAKER		DENOTES WIRE CONTINUES ELSEWHERE
	CAPACITOR		SPLICE
Ω	OHMS		SPLICE IDENTIFICATION
	RESISTOR		OPTIONAL — WIRING WITH / WIRING WITHOUT
	VARIABLE RESISTOR		THERMAL ELEMENT (BI-METAL STRIP)
	SERIES RESISTOR		"Y" WINDINGS
	COIL	88:88	DIGITAL READOUT
	STEP UP COIL		SINGLE FILAMENT LAMP
	OPEN CONTACT		DUAL FILAMENT LAMP
	CLOSED CONTACT		LED LIGHT EMITTING DIODE
	CLOSED SWITCH		THERMISTOR
	OPEN SWITCH		GAUGE
	CLOSED GANGED SWITCH	TIMER	TIMER
	OPEN GANGED SWITCH		MOTOR
	TWO POLE SINGLE THROW SWITCH		ARMATURE AND BRUSHES
	PRESSURE SWITCH		DENOTES WIRE GOES THROUGH GROMMET
	SOLENOID SWITCH		DENOTES WIRE GOES THROUGH 40 WAY DISCONNECT
	MERCURY SWITCH	STRG COLUMN	DENOTES WIRE GOES THROUGH STEERING COLUMN CONNECTOR
	DIODE OR RECTIFIER	INST PANEL	DENOTES WIRE GOES THROUGH INSTRUMENT PANEL CONNECTOR

SAE-Recommended Abbreviations/Acronyms

Term	Abbreviation/ Acronym	Term	Abbreviation/ Acronym
Accelerator Pedal	AP	Inertia Fuel Shutoff	IFS
Air Cleaner	AC	Intake Air	IA
Air Conditioning	A/C	Intake Air Temperature	IAT
Automatic Transmission	A/T		
Automatic Transaxle	A/T	Knock Sensor	KS
Barometric Pressure	BARO	Malfunction Indicator Lamp	MIL
Battery Positive Voltage	B+	Manifold Absolute Pressure	MAP
		Manifold Differential Pressure	MDP
Camshaft Position	CMP	Manifold Surface Temperature	MST
Carburetor	CARB	Manifold Vacuum Zone	MVZ
Charge Air Cooler	CAC	Mass Airflow	MAF
Closed Loop	CL	Mixture Control	MC
Closed Throttle Position	CTP	Multiport Fuel Injection	MFI
Clutch Pedal Position	CPP		
Continuous Fuel Injection	CFI	Nonvolatile Random Access Memory	NVRAM
Continuous Trap Oxidizer	CTOX		
Crankshaft Position	CKP	On-Board Diagnostic	OBD
		Open Loop	OL
Data Link Connector	DLC	Oxidation Catalytic Converter	OC
Diagnostic Test Mode	DTM	Oxygen Sensor	O2S
Diagnostic Trouble Code	DTC		
Direct Fuel Injection	DFI	Park/Neutral Position	PNP
		Periodic Trap Oxidizer	PTOX
Early Fuel Evaporation	EFE	Positive Crankcase Ventilation	PCV
EGR Temperature	EGRT	Power Steering Pressure	PSP
Electronically Erasable Programmable		Powertrain Control Module	PCM
Read Only Memory	EEPROM	Programmable Read Only Memory	PROM
Electronic Ignition	EI	Pulsed Secondary Air Injection	PAIR
Engine Control	EC		
Engine Control Module	ECM	Random Access Memory	RAM
Engine Coolant Level	ECL	Read Only Memory	ROM
Engine Coolant Temperature	ECT	Relay Module	RM
Engine Modification	EM		
Engine Speed	RPM	Scan Tool	ST
Erasable Programmable		Secondary Air Injection	AIR
Read Only Memory	EPROM	Sequential Multiport Fuel Injection	SFI
Evaporative Emission	EVAP	Service Reminder Indicator	SRI
Exhaust Gas Recirculation	EGR	Smoke Puff Limiter	SPL
		Supercharger	SC
Fan Control	FC	Supercharger Bypass	SCB
Flash Electrically Erasable Programmable		System Readiness Test	SRT
Read Only Memory	FEEPROM		
Flash Erasable Programmable		Thermal Vacuum Valve	TVV
Read Only Memory	FEPROM	Third Gear	3GR
Flexible Fuel	FF	Three Way + Oxidation Catalytic Converter	TWC+OC
Fourth Gear	4GR	Three Way Catalytic Converter	TWC
Fuel Pump	FP	Throttle Body	TB
Fuel Trim	FT	Throttle Body Fuel Injection	TBI
		Throttle Position	TP
Generator	GEN	Torque Converter Clutch	TCC
Governor Control Module	GCM	Transmission Control Module	TCM
Ground	GND	Transmission Range	TR
		Turbocharger	TC
Heated Oxygen Sensor	HO2S		
		Vehicle Speed Sensor	VSS
Idle Air Control	IAC	Voltage Regulator	VR
Idle Speed Control	ISC	Volume Airflow	VAF
Ignition Control	IC		
Ignition Control Module	ICM	Warm Up Three Way Catalytic Converter	WU-TWC
Indirect Fuel Injection	IFI	Wide Open Throttle	WOT

STANDARD PREFIXES

Prefix	Symbol	Multiplier	Exponent Form
tera	T	1 000 000 000 000	10^{12}
giga	G	1 000 000 000	10^{9}
mega	M	1 000 000	10^{6}
kilo	k	1 000	10^{3}
deka	da	10	10^{1}
deci	d	0.1	10^{-1}
centi	c	0.01	10^{-2}
milli	m	0.001	10^{-3}
micro	μ	0.000 001	10^{-6}
nano	n	0.000 000 001	10^{-9}
pico	p	0.000 000 000 001	10^{-12}

RESISTOR VALUES

Color	1st & 2nd BAND DIGITS	3rd BAND MULTIPLY BY	4th BAND TOLERANCE ± %
BLACK	0	1	—
BROWN	1	10	—
RED	2	100	—
ORANGE	3	1000	—
YELLOW	4	10000	—
GREEN	5	100000	—
BLUE	6	1000000	—
VIOLET	7	10000000	—
GRAY	8	100000000	—
WHITE	9	1000000000	—
GOLD	—	0.1	5
SILVER	—	0.01	10
NO COLOR	—	—	20

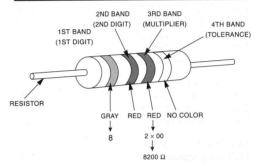

1ST BAND (1ST DIGIT)
2ND BAND (2ND DIGIT)
3RD BAND (MULTIPLIER)
4TH BAND (TOLERANCE)
RESISTOR
GRAY RED RED NO COLOR
8   2 × 00
8200 Ω

CONVERSION CHART

METRIC/U.S. CUSTOMARY UNIT EQUIVALENTS

Multiply:	by:	to get:		Multiply:	by:	to get:

ACCELERATION

| feet/sec² | x 0.3048 | = meters/sec² (m/s²) | | x 3.281 | = feet/sec² |
| inches/sec² | x 0.0254 | = meters/sec² (m/s²) | | x 39.37 | = inches/sec² |

ENERGY OR WORK (watt–second = joule = newton–meter)

foot–pounds	x 1.3558	= joules (J)		x 0.7376	= foot–pounds
calories	x 4.187	= joules (J)		x 0.2388	= calories
Btu	x 1055	= joules (J)		x 0.000948	= Btu
watt–hours	x 3600	= joules (J)		x 0.0002778	= watt–hours
kilowatt–hrs.	x 3.600	= megajoules (MJ)		x 0.2778	= kilowatt–hrs

FUEL ECONOMY AND FUEL CONSUMPTION

| miles/gal | x 0.42514 | = kilometers/liter (km/L) | | x 2.3522 | = miles/gal |

Note:
235.2/(mi/gal) = liters/100km
235.2/(liters/100 km) = mi/gal

LIGHT

| footcandles | x 10.76 | = lumens/meter² (lm/m²) | x 0.0929 | = footcandles |

PRESSURE OR STRESS (newton/sq meter = pascal)

inches Hg(60°F)	x 3.377	= kilopascals (kPa)		x 0.2961	= inches Hg
pounds/sq in	x 6.895	= kilopascals (kPa)		x 0.145	= pounds/sq in
inches H₂O(60°F)	x 0.2488	= kilopascals (kPa)		x 4.0193	= inches H₂O
bars	x 100	= kilopascals (kPa)		x 0.01	= bars
pounds/sq ft	x 47.88	= pascals (Pa)		x 0.02088	= pounds/sq ft

POWER

| horsepower | x 0.746 | = kilowatts (kW) | | x 1.34 | = horsepower |
| ft–lbf/min | x 0.0226 | = watts (W) | | x 44.25 | = ft–lbf/min |

TORQUE

| pounds–inches | x 0.11298 | = newton–meters (N·m) | | x 8.851 | = pound–inches |
| pound–feet | x 1.3558 | = newton–meters (N·m) | | x 0.7376 | = pound–feet |

VELOCITY

miles/hour	x 1.6093	= kilometers/hour (km/h)	x 0.6214	= miles/hour
feet/sec	x 0.3048	= meters/sec (m/s)		x 3.281	= feet/sec
kilometers/hr	x 0.27778	= meters/sec (m/s)		x 3.600	= kilometers/hr
miles/hour	x 0.4470	= meters/sec (m/s)		x 2.237	= miles/hour

COMMON METRIC PREFIXES

mega	(M)	= 1 000 000	or 10^{6}	centi	(c)	= 0.01	or 10^{-2}
kilo	(k)	= 1 000	or 10^{3}	milli	(m)	= 0.001	or 10^{-3}
hecto	(h)	= 100	or 10^{2}	micro	(μ)	= 0.000 001	or 10^{-6}

METRIC/U.S. CUSTOMARY UNIT EQUIVALENTS

Multiply:	by:	to get:			by:	to get:

LINEAR

inches	x 25.4	= millimeters (mm)		x 0.03937	= inches
feet	x 0.3048	= meters (m)		x 3.281	= feet
yards	x 0.9144	= meters (m)		x 1.0936	= yards
miles	x 1.6093	= kilometers (km)		x 0.6214	= miles
inches	x 2.54	= centimeters (cm)		x 0.3937	= inches
microinches	x 0.0254	= micrometers (μm)		x 39.37	= microinches

AREA

inches²	x 645.16	= millimeters²(mm²)		x 0.00155	= inches²
inches²	x 6.452	= centimeters²(cm²)		x 0.155	= inches²
feet²	x 0.0929	= meters²(m²)		x 10.764	= feet²
yards²	x 0.8361	= meters²(m²)		x 1.196	= yards²
acres²	x 0.4047	= hectares (10⁴m²)			
			ha	x 2.471	= acres
miles²	x 2.590	= kilometers² (km²)		x 0.3861	= miles²

VOLUME

inches³	x 16387	= millimeters³ (mm³)		x 0.000061	= inches³
inches³	x 16.387	= centimeters³ (cm³)		x 0.06102	= inches³
inches³	x 0.01639	= liters (L)		x 61.024	= inches³
quarts	x 0.94635	= liters (L)		x 1.0567	= quarts
gallons	x 3.7854	= liters (L)		x 0.2642	= gallons
feet³	x 28.317	= liters (L)		x 0.03531	= feet³
feet³	x 0.02832	= meters³ (m³)		x 35.315	= feet³
fluid oz	x 29.57	= milliliters (mL)		x 0.03381	= fluid oz
yards³	x 0.7646	= meters³ (m³)		x 1.3080	= yards³
teaspoons	x 4.929	= milliliters (mL)		x 0.2029	= teaspoons
cups	x 0.2366	= liters (L)		x 4.227	= cups

MASS

ounces (av)	x 28.35	= grams (g)		x 0.03527	= ounces (av)
pounds (av)	x 0.4536	= kilograms (kg)		x 2.2046	= pounds (av)
tons (2000 lb)	x 907.18	= kilograms (kg)		x 0.001102	= tons (2000 lb)
tons (2000 lb)	x 0.90718	= metric tons (t)		x 1.1023	= tons (2000 lb)

FORCE

ounces—f (av)	x 0.278	= newtons (N)		x 3.597	= ounces—f (av)
pounds—f (av)	x 4.448	= newtons (N)		x 0.2248	= pounds—f (av)
kilograms—f	x 9.807	= newtons (N)		x 0.10197	= kilograms—f

TEMPERATURE

°F -40 0 32 40 80 98.6 120 160 200 212 240 280 320 °F
°C -40 -20 0 20 40 60 80 100 120 140 160 °C

°Celsius = 0.556 (°F − 32)   °F = (1.8 °C) + 32

DECIMAL CONVERSION CHART

FRACTION	INCHES	M/M	FRACTION	INCHES	M/M
1/64	.01563	.397	33/64	.51563	13.097
1/32	.03125	.794	17/32	.53125	13.494
3/64	.04688	1.191	35/64	.54688	13.891
1/16	.6250	1.588	9/16	.56250	14.288
5/64	.07813	1.984	37/64	.57813	14.684
3/32	.09375	2.381	19/32	.59375	15.081
7/64	.10938	2.778	39/64	.60938	15.478
1/8	.12500	3.175	5/8	.62500	15.875
9/64	.14063	3.572	41/64	.64063	16.272
5/32	.15625	3.969	21/32	.65625	16.669
11/64	.17188	4.366	43/64	.67188	17.066
3/16	.18750	4.763	11/16	.68750	17.463
13/64	.20313	5.159	45/64	.70313	17.859
7/32	.21875	5.556	23/32	.71875	18.256
15/64	.23438	5.953	47/64	.73438	18.653
1/4	.25000	6.350	3/4	.75000	19.050
17/64	.26563	6.747	49/64	.76563	19.447
9/32	.28125	7.144	25/32	.78125	19.844
19/64	.29688	7.541	51/64	.79688	20.241
5/16	.31250	7.938	13/16	.81250	20.638
21/64	.32813	8.334	53/64	.82813	21.034
11/32	.34375	8.731	27/32	.84375	21.431
23/64	.35938	9.128	55/64	.85938	21.828
3/8	.37500	9.525	7/8	.87500	22.225
25/64	.39063	9.922	57/64	.89063	22.622
13/32	.40625	10.319	29/32	.90625	23.019
27/64	.42188	10.716	59/64	.92188	23.416
7/16	.43750	11.113	15/16	.93750	23.813
29/64	.45313	11.509	61/64	.95313	24.209
15/32	.46875	11.906	31/32	.96875	24.606
31/64	.48438	12.303	63/64	.98438	25.003
1/2	.50000	12.700	1	1.00000	25.400

Acknowledgments

The publication of a book of this nature would not be possible without the cooperation of many segments of the automotive industry. The author would like to thank all the companies and individuals that helped make this book possible.

3-M Company
AC-Delco
Airsearch Industrial Div.
Airtex Automotive Division
Alloy American Bosch
American Hammered Automotive Division
American Honda Motor Co.
AP Parts Co.
Applied Power, Inc.
Automotive Control System Group
Bear Automotive
Belden Corp.
Bendix
Black & Decker, Inc.
BMW of North America, Inc.
Bonney Tools
Borg-Warner Corp.
Bosch Power Tools
Buick Motor Division
C.A. Laboratories, Inc.
Cadillac Motor Division
Carter Div. of AFC Ind.
Caterpillar Tractor Co.
Champion Spark Plug Co.
Chevrolet Motor Division
Chrysler Motor Corp.
Colt Industries
Cummins Engine Co., Inc.
D.A.B. Industries, Inc.
Dana Corp.
Deere & Co.
Delco-Remy Div. of GMC
Detroit Art Services, Inc.
Detroit Diesel Allison Div.
Duro-Chrome Hand Tools
Edu-Tech—A Division of Commercial Service Co.
Exxon Co. USA
Fel-Pro Inc.
Fiat Motors of North America, Inc.
Florida Dept. of Vocational Education
Fluke Corp.
FMC Corporation
Ford Motor Company
Ford Parts and Service Division

Fram Corp.
Gates Rubber Co.
General Motors Corp.*
GMC Truck and Coach Div.
Gould Inc.
Heli-Coil Products
Helm Inc.
Hennessy Industries
Holley Carburetor Div.
Honda
Hunter Engineering Co.
Ingersoll-Rand Co.
International Harvester Co.
Jaguar
K-D Tools Manufacturing Co.
Kansas Jack, Inc.
Keller Crescent Co.
Kem Manufacturing Co., Inc.
Kent-Moore
Killian Corp.
Lincoln St. Louis, Div. of McNeil Corp.
Lisle Corp.
Lufkin Instrument Div.—Cooper Industries Inc.
Mac Tools Inc.
Maremont Corp.
Marquette Corp.
Maserati Automobiles, Inc.
Mazda Motors of America, Inc.
McCord Replacement Products Division
Mercedes-Benz of North America, Inc.
Minnesota Curriculum Services Center
Mitsubishi Motor Sales of America
Mobile Oil Corp.
Motor Vehicle Manufacturer's Assn.
Motorola
NAPA
National Institute for Automotive Service Excellence
Nichols
Nissan Motor Corp.
Oldsmobile Motor Division
OTC Tools & Equipment
Owatonna Tool Co.
Parker Hannifin Corp.
Peerless Instruments

Peugeot, Inc.
Pontiac Motor Division
Precision Brand Products
Proto Tool Co.
Purolator Filter Division
Quaker State Corp.
Renault USA, Inc.
Robert Bosch Corp.
Rochester Div. of GM
Roto-Master
Saab-Scandia of America, Inc.
SATCO
Saturn Corp.
Sealed Power Corp.—Replacement Products Group
Sears, Roebuck, and Co.
Sellstrom Mfg. Co.
Sem Products, Inc.
Simpson Electric Co.
Sioux Tools, Inc.

Snap-on Tools Corp.
Speed Clips Sales Co.
Stanadyne, Inc.
Stewart-Warner
Subaru of America, Inc.
Sun Electric Corp.
Sunnen Product Co.
Test Products Division—The Allen Group, Inc.
The Echlin Mfg. Co.
The L.S. Starrett Co.
TIF Instruments
Toyota Motor Sales, USA, Inc.
TRW Inc.
Victor Gasket Co.
Volkswagen of America, Inc.—Porsche
Volvo of America
Weatherhead Co.
White Diesel Div.

A special thanks goes to TIF Instruments (800-327-5060), to my wife (Jeanette), and to my children (Danielle, Jimmy, and DJ).

Index-Glossary Reference

This Index-Glossary Reference can be used as a conventional index for finding topics in the body of the textbook. It also provides a method of quickly finding definitions of technical terms.

A **bold typeface** is used to identify the pages that contain definitions. If you need a technical word explained in one or two sentences, simply turn to the page number printed in bold type. The defined term is printed in *italics* in the body of the textbook

The Index-Glossary is educationally superior to a conventional index because it allows you to obtain more information about the term being questioned. You can read the definition in context and then continue to read more on the subject as needed. You can also refer to the illustrations.